🌺 Taylor's
Encyclopedia
of Garden Plants

Taylor's Guides to Gardening

Taylor's
Encyclopedia of
Garden Plants

FRANCES TENENBAUM, Editor

A Frances Tenenbaum Book

HOUGHTON MIFFLIN COMPANY

BOSTON   NEW YORK   2003

ACKNOWLEDGMENTS

I owe a debt of gratitude to the authors and advisers who wrote and contributed to the individual *Taylor's Guides* that are the basis for this encyclopedia. Specifically, my thanks to Kathleen Fisher, *Taylor's Guide to Shrubs*; Nancy J. Ondra, *Taylor's Guide to Roses*; Susan A. Roth, *Taylor's Guide to Trees*; and David C. Michener and Nan Sinton, *Taylor's Guide to Ground Covers*. Above all, I wish to express my thanks to and admiration for Barbara Ellis, the author of *Taylor's Guide to Annuals*, *Taylor's Guide to Perennials*, and *Taylor's Guide to Bulbs*. In addition, she wrote the glossary for this encyclopedia and graciously answered every question I asked.

Visit our Web site: www.houghtonmifflinbooks.com.

Taylor's Guide is a registered trademark of Houghton Mifflin Company.

Library of Congress Cataloging-in-Publication Data

Taylor's encyclopedia of garden plants / edited by Frances Tenenbaum.
     p.   cm.
  ISBN 0-618-22644-3
     1. Plants, Ornamental — Encyclopedias.   I. Tenenbaum, Frances.
  SB403.2 .T39   2003
  635.9′03 — dc21   2002027630

Book design by Anne Chalmers
Typefaces: Minion, News Gothic

Printed in Singapore

TWP 10 9 8 7 6 5 4 3 2 1

Contents

Introduction

ALTHOUGH GARDENING HAS MANY ASPECTS, and gardeners have special interests, the single incontrovertible fact is that everything begins with plants. Whether you are a new gardener or a longtime expert, whether you collect books and articles on your favorite subject or want a single volume that you can refer to today and twenty years from now, you need an encyclopedia of plants. In many ways this book is the culmination of the series of Taylor's Guides that began in the 1980s, inspired by horticulturist Norman Taylor, whose classic garden encyclopedia was first published by Houghton Mifflin in 1936 and last revised in 1956.

As with all of the Taylor's Guides, the aim in this book is to be thorough, accurate, dependable, and useful to North American gardeners. As we have shown in the plant guides, as well as in the other Taylor's books, it is quite possible to make a practical reference book attractive and pleasurable to use. The text is readable, and the pictures and layout are beautiful. Like gardening itself, this book will give you immediate joy as well as long-term rewards.

HOW THE PLANTS ARE ARRANGED

To make this book useful to both experienced and novice gardeners, as well as professionals, the plants are organized alphabetically by genus name. A *genus* is a group of plants that share a certain number of characteristics. Within the genus are *species,* and the species name refers to only one plant. A genus may have a single species or it may include hundreds. The genus *Cornus,* for example, has a number of trees: flowering dogwood, *Cornus florida;* Pacific dogwood, *Cornus nuttallii;* pagoda dogwood, *Cornus alternifolia;* and several others. It also has shrubs, such as red osier dogwood, *Cornus stolonifera,* and the elegant little ground cover *Cornus canadensis,* or bunchberry.

This system of terminology is easier to use than it sounds; to find any of these plants in the encyclopedia, all you need to know is its common name. The index of common names (page 431) will lead you to the botanical name of the genus that the plant belongs to, which you can find listed alphabetically. "Dogwood" or "bunchberry" will lead you to *Cornus,* and there you will find entries for all of the *Cornus* species covered in the book.

Why not arrange the encyclopedia by common names in the first place? The reason is that although common names are often charming and descriptive (and none of us is likely to call a marigold a *Tagetes*), only the botanical name identifies the exact, specific plant. In this book there are at least ten very different plants whose name begins with the word "false," such as false indigo and false Solomon's seal, and five that begin with "glory." "Ironweed" could be *Ostrya,* a tree, or *Vernonia,* a wildflower. Is the plant you admired in a friend's garden love-in-a mist, love-in-a-puff, or love-lies-bleeding? Or might it be bleeding heart? Harry

Physostegia

Franklinia

Lauder's walking stick (named for an early-twentieth-century British comic entertainer) is both descriptive of this corkscrew shrub and easier to remember than *Corylus avellana* 'Contorta'. Poached-egg plant is certainly a more colorful name than *Limnanthes douglasii*. And I'd hate to see names like lion's ear and tidy tips and blue-eyed grass disappear from the gardener's vocabulary. But when you are looking for accurate information, you need to know what plant you are talking about. Is your prince's feather an *Amaranthus* or a *Persicaria?*

Look up any of these names in the index of common names, and you'll be referred to the genus to which the plant belongs. In the entry you'll find a description of the species and an illustration to help you identify the plant in your friend's garden. Should you want to grow it yourself, you'll learn whether it will survive in your climate, how to plant it, and what further information you need to know to succeed with that plant. You'll also find the names of hybrids and cultivars that may be improvements over the species. (In the glossary on page 424, you'll find definitions of the terms *hybrid* and *cultivar* and of many other botanical terms used in this book.)

HOW WE DECIDED WHICH PLANTS TO INCLUDE

In an encyclopedia like this, more is not necessarily better. We have included at least one thousand species of desirable plants for American gardens; to list all available species would require a volume as large and unwieldy as a Manhattan phone book. We have obviously had to make choices, based on the knowledge and experience of the Taylor's Guide editors. For example, you'll find here the dawn redwood, *Metasequoia* — once thought to be extinct but now available as a desirable garden tree — but not the *Sequoia*, the tallest tree in the world, or the massive giant sequoia, *Sequoiaden-*

dron, both of which are recommended mainly for public parks and large estates.

Some plants are not recommended for home gardens because they are invasive, but deciding which ones to eliminate turned out to be a rather complicated issue. A handsome perennial like purple loosestrife *(Lythrum)* does not appear in this book because the plants are such rampant invaders of wetlands that some states actually ban them; even the supposedly sterile cultivars have been found to set seeds. Some popular genera include species that are invasive and species that are not, as well as some that are problematic in one part of the country but not in others. Some common plants that fall into these good/bad categories are privet *(Ligustrum)*, bittersweet *(Celastrus)*, burning bush *(Euonymus)*, barberry *(Berberis)*, and honeysuckle *(Lonicera)*. Before you decide on a plant for your own property, be sure to read the entry for that species. Readers who are concerned about this subject should consult the handbook *Invasive Plants*, published by the Brooklyn Botanic Garden.

HARDINESS

Will the plant you are considering grow where you live? For gardeners, this is the question that matters most. If you do not know the plant zone of your geographic area, look at the U.S. Department of Agriculture Plant Hardiness Zone Map on pages 446–47. The zones range from Zone 1, the coldest, to Zone 11, the hottest. (In a new map, scheduled to be published in 2003, the major changes are the addition of the tropical zones, 12 through 15.) No zones are given for *annual* plants, which live for one growing season only, no matter what the climate. You'll also find some plants listed as *tender perennials.* Although these will live and rebloom in suc-

ABOVE: *Heliopsis*　　　RIGHT: *Celastrus scandens*

ceeding seasons in warm or tropical zones, in most parts of the country they are grown as annuals.

Except for annuals and tender perennials, the plant descriptions give a range of zones. The first number in the range indicates the northern limit of hardiness, while the second is a guideline to how much heat the plant can handle. For example, peach-leaved bell-flower *(Campanula persicifolia),* hardy from Zone 3 to Zone 7, is fairly cold-tolerant: it withstands Zone 3 winters, with average annual minimum temperatures of −30° to −40°F. But it is not particularly tolerant of heat and doesn't grow well in the hot summers characteristic of areas south of Zone 7.

The northern limits of the zone ranges are based on average minimum temperatures taken from 6,700 weather stations and do not include any of the other variables that can affect a plant's hardiness, such as a freak ice storm, an unusually warm winter, a year of drought, or being planted next to a south-facing brick wall. A good predictor of a plant's success in your garden is finding it in other gardens in your area. But the USDA Zone Map is a useful place to start, especially if you are considering a tree or other valuable plant. The second number in the zone range, the southern heat limit, is based on the experience of professional growers and gardeners. If your own garden has a cold microclimate, you may be able to succeed with that Zone 3 to 7 bellflower even if you live in Zone 8.

AT THE VERY LEAST, gardening is an enjoyable pastime; at the most, it is a passion. To all who use this book, we hope it will fulfill your needs and increase your pleasure.

— FRANCES TENENBAUM

🌿 Taylor's
Encyclopedia
of Garden Plants

A

Abelia

ah-BEEL-yuh. Honeysuckle family, Caprifoliaceae.

This genus encompasses up to 30 species of evergreen and deciduous shrubs found on hills and in open woods in Mexico, the Himalayas, and East Asia. Gardeners grow a handful of species and, particularly, the following two hybrids for their glossy green leaves and arching branches. Small pink to white funnel-shaped flowers bloom in mid- to late season, and when they drop, lobed calyxes often remain to extend the season of interest.

HOW TO GROW
Give abelias full sun or partial shade and moisture-retentive, acid soil. They are popular for hedges and work well on banks or in masses. They require minimal pruning but can be pruned hard in spring if they outgrow their space. You can propagate them easily from cuttings or seeds sown as soon as they are collected.

A. 'Edward Goucher'
A semievergreen shrub about 5 feet tall and wide with bumpy-surfaced leaves emerging bronze. The trumpet-shaped flowers are lavender-pink, blooming heavily from early summer until frost, and the sepals are usually two lobed.
Zones 6 to 10.

A. × grandiflora
a. × gran-dih-FLOR-uh. GLOSSY ABELIA. This rounded, many-branched semievergreen shrub grows 6 feet tall and wide, sometimes larger in the South. Flowering begins from midspring to midsummer, depending on the region, and lasts into fall. The lightly scented, pink-tinged white flowers appear on the ends of the arching branches. Rosy sepals with two to five lobes can persist for months after the flowers drop. In the South, so do the lustrous oval leaves, often tinged bronzy purple through winter. Variegated cultivars include the trademarked 'Confetti' and 'Sunrise'.
Zones 6 to 10.

Abeliophyllum

ah-beel-ee-oh-FY-lum. Olive family, Oleaceae.

A single species of deciduous shrub from the hills of Korea, related to forsythia and grown for its fragrant early-spring flowers.

HOW TO GROW
White forsythia needs full sun to flower best, as well as fertile, well-drained soil. After blooming, cut back all stems to strong buds near the ground to encourage a denser, fountainlike shape. Use it in masses, or in a shrub border. Propagate from softwood cuttings or by layering. Buds are less likely to be killed by late frosts than those of true forsythia.

A. distichum
a. DISS-tih-kum. WHITE FORSYTHIA. An open, spreading shrub, 5 feet tall and wide, with arching branches. In late winter or early spring, cross-shaped fragrant white flowers bloom in axillary racemes before the leaves appear. The bare stems and the base of the flower may have a purplish tinge. 'Roseum' has pink flowers.
Zones 5 to 9.

Abelmoschus

ah-bel-MOS-kus. Mallow family, Malvaceae.

The members of this genus of 15 or so heat-loving annuals or tender perennials hail from the tropics of Asia. They bear five-petaled, hibiscus-like blooms singly in leaf axils or in racemelike clusters. (*Abelmoschus* species were all once classified in *Hibiscus*.) Two species of tender perennials, hardy to **Zone 9**, are commonly grown as annuals. Both have handsome, dark green, palmately lobed leaves that lend a tropical air to beds and borders and produce an abundance of flowers, each of which lasts only a day, from late summer to frost. Okra *(A. esculentus),* cultivated for its young seedpods, also is a well-known member of the genus.

HOW TO GROW
Full sun, warm temperatures, and rich, well-drained soil are ideal. Sow seeds indoors in individual peat pots 8 to 10 weeks before the last spring frost date, and germinate at 50° to 55°F. (Indoor sowing is especially helpful north of Zone 6 and in any area where spring is cool and rainy.) Seedlings resent transplanting, so handle them carefully. Plants take about 3 months to bloom from seeds. Feed with a balanced fertilizer in midsummer.

A. manihot
a. MAN-ih-hot. SUNSET HIBISCUS. A shrubby plant reaching 5 to 6 feet in height by summer's end. It bears lush, 1- to 1½-foot-long leaves and pale lemon yellow, 5- to 6-inch-wide flowers with burgundy centers. Tender perennial or grow as an annual.

A. moschatus
a. moe-SHAH-tus. MUSK MALLOW. Compact, bushy plant that stays between 1½ and 2 feet high in northern gardens but reaches 4 feet or more in warm climates. Leaves range from 2 to 3 inches to as much as a foot in length. Showy, 3-inch-wide flowers with white centers come in shades of pink, orange-red, and scarlet. Tender perennial or grow as an annual.

Abelia × grandiflora 'Dwarf Purple'

Abeliophyllum distichum

Abelmoschus moschatus

Abies

AY-beez. Pine family, Pinaceae.

The 50 or so fir species, members of the genus *Abies,* hail from northern or mountainous regions of North America, Europe, Asia, and northern Africa. They are tall symmetrical conifers with dense whorled branches and rigid pyramidal or conical shapes. The mature female cones are squat, sturdy, and showy, standing upright along the high branches. They ripen and fall apart on the tree rather than dropping to the ground, easily distinguishing them from the cones of spruces *(Picea),* which hang down and drop in one piece. Fir needles are more flattened than spruce needles and are blunt tipped and soft to the touch, unlike the spruces' sharp, pointed needles. (Firs are friendly, spruces not.) They grow directly from twigs that either encircle the branch or curve up and away from the underside of the branch. If pulled off, they leave behind a round white depression, another identifying feature.

Firs look best with the lowest branches left to sweep the ground. Be careful how you prune them, because they will not resprout from old, leafless wood.

HOW TO GROW

Firs generally need cool, acid, moist soil and cool temperatures, so they are unreliable performers in much of North America. They

Abies balsamea

are usually pest- and disease-free, although aphids, bagworms, spider mites, and twig blight sometimes can be troublesome, and root rot is common in poorly drained soil. Most firs are grafted to rootstocks of *A. fraseri* or *A. balsamea,* which do not thrive in dry soil or hot summers, so they perform poorly in the South and Midwest. In these regions, choose a fir that is grafted to the more tolerant *A. firma.* Where adapted, firs make gorgeous specimens and screens.

A. balsamea

a. ball-SAM-ee-uh. BALSAM FIR. Growing into a dense, narrow, pointed pyramid that reaches 50 to 70 feet tall and 20 to 25 feet wide, this native is loved for its piny fragrance and is often cultivated as a Christmas tree. The 1-inch-long needles are blunt, rounded, and shiny dark blue-green. They are arranged in two ranks along the side branches. Trunk bark is gray-brown. Cones are 2 to 3 inches long and violet purple. Balsam fir thrives in cool northern climates, but it is the worst performer of any fir in the Upper South, Mid-Atlantic states, and Midwest. Despite this, it is often sold by nurseries in those areas. Use spire-shaped balsam fir as a specimen, with its lowest branches left to sweep the ground. From northeastern North America. **Zones 2 to 5.**

SIMILAR SPECIES

A. balsamea var. *phanerolepis* (Canada fir) is fast growing and produces heavy side branches. *A. fraseri* (Fraser fir) forms a narrow pyramid to 40 feet tall and has very short, glossy, dark green needles. It comes from a more southerly mountainous climate than balsam fir and performs well at high elevations in the South and North, likes moist, well-drained, acid soil, and is a favorite Christmas tree. **Zones 3 to 7.**

A. concolor

a. KON-kuh-lor. WHITE FIR. The most beautiful and adaptable of the firs, this dense, conical tree features horizontal branches and grows 35 to 50 feet tall and 15 to 30 feet wide. White fir makes an elegant, symmetrical specimen reminiscent of Colorado blue spruce. Needles are $1^1/2$ to $2^1/2$ inches long, soft gray-green to silvery blue-green, and curved upward with rounded tips. Trunk bark is smooth and gray, becoming scaly

Abies concolor

with age. Immature cones are purplish, turning light brown and growing to 5 inches long and 2 inches wide when mature.

Use this tree, especially its most silvery cultivars, as an eye-catching specimen in an open area where its lowest branches can sweep the ground. White fir makes a good substitute for Colorado blue spruce in areas where the latter suffers from diseases and insects. Although it tolerates more heat and drought than other firs, it does not tolerate urban conditions. Keep the soil cool and moist with an organic mulch. This is the best fir for the Midwest and East Coast, but it performs best of all in the North and the Pacific Northwest. From high elevations of western North America. **Zones 4 to 8.**

CULTIVARS

'Candicans' has vivid silvery blue or silvery white needles when grown in full sun and forms a narrow, upright pyramid. 'Glenmore' has large, gray-blue needles and a nice compact tree shape. 'Swift's Silver' offers exceptionally silvery needles. 'Violacea' bears bright silvery blue needles.

A. homolepis

a. hoe-moe-LEP-is. NIKKO FIR. Unlike most firs, which are spire shaped, the heat-tolerant Nikko fir starts out pyramidal but matures into a broad-spreading tree that grows 40 to 50 or more feet tall and 30 feet wide. The attractive needles are denser than those of most firs, have notched tips, and are $1/2$ to 1 inch long. They are dark green with two white stripes on their undersides, giving the tree an overall lighter color. Trunk bark is gray but tinged with pink and becomes scaly with age. The 3- to 4-inch-long, ornamental cones are green when young and pale brown when mature. They are borne lower on the tree than those of most firs. Use this distinctive tree for its full silhouette as a specimen or massed for a screen. From Japan. **Zones 5 to 6.**

SIMILAR SPECIES

A. firma (Momi fir), from Japan, is a wide-spreading tree that grows to 50 feet tall and bears glossy, two-tone needles (dark green on top and light green on the undersides). It is the only fir that adapts to heavy, acid soil and heat, making it the best fir for the South. **Zones 6 to 8.**

A. koreana

a. kor-ee-AY-nuh. KOREAN FIR. Korean fir has a compact, wide-

Abies koreana 'Silver Snow'

spreading, pyramidal form and grows slowly to about 30 feet tall and 15 feet wide. The $^1/_2$- to 1-inch-long needles are rich green with two broad silver bands on the undersides, creating a shimmery effect, and are arranged in V-shaped ranks. Trunk bark is dark gray-brown. Cones are red and chartreuse when young and bluish purple when mature. These beautiful cones are profuse even when the tree is young. This species is more heat tolerant than other firs, but it performs best in a cool climate. From southern Korea. **Zones 5 to 7.**

CULTIVARS

'Hortsmann's Silberlocke' is a compact tree that has a silvery effect because its needles twist to expose the silver undersides.

A. nordmanniana

a. nord-man-nee-AY-nuh. NORD-MANN FIR. This handsome tree grows to 60 feet tall and 25 feet wide, producing tiers of down-swept branches. The beautiful, forward-pointing, glossy black-green needles are about $1^1/_2$ inches long and have two white bands on their undersides. Mature cones are 6 inches long and greenish black and have protruding bracts. Trunk bark is very dark gray-black and broken into plates. Locate Nordmann fir as a specimen in a lawn or border where it has plenty of growing room. From the Caucasus Mountains of eastern Europe. **Zones 4 to 7.**

Abutilon

ah-BEW-tih-lon. Mallow family, Malvaceae.

Closely related to hollyhocks and hibiscus, the genus *Abutilon* contains about 150 species of tender shrubs, small trees, perennials, and annuals. These tropical natives, most hardy from **Zone 8 or 9 south,** are grown for their colorful, pendulous, bell- or cup-shaped flowers. The solitary 2- to 3-inch-long flowers appear continuously from spring to fall and have five petals, a calyx that in some forms is also colorful, and a hibiscus-like column of fertile parts at the center. The leaves are simple or lobed and maplelike — thus the common name "flowering maple." Many hybrids and cultivars are available.

HOW TO GROW

Give abutilons full sun or partial shade and rich, well-drained soil. Where hardy, grow them outdoors

as shrubs; in areas where they are marginally hardy, try a site against a south-facing wall for extra winter protection. In the North, grow them in containers and overwinter them indoors in a bright, cool (40° to 45°F) spot, or use as bedding plants replaced annually. Upright types make handsome standards. Water deeply during dry weather and feed pot-grown plants a few times during the summer with a balanced fertilizer. Prune plants to shape in late winter or early spring: cut them back hard if necessary. Pinch to encourage bushy growth. Since young plants bloom best — the older ones become woody — consider growing new ones from cuttings taken annually or every other year. Take cuttings in spring to propagate for garden use or in late summer to overwinter the plants. Hybrids and cultivars do not come true from seed.

A. × hybridum

a. × HI-brih-dum. FLOWERING MAPLE. A shrubby plant reaching 15 feet in height. The pendent, bell- to cup-shaped flowers come in yellow, orange, red, or white. The ovate to lobed, maplelike leaves may be variegated. Cultivars include 'Huntington Pink', which has rich pink blooms; 'Moonchimes', which produces yellow flowers; and 'Souvenir de Bonn', bearing soft orange flowers and white-edged leaves. **Zones 9 to 10.**

A. megapotamicum

a. meg-ah-poe-TAM-ih-kum. TRAILING ABUTILON. A shrubby species with trailing or arching shoots, reaching 6 feet in height and spread. It has bright

Abutilon pictum 'Thompsonii'

green, ovate leaves and pendent flowers with red heart-shaped calyxes and yellow petals. 'Variegatum' has yellow-mottled leaves. **Zones 8 to 10.**

A. pictum

a. PIK-tum. An erect to spreading shrubby species reaching 15 feet in height. It bears ovate to maplelike leaves and yellow to orange flowers with red veins. 'Thompsonii' has pale orange flowers and yellow-mottled leaves. **Zones 8 to 10.**

A. vitifolium

a. vy-tih-FOAL-ee-um. This deciduous shrub from Chile grows quickly up to 15 feet tall and about half as wide. The leaves, which can be 6 inches long, are shaped like grape leaves, so the species gets its name from that genus, *Vitis*. Both leaves and stems are covered with gray down. The five-petaled, saucer-shaped summer flowers can be either white or lavender-blue and droop from long stalks. **Zones 8 to 9.**

Acacia

uh-KAY-shuh. Pea family, Fabaceae.

Sometimes called wattle or mimosa, this is a huge genus of evergreen or deciduous shrubs, trees, and vines hailing from the tropics or warm temperate areas of Australia, Africa, and the Americas. About 30 species are available as seeds or plants. In many species, ferny leaves on young plants give way to flattened leafstalks called phyllodes. The balls or spikes of flowers, always yellow and often fragrant, are sometimes followed by ornamental seedpods.

HOW TO GROW

Acacias like full sun but tolerate poor soil, heat, drought, and wind. If they receive adequate water when planted, they can form deep roots that will help anchor banks and slopes. They can be trained when young as shrubs (by removing the central leader) or trees (by limbing up) and make good screens or windbreaks. The pods attract birds. Propagate from seeds soaked overnight.

A. cultriformis

a. kul-trih-FOR-miss. KNIFE ACACIA. An evergreen averaging about 12 feet tall and wide, this shrub earns its common name from its 1-inch silvery green phyllodes, which are asymmetrical, like a paring knife. The flowers bloom in early to midspring. **Zones 9 to 11.**

A. decora

a. deh-KOR-uh. GRACEFUL WATTLE. A rounded evergreen 6 to 8 feet tall and wide with 2-inch, lance-shaped phyllodes and pro-

Abutilon × hybridum

Acacia cultriformis

fuse, bright yellow, fragrant spring flowers. It takes to shearing for a hedge. **Zones 10 and 11**.

A. greggii

a. GREG-ee-eye. CATCLAW ACACIA. This deciduous native of the southwestern United States and northern Mexico grows 6 to 8 feet tall as a shrub and 10 feet when pruned as a tree. Its finely divided leaves are feathery. The common name comes from the curved thorns that cover the branches. Late-spring bloom sometimes repeats in fall. Needs some extra pruning to reshape the natural form, which is a dense, spreading tangle. **Zones 9 to 10**.

A. redolens

a. REH-doe-lenz. This dense evergreen can grow more than 20 feet tall, has gray-green phyllodes, and bears yellow puffball flowers in spring. Better known than the species may be its sideways-growing cultivar, 'Prostrata', which stays about 2 feet tall but can spread to 15 feet wide. A useful ground cover in poor soil, it is sometimes sold as 'Ongerup'. **Zones 10 and 11**.

A. verticillata

a. ver-tih-sil-LAH-tuh. PRICKLY MOSES. Growing 15 feet tall and wide, this evergreen species is distinguished by dark green ^{3}/4-inch needlelike phyllodes, sometimes in whorls. It has a bushy habit if pruned, but its natural habit is open with twisted branches. Inch-long spikes of yellow flowers bloom in midspring. **Zones 9 to 10**.

Acalypha

ack-ah-LIFF-ah. Spurge family, Euphorbiaceae.

This genus comprises about 450 species of tender shrubs with oval to ovate leaves and tiny, densely packed, petalless flowers in fuzzy, pendent, catkinlike clusters. Flower clusters are either showy — somewhat resembling colorful pipe cleaners — or insignificant. Two species are grown as annuals or tender perennials for the tropical air they add to the summer garden.

HOW TO GROW

Give these tropicals heat, humidity, and full sun or partial shade, along with average to fertile, well-drained soil. Grow them as bedding plants mixed with other annuals or in containers; coarse, well-drained soil is best for con-

Acalypha hispida

tainer culture. Water regularly during the season and feed at least monthly with a balanced fertilizer. Pinch stem tips to encourage branching and shapely, compact growth. Overwinter plants indoors in a fairly warm spot (55° to 60°F at night and up to 10 degrees warmer during the day) in containers or as late-summer cuttings. Prune hard, as necessary, in late winter or early spring.

A. hispida

a. HISS-pih-dah. CHENILLE PLANT, RED-HOT CAT'S TAIL. A shrubby plant reaching 6 feet or more and offering rich green, oval leaves. The showy, crimson to maroon-red, 1-inch-wide flower clusters are from 10 to 20 inches long. Semitrailing forms of this species are available, and these make handsome additions to hanging baskets. Tender perennial.

A. wilkesiana

a. will-kes-ee-AN-ah. COPPER-LEAF, JOSEPH'S COAT. A shrubby plant reaching 6 feet, with variegated oval leaves variously marked with bronze, copper, red, white, and green. The 4- to 8-inch-long flower clusters are green or coppery and relatively insignificant. Tender perennial.

Acanthus

ah-KAN-thus. Acanthus family, Acanthaceae.

From southern Europe comes a plant immortalized on many civic buildings and carved stone pediments — *A. mollis* — one of the nearly 20 species native from the Mediterranean region to Asia. *Acanthus* species are long-lived

perennials with coarsely toothed and often spiny evergreen to semideciduous leaves measuring 2 feet or more long. The showy, two-lipped flowers are arranged on dramatic elongated spikes (with leaflike hoods — bracts to botanists) that look like enormous foxgloves. These spikes are often 3 feet or more tall and long lasting, both in the garden and as cut flowers. The flowers themselves are pale lavender to white, often with purplish veining. The scientific name is very descriptive and means "thorny" or "spiny." No one seems to know where the common name, bear's breeches, came from.

HOW TO GROW

A. mollis and *A. spinosus* are both excellent ground covers with similar cultural requirements. *A. mollis* makes a handsome large-scale ground cover for moist, partially shaded sites. The soil should retain moisture but be well drained. Plants will not tolerate wet, poorly drained soil, especially in winter. In Portugal, where it is native, great stands of *A. mollis* carpet woodland areas and shaded town gardens, where established plants are 3 to 4 feet tall and spread 4 to 5 feet. *A. spinosus* is shorter and grows in full sun to partial shade.

HOW TO USE

A. mollis is one of the finest choices for a sculptural effect. Plant it in bold drifts — 10 or more at a time — in shaded woodland areas or as a magnificent foundation planting around a building that recalls southern European architecture. It looks especially stunning when used in settings where the building architecture is on a grand scale — such as an art museum or on a college campus. In the home garden, the space needs to be appropriate to the scale of the plant. Whereas *A. mollis* is a plant for shade, moist soils, and warm Mediterranean climates (Zones 7 to 9), other *Acanthus* species are more commonly found in gravel gardens, where their spiny leaves blend well with other jagged textures.

A. hungaricus

a. hun-GAH-rih-kus. This species resembles *A. spinosus* but has paler foliage. It makes a handsome, slowly spreading mass and is one of the hardiest selections for northern gardeners. **Zones 6 to 9**.

A. mollis

a. MOLL-iss. BEAR'S BREECHES. This plant's lustrous evergreen fo-

Acanthus mollis

Acca sellowiana

liage (deciduous at the species' northern limit) makes a classic ground cover for shaded sites in Mediterranean-like climates. *A. mollis* may go dormant in hot, humid weather such as that found in the southeastern United States. It is reported invasive in the Pacific Northwest. **Zones 7 to 10.**

A. spinosus

a. spy-NO-sis. Native to southern Europe, this handsome, spreading perennial has dark green, dissected foliage that is somewhat spiny. The hooded, mauve flowers appear in early summer. It is tolerant of more sun than *A. mollis,* but it does not tolerate full afternoon sun. **Zones 5 to 10.**

Acca

ACK-uh. Myrtle family, Myrtaceae.

This genus contains two or three species of evergreen shrubs from dry habitats in South American subtropics. Only one is commonly grown, for its showy midsummer flowers and, in the southern part of its range, edible fruits.

HOW TO GROW
Acca prefers a light, loamy soil in full sun but can tolerate shade where fruiting is not an issue. (Fruit needs temperatures that stay above 40°F.) Sometimes used as a hedge, it tolerates dry, sandy soil and salt spray but not cold wind. Prune lightly after flowering if grown only as an ornamental. Propagate by seeds or semiripe cuttings.

A. sellowiana

a. sel-oh-wee-AY-nuh. PINEAPPLE GUAVA. This native of Brazil and Uruguay grows 8 to 10 feet tall and wide. Its opposite, oval leaves are a lustrous, powdery blue-green and up to 1 1/2 inches long. The late-spring flowers, 1 1/2 inches across, have four thick, cupped petals, white on the back and red inside, with a starburst of showy stamens. The 2-inch egg-shaped fruits are green with a red tinge, maturing to yellow in late summer and early fall. **Zones 8 to 10.**

Acer

AY-ser. Maple family, Aceraceae.

This important genus, which includes some of our most beloved and best-known deciduous landscape trees, contains approximately 124 species. Most hail from North America, Asia, and Europe, with a few from Central America and northern Africa. Leaves are opposite and may be simple, lobed, or compound, with three to seven leaflets. Flowers are arranged in clusters and are not usually showy. Fruits, called samaras, consist of two winged seeds joined together.

Landscape maples can be grouped for convenience into three main types: *small maples, tall shade-tree maples,* and *Japanese maples.* Each group has its own cultural needs and landscape uses. Many of the small garden maples adapt to poor, dry soil and thrive in urban areas. Most shade-tree maples need full sun and moist, rich, acid soil and may develop scorched leaves under drought or hot wind, although some tolerate adverse conditions. Japanese maples prefer humus-rich soil and full sun to partial shade, and they need protection from harsh wind and hot sun.

The small maples make excellent choices as street trees near or under power lines and as ornamentals for small-space gardens, especially where growing conditions are tough. Use tall maples as shade trees to cool the house, yard, or street, keeping in mind that their competitive roots can affect nearby plants. Japanese maples display gorgeous lobed or dissected foliage and ornamental bark; use them as focal points in a garden. Most maples offer unrivaled displays of red, scarlet, or gold foliage in fall.

HOW TO GROW
Because maples are so numerous and so varied and grow in so many different places and under different conditions, their specific requirements, if any, appear at the end of each description.

SMALL MAPLES

A. buergerianum

a. burr-jar-ee-AY-num. TRIDENT MAPLE. Formerly *A. trifidum.* This attractive, rounded, multi-trunked tree grows about 20 to 35 feet tall and 25 feet wide and is quite heat tolerant. Leaves are very glossy dark green with blue-green undersides and measure about 4 inches long. Their three pointed lobes sketch the outline of a tulip. Leaves change color in late fall, turning an excellent dark red and orange. Trunk bark is gray and peels attractively on older trees to reveal a patchwork of orange, gray, and brown underbark. Yellowish green flowers bloom in spring with the new leaves. The red-tinged green samaras ripen to brown by summer's end. Trident maple makes an excellent medium-size street or garden tree where growing conditions are demanding.

Trident maple tolerates urban conditions and neutral to acid soil that is sandy, clayey, or chalky. It is also very tolerant of heat, poor soil, and drought. Train to a single trunk. Pest-free. From China and Japan. **Zones 5 to 8.**

CULTIVARS AND SIMILAR SPECIES
'Streetwise' is a fast-growing selection with reddish purple new growth maturing to dark green and burgundy in fall; grows more upright, with a single trunk; **Zones 6 to 9.** *A. glabrum* (Rocky Mountain maple) is a beautiful 20-foot-tall native with 1- to 3-inch, lobed

MAPLES FOR DIFFICULT PLACES

Acer buergerianum
Trident maple tolerates urban conditions and drought as well as soil that is sandy, clayey, or chalky. A similar species, *A. glabrum,* Rocky Mountain maple, is useful in the North and Mountain States in gravelly or damp areas, on slopes or in shade.

A. campestre
Hedge maple can be used as a patio tree in a difficult spot or as a street tree under power lines. It tolerates heat, poor soil, and urban conditions.

A. tataricum ssp. *ginnala*
Amur maple is a durable, tough tree for cold climates in the Northeast, Midwest, and Mountain States. It can be planted as a hedge or windbreak, and it tolerates poor alkaline soil, road salt, and urban conditions.

A. × freemanii
Freeman maple is a good shade tree for the Upper Midwest and Plains States.

A. negundo
Box elder is valuable for stabilizing streambanks and is useful as a shelterbelt tree in the Midwest and Great Plains, where more desirable trees are unable to survive extreme cold and drought.

A. platanoides
Norway maple, though generally overplanted, is indispensable in the extremely cold, windy, droughty regions of the Midwest, Great Plains, and Mountain States. It tolerates compacted soil, air pollution, and road salt. Select from cultivars rather than unnamed choices.

A. saccharinum
Silver maple is best used for a reclamation project or for a natural site near wetlands. It should not be planted close to a street or house because the branches are weak and easily broken.

or trifoliate, red-veined leaves; red twigs; smooth bark; and clear yellow fall color. It is useful in the North and Mountain States in gravelly or damp areas, on slopes, or in shade; **Zones 3 to 7.**

A. campestre

a. kam-PES-tree. HEDGE MAPLE.
Hedge maples are low-branched,
round-headed trees that reach 35
feet tall and wide. They are often
planted about 10 feet apart to
make a dense screen or windbreak.
Leaves are dull green on top and
hairy on the undersides. They are
2 to 4 inches long and have three
to five rounded lobes. Fall color is
often lackluster but may be a
pleasing yellow in late fall. Bark on
branches is corky and attractive in
winter. Use as a specimen tree in a
small garden, as a patio tree in a
difficult site, as a street tree under
power lines, or as a hedge.

Grow hedge maple in full sun
and almost any soil. This tough
tree tolerates heat; poor, sandy, alkaline soil; and urban conditions.
From Europe and Asia Minor.
Zones 4 to 8.

**CULTIVARS AND SIMILAR
SPECIES**
'Nanum' ('Compactum') is slow
growing and dense, reaching 6 feet
tall. 'Queen Elizabeth' ('Evelyn') is
a fast-growing, upright or oval selection with uniform growth and
excellent gold fall color. 'St. Greg-
ory' is upright or oval and uniform, with deep green, very durable foliage and smooth bark. *A.
miyabei* (Miyabe maple) is a simi-
lar-looking tree from Japan with
larger leaves and scaly trunk bark;
Zones 4 to 7.

A. griseum

a. GRISS-ee-um. PAPERBARK
MAPLE. This slow-growing, upright or oval tree eventually
reaches 20 to 40 feet tall and 15 to
25 feet wide. The shiny, cinnamon
brown bark peels off in large papery curls, even on young trees,
and glistens with a metallic sheen.
The bark makes an outstanding
contribution to the garden
throughout the year, especially in
winter, and is complemented in
other seasons by the compound
leaves, which are formed of three
3- to 6-inch-long, jagged-edged
leaflets. These are dark green in
summer and change in very late
autumn to glowing shades of deep
reddish orange. Locate this lovely
tree in a mixed border or use it as
a patio or courtyard tree, where it
can be seen throughout the year.

Grow in full sun to partial
shade and well-drained, humus-
rich soil with a pH of 5 to 7. It
needs plentiful moisture. Prune
when dormant to remove lower
limbs and reveal attractive bark.
Usually pest-free. From central
China. **Zones 5 to 7.**

**CULTIVARS AND SIMILAR
SPECIES**
A. triflorum (three-flowered maple) has colorful peeling bark,
three-part compound leaves, and
dazzling yellow and scarlet fall
color; grow in full sun to full
shade; **Zones 4 to 8.** *A. maximo-
wiczianum* (*A. nikoense;* Nikko
maple) is similar but with
smooth-edged, three-part compound leaves and smooth, gray to
gray-brown bark. Hybrids of the
two trees are 'Gingerbread', a fast-
growing, heat-tolerant tree with
flaky cinnamon-colored bark and
glowing red and orange fall color,
and 'Cinnamon Flakes', which is
similar but offers red autumn
color in very late fall; both hybrids, **Zones 5 to 8.**

A. tataricum

a. tah-TAR-ih-kum. AMUR MAPLE.
Formerly *A. ginnala.* This very
pretty multitrunked tree has
branches low to the ground and
forms a 15- to 20-foot-tall specimen with a dense, rounded head.
The 1½- to 3-inch-long, dark
green leaves have light green or
gray-green undersides and are divided into three narrow lobes with
toothed edges. Leaf shape varies,
with some trees exhibiting very
feathery leaves. Trunk bark is
smooth and gray with darker
stripes; young twigs are deep reddish purple. Flowers are yellowish
and surprisingly fragrant. Pinkish
red samaras ripen in summer and
look so showy that from a distance
the tree appears to be in bloom
right up to fall, when the foliage
changes to deep red or bright scarlet. This is a tough, durable tree
for cold climates in the Northeast,
Midwest, and Mountain States, although some report it invasive in
the Midwest. Use as a garden or
patio tree, a hedge, or a screen.

Fall color is showiest in full sun.
Although best in well-drained, fertile soil, Amur maple tolerates
poor alkaline soil, road salt, and
urban conditions. It also withstands heavy pruning; plant as a
hedge or windbreak by spacing
trees 10 feet apart and shearing

Acer tataricum

yearly in winter. May be pruned to
a single trunk. To use as a specimen, remove the lower branches.
Numerous seeds may cause a
weed-seedling problem. Susceptible to verticillium wilt. From Asia.
Zones 2 to 7.

**CULTIVARS AND SIMILAR
SPECIES**
The species is variable, so named
cultivars are best. 'Beethoven' is
columnar, with a central leader,
brilliant red samaras, and superior fall color. 'Compactum'
('Bailey Compact') is bushlike,
growing to 10 to 12 feet tall, and
makes an excellent hedge; red fall
color. 'Embers' features brighter
red samaras and scarlet fall color.
'Flame' has dazzling red fall color.
'Mozart' is pyramidal, with a central trunk; striking red samaras
and fall color. 'Red Rhapsody' has
brilliant red fall color. 'Red Wing'
displays very showy red samaras.
Zones 2 to 7.

TALL SHADE-TREE MAPLES

A. × freemanii

a. × free-MAN-ee-eye. FREEMAN
MAPLE. This hybrid of red maple and silver maple was developed at the National Arboretum.
Specimens grow into oval trees
about 50 feet tall with beautiful,
often deeply cut, leaves. Selected
cultivars offer the best of both of
the hybrid's parents: a strong
branch structure, excellent fall
color, and tolerance to adverse
growing conditions. Use Freeman
maple as a shade, lawn, or street
tree (away from power lines) or to
create a woodland effect, especially
in the Upper Midwest and Plains
States, where shade-tree choices
are few.

Grow in full sun and acid to
slightly alkaline soil. Prune if nec-

Acer campestre

Acer tataricum

essary to develop strong branching. The hybrid is subject to disease and insect problems similar to those of red maple. **Zones 4 to 7**.

CULTIVARS

Note: Sometimes nurseries mistakenly sell these cultivars as *A. rubrum*. 'Armstrong Two' is an improved version of 'Armstrong', with a tall columnar shape and dependable yellow-orange fall color. 'Autumn Blaze' is upright or oval and features glowing red fall color and strong branches; it is drought tolerant and nearly seedless. 'Autumn Fantasy' is broadly oval, with large leaves and ruby red fall color. 'Celebration' is seedless (less messy) and has a compact oval shape, very strong branches, and golden yellow to red early-fall color. 'Scarlet Sentinel' is seedless and has a narrow oval or columnar shape, large leaves, and unreliable yellow-orange to scarlet fall color.

A. negundo

a. neh-GOON-doe. B OX E LDER, A SH - LEAVED M APLE. One of those trees that are best appreciated in harsh sites where few other trees flourish, this broad, rounded, open-branched native grows 30 to 50 feet tall and spreads even wider, possessing ragged good looks at maturity. Box elder is among the

few maples with compound leaves, which are divided into three or five 2- to 4-inch-long, pointed leaflets that resemble ash tree leaves. Usually bright green on top with slightly hairy, light green undersides, the leaves also may be attractively variegated. Stems of young branches are green to reddish brown and waxy. Trunk bark is gray-brown and deeply ridged and furrowed. Yellow-green male and female flowers develop in pendulous clusters on separate trees in early spring before the leaves. Dry brown samaras hang on to female trees well into winter and may look messy.

This picturesque tree is native to streambanks and edges of lakes and swamps throughout most of North America. Unfortunately, it is weak wooded and subject to storm damage, making it short-lived, although improved cultivars do not have this problem. Despite its drawbacks, this native is valuable for streambank stabilization or as a shelterbelt tree in the Midwest and Great Plains, where more desirable trees do not survive the extreme cold and drought.

Grow in full sun to light shade; variegated forms need partial or light shade in the South. Box elder is very tolerant of soil type, flourishes in wet or dry sites and in al-

kaline soil, and withstands flooding. Prune when dormant to develop strong branch angles and to thin the crown; prune when mature to reduce wind resistance. Needs regular pruning to remove storm-damaged wood. Box elder bugs are annoying pests that feed on the seeds on female trees and can invade houses in autumn; plant male trees or locate female trees away from buildings and outdoor living areas. Female trees also are messy; choose seedless male types to reduce cleanup. Anthracnose can be a problem during rainy years. From North America. **Zones 2 to 8**.

CULTIVARS AND SIMILAR SPECIES

'Baron' is a male form of the species and seedless. 'Flamingo' is a female with pink new growth that matures to green-and-white variegation; grows to 20 feet tall. 'Kelly's Gold' produces gold leaves in spring, chartreuse in summer. 'Sensation' has a stronger, more uniform shape; grows to 30 feet tall and has brilliant red fall color. 'Variegatum' is a female with irregular white-edged leaves. 'Violaceum' has attractive purplish twigs, purplish male flowers, and no seeds. *A. cissifolium* (ivy-leaved maple) is a drought-tolerant trifoliate maple from Japan; grows to 20 to 30 feet tall; has a spreading mushroom shape, gnarled branches, and glossy dark green leaves that turn brilliant red and yellow in fall; and is uncommon but should be grown more; **Zones 5 to 8**.

A. pensylvanicum

a. pen-sil-VAHN-ih-kum. S TRIPED M APLE, M OOSEWOOD. Naturally growing as an understory tree in tall forests, this flat-topped or rounded maple reaches 20 to 30 feet tall and wide and is valued for its interesting bark. Young trunks and branches have smooth, dark pea green bark with prominent bright white stripes, while twigs are red or reddish brown. Bark on the lower trunks of old trees becomes rough and brown, but branches higher up retain the green-and-white-striped character. Leaves are 5 to 7 inches long and three lobed, in the shape of a tulip cutout. Bright light green during the growing season, they change to an excellent yellow in autumn. Best used in an informal or naturalistic landscape and located where the bark is visible in winter.

Grow in partial or light shade

and humus-rich, moist, well-drained soil. Trees perform poorly in heat and drought. Bark is thin; protect from mechanical injury. Prune as needed to reveal bark. Verticillium wilt, aphids, and scale sometimes are troublesome. From eastern North America. **Zones 3 to 7**.

CULTIVARS AND SIMILAR SPECIES

'Erythrocladum' has scarlet twigs with white stripes and a green trunk with white stripes. *A. capillipes* (snakebark maple) has red young twigs, green-and-white-striped trunk bark, and scarlet fall foliage; **Zones 5 to 7**. *A. davidii* (David maple) is an Asian species with very showy striped bark; performs well in the South; **Zones 7 to 9**. *A. tegmentosum* 'White Tigress' is another Asian species and has smooth, rich green to purple-green bark with white stripes; **Zones 5 to 7**.

A. platanoides

a. plat-an-NOY-deez. N ORWAY M APLE. Widely planted — many say overplanted — in North America, this European maple is a beautiful, dense, round-headed tree that grows to 50 or more feet tall and wide. In spring showy clusters of airy yellow-green flowers cover the tree before the leaves appear. In summer bright green samaras develop and then turn tan before dropping. The lustrous dark green leaves have five pointed lobes and measure 4 to 7 inches across. They become brilliant golden yellow in late fall in the North but drop with little color change in the South.

Despite its beauty, the tree has many drawbacks: its roots are very shallow and feed greedily, robbing garden plants of moisture and nutrients; the shade it casts is so dense that lawn and garden plants struggle in it; and so many seeds develop (on the species) that tree seedlings create a cleanup and weed nuisance. On the other hand, it tolerates poorly drained, compacted soil; road salt; and air pollution and urban conditions.

In some areas, Norway maple has invaded natural areas and may be crowding out native trees. In these areas, choose another tree or plant a seedless form of Norway maple. Despite these drawbacks, Norway maple is an indispensable shade or street tree (away from power lines) in the extremely cold, windy, drought-ridden regions of the Great Plains, Midwest, and Mountain States, where few other tall shade trees will grow. Other trees make better choices elsewhere. From Europe. **Zones 4 to 7**.

CULTIVARS AND SIMILAR SPECIES

Many improved cultivars are available and should be used rather than unnamed choices.

Columnar: 'Cleveland' has upswept branches; grows 50 feet tall and half as wide. 'Columnare' is very narrow, producing dense, erect branches; grows to 35 feet tall and 15 feet wide.

Gold leaves: 'Princeton Gold' is a uniform oval with bright yellow leaves on new growth; similar to 'Sunburst' honey locust (*gleditsia*).

Purplish red summer leaves: 'Crimson Sentry' is columnar, growing to 25 feet tall and 15 feet wide, with blood red foliage all summer. 'Crimson King' is rounded and dense, with dark, blood red foliage all summer. 'Deborah' is oval and has red new growth that turns green in summer. 'Fairview' is a narrower version of 'Deborah'. 'Royal Red' is identical to 'Crimson King' but perhaps more cold hardy.

Variegated leaves: 'Drummondii' has light green leaves with wide white edges; protect from wind.

Cut leaves: 'Oregon Pride' is a rounded tree with deeply cut, lacy leaves.

Especially heat, cold, and drought resistant: 'Alberta Park' resists frost cracking. 'Emerald Luster' has a strong, rounded crown and glossy, cupped leaves. 'Emerald Queen' is fast growing, very tall, and drought tolerant. 'Medallion' has red and gold fall color and is seedless. 'Summershade' is one of the best — very tall with lustrous green, insect-resistant leaves. *A. truncatum* (Shantung maple, purpleblow maple) grows to 25 feet tall; similar to Norway maple but with purplish new growth and orange late-fall color; very heat and drought tolerant; makes an excellent tall maple for the Southwest and Plains States.

Stress-tolerant hybrids of A. platanoides *and* A. truncatum: 'Norwegian Sunset' is a compact, upright oval with purplish new growth and yellow-orange to red fall color. 'Pacific Sunset' grows upright or rounded and is of medium height; purplish new growth and excellent bright red to orange-yellow early-fall color; infertile seeds; excellent in the Midwest. *A. mono* (painted maple) is related to these two trees but in form resembles a large Japanese maple, with

bright light green leaves that may turn orange-yellow in fall; grows to 50 feet tall; **Zones 4 to 7**.

A. pseudoplatanus

a. sue-doe-PLAT-tan-us. SYCAMORE MAPLE. This broadly arching, handsome tree grows 40 to 60 feet tall and has attractive flaking or peeling orange-brown bark. It grows well in difficult sites that challenge other maples, but it may self-seed and become invasive in Zone 6 and warmer. The bold, rounded leaves are about 6 inches across and cut into five lobes, closely resembling sycamore leaves. They are dark green on top and gray-green on the undersides, turning an unremarkable yellow in autumn. Flowers form in large, bright green, pendulous clusters, blooming after the new leaves emerge. Use as a sturdy lawn, park, or street tree or as a seaside tree, as it tolerates salt spray.

Sycamore maple adapts to a wide range of soil, from clay to sand, acid to alkaline, but grows best in a humus-rich site with even moisture. Tolerates road salt. Numerous seeds may require cleanup in early summer and create a weed-seedling problem in beds. Excellent in the maritime climates of the East and West Coasts, but performs poorly in the South. From Europe. **Zones 5 to 7**.

CULTIVARS AND VARIETIES

'Atropurpureum' has green leaves with deep purple undersides. *A. pseudoplatanus* f. *erythrocarpum* has bright red samaras.

A. rubrum

a. RUE-brum. RED MAPLE, SWAMP MAPLE. Pyramidal when young and becoming rounded with age, red maple grows rapidly to 60 to 80 feet tall and 45 feet wide and is one of the most popular landscape maples. In the wild, it usually inhabits wet areas and partly shaded woodlands, but it also can be found in fallow fields and on dry hilltops. In early spring, small, bright red flowers cover the silvery branches before the leaves appear. They are followed by red samaras in early summer. The 2- to 4-inch-wide, dark green leaves are gray-green on their undersides and change to a variable combination of red and yellow in early fall. Autumn color varies from tree to tree; some trees color more consistently and better than others. Red maple makes a good shade or street tree (away from power

lines), although surface roots may interfere with a garden or lawn beneath the tree.

Full sun is best, but this tree tolerates partial sun, a wide range of soils, and air pollution but not salt. Fallen seeds pose a weed-seedling problem; consider seedless forms. Leaf scorch disfigures leaves during hot, windy summers in unprotected sites. Chlorosis develops in alkaline soil. Verticillium wilt and trunk decay are sometimes serious. From eastern North America–Canada to the Gulf Coast. **Zones 4 or 5 to 9**.

CULTIVARS AND VARIETIES

Choose plants adapted to your region for best performance and fall color.

Northeast: 'Autumn Flame' is a rounded, dense, seedless tree with small leaves and long-lasting, bright red early-fall color. 'Embers' is pyramidal and has brilliant red fall color. 'Karpick' is seedless and has a narrow oval shape, red twigs, and gold and red fall color. 'New World' resists potato leafhoppers,

has orange-red fall color, and grows into an upright, spreading or weeping shape; **Zones 4 to 8**. 'Red Sunset' is broadly oval, with wonderful long-lasting, orange-red fall color and scorch-resistant leaves; tolerates flooding.

South: A. rubrum var. *drummondii* is of southern origin, so it colors well in the South and tolerates salty soil. 'Legacy' has an oval outline and strong branches; turns red to yellow-orange in fall. 'October Glory' is rounded, with very late crimson fall color. 'Steeple' has a dense oval or columnar shape, with yellow to orange fall color. Also use 'Red Sunset'.

Midwest: 'Brandywine' is resistant to potato leafhoppers; wine red fall color; **Zones 4 to 8**. 'Doric' forms a narrow column, with very late red to orange fall color. 'Northfire' is broadly oval, with fiery scarlet fall color. 'Scanlon' grows densely upright, with orange fall color. Also use 'New World' and 'Red Sunset'.

Upper Midwest: 'Autumn Spire'

Acer rubrum

is columnar or oval and seedless, offering excellent red fall color. 'Firedance' is oval and seedless and has brilliant red fall color. 'Northwood' is oval or round, with orange-red fall color; seedless and intolerant of flooding. 'Red Rocket' is very narrow and features fiery red fall color; **Zones 3 to 8**. 'Rubyfrost' has strong branches, is drought and cold tolerant, and has bright red fall color. Also use 'Northfire'.

A. saccharinum

a. sak-ah-RYE-num. S ILVER MA-PLE. Native to moist streambanks, lake edges, and floodplains, silver maple is a beautiful oval tree with slightly pendulous branches that grows 60 to 80 feet tall. Older trees can be unsightly and even hazardous due to weak wood and consequent storm damage. The 3- to 5-inch-wide leaves are star shaped and cut into five jagged-edged lobes. The tree's common name comes from the silvery undersides of the light green leaves, which sparkle as they wave in the breeze. Fall color is light yellow. The greenish yellow or red flowers open in late winter or very early spring, creating a pretty effect. Trunk bark is smooth when young but rough and flaky on older trees.

Because branches are easily broken during wind-, rain-, and snowstorms, the tree poses a hazard if planted close to a street or house. Old trees have surface roots that can tear up sidewalks and lawns, and the large seeds and abundant seedlings create a cleanup problem. This fast-growing maple is one of the best shade trees for poor-soil areas, but it should not be planted where stronger trees will grow. It is best planted in natural sites near wetlands, on reclamation projects, or as a landscape tree in the northern Plains and Mountain States, where few other shade trees flourish. Only improved cultivars should be chosen for landscape situations. From eastern North America. **Zones 3 to 9**.

CULTIVARS

'Blair' has shorter limbs that are less prone to breakage. 'Northline' is slow growing and strong, good in the Midwest and Great Plains. 'Silver Queen' features deeply cut leaves with silvery undersides, has stronger upright branching, and is nearly seedless. 'Skinneri' is probably the best form, offering lacy leaves and strong horizontal

Acer saccharum

branches. For improved hybrids, see *A. rubrum*.

A. saccharum

a. SAK-kar-um. S UGAR MAPLE, HARD MAPLE, ROCK MA-PLE. The sugar maple is one of North America's finest trees, its foliage painting the landscape with fiery hues in September and October. It grows into a magnificent, long-lived, 80-foot-tall specimen with a strong, symmetrical, oval silhouette, and its sap is the source of maple syrup. Medium green leaves are broad (to 6 inches across) and star shaped. In autumn they turn scarlet, orange-red, orange, or yellow, depending on sun exposure. Trunk bark is rough and gray. Light yellow flowers bloom before the leaves appear and are followed by tan samaras. Sugar maple makes a stunning shade or background tree with a beautiful winter silhouette, but it casts deep shade and has surface roots that make growing grass around it difficult. It performs poorly in urban conditions with road salt and dry, compacted soil. Some cultivars tolerate heat and drought better than others do. Prune when dormant or in midsummer to maintain a single leader and to develop strong branch angles. From eastern North America–Canada south to Georgia and west to Texas. **Zones 3 to 7**.

CULTIVARS AND VARIETIES

For best performance, choose plants adapted to your region.

North and Northeast: 'Bonfire' is broader than most, fast growing, and heat resistant, with red fall color; likes acid or slightly alkaline soil; resists leafhoppers. 'Goldspire' is very narrow and city tolerant; resists leaf scorch; bright yellow late-fall color. 'Green Mountain' features thick, dark green leaves that do not scald in heat and drought; fall color is golden in alkaline soil and red in acid soil. 'Majesty' forms a narrow oval and has red and orange early-fall color. 'Newton Sentry' forms an extremely narrow column, exhibiting several leaders and gold fall color.

South: 'Legacy' forms a dense oval with thick, scald-resistant, dark green leaves and red, pink, and orange fall color.

Midwest: 'Caddo', a selection from Oklahoma, tolerates drought and alkaline soil; features yellow, orange, and red fall color. 'Commemoration' is vigorous and turns golden yellow-orange in early fall. 'Steeple' grows into a dense column or oval. 'Sweet Shadow' has lacy leaves and yellow fall color. *A. saccharum* ssp. *nigrum* (black maple) is endemic to the Midwest; it is more heat tolerant than the species, with more shallowly lobed, droopy leaves, but just as beautiful. Also use 'Goldspire', 'Green Mountain', 'Legacy', 'Majesty', and 'Newton Sentry'.

Mountain States: Use 'Legacy' and 'Green Mountain'.

Southwest: *A. saccharum* ssp. *grandidentatum*, a naturally occurring form with good fall color, is

heat and drought tolerant. 'Highland Park' is a tight pyramid with tatter-proof foliage and very showy, orange-red fall color. 'Rocky Mountain Glow' has an oval shape, with smaller leaves and coral red fall color. Also use 'Caddo'.

JAPANESE MAPLES

A. japonicum

a. juh-PON-ih-kum. F ULL-MOON MAPLE. This lovely, small, rounded or vase-shaped, multitrunked maple grows 15 to 30 feet tall and makes a stunning garden addition. Its attention-grabbing, rounded, 4-inch-wide leaves have 7 to 11 lobes with jagged edges. Small red flowers in bold, nodding clusters make a pretty show in early spring before the new leaves unfold. Fall color is brilliant scarlet, red, or gold. This is a perfect shade tree for a patio or small garden, or use it in a mixed border. It likes full sun to partial or light shade and evenly moist, rich soil that has a near neutral pH. Mulch the soil to retain moisture. From Japan. **Zones 6 to 9**.

CULTIVARS AND SIMILAR SPECIES

A. japonicum 'Aconitifolium' ('Filicifolium'; fernleaf Japanese maple) has large, rounded leaves that are deeply cut to the base into ferny lobes with jagged edges; leaves are deep green in summer and ruby red and orange in early fall; very cold hardy. 'Vitifolium' leaves are not as deeply divided and appear coarser. *A. circinatum* (vine maple) is native to the Pacific Northwest, tolerates dry shade, and resembles full-moon maple; 'Sunglow' has sunny yellow leaves with a coral tinge that turn yellow and crimson in fall. *A. pseudosieboldianum* (Korean maple) is a small, beautiful tree with glossy green, 9- to 11-lobed leaves; exquisite fall color and white young twigs; **Zones 5 to 7.**

A. palmatum

a. pal-MAY-tum. JAPANESE MAPLE. A small, slow-growing, elegant tree with gorgeous foliage, Japanese maple commands attention wherever it grows. Trees are usually upright or vase shaped with layered branching. They reach 15 to 30 feet tall and have smooth gray trunks and waxy reddish or pea green twigs. The small, 1^{1}/$_{2}$- to 3-inch-wide, star-shaped leaves are cut past their midpoints into five to seven toothed lobes, like the fingers of a glove. Red flowers bloom with the new leaves and are followed by red-tinged samaras. Gardeners are enticed by hundreds of cultivars with more finely cut leaves or distinctive colors. Leaves may be pale green, gold, deep red, dark burgundy, or multicolored. Spring growth is often reddish or brighter colored than summer foliage, which dulls some. In autumn green-leaved types turn gold or yellow, purple- and red-leaved types turn red or scarlet, and gold-leaved forms turn orange or yellow. These small trees are especially lovely in mixed borders and small gardens. Use weeping cut-leaved forms to cascade down a slope or waterfall. Purple-leaved forms contrast beautifully with blue-needled conifers.

Japanese maple needs full sun to partial shade and humus-rich, moist, well-drained soil; mulch to retain soil moisture. For best color, give red-leaved types plenty of sun but protect from hot afternoon rays in exposed sites. Prune deadwood from the interior; thin to expose the trunk and branching pattern. Verticillium wilt can be a serious problem, suddenly killing the tree. From China, Korea, and Japan. **Zones 5 to 8.**

CULTIVARS AND VARIETIES
A number of cultivars are widely available. Specialty catalogs offer rarer types for collectors. 'Aoyagi' (green-bark maple) has pea green young branches, bright green leaves, and yellow fall color. 'Asahi

Acer palmatum

Zuru' has red new growth that changes to green, with pink, red, and white variegations. 'Atropurpureum' is the name used for any form with reddish purple leaves. 'Bloodgood' is the most popular red-leaved form; its deeply incised leaves retain their dark crimson color all summer and turn clear red in fall. 'Burgundy Lace' is a spreading tree that grows to 20 feet tall and has dark purple-red leaves whose lobes are cut all the way to the base. 'Butterfly' features white, pink, and green variegated leaves and is bushy to 10 feet tall. 'Sango-kaku' (coral-bark maple) has striking coral red twigs and pale green leaves that turn yellow in fall; **Zones 6 to 9.** 'Shishigashira' has dark green, curled leaves that turn brilliant orange in fall. 'Trompenburg' bears dark purple leaves that turn scarlet in fall. 'Ukigumo' has orange-red leaves that turn yellow in fall. 'Viridis' offers light green leaves, green branches, and yellow fall color. *A. palmatum* var. *dissectum* (threadleaf maple, laceleaf maple) is a gorgeous, low-spreading or weeping shrub that grows wider than it is tall, with lacy, deeply dissected leaves; may have several twisted trunks that grow to 20 feet with great age. 'Crimson Queen' produces deep burgundy, dissected leaves that turn red in fall. 'Ornatum' has bronze leaves that turn scarlet in fall. 'Seiryu' grows upright to 20 feet, with lacy green leaves and orange-gold fall color.

A. shirasawanum

a. sheer-ah-SAW-ay-num. SHIRASAWA MAPLE. Formerly *A. japonicum* var. *microphyllum*. Very similar to *A. japonicum*, this elegant small tree is vase shaped with layered branches and grows 20 to 30 feet tall. It features rounded, 2- to 5-inch-wide, red-stemmed leaves that are cut into 9 or 11, or even 13, sharply toothed, shallow lobes. A cultivar with yellow-green leaves is particularly beautiful and widely grown. In fall Shirasawa maple's foliage turns clear red, yellow, or orange. In spring pink and creamy yellow flowers bloom as the new leaves unfold, creating a lovely sight. The samaras are quite attractive, too, as they are held upright, an identifying trait. Trunks feature smooth gray-brown bark. Use as a specimen in a shade garden. It needs evenly moist, humus-rich soil. From Japan. **Zones 5 to 7.**

Achillea

ah-KILL-ee-ah. Aster family, Asteraceae.

Long-blooming achilleas, also called yarrows, are perennials that bear dense, flat-topped or slightly rounded clusters of tiny daisylike flower heads. Some 85 species belong to the genus, most flowering from late spring into midsummer. Many also bloom intermittently into fall. The flowers come in yellows, pinks, reds, and white and are borne above mounds of aromatic, feathery leaves that may be green, blue-gray, or gray-green. The botanical name commemorates the Greek god Achilles, who was believed to have used these plants to heal wounds — they have a long history of herbal use.

HOW TO GROW
Give plants full sun and average to poor, well-drained soil. They thrive in dry or sandy conditions but also grow in moist, rich soil provided it is well drained. Too-rich soil encourages lush, rank growth. A site with good air circulation is best. Give yarrows plenty of room to spread at planting time — all the species listed here form clumps 2 feet or more across. Divide clumps in spring or early fall every 3 to 5 years to keep them vigorous. Stake tall cultivars. Remove spent flowers to encourage reblooming. Propagate plants by dividing, by taking cuttings from the base of the plant as shoots

Achillea 'Coronation Gold'

Achillea millefolium

emerge in early spring or in summer, or by sowing seeds.

A. filipendulina

a. fil-ih-pen-due-LEE-nuh. This species produces gray-green leaves and flat-topped 5-inch-wide clusters of golden yellow flowers on 4-foot-tall stems from early summer to fall. 'Gold Plate' bears 6-inch-wide flowers. **Zones 3 to 9.**

A. hybrids

Many popular yarrows are the result of complex crosses. 'Coronation Gold' bears 4- to 5-inch-wide mustard yellow flowers on 3- to 3¹/₂-foot stems all summer long; hardy in **Zones 3 to 9**, it tolerates hot, humid summers. 'Moonshine' has gray-green foliage and sulphur yellow blooms all summer on 1- to 2-foot stems and is best in **Zones 3 to 8**. Galaxy hybrid cultivars, hardy in **Zones 4 to 8**, bear 2- to 4-inch-wide flower clusters all summer on compact 2- to 3-foot-tall plants. Galaxy cultivars include lilac-pink 'Appleblossom' ('Apfelblüte'), red-flowered 'Fanal', and dark red 'Summerwine'.

A. millefolium

a. mil-leh-FOE-lee-um. Vigorous to invasive North American native with flat-topped flower clusters

atop 2-foot-tall plants from early to late summer. Blooms come in pink, red, and pastel shades. Cultivars, which have showier flowers and spread less quickly than the species, include magenta 'Cerise Queen', red 'Fire King', orange-red 'Paprika', and 'Summer Pastels'. **Zones 3 to 9.**

A. ptarmica

a. TAR-mih-kuh. SNEEZEWORT. A weedy 1- to 3-foot-tall species with narrow, lance-shaped leaves and loose sprays of white flowers from early to late summer. Double-flowered cultivars such as 'The Pearl', which bears button-like ³/₄-inch blooms, are the best choices for the garden. **Zones 2 to 9.**

A. tomentosa

a. toe-men-TOE-suh. WOOLLY YARROW. Low-growing mounds of woolly gray-green leaves and 3-inch-wide clusters of yellow flowers on 1-foot-tall stems. Blooms early summer to fall. Plants require perfect drainage, do not tolerate heat and humidity, and are best for rock gardens or other very well drained sites. Woolly yarrow can also be mowed and used as a ground cover in those sites. **Zones 3 to 7.**

Achimenes

ah-KIM-eh-neez. Gesneriad family, Gesneriaceae.

Relatives of such popular houseplants as African violets and Cape primroses (*Streptocarpus* spp.), achimenes are tender bulbs primarily native to Central America. About 25 species belong to the

Achimenes 'Minette'

genus, all of which grow from scaly rhizomes that somewhat resemble caterpillars. They bear showy salverform flowers, meaning each bloom has a tubular base and an abruptly flared and flattened face that has five prominent lobes. Blooms are borne singly, in pairs, or in clusters from summer to fall above ovate, often hairy, dark green leaves with toothed margins. The plants are dormant in winter. In the garden, achimenes are mainly used in containers and hanging baskets, although they also can be grown in shade gardens.

HOW TO GROW

Grow achimenes in pots set in a bright, shaded area protected from direct sun, which will scorch the leaves. They require rich, evenly moist soil and high humidity for best growth. Pot sections of dormant rhizomes in damp peat moss or vermiculite anytime from late winter to late spring, covering to a depth of ¹/₂ to 1 inch. Start them in a humid, warm (65° to 70°F) spot. Water very sparingly until they begin to grow; otherwise the rhizomes will rot. When plants are 2 inches tall, move them to pots or baskets filled with a light, loose medium rich in organic matter such as compost or leaf mold. (Don't pack the medium into the pots.) Continue watering moderately until they are growing actively, then keep them evenly moist. Plants that dry out may enter dormancy prematurely. Pinch to encourage branching. Move containers outdoors when night temperatures remain above 60° to

65°F. Feed every two weeks with a dilute fertilizer. In late summer, gradually reduce watering, then dry the containers out completely. Store the rhizomes, still in their containers, in a cool (50° to 55°F), dry spot. Divide and repot in late winter or spring to repeat the cycle. Propagate by dividing the rhizomes.

A. hybrids

ACHIMENES, MONKEY-FACED PANSY, ORCHID PANSY. Cultivars are much more commonly grown than the species and are available in white, pink, red, blue, purple-blue, and violet. Blooms are 1¹/₂ to 3 inches wide and are borne from summer to fall on arching 1- to 2-foot-long stems. Cultivars include 'Ambroise Vershaffelt', which bears white flowers with purple veins at the throat; 'Blue Sparks', blue flowers; 'Harry Williams', red; 'Peach Blossom', rosy salmon; 'Little Beauty', dark pink; and 'Purple King', red-purple. All are tender plants, surviving outdoors in **Zones 10 and 11.**

Aconitum

ack-oh-NYE-tum. Buttercup family, Ranunculaceae.

The genus *Aconitum* contains 100 species of perennials and biennials commonly called monkshoods or aconites. They are grown for their erect racemes or panicles of showy hooded flowers that bring rich blues and purples to the garden from summer to fall. There also are yellow-flowered monkshoods.

Achillea millefolium 'Paprika'

The showy portion of the flowers actually is made up of five petal-like sepals, including one that forms the hood-shaped topmost "petal" for which the plants are named. The true petals have been reduced to spurlike nectaries. The flowers are borne above clumps of handsome leaves, which usually are deeply cut or lobed in a palmate (handlike) fashion. Another common name, wolfsbane, refers to a more sinister characteristic of these plants: the leaves, roots, flowers, and seeds are all quite poisonous.

HOW TO GROW

Give monkshoods a site in partial or dappled shade and rich, evenly moist but well-drained soil. Plants will grow in full sun, but in southern zones a site with afternoon shade helps plants cope with the heat. Monkshoods won't grow well in areas where night temperatures do not drop below 70°F. A protected site helps prevent the brittle stems from breaking in wind and rain. Plants resent transplanting and can be left in place for many years, so space them generously at

Aconitum napellus

Aconitum napellus

planting time — the species listed here form 2- to 3-foot-wide clumps. Handle the plants carefully: the large, fleshy, tuberlike roots break easily. Since monkshoods emerge late in spring, mark the location of the clumps to avoid digging into them accidentally. Water deeply during dry spells. Feed in spring with a mix of well-rotted manure and compost. Taller monkshoods require staking. Divide plants in spring or fall if necessary or for propagation. Wear rubber gloves when handling the roots (rubbing the plant's sap on skin causes tingling and numbness), and keep hands away from your face, especially your eyes and mouth.

A. × cammarum

a. × cam-MAR-um. BICOLOR MONKSHOOD. Formerly *A. × bicol* to 4-foot-tall hybrid   ue, bluish purple, or   flowers from mid-   Bicolor' bears   e-and-white   Spire' bears   foot   aking.

...aelii

  KELL-ee-eye. AZURE   NKSHOOD. A 3- to 6-foot-tall species with rich violet-blue blooms from late summer through fall. 'Arendsii' bears violet-blue flowers in early to midfall on 3- to 4-foot plants. **Zones 3 to 7.**

A. lycoctonum

a. lie-COCK-ton-um. WOLFS-BANE. Produces yellow or sometimes purple flowers from midsummer to early fall on 2- to 6-foot plants. *A. lycoctonum* ssp. *vulparia* (*A. vulparia*) bears pale yellow flowers. **Zones 4 to 8.**

A. napellus

a. NAP-ell-us. COMMON MONKS-HOOD. An old-fashioned 3- to 4-foot-tall species with dense, showy clusters of dark blue-violet flowers in mid- to late summer. **Zones 3 to 8.**

Acorus gramineus

Acorus

ah-KOR-us. Arum family, Araceae.

Despite the common name "sweet flag," *Acorus* species are more closely related to jack-in-the-pulpits (*Asarum*) than to flags or irises. The two species here are both wetland perennials grown for their attractive clumps of strap-shaped or grasslike foliage. They bear insignificant rounded or club-shaped flowers in brownish green or white that jut out just below the tops of leaflike flower stalks. The plants spread by fleshy, aromatic rhizomes. Sweet flags have a long history of herbal uses. The rhizomes can be dried and ground for use as a fixative in potpourri. The leaves, which have a slightly sweet, spicy fragrance, have been used as a strewing herb.

HOW TO GROW

Select a site in full sun or partial shade with constantly moist or wet soil rich in organic matter. Plants also grow in standing water. Sites in bogs, in wet borders, and along natural ponds are ideal: the plants spread steadily but generally aren't invasive. Divide them every 3 to 4 years to keep the clumps vigorous and to contain their spread. Propagate by division in spring.

A. calamus

a. KAL-ah-mus. SWEET FLAG, SWEET CALAMUS. A deciduous

species forming 2-foot-wide clumps of strap-shaped, ³/₄-inch-wide, 3- to 4-foot-long leaves. 'Variegatus' bears leaves striped lengthwise with cream and white. Plants grow with up to 6 inches of standing water over the rhizomes. **Zones 4 to 11.**

A. gramineus

a. grah-MIN-ee-us. GRASSY-LEAVED SWEET FLAG. An evergreen to semievergreen species with glossy, linear, grasslike leaves that form arching clumps to about 12 inches in height and width. Plants grow with 1 to 2 inches of standing water over the rhizomes. Variegated and dwarf cultivars are available. **Zones 5 to 11.**

Actaea

ack-TEE-uh. Buttercup family, Ranunculaceae.

Members of this genus of eight species of woodland perennials are grown for their foliage and showy fruit rather than their flowers. Commonly known as baneberries because the attractive berries and the roots are extremely toxic if ingested, *Actaea* species bear fluffy racemes of small white flowers in late spring and early summer. The flowers are followed by clusters of round berries that add color to the shade garden in late summer and fall. The plants form handsome 2- to 3-foot-wide clumps of leaves that are divided in a featherlike fashion and have toothed leaflets.

HOW TO GROW

Select a site in partial shade with average to rich, evenly moist soil. Amend the soil with compost or humus at planting time, and water deeply in dry weather. Abundant soil moisture is essential to success in areas with hot summers. To

Acorus gramineus 'Oborozuki'

Actaea alba

propagate, divide plants in spring or sow seeds as soon as they are ripe in fall.

A. alba

a. AL-buh. DOLL'S EYES, WHITE BANEBERRY. Formerly *A. pachypoda*. Native 2- to 4-foot-tall wildflower bearing fluffy, rounded, 2- to 4-inch-long racemes of white flowers well above the foliage. The flower stalks (pedicels) turn red as the 3/8-inch-wide berries ripen to white. **Zones 3 to 7.**

A. rubra

a. RUE-bruh. RED BANEBERRY, SNAKEBERRY. Native 2- to 4-foot-tall wildflower that bears fluffy, rounded, 1 1/4- to 2-inch-long racemes of flowers followed by clusters of round, red, 1/4-inch-wide berries. **Zones 3 to 7.**

Actinidia

ack-tih-NIH-dee-ah. Kiwi family, Actinidiaceae.

Commonly called kiwis, the 40 species that belong to the genus *Actinidia* are woody twining vines. They are hardy or tender and bear simple leaves. In summer, plants produce small, cup-shaped flowers in the leaf axils. Blooms, borne singly or in small clusters, sometimes are fragrant. Edible, many-seeded berries follow the flowers. The best-known species of kiwi is

a vigorous tender vine whose large fuzzy fruits are commonly available in grocery stores. Hardy species bear grape-sized edible fruit. In most cases, both male and female plants are required to produce fruit. One species is grown for its colorful variegated leaves.

HOW TO GROW

Select a site in full sun or partial shade and average to rich, well-drained soil. Plants grown in full sun bear the most fruit. For fruit production, grow one male plant for every few females, or plant a self-fertile cultivar. Kiwis are large, vigorous vines that require a sturdy trellis or arbor for support. For best results, install the support before planting. Prune plants in late winter or early spring to keep them in bounds. For fruit production, use a pruning and training system designed for grapes. Propagate by taking cuttings in summer; bottom heat speeds rooting. Train kiwis over arbors or other structures to shade sitting areas. They also can be grown on fences or trellises as screens or privacy barriers.

A. arguta

a. are-GUE-tuh. HARDY KIWI, TARA VINE. A woody, deciduous climber reaching 20 feet or more in height. Bears dark green, 5-inch-long, toothed leaves. Small clusters of fragrant, 3/4-inch-wide, white flowers appear in early summer. Flowers are followed by smooth-skinned, yellow-green, 1-inch-long fruits on female plants. 'Issai' is a self-fertile cultivar that bears fruit without male and female plants. **Zones 3 to 8.**

A. deliciosa

a. deh-lih-see-OH-suh. KIWI FRUIT, CHINESE GOOSE-BERRY. This vigorous, woody, de-

ciduous vine climbs to 30 feet. Plants bear heart-shaped, 8-inch-long leaves and stems that are covered with red-brown hairs. Small clusters of 1 1/2-inch-wide creamy white flowers that fade to yellow appear in early summer. On female plants flowers are followed by 3-inch-long green-brown fruits covered with bristly brown hairs. Named male and female cultivars are available. **Zones 7 to 9.**

A. kolomikta

a. koe-low-MIK-tuh. VARIEGATED KIWI VINE. A woody deciduous vine that grows to 15 feet and bears rounded, 6-inch-long leaves. When leaves emerge they are green with a purple tinge. As they mature, showy white and pink blotches develop toward the tips of the leaves. In early summer, plants produce small clusters of fragrant, white, 3/4-inch-wide flowers. On female plants, flowers are followed by smooth-skinned, 1-inch-long, yellow-green berries. 'Arctic Beauty', hardy in **Zones 4 to 8**, has purple-tinged leaves that become variegated with purple, pink, and green as they mature. **Zones 5 to 8.**

Adenophora

ah-den-OFF-or-uh. Bellflower family, Campanulaceae.

The nodding flowers of *Adenophora* species, commonly called ladybells, reveal a close kinship with bellflowers (*Campanula* species). *Adenophora* contains 40 species, all perennials with bell- or funnel-shaped flowers that feature a swollen disk surrounding the style, just above the ovary, which distinguishes them from the true bellflowers. Flowers are carried in erect, showy terminal racemes or

Adenophora confusa

panicles and come in shades from pale lavender or white to violet-blue. Most species produce clumps of rounded basal leaves and bear smaller leaves along the flowering stems.

HOW TO GROW

Give ladybells a site in full sun to partial shade with rich, deeply dug, evenly moist, well-drained soil. Plants are deep rooted and resent being disturbed, so prepare the soil thoroughly at planting time. Because of the deep, fleshy roots, the plants seldom tolerate division and are best propagated by cuttings taken from shoots that arise near the base of the plant in late spring. Or propagate by seeds.

A. confusa

a. kon-FEW-suh. COMMON LADYBELLS. An erect 2- to 2 1/2-foot-tall perennial forming 2-foot-wide clumps of toothed, scalloped leaves. Bears loose panicles of 3/4-inch-wide, bell-shaped, purple-blue flowers for three to four weeks in early summer. **Zones 3 to 8.**

Adiantum

ah-dee-AN-tum. Brake fern family, Pteridaceae.

Better known as maidenhair ferns, *Adiantum* species are moisture-loving perennials with branched, delicate-looking fronds with shiny black stems that are divided into three or five featherlike (pinnate) leaflets. Fiddleheads and new leaves often are pink in color. Between 200 and 250 species, both hardy and tropical, belong to this genus. The plants spread via

Actinidia arguta

Adiantum pedatum

creeping rhizomes and in the right site form large lacy-textured mounds of foliage.

HOW TO GROW

Give maidenhairs a site in partial shade with evenly moist, well-drained, slightly acid soil. They will tolerate some sun if soil moisture is plentiful and reliable, but unlike many ferns they do not grow well in deep shade. Propagate by dividing the plants in early spring.

A. pedatum

a. peh-DAY-tum. NORTHERN MAIDENHAIR FERN. A 1- to 1½-foot-tall native North American fern with lacy, flat fronds that are branched in a horseshoelike manner. Western maidenhair *(A. aleuticum,* formerly *A. pedatum* ssp. *aleuticum),* native to western North America and eastern Asia, is a similar species. Both are hardy in **Zones 2 to 8.**

Aegopodium

ee-goe-POE-dee-um. Carrot family, Apiaceae.

Five species of fast-spreading perennials belong to the genus *Aegopodium.* The common names of these plants — bishop's weed and goutweed — suggest the garden-management problems they create when poorly used. Plants have compound leaves with three

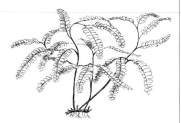

Adiantum pedatum

leaflets and umbels of white flowers in summer.

HOW TO GROW

Select a site in partial to full shade. Although bishop's weed will thrive in any soil, a spot with poor, dry soil where little else will grow is best, and therein lies the benefit of this invasive spreader. Plants easily compete with the roots of such trees as Norway maples, hemlocks, and beeches. However, established plants root very deeply and are difficult to eradicate. Unchecked clumps easily smother less-vigorous plants. Consider a site surrounded by mown lawn on all sides, either alone or under shrubs. To prevent self-sown seedlings, remove the flowers as they fade. *Aegopodium* is an effective plant in urban situations, where tall buildings often result in deep, dry shade. Here paths or sidewalks can offer good barriers to the roving roots of both the species and the variegated forms. To prevent seeding, mow the foliage to the ground in early summer — it will quickly refresh. The variegated form of *A. podagraria* isn't quite as

Aegopodium podagraria

aggressive as the species but still spreads quickly. If variegated plants revert to green or mostly green, promptly dig up reverted portions of the clump and discard them. Otherwise the green portions will overwhelm the remaining variegated ones. Propagate plants by division in spring or fall.

A. podagraria

a. poe-duh-GRAIR-ee-uh. BISHOP'S WEED. Invasive 1- to 1½-foot-tall species with deep, wide-spreading rhizomes. 'Variegatum' bears attractive three-part leaves with irregular creamy white margins and is more commonly grown than the species. **Zones 4 to 9.**

Aesculus

ESS-kew-lus. Buckeye or horse chestnut family, Hippocastanaceae.

This genus contains about 15 deciduous trees and shrubs from southeastern Europe, North America, and eastern Asia. Species from North America are usually called buckeyes; those from other continents are called horse chestnuts. Leaves are opposite, rounded, and boldly cut into five or seven palmate lobes. Tubular flowers bloom in tall spikes. Most species leaf out very early in spring or late winter, their frost-tolerant new growth providing greenery well before other trees do. Although outstandingly beautiful when in bloom in late spring and early summer, most members of this family are messy throughout the growing season, dropping flowers, leaf and twig litter, and nuts. As a group, they are prone to leaf diseases, but some are more resistant than others. All parts of

Aegopodium podagraria

these trees, especially their beautiful nuts, are poisonous to people if eaten, but the nuts provide food for wildlife.

Most buckeyes and horse chestnuts are not fussy as to growing conditions, but good air circulation and even soil moisture discourage leaf diseases. Drought increases unsightly leaf scorch. Use as shade trees or small ornamentals in open or naturalistic areas, with a ground cover planted beneath to absorb the litter and reduce cleanup. Avoid sites near sidewalks, driveways, or patios, and do not plant near playgrounds, where the nuts might tempt children to taste them.

HOW TO GROW

Plant in full sun and evenly moist, well-drained, acid to alkaline soil. *A. × carnea* tolerates drought better than common horse chestnut *(A. hippocastanum)* does. It also suffers somewhat from leaf scorch and mildew during dry spells and leaf blotch and anthracnose during wet spells, but less so than common horse chestnut. Prune low-hanging branches if needed.

A. × carnea

a. × KAR-nee-uh. RED HORSE CHESTNUT. Growing into a dense, rounded, 30- to 40-foot-tall tree, this hybrid of horse chestnut and red buckeye is very showy and disease resistant. Eye-catching

Aesculus × carnea 'Rosea'

Aesculus parviflora

6- to 8-inch-tall spires of rose pink flowers rise up from the branches in late spring. The glossy, dark green leaves are big and bold, divided like fingers into five or seven leaflets. In autumn, spine-covered green fruits drop from the tree and reveal lustrous, chestnut brown nuts. Leaves turn yellow-brown in early fall. **Zones 5 to 7.**

CULTIVARS

'Briotii' has 10-inch-tall, deep rosy red flowers and matures as a smaller tree. 'Fort McNair' has dark pink flowers with yellow throats and resists leaf scorch and leaf blotch. 'O'Neil Red' produces larger (10- to 12-inch-tall), brighter red flowers. 'Plantierensis' has intense rose pink flowers with yellow throats and does not set fruit, so it is less messy.

A. glabra

a. GLAY-bruh. OHIO BUCKEYE. Ohio buckeye is a round-headed native tree with ascending branches that grows to 30 feet tall and inhabits moist areas. Its bright green, 6-inch-wide, five-fingered leaves appear in early spring before most other plants start growing and change color earlier than most trees in fall, turning bright to golden yellow or orange. The slender, 6-inch-tall, greenish yellow flower clusters bloom in mid-spring. Prickly fruits are typical of the family. This adaptable tree has a rugged character with furrowed, corky, gray bark. Makes an outstanding shade tree for extremely cold areas of the Midwest and Mountain States. Adapts well to naturalistic sites and moist areas. Plant small specimens, as this taprooted tree may be difficult to transplant. From midwestern North America. **Zones 3 to 8.**

CULTIVARS AND SIMILAR SPECIES

'Homestead' has spectacular, long-lasting, orange-red fall color. *A. flava* (*A. octandra*; yellow buckeye) is very similar but grows to 80 feet tall and is an elegant tree. It has glossy, green, disease-resistant leaves and spectacular red-orange fall color; 6-inch-tall spires of creamy yellow flowers; and fruits with smooth husks; **Zones 3 to 8.**

A. hippocastanum

a. hip-oh-kas-TAY-num. COMMON HORSE CHESTNUT. This upright or oval tree grows 50 to 75 feet tall and has down-swept branches crowned with spectacular 12-inch-tall candles of creamy, red-blotched flowers in late spring and early summer. The coarse-textured leaves may be 10 inches across and are divided into seven fingerlike leaflets. Fall color is yellowish. Spine-covered, brown fruits drop to reveal glossy, reddish brown nuts. From Europe. **Zones 4 to 8.**

CULTIVARS

'Baumannii' has long-lasting double flowers that do not produce nuts, so it is less messy.

A. parviflora

a. par-vih-FLOR-uh. BOTTLE-BRUSH BUCKEYE. This southern U.S. native shrub spreads so wide — 15 feet compared with a 9- to 12-foot height — that one plant is about all any garden can handle. In a large space, one is a hedge all by itself. The palmately compound leaves have five or seven leaflets up to 9 inches long that turn bright yellow in autumn. The white cylinder flowers, set off by pink stamens and red anthers, are borne in upright clusters up to 1 foot high, appearing in late summer. In warm areas it develops smooth brown fruits. Can be pruned to the ground if desired. **Zones 5 to 8.**

A. pavia

a. paw-VEE-uh. RED BUCKEYE. This multitrunked, round-headed native is a lovely sight when in bloom in spring. It grows to 25 feet tall, with neat, bold-textured, glossy green leaves that sprout very early. In mid- to late spring, 4- to 8-inch-tall spires of slender flowers, which vary from coral pink to bright red, adorn the branches. These tubular blooms attract hummingbirds. Fruit husks are smooth, not spiny, and contain orange-brown nuts. Use red buckeye in a woodland or naturalistic garden or as a small ornamental in a yard. Or mass it as a screen. It does not tolerate drought well. From midwestern and southeastern North America. **Zones 6 to 9.**

Agapanthus

ag-uh-PAN-thus. Lily family, Liliaceae.

Although commonly called lilies-of-the-Nile, the ten species of *Agapanthus* hail from southern Africa, not along the Nile. They are tender perennials, some evergreen, that produce thick, fleshy roots and bold clumps of basal, strap-shaped leaves. Striking, rounded umbels of trumpet-shaped blue, blue-violet, or white flowers appear on erect, leafless stalks above the foliage in summer. The individual flowers may be tubular, bell, or trumpet shaped and consist of six petal-like tepals.

HOW TO GROW

Give agapanthus full sun and fertile, well-drained, evenly moist soil. *Agapanthus* species are hardy perennials from at least **Zone 9 south**; some hybrids, especially deciduous ones, are hardy to **Zone 6** with protection. For plants overwintered outdoors, well-drained soil (sandy soil is ideal) and a consistent cover of mulch are essential. Where they are not hardy, grow these striking plants in large containers or tubs either set on terraces or sunk to the rim in the soil. Or plant clumps in the ground and dig them each fall for overwintering. They bloom best when the roots are slightly crowded. Feed pot-grown plants monthly in early summer until flower buds appear. Water regularly when plants are growing and

Agapanthus hybrid

flowering actively, but gradually withhold water in fall and keep them nearly dry over winter. Overwinter them in a bright, cool (40° to 50°F) spot and water sparingly until active growth resumes in spring. Propagate by dividing the clumps, removing offsets, or sowing seeds. Repot or divide in late winter or early spring as necessary.

A. africanus

a. af-rih-KAH-nus. AFRICAN LILY. Evergreen, clump-forming 2- to 3-foot-tall species that spreads from 1¹/₂ to 2 feet. Bears rounded 6- to 12-inch-wide umbels of dark purple-blue flowers in late summer. Individual blooms are trumpet shaped and 1 to 2 inches long. **Zones 9 to 11**.

A. campanulatus

a. cam-pah-nue-LAY-tus. Deciduous, clump-forming 2- to 4-foot-tall species that spreads from 1¹/₂ to 2 feet. Bears rounded 4- to 8-inch-wide umbels of bell-shaped flowers that are pale to dark purplish blue and ³/₄ to 1¹/₂ inches long. 'Albovittatus' bears white-striped leaves. **Zones 7 to 10**.

A. hybrids

Species and hybrids ranging from 1 to 4 feet in height are available. 'Peter Pan' is a heavy-blooming dwarf cultivar that reaches 18 inches. 'Bressingham White' and 'Snowy Owl' bear white flowers. Headbourne Hybrids have pale blue to violet flowers and are reportedly hardy to **Zone 6**. 'Storm Cloud' bears especially dark purple-blue flowers. Tender perennials, hardy from **Zones 6 to 10**, depending on the selection.

Agastache

ag-ah-STACK-ee. Mint family, Lamiaceae.

Square stems, ovate aromatic leaves, and erect clusters of small, two-lipped flowers characterize the 20 or so species of giant hyssops, also called Mexican hyssops. A few are hardy and suitable for perennial plantings in **Zones 4 and 5**. Several species are hardy from **Zone 7 south** (to 6 with protection). All can be grown as annuals.

HOW TO GROW

Give giant hyssops full sun or very light shade and rich, well-drained soil for best results. Grow them in the ground where they are hardy, but container culture is a good op-

Agastache foeniculum

tion in areas where they are not. They are easy to grow from seeds sown indoors 8 to 10 weeks before the last spring frost date. Germination takes 2 to 4 weeks at 55° to 60°F. For quicker results, and to propagate many of the cultivars, take cuttings or divide plants in spring. To overwinter the plants indoors, take cuttings in late summer.

A. barberi

a. BAR-ber-eye. Bushy 2-foot plants with fragrant, oval leaves. Loose spikes of red-purple flowers from midsummer to fall. 'Tutti-Frutti', with raspberry red flowers, is a popular cultivar. Hardy from **Zone 6 south**, or grow as tender perennial or annual.

A. cana

a. CAY-nuh. WILD HYSSOP, HUMMINGBIRD MINT, MOSQUITO PLANT. Well-branched 2- to 3-foot-tall plant with aromatic leaves and loose 1-foot-long spikes of pink or rose-purple flowers from late summer to fall. **Zones 5 to 10**.

A. foeniculum

a. foe-NIK-yew-lum. ANISE HYSSOP. Anise-scented, 3- to 5-foot plants. Spikes of blue flowers with violet bracts from midsummer to fall. Self-sows. Hardy from **Zone 6 south**, or grow as tender perennial or annual.

A. mexicana

a. mex-ih-KAN-uh. MEXICAN GIANT HYSSOP. Lemon-scented foliage on 2- to 3-foot plants. Spikes of rose-red flowers in mid- to late summer. Hardy from **Zone 7 south**, or grow as tender perennial or annual.

Ageratum

ah-jer-AY-tum. Aster family, Asteraceae.

One member of this group of 40 annuals, perennials, and shrubs from the warmer reaches of North and South America is a popular annual bedding plant. All bear rounded clusters of small, fluffy, buttonlike flowers.

HOW TO GROW

Ageratums thrive in full sun or light shade and rich, moist, well-drained soil. In areas with long, hot summers, partial shade is best. Sow seeds indoors 6 to 8 weeks before the last spring frost date. Seeds can be sown outdoors after frost once the soil is warm, but the seedlings are easily swamped by weeds. When sowing, just press the tiny seeds into the soil surface, as they need light to germinate. Germination takes about 2 weeks

at 70° to 75°F. In areas with mild winters (Zone 9 south), plant in late summer for fall to early-winter bloom. Water during dry weather. Use ageratums as edging plants, in mixed plantings, and as cut flowers. The flowers attract butterflies.

A. houstonianum

a. hous-toe-nee-AN-um. AGERATUM, FLOSS FLOWER. Compact, mound-forming annual with oval leaves that have heart-shaped bases. Lavender-blue, lilac, white, or pink flowers. Many cultivars are available. Dwarf types, from 6 to 8 inches tall, are ideal for edging, including lavender 'Blue Danube' and the Swing and Hawaii Series plants, which come in lavender, pink, or white. 'Blue Horizon', to 18 inches, is a good cut flower and, along with midsize cultivars such as 'Blue Mink', to 12 inches, also well suited for mixed plantings. Warm-weather annual.

Agrostemma

ah-gro-STEM-mah. Pink family, Caryophyllaceae.

Agrostemma contains two to four species of annuals native to poor, dry soil. They have linear to lance-shaped leaves covered with white hairs and solitary, trumpet-shaped, five-petaled flowers. One species is commonly grown.

HOW TO GROW

Select a site in full sun and poor to average, well-drained soil. Sow seeds in early spring while light frost is still possible, several weeks before the last spring frost date, or in late summer or fall in drifts outdoors where the plants are to

Ageratum houstonianum 'Blue Horizon'

Agrostemma githago

Ajania pacifica

grow. Germination takes 2 to 3 weeks. Space closely — at 3 to 4 inches — to help plants support one another, or use pea stakes to keep them erect. Another option is interplanting with shrubs, sturdier annuals, or perennials. Deadheading prolongs bloom. Plants self-sow.

A. githago

a. geh-THAH-go. CORN COCKLE. Gray-green leaves on 2- to 3-foot plants. Showy, 2-inch-wide, magenta to cerise-pink flowers. 'Milas', also sold as 'Rose Queen', is most common. This species has poisonous seeds and is an agricultural weed in some areas. The blooms are attractive to bees and make fine cut flowers. Cool-weather annual.

Ajania

ah-JAN-ee-ah. Aster family, Asteraceae.

The 30 species of *Ajania*, native from central Asia to the Pacific coast of Siberia, were once classified in the genus *Chrysanthemum*. Ajanias are perennials, subshrubs, and shrubs. Foliage is deciduous and lobed or toothed. When crushed, the leaves are fragrant to malodorous, depending on one's interpretation of the complex aromatics. Flowers are clusters of attractive yellow buttons. The generic name commemorates a site in Siberia.

HOW TO GROW

Grow ajanias in full sun to very light shade in poor to average, well-drained soil, or their stems will become leggy and lax. Wet soil in winter is fatal. Ajanias form sprawling masses up to 3 feet across. Plants will become bushier if you severely prune them back in early spring. Flowers bloom in mid- to late fall and help close the season in the garden. Propagate by division in spring or from seeds.

A. pacifica

a. pah-SIFF-ih-kuh. GOLD-AND-SILVER CHRYSANTHEMUM. Formerly *Chrysanthemum pacificum*. Shrubby to mounding 1-foot-tall species spreading by runners to form 3-foot-wide mounds of handsome silver-edged leaves. Bears branched clusters of golden buttonlike flower heads in fall. In the North, plants may not bloom but are still grown for their attractive foliage. **Zones 5 to 9.**

Ajuga

ah-JEW-guh. Mint family, Lamiaceae.

Ajuga species, also called bugleweeds or just plain bugle, are vigorous perennials usually grown

Ajuga reptans

as ground covers for their showy foliage as well as their short, showy spikes of tiny, densely packed, two-lipped flowers. Flowers appear in spring and early summer and range from cobalt blue to bluish purple, as well as pink and white. Most ajugas — there are about 40 species in the genus — have green, spoon-shaped, somewhat spinachlike leaves that are evergreen or semi-evergreen and borne in dense rosettes. Many cultivars have been selected for their handsome variegated leaves, and gardeners treasure these ground-hugging plants more for their foliage and carpeting habit than for their flowers.

HOW TO GROW

While ajugas grow in full sun to full shade, a site with light to partial shade is best. Well-drained, evenly moist, average to rich soil is fine. Be sure to consider the speed at which the plants spread when selecting a site. *A. reptans* spreads via fast-growing stolons, making it a terrific ground cover in the right site or an invasive weed in the wrong one. To keep spreading species in check, install an edging strip between the lawn and the garden. Trimming off wayward stolons also helps. Propagate by dividing the clumps anytime from spring to fall or by potting up individual rosettes of leaves. Or take

Ajuga reptans 'Variegata'

root cuttings from the stolons (cut just below a node). Ajugas are seldom grown from seed because the cultivars must be propagated by cuttings or division.

A. genevensis

a. jen-eh-VEN-sis. BLUE BUGLEWEED, GENEVA BUGLEWEED. A 6- to 12-inch-tall species that spreads gradually by rhizomes to form 1¹/₂-foot-wide clumps. Bears 2- to 4-inch-long spikes of indigo blue flowers in spring. 'Alba' bears white flowers; 'Pink Beauty', pink ones. **Zones 4 to 8.**

A. pyramidalis

a. peer-ah-mih-DAL-iss. PYRAMID BUGLEWEED, UPRIGHT BUGLEWEED. Compact 6- to 10-inch-tall species that forms 1¹/₂- to 2-foot-wide mounds of dark green leaves. Plants produce stolons but are fairly restrained spreaders because the stolons appear only at the end of the season. This species bears dense 4- to 6-inch-tall spikes of purple-blue flowers in spring and early summer. 'Metallica Crispa', a 4- to 6-inch cultivar, has handsome, crinkled, dark green leaves flushed with metallic bronze-purple. **Zones 3 to 8.**

A. reptans

a. REP-tanz. COMMON BUGLEWEED, CARPET BUGLEWEED. Fast-spreading species with ground-hugging rosettes of spoon-shaped leaves that quickly spreads to 3 feet or more. Bears 4- to 6-inch-tall spikes of violet-blue flowers in late spring. 'Catlin's Giant' and 'Jungle Beauty' are large-leaved, vigorous spreaders ideal for covering large areas. Variegated cultivars spread but are less vigorous than green-leaved selections. These include 'Burgundy Glow', with white, pink, and green leaves, as well as 'Silver Beauty', with gray-green leaves edged in white. **Zones 3 to 9.**

Akebia

ah-KEE-bee-ah. Lardizabala family, Lardizabialaceae.

Commonly called chocolate vines or simply akebias, members of this genus are vigorous, woody, twining vines from East Asia. Botanists recognize about five species, which are deciduous, evergreen, or semievergreen, depending on the climate in which they are grown. Akebias have handsome palmate leaves with three, five, or seven

Akebia quinata

leaflets. They bear racemes of flowers in spring. Male and female flowers are borne separately, with female flowers borne toward the base of each cluster and the smaller male flowers toward the tip. The shallowly cup-shaped blooms lack true petals but have three showy petal-like sepals. Fruits are sausage shaped and edible, but plants are self-sterile and often do not produce fruit in cultivation. (Two genetically distinct plants of the same species are required for cross-pollination; two plants of the same clone will be self-sterile.) Hand pollination is best to ensure fruit set.

HOW TO GROW
Plant akebias in full sun or partial shade. Give them a spot with average to rich soil that is evenly moist but well drained. Established plants tolerate both drought and shade. These are fast-growing, vigorous vines that can become very invasive. Train them on arbors, large trellises, or fences or up trees. Akebias also make very fast-growing, dense ground covers. Prune plants as necessary in spring or in early summer after flowering to keep them in bounds. Propagate akebias by stem cuttings taken in summer, by layering in spring or fall, or from seed.

A. quinata
a. qwih-NAY-tah. FIVELEAF AKEBIA. A very vigorous, 20- to 40-foot-tall vine that climbs by twining stems. Plants feature handsome blue-green leaves and clusters of fragrant brown-purple flowers in spring. In the North, this species is deciduous, although foliage remains on the plant until early winter; plants are semi-

evergreen in southern zones. Flowers are followed by purplish, 4-inch-long fruits in fall. **Zones 4 to 8.**

Albizia

al-BIZZ-ee-uh. Pea family, Fabaceae.

This large genus contains about 150 deciduous trees and shrubs, most native to tropical and subtropical areas of Africa, Asia, and Australia. Leaves are alternate and cut into lacy leaflets. Flowers have long stamens and are arranged in fluffy heads. Only one species is commonly grown in North American gardens.

HOW TO GROW
Plant in full sun and well-drained, acid or alkaline soil. Tolerates road salt, drought, and urban and sea-

Albizia julibrissin

shore conditions. Numerous seedlings can be a weed problem in Zone 7 and warmer. Trees are weak wooded and subject to storm damage. Remove deadwood and shorten wide-spreading branches in spring. Highly susceptible to mimosa webworm, which can defoliate the tree, and mimosa wilt, which can kill the tree suddenly; grow resistant cultivars.

A. julibrissin
a. jew-lee-BRIS-in. SILK TREE, MIMOSA. This cold-hardy species grows rapidly into a widespreading, flat-topped, 30-foot-tall specimen with horizontal branches, lacy leaves, and a tropical air. Leaves, which don't emerge until late spring, are 12 to 18 inches long and dissected into tiny leaflets, which fold up at night or when touched. Leaves do not change color in autumn but remain bright green until frost. Powder puff–like flowers cover the tree in mid- to late summer, their color varying from pale to intense pink. Dark brown, 6-inch-long seedpods develop after the flowers. They remain on the tree all winter and may be unsightly. Silk tree has smooth, light brown bark and is often multitrunked. Use as a short-lived lawn or patio tree or near the seashore to cast light shade. Or arrange in a border for an exotic look. This tree is especially valued for its late-season flowers. From the Mideast, Japan, China, and India. **Zones 6 to 9.**

CULTIVARS
'Rosea' has very deep pink flowers. Wilt-resistant cultivars for Zones 7 to 9 include 'Charlotte', with light pink flowers, and 'Tyron', with deep pink ones.

Alcea

AL-see-ah. Mallow family, Malvaceae.

While there are about 60 species of biennials and short-lived perennials in *Alcea* (formerly *Althaea*), only a handful have found their way to gardens. Common hollyhock (*A. rosea*), by far the most popular, is grown for its showy, erect bloom stalks covered with colorful, funnel-shaped flowers that rise above mounds of large, lobed leaves. The flowers attract both butterflies and hummingbirds.

HOW TO GROW
Full sun to light shade and average, well-drained soil suit most *Alcea* species. A site protected from wind is best to help minimize the need to stake. For the showiest display, as well as to curb problems with rust, a common fungal disease, grow these plants as biennials. Some cultivars can be grown as annuals provided they are started indoors in late winter, 6 to 8 weeks before the last spring frost. To grow them as biennials or perennials, sow indoors or out. Once established, hollyhocks survive dry conditions quite well, but for top-notch performance, water deeply in dry weather. Plants growing in rich soil may need staking. To grow hollyhocks as biennials, pull up 2-year-old plants after they have flowered and replace them. Plants self-sow.

A. rosea
a. ROE-zee-uh. COMMON HOLLYHOCK. Erect stems of single or double, 2- to 4-inch-wide blooms in yellow, white, pink, and red.

Alcea rosea 'Chatter's Double'

Alchemilla mollis

Most plants grow 4 to 5 feet tall or taller, but there are dwarf cultivars, such as 2- to 3-foot 'Majorette'. 'Chatter's Double' and 'Powder Puffs' are popular double-flowered forms. 'Nigra' has maroon-black blooms. Single hollyhocks such as 'Country Romance' are ideal for cottage gardens. Short-lived perennial grown as a biennial.

Alchemilla

al-kah-MILL-uh. Rose family, Rosaceae.

Grown as much for their handsome foliage as for their flowers, *Alchemilla* species are commonly called lady's mantles. They are popular ground covers. About 250 species belong to the genus, most of which produce woody rhizomes and lobed, rounded, or kidney-shaped leaves that often are softly hairy. The individual greenish to yellow-green flowers are tiny (from $1/16$ to $1/8$ inch across), but they are borne in large branched clusters that have a frothy appearance and are lovely in flower arrangements.

HOW TO GROW
Select a site in partial shade with rich, evenly moist, well-drained soil. A spot with morning sun and afternoon shade is ideal. In the North, plants can be grown in full sun but will need constantly moist soil for best growth. Heat is a problem in the South (Zones 7 and 8), so give them partial to full shade and make sure the soil remains moist. Water during dry weather, although established plants are fairly drought tolerant. Cut tattered foliage to the ground in midsummer if necessary and water deeply; fresh new leaves will appear in fall. Plants self-sow, and since seeds are produced without pollination, the seedlings are identical to the parent plants. Propagate by division in spring or fall or from seed.

A. alpina
a. al-PIE-nuh. ALPINE LADY'S MANTLE. Ground-hugging 6- to

Alchemilla mollis

8-inch-tall species forming 1- to 2-foot-wide mounds of deeply lobed leaves edged with silver hairs. Bears loose sprays of yellow-green flowers in summer. **Zones 3 to 7.**

A. erythropoda
a. air-ith-roe-POE-duh. Clump-forming 8- to 12-inch-tall species with 1-foot-wide mounds of lobed, sharp-toothed, blue-green leaves. Bears clusters of yellow-green flowers from late spring to summer. **Zones 3 to 7.**

A. mollis
a. MOLL-iss. COMMON LADY'S MANTLE. A 1- to 2-foot-tall perennial forming 2-foot-wide mounds of handsome, pleated, lobed leaves covered with tiny soft hairs. Bears frothy, somewhat sprawling clusters of tiny chartreuse flowers from late spring to early summer. **Zones 4 to 7.**

Allium

AL-ee-um. Lily family, Liliaceae.

While the best-known members of this genus undoubtedly are onions, garlic, leeks, and shallots, *Allium* also contains a wealth of ornamental plants suitable for the flower garden. Commonly called ornamental onions or simply alliums, these bulbs bear showy, rounded flower clusters called umbels atop hollow, unbranched stems. The umbels range from 1-inch pompons to huge 5-inch balls and are carried above the leaves. They can consist of many densely

packed flowers that form a round inflorescence or may have fewer, more loosely arranged blooms. The individual flowers are small and starry or bell shaped with six petal-like tepals. Leaves, which are grassy or straplike and onion scented when bruised, are borne at the base of the plant and often fade as or just after the flowers open.

Alliums grow from tunicate bulbs, although many species have very small bulbs or ones that are barely developed and are borne on a horizontal rhizome. Other species produce bulbs clustered on slender rhizomes. The species with poorly developed bulbs are sold in pots and grown like herbaceous perennials rather than like typical bulbs. Ornamental species with both well- and poorly developed bulbs are listed here. About 700 species belong to this large genus.

HOW TO GROW
A site in full sun with well-drained soil is the rule for most alliums. They grow well in a range of soils — from poor soil to rich, fertile loam — provided it is well drained. They also tolerate relatively dry soil. Plant dormant bulbs in fall with the tops at a depth of about three times the diameter of the bulb. Plant pot-grown clumps of alliums in spring or fall, setting the plants at the same depth at which they were growing in the pot. Tall, nonspreading species look best when planted in clumps with the bulbs fairly close together — space *A. aflatunense* bulbs about 6 inches apart; *A. giganteum*, 1 foot apart. *A. cristophii* also is best spaced 1 foot apart. Space smaller species about 3 to 6 inches apart and container-grown plants a distance of about half their height.

Many species have foliage that dies back just before or after flowering, and the dying foliage can be very unattractive — plus the plants leave a hole to fill in the

Allium 'Globemaster'

garden. Solve this problem either by interspersing the alliums among clumps of annuals or low-growing perennials, shrubs, or ground covers, or by simply planting the alliums behind their companions. Don't cut the foliage back before it yellows completely — it is making food for next year's blooms.

Divide plants in spring or fall if clumps become overcrowded. Propagate by removing offsets from the parent bulbs or dividing the clumps just after they finish flowering. Some species produce bulbils in the flower heads. These are small bulbs that can be planted like seeds and will yield blooming-size plants sooner than seeds would. Bulbils are genetically identical to their parents and can be used to propagate cultivars. Species alliums can be grown from fresh seeds sown outdoors in summer or fall as soon as they are ripe, and some species, including *A. cristophii*, self-sow. Seeds yield blooming-size plants in about 3 years.

A. aflatunense
a. ah-flah-too-NEN-see. PERSIAN ONION. Asian species with rounded 1- to $2^{1}/2$-inch-wide bulbs. Bears round $4^{1}/2$-inch-wide umbels of many densely packed, red-violet flowers on 2- to 3-foot-tall stems. Leaves wither as the flowers open. Seed heads are ornamental. The hybrid 'Purple Sensation', with violet blooms, is usually listed here. Blooms in early summer. **Zones 4 to 8.**

A. atropurpureum
a. ah-tro-pur-PUR-ee-um. Medium-size species with small round bulbs and $2^{1}/2$-inch-wide umbels of densely packed, starry dark purple to purple-maroon flowers on 20-inch-tall stems in summer. **Zones 3 to 8.**

A. caeruleum
a. see-RUE-lee-um. BLUE GLOBE ONION, NODDING ONION. Siberian species with small rounded bulbs and 2-inch-wide

Allium cernuum

Allium karataviense

umbels of 30 to 50 densely packed, starry dark blue flowers on 1- to 2-foot stems in early summer. Requires very well drained soil and a hot site for best results. **Zones 3 to 8**.

A. carinatum
a. kare-in-AY-tum. KEELED GARLIC. Medium-size species with very small egg-shaped bulbs. Bears loose 2-inch-wide umbels of 25 to 30 bell-shaped purple flowers on 1- to 2-foot-tall stems. Usually produces bulbils in the flower clusters. *A. carinatum* ssp. *pulchellum* (also listed as *A. pulchellum*) bears 2¹/₂-inch-wide umbels of reddish violet blooms on 1- to 1¹/₂-foot-tall stalks that lack bulbils. Blooms in midsummer. **Zones 5 to 8**.

A. cernuum
a. SIR-new-um. NODDING ONION, WILD ONION. Native North American species with clusters of very small oval bulbs on short rhizomes. Bears 2¹/₂-inch-wide umbels of from 25 to 40 rose-purple, pink, or white flowers on 1¹/₂- to 2-foot stems in early summer. Both the umbel and the individual flowers are nodding. Foliage remains green until late summer. Grows in shade or sun and tolerates heavy (but not wet) soil or dry sandy conditions. Forms large handsome clumps and naturalizes easily. Self-sows. **Zones 4 to 9**.

A. cristophii
a. krih-STOF-ee-eye. STAR OF PERSIA. Formerly *A. albopilosum*. Striking species with small round bulbs and attractive gray-green leaves that wither as the flowers open. Bears huge ball-like 8- to 12-inch-wide umbels of about 100 starry silvery purple

flowers on 1- to 2-foot stalks in summer. Seed heads are showy, and plants self-sow. **Zones 4 to 8**.

A. giganteum
a. jy-GAN-tee-um. GIANT ONION. Striking, tall species with rounded 2- to 3-inch-wide bulbs. Produces dense, round 4- to 5-inch-wide umbels of 50 to 100 starry rosy purple flowers on 3- to 5-foot-tall stalks. Leaves wither as the flowers open. Bulbs tend to be short-lived in the garden. 'White Giant' bears white flowers. Blooms in summer. **Zones 4 to 8**.

A. hybrids
Many excellent hybrid ornamental onions have been developed. All of the following grow from fully developed bulbs, bear round or nearly round umbels, and bloom in early summer: 'Gladiator' (*A. aflatunense × A. macleanii*), which bears 6- to 8-inch-wide umbels of many rose-violet flowers on 4- to 5-foot-tall stems; 'Globemaster' (*A. cristophii × A. macleanii*), with very long-lasting 10-inch-wide umbels of rich violet flowers on 2- to 3-foot-tall stems and handsome ornamental seed heads; 'Lucy Ball' (*A. aflatunense × A. macleanii*),

Allium moly

bearing 5-inch-wide umbels of 50 or more starry, dark lilac-purple blooms on 3-foot-stems; 'Mars' (*A. stipitatum × A. aflatunense*), bearing 6-inch umbels of red-purple flowers on 3-foot-tall stems; 'Mount Everest', with 6-inch-wide umbels of white flowers on 2- to 3-foot stems; and 'Rien Poortvliet', which bears 6- to 8-inch-wide umbels of rich purple flowers. **Zones 4 or 5 to 8**.

A. karataviense
a. kare-ah-tah-vee-EN-see. TURKISTAN ONION. Dwarf species with 1- to 2-inch-wide bulbs. The 6- to 10-inch-tall plants are grown as much for their foliage as for their flowers. The 4-inch-wide leaves are gray-green to gray-purple and reach 6 to 9 inches long. In early summer, plants bear up to 50 starry pale pink flowers in umbels that range from 3 to 5 or more inches across. Leaves remain attractive for a few weeks after the flowers fade. **Zones 5 to 9**.

A. moly
a. MOLL-ee. LILY LEEK, GOLDEN GARLIC. Charming medium-size species with 1-inch-wide bulbs and showy, loose 2-inch-wide umbels of 20 to 30 star-shaped golden yellow flowers in early summer on ¹/₂- to 1-foot-tall stalks. Needs very well drained soil that is nearly dry after flowering. Tolerates partial shade. Bulbs produce abundant offsets where happy and are good for naturalizing. 'Jeannine' bears 3-inch-wide umbels in early summer on 12- to 16-inch-stalks. **Zones 3 to 9**.

A. narcissiflorum
a. nar-sih-sih-FLOR-um. NARCISSUS ONION. Dwarf species that grows from very small bulbs clustered on a thickened rhizome. Produces pendent 1-inch-wide umbels

of six to ten flowers in summer on 6- to 12-inch-tall stalks. Individual blooms are bell shaped and pinkish purple. Bears blue-green leaves that last through the season. **Zones 4 to 8**.

A. neapolitanum
a. nee-ah-pol-ih-TAH-num. NAPLES ONION, DAFFODIL GARLIC. Formerly *A. cowanii*. Dwarf species that grows from ³/₄-inch-wide bulbs. Bears loose 2-inch-wide umbels of 20 to 30 fragrant white flowers in spring on 6- to 12-inch-tall stems. Leaves wither as the flowers open. **Zones 6 to 10**.

A. nigrum
a. NYE-grum. BLACK ONION. Formerly *A. multibulbosum*. Medium-size species growing from 2-inch-wide bulbs. Produces somewhat flattened 3- to 4-inch-wide umbels of 20 to 30 or more cup-shaped, creamy white flowers on 1¹/₂- to 3-foot-tall stems in early summer. Each flower has a dark green to black ovary in its center, and umbels sometimes contain bulbils. Seed heads are ornamental. **Zones 6 to 10**.

A. oreophilum
a. or-ee-OFF-ih-lum. Formerly *A. ostrowskianum*. Dwarf species growing from very small bulbs that produce loose 1¹/₂-inch-wide umbels of 10 to 15 bell-shaped pinkish purple flowers in early summer on 2- to 8-inch stalks. Leaves wither as the flowers open. **Zones 4 to 9**.

A. rosenbachianum
a. roe-sen-bak-ee-AH-num. A tall species growing from round bulbs less than 1 inch wide. Produces 4-inch-wide umbels of more than 50 star-shaped purple flowers in early summer on 3- to 4-foot-tall stalks. Leaves wither as the flowers open. Seed heads are ornamental. 'Album' bears white flowers. **Zones 4 to 10**.

A. roseum
a. ROE-zee-um. ROSY GARLIC. Medium-size species growing from very small bulbs. Bears loose 1- to 3-inch-wide umbels of 5 to as many as 30 rose pink flowers on 1- to 1¹/₂-foot-tall stems in late spring. 'Grandiflorum' bears 4-inch-wide umbels. **Zones 5 to 8**.

A. schoenoprasum
a. show-no-PRAZ-um. CHIVES. Mounding species producing clumps of long, very narrow,

poorly developed bulbs on short rhizomes. Has edible round leaves that remain green through the summer and are evergreen in warm climates. Bears dense 1-inch-wide cloverlike umbels of 30 or more rosy pink flowers in summer. Clumps reach 1 to 2 feet and spread as far. Tolerates light shade. Cut plants — foliage and all — to the ground after flowering to encourage reblooming and fresh foliage and to discourage reseeding. **Zones 3 to 9.**

A. schubertii
a. shoo-BER-tee-eye. Striking species that grows from a 1¹/₄- to 1¹/₂-inch-wide bulb. Bears huge round umbels that range from 9 to 12 inches in diameter on 1- to 2-foot-tall stems. Pale purple individual flowers are loosely arranged on stalks of different lengths and ¹/₂ inch wide. Leaves wither as the flowers open. **Zones 5 to 10.**

A. senescens
a. seh-NESS-ens. Dwarf species bearing small bulbs clustered on short stout rhizomes. Bears strap-shaped leaves that are evergreen to 25°F and 1-inch-wide umbels of 20 to 30 mauve-pink flowers in mid- to late summer. Plants reach 6 to 12 inches in height and spread slowly into clumps. *A. senescens* ssp. *montanum* var. *glaucum* is grown for its clumps of attractive, twisted silver-blue leaves and pink flowers. **Zones 5 to 9.**

A. sphaerocephalon
a. sphare-oh-SEFF-ah-lon. DRUM-STICK CHIVES. Taller species, reaching 2 to 3 feet, that grows from small bulbs. Produces very dense (nearly solid) 1-inch-wide

Allium triquetrum

umbels of 30 to as many as 100 bell-shaped flowers in midsummer that vary from green to purple or purplish maroon. Umbels may contain bulbils. **Zones 4 to 8.**

A. stellatum
a. steh-LAH-tum. PRAIRIE ON-ION. Native North American wildflower growing from rounded bulbs and producing leaves that die back before the flowers appear. Bears rounded 1- to 2-inch-wide umbels of cup-shaped rose pink flowers from midsummer to fall. **Zones 5 to 9.**

A. tanguticum
a. tan-GOO-tih-kum. LAVENDER GLOBE LILY. Clumping species with small rounded bulbs on branching rhizomes. Bears lavender-blue 2-inch-wide umbels on 2-foot-tall stalks in midsummer. Foliage remains attractive all season. 'Blue Skies' produces light lavender-blue umbels over a long season. 'Summer Beauty' bears dark lavender-blue umbels on 1¹/₂-foot stems. **Zones 4 to 9.**

A. thunbergii
a. thun-BER-jee-eye. Dwarf species with clumps of very small bulbs on branched rhizomes. Bears 1- to 1¹/₂-inch-wide umbels of rose-purple flowers in fall. Plants reach about 8 inches in height, spread slowly to form small clumps, and have grassy foliage that remains green all season. 'Ozawa' bears rosy violet flowers. **Zones 4 to 8.**

A. triquetrum
a. try-KEH-trum. THREE-CORNERED LEEK. Medium-size 8- to 15-inch-tall species growing from small bulbs and producing three-cornered stems and linear leaves. In late spring or early summer, it bears nodding 1- to 3-inch-wide umbels of 5 to 15 bell-shaped, lightly scented white flowers striped with green. Spreads quickly and is good for naturalizing. **Zones 5 to 9.**

A. tuberosum
a. too-ber-OH-sum. GARLIC CHIVES. A species popular in herb and flower gardens alike that grows from poorly developed bulbs clustered on branched rhizomes and forms good-sized clumps. Bears rounded 2-inch-wide umbels of fragrant, starry white flowers on 2-foot plants from late summer to fall. Foliage is edible and remains green all season. Best planted in rich, evenly moist soil. Self-sows with abandon. Deadheading prevents excessive self-seeding; plants can become troublesome weeds. **Zones 4 to 8.**

A. unifolium
a. yew-nih-FOE-lee-um. Formerly *A. murrayanum*. Wildflower native to the Pacific Northwest with small bulbs that are not on rhizomes, but that produces bulblets on short rhizomes. Bears rounded 2- to 2¹/₂-inch-wide umbels of about 20 bell-shaped pink to purplish pink flowers in late spring or early summer on 1- to 1¹/₂-foot-tall stalks. Grassy gray-green leaves wither as the flowers open. Best in moist soil. **Zones 5 to 9.**

A. ursinum
a. ur-SYE-num. RAMSONS, BEAR'S GARLIC, WOOD GARLIC. Fairly dwarf species producing small rounded bulbs on branched rhizomes. Bears flattened 2-inch-wide umbels of 15 to 20 white flowers on 6- to 18-inch-tall stalks in spring. Thrives in partial shade. **Zones 5 to 8.**

Alnus
ALL-nus. Birch family, Betulaceae.

Native to North America and Europe, this genus of deciduous trees and shrubs, commonly called alders, contains 60 species. Leaves are alternate and simple in outline, with coarse teeth along their edges. Flowers are conspicuous male catkins and inconspicuous female catkins that bloom from stalked buds in late winter before the leaves emerge. Female catkins ripen to small, woody cones. Trees in this genus are among the few not in the pea family (Fabaceae) that are able to fix nitrogen from the soil and thus grow readily in poor-soil areas.

HOW TO GROW
Plant in full sun to partial shade. Alders adapt to most soils, even sandy or gravelly sites. Although best in moist to wet sites, they tolerate occasional dryness. They also grow in infertile soil, since they can fix nitrogen. Usually pest-free, but leaf miners and tent caterpillars can be pests.

Allium senescens

Alnus glutinosa

A. glutinosa

a. glue-TIN-oh-suh. BLACK ALDER, EUROPEAN ALDER. This fast-growing tree, which has an irregular oval or pyramidal shape, grows 40 to 50 feet tall and 25 to 40 feet wide. Like its birch relatives, it can bend under the weight of snow without snapping. Leaves are 4 inches long, glossy, dark green, and oval, with toothed undulate margins. They remain green until frost. Young twigs and unfolding leaves are gummy, accounting for the species name. Four-inch-long, yellowish male catkins liven up the tree in late winter before the leaves unfold. Seedpods add a bit of winter interest. Trunk bark is glossy and dark brown, not black. This tree, which has naturalized in the United States, thrives in inhospitable wet sites or in areas that are periodically flooded. Use it as an urban specimen or as a woodland, streambank, or wetland tree; excellent in land reclamation projects. From Europe, northern Africa, and western Asia. **Zones 3 to 7.**

CULTIVARS AND SIMILAR SPECIES

'Aurea' has leaves that emerge yellow and mature to light green. 'Imperialis' has finely cut leaves. 'Pyramidalis' grows into a handsome, narrow pyramid. *A. incana* (gray alder) is similar, with light gray bark and downy, not gummy, shoots; tolerates dry sites in **Zones 2 to 6.**

Alocasia

al-oh-KASE-ee-uh. Arum family, Araceae.

Commonly called elephant's ear, *Alocasia* species are tender perennials that either are rhizomatous or grow from tuberous roots. About 70 species belong to the genus, all native to southern and Southeast Asia. Plants are grown for their large, showy, arrowhead-shaped leaves, which have prominent veins and often are marked with bronze, black, or violet-black. The flowers are relatively insignificant: like those of closely related *Colocasia* species as well as jack-in-the-pulpits *(Arisaema),* they consist of an inflorescence made up of many tiny flowers clustered on a central stalk, called a spadix, that is surrounded by a modified leaf, called a spathe. Contact with the sap may cause skin irritation, and all parts of the plant cause stomach upset if eaten. *Alocasia* species usually are grown in tropical climates or as greenhouse plants, but a few selections have begun to find their way into more northern gardens, where they add a lush, tropical effect during the warm summer months.

HOW TO GROW

Select a site in partial shade with deep, rich, evenly moist soil that is well drained. A sheltered spot is best, and protection from hot sun is essential. Plants thrive in heat

Alocasia 'Hilo Beauty'

and humidity and can be grown outdoors year-round in Zones 10 and 11. In the North, start small plants or tubers indoors before the last frost date, and keep in a warm (70° to 75°F) spot. Move the plants outdoors only after the weather is warm and settled and night temperatures do not dip below 60°F. Sink them into the soil, still in their pots. Keep the soil evenly moist during the growing season. To overwinter, bring the pots indoors and keep the plants in a warm (60°F minimum), humid spot. Keep the soil somewhat drier in winter when plants are resting; mist the foliage to maintain high humidity. Repot, as necessary, in spring. Propagate by dividing the fleshy rhizomes or separating the offsets in spring.

A. hybrids

A variety of hybrids with showy leaves are available. 'Black Velvet' has black leaves with silver veins. 'Hilo Beauty' bears green leaves mottled with cream (or light green). **Zones 10 and 11.**

A. macrorrhiza

a. mak-roe-RYE-zuh. GIANT TARO. A tropical species that can reach 15 feet high and spread to 8 feet or more but is smaller in the North. Bears glossy, arrow-shaped green leaves with leaf blades that range from 2 to 4 feet long. Flowers have a yellow-green spathe. Widely grown in the tropics for its edible rhizomes. 'Variegata' bears leaves blotched with cream, gray-green, and dark green. Plants remain evergreen if temperatures briefly dip to 29°F, and they are killed to the ground but return if exposed to cooler temperatures only for short stretches. **Zones 10 and 11.**

Alstroemeria

al-stro-MAIR-ee-uh. Lily family, Liliaceae.

Commonly known as Peruvian lily or lily-of-the-Incas, *Alstroemeria* species hail from mountainous regions and grasslands in South America. About 50 species make up the genus, all of which produce clumps of tubers or fleshy rhizomes and have thick, fleshy roots. The leaves are linear to lance shaped. Plants produce loose clusters of showy funnel-shaped flowers in summer. Each bloom has six petal-like tepals. Blooms are about 1¹⁄₂ inches long and range from 1¹⁄₂ to 4 inches wide.

HOW TO GROW

Give alstroemerias rich, moist, well-drained soil. In the North (Zones 5 and 6), plant them in full sun, preferably in a protected site such as at the base of a south-facing wall. From Zone 7 south, plant them in light shade. They do not tolerate the extremes of heat and cold characteristic of most gardens in North America and are best in areas with Mediterranean climates — with mild summers and winters. (They are commonly grown as cut flowers in California, for example.) When planting, set the tubers about 8 inches deep, and handle them carefully, as they are brittle and can break. Mulch annually in early summer with compost to keep the soil rich. In areas with hot summers, mulch also helps keep the soil cool and moist and prolongs bloom. Water regularly in dry weather. Deadheading prevents seed formation and directs the plant's energy toward the formation of next year's flowers. Plants resent being disturbed, so

Alstroemeria aurea

do not transplant or divide them unless absolutely necessary, or for propagation. New divisions can be very slow to establish. In the North, protect clumps over winter with a thick layer of coarse mulch such as evergreen boughs, coarse leaves, pine needles, or salt hay. Clumps can be dug for over-wintering indoors: pack them in moist peat moss and store them in boxes or paper bags in a cool (32° to 40°F), frost-free spot. Container-grown plants can be over-wintered dry in their containers.

A. aurea

a. AW-ree-uh. PERUVIAN LILY, LILY-OF-THE-INCAS. Formerly *A. aurantiaca*. A 2- to 3-foot-tall species, spreading to 1½ feet. Bears clusters of orange or yellow flowers with red-striped tepals in summer. 'Lutea' has yellow blooms spotted with brown. **Zones 7 to 10; to Zone 5 with winter protection.**

A. ligtu

a. LIG-too. PERUVIAN LILY, LILY-OF-THE-INCAS. A 1½- to 2-foot-tall species forming 2½-foot-wide clumps. Bears clusters of yellow flowers spotted and streaked with yellow, white, red, or purple in summer. Ligtu Hybrids come in a wide range of pastel shades, with blooms often marked with dark red or black. **Zones 7 to 10; to Zone 5 with winter protection.**

Amaranthus

am-ah-RAN-thus. Amaranth family, Amaranthaceae.

Amaranthus is a cosmopolitan genus comprising 60 species of annuals or short-lived perennials found in wastelands and tilled fields in mild and tropical regions around the globe. While many species are weedy — pigweed *(A. retroflexus)* belongs here — several bring brilliant foliage and/or exotic-looking flower clusters to the garden. They bear alternate leaves and erect or pendent clusters of tiny, densely packed, petalless flowers followed by small, bladder-like fruits.

HOW TO GROW

Plant amaranths in full sun to partial shade and evenly moist, average soil. Foliage types produce larger but less brilliantly colored leaves in rich soil. Sow seeds indoors 6 to 8 weeks before the last frost. Germination takes about a week at 70° to 75°F. Wait until after

Amaranthus tricolor

the last spring frost date, once the weather has settled and the soil has warmed up, to transplant. Outdoor sowing delays bloom but is practical in areas with long growing seasons — roughly from Zone 6 south: sow seeds outdoors after the last frost where plants are to grow. Water during dry weather to prolong flowering. Amaranths lend an exotic, tropical air to beds and borders. The flowers and foliage are effective from midsummer to frost. Plants self-sow.

A. caudatus

a. kaw-DAY-tus. LOVE-LIES-BLEEDING, TASSEL FLOWER. Pale green, ovate leaves on bushy, 3- to 5-foot plants. Showy, pendulous, rope- or tassel-like clusters of flowers at the tips of the stems and in the leaf axils. Some cultivars have red or reddish purple leaves. The seeds are edible, and this species is grown as a grain in portions of South America. The foliage also is edible and is used medicinally in some cultures. 'Love-Lies-Bleeding' bears blood red flower clusters up to 2 feet in length. 'Viridis' and 'Green Tails' have yellow-green

flowers. *A. cruentus*, commonly called prince's feather or purple amaranth, is a somewhat similar species with purplish green leaves and cylindrical flower clusters that are green blushed with red at first and ripen to red-brown, purple, or sometimes yellow. Warm-weather annual.

A. hypochondriacus

a. hi-poe-kon-dree-AY-kus. PRINCE'S FEATHER. Formerly *A. hybridus* ssp. *hypochondriacus*. Bushy, 3- to 4-foot plants with oblong- to lance-shaped, purple-green leaves. The erect, plumelike flower clusters reach 6 inches or more in length. 'Pygmy Torch' is a 1- to 1½-foot cultivar with maroon flowers. Warm-weather annual.

A. tricolor

a. TRY-kuh-lor. JOSEPH'S COAT. Showy, ovate leaves in shades of green, purple, flaming scarlet, and rich maroon on 1½- to 4½-foot plants. Also called Chinese spinach because the young leaves are edible fresh or cooked. Depending on the cultivar, the leaves also may be

marked with rose-pink, gold, yellow, or brown. Insignificant flowers. Cultivars include 'Aurora Yellow', which has a topknot of yellow leaves; 'Flaming Fountains', with narrow scarlet and bronze leaves; and 'Illumination', with bronze lower leaves and flaming red upper ones. Warm-weather annual.

× Amarcrinum

ah-mar-KRY-num. Amaryllis family, Amaryllidaceae.

This hybrid genus, the result of a cross between *Amaryllis belladonna* and *Crinum moorei*, contains a single species grown for its fragrant rose pink, trumpet-shaped flowers. The long-lived blooms are borne in late summer to early fall atop thick, leafless stems and are arranged in clusters, called umbels. Individual flowers have six petal-like tepals. The strap-shaped 1½- to 3-inch-wide leaves can reach 2 feet in length and are evergreen from about Zone 8 south. Plants grow from long-necked tunicate bulbs that are poisonous to rodents. Foliage and flowers also resist deer for the same reason. With time, plants divide to form clumps.

HOW TO GROW

Give plants full sun or partial shade with rich, well-drained soil. They require evenly moist conditions when actively growing from spring to fall and drier conditions when dormant in winter. In the North, grow them in large containers or tubs, where they can be planted with just the base of the bulb (about one-third of it) in the

Amaranthus hypochondriacus

× Amarcrinum memoria-corsii

soil. Give container-grown plants partial shade in summer and feed them weekly during the growing season. Overwinter the bulbs in their containers indoors in a cool (45° to 50°F nights), frost-free spot. While the plants are not growing actively, either keep the soil on the dry side (letting the leaves remain evergreen) or allow it to dry out completely and the leaves to wither away. Where hardy, the plants can be grown outdoors year-round: plant either in late summer or in spring, setting the bulbs with the noses just at the soil surface. Where marginally hardy, mulch them in late fall with evergreen boughs, salt hay, pine needles, or another coarse mulch. Propagate by separating offsets that appear at the base of the bulbs in early spring.

A. memoria-corsii

a. mem-OR-ee-uh-KOR-see-eye. Also listed as × *Crinodonna memoria-corsii*. Vigorous hybrid bearing umbels of 10 to as many as 16 fragrant 3- to 4-inch-wide flowers on 2- to 3-foot-tall stems. **Zones 8 to 10; to Zone 7 with winter protection.**

Amaryllis

am-ah-RILL-iss. Amaryllis family, Amaryllidaceae.

Amaryllis contains a single species, native to South Africa, that is grown for its showy, funnel-shaped blooms, which are borne in late summer and fall. The blooms are produced in umbels of 6 to 12 fragrant pink flowers atop fleshy, leafless stems. The individual flowers, which resemble lilies, have six petal-like tepals, or perianth lobes, that curve backward at the tips. Plants, which grow from a 2- to 4-inch-diameter tunicate bulb, have strap-shaped leaves that appear either in late fall or in late spring and die back in early summer. Like many other members of the amaryllis family, these plants are rodent- and deer-proof because the bulbs and other plant parts are poisonous. Plants of the genus *Amaryllis* are often confused with the bulbs sold for winter forcing and commonly called amaryllis.

HOW TO GROW
Plant *Amaryllis* in full sun or partial shade with average, deeply prepared, well-drained soil. They are quite drought tolerant and happiest in Mediterranean-like climates where warm, dry summers

Amaryllis belladonna

prevail. Plant in late spring or early summer with the tops of the bulbs just under the soil surface. Where they are marginally hardy (**Zones 7 and 8**), plant them in a warm, protected site, such as against a south-facing wall, and set the bulbs 4 to 6 inches deep. Cover them over in winter (especially outdoors in Zone 7) with a coarse mulch such as evergreen boughs, coarse leaves, or salt hay. Where they are not hardy, grow them in large containers or tubs; allow the soil to dry off gradually and then overwinter plants indoors by setting the containers in a cool (40° to 50°F nights), dry place. Or dig the bulbs in fall and store them in dry peat moss or vermiculite over winter. Bulbs are happiest when left undisturbed — both in the ground and in containers. Dig and divide plants when they are dormant for propagation or if they become too crowded.

A. belladonna

a. bel-uh-DON-uh. B ELLADONNA L ILY, M AGIC L ILY, N AKED L ADIES, R ESURRECTION L ILY. A deciduous bulb that produces umbels of 2½- to 4-inch-long trumpets in late summer or early fall atop 1½- to 2-foot-tall stalks. Blooms come in shades from pale to dark pink, and white-flowered cultivars are also available. With time, clumps spread to several feet. **Zones 8 to 10; to Zone 7 with winter protection.**

Amberboa

am-ber-BOH-ah. Aster family, Asteraceae.

This genus of six species of annuals or biennials from the Mediterranean region and central and

western Asia contains one commonly grown annual, a beloved cottage-garden plant and cut flower. All *Amberboa* species bear solitary flower heads with thistle-like centers surrounded by a fringe of showy petals, more properly called ray florets.

HOW TO GROW
A site in full sun with average, well-drained soil suits any of these species, which grow naturally in sandy or gravelly soils. Sow seeds indoors 6 to 8 weeks before the last frost and germinate at temperatures between 55° and 60°F. Or sow outdoors just before the last frost while temperatures are still cool. For continuous bloom, make successive sowings every few weeks throughout the summer. Support plants with pea stakes, and deadhead to prolong bloom. Plants self-sow.

A. moschata

a. moe-SHAH-tah. S WEET S UL-TAN. Formerly *Centaurea moschata*. These 2-foot plants produce gray-green, entire leaves at

Amberboa moschata

the base of the plant and deeply cut ones higher up the stem. The fragrant, 2-inch-wide flowers come in white, yellow, pink, or purple. Cool-weather annual.

Amelanchier

am-eh-LAN-key-er. Rose family, Rosaceae.

About 25 deciduous trees and shrubs native to North America, Europe, and Asia. Several species and cultivars — all very similar — are grown for their starry white early-spring flowers, colorful autumn foliage, and small edible fruits. The trees are valued for their early blooms and graceful smooth-barked trunks. Their common name, "serviceberry" or "sarvice," is attributed sometimes to their early-spring bloom time, which coincided with the ground thawing enough for burials, and sometimes to the berries being used for wine in church. "Shadblow," another common name, refers to the fact that the plant blossoms when the shad are swimming upstream to spawn.

HOW TO GROW
Give serviceberry full sun or partial shade and moisture-retentive but well-aerated acid soil. (*A. alnifolia* is more tolerant of alkaline soil than other species are.) These plants are excellent at the edge of a wood or other moist, natural area such as a streambank, where their delicate flowers will be reflected and birds will flock to their fruits. (The fruits are said to make terrific pies if you can rescue any.) Serviceberries don't tolerate drought or pollution and are susceptible to problems that plague other members of the rose family, such as Japanese beetles.

A. alnifolia

a. al-nih-FOE-lee-uh. A LDER-LEAVED S ERVICEBERRY. Also called saskatoon, this northwest U.S. native is a beautiful suckering shrub averaging 12 feet tall, with 2-inch oval leaves, racemes of ³/4-inch white flowers, red or yellow

Amelanchier laevis

Amelanchier alnifolia

Ammi majus

fall foliage, and purple-black berries. 'Regent' grows only 4 to 6 feet tall and has especially sweet fruit. **Zones 4 to 5.**

A. canadensis

a. kan-uh-DEN-sis. Shadblow. Native to the eastern United States, shadblow forms a thicket of suckering shoots up to 20 feet tall. The 4-inch leaves are initially gray and hairy. The white flowers are in erect racemes more than 2 inches long, followed by ¹/₂-inch blue-black fruits. Fall leaves are yellow, orange, and red. **Zones 4 to 7.**

A. × grandiflora

a. × gran-dih-FLOR-uh. Apple Serviceberry. This naturally occurring hybrid of *A. arborea* and *A. laevis* combines the best qualities of the two species: very large flowers; somewhat downy, purple-tinged new leaves; large fruits; exceptional fall color; and a tall, nonsuckering, single- or multi-trunked form. Trees have an irregular oval shape and reach 25 to 40 feet tall. Leaves mature to dark green, toothed, 3-inch-long ovals that turn orange and red in fall. This hybrid and its lovely cultivars are the showiest of the genus, making them great as street trees or as ornamentals for manicured gardens and landscapes. From North America. **Zones 3 to 8.**

CULTIVARS

'Autumn Brilliance' has strong, storm-resistant branches and brilliant orange-red color. 'Ballerina' bears slightly pendulous flowers and large, juicy berries. 'Brilliance' forms a single trunk and has bright scarlet fall color. 'Cumulus' offers a dense cloud of white flowers and yellow-orange fall color. 'Princess Diana' has brilliant red, long-lasting fall color. 'Robin Hill' blooms very early, with pink buds that open to white flowers;

features gleaming yellow and red fall color and a narrow shape. 'Strata' has horizontally spreading, layered branches.

A. laevis

a. LAY-viss. Allegheny Serviceberry. This multi-trunked native of eastern North America has an upright shape, reaching 25 to 30 feet tall, or even 40 feet tall in a rich, moist site. Large fluffy white flowers decorate the tree with a lacy mantle for a week in early spring. As the flowers mature, new leaves open, emerging glossy and reddish green but maturing to bright green. These round, 1- to 1¹/₂-inch-long leaves sport fine-toothed edges and turn a multitude of glorious colors, including yellow, orange, red, and purple-red, in early fall. The fruits are savored by birds and cooks; plant at least two trees to ensure fruit set. Smooth, dark gray or pinkish gray bark, which becomes scaly on old trees, cloaks the trunks, making for a pretty sight in winter. This delicate-looking tree is lovely naturalized in a woodland or used in a mixed border. It does not tolerate heat or drought. **Zones 4 to 8.**

CULTIVARS AND SIMILAR SPECIES

'R. J. Hilton' has pink-flushed white flowers, extra-sweet fruits, and red fall foliage with orange-yellow veins. 'Snowcloud' offers large flower clusters and scarlet fall color. *A. arborea* (shadblow, downy serviceberry, service tree, Juneberry) is hard to distinguish from *A. laevis,* but its flowers are somewhat smaller; its new leaves emerge downy and silver gray; and it may grow taller, to 40 to 50 feet, and form suckers; **Zones 3 to 8.** 'White Pillar' has a columnar shape, large flower clusters, and scarlet fall foliage.

Ammi

AM-me. Carrot family, Apiaceae.

The lacy, rounded flower heads and deeply cut, fernlike leaves of the 10 or so species of annuals and biennials in this genus are reminiscent of their close relative Queen Anne's lace (*Daucus carota*). Two species grown as annuals make fine cut flowers and additions to beds and borders.

HOW TO GROW

Plant in full sun or partial shade in average to rich, well-drained soil that is evenly moist. Sow seeds outdoors in early spring before the last spring frost date or in fall. Indoors, sow 6 to 8 weeks before the last frost date and transplant after the last frost. Support plants with pea stakes when they are about 4 inches tall.

A. majus

a. MAY-jus. Lace Flower, Bishop's Flower, White Dill. Rounded, 6-inch-wide umbels of tiny white flowers are borne in summer atop 3-foot plants. Cool-weather annual.

A. visnaga

a. vis-NAY-gah. Similar to *A. majus* but with handsome chartreuse flowers. Cool-weather annual.

Ammobium

am-MOE-bee-um. Aster family, Asteraceae.

The botanical name of this genus of Australian perennials says much about the plants' cultivation: it is derived from the Greek words for "sand," *ammos,* and "to live," *bios.* The two or three species feature woolly white, lance-shaped leaves and branched stems with thin, flattened wings. All bear papery flowers, and one species in particular is grown for its daisylike blooms, which are excellent for drying.

HOW TO GROW

A site in full sun with light, well-drained, average soil is ideal. Plants also thrive in dry conditions and soil low in nutrients. Sow seeds indoors 6 to 8 weeks before the last spring frost date. Press the seeds into the surface of a sterile germinating mix amended with

Amelanchier laevis

Ammobium alatum

half clean, washed sand. Germination takes about a week at 55° to 60°F. Or sow outdoors several weeks before the last frost or in fall for bloom the following spring. Although plants are perennials, they are not commonly over-wintered, since they are easy and fast from seeds. To dry the blooms, harvest just before they are fully open and hang in small bunches in a warm, dry place; stems may rot if tied in large bunches. Plants self-sow.

A. alatum

a. ah-LAY-tum. PEARLY EVER-LASTING, WINGED EVER-LASTING. Woolly white leaves are borne on 1¹/₂- to 3-foot plants with branched, winged stems. The daisylike, 1-inch-wide flower heads with orange or yellow centers are surrounded by papery white bracts. Tender perennial grown as a cool-weather annual.

Amorphophallus

ah-mor-foe-FAL-us. Arum family, Araceae.

With common names such as devil's tongue, snake palm, and voodoo lily, it isn't surprising that *Amorphophallus* species make an unusual addition to the garden. Between 90 and 100 species make up the genus, all native to the warm, moist tropics of Africa and Asia. All grow from cormlike rhizomes that in some cases achieve immense proportions: a corm that reached 8 feet at the University of

Wisconsin attracted 25,000 visitors and thousands of flies.

While the exotic blooms certainly are a curiosity, the single, deeply lobed leaf that each corm produces is extremely ornamental and can add a tropical flair to shady summer beds and borders. Corms that have reached flowering size (this may take several years) produce a single inflorescence before the leaf appears. The inflorescence consists of many tiny flowers clustered on a central stalk, called a spadix. The spadix is surrounded by a modified leaf, called a spathe. The exotic-looking blooms somewhat resemble those of calla lilies *(Zantedeschia)* and jack-in-the-pulpits *(Arisaema)*, both close relatives. The fact that *Amorphophallus* blooms are pollinated by flies and other insects attracted to carrion gives a hint to the foul odor emitted by some species. Fortunately the odor is released for a relatively short period — commonly only a few days.

HOW TO GROW
Give these plants a spot in partial to full shade with very rich, evenly moist soil. Roots form on the top of the corm. Where they are hardy, set the corms with the tops at least 4 to 6 inches below the soil surface — deeper in areas where they are only marginally hardy. In northern zones where they are not hardy, grow these plants in containers (set corms with the tops at least 2 to 3 inches deep) for overwintering indoors, or plant directly in the soil and dig the corms in early fall after the foliage fades. Corms develop cup-shaped tops; in areas with wet winters, set them on their

Amorphophallus konjac

Amsonia tabernaemontana

sides to prevent water from collecting. Mark the locations of corms, as plants are very late to emerge in spring. Keep the soil evenly moist while the plants are in leaf, but gradually withhold water later in the summer as they enter dormancy. To overwinter corms indoors, store them in a cool (55° to 60°F) place. Pack the corms in barely moist peat moss; corms of *A. konjac* can be stored on a shelf without any packing. Propagate from seeds or by separating offsets when corms are dormant.

A. konjac

a. KON-jak. DEVIL'S TONGUE, SNAKE PALM, VOODOO LILY, UMBRELLA ARUM. Formerly *A. rivieri*. A 3- to 6-foot-tall perennial bearing a leathery, 12- to 16-inch-long, red-purple spathe surrounding a dark brown spadix. A deeply lobed, brown-green leaf mottled with white follows the flowers. Leaves can reach 3 to 4¹/₂ feet in length. **Zones 7 to 10; to Zone 6 with winter protection.**

Amsonia

am-SO-nee-uh. Dogbane family, Apocynaceae.

Commonly known as bluestar or dogbane, *Amsonia* species are perennials or subshrubs bearing clusters of flowers with funnel-shaped bases and flared, starry faces. The stems contain milky sap, and leaves are lance shaped to ovate or rounded. Some of the roughly 20 species in the genus feature brilliant yellow fall foliage.
HOW TO GROW
Select a site in full sun or partial shade that has average, moist, well-drained soil. Established

plants tolerate some drought. To keep plants that are growing in shade neat looking, cut them back after flowering. Propagate by dividing plants in spring or fall, taking stem cuttings in early summer, or sowing seeds.

A. ciliata

a. sil-ee-AH-tuh. DOWNY BLUESTAR. A 1- to 3-foot-tall species native to the southeastern United States forming 1-foot-wide clumps. Bears threadlike leaves that turn yellow in fall and clusters of pale blue ¹/₂-inch-wide flowers in summer. **Zones 5 to 9.**

A. hubrectii

a. who-BRECK-tee-eye. A 2- to 3-foot-tall species native to the United States forming handsome 3- to 4-foot-wide clumps of very narrow leaves that turn golden yellow in fall. Bears clusters of very pale blue 2- to 3-inch-wide flowers in summer. **Zones 5 to 9.**

A. tabernaemontana

a. tah-ber-nay-mon-TAN-uh. WILLOW BLUESTAR. A 1- to 3-foot-tall species native to the eastern United States forming 2- to 3-foot-wide clumps. Bears lance-shaped leaves that turn yellow in fall and rounded clusters of ¹/₂-inch-wide star-shaped blue flowers in spring and early summer. **Zones 3 to 9.**

Amsonia tabernaemontana

Anagallis

an-ah-GAL-liss. Primrose family, Primulaceae.

Commonly called pimpernel, *Anagallis* species are annuals, biennials, and perennials native to the Mediterranean region and western Europe. Two of the 20 species in the genus are grown as annuals for their dainty blooms. The plants are low growing and have saucer- to shallowly bell-shaped flowers with five lobes, or "petals."

HOW TO GROW
A site with full sun and average, light to sandy, well-drained soil is ideal. Sow seeds outdoors after the last spring frost date. Or sow seeds indoors in individual pots 6 to 8 weeks before the last frost date and germinate at 60° to 65°F. Germination takes about 3 weeks. Transplant with care. Perennial species can be propagated by cuttings taken in spring or early summer. Use pimpernels as edging plants in beds and borders. They also make attractive indoor container plants in winter and spring.

A. arvensis
a. are-VEN-sis. SCARLET PIMPERNEL. A weedy species with ovate leaves and trailing stems that reaches about 6 inches in height. The orange-red, ¹/₂- to ³/₄-inch flowers close in cloudy or cool weather, thus the common name "poor man's weatherglass." *A. arvensis* var. *caerulea* bears blue flowers. Cool-weather annual.

A. monellii
a. mon-ELL-lee-eye. BLUE PIMPERNEL. Ovate to lance-shaped leaves on 1- to 1¹/₂-foot plants.

Anagallis monellii

Bears deep blue, ¹/₂-inch-wide flowers. Flax-leaved pimpernel (*A. monellii* ssp. *linifolia*) has narrow, lance-shaped leaves. A tender perennial (hardy to **Zone 7**) grown as a warm-weather annual.

Anaphalis

ah-NAFF-ah-liss. Aster family, Asteraceae.

Woolly gray-green leaves and rounded clusters of small button-like flower heads characterize *Anaphalis* species, commonly known as pearly everlastings. The flowers, which are excellent for drying, consist of yellow daisylike centers surrounded by white petal-like bracts that have a dry, papery texture. The leaves, which are linear to lance shaped, are covered with woolly hairs that give the foliage its silvery appearance.

HOW TO GROW
Select a site in full sun or partial shade with average to rich, evenly moist soil that is fairly well drained. Unlike many other silver-leaved perennials, pearly everlastings thrive in moist soil; in dry soil, the plants drop their lower leaves and generally look unattractive. To keep these clump-forming plants vigorous, dig and divide the clumps every 3 to 4 years in spring. In addition to division, propagate by cuttings taken from shoots at the base of the plant in spring, from stem cuttings taken in spring or early summer, or by seeds.

A. margaritacea
a. mar-gar-ih-TAY-see-uh. PEARLY EVERLASTING. A 2- to 3-foot-tall, 2-foot-wide species with lance-shaped leaves that are gray-green above and white and woolly beneath. The edges of the leaves

Anaphalis margaritacea

Anchusa capensis

roll upward, giving them a silver-edged appearance. Rounded 6-inch-wide clusters of flowers bloom from midsummer to fall. **Zones 4 to 8.**

A. triplinervis
a. trip-lih-NERV-iss. THREE-VEINED EVERLASTING. A 1- to 2-foot-tall species that spreads from 1¹/₂ to 2 feet and bears gray-green, rounded to spoon-shaped leaves with woolly white hairs. Produces rounded 1¹/₂- to 2-inch-wide clusters of flowers with white bracts from mid- to late summer. **Zones 3 to 8.**

Anchusa

an-KOO-suh. Borage family, Boraginaceae.

This genus contains about 35 species of annuals, biennials, and perennials commonly called anchusas, alkanets, or bugloss. They are grown for their clusters of five-lobed flowers with tubular bases in shades of blue, rich violet, or purple-blue. Leaves are linear to lance-shaped, and some species have leaves and stems covered with bristly hairs.

HOW TO GROW
Give anchusas a site in full sun or light shade with rich, well-drained, evenly moist soil. They do not tolerate drought. Water deeply during dry weather. To maintain the rich soil these plants require, top-dress annually with a balanced fertilizer in spring and again in summer. Cut plants back after the first flush of bloom to encourage a second flush of flowers. Tall plants require staking. Perennial anchusas tend to be short-lived; divide clumps every 2 to 3 years to keep them vigorous. Sow seeds of annual anchusas indoors 6 to 8 weeks before the last spring frost date, or sow outdoors in early spring. Plants self-sow and can become weedy.

A. azurea
a. ah-ZUR-ee-uh. ITALIAN ALKANET, ITALIAN BUGLOSS. Erect, 2- to 5-foot-tall, short-lived perennial forming 2-foot-wide clumps and bearing bristly leaves and stems. Produces showy, loose clusters of ³/₄-inch-wide flowers in early summer. 'Dropmore' bears deep purple-blue flowers on 4-foot plants. 'Little John' is a fairly long-lived 1¹/₂-foot cultivar. 'Loddon Royalist' reaches 3 feet and rarely needs staking. **Zones 3 to 8.**

A. capensis
a. kah-PEN-sis. BUGLOSS, SUMMER FORGET-ME-NOT. Lance-shaped, 5-inch-long leaves on ¹/₂- to 1¹/₂-foot-tall plants. Bears sprays of tiny, ¹/₄-inch, true blue flowers with white throats. Cultivars include 8-inch-tall 'Blue Angel' and 18-inch 'Blue Bird', both with deep, rich blue flowers. Biennial grown as a cool-weather annual.

Andromeda polifolia

Andromeda

an-DROM-uh-duh. Heath family, Ericaceae.

Of this genus's two species of low evergreen shrubs from cool areas of the Northern Hemisphere, one — known as bog rosemary — is commonly grown for its small urn-shaped flowers and needlelike leaves. It is one of those valuable shrubs that take happily to poorly drained areas and are useful for naturalizing.

HOW TO GROW

Bog rosemary needs a shady home in moist, peaty, acid soil. Adding peat to sand will create an ideal medium. This shrub's size makes it useful for a shady rock garden, a pondside bog garden, or the front of a damp, wooded border. Mulch it with leaf mold, and prune after flowering only to keep it shapely. Propagate from softwood cuttings, layering, or suckers.

A. polifolia

a. pawl-ih-FOE-lee-uh. BOG ROSE-MARY. Formerly *A. rosmarinifolia*. Only about a foot tall and 8 inches wide, it may be erect or slightly floppy. The leaves are

pointed and leathery, like the culinary herb rosemary, inspiring its common name. White or pale pink flowers appear in umbels of two to five, in spring to early summer. **Zones 2 to 6.**

Anemone

ah-NEM-oh-nee. Buttercup family, Ranunculaceae.

The genus *Anemone* is a diverse group of about 120 species that bear saucer- to cup-shaped flowers with a boss, or tuft, of showy yellow stamens in the center. The flowers have petal-like sepals instead of true petals and come in shades of pink, rose-red, scarlet, white, and lavender- and violet-blue. Blooms are borne one per stem or in branched clusters and may be single, semidouble, or double. Also called windflowers (the botanical name is from the Greek word *anemos,* meaning "wind"), anemones have attractive, deeply cut, fernlike leaves. Most produce a cluster of leaves at the base of the plant, but some species also have leaves along the wiry flower stems. There are anemones that bloom from spring into early summer; others bloom in late summer and fall. Root systems are diverse, too: while many species grow from rhizomes or fleshy or fibrous roots, others produce woody tubers and are planted and treated like bulbs.

HOW TO GROW

For best results, select planting sites according to when plants bloom. Give spring-blooming species — *A. canadensis* and *A. sylvestris* — a site in partial shade and light, rich, evenly moist soil. Most spring-blooming species also grow in full sun provided the soil remains moist. Spring-blooming

anemones usually go dormant after flowering, and once dormant they tolerate drier conditions. Combine them with other low-growing perennials to fill the space they leave. Divide clumps immediately after the foliage has turned yellow in late spring or early summer to control plants that have spread too far, to relieve overcrowding, or for propagation.

Fall-blooming anemones, often collectively referred to as Japanese anemones, thrive in full sun or partial shade and rich, evenly moist, well-drained soil. These species — *A. hupehensis, A. × hybrida,* and *A. tomentosa* — benefit from a spot with afternoon shade, especially in areas with hot summers. When planting, select the location carefully and dig the soil deeply, as plants will thrive for years in one spot. Keep newly planted clumps well watered the first season or they can succumb to heat and drought. Propagate by dividing the clumps in spring or immediately after they flower in fall or by root cuttings dug in winter or early spring. All anemones grow slowly from seed.

A. apennina

a. ah-pen-NYE-nuh. APENNINE WINDFLOWER. An 8-inch-tall species growing from short creeping rhizomes and spreading to about 1 foot. Bears toothed, lobed, dark green leaves and solitary 1- to 1^1/$_4$-inch-wide flowers in spring that are blue with yellow stamens. **Zones 6 to 9.**

A. blanda

a. BLAN-duh. GRECIAN WINDFLOWER. A 6- to 8-inch-tall species growing from woody, knobby tuberous rhizomes. Bears fernlike leaves and white, pink, or blue 2-inch-wide daisylike flowers in spring. Cultivars include 'Blue

Star', with large blue blooms; 'Pink Star', with pink flowers; 'Radar', with magenta blooms; and 'White Splendour', with large white flowers. **Zones 4 to 8.**

A. canadensis

a. kan-uh-DEN-sis. MEADOW ANEMONE. Vigorous 6- to 8-inch-tall native North American wildflower spreading by rhizomes to 2 feet or more. Bears single 2-inch-wide white flowers from late spring to early summer. **Zones 3 to 7.**

A. coronaria

a. kor-oh-NAIR-ee-uh. FLORIST'S ANEMONE, POPPY ANEMONE. A tender, short-lived 1- to 1^1/$_2$-foot-tall species that grows from stem tubers. In spring, it bears very showy, 2- to 3-inch single or double blooms with black centers in shades of scarlet and violet-blue, as well as white.

Plant the woody tubers 2 inches deep. Plant outdoors in fall in Zones 8 to 10, but in pots or in the spring in the North. (Tubers are sold in fall with spring-blooming bulbs such as daffodils and tulips even in areas where the plants are not hardy.) Give them full sun or partial shade in well-drained, rich, somewhat sandy soil. When planting outdoors in fall, cover the beds with mulch over winter, but remove it in late winter. In the North, treat florist's anemones as annuals: they can be planted in spring, but for best flowering, plant tubers in pots in fall (several tubers per 6- to 8-inch-pot), then overwinter them in a greenhouse, cold frame, sun porch, or other cool, freeze-free spot. Water sparingly at planting time and until foliage appears. Once buds appear, feed each time you water with a dilute liquid fertilizer and keep the soil evenly moist.

Anemone canadensis

Anemone sylvestris

Anemone tomentosa 'Robustissima'

Anemonella thalictroides

Cultivars include the De Caen Hybrids, which are single-flowered types, and the St. Brigid Hybrids, which are double flowered. **Zones 8 to 10.**

A. hupehensis
a. hue-peh-HEN-sis. CHINESE ANEMONE. Handsome 2- to 3-foot-tall species producing 2-foot-wide clumps of three-parted leaves. Bears long-stalked 2- to 2¹/₂-inch-wide flowers in pink or white arranged in umbels of about 12 from midsummer to fall. 'Hadspen Abundance' bears dark reddish pink blooms. *A. hupehensis* var. *japonica,* commonly called Japanese anemone, offers creamy pink flowers on 2- to 4-foot plants. 'Bressingham Glow', 'Pink Shell' ('Rosenschale'), and 'September Charm' are among the many excellent cultivars. **Zones 4 to 8.**

A. × hybrida
a. × HI-brih-duh. JAPANESE ANEMONE, HYBRID ANEMONE. Vigorous 2¹/₂- to 5-foot-tall species spreading by rhizomes to form clumps exceeding 3 feet in width. Bears long-stalked 3- to 3¹/₂-inch-wide flowers in 12- to 18-flowered umbels in shades of pink and white from summer to midfall. 'Honorine Jobert' produces single 2- to 3-inch-wide white flowers on 3- to 4-foot plants. 'Margarete' has semidouble to double deep pink blooms. 'Queen Charlotte' ('Königin Charlotte') bears semidouble 4-inch-wide pink flowers. 'Whirlwind' carries 4-inch-wide semidouble white blooms on 4- to 5-foot plants. **Zones 4 to 8.**

A. nemorosa
a. neh-moe-ROE-suh. WOOD ANEMONE. Vigorous 4- to 10-inch-tall species that spreads by heavily branching rhizomes. Bears leaves with narrow, deeply toothed lobes and white, pale pink, or lavender-blue ¹/₂- to ³/₄-inch flowers in spring. Cultivars include 'Flore Pleno', with double white flowers; 'Robinsoniana', with pale lavender-blue flowers; and 'Rosea', with rose pink blooms. **Zones 4 to 8.**

A. pavonina
a. pah-VOE-nee-nah. Tender 8- to 10-inch-tall species growing from a tuber. Bears deeply lobed leaves and showy, solitary 1¹/₄- to 4-inch-wide flowers in spring in shades of red, pink, and purple. Grow as you would *A. coronaria.* **Zones 8 to 10.**

A. ranunculoides
a. rah-nun-kew-LOY-deez. BUTTERCUP ANEMONE, YELLOW WINDFLOWER. Vigorous, fast-spreading, 2- to 4-inch-tall species that spreads by rhizomes to 1¹/₂ feet or more. Bears deeply lobed leaves and solitary ³/₄- to 1¹/₄-inch-wide blooms with five or six tepals in spring. 'Superba' has bronze-green leaves. **Zones 4 to 8.**

A. sylvestris
a. sil-VES-tris. SNOWDROP ANEMONE. Vigorous 1- to 1¹/₂-foot-tall species that has fibrous roots with a woody base and spreads via root suckers to about 2 feet. Bears single white 2-inch-wide flowers in spring. **Zones 3 to 8.**

A. tomentosa 'Robustissima'
a. toe-men-TOE-suh. GRAPE-LEAF ANEMONE. Well known as a bully in perennial borders — where it quickly stakes its claim to all the territory in sight — this makes an effective woodland edge. It has pink flowers in late summer and attractive foliage throughout the growing season. It does best in moist, organic soils and partial shade, but it will tolerate less-than-ideal situations and spread happily. 'Robustissima' is an especially hardy selection that can be grown in **Zone 4. Zones 5 to 8.**

Anemonella
an-nem-oh-NEL-uh. Buttercup family, Ranunculaceae.

This genus contains a single species native to woodlands in eastern North America — *A. thalictroides,* commonly called rue anemone. It bears cup-shaped flowers that very closely resemble those of its relatives, the true anemones (*Anemone*). Flowers of the two genera both lack true petals; the showy structures called "petals" actually are petal-like sepals surrounding a dainty cluster of stamens in the center of the blooms. The structure of their pistils, the female portion of the flower, differs. While the pistils in *Anemone* flowers consist of three parts — stigma, style, and ovary — *Anemonella* flowers have knoblike stigmas set directly atop the ovary, without a connecting style. Plants grow from tuberous roots and bear dainty dark blue-green leaves that are divided two or three times into rounded, toothed leaflets.

HOW TO GROW
Select a site in partial shade with average to rich, evenly moist soil. The tubers will rot in constantly wet conditions. Plants thrive in woodland gardens, shady rock gardens, and similar sites provided they do not have to compete with aggressive neighbors. Propagate by seed or divide clumps in early spring. When adding this plant to your garden, be sure to purchase nursery-propagated plants — or ones offered by a native plant society or botanical garden — not ones collected from the wild.

A. thalictroides
a. thal-ick-TROY-deez. RUE ANEMONE. A native 4- to 8-inch-tall wildflower with ³/₄-inch-wide flowers that are white or pale pink and appear from spring to early summer above fernlike blue-green leaves. Plants form 1-foot-wide clumps with time. 'Oscar Schoaf' is a double pink cultivar sometimes sold as 'Rosea Flore Pleno' or 'Schoaf's Pink'. **Zones 4 to 8.**

Anethum
ah-NEE-thum. Carrot family, Apiaceae.

Anethum comprises two species of aromatic annuals or biennials with feathery blue-green leaves and umbels of tiny yellow flowers. One species — dill (*A. graveolens*) — is a popular herb that makes a pretty addition to mixed plantings.

Anethum graveolens

HOW TO GROW

Full sun and fertile, well-drained soil that remains evenly moist are all dill requires to grow well. Sow seeds outdoors beginning in early spring, and sow new crops every 3 to 4 weeks to ensure a continuous supply of foliage and flowers. From Zone 9 south, sow outdoors from late summer through winter. Indoors, start seeds 6 to 8 weeks before the last spring frost date and germinate at 60° to 70°F, which takes about 3 weeks. Transplant with care, as the seedlings resent being disturbed. Water regularly during dry weather to keep plants from going to seed. Plants self-sow.

A. graveolens

a. grav-ee-OH-lenz. DILL. Feathery, aromatic leaves and lacy yellow flower clusters on 2-foot plants. 'Fernleaf' is an 18-inch-tall cultivar with long-lasting, bushy foliage. Cool-weather annual.

Angelica

an-JEL-ih-kuh. Carrot family, Apiaceae.

Statuesque short-lived perennials or biennials native to the Northern Hemisphere, *Angelica* species bear pinnately compound leaves ranging from 1 to 3 feet in length. The leaves are divided into large, roughly diamond-shaped leaflets arranged in a pinnate (featherlike) fashion. Flat-topped or rounded umbels of yellow-green or purple flowers are carried above the foliage in summer. There are 30 spe-

Angelica archangelica

cies in the genus, most native to rich, damp woodlands, meadows, or streambanks. The botanical name, derived from the Latin word for "angel," *angelus*, is a reference to the healing properties of the best-known species in the genus, *A. archangelica*.

HOW TO GROW

Give these plants a spot in partial shade with rich, deep, moist soil, which yields the largest plants, although they will tolerate drier conditions. Plants grow in full shade but don't bloom as well. Angelicas are taprooted and resent transplanting. The species listed here are monocarpic, meaning they die after setting seeds. Some gardeners simply grow new plants from seed annually to ensure a continuing supply of plants. (To minimize damage to the taproot, transplant seedlings when they are still small.) Others remove the flower heads as they fade in order to encourage plants to perform more as perennials. Plants treated this way generally bloom for 2 to 3 years. Plants self-sow.

A. archangelica

a. ark-an-JEL-ih-kuh. ARCHANGEL, WILD PARSNIP. Statuesque 6-foot-tall perennial producing 4-foot-wide mounds of pinnate 2-foot-long leaves. Bears rounded 10-inch-wide umbels of tiny greenish yellow flowers on thick, upright stalks from early to midsummer. **Zones 4 to 9.**

A. gigas

a. JEE-gas. Clump-forming 3- to 6-foot-tall biennial or short-lived perennial that spreads to 4 feet and bears 5-inch-wide umbels of tiny purple flowers on purplish red stems in late summer and early fall. **Zones 4 to 9.**

Anisodontea

an-eye-so-DON-tee-ah. Mallow family, Malvaceae.

The 19 species in the genus *Anisodontea* are woody-based perennials or shrubs with sprays of bowl-shaped, five-petaled flowers. Native to South Africa, they bear linear, ovate, or lobed leaves that are evergreen in tropical climates. One species is grown as a tender perennial.

HOW TO GROW

Give these mallow-family plants rich, well-drained soil. They tolerate full sun in areas with cool summers, but a spot with late-

Anisodontea × hypomandarum

afternoon shade is best where summers are warm, because the plants tend to stop blooming during the heat of summer. Water regularly in spring and summer when the plants are growing actively, and feed monthly with a balanced fertilizer. Remove seed heads regularly to keep the plants blooming. Sow seeds indoors in late winter and germinate at 55° to 65°F. Or propagate from cuttings taken in early summer. Grow *Anisodontea* species in mixed plantings or in containers, and overwinter them indoors either as container plants or as cuttings. Gradually withhold water in fall and keep plants on the dry side over winter.

A. × hypomandarum

a. × hi-poe-man-DAIR-um. ROSE MALLOW. A shrub or subshrub, ranging from 3 to 5 feet in height, with ovate, three-lobed leaves. Pale pink, 1- to 1¼-inch-wide flowers with purple veins are borne from spring to fall. Tender perennial or grow as an annual.

Anthemis

an-THEE-mus. Aster family, Asteraceae.

Commonly called dog fennels — or, more poetically, golden marguerites — members of this genus bear cheerful daisylike flowers and aromatic stems and leaves. *Anthemis* contains about 100 species of mound-forming annuals and shrubby perennials that hail from the Mediterranean region, northern Africa, and the Middle East. Although hardy, the two most popular species are short-lived perennials often grown as annuals.

HOW TO GROW

Full sun and very well drained, poor to average soil are fine for golden marguerites, which also thrive in sandy or gravelly soil. The plants tolerate dry soil and are best in neutral to slightly alkaline conditions. Cut them back hard after their first flush of bloom. Plants may need staking. Propagate by dividing clumps in spring, by taking cuttings from shoots at the base of the plants in spring or late summer, or by seeds, although named cultivars do not come true.

A. punctata ssp. cupaniana

a. punk-TAH-tuh ssp. kup-an-ee-AH-nuh. Formerly *A. cupaniana*. Low-growing 1-foot-tall species spreading to about 3 feet. Bears handsome, fernlike, silver-gray leaves and 2½-inch-wide white daisy flowers in early summer. **Zones 6 to 9.**

Anthemis tinctoria

A. sancti-johannis

a. SANK-tee-joe-HAN-iss. GOLDEN MARGUERITE. Clump-forming 2- to 3-foot-tall species spreading to 2 feet. Bears finely cut, fernlike, gray-green leaves and 1¼- to 2-inch-wide buttonlike orange daisies with rounded centers and short petals all summer.
Zones 4 to 9.

A. tinctoria

a. tink-TOR-ee-uh. GOLDEN MARGUERITE. Clump-forming 1½- to 2½-foot-tall species spreading from 2 to 3 feet. Bears pinnate leaves that are gray-hairy underneath and yellow to cream-colored 1- to 1½-inch-wide daisy flowers from summer to fall. Many cultivars are available, including 'Moonlight', with light yellow blooms, and 'Sauce Hollandaise', with pale cream flowers.
Zones 3 to 7.

Anthericum

an-THEER-ih-kum. Lily family, Liliaceae.

Anthericum species are grown for their loose, erect panicles or racemes of small white flowers borne in spring or summer. The flowers consist of six petal-like tepals and are carried on erect stalks above clumps of long, narrow, basal, grasslike leaves. Unlike many other lily-family plants, these plants grow from fleshy or tuberous roots. About 50 species belong to the genus, all of which are native to Europe, Turkey, and Africa.

Anthericum liliago

HOW TO GROW

Select a site in full sun with rich, well-drained soil. Plant the roots in spring, amending the soil with sand and plenty of organic matter. Water regularly when plants are actively growing; they tolerate drier conditions when dormant. Protect clumps from fluctuating winter temperatures by covering them in late fall with a coarse mulch such as evergreen boughs, salt hay, pine needles, or coarse hay. These plants thrive for years without needing to be divided. Dig them in early spring if they become overcrowded or for propagation, or propagate by seeds.

A. liliago

a. lil-ee-AH-go. SAINT BERNARD'S LILY. A 2- to 3-foot-tall perennial with clumps of arching, gray-green, 1½-foot-long grassy leaves. Bears slender 2-foot-long racemes of starry white 1½-inch-wide flowers in late spring or early summer. **Zones 4 to 7.**

A. ramosum

a. rah-MOE-sum. A 2½- to 3-foot-tall perennial producing clumps of arching, gray-green, 1½-foot-long grassy leaves. Bears slender, branched 2-foot-long panicles of starry white 1½-inch-wide flowers in late spring or early summer. Somewhat more heat tolerant than *A. liliago*. **Zones 4 to 8.**

Antirrhinum

an-tir-RYE-num. Figwort family, Scrophulariaceae.

Common snapdragons, with their two-lipped flowers that have delighted children for generations, are by far the best-known members of this genus of 30 to 40 species of annuals, perennials, and tender subshrubs. *Antirrhinum* species bear racemes of tubular, two-lipped flowers and linear to lance-shaped leaves. Members of the genus are native to Europe, North Africa, and North America.

HOW TO GROW

Give snapdragons full sun and soil that is rich in organic matter and very well drained. They are easy from seeds, and many cultivars are available that come true from seed. Sow indoors 8 to 10 weeks before the last spring frost. Use vermiculite or a sterile seed-starting mix, and just press the tiny seeds into the surface of the medium, as light is required for germination. Water from below to

Antirrhinum majus

avoid washing the seeds away and to prevent damping off, which can be a problem. Germination takes 2 to 3 weeks at 55° to 60°F. Seedlings grown in cool conditions — 45° to 50°F at night — are sturdier than ones grown at higher temperatures. In Zones 7 to 9, try growing snapdragons as biennials by sowing seeds in summer. Plant summer-sown seedlings out in fall and mulch them deeply over winter with a loose mulch such as straw or salt hay; some cultivars overwinter better than others.

Indoors or out, when seedlings are about 3 inches tall, pinch out the tips to encourage branching. Deadhead plants regularly to lengthen the bloom season (leave some flowers to set seed if you want the planting to self-sow, although self-sown plants may not resemble their parents). After the first flush of bloom, or when hot weather arrives, cut the plants back hard, water, and feed them lightly with a balanced fertilizer: they will respond with new growth. Snapdragons also can be propagated by cuttings taken in spring or fall. Medium and tall cultivars need staking; install pea stakes or other supports when plants are still relatively small. Use snapdragons in beds and borders as well as the cutting garden. Hummingbirds visit the flowers. Dwarf and trailing cultivars make eye-catching container plants.

A. majus

a. MAY-jus. COMMON SNAPDRAGON. Shrubby plants ranging from 8 inches to 3 feet in height with glossy, lance-shaped leaves. Dense spikes of two-lipped flowers in all colors except true blue, including white, yellow, orange, maroon, pink, red, and fuchsia. Flowers can be a solid color or bicolor. Butterfly snapdragons have flared, open-faced flowers that are single or double. Cultivars in three height categories are available: tall, to 3 feet; intermediate, from 1 to 2 feet; and dwarf, from 8 to 12 inches. Dwarf cultivars include 8-inch-tall 'Bells Mix', 6- to 8-inch 'Chimes Mix', 5-inch 'Floral Showers Mix', and 10-inch 'Tahiti Mix'. 'Sonnet Mix' plants are semidwarf at 14 inches and tolerate windy sites. 'Madame Butterfly Mix' plants feature fully double blooms on 2- to 2½-foot plants. 'Rocket Mix' plants reach 3 feet and are excellent cut flowers. Tender perennial usually grown as a cool-weather annual.

Aquilegia

ack-will-EE-juh. Buttercup family, Ranunculaceae.

Commonly known as columbines, *Aquilegia* species are perennials grown for their graceful flowers borne on wiry stems above mounds of attractive, lacy foliage. Both the botanical and common names refer to the uniquely shaped flowers. *Aquilegia* is from the Latin *aquila*, meaning "eagle," a reference to the spurred petals, while the common name is from the Latin *columbinus*, "like a dove," or *columba*, "dove." When looked at from above, the petals of short-spurred types resemble doves with

Aquilegia canadensis

leaves are shallowly toothed and 2 to 4 inches long. In autumn, white urn-shaped flowers (sometimes tinged pink) appear in 2-inch panicles, while the ¾-inch fruits from the previous year are ripening from yellow to red. Look for 'Compacta', which grows to only 6 to 8 feet tall, or 'Elfin King', which may stop growing at 5 feet. **Zones 7 to 10.**

Arctostaphylos

ark-toe-STAF-ih-los. Heath family, Ericaceae.

Of this genus's 50 species of mostly evergreen shrubs or small trees, primarily from western North America, only a few are beginning to be appreciated by gardeners. In addition to lustrous green leaves, they have urn-shaped flowers and attractive berries. Those categorized as shrubs make good low to medium ground covers on banks or other challenging sites.

HOW TO GROW
Bearberries, or manzanitas, will grow in poor, dry, sandy soil ranging from acid to alkaline, in sun or shade, and tolerate salt and wind but not humidity or boggy soil. They can be difficult to establish. Start shrubs in fall after a good rain, planting those intended as ground covers from quart-sized containers, spaced a foot apart. Pruning shrub tips lightly will encourage growth, but don't prune prostrate branches. Start semiripe cuttings in summer or layer in fall.

A. densiflora 'Howard McMinn'
a. den-sih-FLOR-uh. Sonoma Manzanita cultivar. This native Californian forms a dense mound 5 feet high and 7 feet wide,

Arctostaphylos uva-ursi

with peeling dark red bark and glossy elliptic leaves. Tiny urn-shaped pink to white flowers hang in clusters from late winter to early spring, followed by tiny reddish brown apple-shaped fruits. 'Sentinel' is more erect. **Zones 7 to 10.**

A. manzanita
a. man-zuh-NEET-uh. Common Manzanita. This shrub from the Sierra Nevada and Coast ranges varies from 6 to 20 feet tall and about half as wide, but averages 12 feet high. It is known for its crooked reddish purple limbs. The leaves are wide ovals, while the late-winter flowers bloom in clusters of white or pink, followed in fall by rounded white fruits that turn red. **Zones 8 to 10.**

A. uva-ursi
a. OO-vuh-UR-see. Common Bearberry. Also called kinnikinick, this 6- to 12-inch-high

Arctostaphylos uva-ursi 'Massachusetts'

evergreen ground cover is native to northern California and the Northeast as well as northern Eurasia. It has 1-inch glossy green leaves that turn bronze or red in winter. Clusters of ¼-inch pink-tinged white flowers in mid- to late spring are followed by round, brilliant scarlet berries. Plants usually grow 2 feet across but can spread much wider. An excellent seaside plant that tolerates salt and performs best in dry, sandy soil. Numerous cultivars have been selected. 'Emerald Carpet' tolerates shade, and 'Vancouver Jade' has pink flowers and strong autumn color. Gardeners in the southern United States (Zone 7) should look for 'Massachusetts'. **Zones 2 to 6.**

Arctotis

ark-TOE-tiss. Aster family, Asteraceae.

Commonly called African daisies, the 50 or so species in this genus are annuals and tender perennials, hardy to **Zone 9**. These natives of South Africa grow naturally in dry conditions, producing rosettes of gray- to silvery green leaves that are entire or lobed. The brightly colored daisylike flowers, borne one per stem from midsummer to fall, close at night. The blooms tend to open during sunny or bright weather, and do not open fully on dark days, a characteristic that limits their usefulness as cut flowers. Modern cultivars generally stay open longer than species. Use African daisies as edging plants, in beds and borders, and as container plants. *Arctotis* species also are listed as × *Venidioarctotis* and *Venidium*.

HOW TO GROW
African daisies thrive in full sun and light, very well drained soil that remains evenly moist. Sow seeds indoors 6 to 8 weeks before the last spring frost date at 60° to 70°F; germination generally takes 1 to 2 weeks. Use a sterile seed-starting mix, and barely cover seeds with mix. Water from below, and do not overwater; keeping the soil on the dry side is best, since damping off can be a problem. Transplant seedlings to individual pots as soon as they are large enough to handle. Or sow outdoors after the last frost date once the soil has warmed up a bit. Cuttings taken in spring or fall are a good option for multiplying plants with outstanding colors. The

Arctotis venusta

plants do not grow well in very hot summer weather. Plants self-sow in warm climates.

A. fastuosa
a. fas-tue-OH-suh. Monarch of the Veldt. Formerly *Venidium fastuosum*. A 1- to 2-foot species with silver-white, 5-inch-long leaves that are deeply lobed. Bears orange, 4-inch, daisylike flowers with dark purple or black centers. Tender perennial grown as a warm-weather annual.

A. × *hybrida*
a. × HI-brih-duh. Vigorous, 18- to 20-inch-tall plants with silver-green leaves that have wavy margins. The showy, 3- to 3½-inch daisylike flowers with dark centers and orange-yellow, orange, pink, white, or red rays, or petals, may have dark markings on them. Tender perennial grown as a warm-weather annual.

A. venusta
a. veh-NUE-stuh. Blue-eyed African Daisy. Formerly *A. stoechadifolia*. A 2-foot-tall plant with lobed, dark green leaves that are silvery beneath. Bears white, 3-inch-wide, daisylike flowers with blue centers. Tender perennial grown as a warm-weather annual.

Ardisia

are-DEES-juh. Myrsine family, Myrsinaceae.

Among the 250 evergreen trees and shrubs in this genus, from warm to tropical areas of the Americas and Asia, only a couple are commonly grown in gardens. They are eye-catching throughout the year, with whorls of glossy leaves, star-shaped flowers, and lasting bright red fruits.

Ardisia japonica

HOW TO GROW

Native to damp woods, ardisias need rich, organic, well-drained acid soil and shelter from strong sun and wind. In moist, shady conditions they spread quickly by root runners to form a tall ground cover. Temperatures of 20°F and lower can kill leaves, especially of the variegated varieties, although plants will resprout from the roots. Pruning is minimal, but shrubs may need pinching to keep them from getting leggy. These plants propagate most easily by division but also can be reproduced from stem cuttings collected in early spring or seeds sown in spring.

A. japonica

a. juh-PON-ih-kuh. MARLBERRY. Growing only 18 inches tall or less but spreading indefinitely, this Asian species has glossy, toothed leaves up to 3¹/₂ inches long, held in whorls. The foliage resembles that of a hellebore. Clusters of ¹/₂-inch pink or white star-shaped flowers bloom in late summer, followed by round ¹/₄-inch bright red berries that persist into winter. Marlberry spreads quickly; its value as a ground cover is limited only by its variable cold hardiness. It will not tolerate even moderately dry soils. Variegated forms may have white, cream, yellow, or pink markings. **Zones 7 to 9.**

Arenaria

are-en-AIR-ee-uh. Pink family, Caryophyllaceae.

The genus *Arenaria*, or sandworts, includes more than 250 species of annuals, perennials, and subshrubs native throughout the north temperate regions of the world. The species grown in gardens are usu-

ally perennials. Foliage is green, with the opposite leaves being lanceolate or oblong lanceolate, often awl tipped and slightly prickly. Flowers are typically small and white, creating attractive sprays of bloom.

HOW TO GROW

Arenarias thrive in sunny, well-drained sites. They prefer gritty, sandy, poor soils and blend nicely with rosemary, oregano, and thyme. Planting in rich or moist soils will lead to short-lived plants rather than dense growth. They are an attractive choice to fill between steppingstones, especially in terraces or patios.

A. montana

a. mon-TAHN-uh. EUROPEAN SANDWORT, MOUNTAIN SANDWORT. The grassy, matlike foliage reaches only 4 inches tall and spreads only about 12 inches on lax, trailing stems. Small white flowers appear in spring. Plants need alkaline soil, full sun, and very good drainage to thrive. **Zones 4 to 8.**

Arenaria montana

Argemone

are-GEH-moe-nee. Poppy family, Papaveraceae.

Prickly poppies are well named: they feature poppylike flowers and prickly leaves and seedpods. About 28 annuals and perennials, plus one shrub, belong to this genus of plants native to North and Central America. Blue-green or blue-gray leaves are borne on the somewhat coarse plants, which can be spreading or erect and have yellow or orange sap. Showy, paperlike flowers with four to six yellow, white, or mauve-pink petals appear from summer to fall.

HOW TO GROW

Full sun and poor, well-drained soil are all prickly poppies require. They thrive in alkaline soil and sandy or gravelly conditions; rich soil yields foliage but few flowers. Sow seeds outdoors after the last spring frost date. Or sow indoors in individual pots 6 weeks before the last spring frost date at 55° to 60°F. Germination takes about 2 weeks. Transplant indoor-sown seedlings with care, as they resent being disturbed. Use prickly poppies in rock gardens or raised beds, and give them plenty of space to spread, show off their handsome foliage, and soak up the sun. They also can be used in mixed plantings and allowed to grow up through and fill in around nearby plants. Plants self-sow.

A. grandiflora

a. gran-dih-FLOR-uh. An annual or short-lived tender perennial, hardy from **Zone 8 south**, that forms clumps reaching 5 feet, although plants usually stay around 2 feet in

Argemone mexicana

height. Bears showy, 4-inch-wide, white or yellow flowers, singly or in small clusters. Warm-weather annual.

A. mexicana

a. mex-ih-KAN-uh. MEXICAN PRICKLY POPPY. A sprawling 2- to 3-foot-tall species with spiny, blue-green leaves. Produces solitary, pale lemon to deep yellow flowers from midsummer to frost. 'White Lustre' bears white flowers. Warm-weather annual.

Argyranthemum

are-geh-RAN-thuh-mum. Aster family, Asteraceae.

Sometimes sold as chrysanthemums, members of this genus bear daisy- or chrysanthemum-like blooms from midsummer to frost. The flowers are single or double and come in shades of pink, yellow, and white. The genus contains about 23 species of subshrubs native to the Canary Islands and Madeira, but the plants commonly in cultivation are cultivars, generally of hybrid origin. The plants are erect or spreading and have leaves that are coarsely lobed to very finely dissected. Use them in beds and borders, as well as containers. Most also are suitable for seaside gardens.

HOW TO GROW

A site in full sun with well-drained, moderately fertile soil is ideal. They are hardy only in completely frost-free areas — **Zones 10 and 11**. In areas where they are marginally hardy, try a site against a south-facing wall for extra winter protection, and protect plants with a loose winter mulch such as

Argyranthemum frutescens 'Vancouver'

straw or salt hay; plants killed to the ground may regrow from the base. Propagate by cuttings (cultivars do not come true from seed) taken either in spring for the garden or in late summer for overwintering indoors. Pinch rooted plants to encourage bushy growth. Water regularly when plants are actively growing, and feed regularly; pot-grown plants are best fed weekly or biweekly. Deadhead to prolong bloom. Overwinter plants in a spot that is bright and cool (45° to 50°F nights).

A. frutescens

a. fru-TESS-enz. MARGUERITE DAISY, BOSTON DAISY. Formerly *Chrysanthemum frutescens*. A shrubby species reaching about 2 feet tall and wide. Deeply cut leaves. The species bears ³/4-inch, white, daisylike flowers with yellow centers, but many cultivars of hybrid origin are available. 'Comtesse du Chambourd' bears single white flowers and gray-green leaves. 'Jamaica Primrose' has single, yellow, daisylike blooms. 'Pink Australian' produces double pink flowers. Tender perennial or grow as an annual.

Arisaema

air-ih-SEE-muh. Arum family, Araceae.

The best-known member of this genus is a native North American wildflower commonly called jack-in-the-pulpit, *A. triphyllum*. About 150 species belong here — they are native to North America as well as Japan, China, and the Himalaya. The plants either are tuberous or grow from rhizomes, and they produce their unusual flowers in spring or summer. The inflores-

cence consists of many tiny flowers clustered on a central stalk — the "jack," which is more correctly called a spadix. The spadix is surrounded by a modified leaf — the "pulpit," which is more correctly called a spathe. In most species, the spathe bends over at the tip to shelter and partially enclose the spadix. The flowers are followed by round red berries in fall. Plants bear attractive leaves that are divided or lobed in a palmate fashion.

HOW TO GROW

Select a site in partial shade with rich, moist, well-drained soil. Plant tubers or purchased plants in either fall or spring. For best results, work plenty of compost or other organic matter into the soil at planting time, and mulch to keep the soil moist. Once planted, they require little care. Where they

Arisaema candidissimum

are not hardy, grow *Arisaema* species in containers and overwinter them indoors while still in their pots in a cool (40° to 45°F) spot, keeping the soil just barely moist. Propagate the plants by separating offsets in late summer or fall, before the foliage dies back. Or sow fresh seeds as soon as they are ripe.

A. candidissimum

a. kan-dih-DISS-ih-mum. A 14- to 16-inch-tall species with hooded 3- to 6-inch-long spathes that are greenish at the base and white with pink stripes at the top. Blooms have a sweet scent and appear in early summer. After the flowers appear, plants bear a single leaf with three ovate leaflets. Zones 6 to 9.

A. consanguineum

a. kon-san-GWIH-nee-um. Summer-blooming 2- to 3-foot-tall species bearing hooded 4- to 8-inch-long spathes striped with white and greenish brown. Plants have a single leaf with 10 to 20 leaflets above the inflorescence. Zones 7 to 9.

A. dracontium

a. drah-KON-tee-um. GREEN DRAGON, DRAGON ROOT. A wildflower native to eastern North America that bears green 2- to 3-inch-long spathes in spring. The spathes surround a 4- to 8-inch-long whiplike spadix that extends far beyond the spathe. Plants produce a single leaf divided into 5 to as many as 17 segments that is only

about 1 to 1¹/2 feet tall at blooming time but reaches 2 to 3 feet as the season progresses. Zones 4 to 9.

A. ringens

a. RIN-jenz. An early-summer-blooming 10- to 12-inch-tall species with hooded 4- to 6-inch-long green spathes striped and tipped with purple. Bears a pair of three-leaflet leaves above the spathes. Zones 6 to 9.

A. sikokianum

a. sih-koe-key-AH-num. A 1- to 1¹/2-foot-tall species that in late spring produces a hooded 6- to 8-inch-long purple-brown spathe that surrounds a white club-shaped spadix. Bears two leaves with three or five leaflets. Zones 5 to 9.

A. triphyllum

a. try-FILL-um. Native North American wildflower bearing hooded 4- to 6-inch-long green spathes, often striped with dark purple, in spring and early summer. Produces one or two 3-leaflet leaves and reaches 1 foot. Zones 4 to 9.

Aristolochia

ah-ris-toe-LOW-key-uh. Aristolochia family, Aristolochiaceae.

Commonly called Dutchman's pipes, *Aristolochia* species are grown for their unusually shaped blooms along with their large, often heart-shaped leaves, which make them effective plants for

Aristolochia macrophylla

Armeria maritima

shading and screening. The strange-looking flowers are petalless, but they have a large curved calyx that resembles a pipe because of its inflated base and flaring lip. Flowers come in shades of brown, maroon, purple, or white and are typically marked or mottled in combinations of these colors. They normally are pollinated by flies and other insects attracted to carrion, and most species have foul-smelling flowers. Also called pipevine, calico flower, pelican flower, and birthwort, most Dutchman's pipes are evergreen or deciduous woody twining climbers. A few of the some 300 species in the genus are shrubs or scandent perennials; most are tropical and tender.

HOW TO GROW

Select a site in full sun or partial shade. Dutchman's pipes are best in average to rich soil that is moist and well drained. Plants require a sturdy arbor or other support upon which to climb. These vigorous vines make excellent plants for shading arbors or covering trellises, pergolas, or other structures. Because of their large leaves, they form a solid screen in relatively short order. Prune as necessary in spring to shape plants and direct their growth. Propagate by taking cuttings in midsummer. Dutchman's pipes attract butterflies, specifically pipevine swallowtails.

A. macrophylla

a. mack-roe-FILL-uh. DUTCH-MAN'S PIPE. Formerly *A. durior*. A vigorous woody vine native to the southeastern United States that reaches 25 to 30 feet. Bears heart-shaped, 4- to 12-inch-long leaves. Insignificant 1-inch-wide flowers appear in summer in the leaf axils.

Blooms are greenish and mottled with yellow, purple, or brown. Zones 5 to 8.

Armeria

are-MEER-ee-uh. Plumbago family, Plumbaginaceae.

Dense rosettes of linear or strap-shaped leaves topped by round clusters of tiny flowers characterize the 80 or so species of the genus *Armeria*. Commonly known as sea pinks, thrifts, or simply armerias, they are low-growing evergreen perennials or subshrubs that form attractive mounds or tufts of basal foliage. The globular flower heads come in shades from pink to magenta-purple, purplish red, and white. They are carried above the foliage on thin, leafless, erect stems.

HOW TO GROW

Give armerias a spot in full sun with poor to average soil that is well drained and not too rich. Sandy soil is ideal. These perennials thrive by the ocean and prefer areas with cool summers; in areas with hot summers, give them shade during the afternoon. Propagate by division in early spring, by taking cuttings from shoots that appear at the base of the plants in summer, or by seeds.

A. juniperifolia

a. jew-nip-er-ih-FOE-lee-uh. Formerly *A. caespitosa*. Compact 2- to 3-inch-tall species forming 6-inch-wide mounds of gray-green ¾-inch-long leaves. In late spring and early summer, bears purplish pink ½-inch-wide flower clusters that are held about ¾ to 1 inch above the foliage. 'Alba' has white flowers. 'Bevan's Variety' bears

nearly stemless pink flowers on 2-inch-tall plants. Zones 4 to 8.

A. maritima

a. mah-RIT-ih-muh. SEA PINK, COMMON THRIFT. A variable species with rosettes of 1½- to 5-inch-long leaves that form 1-foot-wide mounds. Produces 1-inch-wide flower clusters in early summer in shades from pink to reddish purple or white on erect 6- to 8-inch-tall stems. 'Alba' features white flowers. 'Dusseldorf Pride' has deep rose pink flowers. 'Vindictive' bears rosy red blooms. 'Rubrifolia' has red-purple foliage and rosy pink flowers. All are hardy in Zones 3 to 8. 'Bees Ruby' produces hot pink 1¼- to 1½-inch-wide flowers on 12-inch-tall stems and is hardy to Zone 6.

Aronia

ah-ROE-nee-uh. Rose family, Rosaceae.

This is a genus of only two species, both deciduous woodland shrubs from the eastern United States and commonly called chokeberry. They are grown primarily for their stunning fall color and berries.

HOW TO GROW

Native to swamps and moist banks, chokeberries adapt to drier soils ranging from neutral to acid, and even to low fertility. Fruiting is best in full sun. They tend to sucker and become leggy, a trait that is less apparent when they are massed for a huge splash of fall color. If you have space to accommodate their inevitable spread,

Aronia arbutifolia
'Brilliantissima'

Aronia arbutifolia

they are ideal for naturalizing. They are prone to insects and diseases that disfigure other members of the rose family. Pruning back by a third or more will control spread and stimulate new growth. Propagate from dormant suckers, soft-wood cuttings in summer, or seeds planted in autumn.

A. arbutifolia 'Brilliantissima'

a. are-bew-tih-FOE-lee-uh. RED CHOKEBERRY CULTIVAR. This selection grows 6 to 8 feet tall and 3 to 5 feet wide and has lustrous, oval, finely toothed 3- to 4-inch leaves that are hairy and gray on the undersides, with autumn leaves predominantly a brilliant red. The late-spring flowers are white and arranged in 2-inch corymbs, upstaged by the abundant bright red fruits, which can be persistent but are a favorite of mockingbirds. This cultivar received a Gold Medal from the Pennsylvania Horticultural Society in 2000. Zones 4 to 9.

A. melanocarpa

a. mel-an-oh-KAR-puh. BLACK CHOKEBERRY. This species is similar to red chokeberry but only 3 to 5 feet tall, spreading to twice as wide. The fall fruits are larger and dark purple. Most cultivars have reddish purple foliage in autumn. 'Autumn Magic' has a mix of red and purple leaves. 'Morton' (trademarked as Iroquois Beauty) is a dwarf growing to 3 feet. Zones 3 to 8.

Artemisia

are-teh-MEE-see-uh. Aster family, Asteraceae.

Grown for their foliage rather than their flowers, artemisias are perennials, annuals, or shrubs usually native to dry or arid habitats in the Northern Hemisphere. About 300 species belong to the genus, and plants may be evergreen or deciduous. Most have aromatic foliage and many feature

Artemisia ludoviciana
'Silver King'

silver or gray-green leaves that may be smooth edged, toothed, or deeply cut and feathery. Artemisias produce tiny insignificant flower heads, typically carried in panicles or racemes but sometimes singly. The flower heads, which usually appear from mid- to late summer, are yellowish or grayish and lack ray florets. In addition to a variety of ornamental perennials, the genus also includes herbs, most notably tarragon (*A. dracunculus*). It also contains some vigorous weeds, such as mugwort (*A. vulgaris*).

HOW TO GROW

A site in full sun with average, well-drained soil will satisfy most artemisias. *A. lactiflora* is an exception: give it full sun and well-drained soil that remains evenly moist. Artemisias tolerate poor, dry conditions; sandy soils; and seaside conditions — most are quite drought tolerant — but heavy, wet soils are generally fatal. *A. stelleriana* is especially tolerant of saline soil and seaside conditions. Some species do not tolerate heat and humidity. Cut plants back hard in late fall or early spring annually, and cut species that tend to flop over during the growing season back hard again in early to midsummer to keep them compact and erect. Divide fast-spreading species, particularly *A. lactiflora* and *A. ludoviciana* and their cultivars, every 2 to 3 years to keep them in check. Propagate by division in spring or fall, by stem or heel cuttings taken in early

Artemisia schmidtiana 'Nana'

summer, or by mallet cuttings in late summer. Artemisias make excellent silvery ground covers in thin, dry soils.

A. abrotanum
a. ah-broe-TAY-num. SOUTHERNWOOD, LAD'S LOVE. Shrubby 3- to 4-foot-tall species that spreads as far to form feathery textured mounds of threadlike, aromatic, pale green to gray-green leaves. **Zones 5 to 8.**

A. absinthium
a. ab-SIN-thee-um. WORMWOOD. Vigorous, shrubby, 2- to 3-foot-tall perennial that spreads as far. Absinthe, an addictive and toxic narcotic beverage popular in certain artistic circles at the end of the 19th century, is derived from this species. Forms mounds of aromatic, deeply divided, silky-hairy leaves. 'Lambrook Silver' produces silver-gray foliage on 2¹/₂-foot plants. **Zones 3 to 9.**

A. annua
a. AN-yew-uh. SWEET WORMWOOD, ANNUAL ARTEMISIA, SWEET ANNIE. Deeply cut, featherlike, green leaves with a sweet fragrance on fast-growing, well-branched plants ranging from 1 to 5 feet or more in height. Bears panicles of tiny yellow flowers. Flowers and foliage are used in herbal preparations, and the dried foliage is popular for use in wreaths because of its sweet fragrance. Hang cut branches in small bunches in a warm, dark, dry place to dry. Cool-weather annual.

A. lactiflora
a. lak-tih-FLOR-uh. WHITE SAGE, WHITE MUGWORT. A 4- to 6-foot-tall species that spreads to

about 4 feet. Bears deeply cut, dark green leaves and handsome creamy white panicles of flowers from late summer to fall that add airy texture to plantings. **Zones 4 to 9.**

A. ludoviciana
a. loo-doe-vish-ee-AH-nuh. WHITE SAGE, WESTERN MUGWORT. Fast-spreading 2- to 4-foot-tall species that forms 2-foot-wide clumps of lance-shaped, silver-white, felted leaves that become greener with age. Plants spread vigorously by rhizomes and can be quite invasive if not divided regularly. 'Silver King' has white leaves. 'Silver Queen', another fast spreader, has larger leaves than the species and reaches about 2¹/₂ feet in height. 'Valerie Finnis' is a 1¹/₂-foot-tall selection that is not invasive but is less tolerant of summer heat and rain than the species. **Zones 3 to 9.**

A. 'Powis Castle'
Shrubby 2- to 3-foot perennial forming handsome, billowing 2- to 3-foot-wide clumps of feathery, aromatic, silver-gray foliage. **Zones 5 to 8.**

A. schmidtiana
a. shmid-ee-AH-nuh. SILVERMOUND ARTEMISIA. Mound-forming 1- to 2-foot-tall perennial with 1¹/₂-foot-wide clumps of feathery, finely cut silver-gray leaves. The clumps often flop open in the center in areas with hot, humid summers. 'Nana' (also sold as 'Silver Mound'), a compact selection, is more common in cultivation than the species. **Zones 3 to 7.**

A. stelleriana
a. steh-lair-ee-AH-nuh. BEACH WORMWOOD, OLD WOMAN, PERENNIAL DUSTY MILLER. Compact 6- to 12-inch-tall species that spreads by rhizomes to about 2¹/₂ feet. Bears deeply lobed, felted white leaves. **Zones 3 to 8.**

Arum

AIR-um. Arum family, Araceae.

Closely related to jack-in-the-pulpits (*Arisaema*), arums — or lords and ladies as they are sometimes called — are tuberous, deciduous perennials native to southern Eu-

Arum italicum 'Marmoratum'

rope, northern Africa, and Asia. About 26 species belong to the genus, most of which bloom in spring or early summer. Most species produce new leaves in fall or early winter that last until about the time the plants bloom, then go dormant. The exotic-looking "flowers" somewhat resemble those of calla lilies (*Zantedeschia*), another close relative, and may have a sweet or unpleasant scent. They are actually an inflorescence consisting of many tiny flowers clustered on a central stalk, called a spadix. The spadix is surrounded by a modified leaf, called a spathe. Showy spikes of red or orange berries follow the flowers in late summer and fall. Leaves may be spear, arrow, or heart shaped and are often attractively marbled. In areas with mild winters, the leaves remain attractive until late spring and add interest to shade and woodland gardens at that time of year. All parts of the plants are poisonous if ingested, and the sap can cause skin irritation.

HOW TO GROW
Select a site in full sun or partial shade with deeply prepared, rich, moist, well-drained soil. A sheltered site is best, especially because it helps protect the foliage in winter. Set tubers with the tops 4 to 6 inches below the soil surface (roots develop from the tops of the tubers). Mark the locations of the plants to avoid digging into them by mistake when they are dormant. Mulch with compost in spring to keep the soil rich and to help retain moisture. In areas where the plants are marginally hardy, cover them with a coarse mulch such as evergreen boughs in late fall. In areas where arums are not hardy, grow them in pots and overwinter them in a cool (40° to 50°F) spot. Propagate by separating offsets or by sowing fresh seeds.

A. creticum
a. KREH-tih-kum. Tuberous, spring-flowering species with arrow-shaped dark green leaves and fragrant flowers. Spathes are yellow or creamy white and are 6 to 10 inches long. Plants range from 1 to 2¹/₂ feet in height. **Zones 8 to 10.**

A. dioscoridis
a. dye-oss-KOR-ih-dis. Tuberous 8- to 12-inch-tall species with spring flowers featuring 6- to 14-inch-long spathes that are deep purple or green and blushed or spotted with maroon. Bears narrow, ar-

Aruncus dioicus

row-shaped leaves. Flowers have an unpleasant scent. **Zones 7 to 9.**

A. italicum
a. ih-TAL-ih-kum. ITALIAN ARUM. Tuberous perennial grown primarily for its handsome, leathery, arrow-shaped leaves that range from 10 to 14 inches long. Bears flowers with pale greenish white, 6- to 16-inch-long spathes in early summer and showy, erect spikes of orange-red berries that are attractive until fall, when the new leaves appear. 'Marmoratum', also sold as 'Pictum', is more commonly grown than the species; it bears leaves netted with pale green or cream veins. **Zones 6 to 9; to Zone 5 with winter protection.**

A. maculatum
a. mak-yew-LAY-tum. LORDS AND LADIES, CUCKOO-PINT, ADAM-AND-EVE. A 12- to 15-inch-tall species that is similar to *A. italicum* but bears glossy, arrow-shaped leaves that usually have black or purple spots and appear in spring with the flowers. Blooms have yellow-green 6- to 10-inch-long spathes usually edged and spotted with purple. Berries are bright red. **Zones 6 to 9.**

Aruncus
ah-RUN-kus. Rose family, Rosaceae.

Aruncus species, or goat's beards, as they are commonly called, are

handsome perennials grown for their clusters of creamy white flowers. While the individual flowers are tiny, they are borne abundantly in branched, airy clusters. Two or three species belong to the genus, all generally bearing male and female flowers on separate plants. (Botanically speaking, *Aruncus* species actually are polygamo-dioecious, rather than dioecious, since plants produce some perfect, or bisexual, flowers as well.) The flowers are carried above attractive mounds of pinnate leaves.

HOW TO GROW
Give goat's beards a site with partial or dappled shade and rich, evenly moist soil. In areas with cool summers they tolerate full sun provided they receive constant soil moisture. In most cases, a site that is shady during the hottest part of the day is best, and constant soil moisture is essential for success in the South. Plants thrive along streams and ponds; in such sites, plant them with the crown a foot or so above the water table. Leaves that develop crisp brown edges are an indication that the soil is too dry. Plants spread by rhizomes to form large handsome clumps. To propagate, divide clumps in spring or early fall, although established plants have deep, woody roots and are quite difficult to dig. Or sow seeds.

A. aethusifolius
a. ee-thew-sih-FOE-lee-us. DWARF GOAT'S BEARD. Clump-forming 8- to 12-inch-tall species that forms 1- to 1¹/₂-foot-wide mounds topped by creamy white flowers from early to midsummer. **Zones 4 to 8.**

A. dioicus
a. die-OH-ih-kus. GOAT'S BEARD. Shrub-sized native North American species that ranges from 3 to 6

feet in height and spreads to 4 feet. Bears plumy 1- to 2-foot-long clusters of creamy white flowers from early to midsummer. **Zones 3 to 7.**

Arundo
ah-RUN-doe. Grass family, Poaceae.

Arundo contains two or three species of grasses, one of which is grown for its distinctive bamboo-like foliage and giant stature. The plants have jointed, reedlike stems with long, broadly linear leaves. They are evergreen in warm climates. Where seasons are long enough, the plants produce fluffy panicles of flowers in fall.

HOW TO GROW
Plant in full sun and average, moist but well-drained soil. Plants tolerate heat and seaside conditions. In warm climates, they can become very invasive (especially in moist soil) and difficult to control, but they are rarely a problem at the northern limits of their hardiness. Cut the plants to the ground in late winter or very early spring, even in areas where they are evergreen. Divide as necessary to keep the clumps a manageable size. Propagate in spring either by division or by cuttings taken from stems at the base of the plant.

A. donax
a. DOE-nax. GIANT REED. Enormous 10- to 25-foot-tall ornamental grass that forms clumps of thick reedlike stems and spreads by rhizomes to form clumps that exceed 5 feet. *A. donax* var. *versicolor*, commonly sold as 'Variegata', is 6 to 12 feet tall and

Aruncus dioicus

Arundo donax 'Variegata'

Asphodelus albus

long racemes of starry bright yellow flowers in late spring or early summer. Blooms are fragrant and 1 inch wide. **Zones 6 to 8; to Zone 5 with winter protection.**

Asphodelus

as-foe-DEL-us. Lily family, Liliaceae.

Native from the Mediterranean region and central Europe to Asia, *Asphodelus* species are grown for their dense, erect racemes of starry, funnel-shaped flowers. The flowers are white or pink and have six petal-like tepals. The leafless flower stalks are borne above clumps of grassy basal leaves. (Species in the closely related genus *Asphodeline* bear flower stalks that have leaves on them.) The genus contains 12 species, including perennials growing from clumps of congested, fleshy rhizomes as well as annuals, biennials, and short-lived perennials with fibrous roots.

HOW TO GROW

Select a site in full sun with average, well-drained soil that is deeply prepared. Established clumps can thrive for years without requiring division or other care. Propagate by dividing the clumps in spring or fall or by sowing seeds.

A. aestivus

a. ESS-tih-vus. A 3-foot-tall species with leathery 1- to 1$^{1}/_{2}$-foot-long linear leaves and racemes of 2- to 3-inch-wide flowers in spring that are white or white flushed with pink. **Zones 7 to 10.**

A. albus

a. AL-bus. A 2$^{1}/_{2}$- to 3-foot-tall species with linear 1- to 2-foot-long leaves and starry white $^{3}/_{4}$- to 1$^{1}/_{2}$-inch flowers with pink veins in early summer. **Zones 7 to 10.**

Aster

ASS-ter. Aster family, Asteraceae.

The colorful blooms of asters are a familiar sight in fall, but this large genus contains a range of perennials that can provide a parade of daisylike flowers beginning in early summer. Some 250 species of annuals, biennials, perennials, and subshrubs belong here, many native to North America. The individual blooms are starry — *aster* is the Latin word for "star" — and like daisies they consist of ray florets, commonly called petals, surrounding dense buttonlike centers of disk florets, which are generally yellow. Flowers usually range from 1 to 2 inches wide and may be single, semidouble, or double. They come in shades of purple, violet, lavender, blue, pink, ruby red, and white. A few species bear solitary flowers (one per stem), but most produce their blooms in loose, showy clusters. Leaves typically are lance shaped. Depending on the species or cultivar, the plants range from under a foot in height to 8 feet or more. Asters grow from creeping rhizomes and form spreading clumps.

Aster novae-angliae

HOW TO GROW

Most asters thrive in full sun and rich, well-drained, evenly moist soil. However, there are species suitable for other sites. *A. cordifolius, A. divaricatus,* and *A. macrophyllus* all grow in partial shade, while *A. ericoides* and *A. lateriflorus* thrive in full sun with very poor soil. *A. alpinus* is best in areas with cool summers. For all species, a site with good air circulation is best, since asters are subject to powdery mildew. Give plants plenty of room to ensure good air circulation; as a general rule, space plants at about half their height. Feed plants in spring with a topdressing of compost, well-rotted manure, or a balanced organic fertilizer. Mulch *A. novae-angliae* and *A. novi-belgii* to help hold moisture in the soil.

To keep plants compact and encourage branching, in spring and again in early summer pinch out the stem tips or cut plants back by one-third to one-half with hedge shears. Do not pinch fall-blooming asters after June 15 from about Zone 6 north, or you may remove the flower buds. In the South, asters can be pinched as late as July 1. Pinch *A. × frikartii* only once in spring, and do not pinch *A. alpinus.* Stake taller-growing species in spring or very early summer. Remove flowers after they fade to curtail self-sowing: hybrid asters do not come true from seed, and seedlings will compete with them. (You may decide to leave self-sown seedlings of species asters, especially in a wild garden.) Most asters need to be divided every 2 to 3 years to keep them vigorous. Propagate by division in spring or from cuttings taken in

spring or early summer. Species can be started from seeds.

A. alpinus

a. al-PIE-nus. ALPINE ASTER. A 6- to 12-inch-tall species, spreading to 1$^{1}/_{2}$ feet. Bears solitary flower heads from early to midsummer in violet purple to lavender, pink, and white. **Zones 2 to 7.**

A. amellus

a. ah-MELL-us. ITALIAN ASTER. A 1- to 2-foot-tall species, spreading to 1$^{1}/_{2}$ feet. Bears loose clusters of 1$^{1}/_{4}$- to 2-inch-wide flower heads in shades from violet, violet-blue, and lilac to pink from late summer to frost. Thrives in alkaline soil. Cultivars include 'Nocturne', with lilac flowers; 'Sonia', pink; and 'Violet Queen' ('Veilchenkönigin'), violet. **Zones 5 to 8.**

A. carolinianus

a. kare-oh-lin-ee-AH-nus. CLIMBING ASTER. Native North American subshrub with long arching branches that reach 5 to 10 feet or more and can be tied to trellises or trained through shrubs. Bears an abundance of solitary, 1-inch-wide, pale pink or purple flower heads in fall. In the North, it can be overwintered as a tender perennial by cuttings taken in late summer. **Zones 6 to 9.**

A. cordifolius

a. kor-dih-FOE-lee-us. BLUE WOOD ASTER, HEART-LEAVED ASTER. Native North American species forming 2- to 5-foot-tall, 2-foot-wide clumps. Bears clusters of $^{3}/_{4}$-inch-wide pale lavender or white flower heads from late summer to fall. **Zones 4 to 8.**

Aster novae-angliae

A. divaricatus

a. dih-vair-ih-KAH-tus. WHITE WOOD ASTER. Native North American species that reaches 1 to 2 feet in height and spreads as far. Produces loose clusters of starry white ³/₄-inch-wide flower heads in abundance from midsummer through fall. **Zones 4 to 8.**

A. ericoides

a. air-ih-KOY-deez. HEATH ASTER. Native North American species ranging from 1 to 3 feet tall and spreading to 2 feet. Bears needlelike leaves and loose clusters of ³/₄-inch-wide white flower heads in abundance from late summer to fall. **Zones 3 to 8.**

A. × frikartii

a. × frih-KAR-tee-eye. FRIKART'S ASTER. A 2- to 3-foot-tall hybrid bearing loose sprays of lavender-blue 2- to 3-inch-wide flowers from midsummer through fall on 1¹/₂-foot-wide plants. 'Mönch' and 'Wonder of Staffa', both lavender-blue, are the most popular cultivars. **Zones 5 to 8.**

A. lateriflorus

a. lah-ter-ih-FLOR-us. CALICO ASTER, STARVED ASTER. North American native reaching 2 to 4 feet in height and spreading from 2 to 3 feet. Bears clouds of starry ¹/₂-inch-wide flower heads in white to pale lavender from midsummmer to fall. **Zones 3 to 8.**

A. macrophyllus

a. mack-roe-FILL-us. LARGE-LEAVED ASTER, BIGLEAF ASTER. Native North American aster reaching 1 to 2¹/₂ feet in height and spreading as far. Bears flat clusters of 1-inch-wide white to pale lavender flower heads from late summer to fall. **Zones 4 to 8.**

A. novae-angliae

a. NO-vay-ANG-lee-eye. NEW ENGLAND ASTER, MICHAELMAS DAISY. Much-hybridized native North American species that grows to 1¹/₂ feet tall and spreads from 2 to 4 feet. Bears showy clusters of violet, purple, lavender, rose-red, pink, or white flowers in fall. Individual flower heads are 1¹/₂ to 2 inches wide, and leaves are lance shaped with lobes that clasp the hairy stem at the base. Cultivars include 'Alma Pötschke' (rose pink), 'Harrington's Pink' (light pink), and 'Hella Lacy' (royal purple). 'Purple Dome' produces mounds of deep purple flowers on compact 1¹/₂-foot plants that do not need staking or pinching. **Zones 3 to 8.**

A. novi-belgii

a. NO-vee BELL-jee-eye. NEW YORK ASTER, MICHAELMAS DAISY. Much-hybridized native North American species ranging from 1 to 4 feet in height and spreading from 2 to 3 feet. Bears showy clusters of lavender-blue, white, ruby red, pink, or purple flower heads in fall. Individual flower heads are 1 to 1¹/₂ inches wide, and leaves are much narrower than those of *A. novae-angliae*. 'Eventide' has semidouble purple blooms. 'Fellowship' bears deep pink 3-inch blooms. Low-growing selections, including 6- to 10-inch white-flowered 'Niobe' and 14-inch lavender-blue 'Professor Anton Kippenberg', do not need staking. **Zones 3 to 8.**

A. tataricus

a. tah-TAR-ih-kus. TARTARIAN ASTER. Robust, strong-stemmed, 5- to 8-foot-tall species spreading to 3 feet or more. Bears large clusters of lavender-blue 1- to 1¹/₄-

Aster novi-belgii

inch-wide flower heads from mid-to late fall. 'Jindai' is a comparative dwarf, reaching only 4 to 5 feet tall. **Zones 2 to 8.**

Astilbe

uh-STILL-bee. Saxifrage family, Saxifragaceae.

Astilbes are clump-forming, rhizomatous perennials that form 1- to 3-foot-tall mounds of handsome, fernlike foliage topped by feathery, plumelike flower clusters that rise several inches above the foliage in late spring and summer. Flowers come in white, shades of pink, ruby red to crimson, and rosy purple. The individual flowers are quite tiny but are borne in abundance in densely packed, branched panicles that may be roughly pyramidal in shape, weeping, or stiffly upright. About 12 species belong to the genus, all native to moist, generally shaded sites in eastern Asia and North America.

HOW TO GROW

Rich, constantly moist, well-drained soil is essential to success with astilbes. Partial shade is best — a site with sun in the morning and shade in the afternoon is ideal. In the North, where summers remain relatively cool, astilbes grow in full sun provided the soil remains moist. In the South, give them partial to full shade. Curled leaves with crispy brown edges signal that plants are receiving too little moisture and too much sun. Provided they are

Astilbe 'Fanal'

planted above the water line, astilbes are good choices for sites along streams and ponds. *A. chinensis* var. *davidii* and *A. chinensis* var. *taquetii* tolerate drier soil and more sun than most astilbes do. Work plenty of compost or other organic matter into the soil at planting time and feed annually in spring by top-dressing with compost or a balanced organic fertilizer. If the woody crowns grow above the soil surface, either top-dress the plants with loose soil to cover them or divide and replant. Water regularly in dry weather, and mulch with chopped leaves or compost to hold in soil moisture. To keep plants vigorous or to propagate them, dig and divide them every 3 to 4 years in spring or early fall.

A. chinensis

a. chih-NEN-sis. CHINESE ASTILBE. Vigorous species that reaches 2 feet tall and spreads as far. It bears pinkish white flowers in late summer. *A. chinensis* var. *davidii* (formerly *A. davidii*) has purple-pink blooms and bronze-tinted leaves and reaches 4 to 6 feet. *A. chinensis* var. *pumila* is a dwarf form with foliage that reaches about 6 inches and erect 10- to 12-inch-tall purplish pink plumes in midsummer to early fall. In shade with abundant moisture plants reach 2 feet or more. *A. chinensis* var. *taquetii* (sometimes listed as *A. taquetii*) and its cultivars 'Purple Lance' ('Purpurlanze') and 'Superba' bear plumes

Astilbe chinensis 'Pumila'

in shades of red-purple from mid-summer to fall on 4-foot-tall plants. **Zones 4 to 8.**

A. hybrids

Astilbes have been heavily hybridized (the species are seldom grown), and many cultivars are available. Hybrids range from 2 to 3 feet in height and spread to about 2 feet. Many feature showy red to bronze foliage in spring. Early- to midseason cultivars bloom in late spring and early summer and include white-flowered 'Deutschland'; pink 'Europa', 'Peach Blossom', and 'Rheinand'; and crimson-rose 'Bremen'. Midseason bloomers include white 'Bridal Veil' and 'Snowdrift', blood red 'Fanal', and carmine-rose 'Federsee'. Late-season cultivars include rose pink 'Cattleya' and scarlet 'Red Sentinel'. All are cultivars of either A. × *arendsii* or A. *japonica*. **Zones 4 to 8; to Zone 3 with winter protection.**

A. simplicifolia

a. sim-plih-sih-FOE-lee-uh. S T A R A S T I L B E . Dwarf 1- to 1¹/₂-foot-tall plants with glossy leaves and loose plumes of flowers in mid- to late summer. 'Gnom', which bears pale pink flowers, reaches only about 6 inches tall. 'Sprite' also produces pale pink flowers and has bronzy foliage. **Zones 4 to 8.**

A. thunbergii

a. thun-BER-jee-eye. Vigorous 3- to 4-foot-tall moisture-loving species

Astilbe chinensis 'Pumila'

that spreads to 3 feet. Its cultivar 'Ostrich Plume' ('Straussenfeder'), with coral pink flowers in mid- to late summer, is most often grown. **Zones 4 to 9.**

Astrantia

ah-STRAN-tee-uh. Carrot family, Apiaceae.

Commonly known as masterworts, *Astrantia* species are clump-forming perennials that make attractive additions to the shade garden. About 10 species belong to the genus, all native to cool, alpine woods and meadows in Europe and Asia. At first glance, the buttonlike flowers do not seem to suggest a relationship to carrots or dill, two other well-known carrot-family plants. However, close inspection reveals that each bloom consists of an umbel of small, tightly packed, five-petaled flowers. The umbels are surrounded by a showy ruff of papery, petal-like bracts. The flowers are borne on branched stems above loose mounds of leaves that are cut or lobed in a palmate fashion.

HOW TO GROW

Plant in partial or dappled shade and rich, evenly moist soil. Plants tolerate full sun provided the soil is very rich and remains evenly moist. Try them along ponds or streams, with the crowns planted above the water table, or in open, moist woodlands. They require cool night temperatures for best performance. Propagate by division in spring or by seeds. Plants self-sow.

A. major

a. MAY-jor. M A S T E R W O R T . Clump-forming 1- to 3-foot-tall perennial producing 1¹/₂-foot-wide mounds of attractive leaves with five to seven toothed lobes. The

³/₄- to 1¹/₄-inch-wide umbels of flowers come in green, pink, or sometimes purplish red and have a ruff of green-veined white bracts beneath them. Blooms early to midsummer. 'Hadspen Blood' bears maroon bracts and flowers. 'Sunningdale Variegated' bears pink flowers and leaves edged in creamy yellow that fades to green. **Zones 4 to 7.**

Athyrium

ah-THY-ree-um. Wood Fern family, Dryopteridaceae.

Athyrium species, commonly called lady ferns, are terrestrial, deciduous perennials with handsome fronds that are once-, twice-, or thrice-cut or divided in a pinnate fashion. The plants grow from rhizomes that either spread slowly to form compact, mounding clumps or grow erect to form crowns. There are 180 species in the genus, 2 of which are commonly grown in gardens.

HOW TO GROW

Select a site in partial to full shade with evenly moist, well-drained soil rich in organic matter. A spot with bright, indirect light or dappled shade under the high branches of oaks or other deep-rooted trees is ideal, as is one with morning sun and afternoon shade. Plants have somewhat brittle fronds that break easily, so keep them away from high-traffic or windy sites. Work plenty of organic matter such as compost or chopped leaves into the soil at planting time. Water deeply during dry weather. A. *filix-femina* has erect rhizomes that gradually grow too far out of the soil. Dig and divide the clumps every few years, and replant the divisions with the crowns at soil level to keep them

Athyrium niponicum

vigorous. To propagate, divide the clumps in spring.

A. filix-femina

a. FEE-lix-FEM-in-uh. L A D Y F E R N , E U R O P E A N L A D Y F E R N . Vigorous 2- to 3-foot-tall species that spreads as far and forms mounds of thrice-cut fronds that taper slightly at the base. Many forms of this fern are available, featuring branched, crested, or plumy fronds. **Zones 4 to 8.**

A. niponicum

a. nih-PON-ih-kum. J A PA N E S E PA I N T E D F E R N . Formerly A. *goeringianum*. Rhizomatous 1- to 1¹/₂-foot-tall Japanese native spreading vigorously to form drifts to 2 or more feet wide. Bears twice-cut fronds variously marked with silver or gray and maroon-purple midribs. A. *niponicum* var. *pictum* (also sold as 'Pictum') is more commonly sold than the species and has leaves splashed with burgundy and silver. **Zones 4 to 9.**

Aubretia

aw-BREE-shah. Cabbage family, Brassicaceae.

Commonly called rock cresses or simply aubretias, *Aubretia* species bear small clusters of four-petaled, cross-shaped flowers in spring. Blooms are carried atop dense mounds or mats of small, hairy,

Astrantia major

Athyrium niponicum var. *pictum*

evergreen leaves that range from oval to oblong and may be toothed. About 12 species of perennials belong to the genus, but gardeners most often grow hybrids, collectively referred to as *A. × cultorum.*

HOW TO GROW

Give aubretias full sun and average, well-drained soil. Neutral to alkaline pH is best, and plants grow well in sandy soil. Clayey soil that is poorly aerated and remains wet for long periods is fatal. Aubretias do not tolerate heat well and are short-lived in the South, although a site with light shade during the afternoon can help them cope. Shear plants after the flowers fade to keep them compact. Especially in hot-summer areas, propagate new plants every 2 to 3 years to keep them vigorous. Propagate by taking cuttings in spring after the flowers fade or by carefully dividing the clumps in spring or fall. Aubretias are easy to grow from seeds, but most cultivated forms do not come true.

A. × cultorum

a. × kul-TOR-um. A U B R E T I A, R O C K C R E S S. Hybrids are sometimes listed as *A. deltoidea,* one of the parent species. These low-growing, mat-forming perennials reach 2 inches in height and spread to 2 feet or more. Hy-

Aucuba japonica

brids bear single or double ¹/₂-inch-wide flowers in shades of pink, purple, mauve, violet purple, magenta, or red in spring. Variegated forms with leaves edged in white or yellow are available. **Zones 4 to 7.**

Aucuba

ah-KOO-buh. Dogwood family, Cornaceae.

There are three or four evergreen, dioecious species in this genus, native from the Himalaya to East Asia. One species is popular in southern gardens for its handsome, leathery, often variegated leaves and shade tolerance. Despite its membership in the dogwood family, the common names "spotted laurel" and "Japanese laurel" more accurately reflect the appearance of its evergreen foliage.

HOW TO GROW

Variegated aucubas, particularly, should have some shade all year. All should have shade in the southern portion of their range and protection from winter sun and wind in the more northerly regions. They tolerate dry soil, heavy clay, air pollution, and salty wind and can even be grown under trees. Use them to brighten dark corners, as an unusual medium-high hedge, or in containers. They need little pruning. Trim hedges in spring to control growth, and remove any solid green branches on variegated selections. Aucubas root easily from cuttings all year.

A. japonica

a. juh-PON-ih-kuh. J A P A N E S E A U C U B A. Usually growing to about 6 feet (occasionally up to 10 feet or more) and slightly nar-

Aubretia × cultorum

Aucuba japonica 'Variegata'

rower, this species bears ¹/₃-inch purple flowers in early to midspring, the males in upright terminal panicles to 4 inches long and the females in shorter panicles in the leaf axils. In midautumn females bear elliptic, bright red, ¹/₂-inch-long fruits, up to five in a cluster. The gold-flecked 'Variegata', or 'Gold Dust', was introduced to the trade before the species. 'Sulfur' ('Sulfurea Marginata') has wide yellow edges. **Zones 7 to 10.**

Aurinia

aw-RIH-nee-uh. Cabbage family, Brassicaceae.

Clump-forming evergreen biennials or perennials, *Aurinia* species are natives of rocky, mountainous areas from southern Europe east to Russia and Turkey. Plants produce low, tufted rosettes of hairy, lance- to spoon-shaped evergreen leaves. The clumps are topped in late spring and early summer by showy, rounded clusters of tiny

four-petaled flowers in yellow or white. One of the seven species in the genus is commonly grown in gardens. It makes a handsome cascading plant.

HOW TO GROW

Select a site in full sun with average soil that is well drained and not too rich. Cut the plants back hard after they flower to keep them neat looking and compact. To propagate, take cuttings in early summer of shoots that have not flowered or divide plants in spring. The plants are easy from seeds, but many cultivars do not come true.

A. saxatilis

a. sax-ah-TILL-iss. B A S K E T - O F - G O L D, C L O T H - O F - G O L D, G O L D D U S T. Formerly *Alyssum saxatile.* Vigorous, mound-forming species with gray-green hairy leaves on 8-inch-tall plants that spread to 1 foot or more. Bears dense, rounded clusters of small, brilliant yellow flowers. 'Citrina' has lemon yellow flowers. **Zones 4 to 8.**

Aurinia saxatilis

Babiana

bah-bee-AH-nuh. Iris family, Iridaceae.

Both the common and botanical names for this genus of 50 to 60 species of South African plants have an unusual derivation. The corms of these plants are a favorite food of baboons, thus the common name "baboon flower." The botanical name comes from the Dutch and Anglicized names for these African primates: *bobbejane* and *babianer*. *Babiana* species bear pleated, lance-shaped leaves and freesia-like spikes of funnel-shaped flowers that come in shades of purple, blue, violet, red, pink, yellow, cream, and white. Flowers appear in spring and often are very fragrant. They are made up of six petal-like tepals.

HOW TO GROW

Select a site in full sun with light, rich, well-drained soil. Plants tolerate poor soil provided it is well drained. A spot with light shade during the hottest part of the day affords beneficial heat protection, however. These plants are best in frost-free regions with dry summers, such as California, where they grow during the winter months and are dormant during the hot, dry summers. However,

Babiana stricta

they can grow in areas with rainy summers provided they are in very well drained soil; a spot in a raised bed or rock garden also is beneficial. In the North, grow babianas in containers or treat the corms as you would gladiolus: plant in spring, dig them after they have entered dormancy in summer or fall, and store them dry over winter in a cool (50° to 60°F), dry, frost-free place. Where hardy, plant corms in late summer or early fall for bloom the following spring, setting them with the tops 4 to 6 inches deep. Where plants are marginally hardy, try deeper planting — from 8 to 10 inches provided the soil is deeply prepared and well drained. (In the wild, they are found at depths up to 1 foot, and corms planted shallowly will gradually move deeper into the soil.) Pots of corms planted in fall and overwintered in a cool greenhouse or sunroom with nighttime temperatures between 40° and 50°F will bloom in early spring. Water regularly when plants are actively growing, and gradually withhold water once the leaves begin to turn yellow. Propagate by separating the offsets.

B. rubrocyanea

b. rue-broh-sy-AN-ee-uh. Low-growing 2- to 8-inch-tall species that bears spikes of five to ten $^3/_4$- to $1^1/_2$-inch-wide red-and-blue flowers in spring. **Zones 8 to 10.**

B. stricta

b. STRIK-tuh. A 5- to 12-inch-tall species with four- to eight-flowered spikes of $^3/_4$- to $1^1/_2$-inch-long flowers in spring in shades of blue, purple, mauve, and yellow. Kew Hybrids bear blooms in a range of pastel colors. **Zones 8 to 10.**

Baccharis

BAK-kar-iss. Aster family, Asteraceae.

There are more than 300 species of trees, shrubs, and perennials in the genus *Baccharis*, and all are native to North and South America. Only a few of the shrubby species are used as ornamentals in warm temperate gardens, and these are highly tolerant of salty soils. Leaves are evergreen, small; flowers are inconspicuous, but their tiny seeds are produced in conspicuous masses of cottony fibers that make an eye-catching sight in early fall. If you don't enjoy this ephemeral mess, nurseries offer seedless male plants.

HOW TO GROW

The species listed here tolerate moderate to poor, sandy or salty soils in full sun. Use them as a windbreak, a seaside planting, or for naturalizing. Do not need pruning but can be cut back by a third to stimulate growth. Sow seeds in spring or take softwood cuttings in summer.

B. halimifolia

b. hal-ih-mih-FOH-lee-uh. GROUND-SEL BUSH. A semievergreen to deciduous shrub reaching 12 feet in height and spread, this species is also called sea myrtle because its 3-inch leaves have an elongated oval shape and leathery texture similar to plants in the genus *Myrica*. The foliage differs in having more prominent, coarser teeth and can be gray-green as well as dark green. The small white flowers bloom in open clusters in late summer, after which female plants develop clouds of unusual silky white seed heads. **Zones 5 to 9.**

Baccharis halimifolia

B. pilularis

pil-yew-LAIR-iss. COYOTE BUSH. Native to dry areas of Oregon and California, this low-spreading shrub is an excellent and reliable ground cover in dry to desert regions of the West. Growing 2 to 3 feet tall and spreading to 10 feet or more, it is often used as a bank stabilizer and a fire-retardant ground cover for large areas. It is also resistant to salt spray. 'Pigeon Point' is larger in all respects, with bright green leaves and a fast-spreading habit. 'Twin Peaks' is also called dwarf coyote bush and spreads quickly into a low (6 to 12 inches tall), wide (6 feet), fire-resistant, drought-tolerant ground cover. This is a male selection, so there is no seed fluff. **Zones 6 to 9.**

Bacopa

bah-KOPE-uh. Figwort family, Scrophulariaceae.

While most of the 56 species in this genus are aquatic perennials commonly called water hyssops, one species suitable for well-drained garden soil is gaining widespread popularity. A tender perennial, commonly referred to simply as bacopa, it is a prostrate plant grown for its small white flowers, which are borne in profusion from early summer through fall. It is especially effective when allowed to cascade over the side of a container or window box.

HOW TO GROW

Give bacopa a spot in full sun to partial shade and rich, well-drained soil. Afternoon shade is beneficial in hot climates. Propagate by taking cuttings in spring or early summer, as the cultivars

Baccharis halimifolia

Bacopa sp. 'Snowflake'

available in the trade do not come true from seed. Water regularly during dry weather; dry soil causes flowers to drop. Feed with a balanced fertilizer a few times during the summer. While the plants are normally grown as annuals, they are perennials hardy from **Zone 9 south** and could be overwintered indoors.

Bacopa sp.

Variously listed as *Bacopa* sp., *Sutera cordata*, and *B. monnieri*. A spreading, well-branched plant with rounded, toothed leaves that reaches only 3 inches tall but spreads from 1 to 1¹/₂ feet. Plants produce an abundance of tubular, white, ³/₄-inch-long flowers with five flared lobes. Two cultivars, 'Snowflake' and 'Snowstorm', are available; 'Snowstorm' is said to be more disease and heat resistant than 'Snowflake'. Tender perennial or grow as an annual.

Ballota

bah-LOT-uh. Mint family, Lamiaceae.

Like their relatives the mints (*Mentha*), *Ballota* species bear aromatic foliage and whorls of two-lipped flowers. The 30 to 35 species in the genus are low-growing perennials or subshrubs native to the Mediterranean region, Europe, and western Asia.

HOW TO GROW

Plant in full sun and poor, dry, well-drained soil. Most are hardy from **Zone 7 south** and are grown as tender perennials elsewhere. Grow plants from cuttings taken in spring or early summer. Or sow seeds indoors in late winter in a sterile, very well drained medium.

Cover the seeds lightly and germinate at 70°F. Where they are not hardy, replace plants annually or overwinter them indoors in pots or by taking cuttings in summer. Use them as foliage plants to fill out garden beds and mixed plantings. They tend to shed leaves in summer, so they aren't the best choices for containers on a patio.

B. pseudodictamnus

b. sue-doe-dik-TAM-nus. FALSE DITTANY. A mound-forming, 2-foot-tall subshrub with woolly white stems and fuzzy gray-green leaves. Whorls of tubular, two-lipped, ¹/₂-inch-long flowers in white or pinkish white. **Zones 7 to 10**, or grow as an annual.

Ballota pseudodictamnus

Baptisia

bap-TEEZ-ee-uh. Pea family, Fabaceae.

Baptisias are long-lived shrub-sized perennials that bear erect, lupinelike racemes of pea-shaped flowers and have attractive, three-leaflet leaves. There are 20 or so species in the genus, all native to North America. Both the botanical name and the common name, false indigo, refer to the fact that members of the genus have been used as dye plants — *bapto* is from the Greek, "to dye" — most notably as a substitute for indigo. All are good cut flowers, and the inflated pods that follow the flowers are effective in dried arrangements.

HOW TO GROW

Select a site in full sun and give blue false indigo (*B. australis*) rich, evenly moist, well-drained soil. The other species are suitable for spots with poor, sandy, or dry soil. All are drought tolerant and difficult to move once established because of their deep taproots. Baptisias also grow in partial shade, but plants bloom less and are more likely to require staking. Select a site with care, since the plants establish slowly and thrive for years without being divided, eventually spreading via rhizomes to form broad 3- to 4-foot-wide clumps. Plants may need staking. Divide them in spring or fall if they outgrow their site or become overcrowded, or for propagation. Or sow fresh seeds.

B. alba

b. AL-buh. WHITE WILD INDIGO. A 2- to 3-foot-tall species from the southeastern United States with racemes of white ³/₄-inch-wide flowers in early summer. 'Purple Smoke' is a pale blue–flowered hybrid with this species and *B. australis*. Prairie Wild Indigo (*B. lactea*, formerly *B. leucantha*), another native species, is similar to *B. alba* but bears white flowers on 3- to 5-foot plants. **Zones 4 to 9**.

Baptisia australis

Baptisia alba

B. australis

b. aw-STRAL-iss. BLUE FALSE INDIGO, PLAINS FALSE INDIGO. Robust, showy, 3- to 5-foot-tall species with blue-green leaves and erect clusters of dark blue 1¹/₄-inch-wide flowers in early summer followed by spikes of inflated blue-black seedpods. **Zones 3 to 9.**

B. bracteata

b. brack-tee-AH-tuh. PLAINS WILD INDIGO, BUFFALO PEA. Formerly *B. leucophaea*. Spreading 1- to 2-foot-tall plant with drooping clusters of creamy white to pale yellow 1- to 1¹/₂-inch-wide flowers. Blooms mid- to late spring. **Zones 3 to 9.**

B. pendula

b. PEN-due-luh. A 2- to 3¹/₂-foot-tall species with blue-gray leaves and erect racemes of 1-inch-wide white flowers in late spring to early summer followed by arching clusters of blue-black seedpods. **Zones 5 to 9.**

B. perfoliata

b. per-foe-lee-AH-tuh. GEORGIA WILD INDIGO. Relatively low-growing 1- to 2-foot-tall species, native to the Southeast, that spreads to about 4 feet. Bears solitary ¹/₂-inch-wide yellow flowers in the leaf axils in early summer. The leaves are round and perfoliate, meaning the stem runs through the center of the leaf. **Zones 5 to 9.**

Bassia

BAH-see-ah. Goosefoot family, Chenopodiaceae.

Although they don't look much alike, *Bassia* (formerly *Kochia*) species are related to beets. The genus contains about seven species with very narrow leaves and inconspicuous flowers. One species is grown for the feathery effect its foliage adds to the garden, as well as its fall color.

HOW TO GROW

Give burning bush (*B. scoparia*) full sun and rich, well-drained soil. Sow seeds outdoors after the last spring frost date. Or sow indoors 4 to 6 weeks before the last frost date and germinate at between 65° and 70°F. Do not cover the seeds, which need light to germinate. Use burning bush as an edging or low, temporary hedge. Plants self-sow and can become weedy, especially in warm climates.

B. scoparia f. trichophylla

b. skoh-PAIR-ee-ah f. try-koe-FILL-uh. BURNING BUSH, SUMMER CYPRESS. Formerly *Kochia scoparia* f. *trichophylla*. A fast-growing shrublike annual ranging from 1 to 5 feet with narrow, lance-shaped leaves that turn scarlet in fall. Warm-weather annual.

Begonia

beh-GOAN-yah. Begonia family, Begoniaceae.

The vast *Begonia* clan contains some 1,300 species — annuals, perennials, shrubs, climbers, succulents, and epiphytes — native to tropical and subtropical regions worldwide. Begonias have fleshy leaves and stems and grow from rhizomes, fibrous roots, or tubers.

Bassia scoparia f. *trichophylla*

Male and female flowers are borne separately, usually on the same plant. (Female flowers have a swollen winged seed capsule directly behind the petals; males don't.) The fleshy leaves vary in shape, size, and color. Rounded and wing-shaped foliage is common. North of Zone 10, most begonias are suitable only for house or greenhouse culture, but a few species are popular perennials grown as annuals or tender perennials. One, *B. grandis*, is a hardy perennial.

HOW TO GROW

This depends on the kind of begonia. Give wax begonias (*B. semperflorens*), which are tender perennials, average to rich, well-drained soil. They tolerate sun to shade; partial shade is best, especially in southern zones, where they struggle with the heat. Keep the soil evenly moist, especially if plants are in full sun. Use wax begonias as edging plants or to add color to shade gardens. Start begonias from cuttings or seeds sown

in early to midwinter. Scatter the dustlike seeds thinly on the surface of a moist, sterile seed-starting mix. Do not cover them with soil, but place a pane of glass or a piece of plastic wrap over the container to keep the medium moist. Germination occurs in 2 to 3 weeks; keep them at 70°F. Propagate from cuttings taken anytime, or divide the clumps. (Double-flowered cultivars must be grown from cuttings or division; they do not come true from seed.) Use wax begonias in containers and hanging baskets, as well as in mixed plantings and as edgings. Overwinter plants by taking cuttings in late summer, digging entire plants, or bringing in containers. Keep them in a sunny spot at temperatures between 60° and 65°F.

Plant hardy begonias in partial to full shade in rich, evenly moist, well-drained soil. To propagate, collect the tiny tubers that appear in the leaf axils in late summer or fall and plant them outdoors where they are to grow, or plant them indoors in late winter in pots. Either way, barely cover them with loose soil. Or start from seeds. Plants also self-sow.

Tuberous begonias are a bit demanding but aren't difficult if you have the right site. They grow best in areas with cool, somewhat humid summers , and are disappointing in areas with dry heat. Grow them in partial shade and loose, well-drained soil rich in organic matter. A site protected from wind is best. Start with firm, solid tubers that do not have soft spots or cuts. Small pink buds may be evident; avoid tubers that have already sprouted. Start tubers in-

doors 8 to 10 weeks before the last spring frost date in flats filled with loose, free-draining potting medium that is barely moist. If buds are not visible on the top of the tubers (the concave side), place them upside down on the surface of the medium and set them in a warm (70° to 80°F), humid place for about a week. After that, check for buds every few days.

Once ¹/₂-inch pink buds appear, plant the tubers with the medium barely covering the tops. Water sparingly until they are growing actively — too much moisture causes rot. Once the tubers are actively growing, keep them evenly moist and set them in a bright spot protected from direct sun. Move started tubers to individual 4- to 5-inch pots when the shoots are about 1¹/₂ inches tall. Move plants to the containers where they will bloom or to shady spots in the garden once the shoots are several inches tall, but keep them indoors until all danger of frost has passed and the soil has warmed. Insert stakes at planting time, otherwise it's easy to damage the tubers. Loosely tie the brittle stems to the stakes with soft yarn or strips of nylon stocking. Propagate from seeds or cuttings of young shoots with a small "heel" of the tuber attached.

To overwinter tuberous begonias, dig the tubers after the first light frost in fall and spread them out, tops and all, in a shady, dry, well-ventilated spot protected from further frosts. Let the tops dry, then shake the soil from the tubers. Store them in a cool (40° to 50°F), well-ventilated, dry place in shallow trays filled with dry peat moss. Or hang them in net bags or pantyhose filled with peat. Check regularly for signs of rot, and discard rotted tubers. Replant as you would new tubers in spring.

B. grandis ssp. evansiana

b. GRAN-diss ssp. eh-van-see-AH-nuh. HARDY BEGONIA. A 2- to 2¹/₂-foot perennial that grows from a small tuber and spreads to 1 foot.

Begonia semperflorens

Begonia hybrid

Begonia × tuberhybrida

Bears arching clusters of pink flowers in late summer or fall above wing-shaped 4-inch-long leaves that are olive green above and usually red beneath. The variety *alba* bears white flowers. **Zones 6 to 10; to Zone 5 with winter protection.**

B. semperflorens

b. sem-per-FLOR-enz. WAX BEGONIA. Fibrous-rooted, mounding, 8- to 12-inch-tall perennial with fleshy stems, fleshy green or bronze leaves, and abundant clusters of white, pink, red, or bicolor blooms. Many cultivars with single or double blooms are available. Tender perennial or warm-weather annual.

B. sutherlandii

b. suh-ther-LAN-dee-eye. SUTHERLAND BEGONIA. A tuberous species bearing pendent clusters of orange 1-inch flowers all summer atop 1- to 2-foot mounds of bright green lance-shaped leaves. Overwinter indoors as houseplants (they are ideal for containers and hanging baskets, as well as shady sites with rich soil) or let plants go dormant and keep them relatively dry and cool, as for conventional tuberous begonias. **Zones 8 to 10; to Zone 7 with winter protection.**

B. × tuberhybrida

b. × too-ber-HI-brih-duh. TUBEROUS BEGONIA. Upright to pendent perennial plants with tuberous roots, fleshy stems reaching 8 to 12 inches, glossy bright to dark green leaves, and showy flowers in shades of yellow, orange, pink, red, salmon, and white. Flowers are single or double and can be 3 inches or more across. 'Clips' and 'Non-Stop' mixes are two strains that come true from seed. **Zones 10 to 11.**

Belamcanda

beh-lam-KAN-duh. Iris family, Iridaceae.

Commonly called blackberry lilies, *Belamcanda* species have irislike fans of sword-shaped leaves that grow from thick, fleshy rhizomes. The plants produce branched clusters of small flowers that have six petals, more properly called tepals. The flowers are followed by showy clusters of shiny blackberry-like fruits.

HOW TO GROW

Select a site in full sun with average to somewhat rich, well-drained, evenly moist soil. Plants

Belamcanda chinensis

grow well in sandy soil. Water during dry weather. Iris borers and the bacterial crown rot that they introduce to bearded irises can also attack blackberry lilies. Prevent them by removing dead or dying leaves and other litter that cover the rhizomes. This will also help control borers and rot on susceptible irises. Propagate by dividing the clumps in spring or early fall or by seeds. Plants self-sow.

B. chinensis

b. chih-NEN-sis. BLACKBERRY LILY, LEOPARD FLOWER. Produces clumps of erect, sword-shaped, 2-foot-tall leaves topped in summer by branched stems of flowers that reach 2 to 4 feet. Flowers are 1 to 2 inches wide and are bright orange or yellow with maroon spots. Beige seed capsules follow the flowers and open to reveal clusters of large shiny black seeds. **Zones 5 to 9.**

Bellevalia

bel-leh-VAH-lee-uh. Lily family, Liliaceae

Native from the Mediterranean region to western Asia, *Bellevalia* species are spring-blooming bulbs bearing flowers that resemble those of their close relatives the grape hyacinths (*Muscari*) and hyacinths (*Hyacinthus*). Plants grow from tunicate bulbs and have long, strap-shaped, green to gray-green leaves that are basal and can extend from 1 to 1½ feet in length. The small bell-shaped flowers have

Bellevalia pycnantha

six lobes and are carried in erect, densely packed racemes. They come in violet-blue, lavender, and white.

HOW TO GROW

Select a site in full sun or light shade with rich, well-drained soil. These are spring-blooming plants that disappear by midsummer, so spots under deciduous trees, which offer full sun before the trees leaf out, are fine. These bulbs are ideal for rock gardens or sunny beds and borders, as they prefer dry soil once they enter dormancy in summer. Plant the bulbs in fall with the tops 2 inches below the soil surface. If clumps become crowded or begin to bloom less, divide them in summer just as the leaves die back. Propagate by separating offsets, by division, or by seeds.

B. hyacinthoides

b. hi-ah-sin-THOY-deez. Formerly *Strangweja spicata*. Produces long strap-shaped leaves through fall and winter and loose, few-flowered racemes of ¼- to ½-inch-wide pale blue flowers in spring on 2- to 6-inch-tall stalks. **Zones 7 to 9.**

B. pycnantha

b. pik-NAN-thah. Also listed as *Muscari paradoxum*. Bears gray-green leaves topped by dense 1-foot-tall clusters of violet-blue flowers edged in yellow. Individual flowers are ¼ inch long and appear in spring. **Zones 5 to 8.**

B. romana

b. ro-MAH-nuh. Formerly *Hyacinthus romanus*. A 12-inch-tall species with loose racemes of ³/₈-inch-long white flowers in spring. **Zones 7 to 9.**

Bellis

BELL-iss. Aster family, Asteraceae.

Of the 15 species of perennials that belong to this genus, one is grown as an annual or biennial. *Bellis* species form rosettes of oval- to spoon-shaped leaves and bear solitary, daisylike flower heads in shades of pink, reddish pink, and white.

HOW TO GROW

Give English daisy (*B. perennis*) full sun or light shade and average to rich, well-drained soil. Plants perform best in areas with cool summers. Although perennial and hardy in **Zones 4 to 8**, they are usually dug and discarded after they bloom. (From Zone 9 south, they are grown as annuals for fall to winter or early-spring bloom.) Sow seeds indoors 8 to 10 weeks before the last spring frost date at 50° to 55°F; germination takes 2 to 4 weeks. Outdoors from Zone 7 north, sow from midsummer to fall for bloom the following year; cover plants with a loose mulch such as straw or salt hay over winter. From Zone 8 south, sow in early spring several weeks before the last spring frost date or in fall. When sowing, just press the seeds into the soil surface, as light aids germination. Water regularly and deadhead plants to prevent self-sowing. Discard plants after they flower, or divide the clumps and raise the divisions in a seedbed, as you would seedlings, for bloom the following year.

B. perennis

b. per-EN-iss. ENGLISH DAISY. Low-growing, 2- to 8-inch-tall stoloniferous perennial with obovate to spoon-shaped leaves. The species bears ¹/₂- to 1¹/₄-inch white to pinkish flowers with yellow centers but is seldom grown. Cultivars, which come true from seed, have large single or double flowers ranging from 1 to 3 inches across in shades of pink, red, and white. Perennial grown as a biennial.

Berberis

BER-ber-iss. Barberry family, Berberidaceae.

This genus encompasses more than 450 species of spiny-stemmed evergreen or deciduous shrubs, commonly known as barberries, from Africa, South America, and the Northern Hemisphere. Many are useful in gardens for fall foliage, colorful fruits, and small yellow or orange spring flowers.

HOW TO GROW

Barberries need well-drained soil in full sun for the best fruit and fall color. Grow them where people will not come in contact with their thorns. The small species are

Berberis darwinii

ideal for rock gardens, the larger ones as barrier hedges. The one thing you don't ever want to do is prune a barberry — the thorns make this a most unpleasant garden task. To propagate, root from softwood cuttings in summer, or sow seeds in fall after removing them from the pulp. *B. vulgaris* (common barberry) is considered an invasive pest by naturalists in 26 states from coast to coast and should be avoided. Also troublesome, from New England west to Wisconsin and south to Tennessee and Kentucky, is *B. thunbergii* (Japanese barberry), of which there are dozens of cultivars widely available. Gardeners who live in the area described should consider other barberries.

B. × chenaultii

b. × shen-OH-ee-eye. CHENAULT BARBERRY. This cold-hardy evergreen hybrid, developed in France in the 1930s, grows 3 to 4 feet tall and slightly wider and bears shiny dark green leaves that turn bronzy red with the first frosts. **Zones 5 to 8.**

B. darwinii

b. dar-WIN-ee-eye. DARWIN BARBERRY. An upright evergreen to 10 feet high and wide and then spreading, with spiny, glossy, 1¹/₂-inch dark green leaves. It bears 2-inch racemes of gold to orange flowers in early spring, then pea-sized dark turquoise berries. **Zones 7 to 9.**

B. gladwynensis 'William Penn'

b. glad-win-EN-sis. The habit is a dense 4-foot mound. High-gloss leaves to 4 inches turn bronze in winter, and some will fall in the northern part of its range. Bright

Berberis verruculosa

yellow midspring flowers are followed by ¹/₂-inch yellow fruits tinged with purple. **Zones 6 to 9.**

B. julianae

b. jool-ee-AY-nee. WINTERGREEN BARBERRY. Forms a mass of upright shoots 8 to 10 feet tall and wide, with spiny, lustrous evergreen leaves that are pale underneath. In late spring it bears clusters of yellow flowers, sometimes tinged red, followed by ³/₈-inch glaucous blue-black fruits. In the northern part of its range, its leaves may show signs of winter damage in exposed areas. Nevertheless, along with *B. × chenaultii*, it is considered the hardiest of the evergreen barberries. **Zones 6 to 9.**

B. koreana

b. kor-ee-AY-nuh. KOREAN BARBERRY. A vigorous deciduous barberry to 6 feet or taller, with many stems and sometimes suckering. Oval 1- to 3-inch leaves turn reddish purple in fall. Midspring yellow flowers appear in 3- to 4-inch racemes and are followed by ¹/₄-inch bright red oval berries. **Zones 3 to 7.**

B. × mentorensis

b. × men-tor-EN-sis. MENTOR BARBERRY. Fast growing and dense, with an upright bearing when young, then becoming more rounded, to 5 feet tall and wider.

Bellis perennis

Bergenia cordifolia

Popular for creating an impenetrable, semievergreen hedge. The dark green leathery leaves show yellow, orange, and red in fall. Yellow spring flowers, solitary or paired, are occasionally followed by reddish brown fruits. **Zones 5 to 8.**

B. × ottawensis 'Superba'

b. × aw-tuh-WEN-sis. A rounded deciduous shrub 6 to 8 feet high and wide, valued for purple-red foliage that turns bright red in fall. The spring flower clusters are pale yellow tinged with red, and berries are ³/₈-inch red ovals. **Zones 5 to 9.**

B. verruculosa

b. veh-rue-kew-LOH-suh. W A R T Y
B A R B E R R Y. Named for the bumps on its stems, this species makes a dense mound 3 to 5 feet high and across, with small evergreen leaves that develop a burgundy tinge in autumn. The solitary golden yellow flowers are followed by glaucous blue-black fruits. **Zones 6 to 9.**

Bergenia

ber-JIN-ee-uh. Saxifrage family, Saxifragaceae.

Grown more for their foliage than their flowers, bergenias produce clumps of leathery, rounded, cabbagelike leaves ranging from 8
to 12 inches long and up to 8 inches wide. The leaves turn from green to bronze-purple or reddish in fall. Most species are evergreen, but the leaves are damaged by harsh winter weather and often are not very ornamental by spring. Dense 5- to 6-inch-wide clusters of small funnel- to bell-shaped flowers appear above the leaves in spring in shades of pink, rose-red, or white. There are from six to eight species in the genus, all of which grow from thick, branching rhizomes that slowly spread into handsome clumps about 1 foot in width. Plants are about a foot tall when not in bloom, up to 1¹/₂ to 2 feet when they are.

HOW TO GROW

Give bergenias a site in partial to dappled shade with well-drained, humus-rich, evenly moist soil. Plants can take full sun in the North provided the soil remains moist. In the South, shade is best, especially in the afternoon. A location sheltered from strong winds helps protect the foliage. Bergenias are ideal for growing along ponds or streams, but plant them above the water table so the soil is not constantly wet. Water during dry weather. Mulch in fall where snow cover is uncertain, and remove damaged foliage in spring. Clumps that have died out in the center need dividing. To propagate, divide plants in spring or fall or take
cuttings (a piece of new rhizome that has a rosette of foliage attached) in spring. Or start from seeds, although hybrids will not come true.

B. ciliata

b. sil-ee-AH-tuh. W I N T E R
B E R G E N I A. Deciduous species with oval or rounded 14-inch-long leaves and pink or white flowers in early spring. **Zones 5 to 9.**

B. cordifolia

b. kor-dih-FOE-lee-uh. H E A R T -
L E A V E D B E R G E N I A. Clumping species with leathery, rounded to heart-shaped, 10-inch-long leaves and rose pink to rose-red flowers in late winter and early spring. *B. crassifolia*, Siberian tea, is a similar species with slightly smaller leaves that are 4 to 7 inches long and have toothed margins. **Zones 3 to 8.**

B. hybrids

Hybrids, selected for either their spring flowers or their fall foliage color, have been derived from heart-leaved bergenia, purple-leaved bergenia (*B. purpurascens*), and other species. 'Baby Doll' has 4-inch-long bronze-tinted leaves and pink flowers. 'Bressingham Ruby' has maroon-red flowers and leaves that turn maroon in fall. 'Bressingham White' bears white flowers. 'Sunningdale' has lilac-
magenta flowers and copper red fall-to-winter foliage. **Zones 3 to 8.**

Bessera

BESS-er-uh. Lily family, Liliaceae.

Two species of wildflowers native to Mexico belong to the genus *Bessera*. Both are tender perennials that grow from corms and produce narrow, grasslike, basal leaves and loose umbels of nodding, somewhat bell-shaped flowers. The individual flowers, which are carried on very thin stems, have six petal-like tepals. Each flower has six stamens that are united for about half their length to form a daffodil-like corona or cup (called a staminal cup) in the center.

HOW TO GROW

Select a site in full sun with average, well-drained soil. Plant the bulbs in spring at a depth of 2¹/₂ to 3 inches. Where hardy, they can be left in the ground year-round and require very little care. Where they are marginally hardy, look for a protected spot such as at the base of a south-facing wall, and protect plants in fall with a heavy layer of coarse mulch such as evergreen boughs, pine needles, salt hay, or coarse leaves. In the North, dig the corms after the first light frosts of fall (earlier if the foliage dies back), dry them off, brush off excess soil, and store them in a cool (40° to 50°F), dry place over winter, as you would gladiolus corms. *Bessera* species also will grow in pots. Propagate by removing the offsets in fall or by seeds.

Bessera elegans

B. elegans

b. EL-eh-ganz. CORAL DROPS. A 2-foot-tall species with grassy 2- to 2½-foot-long leaves. Bears 1½-inch-wide umbels of three to nine scarlet flowers in late summer or early fall. **Zones 9 to 11; to Zone 8 with winter protection.**

Betula

BET-yew-luh. Birch family, Betulaceae.

This genus contains about 60 species of deciduous trees and shrubs native to northern North America, Europe, and Asia. Many have white or colorful peeling bark, making them very popular landscape subjects, although they are all relatively short-lived. Leaves are alternate, pointed, bright green ovals with toothed margins. Flowers are dangling, conspicuous male catkins and upright, inconspicuous female catkins. Since the bark is so ornamental, be sure to locate birches where they can be admired from indoors during winter. Naturalize birches in showy groves in a naturalistic landscape, or use one as a focal point in a more formal garden. Trees that are fertilized in spring and kept well watered resist pests better than neglected or stressed trees do. Do not prune birches in spring, because the bronze birch borer, the trees' most serious pest, is active then and can enter through the wounds.

HOW TO GROW

As a group, birches are highly susceptible to leaf miners and borers and may suffer from drought and heat. North American species are best grown in northern climates and suffer when grown in the South. Asian species are more tolerant and adapt better to poor soil,

Betula nigra

heat, and drought; these should be the choices for warmer regions. See the individual species for special needs.

B. nigra

b. Nye-gruh. RIVER BIRCH. In its native habitat — streambanks and marshy areas — river birch grows into a pyramidal or oval tree with slightly pendulous branches and a single trunk; it reaches 40 to 70 feet tall. In cultivation, it is often grown as a multitrunked clump. The beautiful, exfoliating trunk bark is not white, as on so many birches, but bright reddish brown, varying widely on seed-grown trees. Twigs have glossy, dark brown bark. Cultivars are even showier and tend to have apricot or creamy bark. Leaves are dark green triangles with toothed edges that turn an alluring bright yellow in autumn.

Use this tree in a difficult wet area or natural site, or plant it for winter interest in a garden border. River birch also is very effective planted in groves. From eastern and midwestern North America; **Zones 4 to 9**. It grows best in moist, humus-rich, acid (pH of 6.5 or lower) soil but adapts to clayey soil and wet or periodically flooded sites. Tolerates drought and heat once established. Does not tolerate compacted urban soil. Late-summer pruning is best; sap bleeds in spring. Immune to bronze birch borers and troubled less by other pests than most birches are. Leaf spot may occur in rainy years. Chlorosis due to iron deficiency occurs in alkaline soil.

CULTIVARS AND SIMILAR SPECIES

'Fox Valley' is a dense, compact dwarf, growing only to 10 feet tall. 'Heritage' is a fast-growing (to 50 feet tall) and extremely popular

Betula papyrifera

disease-resistant selection; very showy, creamy white and pinkish tan bark and excellent fall color. *B. albosinensis* (Chinese paper birch) has matte orange-red, orange-brown, and beige-pink peeling bark with white patches; **Zones 5 to 8**. *B. alleghaniensis* (yellow birch) is native to eastern North America; polished bronze, peeling bark and glorious gold fall color; **Zones 4 to 7**. *B. lenta* (sweet birch, cherry birch) is native to eastern North America; glistening, almost black bark and the best golden yellow fall color of any birch; resists bronze birch borers; **Zones 4 to 7**.

B. papyrifera

b. pap-ee-RIFF-er-uh. PAPER BIRCH, CANOE BIRCH. Named for its creamy white bark, which peels off in papery shreds, this native tree is pyramidal when young but becomes irregular or oval when mature; it reaches 50 to 70 feet tall. Until young trees are about 15 feet tall, the bark is brown; thereafter it becomes white with horizontal black markings. Leaves are dark green, oval or triangular, and about 4 inches long,

with coarse-toothed margins. Fall color is an excellent yellow. Often grown in clumps but more stunning as a single specimen, because the trunk is very stout and white. Native Americans used the bark to make canoes.

Plant in full sun in the North and light afternoon shade in the South. Needs even moisture and deep, humus-rich, acid soil. Mulch to keep soil moist, especially in warm areas. Performs poorly in compacted soil, heat, drought, and urban conditions. Less susceptible to insects than is *B. pendula*, which is a better choice in the Midwest, but heat- or water-stressed trees may attract borers and leaf miners. Larvae of the beautiful luna moth feed on the leaves. From northern North America. Best in **Zones 2 to 5**; grow in cool-summer mountain or coastal areas in **Zones 5 to 7**; a better choice than *B. pendula* in the Midwest.

CULTIVARS AND SIMILAR SPECIES

New cultivars that are highly resistant to bronze birch borers and are tolerant of high soil pH include the following: 'Renaissance Compact', which grows into a tight 40-foot-tall oval with shaggy white bark; 'Renaissance Oasis', which is a dense tree with peeling white bark; and 'Renaissance Upright', which is a distinctly narrow form with slightly exfoliating white bark. *B. populifolia* (gray birch) is native to northeastern forests and forms lovely clumps of grayish white, black-marked, slender trunks that grow to 30 feet tall; long, pointed, triangular leaves; resists borers, but leaf miners can be a serious problem; useful in wet or dry areas of **Zones 4 to 6**.

B. pendula (B. alba)
b. PEN-due-luh. EUROPEAN BIRCH. Formerly *B. alba*. Often grown in clumps, this popular species reaches 40 to 50 feet tall and has enchanting chalk white bark, even on young trees. The lower part of the trunk turns rough and black as trees mature. The 2-inch glossy green leaves are oval or triangular, have toothed margins, and turn yellow in autumn. Unless grown in the North and given plenty of moisture and deep, humus-rich acid soil, European birch is short-lived and highly susceptible to bronze birch borers and leaf miners, especially in the southern part of its range. From northern Europe.
Zones 3 to 5.
CULTIVARS
Weeping forms: 'Tristis' is a weeping form with a central leader. 'Youngii' is a weeping, moplike, grafted form that grows to 15 feet

Betula ermanii

Betula pendula 'Youngii'

tall. *Cut-leaved forms:* 'Crispa' has deeply cut leaves; weeping form with a central leader. 'Gracilis' has very deeply cut leaves; weeping, without a central leader, to 20 feet tall. *Purple leaves:* 'Purple Rain' has young purple leaves that mature to bronze-green; orange to copper fall color. 'Crimson Frost' is a hybrid with the following species and has cinnamon-tinged, exfoliating, white bark and purple leaves all summer. *Insect resistant: B. platyphylla* var. *japonica* 'Whitespire Sr.' ('Whitespire' Asian birch) is a desirable drought-resistant cultivar that is highly resistant to bronze birch borers and moderately resistant to leaf miners; pyramidal shape and smooth, chalk-white bark that does not develop until the tree reaches 15 feet tall; **Zones 4 to 7**. 'Dakota Pinnacle' is an excellent, columnar tree for the northern Plains; cold hardy in **Zone 3**.

B. utilis ssp. jacquemontii
b. YEW-til-iss ssp. jack-uh-MONT-tee-eye. WHITE-BARKED HIMALAYAN BIRCH. Formerly *B. jacquemontii*. This fast-growing Asian birch is relatively new to North American gardens. It's a white-barked subspecies of the coppery brown–barked species and is known for having the whitest bark of any birch, making it a dramatic year-round statement in the garden. Its 2¹/2-inch-long, oval leaves are sharply toothed and turn a rich golden yellow in fall. Trees are fast growing, single trunked, and oval in outline, often

with low branches. They can reach 60 feet tall and tolerate slightly alkaline conditions. Some resistance to bronze birch borer and leaf miners. From China and Nepal. **Zones 5 to 8**.
CULTIVARS AND SIMILAR SPECIES
Several named clones exist, such as 'Ghost', 'Silver Shadow', and 'Yunnan' — all probably identical to the subspecies. *B. utilis* (red-barked Himalayan birch) has pale pink to red-brown bark that peels in narrow strips. *B. ermanii* (Erman's birch), from Siberia, has creamy white to pinkish peeling bark with many horizontal markings; rounded green leaves with prominent veins; **Zones 5 to 7**. *B. maximowicziana* (monarch birch)

Bidens ferulifolia

is an Asian species with yellow-white peeling bark; it is less susceptible to borers and more drought tolerant; **Zones 6 to 8**.

Bidens
BYE-denz. Aster family, Asteraceae.

This widely distributed genus contains some 200 species of annuals, perennials, and shrubs with clusters of daisylike flowers. Commonly called tickseeds, sticktights, or burr marigolds, they have simple or pinnate leaves and barbed seeds: the name *Bidens* is from the Latin *bis*, meaning "two," and *dens*, "tooth." Most tend to be weedy plants native to grasslands and wastelands and suitable for wild gardens. One species is grown as an annual or tender perennial.
HOW TO GROW
Give *Bidens* species full sun and evenly moist, average to rich soil that is well drained. Sow seeds indoors 6 to 8 weeks before the last spring frost date and germinate at 55° to 65°F. Or sow outdoors after the last frost date. Or propagate from cuttings taken in spring or late summer to early fall to overwinter the plants indoors. Clumps also can be divided. Plants self-sow.

B. ferulifolia
b. fer-yew-lih-FOE-lee-uh. Spreading, 12-inch-tall perennial hardy from **Zone 8 south** with lacy, deeply divided leaves. Bears golden yellow, 1¹/4- to 1¹/2-inch-wide, daisylike

Bignonia capreolata

flower heads from summer to fall. 'Golden Goddess' bears 2-inch-wide flowers. Tender perennial. Overwinter plants or grow as an annual. Cool-weather annual.

Bignonia

big-NOH-nee-ah. Bignonia family, Bignoniaceae.

A single species of climber belongs to the genus *Bignonia* — *B. capreolata*, a woody vine native to eastern North America. Commonly called cross vine, this species features semievergreen to evergreen leaves and climbs by tendrils tipped with small disks. It is grown for its showy clusters of trumpet-shaped flowers.

HOW TO GROW

Select a site in full sun or partial shade with average to rich soil that is moist and well drained. Plants tolerate full shade but bloom best in sun. They'll also survive periods of wet soil in springtime. Prune plants as necessary in spring to direct their growth and to keep them in bounds. Use cross vine to cover arbors, walls, fences, or other structures. This species also can be used as a ground cover. Propagate

by layering stems in spring or fall or by cuttings in summer.

B. capreolata

b. kah-pre-oh-LAH-tuh. CROSS VINE. This climbing vine ranges from 30 to 60 feet and bears lance-shaped leaves to 7 inches long. Clusters of fragrant, 2-inch-long trumpet-shaped flowers appear in spring. Blooms are red-brown outside and yellow-orange inside. 'Jekyll' bears flowers that are orange on the outside and yellow inside, but are not fragrant. 'Tangerine Beauty', also not fragrant, bears abundant red-orange blooms. **Zones 6 to 9.**

Bletilla

bleh-TIL-uh. Orchid family, Orchidaceae

Bletilla species are deciduous, terrestrial orchids that have pleated, linear to rounded leaves and bear loose racemes of small bell-shaped flowers in spring to early summer. They spread by short rhizomes and produce tuber- or cormlike underground pseudobulbs. About 9 or 10 species belong to the genus, all native to Asia — China, Japan, and Taiwan.

HOW TO GROW

Select a site in partial shade — shelter from hot sun is essential in summer — with rich, evenly moist, well-drained soil. A protected spot is best. Work in plenty of compost or leaf mold at planting time to ensure rich, moisture-retentive soil. Keep the soil evenly moist in summer when plants are actively

growing. Plants also thrive in containers, and container culture is a good option in areas where these orchids are not hardy. Crowded clumps bloom best, so leave plants undisturbed as long as possible — either in the ground or in pots. Where not hardy, overwinter them indoors. In pots, let the soil dry out and the leaves die back, then store them in a cool (50° to 60°F), dry place. Or pack rhizomes in dry peat moss or vermiculite over winter and replant in spring. Propagate by dividing the clumps in early spring.

B. striata

b. stry-AY-tuh. CHINESE GROUND ORCHID, HYACINTH BLETILLA. Formerly *B. hyacinthina*. A 1- to 2-foot-tall spe-

Bloomeria crocea

cies that spreads as far. Bears 1- to 1¹/₂-foot-long lance-shaped leaves. From spring to early summer it produces loose clusters of up to 12 flowers that are 1 inch wide and magenta-pink. *B. striata* f. *alba* bears white flowers. **Zones 7 to 9; to Zone 5 or 6 with winter protection.**

Bloomeria

bloo-MEER-ee-uh. Lily family, Liliaceae.

Three species belong to the genus *Bloomeria*, all perennials that grow from corms and are native to California and Mexico. They are closely related to ornamental onions (*Allium*) and brodiaeas (*Brodiaea*). Plants bear linear, basal leaves and loose, long-stemmed umbels of yellow star- or wheel-shaped flowers that have six petal-like tepals.

HOW TO GROW

Select a site in full sun or partial shade with light, sandy soil with plenty of organic matter. Plant the corms in fall at a depth of 2 to 3 inches. For best effect, arrange them in drifts. Where they are marginally hardy, protect the plants over winter with a coarse mulch such as evergreen boughs, salt hay, or pine needles. Once the plants begin actively growing in spring, keep the soil evenly moist. Like many plants native to the Southwest, bloomerias require dry soil in summer after they go dormant; the corms rot in soil that remains too wet. In the East, where summers are too rainy, and in the North, where winters are too cold, grow these plants in containers. To overwinter container-grown

Bignonia capreolata

Bletilla striata

plants, once they have bloomed and the foliage has died back, set the pots in a dry, well-ventilated spot until fall, then move them to a cool, dry spot. Or dig the corms and store them in dry peat moss or vermiculite in a cool, dry spot. Propagate by removing offsets in summer as soon as the foliage dies back or in fall.

B. crocea

b. KRO-see-uh. GOLDEN STARS. California native wildflower with a single ¹/₂-inch-wide linear leaf that dies down about the time plants flower. Bears loose umbels of showy orangy yellow flowers with darker stripes atop 6- to 12-inch-tall stems in late spring or early summer. Individual blooms are ³/₄ to 1 inch wide and borne on long individual stems. **Zones 9 to 10; to Zone 8 with winter protection.**

Boltonia

bol-TOE-nee-uh. Aster family, Asteraceae.

Native North American wild-flowers, boltonias are large shrub-sized perennials with lance-shaped leaves that bear clouds of tiny daisylike flowers with yellow centers in showy panicles that bloom from late summer to fall. About eight species belong to the genus, one of which is commonly grown in gardens.
HOW TO GROW
Give boltonias the same conditions you would asters: full sun and rich, well-drained, evenly moist soil. They also tolerate drought. The plants are stiff stemmed and generally stand without staking. Divide clumps every 2 to 3 years, and care for and propagate the plants as you would asters.

B. asteroides

b. as-ter-OY-deez. BOLTONIA. Robust, shrubby 4- to 6-foot-tall perennial with narrow blue-green leaves. Bears masses of ³/₄-inch-wide daisies in 4- to 6-inch-wide panicles from late summer to early fall. Flowers have yellow centers and white, pink, or pinkish purple ray florets. 'Pink Beauty' bears pale pink ray florets. 'Snowbank', more often grown than the species, is a 5-foot plant with pure white ray florets. **Zones 3 to 9.**

Borago

boar-AH-go. Borage family, Boraginaceae.

Native to rocky soils in the Mediterranean region and Europe, *Borago* species are annuals and perennials with hairy stems and leaves topped by clusters of nodding, star-shaped flowers. Of the three species in the genus, one is commonly grown as an herb, salad plant, and ornamental.
HOW TO GROW
Full sun to partial shade and average, well-drained soil satisfy common borage (*B. officinalis*). Sow seeds outdoors in spring about a week before the last spring frost date. Or sow seeds in late summer or fall for germination the following spring. Do not cover the seeds, which need light to germinate. Use borage in mixed plantings and the herb garden, as well as in containers. Plants self-sow.

B. officinalis

b. oh-fih-shih-NAL-iss. COMMON BORAGE. A large, vigorous, 2-foot-tall annual with lance-shaped to ovate, hairy, grayish green

Bougainvillea 'Bridal Veil'

Bougainvillea hybrid

leaves. Bears clusters of 1-inch-wide, star-shaped flowers in summer in rich, true blue. There also are white- and pink-flowered forms. Cool-weather annual.

Bougainvillea

boo-gahn-VIL-lee-ah. Four-o'clock family, Nyctaginaceae.

The best known of the 14 species that belong to *Bougainvillea* are woody climbers, although the genus also contains trees and shrubs. All are tropical or subtropical plants with evergreen or semievergreen leaves. They bear small tubular flowers surrounded by three colorful petal-like bracts that are quite showy. Leaves are alternate and usually ovate in shape.
HOW TO GROW
Give bougainvilleas a spot in full sun. Rich soil is ideal, but plants grow in any well-drained soil. They thrive in high humidity in summer, when they are growing actively and need evenly moist soil. Bougainvilleas are climbers with stout thorns that allow them to clamber up rough surfaces, but they cannot attach themselves to arbors, walls, or other flat surfaces. Attach wires or small trellises to larger supports and tie the stems

Boltonia asteroides

Borago officinalis

Bouvardia ternifolia

to the supports as needed. Grow bougainvilleas outdoors year-round in frost-free climates. In the north, they make attractive plants for summer bedding (sink the pots to the rim in the soil) or in large containers. To overwinter, gradually reduce watering beginning in early to mid-fall and keep them in a cool spot (50° to 55°F nights; no more than 60°F during the day). Water just enough to keep the stems from shriveling; plants may lose some leaves. Repot in late winter or spring. Prune plants in spring by removing weak spindly growth and cutting side shoots back hard. Propagate by taking cuttings in early spring or summer; bottom heat speeds rooting.

B. × buttiana

b. × but-tee-AH-nah. Vigorous hybrids (B. glabra × B. peruviana) grown for their large, showy clusters of flowers featuring wavy, $1^1/_2$- to $2^1/_2$-inch-long bracts. Plants climb from 20 to 40 feet. Many hybrids are available in shades of purple, white, apricot, yellow, and red. **Zones 9 to 11.**

B. glabra

b. GLAY-brah. A species from Brazil with showy clusters of flowers with $1^1/_2$- to $2^1/_2$-inch bracts in purple, magenta, or white. Plants climb from 15 to 25 feet. **Zones 9 to 11.**

Bouvardia

boo-VAR-dee-uh. Madder family, Rubiaceae.

The genus *Bouvardia* comprises about 30 species of tender perennials and shrubs native to southern regions of North Amer-ica to South America. They bear ovate to lance-shaped leaves and clusters of tube- to funnel-shaped flowers.

HOW TO GROW
Give *Bouvardia* species full sun and average to rich, well-drained soil that remains evenly moist; a spot with midday shade is best where summers are hot. In frost-free or nearly frost-free climates (roughly Zone 9 south), grow them outdoors as shrubs in mixed plantings. In the North, grow them in containers and overwinter them indoors (in a bright spot with temperatures between 50° and 55°F at night). In summer, water regularly and feed every two weeks when plants are growing and flowering actively; gradually withhold water after they bloom and keep them nearly dry over winter. Since young plants bloom best, replace them annually or every other year. Take stem cut-tings in spring to propagate for garden use or in late summer to overwinter the plants; cuttings root best if given bottom heat. Or take root cuttings in midwinter. *Bouvardia* species are rarely grown from seeds, as cultivars do not come true.

B. ternifolia

b. tern-ih-FOE-lee-uh. SCARLET TROMPETILLA. A 2- to 3-foot shrub with lance-shaped leaves. Bears showy clusters of tubular scarlet flowers from late summer onward. Tender perennial, or grow as an annual.

Brachyscome

brah-key-SKO-mee. Aster family, Asteraceae.

Natives of Australia, New Zealand, Tasmania, and New Guinea, *Brachyscome* (also spelled *Brachycome*) species bear mounds of daisylike flowers with yellow centers and purple, blue, or white petals, more accurately called ray florets. One annual in this genus of 60 to 70 species of annuals and perennials is commonly grown in gardens.

HOW TO GROW
Give Swan River daisy (*B. iberidifolia*) full sun and rich, well-drained soil. Brachyscomes do not perform well in areas with very hot, humid summers. Sow seeds outdoors after danger of frost has passed. Or sow seeds indoors 4 to 6 weeks before the last spring frost date and germinate at temperatures between 60° and 70°F. Water from below and keep the soil on the dry side to avoid damping off. Make successive sowings every 3 weeks for continued bloom. Support plants with twiggy brush. Use Swan River daisies in containers and along the front edges of mixed plantings.

B. iberidifolia

b. eye-ber-id-ih-FOE-lee-uh. SWAN RIVER DAISY. A densely branched, 1- to $1^1/_2$-foot annual with deeply cut, gray-green, nearly fernlike leaves. Bears fragrant, $1^1/_2$-inch-wide, daisylike flowers in purplish blue, white, and pink in summer. Splendour Series cultivars come in white, purple, and lilac-pink with black centers. 'Blue Star' reaches 1 foot and bears purple-blue flowers with pointed petals. Cool-weather annual.

Bracteantha

brack-tee-AN-thuh. Aster family, Asteraceae.

Commonly called strawflowers or everlastings, *Bracteantha* species are perennials and annuals from the scrublands of Australia. Once classified in the genus *Helichrysum*, they bear hairy, lance-shaped to ovate leaves. Their daisylike flowers actually consist of all disk florets — they lack the "petals," or ray florets, of many aster-family plants. The showy "petals" in this case are papery, petal-like bracts in bright yellows, pinks, and white. One of the seven species in the genus is a popular annual and an exceptional dried flower.

HOW TO GROW
Give strawflowers full sun and average to dry, well-drained soil. They thrive in areas with long, hot summers. Sow seeds indoors 6 to 8 weeks before the last spring frost date and germinate at 65° to 70°F. In the South, where summers are long, strawflowers can be sown outdoors in spring. Do not cover seeds, which need light to germinate. Wait to transplant until after the last frost, once the soil has warmed up, and handle plants with care. Tall cultivars require staking. To dry the flowers, pick them before they are fully open, then hang them in small bunches in a warm, dark, dry place.

B. bracteata

b. brack-tee-AY-tuh. STRAW-FLOWER. Formerly *Helichrysum bracteatum*. An annual or short-lived perennial with lance-shaped,

Brachyscome iberidifolia

Bracteantha bracteata

gray-green leaves and papery, 1- to 3-inch-wide flower heads in yellow, pink, red, or white. Dwarf types, including Bright Bikinis Series, reach only 1 foot in height; taller types range from 3 to 5 feet. Warm-weather annual.

Brimeura

brih-mee-YOUR-uh. Lily family, Liliaceae.

Two species belong to this genus in the lily family, both bulbous, spring-blooming perennials native

Brimeura amethystina

to southeastern Europe. They bear loose racemes of dainty, bell-shaped flowers on leafless stalks. The individual flowers are tubular and have six fairly short lobes at the tips. The linear, grasslike leaves are borne at the base of the plant.

HOW TO GROW
Select a site in full sun or light shade with rich, well-drained soil. These are spring-blooming plants that disappear by midsummer, so spots under deciduous trees, which offer full sun before the trees leaf out, are fine. Plant the bulbs in fall with the tops 2 inches below the soil surface. Propagate by dividing the clumps in summer, after the leaves begin to turn yellow but before they disappear completely. Or sow seeds.

B. amethystina

b. am-eh-thiss-TYE-nuh. Formerly *Hyacinthus amethystinus.* Spring-blooming bulbs with 8- to 10-inch-tall racemes of between 6 and 12 pale blue flowers that are tubular to bell shaped and ¹/2 inch long. *B. amethystina* var. *alba* bears white flowers. **Zones 5 to 9.**

Briza

BREE-zah. Grass family, Poaceae.

While the best-known ornamental grasses are perennials, the genus *Briza* contains 2 species of attractive annuals. The 12 to 20 species of *Briza* all bear linear leaves and loose racemes or panicles of spike-

lets ("flowers") that hang from very fine stalks and as a result quake and flutter in the slightest breeze.

HOW TO GROW
Give annual quaking grasses full sun to light shade and average to rich soil that is well drained. Sow seeds outdoors in fall or in spring after the last spring frost date. Or sow indoors in individual pots 6 to 8 weeks before the last frost and transplant with care. Keep plants evenly moist for best results. Use quaking grasses in mixed plantings, or grow them in rows in

Briza maxima

the cutting garden to produce stems for drying. To dry, cut stems when they are either green or have dried to brown. Hang them in a warm, dark place to dry, or stand a bunch in a vase.

B. maxima

b. MAX-ih-muh. BIG QUAKING GRASS. A 1¹/2- to 2-foot annual with loosely branched panicles of nodding, ovate, 1-inch-long spikelets. Flowers are heart-shaped, ¹/2-inch-long spikelets that appear from late spring to late summer and turn from green to red-brown- or purple-flushed, ripening to straw-colored. Warm-weather annual.

B. minor

b. MY-nor. LITTLE QUAKING GRASS. A 6-inch to 1¹/2-foot annual with ovate, nodding, ¹/4-inch-long spikelets in loose panicles. Flowers are small ¹/2-inch spikelets that appear from early summer to fall and ripen from green, often purple-tinged, to pale tan. Warm-weather annual.

Browallia

broh-WAL-lee-ah. Nightshade family, Solanaceae.

The genus *Browallia* contains six species of annuals and tender perennials native to tropical South America and the West Indies. Commonly called browallias or bush violets, they have narrow, ovate to elliptic leaves and trumpet-shaped flowers with five broad lobes, or "petals." Flowers come in shades of purple, blue-violet, and white and will attract hummingbirds.

HOW TO GROW
Plant browallias in full sun or partial shade and rich, well-drained soil. Sow seeds indoors 8 to 10 weeks before the last spring frost date and germinate at 65° to 70°F. When sowing, just press the seeds into the soil surface, as light is required for germination. Seedlings appear in 1 to 3 weeks. Pinch plants several times to encourage branching. In areas with very long summers, it is possible to sow seeds outdoors where the plants are to grow.

B. americana

b. ah-mair-ih-kah-nuh. BROWALLIA, BUSH VIOLET. Formerly *B. elata.* A 1- to 2-foot annual with ovate, somewhat sticky leaves and 2-inch-wide

Browallia speciosa

flowers borne singly or in small clusters. Warm-weather annual.

B. speciosa

b. spee-see-OH-suh. BROWALLIA, BUSH VIOLET, SAPPHIRE FLOWER. A tender, woody-based perennial that can reach 5 feet in the tropics but ranges from 1 to 2 feet when grown in gardens. Ovate to elliptic leaves and 2-inch-wide flowers borne singly or in small clusters. Cultivars include Troll Series plants, which bear their flowers on rounded, compact, 10-inch plants. Tender perennial or warm-weather annual.

Brugmansia

brug-MAN-see-ah. Nightshade family, Solanaceae.

The five species of *Brugmansia* are tender shrubs or trees from South America. Commonly called angels' trumpets and once included in *Datura,* all bear large, pendent, trumpet-shaped flowers that typically have five pointed lobes that are curled back. Flowers are usually fragrant and are borne from late spring or early summer through fall, nearly year-round in frost-free areas. Leaves are oblong to ovate and either entire, toothed, or lobed. All parts of these plants are poisonous if ingested.

HOW TO GROW

Angels' trumpets thrive in full sun or very light shade and rich, well-drained soil. They are huge dramatic plants. In frost-free areas — Zones 10 and 11 — grow them outdoors as shrubs or specimen plants. They can tolerate some wind, drought, and salt, but not pollution. Where they are not hardy, set these striking plants outdoors each spring, and dig them each fall for overwintering. They also grow in very large containers or tubs, but growing in the ground yields the most spectacular plants. Feed plants, especially pot-grown ones, every 2 to 3 weeks from spring to fall, and water regularly when plants are growing and flowering actively. Dig plants in early fall, before frost, keeping as much soil around the roots as possible. Store them in a bright, cool (40° to 50°F), frost-free place, and keep them nearly dry over winter. Plants may lose their leaves but will begin growing in spring when temperatures warm up and watering is resumed. Prune plants as necessary in spring; they withstand hard pruning, to within several inches of the base of the plant. Repot container-grown specimens annually. Propagate *Brugmansia* species by seeds sown in winter or early spring and germinated at 60° to 70°F. Or take softwood or heel cuttings in summer; bottom heat speeds rooting.

B. arborea

b. are-BORE-ee-uh. COMMON AN-GELS' TRUMPET. Also listed as *B. versicolor* and *Datura arborea.* A 6- to 12-foot shrub or tree with fragrant, white, 6-inch-long flowers. Tender perennial.

B. × candida

b. × kan-DEE-duh. ANGELS' TRUMPETS. Formerly *Datura × candida.* A 10- to 15-foot shrub or tree with 6- to 12-inch-long trumpets that are fragrant at night. Flowers come in white, pale yellow, or sometimes pink. Double-flowered forms include 'Double White' and 'Plena'. Tender perennial.

B. sanguinea

b. san-GWIH-nee-uh. RED AN-GELS' TRUMPETS. Also listed as *B. rosei* and *Datura sanguinea.* A 10- to 30-foot shrub or tree with 6- to 10-inch-long, orange-red flowers that are not fragrant. Tender perennial.

B. suaveolens

b. swah-vee-OH-lenz. ANGELS' TRUMPETS. Formerly *Datura suaveolens.* A 10- to 15-foot shrub or tree with 8-inch-long flowers that come in white, yellow, or pink and are fragrant at night. Tender perennial.

Brunfelsia

broon-FEL-see-uh. Nightshade family, Solanaceae.

This is a genus of about 40 species of evergreen shrubs and small trees native to the tropical Americas. It includes only one species that is widely grown by gardeners, indoors and out, for handsome foliage and flowers that change color from the time they open until they drop.

Brugmansia suaveolens

Brunfelsia pauciflora

Buddleia alternifolia

HOW TO GROW

Brunfelsia needs some pampering. Make sure it has rich, moist soil with excellent drainage, and keep it well fed and watered with protection from midday sun. It can be pruned in spring to improve shape or to restrict size. Indoors, give it bright indirect light. Water lightly in winter, then resume feeding and repot if needed in late winter. Propagate from softwood cuttings in spring or summer.

B. pauciflora
b. paw-sih-FLOR-uh. YESTERDAY, TODAY, AND TOMORROW. Formerly *B. calycina*. This bushy shrub ranges in height from 3 to 10 feet, with a width about half that. The oval leaves are 3 to 6 inches long, dark green, leathery, and glossy. From spring through summer it produces cymes of pansy-shaped flowers, 2 inches across, with five wavy petals. The blossoms open purple, fading to lavender and then white, suggesting the plant's common name. Established plants growing in the ground can survive temperatures into the 20s (Zone 9) but will be defoliated. **Zones 9 to 11**.

Brunnera

BRUN-er-uh. Borage family, Boraginaceae.

Brunneras are rhizomatous perennials with dainty panicles of tiny purplish blue flowers in spring borne above mounds of handsome, rounded leaves. Of the three species in the genus, only one is commonly grown in gardens.

HOW TO GROW

Select a site in partial to full shade with rich, evenly moist soil. While plants tolerate drier conditions, moisture yields the largest, most eye-catching leaves. Plants go dormant during drought but reappear the following year. If the clumps die out in the center, dig and divide them. Propagate by division in spring, taking root cuttings in late winter or early spring, or by seeds. Variegated cultivars can be propagated only by division. Plants self-sow.

B. macrophylla
b. mack-roe-FILL-uh. SIBERIAN BUGLOSS. Formerly *Anchusa myosotidiflora*. A 1- to 1¹/₂-foot-tall species forming 1¹/₂- to 2-foot-wide mounds of 6- to 8-inch-long heart-shaped, coarsely hairy leaves. Bears clusters of ¹/₄-inch-

Brunnera macrophylla

wide blue flowers in mid- to late spring. Variegated cultivars include 'Dawson's White', with creamy leaf edges, and 'Langtrees', with silver-spotted leaves. **Zones 3 to 8**.

Buddleia

BUD-lee-uh. Logania family, Loganiaceae.

This is a well-populated genus of about 100 species, mostly evergreen to deciduous shrubs plus a few trees, vines, and herbaceous perennials from Asia, Africa, and the Americas. About a dozen species of these shrubs have made their way to gardens, but only two are widely available. Both have clusters of fragrant flowers on slender, arching branches.

HOW TO GROW

Plant buddleia in full sun and relatively fertile, moisture-retentive soil. It can tolerate some drought but not wet feet. Use it in a shrub or herbaceous border or make it the centerpiece of a butterfly garden. Deadhead it regularly to remove unsightly dead flowers and to encourage more blooms. *B. davidii* is becoming invasive on the East Coast, and any possibility of self-seeding needs to be controlled. After the last frost in spring but before new growth begins, prune this species, which blooms on new growth, back to strong buds near the ground. It can be encouraged to take on either upright or more spreading shapes. *B. alternifolia*, which blooms on the previous season's growth, should be pruned after flowering in summer and can be espaliered or trained to a single stem with attractive peeling bark. Propagate buddleia from seeds or semiripe cuttings in summer.

B. alternifolia
b. al-tern-ih-FOE-lee-uh. FOUNTAIN BUDDLEIA. Slender, arching shoots form a fountain 10 to 12 feet tall and wide with alternate, 3-inch, willowlike gray-green leaves that turn yellow in fall. In midsummer, dense clusters of fra-

Buddleia davidii

Buddleia 'Lochinch'

grant, trumpet-shaped, lilac purple flowers are packed along the slender stems in the leaf axils of the previous season's growth. The leaves of 'Argentea' have silvery white hairs. **Zones 5 to 9.**

B. davidii

b. da-VID-ee-eye. B U T T E R F L Y B U S H. This fast grower sends its shoots up to 10 feet and spreads wider, although it is usually kept to about half that height with annual pruning. The opposite, lance-shaped leaves, up to 10 inches long, are white underneath and appear gray-green from a distance. They often remain on the plant through fall. The strongly honey-scented terminal flowers appear in cone-shaped spikes from mid- to late summer and are butterfly magnets. Sometimes called summer lilac for the frequently lavender flowers of the species, it has cultivars offering numerous other color choices, many with orange eyes: 'Black Knight' (purple-black), 'Dartmoor' (deep lilac, multibranched flower panicles), 'Honeycomb' (yellow), 'Pink Delight' (bright pink), and 'Royal Red' (purple-red). 'Harlequin' has variegated foliage. 'Nanho Blue', 'Nanho Purple', and 'Nanho White' are smaller, at 4 to 5 feet. Will survive to Zone 4 but die to the ground each year. **Zones 6 to 9.**

B. globosa

b. gloh-BOH-suh. O R A N G E B A L L T R E E. This species from Chile and Peru is still difficult to find but is worth seeking for its unusual flowers. For warm-climate gardeners it may offer a noninvasive alternative to *B.*

davidii. Open and lank and ranging from 6 to 15 feet tall, it has deciduous to semievergreen lance-shaped leaves and holds its bright yellow flowers in $^{3}/_{4}$-inch balls. **Zones 7 to 10.**

B. 'Lochinch'

This vigorous hybrid is 6 to 8 feet tall and has a more compact mound shape, gray-green leaves, and lavender-blue flowers. **Zones 6 to 9.**

Bulbine

BUL-bean. Lily family, Liliaceae.

Bulbine species, offering showy racemes of spring or summer flowers, are native to South Af-

Bulbine frutescens

rica, eastern Africa, and Australia. About 30 species belong to the genus, some of which grow from bulbous or tuberous roots. Plants produce clumps of linear to lance-shaped leaves topped by lacy racemes of small star-shaped flowers. The individual flowers, which are arranged in fairly dense racemes, consist of six petal-like tepals. Most species bear yellow flowers.

HOW TO GROW
Select a site in full sun with sandy, well-drained soil. Plants tolerate poor, dry soil. In areas with dry, mild climates, such as southern California, they can be grown outdoors year-round. Elsewhere, grow them in containers. When plants are actively growing, water regularly, but let the soil almost dry out between waterings. Where plants are not hardy, bring containers indoors in fall and overwinter in a cool (40° to 50°F), dry, well-ventilated place. Propagate by rooting offsets produced around the clump or by seeds. Divide plants as necessary in spring.

B. alooides

b. al-oh-OY-deez. A native South African species reaching 1 foot in height and forming clumps of fleshy, lance-shaped leaves. Bears 8- to 12-inch-long racemes of starry yellow $^{1}/_{8}$-inch-wide flowers in late spring. **Zones 10 to 11.**

B. frutescens

b. fru-TESS-enz. Formerly *B. caulescens.* A 1- to 1$^{1}/_{2}$-foot-tall South African species with succulent, lance-shaped leaves and 6- to 12-inch-long racemes of starry $^{1}/_{4}$- to $^{1}/_{2}$-inch-wide flowers in summer. **Zones 10 to 11.**

Bulbinella

bul-bih-NEL-uh. Lily family, Liliaceae.

Bulbinella species, fleshy-rooted perennials native to South Africa and New Zealand, are closely related to *Bulbine*. About 20 species belong here, all producing clumps of succulent, grasslike leaves topped by racemes of flowers in late winter, spring, or summer, depending on the species. Individual flowers are small — usually about $^{1}/_{2}$ inch across — and starry or cup shaped. They are packed very densely into cylindrical racemes. Each flower consists of six petal-like tepals.

HOW TO GROW
Select a site in full sun or partial shade with moist, well-drained soil that has a neutral to acid pH. These are suitable plants for areas with mild winters, such as southern California. *B. hookeri* grows naturally in moist, peaty soil but also tolerates drier conditions. Where plants are marginally hardy, look for a protected, south-facing site and protect them over winter with a thick, coarse mulch of evergreen boughs, pine needles, or salt hay. Where not hardy, grow them in containers overwintered indoors in a cool (40° to 50°F) spot. Amend the soil or potting mix with peat moss to ensure an acid pH and good moisture retention. Propagate by dividing the clumps in fall or by seeds.

B. hookeri

b. HOOK-er-eye. New Zealand native with sword-shaped leaves that reaches 1$^{1}/_{2}$ to 2 feet in height. Bears 1-foot-long racemes of yel-

Bulbinella rossii

low flowers from spring to summer. Best in areas with somewhat cool summers. **Zones 8 to 9**.

B. rossii

b. ROSS-ee-eye. New Zealand native reaching 4 feet in height that bears racemes of yellow flowers in spring. **Zones 8 to 9**.

Bulbocodium

bul-boh-KOH-dee-um. Lily family, Liliaceae.

Two species belong to the genus *Bulbocodium*, both perennials that grow from corms and are native to dry grasslands and meadows in eastern and southern Europe. They are closely related to autumn crocuses (*Colchicum*) and bear their showy flowers quite near the ground. Blooms appear in spring and are borne either singly or in twos or threes. The lance- to strap-shaped leaves appear slightly after the flowers and lengthen after the blooms disappear. Like other lily-family plants, these plants produce flowers that consist of six petal-like tepals.

HOW TO GROW

Select a site in full sun or very light shade with rich, well-drained soil. These plants can be finicky: give them rich soil amended with both leaf mold and grit to ensure moisture retention and good drainage. The soil should remain evenly moist in spring when plants are actively growing. Plant the corms in fall at a depth of 3 inches. Some gardeners replant them in fresh soil every 2 to 3 years to keep the plants vigorous. Propagate by division in early summer, as the plants go dormant; by separating offsets; or by seeds.

B. vernum

b. VER-num. SPRING MEADOW SAFFRON. A 1¹/₂- to 3-inch-tall species with showy rosy purple blooms in spring. Blooms are somewhat crocuslike and have 1¹/₂- to 3-inch-long petals. **Zones 3 to 9**.

Bupleurum

bup-LOOR-um. Carrot family, Apiaceae.

Related to carrots and dill, *Bupleurum* species bear rounded umbels of tiny, star-shaped flowers that are frequently surrounded by leafy bracts. The genus contains about 100 species of annuals,

Bulbocodium vernum

perennials, and shrubs with simple leaves that have parallel veins.

HOW TO GROW

Full sun and average to poor soil satisfy *Bupleurum* species. They tolerate exposed sites as well as dry or rocky soil and are suitable for seaside gardens. The flowers are good for cutting. Sow seeds indoors 6 to 8 weeks before the last spring frost date in individual pots. Transplant with care after the last frost. Or sow outdoors a few weeks before the last frost. Plants self-sow.

B. fruticosum

b. fru-tih-KOSE-um. SHRUBBY HARE'S EAR. A tender 4- to 6-foot-tall shrub, hardy from Zone 7 south, with glossy blue-green leaves. Bears rounded, 1¹/₂-inch-wide umbels of starry yellow flowers from midsummer to fall. **Zones 7 to 10** or grow as an annual.

B. rotundifolium

b. roe-tun-dih-FOE-lee-um. THOROW WAX, THOROUGH WAX. A shrubby 1¹/₂- to 2-foot-tall short-lived perennial. Produces 1¹/₄-inch-wide umbels of yellow-green flowers in summer. The common names refer to the ovate leaves, which appear to surround the stems: *thorow* and *thorough* are Middle English spellings from the Old English *thuruh*, meaning "from end to end" or "through." **Zones 4 to 8**, or grow as an annual.

Buxus

BUCKS-us. Boxwood family, Buxaceae.

Among this genus's 70 species of evergreen shrubs and trees from Europe, Asia, Africa, and Central America, a handful have been cul-

Bupleurum rotundifolium

tivated for their usually small, tough, evergreen leaves and amenability to pruning. Boxwood is notoriously slow growing. Its distinctive aroma and formally pruned shapes are a hallmark of many historic gardens.

HOW TO GROW

Boxwoods need relatively neutral, well-drained soil generously amended with organic matter. They will tolerate full sun but handle stress — drought, dry wind, rapid temperature fluctuations — better in part shade. These conditions, or winter sun, can bronze the leaves. To reduce winter scorching or ice damage, water heavily in fall and tie up branches by spiraling twine around the shrub from the bottom. Mulch in summer to keep the shallow roots cool. Use small boxwoods to edge walkways or formal herb or ornamental beds, and larger ones for hedging or topiary. Prune heavily in early spring, or lightly in summer. Thin the interior annually to prevent fungal diseases. Propagate

from stem cuttings July through December.

B. microphylla

b. my-kro-FILL-luh. LITTLELEAF BOX. Forms a dense mound 3 feet tall and wide, with oblong leaves usually less than 1 inch long. 'Compacta' (sometimes listed as 'Kingsville Dwarf') is slower growing, to only 10 to 12 inches tall and 18 inches wide, with ¹/₂-inch leaves less than ¹/₄ inch wide. 'Green Pillow' grows 2 feet tall and 3 feet wide and has larger leaves. **Zones 6 to 9**.

B. microphylla var. koreana × B. sempervirens

b. my-kro-FILL-uh var. kor-ee-AY-nuh × b. sem-per-VEER-enz. These hybrids are better adapted to the cold, dry, windy winters of the Midwest, most of them growing 2 to 3 feet tall. They include 'Glencoe' ('Chicagoland Green'), 'Green Ice', and 'Green Mountain', which is 5 feet tall and 3 feet wide and may survive in Zone 4. Others, **Zones 5 to 7**.

B. sempervirens

b. sem-per-VIE-enz. COMMON BOXWOOD. A rounded bushy shrub, to 15 feet tall and wide that can be trained as a tree. 'Elegantissima' has creamy white leaf margins. 'Graham Blandy' is narrow and upright at 9 feet by 18 inches. 'Pendula' has weeping branches. 'Suffruticosa', the edging box or dwarf boxwood, has a dense mound form and small round leaves and grows only an inch a year to 3 to 5 feet. 'Vardar Valley' is 6 feet high by 10 feet wide and has blue-green foliage. **Zones 6 to 8**.

Buxus microphylla

Caladium

kah-LAY-dee-um. Arum family, Araceae.

These tender, tuberous perennials from the South American tropics are grown for their large, showy, arrowhead-shaped leaves rather than their flowers. The species are seldom grown; plant breeders have developed a wide variety of hybrids treasured for their brightly patterned foliage variegated in shades of green as well as pinks, rose-reds, maroon, and white. Like other arum-family plants, caladiums bear flowers that are actually an inflorescence consisting of many tiny flowers clustered on a central stalk, called a spadix. The spadix is surrounded by a modified leaf, called a spathe. The blooms somewhat resemble those of calla lilies (*Zantedeschia*) but have a greenish white spathe that isn't showy. While seven species belong to this genus, all of the commonly grown cultivars belong to a single genus, *C. bicolor*.

HOW TO GROW

Select a site in partial to full shade with evenly moist, well-drained soil that is very rich in organic matter. Slightly acid pH is best. In all but the very warmest climates (Zones 10 and 11), start the tubers indoors 8 to 10 weeks before the last spring frost date. Set the tubers close together in flats filled with barely moist vermiculite, and cover the tops with 1 inch of vermiculite. Set the flats in a warm (70° to 85°F), humid place until leaves and roots sprout. Then plant the tubers in individual bulb pans (shallow pots) or group them in large pots. Keep the soil evenly moist, and set them in a bright spot, such as a north or east window. Move the plants outdoors in early summer, once nighttime temperatures remain above 55°F and the soil has warmed to 60°F at a depth of several inches. Either keep them in pots or transplant to a shady spot with rich, moist soil. Bright, dappled shade is best; direct sun will scorch the leaves. Water regularly and feed monthly to encourage large leaves. Remove the flowers as they appear.

These plants can be grown as annuals, but overwintering the tubers isn't difficult. Let the soil dry gradually in fall, dig the tubers before frost, and set them in a warm, dry spot. Clean off soil and remove roots and tops before storing them in sand or vermiculite in a warm (60° to 70°F) place. Pot-grown plants can be stored under similar conditions — just turn the containers on their sides. To propagate, cut the tubers into parts with a knife in spring, then dust the cut pieces with sulfur before potting them up.

C. bicolor

c. BI-kuh-lor. Caladium, Angel Wings, Elephant's Ears. A 1½- to 2-foot-tall species that can spread to 2 feet. Bears arrow-shaped 8- to 12-inch-long leaves and greenish white flowers in spring. Cultivars include 'Candidum', with white leaves netted in green; 'Carolyn Whorton', with pink leaves edged with green and netted with dark pink veins. 'Fanny Munson', with pale pink leaves edged in green and netted with dark pink; 'Little Miss Muffet', an 8- to 12-inch-tall selection with chartreuse leaves spotted with burgundy; 'White Christmas', with white leaves with green midribs and veins; and Florida Series cultivars bear leaves that are thicker and more sun tolerant than those of older cultivars. These include 'Florida Cardinal', with green-edged burgundy leaves; 'Florida Fantasy', with white leaves with red veins that are netted with green; and 'Florida Sunrise', with rose leaves with red main veins and white smaller veins. Tender perennial, hardy in **Zones 10 to 11**.

Calamagrostis

kal-ah-mah-GROSS-tiss. Grass family, Poaceae.

There are some 250 species of *Calamagrostis*, all perennial grasses with linear leaves that bear their tiny flowers in fluffy, airy-textured branched panicles. One species is popular as an ornamental.

HOW TO GROW

Give *Calamagrostis* full sun to light shade and average to rich soil that is well drained and evenly moist. Plants also tolerate a wide range of soils, including heavy clay. Cut the plants to the ground in late winter or very early spring, before new growth appears. Popular *C. × acutiflora* is a sterile hybrid and does not produce seeds, so plants do not self-sow. To propagate, divide the clumps in spring.

C. × acutiflora

c. × ah-kew-tih-FLOR-uh. Feather Reed Grass. Clump-forming hybrid producing arching mounds of 1½- to 3-foot-long leaves and spreading from 2 to 4 feet. Plants are deciduous to semievergreen in the North, evergreen in the South. Clumps are topped by erect 2- to 6-foot-tall panicles of fluffy, silvery brown to purplish flowers in mid- to late summer that fade to buff and last through winter. 'Karl Foerster' bears pinkish bronze panicles that fade to buff. 'Overdam', which has leaves striped with pale yellow or

Caladium

Caladium bicolor

Calamagrostis × acutiflora

cream, is less vigorous and does not do well in hot, humid climates. **Zones 5 to 9.**

Calamintha

kal-ah-MIN-thuh. Mint family, Lamiaceae.

Aromatic leaves and clusters of small, tubular, two-lipped flowers characterize the members of this genus, which contains about eight species of perennials and sub-shrubs. Commonly called cala-mints, they bear small ovate to oblong leaves that usually are toothed. The flowers come in shades of lilac-blue as well as pink and white. The name *Calamintha* is from the Greek *kalos*, meaning "beautiful," and *minthe*, "mint."

HOW TO GROW
Plant calamints in full sun or par-tial shade and average, moist, well-drained soil. They tolerate poorer soils. In areas with humid, wet summers, plant them in raised beds to ensure excellent drainage. Plants spread by rhizomes and form rounded mounds that spread from 1¹/₂ to 2¹/₂ feet. Cut them back after flowering to keep them neat. Cut plants back hard if they become woody. To propagate, di-vide plants in early spring, take cuttings in summer, or sow seeds.

C. grandiflora
c. gran-dih-FLOR-uh. LARGE-FLOWERED CALAMINT. Bushy 1¹/₂-foot-tall perennial bearing loose clusters of ¹/₂- to 1-inch-long pink flowers in summer.
Zones 5 to 9.

Calamintha grandiflora

C. nepeta
c. NEP-eh-tuh. LESSER CALAMINT. Lacy-textured 1- to 1¹/₂-foot-tall perennial with very aromatic, hairy leaves. Bears branched clusters of ¹/₄-inch-long lilac to mauve flowers in summer. 'Alba' has white flowers.
Zones 5 to 9.

Calendula

kah-LEN-du-luh. Aster family, Asteraceae.

Commonly called pot marigolds, *Calendula* species are annuals or woody-based perennials with sin-gle or double daisylike flowers and aromatic leaves. The flowers have petals (more properly called ray florets) in shades of yellow or or-ange, with centers (disk florets) in yellow, orange, purple, or brown. The genus contains some 20 to 30 species native to the Mediterra-nean region and North Africa, one of which is a popular annual.

HOW TO GROW
Full sun or light shade and aver-age, well-drained soil are ideal. Plants tolerate poor, relatively dry soil and are best in areas with cool summers. Sow seeds outdoors sev-eral weeks before the last spring frost date. Or sow indoors 6 to 8 weeks before the last frost date at 45° to 50°F at night and no more than 55° to 60°F during the day;

seedlings grown at warmer tem-peratures tend to be floppy and weak. Sow in a sterile seed-starting medium, and water from below to prevent damping off, which can be a problem. Cover the seeds with soil, as darkness is required for germination, which takes up to 2 weeks. Also sow seeds in midsum-mer for fall bloom. In mild cli-mates (Zone 8 and warmer), sow in late summer for winter and early-spring bloom. If plants begin dying out due to summer heat, cut them back hard, and they will re-sume growth when cooler weather returns.

Use pot marigolds in beds and borders, in containers, and in the

Callicarpa dichotoma

herb garden. The flowers attract butterflies and have edible petals. Add them fresh to salads, or use them as a substitute for saffron and to add color to cakes and other desserts. The flowers are also ideal for cutting.

C. officinalis
c. oh-fih-shih-NAL-iss. POT MARI-GOLD. A fast-growing, 1- to 2¹/₂-foot species with lance- to spoon-shaped leaves and single or double daisylike flowers in shades of yel-low, orange, apricot, or cream. Many cultivars are available, in-cluding the Bon Bon Series, 1-foot dwarf selections, and Prince Se-ries, ideal for cutting at 2 to 2¹/₂ feet tall. Cool-weather annual.

Callicarpa

Kal-Lih-KARP-Uh. Verbena Family, Verbenaceae.

The 140 evergreen and deciduous shrubs in this genus are mainly from the tropics and subtropics, but 4 or 5 cold-hardy deciduous species, commonly known as beautyberries, are grown for their small, usually purple but occasion-ally white fruit clusters.

HOW TO GROW
Give beautyberries moderately fer-tile, well-drained soil in dappled shade or full sun. *C. americana* will even grow under pines, but fruiting is most dramatic when the plants are grouped in full sun in hot climates. Beautiful in a shrub border or open woods. Flowers appear on new growth; pruning low to the ground regularly in early spring will help the plants maintain a compact shape. Propa-gate from softwood cuttings or give seeds warm stratification and plant in spring.

Calendula officinalis

Callirhoe involucrata

C. americana
c. ah-mair-ih-KAH-nuh. A MERICAN BEAUTYBERRY. A coarse and open shrub native from Maryland to Florida, beautyberry can reach 8 feet tall and 6 feet wide, but regular pruning will hold it to half that. The oval, toothed, mid-green leaves may reach 6 inches long. In early to late summer, tiny lavender-pink flowers appear in the leaf axils, followed by bright purple berry clusters. 'Lactea' has white flowers and fruits. **Zones 7 to 10.**

C. bodinieri var. giraldii
c. boh-din-ee-EH-ree var. jeer-ALL-dee-eye. C HINESE BEAUTYBERRY CULTIVAR. This selection of a Chinese variety reaches 6 to 10 feet with arching branches. The showy flowers give way to heavy clusters of 30 to 40 iridescent purple-pink berries encircling the branches. In early spring and fall, leaves have a purple cast. **Zones 5 to 9.**

C. dichotoma
c. dye-KOT-oh-muh. P URPLE BEAUTYBERRY. Fountainlike and branching to the ground, this Asian species grows 4 to 5 feet tall with a wider spread. Amethyst berries appear in September or October on short stalks along the branches, either on bare branches in the North or above the leaves in the South. This species, which has received a Gold Medal from the Pennsylvania Horticultural Society, has a white-fruited form, *C. dichotoma* var. *albifructus*. **Zones 6 to 9.**

C. japonica
c. juh-PON-ih-kuh. J APANESE BEAUTYBERRY. Erect and rounded, to 4 to 6 feet tall and wide, this shrub has arching branches. 'Leucocarpa' has heavy white fruit and yellow fall leaves. *C. japonica* var. *luxurians* has larger leaves and reddish violet fruit clusters. **Zones 5 to 9.**

Callirhoe
kal-ir-HOE-ee. Mallow family, Malvaceae.

The nine species that make up *Callirhoe* are North American perennials most common in the central and southwestern United States. They range from Florida and Illinois west to Texas and Wyoming. They are related to hollyhocks (*Alcea* and *Althaea*). All are low growing and bear very showy flowers. Leaves are alternate and typically deeply cleft. Flowers, inordinately large for the plant size, are visible at a considerable distance and are brilliant wine red, rose, pink, or occasionally white.

HOW TO GROW
Plants of the genus *Callirhoe* are valued ground covers in the south central United States, as they thrive on high summer heat. They need full sun and good drainage. Soil should be more mineral than organic, especially in regions with humid, wet summers, or the plants will rot. The spreading stems do not root (although they carry profuse blooms), so coverage is dependent on establishing numerous perennial crowns.

Callistemon citrinus

C. involucrata
in-vol-yew CRAY-tuh. W INE CUPS. In hot, dry, sunny sites, the sprawling stems display cherry red blossoms that cascade happily through borders and over walls. Native from Texas to Utah and Wyoming, it performs well where summers are dry rather than humid. **Zones 6 to 9.**

Callistemon
kal-LIH-steh-mun. Myrtle family, Myrtaceae.

The name of this Australian genus comes from two Greek words meaning "beautiful" and "stamen." Gardeners on America's West Coast grow many of the 25 species of evergreen trees and shrubs for the flower spikes' colorful and prominent stamens.

HOW TO GROW
Callistemons grow in neutral to acid, moderately fertile soil in full sun. Most need little water, and some species will tolerate alkaline soil and salt. They can be pruned hard when young to be used as hedges or espaliers or to coax them into more treelike shapes. Sow seeds in spring or root semiripe cuttings in late summer.

C. citrinus
c. sih-TRY-nus. C OMMON BOT-TLEBRUSH. Variable shrub to 10 or 15 feet tall and wide. The 4-inch lance-shaped leaves are coppery when new; bright red bottlebrush flower spikes attract hummingbirds in spring and summer. 'Jeffers' grows 6 to 8 feet tall and bears purple-pink flowers. **Zones 8 to 11.**

C. 'Little John'
This dwarf selection, often sold as *C. viminalis* 'Little John', has a rounded form 3 feet tall and wide, with brilliant red flowers that rebloom throughout the year. **Zones 8 to 11.**

C. salignus
c. sal-IG-nus. W HITE BOTTLE-BRUSH. Left to grow as a shrub, this species can reach 15 to 20 feet tall, although it is sometimes trained as a tree. Most gardeners grow it for its stunning new leaves, which verge on magenta. The flowers are cream colored to pale yellow. **Zones 8 to 11.**

Callistephus
kal-ISS-teh-fus. Aster family, Asteraceae.

One species, a popular annual native to China, belongs to this genus: *C. chinensis*, commonly called China aster. It has ovate to ovate-triangular leaves, sometimes coarsely toothed, and daisylike flowers from midsummer to fall. Many cultivars are available with both single and double flowers; the species is seldom grown.

HOW TO GROW
China asters thrive in a site with full sun or partial shade and rich, well-drained, evenly moist soil that is neutral or alkaline. Sow seeds indoors 6 to 8 weeks before the last spring frost date in individual pots. Germination takes 1 to

Callistemon 'Little John'

Callistephus chinensis 'Early Charm Choice'

2 weeks at 65° to 70°F. Transplant with care. Or sow outdoors after the last frost date. For best results, choose disease-resistant cultivars and rotate planting locations annually to avoid problems with soilborne diseases. Space plants generously to ensure good air circulation: they resent hot climates, crowding, poor air circulation, and reflected heat. Water regularly during dry weather, and deadhead to prolong bloom. Use China asters in beds and borders, in containers, and as cut flowers.

C. chinensis

c. chih-NEN-sis. CHINA ASTER, ANNUAL ASTER. A bushy, fast-growing annual with single or double, 3- to 5-inch flowers in shades of violet, lavender, purple, pink, red, white, or yellow. Cultivars in different heights are available: Taller ones, from 1½ to 3 feet tall, are best for cut flowers and include 'Fireworks Mix' and 'Powder Puff Mix'. Use shorter cultivars, including 8-inch-tall Comet Series plants, near the front of plantings and in pots. Cool-weather annual.

Calluna

kal-OO-nuh. Heath family, Ericeae.

There is only one species in this genus of low, evergreen shrubs but more than 500 cultivars. A dominant feature of moors in Europe,

heather is also found from Siberia to the Azores islands in the North Atlantic. The upright but flexible branches have tiny overlapping leaves, often with hairs that give them a gray cast. Some of the little bell flowers never open from bud. Subtle variations in foliage and flower color — white, pink, purple, to red — bring year-round interest to gardens in the ideal climate.

HOW TO GROW

Heather prefers poor, acid soil but must have sharp drainage. Sandy soil amended with peat moss is excellent. It becomes leggy in too much shade but can't tolerate full sun or exposure to wind in the southern portion of its range. It is recommended for coastal locations with moderate winters and

Calluna vulgaris

mild summers. In winter, mulch where snow cover is unreliable. Like other heath-family members, heather is shallow rooted, so weed carefully. After flowering, prune back flowered shoots. Propagate by layering.

C. vulgaris

c. vul-GAIR-iss. SCOTCH HEATHER. Cultivars range from 4 to more than 24 inches tall and spread up to 2 feet across. Most bloom in summer, but some have flowers in December or even January. Flowers are sometimes double, and foliage comes in shades of green or silver, gold or bronze, sometimes taking on a striking red hue in winter. 'County Wicklow' is double pink, 'Gold Haze' has gold

foliage and white flowers, and 'Kinlochruel' is double white. **Zones 4 to 7.**

Calocedrus

kal-oh-CED-druss. Cypress family, Cupressaceae.

Characterized by flat branchlets and scalelike leaves in whorls of four, this genus includes two or three species, all from North America and Asia. Only one, incense cedar, is common as a landscape plant. Widely grown on the West Coast, this adaptable tree should receive more attention in the East, South, and Southwest, where it makes an excellent substitute for two overused plants — arborvitae *(Thuja occidentalis)* and eastern red cedar *(Juniperus virginiana)*. Unlike these two trees, incense cedar has a single leader and short branches that do not split in ice and snow, and its foliage retains its bright green color in winter.

HOW TO GROW

Plant incense cedar in full sun to light shade; provide afternoon shade in the South. It is best in deep, moist, well-drained, acid soil but tolerates clayey and slightly alkaline soil and can take heat, humidity, and urban conditions. Although it withstands drought once established, it grows best with even moisture and does not tolerate wet soil. Shelter from drying wind. Water deeply when young to encourage drought-resistant roots. Plants need no pruning but may be sheared for a hedge; do not remove the lower limbs. Usually pest-free.

C. decurrens

c. dee-KUR-renz. INCENSE CEDAR. Formerly *Libocedrus decurrens*. This narrow, columnar tree reaches 30 to 50 feet tall and 10 feet wide. It has a single straight trunk that tapers to a point and spreads into a wide buttress at its base. Bark is cinnamon brown, deeply furrowed, and shredding, adding an ornamental touch. Emitting a spicy aroma when crushed, the glossy, emerald green foliage is made up of pointed scales and grows in fanlike sprays on short, slightly pendulous side branches that resist snow and ice damage. The distinctive but inconspicuous cones are ¾-inch-long, brown cylinders with several scales that spread open like small flowers in autumn to release the seeds. Use

Calocedrus decurrens

a single plant as a strong, upright accent. The narrow shape also works well planted in a grove or as a tall screen. Although this conifer comes from a cool area, it adapts to many climates. From the mountains of the West Coast of North America. **Zones 6 to 8**.

CULTIVARS

'Columnaris' is narrow and spire-like; the form is usually offered under the species name.

Calocephalus

kal-oh-SEFF-ah-lus. Aster family, Asteraceae.

The 18 species of annuals, perennials, and small shrubs that belong to *Calocephalus* all are native to rocky coastal areas in Australia. Most have leaves that are white and feltlike or woolly, as well as silvery white flower heads. One species, cushionbush (*C. brownii*), is grown for its attractive foliage.

HOW TO GROW

Give cushionbush a site in full sun with sandy, well-drained soil. In warm, dry, frost-free areas (Zone 9 south) grow these plants outdoors year-round as small shrubs. In the North, grow them in containers and overwinter them indoors (in a bright, 40° to 45°F spot), or grow as bedding plants replaced annually. They are generally started from cuttings rather than seeds. Take cuttings from late summer to fall to overwinter plants, and root them in very well drained potting soil at around 50°F. Pinch to encourage bushy growth. Move plants to the garden several weeks after the last spring frost date, once night temperatures do not dip below 50°F. Use cushionbush as an edging plant, or add it to containers or mixed plantings. It is suitable for seaside gardens.

C. brownii

c. BROW-nee-eye.

CUSHIONBUSH. Formerly *Leucophyta browni*. A 1-foot-tall shrub with wiry branches, woolly white linear leaves, and silvery ¹/₂-inch flower heads. Tender perennial, or grow as an annual.

Calochortus

kal-oh-KOR-tus. Lily family, Liliaceae.

Charming wildflowers native to western North America as well as Central America, *Calochortus* species have a variety of common names that refer to their tuliplike flowers: they have been called butterfly tulips, mariposa lilies, globe tulips, fairy lanterns, and sego lilies. The botanical name is from the Greek *kalos,* meaning "beautiful," and *chortus,* "grass." About 60 species belong to the genus, all of which are herbaceous perennials that grow from edible, tunicate bulbs, which once were used as food by Native Americans. Plants bear linear- to lance-shaped leaves that are most often grassy and basal. Flowers, which are borne singly or in clusters, face up, out, or are nodding. They can be cup shaped and tuliplike, rounded and lantern shaped, or bell shaped. Each bloom has three showy petals that usually have prominent markings and/or showy, irislike beards in a contrasting color at the base. These, in nearly all cases, mark the location of a specialized gland called a nectary located near the base of the petal on the inside of the bloom.

HOW TO GROW

Give these plants full sun and very well drained soil. They are happiest and easiest to grow in the West, because warm, dry summers and mild winters suit their tastes. There, they can be naturalized or used in beds and borders or in rock gardens. Plant the bulbs in fall at a depth of 4 to 6 inches. Site selection is the secret to success from the Midwest eastward, where summer rainfall, winter wet, and alternate cycles of freezing and thawing do not suit the plants' natural preferences. (Gardeners in these regions may want to buy new bulbs annually, much like tulips, to ensure an annual display.) Give *Calochortus* species perfectly drained soil — amend with coarse sand or grit as well as organic matter at planting time to ensure both good drainage and moisture retention — and combine them with plants that do not need supplemental watering in the summer. A south-facing site at the

Calocephalus brownii

Calochortus superbus

base of a rock in a rock garden or next to a rock wall helps provide winter protection. Once the ground has frozen, mulch with evergreen boughs, salt hay, or dry, coarse leaves (oak leaves are suitable) to protect the plants from alternate cycles of freezing and thawing. Top the mulch with a weighted-down sheet of plastic mulch to keep the site dry over winter. Propagate by separating offsets in summer or by seeds. Some species produce bulbils in the leaf axils, which also can be planted.

C. albus

c. AL-bus. FAIRY LANTERN, GLOBE LILY. A wildflower, native to California, that ranges from 4 to 20 inches tall. Bears loose clusters of nodding, 1-inch-long, rounded to bell-shaped white flowers in spring and early summer. **Zones 6 to 10.**

C. amabilis

c. ah-MAB-ih-liss. GOLDEN FAIRY LANTERN, GOLDEN GLOBE TULIP. California native wildflower featuring loose clusters of nodding deep yellow blooms with 1- to 1^{1}/4-inch-long petals and prominent green-tinged sepals in spring and early summer. **Zones 6 to 10.**

C. macrocarpus

c. mack-roe-KAR-pus. GREEN-BANDED MARIPOSA. Summer-blooming 8- to 20-inch-tall species native to the West that bears one to three upward-facing, cup-shaped blooms per stem in summer. Blooms are 2^{1}/2 to 3^{1}/2 inches wide and purple with a darker purple ring near the base of the petals. **Zones 6 to 10.**

C. superbus

c. sue-PER-bus. California native wildflower ranging from 1^{1}/2 to 2 feet tall and bearing small loose clusters of upward-facing, cup-shaped, 2- to 3-inch-wide blooms in late spring. Flowers are cream, lavender-blue, or yellow with yellow and maroon at the base of the petals. **Zones 5 to 10.**

C. venustus

c. veh-NOO-stus. WHITE MARIPOSA. A ^{1}/2- to 2-foot-tall native California wildflower with clusters of one to three upward-facing, cup-shaped flowers from late spring to early summer. Blooms are 2 to 3 inches across and come in white or yellow as well as red or

Caltha palustris

purple. Petals are marked with yellow and maroon at the base. **Zones 6 to 10.**

C. vestae

c. VES-tye. Native California wildflower ranging from 1 to 2 feet tall and bearing small clusters of cup-shaped, upward-facing blooms from late spring to summer. Individual blooms are 2 to 3 inches wide and white with yellow and maroon markings at the base of the petals. **Zones 5 to 10.**

Caltha

KAL-thah. Buttercup family, Ranunculaceae.

Commonly known as marsh marigolds, *Caltha* species are moisture-loving perennials bearing loose clusters of showy golden yellow or white flowers in spring. The usually cup-shaped flowers, which appear before the heart- or kidney-shaped leaves emerge, actually lack true petals. Instead they have petal-like sepals. *Caltha* contains

Calycanthus floridus

about 10 species, all rhizomatous perennials.

HOW TO GROW

Select a site in full sun with rich, constantly moist to boggy soil. A spot in the wet soil at the edge of a stream or pond is ideal. *C. palustris* will grow in standing water up to a depth of about 9 inches, although plants do better in shallower water, boggy soil, or even containers in a water garden. For propagation, divide plants in late

summer or very early spring or sow seeds. Plants self-sow.

C. palustris

c. pah-LUS-tris. MARSH MARIGOLD. A 1- to 1^{1}/2-foot-tall species native to North America, Europe, and Asia that spreads to 1 foot. Bears toothed, kidney-shaped leaves and clusters of waxy, golden yellow, 1^{1}/2-inch-wide flowers on 1- to 1^{1}/2-foot-tall stems in spring. 'Flore Pleno' bears double flowers on 10-inch plants. **Zones 3 to 7.**

Calycanthus

kal-ih-KAN-thus. Sweetshrub family, Calycanthaceae.

There are only two species of these deciduous native American shrubs, typically found in woods and along streams, and grown in gardens for their unusual, fruit-scented flowers. Thanks to taxonomists, a scentless Asian species has recently joined them.

HOW TO GROW

Give these shrubs fertile, moisture-retentive soil that is rich in organic matter, in full sun toward the northern part of their range and partial shade in the southern. Site them along a path or near a seating area where their fragrance can be enjoyed. Because they flower on the current season's growth, they can be pruned close to the ground in early spring. Start from stratified seeds. Cuttings show genetic variation; some root

Calycanthus floridus 'Athens'

Camassia cusickii

readily, while others are more difficult.

C. chinensis

c. chih-NEN-sis. CHINESE SPICE-BUSH. Also listed as *Sinocalycanthus chinensis*. Grows 6 to 9 feet tall and bears huge glossy leaves. The 3-inch white spring flowers are tinged with pink and have yellow centers but no fragrance. Zones 7 to 8.

C. floridus

c. FLOR-ih-dus. COMMON SWEETSHRUB, CAROLINA ALLSPICE. Also called sweet bubby and strawberry shrub, this sweetshrub is native from Pennsylvania to Florida. It averages 8 feet tall and spreads 10 feet wide. Dark green leaves up to 5 inches long are rough to the touch and fragrant when crushed, turning yellow in fall. The 2-inch maroon flowers, which have straplike petals and may smell like strawberries, bananas, or pineapples, bloom late spring into early summer. Buy the shrubs in bloom if possible, since some seed-grown plants may be largely lacking in scent. A persistent leathery pod holds numerous dark brown seeds. Zones 5 to 9.

C. occidentalis

c. ox-ih-den-TAL-iss. CALIFORNIA ALLSPICE. This West Coast native is similar to the eastern version but grows larger and has longer leaves. Zones 6 to 9.

Camassia

kah-MASS-ee-uh. Lily family, Liliaceae.

Handsome and easy to grow, camassias are native North American plants that are underused in gardens. The botanical name is derived from Native American words for these plants — camass or quamash. The boiled bulbs, which can reach half a pound or more, were extremely important food plants. Plants grow from rounded, tunicate bulbs and produce grassy clumps of narrow, lance-shaped, basal leaves that are erect and generally 1 to 2 feet long. They bear erect racemes of small starry flowers in spring or early summer that extend well above the foliage. (Heights given below are for plants in bloom.) Like other lily-family plants, their individual flowers consist of six petal-like tepals. Blooms come in shades of blue, violet-blue, cream, and white.

HOW TO GROW

Give camassias a site in full sun or partial shade and rich, well-drained soil. In the wild, most species grow naturally in moist meadows that may be under water for periods of time in spring but that are dry during the summer months. When plants are actively growing in spring, evenly moist conditions are essential, but dry soil in summer after the foliage dies back suits them just fine. Wet, waterlogged soil when plants are dormant — especially in winter — is generally fatal. Plant the bulbs in fall, setting the tops of the bulbs 4 inches below the soil surface. For best effect, arrange them in drifts of a dozen or more, spacing bulbs 6 to 8 inches apart. Camassias produce offsets, which can be used for propagation, but offset production

Camellia japonica

is slow, and clumps are best left undisturbed. Dig and divide in summer just as the foliage dies back for propagation or if clumps show signs of overcrowding such as reduced flowering. Or propagate by seeds. Plants self-sow, and seedlings take 3 to 4 years to bloom.

C. cusickii

c. kew-SIK-ee-eye. CAMASS, CUSICK QUAMASH. A 2- to 3-foot-tall species native to northeastern Oregon. Bears erect, showy $^1/_2$- to $1^1/_2$-foot-long racemes of 30 to as many as 100 starry blue 2-inch-wide flowers in late spring. Zones 3 to 10.

C. leichtlinii

c. lekt-LIN-ee-eye. LEICHTLIN QUAMASH. A 2- to 4-foot-tall species native to the Pacific Northwest. Bears erect $^1/_2$- to 1-foot-long racemes of creamy white flowers in late spring. Individual blooms are 2 to 3 inches wide and 1 to 2 inches long; the petals twist together as they wither. 'Alba' bears single white blooms. 'Blue Danube' (also listed as 'Blau Donau') bears violet-blue flowers. 'Semiplena' features semidouble creamy white flowers on $2^1/_2$- to 3-foot plants. Zones 4 to 10.

C. quamash

c. KWAH-mash. QUAMASH, COMMON QUAMASH. Formerly *C. esculenta*. A 1- to $2^1/_2$-foot-tall species from the Pacific Northwest with 1-foot-long racemes of 10 to 30 flowers in late spring in blue, violet-purple, and white. Individual blooms are 1 to 2 inches wide and are slightly irregular in form — one tepal curves downward and the other five point

up. This species produces offsets more quickly than other camassias do. 'Blue Melody' and 'Orion' produce dark blue flowers. Zones 4 to 10.

C. scilloides

c. sil-OY-deez. WILD HYACINTH, WESTERN CAMASSIA. Formerly *C. fraseri*; *C. hyacinthina*. A 1- to $2^1/_2$-foot-tall species native from Pennsylvania and Minnesota south to Georgia and Texas. Bears 3- to 6-inch-long racemes of 10 to 40 inch-wide flowers in early summer in blue, violet-blue, or white. Zones 4 to 9.

Camellia

kah-MEEL-yuh. Tea family, Theaceae.

This genus comprises more than 250 evergreen shrubs and trees from Asian woodlands. Most popular in gardens are hybrids averaging 15 feet tall to about 10 feet wide. They are cherished in the southern United States for their winter to early-spring flowers, which look like roses from a distance. Most are unscented, but they come in an array of forms: semidouble, double, anemone, peony, and rose, as well as single. Tea is made from one species, *C. sinensis*.

HOW TO GROW

Give camellias deep, rich, acid soil in partial shade. Sun will burn the plants and deep shade will reduce flowering. At the northern range of hardiness, site against a warm wall or other protected place; the shrubs are most subject to winterkill immediately after transplanting from containers. Mulch annually with leaf mold or shred-

Camellia japonica 'Wilmetta'

Campanula carpatica

ded bark. Camellias make show-stopping specimens and hedges. They can be pruned heavily, but late-season fertilization or pruning can heighten vulnerability to frost. Propagate by air layering or from seeds, which appear in 1-inch woody capsules.

C. japonica
c. juh-PON-ih-kuh. Japanese Camellia. The 2- to 4-inch alternate leaves are serrated, leathery, and shiny dark green. The species grows slowly to 10 to 15 feet tall and 5 to 10 feet wide, usually rather pyramidal and formal. The 2- to 5-inch-diameter flowers of red, pink, or white appear singly at the ends of branches and can turn brown and mushy if they bloom during a frost. **Zones 7 to 10**.

C. oleifera
c. oh-lee-IF-er-uh. Tea-oil Camellia. This species stands out for having fragrant flowers and additional cold hardiness. It was used by William Ackerman of the U.S. National Arboretum to breed a line of camellias that can be grown a zone farther north than other types can. All tend to be compact with small leaves and bloom in late fall. They include 'Polar Ice' (white, anemone form), 'Winter's Charm' (lavender-pink, anemone form), 'Winter's Dream' (pink, semidouble), 'Winter's Rose' (pale pink, double rose), and 'Winter's Star' (reddish purple, single). **Zones 6 to 9**.

C. reticulata
c. reh-tik-yew-LAY-tuh. These open and lanky shrubs can grow more than 30 feet tall but are usually about 10 feet tall and 8 feet wide. The name "reticulata" recognizes the net of veins on the dull green leaves. The species, from China, bears single rosy red flowers more than 4 inches across; most of the popular cultivars have even larger semidouble flowers with wavy inner petals. 'Captain Rawes' is a cold-hardy rose-red; 'Crimson Robe' has bright red flowers and is more attractive out of flower than some others. **Zones 8 to 10**.

C. sasanqua
c. sas-SANK-wah. Sasanqua Camellia. A bit smaller at 6 to 10 feet tall, it also has smaller leaves and flowers than *C. japonica*. It is somewhat more open, with fuzzy stems, and is also slightly less cold hardy. The flowers, which bloom in late fall or early winter, are white, single, cup shaped, and fragrant. **Zones 7 to 10**.

Campanula

kam-PAN-yew-lah. Bellflower family, Campanulaceae.

The bellflower clan is a large one, comprising some 300 species of annuals, biennials, and perennials beloved by gardeners for their dainty flowers in shades of blue, lilac, violet, and white. The botanical name translates as "little bell" — *campana* is Latin for "bell" — but in addition to bell shaped, flowers can be star, cup, or saucer shaped. They have five "petals," or lobes, and are usually borne in clusters.

Campanula medium

HOW TO GROW
A site with full sun to partial shade and rich, well-drained, evenly moist soil is ideal. Most bellflowers do not tolerate heat well and grow best in areas where temperatures routinely dip below 70°F at night in summer. They languish and are generally short-lived where daytime temperatures rise above about 90°F. In the South — especially in Zone 8, but also in the hotter portions of Zone 7 — give them a site with partial shade during the hottest part of the day. Water deeply during dry spells, remove spent flowers regularly to extend bloom (deadheading or cutting back some bellflowers encourages repeat bloom), and mulch plants to keep the soil cool.

C. carpatica
c. kar-PAT-ih-kuh. Carpathian Harebell. Clump-forming 8- to 12-inch-tall perennial that spreads from 1 to 2 feet. Bears masses of upward-facing, cup-shaped flowers in blue, violet, or white over a long season from late spring through summer. Reblooms without deadheading. 'Blue Clips' and 'White Clips' are compact cultivars that come true from seed. **Zones 3 to 8**.

C. cochleariifolia
c. cock-lee-uh-ree-ih-FOE-lee-uh. Spiral Bellflower, Fairies' Thimbles. A creeping, mat-forming, 3- to 6-inch-tall plant spreading to 1 foot. Produces nodding lilac-blue to white flowers in summer, borne one per stem. **Zones 5 to 7**.

C. garganica
c. gar-GAH-nih-kuh. Gargano Bellflower. A 5- to 6-inch-tall species that spreads quickly to 1 foot or more. Bears racemes of abundant, $^1/_2$-inch-wide, starry lilac-blue flowers in summer. **Zones 4 to 7**.

C. glomerata
c. glom-er-AH-tuh. Clustered Bellflower. Vigorous 1- to 2-foot-tall perennial that spreads by underground rhizomes to form broad clumps reaching 2 feet or more. Bears rounded clusters of $^1/_2$- to $1^1/_2$-inch-long flowers on erect stems from early to midsummer in shades of violet, lavender-blue, or white. 'Joan Elliott' bears abundant violet purple blooms. Violet purple–flowered 'Superba'

Campanula glomerata

Campanula persicifolia

is especially heat tolerant. 'Crown of Snow' ('Schneekrone') and 'Superba Alba' have white blooms. **Zones 3 to 8.**

C. isophylla

c. eye-so-FILL-uh. ITALIAN BELL-FLOWER, STAR OF BETHLEHEM, FALLING STARS. A trailing, 6- to 8-inch perennial with heart-shaped leaves. Bears loose clusters of saucer-shaped, 1¹/₂-inch flowers in pale blue or white in midsummer. Hardy to **zone 7 or 8,** but often grown as a tender perennial or biennial.

C. lactiflora

c. lak-tih-FLOR-uh. MILKY BELLFLOWER. Erect 3- to 5-foot-tall species forming 2-foot-wide clumps. Bears large branched clusters of white or lavender-blue, 1-inch-long bell-shaped flowers from early to late summer. Established plants do not transplant well; best propagated by seeds sown where the plants are to grow. Self-sows. **Zones 3 to 7.**

C. latifolia

c. lat-ih-FOE-lee-uh. GREAT BELLFLOWER. Vigorous 4- to 5-foot-tall species that spreads rapidly by rhizomes to 3 feet or more. Bears narrow 2- to 3-inch-long bell-shaped flowers in summer in pale lilac-blue to violet or white. Blooms are carried in pairs or

threes along leafy, erect, spikelike racemes. **Zones 3 to 7.**

C. latiloba

c. lat-ih-LOW-buh. Also listed as *C. persicifolia* ssp. *sessiliflora.* Clump-forming 3-foot-tall species producing 1¹/₂-foot-wide mounds. Bears racemes of cup-shaped 1¹/₄- to 2-inch-wide lavender-blue flowers from mid- to late summer that are attached directly to the stalk. **Zones 4 to 7.**

C. medium

c. ME-dee-um. CANTERBURY BELLS. A slow-growing, 1¹/₂- to 3-foot biennial, hardy in **Zones 5 to 8,** with lance-shaped to elliptic leaves. Produces showy racemes of bell-shaped, single or double, 1¹/₂- to 2-inch-long flowers in purple, lavender, white, or pink from late spring to midsummer. Biennial.

C. persicifolia

c. per-sis-ih-FOE-lee-uh. PEACH-LEAVED BELLFLOWER. A 1- to 3-foot-tall species forming 1- to 2-foot-wide clumps. Bears lance-shaped leaves topped by racemes of outward-pointing, 2-inch-wide bell- to saucer-shaped blooms in pale blue, violet-blue, or white from early to midsummer. **Zones 3 to 7.**

C. portenschlagiana

c. por-ten-schlag-ee-AH-nuh. DAL-MATIAN BELLFLOWER.

Mound-forming 4- to 6-inch-tall perennial that spreads rapidly by underground stems to 2 feet or more. Bears evergreen to semi-evergreen leaves and panicles of bell-shaped, 1-inch-wide violet purple flowers from late spring to early summer. A fairly heat-tolerant species. **Zones 4 to 8.**

C. poscharskyana

c. pah-shar-skee-AH-nuh. SERBIAN BELLFLOWER. Vigorous to invasive 6- to 12-inch-tall perennial that spreads by underground runners to form mounds 2 feet or more across. Bears loose, trailing panicles of starry, 1-inch-wide pale blue flowers in early summer. 'Stella' has violet flowers and is somewhat less invasive. **Zones 3 to 7.**

C. pyramidalis

c. peer-ah-mih-DAL-iss. CHIMNEY BELLFLOWER. A short-lived perennial, hardy in **Zones 6 to 8**, that grows to 10 feet in height and has toothed, ovate- to lance-shaped leaves. Bears showy, erect clusters of fragrant, cup-shaped, pale lilac-blue or white flowers from late spring to summer. Biennial.

C. rapunculoides

c. rah-pun-kew-LOY-deez. CREEPING BELLFLOWER. Extremely invasive 2- to 4-foot-tall species that spreads quickly and widely by underground stolons and by self-sowing. Bears one-sided racemes of 1-inch-long violet purple bells in summer. **Zones 3 to 7.**

C. rotundifolia

c. roe-tun-dih-FOE-lee-uh. BLUE-BELL, HAREBELL. Dainty 5- to 12-inch-tall species that spreads as far and is native to North America as well as other parts of the Northern Hemisphere. Bears round basal leaves that die back early in the season and nodding, bell-shaped flowers on slender stems in summer in pale to violet-blue or white. **Zones 2 to 7.**

Campsis

KAMP-sis. Bignonia family, Bignoniaceae.

Commonly known as trumpet vines or trumpet creepers, *Campsis* species are vigorous, fast-growing woody vines that climb to 30 to 40 feet or more. Plants attach themselves to supports by aerial roots along the stems. There are two species of *Campsis*, and gardeners also grow a hybrid between them. Plants bear pinnate leaves consisting of many small leaflets arranged in a featherlike fashion. The flowers, borne in cymes or racemes at the tips of shoots, are trumpet or funnel shaped. The flowers are followed by flattened, beanlike seed capsules.

HOW TO GROW

Select a spot in full sun. Trumpet vines grow in any soil, from poor to rich, but perform best in moderately fertile, well-drained conditions. Plants are extremely rampant in rich soil. Suckers commonly appear near the main plant.

Campsis radicans

Train trumpet vines on sturdy arbors, up walls, and even up into trees. Tie the shoots in place until the rootlets establish a firm grip; after that, they are self-supporting. For best flowering and to keep plants in bounds, prune them back to a few buds in late winter or early spring. (Flowers are produced on new wood produced the current year.) Leave plants unpruned if they are growing up trees or are substantially out of reach. Removing seedpods as they form encourages plants to continue blooming into fall. Propagate by cuttings taken in early to midsummer or by digging up suckers that appear near the base of the plants. The flowers are attractive to hummingbirds.

C. grandiflora
c. gran-dih-FLOR-uh. CHINESE TRUMPET VINE, CHINESE TRUMPET CREEPER. A woody vine reaching 30 feet or more. Bears pinnate, 12-inch-long leaves and clusters of 6 to 12 funnel-shaped, 2- to 3-inch-long flowers with spreading lobes from late summer to fall. Blooms are dark orange to red. This species produces relatively few aerial roots and may need to be tied to supports. **Zones 7 to 9.**

C. radicans
c. RAH-dih-kanz. TRUMPET VINE, TRUMPET CREEPER. A woody vine native to the southeastern United States with pinnate 6- to 15-inch-long leaves. Bears clusters of 4 to 12 trumpet-shaped, 2- to 3-inch-long blooms from midsummer to fall. Flowers are orange, orange-red, or red. 'Flava' has yellow to orange-yellow flowers. **Zones 4 to 9.**

C. × tagliabuana
c. × tag-lee-ah-BWA-nuh. A hybrid species, the result of a cross between *C. grandiflora* and *C. radicans*, grown for its clusters of orange-red flowers. 'Mme. Galen' features very showy, 3-inch-long red-orange flowers from mid- to late summer through early fall. **Zones 5 to 9.**

Canna
KAN-uh. Canna family, Cannaceae.

Once grown primarily for their showy, hot-colored flowers, cannas today are more likely to be treasured for their enormous, often boldly colored leaves. There are about 50 species in the genus *Canna* — the only genus in the canna family — all tender perennials native to Asia and tropical and subtropical portions of North and South America. Plants have fleshy, branching rhizomes and thick roots. They bear large paddle-shaped leaves that generally are 1 to 2 feet long and have a sheath at the base that wraps around the stem. The flowers, which are borne in panicles or racemes, are asymmetrical and come in shades of red, orange, red-orange, pink, and sometimes white. Each bloom has three showy petals as well as a petal-like stamen and petal-like staminodes. Gardeners mainly grow cultivars to add dramatic color to gardens. All cannas lend tropical flair to summer plantings.

HOW TO GROW
Cannas thrive in full sun and well-drained, evenly moist soil rich in organic matter. Wet soil rots the fleshy rhizomes. From Zone 8 south, grow cannas outdoors year-round. In the North, either replace

Canna hybrid

them annually or overwinter the rhizomes indoors. Cannas can be started from seeds, but purchasing rhizomes is faster and the only way to get most of the improved cultivars. Rhizomes should have one or two pointed growing tips and be thick, fleshy, and firm, with no soft spots. From Zone 7 south, plant the rhizomes outdoors, in soil amended with organic matter, after the last spring frost date. In

Canna 'Pretoria'

the North, pot up the rhizomes indoors with the growing tips just under the soil surface. Keep them warm (75°F) and barely moist until they begin to grow, then move them to a sunny spot, keep them evenly moist, and fertilize weekly. Transplant to the garden after the last frost date, once the soil has warmed to about 65°F. Mulch, water regularly, and feed monthly in summer. Deadhead to keep the plants neat looking and to encourage rebloom.

To overwinter, dig them after a light frost and cut back the tops. Store the rhizomes in barely damp vermiculite, peat moss, or sand in a cool (40° to 50°F), dry place. Sprinkle the soil with water occasionally during winter to keep the roots from shriveling. In spring, cut the rhizomes into pieces with two growing points each and start them as you would new rhizomes. (Do not divide the rhizomes in fall before storage, because the cut surfaces tend to rot over winter.) Use cannas in beds and borders, in mass plantings, along foundations or shrub borders, and in tubs or large containers.

C. × generalis
c. × jen-er-AL-iss. CANNA, CANNA LILY. Bold 5- to 6-foot-tall perennials with 1- to 2-foot-long leaves that can be green or are variegated. Showy 1-foot-tall clusters of 3- to 5-inch flowers bloom from midsummer to frost. Many cultivars with solid green leaves and flowers in shades of red, orange, yellow, or pink are available, as well as bicolored ones. Cultivars described as "self-cleaning" drop their blooms naturally as they fade, keeping the plants attractive looking without deadheading.

Standard-size cannas range

Cardamine pratensis

from 4 to 6 feet or more in height by the end of the summer. 'City of Portland' features green leaves and pink flowers, while 'Cleopatra' has green, purple, or purple-and-green-blotched leaves and blooms in various combinations of red, white, and yellow. Standard-size cultivars featuring burgundy foliage as well as showy flowers include 'Durban', with red flowers and leaves striped with orange, yellow, red, and green; 'Phaison' (also sold as 'Tropicana') bears orange flowers and purple leaves striped with yellow and red; 'Pretoria' (also called 'Bengal Tiger'), with orange-yellow blooms and yellow-and-green-striped leaves edged in maroon; and 'Roi Humbert' or 'Red King Humbert', with bronze-purple leaves and red flowers. 'Wyoming' has burnt orange flowers and burgundy leaves. 'Yellow King Humbert' has deep yellow flowers and burgundy leaves.

Dwarf cultivars include 2-foot-tall 'Tropical Rose', with rose pink flowers, and 2¹/₂- to 3-foot-tall Pfitzer Series cultivars, both of which can be grown from seeds. Other dwarf cultivars include 'Apricot Dream', with gray-green leaves and soft salmon flowers with rose throats; 'China Doll', a 3-foot-tall self-cleaning selection with pink blooms and green leaves; and 'Orange Punch', a self-cleaning selection with green leaves and tangerine orange blos-

soms with yellow throats. 'Red Futurity' is a self-cleaning dwarf with bronze-green to black leaves and deep red flowers; 'Rose Futurity', also self-cleaning, bears dark burgundy leaves and rich coral pink and rose flowers. 'Pink Sunburst' is a 3-foot-tall selection with salmon pink flowers and green-and-yellow-striped leaves that have a pink cast. 'Striped Beauty' is a 2- to 3-foot-tall selection with yellow-and-green-striped leaves and red buds opening into yellow flowers with white stripes.

Tender perennial, hardy in **Zones 7 or 8 to 11**.

C. glauca

c. GLAW-kuh. A 4- to 6-foot-tall species with narrow, rounded gray-green leaves that are 1 to 6 inches wide and 1 to 1¹/₂ feet long. Bears small pale yellow flowers with 3-inch-long petals in summer. Tender perennial hardy in **Zones 7 or 8 to 11**.

Cardamine

kar-dah-MIN-ee. Cabbage family, Brassicaceae.

Cardamines, or bittercresses, as they are also called, are annuals, biennials, or perennials bearing clusters of four-petaled flowers in white, pink, lilac, yellow, or red-violet. The leaves are simple, pinnate, or palmate. The genus contains about 150 species, some

persistent weeds, as well as a few worthy garden plants.

HOW TO GROW
Give cardamines partial to full shade and very rich, evenly moist soil. They are best in cool conditions; shade during the hottest part of the day is essential in warm-climate areas. Propagate by division in spring after they flower or sow seeds. *C. pratensis* also can be propagated by leaf cuttings in midsummer or by separating the bulblets or plantlets that appear in the leaf axils.

C. pratensis

c. pray-TEN-sis. LADY'S SMOCK, CUCKOO FLOWER. A 1- to 1¹/₂-foot-tall perennial that spreads by short rhizomes to form 1-foot-wide clumps. Bears rosettes of gray-green to dark green pinnate leaves and panicles of lilac, purple, or white ¹/₂- to 1-inch-wide flowers in late spring. 'Flore Pleno' produces double flowers on 8-inch-tall plants. **Zones 5 to 8**.

Cardiocrinum

kar-dee-oh-KRY-num. Lily family, Liliaceae.

Three species of bulbs from China, Japan, and the Himalaya belong to

this genus, all once classified with the true lilies, or *Lilium* species. They grow from scaly bulbs, as do true lilies, and bear erect stalks of showy, lilylike, trumpet-shaped flowers that are followed by attractive brown seed capsules. The leaves do not resemble those of true lilies, however: they are handsome and broadly heart shaped. The botanical name is taken from the Greek *kardia,* meaning "heart," and *krinon,* a type of lily. *Cardiocrinum* species grow from very large bulbs that are monocarpic, meaning they die after they flower, but the bulbs generally leave plenty of offsets after flowering to replace themselves.

HOW TO GROW
Select a site in partial shade with rich, deeply prepared, moist soil that is well drained. Plants are happiest in the Pacific Northwest, where summers are cool and wet and winters are mild. In the East, look for a cool site that offers protection from winds. Plant the bulbs in fall, setting the tops just under the soil surface. Work plenty of well-rotted manure, compost, or other organic matter deeply into the soil at planting time. Mulch with compost or chopped leaves to keep the soil moist and cool. Water regularly in

Cardiocrinum giganteum

dry weather. Mulch heavily in late fall to protect bulbs over winter. Propagate by separating offsets, which take 3 to 5 years to reach flowering size, or by seeds.

C. cathayanum

c. kah-THAY-ah-num. Formerly *Lilium cathayanum*. A 4¹/₂-foot-tall species native to China bearing heart-shaped, 8-inch-long leaves. In summer, it produces racemes of 4¹/₂-inch-long flowers that are greenish on the outside and creamy white inside with a few purple dots. **Zones 7 to 9.**

C. giganteum

c. jy-GAN-tee-um. Formerly *Lilium giganteum*. A 5- to 12-foot-tall species from China and the Himalaya bearing 1¹/₂-foot-long heart-shaped leaves. Produces erect racemes of up to 20 nodding, 6- to 8-inch-long white trumpets that are striped with maroon inside. Blooms are very fragrant. **Zones 7 to 9; to Zone 6 with winter protection.**

Cardiospermum

kar-dee-oh-SPER-mum. Soapberry family, Sapindaceae.

The 14 species of *Cardiospermum* are perennial, woody-stemmed vines native to the tropics of Africa, India, and the Americas. Commonly called balloon vine or heart seed — *Cardiospermum* is from the Greek *kardia*, meaning "heart," and *sperma*, "seed" — they bear fernlike leaves, insignificant four-petaled flowers, and inflated, ornamental seedpods.

Cardiospermum halicacabum

HOW TO GROW

Give these tender plants full sun and rich, well-drained, evenly moist soil. They need a trellis upon which to climb. Sow seeds indoors 6 to 8 weeks before the last spring frost date. Germination takes 3 to 4 weeks at 65° to 70°F. In areas with long growing seasons, they can be sown outdoors after the last frost date. Water regularly in dry weather. Butterflies will visit the flowers.

C. halicacabum

c. hal-ih-kuh-KAY-bum. Balloon Vine, Love-in-a-puff. A tender, vining, 10- to 12-foot-tall perennial with fernlike, 6- to 8-inch-long leaves. Greenish white, ¹/₄-inch flowers are followed by rounded, ³/₄- to 1¹/₄-inch-wide seedpods that start out green and ripen to brown. Warm-weather annual.

Carex

KARE-ex. Sedge family, Cyperaceae.

Carex is a vast genus of grasslike perennials containing 1,500 or more species, most native to boggy areas and moist woodlands. Most are grown for their colorful, often handsomely variegated foliage, which can be deciduous or evergreen. Sedges differ from grasses in that they have solid, triangular stems, and the sheaths of the leaves, which are borne in threes, completely encircle the stems. "Sedges have edges" is their identifying characteristic. The small green flowers also are quite different. Sedges bear separate male and female flowers that lack sepals and petals. The flowers usually are carried in dense heads or spikes arising from axils of leaves or bracts. Most plants are monoecious, meaning they bear both sexes of flowers on the same plant, sometimes even in different parts of the same inflorescence. Sedges are rhizomatous or clump forming.

HOW TO GROW

Give sedges full sun or partial shade and rich, moist, well-drained soil. *C. elata*, *C. muskingumensis*, and *C. siderosticha* also grow in wet soil. Cut deciduous sedges to the ground in spring. Evergreen and semievergreen species don't require an annual haircut: cut them back every few years as necessary in late spring to remove old or winterburned foliage. To grow, divide the clumps from midspring to early summer.

C. caryophyllea

kare-ee-oh-FILL-ee-uh, commonly ker-ee-oh-fill-EE-uh. 'The Beatles', sporting a texture that resembles the famous four's haircuts, is a low, evergreen sedge that creeps politely along steppingstones and walkways. It grows 3 to 4 inches or more tall. **Zones 7 to 9.**

Carex morrowii 'Gold Band'

C. conica

c. KON-ih-kuh. A 6-inch-tall sedge that forms dense 10- to 12-inch-wide clumps. Bears low, arching, ¹/₈- to ³/₈-inch-wide evergreen to semievergreen leaves. Variegated cultivars are most commonly grown, including white-edged 'Marginata' and 'Snowline'. **Zones 5 to 9.**

C. elata

c. eh-LAH-tuh. Deciduous species forming dense 1¹/₂-foot-wide clumps of arching 1¹/₂- to 2-foot-long leaves that are ¹/₈ to ¹/₂ inch wide. 'Aurea', commonly called Bowles' golden sedge, has golden yellow leaves and is most often grown. This species requires shade and constant moisture in areas with warm summers, although yellow foliage is most pronounced in full sun. **Zones 5 to 9.**

C. glauca

GLAW-kuh. Blue Sedge. This species is a hardy, vigorous, long-lived ground cover that is especially suited for erosion control. It grows 8 to 10 inches tall and spreads in dry to moist soils. Useful in **Zones 5 to 9.**

C. morrowii

c. more-ROE-ee-eye. Evergreen 16- to 20-inch-tall species forming 1-foot-wide clumps of stiff, shiny ¹/₂-inch-wide leaves. Variegated cultivars, including 'Gold Band', with leaves edged in creamy white, are most often grown. **Zones 5 to 9.**

C. muskingumensis

c. mus-king-uh-MEN-sis. Palm Branch Sedge. Deciduous native North American species with erect stems and leaves that spread out horizontally from the stems. Plants reach 2 feet, and clumps spread by rhizomes to 1¹/₂ feet. The species has green leaves, but variegated cultivars, including 'Oehme' and 'Silberstreif', also are available. **Zones 4 to 9.**

C. nigra

NYE-gruh. Black Sedge. This one is noted for its glossy green foliage and black flower spikes. It prefers moist soils and is partial to full shade. **Zones 6 to 9.**

C. oshimensis

c. oh-she-MEN-sis. Deciduous, clumping 16-inch-tall species that forms dense 14-inch-wide mounds of glossy ⁵/₁₆-inch-wide leaves. The variegated cultivar 'Evergold' (sometimes listed as a cultivar of

Carissa macrocarpa

C. hachijoensis), which has leaves with dark green edges and creamy white centers, is most often grown. **Zones 6 to 9.**

C. siderosticha
c. sid-er-oh-STY-kuh. Deciduous species with strap-shaped, 1¼-inch-wide leaves. Clumps reach 8 to 12 inches and slowly creep by rhizomes to form 1½-foot-wide clumps. 'Variegata', with white-margined leaves, is more often grown than the species. **Zones 6 to 9.**

C. tumulicola
too-muh-LIH-koh-luh. This West Coast native has very narrow, dark green leaves. It forms spreading hummocks that reach about 12 inches tall and mass well to form a ground cover. **Zone 7 and warmer.**

Carissa
kah-RISS-uh. Dogbane family, Apocynaceae.

About 20 evergreen shrubs and small trees with often spiny branches compose this genus. The leaves are glossy, and the fragrant flower clusters are followed by bright red berries that turn dark purple.

HOW TO GROW
Grow the species described here in any soil, in full sun for best fruit. It is a good coastal plant since it tolerates sand, salt, and drought, as well as wet conditions. Weed carefully around its shallow roots. Spines make it a good hedge for deterring pets and wild mammals, or it can be espaliered. Sow seeds in spring or propagate by semiripe cuttings in summer. Although this is definitely a tropical species, the sweet-scented flowers induce many gardeners to grow it in a container to overwinter indoors.

C. macrocarpa
c. mack-roe-KAR-puh. NATAL PLUM. A bushy shrub 8 to 18 feet tall, with spines at the end of the twigs as well as along the branches. The 2-inch fragrant white flowers are like jasmine's with five petals, and they bloom throughout the year. You can collect the 1- to 2-inch red berries to make tart sauces and jellies, but birds like them too. There are many prostrate and dwarf forms, and a thornless one, 'Boxwood Beauty'. **Zone 10.**

Carpenteria
kar-pen-TEER-ee-uh. Hydrangea family, Hydrangeaceae.

There is just one species in this genus, an evergreen shrub that in the wild grows only on scrubby slopes and in pine forests in the foothills of California's Fresno County. But it looks born for a garden, with a neat, almost formal habit and anemone-like flowers against glossy leaves.

HOW TO GROW
This shrub can grow in a range of soils in full sun or light shade. With some shade, it will tolerate drought once established. Its deep root system can make it somewhat difficult to transplant, so site it carefully as a hedge or in a border. After it has flowered, prune some of the oldest shoots to the base to restore the plant's shape and to encourage new growth. Propagate by softwood cuttings in summer or by layering.

C. californica
c. kal-ih-FOR-nih-kuh. BUSH ANEMONE. The bush anemone grows slowly to about 6 feet tall and wide and has light brown, peeling bark. The handsome leathery leaves are lance-shaped to narrow ovals 4 to 5 inches long. Fragrant white five-petaled flowers, which bloom mid- to late summer, can be up to 3 inches across. As the common name implies, they look just like anemones, with a cup shape and central yellow boss, or cluster of stamens. **Zones 8 to 10.**

Carpenteria californica

Carpinus
kar-PYE-nus. Birch family, Betulaceae.

This genus includes 30 species of woodland trees and shrubs from Asia, Europe, and North America. Leaves are alternate, simple, and toothed, with prominent veins. Inconspicuous male and female flowers bloom in separate catkins. Fruits are clustered, dry, brown nutlets nestled in pretty bracts; they provide food for birds. Several species tolerate adverse growing conditions.

HOW TO GROW
Plant in full sun to partial shade (*C. caroliniana* tolerates heavy shade) and rich, moist well-drained soil, acid to alkaline. Usually pest-free. May exhibit some leaf scorch during drought. Prune *C. betulus* when young to prevent split-prone low double leaders; train *C. caroliniana* to several strong trunks.

C. betulus
c. BET-yew-lus. EUROPEAN HORNBEAM. This beautiful, symmetrical tree grows 40 to 60 feet tall and wide and forms a stately pyramid, with numerous slender branches radiating from the central trunk when young; it becomes a bit irregular and rounded when old. The tree's silhouette is quite becoming in winter. Leaves are 2 to 3 inches long and have sharp teeth. Their dark green surfaces are beautifully textured with prominent veins. Trunk bark is very smooth and gray and

Carpinus caroliniana var. *virginiana*

attractively marked with longitudinal ridges. In fall, leaves turn a pleasing yellow and then reddish brown, often remaining on young trees through the winter. European hornbeam is an excellent easy-care, medium-size shade tree for formal landscapes. It also can be easily pruned as a screen or hedge. From Europe and Asia Minor. **Zones 5 to 7.**

CULTIVARS

The species is rarely grown. 'Columnaris' grows into a dense spire. 'Fastigiata', the most common form, grows into a very symmetrical oval shape. 'Frans Fontaine' is the narrowest form, reaching 35 feet tall and 15 feet wide. 'Heterophylla' has deeply lobed leaves. 'Pendula' is a dwarf, umbrella-shaped tree that grows to 10 feet tall. 'Purpurea' has reddish purple new foliage that turns green in summer, then orange in autumn.

C. caroliniana

c. kare-oh-lin-ee-AH-nuh. AMERI-CAN HORNBEAM, BLUE BEECH, MUSCLEWOOD. This handsome native matures into a rounded or flat-topped, 20- to 30-foot-tall tree with a single trunk or multiple trunks. The 2- to 3-inch-long leaves are oblong and have sharp points, tiny marginal teeth, and prominent veins. Their pale green color in spring matures to dark blue-green and then becomes red and orange in autumn. From summer to fall, 2½-inch-long clusters of leafy nutlets add a decorative touch. Trunk bark is smooth and slate gray, an excellent winter feature. Use American hornbeam as an understory tree in a woodland or along a stream, as a

Carthamus tinctorius

Carya ovata

shade tree for a small yard, or as a patio tree in a lightly shaded site. Can be pruned as a hedge or screen. The wood is very strong, which makes the tree great for climbing. From eastern North America. **Zones 3 to 9.**

CULTIVARS AND SIMILAR SPECIES

'Fastigiata' is narrower than the species. *C. japonicus* (Japanese hornbeam) is an uncommon tree with large leaves, dull red fall color, and a graceful, spreading vase shape; grows to 25 feet tall and 20 feet wide; **Zones 5 to 8.**

Carthamus

kar-THAM-us. Aster family, Asteraceae.

Spiny-leaved annuals and perennials native to the Mediterranean region and western Asia, *Carthamus* species bear deeply divided leaves and thistlelike flower heads in yellow, red, orange, pink, or violet. One species, which has been grown for centuries as a source of yellow and red dye as well as for its edible seeds, the source of safflower oil, makes an unusual addition to the annual garden.

HOW TO GROW

Carthamus species thrive in full sun and light, dry, poor soil. Plants will not grow well in areas with wet, humid summers. Sow seeds indoors in individual pots 6 to 8

weeks before the last spring frost date at 50° to 60°F. Germination takes 2 to 3 weeks. Transplant with care. Or sow outdoors a few weeks before the last frost while the soil is still cool. Or sow in fall. Grow safflower (*C. tinctorius*) in the herb garden and informal mixed plantings. It also makes a fine dried flower; cut the blooms when they are just open, and hang them in a warm, dry spot.

C. tinctorius

c. tink-TOR-ee-us. SAFFLOWER, FALSE SAFFRON. Spiny, gray-green leaves on 1- to 2-foot plants. Loose clusters of thistlelike flower heads are surrounded by stiff green bracts and have a showy cluster of orange or yellow ray florets at the center. Cool-weather annual.

Carya

KARE-ee-ah. Hickory family, Juglandaceae.

Closely related to the walnuts, the 17 species that make up this family of tall trees hail from North and Central America and Asia. Leaves are large and pinnately compound, creating a bold texture. Flowers are long, slender male catkins and smaller female catkins, which develop in spring with the leaves. Trunk bark is often rough and attractive, giving the trees a lot of character. Some species produce

edible nuts prized by people and wildlife. Unlike walnuts, the husks surrounding hickory nuts split open when they ripen. These trees have deep taproots and are difficult to transplant but are worth saving or establishing in their natural habit, because they provide valuable food for wildlife.

HOW TO GROW

Plant in full sun to partial shade. The trees do best in humus-rich, well-drained soil but tolerate a range of soils and are drought tolerant. Prune in late winter to develop a strong branch structure. Water during drought to avoid hickory bark beetle infestations.

C. ovata

c. oh-VAH-tah. SHAGBARK HICKORY. Growing into a towering, 60- to 80-foot-tall, oval tree with low, down-swept branches, this native is named for its thick gray bark, which peels off in vertical strips, giving the trunk an appealing, shaggy texture. Leaves are a foot long and composed of five tapered, 8-inch-long, rich green leaflets, which turn a glorious golden brown in autumn. The delicious oval nuts are thin shelled and drop from the tree when ripe. Wood from shagbark hickory is used to impart a smoky flavor to barbecue. Use as a nut-producing tree in an unmown area such as a pasture (nuts can be dangerously shot from the blades of a lawn mower), or plant in a naturalistic landscape or woodland where falling nuts won't be a hazard. From eastern North America. **Zones 4 to 8.**

CULTIVARS AND SIMILAR SPECIES

'Pixely' and 'Wilcox' perform well in the Midwest, 'Porter' in the East, 'Harold' in the North, and 'Grangier' in the South. *C. cordiformis* (bitternut hickory) is another fast-growing native; it grows 50 to 75 feet tall and has bitter nuts and bright yellow leaf buds and fall color; **Zones 5 to 8.** *C. illinoinensis* (pecan), another native, grows into an oval, single-trunked, 70- to 100-foot-tall tree with upright branches; its massive trunk is covered with furrowed gray bark; its edible nuts can be hazardous when they fall, and their husks stain everything they touch; weak, brittle limbs can break suddenly; prone to many diseases and insects; **Zones 6 to 9.** *C. laciniosa* (shellbark hickory) is similar to *C. ovata* but has less-shaggy bark; hardy to **Zone 5.**

C

Caryopteris

kare-ee-OP-ter-iss. Verbena family, Verbenaceae.

Six species belong to the genus *Caryopteris*, one of which is a small shrub usually treated as a perennial. *C. × clandonensis* is grown for its frothy, rounded flower clusters that appear in midsummer. The flowers are set against handsome gray-green, fine-textured foliage that emits a pleasant eucalyptus-like fragrance when rubbed.

HOW TO GROW

Select a site in full sun or very light shade with loose, well-drained soil that is not too rich in organic matter. The plants are excellent mixed in an ornamental bed or butterfly gardens or used as a low hedge. Established plants tolerate dry conditions but benefit if watered during droughts. Bluebeard (*C. × clandonensis*) is root hardy to Zone 4, but the shoots are routinely killed to the ground in winter from Zone 6 north, and occasionally in Zone 7. In the North, cut plants to the ground in spring. From Zone 7 south, cut the stems back hard in spring — to within a few inches of the ground — to encourage dense growth and more flowers. After the main flush of bloom, trim off stem tips with spent flower clusters to encourage new shoots and flowers to form. For propagation, dig clumps in spring or fall or root softwood cuttings taken in late spring.

C. × clandonensis

c. × clan-doe-NEN-sis. BLUE-BEARD, BLUE-MIST SHRUB, BLUE SPIREA. Mounding shrub or woody-based perennial reaching 2 to 3 feet in height and spreading as far. Bears aromatic,

Castanea mollissima

broadly lance-shaped leaves and dense, many-flowered clusters of ¹/₂-inch-long flowers both in the leaf axils and on stem tips. Flowers appear from late summer to early fall. 'Blue Mist' bears pale blue flowers. 'Dark Knight' has silvery leaves and violet-blue flowers. 'Worcester Gold' has purple-blue flowers and golden foliage. **Zones 4 to 9**.

Cassia

KASS-ee-uh. Pea family, Fabaceae.

This huge genus encompasses more than 500 species of annuals, herbaceous perennials, and deciduous to evergreen trees and shrubs from throughout the world, primarily the tropics. About half of

these have been recategorized as *Senna* by some taxonomists. Pinnately compound leaves give them a delicate air. Virtually all the shrubs have clusters of yellow to gold pealike flowers.

HOW TO GROW

Give cassia full sun. Many of the shrubs are native to desert areas and will tolerate relatively dry, infertile soil as long as it is well drained. Infrequent but deep watering during drought is a good idea. Pruning needs vary among species. Propagate from seeds or semiripe cuttings collected in summer.

C. artemisioides

c. ar-teh-miss-ee-OY-ih-deez. FEATHERY CASSIA. Also listed as *Senna artemisioides*. This evergreen from Australia grows from 3

to 5 feet tall. It has 1-inch gray needlelike leaves and clusters of six to eight sulphur yellow flowers that bloom from winter to midspring, sometimes continuing into summer. Deadhead or shear lightly to prevent seed formation. **Zone 10**.

C. bicapsularis

c. bye-kap-sue-LAR-iss. Also listed as *Senna bicapsularis*. This evergreen grows to 10 feet tall and has thick, rounded leaflets. Yellow flowers in spiky clusters bloom from midfall to late winter; both flowers and top growth are frequently zapped by frost. **Zone 10**.

C. didymobotrya

c. did-ee-moe-BOH-tree-uh. An evergreen from East Africa with a lanky habit to about 10 feet tall and 2-inch leaflets with up to 16 pairs of leaves. The yellow flowers bloom in upright clusters up to a foot long from early winter until midspring. Best reserved for informal gardens. **Zone 10**.

Castanea

kass-TAY-nee-ah. Beech family, Fagaceae.

Twelve species native to North America, Europe, and Asia make up this genus of nut-bearing trees, the chestnuts. Leaves are alternate, simple, and toothed. Nuts are 1 to 2¹/₂ inches around and enclosed in husks covered with vicious spines. Flowers are born in showy, cylindrical catkins. Unlike most nut trees, chestnuts bear nuts at a young age, about 12 years.

American chestnut (*C. dentata*) was once the most majestic tree of the eastern American forest, with trunks growing to 120 feet tall and 10 feset in diameter. The tree was

Caryopteris × clandonensis

Cassia bicapsularis

Catalpa bignonioides

not only beautiful but also of great economic importance, providing strong lumber and nutritious food for people, farm animals, and wildlife. Unfortunately, a fungus brought into the country from Asia in 1904 virtually wiped out all the mature chestnut trees by the 1930s. This fungus attacks only mature trees that have developed a rough bark; trees whose trunks are blighted and killed can resprout from their roots. Using genes from highly resistant Chinese chestnuts, researchers are close to developing disease-resistant American chestnuts.

Meanwhile, American chestnut can be grown outside its native range (west of the Mississippi) with little fear of blight. And easterners can grow young trees for many years as tall shrubs, cutting back blighted trunks and allowing suckers to grow from the roots. This way, nuts can still be harvested, and the chestnut's gene pool is kept alive.

HOW TO GROW
Plant in full sun and well-drained, slightly alkaline to slightly acid soil. Heat and drought tolerant. Train when young to grow as a single- or multitrunked tree. Moderately resistant to chestnut blight.

C. mollissima
c. mol-LISS-eh-mah. CHINESE CHESTNUT. This dense, rounded tree grows 35 to 40 feet tall and 40 to 50 feet wide, branching close to the ground. Its shape bears little resemblance to the native chestnut, but it does make a good climbing tree for children. The coarse-textured, green leaves are glossy on top and downy on their undersides. Measuring 4 to 8 inches long, they are lance shaped or oblong with toothed margins. Fall color is a coppery yellow. The tree blooms in early summer, covering itself with decorative, upright, yellowish clusters of 5-inch catkins, whose odor may be objectionable and permeate the entire yard. Soft, spiny fruits ripen in early fall and drop to the ground, splitting open to reveal two or three shiny nuts that are not quite as sweet as those of American chestnut. Use the tree for nut-producing shade away from groomed areas, where low branches and falling nuts would be a hazard. From China and Korea. **Zones 5 to 8.**

CULTIVARS AND SIMILAR SPECIES
Plant two cultivars for best nut production: 'Douglass' and 'Dunstad' are hybrids with American chestnut and have excellent blight resistance, a straight trunk to 5 feet, and delicious nuts. *C. sativa* (Spanish chestnut) is almost identical to American chestnut and is commonly grown in the West; **Zones 6 to 8.**

Catalpa
kah-TALL-paw. Bignonia family, Bignoniaceae.

The 11 species belonging to this genus from North America and Asia are cold-hardy trees and shrubs with a decided tropical appearance. The opposite or whorled leaves are large and without teeth, usually unlobed or shallowly lobed. Flowers are two lipped, have ruffled petals, and are arranged in clusters; they ripen into long, beanlike seedpods. Catalpas are valued in the landscape for their showy foliage and flowers, which rise above the leaves in early summer, after most trees have finished blooming.

HOW TO GROW
Plant catalpas in full sun to partial shade. They do best in rich, moist soil, but tolerate almost any soil, wet or dry, acid or alkaline, and salt spray. Prune in winter; train when young to develop a central leader; shorten branches on mature trees to reduce storm damage, as limbs are brittle and may break. *C. speciosa* continually drops small twigs, flowers, and pods; plant a ground cover to absorb the mess. Verticillium wilt, leaf spot, mildew, and catalpa worms may cause problems. It withstands hot, dry climates and urban conditions; good in the Midwest, Plains, and Mountain States.

C. speciosa
c. spee-see-OH-suh. NORTHERN CATALPA, WESTERN CATALPA. Growing into an irregular, rounded tree with a stout trunk and big branches, northern catalpa can grow 40 to 50 feet tall. Its rugged good looks are highlighted by big, shallowly lobed, heart-shaped leaves, which can reach 12 inches long and are arranged opposite each other. They are glossy on top and densely hairy on their undersides. In autumn they usually turn bright yellow. In early summer 2^1/2-inch bell-shaped white flowers with abundant yellow stripes and purple speckles on their throats bloom dramatically above the leaves in 8-inch clusters. The seedpods, which remain on the tree well into winter, are dark brown and slender. They grow to 2 feet long and contain beanlike seeds. Use this tree as a dramatic

Catalpa speciosa

specimen to contrast with fine-textured plants. From southeastern North America. **Zones 4 to 9.**

CULTIVARS AND SIMILAR SPECIES

C. bignonioides (southern catalpa, Indian bean) is a smaller tree, growing 30 to 40 feet tall, and not quite as showy; produces 10-inch-tall spires of numerous 2-inch, purple-and-yellow-speckled, white flowers 2 weeks later than *C. speciosa;* leaves are heart shaped, grow to 8 inches long, and are whorled and less hairy, with a pungent odor; a southeastern native. 'Aurea' has striking chartreuse leaves. 'Bungei' ('Nana'; umbrella catalpa) is a nonflowering dwarf, growing to 14 feet tall, that forms a tight globular head. *C. × erubescens* 'Purpurea' has purplish new growth maturing to dark green and purple-black leaf stems and twigs. **Zones 5 to 9.**

Catanache

kat-ah-NAH-chee. Aster family, Asteraceae.

Commonly called Cupid's darts, *Catanache* species are annuals and perennials native to the Mediterranean region. About five species belong to the genus, one of which — *C. caerulea* — is an old-fashioned summer-blooming perennial. Cupid's darts produce tufts or mounds of grayish green, linear to inversely lance-shaped leaves. Their solitary flower clusters have strap-shaped ray florets, or "petals," and usually come in lavender-blue as well as white or yellow. The blooms somewhat resemble cornflowers (*Centaurea*) or chicory (*Cichorium intybus*) and have a collar of papery, silvery bracts beneath the flowers.

HOW TO GROW

A site in full sun or very light shade with average, well-drained soil suffices for these easy-to-please perennials. *C. caerulea* is best in sandy or dry soils and is short-lived in heavy, clayey conditions. Dividing clumps annually or every two years in early spring or fall keeps them very vigorous. Grow plants from seeds sown indoors in late winter for bloom the first year. Or sow outdoors where plants are to grow in midspring. In addition to division, propagate plants by root cuttings taken in winter.

C. caerulea

c. see-RUE-lee-uh. C u p i d ' s
D a r t. A 1½- to 2-foot-tall perennial that spreads to 1 foot and has grassy 1-foot-long leaves. Plants produce solitary, 1- to 2-inch-wide lilac-blue flower heads atop wiry stems from midsummer to fall. 'Blue Giant' bears dark lilac-blue flowers on 2-foot plants. **Zones 3 to 8.**

Catharanthus

kath-ah-RAN-thus. Dogbane family, Apocynaceae.

This genus contains eight species of annuals and perennials from the island of Madagascar, off the coast of Africa. All bear simple leaves and five-petaled flowers carried singly or in clusters. One species is a popular bedding plant.

HOW TO GROW

Choose a site in full sun to partial shade with average to rich, well-drained, evenly moist soil. Plants thrive in heat and humidity and thus are good choices for southern gardens. They require a long growing season to bloom best.

Catharanthus roseus

Sow seeds indoors in winter, 3 to 4 months before the last spring frost date, at 65° to 75°F. Cover seeds, as darkness aids germination, which takes 2 to 3 weeks. Pinch seedlings to encourage branching, and transplant after the weather is warm and settled. Plants also can be propagated by cuttings taken in spring or early summer. Consider overwintering a plant or two indoors for use as stock plants in spring.

C. roseus

c. ROE-zee-us. R o s e P e r i w i n -
k l e, M a d a g a s c a r P e r i -
w i n k l e. Formerly *Vinca rosea.* A woody-based, 1- to 2-foot perennial hardy only from **Zone 10 south**, with oblong to ovate leaves. Bears flat-faced, trumpet-shaped flowers with five "petals," or lobes, from summer to frost. Flowers come in pale to hot pink, red, or white, commonly with a contrasting eye. Many cultivars are available, including the Pacifica Series and Pretty Series, both of which are compact 12- to 14-inch plants. Tender perennial or warm-weather annual.

Ceanothus

see-an-OH-thus. Buckthorn family, Rhamnaceae.

There are more than 50 deciduous and evergreen shrubs in this genus, mostly from woods or dry slopes in the western United States. The leaves are toothed and veined, and in spring they can be all but smothered under clusters of flowers that range from white through all shades of blue and blue-violet. A couple of species native to the eastern and central United States are considered somewhat less showy but are valuable for dry, infertile soils.

HOW TO GROW

These plants bloom best in full sun but tolerate considerable shade. Sharply draining soil is a must, however. These shrubs most often die from overwatering and related fungal disease and root rot, but they are tolerant of drought and slightly alkaline soil. They fix their own nitrogen and so do not need a fertile site. Give them some protection from cold winds. Low-growing ceanothus are suitable for ground covers or rock gardens, taller ones for shrub borders. Training them against a wall offers shelter from wind and cold. Prune evergreens lightly after flowering; deciduous forms can be cut back close to the ground. The large roots of eastern species can make them hard to transplant when mature. Propagation is difficult.

C. americanus

c. ah-MAIR-ih-KAH-nus. N e w J e r -
s e y T e a. Despite being named for the Garden State (where it was allegedly used as a substitute during the colonists' boycott of British tea), this deciduous species is native from southern Canada to the central and southeastern United States. Low, broad, and dense at 4 feet tall and 5 feet wide, it produces small white flowers in 1- to 2-inch terminal panicles in mid-

Ceanothus griseus var. *horizontalis*

Catanache caerulea

Ceanothus americanus

Ceanothus griseus var. *horizontalis*

summer. The leaves, dark green in summer, may add some yellow to the landscape in fall. A good plant for inhospitable conditions. **Zones 4 to 8**.

C. cultivars

The average cultivar of western species is evergreen and broadly spreading, 5 to 6 feet tall and 10 to 12 feet wide. Some are as low as 1¹/₂ feet and others may grow to 20 feet. Blue flowers range from powder blue through violet and dark indigo, in spiky clusters 3 to 5 inches long in spring. On evergreens the leaves are often glossy and can be toothed much like a holly's. Among the best are 'Concha', which grows to about 7 feet tall and wide, has dense foliage and dark blue flowers, and tolerates water in summer; and 'Ray Hartman', which can reach 20 feet tall, and bears 3-inch leaves and medium-blue flowers in 3- to 5-inch clusters. Gardeners often train it as a small tree. Most ceanothus cultivars, **Zones 8 to 10**.

C. × delilianus 'Gloire de Versailles'

c. × del-il-ee-AH-nus. FRENCH HYBRID CULTIVAR. This is one of the most cold-hardy blue-flowered selections, growing densely to only about 3 feet and bearing finely toothed, deciduous leaves. Light blue flowers appear in 4-inch clusters in axils and on branch tips from midsummer to fall. **Zones 7 to 10**.

C. griseus var. horizontalis

c. GRIS-ee-us var. hoar-ih-zon-TAL-iss. CARMEL CREEPER. This is a low-spreading, evergreen shrub that reaches approximately 2 to 3 feet in height and can spread 10 to 15 feet. It makes an excellent ground cover for slopes and rough

ground, offering glossy, leathery leaves and pale blue flowers in late winter. 'Hurricane Point' and 'Yankee Point' are selections for landscape use. Carmel creeper requires well-drained soil and can be pruned successfully. It does not tolerate the extreme heat of interior southern California. **Zones 9 to 10**.

C. ovatus

c. oh-VAH-tus. INLAND CEANOTHUS. A slightly smaller, denser plant than *C. americanus,* native

Cedrus atlantica 'Glauca'

from New England to the central United States, with shiny leaves, tiny white flowers, and red seed capsules in summer. Provides food for quail and other birds. **Zones 4 to 6**.

C. thyrsiflorus

c. thur-sih-FLOR-us. BLUE BLOSSOM. Native to California and southern Oregon, this is one of the hardiest evergreens, large and vigorous at up to 20 feet tall and wide with arching branches. It combines glossy leaves with 3-inch

spring flower spikes that range from light to dark blue. There is a prostrate form, *C. thyrsiflorus* var. *repens,* as well as a cultivar, 'Skylark', that grows to only 6 feet. **Zones 8 to 10**.

Cedrus

SEED-russ. Pine family, Pinaceae.

Many trees include "cedar" in their names, but *Cedrus* is the genus of the true cedars, which hail from Asia and northern Africa. These very large, long-lived, elegant trees grow rapidly when young and mature into breathtaking silhouettes, which then grow very slowly to a grand size with old age. The stiff needles are arranged singly on young shoots and in clustered whorls on older branches. Cones are large and showy. The species listed here all look quite similar. Use them in large landscapes.

HOW TO GROW
See individual descriptions for specific requirements.

C. atlantica

c. at-LAN-teh-kuh. ATLAS CEDAR. Also listed as *C. libani* ssp. *atlantica.* Stiffly pyramidal and awkwardly angular when young, Atlas cedar becomes beautifully irregular and flat topped, with upward-reaching top branches and horizontally spreading to ascending lower branches. It matures to

Cedrus atlantica 'Glauca'

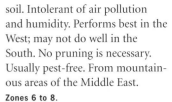

Cedrus libani 'Pendula'

60 feet tall and 30 to 40 feet wide, but it can reach 120 feet tall with great age. Needles are $^3/_4$ to 1 inch long, forming dense tufts on the tops of branches. Their color varies from dark green to blue-green, with the more commonly grown blue Atlas cedar exhibiting stunning silver-blue needles. Female cones are blocky, 3-inch-tall, blue-green cylinders with concave tips. They take 2 years to mature, eventually turning brown. Atlas cedar strongly resembles cedar of Lebanon (*C. libani*) but is taller and has a more open silhouette. It is best planted as a specimen in an open lawn. Although this tree is not particularly cold hardy, it is often sold in borderline areas, where it will not survive an unseasonably cold winter.

Plant in full sun to partial shade. It does best in humus-rich, moist, well-drained, acid soil, but adapts to any well-drained, sandy or clayey, or slightly alkaline soil. Very drought and heat tolerant in deep soil. Shorten long branches when trees are young to encourage resistance to snow and ice damage. Remove multiple leaders if they develop. Leave lower limbs to sweep to the ground or remove them to reveal trunk bark. Sometimes bothered by weevils, tip blight, borers, root rot, and sapsuckers. From northern Africa. **Zones 6 to 9.**

CULTIVARS
'Aurea' has golden yellow new growth and yellow-green older needles; grows slowly to 16 feet tall. 'Glauca' (blue Atlas cedar) has gorgeous, silvery blue needles. 'Glauca Fastigiata' is a dense, narrow, upright tree that reaches 40 feet tall and 10 feet wide; silvery blue needles. 'Glauca Pendula' has silvery blue needles and graceful, weeping branches; must be staked

to create a tree form; grows to 15 feet tall and 20 feet wide.

C. deodara

c. dee-oh-DOOR-uh. DEODAR CEDAR. More graceful and dense when young than Atlas cedar (*C. atlantica*), deodar cedar forms a 50- to 80-foot-tall, 30- to 40-foot-wide pyramid with slightly pendulous, tiered branches and a nodding leader, rather like a hemlock's, which distinguishes it from afar. With age, deodar cedar becomes spreading and flat topped, with the lower branches bowing toward the ground and then turning upward, creating a dramatic silhouette. The blue-green needles are the longest of any cedar's, measuring $1^1/_2$ to 2 inches long, and have a soft, feathery appearance. Female cones are 3 to 4 inches long and pale jade green, maturing to reddish brown after 2 years. This elegant tree is suitable only for a large property and performs well in the South and Southwest.

Grow deodar cedar in full sun and well-drained to dry soil. Tolerates alkaline soil, drought, wind, and heat. If desired, cut back new growth halfway to control the tree's spread. Will not resprout from leafless wood. Usually problem-free, but weevils, canker, and cold can cause tip dieback. From the Himalaya. **Zones 7 to 9.**

CULTIVARS
'Albospicata' has ivory new growth that turns creamy yellow and stands out against bright green older needles. 'Aurea' has yellow new needles that mature to golden green. 'Kashmir' is compact, growing to 20 feet tall; silvery blue-green needles; hardy to **Zone 6.** 'Sander's Blue' is a narrow, bushy form with powder blue new growth that darkens to gray-blue.

'Shalimar' has a graceful, pendulous habit and blue-green needles; hardy to **Zone 6.**

C. libani

c. lib-AHN-eye. CEDAR OF LEBANON. The most cold-hardy species, cedar of Lebanon is tightly pyramidal when young, maturing into an irregular shape with outstretched horizontal branches that sweep the ground. It grows 50 to 60 or more feet tall and wide, has a massive trunk, and often has several leaders. Needles are $^3/_4$ to $1^1/_2$ inches long, stiff, and sharp pointed. They are borne in dense tufts and emerge bright green, contrasting beautifully with the glossy, dark green, older needles. The 4-inch-tall, barrel-shaped cones are purplish when young, turning brown after 2 years. Use this conifer as a specimen in a large landscape; it looks fantastic planted near a reflecting pool or pond.

Plant in full sun. Best in deep, well-drained, fertile soil but adapt well to infertile, dry, or alkaline soil. Intolerant of air pollution and humidity. Performs best in the West; may not do well in the South. No pruning is necessary. Usually pest-free. From mountainous areas of the Middle East. **Zones 6 to 8.**

CULTIVARS
'Pendula' has long, weeping branches and forms a narrow, irregular shape if staked. *C. libani* ssp. *brevifolia* (*C. brevifolia*) (Cypress cedar) has $^1/_2$-inch-long needles and small cones. *C. libani* ssp. *stenocoma* has a more stiffly pyramidal shape and shorter needles; cold hardy to **Zone 5.**

Celastrus

seh-LAS-truss. Staff Tree family, Celastraceae.

Some 30 species belong to the genus *Celastris*, both twining woody vines and shrubs. Plants bear simple, usually toothed, leaves that are deciduous or sometimes evergreen. The flowers, which are borne in clusters, are inconspicu-

Celastrus scandens

C

Celosia argentea 'Century Yellow'

ous and usually greenish white in color. Male and female flowers are borne separately — usually on separate male or female plants, although some species bear male and female flowers in the same cluster. Two species, commonly called bittersweet, are grown for their showy orange-red fall fruit. Both of these bear male and female flowers on separate plants, and female plants are the only ones to produce ornamental fruit. The fruit is attractive to birds, and the clusters of fall fruit are treasured in arrangements.

HOW TO GROW
Give bittersweet a site in full sun or partial shade and average soil. Plants tolerate dry conditions. These vigorous to rampant vines can be trained onto arbors or against a wall, or allowed to scramble over fences, tree stumps, or rock piles. When allowed to climb trees, the twining stems can eventually constrict trunks. For fruit set, a male plant is required for every few females. Prune plants in early spring to keep them in bounds. Propagate by cuttings in summer or by layering in spring or fall; both methods are better than sowing seeds, because it allows for propagation of plants that have previously been identified as male or female. Bittersweets self-sow and spread rampantly, especially *C. orbiculatus*.

C. orbiculatus
c. or-bih-kew-LAH-tus. ORIENTAL BITTERSWEET. A rampant

woody vine that easily climbs 40 to 50 feet or more. Bears rounded leaves with toothed or scalloped edges. Clusters of small green flowers appear in the leaf axils in summer, followed by yellow bead-like fruit on female plants. Fruit opens to reveal pink, orange-red, or red seeds in fall. This species has become an extremely troublesome weed in many areas. It will smother nearby garden plants and is extremely difficult to eradicate. **Zones 4 to 8.**

C. scandens
c. SCAN-denz. AMERICAN BITTERSWEET, STAFF VINE. A native woody vine that climbs 30 to 40 feet or more. Bears oval leaves with toothed edges. Clusters of yellow-green flowers appear in summer at the stem tips. On female plants, flowers are followed by yellow-orange, berrylike fruit that opens to reveal red seeds. **Zones 3 to 8.**

Celosia

seh-LOW-see-uh. Amaranth family, Amaranthaceae.

The best-known *Celosia* species are tender perennials grown as annuals, but this genus of 50 to 60 species also contains shrubs and climbers. All are from the tropics or subtropics, and most have simple, entire leaves. Although the individual flowers are small and chaffy, they are carried in large, showy, plumelike or crested inflorescences. The name *Celosia* is from the Greek *keleos,* for "burnt," and refers to the fiery colors of the flowers and their often flamelike shape.

HOW TO GROW
Give celosias full sun or very light shade and rich, well-drained soil that remains evenly moist. They thrive in hot, humid weather. Sow seeds indoors 6 to 8 weeks before the last spring frost. Cover the seeds with soil, as darkness aids germination, which takes 2 to 3 weeks at 65° to 70°F. Sowing in individual pots is best, because it minimizes transplant shock. For best results, seedlings need to grow unchecked: exposure to cold temperatures, damage to roots during transplanting, and periods of too-dry soil all lead to stunted plants with inferior, undersized blooms. Transplant about 2 weeks after the last spring frost date, once temperatures remain above 40°F at night. Water regularly throughout the

season. Tall cultivars may need staking. Use celosias in beds and borders as well as cutting gardens. They also can be used in containers. Use the flowers fresh or dried. To dry them, harvest just as they fully open, strip off the leaves, and hang in small bunches in a warm, dry place.

C. argentea
c. are-JEN-tee-uh. COCKSCOMB. Formerly *C. cristata.* Two forms of this tender perennial are popular: Cristata Group cultivars bear rounded, crested flower heads that resemble enormous rooster combs or even cauliflowers, while Plumosa Group cultivars have erect, featherlike plumes. Both groups come in oranges, reds, yellows, and creams. Height is an important consideration when picking cultivars because it affects placement. Tall cultivars also are best for cutting and drying. Cristata-type cultivars include 6- to 8-inch Jewel Box Mix and 2¹/₂- to 3-foot-tall Big Chief Mix. Plumosa Group cultivars include the 8-inch Kimono Series, 20-inch 'Apricot Brandy', 2-foot Century Series, and 3-foot Sparkler Series. Warm-weather annual.

C. spicata
c. spih-KAY-tuh. WHEAT CELOSIA. Annuals with lance-shaped leaves on 2-foot plants and erect, wheatlike flower heads in silver-cream and pink. Flamingo Series cultivars are the most widely available. Warm-weather annual.

Celtis

SELL-tiss. Elm family, Ulmaceae.

Seventy species of deciduous and evergreen trees and shrubs make up this genus, which inhabits North and South America. Leaves are alternate, pointed ovals and are usually toothed. Female flowers bloom singly or in pairs at the leaf bases, while male flowers are clustered at the base of the twigs; neither is showy. Fruits are one-seeded sweet berries. Several *Celtis* species make useful and beautiful shade trees for tough sites.

HOW TO GROW
Plant in full sun to partial shade. Best in rich, moist soil but adapts to extremes from wet to dry, acid to alkaline, and clay to sand. Tolerates heat and cold, wind and salt spray. Prune in winter to develop

Celtis occidentalis

Centaurea americana

strong branch angles that resist ice damage. Immune to Dutch elm disease; gall insects may disfigure the leaves but are not lethal. Good in the Plains, Midwest, and Mountain States.

C. occidentalis

c. ox-ih-den-TAL-iss. COMMON HACKBERRY. Pyramidal when young, becoming broad-topped and arching with age, this fast-growing elm relative grows 40 to 50 feet tall and wide. It makes a good substitute for American elm because of its similar mature shape and disease resistance. Leaves are 4 inches long, medium green, oval, and pointed, with tiny teeth along their edges. They turn dull yellow in autumn. Trunk bark is interesting, deeply furrowed, and corky. Green flowers in spring are inconspicuous but ripen into pea-sized purple berries that attract birds and wildlife in fall; these berries may temporarily stain walks and patios. This is a superb, deep-rooted shade tree for almost any location, but it excels in difficult sites where most other trees struggle. From northern and central North America.
Zones 3 to 8.

CULTIVARS AND SIMILAR SPECIES

'Prairie Pride' has thick, wind-resistant leaves; fewer fruits; and a uniform, oval crown. *C. laevigata* (sugar hackberry) has a rounded vase shape with pendulous branches; grows to 40 feet tall, making it an excellent street tree;

leaves are toothless or with a few teeth; bark is smooth and gray, sometimes with many warty projections; good in the South but not in the alkaline soils of the West; Zones 6 to 9. 'All Seasons' has a uniform shape and small leaves with

Centaurea montana

bright yellow fall color. 'Magnifica' is a fast-growing, insect-resistant hybrid with large leaves. *C. sinensis* (Japanese hackberry) is similar to *C. occidentalis*; good in the West; Zones 7 to 9.

Centaurea

sen-TOR-ee-uh. Aster family, Asteraceae.

Better known as cornflowers, knapweeds, or just centaureas, *Centaurea* species bear rounded, thistlelike flower heads with conelike bases made up of scaly, fringed, toothed, or spiny bracts. Each flower head consists of a cluster of small, deeply lobed florets that give the blooms a ragged appearance. Blooms come in colors ranging from deep rich blue to mauve, hot pink, white, pale pink, and yellow. The leaves may be undivided and entire to cut or lobed in a pinnate fashion. About 450 species of annuals, perennials, and subshrubs belong to this genus, most native to dry soils in Europe and the Mediterranean region. A few species are found in North America, Asia, and Australia.

HOW TO GROW

Plant cornflowers in full sun and average to rich, well-drained soil that is evenly moist. *C. montana* also grows in partial shade. Although cornflowers tolerate dry conditions, they perform best if watered during dry weather. Plants may or may not need staking, but in areas with warm summers they usually do. The perennials tend to be short-lived. Regular deadheading encourages new flowers to form. Or cut the plants to within several inches of the ground to eliminate their unsightly, flopping stems and encourage repeat bloom in fall. Both perennials and annuals self-sow.

Sow annual cornflowers, except *C. cineraria*, outdoors on or just before the last spring frost date. In all but the coldest zones, try sowing seeds of annuals outdoors in fall for spring bloom. Indoors, sow in individual pots 6 to 8 weeks before the last frost date and chill the sown pots at 40°F for a week before moving them to a warmer (65° to 70°F) spot for germinating. Sow *C. cineraria* indoors 10 to 12 weeks before the last frost date. Transplant with care. Indoors or out, cover the seeds with soil, as darkness is required for germination.

Use cornflowers in garden beds and borders. They also make fine cut flowers and can be dried. For cutting or drying, harvest when the flowers have expanded fully. *C. cineraria* also is an excellent container plant. Butterflies are attracted to the flowers.

C. americana

c. ah-mair-ih-KAY-nuh. BASKET FLOWER. An annual native to North America with lance-shaped leaves on 3- to 5-foot plants. Bears 4- to 6-inch-wide flower heads in shades of pink, rosy lilac, or white in summer. Cool-weather annual.

C. cineraria

c. sin-er-AIR-ee-uh. DUSTY MILLER. Formerly *C. gymnocarpa*. A tender, 8- to 24-inch-tall perennial or subshrub, hardy from Zone 7 south, grown for its woolly, white fernlike foliage. Remove its clusters of small, mustard yellow flowers. Tender perennial or cool-weather annual.

C. cyanus

c. sy-AN-us. BACHELOR'S BUTTONS, BLUE BOTTLE. An annual with lance-shaped leaves on 1/2- to 2 1/2-foot plants. Bears 1- to

1¹/₂-inch-wide flowers in dark blue, mauve, pink, rosy red, or white from spring to early summer. Cool-weather annual.

C. dealbata
c. deal-BAH-tuh. PERSIAN CENTAUREA. A 2- to 3-foot-tall perennial that spreads to 2 feet. Bears pink 1¹/₂-inch-wide flower heads with white centers in summer. **Zones 3 or 4 to 8.**

C. hypoleuca
c. hi-poe-LOO-kuh. Clump-forming 2-foot-tall perennial that spreads to 1¹/₂ feet. Produces fragrant 2¹/₂-inch-wide pale to dark pink flower heads in summer. 'John Coutts' bears bright rose pink blooms. **Zones 4 to 8.**

C. macrocephala
c. mack-roe-SEFF-ah-luh. GLOBE CENTAUREA, GIANT KNAPWEED. Vigorous 3- to 5-foot-tall perennial that spreads to 2 feet. Produces showy 1¹/₂- to 2-inch-wide blooms with yellow florets and prominent brown conelike bases. Blooms mid- to late summer. **Zones 3 to 7.**

C. montana
c. mon-TAH-nuh. MOUNTAIN BLUET. Vigorous, even weedy, clump-forming perennial that reaches 1¹/₂ to 2 feet and spreads by rhizomes to about 2 feet. Plants produce rich blue 2-inch-wide flower heads in early summer. It prefers cool temperatures and spreads less vigorously in the South than in the North. **Zones 3 to 8.**

Centranthus

sen-TRAN-thus. Valerian family, Valerianaceae.

Native to dry, sunny slopes, often on alkaline soil, *Centranthus* species hail primarily from the Mediterranean region and southern Europe. The genus contains some 8 to 12 species of annuals as well as herbaceous and subshrubby perennials. They bear rounded

Centranthus ruber

Centranthus ruber

clusters of small, spurred, funnel-shaped flowers at the stem tips and in leaf axils. *Centranthus* is from the Greek *kentron,* meaning "spur," and *anthos,* "flower," a reference to the spurred flowers.

HOW TO GROW
Give these plants a spot in full sun with poor to average, well-drained soil. They thrive in poor soils, with pH ranging from slightly acid to alkaline, and also are excellent for planting in walls. Deadhead regularly, and cut plants back by half after flowering if they become floppy. The plants are not long-lived, so plan on replacing them every 3 to 5 years. Established specimens are difficult to move and divide because of their deep roots. Propagate by division in early spring (dig deeply and handle plants very carefully) or seeds. They also self-sow, and seedlings are easy to move.

C. ruber
c. RUE-ber. VALERIAN, JUPITER'S BEARD. Clumping, woody-based perennial that ranges from 1 to 3 feet tall and spreads as far. Bears blue-green lance-shaped leaves and dense, rounded clusters of fragrant ¹/₂-inch-long flowers from late spring through late summer. Blooms are pinkish red, crimson, or white. 'Albus' has white flowers; 'Coccineus', carmine red ones; and 'Roseus', rose pink blooms. **Zones 4 to 8.**

Cephalanthus

seff-al-AN-thus. Madder family, Rubiaceae.

Of about 10 deciduous and evergreen trees and shrubs found in

wetlands in North and Central America, Asia, and Africa, one species, known as buttonbush, is grown in gardens for its small, fragrant, off-white flowers that grow in sputniklike balls.

HOW TO GROW
Soil should be rich and moisture retentive, in full sun. A good plant for a natural pondside. Midsummer flowers appear on the most vigorous young stems. Prune buttonbush to the ground at least every 2 to 3 years when buds swell in spring to keep it from becoming treelike and unkempt. Propagates easily from seeds or soft- or hardwood cuttings.

C. occidentalis
c. ox-ih-den-TAL-iss. BUTTONBUSH. Native from Canada to Florida, this open-branching, usually deciduous shrub averages 6 feet tall and 8 feet wide and has glossy oval or elliptic leaves to 6

inches long. May be evergreen in the southernmost part of its range. The 1-inch ball flowers appear from late summer to fall, depending on heat. Ducks and other waterfowl love to feed on the clusters of nutlets. Look for it at a nursery that specializes in natives. **Zones 5 to 11.**

Cephalotaxus

seff-al-oh-TAX-us. Plum yew family, Cephalotaxaceae.

This genus of small trees and shrubs from Asia contains nine species. Needles are flat, pointed, and usually arranged in two ranks, one on either side of the young branches. The undersides often have silver bands. Female plants produce small, fleshy, plumlike, green fruits. These shade-tolerant trees are not well known but make fine additions to the plant palette in many areas.

HOW TO GROW
Partial to full shade and any moist, well-drained soil, from sand to clay. Winter burn can occur in sunny locations in the North. Needs no pruning, but may be sheared if desired; resprouts from leafless wood. Mites are the worst problem.

C. harringtoniana
c. hair-ring-toe-nee-AH-nuh. JAPANESE PLUM YEW. This dark green, shade-tolerant, deer-proof conifer usually forms a 25-foot-tall pyramid, but some types are low, spreading shrubs. Needles are 1¹/₂ to 2¹/₂ inches long, glossy, very dark green, and arranged in two ranks along the tops of the stems. They are reminiscent of yew nee-

Cephalanthus occidentalis

Cephalotaxus harringtoniana

Cerastium tomentosum

dles, but are much longer and more pointed, and densely cloak the whorled branches. Trunk bark is reddish brown and shredding. Yellowish flowers bloom along the stems in spring. The 1-inch-long, oval, olive-brown fruits ripen to purple in fall. This is a perfect tree for a shade garden or foundation planting. It also looks good planted in groups or as a screen. It tolerates heavier soil and more heat than yews do and is popular in the Southeast. From Japan and China. **Zones 5 to 9**.

CULTIVARS
Cultivars selected for more predictable shape include 'Duke Gardens', 3 to 5 feet tall and wide; and 'Fastigiata', which forms a fat column 10 feet tall and 7 feet wide with longer-leaved bottlebrush branches. 'Prostrata', 2 to 3 feet tall and sometimes slightly wider, received a Gold Medal from the Pennsylvania Horticultural Society.

Cerastium

seh-RAS-tee-um. Pink family, Caryophyllaceae.

Cerastium is a genus of mostly annuals and perennials that form mats or low mounds of simple, often gray-green or silvery leaves and tiny white, usually five-petaled, flowers. The petals have notched tips and typically are carried in small clusters. Between 60 and 100 species belong here, including a few valuable garden plants grown for their starry flowers as well as some troublesome weeds. Mouse-ear chickweed (*C. vulgatum*) is a common lawn weed.

HOW TO GROW
Select a site in full sun with poor to average, very well drained soil. Plants tend to "melt out" in summer in areas with hot weather, so give them light shade in the South, especially during the hottest part of the day. They are quite drought tolerant and grow in almost pure sand, in dry-laid stone walls, and on dry slopes. Shear the plants after the flowers fade. Mow clumps in early spring if overwintered plants look unkempt. Dig and divide them if clumps spread too far. In addition to division, propagate by stem-tip cuttings taken in summer or sow seeds.

C. tomentosum
c. toe-men-TOE-sum. S N O W - I N - S U M M E R. Vigorous to invasive, mat-forming 6- to 10-inch-tall perennial that spreads rapidly and widely, especially in areas with cool, wet summers. Bears woolly, silver-gray, 1-inch-long leaves and clusters of 1-inch-wide white flowers in late spring and early summer. 'Yo-Yo' is a compact 6-inch-tall cultivar that does not spread as quickly. *C. alpinum*, alpine chickweed, is a mat-forming 2- to 6-inch-tall species with small woolly leaves topped by few-flowered clusters of very small white flowers in late spring and early summer. It is less rampant than *C. tomentosum. C. biebersteinii* is a similar species with 1- to 1¹/₂-inch-long silver-gray leaves. **Zones 2 to 7**.

Ceratostigma

sir-rat-oh-STIG-muh. Plumbago family, Plumbaginaceae.

Grown for their flat-faced blue flowers, *Ceratostigma* species are herbaceous perennials, shrubs, and subshrubs that are closely related to, and sometimes called, plumbagos (*Plumbago* spp.).

About eight species belong to the genus, native from tropical Africa to China and India. One species — *C. plumbaginoides* — is a vigorous perennial most often used as a ground cover.

HOW TO GROW
Select a site in full sun with rich, evenly moist but well-drained soil. *C. plumbaginoides* also tolerates partial shade. Established plants tolerate dry soil. Mark the locations of the clumps because plants emerge late in spring. Propagate by division in spring.

C. plumbaginoides
c. plum-bah-gin-OY-deez. P L U M - B A G O, L E A D W O R T. Semiwoody 6- to 12-inch-tall rhizomatous species that spreads quickly to several feet. Features reddish stems, showy clusters of brilliant blue ³/₄-inch-wide flowers from summer to fall, and rounded leaves that turn glowing orange or red in autumn. **Zones 5 to 9**.

Ceratostigma plumbaginoides

Cercidiphyllum

sir-sih-dih-FILL-um.
Cercidiphyllum family,
Cercidiphyllaceae.

This genus contains only one species, a gorgeous tree native to the woodlands of China and Japan.

HOW TO GROW

Plant in full sun except in Zone 8, where partial shade is best. Likes rich, moist, well-drained, acid or alkaline soil; fall color is best in an acid site. Does not tolerate drought when young; best with plentiful moisture. May be trained to a single trunk, but looks best as a multitrunked specimen. Thin and shorten the branches to reduce the possibility of storm damage.

C. japonicum

c. juh-PON-ih-kum. KATSURA TREE. Pyramidal when young, but maturing into a broad-spreading, flat-topped, 40- to 50-foot-tall specimen, katsura tree is an elegant addition to the home landscape. Its delicate-looking, heart-shaped, 3-inch-long leaves emerge reddish purple in spring, mature to bluish green, and change to combinations of glowing orange, gold, and apricot in autumn.

Cercis chinensis

Fallen leaves give off the scent of cotton candy, most noticeable on sunny days. Tiny, red, male and female flowers bloom on separate trees before the leaves unfold in spring. Female trees can be as showy as redbud (*Cercis*) when in bloom and are broader in outline than male trees, which are more narrowly upright. This fast-growing tree is usually multitrunked, with attractive, shaggy, gray-brown bark. Surface roots may interfere with a lawn or garden beneath the tree; plant in a ground cover or a heavily mulched area as a lawn or patio specimen. From Asia. **Zones 4 to 8.**

CULTIVARS

'Pendula' is a graceful weeping tree that grows to 25 feet tall. *C. japonicum* var. *magnificum* 'Pendulum' is a dramatic weeping tree that grows to 50 feet tall with irregular growth and larger leaves.

Cercis

SEER-sus. Pea family,
Fabaceae.

Six species of small trees or shrubs from North America, Asia, and the Mediterranean make up this genus. Heart-shaped leaves, two-lipped flowers blooming in clusters on both old and new wood, and slender seedpods characterize the group. Several species are prized as small, early-blooming landscape trees, and one makes a glorious shrub.

HOW TO GROW

Plant in full sun to light shade. Best in moist, well-drained, deep soil; performs poorly in wet sites. Tolerates acid or alkaline soil. Protect trunk from mechanical injury. Verticillium wilt, canker, leaf spot, leafhoppers, and caterpillars can cause these trees to be short-lived. Best in hot-summer areas.

C. canadensis

c. kan-uh-DEN-sis. EASTERN REDBUD. This rounded or flat-topped tree forms multiple low-branching trunks that mature to 20 to 30 feet tall. In early spring, the leafless gray branches are covered with tight clusters of 1-inch-long, bright purplish pink, pink, or occasionally white blossoms. New leaves emerge reddish purple and quickly mature into 5- to 7-inch-wide, matte green hearts that change to yellow in fall. The bark on the trunk and branches is beautiful — smooth and very dark gray. Flattened, 5-inch-long, brown seedpods decorate the tree in fall and winter. Growing naturally along woodland edges, this pretty little tree adapts well to garden borders and naturalistic landscapes. Plant alone or in groups with a dark background of evergreens to show off the blossoms. From central and eastern North America. **Zones 5 to 9.**

Cercidiphyllum japonicum

Cercis canadensis

'Forest Pansy' has enchanting, glossy, reddish purple leaves in spring that change to dark green in summer if nights are hot, then red and orange in fall. 'Silver Cloud' features white-variegated leaves and flowers more sparsely; grows to 12 feet tall. *C. canadensis* var. *alba* has white flowers and light green leaves. *C. canadensis* var. *texensis (C. reniformis)* is a midwestern variety that grows to 20 feet tall and has smaller, very glossy leaves; the best choice for the Southwest; **Zones 6 to 9**. 'Oklahoma' has deep magenta flowers. 'Texas White' has white flowers. *C. occidentalis* (western redbud) grows to 12 feet tall and tolerates alkaline soil; a better choice than *C. canadensis* for the Pacific Northwest. **Zones 7 to 9**.

C. chinensis

c. chih-NEN-sis. C H I N E S E R E D B U D. A multistemmed shrub with erect branches that are smothered with rosy purple flowers in early spring before the leaves emerge. Generally less than 10 feet tall but can reach 15 feet tall and wide. Immune to canker. 'Avondale' has profuse flowers and performs well in the Pacific Northwest. 'Alba' has white flowers. **Zones 6 to 9**.

Cestrum

SESS-trum. Nightshade family, Solanaceae.

This big genus includes some 175 species of evergreen and deciduous woodland shrubs found from Mexico to South America. About half a dozen are available to gar-

Chaenomeles × superba 'Cameo'

deners. Hummingbirds are passionate about the tubular or funnel-shaped flowers, often powerfully fragrant; the red, white, or purple berries draw other birds as well.

HOW TO GROW

Plant these shrubs in fertile soil, well amended with organic matter, in partial sun or shade. Use them in a border or train them against a wall to protect them from frost, which will often freeze them to the ground. Pinch frequently to maintain an attractive shape, and prune heavily after flowering or fruiting. Propagate from cuttings in summer.

C. nocturnum

c. nok-TERN-um. N I G H T J E S S A - M I N E. An evergreen shrub to 12 feet tall, grown for pale green to ivory flowers that are intensely fragrant at night. They bloom in late summer or early fall in axillary clusters. Where not hardy night jessamines are grown in containers for overwintering indoors. **Zones 10 to 11**.

Chaenomeles

ky-noh-MAY-leez. Rose family, Rosaceae.

All three species of these deciduous, often spiny shrubs, which are known as flowering quinces and are from mountain woods in Asia, have been the object of tinkering by breeders to develop variations on form and flower color. The

Cestrum nocturnum

early-spring blossoms are cup shaped with 5 petals and up to 60 stamens. They can be single or double, solitary or clustered. In autumn they bear green or purple fruits that are aromatic and edible. They sometimes split open; the botanical name means "gaping apple."

HOW TO GROW

Give flowering quince moderately fertile soil. It does best in full sun but tolerates some shade and some lime, as well as pollution and drought. Smaller species can be used for ground cover and underplanting larger shrubs, while upright species can be espaliered. They are not particularly exciting out of bloom. The branches are popular for forcing and arrangements. Prune after flowering, re-

moving at least a third of old branches, to promote the next season's flowering. Propagate from stratified seeds, or from semiripe cuttings in fall.

C. japonica

c. juh-PON-ih-kuh. J A P A N E S E F L O W E R I N G Q U I N C E. This low-growing thorny shrub rarely reaches 3 feet tall but is often twice as wide and bears glossy 2-inch leaves. Flowers are clusters of orange to red in early to midspring. A good choice for northern gardens, where it usually spends winter buried by snow (thus safe from the attention of hungry rabbits). **Zones 5 to 8**.

C. speciosa

c. spee-see-OH-suh. F L O W E R I N G Q U I N C E. This species has variable habit from upright to rounded or spreading, grows 6 to 10 feet or more high and wide, and has shiny brown bark. Flowers are red or orange, with some cultivars offering white, pink, or peach. It makes a good barrier hedge, but visual interest is limited to the flowering season. The sour fruits are cooked for preserves. **Zones 5 to 8**.

C. × superba

c. × sue-PERB-uh. A compact hybrid of *C. speciosa* and *C. japonica*, averaging 5 feet high and 6 feet wide, this shrub is twiggy, thorny, and suckering. Its longer-blooming flowers are 2 inches across and come in a similar range of colors. The fruit is larger and ripens later. Somewhat less drought tolerant. There are a few thornless cultivars, such as 'Cameo' (peachy pink) and 'Pink Lady'. **Zones 5 to 9**.

Chaenomeles speciosa 'Hollandia'

Chamaecyparis

kam-ee-SIP-ah-riss. False
cypress family,
Cupressaceae.

Native to North America and Asia,
the six members of this genus are
usually tall, columnar trees that
thrive in cool, humid climates.
Leaves are tiny scales (sometimes
sharp needles on juvenile trees)
and are arranged in opposite pairs
that create fanlike sprays on the
short branches. Cones are only
about 1/3 inch around and not
very noticeable. They are generally
blue-green when young, with 6 to
12 umbrella-like scales, and ripen
in a year to reddish brown. All
these trees make excellent specimens in a border or arranged as a
screen or in a grove. The dwarf
forms are used for rock gardens or
in shrub borders. They adapt to
container culture if well watered
and fertilized.

HOW TO GROW

See individual descriptions for
cultural requirements.

C. lawsoniana

c. law-son-ee-AY-nah. LAWSON
FALSE CYPRESS, PORT OR-
FORD CEDAR. This pyramidal
or conical evergreen can grow to
60 feet tall and 30 feet wide, although many of its popular
cultivars are smaller. Depending
on the cultivar, the scalelike leaves
vary in color from deep green to
gray-green to golden and have
white marks on their undersides.
They are arranged in flattened
sprays that form vertical or horizontal planes, giving the tree a
very soft, layered appearance.
Trunk is buttressed and has red
bark. Side branches are short and
horizontal to drooping, so the tree
usually resists snow damage. The
widely available colorful forms
make eye-catching specimens that
bring year-round beauty to a garden. The species and its green
cultivars are the best choices for a
screen or hedge.

Plant in full sun to partial
shade; gold forms need full sun.
Needs moist, well-drained loam.
Does not tolerate clayey soil or
drying wind. Performs poorly in
the East; best in the West where it's
cool and moist. May be sheared
for a hedge, but do not cut back to
bare wood, because new shoots
will not grow. Phytopthera fungus
causes root rot in heavy or poorly
drained soil and in hot, humid climates. Mites are a severe problem
in hot, dry sites. From the Pacific
Northwest. **Zones 5 to 8.**

CULTIVARS

'Alumii' forms a narrow, 35-foot-
tall cone; metallic blue new
growth matures to blue-green.

Chamaecyparis obtusa 'Crippsii'

'Dragon Blue' is a compact, upright form with blue-gray needles.
'Ellwoodii' has a dense columnar
shape and reaches 10 to 20 feet tall;
feathery, gray-green, prickly new
growth turns steel blue in winter.
'Golden King' ('Golden Showers')
is a 35-foot-tall pyramid with
slightly pendulous branch tips,
golden yellow outer needles, and
yellow-green inner needles; often
turns deep gold in winter. 'Green
Hedger' is a dense, conical tree
with bright green foliage. 'Lanei'
('Lane') is an upright, compact
form that grows to 15 feet tall;
gold-tipped new foliage and yellow-green older foliage. 'Oregon
Blue' is fast growing, has silvery
blue to blue-gray needles, and resists phytopthera. 'Pendula' has an
upright stem that grows to 30 feet
tall with weeping branches; glossy
needles of variable color.

C. nootkatensis

c. neut-kah-TEN-sis. NOOTKA
FALSE CYPRESS, ALASKA
CEDAR. This beautiful, conical
evergreen has a graceful silhouette.
The main trunk is strong and
straight, with spreading main
branches that swoop downward
and then curve gracefully upward;
side branches hang almost straight
down, creating curtains of weeping foliage. Mature trees reach 40
or more feet tall and 15 to 20 feet
wide. Leaves are usually dark blue-
green or gray-green, sharp-
pointed scales that form fine-textured, flattened sprays. Foliage has
an unpleasant odor when crushed.
Trunk bark is gray-brown or red-
brown and stringy. Cones take 2
years to ripen, unlike those on
other species. Weeping forms
make a wonderful focal point in a
lawn or border. Use nonweeping
forms as a screen. The tree is very
resistant to storm damage.

Plant in full to partial sun or
light shade; best with afternoon
shade in the hottest areas. Needs
plentiful moisture and sandy to
humus-rich, acid soil. Tolerates
heat and humidity and performs
well in the Midwest. Old foliage
may turn brown and remain on
the tree; remove with a strong
spray from a garden hose to improve appearance. Prune carefully,
because it will not resprout from
leafless wood. Usually pest-free,
but scale and bagworms are occasional problems. From coastal
Alaska and the Pacific Northwest.
Zones 5 to 7.

CULTIVARS

'Aurea' forms a slow-growing pyramid with bright yellow new
growth; may be mislabeled as
'Lutea'. 'Glauca' has thick, nodding, blue-green foliage. 'Glauca

Chamaecyparis nootkatensis

Chamaecyparis pisifera

Pendula' is a slender tree with weeping, blue-green foliage. 'Green Arrow' forms a very narrow column with pendulous branches. 'Lutea' has pendulous branches and new growth suffused with gold. 'Pendula' has gracefully weeping, dark green foliage. 'Strict Weeping' is extremely narrow and pendulous. 'Sullivan' is a dense, weeping form that tolerates heavy shade; grows to 20 feet tall.

C. obtusa

c. ob-TWO-sah. HINOKI FALSE CYPRESS. This stunning evergreen forms a 50-foot-tall, 20-foot-wide pyramid, although the commonly grown garden forms are smaller, usually reaching only 25 feet tall and 10 feet wide. The scalelike needles are glossy dark green with white crosses on their undersides, an identifying feature. They form rounded, fan-shaped sprays that give the tree a beautiful texture. The bark on older trunks is reddish brown and shredding. The species makes an excellent tall screen or hedge, while the cultivars create a beautiful focal point in a shrub border or foundation planting.

Plant in full to partial sun; afternoon shade is best in hot areas. Needs moist, well-drained, acid to neutral, sandy to loamy soil. Performs best in humid areas. Foliage may burn in winter wind and sun. Older inner foliage may turn brown without dropping; remove by hand or with a strong spray from a hose to improve appear-ance. Do not prune to bare wood; plants resprout only from wood that contains foliage. Mites may be a problem in hot, dry areas. From Japan and Taiwan. **Zones 5 to 8**.

CULTIVARS
'Aurea' is compact, with bright gold tips on new growth and dark green inner foliage. 'Crippsii' is a broadly spreading, loose pyramid with dense, golden yellow new growth and bright green older foliage. 'Filicoides' (fernspray Hinoki cypress) is an irregular, slow-growing, 10-foot-tall, gaunt pyramid with long, pendulous clusters of green needles. 'Gracilis' ('Nana Gracilis') is the most common dwarf form and very beautiful, bearing dark green, nodding fans of foliage growing slowly to 6 feet or less. 'Gracilis Aurea' has gold-tipped, nodding fans. 'Koster Sport' is a full-size tree with twisted, light green foliage and layered branches. 'Tetragona Aurea' forms a narrow, slow-growing pyramid with bright gold, tufted and twisted branches.

C. pisifera

c. piss-SIF-err-ah. SAWARA FALSE CYPRESS, RETINOSPORA. This broadly conical or pyramidal tree can grow to 60 feet tall and 20 feet wide, although its cultivars are usually smaller and more compact. The species is rarely grown in home landscapes, although its cultivars are commonly found in gardens as medium-size trees and dwarf shrubs. The dark green needles have white markings on their undersides and grow in flattened sprays, but they are quite variable and are found in three distinct shapes: *Filifera types* (threadleaf Sawara cypress) feature closely pressed, scalelike needles that form slender, pendent, cord-like branches. *Plumosa types* (plume Sawara cypress) have sharp, pointed, bright green needles that stand out from the stems, creating a plumed effect. *Squarrosa types* (mossy Sawara cypress) have recurved, pointed, soft, scaly needles that stand away from the stems in a billowy mass.

Plant in full sun and moist, well-drained, humus-rich, acid to neutral soil. Needs plentiful moisture and tolerates only short periods of drought. Performs best in humid climates. Sensitive to road salt. The plumosa and squarrosa types may hold their dead inner needles; remove to improve appearance. Allow branches to remain on the ground for best appearance. Prune carefully, because needles resprout only from older wood containing foliage. Mites are a problem in dry sites. From Japan. **Zones 5 to 8**.

CULTIVARS
Many dwarf, shrublike forms are available. Several are listed below these tree forms. *Filifera types:* 'Filifera' is a slow-growing, broadly conical form with light green needles on long, whiplike branches. 'Filifera Aurea' has bright golden yellow foliage and is a bit smaller than 'Filifera'. 'Lemon Thread' has bright lemon yellow, whiplike branches. *Plumosa types:* 'Plumosa' is a full-size tree with bright green needles. 'Plumosa Aurea' is compact, with golden yellow outer needles that deepen to yellow-green. *Squarrosa types:* 'Squarrosa' forms a densely twiggy, broad cone with billowy sprays of soft, blue-green needles. 'Squarrosa Aurea' has golden foliage. 'Squarrosa Veitchii' is very similar to 'Squarrosa'. *Shrub forms:* 'Filifera Aurea Nana' has delicate threadleaf golden foliage and grows to 3 feet tall. '*Squarrosa Minima*' forms a fluffy globe less than 3 feet across with feathery gray-green foliage.

C. thyoides

c. thigh-OY-deez. ATLANTIC WHITE CEDAR, WHITE FALSE CYPRESS, SWAMP CEDAR. This small to medium-size conifer, which grows naturally in coastal swamps, forms a 40- to 50-foot-tall, slender column that naturally loses its lower branches. It is an excellent choice for difficult wet sites where an evergreen is called for. Needles are blue-green or blue-gray, scalelike leaves with a

Chamaecyparis pisifera

C

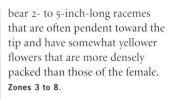

Chamaelirium luteum

conspicuous white gland on the back. They look very much like juniper needles. In fact, the plant closely resembles eastern red cedar (*Juniperus virginiana*). Like juniper, this species' needles often take on a purplish brown hue in winter. When old inner needles die, they turn brown and remain on the tree for another year; remove them to improve appearance. Trunk bark peels in thin shreds and is gray-brown or reddish brown. Fruits are small, pointy, purple cones that turn brown; this helps distinguish the plant from eastern red cedar, which has bright blue-gray, berrylike fruits. This useful native does best in a naturalistic setting in a damp or wet site where other cedars would suffer, but it adapts well to most garden situations.

Plant in full sun to light shade. Best in moist, sandy, acid soil, but tolerates almost any acid soil, sandy to clayey, dry to wet. Usually pest-free. From eastern North America. Zones 5 to 9.

CULTIVARS

Many dwarf, shrublike forms are available. Only tree forms are described here. 'Andelyensis' forms a bright green, 10-foot-tall, narrow column that turns purplish in winter and has numerous cones. 'Ericoides' grows very slowly to 25 feet tall and has blue-gray, needlelike leaves. 'Glauca' has blue-green needles. 'Hopkinton'

has attractive blue-gray needles and is open branched and fast growing.

Chamaelirium

kah-mee-LEER-ee-um. Lily family, Liliaceae.

The genus *Chamaelirium* contains a single species of tuberous peren-

nial that is native to eastern North America. It grows naturally in bogs and moist woodlands and produces rosettes of rounded to spoon-shaped, glossy green leaves that last well into winter. The botanical name comes from the Greek *chamai*, "on the ground," and *lirion*, "lily." While the foliage is primarily basal, the flowers are produced in summer in erect, feathery spikes that can reach 1 to 3 feet. Spikes are cylindrical and densely packed with tiny creamy white flowers that have six narrow petal-like tepals. The species is dioecious, meaning male and female flowers are borne on separate plants.

HOW TO GROW

Select a site in partial shade with rich, moist — even boggy — soil. An acid soil pH is best. Plants withstand considerable sun with consistent moisture. Use this wildflower in moist shade gardens, bog gardens, and natural areas. Propagate by dividing plants in spring or sowing seeds in fall; both male and female plants are required for seed production.

C. luteum

c. LOO-tee-um. DEVIL'S BIT, BLAZING STAR, FAIRY WAND. A native 1- to 3-foot-tall wildflower that bears cylindrical racemes of creamy white 1/4-inch-wide flowers from early to midsummer. Female plants bear 1-foot-long racemes. Male plants

bear 2- to 5-inch-long racemes that are often pendent toward the tip and have somewhat yellower flowers that are more densely packed than those of the female. Zones 3 to 8.

Chamaemelum

kam-eh-MEL-um. Aster family, Asteraceae.

Chamaemelum species bear finely cut, fernlike leaves and daisylike flower heads with yellow centers and white ray florets, or "petals." One of the four species that belong to this genus of aromatic annuals and perennials is the popular herb chamomile, used in teas to soothe one to sleep.

HOW TO GROW

Select a site in full sun with light, well-drained soil. Sandy soil is ideal. These plants are unsuitable where the summers are hot and muggy. Propagate by dividing plants in spring or by seeds. Use division for cultivars, which do not come true from seed.

C. nobile

c. no-BIL-ee. ROMAN CHAMOMILE. Formerly *Anthemis nobilis*. Mat-forming 6- to 12-inch-tall plant that spreads to 1 1/2 feet. Bears threadlike, apple-scented leaves and 1/4- to 1/2-inch-wide daisies in summer on long stalks above the foliage. 'Flore Pleno' bears double white buttonlike

Chamaemelum nobile

Chasmanthe floribunda

Chelidonium majus

blooms on 6-inch plants. 'Treneague' is a compact 4-inch-tall nonflowering cultivar with especially aromatic leaves. It does not withstand more than rare foot traffic when planted as a lawn substitute, but it makes an aromatic carpet between steppingstones. **Zones 6 to 9.**

Chasmanthe

chaz-MAN-thee. Iris family, Iridaceae.

Closely related to *Gladiolus* and *Crocosmia*, *Chasmanthe* species produce fans of erect, sword-shaped leaves and showy, spikelike racemes of flowers in summer. Three species belong to the genus, all native South African perennials that grow from corms. They produce flowers that have curved, tubular to funnel-shaped bases and open into six lobes, or petal-like tepals. The upper tepal is longer than the other five and projects out to form a hood.

HOW TO GROW
Select a site in full sun or partial shade with rich, moist, well-drained soil. *Chasmanthe* species are grown much like gladiolus: plant the corms in spring after the soil has warmed up, setting them 3 to 4 inches deep. For best effect, arrange them in drifts, with corms spaced 3 to 4 inches apart. Water regularly in dry weather. Dig the corms in fall after the first light frost — dig them earlier if the leaves die back. Let them dry for a few hours, brush off excess soil, and store them in paper bags in a cool (40° to 50°F), dry place over winter. Where hardy, the corms can be left in the ground year-

round. In this case, cut back the leaves in late winter. Propagate by separating and planting the offsets in spring or fall or by sowing seeds.

C. aethiopica

c. ee-thee-OH-pih-kuh. A 2-foot-tall species forming clumps of sword-shaped leaves. In spring to early summer, plants produce 6- to 7-inch-long racemes of 3-inch-long red or orange flowers with maroon throats. **Zones 8 to 10.**

C. floribunda

c. flor-ih-BUN-duh. A 2- to 4-foot-tall species producing clumps of sword-shaped leaves and branched 1-foot-long racemes of 3-inch-long yellow or orange flowers in summer. **Zones 9 to 10.**

Chasmanthium

chaz-MAN-thee-um. Grass family, Poaceae.

Chasmanthium contains about six species of perennial grasses native to North and Central America that are commonly called wild oats or wood oats. They bear linear to narrowly lance-shaped leaves and oatlike panicles of flowers. One species is grown as an ornamental grass.

HOW TO GROW
A site in partial shade with rich, moist, well-drained soil is ideal. Plants also will grow in full sun and tolerate dry soil — including dry shade. Cut the plants to the ground in late winter to very early spring. Or, since they self-sow with enthusiasm, cut them back in fall before the seed heads shatter to curtail this tendency. For propagation, divide clumps in spring or early summer, sow seeds, or pot up self-sown seedlings.

C. latifolium

c. lat-ih-FOE-lee-um. NORTHERN SEA OATS. Formerly *Uniola latifolia*. Native North American warm-season grass forming 2- to 3-foot-tall, 2-foot-wide clumps. Has bamboolike leaves and showy,

Chasmanthium latifolium

drooping green seed heads in midsummer that ripen to light brown. **Zones 5 to 9.**

Chelidonium

kel-ih-DOE-nee-um. Poppy family, Papaveraceae.

Chelidonium contains a single species, a biennial or short-lived perennial native to Europe and western Asia that has naturalized throughout North America. Plants bear leaves that are deeply cut in a pinnate fashion and yellow

Chelone lyonii

poppylike flowers in summer. They have orange-yellow sap that can cause skin irritation.

HOW TO GROW
Greater celandine grows in sun or shade and almost any soil, although it is happiest in partial shade in rich, well-drained conditions. The plants do not transplant well, but they grow easily from seeds sown where they are to grow. They self-sow with enthusiasm.

C. majus

c. MAY-jus. GREATER CELANDINE. Clump-forming 1½- to 2-foot-tall species with brittle stems and loose umbels of ¾- to 1-inch-wide bright yellow flowers in summer. 'Flore Pleno' bears double flowers. **Zones 5 to 8.**

Chelone

chee-LOW-nee. Figwort family, Scrophulariaceae.

Both the common and botanical names of these native North American perennials refer to the unusual shape of their tubular, two-lipped flowers. They are commonly called turtleheads, and *Chelone* is the Greek word for "tortoise." Six species belong to the genus, all stiff-stemmed plants with simple, toothed leaves. They bear terminal racemes of pink, purple, or white flowers from late summer to fall. The flowers have a beard on the lower lip.

Chasmanthium latifolium

Chelone lyonii

HOW TO GROW

Plant turtleheads in partial shade or full sun in a site that has deep, rich, moist soil. In the South, constant soil moisture is essential for plants grown in full sun. They grow in heavy clay and also are ideal for the wet conditions of a bog garden. Plants usually stand without staking and spread to form 1¹/₂- to 2-foot-wide clumps. Propagate by dividing the clumps in spring or late fall, taking stem-tip cuttings in late spring or early summer, or sowing seeds.

C. glabra
c. GLAY-bruh. WHITE TURTLEHEAD, SNAKESHEAD TURTLEHEAD. A 3- to 5-foot species with square stems, lance-shaped leaves, and 1-inch-long flowers that are white or white blushed with pink. **Zones 3 to 8.**

C. lyonii
c. lie-OH-nee-eye. PINK TURTLE-HEAD. A 1- to 3-foot-tall species with square stems; ovate, toothed leaves; and purple-pink 1-inch-long flowers that have yellow beards. **Zones 3 to 8.**

C. obliqua
c. oh-BLEE-kwah. ROSE TURTLE-HEAD. A 1¹/₂- to 2-foot-tall species with somewhat rounded stems, broadly lance-shaped toothed or cut leaves, and ³/₄-inch-long dark pink or purple-pink flowers with sparse yellow beards. **Zones 5 to 9.**

Chimonanthus

ky-moe-NAN-thus. Sweetshrub family, Calycanthaceae.

Of this genus's six species of deciduous and evergreen shrubs native to Chinese woodlands, one, known as wintersweet, has been brought to gardens for its exceedingly fragrant flowers that appear on bare branches in early to late winter.

HOW TO GROW
Although wintersweet can tolerate more moisture than most shrubs, it will do best in loamy soil with good drainage, in full sun to partial shade. Site it against evergreens or a wall, outside a window or along a walk where it can be enjoyed on a cold day. Prune off old branches after flowering; hard pruning keeps it from becoming leggy. Sow seeds in May or June or take softwood cuttings in summer.

C. praecox
c. PREE-koks. WINTERSWEET. A deciduous, multistemmed slow grower to an average of 12 feet tall and 10 feet wide. Lance-shaped, 2- to 5-inch glossy leaves turn yellow

Chimonanthus praecox

Chionanthus virginicus

in fall. Outer petals of the 1-inch winter flowers are sulphur yellow and slightly transparent; inner petals are brownish purple. **Zones 7 to 9.**

Chionanthus

ky-oh-NAN-thus. Olive family, Oleaceae.

This genus, which gets its name from Greek words meaning "snow flower," contains more than 100 evergreen and deciduous trees and shrubs from streambanks and other moist areas of the eastern United States and Asia. Two deciduous species of small trees or shrubs are coveted by gardeners because of the dramatic "beards" of white flowers that they sport in late spring, hence their common name, fringe tree. On the females the flowers are followed by dark blue fruits. The elliptic leaves are somewhat glossy and may provide yellow foliage in fall.

HOW TO GROW
Give fringe trees neutral to acid soil that is deep, fertile, and moist but well aerated, in full sun to partial shade. They flower and fruit best where summers are long and hot. Although they require no pruning, they can be limbed up for a more treelike shape. Seeds have double dormancy (needing warm and then cold stratification), so germination takes patience.

C. retusus
c. rey-TUSS-us. CHINESE FRINGE TREE. Growing into a multistemmed, rounded or vase-shaped, 20-foot-tall specimen,

Chinese fringe tree is less commonly grown than the native species but is even more beautiful. Clusters of pure white, fringelike flowers turn the tree into a snowball in early summer — a week later than the native species, because the flowers develop on new wood rather than on the previous year's growth. The tidy, oval leaves are 2 to 4 inches long, glossy on top, and densely hairy on their undersides. They may or may not develop yellow late-fall color. Female trees have purple fruits. Trunk bark is attractive, peeling away to reveal gray, brown, and green patches and eventually becoming furrowed. Use this eye-catching tree for a surprising burst of early-summer color in a border or as a screen. From Asia. **Zones 6 to 9.**

C. virginicus
c. ver-JIN-ee-kus. FRINGE TREE, OLD MAN'S BEARD, GRANCY GRAYBEARD. This rounded, multistemmed, 15- to 20-foot-tall tree blooms and leafs out so late in spring that one begins to wonder whether it is dead just before it suddenly bursts into glorious bloom. The honey-scented, creamy white blossoms are made up of four strap-shaped petals and

Chionanthus virginicus

Chionodoxa forbesii

bloom in dense, 6-inch-long clusters that turn the tree into a billowy cloud for 2 weeks, masking the unfolding leaves. The waxy, dark green, oval leaves are 4 to 8 inches long and have pale undersides and smooth edges. Attractive yellow fall color develops late. Trunk bark is smooth gray, and limbs and twigs have a coarse texture when leafless in winter. Male trees are a bit showier in bloom than female ones, but in fall female trees develop showy blue berries that attract birds. Use as a slow-growing border or patio tree. From southeastern and central North America. **Zones 4 to 9.**

CULTIVARS

'Floyd' is a rare cultivar with very showy male flowers and a dense, upright shape.

Chionodoxa

ky-on-oh-DOX-uh. Lily family, Liliaceae.

Both the common and the botanical names of this genus of easy-to-grow bulbs celebrate their dainty, early-season blooms. They are commonly known as glory-of-the-snow, because the flowers appear in late winter or early spring as snows recede. The botanical name is from the Greek *chion*, meaning "snow," and *doxa*, "glory." Six species belong to the genus, all small bulbous perennials that have tunicate bulbs and produce two or three narrow, linear to strappy leaves. They bear racemes of six-lobed, upward-facing, star-shaped flowers. Blooms often have a white eye and come in shades of rich, true blue as well as pink and white. Individual flowers have six petal-like tepals. The tepals are united at the base to form a short tube; members of the genus *Scilla*, to which these plants are closely related and with which they are often confused, have tepals that are split all the way to the base of the flower.

HOW TO GROW

Select a site with average, well-drained soil that is in full sun or in partial to full shade under deciduous trees so that plants receive full sun in spring when they are actively growing. Plant the bulbs in fall with the bases at a depth of about 3 inches. For best effect, arrange them in drifts — a plant or two here and there will be lost in the spring garden, while plantings of 20 to 50 or more bulbs are stunning. Plants produce offsets freely and also self-sow with enthusiasm: they are ideal for naturalizing and when left undisturbed will form large showy colonies. Propagate by digging and dividing the clumps and/or separating the offsets and seedlings in early summer just as the foliage dies back.

C. forbesii

c. FORBS-ee-eye. GLORY-OF-THE-SNOW. A 4- to 8-inch-tall species producing loose racemes of 4 to 12 flowers in early spring. Individual flowers are blue with white eyes and $1/2$ to $3/4$ inch wide. 'Alba' bears white flowers. 'Pink Giant' produces pink flowers with white centers. **Zones 3 to 9.**

C. luciliae

c. loo-SIL-ee-ee. GLORY-OF-THE-SNOW. A 4- to 6-inch-tall species with racemes of three to six $1/2$- to 1-inch-wide blue flowers with white centers in early spring. **Zones 3 to 9.**

C. nana

c. NAY-nuh. GLORY-OF-THE-SNOW. A 4- to 6-inch-tall species with racemes of two to three $1/4$- to $1/2$-inch-wide blue flowers with white centers in early spring. **Zones 7 to 9.**

C. sardensis

c. sar-DEN-sis. SARDENIAN GLORY-OF-THE-SNOW. A 4- to 6-inch-tall species bearing racemes of 8 to 12 half-inch-wide flowers in early spring. Individual blooms are bluish purple and lack white centers. **Zones 5 to 9.**

Chlidanthus

klih-DAN-thuss. Amaryllis family, Amaryllidaceae.

A single species native to Peru belongs to the genus *Chlidanthus*, a bulb sometimes grown for its fragrant yellow flowers. The botanical name is from the Greek *chlide*, denoting a luxury or costly ornament, and *anthos*, "flower." The lilylike flowers are borne in summer in small clusters of one to four. Individual blooms have a long slender tube at the base and open into six flaring lobes, or petal-like tepals. Plants grow from small tunicate bulbs and produce strap-shaped gray-green leaves that resemble those of daffodils and appear in midsummer either

Chlidanthus fragrans

Choisya ternata

with the flowers or slightly after the flowers open.

HOW TO GROW

Select a site in full sun with moist, well-drained, somewhat sandy soil. In Zones 9 to 11, these plants can be grown outdoors year-round: plant them in spring with about 2 inches of soil over the tops of the bulbs. From Zone 8 north, grow them in pots or plant them outdoors in spring after the last frost date, setting the bulbs with their noses just above the soil surface. Keep the soil barely moist until flowers appear, then water regularly to keep it evenly moist. Pot-grown plants can be kept on a deck or terrace or their pots sunk to the rim in the garden. To overwinter, bring the pots indoors after the first light frost of fall, let them dry out, and store them in a cool (50° to 55°F), dry place over winter. Repot in spring. Or dig bulbs as the foliage dies back in fall and store them in dry peat moss in a cool (50°F), dry spot. Propagate by separating the offsets in spring.

C. fragrans

c. FRAY-grenz. DELICATE LILY, FRAGRANT AMARYLLIS, PERU CHLIDANTHUS. A tender, bulbous perennial bearing lemon-scented, slender-tubed, golden yellow flowers atop 6- to 8-inch-tall stems in summer. Indi-

vidual flowers are 3 inches wide and 4 to 5 inches long. **Zones 9 to 11**.

Choisya

CHOY-zee-uh. Citrus family, Rutaceae.

There are eight or nine species of these evergreen shrubs, which are from canyons and rocky slopes of the southwest United States and Mexico. Only one, called Mexican orange, is commonly cultivated,

both for its attractive foliage and for its long-lasting white clusters of flowers that resemble orange blossoms.

HOW TO GROW

Plant Mexican orange blossom in light but fertile, sharply draining acid soil in full sun. It does best where nights are cool. In hotter areas, give it light shade. It makes a good screen or informal hedge and can be massed or trained against a wall for protection from cold. Make sure that it gets ample air circulation. Prune anytime to reshape; remove old branches to stimulate growth. Propagate from semihard cuttings in summer.

C. ternata

c. ter-NAH-tuh. MEXICAN ORANGE BLOSSOM. This is a compact, moderate grower to 9 feet tall and wide. Glossy, aromatic bright green leaves form fans composed of three leaflets and up to 6 inches across. White 1-inch flowers, which can begin appearing in very early spring and last almost until summer, are in flat-topped clusters at the end of bright green branches. The yellow-green foliage of 5-foot 'Sundance' makes it an outstanding shade plant, although it rarely flowers. **Zones 8 to 10**.

Chrysanthemum

krih-SAN-thuh-mum. Aster family, Asteraceae.

Chrysanthemums bear single, semidouble, or double flower heads made up of dense clusters of tiny flowers, usually called florets. The genus contains about 20 spe-

cies of annuals and perennials. Botanists have reclassified many species once included in *Chrysanthemum*; see the species list at the end of this entry to find them. Until recently, fall mums were classified in the genus *Dendranthema*, but they have been restored to *Chrysanthemum* and are covered here. Whatever they're called, all make rewarding, easily cultivated garden plants.

HOW TO GROW

Choose a site in full sun with average to rich, well-drained soil. Except in areas with cool summers, both of the annual chrysanthemums described here are plants for spring or fall bloom, because they tend to die out when hot weather arrives. Although *C. × morifolium* is a perennial, it is commonly treated as an annual for temporary late-season color.

C. carinatum

c. kar-in-AY-tum. PAINTED DAISY, TRICOLOR CHRYSANTHEMUM. Formerly *C. tricolor*. A fast-growing, well-branched, 2- to 3-foot annual with fernlike leaves and 2½-inch daisylike blooms in shades of red, orange, yellow, maroon, and white. Pull up plants when hot weather arrives. Cool-weather annual.

C. coronarium

c. kor-oh-NAIR-ee-um. CROWN DAISY, GARLAND CHRYSANTHEMUM. A 2½- to 4-foot annual with deeply cut, fernlike leaves. Plants bear yellow, single or double, 1- to 2-inch flowers. The cultivar 'Primrose Gem' bears pale yellow flowers with golden eyes.

Chrysanthemum × morifolium

Chrysanthemum × morifolium

Pull up plants when hot weather arrives. Cool-weather annual.

C. × morifolium

c. × more-ih-FOE-lee-um. MUM, HARDY FALL MUM, GARDEN MUM. Formerly *Dendranthema × grandiflorum*. Clump-forming 1- to 5-foot-tall perennials that spread to 2 feet or more and have lobed, often hairy leaves. They bear late-summer to fall flowers in shades of bronze, purple, yellow, mauve, red, or white. Flower form varies widely and includes single daisies, 1-inch-wide buttons, and enormous doubles that exceed 12 inches in width. All mums start forming flower buds when days begin to shorten in mid- to late July, but cultivars take different amounts of time to come into bloom. Mail-order specialists offer early-, midseason-, and late-blooming cultivars. Early-blooming ones generally bloom in September and are the best choice in areas with very short seasons. Midseason types typically bloom in late September through October; late cultivars after mid-October. Florist mums usually take longer to come into bloom than cultivars grown for garden use and generally don't make good garden plants. Hardiness varies greatly, and depending on the cultivar, fall mums are hardy in **Zones 4 or 5 to 9.**

C. coccineum, see *Tanacetum coccineum*

C. frutescens, see *Argyranthemum frutescens*

C. leucanthemum, see *Leucanthemum vulgare*

C. maximum, see *Leucanthemum × superbum*

C. nipponicum, see *Nipponanthemum nipponicum*

C. pacificum, see *Ajania pacifica*

C. paludosum, see *Leucanthemum paludosum*

C. parthenium, see *Tanacetum parthenium*

C. × superbum, see *Leucanthemum × superbum*

C. weyrichii, see *Dendranthema weyrichii*

Chrysogonum

kry-SOG-oh-num. Aster family, Asteraceae.

A native perennial wildflower, a single species makes up the genus *Chrysogonum*. Found in rich woodlands from Pennsylvania and Ohio south to Florida, it bears starry yellow flowers consisting of five ray florets with yellow "eyes" made up of disk florets. Plants spread moderately by rhizomes and runners, making them excellent ground covers.

HOW TO GROW

Select a site in full sun or partial shade with rich, moist, well-drained soil. Plants also tolerate nearly full shade, although they bloom less. Propagate by dividing clumps in spring or fall, by separating and potting up the runners, or by seeds.

C. virginianum

c. ver-jin-ee-AH-num. GREEN-AND-GOLD, GOLDENSTAR. Creeping 6- to 8-inch-tall perennial with hairy, heart-shaped leaves that spreads to 2 feet. Bears

Chrysogonum virginianum

solitary, star-shaped, 1½-inch-wide yellow flower heads on branched stems from spring to early summer. **Zones 5 to 8.**

Cimicifuga

sim-ih-sih-FEW-guh. Buttercup family, Ranunculaceae.

Commonly known as snakeroots, bugbanes, or black cohosh, *Cimicifuga* species are large perennials native to moist, shady areas in North America, Europe, and Asia. They produce large handsome mounds of compound leaves that are divided two or three times. The tiny flowers lack petals but are borne in graceful, dense, bottlebrush-like wands from midsummer onward. Eighteen species belong to the genus.

HOW TO GROW

Give snakeroots a spot in partial to dappled shade with rich, evenly moist soil. In the North, they will grow in full sun with rich, moist soil, but in southern climates, a spot with consistent soil moisture and shade during the hottest part of the day is essential. Plants are slow to establish and are best left undisturbed once planted. To propagate, divide clumps in fall or in spring. Plants self-sow in a good site.

C. americana

c. ah-mai-rih-KAH-nuh. AMERICAN BUGBANE. An East Coast native that ranges from 2 to 8 feet in height when in bloom and spreads from 2 to 3 feet. Bears 2-foot-long

Cimicifuga racemosa

racemes of creamy white ¼- to ½-inch-long flowers from late summer (midsummer in the South) to fall. **Zones 3 to 8.**

C. racemosa

c. rass-eh-MO-suh. BLACK SNAKEROOT, BLACK COHOSH. A clump-forming, native North American wildflower ranging from 4 to 7 feet tall when in bloom (foliage mounds are about half that height) and spreading from 2 to 4 feet. Bears fluffy, branched racemes of tiny white ¼- to ½-inch-long flowers, which have an unpleasant odor, high above the foliage in midsummer. **Zones 3 to 8.**

C. simplex

c. SIM-plex. KAMCHATKA BUGBANE, AUTUMN SNAKEROOT. A clump-forming perennial that reaches 3 to 4 feet in height and spreads between 2 and 3 feet. Bears arching 3- to 12-inch-long racemes of fragrant ¾-inch-long flowers in fall that are usually unbranched. 'Atropurpurea' bears leaves with a purplish cast. 'Brunette' features brown-purple foliage, purple stems, and 8-inch-long racemes of white flowers with a purple cast. 'White Pearl' bears white flowers on 2- to 3-foot plants. **Zones 4 to 8.**

Cirsium

SIR-see-um. Aster family, Asteraceae.

While the genus *Cirsium* can count pernicious weeds among its 200 species of biennials and perennials — Canada thistle *(C. arvense)* and bull thistle *(C. vulgare)* belong here — it also has at least one species to offer gardeners who love annuals: *C. japonicum.* All members of the genus have spiny, often handsome, leaves and rounded heads of purple, red, pink, yellow, or white flowers that somewhat resemble shaving brushes.

HOW TO GROW

C. japonicum thrives in full sun and poor, average, or rich soil that is moist but well drained. In areas with mild winters, try sowing seeds in late summer to grow it as a biennial. The plants will produce a rosette of leaves in fall and bloom the following year. Elsewhere, sow seeds outdoors about 2 weeks before the last spring frost date. Plants require little care, but deadheading limits their tendency to self-sow. They generally self-sow only in moderation, and unlike weedy thistles, the seedlings are easy to pull up. Use *C. japonicum* in mixed beds, herb gardens, or meadowlike plantings.

C. japonicum

c. juh-PON-ih-kum. PLUMED THISTLE. A 3- to 6-foot biennial or short-lived perennial with deeply cut, thistlelike leaves that are soft to the touch, not spiny. Bears rounded, brushlike, rose pink to lilac-pink flower heads in late summer and fall. Cool-weather annual.

Cistus

SIS-tus. Rock-rose family, Cistaceae.

This genus of about 20 generally low-growing evergreen shrubs from the Mediterranean region has yielded many garden species, appreciated for their spring flowers and tolerance to drought and other adverse conditions. Silky, saucer-shaped flowers with four or five petals may be solitary or bloom in flat-topped clusters, most often white or pink, with bright yellow stamens and sometimes a spot of another color at the base.

HOW TO GROW

Rock roses thrive in moderately alkaline soil of poor to average fertility and a structure that is loose and quickly draining. Most can grow in rocky soil and in salt spray and wind but will react adversely to humidity. They do exceptionally well in the West where summers are dry and winters are relatively warm. These are good fire-retardant plants for high-risk areas, and they also help control erosion when planted on slopes. The informal white or pink flowers are generous in their display, making this an excellent choice for sites near driveways and houses, especially when the plant's fire-retardant qualities are considered. Be prepared to water deeply to establish the plants. Thereafter, they are highly drought resistant and also adapt to desert and coastal situations with saline soils. Cistus can become leggy, so tip-prune frequently, shear lightly, or periodically remove a few older branches. Propagate from seeds or take cuttings in summer.

C. × corbariensis

c. × cor-bah-ree-EN-siss. WHITE ROCK ROSE. Also listed as *C. × hybridus*). Spreading or rounded hybrid, averaging 4 feet high and wide, with fragrant, 2-inch, gray-green wavy leaves. The profuse 1¹/₂-inch late-spring flowers, which open from red buds, are white with yellow centers. **Zones 8 to 10.**

C. ladanifer

c. lah-DAN-if-er. LAUDANUM. Upright species, to 5 feet high and wide, with sticky, aromatic, blue-green leaves to 4 inches long. In early to midsummer it bears white flowers up to 4 inches across, often with a dark red blotch at the base of each petal, on the end of sideshoots. **Zones 8 to 10.**

C. × purpureus

c. × pur-PUR-ee-us. ORCHID ROCK ROSE. A hybrid growing usually 3 feet tall and wide with

Cladrastis kentukea

Cirsium japonicum

Cistus × purpureus

Cistus ladanifer

upright shoots. Cymes of three 3-inch dark pink flowers with a maroon base bloom in summer. **Zones 8 to 10**.

C. salviifolius

sal-vih-FOE-lee-us. SAGE-LEAF ROCK ROSE. This low shrub, 1 to 2 feet tall and up to 6 feet across, has white flowers with yellow markings at the base. Leaves are fuzzy gray-green and about 1 inch long. It makes a very effective ground cover. **Zones 8 to 10**.

C. × skanbergii

c. × skan-BERG-ee-eye. Growing 2 to 3 feet tall but up to 8 feet wide, this hybrid has gray-green lance-shaped leaves. The powder pink 1-inch late-spring flowers bloom in terminal cymes. **Zones 8 to 10**.

Cladrastis

klad-RAS-tis. Pea family, Fabaceae.

A member of the vast pea family, this genus contains only five species native to Asia and North America. Flowers are two lipped and grow in clusters, leaves are pinnately compound, and fruits are flattened seedpods. The native species is almost extinct in the wild, due partly to overlogging, and is gaining popularity as a landscape tree.

HOW TO GROW

Plant in full sun and deep, fertile, well-drained, acid to alkaline soil. Drought tolerant once established, but protect from wind to avoid storm damage. Trees may develop weak branch angles; prune when young to create a strong shape and cable older trees if necessary. Prune in summer to avoid sap bleeding. Usually pest-free, but verticillium wilt and leafhoppers are occasional problems.

C. kentukea

c. ken-TUCK-ee-ay. YELLOW-WOOD. Also listed as *C. lutea*. This round-headed, open-branched native grows 30 to 50 feet tall and may spread even wider. Fragrant 1-inch white flowers in 8- to 14-inch-long wisteria-like clusters decorate the tree in early summer. Foot-long leaves are bright light green and divided pinnately into 7 to 11 leaflets. Fall color is a pleasing soft yellow or apricot. Four-inch-long seedpods ripen in autumn. Trunk bark is smooth and silvery gray, resembling that of a beech tree. When

Clarkia unguiculata

cut, the wood reveals a yellow heart. Tall enough to cast shade and beautiful in flower and foliage, this tree belongs in more landscapes as a lawn or garden specimen. Yellowwood is slow growing and may not bloom until it is 10 or more years old. It often blooms well only in alternate years. From southeastern North America. **Zones 4 to 8**.

CULTIVARS

'Rosea' ('Perkin's Pink') has enchanting, pale rose pink flowers. 'Sweetshade' grows vigorously, has larger flowers and better yellow fall color, and resists leafhoppers.

Clarkia

KLARK-ee-ah. Evening-primrose family, Onagraceae.

Known by an array of common names — including godetia, farewell-to-spring, Rocky Mountain garland, red ribbons, and fairy fans — *Clarkia* species are native to western North America and South America. Formerly known as *Godetia*, the genus *Clarkia* was named for Captain William Clark, of the Lewis and Clark Expedition, and contains 36 species of annuals with slender stems and oval, linear, or elliptic leaves. They are grown for their clusters of funnel-shaped flowers, which have a satiny or crepe-paper texture. Flowers have four petals, but double-flowered forms are also available.

HOW TO GROW

A site with full sun and average, moist, but well-drained soil is ideal. Too-rich soil yields plants with plenty of foliage but few flowers. These plants resent heat and humidity, but a site with light shade, especially in the afternoon, may help them cope in areas with warm summers. In most areas, sow seeds outdoors on or before the last spring frost date. Sow a few weeks before the last frost date in areas with warm summers. From Zone 8 south, sow seeds in fall for late-winter bloom. To lengthen the bloom season, sow new crops of seeds at 2-week intervals until late spring. Or sow indoors 6 to 8 weeks before the last frost in individual pots, and transplant with care. When sowing, just press the seeds into the soil surface, as light is required for germination. Stake with twiggy brush. Use these plants in mixed plantings and combined with other spring-blooming annuals. They make excellent cut flowers and also can be grown in containers.

C. amoena

c. am-oh-EE-nuh. FAREWELL-TO-SPRING, SATIN FLOWER. Formerly *Godetia amoena*. A 2- to 2$^{1}/_{2}$-foot plant with lance-shaped leaves. Clusters of single or double, 2-inch-wide flowers in shades of lavender to lavender- and rose pink in summer. Cool-weather annual.

C. unguiculata

c. un-guih-kew-LAY-tuh. FAREWELL-TO-SPRING. Formerly *C. elegans*. A 1- to 3-foot annual with lance-shaped, elliptic, or ovate leaves. Solitary $^{1}/_{2}$- to 2-inch-wide, single or double flowers in shades from lavender- to rose pink or salmon pink as well as red, red-purple, and white in summer. Cool-weather annual.

Clarkia amoena

Clematis

KLEM-ah-tiss, klem-AT-iss.
Buttercup family,
Ranunculaceae.

The showy blooms of hybrid clematis are a common sight in gardens across the country, but few gardeners appreciate the true diversity and versatility of this genus of prized ornamentals. There are more than 200 species of clematis and literally hundreds of hybrids. By far the best known are the summer-blooming hybrids that bear spectacular single, semidouble, or double blooms ranging from 4 to 8 inches across. There also are clematis with bell- and tulip-shaped flowers, plus species and cultivars with four-petaled dogwoodlike or small starry blooms. These have smaller flowers than the hybrids — between ³/4 inch and 2 inches — but they more than make up the difference in the sheer number of flowers produced. In addition to summer-blooming clematis, there also are spring- and fall-blooming types, as well as selections that rebloom and thus contribute color during two seasons.

All clematis bear flowers that lack true petals — the showy "petals" actually are petal-like sepals. Flowers come in violet, purple-blue, pink, crimson, mauve, white, and even yellow. Many feature a boss of showy anthers in the center of the flower. Blooms are carried singly or in panicles or cymes. The flowers are followed by feathery, silvery seed heads that often are quite ornamental in their own right. Leaves are either undivided or pinnately divided.

Plant size, vigor, and habit also vary. Most large-flowered hybrids range from 6 to 12 feet in height, but some species routinely exceed 20 or even 40 feet. And while the best-known clematis are woody or semi-woody vines, this genus also contains a few herbaceous perennials.

HOW TO GROW

Select a site in full sun or partial shade with well-drained, slightly acid to alkaline soil. Clematis will grow in heavy clay soil; work it deeply and amend with plenty of organic matter at planting time. Ideally, plant clematis in a spot where plants can have their "heads in the sun and feet in the shade." Clematis prefer cool soil conditions (they struggle if soil temperatures exceed about 80°F in sum-

Clematis integrifolia

mer) and the tops bloom best in full sun to partial shade. A spot with dappled to partial shade, particularly during the hottest part of the day, is ideal. Afternoon shade is essential for good performance in areas with hot summers. Large-flowered hybrids especially do not tolerate hot, dry summers well, and shade helps them cope. To give clematis cool soil conditions, look for a spot where the roots will be shaded by low-growing shrubs or perennials that aren't too aggressive, or a spot on the north, or shaded, side of shrubs or even a low wall. Mulch to keep the root run cool, but do not allow mulch to touch the stems, as it leads to rot. Water deeply during dry weather. Feed plants annually in spring by top dressing with well-rotted manure or a balanced organic fertilizer. Once established in a suitable site, clematis are long-lived and easy to grow. Propagate clematis by layering in early spring or by cuttings taken from new shoots at the base of the plant in spring.

Clematis require a trellis or other support. The vines climb by attaching themselves to supports using twining leafstalks. They cannot attach themselves to bare fences or walls or wrap around large supports. Instead, they need strings, lattice, or small supports to cling to. Tie them to trellises with yarn or soft string to get them started. Install trellises or other supports before planting, because it's easy to damage the vines. To train clematis over a tree or shrub, plant it away from the main roots of the woody plant to minimize competition. If the site

is along a wall or building, plant out from the foundation.

PRUNING

Clematis are divided into three general groups by bloom season: early blooming clematis, early large-flowered hybrids, and late-flowering clematis. The bloom-season group a particular species or hybrid is classified in also determines how that plant should be pruned. Clematis hybrids are often the result of complex crosses. Depending on its origin, a particular hybrid may bloom on old wood, meaning the previous season's growth, or on new wood, meaning growth produced during the current season. To determine how to prune an unidentified clematis, watch it closely for a season to see when it blooms and whether the buds are produced on old or new wood. Then prune according to the category that it fits most closely. In northern zones, where

Clematis 'Henryii'

clematis may be killed to the ground each winter, pruning is a moot point: don't grow early-blooming clematis, which bloom only on old wood, and simply remove deadwood in late winter or early spring each year.

Early-blooming Clematis. These bloom on old wood in early spring to early summer, and typically bear flowers that are single or bell-shaped. Prune them immediately after flowering by removing dead or damaged growth and cutting back shoots to shape the plants and keep them in bounds. Plants in this group do not need annual pruning to bloom well.

Early Large-flowered Hybrids. This group consists primarily of large-flowered hybrid clematis, and in terms of bloom time overlaps plants in the early-blooming group. Early large-flowered hybrids bloom from late spring into early summer and also often rebloom in mid- to late summer. The first flush of flowers are produced on old wood; hybrids that rebloom produce a second flush on new wood at the tips of the current year's growth. Some cultivars produce double flowers on the old wood and single flowers on new wood. Plants in this group generally do not need heavy annual pruning to bloom well — just a spring shape-up. In spring before growth begins, prune out all dead or damaged growth. Then cut stems back to a strong set of buds. These plants can also be cut back fairly hard — from 2 to 4 feet above the ground — and they will produce a single flush of growth later in the season on new wood.

Clematis 'Carnaby'

Late-flowering Clematis. This group includes large-flowered hybrids that bloom from summer to early fall, as well as several species that bloom at the same time. Prune them hard annually in early spring, before growth begins, by cutting them down to just above a healthy pair of buds 8 to 12 inches above the ground. Prune herbaceous clematis, such as *C. integrifolia*, in this manner as well; these are perennials, not vines.

C. alpina

c. al-PIE-nah. ALPINE CLEMATIS. Early-blooming clematis. A handsome vine that reaches 10 feet and bears 1- to 3-inch-wide, bell-shaped, blue-and-white blooms in spring and early summer. Flowers are followed by ornamental silky seed heads. Plants may rebloom in summer or fall. Cultivars include 'Helsingborg', with deep blue-purple sepals; 'Pamela Jackson', with deep blue sepals surrounded by a cluster of cream anthers; and 'Willy', with pale pink flowers. Zones 4 to 9.

EARLY LARGE-FLOWERED HYBRIDS

These hybrids range from about 8 to 10 feet in height and bloom from late spring into early summer. They also commonly rebloom in mid- to late summer. Flowers usually are 4 to 5 inches across. Cultivars in this group include 'Barbara Jackman', single mauve-blue; 'Bee's Jubilee', single pale pink flowers with a dark pink stripe down the center of each sepal; 'Belle of Woking', double white; 'Elsa Späth', single purple-blue; 'General Sikorski', single deep purple-blue; 'Henryii', single white; 'Nelly Moser', single, mauve pink; 'Niobe', single red; and 'The President', single deep purple. Most are hardy in Zones 3 or 4 to 8, but some cultivars are less hardy than others. Summer heat is a problem in Zone 9.

C. florida

c. FLOR-ih-duh. EARLY LARGE-FLOWERED HYBRID GROUP. A deciduous or semievergreen species bearing creamy white, 5 1/2-inch-wide flowers in summer. 'Sieboldii' bears white flowers with showy purple anthers. Zones 5 or 6 to 9.

C. heracleifolia

c. her-ah-klee-ih-FOE-lee-uh. TUBE CLEMATIS. Herbaceous Clematis. Sprawling, woody-based perennial or subshrub with toothed, deeply lobed leaves that reaches 2 to 3 feet and spreads to about 3 feet. Bears clusters of tubular, 1 1/4-inch-long pale blue flowers in summer. *C. heracleifolia* var. *davidiana* bears fragrant violet-blue flowers and is more upright than the species. Zones 3 to 8.

C. integrifolia

c. in-teh-grih-FOE-lee-uh. HERBACEOUS CLEMATIS. Mounding, 2-foot-tall perennial that spreads as far. Bears simple, lance-shaped leaves and bell-shaped, 2-inch-long, blue-violet flowers over a long period in summer. Zones 3 to 7.

LATE-FLOWERING HYBRIDS

This group of hybrids, which makes up the bulk of the late-flowering Clematis group, bloom from summer to early fall. Plants range from 6 to about 12 feet and flowers are 4 to 5 inches wide. Cultivars in this group include 'Comtesse de Bouchaud', mauve pink; 'Erest Markham', magenta;

Clematis 'Jackmanii'

Clematis 'Jackmanii'

'Gipsy Queen', violet purple with red anthers; 'Hagley Hybrid', mauve-pink; 'Jackmanii', dark purple'; 'Lady Betty Balfour', purple; 'Polish Spirit', purple-blue; and 'Ville de Lyon', red. Zones 4 or 5 to 9, depending on the cultivar.

C. macropetala

c. mack-roe-PEH-ta-lah. EARLY-BLOOMING CLEMATIS. A vine that reaches 10 feet and bears 3- to 4-inch-wide, lavender- to violet-blue, bell-shaped flowers from spring to early summer. Plants may rebloom in summer or fall. Cultivars include 'Blue Bird', with nodding, mauve-blue flowers; 'Markham's Pink', with clear pink blooms; and 'Rosy O'Grady', with mauve pink blooms. Zones 4 to 9.

C. montana

c. mon-TAN-nuh. EARLY-BLOOMING CLEMATIS. A vigorous, 15- to 45-foot-tall vine bearing an abundance of single, white, 2-inch-wide flowers that resemble dogwood blooms in late spring and early summer. *C. montana* f. *grandiflora* is an exceptionally vigorous selection with 3- to 4-inch-wide white flowers. *C. montana* var. *rubens* produces pink flowers. Cultivars include white-flowered 'Alba'; 'Elizabeth', with fragrant pale pink blooms; 'Mayleen', with 3-inch pink flowers; and 'Tetrarose', which reaches only about 15 feet and boasts pink flowers with yellow anthers. Zones 5 to 9.

C. orientalis

c. or-ee-en-TAL-iss. ORIENTAL CLEMATIS. Late-flowering clematis. A 15- to 20-foot species bearing small, 3-inch-wide, flowers that are bell shaped and yellow from late summer to late fall. Flowers are followed by handsome fluffy seed heads. 'Bill MacKenzie' is most popular. Zones 5 or 6 to 9.

C. recta

c. RECK-tuh. GROUND CLEMATIS. Herbaceous clematis. Clump-forming perennial with compound gray-green leaves. Plants can reach

3 to 6 feet if supported but also can be allowed to sprawl. Bears dense clusters of fragrant, starry, $^3/_4$-inch-wide white flowers summer and fall. The young foliage of 'Purpurea' is reddish purple. **Zones 3 to 7.**

C. spooneri

c. SPOO-ner-eye. Early large-flowered hybrid. A vigorous, 20- to 25-foot vine that bears clusters of 3-inch-wide white flowers with yellow anthers in late spring. 'Rosea' bears pink flowers. **Zones 6 to 9.**

C. terniflora

c. ter-nih-FLOR-ah. SWEET AUTUMN CLEMATIS. Late-flowering clematis. Formerly *C. maximowicziana* and *C. paniculata*. A vigorous to rampant vine that easily climbs from 15 to 20 feet or more. Bears an abundance of star-shaped, white, 3/4- to 1-inch-wide flowers in fall. Flowers are followed by attractive seed heads. Self-sows abundantly. **Zones 4 to 9.**

C. texensis

c. tex-EN-sis. TEXAS CLEMATIS. Late-flowering clematis. This species, native to the Southwest, ranges from 6 to 15 feet. Plants bear bell-shaped, red to red-orange flowers in summer. **Zones 3 to 9.**

C. viticella

c. vih-tih-KEL-luh. ITALIAN CLEMATIS. Late-flowering clematis. A 6- to 12-foot-tall species with bell-shaped, 1$^1/_2$-inch-wide flowers from midsummer to fall in purple-blue or rose-red. Cultivars include 'Betty Corning', pale lilac; and 'Etoile Violette', violet purple. Both are probably of hybrid origin. **Zones 5 to 9.**

Cleome

klee-OH-me. Caper family, Capparidaceae.

The genus *Cleome* includes approximately 150 species of annuals and shrubs distributed in tropical and subtropical regions throughout the world. Most bear palmate leaves with three to seven leaflets, and all have four-petaled asymmetrical flowers that have a spidery appearance, thus the common name "spider flower." Blooms come in pinkish purple, pink, white, or yellowish to greenish and are carried in erect racemes that

Cleome hassleriana

elongate as new flowers open throughout the summer. One species is a popular annual that adds height and airy color to mixed borders. It attracts hummingbirds and butterflies and also makes a stunning cut flower.

HOW TO GROW
A site in full sun with light, rich, well-drained soil is ideal. Sow seeds indoors 6 to 8 weeks before the last spring frost date and germinate at about 65°F. After seedlings emerge, grow them at 70° to 75°F. Some gardeners sow the seeds and then refrigerate the pots for 2 weeks before moving them to a warmer spot. Or sow outdoors after the last frost date, once nighttime temperatures remain above 40°F. Although established plants tolerate dry soil, for best results water regularly during dry weather. Plants self-sow, and seedlings can become a nuisance in warm climates. Deadheading is a tedious task, but it will curtail this tendency.

C. hassleriana

c. hass-ler-AH-nah. SPIDER FLOWER. Sometimes listed as *C. spinosa* or *C. pungens*. A strong-scented annual with palmate leaves that ranges from 3 to 5 or more feet tall. Pink, purple, or white, 1$^1/_4$-inch-wide flowers are carried in large racemes in summer. Several cultivars selected for

color are available, including Queen Series cultivars and white-flowered 'Helen Campbell'. Warm-weather annual.

Clerodendrum

klee-roe-DEN-drum. Verbena family, Verbenaceae.

From this large genus — some 400 trees, shrubs, and vines from tropical and subtropical Asia and Africa — a few are known as houseplants. The two shrub species listed here, called glory bowers, are admired by collectors of unusual plants for their fragrant tubular flowers.

HOW TO GROW
Glory bowers require rich, loamy, moisture-retentive soil in full sun

to partial shade. They also require supplemental water in drought. Shrubs need only minimal pruning except for *C. bungei*, which should be pruned back to near the ground in spring and pinched throughout the season. Start from seeds in spring; propagate from suckers or root cuttings in winter.

C. bungei

c. BUN-gee-eye. GLORY BOWER. This evergreen grows quickly to 6 feet high, spreading by suckers. Hard annual pruning will keep it to a compact 3 to 4 feet. Broad-oval, toothed leaves are 8 to 12 inches long, ringed with purple when young, red-brown and fuzzy underneath, and unpleasantly musky if crushed. The sweet-scented dark pink flowers, tubular with five flaring lobes, bloom from late summer to fall in rounded terminal panicles 6 to 8 inches across. **Zones 8 to 10.**

C. trichotomum

c. try-KOH-toe-mum. HARLEQUIN GLORY BOWER. A deciduous suckering multistemmed shrub or tree 10 to 15 feet tall with oval 5-inch leaves that are soft and hairy. The fragrant white flowers, blooming in clusters up to 8 inches across, are set off by $^1/_2$-inch red calyxes that persist with shiny blue-green fruits. This species can freeze to its base and recover. *C. triochotomum* var. *fargesii*, which may be hardier, is smaller and has green calyxes that turn pink. **Zones 7 to 10.**

Clethra

KLETH-ruh. Summersweet family, Clethraceae.

About a half dozen of this genus's 60 deciduous and evergreen trees and shrubs, native to East Asia and eastern North America, are grown

Clerodendrum bungei

Clethra alnifolia

in gardens for their fragrant racemes of tiny white to pink late-summer flowers.

HOW TO GROW

Clethra takes about anything but alkaline soil — sun or shade, loam or sand, wet conditions or moderate drought. Full sun will produce more flowering. Use clethras in mixed borders, woodland gardens, or masses, or near patios and porches where you can enjoy their pleasant scent. Pruning is unnecessary unless you want to cut back older shoots or remove suckers to control spread. The small seeds may turn black before they are ripe, about midfall, but when ready they germinate readily. Softwood cuttings root easily; hormone treatment may make them more vigorous.

C. acuminata

c. ah-kew-mih-NAY-tuh. CINNAMON CLETHRA. Native from West Virginia to Alabama, it grows lankier than *C. alnifolia* to 12 feet tall and wide, and has leaves to 6 inches long. Terminal racemes 3 to 8 inches long bloom earlier in summer. The cinnamon brown bark may be smooth or exfoliating. Give this species full sun if at all possible. Prune away its lower branches and suckers, or prune it back severely in spring to keep flowers at eye and nose level.
Zones 5 to 8.

C. alnifolia

c. al-nih-FOE-lee-uh. SUMMERSWEET. An upright deciduous eastern U.S. native, to 8 feet tall and wide, with 4-inch oval leaves that sometimes turn yellow in fall. In late summer or early autumn it produces sweetly scented $^1/_2$-inch flowers in upright, 4- to 6-inch racemes. The species is sometimes called sweet pepperbush for the persistent fruit capsules that resemble a string of peppercorns. 'Hummingbird' grows to only 4 feet but flowers heavily. That cultivar received an award from the Pennsylvania Horticultural Society, as did 'Ruby Spice', which has pink flowers that retain their

Clethra alnifolia

color. The pink blooms of 'Rosea' fade to white, while those of 'Fern Valley Pink' are especially fragrant.
Zones 4 to 9.

C. barbinervis

c. bar-bih-NER-viss. JAPANESE CLETHRA. This unusual deciduous Asian species can grow 20 feet tall and wide and has a candelabra-like habit. Leaves, arranged in whorls at the end of branches, can turn red, maroon, and yellow in fall. In late summer, the long dangling flower clusters are slightly arched. Smooth, exfoliating cinnamon-colored bark keeps things interesting in the winter. **Zones 6 to 8**.

Clianthus

klee-AN-thus. Pea family, Fabaceae.

Two tender species, commonly referred to as glory peas, belong to this genus. One, an annual or

Clianthus formosus

short-lived perennial, is native to Australia, while the other, a shrub, to New Zealand. Both are climbing or trailing plants with pinnate leaves with 15 or more leaflets and clusters of extremely showy flowers that have been described as resembling lobsters' claws or parrots' beaks. The pea-like flowers have upturned standards, or petals, and long, curved keels (also petals) that point downward. The botanical name *Clianthus* is from the Greek *kleios*, meaning "glory," and *anthos*, "flower."

HOW TO GROW

Full sun and a warm spot with light, sandy, very well drained soil are essential. Sow seeds indoors and germinate at 55° to 65°F. Grow plants on the dry side: this is especially important with *C. formosus*, which resents overwatering. (Seedlings of this species are commonly grafted onto *Colutea arborescens* rootstocks, because plants grafted in this manner are less susceptible to overwatering.) *Clianthus puniceus*, a tender shrub hardy from about **Zone 7 south**, can be grown from cuttings taken in

summer. In areas where it is marginally hardy, try a site against a south-facing wall for extra winter protection, make sure the soil drains perfectly, and protect plants with loose mulch over winter. Plants killed to the ground will resprout in spring as long as the roots survive. In the North, grow them in containers and overwinter them indoors in a bright, 40° to 45°F spot.

C. formosus

c. for-MOE-sus. GLORY PEA, DESERT PEA. An annual or short-lived perennial that can reach 4 feet on a trellis or other support. Clusters of showy, 2- to 3-inch crimson blooms with purple-black centers appear in summer. Warm-weather annual.

C. puniceus

c. pew-NEE-see-us. PARROT'S BILL, PARROT'S BEAK. A tender shrub that can reach 6 feet. Bears clusters of 3-inch-long red flowers from spring to early summer. Tender perennial.

Clivia

KLIH-vee-uh, KLY-vee-uh. Amaryllis family, Amaryllidaceae.

Clivias are tender perennials from South Africa that have swollen, bulblike bases and fleshy roots. Plants bear handsome, evergreen, generally strap-shaped leaves and showy, tubular to trumpet-shaped flowers. Individual flowers, which are carried in umbels atop thick, leafless stalks, have a short tube at the base and six spreading lobes, or petal-like tepals. They come in shades from orange-red to nearly scarlet as well as yellow and are followed by clusters of round,

Clivia miniata

shiny red berries. Clivias are hardy in only the warmest climates, but they make outstanding plants for large containers and tubs and also are easy-to-grow houseplants.

HOW TO GROW

Give clivias a site in partial shade with rich, well-drained soil. Where they are not hardy, grow them in tubs or large containers. For best results divide the clumps only when the plants show signs of overcrowding. (With time, the fleshy roots will fill up the containers, leaving little room for soil.) Root-bound plants tend to bloom best. Like many South African species, clivias need regular watering from late winter or early spring through summer when they are growing actively and drier conditions when dormant in winter. Gradually dry them off in late summer and fall, and overwinter pot-grown plants in a cool (45° to 50°F), sunny, well-ventilated room or greenhouse. Keep the soil barely moist until growth resumes in late winter or spring. Plants that do not receive a cool, dry dormancy may still flower, but the flower stalks generally fail to elongate, and the blooms are borne down in between the leaves. Propagate by dividing the clumps and potting up the offsets in late winter or early spring. Or sow seeds.

C. miniata

c. min-ee-AH-tuh. A tender, evergreen perennial with arching dark green 2-inch-wide leaves that reach 1½ to 2½ feet in length. Bears clusters of 10 to 20 trumpet-shaped, 2- to 3-inch-long orange, red-orange, or yellow flowers in spring and early summer. Plants

Cobaea scandens

are about 1½ feet tall, with flower clusters extending above the leaves. 'Aurea' ('Citrina') bears yellow flowers. **Zones 10 to 11**.

Cobaea

KOE-bee-ah. Phlox family, Polemoniaceae.

Native from Mexico to South America, the 20 species of *Cobaea* are tender, woody or herbaceous climbers. They have pinnate leaves and produce showy, bell-shaped flowers with five lobes.

HOW TO GROW

A site in full sun with average soil is ideal. Plants require a trellis or other support to climb and need regular watering throughout the growing season. In areas with hot summers, a spot with afternoon shade is best. Sow seeds indoors 8 to 10 weeks before the last spring frost date. (From Zone 9 south, it is possible to sow seeds outdoors where the plants are to grow.) To minimize problems with rot, use a sterile seed-starting mix and set the seeds long edge down, with the upper edge right at the soil surface. Seeds take from 10 to 30 days to germinate at temperatures of 60° to 70°F. Move plants to the garden after the last frost, when temperatures remain above 40°. Pinch seedlings to encourage branching. You can also propagate plants by taking cuttings in summer for overwintering indoors.

C. scandens

c. SCAN-denz. CUP-AND-SAU-CER VINE, CATHEDRAL BELLS. A vigorous tendril climber that can reach 40 feet or

Coix lacryma-jobi

more where hardy (**Zone 10 south**) but is considerably shorter in the North. Bears pinnate leaves with four leaflets and fragrant, 2-inch-long, bell-shaped flowers, each with a ruffled green cup (the calyx) at its base. Flowers open greenish white and age to purple. 'Alba' bears flowers that stay greenish white. Tender perennial, or grow as warm-weather annual.

Coix

KOY-ex. Grass family, Poaceae.

Coix contains five or six species of annuals and perennials native to tropical Asia. All are tall grasses with narrow, lance-shaped leaves that produce separate clusters of male and female flowers. The female flower clusters are decorated with hard, hollow, teardrop-shaped "beads" or "tears," which are actually modified leaf sheaths called utricles that protect the female flowers and seeds. The utricles are used to make necklaces, rosaries, and other decorations.

HOW TO GROW

A site with full sun or light shade and rich, well-drained soil is ideal. Sow seeds indoors 6 to 8 weeks before the last frost. Soak seeds overnight in warm water before sowing, and sow in individual pots. Germination takes 2 to 4 weeks at 60° to 70°F. Transplant after the last spring frost date, once temperatures remain above 45° or 50°F. In areas with long growing seasons, from Zone 8 or 9 south, try sowing seeds outdoors where the

plants are to grow. Water during dry weather. Plants self-sow.

C. lacryma-jobi

c. lah-KRY-mah-JOE-bee. JOB'S TEARS. A 1½- to 3-foot annual with 2-foot-long leaves and jointed stems. Male and female flowers appear in fall. The "tears" on the female spikes are initially green and ripen into hard, shiny, oval to teardrop-shaped, ½-inch-long beads in shades of creamy white, gray, and purple. Warm-weather annual.

Colchicum

KOL-chih-kum. Lily family, Liliaceae.

Commonly known as colchicums or autumn crocuses, *Colchicum* species are grown for their crocuslike flowers that grace the garden in fall. About 45 species belong to the genus, all of which are perennials that grow from corms. Most, but not all, autumn crocuses (or colchicums) bloom from early to late fall and produce lush clumps of basal leaves in spring. The leaves range from strap or lance shaped to rounded and often are pleated or ribbed. The funnel- or goblet-shaped flowers consist of six petal-like tepals. Despite their crocuslike appearance, *Colchicum* species are not closely related to the true crocuses (*Crocus*), which belong in the iris family. *Colchicum* species have six stamens (the male part of the flower), three styles and stigmas (female parts of the flower), and an ovary that is above where the petals are attached. *Crocus* species, on the other hand, have three stamens, one style with three stigmas, and an ovary that is borne beneath where the petals are attached. True crocuses also bear grassy leaves.

HOW TO GROW
For all the species listed here, select a site in full sun or light shade with average, deeply prepared, well-drained soil. Plant the corms in late summer or fall, as early as you can obtain them. Set them with no more than 2 to 3 inches of soil over the tops of the corms. (Have the soil already prepared, and work in plenty of organic matter such as compost, so you can plant as soon as the corms arrive; the corms can bloom even before they are planted.) Space corms 6 to 9 inches apart to accommodate their large leaves. When selecting a site, keep in mind that the large lush clumps of spring foliage these plants produce are quite unattractive when they begin to turn yellow and go dormant in early summer. For this reason, autumn crocuses are best used at the front of informal perennial plantings, mixed borders, shrub borders, and natural areas rather than in neat, formal plantings. Combining them with low perennials or ground covers also helps provide support for the flowers, which tend to flop over. Where happy, autumn crocuses

Colchicum 'Violet Queen'

produce an abundance of offsets and form handsome drifts with time. Divide the clumps every few years when they become crowded. Propagate by separating offsets in summer, just as the foliage dies back, or by seeds.

C. agrippinum
c. ah-grih-PYE-num. A 3- to 4-inch-tall species with clumps of narrow to strap-shaped 6-inch-long leaves. In early fall corms bear one or two funnel-shaped, 2-inch-long, purplish pink flowers checkered with darker pink. **Zones 4 to 8**.

C. autumnale
c. aw-tum-NAL-ee. AUTUMN CROCUS, MEADOW SAFFRON. A 4- to 6-inch-tall species with lance-shaped leaves that can reach 12 to 14 inches in length. In midfall, corms bear one to six pale lavender-pink, 1¹/₂- to 2¹/₂-inch-long flowers. Several cultivars are available, including 'Alboplenum', with double white flowers; 'Album', a single white; and 'Pleniflorum' (also listed as 'Roseum Plenum' and 'Plenum'), with large, double, 2- to 3-inch-long rose-pink flowers. **Zones 4 to 8**.

C. bornmuelleri
c. born-MULE-er-eye. A 4- to 5-inch-tall species with narrowly oval 6- to 10-inch-long leaves. In midfall, corms bear one to six fragrant, funnel-shaped 2- to 3-inch-long blooms that are rose-purple with purplish brown anthers. **Zones 4 to 8**.

C. byzantinum
c. bih-zan-TYE-num. A 4- to 6-inch-tall species with ribbed, rounded to lance-shaped leaves that reach 1 foot in length. In early to midfall, corms bear numerous (up to about 20) 2-inch-long, funnel-shaped, pale pink or lilac-pink flowers. **Zones 4 to 8**.

C. cilicicum
c. sih-LIH-sih-kum. A 4- to 6-inch-tall species with rounded to lance-shaped, 1- to 1¹/₂-foot-long leaves. In fall, each corm produces from 3 or 4 to as many as 25 funnel-shaped, 2- to 3-inch-long rose-purple flowers. **Zones 4 to 8**.

C. hybrids
A variety of showy-flowered hybrids ranging from 5 to 10 inches tall or more have been developed. All produce leaves that can reach 10 inches in length. 'The Giant' is a free-flowering selection that produces 3-inch-long goblet-shaped rose-lilac blooms in early to midfall. 'Lilac Wonder' bears rose-purple 2-inch-long goblet-shaped flowers. 'Violet Queen' bears fragrant, funnel-shaped, 2- to 2¹/₂-inch long violet purple blooms in early fall. 'Waterlily' produces double pinkish lilac blooms with 2- to 3-inch tepals. **Zones 4 to 8**.

C. speciosum
c. spee-see-OH-sum. AUTUMN CROCUS. A 5- to 7-inch-tall species with 7- to 10-inch-long rounded to somewhat lance-shaped leaves. In fall, corms bear one to three 2- to 3-inch-long reddish violet tuliplike blooms with yellow anthers. **Zones 4 to 8**.

Collinsia
kol-LIN-see-ah. Figwort family, Scrophulariaceae.

Most of the 25 species of *Collinsia* are native to the western United States. These relatives of snapdragons (*Antirrhinum*) and foxgloves (*Digitalis*) have ovate to oblong leaves and two-lipped flowers with five lobes, two on the top lip, three on the bottom one. Flowers, which are commonly bicolored, come in

Colchicum speciosum

Collinsia bicolor

C (margin tab)

Colocasia esculenta 'Illustris'

shades of pink, white, blue, lavender-blue, or pinkish purple and are borne in whorls or singly.

HOW TO GROW

Partial shade, especially during the heat of the day, and rich, moist, well-drained soil are best. The plants do not do well in areas with hot, humid summers. Sow seeds outdoors a few weeks before the last spring frost date, when light frost is still possible. Make repeated sowings at 2-week intervals to prolong bloom season. *C. verna* is best in light shade; sow it in fall for spring bloom. Plants tend to sprawl; stake with twiggy brush if you want them to stay more erect. Water during dry weather to prolong bloom. Use *Collinsia* species in mixed plantings and wildflower gardens. They also make excellent cut flowers.

C. bicolor

c. BI-kuh-lor. CHINESE HOUSES. Formerly *C. heterophylla*. A weak-stemmed, 2-foot annual carrying clusters of flowers with white upper lips and rose-purple lower ones. Cool-weather annual.

C. verna

c. VER-nah. BLUE-EYED MARY. A ¹/₂- to 2-foot annual native to rich woods in the East and Upper Midwest. Bears clustered or solitary ¹/₂-inch-long flowers with white upper lips and blue lower ones. Cool-weather annual.

Colocasia

kol-oh-KAYE-see-uh. Arum family, Araceae.

Native to tropical Asia, the six species of *Colocasia* are tender perennials with thick, tuberous roots and large, generally shield- or arrow-shaped leaves. Flowers consist of a spathe and spadix, much like jack-in-the-pulpits (*Arisaema*) and calla lilies (*Zantedeschia*), both close relatives. However, in cultivation these plants seldom bloom, and the one species found in gardens is grown for its huge ornamental leaves. All parts of the plant contain calcium oxalate crystals, which cause long-lasting pain and stomach upset if eaten. These plants are grown for their edible tubers — they are commonly known as taro and dasheen — but the tubers must be cooked thoroughly before they are edible.

HOW TO GROW

Colocasia species are native to swampy areas and require partial shade and deep, rich soil that is wet or at least constantly moist. A sheltered spot is best, because wind will damage the large leaves. Plants thrive in heat and humidity.

They can be grown in containers set in a pond or water garden. In the North, start the tubers indoors in pots 8 to 10 weeks before the last spring frost date, grow them in a warm (70° to 75°F) spot, and transplant outdoors only after the weather is warm and settled. In areas with long growing seasons, plant them directly in the garden after the last frost. Add plenty of organic matter to the soil at planting time. To overwinter the tubers, dig them before the first fall frost, cut off the tops, then dry them for a few hours. Pack them in barely moist sand or peat moss and store them at 40° to 50°F. Use these plants to add a tropical flair to beds and borders, in the bog garden, or in containers.

C. esculenta

c. es-kew-LEN-tuh. ELEPHANT'S EAR, TARO, DASHEEN. Also listed as *C. antiquorum*. A tender 3- to 7-foot perennial with heart- or arrow-shaped 2-foot-long leaves. Bears insignificant flowers. 'Black Magic' bears purple-black leaves. 'Illustris' has purple leaf stalks and green leaves with black-purple veins. **Zones 9 to 11; to Zone 8 with winter protection.**

Commelina

kom-el-EYE-nuh. Spiderwort family, Commelinaceae.

Like their better-known relatives, the spiderworts (*Tradescantia*), *Commelina* species bear three-petaled flowers that each last for less than one day. Unlike spiderworts, which have three similar-size petals, *Commelina* species usually bear flowers that have two petals that are quite a bit larger than the third. About 100 species belong to the genus, which contains annuals as well as perennials that grow from either fibrous or tuberous roots. One species, common day flower (*C. communis*), is a troublesome, fleshy-leaved weed with flowers that have two dark blue petals and one paler blue one. It thrives in shady sites with moist soil, where it self-sows with abandon and also roots at the leaf nodes, as do many other species in the genus. It does not produce tubers.

HOW TO GROW

Give the tuberous species listed here a site with partial shade and rich, well-drained soil. Plant the tubers in spring. In the warmest climates, the plants can be grown

Commelina coelestis

outdoors year-round. In the North, dig the tubers after the first light frosts of fall and overwinter them indoors as you would dahlias — in barely moist peat moss or sand in a cool, dry spot. Propagate by dividing the tubers in spring or by seeds.

C. coelestis

c. koh-LES-tiss. BLUE SPIDER-WORT. A vigorous, tuberous-rooted species that forms 2- to 3-foot-tall, 1¹/₂-foot-wide clumps. Bears fleshy leaves and blue ³/₄- to 1¹/₄-inch-wide flowers from summer to fall. **Zones 9 to 11.**

C. tuberosa

c. too-ber-OH-suh. TUBEROUS DAY FLOWER. A mat-forming 8-inch-tall species native to Central and South America that spreads to several feet. Bears lance-shaped leaves and clusters of greenish flowers striped with blue-purple in summer. **Zones 10 to 11.**

Comptonia

komp-TOE-nee-uh. Wax-myrtle family, Myricaceae.

The single member of this genus is a deciduous shrub known as sweet

Comptonia peregrina

Comptonia peregrina

fern and is native to sandy, peaty, infertile soils of eastern North America. Although not common, it is sought by garden connoisseurs for its shiny, fernlike, aromatic leaves.

HOW TO GROW

An ability to fix its own nitrogen allows sweet fern to thrive in poor to average, sandy or gravelly acid soil, in partial shade to full sun. Add peat to help retain moisture, but sharp drainage is essential. Useful in natural gardens or for holding sandy banks. Sweet fern does not transplant well; buy it as a container-grown shrub. It does not need pruning except for the removal of suckers to control spread. Propagate from rooted suckers in early spring.

C. peregrina

c. pair-eh-GREEN-uh. SWEET FERN. Forms an aromatic suckering shrub 2 to 4 feet high and at least twice as wide. The 4^1/$_2$-inch leaves are ^{1}/$_2$ inch wide and deeply indented, resembling a fern frond but glossy and fragrant when crushed. Inconspicuous yellow-green catkin flowers appear in midspring, followed by brown burlike fruits. Its exclusive spreading roots make it an excellent soil binder and erosion preventer. **Zones 2 to 6.**

Consolida

kon-SOE-lih-dah. Buttercup family, Ranunculaceae.

Commonly called larkspurs and once included in the genus *Delphinium,* the 40 species of

Consolida ajacis

Consolida are annuals from southeastern Europe and the Mediterranean region to central Asia. They bear feathery, deeply cut leaves and spikelike clusters of spurred flowers. One species is a popular annual.

HOW TO GROW

Larkspurs prefer full sun to very light shade and average to rich, well-drained soil. In areas with cool summers, they bloom through much of the growing season, but in the South they provide spring and early-summer bloom, then die out in summer heat and humidity. Sow seeds outdoors in fall or in spring, beginning as soon as the soil can be worked to about 2 weeks before the last spring frost date. Repeated sowings at 3-week intervals lengthen the bloom season. Barely cover the seeds with soil, as darkness is required for germination. Outdoor sowing is generally best, but if you want earlier bloom, try sowing indoors in individual pots 8 to 10 weeks before the last frost date. Set the sown pots in the refrigerator for 2 weeks before moving them to a warmer (50° to 55°F) spot for germination, which takes 2 to 3 weeks. Transplant with care. Stake tall cultivars with twiggy brush, or let them lean on their neighbors.

Convallaria majalis

Water during dry weather. Deadhead to prolong bloom, but let some flowers set seeds, because plants self-sow.

Use larkspur in mixed beds and borders and in cottage gardens. The flowers, which attract hummingbirds, are excellent for cutting and/or drying; tall cultivars are best for these uses. For fresh use, cut just as the lowest blooms on the stalk open. To dry, harvest before the entire spike has opened and hang in bundles in a warm, dry, dark place.

C. ajacis

c. ah-JAY-kiss. LARKSPUR, ANNUAL DELPHINIUM. Formerly *C. ambigua.* Ferny, palmate leaves on 1- to 4-foot plants. Bears branched or unbranched ^{1}/$_2$- to 2-

foot-long flower spikes packed with 1^1/$_2$-inch-wide flowers in shades of blue, violet, lavender, white, or pink. Imperial Series plants are 2 to 3 feet tall and available in separate colors. Dwarf Rocket and Dwarf Hyacinth Series plants range from 1 to 2 feet tall. Cool-weather annual.

Convallaria

kon-vah-LAIR-ee-uh. Lily family, Liliaceae.

Commonly known as lilies-of-the-valley, these lily-family plants bear arching racemes of small, sweetly scented, nodding, bell-shaped flowers. Plants have leaves ranging from ovate-lance-shaped to rounded, and they spread by freely branching rhizomes to form dense mats. Experts differ on whether *Convallaria* contains three species or a single, variable one.

HOW TO GROW

A site in partial shade with evenly moist, rich soil is ideal, although plants grow in full sun (with adequate moisture) to full shade. Established clumps tolerate dry shade, but they will not survive in wet, poorly drained sites. In the South, where plants struggle with the heat, a site in partial to full shade is best. In cooler zones, plants spread vigorously, so keep them away from other perennials or divide clumps frequently to keep them in check. Plant lily-of-the-valley pips — bare-root pieces of the fleshy rhizome that have both growing buds and roots — in fall, late winter, or early spring, ideally before the leaves emerge.

Convallaria majalis

Divide them in summer or fall if they encroach on other plantings, if flowering is reduced because of overcrowding, or for propagation.

C. majalis

mah-JAH-liss. LILY-OF-THE-VALLEY. Vigorous ground-covering perennial that reaches 6 to 9 inches in height and spreads to several feet. Bears one-sided racemes of waxy white $^1/_4$-inch-wide bells in spring followed by round, glossy red berries, which are toxic to humans. 'Fortin's Giant' is a vigorous selection with $^1/_2$-inch-wide flowers on 1-foot-tall plants. *C. majalis* var. *rosea* bears very pale mauve-pink flowers. **Zones 2 to 8**.

Convolvulus

con-VOL-view-lus. Morning-glory family, Convolvulaceae.

About 250 species of annuals, perennials, subshrubs, and shrubs belong to this widely distributed genus, which contains beloved garden annuals as well as notorious weeds — field bindweed (*C. arvensis*) belongs here. These popular garden plants are from the Mediterranean region and North Africa. Plants are erect or have trailing or climbing stems with entire, often heart- or arrow-shaped leaves. The funnel-shaped flowers are borne singly or in clusters.

HOW TO GROW
A warm, protected site in full sun with poor to average or moderately fertile soil is best. Sow seeds indoors in individual pots 6 to 8 weeks before the last spring frost date at 70° to 80°F. In mild areas with long growing seasons (roughly Zone 8 south), gardeners have two growing options: either sow the seeds outdoors after the

Coprosma repens 'Pink Splendor'

last frost date once temperatures remain above 50°F or sow seeds in fall for early bloom the following spring. Before sowing, nick the hard seed coats with a file or soak seeds in warm water for 24 hours. Germination takes 1 to 2 weeks at 55° to 65°F. Perennials and shrubs also can be propagated by cuttings taken in late spring or early summer.

C. cneorum

c. nee-OR-um. SILVERBUSH. Bears lance-shaped, silver-green leaves on mounding 2-foot-tall, 3-foot-wide shrub. Clusters of $1^1/_2$-inch-wide white flowers with yellow centers bloom in spring and summer. **Zones 8 to 10**.

C. sabatius

c. sah-BAY-tee-us. A trailing, 6-inch-tall tender perennial with ovate leaves and lavender-blue,

Convolvulus tricolor

Coreopsis verticillata 'Moonbeam'

funnel-shaped, $^1/_2$- to 1-inch-wide flowers from summer to early fall. **Zones 8 to 9**.

C. tricolor

c. TRY-kuh-lor. DWARF MORNING GLORY. A 1- to $1^1/_2$-foot-tall annual or short-lived perennial, with ovate to lance-shaped leaves. Solitary, $1^1/_2$-inch-wide trumpets in rich blue with yellow-and-white throats appear in summer. Blooms last only a day and close in cloudy weather. **Zones 9 to 10**.

Coprosma

kop-ROZ-mah. Coffee family, Rubiaceae.

Of this genus's roughly 90 species of evergreen shrubs and trees, primarily from New Zealand, several are grown in gardens for their attractive foliage and ability to thrive in difficult situations. Only the species listed here is commonly available.

HOW TO GROW
Grow coprosma in neutral to acid, moderately fertile soil in full sun or partial shade. It is relatively drought tolerant. This taller species makes a good hedge, screen, or espalier. Spreading forms are used as ground covers or to hold banks. Most require frequent pruning, up to twice a year, to keep them from becoming leggy and unkempt. They tolerate seaside sites, where little pruning will be needed. Propagate from semiripe cuttings in late summer.

C. repens

c. REP-enz. MIRROR PLANT. A dioecious shrub that grows rapidly to 10 feet tall and 6 feet wide. In shade it can develop an open, awkward habit unless pruned regularly. The common name comes from the high gloss of its 3-inch

oval or oblong leaves. If you have both male and female plants, the inconspicuous greenish white flowers may be followed from summer to fall by $^1/_2$-inch orange-red, sometimes yellow, berries. There are several variegated forms. **Zones 8 to 10**.

Coreopsis

kore-ee-OP-sis. Aster family, Asteraceae.

Also called tickseeds, coreopsis are long-blooming annuals and perennials that bear daisylike, single or double flowers. From 80 to 100 species belong here, most bearing gold to yellow-orange blooms, but there also are species with pale yellow or pink flowers. The flowers are carried on leafless stems and consist of ray florets (the "petals") surrounding a dense cluster of disk florets (the "eye"). Coreopsis are native to North and Central America and usually have upright stems. The leaves either are simple or are cut in a pinnate or palmate fashion. Both the botanical name and the common name refer to the black seeds that follow the flowers. *Coreopsis* is from the Greek *koris*, meaning "bug," and *opsis*, "resemblance."

HOW TO GROW
Give coreopsis full sun and average to rich, well-drained soil. These heat-loving plants are also happy with some morning shade

Coreopsis grandiflora

Coreopsis auriculata

and afternoon sun. *C. auriculata* and *C. rosea* also grow in partial shade. The plants prefer evenly moist conditions, but once established they withstand considerable drought. Too-rich soil causes them to flop. Deadhead to lengthen the flowering season by cutting off individual blooms or cutting the plants back by about one-third. Allow some flowers to form seeds if you want plants to self-sow. Divide perennials every 2 to 3 years in early spring or early fall to keep them vigorous. Propagate by division, taking cuttings in spring from shoots at the base of the plant or in summer from stem tips, or by seeds.

C. auriculata

c. aw-rick-yew-LAH-tuh. Mouse-ear Coreopsis. Mounding 1- to 2-foot-tall perennial that spreads to about 1 foot by stolons. Bears ovate or lobed leaves and solitary, yellow-orange, 2-inch-wide flowers from late spring to summer. 'Nana' is an 8-inch-tall dwarf cultivar. **Zones 4 to 9.**

C. grandiflora

c. gran-dih-FLOR-uh. Large-flowered Coreopsis. Short-lived 1¹/2- to 3-foot-tall perennial that spreads to about 1¹/2 feet. Bears lance-shaped or palmately lobed leaves and yellow to yellow-orange, 1- to 2¹/2-inch flowers from spring to late summer with regular deadheading. There are single-, semidouble-, and double-flowered cultivars that can be grown from seed. (Many cultivars are hybrids between this species and *C. lanceolata*.) 'Early Sunrise' blooms the first year from seeds sown indoors in midwinter. **Zones 3 or 4 to 9.**

C. lanceolata

c. lan-see-oh-LAH-tuh. Lance-leaved Coreopsis. A 1- to 2-foot-tall species that spreads to 1¹/2 feet and tends to be longer-lived than *C. grandiflora*. Bears lance-shaped leaves and solitary 1¹/2- to 2¹/2-inch-wide flowers from late spring to midsummer. There are single-, semidouble-, and double-flowered cultivars. 'Goldfink' bears 2- to 3-inch-wide flowers on 9-inch plants. **Zones 3 or 4 to 9.**

C. rosea

c. ROE-zee-uh. Pink Coreopsis. Mounding 1- to 2-foot-tall plant spreading to 2 feet or more and especially vigorous in fertile, moist soil. Bears needlelike leaves and small, rosy pink, 1-inch-wide flowers with yellow centers from summer to early fall. **Zones 4 to 8.**

C. tinctoria

c. tink-TOAR-ee-ah. Calliopsis, Plains Coreopsis. An erect, 1- to 4-foot annual with solitary, yellow, 1- to 2-inch-wide daisylike flowers. The species bears bright yellow flowers with maroon centers, but cultivars with petals striped or marked with maroon, dark red, or purple-brown also are available. Warm-weather annual.

C. tripteris

c. TRIP-ter-iss. Tall Tickseed, Atlantic Coreopsis. Native wildflower from the East Coast ranging from 3 to 9 feet in height and spreading to 2 feet or more.

Bears palmately divided, anise-scented leaves and clusters of pale yellow 2-inch-wide flowers from summer to fall. **Zones 3 to 8.**

C. verticillata

c. ver-tih-sil-LAH-tuh. Thread-leaved Coreopsis. A 1- to 2-foot-tall species spreading slowly via rhizomes to form shrubby 2- to 3-foot-wide clumps. Bears pinnate leaves with threadlike leaflets and pale to golden yellow 1- to 2-inch-wide daisies in summer. 'Moonbeam' has pale yellow flowers, reblooms without deadheading, and will flower from early summer to fall. 'Zagreb' bears deep yellow flowers on 1-foot plants. **Zones 3 to 9.**

Coriandrum

kor-ee-AN-drum. Carrot family, Apiaceae.

Two aromatic-leaved annuals native to the Mediterranean region belong to this genus. Both bear deeply divided, ferny leaves and lacy-looking compound umbels of tiny white or pinkish to purplish blooms. One species, *C. sativum*, is known as cilantro when grown for its foliage and coriander when grown for its seeds. Its lacy leaves also make an attractive filler for beds and borders as well as containers.

HOW TO GROW

Full sun or partial shade and average to rich, well-drained soil are ideal. In areas where summers are hot, select a site that receives shade during the hottest part of the day. Sow seeds outdoors after the last spring frost date. When sowing, cover the seeds with soil, as darkness aids germination. Seedlings take about 2 weeks to appear. Sow new crops of seeds every 3 weeks from spring through summer for a continuous supply of leaves. In flower gardens, plants are most effective when grown in drifts of at least three to five plants. Plants self-sow.

C. sativum

c. sah-TIE-vum. Cilantro, Coriander. Bears aromatic, shiny green leaves that resemble flat-leaved parsley on 1- to 2-foot plants. It has lacy, ¹/2-inch-wide umbels of tiny white or pale purple flowers. Cool-weather annual.

Cornus

KOR-nus. Dogwood family, Cornaceae.

Containing many remarkable landscape trees and shrubs and one beautiful ground cover, this large genus encompasses 45 species from Asia and North America. Flowers are dense umbels, often surrounded by showy petal-like bracts, and develop into fleshy berries. Leaves are pointed, smooth-edged ovals with distinctive curving veins and are usually arranged opposite each other. Unfortunately, the magnificent native flowering tree, *C. florida*, is being decimated by anthracnose, a fungal twig blight. Although no other tree can replace its beauty and bloom time, disease-resistant hybrids and other dogwood species should be considered for landscapes in the Northeast and the Mid-Atlantic States. Infected trees

Coriandrum sativum

Cornus florida

should be removed and burned to prevent spread to healthy neighbors.

HOW TO GROW

Dogwoods are adaptable but prefer highly organic, neutral to acid, moist yet well-aerated soil in full sun to partial shade. *C. mas* can take some lime or clay. The species that are grown for colorful winter stems like full sun and tolerate waterlogged soil, making them ideal for pondsides. Their oldest stems should be removed annually, since the best color occurs on new growth. Other species can be sited at the edge of a woodland, or make striking specimens in a lawn, and need little pruning. Dogwood seeds need to be stratified. Softwood cuttings need to overwinter in their propagating medium. Dogwoods grown for colorful twigs can be propagated from suckers.

C. alba
c. AL-buh. TARTARIAN DOGWOOD. With strongly upright stems to 8 to 10 feet tall and spreading about as wide, this species is often called redtwig dogwood because of its bright red winter shoots. The opposite 4-inch leaves turn red or orange in fall. Tiny white flowers bloom in flat 2-inch clusters in late spring to early

Cornus alba

Cornus florida

summer; the fruits are white tinged with blue. This species will sucker and form thickets. May not perform well in the South. There are numerous variegated selections. **Zones 2 to 8.**

C. alternifolia
c. al-tern-ih-FOE-lee-uh. PAGODA DOGWOOD. A large shrub or a small tree, growing 20 feet tall and 35 to 40 feet wide, with wide-spreading horizontal branches, this native has a beautiful layered appearance, like the tiers of a Japanese pagoda. Lacy white flowers bloom in flattened, $2^1/2$-inch-wide clusters above the leaves in late spring and are quite pretty, though not as showy as those of other dogwoods. Unlike most dogwoods, pagoda dogwood has alternate leaves; these 4-inch-long, glossy, dark green ovals turn reddish purple in autumn. The blue-black berries have red stalks and are relished by wildlife. Twigs are glossy purple, and trunk bark is gray, adding to the eye-catching winter silhouette. Use pagoda dogwood as a focal point in a border or shade garden to emphasize its attractive horizontal branching pattern. From eastern North America. **Zones 4 to 7.**

CULTIVARS AND SIMILAR SPECIES
'Argentea' has gorgeous creamy-white-and-green leaves that stand out against a dark background. *C. controversa* (giant dogwood) is

Cornus alternifolia

from Asia and looks similar, bearing 4-inch flower clusters and alternate leaves, but it grows 35 to 50 feet tall and is disease-free; **Zones 6 to 8.** 'June Cloud' has flower clusters that exceed 6 inches across. 'Variegata', with silver-edged leaves, grows 10 to 12 feet tall.

C. amomum
c. uh-MOE-mum. SILKY DOGWOOD. Native to wet areas from Canada to Florida, this somewhat coarse dogwood can grow 10 to 15 feet tall. The off-white flowers bloom in flat-topped clusters in late spring, followed by pale blue berries that turn black if birds don't eat them. Useful for naturalizing, or massing in soils too wet for most other shrubs. **Zones 5 to 8.**

C. canadensis
can-ah-DEN-sis. BUNCHBERRY. Formerly *Chamaepericlymenum canadense*. This much-prized, low-growing dogwood is native to cool northern climates in the United States and Canada, where it grows in acid soils and woodland shade. Reaching only 6 inches tall but speading indefinitely, it makes an attractive ground cover. The showy white flowers are followed by red fruits and dramatic red foliage in fall. Whether naturalized in wild gardens or planted in more formal settings, this tiny, perfectly formed dogwood seems to carry with it the scent of the cool north woods. Difficult to establish in warmer climates.

C. florida
c. FLOR-ih-dah. FLOWERING DOGWOOD. A tree for all seasons, with a beautiful silhouette of undulating horizontal branches, flowering dogwood is a spreading, single-trunked tree that reaches 20 feet tall in the North and 30 feet tall in the South. One of the showiest spring-blooming trees, it produces numerous 2-inch-wide blossoms made up of four notched white, or sometimes pink, bracts that surround a central cluster of small yellow flowers. The bracts

Cornus canadensis

open gradually and are held above the leaves, creating a lacy, layered pattern that lasts for 3 or more weeks if the weather remains cool. Leaves are 5 to 6 inches long and dark green, turning attractive shades of scarlet or wine red in early autumn. Pointed, ¹/₂-inch, red berries ripen in late summer and may last into fall if birds don't eat them. Trunk bark is checkered and gray, rather like alligator hide.

Borers are a serious problem on drought-stressed or injured trees; protect the trunk from mechanical injury, because wounds allow borers to enter. Reduce anthracnose infections by planting flowering dogwood in a location with good air circulation and full sun so that foliage dries quickly, by irrigating without wetting the leaves, and by removing water sprouts and low branches that pick up the fungus from the soil. Control anthracnose infections with well-timed fungicide applications and a low-phosphorus, high-calcium fertilizer. Prune when dormant or in summer. Pink and red forms are less heat resistant and cold hardy. From eastern North America. **Zones 5 to 8.**

CULTIVARS AND SIMILAR SPECIES

White flowers: 'Cherokee Daybreak' has creamy white-margined green leaves and grows upright. 'Cherokee Princess' is strongly horizontal, with 6-inch-wide white blossoms. 'Cloud Nine' flowers profusely, has great red fall color, and blooms when young. 'Gold Nugget' has beautiful gold-margined, green leaves. 'Plena' ('Welch Bay Beauty') bears showy double flowers made up of seven curled bracts. 'Snow Princess' has very large, abundant flowers and

glossy leaves. 'Spring Grove' is a floriferous, wide-spreading tree with 4-inch-wide flowers; resists anthracnose. 'Sterling Silver' has white-and-green-variegated leaves. *Pink to reddish pink flowers: C. florida* var. *rubra* varies from pale to deep pink. 'Cherokee Chief' produces deep reddish pink flowers and red new growth. 'Cherokee Sunset' has multicolored rose- and yellow-and-green-variegated leaves and deep pink flowers. 'Red Beauty' is a compact tree with bright reddish pink bracts. 'Robert's Pink' bears pink flowers and performs well in the Deep South. 'Rubra' blooms pale to medium pink. 'Stokes' Pink' has clear pink flowers and red and purple fall color; excellent in the South. *Other species: C. nuttallii* (mountain dogwood) is native to the West Coast, grows to 60 feet tall, has rounded white flowers with six to eight bracts, and is susceptible to anthracnose; **Zones 7 to 8.**

C. kousa

c. KOO-sah. KOUSA DOGWOOD, JAPANESE DOGWOOD, KOREAN DOGWOOD, CHINESE DOGWOOD. Upright or vase shaped when young, this elegant Asian dogwood eventually spreads horizontally, growing 20 to 30 feet tall and wide. It begins blooming in late spring or early summer, a month after *C. florida.* Its showy bracts open greenish white and mature to pure white, sometimes aging to rose, and last for a month or two, depending on the cultivar. The four petal-like bracts surrounding the yellow flowers are pointed, not notched, and they rise above the branches on 2-inch-tall stems. Leaves are 4 inches long

and glossy green, with long points and curved veins. In late summer, 1¹/₂-inch pink fruits, which ripen to glossy red, dangle from the branches on 4-inch-long stems. These eye-catching fruits stand out gloriously against the green leaves but are soon eaten by birds. Fall color is glossy dark red. As the tree ages, the trunk bark develops into an attractive mixture of brown, gray, and creamy white patches. Tolerates the heat of the Midwest better than *C. florida* does. Plant two trees for best fruit development. Remove lower branches to show off the bark, pruning when dormant. Somewhat susceptible to borers, but immune to anthracnose. From Japan, Korea, and China. **Zones 5 to 8.**

CULTIVARS

Choose named cultivars for best vigor. 'Elizabeth Lustgarten' is a weeping tree that grows to 10 or more feet tall. 'Gold Star' has leaves with a butter yellow central blotch. 'Heart Throb' bears profuse, reddish pink flowers. 'Rosabella' ('Satomi') has deep rose pink, long-lasting bracts. 'Snowboy' offers green leaves with creamy white edges. 'Summer Stars' has showy white bracts for 6 or more weeks. *C. kousa* var. *chinensis* (Chinese dogwood) produces large flowers and is very free flowering; the bracts turn pink as they mature and remain attractive for most of the summer. 'Galilean' has leaves twice as large as the variety and larger flowers; vase shaped or rounded. 'Milky Way' is the same as the variety but is variable. 'Milky Way Select' is more uniform, with a vase shape. 'National' is vase shaped and sports large flowers and fruits. 'Samaritan' has green leaves with creamy white edges and is vigorous.

C. mas

c. maas. CORNELIAN CHERRY, CHERRY DOGWOOD. This late-winter bloomer is a round-headed, low-branched, multitrunked tree or shrub that matures to 20 to 25 feet tall. Because it blooms on leafless branches when most plants are still dormant, it is a beautiful and welcome sight. Unlike those of other popular dogwoods, its flowers don't have showy bracts; instead they are dense, 1-inch clusters of tiny, mustard yellow flowers that turn the tree into a yellow mist for about 3 weeks. Leaves are satiny green and 2 to 4 inches long. They may be purplish in fall or have no appreciable fall color. Dark red, glossy, 1- to ¹/₂-inch berries dangle along the branches in midsummer. Tasting like tart cherries, they are prized in Turkey and Ukraine for juice, sorbet, and preserves, but in North America they are eaten primarily by birds. Trunks of older trees develop an attractive, exfoliating, gray-and-tan bark. The wood is strong; in fact, the Trojan horse may have been made from this wood. Use this lovely tree to brighten the winter landscape in a border where it can be seen from indoors or as you travel to and from the house. Most attractive with an evergreen background or where backlit by the sun. Usually pest-free. Good in the Midwest. From eastern Europe and western Asia. **Zones 5 to 8.**

CULTIVARS AND SIMILAR SPECIES

'Aurea' has golden leaves. 'Elegantissima' features yellow-margined, pink-flushed, green leaves. 'Flava' bears yellow fruits. 'Golden Glory' is pyramidal, growing to 15 feet tall, with abundant flowers. 'Jelico' has oval red

Cornus kousa

Cornus mas

fruits. 'Pioneer' bears 1¹/2-inch-long, tasty fruits. 'Redstone' is vigorous, with very dependable fruit production. *C. officinalis* (Japanese cornelian cherry) looks very similar but blooms a week earlier; its less-tasty berries ripen in early fall, and its trunk bark is more colorful, marked by orange patches; **Zones 6 to 8.**

C. racemosa

c. rass-eh-MOH-suh. GRAY DOGWOOD. An upright species growing 10 to 15 feet high and wide. Multistemmed and suckering, It can be pruned to a single trunk. Opposite 4-inch leaves may turn purple-red. The late-spring flowers are flat white clusters; white berries are borne on red stalks. 'Cayahoga' is pyramidal, grows to 15 feet tall, and makes a good street tree under power lines. 'Ottawa' is columnar and grows to 12 feet tall. A drought-tolerant choice for naturalizing. From the American East and Midwest. **Zones 4 to 8.**

C. × rutgersensis (C. florida × C. kousa)

c. × rut-gurrs-EN-sis. STELLAR DOGWOOD, HYBRID DOGWOOD. First introduced in 1990 by Dr. Elwin R. Orton Jr. of Rutgers University, hybrids between *C. florida* and *C. kousa* are stunning trees that grow vigorously to 20 to 25 feet tall. Tree shape varies from upright to spreading to rounded, depending on the cultivar. Flower shape also varies, with the 2-inch bracts being either narrow and starlike or rounded and overlapping. All cultivars bloom so prolifically that the blossoms almost completely obscure the leaves. The bloom period begins in midspring, about 2 weeks after *C. florida* and 2 weeks before *C. kousa,* and lasts for about 3 weeks. The large, glossy, dark green leaves are 2 to 5 inches long and turn red in autumn. These trees grow more vigorously than *C. kousa* and are highly resistant to both borers and anthracnose. 'Constellation', 'Ruth Ellen', and 'Stardust' may suffer from powdery mildew (others are immune); keep the soil moist and the leaves dry. **Zones 6 to 8.**

CULTIVARS

'Aurora' has large, overlapping, pure white, round bracts with a slight notch and forms a full, bushy, upright tree. 'Celestial' produces oval, pointed, white bracts that touch but do not overlap and forms a rounded tree. 'Constellation' bears delicate, long, nonoverlapping bracts with starry points and forms a narrow tree. 'Galaxy' produces rounded, slightly overlapping, white bracts with a slight point that open first as greenish cups; grows upright. 'Ruth Ellen' blooms a bit earlier than the other cultivars; has horizontal branches and a mounding shape; and has pure white, starlike, pointed bracts. 'Stardust' is a dwarf, growing only to 15 feet tall, with the horizontal form of *C. florida;* it bears rounded, notched, separate bracts and is highly anthracnose resistant. 'Stellar Pink' has broad, pale pink, overlapping, notched bracts and a rounded shape.

C. stolonifera (syn. C. sericea)

c. stoh-lahn-IF-er-uh. RED OSIER DOGWOOD. An eastern U.S. species that may not do well in the heat of the South, it can grow 7 feet tall and 10 feet or more wide, spreading by stolons. Upright twigs range from bright red to a dark purple-red; leaves are opposite, to 5 inches long. The white late-spring flowers are flat 2-inch clusters, and early fall berries are white, sometimes tinged blue. 'Silver and Gold', a Pennsylvania Horticultural Society award winner, has bright yellow stems and leaves with an irregular cream-colored band around the edge. **Zones 2 to 8.**

Corydalis

cor-IH-dah-liss. Poppy family, Papaveraceae.

Corydalis species produce handsome mounds of delicate-looking, ferny foliage and racemes of tubular, spurred flowers in spring. About 300 species, both biennials and perennials, belong to the genus, which was once classified in the fumitory family, Fumariaceae. Corydalis resemble bleeding hearts (*Dicentra* species), but while bleeding hearts have two spurs per flower, corydalis blooms have only one. The perennials grow from rhizomes or tubers.

HOW TO GROW

Give most corydalis full sun to partial shade and rich, well-drained soil. *C. lutea* also grows well in average, well-drained soil as well as the conditions that *C. flexuosa* requires: partial shade and rich, well-drained soil that remains evenly moist. *C. flexuosa* is best in areas with cool summers. Most corydalis resent being transplanted, but they can be dug and divided for propagation in early spring or early fall. Plants self-sow.

C. cava

c. KAY-vuh. FUMEWORT. Also listed as *C. bulbosa.* Tuberous 4- to 8-inch-tall species forming 4-inch-wide mounds of lacy pale green leaves and dense racemes of 1-inch-long rich rosy purple or white flowers in early spring. **Zones 5 to 8.**

C. cheilanthifolia

c. key-lanth-ih-FOE-lee-uh. FERNY CORYDALIS. Produces 10- to 12-inch-tall mounds of very lacy, pinnate leaves that spread as far. Bears dense racemes of ¹/2-inch-long bright yellow flowers from spring to summer. **Zones 3 to 7.**

C. diphylla

c. dye-FILL-uh. Tuberous 4- to 6-inch-tall species that spreads to 4 inches. Bears lacy leaves and loose clusters of six to ten 1-inch-long white flowers with darker red-purple lips in spring. Grows in full sun, although plants tolerate partial shade. Requires very well drained soil and is best for a rock garden. **Zones 5 to 8.**

C. flexuosa

c. flex-yew-OH-suh. BLUE CORYDALIS. Bears 12-inch-tall mounds of glaucous leaves and

Corydalis flexuosa 'Blue Panda'

Corylopsis spicata

racemes of bright blue 1-inch-long flowers from late spring to summer. Plants go dormant after flowering. 'Blue Panda' has sky blue flowers. **Zones 6 to 8**.

C. fumariifolia

c. few-mair-ee-ih-FO-lee-uh. Also listed as *C. ambigua*. A 4- to 6-inch-tall species, spreading to 4 inches, with lacy green leaves topped by spikelike racemes of 1-inch-long blue to purple-blue flowers from late spring to early summer. **Zones 5 to 8**.

C. lutea

c. LOO-tee-uh. YELLOW CORYDALIS. Forms handsome mounds of ferny bluish green leaves that are $1^{1}/_{2}$ feet tall and wide. Foliage remains attractive from early spring through late fall, and even into winter in milder climates. Bears racemes of abundant $^{1}/_{2}$- to $^{3}/_{4}$-inch-long golden yellow flowers over a long season from midspring to early fall. **Zones 5 to 8**.

C. ochroleuca

c. oh-krow-LEW-kuh. Produces 1-foot-tall mounds of ferny leaves that spread as far and are topped by racemes of $^{1}/_{2}$-inch-long white flowers with yellow throats from spring to summer. **Zones 6 to 8**.

C. solida

c. SO-lee-duh. Also listed as *C. halleri, C. transsylvanica*. Vigorous 8- to 10-inch-tall tuberous species forming 8-inch-wide mounds of lacy gray-green leaves. In early spring it bears dense, spikelike racemes of mauve-pink $^{3}/_{4}$-inch-long flowers with spurs that curve downward. 'Beth Evans' has pink blooms. 'George Baker' ('G.P.

Baker') bears rich rose-pink flowers flushed with violet inside. **Zones 5 to 9**.

Corylopsis

kor-ih-LOP-sis. Witch-hazel family, Hamamelidaceae.

This is a small group of deciduous Asian shrubs, commonly called winter hazels, many of which have been tapped by gardeners for their bell-shaped fragrant yellow flowers. These hang from branches in clusters before leaves emerge in early or midspring.

HOW TO GROW

Winter hazels like acidic, fertile, moisture-retentive but well-aerated soil and partial shade. They need protection from wind, hot sun, and late frosts, but rarely require any pruning. They work well in shrub borders but can also deserve specimen status. Propagate by layering or softwood cuttings allowed to overwinter before replanting.

C. glabrescens

c. glab-RES-enz. FRAGRANT WINTER HAZEL. Averaging 10 feet high and wide, this shrub has an open and spreading habit with a somewhat flattened top. The 2- to 4-inch oval leaves are yellow-green to gold in fall. Pale yellow midspring flowers with silky bracts hang in 1-inch racemes. **Zones 5 to 8**.

C. pauciflora

c. paw-sih-FLOR-uh. BUTTERCUP WINTER HAZEL. A dainty spreading shrub, 4 to 6 feet tall and 8 feet wide, with smaller leaves that are silky underneath.

Each inflorescence has fewer pale yellow flowers than *C. glabrescens* does, but each individual flower is larger and more open. **Zones 6 to 8**.

C. spicata

c. spih-KAY-tuh. SPIKE WINTER HAZEL. This species, 6 feet tall and 10 feet wide, is distinguished by crooked branches, and the flowers have pink stamens and darker anthers. New leaves are purple to pink, eventually becoming blue-green. **Zones 5 to 8**.

Corylus

KOR-ih-lus. Birch family, Betulaceae.

Edible nuts are a big draw in this genus, containing about 10 species of deciduous trees and shrubs from North America, Europe, and Asia. The prominent yellow male catkins make them visually appealing as well. Only one tree in the genus, *C. colurna*, or Turkish filbert, is commonly grown as an ornamental.

HOW TO GROW

Give filberts fertile, well-drained soil in full sun or part shade. They adapt well to alkaline soils. In late winter the first year after planting, head back stems of the shrub forms to 2 feet to encourage branching. Then in following winters, head back side shoots and tips by about a third. Removing older branches in the center of the shrub will stimulate growth, reduce chances of disease, and make harvesting easier. Remove vigorous suckers to ground level. Propagate species by stratifying seeds.

C. americana

c. uh-mair-ih-KAH-nuh. AMERICAN FILBERT. This eastern U.S. native is a multistemmed shrub growing to 15 feet tall and 12 feet wide. In early spring it produces prominent yellow-brown male catkins up to 3 inches long. In fall you can collect the $^{1}/_{2}$-inch edible nuts. **Zones 4 to 9**.

C. avellana

c. ah-vel-LAY-nuh. EUROPEAN FILBERT. An upright suckering shrub to 15 to 20 feet tall, this species is often used for commercial nut production. Drooping yellow catkins to $2^{1}/_{2}$ inches appear in late winter. 'Contorta', also called Harry Lauder's walking stick, has twisted, curly stems, good for dried arrangements and winter interest in the landscape. Look for clones of this plant grown from cuttings or layering, since grafted plants will produce uncurly suckers that spoil its silhouette. **Zones 3 to 8**.

Corylus avellana 'Contorta'

Cosmos bipinnatus 'Sonata Pink'

C. colurna

c. koh-LUR-nah. TURKISH FIL-BERT, TURKISH HAZEL. Densely pyramidal when young and eventually maturing into a rounded or oval shape with low-hanging branches, this good-looking tree, which reaches 50 or more feet tall, should be used more often in North American landscapes. Yellowish tan male catkins dangle from the branches in late winter before the leaves unfold. The rounded or heart-shaped leaves are 3 to 6 inches long, rather coarse, glossy, and dark green, with a double row of fine teeth at their margins. Fall color is usually undistinguished. Brown bark exfoliates into an attractive, rough-textured, brown-and-white pattern. Small nuts enclosed in bristly husks ripen in fall and may be messy but are eaten by wildlife. Plant as an easy-care formal lawn, urban, street, or seashore tree. Grow in full sun and any well-drained, acid to alkaline soil. It is drought, heat, and wind tolerant once established and performs well near the seashore, resisting wind and salt spray. Remove lower branches if desired. Eastern filbert blight can be a problem in some areas; otherwise pest-free. From southeastern Europe and southwestern Asia. **Zones 5 to 8.**

C. cornuta

c. kor-NOO-tuh. BEAKED FIL-BERT. A small shrub, 4 to 8 feet tall and wide, native from Canada to Missouri and Georgia, with 1-inch catkins. It gets its common name from a "beak" that forms around the ½-inch nuts. **Zones 4 to 8.**

C. maxima 'Purpurea'

c. MAX-ih-muh. PURPLE GIANT FILBERT. Reaching 20 feet tall and 15 feet wide, this species has larger leaves and fruits, and the cultivar sports dark purple new foliage, with catkins and fruit also purple tinged. **Zones 4 to 8.**

Cosmos

KOZ-mose. Aster family, Asteraceae.

Cosmos contains about 25 species of annuals and perennials native to the southern United States and Central America. All bear daisylike flowers, and most have deeply divided, almost featherlike leaves. The botanical name refers to the attractive flowers of these easy-to-grow plants; it is taken from the Greek *kosmos*, meaning "ornament."

HOW TO GROW

Choose a planting site with full sun and poor to average, evenly moist, well-drained soil. Too-rich soil yields floppy plants and few flowers. Sow seeds outdoors after danger of frost has passed. Or, for earlier bloom, sow seeds indoors 4 to 6 weeks before the last spring frost date. If sowing indoors, place pots in the refrigerator for 2 weeks after sowing, then germinate at between 70° and 75°F. Stake taller types with twiggy brush, or space plants closely so they will support each other. Deadheading lengthens the bloom season. Annuals self-sow. *C. atrosanguineus,* a tender perennial, is hardy from **Zone 7 south**. North of that, dig the roots after a light fall frost, and store them in barely damp vermiculite, peat moss, or sand in a cool (40° to 50°F), dry place, as you would dahlias. Cosmos come in several heights, and all make excellent fillers for the middle or back of a perennial bed or border. All attract butterflies and make outstanding cut flowers.

C. atrosanguineus

c. at-roe-san-GWIH-nee-us. CHOCO-LATE COSMOS, BLACK COSMOS. Formerly *Bidens atrosanguinea.* A 2½-foot-tall, tuberous-rooted perennial. The cup-shaped, 1¾-inch, daisylike flowers have maroon petals, dark red-brown centers, and a slight chocolate fragrance. Tender perennial, or grow as a warm-weather annual.

C. bipinnatus

c. bi-pin-NAY-tus. COSMOS. A 1- to 5-foot annual bearing showy, daisylike, yellow-centered flowers with petals in shades of pink, maroon, crimson, or white. Cultivars with various flower forms and heights are available. 'Seashell Mix' cultivars have rolled petals resembling round shells and reach 3 feet; 'Sonata Mix' and 'Versailles Mix' plants are dwarf, ranging from 1½ to 2 feet. Warm-weather annual.

C. sulphureus

c. sulf-UR-ee-us. COSMOS. A 1- to 6-foot annual with single or double, 1½- to 2½-inch-wide, daisylike flowers in shades of yellow, orange, or orange-red. The Klondike and Ladybird Series are dwarf types, reaching only 14 to 18 inches. Warm-weather annual.

Cotinus

koh-TYE-nus. Cashew family, Anacardiaceae.

This genus contains only two species, both of which are handsome garden plants admired for their foliage and flowers and both commonly called smoke tree. *C. coggygria* is often cut to the ground every year (coppiced) to force vigorous new growth. *C. obovatus* also may be treated this way.

Cotinus coggygria 'Notcutt's Variety'

HOW TO GROW

Plant smoke trees in full sun to light shade and moist, well-drained, sandy to clayey soil. They perform well in alkaline soil and are very drought tolerant. Susceptible to damage during ice storms. Trees will resprout from stumps cut to the ground. Pest-free. From south-central North America. **Zones 4 to 8.**

C. coggygria

SMOKE TREE, SMOKE BUSH. A large shrub or multitrunked small tree growing 15 to 20 feet tall; showier, pink, 4- to 10-inch-long clusters of male and female flowers on the same plant and round leaves. **Zones 4 to 7.** Although it may die to the ground in Zone 4, it will resprout.

CULTIVARS AND SIMILAR SPECIES

'Flame' is a 25-foot-tall hybrid of *C. coggygria* and *C. obovatus* with showy pink flowers and scarlet to orange fall color. 'Grace' is a 20-foot-tall upright hybrid with bronzy pink summer foliage and deep, iridescent, orange-and-red fall color. *C. coggygria* f. *purpureus* has blue-green leaves and pale pinkish purple flowers. 'Pink Champagne' has green leaves and showy, light pink flowers. 'Royal Purple' is the darkest hued, with deep black-purple leaves all summer, red fall color, and burgundy flowers that age to dusty wine-pink. 'Velvet Cloak' has deep red-violet foliage all summer and red fall color. 'Notcutt's Variety' is similar to 'Royal Purple', but the leaves are slightly redder and not as black; flowers are rose pink.

C. obovatus

c. ob-oh-VAH-tuss. AMERICAN SMOKE TREE, SMOKE BUSH. A multitrunked small tree reaching 20 to 30 feet tall, this native forms a round-headed specimen with distinctive 5- to 10-inch-long, oblong leaves that are attached to long petioles. Leaves open pinkish bronze, mature to blue-green, and change to combinations of yellow, red, reddish orange, and purple in fall. In late spring and early summer, the tree is transformed into a smoky cloud when the flowers bloom at the branch tips. The flowers themselves are yellowish and tiny but are grouped into multibranched, 6-inch-long heads that are decorated with plumelike, pinkish gray hairs. Even after the flowers fade or ripen into black seeds, the hairs grow longer and

Cotoneaster dammeri

get showier, creating a "smoky" show that can last for 4 to 6 weeks. Bark is scaly, gray-brown, and attractive in winter. Use this unusual native for a dramatic effect in a lawn, border, or natural area.

Cotoneaster

koh-TOE-nee-ass-ter. Rose family, Rosaceae.

This genus, which deserves an award for most often mispronounced, contains more than 200 deciduous to evergreen shrubs and trees native to temperate areas of Europe, Asia, and North Africa. Bees are drawn to their small white or pink-tinged flowers, which bloom in late spring or early summer, but most species are grown for the berries, usually red or orange.

HOW TO GROW

Give cotoneasters poor to moderately fertile soil in full sun. Most can withstand wind and some drought once established. Evergreens will tolerate shade but will not fruit as heavily. Pruning is not required and can spoil the natural grace of some, but plants can be pruned hard if needed to reshape or increase density. A number of species make excellent ground

Cotoneaster horizontalis

Cotoneaster apiculatus

covers, draping down the sides of raised beds, trained against walls, or used in borders or as hedges. Several species — particularly *C. lacteus, C. microphyllus,* and *C. pannosus* — have become invasive in northern and central California, so gardeners in that state are encouraged to look for substitute shrubs. Cotoneaster can be propagated by hormone-treated softwood cuttings in early summer.

C. adpressus

c. ad-PRESS-us. CREEPING COTONEASTER. A deciduous, compact species with a stiff habit, to 18 inches high and spreading to 6 feet. The leaves have wavy margins and turn red in fall. The white flowers are tipped with pink and are followed by small red fruits. This species is especially tolerant of a wide range of pH and adapts to seaside conditions, although it is prone to spider mites where the weather is hot and dry. **Zones 5 to 8.**

C. apiculatus

c. ah-pik-ew-LAY-tus. CRANBERRY COTONEASTER. Deciduous, low and spreading shrub to 3 feet high and 8 feet wide, similar to *C. adpressus.* Alternate glossy ^{1}/$_2$-inch leaves turn red or bronze-purple in fall. Solitary white flowers are followed by round red ^{1}/$_3$-inch fruits, which it holds in winter. **Zones 4 to 7.**

C. dammeri

c. DAM-er-eye. BEARBERRY COTONEASTER. This 8- to 12-inch-tall evergreen makes a fast-growing ground cover for banks, rocky soil, and other difficult conditions, but after several years it needs pruning to keep it from looking ragged. The fruits, which can be unreliable, look like tiny apples. Cultivars have been selected for vigor, better fruiting, and greater or lower height. **Zones 5 to 8.**

C. divaricatus

c. dih-vair-ih-KAH-tus. SPREADING COTONEASTER. Erect, rounded deciduous shrub that is 6 to 8 feet tall with wider spread. The 1-inch-long, ^{1}/$_2$-inch-wide leaves are especially dark and glossy, turning orange to red in fall, setting off the egg-shaped, dark red, ^{1}/$_3$-inch berries. It is less pest-prone than other cotoneasters. **Zones 4 to 7.**

C. horizontalis

c. hoar-ih-zon-TAL-iss. ROCKSPRAY COTONEASTER. A spreading deciduous species to 3 feet tall and about 6 feet wide. Trained against a wall to accentuate the distinctive

Crambe maritima

herringbone pattern of its branches, it may grow 8 feet high. The leaves turn red in fall and persist into winter. Spring pink-tinged flowers give way to small round red fruits. 'Robustus' is a faster grower. This species is especially prone to diseases such as fire blight and rust. **Zones 5 to 7**.

C. lacteus

c. LAK-tee-us. PARNEY COTONEASTER. Formerly *C. parneyi*. A dense, gracefully arching evergreen 6 to 10 feet tall and wide. The 2-inch leaves have deep veins. White flowers are followed by abundant red fruits in 3-inch clusters. **Zones 7 to 9**.

C. linearifolius

lin-air-ee-FOE-lee-us. THYME-LEAF COTONEASTER . Also listed as *C. microphyllus* var. *thymifolius* and 'Thymifolia'. As the name implies, this dwarf to prostrate Himalayan cotoneaster has small, gray-green leaves and pinkish gray twigs, making it a valuable addition to a mixed ground-cover planting or where a change in scale is needed. **Zones 5 to 8**.

C. lucidus

c. LOO-sih-dus. HEDGE COTONEASTER. An upright, rounded deciduous shrub 6 to 10 feet tall and wide, with yellow and red autumn foliage, pinkish white flattened flower clusters, and round blue-black fruits. **Zones 4 to 7**.

C. multiflorus

c. mul-tih-FLOR-us. MANY-FLOWERED COTONEASTER. This deciduous fountainlike shrub resembles a Van Houtte spirea in flower. It can grow to 15 feet tall

and wide and has gray-green leaves and long arching branches. It holds its showy clusters of 3 to 12 white flowers upright on the stem, which are followed by red fruits. **Zones 4 to 7**.

C. perpusillus

c. pur-PEW-sill-us. Also listed as *C. horizontalis* var. *perpusillus*. A low, ground-hugging plant striking for its red leaf color in fall and orange fruits, as well as the distinctive fish-bone pattern of its branching. Very susceptible to fire blight. **Zones 5 to 8**.

C. procumbens

c. pro-KUM-benz. Also listed as *C. dammeri* 'Streibs Findling'. This ground-hugging shrub is only a few inches tall and has attractive, glossy, evergreen foliage. **Zones 7 to 8**.

C. salicifolius

c. sal-iss-ih-FOE-lee-us. WILLOW-LEAVED COTONEASTER. Also listed as *C. flococcus*. A spreading and arching evergreen, 10 to 15 feet tall, with somewhat hidden woolly 2-inch flower clusters and bright red berries. It may need pruning to keep the base from becoming leggy and can self-sow to become invasive. More desirable are low-growing cultivars, including 'Em-

Craspedia globosa

erald Carpet', 'Repens', and 'Scarlet Leader'. **Zones 6 to 8**.

Crambe

KRAM-bee. Cabbage family, Brassicaceae.

Crambes, or sea kales, as they are also called, are grown for their abundant clusters of small, cross-shaped, four-petaled flowers. They produce large cabbagelike mounds of bold, usually pinnately lobed leaves. About 20 species of annuals and perennials belong to the genus, native primarily from central

Crataegus laevigata

Europe, tropical Africa, and central Asia. The young shoots of one species, *C. maritima*, are sometimes eaten as a vegetable.

HOW TO GROW

A site with full sun and deep, rich, well-drained soil is ideal, although crambes also tolerate poor soil and partial shade. Neutral to alkaline pH is best. Plants die back after flowering, so combine them with annuals to fill the gap in mid- to late summer. They do not tolerate heat and humidity well. The plants are deep rooted and resent transplanting, but they can be divided for propagation if necessary in early spring. Or take root cuttings in late fall or winter or sow seeds.

C. cordifolia

c. Kor-dih-FOE-lee-uh. GIANT KALE, COLEWORT. A giant perennial with heart-shaped, toothed 2-foot-wide leaves forming mounds of foliage that reach about 8 feet tall and can spread to 5 feet. Bears airy 6- to 8-foot-tall panicles of tiny white flowers from late spring to early summer. **Zones 6 to 9**.

C. maritima

c. mah-RIT-ih-muh. SEA KALE. A mounding perennial that reaches 2½ feet tall and spreads to 2 feet. Bears rounded, lobed, blue-green leaves and dense 2-foot-wide racemes of tiny white flowers in early summer. **Zones 6 to 9**.

Craspedia

Krass-PEE-dee-ah. Aster family, Asteraceae.

Craspedia contains about eight species of annuals and tender perennials; all bear rounded, buttonlike flower heads and are native to Australia, New Zealand, and Tasmania. Their blooms consist of disk florets, but no petal-like ray florets, and the flowers are carried on unbranched stalks above a dense rosette of leaves.

HOW TO GROW

A site in full sun and average, well-drained soil is ideal. Sow seeds indoors 8 to 10 weeks before the last spring frost date at 55° to 65°F. Water plants regularly when they are actively growing; if possible, avoid wetting the rosette of foliage. In areas with very mild winters, tender perennial species can be overwintered outdoors; gritty, perfectly drained soil is essential to success, because plants resent wet soil in winter. Use these plants in

Crataegus laevigata

mixed plantings and for dried arrangements. To dry the blooms, harvest as soon as they are fully open, and hang them in bunches in a warm, dry, dark place.

C. globosa

c. gloh-BOH-sah. BACHELOR'S BUTTONS, DRUMSTICKS. A tender perennial, hardy from **Zone 9 south**, with a low rosette of strap-shaped, woolly white leaves and stiff, unbranched flower stems reaching 2 to 3 feet. Rounded, 1¼-inch-wide, mustard yellow flower heads appear in summer. Tender perennial, or grow as a warm-weather annual.

Crataegus

kruh-TEE-gus. Rose family, Rosaceae.

This large genus contains 200 species of trees and shrubs, collectively known as hawthorns, from woodlands and scrubby areas of the north temperate zones. They usually have thorny branches, simple or lobed alternate leaves, small five-petaled flowers borne in dense clusters, and small applelike berries. Most hawthorns make excellent ornamentals for year-round beauty, especially in the North. Like most rose-family members, however, they suffer from many insect and disease problems, including fire blight and cedar-apple rust, a leaf and fruit fungus whose alternate host is the native eastern red cedar *(Juniperus virginiana)*. This leaf disease may defoliate susceptible trees in midsummer. Hawthorns and cedars therefore should not be planted near each other. Despite these drawbacks, hawthorns are valued landscape trees because they bloom in late spring after most other trees, and they are especially cold hardy.

HOW TO GROW

See individual listings for cultural requirements.

C. crus-galli

c. krus-GAL-ee. COCKSPUR HAWTHORN. A spreading tree with dramatic horizontal branches, this small, dense hawthorn grows 15 to 25 feet tall and 20 to 30 feet wide and provides year-round landscape interest. Lacy white flowers with pink anthers bloom in 2- to 3-inch-wide clusters that cloak the tree in late spring along with the young foliage and may have an unpleasant odor at close range. The glossy, wedge-shaped leaves emerge light green, mature to dark green, and turn wine red or scarlet in autumn. The ½-inch, showy berries ripen to dark red in fall and decorate the leafless branches well into winter. Rather lethal-looking, curved, 2-inch or longer thorns arm the branches, although thornless forms are available. This tough tree excels in cold, harsh climates, making it an excellent choice for an impenetrable screen or garden border. Its low-branched shape precludes growing grass or anything but a shade-loving ground cover underneath.

Plant in full sun and any well-drained soil. Withstands urban conditions and air pollution. Fruits are moderately susceptible to rust, but leaves are only slightly affected. From eastern and central North America. **Zones 3 to 6**.

CULTIVARS AND SIMILAR SPECIES

C. crus-galli var. *inermis* is thornless and very resistant to rust. 'Crusader' is denser, growing to 15 feet tall. 'Vaughn' is a hybrid with *C. phaenopyrum;* it has horizontal branches, disease-resistant leaves, and masses of long-lasting orange-red fruits. *C. × lavallei* (Lavalle hawthorn) is an upright hybrid with somewhat larger flowers, scarlet-orange fruits that last through the winter, fewer spines, and rust-resistant foliage; **Zones 4 to 7**.

C. laevigata

c. lee-vih-GAH-tah. ENGLISH HAWTHORN. The most commonly planted of all the hawthorns because it blooms so profusely, English hawthorn is a small, rounded, multitrunked tree that grows 15 to 20 feet tall and wide. Flowers bloom in clusters of 5 to 15 blossoms in midspring with the emerging leaves and may be white or shades of pink or red, with pink or purple anthers. The glossy, 2-inch leaves have three to five shallow lobes with toothed edges and don't change color in fall. The dense zigzagging branches are covered with 1-inch-long thorns. Numerous deep red, ½-inch berries ripen in fall but are not long lasting. English hawthorn makes a grand statement in a spring and fall border, but it is plagued by disease.

Grow in full sun and well-drained soil. Tolerates cold, drought, and clayey soil. Prone to insect and disease problems and sensitive to road salt. Provide good air circulation to reduce leaf diseases. Train to a single trunk and prune off lower branches if desired. From Europe. **Zones 5 to 7**.

CULTIVARS AND SIMILAR SPECIES

'Crimson Cloud' ('Superba') has disease-resistant foliage, very large crimson flowers with white centers, and glossy berries. 'Paul's Scarlet' is widely planted and has large, double, rose-crimson flowers and thornless branches; very susceptible to leaf spot. 'Plena' has large, double, white flowers that age to pink; resistant to leaf spot. *C. × mordenensis* is a cold-hardy, thornless hybrid with double white flowers and sparse scarlet fruits; hardy to **Zone 3**.

Crataegus phaenopyrum

Crepis rubra

'Snowbird' is an upright or oval form. 'Toba' has a rounded shape, and the flowers age from white to pink.

C. phaenopyrum

c. fay-no-PYE-rum. WASHINGTON HAWTHORN. Also listed as *C. cordata*. Growing into a 20- to 35-foot-tall, rounded or pyramidal specimen, this is the largest and latest-flowering of the hawthorns. Clusters of white flowers with yellowish pink anthers bloom in early summer. New leaves open with a reddish cast, mature to dark green, and turn orange, scarlet, or purple in fall. Individual leaves are 1 to 2 inches long and shallowly cut into three to seven lobes with sharp teeth, like a maple's. The glossy, bright red berries last through the winter, adding interest. Trunk and branches sport very sharp, 3-inch-long thorns. Leaves and fruits of Washington hawthorn are less susceptible to disease than those of other hawthorns. This is the best hawthorn for the South.

Plant in full sun and any well-drained soil. Does not tolerate road salt. Prune to a single trunk if desired. Rust-resistant leaves. From eastern North America. Zones 4 to 8.

CULTIVARS
'Princeton Sentry' grows into an upright tree with very showy fruits and few thorns. 'Washington Lustre' has fewer thorns, shinier leaves, and more profuse flowers and fruits than the species.

C. viridis

c. VEER-ih-dis. GREEN HAWTHORN. This native is a tree for all seasons. Vase shaped when young, it matures into a flat-topped, horizontally spreading specimen that grows to 30 feet tall and wide. A profusion of lacy white flowers with yellow anthers bloom in 2-inch-wide clusters in late spring. The wedge-shaped leaves are $^1/_2$ to $3^1/_2$ inches long. They have a fine texture, a glossy sheen, and scalloped edges, and, unlike those of most hawthorns, they are generally disease-free. Fall color is often scarlet or purple. Small, very persistent, scarlet berries ripen in fall and last most of the winter, making an outstanding color statement against the gray bark of the branches. Thorns are about 1 inch long. Mature trees have rough, flaky trunk bark with orange patches. Use as a small garden tree or in groves where it can be seen in winter. Showiest with an evergreen background.

Grow in full sun and almost any soil, well drained to wet. Tolerates drought, wind, and urban conditions. Thin branches and remove water sprouts when dormant. Provide good air circulation. Usually free of fire blight, leaf spot, and insects, although fruits can become diseased. Good in the Midwest. Zones 5 to 9.

CULTIVARS
'Winter King' is an award-winning cultivar noted for its profusion of

Crinum hybrid

very large, long-lasting, red berries and its strong vase shape.

Crepis

KREY-puss. Aster family, Asteraceae.

Commonly called hawk's beards, *Crepis* species are milky-juiced annuals and perennials native to dry, rocky soils in the Northern Hemisphere. About 200 species belong to the genus. All bear flattened, dandelion-like flower heads, usually in shades of yellow or orange, and flattened rosettes of leaves that can be entire or deeply divided. One species native to Italy and Greece is grown as an annual.

HOW TO GROW

Crepis species require full sun and poor to average, well-drained soil. They generally will not grow well in areas with very hot, humid, wet summers. Sow seeds outdoors in early spring, a few weeks before the last spring frost date. Or sow indoors in individual pots 4 to 6 weeks before the last frost date. From Zone 5 south, try sowing seeds outdoors in fall for earlier bloom the following spring. Plants self-sow.

C. rubra

c. RUE-bruh. HAWK'S BEARD, HAWKWEED. A 1- to 1$^1/_2$-foot annual or short-lived perennial, hardy from Zone 5 south, with a rosette of lance-shaped leaves. Bears showy, 1- to 1$^1/_2$-inch flowers in pinkish red from spring to summer. Cool-weather annual.

Crinum

KRY-num. Amaryllis family, Amaryllidaceae.

Crinums are tender perennial bulbs grown for their showy umbels of funnel- or bell-shaped flowers. Flower clusters, which are carried on leafless stalks, contain from 3 or 4 to as many as 20 or more blooms. The individual flowers, which are white or nearly white, often are fragrant. They have six petal-like lobes, or tepals. Shape varies: one common name for these plants is crinum lily, a reference to the lilylike shape of the blooms of some species; another is spider lily, as other species bear flowers with very narrow tepals that create a spidery effect. The plants grow from large tunicate bulbs and produce long (to 3 feet or more), narrow, strap- to

Crinum × *powellii*

sword-shaped leaves that may be deciduous, semievergreen, or evergreen. About 130 species belong to the genus, native to the tropics of both the Old and New Worlds, where they are found growing along streams and the edges of lakes — two other common names for these stunning plants are swamp lily and river lily.

HOW TO GROW

Select a site in full sun or partial shade with very deeply prepared, rich, moist, well-drained soil. Shade during the hottest part of the day is beneficial in areas with hot summers. Outdoors, plant the bulbs in spring with the tip of the bulbs just at the soil surface. Space plants 2 to 3 feet apart; where hardy, they can be grown outdoors year-round and left to establish large clumps. Where they're marginally hardy, select a warm, south-facing site and protect plants over winter with a coarse mulch of evergreen boughs, pine needles, salt hay, or coarse leaves such as oak leaves. In the North, grow these plants in large containers or tubs. When planting in containers, set the bulbs with the long necks and even the top part of the bulb extending above the soil surface. In containers or in the ground, keep the soil evenly moist from spring through fall when plants are growing actively. For best results, feed in-ground plants two or three times during the season; feed container-grown plants weekly or every other week with a dilute balanced fertilizer. To overwinter container-grown plants, move them to a cool (50°F), well-ventilated sunroom or greenhouse *before* the first fall frost. Keep the soil fairly dry while plants are dormant.

Crinums resent root disturbance, so divide or transplant them only if absolutely necessary. Plants may refuse to bloom for several years after being disturbed. Move container-grown plants to larger pots only when they become quite crowded. Propagate by separating the offsets in spring or by sowing seeds.

C. americanum

c. ah-mair-ih-KAH-num. SOUTHERN SWAMP LILY, FLORIDA CRINUM. A native species found in boggy soils from Florida to Texas that spreads by stolons. Bears umbels of three to six fragrant flowers atop thick 1¹/₂- to 2-foot-tall stems from late spring to fall. Individual flowers are 4 to 5 inches

Crocosmia 'Lucifer'

long and have narrow, wide-spreading tepals that are creamy white tinged with purple-brown on the backs. **Zones 9 to 11.**

C. asiaticum

c. ay-see-AT-ih-kum. POISON BULB, GRAND CRINUM. (Some varieties produce poisonous bulbs, other do not, thus the name "poison bulb.") A variable 2-foot-tall species native to the tropics of Asia producing clumps of bulbs and large umbels of 20 or more fragrant white flowers in summer. Individual flowers are spidery, with narrow 3-inch-long tepals. **Zones 8 to 11.**

C. bulbispermum

c. bul-bih-SPER-mum. JAMAICA CRINUM. Formerly *C. longifolium*. A South African native bearing umbels of 8 to as many as 15 fragrant, funnel- to bell-shaped, lilylike flowers on 2- to 4-foot-tall stalks in late summer or early fall. Blooms are 3 inches wide, 3 to 4 inches long, and white or pink on the inside, blushed with red-purple on the outside. **Zones 7 to 10.**

C. hybrids

A variety of attractive hybrid crinums are available. These include 'Bradley', with fragrant rose-pink flowers that have white throats; 'Carolina Beauty', with white flowers; and 'Ellen Bosanquet', with spicy-scented wine red bell-shaped flowers. **Zones 7 to 10.**

C. × powellii

c. × pow-ELL-ee-eye. A hybrid species bearing showy umbels of 8 to 10 fragrant 4-inch-long flowers on 4- to 5-foot-tall stalks in late summer and fall. Blooms are trumpet shaped, 3 to 4 inches long, and pink in color. 'Album' bears white flowers. **Zones 7 to 10.**

Crocosmia

kroh-KOS-mee-uh. Iris family, Iridaceae.

Grown for their arching clusters of trumpet-shaped flowers, crocosmias are perennials native to the grasslands of South Africa. The flowers, which are borne in mid- to late summer, are carried in arching spikes or panicles. They are tubular to funnel shaped with six spreading lobes, or petal-like tepals. Blooms come in shades of orange, red-orange, and yellow. Plants grow from corms and produce 2- to 3-foot-tall clumps of ribbed, linear- to sword-shaped leaves. The botanical name is a reference to the fact that the flowers have a saffronlike fragrance when soaked in water: it is from the Greek *krokos*, meaning "saffron," and *osme*, "smell." While seven species belong to the genus, gardeners primarily grow hybrids.

HOW TO GROW

Select a site in full sun with evenly moist soil that is rich in organic matter. Crocosmias tolerate partial shade in the South. Plant the corms in spring at a depth of 3 to

4 inches, spacing them 4 to 5 inches apart. Plants form dense, good-sized clumps with time. Where they are hardy, grow them outdoors year-round. Where they are marginally hardy, select a warm spot, such as one against a south-facing wall, and protect plants over winter by spreading a thick layer of a coarse mulch such as evergreen boughs, salt hay, pine needles, or coarse leaves after the ground has frozen in fall. (Mulch is especially important the first year; after that only plants in the coldest areas require winter protection.) Where these plants are not hardy, dig the clumps in fall, clean soil off the corms, pack them in dry sand, and overwinter them in a cool (35° to 40°F), dry place. It is best to avoid lifting the corms annually, however, because they will not flower as well. They also can be treated as annuals. Divide the clumps in spring if they become overcrowded and begin to bloom less or for propagation.

C. × crocosmiiflora

c. × kro-kos-mih-FLOR-uh. CROCOSMIA, MONTBRETIA. A vigorous 2- to 3-foot-tall hybrid bearing arching spikes, which may or may not be branched, of 1¹/₂- to 2-inch-long orange or yellow flowers in summer. **Zones 6 to 9.**

C. hybrids

Many cultivars have been selected, including 'Citronella', with yellow blooms; 'Emberglow', with dark red blooms; 'Emily McKenzie', with orange flowers with red-brown throats; 'Jackanapes' (also listed as 'Fire King') and 'Venus', with bicolored orange-red and yellow blooms; 'Jenny Bloom', with pale yellow flowers; and 'Lucifer', with bright red flowers and reportedly hardy to **Zone 5**. **Zones 6 to 9**.

C. masoniorum

c. mah-so-nee-OR-um. A 3- to 4-foot-tall species with pleated leaves and 2-inch-long orange-red flowers in midsummer. **Zones 7 to 9**.

Crocus

KRO-kus. Iris family, Iridaceae.

The cup-shaped blooms of crocuses are a familiar sight from late winter to early spring. Without doubt, hybrid crocuses are the most widely planted, but this genus of 80 species offers gardeners a wealth of charming species that bloom in spring as well as fall. All grow from corms and produce grassy leaves that appear with or just after the flowers. Each corm produces from one to about four or five blooms that lack aboveground stems: the so-called stem that arises from the ground actually is the tubular base of the corolla (petals). The individual flowers, which range from cup to goblet shaped, consist of six petal-like tepals. Spring-blooming crocuses come in shades of yellow, white, purple, and lavender, with many selections bearing bicolored blooms. Autumn-blooming crocuses tend toward shades of rose-purple, purple, and violet. Many selections have showy stamens or styles in contrasting colors.

True crocuses (*Crocus*) are not

to be confused with autumn crocuses (*Colchicum*), which belong to the lily family. For more on the differences between these two genera, see *Colchicum*.

HOW TO GROW

Select a site in full sun with poor to average, sandy or gritty, well-drained soil. Spring-blooming selections tolerate light shade under deciduous trees, where they receive full spring sunshine when they are growing actively. The corms do not do well in clay soils or moist conditions. Most prefer dry soil in summer when they are dormant — some require dry conditions in summer and are best planted in very well drained sites in rock gardens or in containers that can be protected from summer rains. Plant the corms 3 to 4 inches deep. Spring-blooming crocuses are planted in fall, while fall-blooming selections are planted as soon as they are available in late summer or very early fall.

For the longest display of bloom, plant a variety of species and cultivars. The earliest-blooming crocuses include snow crocus (*C. chrysanthus*), *C. tommasinianus*, and cloth-of-gold crocus (*C. angustifolius*), which flower from late winter into early spring. Scotch crocuses (*C. biflorus*) and Dutch crocuses (*C. vernus*) bloom somewhat later, in early to mid-spring. Fall-blooming crocuses include *C. speciosus*, *C. kotschyanus*, *C. medius*, and *C. pulchellus*.

Dutch crocuses (*C. vernus*) are one of the best species for naturalizing in a lawn, but they tend to die out after several years unless the turf is sparse. Replace them as necessary. Other species suitable for naturalizing include *C. biflorus* and *C. tommasinianus*. Do not mow the lawn until after the cro-

Crocus sativus

cus foliage turns yellow and dies back. Naturalizing crocuses in wild gardens as well as beds and borders, rather than in grass, yields longer-lived stands.

Propagate crocuses by separating the offsets just as the leaves turn yellow and the corms go dormant in early summer; most crocuses self-sow and produce abundant offsets where happy.

C. ancyrensis

c. an-see-REN-sis. GOLDEN BUNCH CROCUS. Late-winter- to early-spring-blooming species with 2-inch-tall bright yellow to orange-yellow flowers. **Zones 3 to 8**.

C. angustifolius

c. an-gus-tih-FOE-lee-us. CLOTH-OF-GOLD CROCUS. Formerly *C. susianus*. An early-spring-flowering 2-inch-tall species with orange-yellow flowers marked with maroon-brown on the outside. **Zones 3 to 8**.

C. biflorus

c. bi-FLOR-us. SCOTCH CROCUS. Early-spring-blooming species native from Italy, the Balkans, and southern Ukraine to Iran, not Scotland. Bears white or lilac-blue flowers, usually in pairs, that have yellow throats. The outer petals are sometimes striped with brown-purple. Plants are 2 to 2¹/₂ inches tall in bloom. Vigorous and good for naturalizing. *C. biflorus* ssp. *alexandri* has white flowers striped with purple on the outside. *C. biflorus* ssp. *weldenii* 'Albus' has white flowers. 'Miss Vain' bears fragrant white flowers with pale lilac-blue bases and showy orange styles. *C. biflorus* ssp. *weldenii* 'Fairy' bears white flowers dusted with lavender on the outside. **Zones 3 to 8**.

C. cartwrightianus

c. kart-rite-ee-AH-nus. FALL CROCUS. Fall- to early-winter-blooming 2-inch-tall species bearing fragrant lilac to white flowers with brilliant orange styles on 2-inch plants. Requires very well drained soil and a dry summer dormancy. *C. cartwrightianus* f. *albus* bears white flowers. **Zones 6 to 8**.

C. chrysanthus

c. krih-SAN-thus. SNOW CROCUS. Among the first crocuses to bloom in late winter to early spring. Bears lightly fragrant golden yellow flowers often marked with maroon on the outside and typically featuring showy orange stamens. Plants reach 2 inches tall. Many cultivars are available, including 'Advance', with pale peach-yellow flowers that are white and bluish violet on the outside and feature orange stamens; 'Blue Bird', creamy white inside and violet-blue outside; 'Blue Pearl', soft blue on the outside with a bronze-yellow base and a yellow throat; 'Cream Beauty', creamy yellow on the outside, darker yellow inside, and featuring brilliant orange stamens; 'E.A. Bowles', lemon yellow with bronze-yellow at the base; 'Gipsy Girl', bright yellow striped with bronze-purple; 'Goldilocks', dark yellow with purple-brown at the base; 'Ladykiller', white striped with purple; 'Prins Claus', white flowers with oval blue-purple blotches on the outside of the tepals; 'Prinses Beatrix' ('Princess Beatrix'), blue with rich yellow at the base; and 'Snow Bunting', white streaked with lilac on the outside. **Zones 3 to 8**.

C. etruscus

c. eh-TRUS-kus. Late-winter- to early-spring-blooming 3-inch-tall species with lilac flowers that have yellow throats. The outer tepals are buff to creamy colored on the outside, while the inner ones are lightly veined with purple. 'Zwanenburg' bears lilac-blue flowers. **Zones 5 to 8**.

C. flavus

c. FLAY-vus. Formerly *C. aureus*. Spring-blooming 3-inch-tall species with orange-yellow flowers. **Zones 5 to 8**.

C. goulimyi

c. goo-LIM-ee-eye. FALL CROCUS. Fall-blooming 3- to 4-inch-tall species with rosy lilac flowers. **Zones 3 to 8**.

Crocus ancyrensis

Crocus vernus

C. imperati

c. im-per-AH-tee. ITALIAN CROCUS. Late-winter- to early-spring-blooming species that reaches about 4 inches and bears purple flowers striped with tawny yellow on the outside. 'De Jager' has flowers that are violet purple with a yellow heart and tawny yellow-brown striped with purple outside. **Zones 5 to 8.**

C. korolkowii

c. ko-rol-KOH-vee-eye. CELANDINE CROCUS. Late-winter- to early-spring-blooming species that reaches about 4 inches in bloom and bears golden yellow flowers feathered with brown on the outside. Requires completely dry conditions in summer once plants have gone dormant. **Zones 3 to 8.**

C. kotschyanus

c. kot-skee-AH-nus. Formerly *C. zonatus*. Fall-blooming 2- to 3-inch-tall species with pale violet flowers. Requires dry conditions in summer once plants have gone dormant. **Zones 3 to 8.**

C. laevigatus

c. lee-vih-GAH-tus. Fall- to early-winter-blooming 1¹/₂- to 3-inch-tall species bearing white or lilac flowers that are yellow or tan on the outside and streaked with violet-purple. **Zones 5 to 8.**

C. longiflorus

c. lon-jih-FLOR-us. Fall-blooming 3- to 4-inch-tall species bearing fragrant pale to dark lilac flowers. Requires dry conditions in summer once plants have gone dormant. **Zones 5 to 8.**

C. medius

c. MEE-dee-us. Fall-blooming 3-inch-tall species with pale to dark purple flowers featuring brilliant orange styles. **Zones 3 to 8.**

C. minimus

c. MIN-ih-mus. Late-spring-blooming 3-inch-tall species with rich lilac purple flowers and yellow-buff outer petals marked in dark purple. **Zones 3 to 8.**

C. niveus

c. NIV-ee-us. Fall-blooming 4- to 6-inch-tall species with white or pale lilac flowers featuring showy orange styles. Requires dry conditions in summer once plants have gone dormant. **Zones 5 to 8.**

C. ochroleucus

c. oh-kroh-LEW-kus. Fall-blooming 2-inch-tall species with creamy white flowers that have yellow throats. **Zones 5 to 8.**

C. pulchellus

c. pul-CHEL-us. Fall- to early-winter-blooming 4- to 5-inch-tall species with pale lilac-blue flowers that have yellow throats. **Zones 3 to 8.**

C. sativus

c. sah-TEE-vus. SAFFRON CROCUS. Fall- to early-winter-blooming 2-inch-tall species bearing lilac purple flowers veined in dark purple. The showy red styles are the source of the spice saffron. Plants do not flower well in areas with cool, wet summers. **Zones 5 to 8.**

C. sieberi

c. SYE-ber-eye. Late-winter- to early-spring-blooming 2- to 3-inch-tall species bearing rose-purple flowers with yellow throats. 'Bowles' White' bears white flowers; 'Firefly' has white blooms that are white on the outside and flushed with pale violet on the inside; 'Tricolor' features lilac-blue flowers with golden yellow centers edged in white. **Zones 5 to 8.**

C. speciosus

c. spee-see-OH-sus. FALL CROCUS. Vigorous, fall-blooming 4- to 6-inch-tall species with violet-blue flowers with darker purple-blue veins. **Zones 3 to 8.**

C. tommasinianus

c. tom-mah-sin-ee-AH-nus. Vigorous, late-winter- to early-spring-blooming species that reaches 3 to 4 inches and bears pale lilac to red-purple blooms. Good for naturalizing. 'Barr's Purple' bears violet flowers that are silvery on the outside. 'Ruby Giant' has red-purple flowers. 'Whitewell Purple' bears red-purple blooms. **Zones 3 to 8.**

C. vernus

c. VER-nus. DUTCH CROCUS. Popular spring-blooming species reaching 4 to 5 inches tall and bearing white, pale lilac, or rich purple flowers. Many cultivars are available, including 'Flower Record', with dark purple blooms; 'Jeanne d'Arc', white with a purple base; 'Mammoth Yellow', yellow; 'Pickwick', white striped with purple; and 'Remembrance', violet purple. Vigorous and good for naturalizing. **Zones 3 to 8.**

C. versicolor

c. VER-sih-kuh-lor. Late-winter- to early-spring-blooming 5- to 6-inch-tall species with white flowers sometimes striped with purple on the outside and lemon yellow throats. **Zones 3 to 8.**

Cryptomeria

krip-toe-MIR-ee-ah. Bald cypress family, Taxodiaceae.

This genus contains only one species, which is native to Asia, where it is an important timber tree. It is also a much-loved garden plant in Asia and North America.

HOW TO GROW

Plant in full sun where conditions are cool, but best in partial to light shade in hot areas. Needs fertile,

Cryptomeria japonica 'Sekkan-Sugi'

moist, deep, acid soil. Does not tolerate drought. Performs best in humid areas. Protect from winter wind, especially in the coldest areas. Remove dead inner needles if they are unsightly. Will resprout only from wood that contains needles, but may be pruned for a hedge. Lower limbs may be removed to show off the trunk bark. Usually pest-free, but spider mites, leaf blight, branch dieback, and leaf spot are sometimes disfiguring.

C. japonica

c. juh-PON-ih-kuh. JAPANESE CEDAR, CRYPTOMERIA. This elegant conifer with a tall, straight trunk matures into a pyramidal or conical form that reaches 50 or more feet tall and 25 feet wide, with branches layered from its pointed top right to the ground. The $^1/_4$- to $^3/_4$-inch-long, awl-shaped, four-sided, scalelike needles are bright green or blue-green and slightly twisted. They are arranged spirally in plumelike clusters along slightly pendulous, spreading branches, which gives the tree an unusual and beautiful texture. In winter the foliage of the species turns bronze-blue or reddish, but some cultivars retain their summer color. Trunk bark is

reddish brown and shredding. Cones are dark brown and 1 inch around, with 20 pointed scales. Japanese cedar is one of the best conifers to grow in the South. Use it as a specimen or plant it as a screen or in a grove. Several small cultivars are available. Use them in rock gardens or in a shrub border. They do not do well in containers. From China and Japan. **Zones 6 to 9**.

CULTIVARS

Seedlings are variable and do not always grow into attractive plants; named cultivars are best. 'Benjamin Franklin' grows densely to 40 feet tall; rich green needles and no dead inner foliage; resists fungus; tolerates wind and salt spray. 'Elegans' is very dense and compact, with longer needles and an attractive burgundy-plum color in winter. 'Elegans compacta' is a 3- to 6-foot dwarf. 'Glabrosa Nana' is 2 to 5 feet. 'Lobbii' is compact, with slender twigs and long, deep green needles that are densely compacted at the branch tips and remain green in winter. 'Sekkan Sugi' is a slow-growing, dense tree; creamy to bright yellow new growth. 'Yoshino' is narrow, grows to 30 feet tall, and has bright blue-green foliage all year; no dead inner foliage; resists fungus.

Cunninghamia lanceolata 'Glauca'

Cuphea hyssopifolia

Cunninghamia

kun-ing-HAM-ee-ah. Bald-cypress family, Taxodiaceae.

The three species of this genus, which look rather like the monkey-puzzle tree (*Araucaria araucans*), have flat needles that spread out from the stems in two ranks. Native to eastern Asia.

HOW TO GROW

Plant in full sun or light shade and evenly moist soil. Tolerates urban conditions. Protect from wind in the coldest areas. May form several trunks at ground level; best to prune to one trunk. Unlike most conifers, this one resprouts from leafless wood and even from stumps if cut to the ground. Cones and small deciduous branches require cleanup. Remove old brown needles by hand or with a strong spray from a hose. Usually pest-free.

C. lanceolata

c. lan-see-oh-LAH-tuh. CHINA FIR. This uncommon evergreen is a bold-textured, unique-looking plant with a strong central leader and open, irregular branches that form a broadly pyramidal crown with a rounded top. It reaches 60 feet tall and 30 feet wide. The glossy, blue-green, $2^1/_2$-inch-long needles are broad and flat, with sharp points and two white lines on their undersides. They are arranged in two ranks on either side of the branches, creating a distinc-

tive texture. The prickly, 2-inch-long cones grow in clusters and drop to the ground while still attached to large twigs. Trunk bark is reddish brown and peels in strips. Use this distinctive tree as a specimen on a large property. From China. **Zones 6 to 9**.

CULTIVARS

The species is quite variable. 'Chason's Gift' is fast growing and densely symmetrical. 'Glauca' has dark green needles with a blue cast.

Cuphea

KOO-fee-ah. Lythrum family, Lythraceae.

Some 250 annuals, short-lived perennials, and shrubs native to North, Central, and South America belong to the genus *Cuphea*. All bear tubular flowers either singly or in clusters; most have ovate to lance-shaped leaves and are covered with sticky hairs.

HOW TO GROW

A site in full sun or light shade with average to fertile, well-drained soil satisfies these plants. Sow seeds indoors 10 to 12 weeks before the last spring frost date. Just press the seeds into the soil surface, as light is required for germination, which takes 1 to 2 weeks at 70°F. Once seedlings appear, reduce the temperature to about 60°F. Most of the commonly grown species are tender perennials or tender shrubs, hardy from **Zone 10 south**. Propagate them by

× *Cupressocyparis leylandii*

cuttings taken in late spring or by division. In the North, grow them in containers and overwinter them indoors (in a bright, 60° to 65°F spot), or treat them as bedding plants replaced annually. Use *Cuphea* species as edgings or in beds combined with other annuals. They also make attractive container plants, and hummingbirds visit the flowers.

C. hyssopifolia

c. hiss-up-ih-FOE-lee-ah. MEXICAN HEATHER, HAWAIIAN HEATHER, ELFIN HERB. A bushy, tender, 1- to 2-foot shrub with narrow, lance-shaped leaves. Bears small clusters of pale pinkish purple, pink, or white, ¹/₂-inch-long flowers from summer to fall. Tender perennial, or grow as a warm-weather annual.

C. ignea

c. IG-nee-ah. CIGAR FLOWER, FIRECRACKER PLANT. Formerly *C. platycentra*. A tender, 1- to 2¹/₂-foot shrub or subshrub with lance-shaped to oblong leaves. Showy, tubular, ³/₄- to 1¹/₄-inch-long flowers with red to red-orange calyxes (not true petals) appear singly in the leaf axils from early summer to fall. Blooms have a white edge and two dark purple petals at the tip, making them resemble a lit cigarette. Tender perennial, or grow as a warm-weather annual.

C. × purpurea

c. × pur-PUR-ee-ah. A tender 1- to 2-foot subshrub with lance-shaped or ovate leaves. Clusters of pink to red, 1¹/₄-inch-long flowers appear from early summer to fall. Tender perennial, or grow as a warm-weather annual.

× Cupressocyparis

× kew-press-oh-SYE-par-is. Cypress family, Cupressaceae.

The three hybrid coniferous trees called × *Cupressocyparis* are natural hybrids between species of *Chamaecyparis* and *Cupressus*. They were found growing in England and Wales at the end of the 19th century and are notable for their extremely fast growth, as much as 3 feet a year. The most popular form is Leyland cypress (× *C. leylandii*).

HOW TO GROW

Plant in full sun to partial shade; will be less dense in full shade. Prefers fertile, moist soil. Adapts to acid or alkaline soil. Plentiful

× *Cupressocyparis leylandii*

moisture is best, especially when newly planted. Tolerates heat, salt spray, and seashore conditions. Remove multiple leaders to avoid storm damage. May be sheared in early summer for a formal hedge. Bagworms and canker are serious in some areas. Phytophora root rot is troublesome in wet sites. Excellent in the South. Newly planted trees are susceptible to winterkill in **Zone 6**.

× C. leylandii

× c. lay-LAND-ee-eye. LEYLAND CYPRESS. This vigorous, fast-growing, handsome tree is a hybrid between *Chamaecyparis nootkatensis* (Nootka cypress) and *Cupressus macrocarpa* (Monterey cypress). It has a columnar or narrow, pyramidal shape and reaches 65 feet tall but only 15 feet wide, with dense growth all the way to the ground. It may get even taller with great age. The bright green needles are soft scales that are pressed into ropelike bunches

along the stems and form flattened fans that resemble those of Nootka cypress. Because it grows so fast, this evergreen makes an especially valuable screen or hedge in full sun or partial shade, but it is also a useful focal point in a border or lawn. Where pests and diseases are prevalent, use *Juniperus chinensis* 'Spartan' or *Thuja plicata* 'Hogan' instead for screens and hedges. **Zones 6 to 9**.

CULTIVARS

'Castlewellan' has golden yellow new growth that turns bronze in winter; grows to 20 feet tall. 'Robinson Gold' is more golden and faster growing than 'Castlewellan'. 'Emerald Isle' has very dense, bright green, flattened sprays and reaches 25 feet tall. 'Gold Cup' has gold-tipped new growth. 'Green Spire' is dense and narrowly columnar, with bright green foliage. 'Naylor's Blue' has bright gray-blue, slightly pendulous foliage and loose branching; grows to 35 feet tall; looks more like Monterey cypress than other cultivars do. 'Silver Dust' has lovely foliage with creamy variegation.

Cupressus

kew-PRESS-us. Cypress family, Cupressaceae.

Thirteen to 25 species belong to this genus, which is very similar to

Cupressus arizonica 'Glauca'

Cupressus macrocarpa

Chamaecyparis but has shiny, marble-sized cones that remain on the tree and stay closed for many years. Most *Cupressus* species perform best in the mild climates of the West and Southwest and suffer from disease problems elsewhere.

HOW TO GROW

Plant in full sun and well-drained soil. Tolerates a range of soils, from heavy to light, alkaline to acid. Very drought, wind, and heat tolerant. May be short-lived in the East unless soil is very well drained. Prune to a single leader if necessary. Tolerates heavy pruning or shearing. Mites and bagworms may be a problem. Susceptible to twig blight, but less so than junipers, and suffers from stem canker.

C. arizonica var. *glabra*

c. air-ree-ZON-eh-kuh var. GLAY-bruh. ARIZONA CYPRESS. A fast-growing, dense, pyramidal tree that reaches 35 feet tall and 15 to 20 feet wide, this species is cultivated only in the blue-leaved form described here. Foliage is made up of tiny, sharp-pointed, gray-green or blue-green, white-flecked scales that are pressed against the stems, creating ropelike branches. The bluest cultivars are quite beautiful and very popular. Trunk bark is shiny and reddish brown, like that of a cherry tree, and flaking. Cones are about an inch around, larger than those of *Chamaecyparis*. Arizona cypress makes an excellent, fine-textured screen, windbreak, or specimen in a sunny, dry site and can be used as a substitute for Rocky Mountain juniper (*Juniperus scopularum*) in areas where disease limits its use. From southwestern North America. **Zones 7 to 9.**

CULTIVARS AND SIMILAR SPECIES

'Blue Ice' is a very narrow, conical tree that grows to 30 feet tall and 8 feet wide; powder blue needles and red-tinged twigs. 'Blue Pyramid' has handsome gray-blue needles and forms a compact pyramid, growing to 20 feet tall and 10 feet wide. 'Carolina Sapphire' has bright blue needles and a full shape and is very fast growing. *C. sempervirens* (Italian cypress) is a narrow, columnar tree with dark green needles; grows to 50 feet tall and 3 to 10 feet wide; popular as a dramatic, tall screen in mild, dry climates; **Zones 7 to 11.** 'Glauca' has blue-green foliage.

Cupressus glabra

C. macrocarpa

c. mack-roe-KAR-puh. MONTEREY CYPRESS. This tree has a strong pyramidal shape with a spiky top when young, but it matures into a picturesque, flat-topped specimen with horizontal branches that reaches 40 feet tall and 30 feet wide. When grown on the coast, the tree takes on a rugged, wind-swept look. Canker is a serious problem away from the coast. Foliage consists of tiny, dark green, pointed scales that are closely pressed against the stems and borne in irregular sprays. Leaves are aromatic, releasing a lemony scent when crushed. Trunk bark is reddish brown and ridged. Use as a specimen or screen in the West. Use dwarf forms in borders and foundation plantings. From the West Coast of North America. **Zones 8 to 9.**

CULTIVARS

'Golden Pillar' is a dwarf that forms a compact cone, growing to 15 feet tall; vertical fans of golden outer foliage and chartreuse inner foliage. 'Horizontalis Aurea' form a 20-foot-tall, narrow column with golden foliage.

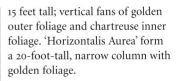

Curcuma

kur-KOO-muh. Ginger family, Zingiberaceae.

Curcuma species are tropical perennials native from India and Malaysia to Australia that grow from thick, fleshy, branching, aromatic rhizomes. Plants have reedlike stems and bear lance- or somewhat paddle-shaped leaf blades. Sometimes called pinecone gingers, they are grown for their large inflorescences, which resemble colorful pinecones: showy, overlapping bracts often hide the true flowers, which are small and tubular and have three petals. The rhizomes of some species have been used as herbs, including *C. longa* (also listed as *C. domestica*), commonly known as turmeric and used both medicinally and in curries. True gingers belong to the genus *Zingiber*, and culinary ginger is *Z. officinale*.

HOW TO GROW

Give these plants partial shade and deeply prepared, moist soil rich in organic matter. They thrive in areas with warm summers and high

Curcuma alismatifolia

Cyclamen coum

humidity and are ideal for gardens in the tropics and subtropics or for adding an exotic touch to more northern gardens in summer. Where hardy, they can be grown outdoors year-round. In the North, plant the rhizomes out in spring after the soil has warmed up. To overwinter, dig the rhizomes after a light frost and cut back the tops. Store the rhizomes in barely damp vermiculite, peat moss, or sand in a cool (55° to 60°F), dry place. Inspect rhizomes occasionally in winter: discard rotted pieces or cut away rotted portions and dust cuts with sulfur; sprinkle the vermiculite with water occasionally during winter to keep the roots from shriveling. Replant in spring. These plants also make excellent year-round container plants; keep them nearly dry in winter. Propagate by dividing the rhizomes in spring.

C. alismatifolia
c. al-iss-mah-tih-FOE-lee-uh. PINECONE GINGER, SIAM TULIP. A 1½- to 2-foot-tall species with dark green leaves and inflorescences of pink bracts. **Zones 8 to 10.**

C. petiolata
c. peh-tee-oh-LAH-tuh. QUEEN LILY. A 2- to 3-foot-tall species with 10-inch-long leaves and 6-inch-long bloom spikes in summer that have tiny ½-inch-long

yellow-and-white flowers surrounded by violet upper bracts and green lower bracts. **Zones 8 to 10.**

C. roscoeana
c. ros-koh-ee-AH-nuh. JEWEL OF BURMA. A 2½- to 3-foot-tall species with oval leaves and erect 8-inch-long spikes in summer with yellow ½-inch-long flowers surrounded by showy orange bracts. **Zones 8 to 10.**

C. zedoaria
c. zeh-doe-AH-ree-uh. PINECONE GINGER. A 3-foot-tall species with handsome 1-foot-long rounded to lance-shaped leaves that have a maroon-brown stripe down the center. In summer, it bears 4-inch-long bloom spikes with green bracts tinged with maroon-red or purple. **Zones 8 to 10.**

Cyclamen

SYE-klah-men. Primrose family, Primulaceae.

Florist's cyclamen are fairly well known to gardeners and nongardeners alike, but this genus also contains several charming hardy species that deserve to be more widely grown. Hardy cyclamen are diminutive versions of the showy florist's pot plants: they grow from rounded tubers that actually are stem tubers rather than

conventional root tubers. Plants have attractive, heart- to kidney-shaped dark green leaves usually handsomely marked with silver. Depending on the species, plants bloom in late winter to early spring or from late summer to fall. Their small pink or white blooms are carried on leafless stalks above the foliage and resemble shuttlecocks: they are solitary and nodding and have five reflexed (backward-pointing) petals that are slightly twisted and are joined in a short tube at the base of the flower. In most species, once the flowers are pollinated the flower stalks (peduncles) coil down to the soil surface to release the seeds. The botanical name refers to this characteristic — it is from the Greek *kyklos,* meaning "circular." About 19 species belong to the genus, most native from Europe and the Mediterranean region to Iran.

HOW TO GROW
For most species of hardy cyclamen, select a site in partial shade with loose soil that is well drained and rich in organic matter. Plant the tubers 1½ to 2 inches deep, spaced 3 to 4 inches apart. When the leaves fade each year, mulch the plants with compost or leaf mold, and mark their locations to avoid digging into them by mistake when plants are dormant. (Fall-blooming species are green from late summer or fall through spring and disappear in summer.)

In areas where cyclamen are marginally hardy, mulch the plants in late fall with evergreen boughs, oak leaves, or another coarse mulch to protect them from winter freezing and thawing cycles. Some species, including *C. creticum,* require dry soil when they are dormant. Grow them in a cold frame or cold greenhouse, or try them in pots sunk to the rim in the soil in summer in a spot that offers excellent drainage, then overwinter the pots in a cold frame or greenhouse where they can be protected from rain during their dormant season. Propagate by seeds; cyclamen tubers grow larger each year but do not produce offsets. Plants may self-sow.

C. cilicium
c. sih-LIH-see-um. A fall-blooming 2-inch-tall species with green ½- to 2-inch-long leaves heavily marked with silver. Bears pink or white ½- to ¾-inch-long flowers with dark red at the base of the petals. Can be grown as above or planted with the tubers at a depth of about 1 inch and given dry conditions after the foliage goes dormant in early summer. Flowers are produced with the leaves. **Zones 5 to 9.**

C. coum
c. KOOM. HARDY CYCLAMEN. A late-winter- to early-spring-blooming 2- to 3-inch-tall species with attractive, rounded, 1- to 2½-inch-long leaves that are either solid dark green or marked with silver; either way, they remain green over winter. Bears ½-inch-long flowers ranging from white to shades of pale to dark pink or pinkish red. Petals have dark reddish pink blotches at the base. Flowers appear with the leaves. **Zones 5 to 9.**

C. creticum
c. KREH-tih-kum. A spring-blooming 2- to 3-inch-tall species with 1½-inch-long gray-green leaves and white to pale pink ½- to 1-inch-long flowers. Plant tubers no more than 1 inch deep, or with the top of the tuber right at the soil surface, and give plants very well drained soil. They require dry soil conditions when dormant. Flowers appear with the leaves. **Zones 7 to 9.**

C. hederifolium
c. heh-der-ih-FOE-lee-um. HARDY CYCLAMEN. Formerly *C. neapolitanum.* Fall-blooming 4- to

Cynara cardunculus

5-inch-tall species bearing dark green 2- to 6-inch-long leaves that may be triangular or heart shaped and often are heavily patterned with silver. Bears 1-inch-long flowers in shades of pink with darker pink blotches at the base of the petals. Flowers appear before the leaves. **Zones 6 or 7 to 9.**

C. persicum

c. PER-sih-kum. FLORIST'S CYCLAMEN. A tender species with 8-inch-tall mounds of dark green 1- to 5-inch-wide leaves often patterned in silver. Bears fragrant $^1/_2$- to 1-inch-long flowers atop the foliage from late winter to early spring. Plant tubers no more than 1 inch deep, or with the top of the tuber right at the soil surface, and give plants very well drained soil. They require cool (55° to 60°F), humid conditions when growing actively and dry soil conditions when dormant in summer. **Zones 10 to 11.**

C. purpurascens

c. pur-pur-ASS-senz. Also listed as *C. europaeum, C. fatrense.* A mid- to late-summer-blooming species that reaches about 4 inches tall. Bears 3-inch-long dark green leaves that are evergreen or sometimes deciduous and may have faint silver markings. Fragrant magenta-pink $^3/_4$-inch-long flowers appear with the leaves. Best in alkaline soil. **Zones 5 to 9.**

C. repandum

c. reh-PAN-dum. HARDY CYCLAMEN. A spring-blooming 4- to 6-inch-tall species with dark green 5-

inch-long leaves spotted or marked with gray-green. Bears fragrant magenta-pink $^3/_4$-inch-long flowers that appear with the leaves. **Zones 7 to 9.**

Cynara

sin-AH-ruh. Aster family, Asteraceae.

Commonly called cardoons or artichokes, thistlelike *Cynara* species are perennials native to the Mediterranean region, northern Africa, and the Canary Islands. They bear clumps of handsome, often gray-green leaves that are cut in a featherlike (pinnatifid) fashion and rounded flower heads that resemble thistles. The flower heads, which have a conelike base consisting of spiny bracts surrounding a dense tuft of soft disk florets, are carried singly or in clusters on stalks above the foliage. About 10 species belong to the genus, one of which is grown primarily for its foliage as a perennial, tender perennial, or annual.

HOW TO GROW

Give cardoons full sun and well-drained, average to rich soil. For best foliage effect, remove flower stalks as they appear. Mulch plants over winter with salt hay or weed-free straw where they are marginally hardy. Propagate by seeds, divide clumps in spring, or take root cuttings in late fall or winter.

C. cardunculus

c. kar-DUN-kew-lus. CARDOON. A large perennial that forms 4-foot-wide clumps of 2-foot-long deeply

cut leaves that are gray-green above and silvery beneath. Bears $1^1/_2$- to 3-inch-wide flower heads on stalks up to 5 feet tall from early summer to fall. **Zones 6 or 7 to 9.**

Cynoglossum

sin-oh-GLOSS-um. Borage family, Boraginaceae.

Cynoglossum contains about 55 species of annuals, biennials, and short-lived perennials. All are characterized by rough, hairy stems and leaves, and sprays of small flowers that resemble forget-me-nots (*Myosotis*). The tubular

to funnel-shaped blooms come in rich, true blue, as well as purple, pink, and white.

HOW TO GROW

A site with full sun to partial shade and average, moist but well-drained soil is ideal. Too-rich soil yields lots of foliage but weak plants and few flowers. Sow seeds indoors 6 to 8 weeks before the last spring frost date. Or sow outdoors several weeks before the last spring frost date. From Zone 5 south, Chinese forget-me-not (*C. amabile*) can be sown in fall and grown as a biennial. Germination takes 1 to 2 weeks at 65° to 75°F; be sure to cover the seeds with soil, as darkness is required for germination. Add these plants to beds and borders and semiwild gardens. Plants self-sow.

C. amabile

c. ah-MAH-bil-ee. CHINESE FORGET-ME-NOT. A $1^1/_2$- to 2-foot biennial producing clumps of hairy, lance-shaped, gray-green leaves. Bears terminal cymes of $^1/_4$- to $^1/_2$-inch flowers in blue or sometimes pink or white in mid- to late summer. 'Blue Showers' bears rich blue flowers; 'Mystery Rose' has soft lilac-pink ones. Biennial or cool-weather annual.

Cypella

sih-PEL-uh. Iris family, Iridaceae.

Native to Central and South America, *Cypella* species are sometimes grown for their unusual-

Cynoglossum amabile

looking irislike flowers. The plants, which grow from elongated tunicate bulbs, bear pleated, lance-shaped leaves. The short-lived flowers are borne singly or in small clusters. Individual blooms consist of six petal-like tepals. The outer tepals are showy and spreading, while the much smaller inner tepals are erect and curve toward the center. Each flower lasts only a day, but blooms in each cluster open in succession and plants produce new clusters from late summer to fall.

HOW TO GROW

Select a site in full sun with average to rich, well-drained soil. Sandy soil is ideal, and plants are best in a warm site. Plant the bulbs at a depth of 3 inches. Where they're hardy, grow them outdoors year-round: plant them in fall and protect the sites with mulch over winter. In the North, plant the bulbs in spring, and overwinter them indoors. To overwinter, dig the bulbs after the first frost in fall, cut off the tops, dry the bulbs off, and dust off excess soil. Or, keep them in pots year-round: gradually withhold water and keep the soil dry in winter. Either way, store them in a cool (40° to 45°F), dry place. Propagate by offsets in late winter or early spring or by seeds.

C. herbertii

c. her-BER-tee-eye. A 1- to 3-foot-tall species native from Brazil south to Argentina. Bears loose clusters of 1¹/₂- to 3-inch-wide flowers with yellowish orange outer tepals and inner tepals spotted or lined with purple. **Zones 9 to 10**.

Cyrilla

HOW TO GROW

sye-RILL-a. Cyrilla family, Cyrillaceae.

The only species in this genus is a deciduous to evergreen shrub that grows naturally from the southeast United States to South America and is commonly known as leatherwood. In a garden it will lend interest throughout the seasons with an attractive foliage pattern and fall color, fragrant flowers, and handsome bark.

HOW TO GROW

Leatherwood should have rich, moisture-retentive, acid soil in full sun or partial shade with shelter from wind. It needs little pruning, although mature plants can sucker. Sow seeds in fall or take semiripe cuttings.

C. racemiflora

c. rass-eh-mih-FLOR-uh. LEATHER-WOOD. This native grows 3 to more than 10 feet tall and wide, smallest where summers are cool. Its leaves, which sometimes appear in whorls, turn orange and red in fall and may linger in the South. The fragrant white flowers are also held in a whorl — a 3- to 6-inch raceme of lizard-tail spikes that bloom in late summer or fall. Removing suckers and lower stems will reveal smooth brown bark

Cypella herbertii

and interesting twisted branches. **Zones 6 to 10**.

Cyrtanthus

sir-TAN-thus. Amaryllis family, Amaryllidaceae.

Commonly known as fire lilies, *Cyrtanthus* species are bulbous plants native to Africa, primarily South Africa. The common name refers to the fact that these plants typically bloom most abundantly after fires sweep through their native habitat. Flowers, which may be fragrant, are borne in umbels atop leafless stalks and either are held horizontally or are pendulous. Individual blooms are tubular or funnel shaped, with a long, narrow, somewhat curved tube and six short petal-like tepals that usually flare out. Typically, the flowers come in shades of red and orange-red. Plants grow from tunicate bulbs that are either underground or partially exposed and bear strap-shaped or linear leaves that may be deciduous or evergreen.

HOW TO GROW

Select a site in full sun with average to rich, well-drained soil. Like many South African species, these plants need regular watering from late winter or early spring through summer when they are growing actively, and drier conditions when dormant in winter. In areas where they are hardy and that offer dry conditions in fall and winter, leave the bulbs in the ground year-round. In areas where they are marginally hardy, look for a protected, south-facing site and mulch plants over winter with evergreen boughs, salt hay, pine needles, or another coarse mulch. In the North and anywhere winters are wet, grow these plants in containers year-round or plant the bulbs in spring after the soil has warmed up and overwinter indoors. They bloom best when left undisturbed, so container culture is the best option in areas where they cannot be left outside year-round. Plant the bulbs in spring, setting them at a depth of 2 to 3 inches. Water regularly in dry weather. Gradually let the soil in containers dry out in fall and store the pots in a cool (40° to 50°F), dry spot over winter. Or dig the bulbs in fall after the first light frost (earlier if the leaves die back) and let them dry in a warm, shady spot for a few hours; brush off excess soil; and store them over winter in a cool, dry place. Propagate

Cyrilla racemiflora

Cyrtanthus elatus

by separating and planting the off-sets in spring or fall or by sowing seeds.

C. elatus

c. eh-LAH-tus. Formerly *C. purpureus*, *Vallota speciosa*. A 1- to 2-foot-tall species with strap-shaped leaves and umbels of two to nine funnel-shaped, 3- to 4-inch-long scarlet flowers in late summer. **Zones 10 and 11**.

Cyrtomium

sear-TOE-mee-um. Wood-fern family, Dryopteridaceae.

Long used as a houseplant with a tropical look, *Cyrtomium* is be-coming more widely used as a shade-loving ground cover in warm climates. The 10 to 12 species are native to warm regions of Asia, Africa, Hawaii, and the Americas. Cyrtomiums, or holly ferns, are related to Christmas ferns *(Polystichum)*. They are erect, with fronds reaching 2 to 3 feet tall. The individual pinnae (sections of the fronds) are relatively large, leathery, and often more than an inch long and nearly as wide. The pinnae are responsible for the common name — they remind observers of holly leaves. The fronds are deciduous at the northern limit of the ferns' growth and evergreen farther south. The botanical name is based on a Greek word meaning "arch" and refers to the curving venation pattern.

HOW TO GROW

Grow cyrtomiums in light to deep shade and an organic soil that does not dry out. Ample moisture is essential to good growth, or the fronds will not survive. Once established and thriving, cyrtomiums spread by spores. Unwanted young plants are easily removed. Hardiness varies by species.

C. falcatum

c. fal-KAY-tum. HOLLY FERN. A stalwart in southern gardens, this species makes a handsome, glossy, evergreen ground cover. It will tolerate drier air and more light than many ferns. Place plants about 18 inches apart and not too deep, and they will quickly fill in. 'Rochfordianum' has coarsely fringed frond segments. **Zones 8 to 10**.

C. fortunei var. intermedia

c. for-TOON-ee-eye var. in-ter-MEE-dee-uh. This variety is said to be hardier than *C. falcatum*. It makes a nicely textured ground cover in a woodland garden. **Zones 7 to 10**.

Cytisus

sye-TISS-us. Pea family, Fabaceae.

Commonly known as broom, about 50 species of deciduous or evergreen shrubs from Europe, western Asia, and northern Africa make up this genus. The palmate leaves are usually opposite and have three leaflets, the flowers are pealike and are followed by linear pods that can be downy.

HOW TO GROW

Broom is tolerant of poor, acidic soil; may become chlorotic in alkaline soil. Tends to be short-lived. Needs minimal pruning, but you can cut back flowered shoots to a new bud or sideshoot if you avoid cutting into old wood. Seeds may need to be soaked in hot water to encourage germination but sometimes self-sow. Take cuttings with a heel in late summer and overwinter in sand. *C. scoparius*, Scotch broom, has become a pest in the West, Northeast, and Mid-Atlantic and should be avoided. *C. × praecox* has become invasive in the West.

C. battandieri

c. bah-ton-dee-AIR-ee. PINEAPPLE BROOM. Deciduous, erect shrub to 15 feet tall and wide with hairy, silver, palmate leaves. Its dense terminal racemes of yellow flowers look and smell like pineapples and are followed by hairy pods. **Zones 7 to 9**.

C. × praecox

c. × PREE-koks. WARMINSTER BROOM. Deciduous and dense shrub, to 4 feet tall and wide, with many long upright shoots and undivided leaves. Midspring flowers are pale yellow. Cultivars offer white, salmon pink, or peach-colored blossoms. **Zones 6 to 9**.

Cyrtomium falcatum

Cytisus × praecox

D

Daboecia

dah-boe-EE-see-a. Heath family, Ericaceae.

Daboecia commemorates St. Daboec of ancient Ireland. Of the two species in this genus, one (*D. cantabrica*) is native to Atlantic Europe from Ireland to Spain, and the other (*D. azorica*) is endemic to the Azores off the coast of Africa. *D. cantabrica* is a small, evergreen, heathlike shrub that reaches 20 inches tall and 2 feet across. It has attractive, bell- or urn-shaped flowers, which are produced in summer in colors from white to purple and mauve. It is useful as a ground cover where heaths and heathers are reliably grown.

HOW TO GROW
Grow daboecias in full sun and organic, acid soils, such as those required for heaths and heathers. They require winter protection with salt hay or evergreen boughs to avoid sunscald. In North America, these plants are best suited to cool maritime climates.

D. cantabrica
d. kan-TAH-brih-kuh. IRISH HEATH, CONNEMARA HEATH. Formerly *Menziesia polifolia*. This native of Atlantic southwestern Europe and Ireland thrives in maritime climates. It does not do well in harsh winter conditions, such as those found in the interior of North America. Where it can be protected, it grows into dense hummocks and can be used to face down larger shrubs in the border. If given good drainage; light, sandy, acid soil; and protection from harsh winter winds, it will flower well. Clip in midspring to encourage growth. *D. cantabrica* f. *alba* has delicate white flowers. 'Buchanan Gold' has cream-variegated foliage. 'Pallida' bears rose pink flowers. 'William Buchanan' is a dense, prostrate selection with deep green leaves and purplish rose flowers. **Zones 6 to 8**.

Dactylorhiza

dak-til-oh-RYE-zuh. Orchid family, Orchidaceae.

This genus contains about 30 species of hardy terrestrial orchids that grow from fingerlike tubers: the botanical name, which refers to the roots, is from the Greek *daktylos*, meaning "finger," and *rhiza*, "root." Commonly called marsh or spotted orchids, *Dactylorhiza* species bear fleshy leaves that are linear or lance shaped and sometimes spotted with purple. They produce showy, erect racemes of densely packed flowers in spring or summer. The individual flowers have showy lower lips and come in shades of rose purple, violet purple, red, pink, and white. Most species are native to Europe, northern Africa, and Asia, but one species is found in North America.

HOW TO GROW
Select a site in partial shade with moist, well-drained soil that is deeply prepared and rich in organic matter. These plants are happiest in areas with cool summers, such as the Pacific Northwest. They can be hard to establish; for best results look for a cool site protected from afternoon sun. Mulch the soil in spring with chopped leaves to keep it moist and cool. Plants resent root disturbance, so once established, transplant or divide them only if absolutely necessary. Propagate by division in spring.

D. maculata
d. mak-yew-LAH-tuh. HEATH SPOTTED ORCHID. A ¹/₂- to 2-foot-tall species with lance-shaped leaves that may be green or spotted with brown or purple. Bears racemes of rose pink, mauve, reddish pink, or white flowers from spring to late summer. **Zones 5 to 8**.

Dahlia

DAHL-ee-ah. Aster family, Asteraceae.

Dahlia contains some 30 species of tuberous-rooted, tender perennials from Central and South America, but gardeners are much more familiar with the hybrids of these popular plants. There are literally thousands to choose from, with showy flowers in an array of shapes and sizes, from enormous doubles 10 inches or more wide to petite daisylike singles. Dahlias bloom from midsummer to frost, and the flowers, which attract hummingbirds, come in all colors except true blue. The plants have fleshy, pinnate leaves that are green or sometimes bronze or maroon.

HOW TO GROW
Give dahlias a site in full sun and rich, well-drained, evenly moist soil. Plants benefit from good air circulation but need protection from wind. They tolerate a site with only a half day of sun but bloom less; in areas with very hot summers, shade during the hottest part of the day is beneficial. Grow dahlias as perennials from Zone 8 south. In the North, grow them as tender perennials overwintered indoors or as annuals.

Most gardeners start dahlias from tubers, which is the only way to acquire most of the improved cultivars. Starting from seed offers the advantage of lots of plants for very little money; sow seeds indoors 4 to 6 weeks before the last spring frost date. To start from tubers, select thick, firm, fleshy tubers that each have a piece of stem attached: the eyes, or growing buds, are on the main stem, not on the tuber itself. Set tubers outdoors no more than 2 weeks before the last frost date (delay planting if the weather has been cold or wet), planting in a 6-inch-deep trench with the eyes pointed up and about 2 inches below the

Daboecia cantabrica

Dactylorhiza maculata

Dahlia 'Coltness' hybrid

soil surface (4 inches in hot climates). For a head start in areas with short seasons, pot up tubers indoors 4 to 6 weeks before the last frost date, with the buds just above the soil surface, and keep in a warm (60° to 75°F), bright spot. Keep the soil barely moist until sprouts appear, which takes 2 to 4 weeks. Move them to the garden after the last spring frost date, and plant them with the tops of the tubers at the soil surface. Dahlias begin flowering about 2 to 2^1/$_2$ months after planting.

For cultivars that will exceed 3 feet in height, install stakes *before* planting. For full-size plants, 6- to 7-foot stakes driven 1^1/$_2$ feet into the ground should suffice. Set the tubers with the eye nearest the stake. When planting individual tubers, pinch off all but two shoots; when planting small clumps of tubers, pinch off all but four to eight. To encourage branching and bushy growth, pinch shoots again when they have two to three sets of leaves. When stems reach 2 feet, begin loosely tying full-size dahlias to their stakes with strips of cloth or nylon stockings. Mulch in early summer and water regularly. Feed plants first after thinning stems, again when buds first appear, and a third time about a month later. Deadheading encourages new flowers to form. To pick dahlias for arrangements, cut them when the flowers are nearly open but still firm in the center.

To overwinter the roots, cut the stalks back to about 6 inches after frost, and dig them up. Shake off the excess soil, and turn the clumps upside down for a few hours to dry. (Attach labels to the clumps as you dig them.) Store them in a well-ventilated, relatively dry, cool (36° to 45°F) spot in boxes of barely moist vermiculite or sand, in paper bags or wrapped in newspaper, or in plastic bags punched with plenty of air holes. High humidity causes rot. Storing the clumps whole is best, but if you divide in fall, dust cuts with sulfur before storage. Inspect monthly for signs of rotting. Trim off rotted spots and dust the cuts with sulfur. Barely mist the tubers if they begin to shrivel.

D. hybrids

Dahlias come in a wealth of sizes, shapes, and heights. Enthusiasts recognize 16 different flower shapes, including cactus, water lily, ball, anemone, collarette, and single dahlias. Size categories range from Giant (or AA) blooms, which exceed 10 inches, to Miniatures, which are 2 inches or less across. For dahlias that produce the most blooms per plant, stick to cultivars with flowers under 6 inches across. If you prefer low-growing plants, look for the word "dwarf" or "bedding" in the description. These will generally range from 1 to 1^1/$_2$ feet tall. (With dahlias the term "Miniature" refers to the flowers only, and Miniatures are as large as other standard-size plants.) Standard-size plants range from 3^1/$_2$ to 6 feet. 'Bambino Mixed' and 'Coltness' hybrids are dwarf plants that can be started from seeds. Seed mixes for full-size plants also are available. Tender perennial, or grow as a warm-weather annual.

Dalea

DALE-ee-uh. Pea family, Fabaceae.

Dalea is a large genus of more than 250 species of annuals, perennials, and low shrubs native to the warmer regions of the Americas. Leaves are alternate and compound. The pealike flowers come in a range of colors. The dry fruits are one- or two-seeded pods and are not ornamental. Only one species, *D. greggii*, is used as a ground cover.

HOW TO GROW
D. greggii requires full sun and very well drained, alkaline soil; in humid conditions it will rot. Low branches will root where they come in contact with the soil, so this plant needs room to spread and make a thick mat: from an initial planting, it will spread to cover 10 feet or more. It prefers hot, dry summers and is drought tolerant once established.

Dalea greggii

D. greggii

d. GREG-ee-eye. TRAILING IN-DIGO BUSH. This low, evergreen (really, ever-gray) shrub is native to Texas and northern Mexico, where it grows in rocky limestone areas. It is attractive and useful for erosion control on slopes and where its silvery gray foliage and pale purple flowers can be appreciated. Do not place it near a sprinkler system. **Zones 8 to 10.**

Daphne

DAF-nee. Leatherwood family, Thymeliaeaceae.

The 70 *Daphne* species, native to Europe, North Africa, and Asia, are small, woody shrubs with deciduous or evergreen, simple, alternate leaves. Small white flowers are borne in late winter to early spring in the leaf axils and have an intensely sweet fragrance. The brightly colored, succulent fruits are extremely poisonous, even lethal, if eaten.

HOW TO GROW
Most daphnes will grow in either full sun or partial shade, and all require fertile, well-amended soil that stays cool and moist at the roots. They have a reputation for being difficult and often die suddenly for unknown reasons after thriving for years. Pruning should be kept to a minimum. Seeds need cold treatment; you can also prop-

Dahlia 'Figurine'

Daphne cneorum 'Ruby Glow'

Darmera peltata

agate daphne by layering in spring or taking soft or semihard cuttings.

D. × burkwoodii

d. × berk-WOOD-ee-eye. BURK-WOOD DAPHNE. This dense, semievergreen, upright hybrid grows 3 to 4 feet tall and wide and is the source of many cultivars. The clusters of sweetly fragrant late-spring flowers (it can rebloom in early fall) are white, sometimes tinged with pink or lavender. The 1½-inch leaves are linear and often variegated. 'Carol Mackie' has cream margins and flowers of palest pink. 'Somerset' is slightly bigger and bears brighter pink flowers. **Zones 4 to 7.**

D. caucasica

d. kaw-KASS-ih-kuh. CAUCASIAN DAPHNE. This deciduous daphne is 4 to 5 feet tall and wide. The intensely fragrant white flowers are heaviest in late spring but can continue sporadically until fall, followed by black or red berries. The pale green leaves are 3 inches long. A Pennsylvania Horticultural Society award winner. **Zones 5 to 7.**

Daphne odora

D. cneorum

d. nee-OR-um. ROSE DAPHNE. Sometimes called garland flower, this tricky rock-garden evergreen grows only 8 inches tall and has ½-inch dark green leaves and branches that trail along the ground or over a wall. The fragrant flowers, which vary from white to rose pink, appear in abundant clusters in late spring, reblooming in late summer. **Zones 4 to 7.**

D. genkwa

d. GENK-wah. LILAC DAPHNE. Clusters of lilac-colored flowers, lacking noticeable fragrance, appear in mid- to late spring before the leaves on this 3- to 4-foot upright shrub. Not as widely available as some other daphnes, it is less heavily branched but provides

Daphne × burkwoodii 'Carol Mackie'

winter interest with its copper bark. **Zones 6 to 8.**

D. mezereum

d. meh-ZEE-ree-um. FEBRUARY DAPHNE. This semievergreen or deciduous daphne may live up to its common name by blooming in late winter, or it may wait until early spring. The clusters of two to four fragrant, rose- or lilac-colored flowers are followed in early summer by red fruits. Usually under 4 feet tall, it grows upright and has pale green or grayish leaves. **Zones 5 to 8.**

D. odora

d. oh-DOR-uh. WINTER DAPHNE. This dense rounded daphne, 4 to 6 feet tall, blooms in late winter or early spring, producing large wonderfully fragrant

purple-pink or white flowers. Considered more shade tolerant but less cold hardy than other daphnes, it has glossy dark evergreen leaves and occasional red berries. **Zones 7 to 9.**

Darmera

dar-MEER-uh. Saxifrage family, Saxifragaceae.

Darmera contains a single species grown primarily for its enormous foliage. The rounded leaves are peltate, meaning the stem is attached in the center of the leaf, much like an umbrella. Plants bear small clusters of dainty flowers that appear before the leaves emerge and grow from thick mats of fleshy rhizomes.

HOW TO GROW
Select a site in full sun or partial shade with rich, constantly moist to boggy soil. A site along a pond or stream or in a bog garden is ideal. Plants tolerate drier conditions but produce smaller foliage and will not be as vigorous. To propagate, divide the clumps in spring or sow seeds.

D. peltata

d. pel-TAH-tuh. UMBRELLA PLANT. Formerly *Peltiphyllum peltatum*. A bold perennial native to the Pacific Northwest that grows to 4 feet tall and 3 to 4 feet wide. Leaves reach 2 feet across and turn brilliant red in fall. Rounded clusters of five-petaled ½-inch-wide flowers appear in late spring. **Zones 5 to 9.**

Datura

dah-TOUR-ah. Nightshade family, Solanaceae.

Commonly called thorn apples or angel's trumpets, *Datura* species are closely related to *Brugmansia* species, which once were classified here. Both bear showy, trumpet-shaped blooms, but those of daturas point up, rather than hang down. Most bear undivided leaves with smooth or wavy-toothed edges and fragrant flowers followed by thorny or spiny seed capsules. The genus contains eight species of annuals and short-lived perennials native to tropical, subtropical, and warm-temperate areas in the Americas. The foliage has an unpleasant scent when bruised, and all parts of the plants are poisonous if eaten. While jimsonweed (*D. stramonium*) is a fairly common North America weed, gardeners grow one species, *D. wrightii*, for its fragrant flowers.

HOW TO GROW

Give *Datura* species full sun and average, well-drained soil. Sow seeds indoors 8 to 10 weeks before the last spring frost date. Germination takes about 2 weeks at 60°F. Transplant with care, as the plants resent having their roots disturbed. In areas with long growing seasons, roughly Zone 9 south, seeds can be sown where the plants are to grow. Plants sprawl, but gracefully, so give them plenty of room. Or give them supports such as small tepees or twiggy brush to encourage them to stand taller. Use them in perennial gardens, shrub borders, or large containers. They are best when used near a terrace or other spot where their nighttime fragrance can be appreciated.

D. wrightii

d. WRIGHT-ee-eye. ANGELS' TRUMPET. Also listed as *D. metel*, *D. meteloides*, and *D. inoxa* ssp. *quinquecuspida*. A 3- to 5-foot annual with felted, wavy-toothed leaves. Bears showy, 5- to 6-inch-long, 6- to 8-inch-wide trumpets in white, white tinged with purple, or pale lilac. Each flower lasts only one night. 'Cornucopaea' has double purple trumpets and purple leaves. 'Evening Fragrance' bears very fragrant white flowers touched with pale lavender. Warm-weather annual.

D. sanguinea, see *Brugmansia sanguinea*

D. suaveolens, see *Brugmansia suaveolens*

Davidia

dah-VID-ee-ah. Tupelo family, Nyssaceae.

This genus contains only one species, a lovely tree that is prized as an unusual specimen.

HOW TO GROW

Plant in partial or light shade and acid, humus-rich, moist, well-drained soil. To reduce storm damage, prune to develop a strong central leader.

D. involucrata

d. in-voh-lew-KRAH-tah. DOVE TREE, HANDKERCHIEF TREE. Growing into an open pyramidal shape, this unique tree reaches 30 to 50 feet tall and is

Davidia involucrata

draped with eye-catching flowers in late spring or early summer. Small, round, yellow flowers are clustered together and have two pure white, papery bracts — one 6 to 8 inches long and the other shorter — suggesting the wings of a dove or a fluttering handkerchief. Unfortunately, this tree may bloom well only in alternate years. The 3- to 7-inch-long leaves are matte green and heart shaped, with toothed margins, red stalks, and downy undersides. Bark is smooth and gray. Fall color is variable, ranging from pastels to fiery shades of red and yellow. Green pearlike fruits, about 1¹⁄₂ inches long, dangle on 3-inch-long stems in summer and fall. From China. **Zones 6 to 8**.

CULTIVARS

D. involucrata var. *vilmoriniana* differs from the species in having almost hairless leaves.

Delosperma

del-oh-SPER-muh. Carpetweed family, Aizoaceae.

Fleshy triangular to cylindrical leaves and daisylike flowers characterize members of this genus of about 150 species native to Africa. Commonly called ice plants, *Delosperma* species are evergreen or semievergreen shrubs or mat-forming perennials. Although the flowers resemble those of daisies and other aster family plants, they actually are single blooms rather than flower heads consisting of many small florets. Blooms are borne singly or in clusters.

HOW TO GROW

Select a site in full sun with very well drained soil. Plants tolerate heat and poor, dry soil. Propagate by cuttings in late spring or summer, or sow seeds.

D. nubigerum

d. new-bih-JER-um. ICE PLANT. A creeping 2- to 3-inch-tall species that forms mats several feet across. Bears narrow, fleshy, 1¹⁄₂-inch-long leaves with warty-looking bumps and orange-red, ³⁄₄-inch-wide flowers in summer. **Zones 6 to 9**.

Delphinium

del-FIN-ee-um. Buttercup family, Ranunculaceae.

Delphiniums are prized by gardeners for their stately flower spikes that come in shades from true sky blue to dark royal blue as well as violet, lavender, pink, mauve, and white. The bloom stalks tower above mounds of maplelike leaves borne from a fleshy crown. About 250 species of

Datura wrightii

Delosperma nubigerum

Delphinium Elatum Group hybrids

annuals, biennials, and perennials belong here, most native to mountainous regions worldwide. They bear flowers in spikes, racemes, or panicles, and the individual blooms consist of five petal-like sepals, one of which forms a spur at the back of the flower, and usually four petals. The most popular delphiniums in gardens are hybrids.

HOW TO GROW

Grow delphiniums in full sun to partial shade in very rich, deeply prepared, well-drained soil. Neutral to alkaline pH is ideal, but plants also grow in slightly acid soil. They thrive in areas with cool summers; where hot summer weather prevails, a site with morning sun and partial or dappled shade during the hottest part of the day is best. Constantly wet soil leads to crown rot and death. A spot with good air circulation helps prevent disease problems, but do protect plants from strong winds. Belladonna Group hybrids tend to be more tolerant of hot summer weather than Elatum Group plants are, and they usually are longer-lived as well. At best, most delphiniums are short-lived perennials.

Dig in compost, well-rotted manure, or other organic matter at planting time, and grade the soil surface so water will not collect on the crowns. Handle the plants with care, as the brittle roots are easy to break. Stake stems when they are about 1 foot tall, water weekly throughout the season, and feed plants in spring and again when the first blooms appear. Remove the flower stalks as they fade, and new spikes may emerge and bloom in late summer or fall. Propagate by sowing seeds or taking cuttings from shoots at the base of the plant in early spring. (Each cutting should have a sliver of the crown attached at the base.)

Belladonna Group hybrids

Also called *D. × belladonna* hybrids. Upright 3- to 4-foot-tall plants forming 1¹/₂-foot-wide mounds of leaves. Produces loosely branched stalks of flowers on wiry stems in early and late summer. Individual blooms are single, are ³/₄ inch wide, and have prominent spurs. 'Bellamosum' bears deep blue flowers. The Connecticut Yankee Series cultivar

Dendranthema weyrichii

'Blue Fountains' is more heat tolerant than most and can be grown in **Zone 8. Zones 3 to 7.**

Elatum Group hybrids

Also called *D. × elatum* hybrids. These are 4- to 6-foot-tall plants that spread from 2 to 3 feet and produce dense spikes of single, semidouble, or double 2¹/₂-inch-wide flowers. They bloom in early and midsummer. Many cultivars are available, including 'Blue Dawn', with pale blue semidouble blooms; 'Butterball', with creamy white flowers; and 'Emily Hawkins', with semidouble lavender blooms. The popular Pacific Hybrids, also sold as Pacific Giants, resemble Elatum Group delphiniums, but are shorter-lived and best grown as annuals or biennials. Pacific Hybrids cultivars usually have Arthurian names, including 'Galahad', 'Guinevere', and 'King Arthur'. **Zones 3 to 7.**

Dendranthema

den-DRAN-thuh-muh. Aster family, Asteraceae.

About 20 species belong to this genus, all of which were once classified as chrysanthemums (*Chrysanthemum*). They bear aromatic, somewhat fleshy leaves that are lobed in a palmate fashion. Daisylike flower heads have white, yellow, or pink ray florets ("petals") and are borne singly or in loose clusters.

HOW TO GROW

Select a site in full sun with rich, moist, well-drained soil. Sandy soil is ideal, and plants tend to be short-lived in heavy clay. Propagate by dividing plants in spring or after they flower in fall, or by sowing seeds.

D. × grandiflorum, see *Chrysanthemum × morifolium*

D. weyrichii

d. way-RICH-ee-eye. Formerly *Chrysanthemum weyrichii*. A 1-foot-tall species that forms 1¹/₂-foot-wide mounds of five-lobed leaves topped with 2-inch-wide daisies in late summer and fall with white or pink ray florets and yellow centers. 'Pink Bomb' bears pink flowers. 'White Bomb' has pink-tinged ray florets. **Zones 3 to 8.**

Dennstaedtia

den-STED-tee-uh. Dennstaedtiaceae.

Of the 70 species of *Dennstaedtia*, most are found in the tropics throughout the world. One species, *D. punctiloba* (hay-scented fern), is a superb ground cover for north temperate woodland gardens. Hay-scented fern is native to

Dennstaedtia punctilobula

Deschampsia cespitosa

open, dry woods and stony forests in eastern and central North America, where it often forms extensive carpets on the forest floor. The slender rhizomes creep just below the soil surface, and from them arise the individual fronds, which can reach 2 feet tall. The fronds are deciduous, soft green, bipinnate, and relatively resistant to breakage.

HOW TO GROW

Grow hay-scented fern in bright shade. Soil should be slightly dry; more mineral than organic; and rocky, stony, or otherwise tending to poor from a garden perspective. Hay-scented ferns will spread over several acres or more if conditions are to their liking. They make an ideal ground cover for naturalized meadow edges that run into woods. Few other plants give such a "been there forever" appearance so quickly to a new planting of shrubs and trees. When they are used in smaller spaces, control may be a problem, although they can be managed if the advancing rhizomes are dug out or blocked with barriers.

D. punctilobula

d. punk-tih-LOW-bew-luh. HAY-SCENTED FERN. This creeping, deciduous perennial has light green fronds that grow 1 to 2 feet tall. The distinctive aroma, often

compared to that of new-mown hay, is released when the foliage is crushed and persists in the dry foliage at the end of the season. Plants thrive in dry, partly sunny woodlands, where they spread to form extensive colonies. **Zones 3 to 8.**

Deschampsia

des-CHAMP-see-uh. Grass family, Poaceae.

Commonly known as hair grass, *Deschampsia* species are clump-forming grasses with threadlike or linear leaves topped by airy panicles of flowers. About 50 species belong to the genus. Most are perennials, although there are some annuals in the genus.

HOW TO GROW

Plant hair grasses in full sun or partial shade and average garden soil. They thrive in moist, even heavy soils as well as in boggy conditions. *D. flexuosa* tolerates dry soils and also grows in dry shade. Neutral to acid pH is best. Hair grasses are cool-season grasses, meaning they grow in late summer or fall when daytime temperatures are between about 60° and 75°F, stop growing over winter, and resume growing in early spring once the weather warms up but before hot summer temperatures arrive.

Cut the plants to the ground in late winter or early spring before new growth begins. Propagate by dividing the clumps in spring or early fall, or sow seeds. Plants self-sow.

D. cespitosa

d. sess-pih-TOE-suh. TUFTED HAIR GRASS. Ornamental grass that forms dense 2-foot-tall clumps of foliage that reach 4 to 5 feet wide. Foliage is evergreen from about Zone 8 south. Bears cloudlike 1¹/₂-foot-long spikelets of flowers from early to late summer. Plants can be 4 feet tall in bloom. **Zones 4 to 9.**

D. flexuosa

d. flex-yew-OH-suh. CRINKLED HAIR GRASS. Compact species forming 1-foot-tall, 1-foot-wide clumps of evergreen or semi-evergreen foliage. Bears airy, 5-inch-long panicles of flowers in early and midsummer. Plants are 2 feet tall in bloom. **Zones 4 to 9.**

Deutzia

DOOT-see-uh. Hydrangea family, Hydrangeaceae.

This genus encompasses more than 60 species of mostly deciduous shrubs from East Asia, grown for their airy sprays of white or pink spring flowers and often delicate, arching habit. Some develop exfoliating bark with age.

HOW TO GROW

Give deutzias full sun or light shade and moderately fertile soil. They tolerate some alkalinity and pollution but not much drought. They can become ragged, so give them a hard pruning to within 6

inches of the ground every two to three years. Propagate by softwood cuttings.

D. crenata 'Nikko'

d. kreh-NAH-tuh. By far the most popular deutzia, sometimes listed under *D. gracilis*, 'Nikko' grows only 2 feet tall but spreads to 4 feet wide, making it excellent in a rock garden or as a ground cover. In late spring the branches drip panicles of starry white flowers, and in fall the dainty leaves turn burgundy. Winner of the Pennsylvania Horticultural Society Gold Medal. **Zones 5 to 8.**

D. gracilis

d. grah-SILL-iss. A bushy shrub gradually growing 3 to 5 feet tall in an erect, graceful mound, its upright panicles or racemes of white flowers are slightly fragrant. **Zones 4 to 8.**

D. × lemoinei

d. × lem-WON-ee-eye. LEMOINE DEUTZIA. A dense shrub growing to an average of 6 feet tall and wide, this hybrid is considered the most reliably cold-hardy deutzia. The pure white flowers bloom in late spring, and the foliage often provides good yellow fall color. **Zones 4 to 8.**

D. × magnifica

d. × mag-NIF-ih-kuh. SHOWY DEUTZIA. This upright hybrid, which grows 6 feet or taller, is considered outstanding for its dense 3-inch panicles of double flowers. **Zones 6 to 8.**

D. scabra

d. SKAB-ruh. FUZZY DEUTZIA. Growing to 8 feet with exfoliating

Deutzia crenata 'Nikko'

bark and reliable blooms, this species is coarser than some others in the genus. **Zones 5 to 8.**

Dianthus

dye-AN-thuss. Pink family, Caryophyllaceae.

Dianthus contains a wealth of charming, old-fashioned garden plants bearing dainty, often spicy-scented flowers over a long season. Blooms come in all shades of pink plus white, maroon, and ruby red. There also are many bicolor forms. Flowers, which appear from late spring into summer, may be single, semidouble, or fully double. The plants are generally low growing and mound shaped and feature attractive blue- or gray-green, lance-shaped to grasslike leaves that are often evergreen. The genus contains more than 300 species of annuals, biennials, perennials, and subshrubs along with thousands of cultivars. The botanical name is from the Greek *dios,* meaning "god," and *anthos,* "flower," or "flower of the gods." The common name "pink" refers not to the color of the flower, but to the fringed or ragged edges of the petals, which look as if they were trimmed with pinking shears.

HOW TO GROW

Give pinks full sun and well-drained, dry to evenly moist soil that is slightly acid to alkaline. They prefer cool conditions, and a site with partial shade during the hottest part of the day provides es-

Dianthus alpinus

sential heat protection and helps keep the plants vigorous.

Perennial species require well-drained conditions, especially in winter. Don't mulch them with organic mulches such as shredded bark, because such materials tend to keep the soil too damp; stone chips are a better option. Use loose soil mixed with compost to cover the shallow feeder roots if they become exposed. Divide clumps every 2 to 3 years in spring to keep them vigorous. Sow seeds indoors 8 to 10 weeks before the last spring frost date at 60° to 70°F. Germination takes 1 to 3 weeks. Transplant with care. Or sow seeds of annual species outdoors a few weeks before the last frost date or, where plants are hardy, in fall for germination the following spring.

Dianthus 'Allwood Pink'

To grow sweet William (*D. barbatus*) as a biennial, sow seeds in late spring or early summer in a nursery bed; transplant to where the plants are to bloom in early fall or the following spring. Take a large ball of soil with each plant, and move them with care. Discard plants after they bloom either the first or the second time.

Perennial species (even those grown as annuals) can be propagated by cuttings taken in summer from nonflowering shoot tips: remove the lowest leaves, root in coarse sand or a 50-50 mix of vermiculite or perlite and coarse sand, and keep the medium barely moist. Use pinks as edging plants for beds and borders, along pathways, and in raised beds. Butterflies visit the blooms, which also make terrific cut flowers.

D. alpinus

d. al-PIE-nus. ALPINE PINK. Mound-forming 3- to 6-inch-tall plant that spreads as far. Bears single 1¹/₂-inch-wide flowers in late spring or early summer. **Zones 3 to 8.**

D. armeria

d. are-MEER-ee-ah. DEPTFORD PINK. A rosette-forming, 16-inch-tall annual or biennial, hardy from **Zone 4 south,** with hairy green

leaves. Bears showy, 3- to 6-inch-wide clusters of ¹/₂-inch, rosy pink flowers in summer. Cool-weather annual.

D. barbatus

d. bar-BAY-tuss. SWEET WILLIAM. A short-lived, 1- to 2-foot-tall perennial with glossy, broad, lance-shaped leaves. Bears showy, 3- to 5-inch-wide, flat-topped clusters of flowers from late spring into early summer. Modern cultivars are usually not fragrant. Flowers come in shades of pale pink to maroon and white; many are bicolors. Where happy, plants self-sow prolifically. To encourage plants to perform as perennials, remove flowers as they fade and divide every 2 to 3 years. Dwarf types, including 6-inch-tall Roundabout Series plants as well as 6-inch 'Wee Willie', are best used as edging plants; taller types are suitable for mid-border and as cut flowers. Hybrid strains such as Ideal Series plants (*D. barbatus* × *D. chinensis*) exhibit more heat tolerance and earlier bloom than the species but are less hardy than *D. barbatus.* Hardy, short-lived perennial or biennial. **Zones 3 to 9.**

D. caryophyllus

d. kare-ee-oh-FILL-us. WILD CARNATION. A tender perennial, hardy from **Zone 7 south,** with flattened, narrow leaves on stiff, 2¹/₂- to 3-foot stems. Bears small clusters of fragrant, 2-inch-wide flowers in summer. This species is the predecessor of the florist's carnation, so be sure to select a cultivar developed for the garden rather than the greenhouse, such as 2- to 3-foot 'Floristan Red' or

Dianthus barbatus

Dianthus barbatus

Digitalis purpurea

can be grown as an annual. Excelsior Hybrids plants reach 5 feet and come in a range of pastel shades. Cool-weather annual, biennial, or short-lived perennial. **Zones 4 to 8.**

Dimorphotheca

dye-more-foe-TEE-kah. Aster family, Asteraceae.

Native to dry, generally sandy areas in South and tropical Africa, *Dimorphotheca* species are shrubby tender perennials closely related to another genus of African plants, *Osteospermum*, whose members once were classified here. Plants in both genera share the common names Cape marigold, African daisy, and star of the veldt. The seven species of *Dimorphotheca* bear aromatic leaves and solitary, daisylike flowers carried atop leafless stems from midsummer to fall. Unlike most other aster-family plants, both the disk florets (the "eye") and the ray florets (the "petals") are fertile.

HOW TO GROW

Full sun and average to poor soil that is light and well drained are ideal. Plants thrive in heat, tolerate dry soil, and perform best in areas with long growing seasons; they do not do as well in areas with hot, humid, rainy summers. In the Southeast, try starting plants indoors early, so they reach blooming size well before heat and humidity set in for the summer. Sow seeds indoors 6 to 8 weeks before the last spring frost date. Germination takes about 2 weeks at 60° to 65°F. Or, from Zone 9 south, sow seeds outdoors where the plants are to grow. Either way, barely cover the seeds with soil; to prevent fungal diseases, try to avoid wetting the foliage when watering. Deadheading prolongs bloom. Use Cape marigolds in containers or add them to mixed plantings in beds and borders. They do not make good cut flowers, since the flowers close during cloudy weather and at night.

Dimorphotheca sinuata

Digitalis purpurea

racemes of 1¹/₂- to 2-inch-long flowers in midsummer that are pale yellow with brown veins on the inside. **Zones 3 to 8.**

D. lutea

d. LOO-tee-uh. A 3- to 4-foot-tall biennial or perennial bearing glossy leaves and then racemes of pale yellow ¹/₂- to 1-inch-long flowers from early to midsummer. **Zones 3 to 8.**

D. × mertonensis

d. × mer-ton-EN-sis. STRAWBERRY FOXGLOVE. A 3-foot-tall perennial that produces racemes of 2¹/₂-inch-long flowers in shades from pinkish to rose pink and white in late spring and early summer. Comes true from seed. **Zones 3 to 8.**

D. purpurea

d. pur-PUR-ee-ah. COMMON FOXGLOVE. A biennial or short-lived perennial ranging from 2 to 6 feet in height. Bears showy spikes of 2- to 2¹/₂-inch-long flowers in rose-purple, white, pink, or creamy yellow. Blooms commonly are spotted with purple inside. 'Foxy' is a 2- to 3-foot-tall cultivar that will bloom the first year from seed and

---

D. pluvialis

d. plu-vee-AL-iss. RAIN DAISY, WEATHER PROPHET. A 1- to 1¹/₂-foot plant with toothed or deeply cut, aromatic leaves. Bears white 2¹/₂-inch, daisylike flowers with a ring of purple around a darker eye. The backs of the petals, which close before rain, also are purple. Warm-weather annual.

D. sinuata

d. sin-yew-AH-tah. STAR OF THE VELDT. A 1-foot species with toothed, lance-shaped, aromatic leaves. Bears 1¹/₂-inch daisylike flowers with purple-brown centers and white, yellow, orange, or pink petals. Warm-weather annual.

Diospyros

dye-OSS-pih-rus. Ebony family, Ebenaceae.

This genus from North America and Asia is known for its edible fall fruits and very strong, beautiful wood. Small blueberry-like flowers and fleshy berries characterize the genus. Native to forests of eastern and central North America, common persimmon is a beloved native that should be preserved in the wild and grown more in landscapes. It is a tough survivor that adapts to urban stress.

HOW TO GROW

Grow in full sun to partial shade. Plants are most vigorous and attractive in rich, moist soil but tolerate poor soil, flooding, drought, heat, and wind. May be difficult to transplant; choose small balled-and-burlapped or container-

---

grown trees. Leaf spot is troublesome in the South.

D. virginiana

d. ver-jin-ee-AH-nuh. COMMON PERSIMMON. Forming a symmetrical pyramid when young and becoming craggier with age, common persimmon reaches 60 to 80 feet tall in good, moist soil and is more shrubby where soil is poor. Female flowers are very fragrant, ³/₄-inch creamy bells and are borne singly. Male flowers are smaller and bloom in clusters of three, usually on separate trees. Female trees produce 1¹/₂-inch green berries that ripen to orange after frost and cling to the bare limbs after the leaves drop. The fruits eventually fall to the ground, causing a litter problem if not immediately gathered to make persimmon pudding or preserves (two midwestern specialties). They also provide valuable food for wildlife. The bold-textured, dark green leaves are 3- to 5-inch-long pointed ovals. Fall color varies from glorious to subdued shades of yellow, gold, and red. This deep-rooted tree is easily recognized by its distinctive trunk bark, which is deeply fissured and cracked into a checkerboard pattern. From eastern and central North America. **Zones 5 to 9.**

CULTIVARS AND SIMILAR SPECIES

'Early Golden' has large, sweet fruits. 'Meader' is self-fertile and bears early-ripening fruits. 'Male' produces no fruits and will pollinate female trees; use it as an urban street tree. *D. kaki* (Oriental

Diospyrus virginiana

persimmon) grows to 30 feet tall and has huge, tasty, orange fruits that ripen in fall after the leaves drop; **Zones 7 to 9.**

Disanthus

dis-AN-thus. Witch-hazel family, Hamamelidaceae.

Brilliant fall color has made a rising star of this deciduous species from the woods and mountains of Asia, the only member of its genus.

HOW TO GROW
Disanthus needs rich, moisture-retentive, slightly acid soil in light shade, especially in the southern part of its range. Plant it as a specimen in a spot where you can admire its autumn show. It won't tolerate wind or drought and may develop fungal diseases in high humidity. It rarely needs pruning. Propagate from seeds or cuttings.

Disanthus cercidifolius

D. cercidifolius

d. ser-sih-dih-FOE-lee-us. The habit is open and upright to 10 feet tall with a rounded crown spreading as wide. The leaves don't look like those of other plants in the witch-hazel family but are heart shaped like those of the unrelated redbud (*Cercis*) and 4 inches across. Blue-green in summer, in fall they may simultaneously show yellow, orange, red, and purple. The spidery purple-red flowers, which appear at the same time, have a slightly unpleasant scent. **Zones 5 to 8.**

Disporum

dye-SPOR-um. Lily family, Liliaceae.

Commonly called fairy bells, *Disporum* species are rhizomatous perennials native to moist woodlands in North America and eastern Asia. Between 10 and 20 species belong to the genus. They bear ovate to lance-shaped leaves and small clusters of flowers that are usually pendent and range in shape from tubular or trumpet shaped to cup shaped. Flower colors include white, greenish yellow, and purplish or brownish red. The flowers are followed by fleshy red, orange, or black berries. Fairy bells are closely related to bellworts (*Uvularia*) and toad lilies (*Tricyrtis*).

HOW TO GROW
Select a site in partial shade with rich, moist, well-drained soil. Plants prefer cool conditions, so a site with afternoon shade is best. Mulch with chopped leaves or other organic matter to keep the soil cool, retain moisture, and add beneficial organic matter. Water during dry weather. To propagate, divide plants in early spring or start from seeds.

D. flavens

d. FLAY-venz. FAIRY BELLS. A clumping 2½-foot-tall species spreading to 1 foot or more. Bears clusters of one to three tubular, pendent, 2-inch-long pale yellow flowers in early spring. Black berries follow the flowers in fall. **Zones 4 to 9.**

D. sessile

d. SES-sil-ee. FAIRY BELLS. A 1- to 2-foot-tall species that slowly forms 2-foot-wide clumps. Bears nearly stalkless leaves and clusters of one to three pendent, tubular 1-inch-long flowers in late spring and early summer. Flowers are creamy white, very pale yellow, or greenish and are followed by black berries in fall. **Zones 4 to 9.**

Dodecatheon

doe-dee-KATH-ee-on. Primrose family, Primulaceae.

Grown for their spring clusters of cyclamen- or shuttlecock-shaped flowers, *Dodecatheon* species are perennials primarily native to North America. About 14 species belong here, found in moist grasslands, alpine meadows, and sometimes woodlands. Commonly known as shooting stars (another common name is American cowslip), they produce a low basal rosette of lance-shaped, spoon-shaped, or rounded leaves topped in spring by umbels of flowers held on leafless stalks high above the foliage. The small pendent flowers have reflexed (backward-pointing) petals and stamens united to form a beaklike projection. Plants go dormant shortly after they finish blooming.

HOW TO GROW
Select a site in full sun or partial shade with rich, moist, well-drained soil. In areas with warm summers, a spot with afternoon shade is best, since plants prefer cool conditions. Mulching helps keep the soil moist and cool. Because the plants go dormant and disappear completely in summer, mark their locations and combine them with other perennials that are not too vigorous or with annuals to fill the gaps they leave. Propagate by division in spring or by seeds.

D. clevelandii

d. cleve-LAN-dee-eye. California native ranging from 12 to 16 inches in height and forming a 6-inch-wide rosette of leaves. Bears umbels of 10 to 20 reddish purple ¾-inch-long flowers in early spring. Requires dry conditions during its summer dormancy. **Zones 5 to 7.**

D. dentatum

d. den-TAH-tum. An 8-inch-tall species native to western North America that forms an 8-inch-wide rosette of leaves. Bears small umbels of up to five ½- to ¾-inch-long white flowers in late

Disporum flavens

Dodecatheon meadia

spring. Best in a spot with moist soil in shade. **Zones 5 to 7**.

D. meadia

d. MEE-dee-uh. COMMON SHOOTING STAR. A clump-forming wildflower native to the edges of woodlands and prairies from the eastern United States west to Texas. Forms low 1-foot-wide rosettes of leaves. Bears clusters of 12 to 15 magenta-pink ¹/₂- to ³/₄-inch-long flowers on 1¹/₂-foot-tall stalks in mid- and late spring. *D. meadia* f. *album* bears white flowers. **Zones 4 to 8**.

Doronicum

doh-RON-ih-kum. Aster family, Asteraceae.

Commonly called leopard's banes, *Doronicum* species are perennials from Europe, Southwestern Asia, and Siberia. About 35 species belong to the genus. Plants are deciduous and go dormant after blooming. They spread by rhizomes or grow from tubers. All bear yellow, daisylike flowerheads composed of many ray florets, the "petals," surrounding slightly dome-shaped yellow centers consisting of densely packed disc florets. Blooms are produced one per stem or in small clusters. Leaves are heart shaped at the base and lance shaped to rounded.

HOW TO GROW

Select a site in partial shade with moist, rich soil. Sandy soil rich in organic matter is ideal. Plants do not tolerate drought. They bloom in spring or early summer, then go

dormant in summer. Propagate by seeds sown in spring or digging and dividing the clumps in fall. Grow leopard's banes in shady borders or wildflower gardens. Overplant them with shallow rooted annuals such as impatiens to fill the gap they leave in summer. The flowers are good for cutting.

D. × excelsum

d. × ex-SEL-sum. A 2-foot-tall hybrid that spreads by rhizomes to form 2-foot-wide clumps. Plants bear toothed leaves and golden yellow, 4-inch-wide flowerheads in spring. Blooms are borne in

Doronicum pardalianches

branched clusters of 3 or 4 blooms. 'Harpur Crewe' is most commonly grown. **Zones 4 to 8**.

D. orientale

d. or-ee-en-TAL-ee. Formerly *D. caucasicum*. A 2-foot-tall rhizomatous species that gradually spreads to form 3-foot-wide clumps. Plants bear golden yellow, 1- to 2-inch wide flowerheads in mid- to late spring. Leaves have slightly scalloped edges. 'Magnificum' bears 1¹/₂- to 2-inch-wide blooms. 'Spring Beauty' ('Frühlingspracht') bears double flowers on 16-inch-tall plants. **Zones 5 to 8**.

D. pardalianches

d. par-dil-ee-AN-kees. GREAT LEOPARD'S BANE. Formerly *D. cordatum*. This rhizomatous species bears pale yellow, 1¹/₂- to 2-inch-wide daisy flowers on branched stems from late spring to midsummer. Blooms are carried above nearly round basal leaves that have heart-shaped bases; rounded to lance-shaped leaves appear on the stems. **Zones 4 to 8**.

Dorotheanthus

dor-oh-thee-AN-thuss. Carpetweed family, Aizoaceae.

Succulent-leaved annuals from South Africa, *Dorotheanthus* species are grown for their showy flowers, which resemble daisies. About 10 species belong to this ge-

Dorotheanthus bellidiformis

nus, all once included in *Mesembryanthemum*. They bear fleshy, linear or spoon-shaped leaves covered with crystal-like lumps called papillae. While the flowers resemble daisies — they have petals surrounding a darker eye — each bloom is actually a single flower. (True daisies and other aster-family plants bear heads that consist of many individual flowers.)

HOW TO GROW

Choose a site with full sun and poor to average, very well drained soil. Poor, sandy soil that is on the dry side is best, although plants will grow in richer soil as long as it is well drained. Sow seeds indoors 8 to 10 weeks before the last spring frost date. Or sow outdoors after the last frost. Either way, just press the seeds into the soil surface. Deadhead to prolong bloom. Sowing new seeds every few weeks also extends the bloom season. Use these plants as temporary ground covers, as edgings, on slopes, and in rock gardens.

D. bellidiformis

d. bell-ih-dih-FOR-miss. LIVINGSTONE DAISY. Formerly *Mesembryanthemum criniflorum*. A 6-inch-tall annual that spreads to 1 foot with fleshy, obovate to spoon-shaped leaves. Bears showy, solitary, 1¹/₂-inch-wide flowers in pink, purple, orange, red, cream, or yellow, sometimes with two-tone petals that create a contrasting eye zone. Warm-weather annual.

Dracocephalum

dray-koh-SEFF-ah-lum. Mint family, Lamiaceae.

This genus contains about 50 species of annuals, perennials, and small shrubs mostly native to Eurasia, as well as North Africa and the northern United States. The plants have square stems — they are related to mints *(Mentha)* — and have entire, toothed, or lobed leaves that are often aromatic. Both the common name, dragon's head, and the botanical name refer to the tubular, two-lipped flowers, which are borne in whorls around the stems: *Dracocephalum* is from the Greek *drakon*, meaning "dragon," and *kephale*, "head."

HOW TO GROW

Give these plants full sun to light shade and average to rich, well-drained soil. (Light shade is beneficial during the hottest part of the day.) Sow seeds outdoors around

Dracocephalum moldavica

the last spring frost date. Or sow indoors 6 to 8 weeks before the last frost date. Pinch seedlings when they are about a month old to encourage branching. Use these plants to fill spaces in beds and borders as well as in wild gardens.

D. moldavica

d. mol-DAV-ih-cuh. MOLDAVIAN BALM, DRAGON'S HEAD. A 1- to 2-foot annual with aromatic leaves native from Europe to Siberia and naturalized in North America. Bears narrow, spikelike racemes of violet-blue or white, 1-inch-long flowers in summer. Warm-weather annual.

Dracunculus

drah-KUNK-yew-lus. Arum family, Araceae.

Dracunculus species are tuberous perennials grown for their exotic, but foul-smelling, blooms. Three species belong to the genus, all native to the Mediterranean region and the Canary Islands. As the common name, dragon arum, suggests, *Dracunculus* species are closely related to arums *(Arum)*. They also are kin to the more familiar jack-in-the-pulpits *(Arisaema)*. The exotic-looking "flowers" actually are an inflorescence consisting of many tiny flowers clustered on a long thick central stalk, called a spadix. The spadix is surrounded by a large showy modified leaf, called a spathe. Leaves are divided into fingerlike lobes (those of arums are always arrow shaped) and may be marbled with white.

HOW TO GROW
Give these plants a spot in full sun or partial shade with rich, well-

drained soil. Plants require soil that is moist in spring and early summer, when they are growing actively, and drier once they go dormant later in the season. Where they are hardy, plant the tubers 6 inches deep in fall; plant them in spring in areas where they are not hardy. In the North, grow these plants in containers or plant directly in the soil and dig the tubers in early fall after the foliage fades. Keep the soil evenly moist while the plants are in leaf, but gradually withhold water later in the summer as they enter dormancy. To overwinter them indoors, either dig the tubers and store them in dry peat moss or store them in pots with the soil kept dry. Either way, keep them in a cool (50° to 55°F), dry place. Propagate by seeds or by separat-

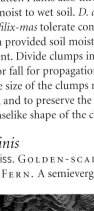

Dracunculus vulgaris

ing offsets when the tubers are dormant in spring or fall.

D. vulgaris

d. vul-GAIR-iss. Formerly *Arum dracunculus*. A spring- or summer-blooming species that normally is about 3 feet tall but can reach 5 feet. Plants spread to about 2 feet and bear 1-foot-long dark green leaves marked with white that have up to 15 lobes. The inflorescence consists of a dark maroon, velvety-textured 1½-foot-long spathe surrounding a nearly black 1-foot-long spadix. **Zones 8 to 10.**

Dryopteris

dry-OP-ter-iss. Wood-fern family, Dryopteridaceae.

Dryopteris species are known by a variety of common names, including shield fern, wood fern, male fern, and buckler fern. The genus contains about 225 species, most native to moist woodlands and boggy sites in the Northern Hemisphere. Plants bear scaly rhizomes that either creep to form small clumps or are erect and form crowns. The pinnate fronds have dense brown, gold, black, or tan scales at the base and usually form vase-shaped clumps.

HOW TO GROW
Select a site in partial shade with moist, well-drained soil rich in organic matter. Plants also thrive in evenly moist to wet soil. *D. affinis* and *D. filix-mas* tolerate considerable sun provided soil moisture is consistent. Divide clumps in spring or fall for propagation, to keep the size of the clumps manageable, and to preserve the handsome vaselike shape of the clumps.

D. affinis

d. aff-IN-iss. GOLDEN-SCALED MALE FERN. A semievergreen

to evergreen species bearing 2- to 3-foot-tall fronds with golden brown scales in vase-shaped clumps that spread to 3 feet. Many forms with crested fronds are available (these come true from spores). 'Cristata', sometimes sold as 'The King', is a popular selection that has 2- to 4-foot fronds with crests at the top of the frond as well as at the tips of the pinnae (leaflets). **Zones 4 to 8.**

D. erythrosora

d. ee-rith-roe-SOR-uh. AUTUMN FERN. An evergreen to deciduous species with 1½- to 2-foot-tall fronds that are bronze- to copper red when they emerge in spring and slowly turn green by summer. Plants spread slowly to form 1½-foot-wide clumps. **Zones 5 to 8.**

D. filix-mas

d. FEE-lix-MAAS. MALE FERN. A deciduous species native to North America as well as Europe and Asia that reaches 3 feet in height and spreads as far. Many forms with crested fronds are available, including 'Cristata' and 'Grandiceps', both of which have crested pinnae (leaflet) tips. **Zones 4 to 8.**

D. intermedia

in-ter-MEE-dee-uh. INTERMEDIATE SHIELD FERN. This attractive species spreads quickly, its fronds reaching 1½ to 2 feet tall. **Zones 4 to 8.**

D. marginalis

mar-jin-AL-iss. MARGINAL WOOD FERN. This eastern North American native spreads slowly while creating dramatic clusters. Fronds are less than 2 feet tall and do not recover well from drought. **Zones 5 to 9.**

Dryopteris marginalis

E

Eccremocarpus

eck-krey-moe-KAR-pus. Bignonia family, Bignoniaceae.

The five species of *Eccremocarpus* are exotic, fast-growing, herbaceous or woody climbers native to Chile and Peru. They bear bipinnately divided leaves, each ending in a tendril. Showy clusters of tubular, hot-colored flowers, which attract hummingbirds, appear throughout the growing season. The botanical name refers to the seedpods that follow the flowers: *Eccremocarpus* is from the Greek *ekkremes*, meaning "pendent" or "hanging," and *carpus*, "fruit." One species is grown as a tender perennial.

HOW TO GROW

A site in full sun and fertile, well-drained soil, preferably on the sandy side, is ideal. Plants require a trellis or other support upon which to climb. They will clamber over brushy twigs and through and over shrubs. From Zone 10 south, grow Chilean glory vine (*E. scaber*) as a perennial; since plants can be killed to the ground and

will resprout from the roots, they may survive the winter a bit farther north if protected by a mound of loose soil over the roots. Sow seeds indoors 8 to 10 weeks or more before the last spring frost date and germinate at 55° to 65°F. Move the plants to the garden a few weeks after the last frost date, once the weather is warm and settled. Propagate by cuttings taken in spring or summer, which can be used to overwinter the plants indoors.

E. scaber

e. SKAY-ber. CHILEAN GLORY VINE. A fast-growing climber that can reach 10 to 15 feet in warm climates but stays somewhat shorter in the North. Bears clusters of tubular 1-inch-long flowers in shades of orange-red, orange, red, pink, or yellow. Tender perennial, or grow as a warm-weather annual.

Echinacea

eck-in-AY-see-uh. Aster family, Asteraceae.

Echinacea species are stalwart, sun-loving native North American wildflowers best known as purple coneflowers. About nine species belong to the genus, all having daisylike flower heads with raised, cone- or pincushion-like centers consisting of spiny yellow-brown or orange disk florets. The ray florets, or "petals," are purple, purple-pink, or white and generally drooping. Flowers appear from early to midsummer atop stiff-stemmed clumps of bristly leaves that range from linear to lance shaped or ovate. The botanical

name refers to the spiny cones: it is from the Greek *echinos*, meaning "hedgehog."

HOW TO GROW

Give coneflowers full sun and well-drained, average soil. They tolerate drought and heat and also bloom in light shade. Plants in shade tend to get leggy, but pinching in spring helps keep them compact. Dig and divide the plants in spring or fall if they die out in the center or outgrow their space. Division offers a fairly easy propagation method, although the plants have deep taproots and are happier if left undisturbed. Or take basal cuttings (cuttings of shoots from the base of the plant) in spring, take root cuttings in fall, or start from seeds. Plants self-sow.

E. angustifolia

e. an-gus-tih-FOE-lee-uh. NARROW-LEAVED CONEFLOWER. Clump-forming 1- to 2-foot plant spreading to 1½ feet. Bears 2-inch-wide flowers in early summer with 1-inch-long rose-pink ray florets. **Zones 3 to 8.**

E. pallida

e. PAL-lih-duh. PALE CONEFLOWER. Clump-forming 3- to 4-foot-tall species that spreads to about 2 feet. In summer, it bears 4- to 6-inch-wide flower heads with

drooping 1½- to 3½-inch-long pale pink ray florets. **Zones 4 to 8.**

E. purpurea

e. pur-PUR-ee-ah. PURPLE CONEFLOWER. Shrubby 2- to 4-foot-tall species that occasionally reaches 6 feet and spreads from 1½ to 2 feet. Bears 1½- to 3-inch-wide flower heads with drooping 1½- to 2½-inch-long ray florets from midsummer to fall. Several cultivars are more compact than the species and bear wider blooms with more horizontal petals than the species. 'Bravado' bears 4-inch-wide flowers on 2-foot plants. 'Leuchtstern' (also sold as 'Bright Star') has purple-red ray florets and reaches about 2½ feet. 'Magnus' produces 7-inch-wide blooms. 'White Lustre' bears white blooms on 3-foot plants, while 'White Swan' reaches 1 to 2 feet. **Zones 3 to 9.**

Echinops

ECK-in-ops. Aster family, Asteraceae.

As their common name suggests, globe thistles are spiny-leaved plants with round, spiny flower heads. Blooms are silvery to metallic blue in color. Like *Echinacea*, *Echinops* takes its name from the Greek word for "hedgehog," in this

Eccremocarpus scaber

Echinacea purpurea

Echinacea purpurea

Echinops ritro

case *echinos,* meaning "hedgehog," and *opsis,* "appearance." About 120 species belong to the genus — annuals, biennials, and perennials that have deep taproots and are found growing naturally in hot, dry areas such as gravelly slopes and grasslands mostly from central and southern Europe to central Asia.

HOW TO GROW
Select a site in full sun with poor to average, well-drained soil. Good drainage is especially important in winter. Established plants are very drought tolerant. Prepare the soil deeply at planting time to ensure adequate drainage, and space plants generously because they resent transplanting and can be left undisturbed for many years. Deadhead to encourage reblooming and to curtail self-seeding. Propagate by washing away some soil from around the base of the plant and slicing off the small side plants that have arisen there, or take root cuttings in spring or fall. Or start from seeds, although cultivars don't come true.

E. bannaticus
e. ban-NAT-ih-kus. A 1¹/₂- to 4-foot-tall species forming clumps that spread to about 2 feet. Bears 1- to 2-inch-wide violet-blue to blue-gray flower heads from mid- to late summer. 'Blue Globe' produces dark violet-blue 2¹/₂-inch-wide flower heads on 3-foot plants and reblooms if plants are cut back hard after the first flush of flowers. 'Taplow Blue' bears 2-inch-wide metallic blue flower heads. **Zones 3 to 9.**

E. ritro
e. REE-tro. SMALL GLOBE THISTLE. Compact 2-foot-tall species spreading to 1¹/₂ feet. Bears 1- to 1³/₄-inch-wide flower heads in mid- to late summer. 'Veitch's Blue' has dark metallic blue flowers on sturdy plants and is an especially good rebloomer.
Zones 3 to 9.

E. sphaerocephalus
e. sphare-oh-SEFF-ah-lus. Large clump-forming species that reaches 6 feet tall and spreads to about 3 feet. Bears silver-gray 1¹/₄- to 2¹/₂-inch-wide flower heads on gray stems in mid- and late summer. **Zones 3 to 9.**

Echium candicans

Echium
ECK-ee-um. Borage family, Boraginaceae.

Native primarily to the Mediterranean region and the Canary Islands, *Echium* species are annuals, biennials, perennials, and shrubs. The 40 species in the genus feature a range of common names, including tower-of-jewels, pride of Madeira, blue devil, and viper's bugloss. The plants produce a rosette of generally narrow leaves that are silvery and hairy or bristly. The rosette is topped by spikes or panicles of funnel- or bell-shaped flowers in shades of violet-blue, purple, white, yellow, or red.

HOW TO GROW
Give these plants full sun and poor to average soil that is well drained. They grow and bloom best in poorer soils that stay on the dry side; rich soil yields rank growth and plants that fail to flower or that produce inferior blooms. They also are best in mild, dry climates, such as coastal California. Sow seeds indoors 8 to 10 weeks before the last spring frost date at 60° to 65°F. Germination takes 1 to 3 weeks. Transplant with care, and do not try to move established plants. Or sow seeds outdoors after the last frost date. All are biennials or tender perennials hardy from about **Zone 9 south**; in areas where they are not hardy, grow them in containers and overwinter them indoors. Where plants are hardy, seeds can be sown in fall for bloom the following year. Plants self-sow, sometimes excessively.

E. candicans
e. KAN-dih-kans. PRIDE OF MADEIRA. A 5- to 8-foot, woody-based biennial with silvery-hairy leaves and dense, cylindrical, 1-foot-long panicles of bluish purple or white flowers in spring and summer. Biennial.

E. pininana
e. pin-ee-NAY-nah. TOWER-OF-JEWELS, PRIDE OF TENERIFE. A 6- to 12-foot biennial or short-lived perennial with a woody base and silvery-hairy leaves up to 3 feet long and a foot wide. Bears dense, cylindrical panicles of purple-blue, ¹/₂-inch-long flowers; panicles can range from 5 to 10 or more feet long, and plants die after flowering. Biennial.

E. vulgare
e. vul-GAIR-ee. VIPER'S BUGLOSS. A 2- to 3-foot biennial with linear to lance-shaped leaves covered with stiff white hairs. Bears dense clusters of violet-blue flowers in late summer. Naturalized in North America. Cool-weather annual.

E. wildpretii
e. wild-PRET-ee-eye. Formerly *E. bourgaenanum.* A woody-based, 4- to 6-foot biennial or short-lived perennial with silvery-hairy, lance-shaped leaves. Bears rounded panicles, up to 3 feet long, of small violet or red flowers. Biennial.

Elaeagnus
eel-ee-AG-nus. Oleaster family, Elaeagnaceae.

A genus of 45 deciduous or evergreen trees and shrubs, primarily from Asia, grown for their silvery leaves, small but intensely fragrant flowers, and berries that attract wildlife.

HOW TO GROW
Plant in full sun and well-drained soil. Several of the Asian species, notably *E. angustifolia* (Russian olive) and *E. umbellata* (autumn olive), have escaped cultivation in many areas, displacing native trees and birds' nesting sites in fields and along streams. They have succeeded in spreading because they are tolerant of wind and poor, dry, even salty soil, as are the other species listed here. They can become chlorotic in highly alkaline soil. They do not need pruning,

Elaeagnus angustifolia

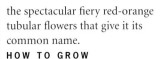

except to remove solid green branches on variegated selections. Propagation is easy by cuttings taken in summer or from rooted suckers.

E. angustifolia

e. an-gus-tih-FOE-lee-uh. RUSSIAN OLIVE, WILD OLIVE. This small, multitrunked tree can fix its own nitrogen from the soil, which means it flourishes in poor-soil sites. It forms a round, dense crown about 20 feet tall and wide, and its willowy leaves create a beautiful, light-reflecting sight. The 3-inch-long, lance-shaped leaves are gray-green on top and silver gray on the undersides and are borne on thorny, silvery twigs and branches. Small, tubular, creamy yellow flowers hide under the leaves but give off a very sweet fragrance that is hard to miss. The flowers are followed in late summer and fall by silvery scaled, yellow berries that attract birds. Trunk bark is shaggy and dark gray to black. Use this tree as a focal point in a border or mixed planting, or plant it as a screen. Russian olive has become a pest, spreading to wild areas in both the eastern and western states, so confine it to urban areas away from natural sites. **Zones 3 to 7**.

CULTIVARS

'King Red' has large burgundy fruits. 'Quicksilver' has extra-silvery foliage.

E. commutata

e. kom-mew-TAY-tuh. SILVER-BERRY. A thicket-forming deciduous shrub 6 to 12 feet tall and wide, this species is native to the American Midwest and eastern Canada. It has reddish brown shoots and broad, elliptic, showy silver leaves. The fragrant silvery yellow-white, 1/2-inch flowers appear in late spring and are followed by red berries. **Zones 3 to 6**.

E. × ebbingei

e. × eb-BIN-jee-eye. This hybrid shrub, 10 to 12 feet tall and wide, has silvery speckled, semievergreen to evergreen leaves. The small creamy flowers appear in fall. 'Gilt Edge' has yellow-gold leaf margins. **Zones 7 to 9**.

Embothrium

em-BOTH-ree-um. Protea family, Proteaceae.

A genus of eight evergreen shrubs and trees from woods of Central and South America. If you have room and the climate for it, the species listed here is worth seeking out and attempting to grow for the spectacular fiery red-orange tubular flowers that give it its common name.

HOW TO GROW

Grow in full sun or partial shade in neutral to acid, moisture-retentive soil where it is protected from wind. Native to the Chilean Andes, it thrives only in relatively mild climates such as that of the Pacific Northwest. It needs little pruning. Sow seeds in spring, or root from greenwood cuttings or suckers.

E. coccineum

e. kok-SIN-ee-um. CHILEAN FIREBUSH. Upright, freely branching and suckering shrub that reaches 10 to 30 feet tall and 15 feet wide. The leathery, narrow oval leaves grow to 4 inches or more. The waxy flowers, which appear in late spring and early summer, are intensely orange-red 2-inch tubes, held in dense terminal and axillary racemes. **Zones 8 to 10**.

Emilia

eh-MIL-ee-ah. Aster family, Asteraceae.

"Flora's paintbrush" and "tassel flower" are two of the common names that have been applied to members of this genus of 24 species of annuals from India, tropical Africa, and Polynesia. They bear tassel- or ball-like heads of brightly colored flowers on wiry

Embothrium coccineum

Emilia coccinea

Enkianthus campanulatus

stems. The blooms consist of all disk florets — they lack the "petals," or ray florets, of many aster-family plants.

HOW TO GROW

Full sun and average, well-drained soil will suffice for these plants. Sow seeds outdoors 2 to 3 weeks before the last spring frost date or, from Zone 8 south, in fall. Or sow indoors 6 to 8 weeks before the last frost. Transplant with care. Either way, barely cover the seeds with soil, as darkness aids germination. Regular deadheading increases bloom. Plants self-sow.

E. coccinea

e. kok-SIN-ee-ah. FLORA'S PAINTBRUSH. Formerly *E. flammea, E. javanica*. A 1¹/₂- to 2-foot annual with a rosette of ovate, toothed leaves. Produces loose clusters of ¹/₂-inch red to red-orange flowers in summer. Cool-weather annual.

Enkianthus

en-kee-AN-thus. Heath family, Ericaceae.

This genus, whose name means "pregnant flower," contains about 10 species of primarily deciduous shrubs and trees from East Asia. They are increasingly making their way into gardens because of their interesting habits, clusters of bell-shaped flowers, and arresting fall color.

HOW TO GROW

Good in open woods with full sun or partial shade in neutral to acid, humus-rich soil. An excellent companion in a shrub border with acid-loving broad-leaved evergreens. Pruning is rarely needed. Propagate from seeds or softwood cuttings.

E. campanulatus

e. kam-pan-yew-LAY-tus. REDVEIN ENKIANTHUS. Generally ranging from 8 to 15 feet tall and wide, this species is narrow and upright with layered branches. The elliptic leaves are held in whorls at the ends of branches and turn bright yellow, orange, and red in fall. The slightly fragrant creamy flowers, which have pink to red veins, hang in graceful clusters of 5 to 15 in late spring as the leaves unfurl. 'Red Bells' has slightly redder flowers and stays somewhat smaller. There are several selections with pink to red flowers. **Zones 5 to 8.**

E. cernuus var. rubens

e. SER-noo-us var. RUE-benz. This variety is 6 to 8 feet tall. Its leaves have a purple tinge in summer and turn purple-red in autumn. The flowers are reddish purple and have toothed lips. **Zones 5 to 8.**

E. perulatus

e. pur-yew-LAY-tuss. WHITE ENKIANTHUS. Still difficult to find, this species grows slowly to 6 feet tall and eventually wider, with a striking layered habit. In late spring, dangling clusters of urn-shaped white flowers bloom before the leaves emerge. The autumn color is intense scarlet. **Zones 5 to 8.**

Epigaea

eh-PIJ-ee-uh. Heath family, Ericaceae.

The three species of *Epigaea* are native to eastern North America, Japan, and the Caucasus. The simple, evergreen leaves are tough as cardboard, only 1 to 3 inches long, and held close to the ground, where they often obscure the prostrate branches. Flowers are tiny, waxy, white or pinkish, and cup shaped. Flowers of the American species *E. repens* bloom in earliest spring and are intensely fragrant. The botanical name means "upon the earth," in reference to the plants' creeping habit.

HOW TO GROW

E. repens (mayflower) has been driven nearly to extinction

Epigaea repens

Epimedium × youngianum

throughout much of its former range, so it is important to obtain this species from nursery-propagated stock. Epigaeas require soil that is highly acid, organic, well drained, and moist — not an impossible combination on rocky faces and slopes in mixed deciduous and coniferous forests. They prefer light shade to filtered sun and despise hot, humid summers, thriving instead in cool climates. Use mayflower as a stunningly fragrant, low, naturalistic, evergreen ground cover, provided you can emulate its natural growing conditions.

E. repens

e. REP-enz. MAYFLOWER, TRAILING ARBUTUS. This evergreen, ground-hugging shrub has branches that root along the stems. The entire colony resents being disturbed, which is why it can be so difficult to transplant to a new site. The fragrant flowers appear in very early spring. Mayflower needs superb drainage and strongly acid soil. **Zones 3 to 6.**

Epimedium

eh-pih-MEE-dee-um. Barberry family, Berberidaceae.

Epimedium species are grown for their delicate sprays of spring flowers, their handsome foliage, and their tough, no-nonsense constitution. Also commonly called barrenworts and bishop's caps (the latter a reference to the flower shape), they bear loose, airy racemes or panicles of ¹/₂- to 1-inch flowers on wiry stems in spring. Blooms have eight sepals, four of which are petal-like, and four true petals that are hooded or spurlike and serve as nectaries. Flowers are white, rose, red, yellow, or bicolored. The wiry-stemmed leaves emerge with or slightly after the flowers. Each leaf consists of several heart-shaped or somewhat triangular leaflets (from three to nine or more) that have either spiny or smooth edges. New leaves are bright green, sometimes

Epimedium × rubrum

marked with bronze or maroon, and they turn darker green and become more leathery as they mature. Epimediums make handsome ground covers or edging plants, bearing their attractive leaves from early spring into late fall and even early winter, and often showing good fall color. Plants described as evergreen or semievergreen generally exhibit this characteristic in areas with mild winters. From about Zone 6 north, the foliage turns brown and curls over winter. The genus contains between 30 and 40 species native to the Mediterranean region and eastern Asia.

HOW TO GROW

Give epimediums partial to full shade and rich, evenly moist soil. They also grow in sun provided the soil is rich and consistently moist. Established plants tolerate dry shade and can compete with the roots of established trees. Epimediums are rhizomatous, and most species spread steadily, but slowly, to form broad 1- to 2-foot-wide mounds. In late winter cut back the old foliage so it will not hide the spring flowers. Propagate by dividing the clumps in spring. Another option is to root individual sections of rhizomes.

E. alpinum

e. al-PIE-num. ALPINE EPIME-DIUM. A 6- to 9-inch-tall species with deciduous leaves and red, nearly spurless flowers in spring. **Zones 3 to 8.**

E. grandiflorum

e. gran-dih-FLOR-um. LONG-SPURRED EPIMEDIUM. Decid-uous 8- to 12-inch-tall species with

large 1- to 1½-inch-wide flowers in white, yellow, pink, or purple, which bloom in spring. 'Crimson Beauty' has coppery red flowers. 'Lilafee' bears purple flowers. 'Rose Queen' bears bronzy young leaves and rose-pink blooms. 'White Queen' bears white flowers. **Zones 4 to 8.**

E. × perralchicum

e. × per-RAL-chee-kum. Vigorous 12- to 16-inch-tall hybrid that spreads to 2 feet or more. Bears evergreen or semievergreen leaves and bright yellow ¾-inch-wide flowers in spring. 'Fröhnleiten' has showy 1-inch-wide blooms. **Zones 5 to 8.**

E. perralderianum

e. per-ral-der-ee-AY-num. A 10- to 12-inch-tall species that spreads to 2 feet or more. Bears evergreen to semievergreen leaves and short-spurred, ¾-inch-wide yellow flowers in spring. **Zones 5 to 8.**

E. pinnatum

e. pin-NAH-tum. An 8- to 12-inch-tall species that has evergreen to semievergreen leaves and ¾-inch-wide yellow flowers with brown-purple spurs in spring. **Zones 4 to 8.**

E. × rubrum

e. × RUE-brum. RED-FLOWERED EPIMEDIUM. An 8- to 12-inch-tall species with deciduous leaves and ¾-inch-wide flowers in spring that are red and pale yellow. **Zones 4 to 8.**

E. × versicolor

e. × VER-sih-kuh-er. BICOLOR EPIMEDIUM. Vigorous 12-inch-tall species with evergreen to

semievergreen leaves and ¼- to ¾-inch-wide flowers in spring that are pinkish red and yellow with red spurs. 'Neosulfureum' has pale yellow flowers. 'Sulfureum' bears flowers that are darker yellow and have longer spurs than those of 'Neosulfureum'. **Zones 4 to 8.**

E. × warleyense

e. × war-lee-EN-see. WARLEY EPIMEDIUM. Vigorous 8- to 12-inch-tall species that bears evergreen to semievergreen leaves and ½-inch-wide brick to orange-red flowers. **Zones 4 to 8.**

E. × youngianum

e. × young-ee-AH-num. YOUNG'S EPIMEDIUM. Compact 6- to 8-inch-tall species that spreads to 1 foot or less and bears deciduous, delicate-looking fernlike leaves and ½- to ¾-inch-wide white or rose-pink flowers in spring. 'Niveum' has white flowers. 'Roseum', sometimes called 'Lilacinum', has pale mauve-pink to lilac flowers. **Zones 4 to 8.**

Eranthis

eh-RAN-thiss. Buttercup family, Ranunculaceae.

Commonly known as winter aconites, *Eranthis* species are among the earliest flowers of spring. Their yellow cup-shaped flowers, each

with a ruff of green beneath the blooms, appear in very early spring — the botanical name is from the Greek *er*, meaning "spring," and *anthos*, "flower." Flowers, which are borne on leafless stems, consist of showy petal-like sepals that are yellow or white. The true petals are reduced to tubular nectaries. The leafy green collar under the blooms is a single, deeply divided leaf; all the other leaves are basal and also deeply divided. Plants grow from short rhizomes that have knobby tubers. About seven species belong to the genus.

HOW TO GROW

Select a site in full sun to partial shade with rich, moist, but not wet, soil. Winter aconites tolerate drier conditions in summer once the leaves have died back. They thrive on the edges of wooded areas under deciduous trees, where they receive full spring sunshine while they are growing actively but are in shade when dormant in summer. Like other vigorous, spring-blooming bulbs such as crocuses, they are ideal for naturalizing or using at the front of lightly shaded beds and borders. Plant tubers 2 inches deep and 3 inches apart in fall. Soak them overnight in warm water before planting. Old tubers that have dried out too much may not grow. Mulch in summer with well-rotted compost to keep the soil rich and

Eranthis hyemalis

moist. Clumps are best left undisturbed once established, and they form large drifts where happy. Dig and divide them in late spring, just as the leaves die down, if they become too crowded or outgrow their space, or for propagation. Plants also self-sow, and seedlings are easy to move.

E. cilicia

e. sil-IH-see-uh. Winter Aconite. A 2- to 3-inch-tall species bearing very finely lobed green leaves tinged with bronze and ³/4- to 1¹/2-inch-wide yellow flowers in early spring. Zones 4 to 9.

E. hyemalis

e. hi-MAL-iss. Winter Aconite. A 2- to 3-inch-tall species with lobed green leaves and ³/4- to 1¹/4-inch-wide yellow flowers in late winter to early spring. Zones 4 to 9.

Eremurus

air-eh-MURE-us. Lily family, Liliaceae.

Both the common and botanical names of *Eremurus* species make reference to the cylindrical racemes of these stately plants. They are commonly called foxtail lilies and desert candles, and the botanical name is from the Greek *eremos*, meaning "solitary," and *oura*, "tail." About 40 to 50 species belong to the genus, all of which grow from fleshy roots that spread out around a central crown. They bear basal, usually strap-shaped, leaves that reach about 1 foot in length and die back after the plants flower. Each crown produces a single, tail-like bloom that consists of literally hundreds of small densely packed flowers that are starry in shape and have

Eremurus himalaicus

Erica carnea 'Pirbright Rose'

prominent, often showy, stamens. Blooms come in shades of pink, yellow, and white and have six petal-like tepals.

HOW TO GROW

Select a site in full sun that is protected from wind and has rich, well-drained soil. Sandy soil is ideal, and plants will not tolerate the poorly drained conditions offered by heavy clay soil. Plant the fleshy roots in fall. Handle them carefully, as they are brittle and easily broken. Prepare the site deeply (to about 2 feet) at planting time. The roots need to be planted at a depth of 4 to 6 inches and require a wide hole so their starfish-like arms can be spread out evenly. Set the roots on top of a layer of coarse sand or grit at the bottom of the hole to ensure excellent drainage. Mark their locations to avoid digging into them by accident when they are dormant either in winter or from late summer onward.

Plants begin growing very early in spring, and late frosts can severely damage the top growth. To protect them, cover the site with a 3- to 4-inch-deep layer of compost, sand, or sawdust in late fall after the ground has frozen to a depth of 1 to 2 inches. In spring, if plants emerge above this layer before the danger of frost has passed, cover the new growth with evergreen branches or coarse leaves (such as oak leaves). Or protect them with large cardboard boxes overnight. Remove the mounds of mulch once danger of frost has passed.

Use foxtail lilies at the backs of perennial borders — they are espe-

cially effective when set against a dark background such as evergreens — and plant them in drifts to emphasize their bold, vertical lines. Leaves die down as the flowers fade, so plant them behind lower-growing perennials to hide the spaces they leave. Foxtail lilies are best left undisturbed once planted. Dig and divide them if necessary for propagation just as the leaves die down. Or start from seeds, which are slow to germinate.

E. himalaicus

e. him-ah-LAY-ih-kus. Himalayan Foxtail Lily. A white-flowered species bearing 3-foot-long racemes of starry 1-inch-wide flowers in late spring and early summer. Plants reach 4 to 6 feet tall in bloom. Zones 5 to 8.

E. × isabellinus

e. × iss-ah-bell-EYE-nus. A hybrid species bearing ¹/2- to 2-foot-long racemes of ³/4- to 1¹/2-inch-wide flowers in early summer in shades of pink, yellow, orange, or white. Plants are 6 to 8 feet tall in bloom. Many cultivars are available, including Reuter Hybrids, which come in a wide range of rich colors. 'Cleopatra' is a Reuter Hybrid with burnt orange flowers. Shelford Hybrids come in reds, pink, orange, yellow, and white. 'Pinokkio' ('Pinocchio') bears bright yellow flowers with orange anthers. 'White Beauty' has white flowers. Zones 5 to 8.

E. robustus

e. roe-BUS-tus. Vigorous species, reaching 10 feet tall in bloom, that

bears 4-foot-long leaves and 3- to 4-foot-long racemes of pale pink 1¹/2-inch-wide flowers with yellow stamens from early to midsummer. Zones 5 to 8.

E. stenophyllus

e. sten-oh-FILL-us. Foxtail Lily. Fairly compact species, to 3 feet in bloom, bearing ¹/2- to 1-foot-long racemes of dark yellow ³/4-inch-wide flowers from early to midsummer. Flowers turn orange and then brown as they fade. *E. stenophyllus* ssp. *stenophyllus* (sometimes listed as *E. bungei*) produces bright yellow flowers on 5-foot-tall plants. Zones 5 to 8.

Erica

AIR-ih-kuh. Heath family, Ericaceae.

More than 700 species of these evergreen shrubs occur in moors and heaths in Europe and temperate parts of Asia and Africa. Most are grown as shrubby ground covers, for their needlelike whorled leaves and terminal racemes of bell-shaped flowers. A collection of species and cultivars provides color through most of the year. There are a few treelike species.

HOW TO GROW

Most heaths demand acidic soils of peat and sand in open sunny sites. They're good for low hedges, for rock gardens, and as companions for azaleas and rhododendrons. Prune spring bloomers after flowering, fall bloomers in spring to about an inch above the previous season's growth. Give tree

Erigeron 'Foerster's Liebling'

heaths a light trim. Propagate by semiripe cuttings or layering.

E. arborea

e. are-BORE-ee-uh. TREE HEATH. This species grows to 12 feet tall and has honey-scented white flowers in spring. Half as tall are *E. arborea* var. *alpina,* which is anise scented and flowers profusely, and 'Albert', which has yellow foliage but rarely blooms. 'Estrella Gold' is chartreuse and 4 feet tall. **Zones 7 to 10.**

E. carnea

KAR-nee-uh. WINTER HEATH. This low evergreen shrub is considered to be the most cold-tolerant species, blooming right through late snows. Leaves are short needles. Flowers are little bells that appear from late winter to early spring. Flower color varies by selection. 'Springwood White' has creamy buds that open to white flowers. It grows vigorously as a ground cover, remaining under 10 inches tall. 'Springwood Pink' is similar but with pink flowers. 'Vivellii' ('Urville') is one of the most striking heaths in the landscape and makes eye-catching masses with its deep red flowers and winter-bronzed foliage. **Zones 5 to 7.**

E. × darleyensis

e. × dar-lee-EN-sis. Tolerant of alkaline soil, this hybrid grows in mounds 2 feet tall, producing white to rosy flowers in late winter or early spring. It performs best in the Southeast. There are many cultivars with slightly varying foliage hues or more predictable bloom colors. **Zones 7 to 8.**

E. vagans

e. VAY-ganz. CORNISH HEATH. Also called wandering heath for the ground-hugging branches that can develop on this 2-foot-tall mound. Purple-pink flowers bloom from midsummer to early fall. **Zones 5 to 8.**

Erigeron

ee-RIDG-er-on. Aster family, Asteraceae.

Commonly called erigerons or fleabanes, *Erigeron* species are annuals, biennials, and perennials with daisylike flowers. There are about 200 species in the genus, native to mountainous regions and dry grasslands, especially in North America. Erigerons usually produce a rosette of simple, lance- to spoon-shaped or oval leaves, although some species also bear leaves along the stems. Their daisylike blooms are single or double and consist of many very narrow ray florets (the "petals") in yellow, purple, white, pink, orange, or violet-blue. The ray florets surround dense, usually yellow, buttonlike centers of disk florets, which produce the seeds. Flowers are borne singly or in small clusters and typically appear in summer.

HOW TO GROW

Give commonly cultivated erigerons, including the species listed here, full sun or light shade and rich soil that is well drained yet remains evenly moist. (Alpine or rock-garden species require extremely well drained soil and are especially intolerant of wet soil in winter.) A spot with shade during the hottest part of the day is beneficial, especially in Zones 7 and 8, to help the plants cope with heat. Taller species and cultivars require staking. Deadhead to encourage repeat bloom. Divide plants every 2 to 3 years in spring or fall to keep them vigorous. Propagate by division, cuttings taken from shoots at the base of the plants in spring, or seeds.

E. hybrids

Most hybrids range from $1^{1}/2$ to 2 feet in height, spread to about $1^{1}/2$ feet, and bloom from early to midsummer. 'Charity' bears semidouble pink flowers; 'Darkest of All' ('Dunkelste Aller') bears semidouble flowers with violet ray florets; 'Foerster's Liebling' bears semidouble, deep reddish pink blooms with yellow centers; 'Gaiety' and 'Pink Jewel' bear pink flowers; 'Prosperity' bears lavender-blue flowers; and 'Summer Snow' ('Sommerneuschnee') bears white flowers. Hardiness varies among the cultivars, but most are hardy from **Zones 4 or 5 to 8.**

E. pulchellus

e. pul-CHELL-us. POOR ROBIN'S PLANTAIN. A 2-foot-tall species that spreads by stolons to about $1^{1}/2$ feet. Bears 1-inch-wide yellow-centered flowers in summer, either singly or in small clusters, with about 60 lavender ray florets. **Zones 4 to 8.**

E. speciosus

e. spee-see-OH-sus. A 2-foot-tall species that spreads as far and bears 1- to 2-inch-wide flower heads in summer with more than 100 lavender-blue ray florets. **Zones 2 to 9.**

Eryngium

eh-RIN-jee-um. Carrot family, Apiaceae.

Commonly called sea hollies, the 230 species of *Eryngium* are annuals, biennials, and perennials native to dry, sandy, or rocky soils primarily in the Mediterranean region, although there also are native North American species. Unlikely-looking relatives of carrots and Queen Anne's lace *(Daucus carota),* they bear leathery, oval-, heart-, or sword-shaped leaves that often are deeply divided and thistlelike with spiny margins. Their tiny flowers are borne in dense, rounded conelike umbels with a ruff of showy, stiff, spiny bracts at the base. Foliage comes in shades of steely blue-gray, gray-green, or silver-green, while flowers are metallic purple-blue or blue-gray.

HOW TO GROW

Most sea hollies thrive in full sun and average, well-drained soil. They tolerate heat, drought, and poor soil, although some species, including *E. agavifolium, E. yuccifolium,* and the biennial *E. giganteum,* thrive in rich, evenly moist, well-drained soil. For all, good soil drainage is essential, especially in winter. Sea hollies have deep taproots and generally resent being disturbed, so select a permanent spot at planting time. Most spread to form $1^{1}/2$- to 2-foot-wide clumps. Propagate by separating small plantlets from the base of

Eryngium yuccifolium

Erysimum cheiri

the clump. Plants also self-sow, and seedlings are easily moved. Sea hollies make excellent cut and dried flowers. For drying, pick just before the blooms have fully expanded, and hang them in a warm, dry, dark place.

E. agavifolium

e. ah-gah-vih-FOE-lee-um. Evergreen species with rosettes of sword-shaped, sharp-toothed leaves and branched 3- to 5-foot-tall stalks of round, 2-inch-long, greenish white flower heads with spiny bracts in late summer. **Zones 6 to 9.**

E. alpinum

e. al-PIE-num. ALPINE SEA HOLLY. A 2-foot-tall species with rosettes of spiny, heart-shaped leaves. From midsummer to fall it bears branched stalks of round 1¹/₂-inch-long flower heads that are metallic blue-gray and have spiny, lacy-looking bracts. **Zones 5 to 8.**

E. amethystinum

e. am-eh-thuh-STY-num. AME-THYST SEA HOLLY. A 2-foot-tall species forming clumps of rounded, pinnately cut, spiny leaves. Bears round, metallic blue, ³/₄- to 1-inch-long flower heads with spiny silver-gray bracts from mid- to late summer. **Zones 3 to 8.**

E. bourgatii

e. bore-GAH-tee-eye. MEDITER-RANEAN SEA HOLLY. A 1- to 2-foot-tall plant with spiny, pinnate leaves with silver veins. From mid- to late summer it bears branched stems of rounded, gray-green, ¹/₂- to 1-inch-long flower heads with a starlike ruff of lance-shaped bracts. **Zones 5 to 9.**

E. giganteum

e. jy-GAN-tee-um. GIANT SEA HOLLY, MISS WILLMOTT'S GHOST. A 3-foot-tall biennial or short-lived perennial with a rosette of heart-shaped, spiny leaves. Bears branched stems of 2¹/₂-inch-long, steel blue flowers surrounded by 2¹/₂-inch-long, spiny, silvery bracts. Biennial or cool-weather annual.

E. planum

e. PLAY-num. FLAT SEA HOLLY. Evergreen 3-foot-tall species with rounded, toothed, and lobed leaves. From midsummer to fall it bears branched stems of rounded, ¹/₂- to ³/₄-inch-long flower heads that are pale steely blue and surrounded by narrow blue-green bracts. **Zones 5 to 9.**

E. yuccifolium

e. yuck-ih-FOE-lee-um. RATTLE-SNAKE MASTER. Native North American species forming 2-foot-tall rosettes of semievergreen, sword-shaped, blue-gray leaves with spiny margins. From mid-summer to fall it bears branched 4-foot-tall stalks of round ³/₄- to 1-inch-long flower heads that are whitish green with very small gray-green bracts. **Zones 4 to 8.**

Erysimum

er-RISS-ih-mum. Mustard family, Brassicaceae.

Grown for their dense clusters of four-petaled flowers, *Erysimum* species are native to well-drained, mostly alkaline soils in Europe, northern Africa, Asia, and North America. About 80 species of well-branched annuals, biennials, and perennials belong to the genus. Commonly called wallflowers, they bear narrow, sometimes toothed, leaves and feature flowers in shades of yellow, orange, red, and lilac- to mauve-pink. Common wallflower (*E. cheiri*) is the best-known species and is grown as either a biennial or a cool-weather annual.

HOW TO GROW

Give common wallflower full sun to partial shade and poor, average, or somewhat rich soil that is well drained. The plants prefer cool temperatures and need to be replaced once hot weather arrives. To grow it as a biennial, sow seeds outdoors in a nursery bed or pots set in a sheltered spot from early to midsummer, then transplant seedlings in midfall to the spots where they will bloom. Or sow indoors in spring 8 to 10 weeks before the last frost date. Damping off is a common problem, so sow in a sterile seed-starting mix, and water from below. Pull up the plants when they have finished blooming. Use wallflowers with other annuals in bedding displays, in containers, and as cut flowers.

E. cheiri

e. CHEE-er-eye. COMMON WALLFLOWER. Formerly *Cherianthus cheiri*. An evergreen, short-lived perennial ranging from 6 to 30 inches in height. Bears dense racemes of fragrant, 1-inch-wide flowers in spring. Many cultivars are available in shades of rich yellow, scarlet, orange-red, pale pink, and lemon yellow. 'Prince Formula Mix' and 'Tom Thumb Mix' are dwarf strains, from 6 to 9 inches tall; Bedder Series plants reach 1 foot. Cool-weather annual.

Erythronium

air-ih-THRO-nee-um. Lily family, Liliaceae.

These charming members of the lily family have a host of common names, including dogtooth violet, trout lily, adder's tongue, and fawn lily. They are grown for their nodding pink, white, yellow, or cream lilylike flowers that are borne in late spring to early summer. Unlike many bulbous plants, erythroniums also have handsome leaves

Erythronium americanum

Erythronium revolutum

that are broad to oval in shape and often mottled with brown or cream. Each bulb produces two or sometimes three leaves. The yellowish white bulbs (which some sources describe as corms) have a membranous covering and are long and tooth- or fang-shaped. They are buried deep in the ground, with unbranched, subterranean stems leading up to the soil surface. Some species spread by offsets and stolons. Flowers are borne on leafless stalks, either singly or in small graceful racemes. Each individual bloom has six petal-like tepals. In some species they are strongly reflexed, meaning curved backward. About 22 species belong to the genus, native to North America, Asia, and Europe.

HOW TO GROW
Select a site in partial or dappled shade with deeply prepared, evenly moist soil rich in organic matter. Plant the bulbs in fall, setting the toothlike roots upright, not lengthwise, with 4 to 6 inches of soil over the tops. Do not let the bulbs dry out before planting; keep them packed in barely damp peat moss or vermiculite and keep them in a cool, shady place. Plant as soon as possible. Mulch plantings with chopped leaves, compost, or shredded bark to keep the soil rich, moist, and cool. Propagate by seeds, which are slow to germinate and reach blooming size, or by dividing clumps in summer immediately after they flower. Plants may self-sow.

E. americanum
e. ah-mair-ih-KAH-num. Yellow Adder's Tongue, Trout Lily. Wildflower native to eastern North America that reaches 3 to 6 inches in height. Bears 6-inch-long green leaves mottled with purple and solitary yellow flowers that are 1 to 2 inches across in spring. **Zones 3 to 9.**

E. californicum
e. kal-ih-FOR-nih-kum. Fawn Lily. A 6- to 14-inch-tall California native with rounded 3-inch-long green leaves lightly marked with brownish green. Bears creamy white 2- to 3-inch-wide flowers in spring, either singly or in racemes of up to three blooms. 'White Beauty' is a vigorous white-flowered selection. **Zones 3 to 9.**

E. dens-canis
e. denz-KAY-niss. European Dogtooth Violet. A 4- to 6-inch-tall species with elliptic 4- to 6-inch-long green leaves marked with purple-brown. Bears solitary 1½-inch-wide flowers in spring in shades of pink, lilac, or white. Many cultivars are available, including 'Lilac Wonder', with purple flowers that have a single brown spot at the base of each petal; 'Pink Perfection', with pink flowers; 'Purple King', with rich purple flowers striped with pale brown and cream in the center; and 'Rose Queen', with rich, deep pink flowers. **Zones 3 to 9.**

E. grandiflorum
e. gran-dih-FLOR-um. A species native to western North America that reaches 6 to 12 inches in height and has solid green 4- to 8-inch-long rounded leaves. Bears yellow 2-inch-wide flowers in spring, either singly or in racemes of up to three. **Zones 4 to 9.**

E. hendersonii
e. hen-der-SO-nee-eye. Dogtooth Violet. Wildflower native to the Pacific Northwest ranging from 6 to 14 inches in height and bearing 4- to 8-inch-long green leaves marked with pale brownish green bands. In spring, it bears 2-inch-wide pale lilac flowers in racemes of up to 10 flowers. Plants prefer a spot that dries out during the summer (when they are dormant). **Zones 3 to 9.**

E. 'Pagoda'
A showy, vigorous hybrid ranging from 6 to 14 inches in height and bearing rounded green leaves heavily marked with bronze. In spring, it produces rich sulphur yellow blooms in clusters of 2 to as many as 10 flowers. **Zones 4 to 9.**

E. revolutum
e. rev-oh-LOO-tum. Western Trout Lily. An 8- to 12-inch-tall species native to the Pacific Northwest that has 6- to 8-inch-long green leaves heavily marked with brown. In spring, it bears 1½- to 3-inch-wide lilac-pink flowers in racemes of up to four blooms. 'Pink Beauty' has deep lilac-pink blooms. **Zones 5 to 9.**

E. tuolumnense
e. too-lum-NEN-see. An 8- to 14-inch-tall California native with rounded 8- to 12-inch-long green leaves. Bears racemes of four to seven yellow 1- to 2-inch-wide flowers in spring. **Zones 3 to 9.**

Escallonia
es-kal-LONE-ee-uh. Currant family, Grossulariaceae.

This genus comprises approximately 50 species of evergreen shrubs, most from South America, grown for their shiny, often aromatic foliage and long-blooming, funnel-shaped, five-petaled flowers.

HOW TO GROW
Escallonia doesn't tolerate highly alkaline soil, temperature extremes, or wind and is suitable primarily for the Northwest or mild coastal regions. (It doesn't mind salt.) It needs full sun and is happy against a sunny wall or in a hedge. Although it doesn't require pruning, it can be pruned hard to correct shape or to restrict growth. Propagate from semihard cuttings.

E. × exoniensis 'Frades'
e. × ek-soh-nee-EN-sis. This hybrid selection is a dense shrub growing 12 or more feet tall and bearing relatively small, glossy leaves. Profuse pink or rosy flowers cover it most of the year. It is often espaliered. **Zones 8 to 9.**

E. × langleyensis 'Apple Blossom'
e. × lang-lee-EN-sis. Apple Blossom Escallonia. Dense but sprawling if not controlled, this shrub grows to 4 or 5 feet tall and produces large leaves. Profuse pale pink flowers with a white eye appear for many weeks from late spring to early fall. **Zones 8 to 9.**

E. rubra
e. RUE-bruh. This upright, compact species grows anywhere from 8 to

Escallonia × *langleyensis* 'Apple Blossom'

Eschscholzia californica

Eschscholzia californica

15 feet tall and bears glossy dark green leaves and profuse 3-inch panicles of deep red flowers. 'C. F. Ball' will stay under 3 feet with some attention. **Zones 8 and 9.**

Eschscholzia

eh-SCHOLT-zee-ah. Poppy family, Papaveraceae.

Wildflowers native to western North America, the 8 to 10 species of *Eschscholzia* are annuals and perennials with finely divided, fernlike leaves and cup-shaped, poppylike flowers. One species, commonly called California poppy, is a popular annual.

HOW TO GROW

Give eschscholzias full sun and poor to average, well-drained soil. Plants grow well in sandy soil; rich soil yields abundant foliage but few flowers. Sow seeds outdoors after the last spring frost date or in fall where winters are mild — roughly Zone 6 south. Or sow indoors 2 to 3 weeks before the last frost date in individual pots. Germination takes 1 to 3 weeks at 60° to 65°F. Transplant with care: direct sowing is generally best to prevent root damage. Deadheading increases flower production, but leave some flowers to encourage self-sowing. Use California poppies in mixed plantings, containers, and rock gardens. They make attractive but short-lived cut flowers.

E. californica

e. kal-ih-FOR-nih-kuh. CALIFORNIA POPPY. A well-branched, mat-forming, 8- to 12-inch annual or short-lived perennial with blue-green, fernlike leaves. Bears showy, 3-inch-wide, four-petaled flowers in orange, yellow, or red that close when the weather is cloudy. Thai Silk Series plants have single or semidouble flowers with ruffled petals in shades of red, pink, yellow, or orange. 'Mission Bells Mix' features semidouble flowers ranging from cream to orange. Cool-weather annual.

Eucharis

YEW-kah-riss. Amaryllis family, Amaryllidaceae.

These handsome bulbs are grown for their clusters of sweetly fragrant, white, daffodil-like flowers. They grow from tunicate bulbs and also feature handsome, broad, hostalike leaves. The flowers have six spreading lobes surrounding a central cup that resembles the cup

Eucharis × grandiflora

of a daffodil. The cup is formed by the filaments of the six stamens, which broaden and join at the base. Flowers are borne in umbels on leafless stalks well above the foliage. The genus contains 17 species of evergreen bulbs native to Central and South America. Despite their common name, Amazon lily, they are not true lilies nor are they native to areas along the Amazon River. Instead they are found primarily in the Andes in Colombia and Peru — as well as in Central America.

HOW TO GROW

Give these tropical plants a spot in partial, dappled shade with average to rich soil that is well drained. They thrive in heat and humidity, but the large leaves burn if exposed to bright sunlight. Amazon lilies can be grown outdoors year-round from Zone 9 south; in the North, plant them in containers or tubs. (Even in Zone 9, protect plants when temperatures threaten to dip below freezing.) They can be kept indoors year-round or moved outdoors during the summer months.

Amazon lilies grow best, and are most effective, in large pots with several bulbs per pot — at least three or four per 8-inch pot, for example. (Planting several bulbs per pot results in a mound of handsome foliage.) The bulbs resent being disturbed, so don't overcrowd when planting, and select containers large enough to allow for several years' growth. Keep the soil evenly moist when they are growing actively, but let the soil stay fairly dry in winter when plants are dormant and stop producing new leaves. (The plants are evergreen, so they never die back, just grow more slowly.) These are heavy feeders: feed weekly or biweekly with a dilute, balanced fertilizer when they are growing actively. Bring container-grown plants indoors before the first frost threatens.

While the main flush of flowers comes in late summer, it is possible to induce a second blooming period in winter by keeping the plants fairly dry for about 6 weeks just after bringing them indoors — water only when the leaves begin to wilt. Then move plants to a warm, humid spot and resume watering and feeding more regularly.

E. × grandiflora

e. × gran-dih-FLOR-uh. AMAZON LILY, EUCHARIST LILY, MADONNA LILY, LILY-OF-THE-AMAZON. Plants grown in gardens as *E. amazonica* fall here. This hybrid bears glossy, dark green, elliptic to ovate leaves that have wavy margins and reach 12 inches in length. Umbels of 3-inch-wide white flowers with a sweet lemony scent appear on 20-inch-tall stems in summer. Foliage mounds are about 1¹/₂ feet tall, and plants reach 2 feet tall in bloom. Tender perennial. **Zones 9 to 11.**

Eucomis

yew-KOH-miss. Lily family, Liliaceae.

Grown for their unusual, long-lasting blooms that resemble pineapples, *Eucomis* species are primarily native to South Africa. Commonly called pineapple flowers or pineapple lilies, they bear cylindrical racemes of small, densely packed flowers in late summer and early fall that are topped by a cluster of leafy bracts that resemble the leaves at the top of a pineapple. The individual flowers are star shaped and have six petal-like tepals that are fused at the base. The glossy green leaves, which usually range from 1 to 2 feet long, are strap to lance shaped and borne only at the base of the plant. About 15 species belong to the genus, all of which grow from large tunicate bulbs.

HOW TO GROW

Give pineapple lilies full sun or partial shade and rich, well-drained soil. Where hardy, plant the bulbs outdoors in fall at a depth of 5 to 6 inches. Like many South African natives, these bulbs require a dry dormant period, so in areas with rainy winters, mulch the plants with evergreen boughs, salt hay, pine needles, or coarse hay, and then top the site with heavy plastic to keep the soil dry. Where they are marginally hardy, look for a warm, south-facing site, such as at the base of a wall, and mulch heavily over winter. In the North, grow these bulbs in containers, setting the bulbs with the noses, or tips, slightly below or just emerging from the soil surface. To overwinter container-grown plants, gradually withhold water toward the end of the season and let the foliage die back, then store them — still in their containers — in a cool (40° to 50°F), frost-free, dry place.

Whether outdoors or in containers, plants are happiest when left undisturbed and will thrive for years without needing division: dig and divide the bulbs or pot them only if they become overcrowded or for propagation. Bulbs can be stored over winter in dry peat moss in a cool (50°F) spot. Propagate by separating the offsets in early fall or just as the foliage dies down in early fall. Or sow seeds.

Eucomis comosa

E. autumnalis

e. aw-tum-NAL-iss. Formerly *E. undulata*. An 8- to 12-inch-tall species with wavy-margined leaves. In late summer and early fall, produces erect, cylindrical 2- to 6-inch-long racemes of greenish white 1-inch-wide flowers. **Zones 8 to 10**.

E. bicolor

e. BI-kuh-lor. A 1- to 2-foot-tall species with wavy-margined leaves. In late summer, bears erect 6-inch-long racemes of pale green 1-inch-wide flowers edged in purple. **Zones 8 to 10**.

E. comosa

e. koh-MOE-suh. PINEAPPLE FLOWER, PINEAPPLE LILY. Formerly *E. punctata*. A 2- to 3-foot-tall species with wavy-margined leaves. Bears erect, cylindrical 1-foot-long racemes of white 1-inch-wide flowers in late summer that are edged in purple and have showy purple ovaries at the center of each flower. **Zones 6 or 7 to 10**.

E. pole-evansii

e. pole-ee-VAN-see-eye. Vigorous 3- to 6-foot-tall species with 2- to 4-foot-long wavy-margined leaves. Bears cylindrical 1¹/₂- to 3-foot-long racemes of greenish white flowers in late summer. **Zones 8 to 10**.

Euonymus

yew-ON-eh-mus. Spindle-tree family, Celastraceae.

Gardeners tend to either hate or love *Euonymus*, which indicates that it includes extremely versatile garden plants that have been inap-

Euonymus fortunei

Euonymus alatus

propriately or excessively used and in some cases become invasive. The 175 or so species are native throughout the North Temperate Zone, with the great majority native from the Himalayas to China, Korea, and Japan. *Euonymus* is related to *Celastrus* (bittersweet), and both genera have species that are now invasive exotic pests throughout North America. *Euonymus* species are woody plants ranging from prostrate, ground-covering shrubs to small trees. Several species develop corky "wings," or ridges, on the twigs and stems. Leaves are simple, alternate or opposite, usually lanceolate or ovate, and less than an inch to 4 inches or more long. The deciduous species typically have spectacular fall colors, as indicated by the common name "burning bush" for *E. alatus*.

HOW TO GROW

As a rule, euonymus should have full sun and moisture-retentive soil. While evergreen species will tolerate some shade, those with variegated foliage won't develop

their best coloration without plenty of sunlight. Use them as specimens, in the shrub border, or in masses. The native species, *E. americanus*, is good for naturalizing where you need some fall interest. None require pruning, but some are prone to scale and fungal diseases. Propagate from ripe seeds, softwood cuttings of deciduous species, and semiripe cuttings of evergreens.

E. alatus

e. ah-LAY-tus. BURNING BUSH, WINGED EUONYMUS. This species has escaped cultivation in the East and Upper Midwest, and even cultivars will self-sow. Gardeners in those regions should avoid it, or choose cultivars that produce little seed. The species grows 10 to 15 feet tall and wide and has 3-inch toothed leaves that turn fuchsia red in fall. Insignificant yellow-green early-summer flowers give way to capsules of orange-red seeds. 'Rudy Haag' grows slowly to 4 to 5 feet but has inconspicuous fruits. **Zones 4 to 8**.

E. americanus

e. ah-mair-ih-KAH-nus. STRAWBERRY BUSH. This native of the eastern United States, 4 to 6 feet tall with a loose suckering habit, is often called hearts-a-bustin' in honor of its surprising fall fruits. Red and bumpy, they split open to reveal orange-red seeds. Not oth-

Euonymus fortunei

erwise showy, so situate it at the edge of a wood or other out-of-the-way spot. **Zones 6 to 9**.

E. europaeus 'Red Cap'

e. your-oh-PAY-us. EUROPEAN SPINDLE TREE CULTIVAR. The species, although not necessarily its cultivars, is invasive in the East and upper Midwest. Growing fast to 12 to 25 feet tall and wide, the cultivar is notable for abundant fall fruits that are reddish pink with exposed orange seeds (arils). **Zones 4 to 7**.

E. fortunei

e. for-TOON-ee-eye. WINTER-CREEPER. This much-used evergreen ground cover spreads rapidly to about 4 to 5 feet, or indefinitely if not pruned. It benefits from annual shearing in spring to control growth, enhance spread, and thicken the mat. This shearing can be done with a power mower. There are numerous selections in the trade, attesting to its wide adaptability. The named cultivars are usually based on foliage differences. 'Acutus' is vigorously prostrate and produces narrow, dark green leaves. 'Coloratus', commonly known as purple wintercreeper, has dark green foliage during the growing season that turns purple or bronze in fall and winter. 'Emerald 'n Gold' has green leaves with yellow margins and some red tints in fall. 'Kewensis' bears tiny leaves (about 1/4 inch long) and forms a nearly flat mat. 'Minimus' has small leaves (slightly larger than those of 'Kewensis') and more vigorous growth overall. 'Silver Queen' bears green leaves with white markings. **Zones 4 to 9**.

E. japonicus

e. juh-PON-ih-kuss. JAPANESE SPINDLE TREE. Growing 12 to 16 feet tall and 6 feet wide, this evergreen species has been the source of a wide array of variegated cultivars. There are dwarf and variegated forms, such as 'Sil-

Eupatorium purpureum

ver King', which grows to 6 feet tall and 3 feet wide and has off-white leaf margins. **Zones 6 to 9**.

Eupatorium

yew-pah-TORE-ee-um. Aster family, Asteraceae.

Commonly known as bonesets or Joe-Pye weeds, *Eupatorium* species are annuals, perennials, subshrubs, and shrubs. There are about 40 species in the genus, and the ones most often grown in gardens are native North American wildflowers. Commonly cultivated species usually have whorls of lance-shaped to wedge-shaped or rounded leaves and bear showy, rounded clusters of small fuzzy flowers in summer and fall.

HOW TO GROW

Select a site in full sun or partial shade with average to rich soil. Evenly moist to wet conditions are ideal and yield the tallest plants, although plants also grow in rich, well-drained conditions. *E. rugosum* is best in partial shade; both it and *E. purpureum* grow well in alkaline soils. Dig plants in spring or fall if they outgrow their space: *E. coelestinum* benefits from being divided every 3 to 4 years, while the other species can thrive for years untouched. Established plants spread to form 3- to 4-foot-wide clumps. Propagate by division in spring or by cuttings taken in early summer. Most species will self-sow or can be grown from seeds, but cultivars should be propagated by cuttings or division.

E. coelestinum

e. soh-les-TEE-num. HARDY AGERATUM, MISTFLOWER. Native North American wildflower ranging from 2 to 3 feet tall. Bears

Eupatorium coelestinum

Euphorbia marginata

slightly hairy leaves and fluffy, flat-topped 2- to 4-inch-wide clusters of lilac-blue flowers from late summer to fall. **Zones 5 to 9**.

E. fistulosum

e. fis-tew-LO-sum. HOLLOW JOE-PYE WEED. A 5- to 10-foot-tall native species with hollow wine-purple stems and rounded 6- to 10-inch-wide clusters of mauve-pink flowers in midsummer. 'Gateway' bears pink flowers on 5-foot black-stemmed plants. **Zones 3 to 8**.

E. maculatum

e. mak-yew-LAH-tum. SPOTTED JOE-PYE WEED. A 4- to 7-foot-tall native species with stems spotted in purple. Bears flat-topped 4- to 6-inch-wide clusters of pale to

dark purple flowers from mid-summer to fall. 'Bartered Bride' has white flowers. **Zones 3 to 7**.

E. purpureum

e. pur-PUR-ee-um. JOE-PYE WEED. Native 3- to 6-foot-tall wildflower with rounded 4- to 6-inch-wide clusters of pale rose-pink or purplish flowers from midsummer to fall. **Zones 3 to 8**.

E. rugosum

e. rue-GO-sum. WHITE SNAKE-ROOT. A native 5- to 6-foot-tall species with brown stems and 2 1/2-inch-wide clusters of white flowers from midsummer to fall. 'Chocolate' bears purple-brown leaves. **Zones 3 to 7**.

Euphorbia

you-FOR-bee-uh. Spurge family, Euphorbiaceae.

An enormous and varied genus, *Euphorbia* contains some 2,000 species of annuals, biennials, perennials, subshrubs, and trees, as well as exotic-looking succulents. Poinsettias (*E. pulcherrima*) and crown-of-thorns (*E. milii*) are well-known houseplants that belong here; several species are easy-to-grow, hardy perennials valued for their spring to summer flowers, their handsome foliage color, or their evergreen leaves. All euphorbias have very small flowers clustered together in an arrangement called a cyathium, in which a

Euphorbia characias ssp. *wulfenii*

single female flower is surrounded by several male flowers. The showy "flowers" of these plants are actually colorful petal-like bracts borne beneath the true flowers. The stems contain milky sap that flows when stems or leaves are cut or damaged and may irritate skin. Sear the stems of cut flowers or dip them in boiling water to seal in the sap.

HOW TO GROW

For most perennial euphorbias, select a site in full sun to partial or light shade with loose, poor to average, well-drained soil; exceptions are noted in the species descriptions below. A site with sun in the morning and dappled shade in the afternoon is suitable for many species. Most euphorbias are very drought tolerant once established. Cut off the flowering shoots at the base of the plant after they have bloomed. Propagate perennials by division, from cuttings of shoots that appear at the base of the plants in spring or early summer, by tip cuttings taken in summer, or by seeds. Sow seeds of annuals indoors 6 to 8 weeks before the last spring frost date. Plants self-sow.

E. amygdaloides var. robbiae

e. ah-mig-dal-OY-deez var. ROE-bee-eye. WOOD SPURGE, ROBB'S SPURGE. Forms 1½- to 2-foot-tall mounds of shiny, handsome evergreen leaves topped by greenish yellow flowers from midspring to early summer. Grow in evenly moist, rich soil in partial to full shade; tolerates dry shade. Spreads vigorously by rhizomes to 2 feet or more. Makes a good ground cover but can become invasive. **Zones 6 to 9**.

E. characias

e. kah-RAH-key-iss. Evergreen 3- to 4-foot-tall species with gray-green foliage that spreads to 4 feet. Bears rounded 4- to 10-inch-long clusters of chartreuse flowers from spring to summer. *E. characias* ssp. *wulfenii* bears showy yellow-green flower heads. **Zones 7 to 10**.

E. cyanthophora

e. sye-an-tho-FOR-ah. ANNUAL POINSETTIA, FIRE-ON-THE-MOUNTAIN, PAINTED LEAF. Sometimes listed as *E. heterophylla*. A shrubby, 1½- to 3-foot annual native to the United States and eastern Mexico. Best known as a Christmas houseplant. Grown for its showy leaves and bracts, which turn bright red at the stem tops like small poinsettias. Warm-weather annual.

E. cyparissias

e. sye-par-ISS-ee-us. CYPRESS SPURGE. This species must be carefully sited to prevent it from becoming weedy due to its running underground stems. It makes an effective mass in dry, gravelly gardens. Reaching just 10 to 18 inches tall, the plant's finely textured, blue-gray foliage makes it look like a tiny cypress. Yellow bracts appear in spring. 'Orange Man' has bracts that turn orange as they age. **Zones 6 to 8**.

E. dulcis

e. DUL-sis. Rhizomatous 1-foot-tall species that forms 1-foot-wide mounds of dark green or bronze-green leaves. Produces small 2- to 5-inch-wide clusters of greenish yellow flowers in early summer. Grow in evenly moist, rich soil in light shade; it also tolerates dry shade. 'Chameleon' has colorful purple-maroon foliage and yellow-green flowers. **Zones 4 to 9**.

E. griffithii

e. grih-FITH-ee-eye. GRIFFITH'S SPURGE. Mounding, shrublike 2- to 3-foot-tall species that spreads to 2 feet and bears dark green lance-shaped leaves that turn red in fall. Produces 4- to 6-inch-long clusters of orange-red flowers in early summer. Needs evenly moist, rich soil in light shade. Tolerates full sun in northern zones, but does not tolerate drought. 'Fireglow' bears showy scarlet-orange flowers. **Zones 4 to 8**.

E. lathyris

e. LATH-er-iss. GOPHER SPURGE, MOLE PLANT, CAPER SPURGE. A 1- to 4-foot biennial with leathery, lance-shaped, gray- to blue-green leaves. Bears 10- to 12-inch-wide umbels of yellow cyathia in summer. Warm-weather annual.

E. marginata

e. mar-jin-AY-tah. SNOW-ON-THE-MOUNTAIN, GHOST WEED. A vigorous 1- to 3-foot-tall annual native to North America. Grown for its white-edged leaves and bracts, which are carried in loose clusters in summer and fall. Warm-weather annual.

E. myrsinites

e. mir-sin-EYE-tees. SPURGE. This classic ground cover can be used to cascade over walls or spill across the ground in sites with very well drained soil and full sun. The fleshy, waxy, blue-green, oval leaves spiral around trailing stems that seldom rise more than 6 inches from the ground. Chartreuse bracts appear in spring. Cut back after bloom to control vigorous self-seeding. **Zones 6 to 9**.

E. palustris

e. paw-LUS-tris. SWAMP SPURGE. This euphorbia revels in wet to moist locations with full sun. As it matures, it may spread into drier and shadier areas nearby. Plants grow 3 to 4 feet or more tall and form extensive colonies. Use them in a grand-scale composition, where their size and acid yellow bracts will show to best advantage. **Zones 5 to 8**.

E. polychroma

e. pol-ee-KROH-muh. CUSHION SPURGE. Formerly *E. epithymoides*. Compact 1- to 2-foot-tall mounding species that spreads to 2 feet. Bears green leaves and bright yellow-green flowers beginning in early spring and lasting to late spring if cool weather prevails. A spot with afternoon shade is best. **Zones 4 to 9**.

Eustoma

yew-STO-mah. Gentian family, Gentianaceae.

There are three species in this genus of annuals, biennials, and short-lived perennials native to the

Eustoma grandiflorum 'Lisa Blue'

Evolvulus glomeratus 'Blue Daze'

Americas. They are taprooted plants with rosettes of leaves topped by cup- or bell-shaped flowers in shades of lavender-blue, purple, pink, rose-purple, or white.

HOW TO GROW
Give these plants full sun and average, moist, well-drained soil. Neutral to alkaline pH is best. They do not grow well in areas with rainy, humid summers and resent transplanting because of their taproots. Sow seeds indoors in individual pots 10 to 12 weeks before the last spring frost date. Press the tiny seeds into the soil surface, as light is necessary for germination. Seedlings germinate in 2 to 3 weeks at 65° to 70°F and are very slow growing. Keep the soil on the dry side to prevent root rot. From Zone 7 south, try sowing outdoors a few weeks before the last frost date. From Zone 8 south, plants also can be grown as biennials: sow seeds in midsummer and move seedlings to the garden in midfall for bloom the following year. Pinch seedlings to encourage branching. Stake them with twiggy brush. Eustomas make excellent cut flowers.

E. grandiflorum
e. gran-dih-FLOR-um. PRAIRIE GENTIAN, TEXAS BLUEBELL. Formerly *Lisianthus russellianus*. A 1- to 3-foot annual or biennial with fleshy gray-green leaves. Bell-shaped, 2-inch-wide flowers with waxy or satiny-textured petals appear in spring and summer. Echo Series plants bear double flowers in a range of colors on 1¹/₂- to 2-foot plants; Heidi Series, on 1¹/₂-foot ones. Mermaid Series plants are dwarf, to 8 inches, and do not require pinching. Cool-weather annual or biennial.

Evolvulus
ee-VOL-vue-lus. Morning-glory family, Convolvulaceae.

There are about 100 species of *Evolvulus*, which are annuals, perennials, and subshrubs native to prairies and plains from North to South America. They bear entire, lance-shaped to ovate, silky-hairy leaves and small wheel- or bell-shaped flowers, either singly or in clusters. Unlike their relatives the morning glories (*Convolvulus* and *Ipomoea*), they do not climb: the botanical name is from the Latin *evolvere*, meaning "to untwist," in recognition of this fact.

HOW TO GROW
Evolvulus species thrive in full sun and poor to average, well-drained soil. Sow seeds indoors 8 to 10 weeks before the last spring frost date. Or take cuttings in spring or early summer to propagate plants for garden use or for overwintering indoors.

E. glomeratus
e. glom-er-AY-tus. A tender perennial or subshrub that's 1¹/₂ to 2 feet high and wide. Bears silky-hairy, silver gray leaves and funnel- or bell-shaped, ¹/₂- to ³/₄-inch-wide lilac-pink or blue flowers. 'Blue Daze', also listed as a cultivar of *E. pilosus*, bears white, hairy leaves and pale blue flowers with white eyes. Tender perennial or warm-weather annual.

Exacum
EX-ah-kum. Gentian family, Gentianaceae.

Some 25 species of tender annuals, biennials, and perennials belong to this genus of plants from the Middle East to India and Sri Lanka. They bear clusters of small wheel- to saucer-shaped flowers, which are fragrant and come in shades of blue and purple, as well as white and pink.

HOW TO GROW
Give exacum a spot in full sun to partial shade and rich, evenly moist, well-drained soil. These plants thrive in heat and humidity, but where summers are hot, they benefit from some shade during the hottest part of the day. Sow seeds indoors at least 10 to 12 weeks before the last spring frost date. Germinate at 65° to 70°F. Water regularly in summer and feed monthly. Exacums are attractive as edging or container plants and

Exacum affine

when combined with other annuals in beds and borders.

E. affine
e. aff-IN-ee. PERSIAN VIOLET. A compact, bushy, 5- to 12-inch-tall annual or short-lived perennial with shiny, rounded leaves. Bears clusters of lightly fragrant, ³/₄-inch flowers with a clump of golden yellow stamens and lavender-blue, pink, or white petals. Midget Series plants are especially compact, to 5 inches. Warm-weather annual.

Exochorda
ex-oh-KOR-duh. Rose family, Rosaceae.

A small group of deciduous shrubs from central and East Asia, these bushes go through a Cinderella-like transformation in spring when they explode with virginal white flowers. The common name, pearlbush, comes from the appearance of their swelling buds.

HOW TO GROW
While they prefer loamy acid soil, most pearlbushes are adaptable. Plant them in a shrub border in full sun or partial shade with plants that provide a longer season of interest, since they are rather nondescript when out of flower. After flowering, cut back a third of the old shoots to promote flowers and to maintain the shape. Propagate by softwood cuttings in summer.

E. giraldii
e. jer-AL-dee-eye. REDBUD PEARLBUSH. Usually up to 10 feet tall and wide, this species from northwest China has pinkish new leaves that retain red veins. The upright clusters of 1-inch flowers bloom in late spring. *E. giraldii* var. *wilsonii* is more upright and has green veins and larger flowers, to 2 inches across. **Zones 6 to 9**.

E. × macrantha 'The Bride'
e. × mak-RAN-thuh. A compact, bushy form with arching branches, this selection rarely grows more than 4 feet tall (the species can grow to 15), although it may spread somewhat wider. In midspring it is smothered in 4-inch racemes of 6 to 10 white flowers. **Zones 4 to 8**.

Exochorda × macrantha 'The Bride'

F

Fagus

FAY-gus. Beech family, Fagaceae.

Ten tree species from the North Temperate Zone belong to this genus. All have smooth gray bark, very pointed leaf buds, pointed oval leaves with smooth or toothed edges, and triangular nuts borne in spiny husks, which provide food for wildlife. Flowers are not showy. European beech is one of the most stately shade trees. Old, magnificent specimens often adorn estates, parks, and campuses.

HOW TO GROW
Plant in full sun to partial shade and moist, well-drained, acid soil. Somewhat drought tolerant. Train to a single leader to prevent breakage from multiple leaders. Leave lower branches on to create a rounded form, or prune them to show off the trunk. Prune when dormant. Leaf spot, mildew, canker, scale, and beech bark disease can be problems.

F. sylvatica
f. sil-VAT-ih-kuh. EUROPEAN BEECH. As a lawn or landscape specimen, this long-lived, majestic tree grows slowly to 50 to 60 feet tall and 35 to 45 feet wide, forming a beautiful rounded pyramid that is quite striking if the lower limbs are left to sweep to the ground. The leaves are arrow shaped, with smooth, undulating edges. They unfold in spring a lovely silvery green, mature in summer to glossy dark green, and turn a warm golden brown in autumn. Leaves sometimes remain on the tree through the winter, turning alluring shades of buff or apricot. Mature trees have massive trunks and branches cloaked in smooth, silver gray bark, making a dramatic silhouette in winter. Use this big tree in a lawn where it has plenty of room to mature. It has shallow roots and casts so much shade that grass will not grow underneath it, but mulch or bare ground is fine, especially if lower limbs are present. From central Europe. **Zones 5 to 8.**

CULTIVARS AND SIMILAR SPECIES
F. sylvatica f. *purpurea* is a seed-grown, purple-leaved form with variable color. 'Aspleniifolia' (fern-leaf beech) has delicately cut leaves. 'Dawyck' ('Fastigiata') is columnar, growing to 60 feet tall and 30 feet wide. 'Dawyck Gold' features golden leaves and a narrow columnar shape. 'Dawyck Purple' is columnar, with purple leaves. 'Pendula' is a glorious weeping tree that grows to 60 feet tall. 'Purpurea Pendula' is a purple-leaved weeping form without a central leader; it reaches only 10 feet tall unless grafted high. 'Riversii' (purple or copper beech) has dark purple leaves all summer. 'Rohanii' resembles 'Riversii' but has ferny leaves. 'Tricolor' ('Roseomarginata') has bright rosy red new growth that matures to purple with pink and creamy white variegations; reaches 30 feet tall. *F. grandifolia* (American beech) is a similar native tree with blue-green toothed leaves, lighter gray bark, and light yellow to golden bronze fall color; it deserves wider use in landscapes, especially in the South, but is not drought tolerant; **Zones 4 to 9.**

Fallopia

fal-LOE-pee-ah. Buckwheat family, Polygonaceae.

Seven species belong to the genus *Fallopia*, all once classified in the genus *Polygonum*. They bear large clusters of tiny, funnel-shaped flowers in late summer. The most commonly planted species — *P. aubertii* — is a rampant vine that can be very hard to control.

HOW TO GROW
Select a site in full sun or partial shade and poor to average soil that is moist but well drained. *P. aubertii* is vigorous and tolerates a wide range of conditions, including dry soil. This species needs a large and sturdy arbor or other structure to climb. It also can be trained over unattractive buildings, rock piles, or other eyesores and will engulf them in short order. Plants spread by underground rhizomes and are difficult to control, since each piece of root will make a new plant. Prune plants hard in spring to keep them in bounds. Propagate by cuttings in summer or division in spring.

F. aubertii
f. aw-BER-tee-eye. SILVER FLEECE VINE, MILE-A-MINUTE PLANT, SILVER LACE VINE. Formerly *Polygonum aubertii, Bilderdykia aubertii*. A rampant twining climber that can

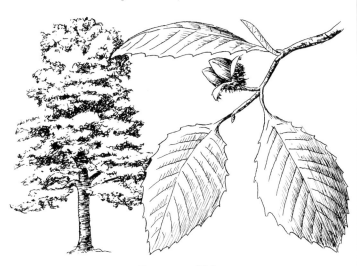

Fagus grandifolia

Fagus grandifolia

Fallopia aubertii

× *Fatshedera lizei*

Fatsia japonica

reach 40 feet. Plants bear heart-shaped leaves and lacy panicles of white to greenish white flowers in late summer and fall. Flowers are followed by small, pinkish white fruits. *F. baldschuanica* (formerly *Polygonum baldschuanica, Bilderdykia baldschuanica*) is a similar species that is equally vigorous. **Zones 5 to 9.**

Fallugia

fal-LOO-jee-uh. Rose family, Rosaceae.

This genus has only one species, a deciduous shrub native to the southwest United States and Mexico and commonly known as Apache plume. It is being eagerly adopted by dry-climate gardeners for its white roselike flowers and interesting seed heads.

HOW TO GROW
Apache plume prefers dry, sandy soil in full sun, and hot, dry sum-mers. Excellent in a shrub or mixed border of other drought-tolerant species. Needs little care of any kind. Propagate by seeds.

F. paradoxa

f. pair-uh-DOKS-uh. APACHE PLUME. Usually 5 to 8 feet tall, it has tiny, pinnately dissected, deep green leaves that are semipersistent. Slightly arching branches peel as they age. The white single-rose flowers last throughout the season, and more interest is provided by the feathery achenes (seedheads) from which it gets its common name. **Zones 6 to 10.**

× Fatshedera

× fats-HED-er-uh. Ginseng family, Araliaceae.

A hybrid between plants in two genera — *Hedera* (ivy) and *Fatsia* — the sole species in this genus is useful for its dramatic foliage and dual nature as a shrub or climber.

HOW TO GROW
Grow in reasonably fertile soil in full sun to moderate shade, as a freestanding shrub or trained against a wall. Does not require pruning except to control growth; you may want to grow it in a container to overwinter as a houseplant. Propagate from softwood cuttings or heel cuttings.

× F. lizei

× f. liz-AY-eye. As a shrub, it forms a loose mound 5 feet high and 10 feet wide, but it will climb to 10 feet if trained as a vine. The leathery, dark green leaves are palmate with five to seven leaflets and up to 10 inches across. In fall, rounded flower panicles are greenish white and sterile. **Zones 8 to 10.**

Fatsia

FAT-see-uh. Ginseng family, Araliaceae.

At most there are three species of these evergreen shrubs or small trees, all from East Asia, grown for their dramatic-looking foliage and autumn flowers and fruits.

HOW TO GROW
Fatsia is adaptable but prefers fertile, quickly draining soil and dappled to deep shade, with protection from cold wind and hot sun. Native to coastal areas, it tolerates salt spray and pollution. Lends a tropical air to swimming pools, patios, and entryways and adapts to container culture. Remove any suckers and prune back hard if plants become spindly. Otherwise prune lightly to retain shape and foliage display. Propagate from seeds or semihard cuttings in mid-summer.

F. japonica

f. juh-PON-ih-kuh. Rounded and suckering, this species grows to 6 to 8 feet tall and wide. The palmate leaves have 7 to 11 deep lobes. Fall flowers are tiny, white, and held in spherical clusters; they are followed by little, round black berries. There are forms with gold- or white-variegated leaves. **Zones 8 to 10.**

Felicia

feh-LEE-see-ah. Aster family, Asteraceae.

Commonly called blue marguerites or blue daisies, *Felicia* species are annuals, perennials, subshrubs, and shrubs native to South and tropical Africa. As their common names suggest, the 80 species in the genus bear daisylike flowers, which have yellow centers, or eyes, and petals in blue, lavender-blue, mauve-blue, or sometimes white.

HOW TO GROW
Blue marguerites thrive in full sun and light, poor to somewhat rich, very well drained soil that remains evenly moist. In frost-free climates — Zone 9 south — they can be grown outdoors as perennials; however, they do not grow well in hot, humid weather and also languish in cold, wet weather. Sow

Fallugia paradoxa

Fatsia japonica 'Variegata'

Felicia amelloides

seeds indoors 6 to 8 weeks before the last spring frost date and germinate at 60° to 70°F, which generally takes 4 weeks. (Indoor sowing gives them a head start in areas where hot summer weather interferes with blooming.) Some gardeners prechill the seeds for 3 weeks to improve germination: sow them 3 weeks earlier and refrigerate the sown pots before moving them to a warmer spot for germinating. Or, in areas with cool summers, sow outdoors after the last frost date. Pinch seedlings once or twice to encourage branching. Take cuttings of perennials in spring to propagate for garden use or in late summer to overwinter the plants indoors. Use blue marguerites near the front of beds and borders as well as to add color to rock gardens. They also are handsome container plants.

F. amelloides

f. am-ell-OY-dees. Blue Daisy. This tender, bushy, 1- to 2-foot subshrub features a rounded habit and ovate leaves. It carries pale to deep blue, ³/4- to 2-inch-wide, daisylike flowers with yellow cen-

ters from summer to fall. Tender perennial or warm-weather annual.

F. bergeriana

f. ber-jer-ee-AY-nah. Kingfisher Daisy. A low-growing annual reaching 8 to 10 inches tall and bearing gray-green, lance-shaped leaves. Produces rich, deep blue, 1¹/2-inch, daisylike flowers with yellow or black centers in summer. Warm-weather annual.

F. heterophylla

f. het-er-oh-FILL-uh. A mounding, 15- to 20-inch-tall annual with lance-shaped, gray-green leaves. Bears ³/4-inch-wide daisies in blue, or sometimes white or pink, in summer. Warm-weather annual.

Festuca

fess-TOO-kuh. Grass family, Poaceae.

The genus *Festuca* contains from 300 to 400 species of deciduous or evergreen perennial grasses commonly called fescues. Apart from the fine-textured lawn grasses, the species most often seen in gardens

Festuca glauca

are clump-forming plants grown for their dense mounds of linear, gray-green or silvery blue leaves.

HOW TO GROW

Select a site in full sun to partial shade with moist, well-drained soil. Good soil drainage is crucial in areas with wet summers. These plants do not grow well where summers are hot and humid, but a site with afternoon shade helps them cope. Cut the plants back to a height of 3 to 4 inches annually in early spring or fall to keep them neat looking. Many gardeners clip off the seed heads when they appear in order to focus attention on the foliage. Divide the clumps every 3 years or so to keep them vigorous. Propagate by division. Plants self-sow and can be grown from seeds, but cultivars do not come true and should be propagated by division.

F. glauca

f. GLAW-kuh. Blue Fescue. Formerly *F. cinerea* and *F. ovina* 'Glauca'. Clump-forming 6- to 12-inch-tall cool-season grass forming evergreen mounds of blue- or silver-green leaves. 'Elijah Blue' offers pale blue leaves on 1-foot-tall plants. 'Sea Urchin' ('Seeigel') forms tight 6-inch-tall mounds of silver-blue leaves. **Zones 4 to 9.**

Ficus

FYE-kus. Mulberry family, Moraceae.

Ficus contains more than 800 species, including the common fig (*F. carica*), the India rubber tree (*F. elastica*), and the bo tree (*F. religiosa*), under which Buddha became enlightened. *Ficus* species are found in all warm regions of the world, with the greatest abundance from India to Polynesia. Most species are shrubs to large forest trees. Only one species, *F. pumila* (creeping fig), is a garden plant for North America. It exhibits potentially unlimited growth in warm gardens. Its climbing habit and small, evergreen leaves make it most unlike a typical fig. As a vine, it clings tenaciously by secreting a tiny amount of latex from the aerial roots, which then dries and helps hold the roots even on the smoothest of surfaces.

HOW TO GROW

Grow *F. pumila* where you want a tough, evergreen climbing vine to cover a concrete wall or an unsightly garage or shed. It will perform best in moist, well-drained, loamy soil and partial shade, and

Ficus pumila

plants will not attach well to extremely hot (such as south- or west-facing) metal surfaces. Creeping fig rarely fruits in North American gardens, but if it does, the fruits are inedible.

F. pumila

f. PEW-mih-luh. Creeping Fig. This warm-climate ground cover makes a uniformly flat mat. It will plaster itself to vertical surfaces or carpet the ground. As the climbing stems mature, they develop many short, woody side branches. The cultivars differ by foliage features. 'Minima' has smaller-than-normal leaves. 'Variegata' has irregular white markings on the leaves. **Zones 8 to 10.**

Filipendula

fill-ih-PEN-jew-luh. Rose family, Rosaceae.

These rose-family members are vigorous perennials bearing plumy flower clusters that resemble astilbes more than they do roses. The individual flowers are tiny and five petaled and come in various shades of pink as well as white. The showy clusters of flowers are

Filipendula rubra

Filipendula rubra

borne above mounds of large, handsome, pinnately divided, lobed leaves. There are about 10 species in the genus, commonly called meadowsweets and queen-of-the-prairie; goat's beards (*Aruncus*) and spireas (*Spiraea*) are both close relatives.

HOW TO GROW
Plant meadowsweets in full sun or light shade and average to rich soil that is moist but well drained. *F. rubra* and *F. ulmaria* will grow in boggy soil. Give *F. vulgaris* a spot in full sun or partial shade, preferably with dry, alkaline soil. Cut plants to the ground if the leaves become tattered looking in summer, then keep the soil moist until new leaves emerge. Divide clumps in spring or fall, as necessary, if they become crowded, begin to flower less, or spread too far. In addition to division, propagate by taking root cuttings in late winter or early spring, or sow seeds.

F. palmata
f. pal-MAY-tuh. SIBERIAN MEAD-OWSWEET. A 3- to 4-foot-tall species that spreads to about 2 feet. Bears frothy 8-inch-wide clusters of pink flowers in midsummer. 'Nana' has fernlike leaves and rose-pink flowers on 2-foot-tall plants. 'Rubra' bears reddish pink blooms. **Zones 3 to 8.**

F. purpurea
f. pur-PUR-ee-uh. JAPANESE MEADOWSWEET. Mounding 3- to 4-foot-tall species that spreads to 2 feet and has large 10-inch-wide leaves. Bears dense 2-inch-wide clusters of hot pink flowers in mid- and late summer. **Zones 4 to 9.**

F. rubra
f. Rue-bruh. QUEEN-OF-THE-PRAIRIE. A native North American wildflower ranging from 6 to 8 feet tall and spreading to 4 feet. Bears mounds of large 8-inch-wide leaves and fluffy 5- to 6-inch-wide clusters of fragrant pink flowers from early to midsummer. 'Venusta' (also sold as 'Venusta Magnifica' and 'Magnifica') has rose-pink flowers. **Zones 3 to 9.**

F. ulmaria
f. ul-MAIR-ee-uh. MEADOW-SWEET, QUEEN-OF-THE-MEADOW. A 3- to 6-foot-tall species forming 2-foot-wide mounds of 8-inch-long leaves. Bears 4- to 6-inch-wide clusters of white flowers in summer. 'Aurea' is grown for its leaves rather than its insignificant flowers, which should be removed. Leaves emerge yellow, then turn to creamy yellow, and finally pale green. **Zones 3 to 9.**

F. vulgaris
f. vul-GAIR-iss. DROPWORT. Compact 2-foot-tall species with 1½-foot-wide rosettes of fernlike leaves. Bears loose 4- to 6-inch-wide clusters of creamy white flowers in early and midsummer. 'Multiplex' (also sold as 'Flore Pleno' and 'Plena') has bronze buds and creamy white, double flowers. **Zones 4 to 9.**

Forsythia
for-SITH-ee-uh. Olive family, Oleaceae.

A genus of seven primarily deciduous shrubs from eastern Asia (with one from southeast Europe), widely grown for their early-spring display of yellow flowers with four flaring petals. The stems leaf out as blossoms fall and, on some forsythias, will root where they touch the ground.

HOW TO GROW
Give forsythia average soil in full sun or dappled shade. It adapts to a wide range of pH and urban insults, such as compacted soil. Grow on a hillside, as a specimen or in masses where its weeping habit can be best displayed. Forsythia is a favorite to force for indoor flowers in late winter. Northern gardeners should select cultivars for bud hardiness. Prune to the ground after flowering or remove the oldest stems. Seeds are not hard to germinate and softwood cuttings root readily, but layering is the easiest route to propagation.

F. 'Arnold Dwarf'
Named at Boston's Arnold Arboretum in 1941, 'Arnold Dwarf' is grown primarily for its stature, only 3 feet tall and about 7 feet wide, and is not a heavy flowerer. The bright green leaves are ser-

Forsythia × intermedia

rated. Good ground cover for banks and other bare areas since it roots itself readily. **Zones 5 to 8.**

F. × intermedia
f. × in-ter-MEE-dee-uh. This hybrid, which averages 10 feet tall, is the source of the most popular cultivars. 'Beatrix Farrand' is relatively upright and is smothered with deep yellow flowers, but it is less bud hardy than some others; 'Lynwood' ('Lynwood Gold') is upright to 7 feet and considered one of the most reliable for uniform bloom on the stems; 'Spectabilis' bears masses of bright yellow flowers in its axils; 'Spring Glory', which has big sulphur yellow flowers, is a good choice for southern gardeners because it needs less cold than others to flower well. **Zones 6 to 9.**

F. ovata
f. oh-VAH-tuh. EARLY FOR-SYTHIA. Compact and blooming earlier than other forsythias, this species is used to breed new cultivars for cold hardiness. 'Northern Sun' grows 8 to 10 feet tall and not quite as wide and has sulphur yellow flowers. **Zones 4 to 8.**

F. suspensa var. sieboldii
f. suh-SPEN-suh var. see-BOLD-ee-eye. WEEPING FORSYTHIA. Left as a shrub, it grows 8 to 10 feet tall and often wider. Some gardeners train its pendulous branches

Forsythia suspensa var. *sieboldii*

Fothergilla major

Fouquieria splendens

Fothergilla major

Fothergilla major

against a wall where the golden yellow flowers can be admired 15 or more feet above the ground. **Zones 6 to 8.**

F. viridissima 'Bronxensis'

f. ver-ih-DISS-ih-muh. GREEN-STEM FORSYTHIA CULTIVAR. A good bank cover, growing only 1 foot tall but 2 to 3 feet wide, with small, serrated, bright green leaves and pale yellow flowers. **Zones 6 to 8.**

Fothergilla

foth-er-GIL-luh. Witch-hazel family, Hamamelidaceae.

In this genus there are just two species, both deciduous shrubs from the eastern United States. In spring they have white, honey-scented bottlebrush flowers. The real show comes in fall, when the foliage turns a rainbow of colors. The leaves, sometimes blue-green, are veined in the same manner as

the related witch hazel (*hamamelis*).

HOW TO GROW
Provide rich, moisture-retentive acid soil in full sun (for best bloom and coloring) or partial shade. Good along foundations or with azaleas and rhododendrons. Fothergilla needs minimal pruning. Propagation is difficult: seeds need double-dormancy treatment; cuttings require bottom heat (for suckers or root cuttings) and mist (for softwood cuttings in summer).

F. gardenii

f. gar-DEEN-ee-eye. DWARF FOTHERGILLA. Usually 3 feet tall and wide, this species sometimes reaches 5 feet. The white flowers, which consist entirely of showy stamens in 1- to 2-inch cylindrical spikes, open in midspring before the leaves. On some selections the foliage is a pronounced blue-green. In fall it turns yellow, orange, and red. 'Blue Mist' won a Gold Medal from the Pennsylvania Horticultural Society. **Zones 5 to 9.**

F. major

f. MAY-jor. LARGE FOTHERGILLA. Up to 10 feet tall and about as wide, this species often has larger flowers than the dwarf species and blooms slightly later, as its leaves are emerging. Its foliage is blue-green in the North,

darker green in the South. It is less drought tolerant than its smaller relative. 'Mt. Airy' was selected for consistent fall coloring, typically including reddish purple, and heavy flowering. **Zones 4 to 8.**

Fouquieria

foh-KEE-ree-uh. Ocotillo family, Fouquieriaceae.

This genus includes about 10 species of deciduous, upright-stemmed succulent or spiny shrubs or trees, native to low arid hillsides of the southwest United States and Mexico. In the desert landscapes where it is at home, it provides a dramatic silhouette and bright tubular flowers.

HOW TO GROW
Grow ocotillo in poor to average, sharply draining sandy soil in full sun. Highlight its shape against the sky or a wall, or plant several as a security hedge or screen. It doesn't tolerate overwatering and rarely needs pruning. After prolonged drought the canes often look dead but will turn green again after a rain. Propagates easily by cuttings.

F. splendens

f. SPLEN-denz. OCOTILLO. This species grows 10 to 25 feet tall, producing numerous white-striped thorny branches in a candelabra shape. It has two types of leaves: 2-inch elliptic leaves and shorter spoon-shaped leaves. These appear after rains and drop in a drought, leaving numerous scars. The narrow bell-shaped

flowers, which bloom after spring and summer rains, are bright red in clusters 4 to 11 inches long, closing at night and attracting hummingbirds by day. **Zones 8 to 11.**

Fragaria

fray-GAIR-ee-uh. Rose family, Rosaceae.

Better known as strawberries, *Fragaria* species are perennials that bear five-petaled, usually white flowers followed by fleshy fruits. One species, alpine strawberry (*F. vesca*), is grown in perennial gardens as an edging plant or ground cover.

HOW TO GROW
Give strawberries full sun or light shade and rich, moist, well-drained soil. Plants tolerate acid conditions but prefer neutral to alkaline pH. Propagate by separating and potting up the plants that form on the ends of the stolons or by sowing seeds.

F. chiloensis

chill-oh-EN-sis. CHILEAN STRAWBERRY. An important parent of our cultivated fruit, this species is also an excellent ground

Fragaria chiloensis

Fragaria 'Pink Panda'

cover, with evergreen foliage that turns dark red in cold weather. The white flowers bloom in spring and are followed by small, red, rather tasteless fruits. Plants spread profusely by runners. **Zones 5 to 10.**

F. 'Pink Panda'

A 4- to 6-inch tall hybrid strawberry with three-part leaves and bright pink, 1-inch-wide flowers borne from late spring through early fall. Plants rarely bear fruit. Can be used as a ground cover, since plants are stoloniferous and easily spread to several feet. They can become invasive. **Zones 5 to 9.**

F. vesca

f. VES-kuh. ALPINE STRAWBERRY, FRAISE DE BOIS. A 6- to 12-inch-tall species with evergreen to semievergreen, three-leaflet leaves. Bears white $^3/_4$-inch-wide flowers from late spring into summer followed by edible red $^1/_2$-inch-long fruits. 'Albicarpa' has white fruits. **Zones 5 to 9.**

Franklinia

frank-LYN-ee-ah. Tea family, Theaceae.

Only one species belongs to this genus, which is related to *Stewartia*. It is a native American tree last seen in the wild in 1803. John Bartram, a botanist from Philadelphia, collected the tree in 1765 in Georgia and named it after Benjamin Franklin. All known specimens are believed to be descendants of the tree he collected.

HOW TO GROW
Franklinia flowers best in full sun, but performs well in light shade. Needs humus-rich, well-drained,

acid soil and plentiful moisture, especially in a sunny site. May be finicky if soil conditions are not right. Can suffer from drought or from root rot in a poorly drained site. Needs no pruning and is usually pest-free.

F. alatamaha

f. al-ah-tah-MAH-ha. FRANKLINIA, FRANKLIN TREE. This graceful, multitrunked tree forms an open pyramid or oval and grows 20 to 30 feet tall and half as wide. The narrow, 6-inch-long leaves are glossy green all summer and turn a rich wine red and gold in autumn. Unusual among trees, franklinia blooms in late summer and fall. Its 3-inch-wide, white, camellia-like flowers open from pearl-like buds when the foliage is still green, and new flowers continue to open even after the leaves have taken on their glorious fall colors. This stunning combination of flowers and fall colors has no equal. The slender trunks and branches have a sinewy shape and are covered with dark gray bark marked with white striations. Use this eye-catching tree in a border or woodland or to cast light shade on a patio, where its silhouette and fall flowers can be readily admired. **Zones 6 to 9.**

Fraxinus

FRAX-in-us. Olive family, Oleaceae.

Some 65 species of woodland trees from North America, Europe, and Asia make up this genus. Leaves are opposite and pinnately compound. Flowers are usually not showy and are borne in clusters in spring or summer. Fruits are sin-

gle-seeded, winged structures and can be messy. Several species are planted as handsome, fast-growing shade trees. Seedless forms are preferred for most landscape situations.

HOW TO GROW
Plant in full sun and deep, moist soil. Tolerates brief flooding and slight drought. Leaf rust, leaf spot, borers, and fall webworms may be troublesome. Dieback (also called ash yellows disease) may be serious. Anthracnose disfigures leaves in wet years. Frost cracking can be a problem in exposed sites in cold-winter areas. To prevent storm damage, prune when young for a strong shape.

F. americana

f. ah-mair-ih-KAH-nuh. WHITE ASH. Pyramidal or oval when young, this fast-growing but strong-wooded tree becomes rounded with age, maturing to 50 to 80 feet tall and wide. Leaves emerge in late spring and are made up of five to nine dark blue-green, sparsely toothed, oval leaflets with white undersides. Fall color develops early and is vivid, including combinations of yellow, orange, and maroon, with the brighter colors usually occurring toward the tree's interior. Flowers are inconspicuous. Female trees produce clusters of 1-inch-long, winged seeds that ripen from green to tan and make a mess when they drop. Seedless cultivars are available. This tree has a more attractive fall color than green ash (*F. pennsylvanica*), but it is not as adaptable to poor soil and is more vulnerable to ash yellows disease. Trunk bark is ash gray with diamond-shaped furrows. Use seedless forms as lawn, park, or street trees where there's plenty of growing room. From eastern and central North America. **Zones 4 to 9.**

CULTIVARS AND SIMILAR SPECIES
'Autumn Applause' is a seedless, compact tree with smaller leaves that turn deep red or mahogany in fall. 'Autumn Blaze' is more drought tolerant; good in the northern Plains. 'Autumn Purple' is seedless and exhibits deep purple fall color. 'Champaign County' is seedless and dense, with bronze fall color; good in the South. 'Chicago Regal' is a symmetrical oval, with excellent fall color. 'Greenspire' is narrow and upright. 'Rosehill' is a seedless, disease-resistant, broad-spreading tree with fiery bronze-red fall color; good in the South. 'Royal Purple' ('Elk Grove') has purple fall color and is hardy to Zone 3. 'Skyline' is a seedless, rounded tree with orange-red fall color. 'Sparticus' has longer-lasting, deep burgundy fall color

Franklinia alatamaha

Fraxinus americana

and a sturdy, uniform pyramidal shape. 'Windy City' is seedless and resists frost cracking. *F. quadrangulata* (blue ash) is a similar native tree with corky twigs; it tolerates drought and alkaline soil; excellent in the northern Plains. **Zones 4 to 9**.

F. pennsylvanica

f. pen-sil-VAHN-ih-kuh G R E E N   A S H , R E D   A S H . This fast-growing shade tree tolerates infertile or alkaline soil, drought, some flooding, and salt. It is narrowly pyramidal with ascending branches when young, but it matures to an upright, spreading tree, 50 to 60 feet tall and wide. The handsome, shiny, dark yellowish green leaves are made up of five to nine pointed, narrow leaflets with jagged edges. In early fall, the foliage turns very bright yellow. Flowers develop into clusters of single-seeded green fruits, which cause a litter and weed-seedling problem. Nonseeding male cultivars are available. Green ash has an overall coarse texture, with strong, bold branching and ash gray, furrowed bark. Use the species for reclamation projects and seedless cultivars as shade trees in areas where cold, poor soil, drought, or flooding precludes the

use of other large trees. From eastern and central North America. **Zones 2 to 9**.

CULTIVARS AND SIMILAR SPECIES

These are all seedless. 'Emerald' has long-lasting, golden yellow fall color and adapts to hot, dry climates. 'Foothills' is especially cold hardy. 'Lednaw' is columnar, growing to 30 feet tall. 'Marshall's Seedless' is identical to the species, except that it usually lacks seeds. The most widely planted form, 'Newport', is an excellent oval tree with a strong central trunk. 'Patmore' has a uniform oval shape with a strong central leader; shiny, dark green leaves; disease resistant. 'Prairie Spire' forms a narrow pyramid. 'Summit' is pyramidal, with golden yellow fall color. 'Urbanite' is pyramidal and especially tolerant of urban settings; thick, shiny, injury-resistant young bark tolerates sunscald; **Zones 5 to 9**. *F. excelsior* (European ash) has 9 to 11 leaflets and yellow-green late-fall color; popular in the Pacific Northwest; **Zones 5 to 8**. 'Aureafolia' has yellow summer foliage. 'Hessii' is a vigorous-growing form with undivided leaves. *F. velutina* (velvet ash) may be a smaller form of green ash that is

Fraxinus velutina

native to the Southwest; adapts well to alkaline soil, drought, and poor drainage; **Zones 7 to 10**.

Freesia

FREE-shuh. FREE-zee-uh. Iris family, Iridaceae.

Popular cut flowers, freesias are treasured for their fragrance as well as their graceful racemes of colorful, funnel-shaped blooms. About six species belong to the genus, all native South African tender perennials that grow from corms. Plants have narrow, sword-shaped or linear leaves that are mostly basal, although a few leaves are borne on the slender, branched flower stems. The flowers are tubular at the base and open to funnel shaped at the top, with six lobes (perianth segments). Hybrids are far more commonly grown than species, and double-flowered forms are available.

HOW TO GROW

Select a site in full sun with average to rich, moist, well-drained soil. Although freesias can be grown outdoors year-round in frost-free climates — southern Cal-

ifornia and the Deep South — they are grown primarily as container plants, especially in greenhouses. They require cool conditions and good air circulation to grow well. In winter, nighttime temperatures need to remain below 50°F, and plants tolerate temperatures to 40°F or lower. When growing freesias outdoors in Zones 10 and 11, schedule planting times so that they will be growing during seasons when temperatures remain cool at night. Plant the corms at a depth of 3 inches in the ground, from $1/2$ to 1 inch deep in containers. Where hardy, plant in late summer or early fall for late-winter or early-spring bloom.

When growing freesias in containers (to be kept indoors in a cool sunroom or greenhouse over winter), plant the corms in fall for bloom the following spring. Or plant them in spring, after danger of frost has passed, for summer bloom. Keep the containers shaded and barely moist until shoots appear. Once the plants are growing actively, keep the soil evenly moist, but not wet, and gradually move them to full sun. Feed container-grown plants weekly. Plants require staking: install stakes and string or brushy twigs when plants are still fairly small. Replace the corms annually, or if you want to save them for next year, continue feeding the plants after the flowers fade, until the leaves turn yellow and die back. Then gradually allow the plants to dry out and store the containers in a cool (40° to 50°F),

Freesia hybrid

Fremontodendron californicum

dry, airy spot. Or clean the soil off the corms and store them in paper bags. Propagate by seeds or by separating offsets.

F. hybrids

A wide variety of freesias have been selected for their fragrant 2-inch-long flowers. Hybrids range from 1 to 1½ feet in height and come in shades of pink, lavender, lilac-blue, red, yellow, creamy white, and orange-red. Many bear bicolor blooms, and double-flowered forms are available. **Zones 10 to 11.**

Fremontodendron

free-mont-oh-DEN-dron. Chocolate family, Sterculiaceae.

This genus is represented by just two species commonly called flannel bushes, which can be considered shrubs or trees, are evergreen to semievergreen, and are native to dry woods and mountainsides in the southwest United States and northern Mexico. They are valued by gardeners for their long-lasting bright yellow flowers and leathery, lobed, deep green leaves that are felted underneath. The blooms are followed by persistent cone-shaped seed capsules covered by reddish brown hairs.

HOW TO GROW
Give flannel bushes dry soil of poor to average fertility, siting them in full sun where they are protected from wind. Provide sharp drainage, such as on a hill-side, with drought-loving companion plants. Flannel bushes are often wall trained, which shows off their handsome foliage and flowers. They tend to be short-lived. Pruning is minimal except for wall-trained specimens. Propagate by seeds (which may benefit from soaking) or from soft or semiripe cuttings taken in summer.

F. 'California Glory'

Vigorous and upright to 20 feet tall and 12 feet wide, with rounded five-lobed leaves. Bright yellow, 2-inch, saucer-shaped flowers with an outer red tinge bloom from late spring into fall. **Zones 8 to 10.**

F. californicum

f. kal-ih-FOR-nih-kum. COMMON FLANNEL BUSH. Differs from 'California Glory' in having smaller lemon yellow flowers that appear all at once in midspring. **Zones 8 to 10.**

F. 'Ken Taylor'

Forms a spreading mound 6 feet tall and 10 feet wide with orange-yellow flowers. **Zones 8 to 10.**

Fritillaria

frih-tih-LAIR-ee-uh. Lily family, Liliaceae.

Fritillaria is a large, diverse genus in the lily family that contains stately plants suitable for beds and borders as well as diminutive species for rock gardens. All of the 100 or so species that belong here grow from bulbs. The bulbs consist either of fleshy, closely fitting scales (sometimes covered with a papery tunic) or of separate, overlapping scales (also thick and fleshy) arranged like those of lily bulbs. Plants produce lance-shaped to grassy leaves and nodding, bell- or funnel-shaped flowers in spring or early summer. Blooms are solitary or borne in erect, unbranched clusters. They consist of six petal-like tepals. Many species bear flowers that are marked with a tessellate, or checkered, pattern of contrasting colors.

HOW TO GROW
The culture of these fascinating plants varies by species, and the genus contains plants that are both easy and difficult to grow. Unless otherwise noted below, give fritillaries a site in full sun or light shade with moist, well-drained soil that is rich in organic matter. Among the easiest, most vigorous species are *F. acmopetala, F. imperialis, F. meleagris, F. persica, F. thunbergii,* and *F. verticillata.* Other species require perfect drainage and dry conditions when dormant. These include *F. affinis, F. aurea, F. hermonis, F. michailovskyi,* and *F. uva-vulpis* — all are good choices for rock gardens and raised beds. If in doubt about whether your garden offers the right conditions, start with a small number of bulbs and experiment to find a suitable site. Knowing the origins of the different species can help with site selection, and they are given in the species descriptions below. Whatever species you grow, keep in mind that the bulbs are fragile and should not be allowed to dry out before planting. Inspect bulbs carefully when you buy, because dried-out bulbs generally will not grow. If you can't plant bulbs immediately, store them in barely moist vermiculite or peat moss.

Plant fritillaries fairly deeply — at least 4 times the height of the bulbs; plant *F. imperialis* with the tops of the bulbs 5 to 6 inches below the surface. Be sure to prepare the soil several inches *below* where the bulbs will sit to provide rich and well-drained conditions. Species with open-crowned, scaly bulbs, including *F. imperialis,* can catch moisture in the top of the bulbs, which causes rot. To prevent this, and also to provide excellent drainage for species that require it, place 2 to 3 inches of sharp sand (also called builder's sand) in the bottom of the planting holes and position the bulbs on their sides when planting. Space *F. imperialis* and *F. persica* about 1 foot apart; smaller species, 3 to 4 inches apart. Mulch plantings with compost or feed with very well rotted manure in spring. For species intolerant of moist soil when they are dormant, plant in a raised bed and be sure to provide loose, gritty, well-drained soil.

Divide established plantings only when they become too crowded. Plants of *F. imperialis* thrive for years without needing to be divided; other species produce good crops of offsets each year and need dividing every 3 to 4

Fritillaria affinis

Fritillaria imperialis

years. Dig them in early summer after the foliage has ripened but before it disappears completely. Propagate by division or seeds.

F. acmopetala
f. ak-moe-PET-ah-luh. A 1- to 1¹/₂-foot-tall species from the eastern Mediterranean region, including Lebanon and southern Turkey. Grows from 1¹/₂-inch bulbs often surrounded by bulblets at the base. Bears 1¹/₂-inch-long, bell-shaped, pale green flowers marked with red-brown in late spring. Although blooms are usually solitary, they are sometimes borne in pairs or threes. **Zones 6 to 8.**

F. affinis
f. aff-IN-iss. RICE-GRAIN FRITILLARY. Formerly *F. lanceolata*. A 1- to 2-foot-tall native of western North America with ³/₄-inch bulbs usually surrounded by many small bulblets at the base. Bears nodding, cup-shaped, greenish white flowers that are marked with red-purple from spring to early summer. Blooms are borne in racemes of 2 or 3 to 10 or more flowers. 'Limelight' has green flowers with a few red-purple specks. 'Vancouver Island' bears maroon-brown blooms checked with green. **Zones 6 to 9.**

F. aurea
f. AW-ree-uh. A 6- to 8-inch-tall species from Turkey with ³/₄-inch bulbs often surrounded by small bulblets at the base. Bears solitary, bell-shaped yellow flowers checkered with orange or red-brown. 'Golden Flag' has bright yellow flowers. Plants require very well drained soil and dry conditions when dormant. **Zones 5 to 8.**

F. biflora
f. bi-FLOR-uh. BLACK FRITILLARY, MISSION BELLS. A 6- to 12-inch-tall California native growing from ³/₄-inch bulbs consisting of about three fleshy, loose scales. In spring, bears stems of 1 to 6, or as many as 12, bell-shaped brown flowers that have a black or purple tinge and are flushed with green. 'Martha Roderick' has red-brown or red-purple blooms with greenish white tips. Plants require perfect drainage and dry conditions when dormant. **Zones 6 to 9.**

F. camschatcensis
f. kam-chat-SEN-sis. BLACK SARANA, BLACK LILY. A 1- to 1¹/₂-foot-tall species native from Alaska and Canada to China and Japan. Grows from a 1-inch-wide bulb consisting of many densely packed scales that often produce many bulblets around the base. In early summer, produces one to eight nodding, cup- to bell-shaped 1¹/₄-inch-long flowers that are black-purple in color. Best in partial shade with rich, moist soil. **Zones 3 to 8.**

F. davisii
f. dah-VIS-ee-eye. FRITILLARY. Species native to Greece that grows from 1-inch-wide bulbs and reaches 6 inches tall. Bears stems of from one to three 1-inch-long, bell-shaped green flowers in spring that commonly have yellow petal edges and checkered brown markings. Plants require perfect drainage and dry conditions when dormant. **Zones 6 to 9.**

F. glauca
f. GLAW-kuh. SISKIYOU LILY. A 5- to 7-inch-tall species found in California and Oregon that grows from very tiny bulbs with two to three scales. In spring, bears solitary, nodding, bell-shaped, 1-inch-wide yellow flowers mottled with brown. 'Goldilocks' bears stems of three to five yellow flowers flushed with green and sometimes flecked with red-brown. Plants require perfect drainage and dry conditions when dormant. **Zones 6 to 9.**

F. hermonis ssp. amana
f. her-MON-iss ssp. ah-MAN-uh. A 6- to 12-inch-tall species from Turkey and Lebanon. Grows from ³/₄-inch bulbs that often are surrounded by bulblets at the base and sometimes produce stolons. In spring, bears 1¹/₂-inch-long green flowers lightly checkered with purple or brown. The inner tepals have purple-brown edges, and flowers are solitary or borne in pairs. Plants require perfect drainage and dry conditions when dormant. **Zones 6 to 8.**

F. imperialis
f. im-per-ee-AL-iss. CROWN IMPERIAL. Vigorous, easy-to-grow, old-fashioned flower, originally native to Asia, that ranges from 2 to 4 feet in height. In early spring, bears umbels of three to as many as eight, downward-pointing 2¹/₂-inch-long flowers topped by a sheaf of leaflike bracts. Bulbs reach about 4 inches in diameter and have a skunklike odor. Orange-, yellow-, and red-flowered forms are available. Cultivars include 'Aurora', with burnt orange flowers; 'Lutea Maxima', with yellow flowers; 'Prolifera' with double orange-red blooms; and 'Rubra Maxima', in bright orange. **Zones 5 to 8.**

F. meleagris
f. mee-lee-AG-riss. CHECKERED LILY, GUINEA-HEN FLOWER, SNAKE'S-HEAD FRITILLARY. An 8- to 12-inch-tall European native growing from 1-inch-wide bulbs consisting of two large scales. Bears nodding, broadly bell-shaped, 1³/₄-inch-long flowers in spring, singly or sometimes in pairs. Flowers can be pinkish purple, red-purple, nearly black, or white and are checked with purple-pink. 'Alba' bears white flowers. **Zones 4 to 8.**

F. michailovskyi
f. mik-ah-LOF-skee-eye. FRITILLARY. A 4- to 8-inch-tall species from Turkey, best in rock gardens or raised beds, that grows from 1-inch-wide bulbs. Bears pendent, broadly bell-shaped, purple-brown flowers edged in yellow in late spring or early summer. Blooms are borne singly or in clusters of up to four. Plants require rich but very well drained soil and dry conditions when dormant. **Zones 5 to 8.**

Fritillaria meleagris

Fritillaria pudica

F. pallidiflora

f. pal-lid-ih-FLOR-uh. FRITILLARY. A vigorous 1/2- to 2-foot-tall species from Siberia and northwestern China. Grows from 1- to 2-inch-wide bulbs and in late spring and early summer bears clusters of six to as many as nine bell-shaped, nodding, creamy yellow flowers blushed with green and sometimes marked with red-brown. Best in partial shade. **Zones 3 to 8.**

F. persica

f. PER-sih-kuh. FRITILLARY. A vigorous, stately species from southern Turkey that produces racemes of 20 to 30 or more mauve-purple flowers on 1- to 3-foot plants in spring. Individual blooms are 3/4 inch long. Bulbs are about 2 inches tall and consist of one large scale and several tightly packed smaller scales. Best in a hot, sun-baked site. **Zones 5 to 8.**

F. pontica

f. PON-tih-kuh. FRITILLARY. A 6- to 8-inch-tall species from the Balkans, including Turkey and Greece, that grows from a 1- to 1 1/4-inch-wide bulb. In spring, produces solitary or sometimes paired flowers that are nodding, bell shaped, and 1 3/4 inches long. Blooms are green with brown or maroon at the base. **Zones 5 or 6 to 8.**

F. pudica

f. PEW-dih-kuh. YELLOW FRITILLARY. Native wildflower from western North America that reaches 3 to 6 inches tall and grows from small disk-shaped bulbs with two to four scales, usu-ally with many small bulblets around the base. Produces pendent, bell-shaped, 1-inch-long flowers in spring that are solitary or carried in pairs. Blooms are golden yellow to orange-yellow. Plants require perfect drainage and dry conditions when dormant. 'Fragrance' bears fragrant yellow flowers. **Zones 4 to 9.**

F. purdyi

f. PUR-dee-eye. A 6- to 8-inch-tall species native to the Southwest that grows from small bulbs that have three to four fleshy scales. Bears from one to four nodding, bell-shaped, 3/4-inch-long whitish to beige flowers veined and mottled with red- or purple-brown. Plants require perfect drainage and dry conditions when dormant. **Zones 5 to 8.**

F. thunbergii

f. thun-BER-jee-eye. Also listed as *F. verticillata* var. *thunbergii*. A 1- to 2 1/2-foot-tall native of China growing from 1 1/2-inch-wide bulbs. Bears loose clusters of two to six bell- to cup-shaped, 1 1/2-inch-long flowers that are creamy white and checkered with pale green. **Zones 6 to 8.**

F. uva-vulpis

f. OO-vah-VUL-pis. FRITILLARY. A 6- to 8-inch-tall species from western Asia, including Turkey, Iraq, and Iran. Plants grow from 1 1/4-inch-wide bulbs that usually produce a few bulblets at the base. In spring, produces solitary, nodding, bell-shaped, 1-inch-long flowers that are purple-brown with yellow edges on the tips of the tepals. Plants require perfect drainage and dry conditions when dormant. **Zones 5 to 8.**

F. verticillata

f. ver-tih-sil-LAH-tuh. A 1- to 3-foot tall species from central Asia and western Siberia that grows from 3/4- to 1 1/2-inch-wide bulbs with two bulb scales. Leaves at the tops of the stems have tendril-like tips. In spring, bears from one to six nodding, bell-shaped, white or yellow flowers flecked with green or purple. **Zones 4 to 8.**

Fuchsia

FEW-shah. Evening-primrose family, Onagraceae.

Best known in North America as greenhouse pot plants, fuchsias are mostly tender shrubs and small trees, plus some climbers and trailers, native to mountainous areas in Central and South America as well as New Zealand and Tahiti. The genus contains some 100 species, and literally thousands of cultivars have been hybridized. They bear entire leaves and showy, often pendulous flowers either singly or in clusters. Shades of pink, purple, and cream predominate, and many bear multicolored blooms.

HOW TO GROW

Give fuchsias partial shade, or morning sun and afternoon shade, as well as rich, well-drained, evenly moist soil. In areas with hot summers, shade is essential, as is regular, even daily, watering. This is especially true for plants grown in containers. Where hardy, grow them outdoors as shrubs or perennials. In the North, grow them as bedding plants replaced annually or as tender perennials overwintered indoors. They make outstanding plants for containers; trailing types are stunning in hanging baskets. Upright types can be trained into handsome standards. The flowers attract hummingbirds. Fuchsias are most often grown from cuttings. Take them in spring to propagate for garden use or in late summer to overwinter the plants. They also can be grown from seeds sown indoors in spring, but cultivars do not come true from seed. Water deeply during dry weather, and feed pot-grown plants weekly during the summer with a balanced fertilizer.

To overwinter, take cuttings, pot up entire plants, or move containers to a bright, cool (40° to 45°F) spot before the first fall frost. Keep them barely moist over winter. Prune overwintered plants to shape them in late winter or early spring; cut them back hard, if necessary, since they bloom best on new wood.

F. × hybrida

f. × HI-brih-duh. COMMON FUCHSIA. Tender, much-hybridized shrub, generally ranging from 1 to 2 feet in height and hardy only in frost-free areas, from **Zone 10 south**, although the plants can regrow from the roots in protected areas somewhat farther north. Bears pendent, tubular flowers that can be single, semidouble, or double and often feature two or more colors. Tender perennial or grow as a warm-weather annual.

F. magellanica

f. mah-jel-LAN-ih-kuh. HARDY FUCHSIA. A tender shrub that can reach 10 feet in frost-free climates but is usually 2 1/2 to 3 feet tall in the North, where it is killed to the ground each winter. Plants are root hardy to **Zone 7**, and with considerable winter protection, they will survive into **Zone 6**. Dainty, red and purple-red, 3/4- to 1 1/4-inch-long flowers appear in summer. 'Aurea' is a semicascading plant with yellow leaves and red flowers. Tender perennial.

Fuchsia × *hybrida* 'Lord Beaconsfield'

G

Gaillardia

gah-LAR-dee-uh. Aster family, Asteraceae.

Commonly called blanket flowers or simply gaillardias, the 30 species in this genus of aster-family plants are annuals, biennials, and perennials primarily native to North America. They bear rosettes of hairy leaves topped by single or double, daisylike flowers in shades of red, red-orange, maroon, or yellow over a long season in summer.

HOW TO GROW
Gaillardias thrive in full sun and average to rich, well-drained soil. They also tolerate poor, dry soil and sandy conditions and are drought and salt tolerant enough for seaside gardens. Too-rich soil yields floppy plants, and heavy clay spells certain death due to root and crown rots, especially in winter. Deadheading encourages repeat bloom and keeps the plants neat looking. Divide perennial plants every 2 to 3 years in early spring to keep them vigorous. Propagate by division, by stem cuttings taken in early summer, or by root cuttings taken in winter.

Sow seeds of annual gaillardias indoors 6 to 8 weeks before the last spring frost date. Or sow them outdoors after the last frost. Either way, since light aids germination, just press the seeds into the soil surface. Plants rebloom without deadheading, but removing the faded flowers promptly keeps the plants neat looking and encourages new buds to form. Gaillardias add summer-long color to beds and borders, wildflower gardens, and containers. Also include them in plantings designed to attract butterflies. They make outstanding cut flowers.

G. aristata

g. air-is-TAH-tuh. BLANKET FLOWER. Native North American perennial wildflower ranging from 2 to 2½ feet tall and spreading to about 2 feet. From summer to fall, bears 4-inch-wide flowers with red-orange centers and yellow petals with lobes at the tips, giving the flowers a ragged appearance. **Zones 3 to 8.**

G. × grandiflora

g. × gran-dih-FLOR-uh. BLANKET FLOWER. A short-lived perennial created by crossing perennial G. aristata and annual G. pulchella, both native North American species. Plants range from 2 to 3 feet tall and spread to about 1½ feet. From early summer to fall they bear showy 3- to 5½-inch-wide flower heads, most often in brilliant combinations of reds, maroons, oranges, and yellows. Dwarf cultivars are especially popular, including 8-inch 'Baby Cole', 12-inch 'Kobold' ('Goblin'), and 14- to 16-inch 'Dazzler'. **Zones 3 to 8.**

G. pulchella

g. pul-CHELL-ah. BLANKET FLOWER, INDIAN BLANKET. An erect, 1- to 1½-foot-tall annual with lance-shaped, grayish green leaves. Bears red, yellow, or red-and-yellow, 2-inch-wide, daisylike flowers with purple-black centers from summer to fall. 'Red Plume' produces rounded, fully double, red flowers on 1-foot plants. Warm-weather annual.

Galanthus

gah-LAN-thus. Amaryllis family, Amaryllidaceae.

The dainty blooms of Galanthus species, better known as snowdrops, are among the earliest flowers to mark the beginning of a new growing season. About 19 species belong to the genus, all hardy perennials native from Europe to Asia that grow from tunicate bulbs and usually produce grassy, strap-shaped leaves. Each bulb normally produces a single pendent bloom on an arching stem. The flowers have six petal-like tepals; the three outer tepals are teardrop shaped and markedly larger than the inner three, which they nearly conceal. Flowers may be all white or green and white in color, and they appear in late winter to midspring. While the botanical name is derived from the Greek gala, meaning "milk," and anthos, "flower," the common name, snowdrop, is thought to have a German derivation. It is from schneetropfen, which were pendants or earrings popular in Germany in the 16th and 17th centuries. Snowdrop bulbs are mildly poisonous, and contact with the foliage can cause skin irritations: their poisonous nature seems to extend to rodents, because these bulbs are generally left alone by mice, voles, and their kin. They are sometimes confused with their close relatives the snowflakes (Leucojum), which bear one to as many as eight flowers per stem and have six tepals of equal size.

HOW TO GROW
Select a site in partial shade with rich, moist, well-drained soil. Snowdrops are best in soil that remains evenly moist, but not wet, in summer. They thrive under deciduous trees and are ideal for naturalizing in shade and woodland gardens as well as along shrub borders. Plant the bulbs in fall, setting them 3 inches deep. Space them at least 3 inches apart because they produce both offsets and self-sown seedlings in abundance and will form nice-size clumps in fairly short order. Clumps can be left undisturbed for years and will become quite large — ones that become too crowded will push bulbs up to the soil surface. (These are easy to pot up for forcing or can be moved to

Gaillardia aristata

Gaillardia pulchella

Galanthus elwesii

a new spot.) Propagate by digging the bulbs in summer just as the foliage dies back. Gardener's lore suggests that snowdrops are happiest when moved "in the green" (with foliage). Or sow seeds.

G. caucasicus

g. kaw-KASS-ih-kus. A 4- to 6-inch-tall species with 5- to 6-inch-long leaves that are about 1 inch wide. From late fall to early spring it bears 1¼-inch-long white flowers with inner tepals dipped in green. **Zones 5 to 9.**

G. elwesii

g. el-WEH-see-eye. GIANT SNOW-DROP. A 5- to 9-inch-tall species bearing fragrant white ³/4- to 1¼-inch-long flowers with green markings on the inner tepals. **Zones 3 to 9.**

G. ikariae

g. ih-KAR-ee-ee. Also listed as *G. latifolius* or *G. ikariae* var. *latifolius*. A 4- to 6-inch-tall plant with broad leaves up to 6 inches long and 1¼ inches wide. Bears ¹/2- to 1¼-inch-long white flowers with green markings on the inner tepals from late winter to early spring. **Zones 3 to 9.**

G. nivalis

g. nih-VAH-liss. COMMON SNOW-DROP. A 4-inch-tall species bearing fragrant white ¹/2- to ³/4-inch-long flowers in late winter to very early spring. Each inner tepal has an inverted green V at the tip. Many cultivars have been selected, but most are very hard to find. 'Flore Pleno' is a vigorous selection with double flowers. 'S. Arnott' ('Sam Arnott'), a vigorous hybrid selection, bears very fragrant 1-to 1¹/2-inch-long flowers with large green V-shaped marks on the inner tepals. 'Viridapicis', also vigorous, has white flowers with green marks on both outer and inner tepals. **Zones 3 to 9.**

G. plicatus

g. plih-KAY-tus. An 8-inch-tall species with ³/4- to 1¼-inch-long white flowers that have a green mark on the tip of each inner tepal. *G. plicatus* ssp. *byzantinus* has green marks on both the tip and the base of the inner tepals. **Zones 3 to 9.**

Galax

GAY-lax. Diapensia family, Diapensiaceae.

Galax consists of one species endemic to the southern Appalachians. It is related to another southern Appalachian native, *Shortia galacifolia* (Oconee bells), which has similar evergreen foliage. *Galax* is a long-lived perennial that grows from a slowly creeping, almost woody rootstock that is technically a stem. Leaves measure up to several inches across and are a dramatic, glossy dark green. The rounded, heart-shaped leaves are held on slender but wiry stalks several inches above the ground. Flowers are tiny, white, and clustered atop leafless racemes that rise well above the foliage. A stand of *Galax* in flower deep in shady woods is stunningly beautiful and not soon forgotten. The botanical name is based on the Greek word for "milk" and probably refers to the appearance of the flowers.

HOW TO GROW

Galax has a reputation as being difficult to establish. It needs deep, organic, acid soil with good moisture and cool woodland conditions for the fibrous roots to become established and thrive. Once

Galax urceolata

Galium odoratum

established, it will persist for decades, spreading to form a solid mass of stunning beauty.

G. urceolata

g. ur-see-oh-LAY-tuh. Formerly *G. aphylla*. A highly desirable ground cover with dark, polished, evergreen foliage that turns coppery red in fall. Its spikes of white, veronica-like flowers light up deep, shady spaces in early summer. Once established, it will spread slowly and indefinitely. Be sure not to let it suffer from drought during its first few seasons. **Zones 5 to 8.**

Galium

GAL-ee-um. Madder family, Rubiaceae.

About 400 species of annuals and perennials belong to the genus *Galium*. Most are weak-stemmed plants with linear leaves arranged in whorls. They bear small tubular flowers that have four or five petal lobes. Although sometimes borne singly, the white, pinkish, or yellow blooms usually are arranged in clusters. One species, *G. odoratum*, commonly known as sweet woodruff, is used as a ground cover in shade.

HOW TO GROW

Give sweet woodruff a spot in partial to deep shade with rich, well-drained soil. Plants also tolerate sandy soil or heavy clay. They spread at a moderate speed; divide them as necessary in spring or fall to keep them in bounds or for propagation.

G. odoratum

g. oh-dor-AH-tum. SWEET WOOD-RUFF, LADIES' BEDSTRAW. Formerly *Asperula odorata*. This European native has been commonly grown as a ground cover in North America for more than a century. Its leaves are used to flavor the "May Wine" traditionally served in open bowls on May Day. The deciduous leaves are bright green at first, acquiring olive green or yellow overtones

G (margin letter)

Galium odoratum

Gardenia augusta

G

through the season. The tiny, star-like flowers are white. Fast spreading in moist, shady sites such as woodland settings, but easy to control, this species also tolerates dry sites, such as under maple trees. **Zones 4 to 8.**

Galtonia

gal-TOE-nee-uh. Lily family, Liliaceae.

Commonly known as summer hyacinths, *Galtonia* species are bulbs native to South Africa. As their common name suggests, they bloom in summer — late summer

Galtonia candicans

to be exact — producing graceful, erect racemes of pendent or nodding, bell-like flowers that are white or tinged with green. The individual blooms are trumpet shaped or tubular and have six lobes. The plants have tunicate bulbs and produce a clump of basal, narrow, lance-shaped leaves that are partially erect. Four species belong to the genus.

HOW TO GROW

Select a site in full sun with rich, well-drained, deeply prepared soil. Unlike many South African natives, summer hyacinths are hardy and thrive in soil that remains moist, but not wet, through the growing season. Plant the bulbs in spring after the last frost date, positioning the bases of the bulbs at least 6 inches below the soil surface: be sure to prepare the soil several inches below that. Plants are happiest when left undisturbed once they are planted, so space them fairly widely — at about 1 foot apart or three to four bulbs per square foot. Where hardy, they can be left undisturbed for years. In areas where they are marginally hardy, protect them over winter with a heavy mulch of evergreen boughs, pine needles, salt hay, or coarse leaves in late fall after the ground has frozen. In the North, either grow these bulbs in large containers, which can be sunk to the rim in the garden in summer, or dig the bulbs in fall after the foliage turns yellow, dry them off for a few hours, brush off excess soil, and store them indoors over winter. In or out of containers, overwinter the bulbs in a cool (35° to 45°F), dry spot. Propagate by digging the clumps in spring or fall and separating the offsets or by seeds.

G. candicans

g. KAN-dih-kans. SUMMER HYACINTH. Formerly *Hyacinthus candicans*. Graceful 3- to 4-foot-tall species that produces erect, showy racemes of 15 to 30 fragrant white 2-inch-long flowers in late summer. **Zones 6 to 10; to Zone 5 with winter mulch protection.** *G. princeps* is a similar species reaching 3 feet in height and bearing 1-inch-long green-tinged white flowers, also in late summer; *G. princeps* is hardy from **Zones 7 or 8 to 10.**

G. viridiflora

g. ver-id-ih-FLOR-uh. A 3-foot-tall species with arching racemes of 15 to 30 pale green, $^3/_4$- to 2-inch-long flowers in late summer. **Zones 7 or 8 to 10.**

Gardenia

gar-DEEN-ee-uh. Coffee family, Rubiaceae.

Even if you don't live where these shrubs will grow outdoors, you know their intensely fragrant, waxy white flowers, probably offered by your nearest garden center as a houseplant. Double forms are employed as corsages. In the garden, they are also prized for their thick, glossy leaves. The approximately 200 members of this genus are evergreen shrubs and trees from tropical Asia and Africa. Most of the widely available cultivars were developed from the single Chinese species listed here.

HOW TO GROW

In the garden, give gardenias dappled to partial shade and provide rich, humusy, neutral to acid soil that retains moisture but drains well. Site them near a sidewalk, deck, or window where the fra-

grance can be savored. They can be espaliered or used as a hedge or screen. Gardenias should be planted shallowly, like azaleas and rhododendrons, or in a container. The roots don't tolerate competition or heavy cultivation, so mulch them well. Feed monthly during the growing season, and lessen disease problems by providing adequate air circulation. Indoors, they are prone to whitefly. Deadhead regularly or prune just lightly in spring, unless espaliered. Sow seeds in spring or root softwood cuttings in summer.

G. augusta

g. ah-GUSS-tuh. Formerly *G. jasminoides*. To more than 30 feet tall in the wild, in the garden this shrub is more often 5 or 6 feet tall and wide, with a dense and rounded habit. The 3-inch glossy, leathery leaves are usually in whorls of three. Thick-petaled white flowers, 2 to 3 inches across, appear from late spring to midsummer. Single forms have a half dozen petals, but double forms with 12 are most popular. 'August Beauty' blooms into fall; 'Mystery' is upright to 8 feet with flowers to 5 inches across; 'Radicans' has small leaves and grows to 1 foot tall and twice as wide; 'Veitchii' grows to 4 feet and flowers profusely from midspring to late fall. **Zones 8 to 11.**

Gardenia augusta

Garrya elliptica

Gaultheria shallon

Garrya

GAIR-ee-uh. Silk-tassel family, Garryaceae.

There are about a dozen species of these evergreen shrubs and trees from the western United States and Mexico, called silk-tassel because of their dramatic winter catkins. Gardeners like them for their handsome foliage and tough nature. The females bear persistent clusters of purple fruits.

HOW TO GROW

Silk-tassel needs only well-drained soil in full sun or partial shade and shelter from cold wind. Unlike many other western natives, the species listed here can use some supplemental water during summer droughts. Try this species for a showy hedge or screen, or as a specimen plant. You will need both male and female shrubs for fruit. Prune lightly to reshape if necessary. Propagate by seeds or semiripe cuttings.

G. elliptica

g. eh-LIP-tih-kuh. SILK-TASSEL TREE. This shrub or small tree grows quickly to 12 feet tall and wide and bears 1¹/₂- to 3-inch leaves that are shiny green on top and fuzzy gray underneath. The thin, drooping, yellow or yellow-green catkins can be up to 8 inches long on male plants, but only about 3 inches on the female, which in early summer develops purple fruit in grapelike clusters. 'James Roof' has striking silver gray catkins, while *G.* × *issaqua-hensis* has dark, glossy foliage. **Zones 8 to 10.**

Gaultheria

gall-THEAR-ee-uh. Heath family, Ericaeae.

Of this genus of almost 200 evergreen shrubs from the Americas, the West Indies, and Asia, a few species are grown in gardens for their combination of leathery leaves, small urn-shaped white flowers, and fleshy, long-lasting seed capsules. One species, wintergreen *(G. procumbens),* is a low-growing ground cover for shade gardens.

HOW TO GROW

Give these shrubs partial shade and acidic peat-rich soil that retains moisture. They can be grown in full sun only where the soil never dries out. Excellent to face down rhododendrons or azaleas, along woodland margins, or in shady rock gardens. They require little pruning except for shaping or to restrict growth. Propagate from suckers or semiripe cuttings in summer.

G. mucronata

g. mew-kron-AH-tuh. This 4-foot-tall, popular suckering shrub from Chile and Argentina has upright shoots and glossy dark green leaves only ³/₄ inch long with a spine at the tip. The urn-shaped white flowers, sometimes tinged pink, are solitary and bloom in late spring to early summer. The ¹/₂-inch fruits can be white or reddish purple. Plant several to ensure fruiting. Cultivars include 'Bell's Seedling' (reliable large, dark red berries), 'Cherry Ripe' (cherry red fruit), 'Mother of

Pearl' (pale pink berries), and 'Snow White' and 'Wintertime' (white berries). **Zones 8 and 9.**

G. procumbens

g. pro-KUM-benz. WINTER-GREEN, CHECKERBERRY. This species is native from eastern Canada south to Michigan and Georgia and grows to less than 6 inches tall. The shiny, dark green 2-inch leaves smell of wintergreen when crushed and blush with the onset of cold weather. Quarter-inch flowers, white with a pink tinge, bloom from midspring through fall, while bright red fleshy seed capsules decorate the plant from midsummer through the following spring. **Zones 3 to 6.**

G. shallon

g. SHAL-lon. SALAL. This western U.S. native suckers to form a thicket 5 feet tall and wide, lower and denser in sun. Red shoots set off the thick, glossy, nearly round 4-inch leaves. Arching 5-inch clusters of pinkish flowers bloom in early summer, followed by small purple-black berries that birds enjoy. **Zones 6 to 8.**

G. × wisleyensis

g. × wiz-lee-EN-sis. An upright, suckering hybrid 4 feet tall and wide with elliptic leaves 1¹/₂ inches long. Two-inch racemes of white flowers bloom in late spring and early summer, followed by 1¹/₄-inch reddish fruits. **Zones 7 to 9.**

Gaura

GAW-ruh. Evening primrose family, Onagraceae.

Gaura species are annuals, biennials, perennials, and subshrubs primarily native to North America. Of the some 20 species in the genus, one is commonly grown in gardens — *G. lindheimeri.* The plants bear mostly basal leaves —

Gaura lindheimeri

usually lance shaped to elliptic or spoon shaped — and small, somewhat star-shaped pink or white flowers carried in spikes or racemes.

HOW TO GROW
Select a site in full sun with moist, well-drained soil. Good soil drainage is essential to success. Plants form deep taproots and are quite drought tolerant (and difficult to dig) once established. They also tolerate heat and humidity as well as light shade. To propagate, take cuttings from shoots that arise at the base of the plant in spring or from stem tips in spring or early summer. Plants also can be divided in spring, but they are best left undisturbed. Or sow seeds.

G. lindheimeri
g. lind-HEIM-er-eye. WHITE GAURA. A shrubby 3- to 4-foot-tall native wildflower with airy, erect panicles of 1-inch-wide white flowers that fade to pink from early summer to fall. 'Corrie's Gold' has leaves edged in gold. 'Siskiyou Pink' bears bright pink flowers. Whirling Butterflies' bears an abundance of white flowers on 2½-foot-tall plants. **Zones 5 to 9**.

Gazania
gah-ZAY-nee-ah. Aster family, Asteraceae.

Gazanias, or treasure flowers as they are sometimes called, are native to tropical Africa, especially South Africa. They bear solitary, hot-colored, daisylike flowers atop leafless stems. The flowers close at night and in cloudy weather. There are 16 or so species of annuals and perennials in this genus,

Gelsemium sempervirens

but most of the plants grown today are hybrids of species such as *G. rigens* and *G. linearis*.

HOW TO GROW
Give gazanias full sun and poor to average, light, very well drained soil. They thrive in heat and dry soil and also tolerate salt spray. They do not bloom well in rich soil and tend to rot in areas with humid, wet summers or constantly wet soil. Grow gazanias as perennials from Zone 8 south. In the North, start them each year from seeds, or overwinter the plants indoors. Sow seeds indoors 6 to 8 weeks before the last spring frost date. Barely cover the seeds with soil, as they need darkness for germination. Seedlings appear in 1 to 3 weeks at 60° to 65°F. Or sow outdoors after the last frost. Deadhead to prolong the bloom season. To overwinter, dig plants before the first hard fall frost and pot them up. Or take cuttings from shoots at the base of the plant in late summer or fall. Keep overwintered plants barely moist. Use gazanias in the front of beds and borders, as edging plants along paths, to add color to rock gardens, and in containers. *G. rigens*, trailing gazania, doesn't flower as prolifically as the commonly grown annual, but it makes an effective hanging plant for containers or window boxes, and it

Gelsemium sempervirens

can be used as a spreading ground cover. They are ideal for seaside gardens and also attract butterflies.

G. hybrids
Tender perennials ranging from 8 to 12 inches with a rosette of spoon-shaped, often lobed leaves. Showy, 3- to 4-inch-wide, daisylike flowers bloom from summer to fall in shades of orange, bronze, gold, yellow, pink, red-orange, or white, sometimes in a solid color but often with bands, stripes, or spots of contrasting colors on the petals. Daybreak Series and Mini-Star Series plants are 8 inches tall, spreading to 10 inches, with flowers that usually have a zone of contrasting color. Sundance Series plants reach 10 to 12 inches. 'Pink Beauty' bears silvery leaves and pink flowers. 'Silverlight' bears bright yellow flowers and woolly white leaves. Tender perennial or warm-weather annual.

Gelsemium
jel-SEE-mee-um. Logania family, Loganiaceae.

Three species belong to the genus *Gelsemium*, all twining climbers with evergreen leaves. They are

grown for their fragrant, funnel-shaped flowers. Flowers are borne in singly or in small clusters. Leaves are simple and borne in pairs.

HOW TO GROW
Select a site in full sun with moist, average to rich soil that is well drained. Plants grow in acid to slightly alkaline pH. They tolerate partial shade but bloom best in sun. They also will grow in poor and even quite sandy soil.

G. sempervirens
g. sem-per-VIE-renz. CAROLINA JESSAMINE. A vigorous, 10- to 20-foot, twining vine, native to the Southeast as well as Central America, with glossy, lance-shaped to narrowly rounded leaves. In late winter and early spring, plants bear fragrant, 1¼-inch-long funnel-shaped flowers that are pale to deep yellow in color. Flowers are carried in clusters or singly, and plants may rebloom sporadically in late summer or fall. **Zones 6 to 9**.

Genista
jen-IS-tuh. Pea family, Fabaceae.

Genista encompasses about 75 usually shrubby species from the Mediterranean region, North Africa, and West Asia. Known commonly as brooms and related to the genus *Cytisus*, these species are arching, branching shrubs formerly used for making dust brooms. They range from almost prostrate shrubs, which are useful as small-scale ground covers, to large shrubs reaching more than 15 feet tall. Unlike *Cytisus* and

Gazania rigens

Gazania rigens var. *leucolaena*

Genista sagittalis

Spartium (Spanish broom), they are not invasive and are good substitutes where those plants are a problem. Leaves are deciduous or semievergreen, small, and have only one or three leaflets each. They may drop during dry weather, and the shrub then continues to photosynthesize using its green stems. Flowers are pealike in size and shape but come in varying shades of yellow and are clustered into small heads. Fruits are not ornamental but are distinctive for their explosive rupture, thus flinging the seeds many feet away from the parent plant. *Genista* is the ancient Latin name for these plants, and the phrase *planta genista* was corrupted into Plantagenet, the family name of a line of English kings.

HOW TO GROW
Grow brooms in full sun, or they will sulk and weaken. The soil must be well drained, as brooms cannot tolerate having even damp feet. Plants are not overly particular as to soil pH, but they do prefer a slightly alkaline condition and low to moderate fertility. They are especially useful for dry climates to control erosion.

G. pilosa 'Vancouver Gold'

g. pil-OH-suh. This selection was introduced by the University of British Columbia Botanical Garden. It grows 4 to 6 inches tall and spreads to 3 feet. Bright yellow flowers cover the branches in spring. It makes a useful ground cover for banks. **Zones 6 to 9.**

G. sagittalis

g. saj-it-TAH-liss. This broom is distinctive at a glance, as the low-lying branches look as if they have been flattened with a rolling pin. It grows to 12 inches tall and spreads modestly, making a small-scale ground cover that can be mixed with other compatible ground covers. Flowers are light yellow and sparse. **Zones 6 to 9.**

G. tinctoria

g. tink-TOR-ee-uh. DYER'S GREENWEED. This shrub is variable in habit, leaf, and flower throughout its natural range, from Europe to the Ukraine. It is spreading or upright to 6 feet and rather spiky, with oblong leaves 1 to 2 inches long. In early summer, bright yellow flowers bloom in upright racemes up to 3 inches high, followed by ¹/₂-inch pods. 'Royal Gold' is 2 feet tall and wide. **Zones 4 to 7.**

Gentiana

jen-shee-AH-nuh. Gentian family, Gentianaceae.

Treasured by gardeners for the rich shades of true blue they bring to beds and borders, gentians also come in shades of violet as well as yellow, white, and red. The plants have simple, often lance-shaped leaves and carry their trumpet- or bell-shaped flowers singly or in clusters. Depending on the species, blooms appear anywhere from spring to fall. The genus contains about 400 species of hardy annuals, biennials, and perennials, which may be deciduous, semievergreen, or evergreen. Most gentians are native to alpine habitats and are suitable only for areas that have cool summers, such as the Pacific Northwest. A few species can be grown successfully over a wider area.

HOW TO GROW
Ideally, gentians prefer a site in full sun with well-drained soil that remains evenly moist. In areas with summers that are warm to hot and dry, however, give them a spot that receives shade during the hottest part of the day. The plants resent disturbance and thrive for years without needing to be divided, so try to select a permanent site. Propagate by carefully dividing the clumps in spring, by lifting and separating offsets in spring, or by sowing seeds.

G. andrewsii

g. an-DREW-see-eye. BOTTLE GENTIAN, CLOSED GENTIAN. A 1- to 2-foot-tall native North American wildflower that spreads from 1 to 2 feet. In late summer, bears clusters of tubular to urn-shaped 1¹/₂-inch-long flowers at the stem tips that never open completely and are dark blue with white on the petal lobes. **Zones 3 to 7.**

G. asclepiadea

g. ah-sklee-pee-ah-DEE-uh. WILLOW GENTIAN. A 2- to 3-foot-tall perennial forming 1¹/₂-foot-wide clumps. Bears narrow, willowlike leaves and 2-inch-long, trumpet-shaped, pale to dark blue flowers in late summer and fall. **Zones 5 to 7.**

G. septemfida

g. sep-tem-FIH-duh. CRESTED GENTIAN. A low-growing 6- to 8-inch-tall species spreading to 1 foot. In late summer, bears clusters of 1¹/₂-inch-long trumpets that are narrowly bell shaped and blue to purple-blue with white throats. **Zones 3 to 8.**

Geranium

jer-AY-nee-um. Geranium family, Geraniaceae.

Commonly called hardy geraniums or cranesbills, *Geranium* species are versatile, long-lived perennials that produce mounds of handsome foliage and loose clusters of five-petaled cup- or saucer-shaped flowers. The leaves are lobed in a palmate fashion and often have toothed or lobed margins. Some species have very lacy-textured foliage. The genus contains about 300 species, including annuals, biennials, and perennials. Perennial species can be hardy or tender and are either herbaceous or, in areas with mild winters, semievergreen to evergreen. Blooms come in shades of pink

Gentiana septemfida

Geranium phaeum 'Samobor'

Geranium endressii

and magenta as well as white, purple, and violet-blue. The main flush of bloom occurs from late spring into early summer, and some geraniums rebloom into fall, especially if the plants are cut back. Some species also feature colorful fall foliage. Too often hardy geraniums are confused with zonal or ivy geraniums (*Pelargonium*), which are popular tender perennials grown as annuals. Hardy geraniums are sometimes dubbed "true" geraniums to distinguish them from their better-known cousins.

HOW TO GROW

Most hardy geraniums thrive in full sun or partial shade and rich, evenly moist, well-drained soil. In most parts of the country, especially the South, shade during the hottest part of the day is best. Taller species tend to flop: either stake them with peabrush or let the plants sprawl. After most of the flowers fade, cut plants to within 1 inch of the ground and a fresh new mound of leaves will arise in a few weeks. Many hardy geraniums need to be divided regularly to look their best, especially *G. endressii*, *G. himalayense*, *G. sanguineum*, and *G. sylvaticum*, which should be divided every 2 to 3 years. Hardy geraniums can be grown from seeds, and plants may self-sow, but most cultivars are best propagated vegetatively — by dividing the clumps in spring or fall, by root cuttings taken in fall, or by cuttings taken in spring from shoots at the base of the plant.

G. × cantabrigiense

g. × kan-tah-brih-jee-EN-see. CAMBRIDGE GERANIUM. Mound-ing 1-foot-tall hybrid with glossy, aromatic leaves that spreads slowly to form dense clumps 2 feet or more in width. Bears clusters of 1-inch-wide purple-pink or white flowers from early to midsummer. 'Biokovo' has white flowers tinged pink and spreads to 3 feet via long runners. **Zones 5 to 8.**

G. cinereum

g. sih-NEER-ee-um. GRAYLEAF CRANESBILL. A 6- to 12-inch species that spreads to 1 foot. Bears gray-green leaves, evergreen in mild climates, and 1-inch-wide purplish pink flowers from late spring to early summer. Requires gritty, very well drained soil. 'Ballerina' produces purplish red flowers with dark eyes all summer long on 4- to 6-inch-tall plants. **Zones 5 to 8.**

G. clarkei

g. KLARK-ee-eye. CLARK'S GERANIUM. Mounding 1½-foot-tall species that spreads quickly by rhizomes to 3 feet or more. Produces deeply cut leaves and abundant, ¾-inch-wide violet purple or white flowers with lilac veins from late spring into early summer. 'Kashmir Purple' has purple-blue flowers with red veins and comes true from seed. 'Kashmir White' bears white flowers with lilac-pink veins and can be grown from seed, though some seedlings will be purple flowered. **Zones 4 to 8.**

G. dalmaticum

g. dal-MAT-ih-kum. DALMATIAN CRANESBILL. Mounding to trailing 4- to 6-inch-tall species that spreads by rhizomes to about 2 feet. Bears soft pink 1-inch-wide flowers in late spring and early summer and has good red-orange fall foliage color that is evergreen in mild-climate areas. Grows well in shade. **Zones 4 to 8.**

G. endressii

g. en-DRESS-ee-eye. ENDRES CRANESBILL. Mounding to sprawling 1½-foot-tall species, evergreen in mild climates, that spreads to about 2 feet. Bears pale pink 1-inch flowers in spring, but blooms all summer (and grows best) in areas with cool temperatures. Tolerates drought. **Zones 4 to 8.**

G. himalayense

g. him-ah-lay-EN-see. LILAC GERANIUM. Clump-forming species with sprawling 1- to 1½-foot-long stems that spread to about 2 feet. Bears violet-blue 2-inch-wide flowers in early summer. Foliage turns orange-red in fall. **Zones 4 to 8.**

G. hybrids

Many outstanding hybrids are available. 'Ann Folkard', a cross between *G. procurrens* and *G. psilostemon*, bears 1½-inch-wide magenta flowers with dark centers from midsummer to fall; features yellow-green leaves and trailing stems that reach about 2 feet in height and scramble and spread to 3 feet or more; Zones 5 to 9. 'Johnson's Blue', a cross between *G. himalayense* and *G. pratense*, bears lavender-blue 1½- to 2-inch-wide flowers in early summer on mounding 1½-foot-tall plants that spread via rhizomes to form 2½-foot-wide clumps; Zones 4 to 8.

G. ibericum

g. eye-BEER-ih-kum. CAUCASUS GERANIUM. Clump-forming 1½-foot-tall, 2-foot-wide species that bears violet 2-inch-wide flowers with dark veins in early summer. **Zones 3 to 8.**

G. macrorrhizum

g. mak-roe-RYE-zum. BIGROOT GERANIUM. Mounding 1½-foot-tall species that spreads vigorously via fleshy, deep roots to 2 feet or more. Bears aromatic leaves and pink to purplish pink 1-inch-wide flowers in spring. Evergreen

Geranium sanguineum var. *striatum*

in mild climates. 'Ingwersen's Variety' has soft pink flowers. Tolerates drought and grows well even in dry shade. **Zones 3 to 8.**

G. maculatum

g. mak-yew-LAY-tum. WILD CRANESBILL, SPOTTED GERANIUM. Native North American wildflower that reaches 1 to 2 feet in height and spreads to about 1¹/₂ feet. Bears pink 1¹/₄-inch-wide flowers from late spring to midsummer. Does best in partial shade in moist, well-drained soil. **Zones 4 to 8.**

G. × magnificum

g. × mag-NIF-ih-kum. SHOWY GERANIUM. Clump-forming 2-foot-tall, 2-foot-wide hybrid (G. ibericum × G. platypetalum) with deeply lobed and toothed leaves. Bears 1¹/₂- to 2-inch-wide violet flowers with darker veins in midsummer and features good fall foliage color. **Zones 4 to 8.**

G. × oxonianum

g. × ox-oh-ee-AH-num. Vigorous 1¹/₂- to 3-foot-tall hybrid (G. endressii × G. versicolor) that spreads from 2 to 3 feet or more. Bears pink 1¹/₂-inch-wide flowers from spring to fall. 'Claridge Druce' is a very vigorous selection with grayish green leaves and rose-pink flowers. 'Wargrave Pink', also vigorous, bears salmon-pink flowers. **Zones 4 to 8.**

G. phaeum

g. FAY-um. DUSKY CRANESBILL, MOURNING WIDOW. Clump-forming 1¹/₂- to 2¹/₂-foot-tall species that spreads as far and bears black-purple, maroon, violet, or white 1-inch-wide flowers with reflexed petals from late spring to early summer. Grows best in partial shade in moist, well-drained soil, but will tolerate dry soil. **Zones 5 to 7.**

G. platypetalum

g. plah-tee-PET-ah-lum. BROAD-PETALED GERANIUM. Clump-forming 1- to 1¹/₂-foot-tall species that spreads about as far. Bears 1¹/₄- to 1³/₄-inch-wide violet-blue flowers from early to midsummer. **Zones 3 to 8.**

G. pratense

g. pray-TEN-see. MEADOW CRANESBILL. Vigorous, clump-forming 2- to 3-foot-tall species forming 2-foot-wide mounds of deeply lobed leaves. Bears blue-violet 1¹/₂-inch-wide flowers in late

Gerbera jamesonii

spring and early summer. **Zones 2 or 3 to 8.**

G. psilostemon

g. sye-LOH-steh-mon. ARMENIAN CRANESBILL. Shrublike 2- to 4-foot-tall species that forms 3-foot-wide clumps. Bears 2-inch-wide magenta flowers with black eyes from early to late summer. Good fall foliage color and evergreen to semievergreen leaves. **Zones 5 to 8.**

G. sanguineum

g. san-GWIH-nee-um. BLOODY CRANESBILL. An 8- to 12-inch-tall species that forms 1-foot-wide mounds of lacy leaves topped by bright pink 1- to 1¹/₂-inch flowers from spring into summer. Leaves turn red in fall. Tolerates drought and does well in shade. 'Album' has white flowers. 'Elsbeth' bears pink flowers with dark veins all summer. 'New Hampshire Purple' bears rose-purple flowers. 'Shepherd's Warning' is compact — from 4 to 6 inches tall. G. sanguineum var. striatum (also listed as G. sanguineum var. lancastriense) produces pale pink flowers on 4- to 6-inch plants. **Zones 3 to 8.**

G. sylvaticum

g. sil-VAT-ih-kum. WOOD CRANESBILL. Bushy, clump-forming 2¹/₂- to 3-foot-tall species with deeply cut leaves and violet-blue 1-inch-wide flowers in early to midspring. Best in partial shade and evenly moist soil. **Zones 3 to 8.**

Gerbera

JER-ber-ah. Aster family, Asteraceae.

While there are some 40 species of tender perennials in this genus, native from Africa to Asia and Indonesia, only one of them is commonly grown in gardens. *Gerbera* species bear solitary, daisylike flower heads above a rosette of pinnate, entire, or toothed leaves that are hairy underneath.

HOW TO GROW

Gerberas require full sun and average to rich, evenly moist, well-drained soil. They do not tolerate wet soil. In areas with very hot summers, partial shade in the afternoon is best. Sow seeds indoors in individual pots 12 weeks before the last spring frost date at 65° to 75°F. When sowing, just press the seeds into the soil surface, as they need light to germinate, which takes 2 to 3 weeks. When transplanting, set the crowns slightly above the soil surface to ensure good drainage. Deadhead regularly, and feed every month to 6 weeks.

Grow gerberas outdoors as perennials from about Zone 8 south; they may survive winters in Zone 7 if they are planted in a protected site and covered with a heavy layer of a dry mulch such as salt hay or weed-free straw. They are often grown as annuals, but older plants bloom best, so the plants are worth trying to overwinter. Plants are deep-rooted and resent transplanting, but container-grown ones can be brought indoors for overwintering: keep plants barely moist and cool (45° to 50°F), and provide sun and good air circulation. They can be propagated by division in spring, as well as from cuttings taken from the base of the plant in summer, which also can be used for overwintering.

Use gerberas as edging plants, in mixed plantings, and in containers that are either set on a terrace or sunk to the rim in soil. They make outstanding, long-lasting cut flowers: cut them after they have fully opened, while the centers are still tight.

G. jamesonii

g. jame-SOH-nee-eye. TRANSVAAL DAISY, BARBERTON DAISY. A tender, 1- to 1¹/₂-foot perennial with deeply lobed leaves that are woolly underneath. Showy, waxy, 3- to 5-inch-wide, single or semidouble, daisylike flowers are carried on leafless stems from early to late summer in shades of orange-red, orange, red, yellow, pink, or cream. Tender perennial, or grow as a warm-weather annual.

Geum

JEE-um. Rose family, Rosaceae.

Geums, sometimes called avens, are rose-family plants with pinnate leaves and small saucer- to bowl-shaped flowers that normally have five petals. Blooms are borne in

Geum chiloense 'Mrs. J. Bradshaw'

shades of orange, red, and yellow as well as cream and pink. They are carried singly or in small clusters and appear from late spring to early summer.

HOW TO GROW
Select a site in full sun with average to rich, evenly moist, well-drained soil. South of Zone 6, a site with afternoon shade is best. Good soil drainage is especially important in winter. *G. rivale* prefers moist or even boggy conditions, however. Plants can be short-lived; divide them every 2 to 3 years to keep them vigorous. Water during dry weather. Propagate named cultivars by division in spring or fall. Seed-grown plants aren't identical to asexually propagated ones, but 'Lady Stratheden' and 'Mrs. J. Bradshaw' can be grown from seeds.

G. chiloense
g. chil-oh-EN-see. GEUM, AVENS. Formerly *G. quellyon*. Clump-forming 1½- to 2-foot-tall species that spreads to about 2 feet. Bears deeply lobed, toothed leaves and clusters of saucer-shaped, 1½-inch-wide red flowers in summer. 'Fire Opal' has semidouble red-orange blooms. 'Lady Stratheden' bears semidouble golden yellow blooms. 'Mrs. J. Bradshaw' produces 1¾-inch-wide scarlet blooms. **Zones 4 to 7 or 8.**

G. coccineum
g. kok-SIN-ee-um. GEUM, AVENS. Formerly *G. × borisii*. A clump-forming 1- to nearly 2-foot-tall species with saucer-shaped, 1½-inch-wide orange-yellow flowers from late spring to midsummer. **Zones 4 to 7 or 8.**

G. rivale
g. rih-VAL-ee. WATER AVENS, INDIAN CHOCOLATE. A ½- to 2-foot-tall species spreading from 1 to 2 feet. Bears pendent, bell-shaped ¾-inch-wide flowers from late spring to midsummer that have purple-pink petals and red-brown sepals. **Zones 3 to 8.**

G. triflorum
g. try-FLOR-um. PRAIRIE SMOKE, PURPLE AVENS. Native North American wildflower that creeps to form 1½-foot-tall, 1-foot-wide mounds of ferny gray-green leaves. In summer, bears 1½-inch-wide flowers with creamy petals and long purple bracts followed by plumy, silvery pink seedpods that have a fuzzy, smokelike appearance. **Zones 1 to 7.**

Gilia
GILL-ee-ah. Phlox family, Polemoniaceae.

There are some 25 to 30 species of *Gilia* native primarily to western North America. Most are annuals, although the genus contains some biennials and perennials. They have deeply divided, feathery leaves and tube-, funnel-, or bell-shaped flowers borne singly or in loose clusters.

HOW TO GROW
Full sun and average, well-drained soil are ideal. These plants are best for areas with cool summers or when started early enough so they bloom before hot weather arrives, since they do not tolerate heat and humidity. They will grow in very sandy soil. Sow seeds outdoors 2 to 3 weeks before the last spring frost date, or in fall in areas with mild winters — roughly Zone 8 south. Or sow indoors 6 to 8 weeks before the last frost and germinate at 50° to 65°F (although outdoor sowing is usually best). Stake plants with twiggy brush. Use gilias in drifts in mixed plantings. They also attract hummingbirds and butterflies and make lovely cut flowers. Plants self-sow.

G. capitata
g. kah-pih-TAH-tah. QUEEN ANNE'S THIMBLES. A feathery-leaved, 1½- to 2-foot-tall annual. Bears rounded, 1-inch-wide clusters of small lilac-blue flowers in summer. Cool-weather annual.

G. tricolor
g. TRY-kuh-lor. BIRD'S EYES. A 1- to 1½-foot-tall annual with

Gillenia trifoliata

fernlike, deeply cut leaves. Lilac- to violet-blue, ½- to ¾-inch-wide flowers, each with an orange or yellow center and purple-blue spots, are borne from spring to late summer either singly or in small clusters. Cool-weather annual.

Gillenia
gih-LEN-ee-uh. Rose family, Rosaceae.

Two species of native North American woodland perennials belong to this rose-family genus. Both are shrubby, spring-blooming perennials with palmate, three-leaflet leaves with toothed margins. The leaves have stipules (leaflike appendages) at the base of the leaf stalks, which offer the

Gilia tricolor

easiest way to distinguish the two species. The white or pale pink flowers are borne in loose panicles and have five lance-shaped to linear petals.

HOW TO GROW
Select a site in partial shade with rich, moist, well-drained soil that has a slightly acid to neutral pH. Established plants tolerate drought. *Gillenia* species will grow in full sun if the soil is consistently moist or if they have shade during the hottest part of the day. They spread slowly by rhizomes, but seldom need dividing. To propagate, divide plants in spring or fall, or sow seeds.

G. stipulata
g. stip-yew-LAH-tuh. AMERICAN IPECAC, INDIAN PHYSIC. Also listed as *Porteranthus stipulatus*. A 1- to 3-foot-tall species that spreads to about 2 feet. Bears broadly ovate, toothed stipules that are leaflike and remain on the plant. Flowers, borne in spring to early summer, are white to pale pink and 1 inch wide. **Zones 5 to 8.**

G. trifoliata
g. try-foe-lee-AH-tuh. BOWMAN'S ROOT, INDIAN PHYSIC. Also listed as *Porteranthus trifoliata*. A 2- to 4-foot-tall species forming 2-foot-wide clumps of bronzy green leaves bearing small awl-shaped stipules that drop off the plant. Bears starry 1- to 1½-inch-wide flowers with pinkish calyxes from late spring to early summer. **Zones 4 to 8.**

ennial or annual, with blue-green leaves. Bears 2-inch-wide yellow to orange flowers in summer. Biennial or cool-weather annual.

Gleditsia

gleh-DIT-see-ah. Pea family, Fabaceae.

Hailing from Asia, North and South America, and Africa, the 14 species of trees in this genus are thorny and have feathery, pinnately compound leaves and beanlike seedpods. The genus contains only one garden tree, a North American native, which is popular because of the dappled shade it casts.

HOW TO GROW
Plant in full sun. Adapts to almost any soil, wet or dry, but does best in rich, moist soil with a pH of 6 to 8. Tolerates drought and road salt. Insects and diseases can be serious problems. Webworms, spider mites, and borers are common, as are leaf spot, mildew, and rust. Performs poorly in the heat and humidity of the Southeast.

G. triacanthos var. inermis
g. try-ah-KAN-thoss var. in-ERR-miss. THORNLESS HONEY LOCUST. Broadly spreading with horizontal branches, this elegant, fast-growing tree reaches 35 to 70 feet tall and wide. Foliage is delicate and lacy, consisting of compound leaves divided into 20 to 30 half- to 1-inch-long, lance-shaped, bright green leaflets. Leaves are divided twice on young, vigorous trees; once on mature trees. Fall

color is a pleasing yellow. Leaflets are so small when they drop in fall that they require little cleanup. By contrast, the 12-inch-long, twisted, dark brown seedpods are a nuisance when they drop in early winter. Clusters of inconspicuous greenish flowers bloom in spring and have a sweet, intense fragrance. Vicious, branched, 3- to 6-inch-long thorns arm the trunk and branches of the species, but this variety and most cultivars are thornless and seedless. Honey locust is a valued landscape tree because it casts light shade and does not have competitive roots, so lawn and garden plants thrive under it. From southeastern and south-central North America. Zones 4 to 9.

CULTIVARS
These are all thornless and mostly seedless. 'Christie' is fast growing and rounded, with horizontal branches. 'Continental' is narrow, with large leaves. 'Halka' is very vigorous and fast growing, with horizontal branches. 'Imperial' is compact and rounded or spreading, with dainty leaves. 'Moraine' has dark green leaves, is vase shaped, and has excellent resistance to webworms. 'Rubylace' has ruby-red new growth that turns bronze-green in summer; susceptible to webworms. 'Shademaster' has dark green leaves, a vase shape with slightly pendulous branches, and a straight trunk. 'Skyline' has dark green leaves, a broad pyramidal shape with a straight trunk, and golden fall color. 'Spectrum' has bright gold leaves in spring and summer and a rounded form

with strong branches. 'Summer Lace' is tall and has light green new growth maturing to dark green. 'Sunburst' has bright yellow new growth at the branch tips all summer and yellow-green older leaves; has a broad, pyramidal, irregular shape; and is susceptible to webworms. 'True Shade' is rounded, with upright branches, and has golden fall color.

Globba

GLOB-buh. Ginger family, Zingiberaceae.

Native to Southeast Asia, *Globba* species are heat-loving, tropical plants grown for their racemes of exotic-looking flowers that are erect or arching and then pendulous. Each individual flower has a long slender tube; three lobes or "petals," one of which forms a spur; and a large lip. There is a showy bract at the base of each flower. Plants grow from slender, branching rhizomes and produce oblong or lance-shaped leaves arranged in two ranks up the reedlike stems. About 70 species belong to the genus.

HOW TO GROW
Give these plants partial shade and deeply prepared, moist soil rich in organic matter. They thrive in ar-

Globba winitii

eas with warm summers and high humidity and are ideal for gardens in the tropics and subtropics as well as for adding an exotic touch to more northern gardens during the summer months. Where hardy, grow them outdoors year-round. In the North, plant the rhizomes out in spring after the soil has warmed up and overwinter them indoors by digging the rhizomes after a light frost and cutting back the tops. Store the rhizomes in barely damp vermiculite, peat moss, or sand in a cool (55°F), dry place. Inspect rhizomes occasionally in winter. Discard rotted pieces or cut away rotted portions and dust cuts with sulfur; sprinkle the vermiculite with water occasionally during winter to keep the roots from shriveling. Replant in spring. Or, grow these plants in containers year-round; keep them nearly dry and set them in a cool (60°F) spot in winter. Propagate by dividing the rhizomes in spring. While they seldom produce seeds, bulbils are often produced along the flower stems among the bracts.

G. winitii
g. wih-NIT-ee-eye. A 2- to 3-foot-tall species native to Thailand that spreads by fleshy rhizomes to 2 feet or more. Leaves are 8 inches

Gleditsia triacanthos var. *inermis*

Gloriosa superba 'Rothschildiana'

long and lance shaped with heart-shaped bases. Bears pendent 6-inch-long racemes of yellow flowers with mauve-pink or purple-pink bracts. **Zones 8 to 11; to Zone 7 with a very heavy winter mulch.**

Gloriosa

glor-ee-OH-suh. Lily family, Liliaceae.

As the common names "climbing lily" and "glory lily" suggest, *Gloriosa* species are climbers that bear spectacular flowers. The botanical name also celebrates the exotic blooms of these tender perennials: it is from the Latin, *gloriosus,* meaning "splendid." The genus contains one very variable species that grows from slender, brittle, fleshy tubers. The plants produce ovate- to lance-shaped leaves that have tendrils at the tips. The flowers come in red or yellow or combinations of the two colors and have six petal-like tepals. The tepals are reflexed, meaning they point backward, and the flowers have been described as resembling butterflies. The tepals usually have wavy or crisped margins, and the flowers also feature six long,

prominent spidery stamens along with a long pistil.

HOW TO GROW

Select a site in full sun with rich, well-drained soil. Where hardy, these plants can be grown outdoors year-round; in areas where they are marginally hardy, look for a protected, south-facing site and mulch heavily over winter with evergreen boughs, pine needles, or salt hay. When selecting a site, try to follow the old adage commonly applied to clematis, and plant with the "head in the sun and feet in the shade." This refers to the fact that plants prefer cool soil conditions, while the tops bloom best in full sun to partial shade. Look for a spot where the roots will be shaded by low-growing shrubs or perennials that aren't too aggressive, or on the north, or shaded, side of shrubs or a low wall. Mulch also helps keep the roots cool. Like clematis, these plants require a trellis or other support so the vines can climb into the sunlight.

In the North, grow climbing lilies in containers or plant the tubers outdoors in spring on or slightly after the last frost date. In Zone 6 and north, start tubers indoors several weeks before the last

frost date to give them a head start. Plant the tubers horizontally or at a slight angle with the tips 2 to 3 inches beneath the soil surface; just barely cover the tops of the tubers when planting in containers. Always handle the tubers carefully, as they are extremely brittle. To overwinter, dig tubers in fall after the first light frost and store them in dry peat moss or sand at a temperature of about 60°F. Or overwinter container-grown plants by allowing the soil to dry out and store them pot and all in a cool, dry place. Propagate by separating the tubers in spring.

G. superba

g. sue-PER-buh. CLIMBING LILY, GLORY LILY. Plants once classified as *G. carsonii, G. lutea, G. minor, G. rothschildiana,* and *G. simplex* all belong here. A climbing, tuberous perennial that can reach 6 feet in areas with long growing seasons. Bears 2- to 4-inch-wide flowers with red or purple tepals that often have yellow margins. 'Citrina' bears orangy yellow flowers. 'Rothschildiana' features 3- to 4-inch-wide flowers with scarlet tepals that have yellow bases and edges. **Zones 8 to 10; to Zone 7 in a protected site with winter mulch.**

Gomphrena

gom-FREE-nah. Amaranth family, Amaranthaceae.

While gomphrenas bear flowers that resemble clovers, their blooms have a decidedly uncloverlike tex-

ture: they are composed of dense clusters of stiff, papery, brightly colored bracts borne beneath tiny, insignificant flowers. The plants flower from summer to frost and have softly hairy, lance-shaped to oval leaves. There are about 90 species in the genus — mostly annuals, but some perennials. They are native to Central and South America as well as Australia.

HOW TO GROW

Full sun and average, well-drained soil are ideal. Gomphrenas thrive in hot weather and tolerate dry soil. Sow seeds indoors 6 to 8 weeks before the last spring frost date at 70° to 75°F. Germination takes 1 to 2 weeks. Water from below, and keep the soil barely moist, never wet. Or sow outdoors after the last spring frost. Either way, barely cover the seeds with soil, as darkness is required for germination. Pinch seedlings to encourage branching. Although the plants tolerate dry soil, water during dry weather for best performance. Use gomphrenas in plantings of annuals, as an edging for perennial gardens, and in containers. They make excellent cut or dried flowers and also attract butterflies. For drying, cut the blooms just as they open fully, and hang in bunches in a warm, dry, dark place.

G. globosa

g. gloh-BOE-sah. GOMPHRENA, GLOBE AMARANTH. A 1- to 2-foot-tall annual with oval to oblong, 1¹/₂-inch-long flower heads in shades of pink, purple, or white. 'Buddy' bears purple flowers on 6-inch-tall plants. Gnome Series

Gomphrena globosa

plants also are 6 inches tall and come in pink, white, and shades of purple. Warm-weather annual.

G. haageana

g. hog-ee-AY-nah. GOMPHRENA, GLOBE AMARANTH. A 2-foot-tall annual with round, 1½-inch-wide flower heads in shades of pale red to reddish orange. 'Lavender Lady' bears pale purple flowers; 'Strawberry Fields', red ones on 30-inch plants. Warm-weather annual.

Grevillea

greh-VILL-ee-uh. Protea family, Proteaceae.

A genus of 250 Australian evergreen shrubs and trees grown for their clusters of slender, tubular flowers that split and curve backward and long styles that give them a spidery look. The foliage is often fine and needlelike.

HOW TO GROW

Give grevillea moderately fertile, neutral to acid soil in full sun. Tolerates drought and heat but not salt or high levels of phosphorus. Larger species are useful as specimens, against a wall, or in borders with other large shrubs. Use smaller ones at the front of a border to face down bigger shrubs, or in a rock garden. Needs minimal pruning. Propagate from semihard cuttings in summer.

G. banksii

g. BANK-see-eye. RED-FLOW-ERED SILKY OAK. This large shrub or small tree averages 12 to 15 feet tall and not quite as wide.

Leaves are 4 to 10 inches long, deeply lobed and silky gray underneath. The dark red flowers bloom in 3- to 7-inch erect racemes, mainly in spring but intermittently all year. **Zones 10 and 11**.

G. 'Canberra Gem'

Vigorous and rounded, from 6 to 8 feet high and sometimes wider, this shrub bears linear leaves and waxy, bright pink flowers that may bloom heavily into summer. **Zones 9 to 11**.

G. rosmarinifolia

g. rose-mair-reen-ih-FOE-lee-uh. Compact shrub, 5 to 6 feet tall and wide, with linear leaves that look like those of rosemary. Bears 3-

Grewia occidentalis

inch racemes of red and cream (occasionally pink or white) flowers from autumn into early spring. **Zones 9 to 11**.

Grewia

GREW-ee-uh. Linden family, Tiliaceae.

The 150 deciduous and evergreen trees, shrubs, and climbers in this genus are native to Australia, Africa, and Asia. The South African species listed here is grown for its small mauve flowers and adaptability to a wide variety of uses.

HOW TO GROW

Give grewia fertile, moisture-retentive soil in full sun or partial shade. It tolerates some wind and salt but not drought. Occasional light pruning will increase its bushiness, and it can be pruned hard to control its size or shape. Prune it to grow vertically in a treelike shape, as an espalier, or across an arbor. Train it to grow horizontally as a bank cover, or shear it as a hedge or even a topiary. If you want it to serve in several of these capacities, propagate it from cuttings collected in spring.

G. occidentalis

g. ox-ih-den-TAL-iss. LAVENDER STARFLOWER. If left unpruned, lavender starflower grows to 10 feet or more with similar spread. The 3-inch oval leaves have rounded teeth. In summer, star-shaped pink-and-purple flowers

with yellow centers bloom in axillary cymes. They are followed by 1-inch four-lobed fruits that are gold and then purple. **Zones 8 to 11**.

Gymnocladus

jim-no-CLAY-duss. Pea family, Fabaceae.

Closely related to *Gleditsia*, this genus of trees with compound leaves contains several species from eastern Asia and one from North America. Only the native species is grown here as an ornamental.

HOW TO GROW

Plant in full sun and humus-rich, moist soil. Tolerates drought and occasional wetness. Adapts to urban conditions and a soil pH of 6 to 8. Train to a strong branch structure when young. Prune in summer to avoid bleeding sap. Pest-free.

G. dioicus

g. die-OH-ih-kuh. KENTUCKY COFFEE TREE. A tough tree for difficult, drought-prone sites, Kentucky coffee tree possesses a craggy oval form, silvery twigs, and ascending branches. It reaches 50 to 70 feet tall and 40 to 50 feet wide. Leaves are doubly compound, measuring up to 3 feet long and 2 feet wide, and consist of a hundred or more 2- to 4-inch-long, pointed leaflets. The pinkish purple leaflets unfold in late spring after most other trees have leafed out, mature to dark blue-green in

Grevillea rosmarinifolia

summer, and turn pastel yellow in autumn. Showy, 12-inch-long panicles of fluffy, greenish white, fragrant flowers bloom on female trees in spring. Male trees have smaller flowers. Six-inch-long, wide, reddish brown seedpods containing large seeds develop on female trees and hang on through the winter. The seeds are poisonous when raw, but European colonists roasted them and used them like coffee. Trunk bark is dark brown and deeply furrowed, with curled ridges. Use this bold, picturesque tree for shade on large properties where its messy habits will not be a problem and its lovely silhouette can be viewed against the sky. From southeastern and midwestern North America. **Zones 3 to 8.**

CULTIVARS

'Espresso' is vase shaped and seedless. 'Prairie Titan' is pyramidal, vigorous, and seedless.

Gypsophila

jip-SOF-ih-luh. Pink family, Caryophyllaceae.

Best known as baby's breaths, *Gypsophila* species are annuals and perennials native from the Mediterranean region to central Asia. Most of the 100 species in the genus are found on dry, rocky, or sandy soil that is alkaline in pH. Plants bear lance-shaped to linear gray-green leaves and clouds of tiny five-petaled white or pink flowers that are star or trumpet shaped. The botanical name is from the Greek *gypsos,* meaning "chalk," and *philos,* "loving," and refers to the preference some species have for alkaline soils rich in

chalk, a soft form of limestone rich in calcium carbonate.

HOW TO GROW

Give baby's breaths full sun or very light shade and rich, evenly moist, very well drained soil. Deeply prepared soil is best, because the perennial species have deep, wide-ranging roots and deep digging improves soil drainage. Wet soil in fall and winter leads to crown rot, and plants in poorly drained conditions tend to be short-lived. *G. paniculata* tolerates slightly acid soil (only to pH 6.5), but plants tend to be short-lived in such conditions and are best in neutral to alkaline soil, pH 7.0 to 7.5. *G. repens* grows well in acid or alkaline soils. Cutting bloom stalks to the ground as the flowers fade — or shearing *G. repens* — encourages rebloom. The perennial species have deep root systems are best left undisturbed once planted. Propagate *G. paniculata* cultivars by cuttings in early summer. *G. repens* can be divided in early spring or in midsummer, after flowering. Or sow seeds.

To grow annual baby's breath (*G. elegans*), sow seeds outdoors a few weeks before the last spring frost date, or sow indoors 6 to 8 weeks before the last frost date; outdoor sowing is generally best. In areas with mild winters, sow seeds outdoors in fall. For continued bloom, sow new crops every 2 to 3 weeks until midsummer. Support tall cultivars with twiggy brush. Cut plants back hard after the first flush of bloom to encourage a second round of flowers. Use annual baby's breath as an airy filler in mixed plantings. It is a good cut flower but unlike *G. paniculata* does not dry well.

Gymnocladus dioicus

G. elegans

g. EL-eh-ganz. ANNUAL BABY'S BREATH. A well-branched, 1- to 2-foot annual with gray-green leaves. Produces masses of tiny, 1/2-inch, star-shaped flowers in white or pink in summer. 'Covent Garden' is an 18-inch-tall cultivar developed for use as a cut flower. 'Early Summer Lace' bears flowers in white and shades of pink. Cool-weather annual.

G. paniculata

g. pan-ick-yew-LAH-tuh. BABY'S BREATH. A shrubby perennial forming 2- to 4-foot-wide clumps that range from 2 to 4 feet tall when in bloom. Bears cloudlike panicles of tiny white or pink flowers from mid- to late summer. Full-size plants need staking, but dwarf cultivars, which are about 2 feet tall, do not. Dwarf types include 18-inch 'Pink Fairy' and 15-inch-tall 'Viette's Dwarf'. 'Perfecta' is a robust 3- to 4-foot double-flowered cultivar. 'Snowflake', another double, reaches 3 feet. **Zones 3 to 9.**

G. repens

g. REP-enz. CREEPING BABY'S BREATH. A 4- to 8-inch-tall perennial spreading to form 1-foot-wide mats of bluish to gray-green semievergreen leaves. Bears loose, broad clusters of 1/2-inch-wide pink or white flowers from early to midsummer. **Zones 4 to 8.**

Gypsophila elegans

H

Habranthus

hah-BRAN-thus. Amaryllis family, Amaryllidaceae.

Habranthus contains 10 species of bulbs native to South America that are grown for their funnel-shaped flowers. The blooms, which are carried on leafless stalks, usually are solitary, or sometimes are borne in pairs. They stick out at an angle from the stalk; the blooms of closely related *Zephyranthes* point upward. The flowers have six petal-like tepals and are followed by conspicuous black seeds. Habranthus grow from tunicate bulbs and bear grassy, linear, basal leaves that are either evergreen or deciduous, in which case they appear with or just after the flowers. The botanical name is from the Greek *habros*, meaning "graceful," and *anthos*, "flower."

HOW TO GROW

Select a site in full sun with deeply prepared, rich, well-drained soil. Neutral to alkaline soil pH is best. Where hardy, these bulbs can be grown outdoors year-round. They prefer a warm site, and where they are marginally hardy, a protected spot at the base of a south-facing wall is best. They require fairly dry soil in winter when they are dormant, so where wet winter conditions might be a problem, plant them in raised beds or rock gardens and amend the soil with grit when planting to improve drainage. In the North, grow them in containers, moving the plants outdoors for summer and indoors in fall for overwintering. In containers or in the ground, plant the bulbs in spring, setting them with the necks above the soil surface. Keep the soil nearly dry until plants sprout, then keep the soil evenly moist once plants are growing actively. Gradually withhold water as the leaves begin to die back. To overwinter bulbs indoors, bring the containers indoors after the foliage has died back and keep them in a cool (45° to 50°F), dry place. The soil should remain nearly, but not completely, dry. Plants can remain in the same containers for several years. Propagate by offsets in late winter or early spring or by seeds. Where hardy, plants often self-sow.

H. robustus

h. roe-BUS-tus. Formerly *Zephyranthes robusta.* An 8- to 12-inch-tall species from Brazil and Argentina with grassy leaves that appear about the time the flower stalks emerge. Bears solitary, 2¹/₂-inch-wide pale pink flowers in summer. **Zones 7 to 11**.

H. tubispathus

h. too-bih-SPAY-thus. Formerly *H. andersonii, H. texanus, Zephyranthes andersonii.* A 4- to 6-inch-tall species found from Texas south to Argentina and Chile. Bears leaves that emerge after the flower stalks and solitary 1-inch-wide trumpets in summer in shades of yellow, orange, or orange-red. **Zones 9 to 11**.

Haemanthus

hee-MAN-thus. Amaryllis family, Amaryllidaceae.

Considering the common name "blood lily," it's not surprising *Haemanthus* species produce exotic-looking blooms. About 21 species belong to this genus, all tender perennials that have tunicate bulbs and are native to Africa, especially South Africa. They bear umbels of tiny, tightly packed flowers that resemble a shaving brush or a rounded paint brush. The umbels are surrounded by showy petal-like bracts (technically these are spathe valves) that make the clusters of flowers look as if they were a single bloom. The botanical name refers to the red color of the bracts of some species: it is from the Greek *haima*, meaning "blood," and *anthos*, "flower." The individual flowers in the umbels have six petal-like tepals. They also have six showy, protruding stamens that add to the brushlike appearance. Plants have deciduous or evergreen leaves that are arranged in two ranks, or rows; range from strap shaped to rounded; and vary from 1 to about 1¹/₂ feet long. Flowers are followed by showy, round berries.

HOW TO GROW

Select a spot in partial shade with rich, well-drained soil. Neutral to alkaline soil pH is best. Like many South African natives, blood lilies require evenly moist soil when they are growing actively and dry conditions when dormant. Dormancy period varies from species to species. Plant the bulbs in fall with the necks just above the soil surface. Grow these bulbs in containers in all but Zone 10 or 11 gardens that can offer dry conditions when the plants are dormant. Water regularly when the plants are growing actively. As the leaves of deciduous species turn yellow, gradually withhold water. Keep evergreen species just barely moist

Habranthus robustus

Haemanthus albiflos

Hakonechloa macra 'Aureola'

when they are dormant; deciduous species can be stored dry. Overwinter them in a spot that does not drop below about 50°F. Plants resent having their roots and bulbs disturbed, and they thrive for years without needing to be divided. Also, container-grown blood lilies bloom best when they are pot-bound, so repot only if necessary just when new growth resumes. Propagate by separating offsets in early spring or by seeds.

H. albiflos

h. AL-bih-floss. SHAVING-BRUSH PLANT, WHITE PAINT-BRUSH. Evergreen 6- to 12-inch-tall species with strap-shaped leaves that rests in summer. In fall, new leaves appear along with brushlike 2- to 3-inch-wide umbels of up to 50 white flowers surrounded by white bracts with green veins. The flowers are followed by white to red berries. **Zones 10 and 11**.

H. coccineus

h. kok-SIN-ee-us. BLOOD LILY, CAPE TULIP. Deciduous 10- to 14-inch-tall species with elliptic to strap-shaped leaves. Dormant until mid- to late summer. From late summer to fall, shortly before the leaves appear, plants produce 2- to 4-inch-wide umbels of up to 100 densely packed red flowers with yellow stamens that are surrounded by eight very showy,

waxy red bracts. The flowers are followed by clusters of white to pink berries. **Zones 10 to 11**.

Hakonechloa

hah-koh-neh-KLOH-uh. Grass family, Poaceae.

A handsome ornamental grass native to Japan is the only species in this genus. Commonly known as Hakone grass, it produces mounds of arching, bamboolike foliage and small panicles of flowers borne among the leaves in mid- to late summer. The botanical name combines the Greek *chloa*, meaning "grass," with *hakone* for Mount Hakone, one of the mountains on Japan's main island, where the grass is found.

HOW TO GROW

Select a site in partial shade with rich, evenly moist, well-drained soil. Although this is a warm-season grass, the plants grow best in cool, moist conditions. In areas with cool summers, plants thrive in full sun, but where summers are hot, partial shade is best. Variegated cultivars usually are most

colorful in partial shade. The plants spread gradually, but not invasively, by rhizomes. Cut the foliage back in spring. To propagate, divide plants in spring. The species can be grown from seeds, but variegated cultivars do not come true.

H. macra

h. MAK-ruh. HAKONE GRASS. Handsome 1½- to 2-foot-tall grass forming 2-foot-wide mounds of arching, linear, bamboolike leaves. 'Aureola' bears stunning green-and-yellow-striped leaves. **Zones 5 to 9**.

Halesia

Hah-LEE-zee-ah. Styrax family, Styracaceae.

This genus contains five species of trees and shrubs from North America and China. All have white, bell-shaped flowers in spring; dry, silvery, winged seed capsules; and alternate, toothed leaves.

HOW TO GROW

Plant in full sun to partial shade and humus-rich, well-drained, acid soil. Provide plentiful moisture, especially if grown in the sun. Sensitive to drought; benefits from an organic mulch. Prune immediately after flowering, removing lower limbs and training to a single trunk when young if desired. Pest-free, but becomes chlorotic in alkaline soil.

H. carolina

h. kare-oh-lie-nuh. CAROLINA SILVERBELL. Formerly *H. tetraptera*. This charming spring bloomer has a broad, rounded shape with low, horizontal or ascending branches and several trunks. It reaches 20 to 30 feet tall and 35 feet wide. Bell-shaped, 1-

inch-long, snow-white blossoms dangle in delicate clusters from the undersides of the tree's branches for 2 weeks in mid- to late spring. The dark yellow-green, oval leaves have pointed tips and measure 4 inches long. Fall color develops early and is a pleasing yellow. The 2-inch-long fruits have four wings and are subtle but pretty in fall, ripening from green to tan. Trunk bark has white furrows and gray-brown plates. A graceful tree that is beautiful when planted on a hillside and viewed from below. From southeastern North America. **Zones 5 to 9**.

CULTIVARS AND SIMILAR SPECIES

H. diptera (two-winged silverbell) flowers 2 weeks later than *H. carolina* and has two-winged seeds. *H. diptera* var. *Magniflora* bears large, showy flowers. *H. monticola* (mountain silverbell) is very similar to *H. carolina* but grows to 60 feet and has larger flowers and leaves and a strong central leader.

Hamamelis

ham-uh-MEL-iss. Witch-hazel family, Hamamelidaceae.

You may be more familiar with these plants for the soothing, astringent extract made from their bark. Their common name, "witch hazel," comes from an Anglo-Saxon word, *wych*, meaning "to bend" and referring to the plants' former use in dowsing for water. As an ornamental, witch hazel has an equally valuable role to play. There are only five species, from North America and eastern Asia — all deciduous and ranging in habit from spreading shrubs to small trees — but many garden-worthy hybrids and cultivars. Their fragrant, straplike flowers bloom in what are often the bleakest weeks of fall or winter, and the autumn foliage can be colorful as well. The leaves have shallow teeth and paired veins.

HOW TO GROW

Give witch hazel moisture-retentive, moderately fertile soil in full

Halesia carolina

Halesia carolina

Hamamelis virginiana

Hamamelis mollis

sun or partial shade. *H. vernalis* may tolerate some alkalinity, but most species prefer acid soil. Take note of the bloom time of the variety you choose, and site it to catch morning or evening sun where it can be seen from a window or frequently used path. Branches can be forced to bloom indoors. Pruning should be minimal, but you can control size and shape by pinching. Seeds take a full year to ripen after the flowers bloom, then "explode" from the pod, so they need to be closely monitored if you want to collect them. The seeds require warm and then cold stratification to germinate. Witch hazels can also be propagated from cuttings taken in midspring.

H. × intermedia

h. × in-ter-MEE-dee-uh. A hybrid that may grow 15 to 20 feet tall, often spreading wider, upright and sparsely branched. The flowers, which appear in mid- to late winter on bare branches, are not as fragrant as those of most species. Fall foliage is yellow on yellow-flowered plants but can be reddish purple on the red-flowered forms. Flowers of 'Arnold Promise' are large and bright yellow. Those of 'Diane' (a Pennsylvania Horticultural Society award winner) are red. 'Jelena' bears flowers that are red at the base, fading to orange and then yellow at the tips. 'Ruby Glow' blooms reddish copper. **Zones 5 to 9**.

H. mollis

h. MOLL-iss. CHINESE WITCH HAZEL. A compact species, 10 to 15 feet tall, spreading to 20 feet or more. Its yellow flowers, with reddish brown calyx cups, are especially fragrant and appear in late winter or early spring. Fall foliage ranges from clear yellow to orange-yellow. 'Pallida' has pale yellow flowers and has been honored by the Pennsylvania Horticultural Society. **Zones 5 to 9**.

H. vernalis

h. ver-NAL-iss. VERNAL WITCH HAZEL. A native of gravelly streambanks in the Ozarks, usually about 10 feet tall and spreading

Hamamelis × intermedia 'Arnold Promise'

wider, this species is multi-stemmed and may sucker heavily to form colonies. The red to yellow flowers, which bloom in late winter as the persistent leaves finally begin to fall, are generally considered the most fragrant of all. Autumn foliage is bright yellow. **Zones 4 to 8**.

H. virginiana

h. ver-jin-ee-AH-nuh. COMMON WITCH HAZEL. A widespread eastern native, this understory shrub is usually 15 to 20 feet tall, somewhat less in width. The habit is open crowned with crooked branching that adds to winter interest. Fragrant yellow flowers appear late fall to early winter, sometimes hidden by the leaves as they turn yellow. **Zones 3 to 8**.

Hebe

HEE-bee. Figwort family, Scrophulariaceae.

This genus, named for Hebe, the Greek goddess of youth, contains about 100 species of evergreen shrubs, mostly from coastal areas of New Zealand. Many are low growing or prostrate, and in mild areas they make good ground covers or rock-garden plants. Often called shrubby veronicas, for their spiky flowers' resemblance to those of that more herbaceous genus, they sometimes have colored or variegated foliage.

HOW TO GROW

Hebes need a cool maritime climate without bitterly cold winters. Such conditions are found throughout much of the Pacific Coast. Some species are tolerant of the more humid summer conditions along the Gulf and southern Atlantic coasts. Give hebes good

Hebe speciosa 'Violacea'

drainage in full sun; partial shade is better in the hottest part of their range. Soil should be poor to average, neutral to alkaline. They tolerate pollution, salt, and coastal wind but not dry heat. The largest species listed here can be used as low hedges as well as rock garden plants. Deadhead; prune lightly if needed. Propagate semiripe cuttings with bottom heat, in late summer.

H. 'Alicia Amherst'

Upright to about 4 feet tall, this cultivar has glossy 4-inch leaves. Somewhat hardier than other hebes, it produces 3-inch racemes of deep violet flowers in late summer or fall. **Zones 9 and 10**.

H. 'Amy'

Growing to 4 feet tall, 'Amy' has bronze-purple foliage in winter and on new growth. Violet-purple flowers in 2-inch spikes bloom in late summer. **Zones 9 and 10**.

H. 'Autumn Glory'

Spreading and 2½ feet tall, this cultivar bears leaves that have reddish purple edge and bright purple flowers that bloom from midsummer into winter. **Zones 9 and 10**.

H. diosmifolia

h. dye-ahs-mih-FOE-lee-uh. This rounded shrub grows 2 to 5 feet tall and wide, with its leaves smaller than those of most species, 1 inch or less long and ¼ inch wide. Rounded clusters of white to lavender flowers bloom in summer at the branch tips. **Zones 9 and 10**.

H. glaucophylla

h. glaw-koh-FYE-luh. This low shrub tends to stay under 12 inches tall but spreads farther. It has dense,

Hedera canariensis 'Gloire de Marengo'

gray-green leaves and white flowers. **Zones 8 to 10.**

h. pinguifolia

h. pin-gwih-FOE-lee-uh. 'Pagei' is a mounding shrublet that reaches 18 inches tall and is frequently planted in large landscapes but can be massed for smaller applications. The petite, blue-gray foliage shows off the white flowers in early summer. 'Sutherlandii' masses well and is a relatively new introduction from New Zealand. **Zones 8 to 10.**

H. speciosa

h. spee-see-OH-suh. A rounded shrub 3 to 6 feet tall, this species has large glossy leaves up to 4 inches long and 2 inches wide. The summer flower spikes are brilliant hues of cerise to purple. **Zones 9 and 10.**

H. 'Youngii'

Also listed as *H.* 'Carl Teschner.' This exceptionally fine ground-covering hebe has tiny, dark green leaves and is covered with small purple-and-white flowers in summer. **Zones 8 and 9.**

Hedera

HED-er-uh. Ivy family, Araliaceae.

Most North American gardeners know the common ivy, *H. helix,* the hardiest of the 15 species native from western Europe to Japan. These evergreen, woody vines have alternate, often lobed leaves. There are hundreds of named selections based on minor but attractive variations in leaf shape, size, mottling, and variegation. Hederas have contrasting juvenile and adult foliage. As long as the plant is vining, the leaves are juvenile. In mature plants, woody, nonclimbing branches grow out from the main vine mass. It is these branches that have the adult foliage, as well as the insignificant greenish white flowers and dark fruits. Fruits are very attractive to birds. Given the plants' ability to colonize large areas, they are invasive in the Pacific Northwest and parts of the South.

HOW TO GROW

Ivy is not particular as to soil, site, or growing conditions, provided its very basic needs are met. Ivy prefers organic, moist soil and partial shade. Given those conditions, it will grow extensively onto adjacent walls, tree trunks, signs, or other stationary objects. Plants will tolerate very poor soils as long as they are not dry. Variegated plants need sun to develop their coloration fully.

H. canariensis

h. kan-are-ee-EN-sis. ALGERIAN IVY. Native to the Canary Islands, off the coast of northern Africa, this species has large, glossy, evergreen foliage that creates a coarse texture and looks best at a distance. Plants can be mowed occasionally to maintain tidiness. This plant is very adaptable, as seen by its use along California freeways. 'Gloire de Marengo' ('Variegata') has elegant foliage with gray, green, and white markings. **Zones 8 to 10.**

H. colchica

h. KOLE-chi-kuh. PERSIAN IVY. This species is hardier than *H. canariensis.* 'Dentata' has leaf peti-oles flushed with purple. 'Dentata Variegata' has leaves with gray-green and primrose yellow markings. 'Sulphur Heart' ('Paddy's Pride') reverses the above patterns, with leaf veins and centers in creamy yellow. **Zones 7 to 10.**

H. helix

h. HEE-liks. ENGLISH IVY. This is the hardiest ivy. At its northern limit, it should be grown on north-facing slopes, sides of buildings, and similar areas protected from winter sun. There are hundreds of named cultivars in the trade, distinguished by leaf shape, size, glossiness, and color. 'Baltica' is dark green with white veins and is the hardiest selection, having been found originally near the Baltic Sea. 'Buttercup' has small yellow leaves and requires some sun for best color. 'Gold Heart' bears green leaves with pale-colored centers. 'Needlepoint' has small, green, sharply pointed leaves and needs some shade; it is popular in the South. 'Sagittifolia' produces grayish green, arrow-shaped leaves. 'Spetchley' has tiny leaves and forms a dense cover; it is superb for small areas. **Zones 4 to 9.**

Hedychium

heh-DEE-kee-um. Ginger family, Zingiberaceae.

Hedychium species, commonly known as gingers or ginger lilies, are tender perennials that grow from fleshy, branching rhizomes. About 40 species belong to the genus, nearly all native to the tropics of Asia, especially India. One species is native to Madagascar. Plants bear reedlike stems with large lance-shaped leaves arranged in two rows, or ranks, up the stems. The flowers often are fragrant and are carried in showy, dense, spike-like racemes. Individual blooms are two-lipped and tubular to somewhat trumpet shaped and come in white as well as shades of yellow and orange-red.

HOW TO GROW

Give these tropical plants a spot in full sun to partial shade and deeply prepared, moist soil that is rich in organic matter. They thrive in areas with warm summers and high humidity and are ideal for gardens in the tropics and sub-tropics or for adding an exotic touch to more northern gardens in summer. Where hardy, grow them outdoors year-round. Plant the tubers just below the soil surface. Where marginally hardy, look for a warm, sheltered spot, such as at the base of a south-facing wall, and mulch plants heavily over winter. In the North, plant the rhizomes out in spring after the soil has warmed up. In Zone 7 and north, start the rhizomes indoors several weeks before the last spring frost date to give them a head start. Or, grow these plants in containers year-round.

To overwinter, either bring con-

Hedychium coccineum

tainers indoors or dig the rhizomes after a light frost and cut back the tops. Overwinter the plants right in the pots — keep the soil nearly dry in winter — or store the rhizomes in barely damp vermiculite, peat moss, or sand in a cool (50° to 55°F), dry place. Inspect rhizomes occasionally in winter: discard rotted pieces or cut away rotted portions and dust cuts with sulfur. Occasionally sprinkle the vermiculite or other medium used to pack them with water to keep the roots from shriveling. Replant in spring. Propagate by dividing the rhizomes in spring.

H. coccineum

h. kok-SIN-ee-um. RED GINGER LILY, SCARLET GINGER LILY, ORANGE BOTTLE-BRUSH GINGER. A 6-foot-tall species with fragrant 10-inch-long flower clusters from late summer to fall in shades of red, orange-red, orange, pink, or white. **Zones 8 to 10.**

H. coronarium

h. kor-oh-NAIR-ee-um. GARLAND FLOWER, WHITE GINGER LILY. A 3- to 6-foot-tall species with extremely fragrant 8-inch-long racemes of white flowers with a touch of yellow at the base of the petals from mid- to late summer. *H. coronarium* var. *chrysoleum* and its cultivar 'Yellow Spot' bear flowers with yellow blotches at the base. Best in partial shade. **Zones 7 to 11.**

H. gardnerianum

h. gard-ner-ee-AH-num. KAHILI GINGER. A 4- to 6-foot-tall spe-

cies. From late summer to fall, it bears 10- to 12-inch-long racemes of fragrant yellow flowers that have showy red stamens. **Zones 8 to 11.**

H. greenii

h. GREE-nee-eye. A 4- to 6-foot-tall species with maroon stems and green leaves tinged with maroon on their undersides. In summer, it bears 5-inch-long racemes of bright red flowers that are not fragrant. **Zones 7 or 8 to 11.**

H. hybrids

A variety of ginger hybrids have been introduced to the market. 'Anne Bishop' bears showy, fragrant orange flowers in summer. 'Elizabeth' has raspberry pink flowers. 'Kinkaku' is a vigorous selection with very fragrant peach-colored flowers. 'Lemon Beauty' bears fragrant yellow flowers. Hybrids are hardy from **Zones 7 or 8 to 11.**

Helenium

hel-EE-nee-um. Aster family, Asteraceae.

The genus *Helenium* contains about 40 species of annuals, biennials, and clump-forming perennials that grow naturally in areas with moist soils and along woodland edges. The perennials in the genus are prized for their late-season daisylike flower heads in shades of yellow, orange, bronze, and red. The flower heads consist of ray florets, commonly called petals, surrounding dense, buttonlike centers of disk florets.

Helianthemum 'Wisley Pink'

Leaves usually are ovate to inversely lance shaped. Although called sneezeweeds, the plants do not cause sneezing, but contact with the foliage can cause an allergic skin reaction, and all parts of the plants are poisonous if eaten. The botanical name honors Helen of Troy, but these plants are native to North and Central America.

HOW TO GROW

Give sneezeweeds full sun and rich, evenly moist, well-drained soil. *H. autumnale* also grows in constantly moist to wet conditions, while *H. hoopesii* tolerates dry soil. Feed plants in spring with a balanced organic fertilizer or a topdressing of compost or well-rotted manure. Water during dry weather. Taller-growing cultivars require staking. Pinching in midsummer reduces the ultimate height of the plants and keeps them compact. Sneezeweeds perform best when divided frequently: dig them every 3 to 4 years in spring. Propagate named cultivars by division in early spring or by cuttings taken from shoots at the base of the plant in spring or early summer. The species are also easy to propagate from seeds.

H. autumnale

h. aw-tum-NAL-ee. COMMON SNEEZEWEED. Native North American perennial ranging from 2 to 5 feet tall and forming 2- to 3-

foot-wide clumps. From late summer to fall, it bears 2- to 3-inch-wide yellow flowers with brown centers and wedge-shaped petals that are toothed at the ends. Cultivars are more often grown than the species. Cultivars that stay under 3 feet include yellow-flowered 'Butterpat'; bronze-red 'Crimson Beauty'; and early-blooming, coppery red 'Moerheim Beauty', which blooms from early to late summer. 'Zimbelstern', which bears yellow-brown flowers on 4-foot plants, also blooms early — from mid- to late summer. 'Brilliant', a 4- to 5-foot cultivar, produces bronze-red flowers in late summer. 'Kugelsonne' is a strong-stemmed 5-foot cultivar with yellow flowers. **Zones 3 to 8.**

H. hoopesii

h. HOOPS-ee-eye. ORANGE SNEEZEWEED. A 2- to 3-foot-tall North American native forming 2-foot-wide clumps. Bears yellow to orange 3-inch-wide flowers in early to midsummer. **Zones 3 to 7.**

Helianthemum

hee-lee-AN-thuh-mum. Rock-rose family, Cistaceae.

The 110 species of *Helianthemum* are native from Europe, the Mediterranean region, and northern Africa to central Asia. They are shallow-rooted, dwarf or prostrate shrubs with evergreen or semievergreen leaves that usually measure less than 1 inch long. Leaves are elliptic and vary in grayness. Flowers measure up to 1 inch or more across, have five petals (double forms exist), and look like miniature wild roses — hence the common names "sun rose" and "rock rose." Each flower lasts only

Helenium autumnale 'Butterpat'

Helenium autumnale

a day, but numerous flowers are carried on each flower stalk, so the blooming period spans several weeks. Colors are in warm sunset shades of yellow, orange, copper, pink, and white. The botanical name is Greek and means "sun flower."

HOW TO GROW

Helianthemums make excellent ground covers on dry sunny banks where they will not be subject to winter wet collecting around their stems and roots. They are not particular about soil pH, but they do dislike humidity and are adapted to the kind of dry summers typical of the American West and Mediterranean climates. For best growth as a ground cover, shear plants lightly after bloom to encourage spreading and branching.

H. hybrids

Most of the best selections are hybrids, commonly listed as *H. nummularium* hybrids. They differ in foliage grayness and flower color. 'Brunette' bears green leaves and dark orange flowers. 'Mesa Wine' has dark green leaves and dark red flowers. 'Saint Mary's' has dark green leaves and white flowers. 'Stoplight' features grayish green leaves and red flowers. 'Wisley Pink' produces gray foliage and pink flowers. 'Wisley Primrose' has gray-green foliage and pale yellow flowers. **Zones 6 to 9.**

Helianthus

hee-lee-AN-thuss. Aster family, Asteraceae.

Known by gardeners and nongardeners alike as sunflowers, *Helianthus* species are annuals and perennials native to North, Central, and South America. The genus contains about 70 to 80 species of usually tall, often coarse plants with showy, daisylike flowers in shades of yellow and gold. The flowers, borne from summer to fall, consist of ray florets, or "petals," surrounding dense centers of disk florets, which produce the seeds. Sunflowers have large, coarse leaves that are oval or lance or heart shaped. Both the common and botanical names celebrate the fact that these are plants for full sun: *Helianthus* is from the Greek *helios*, meaning "sun," and *anthos*, "flower."

HOW TO GROW

Full sun and average soil that is moist but well drained are all these plants require. A few species

Helianthus annuus

of perennials — *H. angustifolius, H. decapetalus, H. divaricatus,* and *H. strumosus* — thrive in sites that receive shade for part of the day or high, dappled shade (but good light) all day. *H. angustifolius, H. decapetalus,* and *H. maximiliani* also grow in wet soil. Pinch stem tips once in early summer or midsummer — or both times — if you want to curtail height and encourage branching. Plants growing in shady or windy spots may need staking.

Sow annual sunflowers outdoors after danger of frost has passed. Or sow into individual pots indoors 4 to 6 weeks before the last spring frost date at 65° to 70°F. Germination takes about 2 weeks. Sunflowers are large plants best kept away from less vigorous

Helianthus maximiliani

neighbors; also, their roots give off a chemical that inhibits growth of some plants. Plant them in drifts at the back of borders and along fences, as accents, or in gardens designed to attract birds or butterflies.

H. angustifolius

h. an-gus-tih-FOE-lee-us. SWAMP SUNFLOWER. A 4- to 8-foot-tall North American native species with lance-shaped leaves and branched clusters of yellow 3-inch-wide flower heads with purple to brown centers from early to midfall. **Zones 6 to 9.**

H. annuus

h. AN-yew-us. ANNUAL SUNFLOWER, COMMON SUNFLOWER. A vigorous, fast-grow-

Helianthus salicifolius

ing annual with roughly hairy, heart-shaped leaves that can range from 1 to 15 feet tall, depending on the cultivar. Flowers are single, semidouble, or double and range from 4 to 12 inches across or more. Many cultivars are available. Two developed for seed production are 6-foot-tall 'Mammoth Russian' and 11-foot 'Russian Giant'; both bear 10- to 12-inch-wide yellow flowers. 'Holiday' offers 3- to 5-inch, classic yellow sunflowers on well-branched, 5- to 7-foot plants. 'Valentine' bears lemon yellow, 5- to 6-inch-wide, dark-centered flowers on 5-foot plants. Dwarf cultivars include golden yellow, 10- to 15-inch-tall 'Big Smile' and 3-foot-tall 'Teddy Bear', which has double, golden yellow flowers. 'Autumn Beauty' bears 8-inch-wide blooms in shades of yellow, bronze, maroon, and purple-red on well-branched, 5-foot plants. 'Velvet Queen' produces burgundy and maroon, 5-inch flowers on 5-foot plants. Warm-weather annual.

H. argophyllus

h. are-go-FILL-us. SILVER-LEAVED SUNFLOWER. A 3- to 6-foot annual native from Texas to Florida with heavily branched stems and white, silky-hairy, oval leaves. Bears 3-inch-wide flowers with yellow petals and dark purple centers. Warm-weather annual.

H. debilis ssp. cucumerifolius

h. deh-BILL-iss ssp. kew-kew-mer-ih-FOE-lee-us. CUCUMBER-LEAVED SUNFLOWER. A 3-foot-tall annual native from Texas to Florida with hairy, toothed leaves and stems mottled in purple. Bears 5- to 6-inch-wide yellow flowers. 'Italian White' produces white to creamy yellow, 4- to 5-inch-wide flowers on well-branched, 4- to 5-foot-tall plants. Warm-weather annual.

H. decapetalus
h. dek-ah-PET-ah-lus. Thin-leaved Sunflower. Rhizomatous 4- to 5-foot-tall North American native bearing yellow 2- to 3-inch-wide flower heads with yellow centers from late summer to midfall. **Zones 4 to 8.**

H. divaricatus
h. dih-vair-ih-KAH-tus. Woodland Sunflower. A 2- to 6-foot-tall North American native with yellow 2-inch-wide flower heads with yellow centers from midsummer to midfall. **Zones 3 to 8.**

H. maximiliani
h. max-ih-mil-lee-AN-ee. Maximilian Sunflower. A 4- to 10-foot-tall North American native with clusters of 2- to 3-inch-wide yellow flowers with brown centers from late summer to fall. Will grow in wet soil. **Zones 3 to 8.**

H. × multiflorus
h. × mul-tih-FLOR-us. Many-flowered Sunflower. A 3- to 5-foot-tall hybrid *(H. annuus × H. decapetalus)*. Bears golden yellow flowers, to 5 inches across, from late summer to midfall. Double-flowered cultivars, including 'Flore Pleno' and 'Loddon Gold', are available. **Zones 5 to 9.**

H. salicifolius
h. sah-lih-sih-FOE-lee-us. Willow-leaved Sunflower. A 3- to 7-foot-tall North American native with clusters of golden yellow 2- to 3-inch-wide flowers from early to midfall. **Zones 3 or 4 to 8.**

H. strumosus
h. strew-MOE-sus. Pale-leaved Wood Sunflower. A 3- to 6-foot-tall North American native bearing yellow 4^1/$_2$-inch-wide flowers with yellow centers from midsummer to early fall. **Zones 4 to 9.**

H. tuberosus
h. too-ber-OH-sus. Jerusalem Artichoke. Extremely vigorous to invasive, rhizomatous 5- to 10-foot-tall North American native producing edible, potato-like tubers. Bears 4-inch-wide flower

Helichrysum italicum ssp. *serotinum*

heads with yellow petals and centers in fall. **Zones 4 to 9.**

Helichrysum
hel-ih-KRY-sum. Aster family, Asteraceae.

The genus *Helichrysum* comprises some 500 species of annuals, perennials, and subshrubs with woolly or hairy leaves and yellow to golden flower heads. Unlike those of many aster-family members, the blooms have only disk florets — they lack true "petals," or ray florets. Instead many have colorful, papery, petal-like bracts that surround the flower heads. Others are grown primarily for their silvery gray foliage.

HOW TO GROW
Give these plants a site in full sun with poor to average, well-drained soil. Sow seeds of annuals indoors 6 to 8 weeks before the last spring frost date at 65° to 70°F. Just press the seeds into the soil surface, as they need light to germinate; germination takes 1 to 3 weeks. Perennial species can be replaced annually, but they likewise are easy to grow from cuttings taken in summer, which can be used to overwinter the plants. They also can be propagated by division in spring. Water during very dry weather. Trim species grown for foliage as needed to keep them shapely. On species grown for foliage, many gardeners remove the flowers as they appear. Use *Helichrysum* species as fillers in low mixed plantings, as edging plants or in containers.

H. italicum ssp. *serotinum*
h. ih-TAL-ih-kum ssp. ser-oh-TYE-num. Curry Plant. Formerly *H. serotinum*. A tender, densely

branched, 1^1/$_2$-foot subshrub with narrow, grayish white, woolly leaves that have an intense, currylike fragrance but no culinary value. Clusters of tiny, ^{1}/$_8$-inch, bottlebrush-like, golden yellow flowers appear from summer to fall. **Zones 7 to 10**, or grow as a warm-weather annual.

H. petiolare
h. pet-ee-oh-LAH-ree. Licorice Plant. This tender evergreen shrub from South Africa is often grown as an annual. It makes a good plant for a hanging basket because of its trailing stems, which can reach 4 feet long, and what look like stacks of woolly gray, heart-shaped leaves that smell slightly of licorice when crushed. The flowers are insignificant. 'Limelight' has chartreuse foliage, and the leaves of 'Variegata' are marked with white. **Zones 10 and 11**, or grow as a warm-weather annual.

Helictotrichon
hel-ick-toe-TRY-kon. Grass family, Poaceae.

Of the 50 species of clump-forming grasses in this genus, one species, commonly known as blue oat grass, is grown as an ornamental. *Helictotrichon* species bear linear green or gray-blue leaves and erect panicles of flattened flower spikelets.

HOW TO GROW
Select a site in full sun to light shade with poor to average, well-drained soil. Plants may succumb to root rot in heavy clay and do not grow well in areas with hot, humid summers. Cut back plants in early spring. For propagation,

Helictotrichon sempervirens

divide clumps in spring or sow seeds.

H. sempervirens
h. sem-per-VIE-renz. Blue Oat Grass. Clump-forming, cool-season grass with 2-foot-tall, 2-foot-wide clumps of erect, evergreen to semievergreen leaves that are gray-blue. Bears 3- to 4-foot-tall spikes of yellow oatlike seed heads in early summer. **Zones 4 to 9.**

Heliopsis
hee-lee-OP-sis. Aster family, Asteraceae.

Commonly called oxeyes, false sunflowers, and sunflower heliopsis, *Heliopsis* species are native North American wildflowers that bear sunflower-like flower heads with golden yellow ray florets (the "petals") and centers (or "eyes") with darker yellow disk florets. About 12 or 13 species belong to the genus, all perennials native to dry prairies and woodlands. The plants are coarsely branched and bear ovate to lance-shaped leaves with toothed margins. Oxeyes differ from true sunflowers *(Helianthus)* in that their ray florets are fertile rather than sterile. The botanical name is from the Greek *helios*, meaning "sun," and *opsis*, "resembling."

Heliopsis helianthoides

Heliopsis helianthoides

HOW TO GROW

Select a site in full sun or partial shade with average to rich soil. Evenly moist, well-drained soil is best, but plants tolerate dry conditions. Pinch and deadhead oxeyes just as you would sunflowers. Plants growing in rich, moist soil may need dividing frequently, about every 2 to 3 years. Propagate by dividing the clumps in spring or fall or by sowing seeds.

H. helianthoides

h. hee-lee-an-THOY-deez. OXEYE. A 3- to 6-foot-tall North American native wildflower spreading from 2 to 4 feet. It bears yellow $1^1/2$- to 3-inch-wide flower heads from midsummer to early fall. *H. helianthoides* ssp. *scabra* is more compact than the species — to about 3 feet — and a better garden plant. Its cultivars 'Gold Greenheart' ('Goldgrünherz'), which bears lemon yellow flowers; bright yellow 'Light of Loddon'; and golden yellow 'Sommersonne' ('Summer Sun') are all good choices with semidouble or double flowers. **Zones 4 to 9.**

Heliotropium

hee-lee-oh-TROW-pee-um. Borage family, Boraginaceae.

Heliotropium contains some 250 species of annuals, perennials, subshrubs, and shrubs with entire, roughly hairy leaves and flattened to rounded clusters of small, funnel-shaped flowers in shades of lavender, purple, white, or sometimes yellow. They are native to tropical and subtropical regions in the Americas as well as the Canary Islands and islands of the Pacific. One species is a popular tender perennial or annual grown for its richly fragrant flowers.

HOW TO GROW

Select a site in full sun or partial shade with rich, well-drained soil. In areas with hot summers, a site with afternoon shade is best. Sow seeds indoors 10 to 12 weeks before the last spring frost date at 70° to 75°F. Germination takes 4 to 6 weeks. Pinch seedlings and young plants to encourage branching and bushy growth. Move them outdoors a few weeks after the last frost date, once the soil has warmed to about 60°F and the weather has settled. Water regularly and feed plants monthly, especially container-grown ones. Deadheading prolongs bloom.

Heliotropium arborescens 'Marine'

Grow heliotropes *(H. arborescens)* as bedding plants replaced annually, or overwinter them indoors in a bright, cool (50° to 55°F) spot. Even in Zone 10, they need protection from the coldest temperatures. Seed-grown plants are slow and will vary in fragrance and color; for uniform plants and quick results, propagate by cuttings. Take them in late summer for overwintering indoors, or bring in whole, container-grown plants to use as stock plants for cuttings in spring. Prune to shape plants in late winter or early spring: cut them back hard if necessary.

Use heliotropes in containers and mixed plantings; dwarf types are good edging plants. They can also be grown as standards or shrubs overwintered indoors. Their flowers attract butterflies.

H. arborescens

h. are-bore-ESS-enz. HELIOTROPE, CHERRY PIE. A tender shrub that can reach 4 feet but is considerably shorter in containers, this species produces oval to lance-shaped, dark green leaves. Bears showy, 3- to 4-inch-wide clusters of tiny flowers in lavender, violet, or white in summer. Many, but not all, cultivars have a rich vanilla-like fragrance. 'Marine' is a dwarf, $1^1/2$-foot-tall cultivar. Tender perennial, or grow as a warm-weather annual.

Helleborus × hybridus

Helleborus

hel-eh-BORE-us. Buttercup family, Ranunculaceae.

Long-lived, shade-loving hellebores are treasured by gardeners not only for their early-season bloom but also for their handsome evergreen or semievergreen foliage. About 15 species belong to the genus, all perennials — several with shrubby habits. They have leathery, usually dark green leaves divided into lobes or leaflets that often are toothed. The flowers are borne singly or in small clusters in winter and early spring and come in subtle shades of cream, purple, dusty mauve, cream-pink, and green. The showy parts of the flowers are not true petals but petal-like sepals, which remain attractive for 2 to even 4 months as seed capsules form. All parts of the plants are poisonous if ingested, and the sap from bruised leaves can cause a skin rash in some individuals.

HOW TO GROW

Plant hellebores in light to full shade with rich, evenly moist, well-drained soil. Neutral to slightly alkaline pH is best, although *H. × hybridus* tolerates slightly acid soil. A sheltered site protected from winter winds helps keep the evergreen foliage at its best. On shrubby species, which have biennial stems (they produce foliage the first year, flowers the second), cut back the stems that have already bloomed to make room for new growth. Leave some stems if you want seedlings.

Once planted, hellebores are best left undisturbed and thrive for years without needing division. Established clumps spread from about 1 to 1½ feet. If you must move them, or want to divide the clumps, dig them in spring after flowering. Handle the plants carefully. Do not divide *H. argutifolius* or *H. foetidus:* the rhizomes of these shrubby species are very short, and division is nearly always fatal. The easiest way to propagate hellebores is to dig self-sown seedlings in spring or summer and replant them.

H. argutifolius

h. are-goo-tih-FOE-lee-us. CORSICAN HELLEBORE. Shrubby species that ranges from 1½ to 2 feet in height and bears clusters of nodding, pale green, bowl-shaped, 1- to 2-inch-wide flowers from late winter to early spring. **Zones 6 or 7 to 9.**

H. atrorubens

h. ah-trow-ROO-benz. A 1-foot-tall perennial bearing purple-blushed leaves and small clusters of purple, saucer-shaped, 1½- to 2-inch-wide flowers from late winter into spring. **Zones 5 to 9.**

H. foetidus

h. FEH-tid-us. STINKING HELLEBORE. Shrubby species ranging from 1½ to 2 feet tall and bearing handsome, deeply cut leaves with narrow leaflets. Leaves have an un-

pleasant scent when crushed. Produces large showy clusters of nodding, bell-shaped ½- to 1-inch green flowers from midwinter to early spring. **Zones 6 to 9; to Zone 5 with winter protection.**

H. × hybridus

h. × HI-brih-dus. LENTEN ROSE. Often listed as *H. orientalis.* A 1- to 1½-foot-tall perennial with leathery leaves and loose, showy clusters of outward-facing, saucer-shaped, 2- to 3-inch-wide flowers. Blooms come from late winter to early spring in shades of cream, greenish white, white, purple, or mauve. **Zones 4 to 9.**

H. niger

h. NYE-jer. CHRISTMAS ROSE. A low-growing 12- to 15-inch-tall species with saucer-shaped, 2- to 3-inch-wide flowers that are white or white flushed with pink. Blooms are borne one per stem or occasionally in clusters of two or three. Plants can bloom beginning in early winter but generally flower in early spring. **Zones 4 to 8.**

H. purpurascens

h. pur-pur-AS-scens. A 4- to 12-inch perennial with loose clusters of cup-shaped, 1½- to 3-inch flowers from midwinter to early spring in shades of purple or pinkish purple flushed with green. **Zones 5 to 8.**

Hemerocallis

hem-er-oh-KAL-iss. Lily family, Liliaceae.

Hemerocallis species, better known as daylilies, are versatile, long-lived perennials grown for their colorful, trumpet-shaped flowers carried on erect stalks, called scapes. Blooms are borne from 1 to as much as 7 feet above low clumps of long, arching, sword-shaped or

grassy leaves that are arranged in fans. The flowers have six petals (more correctly called tepals because three are true petals and three are petal-like sepals) and last for only a day. The botanical name commemorates the fleeting nature of the blooms; it's from the Greek *hemera*, meaning "day," and *kallos*, "beauty." While only about 15 species belong to the genus — all native to China, Japan, and Korea — thousands of cultivars are available. Better selections produce a wealth of buds and bloom over a period of 3 to 4 weeks in summer. The plants have thick, fibrous roots with fleshy, tuberlike swellings on them. Well-formed clumps of standard-size plants spread 2 to 4 feet, with the foliage ranging from about 1 to 2 feet in height. Small daylily cultivars spread from 1 to 2 feet.

HOW TO GROW

Select a site in full sun or light shade and average to rich soil that is well drained and evenly moist. Modern hybrids bloom best with 8 hours of full sun but can make do with less. Daylilies tolerate poor soil and drought but do not bloom as abundantly. Too-rich soil leads to foliage production at the

Hemerocallis 'Living Color'

expense of flowers. Plants bloom best when the soil remains evenly moist, so water during dry weather. Remove faded blooms regularly to keep plants attractive and prevent the limp, old flowers from interfering with new ones that are opening. (Tetraploid daylilies, which bear thick blossoms, are especially notorious for needing regular deadheading.) Pick off any seedpods that begin to form — cultivars do not come true from seed. Remove bloom stalks after the last flowers fade. Divide plants in early spring or early fall when the clumps become crowded, begin to bloom less, or outgrow their space, or for propagation. When you plant daylilies, be aware that the plants in partial shade or the shadow of a building will turn toward the light, so if you want to see the flowers, make sure the prevailing light is behind you.

H. citrina

h. sih-TREE-nuh. CITRON DAYLILY. Vigorous, heavy-blooming, herbaceous species reaching about 4 feet in bloom. Produces fragrant, pale lemon yellow, 3½- to 5-inch-wide trumpets in summer. **Zones 5 to 9.**

H. fulva

h. FUL-vuh. TAWNY DAYLILY. A 3-foot-tall nonnative roadside flower originally from eastern Asia with semievergreen leaves and rusty orange 2½- to 4-inch-wide flowers in summer. 'Flore Pleno' bears double flowers. **Zones 2 to 9.**

H. hybrids

Hybrid daylilies are far more commonly grown than the species and come in many colors, shapes, and

Hemerocallis 'Gentle Shepherd'

Hemerocallis 'Stella de Oro'

H

Hesperis matronalis

sizes. Colors include peach, apricot, yellow-orange, maroon, orange-red, buffy orange, pinkish lavender, plum, and pale yellow or pink blooms that are nearly white. 'Gentle Shepherd' is a midseason cultivar with handsome near-white to ivory blooms. Blooms may be a solid color or feature contrasting colors. Shapes include classic trumpets and recurved blooms with petals curving back to form an almost flat face, as well as spider- and star-shaped blooms with narrow, widely spaced petals. Some are fragrant.

Diploid daylilies have two sets of chromosomes; tetraploids, four — twice the normal number. Tetraploids, which often have ruffled or frilled petal edges, usually are larger plants than diploids, with bigger, more brightly colored flowers. So-called miniature daylilies bear flowers under 3 inches across, often on full-size plants. The term "dwarf" is sometimes used to indicate small plants. 'Mini Pearl' bears 3-inch flowers on 16-inch plants, while 'Peach Fairy' bears 2¹/₂-inch flowers on 26-inch plants. Both are miniatures.

Daylilies are also classified by bloom season, and selecting a mix of early, midseason, and late cultivars extends the bloom season. Reblooming daylilies produce a main flush of bloom that is followed by additional spikes later in the season. 'Eenie Weenie', 'Happy Returns', 'Little Grapette', and 'Par-

don Me' are rebloomers. Ever-bloomers, such as 'Stella de Oro', flower continuously through the season after a first main flush of bloom.

Hybrids may be deciduous (also called dormant), semievergreen, or evergreen. The leaves of evergreen types remain green all winter in the South; protect them with a layer of mulch in winter in Zone 6 and the northern part of Zone 7. Semievergreens are deciduous in the North, semievergreen in the South. Deciduous types go dormant in fall and return in spring wherever they are grown.

Hardiness and heat tolerance vary, so buy from a local grower or mail-order supplier in a climate similar to your own. Cultivars that have received the Stout Medal from the American Hemerocallis Society include 'Barbara Mitchell' (ruffled orchid pink), 'Ed Murray' (deep red), 'Fairy Tale Pink' (ruffled pink), 'Mary Todd' (ruffled yellow), and 'Ruffled Apricot'. **Zones 3 to 10**.

H. lilioasphodelus

h. lil-ee-oh-ass-foe-DEL-us. LEMON LILY. Formerly *H. flava*. Vigorous, semievergreen 3-foot-tall species bearing fragrant lemon yellow, 3¹/₂-inch-wide flowers in late spring or early summer. **Zones 3 to 9**.

Hesperis

HESS-per-iss. Cabbage family, Brassicaceae.

Loose clusters of fragrant, four-petaled flowers characterize the 30 species of biennials and perennials in this genus of plants native from Europe to China and Siberia. The botanical name commemorates the fact that the flowers are most fragrant near nightfall — *Hesperis* is from the Greek *hespera*, meaning "evening." One species has naturalized in eastern North America and is a popular addition to wildflower gardens.

HOW TO GROW

A site with partial shade and rich, evenly moist, well-drained soil is best for dame's rocket (*H. matronalis*). Plants grow in full sun with even moisture and also tolerate full shade. Sow seeds outdoors in spring or from midsummer to fall where the plants are to grow. Or sow seeds indoors 8 to 10 weeks before the last spring frost date. When sowing, just press the seeds into the soil surface, as they need

light to germinate. Germination takes about 3 weeks at 70° to 75°F. Plants self-sow; cut back plants after they have set seed. Or propagate by cuttings taken in spring from shoots at the base of the plant. Use dame's rocket in wildflower gardens and other semiwild plantings, as well as to attract moths.

H. matronalis

h. may-tro-NAL-iss. DAME'S ROCKET, SWEET ROCKET. A 2- to 3-foot biennial or short-lived perennial with toothed, ovate to oblong leaves. Carries loose clusters of 1¹/₄- to 1¹/₂-inch-wide, four-petaled flowers in white or pinkish purple from late spring to midsummer. Biennial. **Zones 4 to 9**.

Heteromeles

heh-ter-oh-MEEL-es. Rose family, Rosaceae.

Once classified among the photinias, popular shrubs in the Southeast, this evergreen shrub native to southern California now has its own genus. Although it has other merits, it is grown primarily for bright berries that are attractive to wildlife.

HOW TO GROW

Give this plant well-drained soil in full sun or partial shade. Fairly tolerant of both wind and drought, it looks better if it gets some supplemental water in summer but will develop root rot if the soil is too wet. Use it for screening or plant it

Heteromeles arbutifolia

on a slope. It needs minimal pruning, but removing old branches will encourage the production of more berries. Propagate from seeds or cuttings.

H. arbutifolia

h. are-bew-tih-FOE-lee-uh. CHRISTMAS BERRY. Also called toyon and California holly, this dense shrub will grow 25 feet high in its native chaparral but usually remains under 10 feet tall in gardens. The glossy, leathery, dark green leaves are 2 to 4 inches long and sharply toothed. Small white flowers appear in flat terminal clusters in early to midsummer. The bright red egg-shaped berries that inspired its common name appear from November through January. **Zones 8 to 10**.

Heuchera

HEW-ker-uh. Saxifrage family, Saxifragaceae.

Heuchera species are native North American plants once grown solely for their airy sprays of tiny colorful flowers. Today heucheras

Heuchera sanguinea

are just as likely to be planted for their ornamental foliage. About 55 species of evergreen or semi-evergreen perennials belong to the genus, all forming mounds of rounded to heart-shaped leaves and delicate-looking panicles or racemes of tiny, sometimes petal-less flowers on erect stems above the foliage. Some heucheras have colorful bell- or funnel-shaped flowers, in which case the showy part of the flower is a five-lobed calyx. Others have inconspicuous blooms. Common names reflect this distinction: heucheras grown for their flowers are commonly called coralbells, while those grown for their foliage are typically referred to as alumroots or simply heucheras. Hybrid heucheras have all but replaced the species in cultivation.

HOW TO GROW

Select a site with rich, evenly moist, well-drained soil. Although plants will grow in full sun to full shade, a site with morning sun and afternoon shade is often the best choice. Heucheras take a season or two to settle in after planting. Water regularly during dry weather, and mulch plants with chopped leaves to keep the soil moist and rich. Deadhead coralbells (*H.* × *brizoides* and *H. sanguinea*) to encourage new flowers to form. Some gardeners remove the flowers of foliage heucheras when they appear. Heucheras have shallow, woody roots and are frequently heaved out of the soil in winter by cycles of freezing and thawing. Check plants during mild spells in winter and reset them if necessary or

cover the crowns with mulch. All can be grown into Zone 3 with a protective winter mulch of evergreen boughs or salt hay. Divide plants in spring about every 4 or 5 years, especially clumps that have congested, woody crowns that have risen above the soil surface. Propagate plants by division or by cutting off and planting individual "branches" or sections of the woody roots in spring or early summer. Most heuchera cultivars do not come true from seed, but some self-sow, and self-sown seedlings may or may not be attractive. Remove the flowers if you want to discourage this or rogue out unattractive seedlings.

H. americana

h. ah-mair-ih-KAH-nuh. AMERICAN ALUMROOT. Native perennial grown for its low, 6- to 12-inch-tall and 1-foot-wide mounds of handsome rounded leaves that are marbled and veined with purple-brown when young. Bears 1¹/₂-foot-tall panicles of brown-green flowers in early summer. **Zones 4 to 8.**

H. × brizoides

h. × briz-OY-deez. HYBRID CORALBELLS. A group of low-growing hybrids (crosses between *H. americana, H. micrantha*, and *H. sanguinea*) with 6-inch-tall, 1- to 1¹/₂-foot-wide mounds of lobed and scalloped evergreen leaves. Plants bear airy 1¹/₂- to 2¹/₂-foot-tall clusters of tiny ³/₈- to ¹/₂-inch-long flowers from late spring into early summer in shades of pink, coral, red, rose-red, or white. *H.* × *brizoides* cultivars tend to be more

Heuchera × *brizoides*

heat tolerant than *H. sanguinea* cultivars, making them better choices for southern gardens. Cultivars include 'Chatterbox' (rose-pink), 'Firebird' (scarlet), 'Firefly' (vermilion red), 'June Bride' (white), 'Mt. St. Helens' (brick red), 'Raspberry Regal' (raspberry red with marbled leaves), and 'Rosamundi' (coral pink). **Zones 4 to 8.**

H. hybrids

Heuchera hybrids form 1-foot-tall, 1¹/₂-foot-wide mounds of showy lobed and/or ruffled leaves that are 3 to 6 inches long. Leaves can be green with gray and silver overtones and veins, purple-brown with metallic mottling, rose-burgundy with silver overtones and purple veins, and green with purple-red mottling. New leaves are the most colorful and are produced all season long, although the color may fade during the hottest part of the summer. Clusters of tiny white, greenish white, or pinkish flowers appear in early summer above the foliage on 1- to 2-foot-tall stalks. Cultivars include 'Chocolate Ruffles', 'Chocolate Veil', 'Dale's Strain', 'Garnet', 'Persian Carpet', 'Pewter Veil', 'Ruby Ruffles', and 'Velvet Knight'. **Zones 4 to 8.**

H. micrantha

h. my-KRAN-thuh. Mound-forming native North American species with 1-foot-tall, 1¹/₂-foot-wide mounds of silver-gray marbled,

ovate to heart-shaped leaves. Bears loose 2- to 3-foot-tall panicles of tiny white to pink-flushed flowers in early summer. *H. micrantha* var. *diversifolia* 'Palace Purple' has shiny, metallic bronze-red leaves and greenish white flowers. **Zones 4 to 8.**

H. sanguinea

h. san-GWIN-ee-uh. CORALBELLS. Native wildflower with low 6-inch-tall, 10- to 12-inch-wide mounds of kidney-shaped leaves. Bears loose 1- to 2-foot-tall panicles of tiny red, pink, or white flowers in summer. Many cultivars are now listed under *H.* × *brizoides* to reflect their hybrid origin. Cultivars include 'Cherry Splash' (rose-red), 'Coral Cloud' (coral red), 'Pluie de Feu' (red), 'Splendens' (scarlet red), and 'White Cloud' (white). **Zones 4 to 8.**

× *Heucherella*

× hew-ker-ELL-uh. Saxifrage family, Saxifragaceae.

Plants in this hybrid genus are commonly called foamy bells, a name derived from the parent species used to create it: coralbells (*Heuchera*) and foamflower (*Tiarella*). Foamy bells produce mounds of evergreen, heart-shaped or broadly ovate leaves topped by loose panicles of tiny pink or white flowers from spring to fall.

Heuchera micrantha 'Palace Purple'

× Heucherella alba 'Bridget Bloom'

HOW TO GROW

Select a site in full sun or partial shade with light, rich soil that is moist but well drained. Neutral to slightly acid pH is best. Plants also grow in full shade, but they do not tolerate heat and humidity and are not long-lived in southern gardens. To propagate, divide plants in spring or fall or sever and pot up runners that appear. They do not set seeds.

× H. alba

× h. AL-buh. FOAMY BELLS. Clump-forming perennial that develops low 12-inch-wide mounds topped by airy 16-inch-tall panicles of $^1/8$- to $^1/4$-inch-long white flowers from late spring to fall. 'Bridget Bloom' has whitish pink flowers. 'Pink Frost' bears pink flowers on 2-foot stalks. **Zones 5 to 8.**

× H. tiarelloides

× h. tee-ah-rell-OY-deez. FOAMY BELLS. Hybrid spreading by stolons to form 1$^1/2$-foot-wide clumps topped by 1$^1/2$-foot-tall panicles of $^1/8$-inch-long flowers in spring and early summer. Plants may rebloom in fall. **Zones 5 to 8.**

Hibiscus

hy-BISS-kus. Mallow family, Malvaceae.

Both hardy and tender plants belong to the genus *Hibiscus* — over 200 species of annuals, perennials, shrubs, and trees are found here. They bear showy, funnel-shaped flowers, each with a prominent central column consisting of the stamens and pistil. The flowers have five petals and are borne either singly or in clusters. The leaves are entire to palmately lobed.

HOW TO GROW

All hibiscus species thrive in full sun, warm temperatures, and rich, well-drained soil. *H. coccineus* likes wet to boggy soil. For annual hibiscus, sow seeds outdoors after danger of frost has passed and the soil has warmed. Since plants take about 3 months to bloom from seeds, they need a head start in northern gardens, roughly Zone 6 north. Where seasons are short, sow indoors in individual peat pots 8 to 10 weeks before the last spring frost date at 50° to 55°F. Transplant after the weather has settled in spring (especially north of Zone 6 and in any area where spring is cool and rainy). Seedlings resent transplanting, so handle

Hibiscus rosa-sinensis 'Euterpe'

them carefully. Feed with a balanced fertilizer in midsummer. Annuals self-sow in mild climates. Grow Chinese hibiscus (*H. rosa-sinensis*) outdoors as a shrub in Zones 10 and 11; in areas where plants are marginally hardy, try a site against a south-facing wall for extra winter protection. In the North, grow Chinese hibiscus in containers and overwinter indoors in a bright, cool (40° to 45°F) spot; prune in spring as needed to shape. Feed container-grown plants monthly. Water all hibiscus regularly and deeply in dry weather. Hummingbirds will visit hibiscus flowers.

H. acetosella

h. ah-see-toe-SELL-ah. Formerly *H. eetveldeanus.* An annual or short-lived tender perennial with lobed, maplelike leaves that ranges from 2 to 5 feet tall. Carries yellow or purple-red, 2$^1/2$- to 4-inch-wide flowers in late summer and fall, but only in areas with very long growing seasons. A maroon-purple–leaved cultivar sold under the names 'Red Shield' and 'Red Sentinel' is grown for its handsome foliage. Tender perennial or warm-weather annual.

H. coccineus

h. kok-SIN-ee-us. SCARLET ROSE MALLOW, SWAMP ROSE MALLOW. North American native perennial with a woody base that reaches 5 to 10 feet in height and forms 4-foot-wide clumps. Bears lacy, palmately lobed leaves with linear leaflets and deep red 6-inch-wide flowers from summer to fall. **Zones 6 to 11.**

H. moscheutos

h. moe-SHOO-tos. COMMON ROSE MALLOW, COMMON MALLOW. Vigorous North American native perennial ranging from 4 to 8 feet in height and forming 3-foot-wide clumps. Bears ovate to lance-shaped, shallowly lobed leaves and funnel-shaped 8- to 10-inch-wide flowers in summer in red, pink, or white. Compact 2- to 2$^1/2$-foot-tall Disco Belle Series plants have 9-inch-wide flowers. Pink-flowered 'Lady Baltimore' and scarlet-flowered 'Lord Baltimore' bear 10-inch-wide flowers on 4-foot plants. Both Disco Belle and Baltimore cultivars come true from seed. **Zones 5 to 10.**

H. rosa-sinensis

h. ROE-suh-sih-NEN-sis. CHINESE HIBISCUS. This rounded, sub-tropical evergreen species averages 10 feet tall and not quite so wide, although most cultivars grow from 6 to 8 feet tall. The glossy dark green, oval to lance-shaped leaves are up to 6 inches long. From summer through fall, five-petaled red flowers 4 inches in diameter appear in the leaf axils. Cultivars in single or double forms can be white, yellow, orange, or pink and 5 to 8 inches across. Some gardeners grow this tender species as an annual or in containers for overwintering indoors. Just a few of the many choices include 'All-Aglow', with orange edges verging to yellow and a pink halo around a white center; 'Cooperi', which has red flowers but is grown primarily for its white, pink, and green foliage; and 'Hula Girl', long blooming and narrow with red-throated bright yellow flowers. **Zones 9 to 11; may be root hardy to Zone 8.**

H. syriacus

h. sear-ee-AY-kuss. ROSE OF SHARON. This deciduous upright shrub grows to 10 feet tall and 6 feet wide with erect branches. The

Hibiscus syriacus 'Diana'

4-inch toothed leaves are often three-lobed, and the 2- to 4-inch axillary flowers, which bloom from midsummer into early autumn, can be white, rosy pink, or lavender with a red center. In the heat of late summer plants can develop powdery mildew where humidity is high and attract mites in dry conditions. The species self-sows readily and is making its way onto lists of invasives in the Southeast, Mid-Atlantic, and Midwest. Popular selections, which may volunteer less eagerly, include 'Aphrodite' (dark pink), 'Diana' (pure white; a Pennsylvania Horticultural Society award winner), 'Helene' (white with a red, radiating eye spot), and 'Minerva' (lavender with a dark red eye). **Zones 5 to 9.**

H. trionum

H. try-ON-um. FLOWER-OF-AN-HOUR. A 1- to 2-foot-tall annual or tender, short-lived perennial that has become a weed in some parts of North America. It bears palmate, three- to five-lobed leaves and from summer to fall carries an abundance of 2- to 3-inch-wide, brown-centered yellow flowers that last a day or less. Tender perennial or warm-weather annual.

Hippeastrum

hip-ee-AS-trum. Amaryllis family, Amaryllidaceae.

Widely known as amaryllis, *Hippeastrum* species are grown for their showy, trumpet- or funnel-shaped flowers. The lilylike flowers are produced in umbels atop leafless stems. They have six petal-like tepals. Plants grow from tunicate bulbs and bear basal leaves

Hippeastrum hybrid 'Red Lion'

that are linear to lance shaped. While the species are native to Central and South America — about 80 species belong here — most gardeners are familiar with the large-flowered hybrids sold for growing indoors in pots.

HOW TO GROW

Outdoors, give these plants a site in full sun to partial shade with deeply prepared, rich, well-drained soil. Where hardy, plant the bulbs in spring or fall with 2 to 3 inches of soil over their tops: be sure the basal plate of the bulb is beneath the frost line. Protect them with evergreen boughs, pine needles, or salt hay over winter.

In most of the country, these showy bulbs are grown in containers: plant them in winter or early spring. Select a pot that is 2 inches larger than the diameter of the bulb (to allow for 1 inch of space between the bulb and the pot all the way around). Position the bulbs so that the top two-thirds is above the soil surface. Keep the soil barely moist and set the pots in a cool (55° to 60°F) room until

leaves or a flower bud appears to signal that the bulbs are growing actively. Then move the pots to a warmer spot and water regularly. Once the bulbs flower, remove the flower stalks and feed with a dilute, balanced fertilizer every 2 weeks until mid- to late summer. Then begin to withhold water gradually to encourage the leaves to go dormant. (If the soil remains moist, the leaves will be evergreen and plants will be less likely to flower again.) Some gardeners let the leaves be cut back by a light fall frost. Once the leaves die back, store the bulbs dry, still in their pots, at about 55°F. Let them rest for at least 8 weeks. Top-dress the bulbs in midwinter and begin watering again — very cautiously at first until the plants are growing actively.

Bulbs are easy to bloom the year they are purchased (the flower buds are already formed in the bulbs when you buy them) but often do not bloom the following year. That's because these plants have permanent, perennial roots and resent root disturbance. Bulbs usually have few, if any, roots when they are offered for sale, and

after flowering the first year they spend their energy replacing them. To minimize root disturbance in subsequent years, repot bulbs only as necessary — every 3 to 4 years — and when topdressing, disturb them as little as possible. When growing these plants in the ground, dig them only if absolutely necessary. Propagate by removing offsets in fall.

H. hybrids

A wide variety of hybrids are offered for sale. Large-flowered types bear umbels of up to four flowers in early spring that are 4 to 6 inches across, and the largest bulbs can produce two flowers on 1- to 2-foot-tall stalks. Cultivars include 'Apple Blossom', with white, pink-tinged flowers; 'Jaguar', with red blooms, green at the center, striped with white; 'Picotee', with white flowers with a thin red edge; and 'Red Lion', bright red. Miniature-flowered cultivars bear 3- to 4-inch-wide blooms on 1-foot-tall stalks. Miniature-flowered cultivars include 'Fairy Tale', with raspberry pink blooms displaying white veins; 'Pamela', with orange-red blooms; and 'Scarlet Baby', with scarlet flowers. **Zones 8 to 10.**

H. papilio

h. pah-PIL-ee-oh. BUTTERFLY AMARYLLIS. An evergreen species that reaches 2 feet in height. Bears umbels of two or three 3½-inch-wide flowers in late winter. Blooms are creamy white heavily striped with maroon and have green throats. **Zones 10 and 11.**

Hippophae

hip-POFF-ay-ee. Oleaster family, Elaeagnaceae.

This genus is made up of three species of deciduous, dioecious shrubs and trees from coastal areas

Hippeastrum papilio

Hippophae rhamnoides

and riverbanks in Asia and Europe. Not well known, it offers great potential for growing in seaside gardens and roadside plantings, as well as for ornamental attributes such as narrow silvery leaves and persistent orange fruits.

HOW TO GROW

This plant needs full sun. While happy in poor, sandy soil it probably will do better with some organic matter to keep its roots cool. Sea buckthorn withstands salt, is useful for stabilizing dunes and riverbanks, and will lend winter color to naturalized areas. Not a selection for small gardens; you'll need both male and female plants in order to enjoy the colorful fruits. Rarely needs pruning. Propagate from cold-treated seeds, root cuttings, layering, or suckers.

H. rhamnoides

h. ram-NOY-deez. S E A
B U C K T H O R N. Variable in size but averaging 20 feet tall and wide, this large shrub or small tree has an irregular open shape and a suckering tendency. The 1- to 3-inch willowlike leaves are gray-green and silvery, borne on spiny branches. Inconspicuous yellow-green spring flowers give way to bright orange, round to oval berries on the females. **Zones 3 to 8**.

Holodiscus

hol-oh-DIS-kuss. Rose family, Rosaceae.

There are eight deciduous shrubs in this genus, with most of those available for gardeners native to dry woods of the western United States. They are closely related to spirea (*Spirosa*) but bloom later, producing graceful white flower plumes almost a foot long in summer.

HOW TO GROW

Give holodiscus rich, fertile, moisture-retentive soil in full sun to partial shade. They are ideal for naturalizing in the West, since they can attract birds and need little care. They do not require pruning, but cutting out older stems after they flower will promote growth. Propagate by seeds, semiripe cuttings in summer, or layering.

H. discolor

h. DISS-kuh-lor. O C E A N S P R A Y. Vigorous and upright, this species ranges from 3 feet tall in dry soil to 20 feet in rich soil, with arching branches. The triangular 3-inch leaves are wrinkled above, white and fuzzy underneath, and have four to eight lobes. The individual flowers are tiny and cup shaped, appearing in pendulous clusters at the branch tips for many weeks in late spring to early summer.
Zones 6 to 9.

Homeria

hoe-MAIR-ee-uh. Iris family, Iridaceae.

These South African natives, commonly known as Cape tulips, are grown for their clusters of fragrant, cupped, tuliplike flowers. While each bloom lasts only a day, they are borne in fairly good-size clusters and open in succession for several weeks from spring to summer. About 31 species belong to the genus, all of which grow from

Homeria collina

corms. Some species have become widely naturalized in Australia. They bear leaves that are mostly basal and range from linear to strap shaped. The leaves of some species are poisonous to livestock.

HOW TO GROW

Select a site in full sun with rich, well-drained soil. Like many South African species, Cape tulips need evenly moist soil while they are growing actively and dry conditions when they are dormant. Where hardy, plant the corms outdoors in fall at a depth of 4 inches. Amend the soil with grit or sharp sand to provide very good drainage. Where they are marginally hardy, look for a warm, south-facing site and protect plants over winter with evergreen boughs, pine needles, salt hay, or another coarse mulch. In the North, grow them in containers. To overwinter them, gradually reduce watering after the flowers fade. Store the corms completely dry — in or out of the pots — in a cool (40° to 45°F) place. Propagate by separating the offsets just as the leaves die back.

H. collina

h. koh-LYE-nuh. C A P E T U L I P. Formerly *H. breyniana*. A 6- to 16-inch-tall species with leaves that are poisonous to livestock. From spring to summer it bears fragrant, cup-shaped, 3-inch-wide flowers that are pink, peach-pink, or yellow. **Zones 9 to 11**.

Hordeum

HOAR-day-um. Grass family, Poaceae.

Some 20 species of annuals and perennials belong to this genus, including the agricultural crop barley. *Hordeum* species have narrow leaves and rounded, plumy flower heads. One species is commonly grown as an ornamental grass and is used in dried flower arrangements.

HOW TO GROW

Full sun and average, well-drained soil suffice for these easy-to-grow plants. Sow seeds outdoors a few weeks before the last spring frost date or in late fall for germination the following spring. (Plants resent transplanting and are best started outdoors where they are to grow.) To use the flower heads of squirrel-tail grass (*H. jubatum*) for drying, cut them just before the flower buds open and hang them in small bunches in a warm, dry, dark place. This species also adds attractive texture to mixed beds and borders. Plants self-sow and can become weedy.

Holodiscus discolor

Hordeum jubatum

H. jubatum

h. jew-BAY-tum. SQUIRREL-TAIL GRASS, FOX-TAIL BARLEY. A 2-foot-tall annual or perennial grass, hardy from Zone 4 south, with arching leaves. Bears feathery, 5-inch-long flower spikes that are green flushed with pale pink or purple and ripen to beige. **Zones 4 to 8.**

Hosta

HOSS-tuh. Lily family, Liliaceae.

Hostas, or plantain lilies, as they are sometimes called, are tough, shade-loving perennials that produce lush mounds of handsome, often variegated leaves and racemes of trumpet-shaped flowers. There are about 70 species in the genus and hundreds of cultivars. Leaves can be heart shaped, nearly round, or lance shaped, and from 1 inch long to as much as 12 inches or more. Foliage color is quite variable: leaves can be solid dark to mid-green, chartreuse, blue-green, blue-gray, or variegated. Leaf texture varies

Hosta 'Krossa Regal'

from smooth or ribbed to deeply corrugated. The 1- to 2-inch-long flowers, which are borne on erect spikes that rise above the mounds of leaves, come in white, pale lavender, and deep purple. Flowering time is variable — from late spring to fall — and depends on the parentage of the particular cultivar. Funkia, another common name, is a former botanical name.

HOW TO GROW

Ideally, select a site in light to full shade with rich, evenly moist soil. A site with a few hours of morning sun and shade for the rest of the day is fine. In the South, shade during the hottest part of the day is essential for success. Blue-leaved cultivars generally retain their color best in cool, shady spots that receive good light but no direct sun, while a spot in bright, dappled shade brings out the best color in variegated cultivars. Golden-leaved cultivars tolerate considerable sun but still benefit from shade during the hottest part of the day. Plants are fairly drought tolerant but grow best (and largest) with even moisture. They grow in heavy clay as well as constantly moist conditions, and they can be planted along streambanks, bogs, and ponds, provided the crowns are set above the water line. Hostas can emerge late in spring, so mark the location of the clumps at planting time. They take from two to four seasons after planting to become established and reach their full size. Cut the bloom stalks back to below the foliage as the flowers fade.

Plants grow well for years without needing to be divided. Dig plants in spring before the leaves unfurl or in early fall for propagation or to move a clump. Another propagation option is to dig a plant or two from the edge of an

existing clump by severing it with a sharp spade. Hosta cultivars do not come true from seed, but they will self-sow (remove flower stalks to prevent this).

H. fortunei

h. for-TOON-ee-eye. Sometimes listed as *H.* 'Fortunei'. A 1½- to 2-foot-tall species spreading from 2 to 3 feet. Bears clumps of 8- to 12-inch-long leaves topped with mauve flowers on 2½-foot-tall stalks in summer. 'Albomarginata' has white margins. 'Aureomarginata' has dark green leaves with yellow margins. **Zones 3 to 8.**

H. hybrids

Hosta hybrids range from 2 inches to more than 3 feet in height and form dense clumps that spread one and a half to two times as far as they are tall. Unless otherwise noted, plants have pale lavender flowers in midsummer. All are hardy in **Zones 3 to 8.**

LARGE CULTIVARS

These form 2½- to 3-foot-tall clumps and spread from 3 to 4 feet

Hosta 'Francee'

Hosta plantaginea

or more. 'Black Hills' has corrugated dark green leaves and pale lavender flowers in late spring to early summer. 'Blue Angel' bears blue-gray heart-shaped leaves and white flowers in midsummer. 'Blue Umbrellas' has heart-shaped blue to blue-green leaves that turn green by midsummer and pale lavender flowers in early summer. 'Krossa Regal' produces vase-shaped clumps of ribbed blue-gray leaves and lavender flowers in mid- to late summer. 'Regal Splendor' has vase-shaped clumps of ribbed blue-gray to gray-green leaves variegated with creamy white and yellow. 'Sagae' (formerly *H. fluctuans* 'Variegata') bears blue-gray creamy-edged leaves and white flowers in mid- to late summer. 'Sum and Substance' features heart-shaped yellow-green leaves and pale lilac flowers in mid- to late summer.

MEDIUM CULTIVARS

These range from 1 to 2 feet in height and spread from 1½ to about 3 feet. 'Abba Dabba Do' has green leaves edged in yellow. 'Birchwood Parky's Gold' produces green-gold heart-shaped leaves. 'Blue Cadet' has heart-shaped blue-green foliage. 'Blue Wedgwood' has blue-gray-green wedge-shaped leaves. 'Brim Cup' bears puckered, cupped, dark green leaves with white margins. 'Francee' has dark green heart-shaped leaves that have white margins and also bears handsome lavender flowers in summer. 'Golden Tiara' features small round to heart-shaped green leaves with irregular golden margins. 'Gold Standard' has golden, green-edged leaves. 'Great Expectations' produces yellow leaves that have blue-green edges and gold centers turning to creamy white by midsummer and white flowers in early summer. 'Halcyon' has rounded blue leaves. 'Undulata', often listed as *H. undulata*, bears rounded lance-shaped leaves that have very wavy margins and are splashed and striped with pale yellow and/or white; it bears pale lilac purple flowers in early and mid-

Hosta plantaginea

summer. 'Wide Brim' has green leaves that have wide creamy white margins. 'Zounds' has puckered golden yellow leaves and white flowers in early summer.

SMALL CULTIVARS

All of these are under 1 foot in height and spread from 1¹/₂ to 3 feet. 'Chartreuse Wiggles' has lance-shaped, yellow-green, wavy-margined leaves and lavender late-summer flowers. 'Ginkgo Craig' bears lance-shaped dark green leaves edged in white and lavender flowers in late summer. 'Gold Edger' has heart-shaped chartreuse leaves. 'Kabitan' features lance-shaped yellow leaves with dark green margins. 'Little Aurora' bears round gold leaves. And 2-inch-tall 'Tiny Tears' has dense clumps of green heart-shaped leaves.

H. lancifolia
h. lan-sih-FOE-lee-uh. A species growing to more than 1 foot tall that spreads quickly. The glossy, relatively narrow leaves are dark green. Lavender-violet flowers appear in late summer. Zones 3 to 8.

H. montana
h. mon-TAHN-uh. A 2- to 2¹/₂-foot-tall species with deeply ribbed leaves that forms 3-foot-wide mounds. Bears white flowers in early summer on 3-foot-tall scapes. 'Aureomarginata' has dark green leaves with irregular yellow margins. 'Mountain Snow' has white-margined leaves. 'On Stage' bears green leaves with gold to white centers. Zones 3 to 8.

H. plantaginea
h. plan-tuh-JIN-ee-uh. AUGUST LILY. A 2- to 2¹/₂-foot-tall species producing 3-foot-wide clumps of heart-shaped green leaves and showy racemes of large, very fra-

grant white flowers on erect stalks high above the foliage in late summer. 'Aphrodite' bears double flowers. Zones 3 to 8.

H. sieboldiana
h. see-bold-ee-AH-nuh. Vigorous 2- to 2¹/₂-foot-tall species forming 4-foot-wide mounds of heart-shaped, puckered, gray-green leaves. Bears dense racemes of pale lilac-white flowers just above the foliage in early summer. *H. sieboldiana* var. *elegans*, also sold as 'Elegans', has very puckered blue-gray leaves. 'Frances Williams' produces 2-foot-tall clumps of blue-green leaves with irregular greenish yellow edges. Zones 3 to 8.

H. tokudama
h. tow-koo-DAH-muh. A 1¹/₂-foot-tall species forming 3-foot-wide clumps of heart-shaped, heavily puckered leaves. Bears white flowers in summer. 'Aureonebulosa' has yellow-green leaves with irregular blotches and margins of

Houttuynia cordata 'Chameleon'

blue-green. 'Flavocircinalis' has blue-green leaves with irregular yellow-green margins. Zones 3 to 8.

H. venusta
h. veh-NOO-stuh. A dwarf species with 4-inch-tall clumps of heart-shaped leaves that spread to about 10 inches. Bears pretty lavender flowers on 1- to 1¹/₂-foot-tall stalks in midsummer. Zones 3 to 8.

H. ventricosa
h. ven-trih-KOH-suh. A 1¹/₂- to 2-foot-tall species forming 3-foot-wide clumps of dark, glossy green leaves and handsome dark purple flowers in late summer. 'Aureo-maculata' bears leaves with green edges and a central yellow blotch; its leaves fade to yellow-green in summer. 'Aureomarginata' has leaves variegated with yellow and cream. Zones 3 to 8.

Houttuynia
hoo-too-IN-ee-uh. Lizard's tail family, Saururaceae.

Ask someone to crush a leaf of houttuynia and watch his or her reaction — depending on who describes it, houttuynia is foul-smelling or has a strong, bitter orange fragrance. Native from Japan to the Himalayas of China and India, the single species in the genus is an aggressive perennial in marshy aquatic sites and moist soils and spreads rapidly by subterranean stems. Its leafy stems typically grow to 18 inches or more tall. The alternate leaves are often heart shaped. The small, yellowish

Humulus japonicus 'Variegatus'

flowers are visible above four showy, white bracts. Houttuynias are seriously invasive pests in moist soils and wetlands and should be considered for use only where they can be controlled, such as by planting in sunken tubs and liners. When grown in drier garden soils, however, houttuynias are likely to die out within a few years.

HOW TO GROW

Select a site in full sun or partial shade with average to rich soil. Plants prefer evenly moist conditions and will grow in boggy soil as well as shallow standing water, but in such sites they are especially invasive. The variegated form tends to revert to green, especially in too much shade: rogue out reverted plants regularly. Propagate by division in spring or by cuttings taken in late spring or early summer.

H. cordata
h. kor-DAH-tuh. The wild form of the species is rarely seen in gardens because of its weedy nature. 'Chameleon', also sold as 'Tricolor', has orange, red, green, and cream leaf markings and is highly ornamental but when planted in sites with moist soil and partial shade to morning sun, it will spread rampantly. It is best reserved for large containers, where its brilliantly colored foliage can be enjoyed under optimum control. 'Flore Pleno' has green foliage and creamy white, double-bracted

flowers, almost like those of a miniature gardenia. It is a less vigorous spreader. **Zones 6 to 9.**

Humulus

HEW-mew-lus. Hemp family, Cannabidaceae.

The two species that belong to this genus are the vines commonly called hops. They feature attractive, deeply lobed, palmate leaves and bear male and female flowers on separate plants. One species, Japanese hops *(H. japonicus)*, is commonly grown as an annual.

HOW TO GROW
Give Japanese hops full sun or partial shade and average to rich, evenly moist but well-drained soil. It also needs a sturdy trellis upon which to climb. Sow seeds indoors 8 to 10 weeks before the last spring frost date, and place the sown pots in the refrigerator for 2 to 3 weeks before moving them to a warmer (70° to 75°F) spot for germinating. Germination takes 3 to 4 weeks. Or sow seeds outdoors in spring a few weeks before the last frost date, or in fall for germination the following spring. Or propagate by cuttings taken in spring or summer. Plants self-sow and can become weedy; pull up unwanted seedlings as they appear. Use this vigorous vine to create temporary privacy screens, or train it over an arbor to add shade to a sitting area.

H. japonicus

h. juh-PON-ih-kus. JAPANESE HOPS. A vigorous, tender perennial climber that can reach 10 feet or more in a single season. Lobed, maplelike leaves and small, oval spikes of greenish flowers appear

from mid- to late summer. Plants self-sow abundantly from about Zone 4 south. 'Variegatus' features leaves streaked and mottled with white and comes true from seed. Cool-weather annual.

Hunnemannia

hun-eh-MAN-ee-ah. Poppy family, Papaveraceae.

Only one species belongs to the genus *Hunnemannia,* a tender perennial native to Mexico commonly called Mexican tulip poppy. It closely resembles California poppy *(Eschscholzia)* and has deeply divided, blue-green leaves and glossy, cup-shaped, four-petaled flowers, borne from summer to fall. Botanists distinguish plants in the two genera because *H. fumariifolia* has separate sepals, while in *Eschscholzia* species they are united to form a cap.

HOW TO GROW
Plant Mexican tulip poppies in full sun and average, well-drained soil. They thrive in heat and do not tolerate shade or wet soil. Sow seeds outdoors in spring several weeks before the last frost date. Or sow indoors in individual pots 6 to 8 weeks before the last frost date at 55° to 60°F. Germination takes 2 to 3 weeks. Handle the plants carefully at transplanting, as they resent root disturbance; for this reason, they aren't generally overwintered. Use tulip poppies in mixed plantings in beds and borders as well as in containers. They also make excellent cut flowers.

H. fumariifolia

h. few-mair-ee-ih-FOE-lee-ah. MEXICAN TULIP POPPY, MEXICAN GOLDEN-CUP. A tender,

Hyacinthoides hispanica

2- to 3-foot perennial with ferny, blue-green leaves. Bears 2- to 3-inch-wide, golden yellow flowers with glossy petals from midsummer to frost. Tender perennial grown as a cool-weather annual.

Hyacinthoides

hy-ah-sin-THOY-deez. Lily family, Liliaceae.

Hyacinthoides contains three or four species grown for their charming racemes of spring-borne flowers that come in shades of blue, lavender, violet, pink, and white. The small bell-shaped flowers have six lobes, petal-like tepals that are united at the base. Some species are fragrant. Plants grow from tunicate bulbs that are renewed annually, meaning new bulbs are formed each year to replace the old one that dies. They bear basal, strap- to lance-shaped or linear leaves. *Hyacinthoides* species are closely related to *Scilla* and native to western Europe and northern Africa. They also were once classified in *Endymion.* Some gardeners develop skin allergies if they come in contact with the foliage or flowers.

HOW TO GROW
Select a site in partial or dappled shade with average to rich, moist, well-drained soil. The plants also tolerate full sun and thrive under deciduous trees, where they receive a good amount of sunshine in spring when they are growing actively. Plant the bulbs in fall at a depth of 3 inches. Since plants

produce abundant offsets and can be left in place for many years without needing to be divided, space them generously — about 6 inches apart. Divide clumps only if they become overcrowded and begin to bloom less. Plants also self-sow and are ideal for naturalizing in wild and woodland gardens, where they will form large handsome clumps with time. They also can be naturalized in grass. Because *Hyacinthoides* renew their bulbs yearly, the bulbs of established clumps are quite deep in the soil. Propagate by separating the offsets in early summer as the foliage dies down or from seeds.

H. hispanica

h. hiss-PAN-ih-kuh. SPANISH BLUEBELL. Formerly *H. campanulata, Endymion hispanicus, Scilla campanulata. S. hispanica.* Vigorous 10- to 14-inch-tall species with large clumps of glossy leaves topped by showy racemes of 6 to as many as 15 bell-shaped, unscented, lavender-blue ³/4-inch-long flowers in spring. 'Excelsior' has lavender-blue flowers striped with pale blue. 'Rosabella' bears violet-pink flowers. White- and pink-flowered cultivars also are available. **Zones 4 to 9.**

H. italica

h. ih-TAL-ih-kuh. ITALIAN SQUILL. Formerly *Endymion italicus, Scilla italica.* Dainty 4- to 8-inch-tall species with dense, somewhat rounded racemes of 6 to as many as 30 bell-shaped,

Hunnemannia fumariifolia

H

Hyacinthus orientalis

1/2-inch-long flowers that face upward. Blooms are blue or sometimes white and appear in spring. **Zones 4 to 9.**

H. non-scripta

h. non-SKRIP-tuh. ENGLISH BLUEBELL, HAREBELL. Formerly *Endymion non-scriptus*, *Scilla non-scripta*, *S. nutans*. Vigorous 8- to 12-inch-tall species that bears racemes of 6 to 12 lavender-blue flowers in spring arranged all on one side of the raceme. The individual flowers are narrowly bell shaped, are 1/2 to 3/4 inch long, and have tepals that are very curled back at the tips. **Zones 4 to 9.**

Hyacinthus

hy-ah-SIN-thus. Lily family, Liliaceae.

These familiar spring-blooming bulbs are prized for their intensely fragrant flowers. While three species belong to the genus, by far the best-known plants that belong here are cultivars of common hyacinths (*H. orientalis*), also called Dutch hyacinths. These well-known garden plants produce erect, cylindrical trusses of flowers in shades of pink, lilac-blue, violet, yellow, or white. The blooms are carried on thick stalks above basal, strap-shaped leaves. Individual flowers are bell shaped and have

six petal-like tepals. The tepals are united for about half to two-thirds the length of the flower and have tips that flare widely or curve backward. Some gardeners develop a skin rash when they come in contact with the foliage of these plants.

HOW TO GROW

Select a site in full sun or partial shade with average to rich, well-drained soil. Plant the bulbs in fall at a depth of 4 to 5 inches deep — to 6 or even 8 inches deep at the northern limit of their hardiness. In the North, cover plantings with evergreen boughs, salt hay, or another loose mulch to protect the shoots when they emerge in spring. Remove the mulch after the danger of hard frost has passed. Plants produce the largest blooms the first spring and smaller, looser spikes thereafter — many gardeners consider the blooms borne in later years to be more natural-looking and graceful. When the leaves emerge in spring, feeding plants with a top-dressing of well-rotted manure or a balanced organic fertilizer helps keep the blooms large. For formal plantings with exhibition-size blooms, replace the bulbs annually (bulbs that have already bloomed can be moved to less formal areas of the garden). Propagate by separating the offsets in summer just as the leaves die down.

H. orientalis

h. or-ee-en-TAL-iss. HYACINTH. The species that yielded the many cultivars grown today bears loose 8- to 12-inch-tall racemes of 2 to as many as 40 bell-shaped, extremely fragrant flowers that usually are violet-blue. Many cultivars are available, among them: 'Amethyst', lilac purple; 'Blue Jacket', dark violet-blue; "Carnegie', creamy white; 'City of Haarlem', primrose yellow turning to creamy white; 'Delft Blue', pale lilac-blue; 'Jan Bos', pinkish red; 'Lady Derby', pale pink; 'Pink Pearl', deep pink with pale pink edges; and 'White Pearl', white. **Zones 5 to 9; to Zone 4 with deep planting.**

Hydrangea

hy-DRAN-juh. Hydrangea family, Hydrangeaceae.

Hydrangeas are an old-fashioned favorite, some form of which is always being newly discovered by gardeners. They offer flowers that range from buxom white belles to lacy sapphire "caps," as well as species with burgundy fall foliage and furrowed bark. The genus includes two dozen species of deciduous and evergreen shrubs and climbers from East Asia and the Americas. Flowers of all the common shrub species are good for drying indoors.

HOW TO GROW

Give hydrangeas fertile, moisture-retentive soil in full sun to partial shade. These species are all fast growers but vary in their tolerance to sun, wind, salt, and drought and in their pruning requirements. See individual species listings. You can start them from seeds in spring, but they are easy to root from softwood cuttings in early summer.

H. anomala ssp. petiolaris

h. ah-NOM-ah-luh ssp. pet-ee-oh-LAIR-iss. CLIMBING HYDRANGEA. Though this hydrangea will grow very little for the first year or two, it is establishing an impressive root system. After this, it will grow at a remarkable rate, climbing trees and walls and clambering with agility over tree stumps and rocks. It prefers partial shade or woodland conditions. The creamy white flower heads develop with maturity. **Zones 5 to 9.**

H. arborescens 'Annabelle'

h. are-bore-ESS-enz. SMOOTH HYDRANGEA CULTIVAR.

Hydrangea macrophylla

Quickly reaching 3 to 5 feet tall and wide with a suckering habit, this rounded shrub species is considered coarse by some, but the cultivar is noteworthy for its summer flowers carried in rounded clusters up to 12 inches in diameter. In hot summer areas it needs shade and supplemental water. Prune back to low buds in late winter. **Zones 4 to 9.**

H. macrophylla

h. mak-roe-FILL-uh. BIG-LEAF HYDRANGEA. There are two forms, both averaging 6 feet tall and 8 feet wide. The hortensias have large heavy "mopheads" of sterile flowers, while the lacecaps are airy wheels of tiny fertile flowers surrounded by showier sterile flowers. The blooms, which begin appearing in midsummer, are generally blue if the plants are growing in soil with a pH of 5.5 or less, purple in slightly acid soil, or pink if grown in neutral to slightly alkaline soil. Hydrangeas may become chlorotic if the soil is strongly alkaline. There are some white-flowered cultivars. Leaves are 4- to 8-inch toothed ovals, somewhat waxy. This species thrives in the wind and salt of coastal areas but wilts rapidly in a drought. To keep the plant tidy, prune back the previous season's flower heads to the stem's uppermost bud in late winter. 'Blue Bil-

Hydrangea quercifolia

Hydrangea macrophylla 'Nikku Blue'

low', which has sapphire blue lacecap flowers, is a Pennsylvania Horticultural Society award winner. **Zones 6 to 9**.

H. paniculata

h. pan-ick-yew-LAH-tuh. PANICLE HYDRANGEA. Upright and somewhat coarse in texture, but with branches that arch over gracefully, particularly while in bloom. Ranging in size from 10 feet tall to as much as 20 feet with an equal spread, these plants are sometimes trained to a treelike form. The cone-shaped, summer-

Hydrangea paniculata 'Grandiflora'

through-fall flower panicles are 6 to 8 inches long, fading from cream colored to rosy pink. This species is more cold and drought tolerant than *H. macrophylla*. It blooms on new wood and may be pruned in early spring, leaving just a few buds if you want to force larger flowers and a bushier habit. 'Grandiflora', the "peegee" hydrangea, is the most commonly available. 'Tardiva' is a more diminutive form that flowers a bit later. 'Unique' grows 10 to 13 feet tall and bears pure white flower panicles up to 16 inches long. **Zones 4 to 8**.

H. quercifolia

h. kwer-sih-FOE-lee-uh. OAKLEAF HYDRANGEA. The common name comes from the lobed leaves, which can be 8 inches long and turn mahogany red in fall, remaining on the plant for many weeks. The late-spring flowers, held in upright panicles to 12 inches high, emerge white and color pink before fading to brown. Winter interest is provided by exfoliating bark. Up to 8 feet tall and wide, oakleaf hydrangea prefers more shade than others. Although said to flower from buds produced the previous season, in reality it can bloom after being killed to the ground by frost. Doesn't require pruning at all, but a proportion of old growth can be removed to re-

shape or rejuvenate it. 'Snow Flake' and 'Snow Queen' are considered more floriferous than the species. **Zones 5 to 9**.

Hymenocallis

hy-men-oh-KAL-iss. Amaryllis family, Amaryllidaceae.

Commonly known as Peruvian daffodils, spider lilies, or basket flowers, *Hymenocallis* species are tender bulbs grown for their umbels of fragrant flowers that resemble daffodils. The flowers typically are white and have six wide-spreading petal-like tepals that are joined at the base. The tepals usually are narrow, somewhat curled, and spidery in appearance. They surround a daffodil-like cup that is called a staminal cup because it is formed by six stamens that are fused at the base. (A close look at the flowers reveals the stamens protruding from the edge of the cup.) The basal, strap-shaped leaves can be deciduous or evergreen.

About 40 species belong here, all native from the southern United States to South America. Several were once classified in the genus *Ismene*. Species that once belonged to *Ismene* (including popular *H. narcissiflora*) have larger staminal cups — from 1$\frac{1}{2}$ to 3 inches long — than other members of the genus. These species are commonly referred to as basket flowers, or ismenes, and bloom in summer. Species with smaller staminal cups — under 1$\frac{1}{2}$ inches — are commonly called spider lilies; these plants bloom in winter, early spring, or summer.

HOW TO GROW

Select a site in full sun or partial shade with rich, evenly moist, well-drained soil. Evergreen species, including *H. caribaea* and *H. harrisiana*, are best in areas with hot, humid summers and frost-free winters, where they can be grown outdoors year-round. They also can be grown in large containers; to overwinter container-grown evergreen species indoors, keep them in a humid spot where temperatures do not drop below 55°F and water just enough to keep the foliage from wilting. Where they are hardy, deciduous species, including *H. × festalis* and *H. narcissiflora*, also can be grown outdoors year-round. These are the species most often seen in the North, because bulbs planted outdoors in late spring bloom quickly

— by early to midsummer — and are easy to dig and overwinter indoors.

To grow any of these species outdoors in the ground, plant the bulbs in late spring or early summer after the soil has warmed up. Set the tips of the bulbs 3 to 4 inches below the soil surface — slightly deeper if you are trying to grow them outdoors year-round at the northern limit of their hardiness. In containers, plant bulbs with the necks above the soil surface. For any of the species, keep the soil evenly moist while they are growing actively. Feed container-grown plants every other week with a dilute, balanced fertilizer.

Dig deciduous species after a light fall frost or when the foliage turns completely yellow. Try to dig the bulbs with as many undamaged roots as possible. Set the bulbs upside down to dry them off (this ensures that moisture from the foliage will drip away from the bulbs). Store the bulbs in nearly dry peat moss or vermiculite in a cool (55° to 60°F), dry spot. Propagate by separating the offsets in spring.

H. caribaea

h. kah-ree-BAY-uh. SPIDER LILY. Formerly *Pancratium caribaeum*. Evergreen 2-foot-tall species native to the West Indies. Produces umbels of 8 to 12 fragrant 6-inch-wide white flowers with $\frac{3}{4}$- to 1-inch-long staminal cups. Blooms are borne from summer to fall. **Zones 10 and 11**.

H. × festalis

h. × fes-TAL-iss. BASKET LILY, PERUVIAN DAFFODIL. Formerly *Ismene × festalis*. *H. longipetala* × *H. narcissiflora* hybrid. A 1$\frac{1}{2}$- to 2$\frac{1}{2}$-foot-tall deciduous species bearing umbels of two to five fragrant white 3- to 6-inch-wide flowers in late spring or summer. The individual flowers

Hymenocallis harrisiana

Hymenocallis 'Sulphur Queen'

have very narrow tepals and large showy 2-inch-long staminal cups. 'Zwanenburg' bears large flowers with cups that have scalloped edges. **Zones 8 to 10; to Zone 7 with heavy winter mulch.**

H. harrisiana
h. har-ih-see-AH-nuh. SPIDER LILY. Formerly *Ismene harrisiana*. Deciduous 1-foot-tall species native to Mexico. Bears umbels of up to six starry white flowers tinged with green that have 3-inch-long tepals and short staminal cups. **Zones 9 to 11.**

H. narcissiflora
h. nar-sis-ih-FLOR-uh. PERUVIAN DAFFODIL, BASKET LILY. Deciduous 2-foot-tall species bearing umbels with two to five very fragrant white flowers sometimes striped with green. Flowers are borne in summer and are 4 inches wide with 2-inch-long cups. **Zones 8 to 11.**

H. 'Sulphur Queen'
A deciduous 2-foot-tall hybrid grown for its umbels of up to six fragrant yellow flowers with green-striped throats. Blooms are about 6 inches wide and appear from late spring to summer. **Zones 9 to 11.**

Hypericum

hy-PAIR-ih-kum. Mangosteen family, Clusiaceae.

The yellow flowers of these shrubs are unavoidable in the Pacific Northwest, where they thrive in the mild conditions. The genus contains more than 400 species of annuals, perennials, and deciduous or evergreen shrubs and small trees, grown primarily for the

bright yellow flowers with starry stamens. A weedy Eurasian species, *H. perforatum*, is the source of a popular herbal antidepressant that goes by the common name for most of the genus, St. Johnswort.

HOW TO GROW
Most St. Johnsworts, except for *H. frondosum*, are suited primarily to mild climates. Some will tolerate poor or heavy clay soils but succumb to heat and humidity or cold wind. Most species need excellent drainage and full sun, with minimal pruning. An exception is *H. calycinum*, which can be severely pruned or even mowed to the ground in spring. Other species are planted as tall ground covers, as rock-garden plants, and for facing down taller shrubs. Propagate from seeds or softwood cuttings in summer.

H. calycinum
h. kal-ih-SYE-num. AARON'S BEARD. In the Northwest, this species is an almost ubiquitous ground cover along highways and in other public plantings. Evergreen or semievergreen and 1 to 2 feet tall, it spreads by stolons and often becomes invasive. It tolerates shade, where the 4-inch leaves become more yellow-green. Bright yellow saucer flowers 3 to 4 inches across bloom throughout the summer. **Zones 5 to 9.**

H. frondosum
h. fron-DOE-sum. GOLDEN ST. JOHNSWORT. A deciduous southeastern U.S. native growing 3 to 4 feet high and wide, upright and rounded with exfoliating bark and 2¹/₂-inch blue-green oblong leaves. The summer flowers, 1 to 2 inches across, have a dense mass of stamens and are followed by reddish brown seedpods. 'Sunburst' is

Hypericum 'Hidcote'

Hypoestes phyllostachya 'Pink Splash'

tolerant of Midwest conditions and compacted clay soil. **Zones 6 to 8.**

H. 'Hidcote'
Taxonomists can't decide if this popular St. Johnswort is a hybrid or a selection of *H. patulum*. Gardeners need only know that it is a dense, bushy evergreen to 5 feet tall and wide with lance-shaped dark green leaves and golden yellow flowers up to 3 inches across, often blooming from summer into fall. **Zones 6 to 9.**

H. kalmianum
h. kal-mee-AN-um. KALM'S ST. JOHNSWORT. This cold-hardy species, native to southern Canada and the Upper Midwest, is a dense evergreen growing 2 to 3 feet tall. Bears blue-green leaves in summer and clusters of three 1-inch flowers in midsummer. **Zones 4 to 7.**

H. patulum
h. PAT-yew-lum. GOLDEN CUP. Semievergreen to evergreen, this Chinese species grows up to 4 feet tall and spreads to 5 feet. The 2-inch flowers bloom singly or in flat clusters in midsummer. **Zones 7 to 9.**

Hypoestes

hy-poe-ESS-tees. Acanthus family, Acanthaceae.

There are about 40 species of *Hypoestes*, which are tender perennials, subshrubs, and shrubs from South Africa, Madagascar, and Southeast Asia. They bear ovate, sometimes toothed, leaves and small spikes of two-lipped flowers from late summer to frost. One species is grown as a foliage plant, both indoors as a houseplant and outdoors as a foliage accent in bedding displays.

HOW TO GROW
Give these plants a site in partial shade and rich, evenly moist, well-drained soil. Sow seeds indoors 10 to 12 weeks before the last spring frost date. Plants are fast and easy to grow from cuttings taken in spring or summer. Pinch plants to encourage branching and bushy growth. Grow them as bedding plants replaced annually or as tender perennials — keep plants in containers so they are easy to bring in, take cuttings in late summer, or dig the plants and pot them up for overwintering. Feed container-grown plants monthly during the growing season. Use these plants to add foliage color to shady plantings and mixed containers.

H. phyllostachya
h. fill-oh-STAY-kee-ah. POLKA-DOT PLANT, FRECKLE FACE. A 1-foot-tall subshrub with ovate leaves spotted with pink. Bears tiny spikes of pink to lilac flowers in summer and fall. 'Confetti Mix' produces plants spotted with pink and white. 'Splash' has leaves heavily dotted with large spots of bright pink. Tender perennial or warm-weather annual.

Iberis

eye-BEER-iss. Cabbage family, Brassicaceae.

Better known as candytufts, *Iberis* species are annuals, perennials, and subshrubs grown for their rounded clusters of flowers. They bear linear to ovate leaves, and their showy flower clusters, which are sometimes fragrant, are made up of tiny four-petaled flowers. The genus contains about 40 species that thrive in alkaline, fast-draining soils and are found from Spain and southern Europe through North Africa to Turkey and Iran.

HOW TO GROW

Plant candytufts in a site with full sun or very light shade and average, well-drained soil. Wet soil, especially in winter, leads to root rot and death. Immediately after perennial candytufts have flowered, cut plants back by one-third to remove spent blooms and to encourage branching. Every 2 to 3 years, cut them back hard — by about two-thirds — to keep growth compact and dense. Plants seldom need dividing, but dig them in spring immediately after they flower to propagate them or if they outgrow their space.

Sow seeds of annual candytufts outdoors after danger of frost has passed. From Zone 8 south, an-nual candytufts can be sown in late summer or early fall for bloom the following year. Or sow seeds indoors in individual pots 6 to 8 weeks before the last spring frost date at 65° to 70°F. Germination takes 2 to 3 weeks. Transplant with care. Sow new crops every 2 weeks until midsummer for continued bloom. Deadhead to prolong bloom, and pull up plants once they begin to die. Plants self-sow in mild climates.

I. amara

i. ah-MAR-uh. ROCKET CANDYTUFT. A 6- to 18-inch-tall, branching annual with spoon-shaped leaves. Bears rounded, 4- to 6-inch-tall clusters of mildly fragrant white to lilac-white flowers in summer. 'Giant White Hyacinth Flowered' features good fragrance and is an especially good cut flower. Cool-weather annual.

I. saxatilis

i. sax-ah-TILL-iss. ROCK CANDYTUFT, PERENNIAL CANDYTUFT. Woody-based 3- to 6-inch-tall subshrub spreading to about 1 foot. Bears evergreen, needlelike leaves and flat-topped 1^1/$_4$- to 1^1/$_2$-inch-wide clusters of white flowers in midspring. **Zones 2 to 7.**

I. sempervirens

i. sem-per-VIE-renz. PERENNIAL CANDYTUFT, COMMON CANDYTUFT. Woody-based 6- to 12-inch-tall evergreen subshrub spreading to 1^1/$_2$ feet. Bears very dark green 1- to 1^1/$_2$-inch-long leaves and 1^1/$_2$- to 2-inch-wide clusters of tiny white flowers in midspring. 'Autumn Beauty' and 'Autumn Snow' both bloom in spring and again in fall. 'Little Gem' is a dwarf 5- to 8-inch cultivar. **Zones 3 to 9.**

I. umbellata

i. um-bell-AY-tuh. GLOBE CANDYTUFT. A mounding, well-branched 6- to 12-inch annual with linear to lance-shaped leaves. Flattened, 2-inch-wide clusters of fragrant flowers appear in shades of white, pink, lilac, purple, or red in summer. 'Flash Mix' plants come in an especially wide range of colors. Cool-weather annual.

Ilex

EYE-lex. Holly family, Aquifoliaceae.

Ilex is a large genus comprising more than 400 species of evergreen and deciduous shrubs, trees, and climbers from temperate to subtropical climates. Hollies, as they are commonly called, offer glossy leaves that sparkle in the sun and bright berries for the birds.

HOW TO GROW

Most hollies prefer acid soils but are otherwise varied in their preferences — from rich humus to sand to waterside conditions — and somewhat adaptable. As woodland natives they tolerate shade, but variegated species in particular do best in full sun. Un-

Iberis sempervirens

Ilex aquifolium 'Aureomarginata'

Ilex aquifolium 'Flavescens'

yellow-green, unscented flowers, 1 inch across and composed of 30 narrow petals, appear in the leaf axils. **Zones 7 to 9.**

I. floridanum

i. flor-ih-DAY-num. FLORIDA AN-ISE. Also called purple anise, this native of Florida and Louisiana grows upright and compact from 5 to 10 feet tall, occasionally suckering. Dark green 2- to 6-inch leaves held in whorls are similar to a rhododendron's. In midspring it produces 1- to 2-inch fragrant flowers with up to 30 maroon petals. **Zones 7 to 9.**

I. henryi

i. HEN-ree-eye. HENRY ANISE TREE. A western Chinese species forming a dense pyramid 6 to 10 feet tall, with whorls of lustrous dark green leaves. The midspring flowers are 1 inch across, have 15 to 20 dark pink to red petals. **Zones 8 to 9.**

I. parviflorum

i. par-vih-FLOR-um. SMALL AN-ISE. Native to Florida and Georgia, small anise is similar to *I. Henryi* but taller at 15 to 20 feet and sometimes suckering. Leaves are olive green, and the midspring flowers that inspired the common name are only $^1/_2$ inch across. Tolerant of more sun and drier soils. **Zones 7 to 9.**

Impatiens

im-PAY-shens. Balsam family, Balsaminaceae.

The genus *Impatiens* contains about 850 species of annuals, perennials, and subshrubs with brittle, succulent stems; fleshy leaves; and spurred, asymmetrical

Impatiens balsamina

flowers. The flowers have five petals, although the lower petals on each flower are fused together to form two lobed pairs. Cultivated forms of impatiens bear single or double flowers; in some species they are hooded. In addition to beloved garden annuals, the wildflower jewelweed (*I. capensis*) belongs here. It is also called touch-me-not, a name that celebrates another characteristic of all impatiens: the seeds are contained in an explosive capsule that flings seeds in all directions when touched. Hummingbirds visit many species of impatiens.

HOW TO GROW

Give impatiens partial to full shade and rich, evenly moist, well-drained soil. New Guinea impatiens grow best in full sun to very light shade. Sow seeds indoors 8 to 10 weeks before the last spring frost date. Germination takes 2 to 3 weeks at 70° to 75°F (germinate garden balsam, *I. balsamina*, slightly cooler — 60° to 65°F). Use a sterile seed-starting mix, and just press the seeds into the soil surface, since light aids germination. To combat damping off, which can be a problem, water only from below, but provide high humidity by covering the pots with plastic until seedlings appear. Do not set plastic-covered pots or flats in sun, since they can quickly overheat. Grow seedlings at around 60°F. Transplant to the garden several weeks after the last spring frost date, once night temperatures remain above 50°F. Perennials, including New Guinea impatiens and garden impatiens (*I. wallerana*), are easy to propagate by cuttings taken in spring or summer. They can be grown as bedding plants replaced annually or as tender perennials: to

Impatiens New Guinea hybrid

overwinter them, take cuttings, dig and pot up plants, or keep them in containers.

Use impatiens to add summer-long color to shade gardens, either planted in large drifts or interspersed among perennials, as well as in containers. Dwarf types make excellent edgings for paths and beds. Some species, especially *I. balsamina*, self-sow.

I. balsamina

i. bal-sah-MEE-nah. GARDEN BALSAM. A 1- to 2$^1/_2$-foot-tall annual with lance-shaped leaves and single or double flowers borne along the main stem in the leaf axils from summer to early fall. Flowers come in shades of pink, white, red, and purple. Camellia-flowered Series plants are 5 feet tall and double flowered. Tom Thumb Series plants are 8 to 12 inches tall. Warm-weather annual.

I. glandulifera

i. gland-yew-LIF-er-ah. HIMALAYAN JEWELWEED. Formerly *I. roylei*. A somewhat coarse, 1- to 3-

Impatiens walleriana

foot annual with ovate to lance-shaped leaves. Bears clusters of fragrant, 1$^1/_2$-inch-long, lavender to rose-purple flowers. This species is native to the Himalaya but has naturalized in North America. Warm-weather annual.

I. New Guinea hybrids

Hybrid, tender, subshrubby perennials developed by crossing various species from New Guinea, including *I. schlecteri*. They bear lance-shaped leaves on 12- to 14-inch-tall plants that can be green, bronze, or variegated with yellow or cream. Flat-faced, 2- to 2$^1/_2$-inch-wide flowers appear from summer to frost in shades of rose, red, salmon, lilac-pink, and white. Many cultivars are cutting-propagated, but 'Spectra Mix' is a strain that comes true from seed. Tender perennial or warm-weather annual.

I. walleriana

i. wall-er-ee-AH-nah. GARDEN IMPATIENS, BUSY LIZZIE, PATIENCE PLANT. Tender, subshrubby, $^1/_2$- to 2-foot-tall perennial with rounded to lance-shaped, green leaves that may be flushed with bronze. Showy, flat-faced, single or double, 1- to 2$^1/_2$-inch-wide flowers are borne in abundance from summer to frost. Many cultivars are available, most mixes with a wide range of colors, including pale and dark pink, lav-

Incarvillea delavayi 'Snowtop'

Indigofera kirilowii

ender, rose, white, salmon, red, and orange-red; bicolors also are available. A large percentage of Confection Series plants are double-flowered plants. Mini-Hawaiian Series plants are miniature and well-branched and bear leaves and flowers under 1 inch. Super Elfin Series plants are 6 inches tall. Tender perennial or warm-weather annual.

Incarvillea

in-kar-VIL-lee-uh. Bignonia family, Bignoniaceae.

Grown for their showy clusters of trumpet-shaped flowers, *Incarvillea* species are annuals and taprooted perennials native to Asia. While trumpet-shaped blooms of the most commonly grown species in this genus have earned it the name "hardy gloxinia," these members of the bignonia family actually are more closely related to trumpet vines (*Campsis*) and Chilean glory vine (*Eccremocarpus scaber*) than to gloxinias. All of the 14 species that belong to this genus bear racemes or panicles of tubular two-lipped flowers that have five spreading lobes, or "petals." The flowers are borne above mounds of handsome leaves divided in a featherlike (pinnate or pinnatisect) fashion.

HOW TO GROW

Select a site in full sun that is shaded during the hottest part of the day. Rich, moist, well-drained soil is ideal. Since incarvilleas do not tolerate soil that is very wet in winter, a well-drained site, such as a raised bed, is best. Plant the crowns (composed of thick, fleshy roots) in spring, setting the crown about 1 inch below the soil surface. Handle them carefully to avoid breaking the brittle roots. Amend the soil with coarse sand or grit if winter moisture might be a problem. Incarvilleas are best left undisturbed once planted, as they resent root disturbance. In areas where they are marginally hardy, mulch plants in late fall with evergreen boughs, pine needles, salt hay, or another coarse mulch. Plants also thrive in containers, which can be overwintered in a cool (40° to 50°F) spot and kept on the dry side. Or dig the roots and store them in dry peat moss in a cool spot over winter. Propagate by seeds, by carefully digging and dividing the clumps, or by rooting shoot cuttings of stems that arise at the base of the plant in spring.

I. delavayi

i. deh-LAV-ay-eye. HARDY GLOXINIA. Handsome, taprooted 1- to 2-foot-tall perennial forming 1-foot-wide rosettes of pinnate leaves with coarsely toothed leaflets. From early to midsummer plants bear showy racemes of up to 10 pink 3-inch-wide flowers with yellow throats. 'Snowtop' is a white-flowered cultivar. Zones 6 to 10.

Indigofera

in-dig-OFF-er-uh. Pea family, Fabaceae.

Indigofera is an enormous genus of nearly 800 species of perennials and shrubs native to warm zones throughout the world. It is in the pea family with *Trifolium* (clover) and *Lupinus* (lupines). The deciduous leaves are compound and have numerous leaflets, including one at the tip. Flowers are less than an inch long, pealike, and rose or pink. The small flowers appear in spikelike clusters that are produced all along the stem. One nonornamental species, *I. tinc-*toria, is a traditional source of the blue dye indigo. The botanical name is Latin and means "bearing indigo."

HOW TO GROW

Grow indigoferas in full sun. They are very deep rooted and demand a well-drained but fertile loam that is neutral to slightly alkaline. They may die back to the ground in cold winters but can be cut back and will return to flower on new wood. Indigoferas develop a strong crown at ground level, which must be mulched or covered to prevent damage in severe winters near the northern limit of their range. Like many members of the pea family, plants may sulk if moved after becoming established. Their ability to fix nitrogen and their suckering growth make them excellent bank stabilizers that also improve the site for companion plants.

I. incarnata

i. in-kar-NAH-tuh. This low shrub produces fountains of branches that bear light pink flowers in late spring. Plants mature to under 2 feet tall but are many times wider. Zones 7 to 10.

I. kirilowii

i. kir-uh-LOW-ee-eye. Smaller and hardier than *I. incarnata*, this slowly spreading shrub has pink cotton-candy flowers. Zones 6 (with proper siting) to 10.

Inula

IN-yew-luh. Aster family, Asteraceae.

The genus *Inula* contains about 100 species, mostly perennial herbs and shrubs that bear showy, daisylike flower heads in shades of orange-yellow to yellow. The blooms are carried singly or in clusters and consist of a central "eye" of closely packed disk florets surrounding numerous, narrow ray florets, or "petals," that in some species are nearly threadlike.

HOW TO GROW

Select a site in full sun with rich, moist soil that is well drained. *I. helenium* and *I. hookeri* grow in partial shade. *I. magnifica* grows in wet and even boggy conditions and also tolerates partial shade. Taller species generally need staking. To propagate, divide the clumps in spring or fall or sow seeds.

I. ensifolia

i. en-sih-FOE-lee-uh. SWORD-LEAVED INULA. A 1- to 2-foot-tall species that spreads to about 1 foot. Bears narrow, lance-shaped leaves and small clusters of 1- to 2-inch-wide golden yellow flowers in mid- to late summer. Zones 4 to 9.

I. helenium

i. hel-EE-nee-um. ELECAMPANE. Robust 3- to 6-foot-tall herb (the dried roots were once used as an expectorant) forming low 3-foot-wide clumps of ovate, toothed, 32-inch-long leaves. Bears 3-inch-

Inula ensifolia

Ipheion uniflorum 'Wisley Blue'

wide yellow flowers, either singly or in small clusters, in mid- to late summer. **Zones 5 to 8.**

I. hookeri

i. HOOK-er-eye. A 2- to 2¹/₂-foot-tall species with lance-shaped leaves and pale yellow 1¹/₂- to 3-inch-wide flowers borne singly or in small clusters in late summer and fall. **Zones 4 to 8.**

I. magnifica

i. mag-NIF-ih-kuh. Vigorous 5- to 6-foot-tall species forming 3-foot-wide clumps of rounded 10-inch-long leaves. Bears clusters of 6-inch-wide daisies in late summer. **Zones 5 to 8.**

Ipheion

IF-ee-on. Lily family, Liliaceae.

One species in this genus of 10 is cultivated — *I. uniflorum*, commonly known as spring starflower. It bears starry, fragrant blooms in spring and like all the members of this genus, it grows from small tunicate bulbs. Bulbs usually produce a single flower stalk, sometimes two, with one or two upward-facing flowers. The individual flowers have a salverform shape, meaning they have a slender tube with a flared and flattened face. Like other lily-family plants, the flowers have six lobes, or petal-like tepals. *Ipheion* species are native to South America. Plants produce basal, linear leaves that have a garlicky odor when bruised.

HOW TO GROW

Give spring starflowers a site in full sun with average soil that is moist and well drained. Where hardy, plant the bulbs in late summer or early fall, positioning the tops of the bulbs 3 inches below the soil surface. Where marginally hardy, look for a protected site, such as at the base of a south-facing wall, and protect the bulbs with a coarse winter mulch of evergreen boughs, pine needles, salt hay, or coarse leaves such as oak leaves from late fall through winter. These plants also are good candidates for growing in containers: pot the bulbs in fall with the tips about ¹/₂ inch under the soil surface. Hold them in a cool (40° to 45°F) room or cold frame and keep the soil just barely moist. After plants have bloomed, water and feed regularly until the leaves turn yellow, then store them nearly dry until the following year. Repot in fall as necessary.

Spring starflowers grown in the ground can be left for years without needing to be divided. Dig the clumps in summer, just as the leaves disappear, if they become overcrowded and begin to bloom less, or for propagation. Or propagate by seeds.

I. uniflorum

i. yew-nih-FLOR-um. S P R I N G S T A R F L O W E R. Formerly *Tristagma uniflorum*. A 6- to 8-inch-tall species bearing starry, fragrant 1¹/₂-inch-wide flowers in spring. Blooms are normally pale blue with darker blue midribs. 'Rolf Fiedler' is a 4- to 5-inch-tall hybrid with rich blue flowers that have overlapping tepals. 'Wisley Blue' bears darker purplish blue flowers. **Zones 6 to 9.**

Ipomoea

eye-poe-MEE-ah. Morning-glory family, Convolvulaceae.

Ipomoea is a large and diverse genus consisting of about 500 species. The best-known garden plants are climbing annuals and tender perennials — the botanical name is from the Greek *ips*, meaning "worm," and *homoios*, "resembling" — but the genus also contains nonclimbing annuals and perennials along with a few shrubs and trees. Botanists have classified and reclassified the plants contained here, so several species are still listed under other names. Closely related to *Convolvulus* species, *Ipomoea* species bear funnel- or bell-shaped flowers, either singly or in clusters in the leaf axils. Hummingbirds are attracted to the blooms, especially of red-flowered species and cultivars.

HOW TO GROW

A site in full sun and average, well-drained, evenly moist soil is ideal. Most ipomoeas require strings, a trellis, or other support upon which to climb. Sow seeds indoors in individual pots 6 to 8 weeks before the last spring frost date. Germination takes from 1 to 3 weeks at 65° to 70°F. Seedlings need a stake to climb on even when they are still fairly small; otherwise the vines will become entangled. Transplant a few weeks after the last frost, once temperatures remain above 45°F. Or sow outdoors 2 weeks after the last frost date. Install the required trellis *before* outdoor sowing. Either way, to speed germination, carefully nick the seed coats with a knife or file and/or soak the seeds for 24 hours in warm water before sowing. In addition to seeds, perennial types can be propagated by cuttings taken in spring or summer, which can be used to overwinter the plants, if desired.

Use these plants to climb and cover all manner of structures,

Ipomoea lobata

Ipomoea tricolor 'Heavenly Blue'

Ipomoea nil 'Early Call'

from deck railings and fences to trellises. They also can be trained over shrubs. Some, including foliage cultivars of *I. batatas,* are effective clambering among perennials and annuals in mixed plantings or in containers.

I. alba

i. AL-buh. MOONFLOWER. Formerly *Calonyction aculeatum, I. bona-nox.* A tender perennial climber that can reach 15 feet in a single season. Produces large, rounded leaves with heart-shaped bases. Bears fragrant, white, 5- to 5¹/₂-inch-wide flowers that open at dusk from early or midsummer to frost. The flowers attract night-flying moths. Warm-weather annual or tender perennial.

I. batatas

i. bah-TAH-tas. SWEET POTATO. A tender perennial grown in food gardens for its fleshy, sweet, edible roots. Plants can climb or spread 10 feet or more in a single season, and to 20 feet or more in frost-free climates. They bear rounded to heart-shaped leaves that can be entire or lobed and 1-inch-wide, pale purple flowers in summer. While even cultivars developed for vegetable gardens have attractive foliage, often flushed with purple, several are grown for their leaves alone: 'Blackie' bears dark purple-black, maplelike leaves; 'Margarita' has chartreuse, heart-shaped leaves; 'Pink Frost' has arrow-shaped leaves marked with green, white, and pink, which require protection from direct sun. All are hardy from **Zone 9 south** and produce tubers, which can be dug before frost and used to overwinter the plants farther north. Warm-weather annual or tender perennial.

I. coccinea

i. kok-SIN-ee-ah. RED MORNING GLORY, STAR MORNING GLORY. Formerly *Quamoclit coccinea.* A vigorous 6- to 12-foot annual climber with ovate or deeply toothed leaves. Bears small clusters of scarlet, ³/₄-inch-wide trumpets in summer. Warm-weather annual.

I. hederacea

i. hed-er-AY-see-ah. Formerly *Pharbitis hederacea.* A 6- to 10-foot annual climber with rounded, three-lobed leaves. Bears small clusters of ³/₄- to 1¹/₂-inch-wide, blue, purple, or purple-red flowers in summer. 'Fugi Mix' and 'Ro-man Candy' feature variegated leaves. Warm-weather annual.

I. lobata

i. low-BAH-tah. SPANISH FLAG, EXOTIC LOVE. Formerly *I. versicolor, Mina lobata. Quamoclit lobata.* A tender perennial climber most often grown as an annual that ranges from 6 to 15 feet in height. Bears lobed leaves and dense, one-sided racemes of slightly curved, narrow, tubular flowers that are ¹/₂ to ³/₄ inch long. Buds and flowers initially are red but turn orange, yellow, and then cream as they age. 'Citronella' bears lemon yellow flowers that age to white. Tender perennial or warm-weather annual.

I. × multifida

i. × mul-TIFF-ih-dah. CARDINAL CLIMBER. A 3- to 6-foot annual climber, the result of a cross between *I. coccinea* and *I. quamoclit.* Bears deeply lobed leaves and crimson, 1-inch-wide, salverform flowers. Warm-weather annual.

I. nil

i. NIL. MORNING GLORY. Formerly *I. imperialis.* A vigorous annual or tender, short-lived perennial that can reach 15 feet in a single season. Bears ovate, sometimes lobed, leaves and 2- to 4-inch-wide, white-tubed flowers in shades of pale to deep blue, red, purple, or white from midsummer to fall. 'Early Call Mix' is fast from seeds and a good choice for areas with short growing seasons. 'Chocolate' bears pale red-brown flowers. Platycodon Series plants have purple, red, or white, single or semidouble flowers. 'Scarlett O'Hara' bears red flowers. Warm-weather annual.

I. purpurea

i. pur-PUR-ee-ah. COMMON MORNING GLORY. Formerly *Convolvulus purpureus* and *Pharbitis purpurea.* A 6- to 10-foot annual climber with broad, rounded to lobed leaves and trumpet-shaped, 2¹/₂-inch-wide, white-throated flowers in shades of blue, purple-blue, pink, red, or white in summer; white flowers with stripes of color also are available. Warm-weather annual.

I. quamoclit

i. KWAM-oh-klit. CYPRESS VINE, STAR GLORY. Formerly *Quamoclit pennata.* A 6- to 20-foot annual climber with deeply cut leaves. Bears scarlet, ³/₄-inch-wide flowers in summer. Warm-weather annual.

I. tricolor

i. TRY-kuh-lor. MORNING GLORY. Formerly *I. rubrocaerulea.* A vigorous annual or short-lived tender perennial reaching 10

Ipomopsis rubra (see page 210)

Iresine lindenii

to 12 feet in a season. Bears 3-inch-wide flowers with white throats in shades from pale blue to purple in summer. 'Crimson Rambler' has red flowers with white throats. 'Heavenly Blue' bears sky blue flowers with white throats. 'Pearly Gates' bears white flowers. Warm-weather annual.

Ipomopsis

ip-oh-MOP-sis. Phlox family, Polemoniaceae.

This genus contains 24 species of annuals, biennials, and perennials, plus one shrub, that were once included in the genus *Gilia*. Most are native to western North America, although standing cypress *(I. rubra)* is native from South Carolina and Florida to Texas. They bear entire to deeply cut, feather-like leaves and showy clusters of tubular flowers in shades of red, pink, violet, yellow, and white.

HOW TO GROW

Plant in full sun and average, very well drained soil. The species discussed here thrive in sandy soil. They can be grown as annuals or biennials, but growing them as biennials yields the showiest flower display and is the best option where plants are hardy. To grow them as annuals, sow seeds outdoors 2 to 3 weeks before the last spring frost date; sow in fall in areas with mild winters (from Zone 6 south). Or sow indoors 6 to 8 weeks before the last frost date, and germinate at 50° to 65°F, although outdoor sowing is usually best. To grow them as biennials, sow seeds outdoors in mid- to late summer. Keep the soil on the dry side, since wet conditions lead to root rot, especially in winter. Use these plants in drifts in mixed plantings as well as wild gardens. The flowers attract hummingbirds as well as moths and also make attractive additions to bouquets. Plants self-sow.

I. aggregata

i. ag-greh-GAH-tuh. SKYROCKET, SCARLET GILIA. A 2-foot-tall biennial bearing large panicles of tubular to funnelform, $^1/_4$- to $1^1/_2$-inch-long flowers in red, pink, yellow, or nearly white. **Zones 6 to 9**.

I. rubra

i. RUE-bruh. STANDING CYPRESS. A 3- to 6-foot biennial with feathery leaves and narrow panicles of scarlet flowers dotted with red and yellow inside. **Zones 6 to 9**.

Iresine

EYE-reh-sine. Amaranth family, Amaranthaceae.

Colorful foliage is the hallmark of *Iresine* species, which are commonly referred to as blood leaf. About 80 species of plants native to South America and Australia belong to this genus, including both erect and climbing annuals and tender perennials, as well as subshrubs. They bear simple, unlobed leaves that often are brilliantly marked with red or yellow. The insignificant flowers are white or greenish.

HOW TO GROW

Full sun and rich, evenly moist, well-drained soil are best. Plants grow in partial shade but show best leaf color in sun. Since asexual propagation yields uniform-looking plants identical to their parents, cuttings are the best choice for propagation. Grow blood leaves as bedding plants replaced annually or as tender

Bearded iris

perennials. If you start from seeds, sow indoors 8 to 10 weeks before the last spring frost date and germinate at 55° to 60°F. Take cuttings anytime. Move plants to the garden several weeks after the last frost date, once temperatures consistently stay in the 50s. Water regularly and feed monthly during the growing season. Pinch regularly to encourage branching and bushy growth. To overwinter plants indoors, take cuttings in late summer, and keep them on the dry side.

Use blood leaves as edging plants or to add season-long foliage color to beds and borders. They tolerate shearing and thus make a good edging for knot gardens, and also are used in carpet-bedding displays.

I. herbstii

i. HERB-stee-eye. PAINTED BLOOD LEAF, BEEFSTEAK PLANT, CHICKEN GIZZARD. A well-branched, bushy annual or short-lived tender perennial that can reach 5 to 6 feet in the tropics

Iris bearded hybrids

Ipomopsis rubra

Iris ensata

but is usually a foot tall when grown in the North. Rounded, waxy, 2¹/₂- to 3-inch-long leaves are variegated or have contrasting veins: colors include green, yellow, red, purple-red, and orange-red. The leaf surface may be puckered. 'Aureoreticulata' features green leaves with yellow veins. 'Brilliantissima' has shocking red-pink leaves blotched with purple-brown. Tender perennial or warm-weather annual.

I. lindenii
i. lin-DEN-ee-eye. BLOOD LEAF. A tender perennial that can reach 3 feet in the tropics but is considerably shorter in northern gardens. Grown for its glossy, ovate to lance-shaped, dark red leaves, leafstalks, and stems. Tender perennial or warm-weather annual.

Iris

EYE-riss. Iris family, Iridaceae.

Named in honor of the mythological Greek goddess Iris, who rode to earth on a rainbow, *Iris* is a vast genus containing about 300 species — both perennials and bulbs — along with thousands of cultivars. All bear flowers with six petals, three of which point up or out and are called standards, and three of which point out or down and are called falls. Generally the flowers are borne in small clusters and the buds open in succession, a characteristic that lengthens the display from each flower stalk. The foliage is sword shaped, strap shaped, or grassy. While some rhizomatous species spread widely, others form dense, grasslike clumps.

HOW TO GROW
The ideal site for irises varies according to species. Plant bearded irises in full sun and average to rich, well-drained soil from midsummer to early fall, setting the tops of the fleshy rhizomes just above the soil surface. Rhizomes planted too deeply or covered with mulch are susceptible to rot. Tall bearded cultivars may need stak-

Iris ensata

ing. Cut back and destroy old foliage and rake up debris around the plants in fall to help control iris borers. Dig and divide bearded irises every 3 years in midsummer or early fall to keep them healthy and vigorous, as well as for propagation. (Discard spongy, old portions along with any rhizomes infested with fat, fleshy iris borer larvae or any that smell or are slimy, both signs of bacterial soft rot.) Cut the leaves back by two-thirds, then replant. Water deeply to settle the plants in the soil, and every 10 days to 2 weeks for the rest of the growing season if the weather is dry. Established plants are quite drought tolerant. See the individual descriptions below for recommended care for other species.

I. bearded hybrids
Sometimes listed as *I. germanica*, these hybrids bloom in late spring or early summer with flowers that have fuzzy beards at the top of each fall. They come in various heights and flower sizes, although tall bearded irises, with 4- to 8-inch-wide blooms atop 27-inch-tall plants, are by far the best known. Other size classes can be as small as 8 inches in height and bloom at slightly different times. Hundreds of cultivars are available in colors from white and pale yellow through peach, pink, raspberry, bronze-red, lilac, purple, and violet-blue to chocolate brown and red-black. The falls and standards may be the same color, be contrasting solid colors, or have margins or mottling in contrasting colors. Many are fragrant. Winners of the American Iris Society's Dykes Medal are all good cultivars, including 'Beverly Sills' (pink),

'Bride's Halo' (white and lemon yellow), 'Dusky Challenger' (purple and violet), 'Edith Wolford' (yellow and blue-violet), 'Hello Darkness' (violet-black),'Honky Tonk Blues' (blue and white), 'Jessy's Song' (white with red-violet, and lemon yellow beards), 'Silverado' (silvery lavender-blue), and 'Victoria Falls' (blue and white). **Zones 3 to 9**.

I. bucharica
i. boo-KAR-ih-kuh. An 8- to 16-inch-tall species that belongs to a group called Juno irises, because it has bulbs with fleshy roots attached; handle them carefully at planting time (and when transplanting) to avoid breaking the brittle roots. Bears creamy white and yellow flowers that are 2 to 2¹/₂ inches wide in spring. Best for dry, well-drained spots in full sun and good for rock gardens. **Zones 5 to 9**.

I. cristata
i. kris-TAH-tuh. CRESTED IRIS. Clump-forming 4- to 8-inch-tall native North American wildflower that spreads via fleshy rhizomes to form 1¹/₂- to 2-foot-wide mats. In late spring it bears pale lavender-blue or white 1¹/₂- to 2-inch-wide flowers with yellow or orange crests on each fall. Grows in partial to full shade and rich, evenly moist, well-drained soil with a slightly acid pH. Divide the clumps in early spring as necessary or for propagation. **Zones 3 to 9**.

I. danfordiae
i. dan-FOR-dee-ee. DANFORD IRIS. A 3- to 6-inch-tall species classified as a reticulated iris because of the brown netlike covering on the bulbs. Bears fragrant yellow 2-inch-wide flowers with brown spots in late winter or early spring. Plant the bulbs with the tops a full 4 inches below the soil surface to discourage them from breaking into many bulblets that are too small to flower. They require warm, dry soil during summer, when they are dormant. **Zones 5 to 8**.

I. Dutch hybrids
Dutch irises are 15- to 30-inch-tall plants that belong to a group called the xiphium irises, which also contains Spanish and English irises. *I. xiphium* played a major role in the development of Dutch irises. They produce 3- to 3¹/₂-inch-wide flowers in shades of white, yellow, or violet from late spring to early summer. Gardeners who want reliable bloom each year often grow these irises as annuals.

Iris Louisiana hybrid

Iris sibirica

They make excellent cut flowers, although cutting generally removes enough foliage that the plants won't return the following year. **Zones 6 to 9.**

I. ensata

i. en-SAH-tuh. J A P A N E S E I R I S. Formerly *I. kaempferi*. Sturdy perennial forming 2¹/₂- to 3-foot-tall clumps of grasslike leaves that spread to 2 feet via short rhizomes. Bears beardless, flat 4- to 8-inch-wide flowers in early to midsummer in shades of violet-blue, purple, lavender-blue, white, rose pink, or wine red. Blooms are single or double and have large falls with standards that point downward. Select a site in full sun to partial shade with very rich, acid soil — pH 5.5 to 6.5. It requires constantly moist to even boggy

Iris versicolor

soil in spring and summer but needs drier conditions in winter. Divide clumps in early spring or early fall every 3 to 4 years. **Zones 4 to 9.**

I. foetidissima

i. feh-tih-DISS-ih-muh. S T I N K I N G I R I S. Unusual 1- to 3-foot-tall species that spreads to 1¹/₂ feet. Bears dull purple flowers in early summer followed by showy scarlet seeds in fall. Plant in partial to full shade in evenly moist, well-drained soil that is rich in organic matter. **Zones 7 to 9; to Zone 6 with protection.**

I. histrioides

i. hiss-tree-OY-deez. A 4- to 6-inch-tall species classified as a reticulated iris because of the brown netlike covering on the bulbs. Bears violet-blue 2¹/₂- to 3-inch-wide flowers in early spring. Best in rich, well-drained soil. Good for naturalizing, but the bulbs may break up into many small bulbs that take several years to achieve flowering size. 'Frank Elder' bears pale violet-blue flowers with darker stripes and a yellow crest on the falls. 'George' offers especially fragrant purple blooms.

'Katharine Hodgkin' has yellow flowers blushed with pale blue and veined and dotted with dark blue. **Zones 4 to 9.**

I. latifolia

i. lat-ih-FOE-lee-uh. E N G L I S H I R I S. Formerly *I. xiphioides*. A 20-inch-tall hybrid that bears 4- to 5-inch-wide flowers in midsummer in shades of violet-blue, purple, white, or lilac-rose. Grow it in full sun or partial shade with rich, well-drained soil that is constantly moist. The plants are difficult to accommodate in much of North America but are relatively easy in the Pacific Northwest and Northeast. Where conditions suit them, they are longer-lived than Dutch and Spanish irises. 'Isabella' bears lilac-rose blooms. 'Mansfield' has purple flowers with a violet-blue blotch and white stripes. 'Mont Blanc' bears white flowers blushed with lilac. **Zones 5 to 8.**

I. Louisiana hybrids

L O U I S I A N A I R I S E S. Hybrid irises derived from several native species ranging in height from 1¹/₂ or 2 feet to 5 feet and spreading to 3 feet or more via wide-spreading rhizomes. They bear flowers in shades of purple to blue-black, sky blue, vermilion red, or violet from midspring to early summer. Plant in full sun to partial shade and very rich, constantly moist to wet soil with an acid pH. They also grow in rich, well-drained soil that remains evenly moist. **Zones 6 to 11**, but hardiness varies depending on the cultivar, and some are hardy to **Zone 4 with winter protection.**

I. pseudacorus

i. sue-dah-KOR-us. Y E L L O W F L A G. Vigorous 3- to 4-foot-tall species that spreads as far. Produces clumps of sword-shaped leaves topped by bright yellow 2¹/₂-inch-wide flowers in early summer. Grows in full sun or light shade in a range of soils, from evenly moist to well-drained to constantly wet or boggy, as well as with up to 10 inches of water over the crowns. **Zones 4 to 9.**

I. pumila

i. PEW-mih-luh. D W A R F B E A R D E D I R I S. This low European and Asian iris grows to only 5 inches tall and spreads to form masses. Several color selections exist in purple, blue, yellow, and cream. **Zones 4 to 8.**

I. reticulata

i. reh-tik-yew-LAH-tuh. A 4- to 6-inch-tall species with bulbs that have a netted tunic and grasslike, four-angled leaves. Bears fragrant 2-inch-wide flowers in late winter to early spring in shades of blue or purple. Good for naturalizing, but may not return reliably in areas with hot, wet summers. Several cultivars are available, including 'Cantab', pale blue with a pale yellow blotch on each fall; 'Harmony', deep blue blooms and yellow blotches; 'J.S. Dijt', purple with red-purple falls that are borne late; 'Natascha', pale blue, nearly white, with an orange blotch on each fall; and 'Purple Gem', violet-purple with plum purple falls and purple blotches edged in white. **Zones 3 to 8.**

I. sibirica

i. sye-BEER-ih-kuh. S I B E R I A N I R I S. A 1- to 3-foot-tall clump-forming species spreading to 2 feet. Produces clumps of handsome, grassy leaves and beardless 3-inch-wide flowers in early summer in shades from violet-blue, blue, and purple to white or yellow. Many cultivars are available, including ones with bicolor blooms. Plants grow in full sun to light shade and evenly moist, well-drained, or constantly wet soil. They also grow with up to 2 inches of standing water over the crowns. 'Butter and Sugar' bears white-and-yellow blooms. 'Caesar' has violet-purple blooms. 'Super Ego' features pale blue flowers with darker violet-blue falls. 'White Swirl' bears white flowers that have yellow centers. Plants take a season or two to become established and resent being disturbed. Divide them in early spring or early fall only when they become so very crowded that blooming is reduced or for propagation. **Zones 2 to 9.**

I. tectorum

i. tek-TOR-um. R O O F I R I S. A 10- to 16-inch-tall species spreading by fleshy rhizomes to form broad 1¹/₂-foot-wide clumps. Bears crested 2- to 5-inch-wide flowers in lavender or white in late spring or early summer. Select a site in full sun or partial shade with rich, evenly moist, well-drained soil. Also tolerates dry soil in shade. Divide immediately after flowering every 3 to 5 years when clumps become overcrowded or for propagation. Set the rhizomes with the tops just above the soil surface. **Zones 5 to 9**.

I. versicolor

i. ver-sih-KUH-lor. BLUE FLAG. A native North American wildflower ranging from 2 to 2¹/₂ feet in height and spreading to 2 to 3 feet. Bears blue-violet or purple 2- to 3-inch-wide flowers in early to midsummer. **Zones 2 to 9**. Southern blue flag (*I. virginica*) is a similar native species hardy in **Zones 7 to 11**. Both species grow in full sun in constantly moist soil or standing water.

I. xiphium

i. ZIFF-ee-um. SPANISH IRIS. The Spanish irises grown in gardens are hybrids, similar to Dutch irises, that bear white, yellow, or violet flowers on 15- to 30-inch plants. They bloom from late spring to early summer, about 3 weeks after Dutch cultivars. Gardeners who want reliable bloom each year often grow these irises as annuals. All make excellent cut flowers, although cutting generally removes enough foliage that the plants won't return the following year. **Zones 6 to 9**.

Itea

eye-TEE-uh. Currant family, Grossulariaceae.

A genus of about 10 species of shrubs from the eastern United States and East Asia, grown for their catkinlike panicles of small white flowers and either evergreen leaves similar to a holly's (*Ilex*) or deciduous leaves with colorful fall foliage.

HOW TO GROW
The two readily available species are quite different in appearance and cultural needs; see the individual listings. Both propagate easily from cuttings or suckers.

I. ilicifolia

i. il-ih-sih-FOE-ee-uh. This Chinese evergreen grows 10 to 12 feet tall and has spiny, lustrous, dark green hollylike leaves 2 to 4 inches long. The tiny greenish white flowers appear in slender racemes from mid- to late summer. It needs fertile, moist soil in partial shade and out of the wind and requires minimal pruning. **Zones 8 to 9**.

I. virginica

i. ver-JIN-ih-kuh. VIRGINIA SWEETSPIRE. An eastern U.S. wetland plant growing to 5 feet tall

Itea virginica

and easily suckering twice as wide, this species is adaptable to drought and almost any other hardship, although it flowers and colors best in moist, fertile soil and full sun. Autumn foliage can be a spectacular mix of red and reddish purple, sometimes with orange or yellow. Excellent at the edge of a wood or pond, or in a border. On mature plants, cut back about one-third of oldest shoots to stimulate new growth. 'Henry's Garnet', which received a Gold Medal from the Pennsylvania Horticultural Society, has large flowers and outstanding fall color. **Zones 6 to 9**.

Ixia

IKS-ee-uh. Iris family, Iridaceae.

Ixia species, commonly called ixias, corn lilies, or wand flowers, are South African plants that grow from small corms. They are prized for their showy clusters of star-shaped flowers borne on thin, wiry stems. The plants flower from spring to summer and come in a range of bright colors. Blooms often feature an eye, or center, in a contrasting color. The individual blooms have six petal-like tepals. The flowers can be arranged in loose, graceful spikes or in fairly congested, rounded clusters. The grasslike leaves are mostly basal, although small leaves are borne on the stems, and they are arranged in two ranks, or rows. From 40 to 50 species belong to this genus.

HOW TO GROW
Give ixias a site with full sun and rich, well-drained soil. Where hardy, they can be grown outdoors year-round. Like many South African species, they prefer dry soil conditions when dormant. Especially in areas with wet winters, a

site with very well drained soil (such as a raised bed) is essential. When growing these corms outdoors year-round, plant them in fall at a depth of 3 to 6 inches. Where they are marginally hardy, look for a protected spot, such as at the base of a south-facing wall, and mulch heavily in fall with a coarse mulch such as evergreen boughs, salt hay, or pine needles.

Where ixias are not hardy, treat the corms like those of gladioli: plant outdoors in spring after all danger of frost has passed at a depth of 3 to 6 inches, then dig the corms in summer after the leaves have died back. Store them dry in net or paper bags in a cool (50° to 60°F), dry, well-ventilated spot. Or grow them in containers by potting the corms in spring (or in late summer for bloom the following year). In pots, set the corms at a depth of about 1 inch. Water carefully until the plants begin to flower: the soil should stay barely moist, never wet or completely dry. Replace the corms annually or, to hold them for another year's bloom, continue watering after plants flower and feed every other

week with a dilute, balanced fertilizer. When the leaves begin to turn yellow and die back gradually, dry off the plants and store the containers in a relatively cool, dry, airy spot. Or clean the soil off the corms and store them in paper bags. Repot in spring. Propagate by seeds or by separating offsets in late summer just as the leaves die down.

I. hybrids

HYBRID CORN LILY, HYBRID WAND FLOWER. Many hybrids have been selected. Most are 12- to 16-inch-tall plants with 1¹/₂- to 3-inch-wide blooms from spring to summer. 'Blue Bird' bears white flowers with dark purple centers, and the outer petals have a violet purple streak and purple tip. 'Mable' has magenta-pink flowers. 'Marquette' features yellow flowers with purple-red centers and petal tips. 'Panorama' bears hot pink flowers with purple centers. 'Rose Emperor' has rose-pink flowers with magenta centers. **Zones 9 to 11; to Zone 8 with winter protection**.

I. maculata

i. mak-yew-LAH-tuh. A 6- to 20-inch-tall species bearing spikes of 2¹/₂-inch-wide flowers from spring to early summer. Blooms are yellow or orange and have dark purple to purple-black centers. **Zones 9 to 11; to Zone 8 with winter protection**.

I. viridiflora

i. ver-id-ih-FLOR-uh. GREEN-FLOWERED CORN LILY. A 1- to 2-foot-tall species bearing spikes of 12 or more pale green flowers with black centers rimmed in violet-purple from spring to summer. **Zones 9 to 11; to Zone 8 with winter protection**.

Ixia viridiflora

J

Jasminum

JAS-min-um. Olive family, Oleaceae.

This genus boasts about 200 evergreen and deciduous shrubs and climbers primarily from Europe, Asia, and Africa. The temperate shrubs are cultivated for their yellow, usually fragrant flowers.

HOW TO GROW

Jasmines are often wall trained, which gives them extra warmth, or incorporated into mixed borders. Plant them in fertile, well-drained soil in full sun or partial shade. Prune off flowered shoots and remove about one-third of old shoots from established plants to encourage new growth. Propagate from semiripe cuttings.

J. floridum

j. FLOR-ih-dum. SHOWY JASMINE. An evergreen to semi-evergreen from China growing to 5 feet tall. The lustrous dark green leaves have three to five leaflets, and the yellow five-lobed flowers bloom in cymes from mid- to late spring. Zones 8 to 10.

J. humile

j. HEW-mil-ee. ITALIAN YELLOW JASMINE. An evergreen similar to *J. floridum* but more upright, to about 6 feet, and having less glossy leaves. Commences blooming later with slightly fragrant flowers. 'Revolutum' may be more cold hardy. Zones 8 to 10.

J. mesnyi

j. MEZ-nee-eye. PRIMROSE JASMINE. Forms an evergreen mound to 8 feet high and half as wide, with trailing branches and double flowers in early spring. Good for training against a wall. Zones 8 to 10.

J. nudiflorum

j. noo-dih-FLOR-um. WINTER JASMINE. Deciduous arching or climbing shrub, 4 feet high and 6 feet wide if grown in a border or down a bank, up to 10 to 12 feet high if trained against a wall. The bright yellow axillary flowers are 2-inch tubes with spreading lobes 1 inch across, appearing for a long period in late winter before the foliage. Zones 6 to 9.

Juglans

JEW-glanz. Walnut family, Juglandaceae.

The trees of this genus are closely related to hickories. They have large, pinnately compound, alternate leaves and male and female flowers on the same tree. Some species have edible nuts and are valued for their wood. Members of this genus, especially black walnut and butternut, exude a toxic chemical called juglone from their roots that inhibits the growth of some plants. Grass grows well near walnut trees, but many garden plants, such as asparagus, tomatoes, potatoes, eggplants, blueberries, mountain laurel, red pine, apples, rhododendrons, azaleas, hydrangeas, peonies, chrysanthemums, and columbines, do not. The area of toxicity usually extends within a radius of 50 to 60 feet from the trunk, but it can extend up to 80 feet. Leaves contain lower concentrations of the toxin and can be composted and used in the garden, because the toxin breaks down quickly when exposed to air and water. Bark and wood chips need to be aged for 6 months before garden use.

HOW TO GROW

Plant in full sun and deep, rich, moist soil. Tolerates somewhat drier sites.

J. nigra

j. NYE-gruh. BLACK WALNUT. A tall native with a wide-spreading, ruggedly picturesque outline, black walnut grows to 75 feet tall and almost as wide. Dark green leaves emerge in late spring and are divided like large feathers into pointed, 5-inch-long leaflets. They lack a terminal leaflet, are aromatic when crushed, and turn yellowish in late summer or early autumn before dropping. Leaves fall apart and pose little cleanup problem, although the long central rachis (leaf stem) must be raked up. Edible nuts enclosed in green, 2-inch, round husks drop in autumn, posing a hazard and a cleanup problem if the tree is near a walkway, driveway, or lawn. The nuts are valued food for people and wildlife, but the husks are hard to remove and can stain hands and clothing. Trunk bark is brown and thickly furrowed. The beautiful, fine-grained wood is

Jasminum nudiflorum

Juglans nigra (flowers)

valued for furniture making. Save native trees in a natural landscape and locate young trees in a large field, pasture, park, or open lawn, where they will hold the soil and provide light shade. From eastern and central North America. **Zones 4 to 9.**

CULTIVARS AND SIMILAR SPECIES

J. cinerea (butternut) is similar, but its leaves have a terminal leaflet and it is more cold hardy; **Zones 3 to 7.** *J. regia* (English walnut) is a smaller tree grown commercially for its easier-to-shell nuts; hardy to **Zone 7.** 'Carpathian' is hardy to **Zone 6.**

Juniperus

jew-NIP-er-us. Cypress family, Cupressaceae.

This large and variable genus contains about 60 species from North America, Asia, and Europe, many of them important landscape trees, shrubs, and ground covers. Young plants have sharp-pointed, needlelike foliage, while mature plants usually feature scalelike foliage. Some cultivars have both juvenile and adult foliage at the same time; others keep the juvenile form throughout their lives. Fruits are technically cones but look like berries and are usually dark gray-blue.

TREES

HOW TO GROW

Full sun and average to sandy, well-drained, alkaline to slightly

Juniperus virginiana 'Grey Owl'

acid soil suit most junipers. They adapt to moist or dry conditions and rocky soil, but fare poorly in heavy soil. They also tolerate heat and drought. Juniper blight and cedar-apple rust can be serious problems in humid areas.

J. scopulorum

j. skop-yew-LOR-um. ROCKY MOUNTAIN JUNIPER, WESTERN RED CEDAR. Forming a narrow pyramid with several 30- to 40-foot-tall trunks, this western native has cultivars that are smaller and more compact. Leaves are scalelike and green or blue-green; they keep their color in winter, unlike eastern red cedar (*J. virginiana*). Trunks are covered with reddish brown, shredding bark. This drought-tolerant evergreen is useful as a fine-textured, vertical accent or screen in Xeriscape gardens or areas with

low rainfall. It performs poorly in areas where rainfall and humidity are high, such as the Southeast. From the Rocky Mountains. **Zones 3 to 6.**

CULTIVARS

'Blue Heaven' ('Blue Haven') is a disease-resistant, bright blue, 20-foot-tall pyramid. 'Blue Trail' is a silver-blue, 18-foot-tall column. 'Medora' forms a very narrow, dense, blue-green column that is especially tolerant of cold and drought. 'Moonglow' is a dense, 20-foot-tall, silver-blue pyramid. 'Skyrocket' makes an extremely narrow, silver-blue column that grows to 15 feet tall and 2 feet wide; susceptible to storm damage. 'Sutherland' is a silvery green, 18-foot-tall column. 'Tolleson's Blue Weeping' has silver-blue foliage and gracefully arching, wide-spreading branches; grows to 20 feet tall and wide if the central trunk is staked. 'Welchii' forms a dense, 12-foot-tall, blue-green cone. 'Wichita Blue' is a brilliant blue, 20-foot-tall, 6-foot-wide pyramid; susceptible to disease.

J. virginiana

j. ver-jin-ee-AH-nuh. EASTERN RED CEDAR. Forming a 50-foot-tall, 10- to 20-foot-wide pyramid or column, this adaptable native is common in the wild but is not well known in gardens. The dark green foliage has a strong cedar fragrance when crushed. It is needlelike on young plants, changing to scalelike with maturity. Foliage turns brownish green in winter, although improved cultivars have a more attractive winter color. Trunk bark is shredding and reddish brown. Female trees produce clusters of eye-catching, waxy blue fruits, which provide food for birds and other wildlife. This underused tree makes an easy-to-

Juniperis chinensis 'Torulosa'

grow screen or windbreak, especially in poor-soil sites in the East and Midwest. It grows best in moist sites but tolerates drought, road salt, salt spray, and seashore and urban conditions. It is usually pest-free, but mites may be a problem in very hot, dry locations. Twig blight is a problem in wet areas. Eastern red cedar also is the alternate host for cedar-apple rust, which can disfigure the tree and seriously hurt nearby apples, crab apples, and hawthorns. Do not plant within a mile of an apple orchard. From eastern North America. **Zones 3 to 9.**

CULTIVARS

'Burkii' has steel blue needles that turn an attractive purplish color in winter; grows 10 to 25 feet tall. 'Canaerti' is a dark green form with copious berries; pyramidal, growing to 25 feet tall. 'Emerald Sentinel' forms a deep green, 20-foot-tall, 4-foot-wide column. 'Princeton Sentry' is a blue-green, very narrow, 25-foot-tall column. *Upright cultivars:* 'Blue Point' makes a vivid blue-green, 12-foot-tall, 8-foot-wide column. 'Hetzii Columnaris' is a bright green, 15-foot-tall, 5-foot-wide column. 'Keteleeri' forms a 30-foot-tall cone with dense, vivid light blue-green foliage.

SHRUBS

HOW TO GROW

Shrub junipers are ubiquitous because they tolerate almost any soil type — acid or alkaline, sandy or clay — except waterlogged. They can survive drought and wind and some salt. Give them full sun, as they may become too open in shade. Small varieties can be used in rock gardens and containers, or to provide an evergreen accent among perennials. Try taller selections as hedges, in shrub borders, or as specimens. Juniper blight can cause tip dieback on many types, and bagworms are often a serious problem.

J. chinensis

j. chih-NEN-sis. CHINESE JUNIPER. Although it's a 60-foot tree

Juglans nigra

in northern Asia, its native habitat, Chinese juniper's cultivars are popular small garden plants. 'San Jose' is a creeper that reaches 12 to 18 inches tall and more than 6 feet wide, with irregular branching. Needles are a muted sage green. 'Sea Spray' grows to 15 inches tall and more than 5 feet across and has blue-green foliage. *J. c.* var. *sargentii*, Sargent juniper, is a ground-covering juniper native to coastal northern Japan. It will grow in almost pure sand. Plants are 1¹/₂ to 2 feet tall and spread to 9 feet. Needles are blue-green. **Zones 4 to 9.**

J. communis

j. kuh-MEW-niss. COMMON JUNIPER. This species is native to cold and temperate regions of Asia, Europe, and North America, with outlying populations high in the mountains far south of its typical range. It does not perform well where summers are hot and muggy. 'Effusa' is a low grower that spreads to 4 feet across. It has green foliage with silver stripes on

Juniperus horizontalis

the underside. Its "berries" are the critical flavoring for gin. **Zones 2 to 6.**

J. conferta

j. kon-FUR-tuh. SHORE JUNIPER. Although the species grows wild only on the islands of Japan and on Sakhalin (a Russian island north of Japan), its cultivars grow well in warmer climates in sandy soils. 'Blue Pacific' is a low-growing and relatively heat-tolerant form that grows to 12 inches tall and 6 feet across. Its needles are blue-green. 'Emerald Sea' is dense, low, and relatively salt tolerant. Its emerald green needles have a gray band. **Zones 6 to 8.**

Juniperus sabina

J. horizontalis

j. hoar-ih-zon-TAL-iss. CREEPING JUNIPER. This North American native grows wild from the Atlantic to the Pacific in northern regions, and some wild populations grow even in Zone 2. All forms are low growing and spread 5 to 10 feet over time. 'Andorra Compacta' grows to 18 inches tall and has dense, gray-green foliage that bronzes in winter. 'Bar Harbor' was originally collected near its namesake town in coastal Maine. Its creeping stems have short side branches that grow up to 10 inches tall. Foliage is blue-gray. 'Blue Chip' is a low spreader with blue foliage on short, upright tips that become purplish in winter. 'Wiltonii' is a classic selection from coastal New England. It is very flat — rarely more than 6 inches tall — and dense. Needles are silvery green with a tinge of purple in winter. This cultivar performs relatively well in the Deep South. **Zones 4 to 9.**

J. × pfitzeriana

j. × fitz-er-ee-AY-nuh. PFITZER JUNIPER. Formerly *J. × media*. This widely planted variety is a hybrid of *J. sabina* and *J. chinensis*, looking much like the former (with 45-degree branches) but sometimes listed as a cultivar of the latter. Growing about 5 feet tall and 10 feet wide, it has scalelike, diamond-shaped, sage green leaves and round, dark purple cones. It performs well in both the North and the South. Cultivars include 'Monlep' (trademarked as Mint Julep), which is slightly more compact and has a fountainlike habit and fine foliage; and 'Sulphur Spray', which is about 20 inches tall by 4¹/₂ feet wide and

has soft green foliage tipped with yellow when new. **Zones 4 to 9.**

J. procumbens 'Nana'

j. proh-KUM-benz. JAPANESE GARDEN JUNIPER. Forms a ground-hugging mat 1 foot tall and 4 to 6 feet wide (possibly 10 feet or more after many years) with upturned, spray-shaped branches that form layers. The blue-green foliage often turns somewhat purple in winter. **Zones 5 to 9.**

J. sabina

j. suh-BEE-nuh. SAVIN JUNIPER. This species from the mountains of Europe and Asia grows 4 to 6 feet tall and 5 to 10 feet wide with stiffly upturned branches. Among its many low-growing cultivars are 'Broadmoor', growing 2 to 3 feet tall and 10 feet wide with gray-green foliage; and 'Monna' (trademarked as Calvary Carpet), truly carpetlike at 6 to 8 inches high and 10 feet wide. Both are considered blight resistant. **Zones 4 to 7.**

J. sargentii 'Glauca'

j. sar-JEN-tee-eye. BLUE SARGENT JUNIPER. Grows 30 inches tall by 10 feet wide with upright branching and has blue-green, camphor-scented foliage that is disease resistant. **Zones 3 to 9.**

J. squamata 'Blue Star'

j. skwah-MAH-tuh. BLUE STAR JUNIPER. This popular cultivar of the singleseed or flaky juniper from Asia forms a pincushion-shaped mound about 3 feet tall and wide and has silver-blue needles that may turn somewhat purple in winter. Does not perform well in heat and humidity. **Zones 4 to 7.**

Juniperus scopulorum

K

Kaempferia

kemp-FAIR-ee-uh. Ginger family, Zingirberaceae.

Kaempferia species are tender perennials native to tropical portions of Asia that grow from thick, fleshy rhizomes; some species have aromatic tubers. They bear rounded leaves that are either clustered at the base of the plant or borne in two rows, or ranks, up short stems. The flowers, which are borne on either leafy or scaly spikes, appear either with the leaves or before the leaves emerge. Each flower has a bract at the base, and individual blooms have three petals with a lower lip that is deeply split into two lobes. About 40 species belong to the genus. The roots of some species are used medicinally and to flavor foods.

HOW TO GROW

Give these plants partial shade and deeply prepared, moist soil that is rich in organic matter. They thrive in areas with warm summers and high humidity and are ideal for gardens in the tropics and subtropics or for adding an exotic touch to more northern gardens. Where hardy, they grow outdoors year-round. In the North, plant the rhizomes out in spring after the soil has warmed up and overwinter them indoors. To overwinter, dig the rhizomes after a light frost and cut back the tops.

Store the rhizomes in barely damp vermiculite, peat moss, or sand in a cool (55°F), dry place. Inspect rhizomes occasionally in winter. Discard rotted pieces or cut away rotted portions and dust cuts with sulfur; sprinkle the vermiculite with water occasionally during winter to keep the roots from shriveling. Replant in spring. Or grow these plants in containers year-round; keep them nearly dry and in a cool spot over winter. Propagate by dividing the rhizomes in spring.

K. pulchra

k. PUL-kruh. GINGER LILY. A low-growing species that reaches about 6 inches tall and spreads to 12 inches. Bears handsome, rounded leaves marked with dark green and silver-green. Short spikes of 2-inch-wide lilac or lilac-pink flowers appear among the leaves in summer. **Zones 10 to 11.**

K. roscoeana

k. ros-koh-ee-AH-nuh. DWARF GINGER LILY, PEACOCK LILY. A 6-inch-tall species that spreads to about 8 to 10 inches. Bears two rounded, dark green leaves that are handsomely marked with lighter green on top and tinged with red-purple underneath. From summer to fall, plants produce short spikes of 2-inch-wide white flowers among the leaves. **Zones 10 and 11.**

K. rotunda

k. roe-TUN-duh. RESURREC-TION LILY. A 6-inch-tall species spreading to 1½ feet. Bears 16-inch-long lance-shaped leaves that are silvery green on top and flushed with purple beneath. Spikes of up to six fragrant white 2-inch-wide flowers with purplish bracts appear before the leaves. **Zones 10 and 11.**

Kalmia

KAL-mee-uh. Heath family, Ericaceae.

When not in flower, the laurel-like leaves of these species look a lot like those of the related rhododendron. But the blossoms of these species are cup shaped with stamens radiating to anther sacs in the flower wall. Dark dots around these sacs inspired the common name "calico bush" for one species. The taut stamens "shoot" pollen onto visiting bees. There are seven species of these evergreen shrubs, at home in woods and meadows primarily in North America.

HOW TO GROW

Grow kalmias in fertile, humus-rich, acid soil in partial shade. Growing naturally on slopes, they need a well-draining but moisture-retentive situation in the garden. Excellent for woodland gardens or shady shrub borders. They

don't need regular pruning, but leggy plants can be pruned hard to stimulate new growth. Propagation is difficult.

K. angustifolia

k. an-gus-tih-FOE-lee-uh. SHEEP LAUREL. Native to the eastern United States and Canada, this shrub averages 2 feet high and spreads by stolons to 10 feet wide. The oblong, leathery leaves are 2 inches long in whorls of three. The early-summer, saucer-shaped flowers range from lavender-pink to burgundy, rarely white, and are carried in 2-inch clusters. **Zones 2 to 7.**

K. latifolia

k. lat-ih-FOE-lee-uh. MOUNTAIN LAUREL. This better-known eastern U.S. native grows slowly to 10 feet tall and wide, fairly rounded and dense at first and then more open and showing gnarled branches. The leathery leaves are up to 5 inches long. The cup-shaped "calico flowers" with 10 stamens are usually pink in bud and open to white but can open deep pink. Among the many cultivars are forms with red buds opening to pink ('Olympic Fire', 'Richard Jaynes'), interior bands ('Bullseye'), or stars ('Carousel'). **Zones 4 to 9.**

Kerria

KAIR-ee-uh. Rose family, Rosaceae.

There is just one species in this genus, a deciduous shrub from Asia with cheery golden yellow flowers and bright green stems that provide winter interest.

Kaempferia pulchra

Kalmia latifolia 'Carousel'

Kalmia latifolia

Kerria japonica

HOW TO GROW

Give kerria moderately fertile soil in full sun to full shade. Partial shade will keep the flowers from fading. Good for awkward narrow spaces, massing, or in shrub or mixed borders. Prune out dead branches and trim back a portion of flowered branches to keep under control. Suckers can pop up a couple of feet from the parent plant, but the species is not invasive. Pull up the suckers, or use them for easy propagation.

K. japonica

k. juh-PON-ih-kuh. JAPANESE KERRIA. The upright, arching, bright green branches grow 5 to 6 feet tall and can sucker to form a mass 6 or more feet across. Bright green leaves, doubly toothed and slightly pleated, grow to 4 inches long. Golden yellow, five-petaled flowers that are 1¹/₂ inches across appear in midspring and sporadically throughout the season. 'Picta' has white leaf margins. 'Pleniflora' is a double-flowered form with 1- to 2-inch pompon blooms. **Zones 4 to 9.**

Kirengeshoma

kih-ren-guh-SHOW-muh. Hydrangea family, Hydrangeaceae.

Two species of perennials native to Japan and Korea belong to the genus *Kirengeshoma*. They bear branched clusters of nodding, tu-

Kerria japonica 'Pleniflora'

bular to bell-shaped blooms above mounds of large maplelike leaves.

HOW TO GROW

Select a site in partial shade with rich, evenly moist soil with an acid pH. Clumps are best left undisturbed, so try to pick a permanent site and prepare the soil deeply at planting time by adding plenty of compost or other organic matter. To propagate, carefully dig and divide the plants in spring.

K. palmata

k. pal-MAY-tuh. YELLOW WAX BELLS. A 3- to 4-foot-tall species that forms 2¹/₂- to 4-foot-wide clumps. Bears 5- to 8-inch-long palmately lobed leaves and pale yellow, waxy-textured, 1¹/₂-inch-long flowers in late summer and early fall. **Zones 5 to 8.**

Knautia

NAW-tee-uh. Teasel family, Dipsacaceae.

Knautia contains 40 or more species of annuals and perennials

sometimes grown for their pincushion-like flower heads that resemble scabiosas *(Scabiosa)*. The flowers are bluish lilac or red-purple and are carried in loose, branched clusters above rosettes of leaves that are simple or lobed in a pinnate manner.

HOW TO GROW

Select a site in full sun with average to rich, well-drained soil. Neutral to alkaline pH is best. Plants are short-lived, especially in areas with hot, humid summers. They tend to flop in midsummer in hot climates: cut them back in spring to keep them compact and prevent this. Propagate by taking cuttings

from shoots that appear at the base of the plant in spring or by seeds.

K. macedonica

k. mah-sih-DON-ih-kuh. Formerly *Scabiosa rumelica*. Clump-forming 2- to 2¹/₂-foot-tall perennial spreading to about 1¹/₂ feet. Bears purple- to maroon-red, ¹/₂- to 1¹/₂-inch-wide flower heads from mid- to late summer. **Zones 4 to 8.**

Kniphofia

nih-FOE-fee-uh. Lily family, Liliaceae.

Kniphofia species bear erect spikes of flowers aptly described by the common names "torch lilies," "red-hot pokers," and "poker plants." The blooms consist of densely packed, tubular flowers above clumps of grassy evergreen or deciduous leaves. They usually are pendent but sometimes are held erect and come in fiery oranges, reds, and yellows as well as pale yellows, cream, and shades of pink. About 70 species — all perennials — belong to the genus.

HOW TO GROW

Give torch lilies full sun and average to rich soil that is evenly moist but well drained. Good soil drainage is especially important in winter. Plants do well in sandy soil. Cut the flower stalks to the ground after the blooms fade; cut the fo-

Kirengeshoma palmata

Knautia macedonica

Kniphofia uvaria

liage back by half in late summer if it becomes unkempt looking. Plants resent being disturbed and can be left for years without needing division. Divide them in spring if they become crowded or outgrow their space, or for propagation. To make divisions without disturbing the thick rhizomes and fleshy roots, try severing offsets from the outside of the clumps in spring. Or sow seeds, although cultivars do not come true.

K. uvaria

k. yew-VAIR-ee-uh. COMMON TORCH LILY. A clump-forming perennial with roughly 2-foot-tall, 2-foot-wide mounds of grassy evergreen leaves. Bears spikes of red-orange and yellow flowers from early to late summer. Plants are 2 to 4 feet tall in bloom. Many cultivars are available. 'Little Maid' bears yellow blooms on $1^{1}/_{2}$- to 2-foot plants. 'Primrose Beauty' has yellow blooms. 'Royal Standard' bears spikes of scarlet buds that open into yellow flowers. **Zones 5 to 9**.

Koelreuteria

kohl-rue-TEER-ee-ah. Soapberry family, Sapindaceae.

This small genus is made up of four or five species from Asia. These trees are characterized by their showy yellow blossoms, pinnately or bipinnately compound leaves, and papery seedpods. Though not pests, some species

have reseeded and naturalized in some parts of the country.

HOW TO GROW

Plant in full sun and almost any well-drained soil, including alkaline soil. Tolerates drought, heat, road salt, and urban conditions. The numerous seeds can cause a weed-seedling problem if the tree is sited near a garden bed; best in a lawn where seedlings can be mown. Prune when dormant to develop a strong branch structure and to remove lower limbs that may die naturally from lack of light. May be weak wooded if not properly pruned. Usually pest-free.

K. paniculata

k. pan-ick-yew-LAH-tuh. GOLDEN-RAIN TREE. This large flowering tree forms a rounded crown and reaches 30 to 40 feet tall and wide. Airy, 15-inch-long panicles of tiny, starlike, yellow blossoms bloom at the branch tips for several weeks in mid- to late summer. Clusters of 1- to 2-inch seedpods ripen from green to pinkish tan in fall, resembling Japanese lanterns. The large, compound leaves emerge with a pinkish or reddish purple tinge and become bright green in summer, changing to variable shades of orange, gold, and yellow in autumn. Made up of 7 to 17 leaflets with deeply jagged lobes, the 15-inch-long leaves have a bold, exotic texture. Goldenrain tree makes a fine shade tree for a lawn or patio or a good street tree away from power lines or near the seashore. From China, Japan, and Korea. **Zones 5 to 9**.

Koelreuteria paniculata 'September Gold'

CULTIVARS AND SIMILAR SPECIES

'Rose Lantern' blooms late and has rose pink seedpods. 'September' ('September Gold') has larger flowers and blooms later than the species, in late summer or early fall; **Zones 6 to 9**. *K. bipinnata* (Chinese goldenrain tree) grows larger and has more delicate-looking foliage, with 50 unlobed leaflets; flowers are not as showy and bloom in late summer; seedpods are a showy pink; **Zones 7 to 9**.

Kolkwitzia

kolk-WIT-zee-uh. Honeysuckle family, Caprifoliaceae.

This genus contains only a single species of deciduous shrub from a single province in China. Commonly known as beautybush, it is grown for clusters of pink bell-shaped flowers in mid- to late spring.

HOW TO GROW

Beautybush prefers fertile, loamy, well-drained soil in full sun but adapts to a wide pH range. It becomes rangy and ragged, so is best situated where it can be somewhat hidden in a shrub border. Prune flowered shoots after blooming is over, and remove a third of old growth annually. Propagate from softwood cuttings.

K. amabilis

k. ah-MAB-ih-liss. BEAUTYBUSH. A deciduous shrub with an erect and arching habit similar to forsythia, reaching 6 to 10 feet tall and spreading wider if given space. The dull green leaves, 1 to 3 inches long, may turn slightly yellow or red in fall. The $^{1}/_{2}$-inch midspring flowers, which are flaring pink bells with yellow throats, bloom in clusters up to 3 inches across. **Zones 4 to 8**.

Kolkwitzia amabilis

L

Lablab

LAB-lab. Pea family, Fabaceae.

The one species that belongs to this genus — *L. purpureus* — is a tender, climbing perennial known under such common names as hyacinth bean, bonavist, lablab, and Indian or Egyptian bean. It is widely grown from North Africa to India for its edible beans and pods, but in North America it is primarily appreciated as an ornamental because of its rose-purple flowers and glossy purple-maroon fruit.

HOW TO GROW

Full sun and average to rich, well-drained soil are ideal. Plants need strings, netting, or a trellis upon which to climb. Sow seeds indoors in individual pots 6 to 8 weeks before the last spring frost date at 65° to 75°F. Germination takes 2 weeks. Or, in areas with long growing seasons — roughly Zone 7 south — sow outdoors after the last frost, once the soil has warmed to 60°F. Soak seeds in warm water for 24 hours before sowing, and barely cover them with soil. Plants tolerate poor, dry soil, but for best growth water regularly and feed once or twice when the plants are still small to give them a good start. Use hyacinth beans to decorate trellises, walls, pergolas, and railings. They are effective when combined with other annual vines.

L. purpureus

l. pur-PUR-ee-us. HYACINTH BEAN, LABLAB. Formerly *Dolichos lablab*, *D. purpureus*. A vigorous, fast-growing, tender vine, ranging from 6 to 20 feet in height and hardy only in **Zones 10 and 11**. Bears palmate leaves and clusters of fragrant, rose-purple, 1/2- to 1-inch-long, pealike flowers. The flowers are followed by flat, glossy, maroon-purple pods that are quite showy. The pods and beans are edible, but strong-tasting, and dry beans can cause an allergic reaction in some people; soak the beans in hot water and discard the water to eliminate this danger. Tender perennial, or grow as a warm-weather annual.

Laburnum

lah-BURR-num. Bean family, Fabaceae.

The two small European trees that make up this genus feature clusters of yellow flowers, trifoliate leaves, and narrow seedpods. All plant parts, especially the seeds, are poisonous if eaten. A very showy hybrid of the two species is grown most frequently.

HOW TO GROW

Plant in full sun with light afternoon shade in hot climates; best where summers are cool. Likes humus-rich, moist, well-drained soil; tolerates alkaline soil. Protect from wind and full sun in winter. Prune in summer (to avoid bleeding sap) to develop a main leader. Twig blight, aphids, and mealybugs can be troublesome.

L. × watereri

l. × WAH-ter-er-eye. GOLDEN CHAIN TREE, WATERER LABURNUM. This small, spring-blooming tree, a showy hybrid of *L. anagyroides* and *L. alpinum*, has a stiff, upright or oval form and grows to 15 feet tall and 12 feet wide. For two weeks in late spring and early summer it is decked out with 12-inch-long or longer, wisteria-like chains of golden yellow flowers. Leaves are bright green and dainty, made up of three pointed, 3-inch leaflets, which close up at night. Leaves drop in fall with little color change. Bark on new shoots, trunk, and branches is smooth and olive green. Produces few seedpods. This tree is often short-lived, but it is worth planting in a spring border or foundation planting, where it will garner a lot of attention.

Zones 6 to 7; to Zone 8 where summers are cool.

CULTIVARS AND SIMILAR SPECIES

'Vossii' is the most widely grown cultivar because of its 2-foot-long flower clusters. *L. alpinum* (Scotch laburnum) has 10- to 16-inch-long

Lablab purpureus

Laburnum × watereri

Lachenalia aloides

flower clusters in early summer, shiny green leaves, and shiny seedpods. 'Pendulum' is a weeping, 10-foot-tall form with 1-foot-long flower clusters. *L. anagyroides* (common laburnum) has 6- to 12-inch-long flower clusters in late spring, matte green leaves, and hairy round seedpods.

Lachenalia

lak-eh-NAIL-ee-uh. Lily family, Liliaceae.

Commonly called Cape cowslips, *Lachenalia* species are tender, bulbous perennials native to South Africa grown for their showy, erect spikes or racemes of flowers that appear from fall to spring. The flowers, which are carried on leafless, often mottled stems, are nodding, are held horizontally, or point upward. Individual blooms are bell shaped or tubular to cylindrical and have six petal-like tepals. The tepals are arranged in two whorls, with three outer ones that usually are shorter, are somewhat swollen at the tips, and form a fleshy cup or tube. The three inner tepals are longer, and usually wider, and they often feature tips that are a contrasting color and may be recurved. About 90 species

belong to the genus, all of which grow from fleshy, tunicate bulbs and produce basal leaves that often are spotted or mottled.

HOW TO GROW

Select a site in full sun with light, rich, well-drained soil. A spot with light shade during the hottest part of the day is best, because it protects plants from heat. Plants require very well drained soil, so if drainage might be a problem, select a spot in a raised bed or rock garden and/or amend the soil with plenty of coarse sand or grit at planting time. Like many South African natives, Cape cowslips are ideal for areas that have Mediterranean climates (such as southern California), characterized by dry summers and mild winters. There, they grow and bloom during the winter months and are dormant during the hot, dry summers. Elsewhere, grow them in containers.

In the ground or in containers, plant in late summer or fall. When planting in the ground, set the bulbs at a depth of 3 inches; in containers, set them with the tips just under the soil surface. Water the containers and then hold them over winter in a cool spot (45°F nights; 55°F days) that is well ventilated. Keep the soil just barely moist until the plants begin grow-

ing actively; after that, keep the soil evenly moist but never wet. Feed container-grown plants weekly during the growing season. After they bloom, continue watering until the foliage begins to turn yellow, then gradually withhold water. Store the containers in a cool, dry, shady place until late summer, then move them to your overwintering spot in fall to repeat the process. Repot, as necessary, in late summer. Propagate by separating the offsets.

L. aloides

l. al-OY-deez. CAPE COWSLIP. Formerly *L. tricolor*. A 6- to 12-inch-tall species with broadly lance-shaped, 8-inch-long leaves spotted with dull red-purple. In late winter or spring it bears erect racemes of 10 to 20 pendent, tubular, 1- to 1½-inch-long flowers that are rich yellow with scarlet at the top and bottom. 'Nelsonii' has golden yellow flowers and leaves that are not spotted. 'Pearsonii' bears red-orange buds that open into yellow-orange flowers with red-orange bases and leaves mottled with brown. **Zones 9 and 10**.

L. bulbifera

l. bul-BIF-er-uh. CAPE COWSLIP. Formerly *L. pendula*. A 1-foot-tall species with ovate to lance- or strap-shaped leaves that are either all-green or spotted with brownish purple. Bears loose racemes of pendent, 1½-inch-long, red or orange flowers with green and purple tips. **Zones 9 and 10**.

Lagenaria

lah-jen-AIR-ee-uh. Squash family, Cucurbitaceae.

Lagenaria species, commonly known as bottle gourds, often are overlooked by gardeners interested in growing ornamentals. These climbing or sprawling plants feature large leaves that are rounded to heart shaped, or sometimes lobed. They climb via tendrils and bear separate male and female five-petaled flowers. Flowers are followed by fruits that can exceed 3 feet in length. The botanical name is from the Greek *lagenos*, meaning "flask." Of the six species of annuals and perennials in the genus, one is grown for its variously shaped fruits, which can be dried and used to make items such as birdhouses, dried-flower vases, toys, musical instruments, and serving containers and utensils.

HOW TO GROW

Full sun; rich, well-drained soil; and plenty of space will satisfy gourds. In areas with long growing seasons, the vines can climb or spread to 30 feet in a single season. Sow seeds indoors in individual pots no more than 4 weeks before the last spring frost date. Germination takes about 1 week if the soil is kept warm, about 75°F. Transplant with care after the last frost date, once the weather has settled and the soil has warmed up to at least 50°F. In areas with long growing seasons, sow seeds outdoors after the soil has reached 60°F. Larger gourds require a longer season to set and ripen fruit: birdhouse gourds can be direct-sown from about Zone 7 south, while kettle gourds should be given a head start indoors from about Zone 8 south. Use gourds as fast, temporary, inexpensive ground covers in new gardens and under shrubs. They will climb trees and trellises if permitted; just don't let them engulf shrubs you value. They also will cover eyesores.

The best way to dry the gourds is to wait until they turn brown on the plants and then cut them with several inches of stem attached. If frost threatens, however, harvest immediately. Spread them out in a dry, warm (70°F or warmer), airy spot until they turn light brown or straw-colored and are light in weight. This can take several months for larger types. Handle undried gourds carefully, as they break easily and bruised spots tend to rot during the drying process. Some experts wipe down the out-

Lagenaria siceraria

L

side of the gourds every few weeks with a 10 percent bleach solution (1 part bleach to 9 parts water). Inspect the drying gourds regularly, and discard any that show signs of rot.

L. siceraria

l. sis-er-AIR-ee-uh. BOTTLE GOURD, WHITE-FLOWERED GOURD, CALABASH. A vigorous climbing annual, to 30 feet, with heart-shaped leaves, white flowers, and fruit in various shapes and sizes. Cultivars are named by the shapes of the fruit, or gourds: 'Birdhouse', 'Hercules Club', 'Kettle', and 'Long-handled Dipper' are a few of the cultivars/shapes available. Warm-weather annual.

Lagerstroemia

lay-gurr-STREE-mee-uh. Loosestrife family, Lythraceae.

This genus of at least 35 species of trees and shrubs, mostly from tropical Asia, offers several outstanding flowering trees for southern landscapes. The species described here is an extremely popular landscape plant in the Deep South, along the Gulf Coast, and in California. Recent hybrids made at the National Arboretum have extended the hardiness range and increased the disease resistance of this remarkable tree.

HOW TO GROW

Plant in full sun to partial shade; flowers best in sun. Needs moist, well-drained, loamy or clayey soil with a pH of 5 to 6.5. Tolerates heat and drought once established. Train to several strong trunks. Withstands heavy pruning and blooms on new growth. Can be cut to the ground and treated as a shrub where winter cold kills the tops, but do not head back branches to stumps, which will turn this lovely tree into an unattractive lollipop. Clip off faded blossoms to encourage repeat bloom through the summer and fall. Older types suffer from mildew, aphids, and black soot fun-

Lagerstroemia indica

gus; hybrids are immune to powdery mildew.

L. indica

l. IN-dih-kuh. CRAPE MYRTLE. A shrub or tree for all seasons, crape myrtle forms a multitrunked, upright or spreading specimen that reaches 15 to 25 feet tall and half as wide. Sumptuous, 6- to 20-inch-long clusters of pink, purple, lavender, or white flowers with crinkled petals and yellow markings bloom from early summer to fall, depending on the cultivar. New genetic dwarves are only 2 feet by 3 feet. The shiny, oval leaves are 1 to 3 inches long and arranged in whorls of three. They emerge with a reddish tinge and turn deep green in summer. Fall color is superb, including light-reflecting combinations of yellow, gold, scarlet, orange, maroon, and red. The attractive trunk bark of the species peels to reveal a gray-and-cream patchwork in trees 3 to 5 years old. Hybrids have orange and cinnamon-brown mottled bark. Locate this outstanding tree in a border or foundation planting where it can be seen throughout the year. Or use it to shade a patio or as a street tree under power lines. Excellent planted in groups or allées. From China, Korea, and India.

Zones 7 to 9.

CULTIVARS AND SIMILAR SPECIES

'Centennial Spirit' features dark rose-red flowers and an upright form. 'Near East' has unique peach flowers and a loose, irregular growth habit. 'Potomac' has medium pink flowers, orange fall color, and an excellent form. 'Regal Red' offers dark rose-red blossoms, red-orange fall color, and a broad shape. 'Seminole' has medium pink flowers and yellow fall color, grows to 15 feet tall, and is mildew resistant. 'Twilight' bears heavy clusters of purple blossoms; a vigorous grower. Hybrids of *L. indica* and *L. fauriei*, a rarely grown white-flowered species, are extremely popular, mildew-resistant plants with excellent bark and flowers; they are **top hardy in Zones 7 to 9; root hardy in Zone 6.**

Miniature and dwarf shrubs include 'Chickasaw' (lavender-pink) and 'Pocomoke' (deep rosy pink). Semidwarf forms growing to 12 feet or less include 'Acoma' (white), 'Hopi' (light pink), 'Tonto' (fuchsia), and 'Zuni' (lavender).

Intermediate trees (12 to 20 feet tall): 'Apalachee' is columnar, with light lavender blossoms, cinnamon brown bark, and orange fall color. 'Osage' is broadly rounded, with light pink reblooming flowers, chestnut brown bark, and red fall color. 'Sioux' has a tight vase shape, medium pink blossoms, and intense red fall color. 'Tuskegee' has dark red-pink flowers, tan-and-gray-mottled bark, orange-red fall color, and horizontal branches.

Tall trees (20 to 35 feet tall): 'Biloxi' features an open vase shape, pale pink flowers, brown-mottled bark, and orange-red fall color. 'Miami' has dark coral pink flowers, dark chestnut brown bark, and red-orange fall color. 'Muskogee' is a spreading type with light lavender-pink flowers, gray-and-tan-mottled bark, and bright red-orange fall color. 'Natchez' has a broad shape, reblooming white flowers, cinnamon-brown mottled bark, and orange and red fall color.

Lagurus

LAG-ur-us. Grass family, Poaceae.

One annual species belongs to this genus: hare's tail grass (*L. ovatus*), a native of sandy soils in the Mediterranean region. It is grown for its fluffy, rounded flower heads, which both the common and botanical names commemorate. *Lagurus* is from the Greek *lagos*, meaning "hare," and *oura*, "tail."

HOW TO GROW

Select a site with full sun and poor to average soil that is light, even sandy, and very well drained. Plants tolerate dry soil. Sow seeds indoors 6 to 8 weeks before the last spring frost date at 55°F. Germination takes 2 to 3 weeks. Or sow outdoors 2 to 3 weeks before the last frost date where the plants are to grow. In mild climates — roughly Zone 7 south — sow seeds outdoors in late summer or fall for bloom the following year. Use hare's tail grass as an edging plant, in mixed plantings, and in con-

Lagerstroemia 'Tonto'

Lagurus ovatus

tainers. It makes an attractive cut or dried flower. Harvest the flower heads just before they mature (either cut them or pull up the plants), and hang in a warm, dry place. Plants self-sow.

L. ovatus
l. oh-VAH-tus. HARE'S TAIL GRASS. A clumping annual, to 20 inches in height, with narrow leaves. In summer, plants bear greenish white, 2¹/2-inch-long plumes that may be tinted with purple; they ripen to creamy tan. 'Nanus' is 5 inches tall. Warm-weather annual.

Lamium

LAY-mee-um. Mint family, Lamiaceae.

Lamium contains a variety of garden-worthy perennials commonly known as dead nettles. There are about 50 species of perennials and

Lamium maculatum

seldom-cultivated annuals in the genus, all with square stems and mostly ovate to kidney-shaped leaves. They bear small two-lipped flowers either singly or in whorls on short, dense spikes. Most cultivated forms are valued for their handsome, variegated foliage and their usefulness as a ground cover that will withstand dry shade.

HOW TO GROW
Select a site in partial to full shade with average to rich, moist, well-drained soil. Lamiums will grow in sun with constantly moist soil. Keep the species listed here away from less vigorous perennials, because they spread quickly by rhizomes and/or stolons to form mounds to 3 feet or more across. Shear plants in midsummer if they become ragged looking. Divide plants as necessary to contain their spread. To propagate, divide the clumps in spring or fall or take cuttings of nonflowering shoots in early summer. Dead nettles are seldom grown from seeds since variegated forms do not come true. Plants often self-sow.

L. galeobdolon
l. gah-lee-OB-doe-lon. YELLOW ARCHANGEL. Formerly *Galeobdolon luteum, Lamiastrum galeobdolon*. Vigorous 2-foot-tall species that spreads quickly by rhizomes and stolons. Has the ability to carpet large open spaces and banks as a soil binder. Bears ovate to diamond-shaped, toothed leaves and spikelike whorls of yellow ³/4-inch-long flowers in summer. 'Hermann's Pride' has silver-

Lantana camara 'Radiation'

streaked leaves and is less invasive than the species. **Zones 4 to 8**.

L. maculatum
l. mak-yew-LAY-tum. SPOTTED DEAD NETTLE. An 8- to 10-inch-tall species bearing toothed leaves with heart-shaped bases and whorls of ³/4-inch-long red-purple flowers in summer. 'Beacon Silver' has silver leaves with green margins and pink flowers. 'Beedham's White' bears chartreuse leaves and white flowers. 'White Nancy' has silver leaves with green edges and white flowers. **Zones 3 to 8**.

Lantana

lan-TAN-ah. Vervain or Verbena family, Verbenaceae.

Showy, domed clusters of flowers characterize the cultivated

Lamium maculatum

lantanas, or shrub verbenas as they are sometimes called. Some 150 species of tender shrubs and perennials, native to the Americas and South Africa, belong to this genus, but gardeners primarily grow cultivars of two species. *Lantana* species bear simple, toothed, wrinkled leaves and dense clusters of salverform flowers, which have a slender tube with a flared, flattened face. The flowers, which attract both hummingbirds and butterflies, have five lobes and are arranged in rounded or flattened heads.

HOW TO GROW
Full sun and poor to average, well-drained soil are ideal. Lantanas are hardy in **Zones 10 and 11**, where they can be grown outdoors as shrubs (they survive a light frost but not a hard freeze). In areas where they are marginally hardy, try a site against a south-facing wall for extra winter protection, and cover them when frost threatens. North of Zone 10, grow them as bedding plants replaced annually or as tender perennials kept in containers and overwintered indoors in a bright, cool (40° to 45°F) spot. Sow seeds indoors 12 to 15 weeks before the last spring frost date. Germination takes 6 to 8 weeks at 70° to 75°F. Soak seeds in warm water for 24 hours before sowing. Pinch seedlings to encourage branching. Transplant to the garden after the last frost date once the soil has warmed to 50°F. Lantanas are also easy to grow from cuttings taken in spring or summer, and cuttings are best if you want a particular color, since cultivars do not come true from seed. (Seeds yield plants in a mix of colors.) Consider buying or overwintering a stock plant from which to take cuttings.

Larix larcinia

Water deeply during dry weather, and feed pot-grown plants monthly in summer. Prune to shape plants in late winter or early spring; cut them back hard, if necessary. Use lantanas as bedding plants or in containers either set on terraces or sunk to the rim in the soil.

L. camara
l. kam-AH-rah. LANTANA. A tender, 3- to 6-foot shrub with ill-smelling, slightly toothed leaves. Bears 1- to 2-inch-wide flower heads of $^1/_3$-inch-wide blooms in shades of yellow, pink, cream, red, lilac, or purple, often with multiple colors in each head. Grows well in dry or semidesert areas. Keep it out of Hawaii, where it is a noxiously invasive plant. Tender perennial or warm-weather annual.

L. montevidensis
l. mon-teh-vih-DEN-sis. WEEPING LANTANA. A tender, spreading $^1/_2$- to 3-foot-tall shrub that can be used to form a dense ground cover. Bears ovate to lance-shaped, coarsely toothed leaves and $^3/_4$- to $1^1/_4$-inch-wide clusters of $^1/_2$-inch-wide, rose-lilac flowers. Tender perennial or warm-weather annual.

Larix
LAR-iks. Pine family, Pinaceae.

Related to pines and spruces, this genus of 10 species from the cold regions of the Northern Hemisphere is unusual in that its members drop their needles in fall and stand bare limbed all winter. Needles are borne in whorls on short, spurlike shoots along the horizontal branches. These trees also have wonderful fall color. Three larch species are useful garden plants.

HOW TO GROW
Plant in full sun and moist, well-drained, deep, humus-rich, acid soil. Does not tolerate alkaline or clayey soil or air pollution. Resists storm damage. Prune in summer. Pests include larch casebearers, gypsy moths, Japanese beetles, and canker.

L. decidua
l. deh-SID-yew-uh. EUROPEAN LARCH. With a tall straight trunk, a slender crown, and whorls of horizontal branches, this tree grows into a distinct, dense cone, reaching 75 feet tall and 25 feet wide. The $1^1/_2$-inch-long needles grow in clusters of 30 to 40 on short, brownish black shoots. They are bright light green in spring, mature to darker green in summer, and turn a glorious deep ocher before dropping in autumn. Bark exfoliates and is deeply fissured, revealing a gray-brown and reddish brown pattern. The clustered, 1- to 2-inch-long cones are violet purple in spring and mature to woody brown. They have overlapping scales and stand straight up on the branches, looking showy all year. European larch makes a fine, strong-limbed screen or specimen for a large property in a cold climate. From Europe. **Zones 2 to 6.**

CULTIVARS
'Varied Directions' is a vigorous hybrid with irregular, arching branches; use as an unusual specimen.

L. kaempferi
l. KAMP-fur-eye. JAPANESE LARCH. Pyramidal, with slightly pendulous, horizontal branches and a straight, massive trunk, this picturesque tree grows 70 to 90 feet tall and 35 to 40 feet wide and has an open silhouette. The 1-inch-long needles grow in tufts of 40 on short, reddish brown spurs. They are brilliant green in spring; mature to deep blue-green in summer, with two white bands on their undersides; and turn glorious shades of gold and orange in fall. The scales of the $1^1/_2$-inch-long cones are rolled back, creating a showy rosette. Do not remove lower branches; allow a skirt of branches to form near the ground. Makes an excellent specimen or screen. From Japan. **Zones 4 to 6.**

CULTIVARS
'Blue Rabbit' has blue needles and a narrow shape. 'Pendula' is irregularly weeping, growing to 60 feet tall.

L. larcinia
l. lar-SIN-ee-uh. AMERICAN LARCH, TAMARACK. Growing 40 to 80 feet tall and 15 to 30 feet wide, with a slender trunk and horizontal branches with drooping branchlets, this tree forms an open pyramid that is usually narrower than that of other larches. New growth is bright lime green, matures to blue-green, and turns a very clear golden yellow in fall. The 1-inch-long needles are borne in tufts of 12 to 30. Cones are only about $^1/_2$ inch around, the smallest of any conifer. They hang down from the branches but are hidden by the needles. This very cold hardy, strong-wooded tree grows naturally in boggy soil. Best as a specimen or screen on a large property and very useful in a wet site beside a stream or pond that may flood in spring. Not heat tolerant; prefers a mountain climate. From northern North America. **Zones 2 to 6.**

SIMILAR SPECIES
L. occidentalis (western larch) is a slender tree with a massive trunk, grass green needles, and 2-inch cones; native to western North America.

Lathyrus
LATH-ur-us. Pea family, Fabaceae.

Lathyrus species are annuals and perennials with showy, butterfly-like flowers botanists describe as

Lathyrus odoratus

Laurus nobilis

papilionaceous: they have a large upright petal, called a banner or standard, and two side, or wing, petals. The two lower petals are joined at the base to form a sheath, called a keel. Many of the 150 species in the genus climb by means of tendrils on the leaves, which are divided into leaflets in a pinnate fashion.

HOW TO GROW

Select a spot in full sun or light shade with rich, well-drained soil. Both *L. grandiflorus* and *L. latifolius* require a trellis or other support. Or train them up shrubs or leave them to sprawl. Plants resent being disturbed, although they can be propagated by division in early spring.

Annual sweet peas (*L. odoratus*) are best in areas with cool summers, although in the South they can be grown for winter or spring bloom; pull them up and replace them once hot weather arrives and they begin to languish. Sow seeds outdoors in early spring as soon as the soil can be worked, about 5 weeks before the last spring frost date. Or sow indoors 6 to 8 weeks before the last frost. Germination takes 2 to 3 weeks at 55° to 60°F. Either way, to speed germination, nick the hard seed coats with a file or knife and/or soak them in warm water for 24 hours before sowing. Climbing types require twiggy brush, strings, or a trellis. Deadheading prolongs blooming. Feed monthly.

L. grandiflorus

l. gran-dih-FLOR-us. EVERLASTING PEA, PERENNIAL PEA, TWO-FLOWERED PEA. A climber reaching about 5 feet with support and spreading by suckers to form loose, sprawling clumps.

In summer it bears unwinged stems and two- to sometimes four-flowered racemes of 1 1/2-inch-wide blooms in pinkish purple to pinkish red. **Zones 6 to 9.**

L. latifolius

l. lat-ih-FOE-lee-us. EVERLASTING PEA, PERENNIAL PEA. A climber reaching 5 to 6 feet with support. Bears winged stems, blue-green leaves, and racemes of 5 to 15 flowers in summer to early fall. Blooms are pink to rose-purple and about 1 1/2 inches wide. Cultivars include white-flowered 'Albus' and 'White Pearl', and 'Blushing Bride', with white blooms flushed with pink. All come true from seed. **Zones 5 to 9.**

L. odoratus

l. oh-dor-AH-tus. SWEET PEA. A bushy or climbing annual with winged stems that can reach as much as 6 to 8 feet tall. Bears small clusters of fragrant, 1 1/2- to 2-inch-wide flowers in shades of lavender, rose-pink, purple-pink, white, or purple. Standards and keels may be the same or different colors. Old-fashioned cultivars are more likely to be fragrant; modern ones have been selected for range of color, size of flowers, and habit, rather than fragrance. 'Old Spice Mix' and 'Painted Lady' are two old cultivars that bear fragrant, 1-inch blooms and climb to 5 to 6 feet. Knee-hi Group plants are dwarf, ranging from 1 1/2 to 2 feet tall; tendril-less Explorer Group plants grow to 14 inches. Cool-weather annual.

L. vernus

l. VER-nus. SPRING VETCHLING. Clump-forming 1- to 1 1/2-foot-tall perennial that spreads

as far. Bears racemes of 3 to 15 purple-blue 3/4-inch-wide flowers in spring. 'Rose Fairy' has 3-inch-wide magenta blooms. **Zones 5 to 9.**

Laurus

LAW-rus. Laurel family, Lauraceae.

There are just two evergreen shrubs or trees in this genus, one of which is known to most of us primarily for the tough bay leaves that are used in cooking. Those who can grow it outdoors employ it in formal gardens.

HOW TO GROW

Most gardeners grow sweet bay in a container, either as a year-round houseplant or to overwinter indoors. It needs full sun, consistent moisture with excellent drainage, and good air circulation. The persistent leaves benefit from an occasional shower or sponge bath. Scale may be a problem indoors. Outdoors, in a formal setting or an herb garden, it can tolerate partial shade and hard pruning into a standard or other form, or it can be allowed to take on its natural pyramid shape. Easily propagated from midsummer cuttings.

L. nobilis

l. no-BIL-iss. SWEET BAY. Sometimes called bay laurel, this is the plant whose branches were used in antiquity to honor Olympians and other heroes. Outdoors it may grow to 20 to 30 feet tall, even to 50 feet in the warmest part of its range, but 5 to 10 feet is a maximum for an indoor-outdoor existence. It may produce inconspicuous yellow-green flowers followed by 1/2-inch purple or black berries. Of Mediterranean origin, sweet bay may die to the ground but resprout in the southern part of Zone 8. **Zones 9 to 11.**

Lavandula

lah-VAN-dew-luh. Mint family, Lamiaceae.

Although lavenders are actually shrubs and subshrubs rather than herbaceous perennials, most gardeners consider them classic components of sunny perennial and herb beds. All bear aromatic, linear to oblong or needlelike leaves that may be simple, toothed, or pinnately lobed or cut. The tubular, two-lipped flowers, borne in dense spikes, are often used for potpourris, sachets, and cosmetics. About 25 species native to dry, sunny sites mostly in the Mediterranean region belong to the genus, whose name comes from the Latin word meaning "to wash."

HOW TO GROW

Plant lavender in full sun and poor to rich soil that is quite well drained. Plants also tolerate very light shade, although they are leggier and bloom less. Wet soil is fa-

Lavandula angustifolia

Lavandula angustifolia

tal. A spot protected from winter winds is best in Zone 5 and colder parts of Zone 6. Established plants are quite drought tolerant and best left unmulched during the growing season. In the North, after the soil freezes in fall, mulch around the plants to protect the roots (use a loose, free-draining material), and consider covering plants with cut evergreen boughs in late fall. If desired, cut or shear off spent flower spikes after the main flush of bloom in summer. To keep plants bushy, prune annually (or at least every few years) in spring just as the new growth begins or in summer either as you cut flowers or immediately after the main flush of bloom. To propagate, take heel cuttings in mid- to late summer or try dividing in spring or fall, but established plants resent disturbance and it's best to leave them alone.

L. angustifolia

l. an-gus-tih-FOE-lee-uh. COMMON LAVENDER, ENGLISH LAVENDER. Evergreen 2- to 3-foot-tall shrub that forms 3- to 4-foot-wide mounds of aromatic, needlelike, gray-green to silvery leaves. Bears erect 2- to 3-inch-long spikes of tiny, fragrant, lavender purple flowers in summer. 'Hidcote' is a compact 1¹/2- to 2-foot-tall selection with dark purple flowers. 'Jean Davis' bears pale pink flowers. 'Munstead' reaches about 1¹/2 feet. 'Nana Alba' bears white flowers on 1-foot-tall plants. **Zones 5 to 9.**

L. dentata

l. den-TAH-tuh. FRINGED LAVENDER. Probably the tallest of the garden lavenders, reliably growing to 3 feet tall and spreading to 5 feet. Sweetly scented, it gets its common name from the bumpy appearance of its toothed gray-green leaves. The flowers are pale lavender with purple bracts. **Zones 8 to 9.**

L. × intermedia

l. × in-ter-MEE-dee-uh. These hybrids, less than 2 feet tall and wide,

have broad, hairy leaves; long stems; and relatively open flower spikes. **Zones 5 to 8.**

L. stoechas

l. STOY-kus. FRENCH LAVENDER. This compact, 2-foot-tall species gets both its botanical and common names from its origin on the French Mediterranean Îles d'Hyères, once known as the Stoechades. From late spring through summer, it bears tiny dark purple flowers arranged in a rectangular cone and topped with upright lavender-pink bracts, especially showy in *L. s.* ssp. *pedunculata*. The aroma is more camphorous than that of other lavenders. **Zones 8 and 9.**

Lavatera

lah-vah-TAIR-uh. Mallow family, Malvaceae.

Some 25 species of annuals, biennials, perennials, subshrubs, and shrubs belong to this widely distributed genus. Most *Lavatera* species are plants of dry, rocky soils found from the Mediterranean region to Russia, central Asia, Australia, and California. They are grown for their showy, five-petaled saucer- or funnel-shaped flowers that resemble small hibiscus and come in shades of pink and white. Leaves usually are lobed in a palmate fashion.

HOW TO GROW

Full sun and average, well-drained soil are ideal. Too-rich soil yields abundant foliage but few flowers. Plants may need staking. Propa-

Layia platyglossa

gate by taking cuttings from shoots that arise at the base of the plant in spring, by stem cuttings in early summer, or by sowing seeds. Sow seeds of annuals outdoors where the plants are to grow a few weeks before the last spring frost date, when the soil is still cool.

L. maritima

l. mah-RIT-ih-muh. TREE MALLOW. Evergreen shrub to 6 feet tall and 3 feet wide, with gray-green lobed leaves. Throughout summer, it produces pale pink flowers, 2 to 3 inches across, with notched petals. The veins and base of each petal are magenta. **Zones 8 to 10.**

L. thuringiaca

l. thur-in-jee-AH-kuh. TREE MALLOW, TREE LAVATERA. Shrubby 5- to 6-foot-tall perennial that forms 5- to 6-foot-wide clumps. Bears funnel-shaped 2- to 2¹/2-inch-wide flowers in summer

either singly or in loose clusters. 'Barnsley' produces pink 3-inch-wide flowers on 6-foot plants. 'Shorty' bears rose-pink 2-inch-wide flowers on 3-foot plants. **Zones 7 to 9; to Zone 6 with winter protection.**

L. trimestris

l. try-MES-tris. LAVATERA, TREE MALLOW. A 2- to 4-foot-tall, well-branched annual. Bears funnel-shaped, 3- to 4-inch-wide flowers singly in leaf axils. Flowers come in white and pale to reddish pink. 'Mont Blanc' and 'Mont Rose' are compact 2-foot-tall cultivars. 'Silver Cup' bears rose-pink flowers on 3-foot plants. Cool-weather annual.

Layia

LAY-ee-ah. Aster family, Asteraceae.

The genus *Layia* contains 15 species of annuals native to the western United States, primarily California. Commonly called tidy tips, they bear narrow, toothed to pinnately lobed leaves. The daisylike flower heads have yellow centers, and the petals, more properly called ray florets, are toothed at the tip and come in yellow or white, as well as yellow with white tips.

HOW TO GROW

Give tidy tips a site with full sun or light shade and poor to average, moist but well-drained soil. Plants thrive in sandy soil, and very rich conditions yield floppy growth. They also grow best in areas with cool summers; where hot summers prevail, start seeds indoors to give plants a chance to bloom before hot weather sets in. Sow seeds outdoors where the plants are to grow after the last spring frost date. Or sow indoors 6 to 8 weeks

Lavatera trimestris 'Silver Cup'

Ledum glandulosum

Leiophyllum buxifolium

before the last frost date at 70° to 75°F. Germination takes 1 to 3 weeks. In mild climates — roughly Zone 7 south — sow seeds in fall for bloom the following spring. Water during very dry weather. Use tidy tips in mixed plantings, on banks, and in rock gardens. They make excellent cut flowers.

L. platyglossa

l. plah-tee-GLOSS-uh. TIDY TIPS. Formerly *L. elegans*. A 1- to 1¹/₂-foot-tall annual with featherlike, slightly hairy, gray-green leaves. Bears 2-inch-wide daisies with golden yellow centers and yellow petals tipped with white from summer to fall. Cool-weather annual.

Ledum

LEE-dum. Heath family, Ericaceae.

This genus is made up of four species of evergreen shrubs, native to marshes and other wet habitats throughout the Northern Hemisphere. The species listed here offer northern gardeners a rare opportunity to grow a broad-leaved evergreen. The leaves are aromatic, while the five-petaled white flowers have prominent stamens and are borne in long-lasting clusters.

HOW TO GROW

Ledums are happy only in areas with cool summers. There they can grow in full sun or partial shade, as long as they have soil that is rich, acidic, and moisture retentive but well aerated. Peat moss and sand make an ideal mix. Mulching generously will help keep roots moist and cool. Site these little shrubs in a rock garden

or with their relatives, the heaths and heathers. Deadheading after bloom is a good practice. Seeds will germinate readily if sown on peat. You can also propagate ledum from semiripe cuttings in late summer or by layering.

L. glandulosum

l. gland-yew-LOH-sum. TRAPPER'S TEA. This western U.S. native can grow to 5 feet but is more often about 3 feet tall, bearing clusters of white flowers in late spring. **Zones 2 to 6.**

L. groenlandicum

l. groon-LAN-dih-kum. LABRADOR TEA. Native to Greenland, Alaska, and Canada, this shrub is bushy and round to 3 feet tall and 4 feet wide. Rusty fuzz covers new shoots and the undersides of the leaves, which are narrow ovals with edges curled under, 2 inches long. The ¹/₂-inch white flowers bloom in late spring. 'Compactum' grows only 1 foot tall. **Zones 2 to 6.**

L. palustre

l. pal-US-tree. WILD ROSEMARY. Differs from *L. groenlandicum* in having a more erect habit, ranging in height from 1 to 4 feet. The tiny leaves are covered with fuzz. **Zones 2 to 6.**

Leiophyllum

Lye-oh-FILL-um. Heath family, Ericaceae.

The only species in this genus, commonly known as box sand myrtle, is a suckering evergreen shrub native to woodlands in the eastern United States, often found on mountain slopes. The leaves are small and dainty. In spring, frothy

clouds of white flowers open from pink buds.

HOW TO GROW

Give box sand myrtle full sun to partial shade and acid soil that combines peat moss and sand for moisture retention with good drainage. Keep the soil moist. Does best where nights are cool. Its low habit makes it ideal for rock gardens, or for facing down azaleas and rhododendrons. To propagate, sow the tiny seeds on peat moss, collect softwood cuttings in late summer, or divide suckers.

L. buxifolium

l. bux-ih-FOE-lee-um. BOX SAND MYRTLE. Native from New Jersey into the Carolinas and Kentucky, box sand myrtle averages 18 inches tall but can range in habit from erect to almost a ground cover. It tends to spread and sprawl to 4 feet or more wide. The ¹/₂-inch, shiny dark green leaves bronze in winter. Small white flowers retain a pink edge when they open in May and June. It does well in mountainous parts of the South, but in lower elevations it may suffer from heat. **Zones 5 to 8.**

Leonotis

lee-oh-NO-tis. Mint family, Lamiaceae.

Native mostly to South Africa, the 30 species of *Leonotis* are square-stemmed annuals, perennials, subshrubs, and shrubs with aromatic, lance-shaped to ovate leaves. They bear clusters of showy, two-lipped flowers in tiers at the leaf nodes along upright stems, with each tier consisting of densely clustered flowers arranged

around the stem. The blooms come in red-orange, scarlet, and orange, as well as white. Both the common name, lion's ear, and the botanical name, which is from the Greek *leon*, meaning "lion," and *ous*, "ear," refer to the notion that the flowers' corollas (petals) resemble lion's ears.

HOW TO GROW

Give lion's ears a site in full sun or partial shade and average, well-drained soil. Good choices for seaside gardens, they can be grown outdoors in Zones 10 and 11. In the North, grow them as bedding plants replaced annually or as tender perennials overwintered indoors in a bright, cool (50° to 65°F) spot. Sow seeds indoors 8 to 10 weeks before the last spring frost date at 55° to 65°F. Or start them from cuttings taken in spring or summer, which can be used to propagate the plants for

Leonotis leonurus

the garden or for overwintering. Pinch seed-grown or young cutting-grown plants to encourage branching. Transplant to the garden after the last frost date, once the soil has warmed to 50°F. Water regularly in dry weather. Stake as necessary. Prune to shape plants in late winter or early spring: cut them back hard if necessary. Use lion's ears in mixed beds and borders or in containers, either set on terraces or sunk to the rim in the soil.

L. leonurus

l. lee-oh-NUR-us. LION'S EAR. A tender shrub that can reach 6 feet tall but is considerably smaller in the North. Bears aromatic, lance-shaped leaves and 2¹/₂-inch-long, orange-red to scarlet flowers in fall and will continue to bloom into winter if you bring it indoors. Tender perennial.

L. ocymifolia

l. ah-sim-ih-FOE-lee-uh. LION'S EAR. A tender perennial that can reach 10 feet tall but is smaller in the North. Bears ovate, aromatic leaves with toothed margins and whorls of 1¹/₂-inch-long orange flowers in late summer and fall. Tender perennial.

Leptospermum

Lep-toe-SPUR-mum. Myrtle family, Myrtaceae.

This genus includes about 80 species of evergreen trees and shrubs primarily from Australia. About half a dozen species are grown in gardens for their small but profuse spring flowers and aromatic foliage. The common name, tea tree, comes from Captain James Cook's brewing of the leaves to prevent scurvy among his sailors. Don't confuse this tea tree with *Melaleuca* species, another genus from Down Under. Those leaves are distilled into an oil used externally in herbal medicine, but one species, *M. quinquenervia*, has wreaked environmental havoc in Florida.

HOW TO GROW

Give New Zealand tea tree fertile acidic soil that is moisture retentive but drains well. It tolerates seaside conditions but not cold wind or a combination of heat and humidity. It can become chlorotic in high-pH soils. Give shrubs a light to medium pruning in spring if needed to maintain shape, which should be graceful rather than formal; don't cut into

bare wood. Used in mild climates as a hedge or screen, in Zone 8 it is sometimes grown in a container for overwintering indoors, then moved outdoors to a deck or in a border so its heavy spring flowering can be appreciated. Propagate in summer from semiripe cuttings.

L. scoparium

l. skoh-PAH-ree-um. NEW ZEA-LAND TEA TREE. A compact shrub that grows 6 to 10 feet tall with an upright habit and dense branches of small, almost needlelike, aromatic leaves. Gardeners grow not the species but cultivars, which offer profuse displays of ¹/₂-inch flowers, many of them double, in late winter or late spring. They include 'Helene Strybing' (deep pink spring flowers; somewhat silver leaves with a graceful, more open habit), 'Nanum Tui' (a 2-foot dwarf with a cushion shape and pale pink single flowers, darker in the middle), 'Pink Pearl' (6 to 10 feet tall with pink buds that open to double white or pink flowers), 'Red Damask' (large, double cherry red flowers from midwinter to spring with leaves tinged reddish purple), 'Ruby Glow' (compact to 6 to 8 feet tall with profuse double red

flowers in winter and spring and bronzy foliage), and 'Snow White' (2 to 4 feet tall and spreading with double white, dark-green-centered flowers winter to spring). **Zones 9 to 10.**

Lespedeza

Les-peh-DEEZ-uh. Pea family, Fabaceae.

This genus comprises 40 species of perennials, subshrubs, and shrubs native to the eastern United States, Asia, and Australia. Commonly called bush clovers, they are grown for their clusters of bright pealike flowers and are often grown as perennials in the northern part of their range. Their arching branches provide winter interest.

HOW TO GROW

If bush clover has good drainage and full sun it will tolerate any soil and actually prefers somewhat sandy soil of low fertility. Where it doesn't die to the ground over winter, it needs a hard pruning in early spring to keep it from becoming unkempt. Site it among other plants in a border; it is late to leaf out in spring but will provide color when other flowers have faded. It's also a magnet for bees and other pollinators. Propagate

Lespedeza thunbergii 'White Fountain'

from seeds soaked in hot water, from softwood cuttings, or by dividing clumps in spring.

L. bicolor

l. BI-kuh-lor. SHRUB BUSH CLO-VER. This Asian species grows 6 to 8 feet tall and wide with arching shoots. The palmate, three-part leaves are dark green. Magenta-pink flowers bloom in racemes up to 5 inches long from the upper leaf axils in late summer. Root hardy in **Zones 4 to 8.**

L. thunbergii

l. thun-BER-jee-eye. BUSH CLO-VER. Also from Asia but less cold hardy, this species is considered more ornamental than *L. bicolor*. In late summer or early fall, rosy purple flowers bloom in racemes up to 2 feet long at the ends of long, graceful, arching branches. 'Alba' has white flowers, and 'Gibraltar', a vigorous selection, bears deep pink blooms. **Zones 5 to 8.**

Leucanthemum

loo-KAN-thuh-mum. Aster family, Asteraceae.

The genus *Leucanthemum* contains 26 species of annuals and perennials, many of which once belonged to the genus *Chrysanthemum*. They bear daisylike flower heads and entire to deeply lobed, toothed, or scalloped leaves. The flowers, which are solitary and

Leptospermum scoparium 'Ruby Glow'

Leucanthemum × superbum

borne at the stem tips, generally have white ray florets, or "petals," surrounding yellow centers consisting of densely packed disk florets.

HOW TO GROW

Select a site in full sun with average to rich, well-drained soil. Well-drained conditions are especially important in winter, since water collecting around the crowns causes rot. Plants may need staking. *L. × superbum* also grows in light shade and tolerates somewhat dry, sandy soil and seaside conditions, but it tends to be short-lived, especially in hot climates. Regular deadheading lengthens bloom time. Cut *L. vulgare* to the ground after flowering to encourage repeat bloom and discourage abundant self-seeding. Divide plants in spring every 2 to 3 years, because the clumps tend to die out in the center. In addition to division, propagate by cuttings taken from shoots at the bottom of the plant in spring or by seeds.

L. paludosum

l. pal-yew-DOE-sum. Formerly *Chrysanthemum paludosum, Hymenostemma paludosum, Melampodium paludosum*. A bushy, spreading, 2- to 6-inch-tall annual with spoon-shaped leaves. Bears masses of solitary, $^3/_4$- to $1^1/_4$-inch-wide, daisylike flowers with white petals and yellow centers in summer. Cool-weather annual.

L. × superbum

l. × sue-PER-bum. SHASTA DAISY. Formerly *Chrysanthe-*

mum maximum, C. × superbum. Clump-forming 1- to 4-foot-tall hybrid species that spreads to about 2 feet. Bears single, semidouble, or double 2- to 5-inch white daisies on stiff stems from early summer to early fall. Many cultivars are available. 'Aglaia' produces semidouble flowers with fringed ray florets. 'Little Miss Muffet' is 8 to 12 inches tall and does not need staking. 'Snow Lady' is a 1- to $1^1/_2$-foot-tall plant that blooms the first year from seed. 'Alaska' is hardy to **Zone 3**; **Zones 4 to 8**.

L. vulgare

l. vul-GAIR-ee. OXEYE DAISY. Formerly *Chrysanthemum leucanthemum*. Weedy, vigorous 1- to 3-foot-tall species spreading by rhizomes to form 2- to 3-foot-wide clumps. Bears white 1- to 2-inch-

wide daisies with yellow centers in late spring and early summer. **Zones 3 to 8**.

Leucojum

loo-KOH-jum. Amaryllis family, Amaryllidaceae.

Commonly known as snowflakes, *Leucojum* species are spring- or fall-blooming bulbs grown for their dainty, nodding, bell-shaped flowers. About 10 species belong to the genus, all of which grow from tunicate bulbs and are native to western Europe, the Middle East, and northern Africa. The plants bear basal, strap-shaped to linear leaves and produce their flowers atop erect, leafless stalks with one to as many as eight flowers carried per stalk. The flowers are white and have six petal-like tepals. *Leucojum* species are closely related to snowdrops *(Galanthus)*, which bear their flowers singly, or sometimes in pairs. (In some areas *Leucojum* species also are commonly called snowdrops.) In *Galanthus*, the three outer tepals are markedly larger than the inner three, which they nearly conceal, while in *Leucojum* all six are of equal size.

HOW TO GROW

For *L. aestivum* and *L. vernum*, select a site in full sun or partial shade with rich, moist, well-drained soil. They are best in a spot that is protected from hot afternoon sun and prefer soil that remains evenly moist, but not wet, in summer. Mulch the plants with compost or chopped leaves in summer to keep the soil moist, rich, and cool. Both species are ideal for naturalizing in dappled shade and along shrub borders. *L.*

Leucojum vernum

autumnale can be trickier to establish but is well worth the effort. Give it full sun or very light shade and perfectly drained soil that is rich in organic matter. This species is native to dry, sandy soils, so plant it in raised beds or rock gardens that offer good drainage, and amend the soil at planting time with plenty of coarse sand or grit. When planting any of the species, plant the bulbs in late summer or early fall, as early as you can buy them. Set them with the tops 2 inches below the soil surface. Snowflakes may take a year or two to become established and begin to bloom happily, and once planted they are best left undisturbed. Propagate by digging the clumps and separating the offsets in late spring or early summer just as the foliage dies back. Or sow seeds.

L. aestivum

l. ESS-tih-vum. SUMMER SNOWFLAKE. A $1^1/_2$- to 2-foot-tall species with $1^1/_2$-foot-long leaves. Bears dainty stems of three to as many as eight bell-shaped, $^3/_4$-inch-long and 1-inch-wide white flowers with a green spot on each tepal. Despite the common name, and the fact that *aestivum* is from the Latin for "summer," plants bloom in spring. Flowers are faintly fragrant. 'Gravetye Giant' reaches 3 feet tall and bears 1- to $1^1/_2$-inch-long flowers. **Zones 4 to 9**.

L. autumnale

l. aw-tum-NAL-ee. AUTUMN SNOWFLAKE. A dainty 4- to 6-inch-tall species that bears threadlike or grassy leaves. Sprays of two to four bell-shaped, $^1/_2$- to $^3/_4$-inch-long white flowers tinged with pink appear in late summer or early fall. **Zones 5 to 9**.

L. vernum

l. VER-num. SPRING SNOWFLAKE. An 8- to 12-inch-tall species bearing strap-shaped 10-inch-long leaves. In early spring, produces erect stems with one or sometimes two bell-shaped, 1-inch-long white flowers that have a green spot at the tip of each petal. **Zones 4 to 8**.

Leucophyllum

loo-koh-FILL-um. Snapdragon family, Scrophulariaceae.

From the 12 species of these evergreen shrubs, native to the Ameri-

Leucophyllum frutescens

can Southwest, several species and hybrids are being brought into gardens because of their adaptability to drought and for their silvery foliage, which contrasts with their bell-shaped summer flowers.

HOW TO GROW
These shrubs thrive in the dry soil and air of their native landscape. They're outstanding in a border of other drought-tolerant shrubs or herbaceous perennials. In the humid Southeast, where they are often grown as hedge plants, they are prone to pests and diseases, particularly scale. Give them excellent drainage in full sun, preferably in slightly acid soil. They tolerate salt as well as hard pruning when reshaping is needed. Excellent in a border or as an unusual hedge. Propagate from cuttings.

L. candidum
l. KAN-dih-dum. VIOLET SILVER-LEAF. Also called dwarf silverleaf sage, this Texas native grows to 3 feet tall and has silvery foliage. 'Thundercloud' has profuse dark purple flowers and a rounded, compact habit. **Zones 8 to 10.**

L. frutescens
l. fru-TESS-enz. TEXAS SAGE. Also called Texas ranger or cenizo, this is the most commonly grown species of *Leucophyllum*. It will reach 5 to 8 feet tall and wide with open branching. The silvery, woolly leaves are $^1/_2$ to 1 inch long, while the 1-inch flowers are magenta tubular bells. Cultivars include 'Green Cloud', with green leaves and purple flowers; 'Rain Cloud' (a hybrid with *L. minus*), with gray leaves and lavender-blue flowers; and 'White Cloud', with gray leaves and white flowers. **Zones 8 to 10.**

Leucothoe
loo-KOH-thoh-ee. Heath family, Ericaceae.

This genus comprises approximately 45 species of evergreen and deciduous shrubs from wetlands and woodlands, primarily in the

Leucophyllum frutescens

United States and Japan. Half a dozen species are prized in woodland gardens for their graceful, often arching shape, with branches of some species forming a zigzag. The shiny, leathery leaves are frequently colored bronze or purple in spring and fall; the white urn-shaped flowers bloom in racemes. The botanical name recalls one of the brutal myths of ancient Greece, where Leucothea, daughter of a Babylonian king, offends her father and is buried alive for her intransigence. Apollo, horrified by this punishment (and most likely with a significant role in her demise), transforms her into a shrub. Since this particular shrub was unknown to the ancient Greeks, the name was probably used originally for a different genus.

HOW TO GROW
Like other members of the heath family, leucothoe needs rich, acid, moisture-retentive soil that has been well amended with organic matter, and it prefers partial to full shade. It does not tolerate drought, heat, drying winds, or soggy soil. These shrubs are good for facing down rhododendrons and other larger relatives, or for use in rock gardens, on slopes, or as edging to help define paths. Pruning is the key to keeping these

Leucothoe axillaris

plants attractive. Cut them back hard after they flower. The leaves are often heavily defaced by leaf spot when cultural conditions aren't ideal. Propagate from semihardwood or hardwood cuttings treated with hormone powder.

L. axillaris
l. ax-il-LAIR-iss. COAST LEUCO-THOE. Growing 2 to 4 feet tall and half as wide, this evergreen bears lustrous leaves to 5 inches long on arching branches. New foliage is bronzed, turning somewhat purple in fall. The white

Leucothoe axillaris

flowers bloom in midspring. **Zones 6 to 8.**

L. fontanesiana
l. fon-tan-ee-see-AY-nuh. DROOP-ING LEUCOTHOE. Also called doghobble and fetterbush, this southeastern U.S. native evergreen is the most commonly grown species of *Leucothoe*. It reaches 3 to 6 feet tall and wide, its arching branches forming a fountainlike shape. The pointed leaves are 3 to 6 inches long. Dangling flower clusters appear midspring in 3-inch racemes. Drooping leucothoe must have shade in the southern portion of its range. It is sometimes pruned as a ground cover. Among cultivars selected for colored or variegated foliage are 'Girard's Rainbow', which is mottled with pink and cream; and 'Scarletta', with leaves that are scarlet when young, bronze in autumn. **Zones 5 to 8.**

L. keiskei
l. KEES-kee-eye. KEISK'S LEU-COTHOE. A dwarf evergreen from Japan with red spring growth, turning purple-red in fall, and large flowers that bloom in early to midsummer. **Zones 5 to 8.**

L. populifolia
l. pop-yew-lih-FOE-lee-uh. FLORIDA LEUCOTHOE. Now reclassified in the *Agarista* genus with two natives of Brazil, this species is still usually sold under its former name. An evergreen native from South Carolina to Florida, it has especially graceful drooping branches. Although it can grow 8 to 12 feet tall, it tolerates severe pruning. New reddish growth turns rich, glossy green. In the humid South, it resists leaf spot better than other species do. The fragrant flowers droop from leaf axils in late spring. Tends to sucker; a good choice for shady banks. **Zones 7 to 9.**

L. racemosa
l. rass-eh-MOE-suh. SWEETBELLS LEUCOTHOE. A deciduous species native from Massachusetts to

Leucothoe fontanesiana

Lewisia cotyledon

Florida, usually suckering and 4 to 6 feet tall and wide. The 2-inch leaves are slightly toothed and may turn brilliant scarlet in fall before dropping. The cylindrical flowers, in racemes to 4 inches long, may be tinged with pink when they appear in mid- to late spring. **Zones 5 to 9**.

Lewisia

lew-ISS-ee-uh. Portulaca family, Portulacaceae.

Native to western North America, *Lewisia* species are low-growing perennials forming rosettes or tufts of fleshy deciduous or evergreen leaves. They produce clusters of funnel-shaped pink, magenta, white, orange, or yellow flowers in spring or summer. About 20 species, all perennials, belong to the genus.

HOW TO GROW

Give evergreen species, including *L. cotyledon*, a site in light shade with fairly rich, very well drained soil that has an acid to neutral pH. Grow deciduous species and hybrid lewisias in full sun, also with perfect drainage. Constantly damp soil around the crowns and fleshy rootstocks of these plants is fatal, as is wet soil in winter. To help im-prove drainage, mulch around the crowns with granite chips or coarse grit. Lewisias are ideal for rock gardens, or along rock walls, gravel paths, or other spots with very well drained soil. Propagate by severing offsets that appear in summer or by seeds.

L. cotyledon

l. koh-teh-LEE-don. Evergreen perennial with a low, leafy rosette that can reach 10 inches wide. Bears 8- to 12-inch-tall clusters of 1-inch-wide funnel-shaped flowers from spring to summer in pink, white, cream, or yellow, often striped or marked with a second color. **Zones 6 to 8**.

Leycesteria

lye-sess-TEER-ee-uh. Honeysuckle family, Caprifoliaceae.

Of this genus's six species of deciduous shrubs native to the Himalayas and China, one or two are grown in gardens for their showy wine red bracts and ¹/₂-inch reddish purple berries that attract birds.

HOW TO GROW

For best flower and fruit color, give these shrubs full sun in rich, well-amended, moisture-retentive soil. They will tolerate some drought as well as wind. Prune hard in late winter to maintain shape and stimulate colorful new growth. *Leycesteria* may die back in winter but will regrow in spring, even if killed to the ground. It looks best in an informal situation, such as a relaxed shrub border or wildlife garden. Propagates easily from seeds planted in a mix of peat moss and sand.

L. formosa

l. for-MOE-suh. PHEASANT-EYE. The stems of this shrub, also called Himalayan honeysuckle, are hollow canes similar to bamboo and remain blue-green through winter. They grow 6 feet tall and sucker as wide. The leaves, up to 7 inches long, have small teeth and heart-shaped bases and taper to a point. In late summer to fall, drooping

Leycesteria formosa

spikes up to 4 inches long bear small white flowers in deep red bracts, followed by red berries. **Zones 7 to 10**.

Liatris

lee-AY-tris. Aster family, Asteraceae.

Commonly called gayfeathers or blazing stars, *Liatris* species are native North American perennials that produce erect feather- or wandlike spikes or racemes of flowers that open from the top of the stalk down. Each fuzzy-textured wand consists of many buttonlike flower heads arranged along the stalk. The individual flower heads are made up of all tubular disk florets (they lack ray florets, or "petals") and come in shades of pinkish purple, purple, and white. The plants produce clumps of linear to lance-shaped leaves at the base, with smaller leaves growing up the flower stalks. They grow from thick roots with swollen, flattened stems that are tuber- or cormlike. About 40 species belong to the genus.

HOW TO GROW

Select a site in full sun with average to rich, well-drained soil. Unlike other gayfeathers, which succumb to crown rot in damp soil, *L. spicata* also grows in evenly moist soil. *L. aspera* and *L. punctata* are suitable for sites with dry, well-drained soil. Too-rich soil leads to plants that require staking. Established plants of all species are quite drought tolerant and can remain undisturbed for years. Divide plants, which generally form 1¹/₂- to 2-foot-wide clumps, only if they outgrow their space or die out in the center. Propagate by dividing the clumps or separating the tubers in early spring or fall or by seeds. Several cultivars, including *L. spicata* 'Kobold', come true from seed.

L. aspera

l. ASS-per-uh. ROUGH BLAZING STAR, ROUGH GAYFEATHER. A 3- to 6-foot-tall species with tuberous roots. Bears 1¹/₂- to 3-foot-long spikes of ³/₄- to 1-inch-wide lavender-purple flower heads in late summer and early fall. **Zones 3 to 9**.

L. punctata

l. punk-TAH-tuh. DOTTED BLAZING STAR. Compact 6- to 14-inch-tall species with tuberous roots. Bears dense 6- to 12-inch-

Liatris punctata

long spikes of small ¹/₈-inch-wide rosy purple flower heads in late summer. **Zones 2 to 8.**

L. pycnostachya

l. pik-no-STAY-kee-uh. KANSAS GAYFEATHER, PRAIRIE BLAZING STAR. A 3- to 5-foot-tall species bearing 1- to 2¹/₂-foot-long spikes of densely packed ¹/₂-inch-wide mauve-purple flower heads in midsummer. **Zones 3 to 9.**

L. scariosa

l. scare-ee-OH-suh. TALL GAY-FEATHER. A 2¹/₂- to 3-foot-tall species with 1- to 1¹/₂-foot-long spikes of pale purple 1-inch-wide flower heads in late summer and early fall. **Zones 4 to 9.**

L. spicata

l. spih-KAY-tuh. SPIKE GAY-FEATHER. Handsome 2- to 5-foot-tall species with erect 1¹/₂- to 2-foot-long spikes of densely packed ¹/₂-inch-wide pinkish purple flower heads from mid- to late summer. Compact, mauve-violet–flowered 2- to 2¹/₂-foot-tall 'Kobold' (also sold as 'Gnome') is the most widely available cultivar. 'Floristan White' has white flowers on 3-foot plants. **Zones 3 to 9.**

Ligularia

lig-yew-LAIR-ee-uh. Aster family, Asteraceae.

Ligularia species are bold, sometimes coarse-looking perennials native to central and eastern Asia. They produce 2- to 3-foot-tall mounds of large, rounded to kidney-shaped or lobed leaves that are 1 foot or more in length. The foliage is topped in summer by tall, erect spikes or rounded clusters of golden yellow to orange daisylike flowers. About 150 species belong to the genus.

HOW TO GROW
Select a site in light to partial shade with very rich soil that remains constantly moist. A spot with shade from midday to early afternoon is best, since plants wilt dramatically during the heat of the day if soil moisture is inadequate. A site protected from wind is best. Plants can be left undisturbed for years without needing to be divided. They form 3- to 5-foot-wide mounds of foliage. To propagate, divide clumps in spring or fall.

L. dentata

l. den-TAH-tuh. BIG-LEAVED LIGULARIA, GOLDEN GROUNDSEL. Formerly *L. clivorum, Senecio clivorum.* Clumping species producing kidney- to heart-shaped leaves and flattened clusters of yellow-orange 4-inch-wide daisylike flowers from summer to early fall. Leaf and flower stalks are red, and plants are from 3 to 5 feet tall in bloom. 'Desdemona' bears orange flower heads and brown-green leaves that are purple-maroon underneath. Hybrid 'Gregy-nog Gold' has pyramidal clusters of orange-yellow flowers. 'Othello' produces purple-green leaves that are purple-red underneath. **Zones 4 to 8.**

L. przewalskii

l. she-VALL-skee-eye. Formerly *Senecio przewalskii.* Clumping species with mounds of toothed leaves irregularly cut in a palmate fashion. Bears erect, lacy-textured 6-foot-tall racemes of ³/₄-inch-wide flower heads from early to late summer. **Zones 4 to 8.**

L. stenocephala

l. steh-no-SEFF-uh-luh. Clumping species bearing toothed, triangular leaves with heart-shaped bases and erect 5-foot-tall racemes of 1¹/₂-inch-wide yellow flower heads in late summer. 'The Rocket' reaches 6 feet tall and bears lemon yellow flowers. **Zones 4 to 8.**

Ligustrum

lih-GOOS-trum. Olive family, Oleaceae.

Of this genus's roughly 50 species of deciduous to evergreen shrubs

Ligustrum obtusifolium

and trees native to Europe, Asia, and Australia, about 10 are commonly used as hedges and screens. The fragrant white or cream-colored flowers are often pruned off in creating formal hedge shapes. If left unpruned, they are followed by blue-black or dark gray fruits. Some of the species, notably *L. sinense* (Chinese privet), have escaped into natural areas, especially in the Mid-Atlantic and Southeast. That species is no longer recommended, and others should be chosen with care.

HOW TO GROW
Privets are popular because they are trouble-free in a wide range of conditions. (As with other plants, this is also what has led to their becoming invasive.) They grow quickly; thrive in almost any soil in full sun or partial shade; and tolerate pollution, salt, and drought, but not soggy soil. Prune after flowering; if flowers aren't desired, prune in spring and early fall. Privets propagate easily from softwood cuttings.

L. amurense

l. am-ur-EN-see. AMUR PRIVET. A deciduous Chinese species growing 12 to 15 feet tall and 9 to 12 feet wide. Bears 1- to 2-inch dull green leaves and four-lobed white flowers that bloom in racemes in late spring, followed by persistent black berries. **Zones 4 to 7.**

L. japonicum

l. juh-PON-ih-kum. JAPANESE PRIVET. An evergreen, to 12 feet tall and usually 8 feet wide, with

Ligularia stenocephala 'The Rocket'

thick, shiny, rounded 2- to 4-inch leaves, paler underneath. Pyramid-shaped panicles of heavily perfumed white flowers bloom for several weeks in midspring. Popular for southern gardens, sometimes pruned as a tree. The dark berries are flat and waxy. Cultivars include variegated and curly-leaved forms. **Zones 7 to 10.**

L. obtusifolium

l. ob-too-sih-FOE-lee-um. BORDER PRIVET. A deciduous, multi-stemmed, twiggy shrub to 12 feet tall and wide. The leaves often turn purple in fall, and the early to midsummer flowers nod from side branches. *L. o.* var. *regelianum* (Regel privet) is even more strongly horizontal, with hairier leaves that are held in a flat plane. **Zones 4 to 7.**

L. ovalifolium

l. oh-val-ih-FOE-lee-um. CALIFORNIA PRIVET. This Japanese species got its common name from popularity as a hedge in California. Also called oval-leaved privet, it is a deciduous to semievergreen shrub forming thickets of upright stems to 15 feet with shiny dark green leaves. Erect terminal racemes of white flowers bloom in early to midsummer. Usually sheared when planted as a hedge. There are many variegated forms. **Zones 5 to 8.**

Lilium

LIL-ee-um. Lily family, Liliaceae.

Showy, exotic-looking lilies are among the most dramatic flowers grown in gardens. *Lilium* species often are referred to as true lilies because literally hundreds of plants share their common name, including daylilies (*Hemerocallis*), magic lilies (*Lycoris*), and trout lilies (*Erythronium*). True lilies bear their large flowers on erect unbranched stems and have individual blooms that consist of six petal-like tepals. The blooms may point up, out, or down. Flower shapes vary as well: lilies can bear blooms that are trumpet, star, cup, bowl, funnel, or bell shaped. Lilies with recurved or reflexed blooms have tepals that curve back from the center of the flower toward the stem. Blooms come in fiery hues such as orange, red, hot pink, and yellow as well as pastel pinks, rose-reds, cream, and white. The leaves are narrow and lance shaped or grassy and borne up the stems.

Lilium candidum

Lily bulbs consist of fleshy, overlapping scales that are attached at the base of the bulb but loose at the top. (The scales are not tightly packed and are covered with a papery protective tunic, as are bulbs of daffodils and tulips, which grow from tunicate bulbs.) Lilies also may produce bulbs at the ends of rhizomes or stolons.

There are about 100 species of lilies, numerous hybrid groups, and countless cultivars within those groups. The North American Lily Society has divided the hybrids into eight divisions based on the origin of the plants along with the shape and position of the flowers, plus a ninth division for the true species. Today hybrids are grown more commonly than the species, although species lilies are still popular. Not only are hybrids showy, vigorous, and easy to grow, but most are resistant to common lily diseases, including the viruses that made garden lilies the sickly, problem-prone plants they were 50 years ago.

HOW TO GROW

In general, give lilies a spot in full sun with rich, evenly moist, well-drained soil. Several species thrive in partial shade, however, and a spot that receives shade during the hottest part of the day protects plants from heat and helps prolong bloom. Look for a site sheltered from strong winds, which

Lilium Candidum hybrid

can blow over the plants or break them off at the base. Lilies need plenty of soil moisture during the growing season, but their bulbs rot if the soil remains too wet. Well-drained soil is essential in winter when the bulbs are dormant. Like clematis, lilies like their heads in the sun and their feet in the shade. Look for a spot where the bulbs will be shaded by nearby shallow-rooted perennials. Lilies that tolerate partial shade include Martagon

Lilium 'African Queen'

hybrids (Division 2), American hybrids (Division 4), *L. canadense*, *L. henryi*, *L. pardalinum*, *L. speciosum*, and *L. superbum*. These still need good light to bloom well, and a site with morning sun and afternoon shade is ideal. Or grow them in bright, dappled, all-day shade.

By selecting plants from several different divisions, it's possible to have lilies in bloom from early summer (mid- to late June) right through fall (October). Bloom peaks in midsummer, from July to August, in most areas. Expect bloom times to overlap — lilies that bloom in early summer won't be finished when the earliest midsummer bloomers begin. Also, cultivars in each division can bloom at different times. For example, early- to midseason-blooming Asiatic lilies can flower in mid-June, late June, or July. So, the wider the range of lilies you select, the longer, as well as more consistent and varied, the bloom season you can achieve from these garden aristocrats. *Note:* When purchasing bulbs of native lily species, ask about the origin of the bulbs you buy. Look for a source

Lilium canadense

that offers nursery-propagated plants: do not buy wild-collected bulbs, as collectors devastate native populations.

Inspect lily bulbs carefully before you buy, or before you accept a mail-order shipment. They should have plump, fleshy scales and, ideally, should have fleshy roots attached to the bottom of the bulb. (Some dealers cut off the roots before shipment, but bulbs with roots generally recover from shipping and transplanting more quickly.) Always handle the bulbs carefully, as they are easily bruised or damaged. They also dry out easily. Reject bulbs that have dry, withered scales or roots, as well as any that have signs of rot or mold. Some garden centers offer clumps of potted lilies. Although these are usually more expensive than bulbs, and you may have a more limited choice of cultivars, potted lilies get off to a fast start in the garden.

Plant bulbs in early spring or in fall up to about a month before the first fall frost date, as soon as possible after you buy them. Unlike hardy spring bulbs such as daffodils, lily bulbs are not completely dormant when they are shipped. The bulbs come packed in moist peat moss or other material; do not allow them to dry out before planting. If you can't plant right away, store the bulbs in the refrigerator or a dark, cool (40°F) place. Prepare the soil before you plant — and ideally before you buy — by working compost, leaf mold, or other organic matter into the soil to a depth of 2 feet. Planting depth varies: in general, plant lily bulbs with the tops at a depth of two to three times the height of the bulb — that usually translates to a depth of 6 to 9 inches. Plant smaller bulbs slightly closer to the surface. Many lilies produce roots along the stem *above* the bulb, which help anchor the plant, and deep planting encourages this. *L. candidum* and *L. × testaceum* are the exceptions to the deep planting rule: plant them with only 1 inch of soil over the noses of the bulbs. Space all lilies 1 to 1¹/₂ feet apart, and for best effect, plant them in clumps of at least three to five. Mark the locations of the bulbs to avoid digging into them by accident.

Once planted, many lilies thrive for years with only minimal care. When new growth emerges in spring, feed the plants with well-rotted manure or a balanced organic fertilizer. Taller lilies require staking: insert stakes in spring when the new growth is about 1 foot tall and loosely tie the stems to the stakes with soft yarn or strips of nylon stockings. Mulch the plants to control weeds and to keep the soil cool, but keep mulch away from the stems to prevent rotting. When plants are actively growing, water them deeply whenever the weather is dry. As the flowers fade, deadhead them to direct the plant's energy into next year's flowers. Let species lilies set some seeds if you want to save them or let plants self-sow; hybrids generally don't come true from seed. Dig and destroy stunted plants or plants with leaves that are mottled with yellow, as these symptoms indicate plants that are infected with viral diseases. Cut stalks to the ground in fall.

Divide clumps in early spring or late summer to early fall for propagation, if they outgrow their space, or if they become overcrowded, a condition signaled by lots of stems but relatively few flowers. Be sure to dig very deeply around the edges of the clump to avoid slicing into the bulbs by mistake. Some lilies produce pea-sized purple-black bulbils in the leaf axils; others produce small bulblets near the base of the stems, under the soil just above the bulbs. To use these for propagation, plant them in pots or in a nursery bed at a depth of two to three times their height. Scaling is another method used to propagate lilies. Dig up a bulb immediately after the flowers fade and pull off a few of the thick scales on the outside, near the base of the bulb. Replant the parent bulb. Dust the scales with sulfur and plant them immediately, pointed end up, in a flat filled with moist, soilless mix. Cover the flat with a plastic bag suspended on a wire frame and set it in a shady, protected spot outdoors or a warm, bright place indoors out of direct light. Keep the medium moist but not wet. In 6 to 8 weeks, the scales should produce small bulblets at their bases, which can be potted up.

Divisions and species are listed separately below.

DIVISIONS

ASIATIC HYBRIDS (DIVISION 1)

Early to midsummer bloomers, Asiatic hybrids bear 4- to 6-inch-wide flowers on 2- to 5-foot-tall plants. They are hybrids of several Asian species, including *L. bulbiferum, L. cernuum, L. concolor, L. davidii, L. lancifolium,* and *L. maculatum.* Flowers can point up, out, or down and are not fragrant. They come in a wide range of colors, including orange, yellow, red, pink, purple, cream, and white, and can be a solid color or two-tone. Many have spots in contrasting colors. Asiatics seldom need staking and are vigorous, long-lived plants that form clumps in the right site — well-drained soil in full sun. Cultivars include 'America', deep burgundy red; 'Avignon', bright red-orange; 'Citronella', lemon yellow with recurved tepals speckled with pale reddish or black spots; 'Connecticut King', deep yellow; 'Côte d'Azur', pale pink with recurved tepals; 'Enchantment', orange with brownish speckles; 'Fire King', red-orange with recurved tepals and centers spotted with purple; 'Jetfire', rose-pink with yellow centers; 'Mont Blanc', white lightly spotted with brown; and 'Montreux', deep rose-pink. 'Tiger Babies' bears small peachy salmon flowers with recurved, heavily spotted tepals. Mid-century and Harlequin hybrid lilies also are Asiatics. **Zones 3 to 8**.

MARTAGON HYBRIDS (DIVISION 2)

Early to midsummer bloomers derived primarily from *L. martagon,* commonly known as Turk's-cap lily, which bears nodding, purple-pink, 2-inch-wide flowers with recurved petals and dark spots on 3- to 6-foot-tall plants. *L. martagon* var. *album* has white flowers. Martagon hybrids also are called Turk's-cap hybrids and bear racemes of nodding 3- to 4-inch

Lilium canadense

Lilium Asiatic hybrids

flowers with recurved tepals on 3- to 6-foot plants. The species and many of the cultivars have an unpleasant scent. Martagon lilies include the Backhouse hybrids, including 'Mrs. R.O. Backhouse', which bears orange-yellow flowers flushed with pink, as well as the Paisley and Marhan hybrids. Both *L. martagon* and the Martagon hybrids grow in full sun to partial shade. They tolerate a wide range of well-drained soils, from acid to slightly alkaline. **Zones 3 to 8.**

CANDIDUM HYBRIDS (DIVISION 3)

Early to midsummer bloomers derived from *L. candidum* as well as other species. *L. candidum*, commonly known as Madonna lily, bears fragrant, waxy white, 2- to 3-inch-long flowers in clusters of 5 to 20 blooms on 3- to 6-foot-tall plants. Candidum hybrids bear erect clusters of 4- to 5-inch flowers on 3- to 4-foot plants. Blooms come in deep red, yellow-orange, and pale yellow to tan. Candidum hybrid cultivars, which are not as commonly offered as Asiatics and Orientals, include 'Apollo', with tan flowers flushed with apricot, and 'Zeus', which bears red flowers. Nankeen lily (*L. × testaceum*), with yellow-orange flowers, also is classified as a Candidum. Unlike most lilies, *L. candidum* and Candidum hybrids should be planted with no more than 1 inch of soil over the tops of the bulbs. When planted in fall, they produce a low clump of evergreen leaves before winter. Grow in neutral to slightly alkaline soil. **Zones 4 to 9.**

AMERICAN HYBRIDS (DIVISION 4)

Early to midsummer bloomers, American hybrids were developed by crossing a variety of native North American species, including well-known Canada lily (*L. canadense*) as well as a number of West Coast natives. They bear clusters of 4- to 6-inch flowers with recurved or sometimes funnel-shaped flowers. The 4- to 8-foot

plants require acid soil rich in organic matter. Partial shade is best, especially during the hottest part of the day. Cultivars include the Bellingham hybrids, such as 'Buttercup', a yellow flower spotted with maroon, and yellow-orange 'Shuksan'. **Zones 5 to 8.**

LONGIFLORUM HYBRIDS (DIVISION 5)

Early to midsummer bloomers derived primarily from *L. longiflorum*, or Easter lily, and *L. formosanum*. *L. longiflorum* bears fragrant white 7-inch-long trumpets on 1½- to 3½-foot-tall plants. While the species is not usually considered a garden plant — it is normally hardy only in **Zones 7 to 9** and is grown primarily in pots — the cultivar 'Mount Everest' bears fragrant white flowers and can be grown in Zones 5 to 8. Give it a spot in partial shade. Longiflorum hybrids tolerate alkaline soil.

TRUMPET AND AURELIAN HYBRIDS (DIVISION 6)

Mid- to late-summer bloomers derived from a variety of Asiatic species, including *L. regale*, *L. henryi*, and *L. sargentiae*. Many of the lilies in this division have classic trumpet-shaped blooms, but cultivars with bowl-shaped, flat-faced, or recurved blooms also are included here. The flowers, borne in clusters, usually are fragrant and generally face outward or are nodding. Colors include red, pink, gold, yellow, orange, and white; some are purple-red, brown, or green on the back or outside of the flower. Plants range from 4 to 8 feet tall and nearly always require staking. Cultivars include 'African Queen', with fragrant trumpets that are brown-purple on the outside and golden to orangy yellow inside; 'Black Dragon', which bears fragrant trumpets that are dark purple-red outside and white inside; 'Bright Star', with fragrant creamy white blooms that have recurved tepals; and 'Copper King', with fragrant apricot orange trumpets with recurved tepals; Golden Splendor Group cultivars also fall here. **Zones 4 to 8.**

ORIENTAL HYBRIDS (DIVISION 7)

Mid- to late-summer bloomers with showy, fragrant flowers that can reach 10 inches across. These

are derived primarily from Asian species such as *L. auratum*, *L. japonicum*, and *L. speciosum*. The blooms typically are bowl shaped, flat faced, or recurved, but trumpet-shaped Orientals have also been developed. White, pink, rose-red, and dark maroon-red are common colors; many cultivars feature flowers striped with yellow or spotted with red. Plants range from 2 to 8 feet tall, and the taller-growing cultivars generally require staking. Cultivars include 'Black Beauty', with fragrant, dark raspberry pink blooms that have recurved tepals edged in white; 'Casa Blanca', with fragrant, pure white, bowl-shaped blooms; 'Star Gazer', with rose-red blooms spotted with darker red; and 'Tom Pouce', with pink tepals that have recurved tips and a yellow midrib. **Zones 4 to 8.**

OTHER HYBRIDS (DIVISION 8)

This is a catchall division of hybrids that have parents in more than one division — an Oriental hybrid crossed with a Trumpet hybrid, for example. The cultivar 'Leslie Woodruff' is one example. It bears dark red flat-faced flowers that have a light fragrance and slightly recurved tepals tipped in white. 'Scheherazade' bears dark red flat-faced flowers edged in yellow that have recurved tepals tipped in white. Both are late-season bloomers. **Zones 5 to 8.**

SPECIES

Division 9 includes all true species lilies.

L. auratum

l. aw-RAH-tum. GOLDBAND LILY. Mid- to late-summer- or fall-blooming species with fragrant, 12-inch-wide, bowl-shaped flowers that usually face outward. Blooms are white with a yellow stripe on each recurved tepal and borne in clusters of about 12. Plants range from 2 to 5 feet tall. Susceptible to viral diseases. Requires well-drained, acid soil; wet soil in winter is fatal. **Zones 5 to 8.**

L. bulbiferum

l. bul-BIF-er-um. ORANGE LILY, FIRE LILY. A species that blooms in midsummer, producing one- to five-flowered clusters of erect, bowl-shaped, 4- to 6-inch-wide, orange-red flowers that have tepals spotted with maroon or maroon-black. Produces bulbils in the leaf axils. **Zones 3 to 8.**

Lilium auratum

Lilium pardalinum

L. canadense

l. kan-uh-DEN-see. CANADA LILY, MEADOW LILY. Mid- to late-summer-blooming lily that is a native North American wildflower that spreads via rhizomatous bulbs. Bears yellow-orange 3-inch-wide flowers on 3- to 6-foot-tall plants. Flowers are pendent, have slightly recurved tepals, and are spotted with maroon. Grows in damp to evenly moist, acid soil in full sun or partial shade. **Zones 3 to 7.**

L. candidum

l. kan-DEE-dum. MADONNA LILY. *See* Candidum hybrids.

L. cernuum

l. SIRN-yew-um. NODDING LILY. A midsummer bloomer that produces racemes of 6 to 12 or more fragrant, pendent, $1^{1}/_{4}$- to 2-inch-wide blooms in lilac, lilac-pink, or purple. Tolerates alkaline soil but best in peaty, acidic conditions. **Zones 2 to 6.**

L. columbianum

l. koh-lum-bee-AH-num. COLUMBIA TIGER LILY, OREGON LILY. A 5-foot-tall species native to the Pacific Northwest. Bears clusters of 6 to 10 or more pendent 2-inch-wide flowers with recurved tepals. Blooms are yellow to orange-red in color and spotted with maroon. **Zones 5 to 8.**

L. concolor

l. KON-kuh-lor. STAR LILY, MORNING STAR LILY. A 3-foot-tall species that blooms in midsummer and bears clusters of up to 10 erect, star-shaped, $1^{1}/_{2}$-inch-wide scarlet flowers. **Zones 3 to 7.**

L. davidii

l. dah-VID-ee-eye. A 3- to 4-foot-tall midsummer bloomer that bears clusters of 10 to as many as 20 red 3-inch-wide flowers with recurved tepals and purple-black spots. Bulbs may spread by stolons. **Zones 3 to 7.**

L. formosanum

l. for-moe-SAH-num. FORMOSA LILY. Late-summer- to fall-blooming species bearing 3- to 8-inch-long, trumpet-shaped white flowers on 4- to 7-foot-tall plants. Susceptible to viral diseases. Requires evenly moist, acid soil and spreads via rhizomatous bulbs. Plants are easy and fast from seeds sown indoors in midwinter; seedlings can begin blooming the first year from seed. *L. f.* var. *pricei* is a dwarf form that reaches about 2 feet in height. **Zones 5 to 9.**

L. grayi

l. GRAY-eye. ORANGE BELL LILY, GRAY'S LILY. A native wildflower from the eastern United States that bears clusters of up to 12 fragrant, nodding, $2^{1}/_{2}$-inch-long red flowers that are paler yellowish red inside and spotted with purple. Requires moist, acid soil. **Zones 4 to 7.**

L. henryi

l. HEN-ree-eye. HENRY LILY. Mid- to late-summer-blooming species producing $2^{1}/_{2}$- to 3-inch-wide orange flowers with recurved tepals spotted with maroon. Blooms are borne in clusters of 10 to 20 on 3- to 10-foot plants. Grows in partial shade in neutral to alkaline soil. Self-sows, and seedlings bloom in about 3 years. **Zones 4 to 8.**

L. lancifolium

l. lan-sih-FOE-lee-um. TIGER LILY. Formerly *L. tigrinum*. Orange-red 5- to 9-inch-wide flowers with dark purple-black spots in late summer to fall on 3- to 5-foot plants. Grows in evenly moist acid to slightly alkaline soil. Plants can be infected with viral diseases without showing symptoms. To avoid spreading viral diseases to other lilies, buy certified virus-free bulbs. **Zones 3 to 9.**

L. longiflorum

l. lon-jih-FLOR-um. *See* Longiflorum hybrids

L. martagon

l. MAR-tah-gon. *See* Martagon hybrids

L. pardalinum

l. par-dah-LYE-num. LEOPARD LILY, PANTHER LILY. A 5- to 8-foot-tall species native to the western United States. Bears clusters of up to 10 nodding $3^{1}/_{2}$-inch-wide flowers in midsummer. Blooms are orange-red to red in color, spotted with maroon, and have recurved tepals. Best in moist soil in full sun. Tolerates alkaline soil. **Zones 5 to 8.**

L. philadelphicum

l. fil-ah-DEL-fih-kum. RED LILY, WILD ORANGE LILY, WOOD LILY. A 1- to 3-foot-tall species native to eastern North America. In midsummer, bears racemes of one to three upward-facing, orange-red, 3- to 4-inch-wide, bowl-shaped flowers with slightly recurved tepals spotted with maroon. **Zones 2 to 6.**

L. pumilum

l. pew-MIL-um. CORAL LILY. Formerly *L. tenuifolium*. Early- to midsummer-blooming species bearing fragrant 2-inch-wide scarlet flowers with recurved tepals on 1- to 2-foot-tall plants. Full sun to partial shade. Requires acid soil. Bulbs are short-lived, lasting 2 to 4 years, but plants self-sow. Deadheading prolongs the life of the bulbs, but leave some flowers to form seedpods. **Zones 3 to 7.**

L. regale

l. reh-GAL-ee. REGAL LILY, ROYAL LILY. Mid- to late-summer-blooming species bearing clusters of up to 25 fragrant, 6-inch-long, trumpet-shaped flowers on 2- to 6-foot-tall plants. Blooms are white inside and purple to wine colored on the outside. Vigorous and easy in well-drained soil but will not grow in very alkaline conditions. Plants emerge early in spring and can be killed by late frosts. Cover emerging plants with bushel baskets or burlap if a late frost threatens. Self-sows, and seedlings begin blooming in about 2 years. **Zones 3 to 8.**

L. speciosum

l. spee-see-OH-sum. JAPANESE LILY. Mid- to late-summer-blooming species bearing clusters of about 12 fragrant 7-inch-wide flowers on 3- to $5^{1}/_{2}$-foot-tall plants. Blooms, which may face out or down, have recurved petals and come in pale pink or white, usually flushed deeper pink in the center and spotted with red. *L. s.* var. *rubrum* has deep pink flowers. A vigorous species that grows in full sun or partial shade and requires rich, evenly moist, very well drained, acid soil. Wet soil in winter is fatal. Susceptible to viral diseases and has been largely replaced by the Oriental hybrids. **Zones 4 to 8.**

L. superbum

l. sue-PER-bum. AMERICAN TURK'S-CAP LILY. Mid- to late-summer-blooming species native to North America. Bears clusters of up to 40 orange-red 3-inch-wide flowers with recurved tepals that are spotted with maroon on 4- to 8-foot-tall plants. Grows in damp to evenly moist, acid soil in full sun or partial shade. Established plants tolerate drought. Spreads via rhizomatous bulbs. **Zones 4 to 9.**

Limnanthes

lim-NAN-theez. Meadow-foam family, Limnanthaceae.

Native wildflowers from the western United States, *Limnanthes* species bear cup-shaped, five-petaled flowers and deeply cut, featherlike leaves. Of the 17 species in the genus, all low-growing annuals, one is cultivated.

HOW TO GROW
Choose a planting site with full sun or partial shade and rich, moist, well-drained soil. Sow seeds outdoors where the plants are to grow several weeks before the last spring frost date, while the soil is still cool and light frost is possible. Seeds germinate in about 3 weeks. In areas with mild winters — roughly Zone 7 south — sow seeds in fall for spring bloom; protect them with a light mulch of weed-free straw over winter. Plants grow best in areas with cool summers and die or languish when hot weather arrives. Use these plants for early color in mixed beds and borders. Plants self-sow.

L. douglasii
l. dug-LASS-ee-eye. FRIED EGGS, MEADOW FOAM, POACHED-EGG PLANT. A spreading annual with fleshy, feathery leaves that

Limnanthes douglasii

can reach 6 inches in height and width. Bears masses of fragrant, 1-inch-wide, golden yellow flowers with white-edged petals from summer to fall. Cool-weather annual.

Limonium

lih-MOE-nee-um. Plumbago family, Plumbaginaceae.

Limonium species are commonly known as sea lavenders or statice, the latter a former botanical name

Limonium latifolium

for this genus of 150 species of perennials and subshrubs, along with some annuals and biennials. Most produce a rosette of leaves clustered at the base of the plant. Leaf shape ranges from simple and entire to deeply lobed and featherlike. Plants produce small spikes of small papery flowers in summer and fall that are arranged in larger panicles.

HOW TO GROW
Provide full sun or partial shade and average to rich, well-drained soil. Perennial sea lavenders and annual statice are good plants for sandy soils and seaside gardens. Sea lavender (*L. latifolium*) grows from a woody crown and is deep rooted: plants are slow to establish and best left undisturbed once planted. Propagate by severing small new crowns that arise around the outside of the main plant in spring (be sure to get some roots) or by seeds. Sow statice seeds indoors 6 to 8 weeks before the last spring frost date at 65° to 75°F. Germination takes 2 to 3 weeks. Or sow outdoors after the last frost date. Statice is an ideal candidate for cutting gardens and is a top-notch dried flower. Harvest when most of the flowers in the spray have opened fully, and hang in small bunches in a warm, dark place to dry.

L. latifolium
l. lat-ih-FOE-lee-um. SEA LAVEN-DER. A perennial bearing low 1½-foot-wide rosettes of spoon-shaped leaves topped by airy, branched, 2- to 2½-foot-tall clus-

ters of tiny ¼-inch-long pale lavender to bluish purple flowers in late summer. **Zones 3 to 9.**

L. sinuatum
l. sin-yew-AH-tum. STATICE. A 1½-foot-tall tender perennial, hardy from **Zone 8 south**, and grown as an annual farther north, with showy clusters of brightly colored, ½-inch-long, funnel-shaped flowers in shades of violet, lavender, yellow, pink, orange, salmon, or white. Pacific or California Series plants feature cultivars in separate colors, including 'American Beauty' (deep rose) and 'Gold Coast' (deep yellow). Warm-weather annual.

Linanthus

lih-NAN-thus. Phlox family, Polemoniaceae.

Some 35 species of annuals and perennials belong to the genus *Linanthus*, once included in *Gilia*, a closely related genus. Native to the western United States, Mexico, and Chile, they bear deeply cut leaves and bell- to funnel-shaped, five-petaled flowers. The flowers come in shades of blue, lavender, white, pink, or yellow and somewhat resemble flowers of *Linum* species, commonly known as flax. The botanical name commemorates this resemblance: it is from the Greek *linon*, meaning "flax," and *anthos*, "flower."

HOW TO GROW
Full sun and average, well-drained soil are ideal. These plants grow well in sandy soil and are best for areas with cool summers; or start them early enough to bloom before hot weather arrives, since they do not tolerate heat and humidity.

Linanthus grandiflorus

Linaria maroccana

Sow seeds outdoors where the plants are to grow 2 to 3 weeks before the last spring frost date or in fall in areas with mild winters — roughly from Zone 7 south. Or sow indoors in individual pots 6 to 8 weeks before the last frost date, at 50° to 65°F, but outdoor sowing is usually best. Stake plants with twiggy brush. Use *Linanthus* species in drifts in mixed plantings or wild gardens. They also make attractive cut flowers. Plants self-sow.

L. grandiflorus
l. gran-dih-FLOR-us. Mountain Phlox. A 1- to 2-foot annual with dense heads of 1¼-inch-wide flowers in shades of purplish pink, lavender, or white in spring and summer. Cool-weather annual.

L. nuttallii
l. nut-TAL-lee-eye. A 4- to 8-inch-tall tender perennial, hardy from Zone 8 south. Bears clusters of funnel-shaped, white, ½-inch-wide flowers in summer. Cool-weather annual.

Linaria
lin-AIR-ee-ah. Figwort family, Scrophulariaceae.

Sometimes called spurred snapdragons, *Linaria* species have two-lipped flowers with jaws that open like snapdragons (*Antirrhinum*) but with a spur at the base. The genus contains about 100 species of annuals, biennials, and perennials with ovate, linear, or lance-shaped leaves and erect or trailing stems. Their flowers are carried in erect racemes from spring to fall and come in shades of yellow, orange, white, pink, purple, and red.

HOW TO GROW
Linarias thrive in full sun and average to rich soil that is light and well drained. Most linarias are plants of dry, sandy or rocky soil; they don't tolerate wet soil. Sow seeds of annual *L. maroccana* outdoors where the plants are to grow a few weeks before the last spring frost date. Or sow indoors 6 to 8 weeks before the last frost date at 55° to 60°F. Germination takes 2 weeks. Water plants during dry weather. Propagate perennial *L. purpurea* by dividing plants in spring, by taking cuttings of shoots that arise at the base of the plant in spring, or by seeds. Cut both types back after the first flush of bloom to encourage new flowers to form. Use linarias in mixed plantings and wild gardens. They attract hummingbirds and make excellent cut flowers. Plants self-sow.

L. maroccana
l. mah-rok-AN-ah. A ½- to 2-foot-tall annual from Morocco with linear leaves and loose clusters of ½-inch-long flowers in violet purple, lavender, pink, white, yellow, or orange. The lower lip, called the palate, is usually marked with yellow or orange. 'Fairy Bouquet' bears ¾-inch flowers on 9-inch plants in a range of colors. Cool-weather annual.

L. purpurea
l. pur-PUR-ee-uh. Purple Toadflax. A 3-foot-tall perennial that spreads to about 1 foot.

Bears airy racemes packed with tiny ½-inch-long purple flowers from early summer to fall. 'Canon J. Went' has pink flowers and comes true from seed if grown away from the species. **Zones 5 to 8.**

Lindera
lin-DAIR-uh. Laurel family, Laureaceae.

This genus includes about 80 species of dioecious, deciduous or evergreen shrubs and trees that occur naturally in moist woods and along hillside streams in North America and East Asia. Only two or three of these species, known as spicebush, are cultivated, but they have year-round appeal. The foliage is aromatic and often brightly colored in fall, with attractive fruit on female plants. Tiny yellow-green flowers appear on naked branches in early spring.

Lindera obtusiloba

HOW TO GROW
Spicebush must have the same moisture-retentive, well-aerated, organically rich soil it enjoys in the wild, but it adapts to a wide range of pH. Give it full sun in the North, partial shade in the South. The fibrous roots require steady supplemental moisture when these shrubs are newly transplanted. You will need plants of each sex in order to have berries, which are handsome in wildlife and woodland gardens. Keep them near the beaten path, though, where you can brush against the fragrant leaves. Propagate by cleaning seeds and giving warm treatment followed by cold treatment.

L. benzoin
l. BEN-zoh-in. Spicebush. Often found on moist limestone outcrops from Canada to Florida and Texas, this deciduous shrub nevertheless thrives in more acidic conditions. It grows 6 to 12 feet tall and wide, denser in sun and more open in shade. In early spring the bare branches are covered with clusters of small yellow-green flowers. When crushed, the light green oblong leaves, berries, and stems emit a spicy scent. In early fall, bright red berries ripen on female plants and attract birds, while leaves turn bright yellow. **Zones 5 to 9.**

L. obtusiloba
l. ob-tuss-ih-LOH-buh. Japanese Spicebush. This deciduous Asian species can grow larger than *L. benzoin*, up to 20 feet tall and wide but usually much smaller. In autumn it has more uniform, lasting, golden yellow coloration, even in shade. Leaves are frequently lobed. The foliage and the fruits, which turn from red to shiny black, are less heavily scented than those of the native species. **Zones 6 to 8.**

Linum
LYE-num. Flax family, Linaceae.

This genus contains some 200 species of annuals, biennials, perennials, subshrubs, and shrubs commonly called flax. They bear simple, generally narrow leaves and clusters of five-petaled, funnel- to saucer-shaped flowers. Flowers come in blue, lavender, white, yellow, red, and pink. Common flax (*L. usitatissium*), the source of the fiber from which

Linum perenne

linen is made, belongs here; the botanical name is the Latin word for that plant.

HOW TO GROW

Full sun and average to rich, light, well-drained soil are ideal. Excellent drainage is essential and wet soil in winter is fatal. Perennial species tend to be short-lived, but they self-sow. Propagate by division in spring or fall or by seeds. Sow seeds of annuals outdoors where the plants are to grow a few weeks before the last spring frost date. They also can be started in individual pots 6 to 8 weeks before the last frost date, but outdoor sowing is generally best. Or, where winters are mild — roughly Zone 7 south — sow outdoors in late summer or fall for bloom the following year. Use flaxes in mixed plantings with annuals or perennials. They do not make good cut flowers, as they wilt quickly after picking. Plants self-sow.

L. flavum

l. FLAY-vum. GOLDEN FLAX, YELLOW FLAX. Woody-based 1- to 1½-foot-tall perennial that spreads about as far. Bears clusters of 1-inch-wide, funnel-shaped yellow flowers in summer. 'Compactum' produces a 6- to 9-inch mound of flowers. **Zones 4 to 7.**

L. grandiflorum

l. gran-dih-FLOR-um. FLAX. A 1½- to 3-foot annual with gray-green leaves. Bears saucer-shaped, 1½- to 2-inch-wide flowers in shades of lilac-blue, red, white, or pink. Cool-weather annual.

L. narbonense

l. nar-boh-NEN-see. NARBONNE FLAX. Long-lived 1- to 2-foot-tall species forming 1½-foot-wide clumps. Bears small clusters of saucer-shaped, 1½-inch-wide blue flowers with white eyes from early to midsummer. 'Heavenly Blue' produces rich blue flowers on 1½-foot plants and is less likely to flop than the species. **Zones 6 to 9; to Zone 5 or even Zone 4 with winter protection.**

L. perenne

l. per-EN-ee. PERENNIAL FLAX. Wiry-stemmed, heat-tolerant, 1- to 1½-foot-tall species that spreads to about 1 foot. Bears panicles of rich blue ¾- to 1-inch-wide flowers, which lack white eyes, from early to midsummer. **Zones 4 to 8.**

Liquidambar

lih-quid-AM-bar. Witch-hazel family, Hamamelidaceae.

Four species of deciduous tall trees belong to this genus, which is characterized by aromatic, star-shaped leaves; inconspicuous flowers; and spiky, dry seed balls. Juice or gum from these trees has been used as perfume, incense, and chewing gum. The species native to North America makes an excellent shade tree renowned for its long-lasting fall foliage.

HOW TO GROW

Plant in full sun to partial shade and humus-rich, moist soil with a pH of 7.5 or lower. Tolerates drought and poorly drained soil. Needs little or no pruning to develop a strong branch structure; remove lower limbs if desired. Usually pest-free. Larvae of the luna moth feed on the leaves.

L. styraciflua

l. stye-rah-sih-FLEW-ah. SWEET GUM, GUM TREE. Named for the aromatic gummy resin that

Liquidambar styraciflua

bleeds from its wounded bark, sweet gum forms a narrow pyramid with slightly pendulous branches when young and changes to a rounded tree with a tall, straight trunk and massive branches when mature. It grows 65 to 70 feet tall and 40 to 50 feet wide. The star-shaped, glossy, dark green leaves measure 7 inches long and have five to seven pointed lobes. Fall color develops late and is a combination of yellow, scarlet, and deep purple, with the brightest hues on the tree's interior. Trunk bark is deeply furrowed; twigs are silvery and often feature corky ridges. Fruits are round, spiny, 1-inch-wide, tan seed heads that remain on the tree through the winter and drop in spring, creating a bit of a mess. Use this attractive tree to shade a house, park, or street. Reduce cleanup by planting a ground cover to absorb the fruits, or choose a fruitless form. From eastern and central North America. **Zones 5 to 9.**

CULTIVARS

'Burgundy' forms a wide column and has long-lasting, deep purplish red fall leaves, which can remain on the tree into early winter. 'Corky' is an upright, fruitless form with very corky young branches. 'Festival' has a narrow shape and apricot, peach, and red fall color; **Zones 6 to 9.** 'Gold Dust' ('Variegata') has bright gold-and-green-variegated leaves and pink and wine red fall color. 'Moraine' is pyramidal, with burgundy fall color. 'Palo Alto' also is pyramidal, with orange-red fall color; **Zones 6**

to 9. 'Rotundiloba' is narrowly pyramidal and fruitless; unusual round-lobed leaves; yellow and purple late-fall color; **Zones 6 to 9.** 'Worpelsdon' has rich purple, orange, and yellow fall color; noncorky twigs; and multilobed leaves.

Liriodendron

lear-ee-oh-DEN-dron. Magnolia family, Magnoliaceae.

Two species of deciduous trees belong to this genus, one from Asia and one from North America. The North American species is a noble tree of the eastern forests — perhaps the tallest native tree east of the Mississippi, reaching 200 feet tall in the forest. Although this is a common landscape tree, the Asian species is rare.

HOW TO GROW

Plant in full sun to partial shade and humus-rich, deep, well-drained soil. Best with plentiful moisture, especially when young; not very drought tolerant. Train to a strong central leader; trees with multiple leaders are prone to storm damage. Aphids and associated sooty mold may be a nuisance.

L. tulipifera

l. too-lip-IF-er-uh. TULIP TREE, YELLOW POPLAR. This magnificent tree is pyramidal when young but becomes towering and wide spreading when mature, with a massive trunk and several large, outstretched branches high on the

Liquidambar styraciflua

Liriodendron tulipifera

trunk. It grows 70 to 90 feet tall and 35 to 50 feet wide. Leaves measure 3 to 5 inches across and have an unusual blocky shape, with shallow lobes. Borne on long stems, they flutter in the wind. They are bright yellow-green in spring, dark green in summer, and vibrant yellow in late autumn. In late spring, the 2-inch, upright flowers, which are reminiscent of tulips, bloom at the branch tips. Their orange-marked, yellowish green petals attract humming-birds. Although the flowers are quite pretty, they are not profuse enough to put on a show, and because they bloom high up in the tree, they are easy to overlook. Conelike seedpods develop in fall but are not noteworthy. Trunk bark is gray-brown and furrowed. This is a good-looking shade tree for a large property or a natural landscape. From eastern and central North America. **Zones 5 to 9.**

CULTIVARS AND SIMILAR SPECIES

'Arnold' ('Fastigiatum') is narrow, with upright branches. 'Majestic Beauty' ('Aureomarginatum') has smaller leaves than the species, and the leaves have wide, bright

Liriope muscari 'Big Blue'

golden green margins in spring, turning solid green by midsum-mer. *L. chinense* (Chinese tulip tree) has greenish flowers and 10-inch-long or longer, deeply lobed leaves with pinched "waists" and pale undersides; grows to 60 feet; **Zones 6 to 8.**

Liriope

lih-RYE-oh-pee. Lily family, Liliaceae.

Most of the genus *Liriope*, with their grassy, evergreen foliage, provide a neat ground cover under trees and in shaded areas. The name "lilyturf" is applied to any of the five or six species of *Liriope*, which are all native to China, Ja-

pan, and Vietnam. They are often confused with members of the genus *Ophiopogon* (mondo grass). From a gardener's perspective, *Liriope* is hardier and has longer leaves, and the flowers are carried above the foliage. Leaves of *Liriope* range from only a few inches to nearly 18 inches long and from less than 1/4 inch to more than 1 inch wide. Foliage is evergreen, except at its northern limit, where it becomes semievergreen in winter. Leaves form loose tussocks on the underground rootstock, and several of the species spread by runners. Flowers, which are a bonus rather than the main attraction, resemble grape hyacinths *(Muscari)*. They are followed by small, glossy, black berries.

HOW TO GROW

Lilyturf thrives in loose, rich, moist, acid soils, but it is amazingly tolerant of a broad range of soil textures. Its extensive root system develops nutrient- and water-storing nodules, so the plants are capable of withstanding drought, although they do better with periodic watering. Mow or shear in early spring to maintain a neat appearance. At its northern limit, lilyturf does best in partial shade to prevent winter sunscald. Once established, it is a low-mainte-nance ground cover that can last for years. However, it is not a substitute for lawn if the intention is to walk on it with any regularity.

L. muscari

l. mus-KAR-ee. BIG BLUE LILYTURF. Tuberous-rooted 1- to 1 1/2-foot-tall perennial that spreads slowly to about 1 1/2 feet. Bears 1- to 1 1/2-inch-wide ever-

Liriope muscari

green leaves and spikes of tiny lilac-purple or white flowers above the leaves in fall. 'Big Blue', from 8 to 10 inches tall, has violet-purple flowers and dark green leaves. 'John Burch' bears gold-edged leaves. 'Variegata' has leaves edged in creamy white, and it spreads relatively slowly. **Zones 6 to 9.**

L. spicata

l. spih-KAH-tuh. CREEPING LILY-TURF. Semievergreen 1 to 1 1/2-foot-tall species with 1/4-inch-wide leaves that spreads fairly quickly by rhizomes to form 1 1/2- to 2-foot-wide mats. Use it on banks and where a vigorous weed-free ground cover is desired. Bears pale lavender or white flowers in late summer. **Zones 5 to 10.**

Lithodora

lith-oh-DOR-uh. Borage family, Boraginaceae.

This genus contains seven species of evergreen shrubs from south-west Europe and the Mediterra-nean region, grown primarily as rock-garden plants for their

Liriodendron tulipifera

Lithodora diffusa

ground-hugging form and terminal flat-topped clusters of intense blue (occasionally white), tubular summer flowers. These plants were formerly classified as *Lithospermum*.

HOW TO GROW

Give *L. diffusa*, the most commonly available species, neutral to alkaline soil with excellent drainage in full sun. Prune lightly after flowering. Propagate from semiripe cuttings in summer.

L. diffusa

l. dif-FEW-suh. A prostrate shrub usually 6 inches tall and spreading to 2 feet wide with narrow, oblong, hairy leaves to 1¹/₂ inches long. 'Grace Ward' and 'Heavenly Blue' are covered with azure blue, funnel-shaped, ¹/₂-inch flowers for a long period in late spring and summer. **Zones 6 to 8.**

Lobelia

low-BEE-lee-uh. Bellflower family, Campanulaceae.

While most of the 365 to 370 species in this diverse genus are annuals and perennials, *Lobelia* also contains shrubs, treelike plants, and even an aquatic species that grows partially submerged. Most are native to the Americas; the treelike species, which can reach 10 to 30 feet, are from East Africa. All produce simple leaves and tubular flowers that are slit almost to the base to form two lips. The top lip has two lobes; the bottom one, three. Flowers are borne singly or in erect racemes or panicles and come in shades of blue, lilac, violet, red, pink, white, and yellow.

HOW TO GROW

Plant the commonly grown perennial species — *L. cardinalis, L. siphilitica,* and related hybrids — in light to partial shade and rich, constantly moist soil. With consistent soil moisture they tolerate full sun in areas with cool summers. For best results, plant them in marshy spots or along streams or ponds. Plants are short-lived, but they self-sow where happy.

Lobelia cardinalis

Lobelia siphilitica

Clumps spread to about 1 foot. To keep them vigorous, dig clumps every 2 to 3 years in spring or early fall and replant the new rosettes of leaves that arise around the old rootstock.

L. cardinalis

l. kar-dih-NAL-iss. CARDINAL FLOWER. A 2- to 4-foot-tall native North American wildflower bearing erect racemes of scarlet 2-inch-long flowers in summer and early fall. 'Rosea' has rose-pink blooms. 'Ruby Slippers' bears ruby red flowers. **Zones 2 to 9.**

L. erinus

l. er-EYE-nus. EDGING LOBELIA. A popular, much-hybridized, trailing or bushy tender perennial from South Africa, commonly grown as an annual. Plants range from 4 to 9 inches tall and bear

Lobelia cardinalis

linear leaves sometimes flushed with maroon-bronze. Produces small clusters of ¹/₂-inch flowers from early summer to frost. Cascade Series cultivars are trailing 8-inch-tall plants suitable for baskets. Rainbow Series plants are 5 inches tall and excellent for edging. They include 'Crystal Palace', with blue flowers and bronze leaves; 'Rosamund', with cherry red, white-eyed flowers and green leaves; and 'White Lady', with white flowers and green leaves. Warm-weather annual.

L. siphilitica

l. sih-fih-LIT-ih-kuh. GREAT BLUE LOBELIA. A 2- to 4-foot-tall native North American wildflower bearing dense racemes of blue 1- to 1¹/₂-inch-wide flowers from late summer to fall. *L. s. f. albiflora,* also sold as 'Alba', has white flowers. **Zones 4 to 8.**

L. × speciosa

l. × spee-see-OH-suh. HYBRID CARDINAL FLOWERS. A catch-all for the many hybrid perennials available, which range from 2 to 4 feet tall and bloom from summer to fall. 'Bee's Flame' features red-purple leaves and crimson red flowers. 'Queen Victoria' bears bronze-red leaves and scarlet flowers. **Zones 5 to 9.**

Lobularia

lob-yew-LAIR-ee-ah. Cabbage family, Brassicaceae.

Dense, rounded clusters of fragrant flowers characterize the five species that belong to this genus of plants native to the Mediterranean

region and Canary Islands. They bear narrow, simple leaves and grow in sunny, dry spots with rocky or sandy soil. One species, *L. maritima*, better known as sweet alyssum, is a popular annual.

HOW TO GROW

Give sweet alyssum full sun or partial shade and average, well-drained soil. It grows well in evenly moist soil but also tolerates dry conditions. Sow seeds indoors 6 to 8 weeks before the last spring frost date at 65° to 70°F. Germination takes 1 to 2 weeks. Or sow outdoors where the plants are to grow several weeks before the last frost date, when the soil is cool and light frost is still possible. Or sow in fall for spring bloom the following year. When sowing, just press the seeds into the soil surface, as light is required for germination. Water regularly for best performance. Shear plants back by one-half after the first flush of bloom to encourage new flowers to form. Use sweet alyssum as a ground cover, in mixed plantings, in containers, as an edging, and in paving cracks. It is a good choice for seaside gardens. Plants self-sow.

L. maritima

l. mah-RIT-ih-muh. SWEET ALYSSUM. Formerly *Alyssum maritimum*. A spreading, well-branched, 2- to 12-inch-tall annual with linear, gray-green leaves. Bears masses of rounded, 1- to 3-inch-wide clusters of tiny, four-petaled flowers in white as well as shades of pink, rose-red, violet, and lilac from spring to fall. Many cultivars are available, including

Lobularia maritima 'Snow Crystal'

white-flowered, 3- to 4-inch-tall 'Carpet of Snow' and 'Snow Cloth'; Basket Series, which are 4-inch plants available in separate colors or a mix; 4-inch 'Rosie O'Day', with rose-pink blooms; and purple-flowered, 4-inch 'Royal Carpet'. Cool-weather annual.

Lonas

LOW-nas. Aster family, Asteraceae.

Despite its common name, African daisy, the one species that belongs in this genus is an annual from the Mediterranean region. Another common name, yellow ageratum, is perhaps more apt: it bears dense clusters of buttonlike flower heads consisting of all disk florets — they lack the "petals," or ray florets, of many aster-family plants. The foliage is deeply divided and featherlike.

HOW TO GROW

Choose a site with full sun and average, well-drained soil. Plants tolerate dry soil but flower better in evenly moist conditions. Sow seeds indoors 8 to 10 weeks before the last spring frost date at 60° to 65°F. Or sow outdoors after the last frost date, once the soil has warmed up a bit. Either way, barely cover the seeds with soil, as darkness is required for germination. Yellow ageratum makes an unusual addition to mixed plantings and also is an outstanding cut or dried flower. Harvest

Lonas annua

the blooms as soon as they are fully open, and hang them in bunches in a dark, warm, airy spot to dry.

L. annua

l. AN-yew-uh. YELLOW AGERA-TUM, AFRICAN DAISY. Formerly *L. inodora*. A 1-foot-tall annual with dense, rounded, 3- to 5-inch-wide clusters of small, round, buttonlike flower heads. Warm-weather annual.

Lonicera

lon-ISS-er-uh. Honeysuckle family, Caprifoliaceae.

Better known for the vining members among its 180 species, this genus from throughout the Northern Hemisphere also includes deciduous and evergreen shrubs. Honeysuckles are grown primarily for their tubular, usually fragrant flowers. The berries are popular with birds. But like the common honeysuckle vine, *L. japonica*, many of the shrub species (notably *L. maackii* and *L. tatarica*) have become widely invasive. In most of the country, less troublesome shrubs and vines should be substituted.

HOW TO GROW

Honeysuckles have become invasive because they are so easy to grow, adapting to almost any relatively moisture-retentive, well-drained soil. They bloom best in full sun but also grow in heavy shade, leafing out before taller plants and getting a jump start on the season. If the plants become overgrown, they can be pruned to the ground and will develop new shoots. Use them as hedges, in the shrub border, in wildlife gardens, or massed for winter or early-spring fragrance. The vines are excellent bank holders or covers for unsightly fences. They also can be trained over shrubs.

L. × brownii

l. BROW-nee-eye. SCARLET TRUMPET HONEYSUCKLE. This hybrid, the result of a cross

Lonicera × heckrottii

Lonicera × brownii

between *L. hirsuta* and *L. sempervirens*, is a twining vine that climbs to about 12 feet. Plants bear pairs of oval, blue-green leaves that are either deciduous or semievergreen. In summer, clusters of 1½-inch-long, tubular, scarlet or orange flowers appear at the stem tips. Flowers are slightly fragrant. 'Dropmore Scarlet' bears showy, bright red trumpets over a long season. **Zones 4 to 9.**

L. fragrantissima

l. fray-gran-TISS-ih-muh. WINTER HONEYSUCKLE. Growing 8 to 10 feet tall and wide, winter honeysuckle is somewhat rounded and holds its broad, oval, 1- to 3-inch leaves late into winter. Half-inch two-lipped flowers are cream

tinged with pink and open as early as January and as late as April, more fragrant than pretty. The dark red berries are hidden by the foliage. **Zones 4 to 10.**

L. × heckrottii

l. × heck-ROT-tee-eye. GOLD-FLAME HONEYSUCKLE. This twining climber, the result of a cross between *L. americana* and *L. sempervirens*, has pairs of rounded deciduous or semievergreen leaves that are blue-green in color. Plants reach 10 to 20 feet if given support, but they can be allowed to sprawl over low walls or climb shrubs. Clusters of tubular, lightly fragrant, two-lipped flowers are borne in early summer and sporadically into fall on the tips of

Lonicera sempervirens

L

Loropetalum chinense 'Burgundy'

the new growth. Flower buds are red and open into red-and-yellow flowers. **Zones 5 to 9.**

L. japonica

l. juh-PON-ih-kuh. JAPANESE HONEYSUCKLE. This rampant weedy vine with fragrant flowers has been grown throughout North America for well over a century and is an established plant in many regions — so much so that most people mistake it for a native. Once given a toehold in the garden, it is extremely hard to eliminate. The species is widely available, as are several named selections. 'Aureoreticulata' ('Variegata') has yellow-veined leaves and grows more slowly; it is slightly less hardy, to **Zone 5.** 'Halliana' is evergreen in mild climates and semievergreen otherwise. It spreads by stems that root as they touch the ground and is very fast growing and often invasive. It has been widely used as a bank cover throughout most of the warmer regions of North America. 'Purpurea' has purple-tinged leaves. **Zones 4 to 9.**

L. nitida

l. NIT-ih-duh. BOXLEAF HONEY-SUCKLE. An evergreen species cultivated as a fast-growing, easily pruned, salt-tolerant hedge, rather than for its inconspicuous flowers. Reaches 10 feet tall but is usually kept lower. The common name reflects the leaf shape, similar to that of boxwood. The dark blue fruits are round and translucent but rarely produced. Shiny leaves may bronze in winter. Cultivars include 'Baggesen's Gold', which has golden foliage. **Zones 7 to 9.**

L. periclymenum

l. per-ih-kli-MEH-nee-um. WOOD-BINE HONEYSUCKLE, WOOD-BINE. A deciduous twining climber ranging from 10 to 20 feet in height. Bears rounded leaves and clusters of very fragrant, white to yellow flowers that may be flushed with red from mid- to late summer. 'Graham Thomas' produces white flowers that age to yellow over a very long bloom season. 'Serotina' features white flowers streaked with red-purple over a long season. **Zones 5 to 9.**

L. pileata

l. pil-ee-AY-tuh. PRIVET HONEY-SUCKLE. A semievergreen with a graceful, spreading, horizontal habit to 3 feet tall and more than twice as wide. Similar to *L. nitida* except that the leaves are elongated and larger. It does not perform well in the South but does tolerate seaside conditions. **Zones 6 to 8.**

L. sempervirens

l. sem-per-VIE-renz. TRUMPET HONEYSUCKLE, CORAL HONEYSUCKLE. A native 10- to 20-foot vine that is deciduous or semievergreen. Plants bear rounded leaves and clusters of trumpet-shaped flowers that are not fragrant in shades of orange-red, red, or yellow. Flowers are borne in early summer and sporadically into fall on the tips of the new growth. *L. s.* f. *sulfurea* bears yellow flowers. **Zones 4 to 9.**

L. xylosteum

l. zy-LOSS-tee-um. EUROPEAN FLY HONEYSUCKLE. Forms a mound 10 feet tall and wide with arching branches. The gray-green leaves are slightly fuzzy, and the creamy white flowers are followed by dark red berries. Good selection for the Midwest and Plains. 'Emerald Mound' grows to only 3 feet tall and 5 feet wide and has bluish green foliage. **Zones 4 to 6.**

Loropetalum

lor-oh-PET-uh-lum. Witch-hazel family, Hamamelidaceae.

This genus contains only one small evergreen species from Asia, grown for its compact size, graceful form, and unusual early-season flowers. Cultivars offer the bonus of colorful foliage.

HOW TO GROW

Loropetalum needs organically rich, moist, well-drained, acid soil in full sun or partial shade. It tolerates heavy pruning and can be espaliered, but otherwise loses its appealing natural shape with anything but a light trim after flowering. Plant against a sunny wall or in a shrub border. Pink-flowered forms make a striking echo for similarly colored tulips. Needs mild winters and hot summers. Cuttings need hormones and mist to root; bottom heat may prevent rotting.

L. chinense

l. chih-NEN-see. CHINESE FRINGE-FLOWER. Grows 6 to 10 feet tall and wide, with an irregular fountain or vase shape. The spidery white flowers, similar to those of witch hazel (*Hamamelis*), appear in early spring. Several forms with purple flowers and purple-tinged leaves include *L. c.* var. *rubrum*, 'Blush', 'Burgundy' (with leaves that develop orange or red streaks in fall), and 'Zhuzhous Fuchsia' (said to be the best at maintaining maroon color through summer heat). Plants have occasional light rebloom in fall. The species is considered hardier than the red-foliaged varieties, possibly into **southern Zone 6 with protection. Otherwise, Zones 7 to 10.**

Lotus

LOW-tus. Pea family, Fabaceae.

Lotus species are annuals, perennials, and subshrubs, primarily native to the Mediterra-

Lotus berthelotii

Lunaria annua

nean region, and are no relation to the water-garden plants commonly called lotuses (*Nelumbo*). Some 150 species belong here, all bearing leaves divided into three or more leaflets and pea-shaped flowers. Flowers are most often carried in clusters but also singly or in pairs.

HOW TO GROW

Select a site with full sun and average, well-drained soil. These plants tolerate a wide range of soils, including dry and sandy as well as alkaline to acid. Somewhat dry soil is better than moist conditions. Plants are typically grown from cuttings rather than seeds. Sow seeds indoors 8 to 10 weeks before the last spring frost date at 65° to 75°F. Grow *Lotus* species as bedding plants replaced annually or tender perennials. Take cuttings in summer for garden use or to overwinter the plants indoors. Over winter, keep plants in a bright, cool (50°F), well-ventilated spot. Prune in spring as necessary, and replace plants that become too woody. Use these plants in containers, baskets, and mixed plantings.

L. berthelotii

l. ber-theh-LOW-tee-eye. Lotus Vine, Parrot's Beak, Coral Gem. A trailing, tender subshrub, hardy from about **Zone 9 south**, that reaches 6 to 8 inches in height but can spread several feet. Bears bunches of silver-green, needlelike leaves and orange-red to scarlet, 1¼- to 1½-inch-long flowers with black centers. Flowers are carried singly or in pairs from spring to summer. *L. maculatus* is a similar species that produces 1-inch-long yellow flowers tipped with red-orange or red. Tender perennial or warm-weather annual.

Lunaria

loo-NAIR-ee-ah. Cabbage family, Brassicaceae.

Commonly called honesty, money plant, silver dollar, and just simply lunaria, the three species that belong to this genus are annuals, biennials, or perennials native from Europe to western Asia. They bear toothed, heart-shaped to somewhat triangular leaves and showy racemes of four-petaled, cross-shaped flowers from late spring to summer. The flowers are followed by sprays of round, flat seedpods, called siliques, that split along their edges. When the walls, or valves, fall off, they reveal the silvery, papery partitions that make these plants valued additions to dried arrangements.

HOW TO GROW

Plant lunarias in full sun or partial shade and rich, evenly moist, well-drained soil. Sow seeds outdoors anytime from a few weeks before the last spring frost date to early fall. Or sow indoors 6 to 8 weeks before the last frost date, although outdoor sowing is generally best. Money plant (*L. annua*) produces foliage the first year and blooms the second. To use the seedpods for dried arrangements, harvest them just as they begin to turn from green to brown, and gently loosen the valves covering the silvery partitions by rubbing them between your fingers. Leave some seeds to ripen on the plants, as plants self-sow. Use lunarias in shade gardens, along shrub borders, and in semiwild areas.

L. annua

l. AN-yew-uh. Money Plant, Honesty. A ½- to 1-foot-tall biennial — to 3 feet in bloom — with ½-inch-wide, rose-purple or sometimes white flowers. 'Variegata' bears handsome, white-edged leaves, which are evergreen, and red-purple flowers and comes true from seed. Biennial. **Zones 5 to 9**.

Lupinus

loo-PIE-nus. Pea family, Fabaceae.

Lupines are annuals, perennials, subshrubs, and shrubs with palmate leaves and showy clusters of pealike flowers. The flowers, which are borne in spikelike panicles or sometimes whorls, have an upright petal, called a standard; two side or wing petals; and two lower petals joined at the base to form a sheath, called a keel. About 200 species belong to the genus, most native to the Americas, the Mediterranean region, and North Africa.

HOW TO GROW

Select a site with full sun and average to rich, well-drained soil. Most lupines need cool, moist conditions — they thrive in the Pacific Northwest and in coastal New England — and usually fail or are short-lived in hot, humid climates. They resent root disturbance, so select a permanent location at planting time. Propagate by seeds sown in individual pots and transplant with care, or take cuttings from shoots at the base of the plant in spring. Plants self-sow.

L. hartwegii

l. hart-WEDGE-ee-eye. A 2- to 3-foot-tall annual with dense, 8-inch-long spikes of flowers from summer to fall. Blooms are ½ inch long and pale lavender-blue with a rose-pink blush on the upright standards. Cool-weather annual.

L. hybrids

These are 3- to 5-foot-tall plants with erect, densely packed spikes

Lupinus Russell hybrid

Lupinus texensis

of flowers in early and midsummer. Blooms come in purple, violet, yellow, pink, red, and white. The popular Russell hybrids are 2¹/₂ to 3 feet tall and are hardy in **Zones 3 or 4 to 8,** but are best treated as annuals **south of Zone 6** in eastern and central states.

L. luteus

I. LOO-tee-us. YELLOW LUPINE. A 2-foot-tall annual with 10-inch-long spikes of golden yellow, ¹/₂- to ³/₄-inch-long flowers in summer. Cool-weather annual.

L. nanus

I. NAY-nus. SKY LUPINE. A bushy, 1¹/₂- to 2-foot annual with 8-inch-long spikes of lavender-blue, white, or bicolor, ¹/₂-inch-wide flowers in summer. Cool-weather annual.

Luzula nivea

L. perennis

I. per-EN-iss. WILD LUPINE. A 2-foot-tall species native from Florida to Maine that forms 1¹/₂-foot-wide clumps. Bears 6- to 12-inch-long spikes of blue or sometimes pink or white ¹/₂-inch-long flowers in early summer. **Zones 4 to 9.**

L. polyphyllus

I. pol-ee-FILL-us. A 3- to 5-foot-tall species native to western North America that spreads to about 2¹/₂ feet. Bears 1- to 1¹/₂-foot-long spikes of lilac-blue ¹/₂-inch-long flowers in summer. Blooms are sometimes white or pink. **Zones 3 to 7.**

L. texensis

I. tex-EN-sis. TEXAS BLUEBONNET. A 10- to 12-inch annual with dense, 3-inch-long racemes of blue to violet-blue ¹/₂-inch-wide flowers in summer. Cool-weather annual.

Luzula

LOOZ-yew-luh. Rush family, Juncaceae.

The 80 species of *Luzula* are found throughout the Northern Hemisphere, especially in Europe and Asia. These wood rushes are related to the true rushes *(Juncus),* which are denizens of moist or wet meadows and waterways. All luzulas are deciduous perennials with straplike leaves. Flowers are much-reduced, wind-pollinated affairs that are grouped into small, angular masses reminiscent of cleaning brushes. The fruiting structures have a subtle appeal all their own.

Lychnis coronaria

HOW TO GROW

Wood rushes are sturdy, trouble-free plants that make excellent ground covers for difficult sites. They add a unique textural effect to shady gardens, and some species are tolerant of the thin, rocky soils found in some forested regions. They require dappled or partial shade, as would be found in the forest, where sunlight is filtered to the forest floor for only minutes at a time. Well-drained, organic-rich soil is best for the woodland species. Specialty nurseries may offer species from rockier, more exposed sites.

L. luzuloides

I. looz-yew-LOY-deez. Makes a dense, sprawling, matlike ground cover in shady sites with moist or dry soil. **Zones 3 to 8.**

L. nivea

I. nih-VEE-uh. SNOWY WOOD RUSH. The hairy leaves are up to 1 foot long, and the flowers have a whitish cast. Seed heads are cottony. **Zones 4 to 8.**

L. sylvatica

I. sil-VAT-ih-kuh. GREATER WOOD RUSH. This species has broad, glossy green leaves about 1 foot long. It masses well in semishade and most soils. Flowers have a tan cast. There are several selections for leaf color. 'Aurea' has yellow-chartreuse leaves reminiscent of the color of almost-ripe lemons. It is a bright addition to woodland

gardens, where it will form a pool of light in shaded situations. 'Variegata' has evergreen foliage with narrow, creamy bands on the edges. It spreads slowly. **Zones 5 to 8.**

Lychnis

LICK-niss. Pink Family, Caryophyllaceae.

Lychnis contains some 15 to 20 species of biennials and perennials bearing five-petaled flowers that have tube-shaped bases and flattened faces with petal lobes that are rounded, notched, or sometimes fringed at the tips. Flowers are carried singly on branched stems or in small rounded clusters. The plants have rounded, often hairy leaves. *Lychnis* species are quite similar to *Silene* species and share the common names "campion" and "catchfly." It's no wonder they look so similar, since the two genera differ only in the number of styles (the narrow stalk that joins the stigma and ovary of a pistil, the female part of a blossom) in the flowers. *Lychnis* species have five, or sometimes four styles, while *Silene* species have three or sometimes four. *Saponaria,* another similar species commonly called soapwort, has flowers with two styles.

HOW TO GROW

Select a site in full sun or partial shade with light, average to rich, well-drained soil. In areas with hot summers, a spot that receives afternoon shade is best. *L. chalcedonica* and *L. viscaria* are best in rich, evenly moist soil, while *L. × haageana* requires constant moisture for best growth. Gray-leaved *L. coronaria* exhibits the best foliage color when grown in dry soil. Perennial catchflies tend to be short-lived, but they self-sow. Taller species require staking. Divide them every 2 to 3 years in spring to keep the clumps vigorous and for propagation. Or sow seeds.

L. × arkwrightii

l. × ark-RYE-tee-eye. A R K - W R I G H T ' S C A M P I O N . A 1½- to 2-foot-tall species that spreads to about 1 foot. Bears brownish green leaves and clusters of starry, orange-red, 1½-inch-wide flowers in early to midsummer. 'Vesuvius' has scarlet-orange flowers and dark brown-green leaves. **Zones 4 to 8.**

L. chalcedonica

l. chal-sih-DON-ih-kuh. J E R U S A L E M C R O S S , M A L T E S E C R O S S . A 3- to 4-foot-tall species that spreads to about 1 foot. Bears rounded clusters of star-shaped ½-inch-wide flowers with deeply notched petals in early to midsummer. Blooms are brilliant scarlet. 'Alba' has white flowers. 'Rosea' has pink blooms. **Zones 4 to 8.**

L. coronaria

l. kor-oh-NAIR-ee-uh. R O S E C A M - P I O N , M U L L E I N P I N K , D U S T Y M I L L E R . A 2½- to 3-foot-tall biennial or short-lived perennial that spreads to 1½ feet with rosettes of woolly silver gray leaves. Carries branched clusters of 1- to 1¼-inch-wide flowers with rounded, notched petals in mid- to late summer in magenta-pink or white. 'Angel's Blush' bears white flowers with bright pink eyes. **Zones 4 to 8.**

L. × haageana

l. × hah-jee-AH-nuh. A 1½- to 2-foot-tall hybrid that spreads to about 1 foot. Bears loose clusters of brilliant red or orange-red flowers in summer. **Zones 4 to 8.**

L. viscaria

l. vis-KAR-ee-uh. G E R M A N C A T C H F L Y . A 1- to 1½-foot-tall species that spreads as far. Bears loose, spiky clusters of purplish pink ¾-inch-wide flowers in early and midsummer. 'Alba' has white flowers. 'Fire' ('Feuer') bears red, sometimes double flowers. **Zones 3 or 4 to 8.**

Lycoris

lye-KOR-iss. Amaryllis family, Amaryllidaceae.

Native to China and Japan, *Lycoris* species are grown for their showy clusters of flowers borne from spring to fall, depending on the species. From 10 to 12 species belong to the genus, all perennials that grow from tunicate bulbs and produce linear to strap-shaped leaves. The flowers are borne in umbels atop fleshy, leafless stems, and the blooms appear when the leaves are dormant — the common name "magic lily" refers to this characteristic, since the bloom stalks seem to arise suddenly from bare ground. The leaves either die back before the flowers emerge or appear after the flowers fade. The individual flowers have six petal-like tepals and six prominent stamens that stick out. The tepals, which are joined together only at the base to form a short tube, are recurved and spreading. Blooms either have broad tepals (so the blooms resemble lilylike trumpets) or are spidery looking. Species with spidery blooms have narrow, strongly reflexed tepals with wavy edges along with prominent stamens.

HOW TO GROW

Select a site in full sun or partial shade with deeply prepared, rich, well-drained soil. Where hardy, plant the bulbs in fall with the tops of the bulbs 4 to 6 inches below the soil surface, and space them about 9 inches apart. Mark the location of the plants so you don't dig into them by accident after the foliage dies back in spring. Where they are marginally hardy, protect the plants in late fall with a dry winter mulch of evergreen boughs, salt hay, pine needles, or coarse leaves, such as oak leaves. Top-dress before the foliage emerges with a balanced organic fertilizer. Outdoors, combine *Lycoris* species with perennials such as hostas or low-growing as-ters, which will provide a foil for the blooms. Or overplant the bulbs with annuals.

Where they are not hardy, grow *Lycoris* in containers with the tops of the bulbs set just at the soil surface. When container-grown plants are growing actively, keep the soil evenly moist and feed every other week with a dilute, balanced fertilizer. Gradually withhold water as the leaves turn yellow and die back. Let the soil dry out completely, then overwinter the bulbs indoors — still in their containers — in a cool (45° to 50°F), dry spot. Container-grown plants need repotting only every few years. Outdoors, undisturbed plants gradually form large clumps. They can be propagated by separating the offsets, but plants are best left undisturbed as long as possible. (Disturbing them can prevent their flowering for one or two seasons). Or propagate from seeds.

L. albiflora

l. al-bih-FLOR-uh. A 1½-foot-tall species that bears umbels of four to six white flowers in late summer and early fall. Individual blooms are 1½ to 2 inches long and spidery in appearance, with reflexed, wavy-margined tepals. Leaves appear after the flowers. This species is similar to *L. radiata* and may well be a variety of that species. **Zones 9 to 10.**

L. aurea

l. AW-ree-uh. G O L D E N S P I D E R L I L Y , G O L D E N H U R R I C A N E L I L Y . A 2-foot-tall species that bears umbels of five or six golden yellow flowers in late spring or summer. Individual blooms are 4 inches wide and spidery in appearance, with wavy-margined

Lycoris radiata

Lycoris radiata

Lycoris squamigera

Lysimachia clethroides

tepals reflexed at the tips. Leaves appear after the flowers. **Zones 8 to 10.**

L. radiata

l. ray-dee-AH-tuh. RED SPIDER LILY. A 1- to 2-foot-tall species that bears umbels of four to six deep red or deep pink flowers in late summer and early fall. Individual blooms are 1½ to 2 inches long and spidery in appearance, with very reflexed tepals that have wavy margins. Leaves appear after the flowers. **Zones 8 to 10.**

L. sanguinea

l. san-GWIH-nee-uh. A 1½- to 2-foot-tall species bearing umbels of about six funnel-shaped red flowers in late summer and early fall. Individual blooms are 2 to 2½ inches long and have slightly reflexed tips. **Zones 9 to 10.**

L. squamigera

l. skwa-mih-JEER-uh. HARDY AM-ARYLLIS, MAGIC LILY, RES-URRECTION LILY. A 1½- to 2-foot-tall species bearing umbels of

six to eight fragrant, pale to rich pink flowers in summer. Individual blooms are lilylike and 3 to 4 inches long and have fairly broad tepals that are reflexed at the tips. Leaves appear in spring, before the flowers. **Zones 6 to 10; to Zone 5 with winter protection.**

Lysimachia

lih-sih-MOCK-ee-uh. Primrose family, Primulaceae.

About 150 species of perennials and shrubs belong to the genus *Lysimachia*. The perennials range from erect, clump-forming plants to creeping species suitable for use as ground covers. They bear five-petaled flowers that usually are yellow or white and range from starry to cup or saucer shaped.

Blooms are carried singly or in racemes or panicles. Leaves are simple. Commonly called loose-strifes, *Lysimachia* species are not to be confused with purple loosestrifes *(Lythrum)*, which are perennials that have become noxious weeds in many areas.

HOW TO GROW

Select a site in full sun or partial shade with rich, well-drained, evenly moist soil. Loosestrifes are excellent choices for bog gardens, along ponds or other water features, and in moist borders, since they tolerate constantly moist soil. Dry soil slows their growth, and they do not tolerate drought. Most spread vigorously by rhizomes and can become invasive. To propagate, or to control their spread, divide plants in spring or fall or root cuttings in spring or summer. Plants self-sow.

L. ciliata

l. sil-ee-AH-tuh. FRINGED LOOSE-STRIFE. A 1- to 3-foot-tall species that spreads by rhizomes to form clumps 2 feet or more in width.

Bears star-shaped, 1-inch-wide yellow flowers that are solitary or paired in the leaf axils in midsummer. 'Purpurea' has purple-black leaves. **Zones 3 to 9.**

L. clethroides

l. kleth-ROY-deez. GOOSENECK LOOSESTRIFE. Rhizomatous 3-foot-tall species that spreads vigorously and quickly to form broad clumps several feet across. Bears dense, curved racemes of ½-inch-wide white flowers from mid- to late summer. **Zones 3 to 9.**

L. nummularia

l. num-yew-LAIR-ee-uh. CREEPING JENNY. Mat-forming 2- to 4-inch-tall perennial that spreads quickly to several feet by stems that root as they touch the soil. Bears rounded, evergreen to semievergreen leaves and solitary yellow 1-inch-wide flowers in summer. 'Aurea' has yellow foliage and spreads somewhat more slowly than the species. **Zones 3 to 8.** *L. japonica* 'Minutissima' is another creeping, prostrate selection that stays under 2 inches tall and bears small cup-shaped yellow flowers in summer; **Zones 4 to 9.**

L. punctata

l. punk-TAH-tuh. WHORLED LOOSESTRIFE. Handsome 3-foot-tall species spreading to 2 feet or more by rhizomes. Bears erect stems with whorls of yellow 1-inch-wide flowers in early summer. Plants can become invasive and need to be divided regularly. **Zones 4 to 8.**

Lysimachia nummularia

Lysimachia punctata

M

Maackia

MACK-ee-ah. Pea family, Fabaceae.

This genus from eastern Asia contains about eight tree species, which are closely related to *Cladrastis*, another genus of summer-blooming trees.

HOW TO GROW

Plant in full sun and any well-drained soil, light to heavy, acid to alkaline; grows best in moist loam. Very drought tolerant. When using it as a street tree, remove lower limbs when the tree is young to allow traffic to pass beneath it as it ages. Large pruning cuts are slow to heal.

M. amurensis

m. am-ore-EN-sis. AMUR MAACKIA. This little-known tree grows 20 to 35 feet tall and 25 to 50 feet wide, with a rounded, spreading shape. It deserves wider planting, especially as a street tree. Eight-inch-long, upright flower clusters appear at the branch tips in late summer. They consist of small, creamy white, blue-marked, pealike blossoms with a pleasant grassy fragrance. The compound, gray-green to dark olive green leaves are 8 to 12 inches long and made up of seven to eleven 1- to 3-inch-long, oval, pinnate leaflets with smooth margins. Foliage drops with little color change in fall. The shiny, bright amber bark peels off in attractive curls all year. Flat, 2- to 3-inch-long seedpods develop in autumn. Use this species as a street or urban tree in a tough site or enjoy it in your yard as an easy-care shade tree. From Manchuria, Korea, and Japan.
Zones 3 to 7.

CULTIVARS AND SIMILAR SPECIES

'Starburst' has especially showy flowers. *M. chinensis* (Chinese maackia) is a similar, showier, smaller tree with silvery new leaves; often mislabeled and sold as *M. amurensis*; Zones 4 to 7.

Machaeranthera

mat-cheer-AN-ther-uh. Aster family, Asteraceae.

These natives of western North America bear daisylike flower heads, either singly or in clusters, and leaves with spiny tips and margins that often are toothed or pinnately lobed or cleft. There are about 26 species in the genus, most native to plains and prairies with dry, well-drained soil.

HOW TO GROW

Give Tahoka daisy (*M. tanacetifolia*) full sun or light shade and average to rich, well-drained soil. Plants are best in areas with cool summers; a spot with light shade during the hottest part of the day may help them cope with hot weather, but they tend to be short-lived in hot, humid climates. Sow seeds indoors 8 to 10 weeks before the last spring frost date, and chill the sown pots in the refrigerator for 2 weeks before moving them to a warmer (50° to 60°F) spot for germination, which takes 3 to 4 weeks. Or sow outdoors in spring a few weeks before the last frost date or in early fall for bloom the following year. Either way, just press the seeds into the soil surface. Use Tahoka daisies in wild gardens and mixed plantings. They make excellent cut flowers.

M. tanacetifolia

m. tan-ah-see-tih-FOE-lee-ah. TAHOKA DAISY. Formerly *Aster tanacetifolius*. A bushy, 1- to 2-foot annual or biennial with abundant, 2-inch-wide, daisylike flowers with yellow centers and pale purple "petals," or ray florets. Biennial or cool-weather annual.

Macleaya

mah-KLAY-uh. Poppy family, Papaveraceae.

Macleaya species, commonly known as plume poppies, are bold, vigorous perennials with handsome, heart-shaped, palmately lobed leaves and large, airy, plumy-textured panicles of tiny flowers. The individual flowers are ½ inch long and have two to four sepals surrounding a cluster of stamens. Stems and leaves exude yellow sap when cut. Three species belong to the genus, and all are large plants that easily reach 8 feet in height and spread vigorously by rhizomes to form clumps that are 4 feet across or more.

HOW TO GROW

Select a site in full sun with average soil that is moist but well drained. Plants also grow in partial shade and tolerate most soils, including drier ones, although this restricts their height. Give them plenty of room to spread, and plan on managing the amount of space they occupy by digging up plants and rhizomes that pop up where they are not wanted. Planting in a large container, either above ground or sunk in the soil, also offers a way to control their spread. Another option is a site bordered on two or more sides by a wall or other barrier. To propagate, divide the clumps in spring or fall, pot up plants that appear along rooted rhizomes, or take root cuttings in winter.

M. cordata

m. kor-DAH-tuh. PLUME POPPY. Formerly *Bocconia cordata*. Rhizo-

M

Maackia amurensis

Maackia chinensis

Machaeranthera tanacetifolia

Macleaya cordata

Magnolia × soulangeana

matous perennial with lobed, 10-inch-long, gray- to olive green leaves that are white beneath. Bears 1-foot-long plumes of creamy flowers that have 25 to 40 stamens from mid- to late summer. *M. × kewensis* 'Flamingo' bears pink buds and pinkish tan flowers. All are hardy in **Zones 4 to 9**.

Magnolia

mag-NO-lee-ah. Magnolia family, Magnoliaceae.

This large, ancient genus of deciduous and evergreen trees and shrubs contains 80 to 100 species from Asia and North America. Most produce exquisite, many-petaled flowers with clusters of stamens and pistils in the center and handsome foliage. Buds are often silvery, furry, and quite attractive. Fruits are coblike seedpods with red seeds and can be eye-catching in autumn. Many species and hybrids are favorite garden trees. The Asian species usually bloom on bare branches in late winter or early spring, making them among the first trees to bloom. The North American species bloom in summer.

HOW TO GROW

Plant in full sun to partial shade and deep, loamy, slightly acid soil. Keep moist and mulched after transplanting. Magnolias are somewhat difficult to transplant because of their wide-spreading roots. Container-grown trees planted in spring do better than balled-and-burlapped ones. All prefer undisturbed soil.

DECIDUOUS MAGNOLIAS

M. acuminata

m. ah-kew-mih-NAY-tuh. CUCUMBER TREE. One of the tallest deciduous magnolias, this pyramidal tree becomes wide spreading with age and reaches 80 feet tall and 60 feet wide. The 3-inch-wide, greenish yellow flowers (brighter yellow in the cultivars) are sprinkled all over the branch tips in late spring and early summer. These flowers develop into upright green fruits that look like cucumbers and turn deep pink in autumn. They provide food for wildlife. Leaves are somewhat heart shaped, measuring up to 10 inches long and half as wide, with a pointed tip and wavy edges. They are dark yellow-green on top and light green on the undersides and may turn pale yellow in late fall. Bark is smooth and gray when young, with the lower trunk becoming ridged and brown with age. This great-looking, cold-hardy tree is an excellent shade tree for a lawn or park. It does not tolerate drought or excessive moisture, however. Prune when young to develop a strong structure; pruning wounds do not heal readily. From eastern North America. **Zones 4 to 8**.

CULTIVARS AND SIMILAR SPECIES

M. a. var. *subcordata* (yellow cucumber tree) is smaller and features very pretty, canary yellow flowers. 'Golden Glow' has bright yellow flowers. 'Elizabeth' is a very showy hybrid of *M. a.* var. *subcordata* and *M. denudata;* has 7-inch, creamy yellow flowers on bare branches in late spring; resembles a pale yellow–flowered, 15- to 20-foot-tall saucer magnolia; **Zones 5 to 8**. 'Butterflies' has 4- to 5-inch butter yellow flowers. 'Yellow Bird' has later, bright yellow blossoms. *M. macrophylla* (bigleaf magnolia), from the Southeast, grows 30 to 40 feet tall; huge, oblong, tropical-looking leaves up to 3 feet long; fragrant, white, dark-centered, 8- to 20-inch-wide flowers; **Zones 5 to 9**.

M. liliiflora

m. lil-ih-FLOR-ah. LILY-FLOWERED MAGNOLIA. Formerly *M. quinquepeta*. This multistemmed magnolia grows to 12 feet tall and wide and blooms in mid- to late spring (later than most deciduous Asian magnolias) as the leaves are unfolding. It bears 4-inch-wide flowers with six slender petals that are white inside and purple outside. Leaves are oval and pointed, dark green on top and light green on their undersides. Although this species makes a fine specimen, it's often used in hybridizing to combine a later bloom time with other desirable characteristics. Hybrids with *M. stellata* produce flowers late enough in spring to avoid frost damage but still bloom on bare branches so that the magnificent effect is unsullied. Their only drawback is that they bloom so late that they compete with other flowering trees. The National Arboretum has developed eight shrubby, 15- to 20-foot-tall, very late blooming hybrids between *M. liliiflora* and *M. stellata,* collectively called the Kosar hybrids or the Little Girl Series. From China. **Zones 6 to 9**.

CULTIVARS

'Nigra' has larger and later, deep purple flowers. The most treelike Kosar hybrids are hardy to **Zone 5** and include the following: 'Ann' blooms the earliest, with cinnamon-scented, reddish pink flowers. 'Betty' is similar to 'Ann' but blooms later, with 8-inch, purple flowers. 'Pinkie' is the latest bloomer, with pastel pink, 6-inch flowers. 'Ricki' has flowers whose petals are wine red outside and lavender-pink inside. 'Susan' bears reddish purple flowers with slightly twisted petals.

Magnolia stellata

M. × loebneri

m. × LOBE-nerr-eye. LOEBNER MAGNOLIA. This hybrid of *M. kobus* and *M. stellata* is a rounded, wider-than-tall tree that blooms in early spring. It reaches 30 feet tall. Even young plants bloom profusely, producing white or pink flowers with 12 or more strap-shaped petals on bare branches in late winter or early spring. Leaves are mid-green, oval, and up to 6 inches long. Site this small tree in a bed or border planted with early bulbs such as *Chionodoxa* or *Scilla siberica*, which bloom at the same time. **Zones 4 to 9**.

CULTIVARS

'Ballerina' is a late-blooming form that has very fragrant, pure white flowers with 30 petals. 'Leonard Messel' bears lovely pink flowers that open from dark purplish pink buds and have crinkled petals. 'Merrill' is upright, reaching 25 feet tall; 15-petaled, white flowers are flushed pink at the base. 'Spring Snow' blooms late enough to escape most unexpected frosts and has pure white flowers with 15 to 20 wide petals.

M. × soulangeana

m. × sue-lan-jee-AY-nah. SAUCER MAGNOLIA. A hybrid of *M. denudata* and *M. liliiflora* dating back to the 1800s, saucer magnolia is the most commonly planted deciduous magnolia — which does not decrease the wonder of its

Magnolia liliiflora × stellata 'Randy'

early-spring bloom one iota. It grows into a rounded, low-branched tree, 20 to 30 feet tall and wide. Magnificent saucer-shaped, 5- to 10-inch blossoms made up of nine satiny white, pink, purple, or bicolored petals decorate the branches in profusion before the leaves emerge in early spring. The dark green, smooth-edged, 6-inch-long, oblong leaves have a bold texture. They turn golden brown in fall. Trunk and branches feature smooth gray bark, and twigs are adorned with lovely, fur-covered flower buds in winter, making this open-branched tree an attractive winter specimen. Use it in a border or lawn or to shade a patio. Combine with daffodils, which bloom at the same time. **Zones 5 to 9**.

CULTIVARS

'Alba Superba' has large white flowers that are sometimes flushed pink at the base. 'Alexandrina' has large, early-blooming flowers whose petals are white inside and purple-pink outside. 'Bronzzonii' is an upright form with 10-inch, white flowers. 'Lennei' is an open, shrubby form with enormous, later-blooming, globular flowers that are magenta-purple outside, white inside; **Zone 4**. 'Rustica Rubra' has a treelike form; flowers are rose-red outside and white inside.

M. stellata

m. steh-LAH-tah. STAR MAGNO-LIA. Formerly *M. tomentosa*. This multistemmed, rounded, large shrub or small tree grows 15 to 20 feet tall and features very early, starry white flowers that cover bare branches in late winter or early spring, about a week before

Magnolia grandiflora

M. × soulangeana blooms. The fragrant, 3- to 4-inch-wide flowers consist of a dozen or more strap-like, white or pale pink petals surrounding a yellow center. In some areas, a late frost can ruin the flowers without harming the tree. The oblong leaves are 2 to 4 inches long and dark green, with a finer texture than those on most magnolias. They often turn yellowish in autumn. The smooth, silver gray branches are decorated with furry silver buds in winter. Use this lovely early bloomer in a border or foundation planting, sited where it can be enjoyed from inside or as you go in and out of the house. It performs well in hot climates. From Japan. **Zones 5 to 9**.

CULTIVARS AND SIMILAR SPECIES

'Centennial' has 5-inch, pink-tinged, white flowers with 30 petals. 'Rosea' is pale pink. 'Royal Star' has pink buds that open to white blossoms with 30 petals; late blooming. 'Waterlily' is bushy and late flowering, its blooms having 14 or more white petals that open from pink buds. *M. kobus* (Kobus

magnolia) is a similar multi-trunked tree that grows to 40 feet tall; has 4-inch flowers with nine white petals and a faint purple marking; **Zones 5 to 8**.

EVERGREEN MAGNOLIAS

The following species are summer-flowering landscape trees that are especially useful in the South.

M. grandiflora

m. gran-dih-FLOR-uh. SOUTHERN MAGNOLIA, BULL BAY. One of the most magnificent trees in the southern landscape, this rounded or pyramidal tree can grow 60 to 80 feet tall and 30 to 50 feet wide, although popular cultivars may be smaller. The 4- to 12-inch-long, leathery leaves are oblong and pointed, often with dense gray or rust-colored fuzz coating their undersides. During summer and early fall, large, cup-shaped, creamy white flowers dot the tree. These 6- to 12-inch-wide blossoms emit a heady lemony fragrance. Seed-grown trees may not flower for decades, so it's best to purchase named cultivars. The 2- to 5-inch-long, beige or red seedpods develop in late summer and fall, then split open to reveal red seeds. Trunk bark is smooth gray on young trees and scaly on mature trees. Plant southern magnolia as a specimen where it has plenty of room to grow and where its dense shade will be welcomed. It tolerates wet sites. Allow lower limbs to sweep to the ground or prune off as desired. Older leaves and seedpods drop in autumn and winter, requiring cleanup. Limbs may break during ice storms. From southeastern North America. **Zones 7 to 9**.

CULTIVARS

'Little Gem' is a shrubby dwarf that reaches 20 feet tall. 'Majestic Beauty' is a full-size tree with 12-

Magnolia grandiflora

inch flowers and large leaves with green undersides. 'St. Mary' is a slow-growing, compact form that grows to 20 feet tall; 5-inch flowers bloom profusely even on young trees. 'Samuel Sommers' has 14-inch flowers and grows to 30 feet tall. Cold-hardy forms for **Zones 6 to 9**: 'Bracken's Brown Beauty' has 6-inch flowers and small leaves whose undersides are densely covered with rust-colored hairs; grows to 30 feet tall; may suffer winter leaf damage in Zone 6 during severe winters. 'Edith Bogue' is a compact, pyramidal form that grows to 30 feet tall; narrow leaves have light tan undersides; the most cold-hardy form. Spring Grove Series plants are cold hardy. 'Victoria' has broad, lustrous leaves with green undersides; grows to 20 feet tall.

M. virginiana

m. ver-jin-ee-AH-nuh. SWEET BAY MAGNOLIA. This graceful, shrubby or multitrunked tree forms an open-branched, rounded or oval specimen that can reach 50 feet tall in the South, where it is fully evergreen. In the coldest parts of its range, it is semievergreen and reaches only 20 feet tall. In spring the new leaves emerge silvery green on green twigs and mature to a shiny dark green with white-haired undersides. These 5-inch-long, oblong leaves create a shimmery effect in a breeze. The lemon-scented, 2- to 4-inch flowers have 9 to 12 creamy white petals and bloom at the branch tips for a month or so in early summer. They develop into green fruits that look like small cucumbers until they turn red in fall and split open to reveal orange-red seeds. Sweet bay magnolia makes an excellent understory tree in a woodland garden. It tolerates wet or swampy sites. From southeastern North America. **Zones 5 to 9**.

CULTIVARS

M. v. var. *australis* is the tall southern type. 'Henry Hicks' is the most cold-hardy form, and its leaves remain evergreen in the North. 'Willowleaf' has very narrow leaves.

Magnolia stellata 'Rosea'

M

Mahonia

mah-HOE-nee-uh. Barberry
family, Berberidaceae.

This genus of some 70 evergreen
shrubs, native to North and South
America and East Asia, includes
several species that are popular in
gardens, especially those with an
abundance of shade. They have
eye-catching, usually spiky foliage;
clusters or spikes of yellow flowers;
and, often, colorful berries.

HOW TO GROW

Most mahonias do best in partial
or even full shade, especially if the
soil is at all dry. The soil should be
acidic and full of humus, but well
aerated. Most need protection
from drying winds. Mahonias are
perfect for woodland gardens,
shady foundation areas, or borders. Site spiky varieties away from
paths, or use them as security
hedges. Prune off shoots that are
leggy above foliage, or that otherwise spoil the shape. Propagate
from stratified seeds, semiripe cuttings in autumn, or suckers.

M. aquifolium

m. ah-quih-FOE-lee-um. OREGON
GRAPE-HOLLY. Up to 6 feet or
taller, this Northwest native will
sucker and spread to 5 feet. Leathery, spiny compound leaves with
up to 12 leaflets on a side emerge
light green or bronze and become
shiny dark green, bronzing again
in fall. The clusters of early- to
midspring yellow flowers are followed in summer by grapelike
clusters of blue fruits that remain
through winter. Cultivars include
'Apollo' (2-foot ground cover with
golden orange flowers), 'Atropurpurea' (another low grower with
reliable red-purple fall color),

Mahonia bealei

'Compactum' (dwarf with leaves
that bronze), 'Mayhan Strain'
(about 3 feet tall with fewer,
closely spaced leaves), 'Moseri'
(colorful new growth), and
'Smaragd' (trademarked as Emerald, with bronzy fall leaves and
flower clusters to 4 inches long).
Zones 5 to 8.

M. bealei

m. BEE-lee-eye. LEATHERLEAF
MAHONIA. From China, this
species grows to 12 feet tall and has
foot-long leaves composed of up
to 15 spiny leaflets. Fragrant lemon
yellow flowers appear on spikes in
late winter to early spring, followed by powdery bright blue berries that birds may harvest.
Zones 7 to 9.

M. fortunei

m. for-TOON-ee-eye. CHINESE
MAHONIA. An erect and somewhat stiff species to 6 feet tall,
whose slender leaflets are more
ferny and less spiky than those of
other species. The yellow flowers
are borne in upright racemes in
late summer or early fall. Berries
seldom appear. **Zones 8 to 9; to Zone
7 with winter protection.**

M. japonica

m. juh-PON-ih-kuh. JAPANESE
MAHONIA. Similar to *M. bealei*
but usually only 6 feet tall and

Mahonia repens

spreading half again as wide, with
flowers more relaxed than upright
and brighter yellow. The oval berries are bluish purple. **Zones 7 to 8.**

M. nervosa

m. ner-VOH-suh. CASCADES
MAHONIA. Sometimes called
longleaf mahonia, this 12- to 18-
inch suckering shrub is native
from British Columbia to northern California. The thick, glossy
gray-green leaves are bristly and
have 11 to 23 leaflets up to 3 inches
long. A good ground cover with
the habit of a stiff fern. Flowers
bloom in upright clusters in mid-
to late spring, followed by purple-
blue berries. **Zones 5 to 7.**

M. repens

m. REP-enz. CREEPING MA-
HONIA. Also called dwarf Oregon grape-holly, this cold-hardy
ground cover is native from
northern Mexico and California to
British Columbia and east to the
Rockies. Rarely growing much
higher than 1 foot, it spreads by
underground stolons to 2 to 3 feet
across. The somewhat dull, blue-
green spiny leaves turn purple-
bronze in winter. Yellow flowers
are borne in 1- to 3-inch racemes
in midspring, and blue-black berries develop in late summer.
Zones 4 to 7.

M. × wagneri 'King's Ransom'

m. × WAG-ner-eye. An upright form
to 6½ feet, with 8-inch, dark blue-
green leaves, dense terminal
racemes of spring flowers, and
powdery blue-black berries. De-

velops bronzy, red-purple color in
winter. Leaves of 'Undulata' have
wavy margins. **Zones 6 to 8.**

Maianthemum

may-AN-thuh-mum. Lily-of-the-
valley family, Convallariaceae.

Maianthemum (false lily-of-the-
valley) is a small genus found in
cold and cool regions of North
America, Asia, and Europe. It is
closely related to *Convallaria* (true
lily-of-the-valley), but it is far
more cold tolerant and much
smaller in stature. *Maianthemum*
forms extensive colonies in suitable conditions, as the slender
stems spread just under the soil
surface. Leaves are deciduous, often borne only one or two per
stem, and usually less than 3
inches long. Flowers are very
small, and unlike the true lily-of-
the-valley, where flowers are pendent from the arching flower
stalks, they are clustered into attractive bottlebrush formations at
the tips of the stems. They are
mildly fragrant, and when large
colonies are in bloom, the forest
floor looks as if it has low drifts of
flowers strewn across it. Fruits are
small berries and rarely seen.

HOW TO GROW

Maianthemum thrives in cool
woodland conditions. The eastern
American species (*M. canadense*)
is native from near-arctic regions
to cool woodlands in the southern
Appalachian Mountains, while the
western species (*M. kamtscha-
ticum*) is native from Alaska south
to California. For best growth,
provide plants with a rich, moist

Mahonia aquifolium 'Emerald'

Maianthemum canadense

(but not wet), woodland or naturalistic site. Establishing "sods" purchased from reputable nurseries produces quicker results than planting small starts. Protect plants from dry exposures and foot traffic, as they are unforgiving of being walked on. They do not do well where summers are hot and muggy.

M. canadense

m. kan-uh-DEN-see. FALSE LILY-OF-THE-VALLEY. This species has charmed viewers for centuries. Pierre Rédouté, the famous French botanical artist of Napoleon's wife, Josephine, gave this equal treatment in his work on lilies. Only 6 inches tall but spreading quietly by rhizomes, it produces lovely, heart-shaped leaves that clasp the stems. Spikes of little white flowers are followed by red fruits. The species thrives in cool, damp, shaded, acid, woodland soils. **Zones 3 to 7.**

M. kamtschaticum

m. kampt-CHAH-tih-kum. DEER-BERRY. Similar to *M. canadense* but larger, deerberry inhabits moist coastal woodlands from Alaska south to northern California. In the garden, it forms extensive colonies from creeping rhizomes when its woodland conditions are met. Hardy in maritime climates in **Zones 4 to 8.**

Malcolmia

mal-KOL-mee-uh. Cabbage family, Brassicaceae.

Commonly called stocks, *Malcolmia* species bear racemes of four-petaled, cross-shaped flowers in shades of pink, purple, white, and red from summer to fall. The genus contains about 35 species of annuals and perennials native from the Mediterranean region to central Asia — not Virginia, as the common name of *M. maritima* might suggest.

HOW TO GROW

Full sun to light shade and average to rich, well-drained soil are ideal. Neutral to slightly alkaline pH is best. Stocks are best in areas with cool summers and are especially intolerant of warm nighttime temperatures. A spot with light shade during the hottest part of the day is preferable. Sow seeds outdoors a few weeks before the last spring frost date, simply raking them into the soil surface. For continued bloom in cool climates, sow new crops every 4 weeks through late summer. Or sow outdoors in fall for bloom the following year. In areas with hot, humid summers,

Malcolmia maritima

Malus floribunda

start them early enough to bloom before hot weather arrives. Use stocks in mixed beds and borders, along pathways, and in cracks between paving. They are good choices for seaside gardens. Plants self-sow.

M. maritima

m. mah-RIT-ih-muh. VIRGINIA STOCK. A ½- to 1½-foot-tall annual with oval, softly hairy, gray-green leaves. Bears loose spikes of fragrant, purplish pink, pink, lavender, red, or white flowers. Cool-weather annual.

Malus

MAL-us. Rose family, Rosaceae.

This genus contains 35 species of deciduous trees and shrubs from Asia, Europe, and North America, including apples, which are generally orchard trees grown for their large edible fruits, and crab apples, which are primarily ornamental, although their much smaller, showy fruits are edible (though not always palatable). Both apples and crab apples have clustered, five-petaled blossoms with 15 to 20 yellow stamens in the center. They typically begin blooming before the leaves unfold and are later joined by the young greenery. Blossoms often open from pink or red buds and change to paler shades after opening, creating a beautiful pink cloud lasting several weeks. The Asian crab apple species are usually preferred for ornament, because their fruits are more colorful and last into winter, providing food for birds. Crab apples are favorite spring-flowering trees in the North and Midwest, where cold winters and heavy soil prevent other spring bloomers from performing well.

Because the genus is subject to numerous serious diseases and insects, which vary from region to region and year to year, it's best to choose disease-resistant cultivars adapted to your area. Four diseases are serious. Apple scab, a fungus characterized by black sooty spots on leaves and corky spots on fruits, may defoliate trees in summer. Although it is unsightly, it is not lethal. Fire blight is a bacterium that turns twigs and branches black, eventually killing

M

Malus sargentii

the tree. Cedar-apple rust is a fungus that creates rusty, corky spots on leaves and, if serious, can defoliate the tree. The fungus must have native cedars and junipers (*Juniperus scopulorum*, *J. virginiana*, or *J. horizontalis*) as alternate hosts to complete its life cycle, so do not plant susceptible crab apple cultivars within a mile of junipers. Powdery mildew is a white fungus that attacks leaves, flowers, and fruits during warm, humid weather and is unsightly.

The *Malus* species hybridize easily, resulting in an enormous number of horticultural selections. Older cultivars of hybrid crab apples were selected primarily for blossom size and color, not disease resistance or fruit size and color. Fruits of these older cultivars may be more than 1/2 inch around and drop in fall; they are quite messy and can cause a slippery hazard on sidewalks. Better are newer cultivars that are disease resistant and offer numerous fruits measuring less than 1/2 inch or that remain on the branches into winter, adding color to the winter landscape. These fruits are just the right size for birds, and if they do fall, they are not messy. When selecting a crab apple, choose one based on size, shape, and fruit color rather than flower color. Be sure to avoid the inferior older cultivars; many are still sold even though much better choices are available. Some of the worst are 'Almey', 'Bechtels', 'Eleyi', 'Evelyn', 'Flame', 'Hopa', 'Radiant', 'Red Silver', 'Sparkler', and 'Vanguard'.

HOW TO GROW

Plant in full sun and well-drained, acid or alkaline, loamy or clayey soil. For susceptibility to diseases, see individual entries.

M. baccata

m. bah-KAH-tuh. SIBERIAN CRAB APPLE. This round-headed, wide-spreading species is one of the largest crab apples, reaching 20 to 50 feet tall. In midspring the profuse pink flower buds open into very fragrant, white, five-petaled flowers. Leaves are bright green. Fruits are small, about 1/8 inch around, but are profuse and a very showy, glossy red. They persist on the bare branches through most of the winter. Use this large, very cold hardy crab apple as a lawn, border, or street tree. Susceptible to scab and sometimes fire blight. From northeastern Asia. **Zones 3 to 7.**

CULTIVARS

'Columnaris' has creamy white buds that open to white blossoms and large, red-blushed, yellow fruits; columnar to 30 feet. 'Jackii' blooms and fruits well annually; purplish red, 1/2-inch fruits; resists scab and fire blight; **Zone 2.** 'Walters' is one of the best gold-fruited crab apples; pink buds open to white flowers; 1/2-inch fruits last all winter, changing from gold to bright amber; rounded and growing to 30 feet tall; resists scab and fire blight. Rosybloom crab apples are hybrids with reddish purple flowers; leaves are purple in spring, very dark green in summer, and orange-red in fall; most are very susceptible to scab. 'Adams' has deep reddish pink buds and crimson flowers that fade to pink; very persistent, 1/2-inch, glossy red fruits; broadly rounded and grow-

ing 20 to 25 feet tall; scab resistant. 'Indian Summer' has ruby red buds that open to light magenta flowers; very persistent, 5/8-inch, bright oxblood red fruits; rounded and growing to 18 feet tall; scab resistant. 'Prairiefire' is highly scab resistant and one of the best cultivars; grows into a rounded, 20-foot-tall tree; purple-red flowers and leaves that turn orange-red in fall; persistent, 1/2-inch, oxblood red fruits that turn maroon in winter. 'Weeping Candied Apple' is stiffly weeping, growing to 15 feet tall; large crimson flowers; 1/2-inch, oxblood red fruits last all fall and winter; green foliage with red veins and light red undersides; scab resistant.

M. floribunda

m. flor-ih-BUN-duh. JAPANESE FLOWERING CRAB APPLE. This species is extinct in the wild but is still commonly grown in gardens around the world. A beautiful, disease-resistant tree with horizontal branches and a dense, rounded head, it reaches 20 feet tall and 30 feet wide. Blanketed with clusters of deep reddish pink flower buds that open into 1-inch-wide, fragrant, pink flowers that fade to white, the tree is a sight to behold for 2 or more weeks in early to midspring. The 3-inch, oval leaves are dark green and sometimes slightly lobed. Yellow, 1/3-inch fruits adorn the tree in fall and turn reddish amber after a freeze, but they are quickly eaten by birds and squirrels. Fall color is negligible. This tree is a parent of many hybrid crab apples, which may be rounded, spreading, vase shaped, or even columnar and usually grow 8 to 25 feet tall. The best ones feature red, pink, or

white blossoms; disease-resistant green or purple foliage; and attractive red, orange, or golden yellow fruits that persist on bare winter branches and are not messy.

Plant in well-drained, acid, loamy or clayey soil; tolerates alkaline soil. Fruits are not messy. Seedlings create a minor weed-seedling problem. Prune to a single leader with a good branch structure when young. Remove suckers and water sprouts as needed. The species is moderately resistant to scab, rust, and mildew; fire blight is rarely a problem. Susceptibility to diseases varies widely among cultivars, but all diseases are worse in the South. The species is hardy in **Zones 4 to 8**; some cultivars perform in **Zone 3.**

CULTIVARS

These are all disease-resistant hybrids with long-lasting, nonmessy fruits. 'Amberina' has crimson buds that open to blush pink blossoms; 3/8-inch, cardinal red fruits turn oxblood red in winter; fall foliage is red and gold; upright oval, growing 10 to 12 feet tall. 'Coral Cascade' has deep coral red buds that open to blush white flowers; 1/2-inch fruits are persistent and coral-orange; semiweeping to arching tree that reaches 15 feet tall. 'Harvest Gold' features cardinal red buds opening to pink flowers that fade to white; late-ripening, 1/2-inch fruits on red stems; grows upright to 20 feet tall; tolerates road salt; one of the showiest crab apples in winter. 'Red Jewel' has dawn pink buds opening to white flowers; 1/2-inch fruits are currant red in fall and amber in winter; glossy leaves may turn yellow in fall; upright and spreading, growing to 15 feet tall. 'Red Swan' is an improved 'Red Jade' with

Malus sargentii (berries)

smaller, brighter crimson fruits and extremely weeping branches; rose-pink buds open to white, bell-shaped blossoms; grows to 10 feet tall. 'Sugar Tyme' has pale pink buds that open to fragrant white flowers; very showy, ³/4-inch, red fruits may be messy if the tree is not planted in a ground cover; golden yellow fall color; grows to 18 feet tall. 'White Angel' has pale pink buds opening to pure white blossoms; heavy crops of ¹/2- to ³/4-inch, glossy red berries; vase shaped and growing to 20 feet tall.

M. hupehensis

m. who-puh-HEN-sis. TEA CRAB APPLE. This widely grown species is a graceful, vase-shaped, open-branched tree that reaches 20 to 25 or more feet tall and wide. The deep pink flower buds open to 1¹/2-inch, blush pink blossoms that fade to white and have a lovely scent, turning the tree into a cumulus cloud in early to midspring. The deep green, 4-inch leaves are oval or elliptic and pointed, with toothed edges. They are rarely marred by disease. The showy, ¹/2-inch fruits are yellow

with a rosy blush, changing to red. This tree's shape makes it a good street tree under power lines. Or use it as a patio or border tree where people can walk under its branches. Highly resistant to scab but slightly susceptible to fire blight. From Asia. **Zones 4 to 8.**

CULTIVARS
'Cardinal' is a broad form that grows to 15 feet tall; bright rose-red flowers; small, deep red fruits; red-tinged summer leaves. 'Strawberry Parfait' is a 25-foot-tall, vase-shaped hybrid; fragrant pink flowers with rosy margins; leaves emerge reddish purple and mature to dark green; ³/4-inch fruits are yellow with a red blush or glossy orange-red.

M. sargentii

m. sar-JEN-tee-eye. SARGENT CRAB APPLE. This small crab apple is a moundlike, spreading tree with a single trunk that grows to only 10 feet tall and 15 feet wide, although it is often grafted to a 6-foot trunk to make it taller. In midspring the pale pink flower buds open to very fragrant, 1-inch-wide, white flowers, turning the

tree into a snowball. Numerous bright red, ¹/3-inch fruits stand out in autumn against yellow leaves and hang on well into winter, making this one of the best fall performers among the crab apples. Leaves are dark green and slightly lobed. Some trees bloom and fruit well only in alternate years; others bear annually. The tree is popular because of its unique shape and tidy size. It works well in a foundation planting or border, where it will add interest. Does not hybridize readily and comes true from seed. Resistant to scab. From Japan; not known in the wild. **Zones 4 to 8.**

CULTIVARS
'Firebird' bears ¹/2-inch fruits that keep their red color exceptionally well in winter. 'Pink Princess' has rose-pink flowers and purple-bronze foliage. 'Rosea' has larger, dark pink buds opening to white flowers and large fruits. 'Tina' is smaller but is usually grafted to a trunk to reach 16 feet tall. 'Jewelberry' is a 6- to 7-foot-tall hybrid that looks much like M. sargentii but blooms and fruits annually. 'Mary Potter' is another hybrid that looks like a larger, more horizontally branched M. sargentii.

M. × zumi 'Calocarpa'

m. × ZOO-mee. ZUMI CRAB APPLE, REDBUD CRAB APPLE. This disease-resistant tree, a hybrid of M. baccata var. mandschurica and M. sieboldii, is a rounded, horizontally spreading form that grows to 15 feet tall and 25 feet wide and is one of the best crab apples for fall display. It has abundant, large, white flowers that open from pink buds in late spring, later than most crab apples. Leaves are 3¹/2-inch-long, dark green ovals, often lobed, that may turn golden orange in fall. The glossy, cherry red, ¹/2- to ³/4-inch fruits, which hang from 1¹/2-inch-long stems, persist through the winter, making this tree and its hybrids some of the best for a year-round landscape effect. The species tends to bloom and fruit well every other year, but the cultivars do so annually. Use this eye-catching tree where it can be appreciated throughout the year, especially in fall and winter. Do not confuse it with M. 'Zumi', which is a less desirable tree. Very scab resistant. **Zones 4 to 8.**

CULTIVARS
These hybrids are like the species in flower and fruit unless noted.

'Bob White' bears ¹/2-inch, persistent, yellow fruits; rounded and dense to 20 feet tall; alternate bearer. 'Donald Wyman' has rose-pink flower buds, ¹/2-inch cardinal red fruits, and bronze-yellow fall color; rounded to 20 feet tall; susceptible to scab in some areas. 'Ormiston Roy' features red buds opening to white flowers and ¹/2-inch, red-blushed, orange-yellow fruits that are amber through the winter; grows 20 to 25 feet tall. 'Professor Sprenger' has cardinal red buds opening to white flowers and unusual, brilliant orange-red, ⁵/8-inch fruits; rounded and upright to 35 feet tall; **Zones 3 to 7.** 'Snowdrift' bears orange-red fruits; rounded to 20 feet tall. 'Volcano' has red buds opening to white flowers, orange-red fruits, and golden yellow with orange fall color; grows upright to 10 feet tall. 'White Cascade' produces pink buds opening to white flowers and buttercup yellow fruits that turn amber in winter; grows to 15 feet tall, with gracefully weeping branches. 'Winter Gem' is an upright form. 'Winter Gold' has deep carmine buds opening to white flowers and orange-blushed, yellow fruits; broadly pyramidal to 20 feet tall.

M

Malva

MAL-vuh. Mallow family, Malvaceae.

Closely related to *Hibiscus, Malva* species are annuals, biennials, or perennials commonly known as mallows. About 30 species belong to the genus, all bearing five-petaled, cup- or saucer-shaped flowers with petals that are somewhat squared off at the ends. Blooms are borne singly, in clusters at the leaf axils, or in racemes. They come in shades of rose and pink as well as blue, purple, and white. Leaves are rounded or heart to kidney shaped and either entire or variously toothed and lobed.

HOW TO GROW
Select a site in full sun with average to moderately rich, well-drained soil. Mallows tolerate partial shade and perform better in cooler zones than they do in the warm, humid South. Stake the clumps to keep them erect. Plants tend to be short-lived, but they self-sow. Propagate by taking cuttings from shoots at the base of the plant in spring, taking tip cuttings in early summer, or sowing seeds.

Malva alcea 'Fastigiata'

M. alcea

m. al-SEE-uh. HOLLYHOCK MALLOW. A 2- to 4-foot-tall species that forms 2-foot-wide clumps. Bears funnel-shaped 1^1/$_2$- to 2-inch flowers with notched petals from early summer to fall both in the leaf axils and in racemes. *M. a.* var. *fastigiata* (also sold as 'Fastigiata'), more commonly grown than the species, bears rose-pink 2-inch-wide flowers on erect 2^1/$_2$- to 3-foot-tall plants. **Zones 4 to 9**.

M. moschata

m. moe-SHAH-tuh. MUSK MALLOW. A 3-foot-tall species that forms 2-foot-wide clumps. Bears clusters of pale pink or white, 2- to 2^1/$_2$-inch-wide, saucer-shaped flowers from early summer to fall. **Zones 3 to 7**.

M. sylvestris

m. sil-VES-tris. TREE MALLOW, CHEESES. Woody-based 3- to 4-foot-tall perennial sometimes grown as a biennial. Plants form 2-foot-wide clumps and bear clusters of funnel-shaped, pinkish purple, 2^1/$_2$-inch-wide flowers with notched petals from late spring or early summer to fall. *M. s.* f. *alba* (also sold as 'Alba') bears white flowers. 'Primley Blue' has pale blue flowers on 2-foot plants. 'Zebrina' produces white to pale pink flowers striped with dark pink on 2- to 3-foot plants. **Zones 4 to 8**.

Mandevilla

man-deh-VILL-ah. Dogbane family, Apocynaceae.

For the most part, *Mandevilla* species are woody-stemmed or perennial climbers, often with tuberous

Mandevilla × *amoena* 'Alice DuPont'

roots. About 120 species native to Central and South America belong here. They have simple leaves, have milky sap in their stems, and bear funnel-shaped flowers with five broad "petals," or lobes, either singly or in small racemes.

HOW TO GROW

Give mandevillas full sun to light shade and average to rich soil that is moist but well drained. A site with dappled shade during the hottest part of the day is beneficial. They require a trellis or other support upon which to climb. Where hardy — in **Zones 10 and 11** — grow these plants outdoors. In the North, grow them in large containers and treat them as tender perennials or as annuals. Start plants from cuttings taken in late spring or summer. Or sow seeds at 65° to 70°F in spring. When plants are growing actively, water regularly and feed monthly. Bring container-grown plants indoors before the first fall frost and overwinter indoors in a sunny, warm (60° to 65°F) spot. Prune overwintered plants in late winter or early spring; cut them nearly to the ground, if necessary, and they will produce new shoots from the base of the plant that will still bloom the same year. Water moderately during winter.

M. × amoena 'Alice DuPont'

m. × ah-MEE-nah. A woody-stemmed climber that can reach 20 feet or more in frost-free regions but is considerably shorter when grown in the North. Bears racemes of up to 20 funnel-shaped, 3- to 4-inch-wide, rich

Matteuccia struthiopteris

pink flowers. Tender perennial, or grow as a warm-weather annual.

Matteuccia

mah-TOO-see-uh. Wood-fern family, Dryopteridaceae.

There are only two or three species of *Matteuccia*, and yet they are ubiquitous in most of the Northern Hemisphere. *Matteuccia* (ostrich fern) is related to *Dryopteris*

(wood fern), *Onoclea* (sensitive fern), and *Athyrium* (lady fern). Ostrich ferns have dramatic, bold fronds that grow up to 5 feet tall in favorable conditions but are usually somewhat shorter. Fronds are deciduous and rise in clusters or crowns from the rootstocks. Rootstocks produce vigorous stolons that in turn produce new crowns, gradually making great swaths of plants. Spores are produced on separate brown fronds that never turn green.

HOW TO GROW

Ostrich ferns need partial shade and cool, damp to wet, highly organic, acid soil, such as that found on streambanks, alongside ponds, and in wet woodlands of the far north. In gardens, they must have ample water and should be protected from strong winds, or the fronds will break. Use as a ground cover in naturalistic settings or as a dramatic foil to a major water feature. When conditions are ideal, this fern will form extensive colonies.

M. struthiopteris

m. stru-thee-OP-ter-iss. OSTRICH FERN. This architectural fern makes a magnificent, deciduous, ground-covering mass that spreads by rhizomes. Typically

Matthiola incana

M

grows 3 to 5 feet tall and spreads indefinitely. **Zones 2 to 6**.

Matthiola

mat-thee-OH-luh. Cabbage family, Brassicaceae.

Commonly called stock, *Matthiola* species are closely related to wallflowers *(Erysimum)* and bear dense racemes of sweetly scented, four-petaled flowers and lance-shaped or lobed leaves. Two of the 55 species of annuals, biennials, perennials, and subshrubs that belong to the genus are commonly grown in gardens.

HOW TO GROW

Full sun to light shade and average to rich, well-drained soil are ideal. Neutral to slightly alkaline pH is preferable. Stocks are best in areas with cool summers and are especially intolerant of warm nighttime temperatures. Sow seeds indoors 6 to 8 weeks before the last spring frost date at 50° to 65°F. Germination takes 1 to 3 weeks. To prevent damping off, sow in a sterile seed-starting mix, water only from below, and let the medium dry out slightly between waterings. Or sow outdoors after the last frost date. When sowing, simply press the seeds into the soil surface, as light is required for germination. From Zone 9 south, also sow seeds from late summer to early fall for bloom the following spring. Use stocks in mixed beds and borders as well as in containers, especially in spots where their fragrance can be enjoyed. They make excellent cut flowers and are good choices for seaside gardens.

M. incana

m. in-KAH-nah. COMMON STOCK, GILLYFLOWER. A ¹/₂- to 3-foot-tall tender perennial or subshrub, hardy only in **Zones 7 and 8**, with felty, gray-green leaves. Bears dense, erect clusters of spicy-scented, single or double, 1-inch-wide flowers in shades of pink, white, red, mauve, or purplish pink. 'Ten-Week Mix' plants are quicker to bloom than many cultivars and are a good choice for most North American gardens, where plants decline when hot weather arrives. Tender perennial, or grow as a cool-weather annual.

M. longipetala ssp. bicornis

m. lon-gih-PET-ah-lah ssp. bi-KORN-iss. NIGHT-SCENTED STOCK. A 1- to 1¹/₂-foot-tall annual with loose racemes of ³/₄-inch, pink,

mauve, or purple flowers that release their strong, sweet fragrance at night. Cool-weather annual.

Maurandella and Maurandya

mawr-ran-DELL-ah, maw-RAN-dee-ah. Figwort family, Scrophulariaceae.

The tender perennials in these two closely related genera formerly belonged to *Asarina*. *Maurandella* contains one species native to the southwestern United States and Mexico, and *Maurandya* contains two species found from Mexico through Central America. Plants in both genera bear two-lipped, tubular to trumpet-shaped blooms in summer and fall.

HOW TO GROW

Select a site with full sun and average soil that is moist but well drained. Dappled shade during the hottest part of the day is beneficial, as is neutral to slightly alkaline pH. Where hardy — from **Zone 9 south** — grow these plants outdoors year-round. In the North, grow them as bedding plants replaced annually or as tender perennials overwintered in a sunny, cool (55° to 60°F) spot. Sow seeds indoors about 12 weeks before the last spring frost date at 55° to 60°F. Or start plants from cuttings in spring or in midsummer to overwinter them. Water regularly and feed monthly during the growing season. Keep plants slightly dry over winter. Use these plants to cover trellises or other supports.

Maurandella antirrhiniflora

m. an-tih-rye-nih-FLOR-uh. VIOLET TWINING SNAPDRAGON. For-

Mazus repens

merly *Asarina antirrhiniflora*. A 3- to 6-foot, wiry-stemmed climber with shallowly lobed, ovate to triangular leaves. Bears tubular to trumpet-shaped, 1³/₄-inch-long flowers with flaring purple or violet lobes. Tender perennial, or grow as a warm-weather annual.

Maurandya scandens

m. SCAN-denz. CHICKABIDDY, CREEPING GLOXINIA. Formerly *Asarina scandens*. A 6- to 15-foot, woody-based perennial with angular, heart-shaped to roughly arrowhead-shaped leaves. Bears 1¹/₂- to 2-inch-long, trumpet-shaped flowers with flaring violet, lavender, or pink lobes. *M. barclayana* is a similar species.

Tender perennial, or grow as a warm-weather annual.

Mazus

MAY-zus. Figwort family, Scrophulariaceae.

Of the 30 or so species of annuals and prostrate perennials that belong to this genus, one species — *M. repens* — is commonly grown in gardens as a mat-forming ground cover. Members of the genus bear linear, rounded, or spoon-shaped leaves and tubular flowers with large spreading lower lips that have three lobes.

HOW TO GROW

Select a site in full sun or partial shade with average to somewhat rich, moist but well-drained soil. Plants do not tolerate constantly wet soil. In the South, a site with shade during the hottest part of the day is best. *M. repens* spreads widely by rhizomes that root where they touch the soil and will overwhelm less aggressive plants. To propagate, divide the clumps in spring or anytime during the growing season, or take cuttings.

M. repens

m. REP-enz. Mat-forming 2-inch-tall species that spreads to 1 foot or more. From late spring to summer it bears few-flowered racemes of ¹/₂- to ³/₄-inch-long purple flowers

Maurandya scandens

Melianthus major

with yellow and white spots on their lower lips. 'Albus' has white flowers. **Zones 5 to 8.**

Melianthus

mel-ee-AN-thus. Melianth family, Melianthaceae.

Handsome foliage and nectar-rich flowers are the hallmark of the six species of tender evergreen shrubs in the genus *Melianthus*. All are native to South Africa and bear aromatic leaves that are pinnately divided into toothed leaflets. The common name "honey bush" refers to the fact that their small flowers, which are carried in erect racemes, bear copious amounts of nectar. The botanical name refers to this characteristic as well — it is from the Greek *meli*, meaning "honey," and *anthos*, "flower."

HOW TO GROW

Melianthus species are best in full sun and average to rich, well-drained soil that remains evenly moist but is never wet. Where hardy, grow them outdoors as perennials or shrubs. Plants killed to the base in winter will resprout from the roots, performing as perennials rather than shrubs, provided temperatures don't fall much below 23° to 25°F and they are protected with a thick, dry mulch such as salt hay or weed-free straw over winter. Wet soil in winter may kill the plants, though. Where hardy, they will spread vigorously by suckers. In the North, grow them as tender perennials and overwinter them indoors, or treat them as annuals. Sow seeds indoors 8 to 10 weeks before the last spring frost date at 55° to 65°F. Or take cuttings from shoots at the base of the plant in spring or summer. The plants also can be propagated by division or by digging up suckers that appear near the plants in spring. Bring plants in before hard frost in fall, and keep them barely moist over winter in a bright, cool (55° to 65°F) spot. *Melianthus* species are handsome container plants and also are effective as foliage accents in beds and borders.

M. major

m. MAY-jor. HONEY BUSH. A 6- to 10-foot tender shrub with arching, featherlike, gray-green leaves that are 1 to 1¹/₂ feet long and have up to 17 sharply toothed leaflets. Bears 1- to 2-foot-long racemes of small, red-brown, ill-scented flowers from spring to midsummer, which are followed by attractive, green, bladderlike seedpods. **Zones 8 to 10**, or grow as a warm-weather annual.

Mentzelia

ment-ZEE-lee-ah. Loasa family, Loasaceae.

Native from the southwestern United States to Mexico and the West Indies, *Mentzelia* species bear poppylike orange, yellow, or white flowers with 5 to 10 petals. Commonly called blazing stars, there are 60 species of annuals, biennials, and subshrubs in the genus. One species is widely grown for its handsome foliage and fragrant flowers.

HOW TO GROW

Full sun and average, well-drained soil are ideal. A warm, protected site is best. *Mentzelia* species are taprooted and resent transplanting, so sow seeds outdoors after the last spring frost date. From

Mentzelia lindleyi

Mertensia pulmonarioides

Zone 9 south, sow outdoors in fall or very early spring. Or try starting seeds indoors in individual pots 6 to 8 weeks before the last frost date, and transplant with care. Cut plants back to about 2 inches after the first main flush of bloom; regular watering also encourages repeat bloom. Use these plants in mixed beds and borders as well as wild gardens.

M. lindleyi

m. LIND-lee-eye. BLAZING STAR. Formerly *Bartonia aurea*. A well-branched, ¹/₂- to 2-foot-tall annual with deeply cut, featherlike leaves. Bears golden yellow, 2- to 3¹/₂-inch-wide flowers that are fragrant at night. Cool-weather annual.

Mertensia

mer-TEN-see-uh. Borage family, Boraginaceae.

Some 50 species belong to the genus *Mertensia*, all perennials, about half of which are native North American wildflowers. They bear loose clusters of pendent, bell-shaped or tubular flowers that have five lobes and rounded to lance-shaped leaves. Blooms commonly come in shades of blue to purple, as well as white and sometimes pink.

HOW TO GROW

Select a site in sun or shade with rich, evenly moist, well-drained soil. *M. pulmonarioides* goes dormant and disappears after flowering in spring, so pick a spot where you will not dig into its stout, fleshy, carrotlike rootstocks by mistake. When adding native mertensias to your garden, look for garden-grown or nursery-propagated plants: avoid wild-collected ones. You may be able to acquire these plants from a neighbor's garden or at a local native-plant sale, such as one held by a local botanical garden or conservation organization. To propagate, dig the clumps in early summer before the leaves disappear completely. Plants self-sow, and seedlings are easy to move in spring.

M. pulmonarioides

m. pul-moe-nair-ee-OY-deez. VIRGINIA BLUEBELLS, VIRGINIA COWSLIP. Formerly *M. virginica*. A 1- to 2-foot-tall wildflower native to the eastern half of North America that grows from fleshy white carrotlike roots and spreads to 1 foot. Produces mounds of bluish green leaves, and in spring bears nodding clusters of pink buds that open into pale lilac-blue to purple-blue, ³/₄- to 1-inch-long bells. **Zones 3 to 9.**

Metasequoia

met-ah-seh-KOY-ah. Bald-cypress family, Taxodiaceae.

Twenty million years ago, when dinosaurs were becoming extinct, dawn redwoods (*M. glyptostroboides*) grew throughout most of the Northern Hemisphere. They, too, became known only from fossil records and were thought to be extinct until the 1940s, when a forester discovered 3 trees growing beside a rice paddy in central China. Seeds of this deciduous conifer were eventually gathered

Metasequoia glyptostroboides

from another grove nearby containing 1,500 trees and distributed to arboretums and eventually homes and parks around the world. This is a single-species genus.

HOW TO GROW

Plant in full sun. Best in moist, well-drained, slightly acid soil but adapts to a wet site at a pond's edge. Does not tolerate drought. Growth stops in late fall, and the tree can be injured by early frost; avoid planting in frost pockets. All lower branches should remain on the tree, which will form a new leader if it is injured. It responds to shearing during midsummer. Usually pest-free, but mites are sometimes problematic in dry soil.

M. glyptostroboides

m. glip-toe-stroh-BOY-deez. DAWN REDWOOD. This magnificent tree forms a commanding, tall, narrow cone with a strong, tapering central leader; upright branches; and a buttressed and fluted trunk. It grows 80 to 120 feet tall and 20 to 40 feet wide.

Leaves are flattened, ¹/₂-inch-long needles that are arranged in opposite pairs on the branchlets and create a soft, feathery look. Foliage emerges bright green in early spring, matures to dark green, and turns red-brown or orange in late fall before all the needles drop. (Individual leaves don't actually drop off but fall while still attached to 3-inch-long, green-barked, deciduous branchlets.) The tree then stands leafless throughout the winter. Reddish brown or bright orange shredding bark covers the attractive trunk. Cones are brown and 1 inch around and persist throughout the winter, clustered in long, cascading bunches. Dawn redwood can be distinguished from bald cypress (*Taxodium distichum*) by its large winter buds and oppositely arranged needles; bald cypress has very small buds and alternately arranged needles. This very fast growing tree can add 3 feet of new growth each year and makes an excellent screen. Where space allows, it is beautiful planted in a

grove. It also can be used as a street tree, except under power lines. From China. **Zones 5 to 8**.

CULTIVARS

'National' forms an extremely narrow spire. 'Sheridan Spire' is a narrow pyramid with more compact growth.

Michauxia

mih-SHOW-ee-ah. Bellflower family, Campanulaceae.

Stunning but little known to American gardeners, the seven species of *Michauxia* are native to well-drained, rocky soils from the eastern Mediterranean region to southwestern Asia. They are biennials or short-lived perennials with a rosette of irregularly toothed or lobed leaves and tall spikes or racemes of blue or white flowers. While their relatives the bellflowers (*Campanula*) bear flowers with 5 lobes, or "petals," *Michauxia* species have flowers with 7 to 10 lobes.

HOW TO GROW

Give these plants full sun and average, well-drained soil with a neutral to alkaline pH. They grow well in sandy or stony soil and need a spot protected from wind. Sow seeds indoors 8 to 10 weeks before the last spring frost date at 70°F. Or sow outdoors on the last spring frost date either where the plants are to grow or in a nursery bed. (Move seedlings sown in a nursery bed to where they are to flower in fall or the following spring.) Water regularly in dry weather. Plants are hardy from **Zone 7 south**; protect them in the garden over winter with a dry mulch such as evergreen boughs or salt hay. In the North, keep

plants in pots the first year and overwinter them indoors in a cool, sunny spot or in a cold frame. Use *Michauxia* species in beds and borders and along the front of shrub plantings. Plants die after flowering, either the second or third year from seed, but they may self-sow.

M. tchihatchewii

m. chat-CHEFF-ee-eye. A tender, 5- to 7-foot perennial with lance-shaped, toothed leaves. Each rosette of leaves produces a stiff, branched raceme of 1¹/₄-inch-wide white flowers with slightly reflexed petals in midsummer. Biennial. **Zones 7 to 10**.

Michelia

my-KEE-lee-uh. Magnolia family, Magnoliaceae.

At the turn of the 20th century, this shrub was all the rage in the South because of its fruit-scented blossoms. It arrived in the United States from China a century earlier. There are 45 evergreen trees and shrubs in this genus, most from Southeast Asia, but banana shrub, the one described here, is the only one common to gardens. When out of bloom it offers handsome foliage.

HOW TO GROW

Give banana shrub acid sandy loam, well amended with organic matter, that retains moisture and drains well. It will grow in full sun but partial shade is best. Mulch with leaf mold to further improve moisture retention; protect it from cold, drying winds. It needs little pruning, but it can be espaliered. Plant near a path, patio, or entrance to make the most of its fra-

Michauxia tchihatchewii

Michelia figo

grance. Propagate from semiripe summer cuttings treated with hormones.

M. figo

m. FYE-goh. BANANA SHRUB. A rounded and dense shrub to 2 feet high and wide. Its stems are covered with tan down as are new leaves, which mature to a leathery, glossy green with paler undersides. The magnolia-like midspring flowers are yellow-green tinged with purple and smell richly of fruit. **Zones 8 to 10; to Zone 7 with winter protection.**

Microbiota

my-kro-BY-oh-tuh. Cypress family, Cupressaceae.

Microbiota contains one species, a low-growing, needled, coniferous shrub that is often less than 2 feet tall and spreads beautifully to several feet wide. It is native to mountain ranges near Russia's Pacific coast, an area mistakenly called Siberia in most American references. This gives rise to the common names "Siberian cypress" and "Siberian carpet juniper." Foliage is juniper-like and ranges from bronzy green to olive green. Seeds are borne singly, each in its own fragile wooden cone that soon breaks apart.

Microbiota decussata

HOW TO GROW

Grow *Microbiota* in partial shade to full sun where a juniper-like texture is desired. It will grow well in more shade than junipers can tolerate, however. Foliage typically turns bronze or purple in winter — especially when planted in full sun — then greens back up the following spring. Use as a ground cover near walkways (it is not as prickly as junipers) and on slopes.

M. decussata

m. deh-koo-SAH-tuh. SIBERIAN CARPET JUNIPER. This hardy, evergreen, ground-covering shrub is less than 3 feet tall but spreads widely. In the landscape, it looks like a juniper growing in partial shade and makes a wide, lacy mass. **Zones 3 to 7.**

Mimulus

MIM-yew-lus. Figwort family, Scrophulariaceae.

Commonly called monkey flowers, *Mimulus* species are annuals, perennials, and shrubs with tubular, two-lipped flowers. There are about 150 species in the genus, mostly native to damp areas in the Americas as well as Africa, Asia, and Australia. They bear linear to nearly round leaves that can be toothed or lobed and carry snapdragon-like flowers with five lobes, or "petals." Plants bloom from spring to fall in shades of red, pink, yellow, and orange, and the flowers are often spotted with contrasting colors. Both the common and botanical names refer to the cheerful, funny-faced flowers: *Mimulus* is from the Latin *mimus*, variously translated as "little buffoon" or "mimic actor."

HOW TO GROW

Grow the species described here in full sun to partial shade and rich, moist to wet soil. These plants grow best in areas with cool, wet summers. In areas with hot summers, give them a site that receives dappled shade in the afternoon. Sow seeds indoors 14 to 15 weeks before the last spring frost date, merely pressing the seeds into the soil surface, and chill the sown pots in the refrigerator for 3 weeks before moving them to a warmer (70°F) spot for germinating, which takes 1 to 3 weeks. Pinch plants to encourage branching and bushy growth. Water regularly, especially in hot weather; the soil should never dry out. Deadhead to encourage new flowers to form. Monkey flowers can be propagated by division in spring and by cuttings in spring or summer, which can be used to overwinter the plants. Or keep plants in pots year-round and simply sink them to their rims in the soil in summer. In winter, keep them in a sunny, well-ventilated, cool (50°F) spot. Use *Mimulus* in moist beds and borders, bog gardens, and containers. The flowers attract hummingbirds. Plants self-sow.

M. × hybridus

m. × HI-brih-dus. HYBRID MONKEY FLOWER. Well-branched, 6- to 12-inch tender perennial, hardy from **Zone 7 south**. Bears tubular flowers with flared, 2-inch-wide faces, usually in shades of oranged-red, red, or yellow, often spotted with a contrasting color. Tender perennial, or grow as a cool-weather annual.

M. luteus

m. LOO-tee-us. YELLOW MONKEY FLOWER, MONKEY MUSK. A vigorous, 1-foot-tall tender perennial, hardy from **Zone 7 south**. Bears broadly ovate, toothed leaves and pairs of $^3/4$- to 2-inch-long yellow flowers with

Mimulus × hybridus

Mirabilis jalapa

red- or purple-red-spotted throats and petals from late spring to midsummer. Tender perennial, or grow as a cool-weather annual.

Mirabilis

meer-AB-il-iss. Four-o'clock family, Nyctaginaceae.

Mirabilis contains some 50 species of annuals and tender, tuberous-rooted perennials native to the Americas. They bear ovate leaves and trumpet-shaped flowers that have long tubers and flared, flattened faces that have five spreading lobes, or "petals," as they are usually called. One species, a tender, tuberous-rooted perennial, is a popular, old-fashioned plant. The botanical name for the genus is the Latin word meaning "wonderful."

HOW TO GROW

Full sun to partial shade and average, well-drained soil are ideal. Start four-o'clocks from seeds sown outdoors on the last spring frost date or indoors 6 to 8 weeks before the last frost date at 55° to 65°F. Germination takes 1 to 3 weeks. From Zone 7 south, sow seeds outdoors in fall for bloom the following year. Either way, just press the seeds onto the soil surface, as light is required for germination. For best bloom, water regularly and feed monthly. North of

Zone 10, grow these plants as bedding plants replaced annually or as tender perennials: either start new plants from seeds each year, or dig the tuberous roots after a light fall frost and store them in barely damp vermiculite, peat moss, or sand in a cool (40° to 50°F), dry place, as you would dahlias. In Zones 10 and 11, grow them outdoors year-round as perennials. Where they are marginally hardy, mulch heavily in fall.

M. jalapa

m. jah-LAH-puh. FOUR-O'CLOCK, MARVEL OF PERU. A bushy 2-foot-tall perennial, hardy from **Zone 10 south** but often forming self-sowing colonies north of that zone. Bears ovate leaves and fragrant 2-inch-long flowers in pink, red, magenta, yellow, or white, sometimes with stripes or other markings of more than one color on each flower. Flowers on the same plant can be different colors. Plants bloom from midsummer to fall, and each flower opens in the afternoon and dies by morning. **Zones 10 and 11**.

Miscanthus

mis-KAN-thus. Grass family, Poaceae.

Commonly called eulalia grass, Japanese silver grass, or simply miscanthus, *Miscanthus* species are deciduous or evergreen grasses native from Africa to eastern Asia. From 17 to 20 species belong to the genus, all of which have reedlike stems with linear or narrowly lance-shaped leaves. (The leaves often are sharp edged: although they don't cut deeply, long sleeves and gloves are advisable when working around these plants.) The plants are topped by dense, airy panicles of tiny flowers in summer and fall. Miscanthus are especially valued for their four-season interest: foliage and flowers ripen to shades of tan and brown and add texture and color to the winter landscape.

HOW TO GROW

Select a site in full sun with average soil that is moist but well drained. Give plants plenty of room at planting time, as mature clumps can be 6 feet or more across. Let the foliage stand over winter, then cut plants to the ground in late winter or early spring. Miscanthus are warm-season grasses, so they are late to start growth in the spring. Divide

Miscanthus sinensis

clumps in early spring (use an ax or mattock) for propagation or to control their size; overgrown clumps tend to flop over in summer and also to die out in the center. *M. sinensis* and its cultivars (as well as other species) can become invasive because of prolific self-sowing. Old-fashioned cultivars ('Gracillimus', 'Variegatus', and 'Zebrinus', for example) usually require a very long, hot summer to bloom at all, and for these self-sowing has not been much of a problem. New, early-blooming selections, developed so gardeners in cool northern zones can enjoy the flowers, can self-sow with abandon in areas with warm, wet summers, including the Southeast and the Mid-Atlantic States. There, they have escaped cultivation and naturalized both in and out of gardens.

M. sinensis

m. sih-NEN-sis. EULALIA, JAPANESE SILVER GRASS. Shrub-sized grass forming vase-shaped 3- to 5-foot-tall clumps of foliage that spread from 4 to 6 feet. Bears plumy purplish flowers from summer to fall that range from 6 to 10 inches tall. Flowers and foliage turn light tan and stand through winter. 'Gracillimus', commonly called maiden grass, forms rounded 4½- to 5-foot-tall mounds of fine-textured leaves and bears coppery red blooms in midfall. 'Morning Light' produces rounded mounds of fine-textured silvery leaves with white edges and reddish flowers and does not flop over in summer. Variegated cultivars include white-striped 'Variegatus', which reaches 7 feet and needs staking to remain erect, and 'Zebrinus', commonly called zebra grass, a 6- to 9-foot cultivar with pale yellow bands across the leaves. 'Strictus', commonly called porcupine grass, is similar but less likely to flop in summer. *M. s.* var. *condensatus* 'Cabaret' is a 6- to 9-foot late-blooming selection with a broad band of creamy white in the center; it seldom needs staking. 'Purpurascens', also sold as *M.*

Miscanthus sinensis 'Zebrinus'

s. var. *purpurascens*, is a 3- to 4-foot hybrid (to 6 feet in bloom) grown for its late-summer flowers and brilliant red fall foliage. **Zones 4 to 9**.

Mitchella

mit-CHEL-luh. Madder family, Rubiaceae.

Two species, one native to North America and one to Japan, belong to this genus named in honor of Dr. John Mitchell, an early American botanist. Both are woodland species with trailing stems and evergreen, ovate to lance-shaped leaves. They bear pairs of small funnel-shaped flowers followed by red berries.

Mitchella repens

M

Molinia caerulea

HOW TO GROW

Select a site in dappled or partial shade with rich, evenly moist, well-drained, acid soil. Since the species in cultivation — *M. repens* — is a native perennial, make sure to buy nursery-propagated plants rather than ones dug from the wild. *M. repens* spreads steadily but slowly, by rooting at leaf nodes, and more aggressive ground covers will overwhelm it. To propagate, divide the clumps in spring or pot up rooted sections of the stems.

M. repens

m. REP-enz. PARTRIDGE BERRY, TWIN BERRY, RUNNING BOX. Prostrate, mat-forming 1- to 2-inch-tall perennial that spreads to 1 foot or more. Bears glossy dark green leaves with white veins and 1/2-inch-long white flowers in early summer followed by round 1/2-inch-wide red berries. **Zones 4 to 9.**

Molinia

moe-LIN-ee-uh. Grass family, Poaceae.

Of the two species that belong to the genus *Molinia*, one is grown as an ornamental grass for its handsome clumps of fine-textured leaves and showy flower panicles that are held well above the foliage. Both species are native to moist moors, heaths, and lake shores from Europe to western Russia, Turkey, China, and Japan.

HOW TO GROW

Select a site in full sun to partial shade with poor to average, moist, well-drained soil. *M. caerulea* is best in areas with cool, moist summers; plants don't flower well in hot, and especially dry, weather. In areas where hot weather may be a problem, select a spot with shade during the hottest part of the day. Plants take a year or two to become established and bloom well. The flowers and foliage break off in late fall or early winter, so plants do not need to be cut back in spring. Propagate by dividing

Moluccella laevis

the clumps in spring or by seeds, although cultivars do not come true.

M. caerulea

m. see-RUE-lee-uh. PURPLE MOOR GRASS. Clump-forming, warm-season grass producing mounds of linear leaves 1 to 2 feet tall and wide topped by airy spikes of purplish flowers in early to midsummer that are 2 to 4 feet tall. Flowers fade to yellow-brown and are handsome through fall. *M. c.* ssp. *arundinacea* 'Karl Foerster' has 2 1/2-foot-long leaves and

reaches 5 to 7 feet in bloom. 'Variegata' forms 2-foot mounds of white-striped leaves. **Zones 5 to 9; to Zone 4 with winter protection.**

Moluccella

mol-yew-CHELL-ah. Mint family, Lamiaceae.

Square stems and two-lipped, tubular flowers identify the four species of *Moluccella* as relatives of mints *(Mentha)* and salvias *(Salvia)*. All are annuals or short-lived perennials native from the Mediterranean region to northwestern India. From summer to fall, they bear erect stalks of fragrant but insignificant flowers, each surrounded by a large, showy, saucer- or cup-shaped calyx.

HOW TO GROW

Select a site in full sun to light shade and poor to average, well-drained soil. Plants grow well in sandy soil. Sow seeds indoors in individual pots 8 to 10 weeks before the last spring frost date, and chill the sown pots in the refrigerator for 2 weeks before moving them to a warmer (60°F) spot for germinating, which takes 1 to 4 weeks. Or, from about Zone 5 south, sow outdoors a few weeks before the last frost date. In areas with mild winters — Zone 6 or 7 south — sow outdoors in fall for bloom the following year. When sowing, just press the seeds into the soil surface, as light is necessary for germination. Water regularly during dry weather. Use these

Monarda didyma 'Cambridge Scarlet'

plants near the middle or back of beds and borders and in cottage-style gardens. Stake them when they are still small; otherwise they tend to sprawl. They make excellent cut and dried flowers. For fresh use, cut them when they have reached the desired length. For drying, cut when still green or once they begin to turn beige. Plants may self-sow.

M. laevis

m. LAY-vis. BELLS OF IRELAND, SHELL FLOWER, MOLUCCA BALM. A 2- to 3-foot-tall annual with ovate, scalloped leaves. Bears erect, 1-foot-long stalks of tiny, fragrant, white flowers surrounded by cup-shaped, pale green calyxes, which turn papery once seeds form. Cool-weather annual.

Monarda

moe-NAR-duh. Mint family, Lamiaceae.

Also called bergamots and horsemints, bee balms feature fragrant foliage and showy, ragged-looking clusters of two-lipped, tube-shaped flowers. The flower clusters, which are popular with hummingbirds, often are surrounded by a collar of showy bracts. Blooms come in red and various shades of pink, as well as purple, violet, and white. Bee balms have lance-shaped to oval leaves that are usually toothed and square stems. They spread by fast-creeping rhizomes to form broad clumps. All of the 15 species in the genus are native North American wildflowers.

HOW TO GROW
Plant bee balms in full sun or light shade in a site with evenly moist,

Morus alba

well-drained soil. *M. didyma* requires rich, evenly moist soil but good drainage. *M. fistulosa* and *M. punctata* tolerate average to rich soil as well as drier conditions. To help combat powdery mildew, select a site with good air circulation and choose mildew-resistant cultivars. Deadhead flowers to encourage plants to rebloom. Divide the clumps in spring or early fall every 2 to 3 years to keep them vigorous and control their spread. (The plants are especially aggressive in rich, moist soil; all easily spread to 3 feet or more.) Propagate by division, by taking cuttings in spring from stems that arise at the base of the plant, or by seeds,

although most cultivars do not come true.

M. didyma

m. DID-ih-muh. BEE BALM, BERGAMOT, OSWEGO TEA. Rhizomatous 2- to 4-foot-tall perennial that bears aromatic leaves and whorls of scarlet or pink flowers from mid- to late summer. Mildew-resistant cultivars include red-flowered 'Jacob Cline', pink 'Marshall's Delight', and lilac purple 'Prairie Night' ('Prärienacht'). 'Petite Delight' is mildew resistant and reaches only 12 to 15 inches in height. Popular 'Cambridge Scarlet' produces stunning red flowers but is not mildew resistant. 'Panorama Mix', which comes true from seed, produces plants with red, pink, and salmon flowers. **Zones 4 to 8**.

M. fistulosa

m. fiss-tue-LOH-suh. WILD BERGAMOT. A 3- to 5-foot-tall species with leaves that are less susceptible to mildew and clusters of 1/2-inch-long lavender-pink flowers in mid- to late summer. **Zones 3 to 9**.

M. punctata

m. punk-TAH-tuh. SPOTTED BEE BALM, SPOTTED HORSE-MINT. A 1- to 3-foot-tall annual, biennial, or perennial with whorls of 1/2- to 1-inch-long yellow

flowers with a collar of pink to purplish bracts from midsummer to early fall. **Zones 4 to 9**.

Morus

MOOR-us. Mulberry family, Moraceae.

This genus contains 7 to 12 species, all used in Asia to host silk-producing caterpillars. *M. alba* has been used in China for nearly 4,000 years for silk production. All species produce tasty fruits that resemble blackberries but are too fragile and soft to be marketable.

HOW TO GROW
Plant in partial to full sun and any soil, wet to dry, acid to alkaline. Tolerates heat, drought, road salt, and seashore conditions. Fruit drop can be annoying, and bird-distributed seeds may cause a weed-seedling problem. Susceptible to storm damage and numerous insect pests.

M. alba

m. AL-buh. WHITE MULBERRY. This sturdy, adaptable, small shade tree forms a rounded head and grows 30 to 40 feet tall and wide. It is weak wooded and can sucker badly, so it is suitable for only the most hostile environments, where more attractive trees do not prosper. Flowers bloom in spring but usually go unnoticed, except by

Monarda didyma

Muscari azureum

some allergy sufferers who react to the pollen. Leaves are quite variable and may be lobed or unlobed, but they are typically a lustrous dark green and measure 2 to 7 inches long. Fall color is often a nice yellow. Clusters of pink to purple, 1/2- to 1-inch, blackberry-like fruits ripen in summer. These berries are very messy, staining sidewalks and outdoor furniture, but they are so relished by birds that if you have a home orchard, you might wish to plant several mulberries to lure birds away from your cherries, apples, or blueberries. Otherwise, plant one of the fruitless forms. This unfussy, fast-growing tree has orange-brown bark and grows very well in the harsh climates of the Southwest, Midwest, and Plains, where few trees flourish. It is best limited to use as a quick-growing shade tree or screen in these regions. From China. **Zones 5 to 9.**

CULTIVARS

'Chaparral' features slender, twisted branches that cascade to the ground and deeply cut leaves; grows 8 to 20 feet tall, with a beautiful silhouette; fruitless. 'Fan-San' is fruitless and has very shiny, lobed leaves. 'Kingan' is fruitless and very durable under stressful conditions. 'Mapleleaf' is fruitless

and has large lobed leaves. 'Pendula' is identical to 'Chaparral' but produces fruit. 'Stribling' is fruitless and noted for its excellent yellow fall foliage.

Muscari

mus-KAR-ee. Lily family, Liliaceae.

Commonly known as grape hyacinths, *Muscari* species are beloved for their dainty, grapelike clusters of small flowers, which are borne in early to midspring. About 30 species belong to the genus, all of which grow from tunicate bulbs and have grassy, somewhat fleshy, basal leaves that usually range from 1 to 1 1/2 feet in length. Leaves may be inversely lance shaped (oblanceolate), linear, or narrowly spoon shaped; in all cases they are quite narrow. These bulbous perennials are native to the Mediterranean region as well as southwestern Asia. Although in all cases the individual flowers are tiny — usually 1/8 to 3/8 inch long — the racemes are quite showy because the individual flowers are erect and densely packed. Several species bear sterile flowers at the tops of the racemes that are paler in color than the fertile ones. Flowers

usually come in shades of violet, purplish blue, pale blue, and white. They may be bell or urn shaped as well as nearly round or tubular, and the flowers may point up, out, or down. Most species bear blooms that have constricted mouths, and it is this characteristic that distinguishes them from their close relatives the true hyacinths (*Hyacinthus*), which have flowers with wide-open throats. Grape hyacinths also have much smaller flowers than true hyacinths. The botanical name is from the Latin *moschus*, meaning "musk," and refers to the fragrance of some species.

HOW TO GROW

Select a site in full sun or light shade with rich, well-drained soil. These are spring-blooming plants that disappear by midsummer, so spots lightly shaded under deciduous trees generally are fine because they offer full sun before the trees leaf out. Plant the bulbs in late summer or early fall at a depth of 3 to 4 inches. Some species produce offsets in abundance and others do not; some species also self-sow. *M. armeniacum*, *M. botryoides*, and *M. neglectum* can propagate themselves to the point of being invasive; because of their vigor, they also are excellent for naturalizing. While the foliage of all species dies back in midsummer, *M. armeniacum* produces new leaves again in fall. Many gardeners use this characteristic to

advantage by overplanting other, more expensive spring bulbs with this species: the fall grape-hyacinth foliage marks the location of the other bulbs and eliminates the danger of digging into established clumps. Propagate grape hyacinths by dividing the clumps in summer, after the leaves turn yellow but before they disappear completely.

M. armeniacum

m. are-men-ee-AH-kum. G R A P E H Y A C I N T H . A vigorous 4- to 8-inch-tall species producing dense, cylindrical 1- to 3-inch-long racemes of fragrant, violet-blue, urn-shaped to tubular flowers in spring. The individual flowers have white around the mouth. Cultivars include 'Argaei Album', with white flowers; 'Blue Spike', with double blue flowers; 'Cantab', with large, extra fragrant, blue flowers; 'Christmas Pearl', an early-blooming cultivar with light violet-blue flowers that open in early spring; and 'Fantasy Creation', an 8-inch-tall selection with tight racemes of double violet-blue flowers. **Zones 4 to 8.**

M. aucheri

m. AW-cher-eye. Formerly *M. lingulatum*. A 4- to 6-inch-tall species bearing dense, cylindrical, 1/2- to 1 1/2-inch-long racemes in spring. Individual flowers are rounded-tubular, are rich blue in color, and have white or paler blue at the mouth. The racemes usually

Muscari botryoides

Myoporum parvifolium

have a number of pale blue sterile flowers at the top. 'Tubergenianum' (formerly *M. tubergenianum*) is a vigorous 8-inch-tall selection with a conspicuous cluster of pale blue sterile flowers at the top. **Zones 6 to 9.**

M. azureum

m. ah-ZUR-ee-um. Formerly *Hyacinthus azureus, Hyacinthella azurea, Pseudomuscari azureum.* A dainty 3- to 6-inch-tall species bearing racemes of bell-shaped flowers in spring that have nearly unconstricted mouths. Blooms are sky blue with a darker blue stripe on each lobe. *M. a.* f. *album* bears white flowers. **Zones 4 to 9.**

M. botryoides

m. boh-tree-OY-deez. GRAPE HYACINTH. A 6- to 8-inch-tall species bearing dense 1- to 2-inch-long racemes of flowers in spring that have a fruity fragrance. Individual flowers are bright blue and urn shaped with white mouths. *M. b.* f. *album* bears fragrant white flowers. **Zones 3 to 8.**

M. comosum

m. koe-MOE-sum. TASSEL GRAPE HYACINTH. Formerly *Leopoldia comosa.* An 8-inch to 2-foot-tall species that in spring bears $2^1/2$- to 12-inch-long racemes of nodding, fertile, urn-shaped flowers topped by tassel-like clusters of upward-facing, nearly round, sterile flowers. The fertile flowers are olive-brown with creamy or yellow-brown lobes, and the sterile flowers are bright violet-purple. 'Plumosum', commonly sold as feather hyacinth and sometimes listed as 'Monstrosum' as well as *M. plumosum,* bears racemes of all-sterile violet-blue flowers that have threadlike tepals. **Zones 4 to 9.**

M. latifolium

m. lat-ih-FOE-lee-um. An 8- to 12-inch-tall species bearing 1- to $2^1/2$-inch-long racemes of urn-shaped, dark violet-blue, fertile flowers topped by a cluster of paler sterile flowers. **Zones 4 to 8.**

M. macrocarpum

m. mak-roe-KAR-pum. Formerly *M. moschatum* var. *flavum, M. muscarimi* var. *flavum.* A 4- to 6-inch-tall species bearing $1^1/2$- to $2^1/2$-inch-long racemes of fragrant, tubular, $3/4$-inch-long flowers that point outward. The buds are purple-brown and open into yellow-green flowers. In order to flower well, this species requires hot, dry conditions in summer when it is dormant. **Zones 7 to 9.**

M. neglectum

m. neh-GLEK-tum. MUSK HYACINTH. Formerly *M. racemosum.* A 4- to 8-inch-tall species that often produces leaves in fall. In spring, bears dense $1/2$- to 2-inch-long racemes of dark violet-blue urn-shaped flowers with white mouths. **Zones 4 to 8.**

Myoporum

my-OH-por-um. Myoporum family, Myoporaceae.

The 30-plus species of *Myoporum* are evergreen shrubs or small trees native from warm regions of East Asia, across the tropical islands of the Pacific, to Australia and New Zealand. Leaves are alternate, range from less than $1/2$ inch to more than 3 inches long, and have very small, clear or colored spots that can be seen when held up to the light. The small flowers are usually white and have five petal lobes. They are followed by dark, berrylike fruits that are dispersed by birds. The botanical name is Greek for "closed pores," in reference to the tiny spots on the leaves.

HOW TO GROW

Myoporums require full sun and good drainage. They are very tolerant of seaside conditions but will do best if provided with supplemental water during dry periods. Ground-covering myoporums are very low and thornless. They will not tolerate foot traffic. Useful in maritime and arid areas.

M. parvifolium

m. par-vih-FOE-lee-um. This prostrate shrub hails from the interior of Australia. It grows only 6 to 8 inches tall but can spread to more than 12 feet. It is popular as a heat-tolerant ground cover from southern California to Arizona, both in desert regions and along the coast, where it looks good with occasional watering. 'Putah Creek' has larger foliage than the species and is taller, reaching nearly 2 feet. It has white flowers in summer, followed by purple berries. 'Tucson' has small, bright green leaves and makes a dense ground cover. **Zones 9 and 10.**

Myosotis

my-oh-SO-tis. Borage family, Boraginaceae.

Myosotis species, commonly known as forget-me-nots, are erect or sprawling annuals, biennials, and perennials with hairy leaves and clusters of tiny flowers in shades of blue, violet, pink, and white. The trumpet- to funnel-shaped blooms have five "petals," or lobes; flat faces; and a contrasting yellow or white eye. Some 50 species belong to this widespread genus: plants are native from woods, meadows, and boggy spots mostly in Europe and New Zealand but also in Asia and North and South America.

HOW TO GROW

Select a site in full sun or light shade with well-drained, moist soil. *M. scorpioides* requires constantly moist to wet soil for good performance, and it also will grow in standing water up to a depth of 4 inches. Shade during the hottest part of the day is best in hot climates. Propagate by sowing seeds where they are to grow or by dividing the plants in spring. Cut back *M. sylvatica* or pull plants up after flowering to prevent excessive self-sowing.

M. scorpioides

m. scor-pee-OY-deez. TRUE FORGET-ME-NOT, WATER FORGET-ME-NOT. Moisture-loving 6- to 12-inch-tall perennial that spreads to about 1 foot. Bears ovate leaves and clusters of $1/4$-inch-wide blue flowers with yellow eyes in early summer. 'Sapphire' produces brilliant blue flowers on compact plants. **Zones 5 to 9.**

M

Myosotis sylvatica 'Ultramarine'

Myrica pensylvanica

M. sylvatica

m. sil-VAT-ih-kuh. FORGET-ME-NOT, WOODLAND FORGET-ME-NOT. A 5- to 12-inch-tall biennial or short-lived perennial producing tufts of ovate or lance-shaped gray-green leaves. Bears clusters of tiny 3/8-inch-wide, saucer-shaped flowers in shades of blue, pink, or white in spring and early summer. Many cultivars are available. Ball Series plants are compact and 6 inches tall; Victoria Series plants reach only 4 inches. 'Ultramarine' reaches 6 inches and bears indigo blue flowers. Zones 5 to 9.

Myrica

MIR-ih-kuh, my-REE-kuh. Bayberry family, Myricaceae.

The 50 evergreen and deciduous species of this genus are found in moist or coastal habitats throughout the world. About half a dozen shrubs and small trees in the genus are grown in gardens for their aromatic foliage and attractive small berries, which appeal to birds. The flowers are inconspicuous catkins.

HOW TO GROW

Wax myrtles or bayberries vary in their requirements but are frequently chosen for their ability to withstand challenging situations such as salt spray, drought, or boggy sites. This genus offers a good example of regional genetic variation. To ensure cold hardiness, look for plants grown locally or farther north, as *M. cerifera* raised in Florida, for example, may die in a cold Georgia winter. Its coastal origins make it tolerant of less than ideal soil conditions, although it's best to provide humusy, well-draining soil in full sun or partial shade. Myricas are useful as screens, hedges, or background plantings or for naturaliz-ing. They require little pruning, but they respond well to cutting back if you want to control size or shape. Propagate from seeds by first removing their waxy coating; two months' cold stratification may help. Propagate *M. cerifera* from semihardwood cuttings in early summer or root cuttings in winter.

M. californica

m. kal-ih-FOR-nih-kuh. CALIFORNIA BAYBERRY. Native from southern California to Washington State, this species can reach 20 feet or more tall when grown away from coastal winds but can also remain under 10 feet. It is often multitrunked, and its branches are dense with glossy, toothed, dark green leaves 2 to 4 inches long. The small purple fruits are persistent if not removed by birds. Tolerates salt, drought, and sandy soil. Zones 6 to 10.

M. cerifera

m. ser-IF-er-uh. SOUTHERN WAX MYRTLE. This Southeast native evergreen, also called candleberry, can grow more than 30 feet tall in the wild but usually remains 10 to 15 feet tall in a garden. The fragrant, usually narrow, olive green

Myrica cerifera

leaves are dotted with resin glands on the underside. Tiny blue-gray berries, almost white with wax, cover the stems in fall and winter. Too much shade may make it leggy, but it takes well to pruning, which will expose handsome, smooth, muscular gray bark. It tolerates infertile soil, wet or dry, and possibly a wider pH range than *M. pensylvanica*. Zones 7 to 10.

M. gale

m. GALL-ee. SWEET GALE. This deciduous shrub from Europe, Asia, and cold boggy areas of North America suckers and forms low thickets less than 4 feet high. Male plants have yellow-brown catkins in mid- to late spring, followed by round yellow-brown fruits on the female plants. Fragrant, glossy leaves are dark bluish green. It tolerates saturated soils. Zones 1 to 6.

M. pensylvanica

m. pen-sil-VAHN-ih-kuh. BAYBERRY. Native from the northeastern United States to the Mid-Atlantic, this species is deciduous in the North and evergreen in the southern parts of its range. It averages 9 feet tall and suckers to form rounded colonies. The fragrant, leathery leaves are gray-green to olive and dotted with resin glands on the undersides. Males bear tiny yellow-green flowers, and the females produce equally small blue-gray waxy berries that may last from September to spring. It tolerates soil that is wet or dry, sand or clay, salty or infertile, but it may become chlorotic in alkaline soil. Zones 3 to 6.

Myrtus

MUR-tus. Myrtle family, Myrtaceae.

There are only two species of these evergreen shrubs from North Africa and southern Europe. One of them is popular in mild climates for its aromatic foliage — similar to that of boxwood *(Buxus)* and often trained in a similar manner — as well as its attractive white flowers and berries.

HOW TO GROW

Common myrtle is not particular about soil as long as its drainage is excellent. It does well in full sun or light shade and can be pruned to almost any shape, including espalier, topiary, or limbed up as a tree to expose the attractive branches. In the colder part of its range, plant it against a sunny wall with shelter from wind. It also can be grown as an indoor-outdoor plant, in a loam-based medium with even moisture. Scale and mealybugs, which can be a problem indoors, should be wiped with cotton swabs dipped in neem or denatured alcohol. Propagate from semiripe cuttings in summer.

M. communis

m. kuh-MEW-niss. COMMON MYRTLE. Upright and bushy, this Mediterranean native usually grows 10 to 12 feet tall and wide but can become much larger with a more arching habit. Its pointed oval leaves, glossy and dark green, are 2 inches long and fragrant when crushed. The late-summer solitary flowers are fragrant, white, and 3/4 inch across with five petals and a starry brush of stamens, followed by elliptic 1/2-inch blue-black berries. 'Microphylla' is a dwarf form with especially tiny leaves. There are other compact forms as well as variegated selections. Zones 8 to 11.

Myrtus communis

Myrtus communis

N

Nandina

nan-DEEN-uh. Barberry family, Berberidaceae.

This genus contains a single species of evergreen shrub from China and Japan, grown widely in gardens for its graceful habit and foliage — often bronze-red when young and again in fall. It also features white flower clusters and, especially, red berries that persist through winter.

HOW TO GROW

Nandina will thrive in any moderately fertile soil in sun or shade, although it will produce the most berries if given full sun and kept relatively moist. Use it in masses, as contrast with heavier-foliaged plants, for narrow spaces, and to provide winter interest. Can be pruned to the ground; yearly pruning out of old canes will keep growth dense rather than leggy. Propagate by dividing clumps.

N. domestica

n. doe-MES-tih-kuh. HEAVENLY BAMBOO. Unbranched stems to 6 feet tall form clumps similar to bamboo, with leaves divided into slender leaflets. The late-spring or early-summer flowers are white and borne in foot-long panicles. But they are outdone by the heavy clusters of red berries that last from early autumn through winter, often against bronze-purple or red foliage. Cultivars include 'Alba' (white berries), 'Firepower' (bright red winter foliage), 'Gulf Stream' (mounded form to 3 feet, red leaves in winter), 'Harbour Dwarf' (suckering form to 3 feet, graceful, with smaller flower clusters), 'San Gabriel' (under 2 feet tall with narrow leaflets, less cold hardy), 'Umpqua Warrior' (erect, 4 to 6 feet tall), and 'Wood's Dwarf' (very compact at 2 feet, red winter foliage). Often killed to the ground or winterburned in Zone 6. **Zones 7 to 10**.

Narcissus

nar-SIS-sus. Amaryllis family, Amaryllidaceae.

Although nearly everyone is familiar with the golden yellow trumpets of daffodils in spring, this genus offers flowers in a remarkably wide range of shapes, sizes, and even colors. All daffodils grow from tunicate bulbs and bear strap-shaped leaves that begin poking above the soil surface in winter, generally after a spell of mild weather. The bulbs and all parts of the plants are poisonous, and thus are left alone by deer as well as mice and other rodents. The flowers consist of a central trumpet or cup, properly called a corona: the corona is referred to as a trumpet if it is long and a cup if it is short. The corona is surrounded by six "petals," more properly called perianth segments, that are collectively called the perianth.

The most common flower colors are yellow, orange, and white, but there also are pink daffodils, which generally emerge yellow and turn pink as they mature. Many cultivars feature bicolor blooms — a yellow perianth with an orange cup or trumpet, for example. Bloom season varies, too, and cultivars are generally rated as early, midseason, or late blooming. By planting some that fall into each category, it's possible to have daffodils in bloom for 3 months or more in spring. While all *Narcissus* species are commonly called daffodils, dwarf daffodils with small cups are sometimes referred to as jonquils.

There are about 50 species of daffodils as well as literally thousands of cultivars, which are much more commonly grown in gardens today than the species. These have been divided into 12 divisions based on flower shape and origin, and catalogs and well-labeled nursery displays refer to these divisions when describing their offerings. While you don't necessarily need to know the names of the divisions, knowing they exist will help you make good choices. If you select cultivars from several different divisions, you'll be ensured of an interesting variety of flower shapes and sizes, for example. Most full-size daffodils are $3^{1}/_{2}$ to $4^{1}/_{2}$ inches across, but there are tiny $1^{1}/_{2}$-inch-wide selections. Flowers can be single or double, and a single bulb can bear 1 or up to 20 flowers per stem. Plant sizes vary, too: full-size daffodils are usually 18 inches tall, but there are tiny miniatures that range from 4 to 6 inches. In addition, cultivars in the different divisions tend to bloom at similar times, so choosing cultivars from several different divisions also helps extend the bloom season.

HOW TO GROW

Plant daffodils in full sun to partial shade. A site shaded by deciduous trees is fine, because it provides full sun in spring while the plants are growing actively, and shade isn't a problem once the leaves ripen and the plants are dormant. Well-drained soil is essential: the bulbs of nearly all daffodils rot in damp soil. Beyond that, daffodils aren't particular: they'll grow in sandy to loamy soil and tolerate acid to alkaline conditions — pH 5.0 to 8.0. Ideally, the soil should be evenly moist from fall to spring and drier during summer.

Plant the bulbs in fall. Early planting is best, because it gives the bulbs time to grow roots before cold weather arrives. Bulbs are graded and priced according to size. Landscape-sized or "round" bulbs are 3 years old and produce one or more flower stems the first year. They are the least expensive and generally a good buy. Double-nose or bedding-sized bulbs are 4 years old and usually produce two flower stems the first year. Exhibition-sized or triple-nose bulbs are 5 years old and produce three or more flower stems.

Proper planting depth varies according to the size of the bulbs: plant two to three times as deep as the bulbs are tall, generally with the shoulder of the bulb (the point where it swells out from the nose, or top) 4 to 6 inches below the soil surface. Space large hybrids 6 to 10

Nandina domestica

Narcissus 'Dream Castle'

Narcissus 'Romance'

inches apart; miniatures, slightly closer. Bulbs planted at the wider spacing look sparse at first, but they fill in and need dividing less frequently. If you have heavy, wet soil, dig in lots of organic matter such as compost or leaf mold to improve drainage. In this case, planting on the shallow side is best. Planting in raised beds filled with improved soil is another option for dealing with heavy clay and poorly drained sites.

Daffodils need minimal care once they are planted. The plants survive just fine without watering, but if the weather is unusually dry in spring or fall, weekly watering (1/2 inch per week) is beneficial. Let the leaves ripen for 6 to 8 weeks after the flowers fade so they can make food to support next year's flowers. Where they are marginally hardy, cover the plants in late fall with a coarse mulch of evergreen boughs, salt hay, coarse leaves (such as oak leaves), or pine needles. Propagate by digging the clumps just as the foliage disappears in midsummer and separating and replanting the offsets.

Divisions and species are listed separately below.

DIVISIONS

TRUMPET CULTIVARS (DIVISION 1)

These bear one flower per stem, with a trumpet (corona) as long as or longer than the "petals," or perianth segments. Trumpet hybrids bloom in early to midspring and range from 12 to 20 inches tall. 'King Alfred', introduced in 1899, is one of the best-known cultivars that fall here. It bears all-yellow flowers with pointed perianth seg-

ments that are slightly twisted at the tips. Other all-yellow cultivars include 'Arctic Gold', 'Dutch Master', 'Golden Harvest', 'Marieke', 'Unsurpassable', and lemon yellow 'Lemon Glow'. All-white-flowered cultivars include 'Beersheba', 'Empress of Ireland', 'Rashee', and 'Mount Hood', which bears flowers slightly blushed in yellow when they open. Among the outstanding bicolor cultivars are 'Honeybird', pastel yellow perianth and creamy white, yellow-rimmed trumpet; 'Las Vegas', creamy white perianth, yellow trumpet; and 'Spellbinder', yellow perianth, greenish yellow cup that matures to white.

This division also contains miniatures, including 8-inch-tall 'Little Beauty', white perianth, yellow trumpet; 'Little Gem', 6 inches, with all-yellow blooms; 'Midget', a 3- to 4-inch-tall selection with yellow blooms; and 'Topolino', an 8- to 10-inch-tall cultivar with a white perianth and a yellow trumpet. **Zones 4 to 8; to Zone 3 with winter protection.**

LARGE-CUPPED CULTIVARS (DIVISION 2)

Sometimes called long-cupped daffodils, these bear one flower per stem with a cup (corona) that is more than one-third the length of the "petals," or perianth segments, but not as long as the perianth segments. These cultivars usually bloom in midspring and range from 10 to 20 inches tall. Many cultivars are available. All-yellow selections include 'Carlton', a fragrant, vigorous selection good for naturalizing even in the South, and 'Gigantic Star', with fragrant, rich yellow blooms. All-white se-

lections include 'Easter Moon' and 'White Plume'.

Bicolors are especially popular in this division and among these are 'Fortissimo', yellow perianth, orange cup; 'Ice Follies', white perianth, yellow cup; 'Peaches and Cream', creamy white perianth, pale peach-pink cup; 'Pink Charm', white perianth, with a white cup that has a dark pink band; 'Redhill', creamy white perianth blushed with yellow, red cup; 'Romance', white perianth, rose-pink cup; 'Salome', white perianth, pink cup rimmed with gold; and 'Scarlet O'Hara', yellow perianth, red cup. **Zones 4 to 8; to Zone 3 with winter protection.**

SMALL-CUPPED CULTIVARS (DIVISION 3)

Also called short-cupped daffodils, these cultivars bear one flower per stem with a cup (corona) that is equal to or less than one-third the length of the "petals," or perianth segments. These cultivars usually bloom from mid- to late spring and range from 14 to 18 inches in height. Cultivars include 'Barrett Browning', white perianth, orange-red cup; 'Barrii Conspicuus', an old cultivar introduced in 1869 with a yellow perianth and yellow, red-banded cup; 'Birma' and 'Sabine Hay', both with a yellow perianth and coral red cup; 'Queen of the North', white perianth, small pale yellow cup; 'Sinopel', white perianth, lime green cup; and all-white 'Dream

Castle'. **Zones 4 to 8; to Zone 3 with winter protection.**

DOUBLE CULTIVARS (DIVISION 4)

As their name suggests, these daffodil cultivars bear double flowers — the corona and/or the "petals" (perianth segments) may be doubled. Flowers are either solitary or borne more than one bloom per stem. Plants range from 14 to 18 inches in height. Double cultivars that bear solitary blooms include 'Acropolis', fragrant white blooms flecked with red in the center; 'Flower Drift', creamy white flecked with yellow-orange in the center; 'Honolulu', fragrant white flowers with red petaloids in the center; 'Manly', pale yellow with rich orange in the center; 'Petit Four', creamy white flowers with apricot centers; 'Delnashaugh', white flowers with apricot-pink segments in the center; and 'Tahiti', yellow petals interspersed with bright orangy red segments.

Among the doubles that bear more than one flower per stem are 'Bridal Crown', clusters of two to three fragrant white flowers with orange-yellow segments interspersed, hardy in **Zones 4 to 9**; 'Cheerfulness', clusters of two to three fragrant white flowers flecked with yellow, hardy in **Zones 4 to 9**; 'Sir Winston Churchill', clusters of three to five fragrant, creamy white flowers with orange-flecked segments at the center; and 'Yellow Cheerfulness', with clusters

Narcissus 'Petrel'

Narcissus 'Broadway Star'

of two to three yellow blooms, hardy in **Zones 3 to 9**. Early-flowering 'Rip van Winkle' (also listed as *N. minor* ssp. *pumilus* 'Plenus' and *N. pumilus* 'Plenus') is a 4- to-6-inch-tall miniature with yellow dandelion-like blooms that have many pointed perianth segments and green interspersed with the yellow. Hardiness of double cultivars varies: unless otherwise noted, the ones listed here are hardy in **Zones 4 to 8; to Zone 3 with winter protection**.

TRIANDRUS CULTIVARS (DIVISION 5)

Triandrus daffodils feature umbels of two to six small nodding flowers that usually have short cups and reflexed "petals," or perianth segments. These cultivars bloom in mid- to late spring. Plants are 12 to 14 inches tall. Cultivars include 'Hawera', an 8-inch-tall miniature with clusters of three to five yellow flowers; 'Petrel', with clusters of three to five extremely fragrant white flowers that have bell-shaped cups; 'Stint', with clusters of three to five lemon yellow flowers; and 'Thalia', with clusters of two to three fragrant white flowers. **Zones 4 to 9**.

CYCLAMINEUS CULTIVARS (DIVISION 6)

Solitary flowers and reflexed "petals," or perianth segments, characterize cyclamineus cultivars. The flowers usually have a long trumpet and point down at an acute angle from the stem. These bloom in early to midspring and are 10 to 14 inches tall. Cultivars include 'Beryl', an 8-inch-tall selection with a yellow perianth and yellow cup banded in orange; 'Foundling', white perianth, apricot-pink cup; 'Jack Snipe', white perianth, yellow cup; 'Jetfire', yellow perianth, orange-red cup; and 'Peeping Tom', a vigorous all-yellow selection. **Zones 4 to 9**.

JONQUILLA CULTIVARS (DIVISION 7)

Jonquilla daffodils feature umbels of one to five flowers with small cups and spreading "petals," or perianth segments. They bloom in mid- to late spring and often have fragrant flowers. Jonquilla cultivars have nearly cylindrical leaves. Plants are 12 to 16 inches tall. Cultivars include 'Baby Moon', an 8-inch-tall miniature with clusters of several all-yellow flowers per stem; 'Bell Song', with clusters of three to five fragrant flowers with creamy white perianths and rose pink cups; 'Chit Chat', a miniature from 3 to 4 inches tall with prolific clusters of yellow flowers; 'Curlew', clusters of fragrant white flowers that open creamy yellow; 'Quail', clusters of two to four bronzy yellow blooms; 'Stratosphere', with two to three fragrant golden yellow flowers per stem; 'Sundial', an 8-inch-tall miniature with clusters of fragrant golden yellow flowers that have nearly flat cups; and 'Sweetness', with very fragrant golden yellow flowers produced one or two per stem. **Zones 4 to 9**.

TAZETTA CULTIVARS (DIVISION 8)

These small-flowered daffodils produce umbels of 3 or 4 to as many as 20 flowers that have small cups and broad "petals," or

Narcissus 'Actaea'

perianth segments. The flowers are very fragrant. Tazetta cultivars are good daffodils for southern gardens. They range from 12 to 16 inches in height. Cultivars include 'Avalanche', with clusters of 15 to 20 fragrant flowers with white perianths and yellow cups, **Zones 6 to 9**; 'Geranium', with clusters of three to five fragrant flowers that have white perianths and orange-red cups, **Zones 4 to 9**; 'Scarlet Gem', with clusters of three to five flowers with yellow perianths and red-orange cups, **Zones 5 to 9**; and 'Silver Chimes', with 8 to 10 fragrant white flowers per stem, **Zones 6 to 9**. 'Canaliculatus' is a 4- to 6-inch-tall miniature with four to seven fragrant flowers per stem that have white perianths and yellow cups; hardy in **Zones 6 to 10**, it is best in a spot that remains hot and dry in summer. Hardiness varies widely in this group, from **Zones 4, 5, or 6 to 9, depending on the cultivar.**

Narcissus 'Tête-à-tête'

POETICUS CULTIVARS (DIVISION 9)

Tiny disk-shaped red-rimmed cups and broad white "petals," or perianth segments, characterize poeticus cultivars. The flowers are fragrant and usually borne one per stem. Poeticus cultivars bloom from mid- to late spring and range from 14 to 18 inches tall. The most commonly grown cultivar is 'Actaea', with sweetly fragrant flowers that have broad white perianth segments surrounding a yellow cup edged in dark red. 'Cantabile' bears small fragrant flowers with a white perianth and a green-and-yellow cup edged in red. **Zones 3 to 7**.

WILD SPECIES (DIVISION 10)

This division includes all the species daffodils and their variants, several of which are described below under "Species."

SPLIT-CORONA CULTIVARS (DIVISION 11)

Split-corona daffodils usually bear solitary flowers that are characterized by a trumpet or cup (corona) that is split for more than half its length. These cultivars bloom from mid- to late spring. Plants range from 14 to 18 inches tall. Cultivars include 'Blanc de Blancs', with all-white flowers and a split cup (blushed with yellow when it opens) that lies flat against the perianth; 'Cassata', with a white perianth and yellow cup that matures to white; 'Colblanc', with a white perianth and a green cup; 'Orangery', with white petals and a wavy-edged tangerine cup; 'Palmares', with a white perianth and a frilly salmon pink cup; and 'Printal', with a white perianth and a frilly yellow cup. 'Broadway Star'

N

Narcissus bulbocodium

has white petals surrounding a split cup that forms an orange star in the center, and 'Papillon Blanc' has a white perianth with a white cup marked with green and yellow. **Zones 4 to 7.**

MISCELLANEOUS DAFFODILS (DIVISION 12)
This division contains a variety of daffodils that do not fit into other divisions. Several miniatures fall here. 'Jumblie', a 5- to 6-inch-tall selection, bears clusters of several small flowers that have very reflexed yellow perianth segments surrounding orange-yellow cups; hardy in **Zones 4 to 9.** 'Quince', a 5- to 6-inch-tall selection, bears clusters of three to four flowers with very reflexed sulphur yellow perianth segments and dark yellow cups; hardy in **Zones 4 to 9.** 'Tête-à-Tête' is a 5- to 6-inch-tall cultivar with yellow flowers, usually borne in pairs; hardy in **Zones 4 to 9.**

SPECIES

N. bulbocodium
n. bul-buh-KOH-dee-um. HOOP PETTICOAT DAFFODIL. A diminutive 4- to 6-inch-tall species with nearly round, grasslike leaves. In midspring, bears yellow 1¹/₂-inch-wide flowers with tiny, twisted, pointed perianth segments and a megaphone-shaped trumpet. *N. b.* ssp. *conspicuus* is a vigorous form with deep yellow flowers. **Zones 4 to 8.**

N. jonquilla
n. jon-KWIL-luh. WILD JONQUIL. A 12-inch-tall species bearing rounded leaves and very fragrant flowers in late spring. The golden yellow flowers are 1¹/₄ inches across and have pointed perianth segments and a small flat cup. **Zones 5 to 9.**

N. × medioluteus
n. × meh-dee-oh-LOO-tee-us. PRIMROSE PEERLESS NARCISSUS, POETAZ NARCISSUS, TWIN SISTERS NARCISSUS. Formerly *N. × biflorus.* An *N. poeticus* × *N. tazetta* hybrid. This 10- to 12-inch-tall hybrid blooms in very late spring and usually bears two 1¹/₄- to 2-inch-wide flowers per stalk. Individual blooms have a white perianth and a small yellow cup. **Zones 3 to 8.**

N. minor
n. MY-nor. Sometimes listed as *N. nanus.* A dainty 4- to 6-inch-tall species bearing 1¹/₄-inch-wide yellow flowers in early spring that point slightly downward. **Zones 5 to 8.**

N. obvallaris
n. ob-val-LAR-iss. TENBY DAFFODIL. Also listed as *N. pseudonarcissus* ssp. *obvallaris.* A vigorous 12-inch-tall species bearing golden yellow 1¹/₂-inch-wide flowers in early spring that face upward. **Zones 3 to 8.**

N. × odorus
n. × oh-DOR-us. CAMPERNELLE JONQUIL. Sometimes listed as *N. campernelli.* An *N. jonquilla* × *N. pseudonarcissus* hybrid. A 10- to 12-inch-tall hybrid bearing one or two very fragrant yellow flowers per stem in early spring. Blooms are 1¹/₂ inches across and have narrow perianth segments surrounding a large cup. 'Plenus' bears double flowers. **Zones 5 to 8.**

N. poeticus
n. poe-EH-tih-kus. POET'S NARCISSUS. An 8- to 20-inch-tall species bearing very fragrant, solitary flowers in late spring. Individual blooms are 1³/₄ to 3 inches across and have a white perianth with a very small yellow red-rimmed cup. 'Plenus' (also listed as *N.* 'Albus Plenus Odoratus') bears fragrant double white flowers. *N. p.* var. *recurvus,* commonly called pheasant's eye, bears 1¹/₂-inch-wide flowers with a white perianth and a yellow red-rimmed cup. Unlike other daffodils, *N. poeticus* and its cultivars tolerate moist to wet soil in winter and spring and fairly damp conditions in summer. **Zones 3 to 7.**

N. tazetta
n. tah-ZET-tuh. POLYANTHUS NARCISSUS. A variable 6- to 20-inch-tall species bearing umbels of about 4 to as many as 15 very fragrant blooms in late winter or very early spring. Individual flowers are 1¹/₂ inches across and have a white perianth with a yellow cup. Paperwhite narcissus belong here; these bear clusters of fragrant white flowers and are commonly forced in water. **Zones 7 or 8 to 9.**

N. triandrus
n. tree-AN-drus. ANGEL'S TEARS. A dainty 4- to 10-inch-tall species bearing nodding, creamy white flowers in umbels of one to as many as six blooms in midspring. Individual blooms are 2¹/₂ inches wide and have reflexed perianth segments surrounding a rounded cup. **Zones 4 to 9.**

Nectaroscordum
nek-tah-roe-SKOR-dum. Lily family, Liliaceae.

Nectaroscordum species bear clusters of flowers that resemble those of ornamental onions, and, in fact, the three species in this genus were once classified in *Allium.* The botanical name refers to the fact that all parts of these plants smell strongly of garlic when bruised — it is from the Greek *nektar,* meaning "nectar," and *skordon,* "garlic." The nodding, bell-shaped flowers, which are borne in loose umbels, appear in summer. Like alliums, plants bear individual flowers that are small and have six petal-like tepals. Plants grow from tunicate bulbs and have grassy, linear leaves that emerge in spring and die back as the flowers fade or shortly after they fade.

HOW TO GROW
Select a site in full sun or partial shade with average to rich, well-drained soil. Combine these plants with low-growing annuals or perennials to hide the foliage as it fades. Plants are good for naturalizing, but they self-sow, sometimes with abandon, and can become invasive. Propagate by seeds, or dig the bulbs in summer as the leaves fade and separate the offsets.

Nectaroscordum siculum

N. siculum

n. SIK-yew-lum. HONEY GARLIC.
Formerly *Allium siculum*. A vigorous 3- to 4-foot-tall species with linear leaves that have a sharp keel along one side. In summer, plants bear umbels of 10 to as many as 30 nodding, creamy white, $^1/_2$- to 1-inch-long flowers that are flushed with pink or purple-red and greenish at the base. *N. s.* ssp. *bulgaricum* (formerly *N. discoridis, Allium bulgaricum*) bears creamy white flowers that are green at the base and flushed with purple.
Zones 6 to 10.

Nemesia

neh-MEE-see-ah. Figwort family, Scrophulariaceae.

Nemesia contains some 50 species of annuals, perennials, and subshrubs native to South Africa, where they are found in scrubby, disturbed sites inland as well as sandy soils near the coast. They bear showy, spurred or pouched, two-lipped flowers either singly or in small racemes. The flowers have four upper lobes, or "petals," and one or two large, flared lower ones.

HOW TO GROW

These plants require full sun and average to rich, well-drained soil that remains evenly moist. They are best in areas with mild summers and need cool nighttime temperatures to bloom well. To prolong bloom in hot climates, give them dappled shade in the afternoon. Sow seeds indoors 8 to 10 weeks before the last spring frost date at 55° to 65°F. Germination takes 1 to 3 weeks. To prevent damping off, sow in a sterile seed-starting mix, water only from below, and let the medium dry out

Nepeta × faassenii (see page 274)

slightly between waterings. Pinch to encourage bushy growth. Transplant with care, as the roots are brittle. In areas with mild summers, such as the Pacific Northwest, sow outdoors after the last frost date, and sow new crops every 6 weeks through late summer. Water regularly. Use nemesias in mixed beds and borders and in containers. They are good choices for seaside gardens in areas with cool summers.

N. strumosa

n. strew-MOE-suh. A 6- to 12-inch-tall annual with toothed or entire, lance-shaped, hairy leaves. Bears racemes of 1-inch-wide flowers in shades of red, pink, yellow, lavender-blue, purple, or white in mid-

and late summer. Flowers may be a solid color or bicolor, with upper and lower lips in contrasting colors. Cool-weather annual.

Nemophila

nem-oh-FILL-ah. Water-leaf family, Hydrophyllaceae.

Native to western North America, the 11 species of *Nemophila* are spreading or prostrate annuals with saucer- or bell-shaped, five-petaled flowers in shades of blue or white.

HOW TO GROW

Full sun or partial shade and rich, moist, well-drained soil are ideal. Although these plants tolerate full sun in areas with cool summer weather, a site that receives dappled shade is best in areas where summers bring heat and humidity. They stop blooming once warm, humid weather arrives. Where hot summers prevail, start seeds indoors 6 to 8 weeks before the last spring frost date to give plants a chance to bloom before torrid weather sets in. Germination takes 1 to 3 weeks at 55°F. Or sow seeds outdoors several weeks before the last frost date. In mild climates — roughly Zone 7 south — sow seeds in fall for bloom the following spring. Water regularly and mulch to keep the soil cool. Use nemophilas in mixed plantings and in wildflower gardens. Plants self-sow.

N. maculata

n. mak-yew-LAH-tuh. FIVE-SPOT.
A fleshy-stemmed, 6- to 12-inch-tall annual with pinnate leaves. In summer it carries $1^3/_4$-inch-wide flowers that are white with a purple spot at the tip of each petal. Cool-weather annual.

N. menziesii

n. men-ZEE-see-eye. BABY BLUE EYES. A spreading, 8-inch-tall annual with pinnate leaves. Usually bears $1^1/_2$-inch-wide blue flowers with lighter blue centers, but forms with white or pale blue flowers are available, as well as ones spotted, blotched, or striped with dark blue or violet. Cool-weather annual.

Nemesia strumosa

Nemophila menziesii

Nepeta

NEP-uh-tuh. Mint family, Lamiaceae.

Commonly called catmints, *Nepeta* species have aromatic gray-green leaves, square stems, and showy spikes of small two-lipped flowers, primarily in shades of lavender, purple, violet, and white. About 250 species belong to the genus, and most are perennials, although there are a few annuals. Leaves are ovate to lance shaped and have entire, toothed, or scalloped edges; some species have hairy leaves. Catnip (*N. cataria*) is the member of the clan that has an intoxicating effect on cats. Commonly grown in herb gardens, it has a long history of herbal use but is not especially ornamental. Catmints, which are ornamental and popular in flower gardens, have less effect on cats.

HOW TO GROW

Grow catmints in full sun or light shade and average, well-drained soil. They thrive in drier sites than many commonly grown perennials, and damp soil leads to crown rot and death. Catmints can be short-lived in the South and are best in a spot with shade during the hottest part of the day in hot-summer areas. *N. nervosa* is the most heat-tolerant selection. Taller-growing catmints may need staking but also are attractive when simply allowed to flop. Shear plants back hard — by one- to two-thirds — after the main flush of flowers fades to encourage fresh new foliage and renewed flowering until frost. Divide clumps in spring or fall if they outgrow their site or begin to look less vigorous, or for propagation. Or, propagate

Nerium oleander 'Tangier'

by taking cuttings in summer. *N. cataria* can be grown from seeds and self-sows with abandon unless deadheaded, but none of the commonly grown ornamentals come true (*N.* × *faassenii* plants are sterile and thus produce no seeds).

N. cataria

n. kah-TAR-ee-uh. CATNIP. Clumping 3-foot-tall perennial with aromatic gray-green woolly leaves that spreads to about 1¹/₂ feet. In summer and fall it bears spikes of small white flowers spotted with purple. Zones 3 to 7.

N. × faassenii

n. × fah-SEN-ee-eye. NEPETA, CATMINT. Formerly *N. mussinii.* Clump-forming 1- to 2-foot-tall hybrid that forms 1¹/₂-foot-wide mounds of aromatic, hairy, silvery gray-green leaves. Bears spikes of lavender-blue ¹/₂-inch-long flowers from early summer to fall. 'Snowflake' and 'White Wonder' have white flowers. 'Dropmore' has larger leaves and flowers than the species and is a more erect, 2-foot-tall selection. 'Six Hills Giant', a popular cultivar of uncertain parentage, reaches 3 feet in height and bears showy spikes of violet purple flowers. Zones 4 to 8; to Zone 3 with winter protection.

N. govaniana

n. go-van-ee-AH-nuh. YELLOW CATMINT. Formerly *Dracocephalum govanianum.* A 3-foot-tall clump-forming species that spreads to about 2 feet. Bears large, aromatic, 4-inch-long leaves and loose racemes of pale yellow, 1¹/₄-inch-long flowers from midsummer to fall. Zones 5 to 9.

N. nervosa

n. ner-VOH-suh. VEINED NEPETA. Mounding 1¹/₂- to 2-foot-tall species that spreads to about 2 feet. Bears mildly aromatic gray-green leaves with prominent veins and dense racemes of purple-blue ¹/₂-inch-long flowers from midsummer to fall. Zones 5 to 9.

N. sibirica

n. sye-BEER-ih-kuh. SIBERIAN CATNIP. Formerly *N. macrantha, Dracocephalum sibiricum.* A 3-foot-tall species with lance-shaped dark green leaves that spreads to 2 feet. Bears racemes of 1¹/₂-inch-long lavender-blue flowers in summer. Zones 3 to 9.

Nerine

neh-REE-nee. Amaryllis family, Amaryllidaceae.

Grown for their showy fall flowers, nerines are tender bulbs native to southern Africa. About 30 species belong to the genus, all growing from tunicate bulbs and producing strap-shaped, deciduous leaves that appear either with the flowers or soon after the flowers open. The flowers are produced in umbels of 2 to more than 20 blooms atop fleshy, leafless stems. They have six petal-like tepals. The narrow tepals are joined together only at the base to form a short tube and either stick out straight or spread widely. As a result, the blooms either resemble loose, lilylike trumpets or are spidery in appearance. Species with spidery blooms have narrow, strongly

Nerine bowdenii

Nerium oleander

reflexed tepals with wavy edges along with prominent stamens.

HOW TO GROW

Give nerines full sun and rich, very well drained soil. Where they are hardy, plant the bulbs outdoors in spring at a depth of 5 to 6 inches and space bulbs about 5 inches apart. Like many South African natives, these bulbs require a mild climate with a dry dormant period. In areas with dry summers and nearly frost-free winters, they are easily satisfied: they are dormant in summer, and leaves appear in fall and last partway though winter. Where they are marginally hardy or may be exposed to too much summer rain, look for a warm, south-facing site, such as at the base of a wall, with very well drained soil, and in late fall protect the plants with a heavy, coarse mulch such as evergreen boughs, pine needles, or salt hay. Or, grow these bulbs in containers, planting the bulbs in spring or early summer with the top half above the soil surface.

Soak the soil at planting time, then water very sparingly until the leaves appear in late summer — the soil should remain nearly, but not completely, dry. Water regularly when plants are growing actively. Plants prefer cool temperatures, but bring them indoors before temperatures dip much below 50°F at night in fall. Begin to withhold water when the leaves start to turn yellow, then store the bulbs — still in their containers — in nearly dry soil in a cool (35° to 50°F), dry place. Bulbs also can be dug and stored out of the ground in a cool, dry place but generally do not perform as well. That's because whether outdoors or in containers, plants are happiest when left undisturbed and will thrive for years without needing division: dig or pot on the bulbs only if they become overcrowded or for propagation. Container-grown plants bloom best when slightly pot-bound; top-dress the containers annually in late summer to replenish the soil, but try to disturb the roots as little as possible. Propagate by separating the offsets in fall as the leaves die back or by seeds.

N. bowdenii

n. bow-DEH-nee-eye. NERINE. Native South African species reaching 1¹⁄₂ feet in height. Bears umbels of six or seven funnel-shaped, 3-inch-long pink flowers in fall. Blooms have a musky scent and wavy-edged tepals. 'Pink Triumph' bears dark pink blooms. **Zones 8 to 10; to Zone 7 with heavy winter protection.**

N. sarniensis

n. sar-nee-EN-sis. GUERNSEY LILY. A 1¹⁄₂-foot-tall species native to South Africa and naturalized on the island of Guernsey in the English Channel. In fall it bears umbels of 5 to as many as 20 orange-red to red flowers that are 1¹⁄₄ to 1¹⁄₂ inches across and have wavy-margined, reflexed tepals and showy, protruding stamens. This species is highly variable and is one parent of many hybrids that range in color from rose, salmon pink, and pale pink to scarlet, orange-red, and white. **Zones 8 to 10.**

Nerium

NEE-ree-um. Dogbane family, Apocynaceae.

There is only one species in this genus, an evergreen shrub or small tree found from the Mediterranean region to western China and commonly called oleander. Many cultivars have been developed for gardeners who live in similarly mild climates, where the shrubs

Nicandra physalodes (see page 276)

produce long-blooming terminal clusters of five-petaled flowers.

HOW TO GROW

Oleanders are tolerant of soils that are dry, salty, or waterlogged, and they thrive in the bright, reflected light typical of waterside or desert gardens. They will also tolerate light shade and are deer-proof. They can be pruned as single- or multiple-trunked trees, grown in containers and pruned as standards, or allowed to sucker as a screen or border. In early spring, prune back flowered wood, cutting a proportion of stems to the ground. Other branches can be pruned lightly to restrict size. Pull out any unwanted suckers. Oleanders are easily propagated from seeds or softwood cuttings.

N. oleander

n. OH-lee-an-der. OLEANDER. Oleander is broad, round, and suckering from 8 to 12 feet tall and wide unless pruned, with stout stems and leathery lance-shaped leaves to 4 inches long. The clusters of pinwheel flowers, usually pink in the species, can start blooming in late spring and last well into fall. They are followed by 6-inch seedpods. All parts of the plants are poisonous, and even smoke from the wood can cause irritation. Cultivars have single or double flowers in white, peach, pink, yellow, or red, and many have been chosen for more compact habits. Popular selections include 'Calypso' (single, cherry red), 'Hardy Pink' (single, salmon pink), 'Hardy Red' (single, red), 'Hawaii (single, salmon pink with yellow throat, compact), 'Petite Pink' (grows only 3 to 4 feet tall), 'Sister Agnes' (white, found in both single and double forms, fast growing), and 'Tangier' (single, pale pink, 4 to 6 feet). **Zones 8 (south) to 11.**

Neviusia

nev-ih-YEW-see-uh. Rose family, Rosaceae.

This genus contains only two rare species of deciduous suckering shrubs. The better known *N. alabamensis* is native to the southeast United States, while the other species, *N. cliftonii*, has been more recently discovered in California. Much like a spirea (*Spiraea*) in habit, they are covered with starry balls of white flowers in mid-spring.

HOW TO GROW

N. alabamensis does best in moisture-retentive, well-drained loam but adapts fairly well to less ideal situations in full sun or partial shade. Grow as a specimen or in the shrub border. Prune assertively after flowering to keep it from becoming shaggy. Propagate from softwood cuttings or divide suckers.

N. alabamensis

n. al-uh-bam-EN-sis. ALABAMA SNOW-WREATH. Native to isolated areas of the mid-South, this shrub has erect, arching stems to 6 feet high and spreads at least as wide, eventually developing a rounded habit. The spade-shaped leaves are serrated. The unusual

Neviusia alabamensis

Nicotiana alata 'Nicki Bright'

Nicotiana alata

flowers that open at night on 4- to 5-foot plants. Cultivars are usually 1¹/₂ to 2 feet tall and have flowers in shades of pink, red, white, and chartreuse. They remain open in the daytime but usually are not fragrant. Nicki Series plants bear fragrant flowers in a range of colors on 1¹/₂-foot plants. Warm-weather annual.

N. langsdorffii
n. langs-DORF-fee-eye. FLOWERING TOBACCO. A 5-foot-tall annual with large ovate leaves and airy clusters of small, 2-inch-long, green flowers with tubular bases and bell-like faces. Warm-weather annual.

N. × sanderae
n. × SAND-er-eye. FLOWERING TOBACCO. A tender, 2-foot-tall perennial, grown as an annual, with rounded, wavy-edged leaves and loose panicles of trumpet-shaped, 2-inch-wide flowers in shades of red, pink, purple-pink,

showy white midspring flowers consist entirely of feathery stamens. **Zones 4 to 8**.

Nicandra
nye-KAN-drah. Nightshade family, Solanaceae.

Only one species belongs to this genus, *N. physalodes,* an old-fashioned annual grown for its bell-shaped flowers, which are followed by berries encased in inflated, papery, green calyxes. Apple of Peru, one common name for the plant, celebrates its origin in that country and also calls attention to the ornamental fruit. It is also sometimes called shoo-fly plant, because old-time gardeners believed it repelled flies.

HOW TO GROW
Select a planting site with full sun or partial shade and rich, moist, well-drained soil. Plants thrive in heat and humidity. Sow seeds indoors 6 to 8 weeks before the last spring frost date at 60° to 65°F. Germination takes 2 to 3 weeks. Or sow seeds outdoors, either a few weeks before the last frost date or in fall for germination the following spring. Use apple of Peru in mixed plantings and informal, cottage-style or wild gardens. The decorative fruit is attractive in dried arrangements. Plants self-sow and can become weedy in warm climates.

N. physalodes
n. fye-sal-OH-deez. APPLE OF PERU, SHOO-FLY PLANT. A well-branched, 2- to 3-foot-tall annual with rounded, wavy-margined leaves. Bears short-lived,

1¹/₂-inch-wide, shallowly bell-shaped flowers from summer to fall. The flowers, borne in abundance, are light purple-blue and are followed by inedible berries in lantern-shaped calyxes. Warm-weather annual.

Nicotiana
nih-koh-shee-AH-nah. Nightshade family, Solanaceae.

The ornamental members of this genus are commonly known as flowering tobaccos or simply nicotianas. Some 67 species of annuals, biennials, perennials, and shrubs belong here, including the commercial crop tobacco *(N. tabacum)*. Native to tropical regions in the Americas as well as Australia, they bear undivided leaves, often covered with sticky hairs, and clusters of flowers with narrow, tubular bases and flaring, flat- to cup-shaped faces from summer to frost. Many nicotianas have flowers that open only in late afternoon or early evening and are fragrant at night.

HOW TO GROW
Select a site with full sun or partial shade and rich, evenly moist, well-drained soil. A site with dappled afternoon shade is beneficial in areas with hot summers. Sow seeds indoors 6 to 8 weeks before the last spring frost date at 70° to 75°F. Germination takes 2 to 3 weeks. Or sow outdoors after the last frost date. Either way, just press the tiny seeds into the soil surface, as light is required for germination. Water during dry weather. Deadhead to keep plants neat-

looking and to encourage new flowers to form. Add nicotianas to mixed plantings, and site fragrant types close to sitting areas where you can enjoy them after dark. The flowers attract moths and hummingbirds. Plants self-sow.

N. alata
n. ah-LAH-tuh. FLOWERING TOBACCO. This short-lived, 1¹/₂- to 5-foot tender perennial, hardy in **Zones 10 and 11** and grown as an annual, bears ovate to spoon-shaped leaves and 4-inch-long flowers. The species bears very fragrant, greenish white or yellowish

Nierembergia caerulea

or white. Heat-resistant Domino Series plants are 1 to 1¹/₂ feet tall. Warm-weather annual.

N. sylvestris
n. sil-VES-tris. FLOWERING TOBACCO. A 3- to 5-foot annual or short-lived perennial, hardy in **Zones 10 and 11**, with a rosette of large, rounded leaves up to 3 feet long. Bears clusters of fragrant, white, 3¹/₂-inch-long trumpets. Warm-weather annual.

Nierembergia
near-em-BER-jee-uh. Nightshade family, Solanaceae.

Commonly called cup flowers, *Nierembergia* species are slender-stemmed annuals, perennials, and subshrubs with upturned, cup- or bell-shaped flowers and entire, often spoon-shaped or linear leaves. Some 20 species native to South America belong here.

HOW TO GROW
Full sun and rich, evenly moist, well-drained soil are ideal for all but *N. repens,* which prefers dry, even sandy, conditions. Partial shade in the afternoon is best in areas with hot summers. Sow seeds indoors 8 to 10 weeks before the last spring frost date at 55° to 65°F. Germination takes 2 to 4 weeks. Or sow outdoors in spring a few weeks before the last frost date or in fall. Water regularly, especially in hot weather. Perennials can be propagated by cuttings in summer or early fall. Species covered here are hardy from **Zone 7 south**. Use cup flowers in contain-

Nigella hispanica 'Curiosity'

ers and mixed plantings. *N. repens* also looks great in cracks between paving stones, as an edging or ground cover, and in rock gardens, but where hardy it can become invasive.

N. caerulea
n. see-RUE-lee-uh. Formerly *N. hippomanica* var. *violacea.* A well-branched, 8-inch-tall tender perennial with cup-shaped, lavender-blue, ³/₄-inch flowers in summer. Tender perennial, or grow as a cool-weather annual.

N. repens
n. REP-enz. WHITE CUP. A creeping, mat-forming tender perennial that reaches 2 inches in height and spreads to 2 feet or more. Bears white, 1- to 2-inch-wide, bell-shaped flowers with yellow centers in summer. Tender perennial, or grow as a cool-weather annual.

N. scoparia
n. skoh-PAH-ree-uh. Formerly *N. frutescens.* A shrublike, 1¹/₂- to 3-foot-tall tender perennial with pale lilac-blue, 1-inch-wide, tubular flowers with yellow centers. Tender perennial, or grow as a cool-weather annual.

Nigella
nye-JEL-ah. Buttercup family, Ranunculaceae.

Nigella contains 20 species of bushy annuals native to the Mediterranean region and western Asia. They bear deeply cut, feathery leaves and flowers in shades of lavender-blue, purple, pink, and white. The flowers have 5 petal-like sepals and from 5 to 10 true petals, which are somewhat smaller. In some species, the flowers are surrounded by a ruff (technically called an involucre) of branched, threadlike, green bracts, a characteristic that leads to the common name "love-in-a-mist." The flowers, borne in summer, are followed by inflated seed capsules that are often used in dried arrangements.

HOW TO GROW
A site with full sun and average, well-drained soil is all these easy-to-grow plants require. They are happiest in cool weather. Sow seeds outdoors several weeks before the last spring frost date, barely covering the seeds with soil. Or sow indoors in individual pots 6 to 8 weeks before the last frost

Nipponanthemum nipponicum

date at 65° to 70°F, although outdoor sowing is generally best. For continued bloom in cool climates, sow new crops every 4 weeks through late summer. Or sow outdoors in fall for bloom the following year. Water during dry weather. Deadheading prolongs bloom but prevents the formation of the ornamental seedpods. Use nigellas in mixed beds, as fillers among perennials, or as cut flowers, or dry the seedpods. Plants self-sow.

N. damascena
N. dam-ah-SEEN-uh. LOVE-IN-A-MIST, DEVIL-IN-A-BUSH. A 1¹/₂- to 2-foot annual with 1³/₄-inch-wide flowers in shades of lavender-blue, purple, violet, pink, rose-red, or white. The flowers are surrounded by a showy involucre of branched, threadlike bracts. Plants in the Persian Jewels Series are 16 inches tall and come in an array of rich colors. Cool-weather annual.

N. hispanica
n. hiss-PAN-ih-kuh. FENNEL FLOWER. A 1¹/₂-foot annual with deeply cut but not threadlike

leaves and 2¹/₂-inch-wide, blue, faintly fragrant flowers with maroon-red stamens that lack an involucre of bracts. Cool-weather annual.

Nipponanthemum
nip-oh-NAN-thuh-mum. Aster family, Asteraceae.

Nipponanthemum contains a single species once classified in the vast genus *Chrysanthemum.* A herbaceous perennial or subshrub native to sandy, coastal regions in Japan, it bears daisylike flowers and aromatic leaves.

HOW TO GROW
Select a site in full sun with average, very well drained soil. Plants thrive in sandy soils. Pinch stem tips in spring to encourage branching. In areas where plants are not killed to the ground over winter, in early spring cut them nearly to the ground to keep them from becoming leggy and falling open at the centers of the clumps later in the season. Propagate by dividing the clumps in spring or by seeds.

N

Nolana paradoxa 'Blue Bird'

N. nipponicum

n. nih-PON-ih-kum. NIPPON DAISY. Formerly *Chrysanthemum nipponicum.* A somewhat shrubby 2-foot-tall perennial that spreads as far and bears toothed, spoon-shaped, dark green leaves and 2¹/₂-inch-wide daisylike flowers in fall that have white ray florets ("petals") surrounding yellow centers. **Zones 5 to 9.**

Nolana

no-LAH-nah. Nightshade family, Solanaceae.

Commonly called Chilean bellflowers, the 18 *Nolana* species are all native to Chile and Peru. They are well-branched, prostrate or sprawling annuals, perennials, and subshrubs with simple, sometimes fleshy leaves; many are covered with sticky hairs. Their flowers, which open only in sunny weather, are bell shaped; have five "petals," or lobes; and come in shades of lavender-blue, purple, pink, or white. Some experts classify *Nolana* in the nolana family, Nolanaceae.

HOW TO GROW

Full sun and average, well-drained soil are ideal. These plants grow well in poor, somewhat dry soil and are best in areas with cool summers, where they are suitable for seaside gardens. Sow seeds outdoors several weeks before the last frost date. Or sow indoors 6 to 8 weeks before the last spring frost date at 60°F. Established plants need watering only during very dry weather. Use Chilean bellflowers as edging plants, in mixed plantings, and in containers.

N. humifusa

n. hew-mih-FEW-suh. A spreading, 6-inch-tall tender perennial or subshrub, hardy from **Zone 9 south,** that can spread to 1¹/₂ feet. Carries 1-inch-wide, lilac-blue flowers with white throats and darker purple streaks in summer. Tender perennial, or grow as a cool-weather annual.

N. paradoxa

n. pair-ah-DOX-uh. An 8- to 10-inch-tall annual or tender perennial, hardy from **Zone 9 south,** bearing 2-inch-wide, purple-blue flowers with yellow throats and white eyes.

Nyssa sylvatica

Tender perennial, or grow as a cool-weather annual.

Nyssa

NIH-suh. Tupelo family, Nyssaceae.

Most of the 5 to 10 species of deciduous trees in this genus are native to wet sites. They are grown in gardens for their outstanding fall color and easy-care nature. The most widely grown species, *N. sylvatica,* is highly attractive to bees when in bloom and is the source of the prized tupelo honey.

HOW TO GROW

Plant in full sun to partial shade and moist, humus-rich, acid soil. Tolerates wet and dry conditions but not alkalinity. Plant small trees, since the taproot makes large trees difficult to transplant. Prune lower limbs in fall if desired. Remove suckers. Usually pest-free.

N. sylvatica

n. sil-VAT-ih-kuh. BLACK GUM, SOUR GUM, PEPPERIDGE, TUPELO. On Martha's Vineyard, but apparently nowhere else, this is called the beetlebung tree. The wood was used to plug the bung holes of casks. With a strong pyramidal shape, a central leader, and horizontal to ascending branches when young, this beautiful native tree eventually becomes irregular or rounded and matures to 30 to 50 feet tall and 20 to 30 feet wide. Producing the most reliable and outstanding fall color of all our native trees (although color is not always dependable in the South), black gum should be grown more in home gardens. Leaves are pointed ovals, 3 to 6 inches long, and a highly polished dark green in summer. They change color over a long season, first turning yellow, then orange and scarlet, and finally deep red or maroon before falling in late autumn. The spring flowers go unnoticed except by bees, but the clusters of deep blue berries on female trees look spectacular in fall when they ripen against the red leaves. Birds quickly eat the berries. Trunk bark is patterned into rough, chunky, dark gray checkers, while limbs are silvery gray. Use this medium-size tree in a lawn or border, or plant it in groups in a naturalistic garden or wet site. From eastern and central North America. **Zones 5 to 9.**

CULTIVARS

'Miss Scarlet' has outstanding red fall color and large blue berries.

Nyssa sylvatica

Oemleria

om-LEER-ee-uh. Rose family, Rosaceae.

This genus contains a single species of deciduous, dioecious shrub native to western North America and commonly called Oso berry. Closely related to the plum (*Prunus*), it is one of the first plants of the growing season to leaf out and bloom, with dangling flowers that smell of almonds, followed by dark blue fruits.

HOW TO GROW

Oso berry is easy to grow in any moderately moist, fertile soil with good drainage, in full sun or partial shade. Both male and female shrubs are needed to produce fruit. Grow it in a shrub border or use for naturalizing. Head back stems or remove suckers to restrict growth. If you want more flowers and fruit, prune old flowered shoots to the ground. Propagate from softwood cuttings in early summer or by separating suckers.

O. cerasiformis

o. seh-rass-ih-FORM-iss. OSO BERRY, INDIAN PLUM, OREGON PLUM. Upright, eventually arching shoots to 8 feet tall can sucker to form a thicket 12 feet across. The lance-shaped leaves, to 3¹/₂ inches long, are dark green and glossy above, gray-green and somewhat fuzzy underneath.

Drooping 4-inch racemes of tiny, fragrant, bell-shaped white flowers appear just after the leaves in late winter or earliest spring. Female shrubs then bear oval ³/₄-inch blue-black fruits. **Zones 6 to 9.**

Oenothera

ee-NOTH-er-uh, ee-no-THAIR-uh. Evening-primrose family, Onagraceae.

The 125 species in this genus are commonly called sundrops, evening primroses, golden eggs, or just oenotheras. They are annuals, biennials, and perennials mostly native to North America (a few species are from South America) that bear showy, sometimes fragrant flowers in brilliant yellow, white, or pink. Blooms are borne singly or in clusters, have four petals, and usually are saucer to cup shaped. They open in either the morning or the evening, depending on the species. Although individual flowers fade quickly, they are produced in abundance over a long season in summer.

HOW TO GROW

Select a site in full sun with poor to average, well-drained soil. Sundrops resent wet soil, especially in winter, but tolerate dry, rocky conditions. Too-rich soil yields lots of foliage but few flowers and also leads to short-lived plants. *O. fruticosa* and its cultivars tolerate richer soil than other species and are suitable for planting in beds and borders with well-drained, evenly moist soil. Some species, especially *O. speciosa*, can be invasive. Many oenotheras have taproots and resent being disturbed. Divide clumps in early spring or late summer only if they outgrow their space or begin to lose vigor, or for propagation. Or propagate by removing offsets from the outside of the clumps, by taking stem cuttings in spring or early summer from shoots at the base of the plant, by taking root cuttings in fall from roots that run along the soil surface, or by sowing seeds. Some species self-sow.

O. biennis

o. bi-EN-nis. EVENING PRIMROSE. A 3- to 5-foot annual or biennial, hardy in **Zones 4 to 8**, with a rosette of lance-shaped, somewhat sticky, toothed leaves. Carries fragrant, bowl-shaped, 2-inch-wide flowers that open pale yellow and age to gold from summer to fall. Biennial or cool-weather annual.

O. caespitosa

o. sess-pih-TOE-suh. TUFTED EVENING PRIMROSE. A 4- to 8-inch-tall biennial or perennial that spreads as far. Bears richly fragrant, 4-inch-wide white flowers in summer that open at sunset and fade to pink and die on the following morning. **Zones 4 to 8.**

O. fruticosa

o. fru-tih-KOH-suh. COMMON SUNDROPS. Clump-forming 1- to 3-foot-tall perennial or biennial that spreads to 1 foot. Bears racemes of deep yellow 1- to 3-inch-wide flowers from late spring through summer. Plants once sold as *O. tetragona* have been moved here and are currently listed as *O. f.* ssp. *glauca*. Compact cultivars, which range from 1¹/₂ to 2 feet tall, make outstanding garden plants. These include 'Summer Solstice' ('Sonnenwende'), which blooms from early summer to fall and features maroon fall foliage, and 'Youngii', which blooms from early to midsummer and has scarlet autumn leaves. **Zones 4 to 8.**

O. macrocarpa

o. mak-roe-KAR-puh. OZARK SUNDROPS, MISSOURI EVENING PRIMROSE. Formerly *O. missouriensis*. A 6-inch-tall perennial with trailing stems that spread to 2 feet. Bears solitary, 5-inch-wide yellow flowers from late spring to fall. **Zones 5 to 8.**

O. perennis

o. per-EN-iss. SUNDROPS, NODDING SUNDROPS. An 8-inch-tall perennial that spreads to about 1¹/₂ feet. Bears loose racemes of funnel-shaped, ³/₄-inch-wide

O

Oemleria cerasiformis

Oenothera biennis var. *canescens*

Oenothera speciosa 'Siskiyou Pink'

yellow flowers in summer.
Zones 5 to 8.

O. speciosa

o. spee-see-OH-suh. SHOWY EVE-
NING PRIMROSE. Vigorous 1-
foot-tall perennial that spreads
rapidly by runners to form drifts
that easily exceed 2 to 3 feet. Bears
solitary, cup-shaped 1- to 2¹/₂-
inch-wide flowers from early summer to fall. The species has white
flowers, but pink-flowered forms
such as 'Rosea' are most often
grown. 'Siskiyou Pink' bears 2-
inch flowers on 10-inch plants.
Zones 5 to 8.

Omphalodes

om-fah-LOH-deez. Borage
family, Boraginaceae.

Grown for their forget-me-not–
like flowers, the 28 species of
Omphalodes are annuals, biennials,
and perennials native to Europe,
northern Africa, Asia, and Mexico.
They bear simple, oblong to ovate
leaves and blue or white flowers,
which are usually carried in small
terminal clusters. The flowers have
five lobes, or "petals"; flat faces;
and a paler-colored eye in the center. Both the botanical name and
the common names "navelwort"
and "navelseed" refer to the seeds,
which are actually nutlets that
have a depressed spot on them:
Omphalodes is from the Greek
omphalos, meaning "navel," and
oides, "resembling."

HOW TO GROW
Select a site in partial shade with
rich, moist, well-drained soil. *O.
linifolia* needs full sun. *O. verna*
tolerates dry soil but performs
better with even moisture. Established plants (especially of *O.
cappadocica*) resent being disturbed but can be divided in early
spring for purposes of propagation. Or sow seeds. Plants self-sow.

O. cappadocica

o. kah-pah-DOE-sih-kuh. NAVEL-
WORT, BLUE-EYED MARY. A
rhizomatous 10-inch-tall perennial
that forms 1¹/₂-foot-wide clumps.
It bears ¹/₄-inch-wide clear blue
flowers with white eyes in early
summer. 'Starry Eyes' has deep
blue flowers edged with white.
Zones 6 to 8.

O. linifolia

o. lin-ih-FOE-lee-uh. VENUS'S
NAVELWORT. A 1- to 1¹/₂-foot-
tall annual with spatula-shaped
leaves and airy, terminal racemes
of faintly scented, white or pale
blue, ¹/₂-inch-wide flowers from
spring to summer. Cool-weather
annual.

O. verna

o. VER-nuh. BLUE-EYED MARY,
CREEPING FORGET-ME-NOT.
Stoloniferous 8-inch-tall perennial
that forms 1-foot-wide clumps.
Bears racemes of bright blue ¹/₂-
inch-wide flowers in spring. 'Alba'
has white flowers. **Zones 6 to 9.**

Onoclea

oh-no-CLAY-uh. Wood-fern
family, Dryopteridaceae.

A single species belongs to this genus in the wood-fern family —
sensitive fern (*O. sensibilis*). Native
to eastern Asia as well as eastern
North America, it produces
spreading clumps of coarse-looking, roughly triangular fronds. The
common name refers to the fact
that the fronds turn yellow at the
first fall frost.

HOW TO GROW
Sensitive fern grows in a wide
range of conditions, from full sun,
provided the soil remains moist, to
shade. It thrives in constantly wet,
even swampy soil as well as in dry
conditions and also flourishes in
the moist, well-drained soil of the
average fern garden. The plants
spread steadily by branched rhizomes to form dense, broad
clumps. To propagate, as well as to
keep clumps from spreading too
far, divide them every 2 to 3 years.

O. sensibilis

o. sen-sih-BIL-iss. SENSITIVE
FERN. Vigorous 1- to 3-foot-tall
native fern that easily spreads to 3
feet or more. Bears roughly triangular, pinnate fronds with wavy-
edged leaflets or lobes sometimes
cut all the way to the main stem
and sometimes nearly to the main
stem. Separate dark brown, fertile
fronds with beadlike leaflets hold
the spores. **Zones 2 to 10.**

Onopordum

on-oh-POR-dum. Aster family,
Asteraceae.

Sometimes called cotton thistles
because their leaves and stems are
covered with woolly, cobweblike
hairs, the 40 species of *Onopordum* are biennials native to Europe, the Mediterranean region,
and western Asia. They produce
deeply lobed, spiny leaves as well
as winged, branched stems that
also are spiny. The flowers are
round and thistlelike, with spiny
bases, and come in shades of purple, purplish pink, pink, violet, or
sometimes white. The botanical
name sometimes is spelled
Onopordon.

HOW TO GROW
Select a site in full sun to light
shade with rich, evenly moist,
well-drained soil. Cotton thistles
grow well in heavy soils; neutral to
slightly alkaline pH is best. Sow
seeds outdoors after the last spring
frost date. Sow either where the
plants are to bloom or into a nursery bed, and move the plants to

Omphalodes cappadocica 'Starry Eyes'

Onoclea sensibilis

Onopordum acanthium

their final location in fall or the following spring. Or sow indoors 8 to 10 weeks before the last frost date at 55° to 60°F. Use drifts of these thistles at the back of informal perennial gardens and in semiwild plantings. Deadhead regularly in order to curtail self-sowing, and cut plants down after they finish flowering.

O. acanthium

o. ah-KAN-thee-um. COTTON THISTLE, SCOTCH THISTLE, A taprooted biennial with a rosette of spiny, deeply cut, gray-green, foot-long leaves. Bears erect, branching stems ranging from 3 to 9 feet in height with 1¹/₂- to 2-inch-wide, pale rose-purple or white flower heads in summer. Biennial.

Ophiopogon

oh-fee-oh-POE-gon. Lily family, Liliaceae.

Ophiopogon species are evergreen perennials commonly known as mondo grass. They also are sometimes called lilyturf, a common name that indicates their close resemblance to another popular genus that shares that common name, *Liriope*. There are some 50 species of *Ophiopogon*, all native to eastern Asia. All produce clumps of grasslike leaves topped with racemes of tiny flowers in summer. The flowers, which are mostly hidden by the leaves, are followed by round, glossy, blue or black berries.

HOW TO GROW
Select a site in full sun or partial shade with rich, moist, well-drained soil. *O. japonicus* and *O. planiscapus* are both rhizomatous and spread steadily to form 1-foot-wide clumps. *O. japonicus* has fleshy, tuberous roots, and established plantings are quite drought tolerant. Propagate by digging and dividing the clumps in spring or by seeds.

O. japonicus

o. juh-PON-ih-kus. MONDO GRASS. An 8- to 12-inch-tall species with tuberous roots that forms handsome clumps of grassy leaves. Bears 2- to 3-inch-long racemes of bell-shaped ¹/₄-inch-

Ophiopogon planiscapus

wide flowers in summer followed by blue-black berries. 'Compactus' is only 2 inches tall. 'Variegatus' has white-striped leaves. **Zones 7 to 10.**

O. planiscapus

o. plan-ih-SCAPE-us. An 8-inch-tall species that bears grassy, dark green leaves and 1- to 3-inch-long racemes of bell-shaped, ¹/₄-inch-long, purplish white flowers. Blooms in summer. 'Nigrescens' (also sold as 'Black Dragon' and 'Ebony Knight') is grown for its nearly black leaves. It makes a most unusual ground cover, but it spreads very slowly. **Zones 6 to 10.**

Opuntia

oh-PUN-tee-uh, oh-PUN-shah. Cactus family, Cactaceae.

Native to North, Central, and South America, *Opuntia* species are succulent, perennial cacti from a wide range of habitats. About 200 species belong here. All lack true leaves and instead produce fleshy branches that are either flat and padlike or rounded. Whatever their shape, the fleshy branches are well armed with barbed spines, which can be large or very small and hairlike. *Opuntia* species bear showy bowl-shaped flowers in summer that open during the day. The common name "prickly pear" refers to the spiny, rounded fruits that follow the flowers. The "pears" of some species, which also are called tunas and Indian figs, are edible; in some cases they turn a handsome red when ripe.

HOW TO GROW
Select a site in full sun with sandy or gritty soil that is fairly rich in organic matter and very well drained. Wet soil, especially in winter, is fatal. When siting plants, be sure to consider the spines, which will pierce and/or work their way through gloves: keep plants away from areas where unwary visitors may come in contact with the spines, and weed thoroughly before planting to avoid problems later. *O. compressa* is an excellent container plant and also

Ophiopogon japonicus

Opuntia compressa

a good choice for planting along the top of a rock wall where drainage is excellent. Propagate it by dividing the clumps in spring or rooting the individual flattened pads. Wrap the pads in folded pieces of newspaper to avoid contact with the spines.

O. compressa

o. kom-PRESS-uh. HARDY CACTUS. Formerly *O. humifusa*. A 4- to 12-inch-tall species that forms 3-foot-wide clumps and is native from Montana and Massachusetts south to Florida and Texas. Plants bear fleshy, rounded, gray-green pads with brown spots, called areoles, that carry the tiny barbed spines. Some selections also bear larger white spines with black tips. Produces showy 2- to 2¹/₂-inch-wide yellow flowers, which may have red centers, from late spring to early summer. The 1¹/₂-inch-long "pears" ripen to red or purplish and are edible. The pads are limp during the winter. **Zones 4 or 5 to 9.**

Ornithogalum

or-nith-oh-GAL-um. Lily family, Liliaceae.

Commonly known as stars-of-Bethlehem, *Ornithogalum* species are hardy and tender bulbs primarily native to South Africa and

Opuntia compressa

the Mediterranean region. Plants grow from tunicate bulbs and bear basal leaves that range from narrow and linear to rounded. Depending on the species, plants bloom from late winter to spring or summer. They produce starry, usually white flowers that are carried in either erect, spikelike racemes or rounded racemes that resemble umbels or corymbs. Individual blooms consist of six petal-like tepals. The outer tepals are often striped with green on the outside.

HOW TO GROW

Select a site in full sun or light shade with average to rich, well-drained soil. Where they're hardy, plant the bulbs outdoors in fall, setting them at a depth of 4 inches. The two most commonly grown species — *O. nutans* and *O. umbellatum* — are fairly hardy and suitable for naturalizing in grass, along shrub borders, and in other semiwild areas. Because of their abundant offsets, both can become invasive (*O. umbellatum* tends to be more invasive). Where marginally hardy, look for a warm, south-facing site with very well drained soil and mulch heavily in late fall with evergreen boughs, salt hay, pine needles, or another coarse mulch. Where these plants are not hardy, or in areas where too much summer rain may cause them to rot, plant them outdoors in spring after the soil has warmed up or grow them in containers. Overwinter the plants either by digging the bulbs as they go dormant in late summer or fall or by allowing the soil in the containers to dry out and storing them in a cool (50°F), dry spot. Container-grown plants can be brought indoors be-

Ornithogalum dubium

fore the first frost to finish blooming indoors, then gradually allowed to dry out for overwintering. Propagate by separating the offsets in fall or early spring or by seeds.

O. arabicum

o. ah-RAB-ih-kum. STAR-OF-BETHLEHEM. A 1- to 3-foot-tall species native to the Mediterranean region. Bears rounded racemes of 6 to 25 cup-shaped, 1¹/₂-inch-wide, pearly white flowers that have a prominent black ovary in the center. Blooms appear in early summer and have a rich, fruity fragrance. **Zones 8 to 10.**

O. balansae

o. bah-LAN-see. Sometimes listed as *O. oligophyllum*. A diminutive 3-inch-tall species native to the Bal-

kans, Turkey, and the Republic of Georgia. In early spring, bears rounded racemes of two to five cup-shaped, 1¹/₄-inch-wide white flowers that are green on the outside. **Zones 5 or 6 to 10.**

O. dubium

o. DOO-bee-um. STAR-OF-BETHLEHEM. Formerly *O. florescens*, *O. triniatum*. An 8- to 12-inch-tall species from southern Africa. From late winter to early spring, bears racemes of up to 25 cup-shaped 1-inch-wide flowers in shades of golden yellow, orange, red, or sometimes white. **Zones 8 to 10.**

O. nutans

o. NEW-tans. NODDING STAR-OF-BETHLEHEM. An 8- to 18-inch-tall species from Europe and southwestern Asia that is naturalized in parts of North America. In spring, bears one-sided racemes of about 20 fragrant, funnel-shaped, slightly downturned white flowers that are striped with green on the outside. **Zones 5 to 10.**

O. saundersiae

o. sawn-DER-see-ee. GIANT CHINCHERINCHEE. A 2- to 3-foot-tall species from southern Africa. From late winter to early spring, bears rounded racemes of cup-shaped, ³/₄- to 1-inch-wide, white or creamy white flowers. **Zones 7 or 8 to 10.**

O. thyrsoides

o. thyr-SOY-deez. CHINCHERINCHEE. A 1- to 2-foot-tall South African native. Bears dense racemes of many starry, cup-shaped ³/₄-inch-wide flowers in

spring and early summer that are white with creamy or greenish bases. **Zones 7 or 8 to 10.**

O. umbellatum

o. um-bel-LAH-tum. STAR-OF-BETHLEHEM. A vigorous 6- to 12-inch-tall species native to the Mediterranean region. Bears rounded racemes of starry white ³/₄-inch-wide flowers in early summer that have a broad stripe of green on the backs of the tepals. May be invasive. **Zones 4 to 9.**

Osmanthus

oz-MAN-thus. Olive family, Oleaceae.

The botanical name comes from Greek words for "fragrant" and "flower," and the minuscule blossoms are often intensely fragrant far out of proportion to their size. This is a group of about 20 evergreen shrubs and trees from the southeast United States, East Asia, and the Middle East. The flowers, which bloom in spring or fall depending on the species, are often hidden by the dense, glossy foliage. They are followed by usually persistent, ¹/₂-inch blue-black berries.

HOW TO GROW

Osmanthus does best in soil that is acidic, fertile, moist, and well drained. It tolerates some clay or alkalinity but not prolonged drought. Although it can be grown in full sun or partial shade, the foliage may burn if exposed to winter sun and wind. Ideal for hedges and screens, or along walks and entryways where its fragrance can be appreciated. It can take fairly heavy pruning, after flowering, but doesn't require it. Propagate from semiripe cuttings in late spring or early summer.

O. americanus

o. ah-mair-ih-KAH-nus. DEVIL-WOOD. Native to swampy areas of the southeastern United States, devilwood is unlike other osmanthus in having a more open and loose habit and untoothed leaves. From 2 to 4 inches long, they are lance shaped and shiny

Osmanthus fragrans

Ornithogalum arabicum

olive green. It can grow 15 to 20 feet tall. The aromatic white flowers bloom in midspring. Considered the most cold-hardy species. **Zones 6 to 9.**

O. delavayi
o. del-AH-vay-eye. DELAVAY OSMANTHUS. A Chinese species growing slowly to 6 to 10 feet (although some have reached 20 feet), often broader, and rounded. The 1-inch lustrous leaves are toothed, and the fragrant white flowers with reflexed petals are borne profusely in midspring. It produces clusters at the ends of branches as well as in leaf axils, where other osmanthus flowers are often hidden. **Zones 7 to 9.**

O. × fortunei
o. × for-TOON-ee-eye. FORTUNE'S OSMANTHUS. This hybrid of *O. heterophyllus* and *O. fragrans* grows slowly to 15 to 20 feet high but is usually kept smaller. The 4-inch leaves are toothed like a holly's, and the fragrant flowers bloom in early to midautumn. Retains its deep green color in hot sun better than some other species. 'San Jose' has narrower leaves. **Zones 7 to 9.**

O. fragrans
o. FRAY-grenz. SWEET OLIVE. Also called fragrant tea olive, this Asian species can be a huge shrub at 20 to 30 feet tall and wide but is usually about half that size. The shiny green leaves are finely toothed or untoothed and up to 5 inches long. The flowers, considered the most fragrant of the genus, bloom from early fall and sporadically through winter. *O. f. f.*

aurantiacus has yellow-orange flowers. **Zones 8 to 10.**

O. heterophyllus
o. het-er-oh-FILL-us. FALSE HOLLY. A Japanese species that will grow to 20 feet tall but is usually less than 10 feet high and slightly narrower. Very dense and rounded, it earned all of its common names — the others being holly olive, holly osmanthus — from the resemblance of its leaves to those of many *Ilex* species: shiny, leathery, and spiny when young, less so as they mature. The intensely fragrant, four-petaled white flowers bloom in early to midautumn, almost hidden by the foliage. Cultivars include 'Goshiki' (leaves flecked with yellow), 'Gulftide' (to 15 feet tall and cold tolerant, with shiny, spiny leaves), 'Purpureus' (dark purple new leaves, retaining a purple tint), 'Rotundifolius' (spineless, slow growing), and 'Sasaba' (very spiny, to 4 feet, less cold tolerant). **Zones 6 to 9.**

Osmunda

oz-MUN-duh. Flowering-fern family, Osmundaceae.

Osmunda species are vigorous, stately ferns that have featherlike, once- or twice-cut fronds and grow from a thick mat of horsehairlike roots. The fiddleheads and leaf stalks are densely covered with hair. The common name "flowering fern" refers to the manner in which the spores are borne. They are produced either on separate, specialized, often cinnamon-colored or brown fronds or on sepa-

rate leaflets (pinnae) on the main fronds. In either case, spore-bearing parts lack leafy tissue altogether. Plants range from 2 to 5 feet or more in height. About 12 species belong to the genus.

HOW TO GROW
Select a site in partial shade with rich soil that ranges from evenly moist and well drained to constantly moist or wet. Site these plants beside a pond or stream, or in a bog garden; *O. regalis* will grow in shallow standing water. Acid pH is best. Most species — especially *O. regalis* — grow well in full sun provided water is plentiful. *O. claytoniana* tolerates dry conditions as well as considerable sun or shade. To propagate, divide the clumps in spring or fall.

O. cinnamomea
o. sin-uh-MOE-mee-uh. CINNAMON FERN. A native North American fern that reaches 3 feet and spreads to form 2-foot-wide clumps. It has twice-cut fronds that taper somewhat at the base and have woolly tufts at the base of the leaflets. Plants produce tall, fertile fronds in late spring that turn cinnamon brown after the spores are shed. **Zones 2 to 10.**

O. claytoniana
o. klay-toe-nee-AH-nuh. INTERRUPTED FERN. A native North American species with 2- to 4-foot-tall fronds that resemble those of *O. cinnamomea*. This species does not bear specialized fertile fronds; instead, fronds have specialized brown, spore-bearing leaflets that "interrupt" the frond. **Zones 2 to 8.**

O. regalis
o. reh-GAL-iss. ROYAL FERN, FLOWERING FERN. A 5- to 6-foot-tall species that spreads as far and bears somewhat coarse-looking, twice-cut fronds with widely spaced oval leaflets. It produces fronds with tassel-like tips (about one-quarter of the frond) that are covered with showy brown clusters of spores. **Zones 2 to 10.**

Osteospermum

oss-tee-oh-SPER-mum. Aster family, Asteraceae.

Grown for their showy, daisylike flowers in shades of yellow, white, or pink, *Osteospermum* species are native from South Africa to the Arabian Peninsula. About 70 species of annuals, perennials, and subshrubs belong to the genus.

Osmunda cinnamomea

They are closely related to *Dimorphotheca* species, and plants in both genera share the common names "Cape marigold," "African daisy," and "star of the veldt." Like many other aster-family plants, *Osteospermum* species produce flowers consisting of sterile, petal-like ray florets (the "petals") around a dense cluster of fertile disk florets (the "eye"), which produce the seeds. (*Dimorphotheca* species bear fertile ray florets.) The flowers are borne from midsummer to fall. The leaves are narrow to oval with lobed, toothed, or entire margins.

HOW TO GROW
Select a site in full sun and average to poor soil that is light and well drained. Plants thrive in heat, tolerate dry soil, and perform best in areas with a long growing season; they do not do as well in areas with hot, humid, rainy summers. Sow seeds indoors 6 to 8 weeks before the last spring frost date at 60° to 65°F. Germination takes

Osmanthus delavayi

Osmunda cinnamomea

O

Osteospermum 'Burgundy Mound'

about 2 weeks. Or, from Zone 9 south, sow seeds outdoors. Either way, barely cover the seeds with soil, and try to avoid wetting the foliage when watering, to prevent fungal diseases. Deadheading prolongs bloom. Perennials can be propagated by cuttings taken in spring or summer. Try over-wintering plants in a sunny, well-ventilated, cool (50°F) spot: they require very well drained soil that is evenly moist but never wet. Prune in spring. Use osteo-spermums in containers, or add them to mixed plantings in beds and borders.

O. ecklonis

o. eck-LON-iss. A sprawling subshrub with gray-green leaves, this species can range from 2 to 5 feet tall and spread to 4 feet. Bears 2- to 3-inch-wide, daisylike flowers with violet-blue centers and white petals that are violet-blue on the undersides. 'Silver Sparkler' has 3-inch-wide flowers and white-edged leaves. Tender perennial or warm-weather annual. **Zones 10 to 11**.

O. fruticosum

o. fru-tih-KOH-sum. FREEWAY DAISY. Frequently planted along highways in southern California, this perennial species has thick, mat-forming stems that are less than 12 inches tall but spread to 4 feet or more. It is considered relatively fire retardant and salt tolerant. The foliage is evergreen, and stems root as they trail. Cultivars include white-flowering selections under names such as 'Hybrid White', 'Snow White', and 'White Cloud'. Purple-flowering selections

are sold as 'African Queen', 'Nairobi Purple', and 'Tresco Purple'. **Zones 9 to 10**.

O. jucundum

o. juh-KUN-dum. Formerly *Dimorphotheca barberae*. A mounding, ¹/₂- to 2-foot tender perennial with gray-green leaves and 2-inch-wide, magenta-purple daisies with petals that are darker on the undersides. Warm-weather annual or tender perennial. **Zones 9 to 10**.

Ostrya

oss-TRY-ah. Birch family, Betulaceae.

This genus contains 8 to 10 species of deciduous trees from the woodlands of North and Central America, Europe, and Asia. They have simple, oval or lance-shaped leaves and male and female catkins on the same tree. Fruits with distinctive papery bracts identify these species, distinguishing them from the genus *Carpinus,* to which they are related. They are excellent performers in shady gardens.

HOW TO GROW

Very adaptable, growing in full sun to shade and almost any soil, except for wet sites, ostrya tolerates moderate drought and all urban conditions except road salt. Somewhat difficult to transplant, so choose small container-grown trees. Pest-free except for gypsy moths, which love it.

O. virginiana

o. ver-jin-ee-AH-nuh. IRONWOOD, HOP HORNBEAM. Forming a strong central leader and growing 30 to 40 feet tall and even wider

when situated in full sun, ironwood remains pyramidal and shorter when grown in shade. Its 2- to 5-inch-long, toothed leaves are pointed, light green ovals that feel like thin felt and turn golden yellow in fall. The unopened buds of the catkins provide winter interest but are obscured by new leaves when the buds expand and bloom. In summer, pale green clusters of hoplike, papery capsules hang from the undersides of the branches, adding interest, and the nuts they enclose provide food for wildlife. Like its relative hornbeam *(Carpinus caroliniana),* ironwood has extremely hard wood. Reddish, shredding bark decorates the trunks and branches of older trees, eventually becoming very dark on the lower trunk. This fine-textured, slow-growing tree works well as an understory tree in a woodland or shaded garden. Save this native species during development. From most of North America, except the extreme Southeast. **Zones 3 to 9**.

SIMILAR SPECIES

O. carpinifolia (European hop hornbeam) is hardy to **Zone 5** and is almost identical to the American species.

Oxalis

ox-AL-iss. Oxalis or Wood-sorrel family, Oxalidaceae.

Oxalis is a large, diverse genus of annuals and perennials (both hardy and tender) as well as a few shrubby species. Primarily native to Africa and South America, they are commonly called wood sorrels or simply oxalis. Plants have bulbous, rhizomatous, tuberous, or fibrous roots. While most species bear shamrocklike, 3-leaflet leaves, there are also wood sorrels with up to 20 or more leaflets. All have leaves with leaflets arranged in a palmate fashion. Many species have leaves that fold downward at night. The small flowers have five rounded petals and are solitary or borne in clusters (umbel-like cymes). Not surprising for a large genus — about 500 species belong here — *Oxalis* contains some attractive garden plants as well as some pesky weeds, including creeping wood sorrel *(O. corniculata),* and common or yellow wood sorrel *(O. stricta,* formerly *O. europaea).*

HOW TO GROW

Select a site in full sun to partial shade with sandy to gritty soil that is well drained. Outdoors, most

wood sorrels are happiest in Mediterranean-like climates, characterized by cool summers, mild winters, and alternating seasons of wet and fairly dry weather. (Plants tolerate dry soil in summer, but they are best with a little moisture.) Nevertheless, most are easy to grow elsewhere. Where summers are hot, look for a cool, north-facing site or one that receives shade during the hottest part of the day. Where winters are wet, grow them in raised beds or rock gardens with very well drained soil: wet feet in winter spells disaster. At the northern limits of their hardiness, protect plants over winter with a coarse mulch such as evergreen boughs, pine needles, or salt hay. The tuberous and bulbous species listed here need a rest period, and most are deciduous. (*O. regnellii,* for example, will keep its leaves over winter if grown indoors as a houseplant or can be allowed to dry out like the other species, as described below.)

To grow wood sorrels in containers, plant the tubers or bulbs in pots or bulb pans (shallow pots) at the beginning of their growing season — spring for the species listed here, except for spring-blooming *O. adenophylla,* which should be started in a cool greenhouse in fall. Soak the soil at potting time, then water very sparingly until leaves emerge and the plants begin growing actively. Keep the soil evenly moist and feed regularly throughout the growing season. Plants grow best in cool conditions, so protect them from the hottest sun of the day. In late summer or fall, gradually withhold water as the leaves

Ostrya virginiana

Oxalis bowiei

begin to die back. Store the bulbs or tubers — still in their pots — in completely dry soil in a cool (40° to 50°F), dry spot. Repot in spring. Propagate by separating the offsets or dividing the tubers in early spring.

O. adenophylla

o. ah-den-oh-FILL-uh. Wood Sorrel, Oxalis. A 4-inch-tall South American species that grows from a tuberous, scale-covered base with leaves that have 9 to 20 or more inversely heart-shaped leaflets. In late spring, bears solitary, 1-inch-wide funnel-shaped flowers that are pale purplish pink with white throats and darker purple-pink veins. **Zones 6 to 8.**

O. bowiei

o. BOH-wee-eye. Wood Sorrel, Oxalis. Formerly *O. purpurata* var. *bowiei*. An 8- to 10-inch-tall South African species that grows from tunicate bulbs and has leathery, cloverlike, three-leaflet leaves that are green above and sometimes purple below. Bears clusters (umbel-like cymes) of 3 to 12 funnel-shaped 1½-inch-wide flowers from summer to fall that are purple-pink to rose-red with green throats. **Zones 8 to 10.**

O. depressa

o. deh-PRESS-uh. Formerly *O. inops*. A bulbous South African species that reaches 4 inches in height and bears gray-green three-leaflet leaves that have triangular leaflets and sometimes dark spots. In summer, bears solitary, funnel-shaped, ³/₄-inch-wide, dark rose pink to purple-pink flowers that have yellow throats. **Zones 5 to 9.**

O. lasiandra

o. lah-see-AN-druh. A bulbous 5- to 12-inch-tall species from Mexico with green leaves that have 5 to 10 narrow, wedge-shaped to straplike leaflets. From summer to fall, bears umbels of 9 to 25 or more trumpet-shaped ³/₄-inch-wide flowers that are red or violet with a yellow throat. Plants produce a thick taproot that is covered with small scaly bulbils near the top. **Zones 7 to 10.**

O. purpurea

o. pur-PUR-ee-uh. Wood Sorrel, Oxalis. A variable 4-inch-tall bulbous South African species with three-leaflet leaves. Leaflets range from diamond shaped to rounded and dark green above, purple beneath. Solitary, funnel-shaped flowers, borne in summer to fall, are 1¼ to 2 inches across. They have a yellow throat and come in rose-purple, rose-pink, pale to deep violet, cream, and white. **Zones 9 to 10.**

O. regnellii

o. reg-NEL-lee-eye. Wood Sorrel, Oxalis. A 4- to 10-inch-tall South American species with scale-covered rhizomes. Bears three-leaflet leaves with triangular-shaped leaflets that are green above and burgundy on the undersides. Flowers, borne in three- to seven-flowered umbels, are ³/₈ to ³/₄ inch across and white or very pale pink in color. *O. r.* var. *triangularis* bears rich burgundy leaves and pale pink flowers. **Zones 7 to 10.**

O. tetraphylla

o. teh-trah-FILL-uh. Wood Sorrel, Oxalis, Good Luck Plant. Formerly *O. deppei.* A 6-inch-tall bulbous species from Mexico with leaves that have four leaflets that range from triangular to strap shaped and usually are marked with purple at the base. In summer, bears clusters (umbel-like cymes) of 4 to 12 funnel-shaped, ³/₄- to 1¼-inch-wide, red-purple to rich rose-pink flowers that have yellow-green throats. 'Alba' has a white triangle on the leaves and pink flowers. 'Iron Cross' has burgundy cross-shaped blotches at the bases of the leaflets and hot pink flowers. **Zones 7 to 10.**

O. versicolor

o. VER-sih-kuh-lor. Candycane Sorrel. A bulbous 3-inch-tall species from South Africa with three-leaflet leaves that have linear leaflets. From late summer to winter, bears solitary, funnel-shaped, ³/₄- to 1¼-inch-wide white flowers that are edged in either red or violet purple on the back. **Zones 9 to 10.**

Oxydendrum

ox-ee-DEN-drum. Heath family, Ericaceae.

Related to heaths, heathers, azaleas, rhododendrons, and other acid-loving plants, this genus con-tains only one species, a deciduous tree native to the woodlands and streambanks of eastern North America commonly called sourwood. It is a valuable landscape tree because of its unusual bloom time and outstanding fall color.

HOW TO GROW

Although sourwood will grow in full sun to partial shade, blooms more profusely and has better fall color when planted in sun. Likes moist, well-drained, fertile, acid soil. Somewhat drought tolerant, but keep it well watered in hot climates. Sensitive to air pollution. Branches sweep low to the ground; prune if desired. Usually problem-free.

O. arboreum

o. are-BORE-ee-um. Sourwood, Sorrel Tree. A tidy, summer-blooming tree, sourwood has a py-ramidal shape with low ascending branches and grows 25 to 35 or more feet tall and 15 to 20 feet wide. In midsummer this native is adorned with 10-inch-long, nodding clusters of creamy white, bell-shaped flowers. The flowers ripen to buff-colored seedpods, which are quite attractive from late summer through winter. The 4- to 8-inch-long, lance-shaped or oblong leaves are glossy dark green and turn showy shades of yellow, scarlet, and burgundy in early to midfall. Trunk bark is dark gray and deeply furrowed into blocks. This tree's shape makes it an excellent candidate for a small property, in a lawn, border, or foundation planting or grouped in a woodland setting. 'Chameleon' exhibits consistent fall color in various flaming shades. From eastern North America. **Zones 5 to 9.**

Oxydendrum arboreum

Oxydendrum arboreum

O

P

Pachysandra

pak-ih-SAN-druh. Box family, Buxaceae.

One of the ubiquitous ground covers in the eastern United States, *Pachysandra* species are excellent workhorse plants. Only two of the four or five species are seen in cultivation, and one, *P. terminalis,* is the most frequently grown. Pachysandras are native mostly to East Asia, with one species, *P. procumbens,* native to the Appalachian Mountains. They are deciduous or evergreen perennials. Leaves are up to 3 inches long and elliptical or oval. Flowers are individually tiny, off-white, and presented on short flower stalks, resembling stubby, worn-out, white bottlebrushes.

HOW TO GROW

Pachysandras require at least partial shade. They thrive in the filtered light of large, high-branched trees. Soil should be moisture retentive and slightly to strongly acid. Once established, pachysandras are extremely tolerant of neglect, and colonies will slowly spread to the limits of the suitable conditions. At their northern limit, they need to be sited out of strong winter sun.

P. procumbens

p. pro-KUM-benz. ALLEGHENY SPURGE. This species grows 8 to 12 inches tall and very slowly spreads as much as 2 to 4 feet. Leaves are a matte green with earth tones and become evergreen at the southern limit of the species' range. Spikes of pale creamy white or greenish white flowers appear before the new leaves. This is an attractive, underused, slow-

Pachysandra terminalis

growing woodlander appropriate as a small-scale ground cover. **Zones 5 to 9.**

P. terminalis

p. ter-min-AL-iss. PACHYSANDRA. If this plant were rare or difficult to grow, it would be highly sought after. But sometimes a plant is too successful, and pachysandra suffers low esteem because of overuse. It forms a dense, spreading, evergreen ground cover. Leaves are dark green. The tiny white flower spikes appear in spring. This species thrives in acid soil, shade, and woodland conditions in northern North America. 'Green Sheen' has glossy, almost varnished, foliage. 'Kingwood' has medium-green leaves with deeply cut teeth at the leaf tips. 'Silver Edge' bears gray-green foliage edged with creamy white; it is slow to establish and spread. **Zones 4 to 9.**

Paeonia

pay-OH-nee-uh. Peony family, Paeoniaceae.

Grown for their showy, often fragrant flowers, peonies are herbaceous perennials, shrubs, or subshrubs. About 30 species belong to the genus, most native from Europe to eastern Asia. Flowers are cup, bowl, or saucer

Pachysandra terminalis 'Variegata'

shaped. Single-flowered peonies have 5 to 10 petals surrounding a central boss, or cluster, of showy yellow or cream-colored stamens. Double-flowered forms either lack stamens altogether or have a few hidden among showy, sterile petal-like structures called staminodes. Plants bear handsome, deeply cut leaves.

HERBACEOUS PEONIES

Herbaceous peonies, which die to the ground each year, are the best known. They bloom from late spring to early summer, and their dark to bright green leaves remain attractive all season.

HOW TO GROW

Plant herbaceous peonies in full sun and average to rich, well-drained soil. They do not tolerate poorly drained soil. Plants flower, although less abundantly, in light shade. In the South (Zone 7, and especially Zone 8), summer heat and humidity are a problem, so look for a cool site with afternoon shade. Plants still may be short-lived or fail to bloom in the warmest parts of Zone 8. Select a site with care, because peonies are deep-rooted plants with thick, fleshy roots and almost woody crowns. They grow best if planted in a permanent location, and plants thrive for years without needing to be divided.

Peonies are commonly sold as bare-root plants, with three to five eye, or bud, divisions for planting

in mid- to late fall. Container-grown peonies can be planted in early spring. Peonies buried too deeply will not bloom: in northern zones, plant bare-root plants with the buds *no more than* 2 inches below the soil surface. In central portions of the country, 1 inch deep is fine, while in the South, even shallower planting is best. When in doubt, plant more shallowly. Feed plants annually each spring with a topdressing of well-rotted manure, compost, or a balanced organic plant food. Most peonies need staking, but single-flowered cultivars, especially those described as "strong stemmed," often stand without staking. Divide in late summer or early fall, either for propagation or to separate large overcrowded clumps.

P. hybrids

COMMON GARDEN PEONY. Most commonly cultivated peonies are hybrids that range from 1¹/₂ to about 3 feet in height and form handsome 3- to 4-foot-wide clumps. Hundreds of cultivars are available in colors from white to red, including pure white, ivory, cream, pale yellow, pale pink, rose pink, crimson, and maroon. Flowers may be single, semidouble, double, or Japanese type (with a ring or two of petals around a cluster of modified petal-like stamens and carpels). Peonies with a dense, rounded center are called "bombs" or "anemones." Early-, midseason-,

Paeonia hybrids

and late-blooming cultivars are available.

Early cultivars include 'America', single with red flowers and golden stamens; 'Bowl of Beauty', Japanese type with rose-pink outer petals and creamy white centers; 'Festiva Maxima', double with very fragrant white flowers flecked with red; 'Krinkled White', single with white crepe paper–textured petals and showy yellow stamens; 'Miss America', semidouble with white petals and gold stamens; 'Monsieur Jules Elie', double with fragrant rose-pink flowers; and 'Scarlett O'Hara', an early single with vibrant red flowers and yellow centers.

Midseason cultivars include 'Bowl of Cream', double with white flowers; 'Do Tell', Japanese type with pale pink outer petals and cream, pink, and rose-red centers; 'Kansas', double with red flowers; 'Mrs. F. D. Roosevelt', double with fragrant shell pink blooms; 'Pink Lemonade', anemone or bomb with pink outer petals surrounding a dense cluster of pink, cream, and yellow petals; 'Raspberry Sundae', anemone or bomb with pale pink outer petals and a dense center of darker pink petals rimmed with creamy white petals; and 'Seashell', a single with shell pink flowers.

Late cultivars include 'Nippon Beauty', Japanese type with dark red blooms; and 'Sarah Bernhardt', a double with fragrant shell pink blooms occasionally flecked with red. **Zones 3 to 8.**

P

P. lactiflora

p. lak-tih-FLOR-uh. COMMON PEONY. A parent of hybrid herbaceous peonies that reaches about 2 feet in height and bears fragrant, single 3- to 4-inch-wide flowers in early summer. Blooms are usually white but sometimes pink or red. **Zones 2 to 8.**

P. officinalis

p. oh-fih-shih-NAL-iss. COMMON PEONY, MEMORIAL DAY PEONY. A parent of today's hybrid herbaceous peonies that reaches 2 feet in height and bears red flowers in early summer. 'Rosea Superba' has double pink blooms; 'Rubra Plena', double red ones. **Zones 3 to 8.**

P. tenuifolia

p. ten-yew-ih-FOE-lee-uh. FERNLEAF PEONY. A 2-foot-tall species with finely divided, fernlike leaves and single, ruby red, 3-inch-

Paeonia tenuifolia

wide flowers from mid- to late spring. 'Rubra Plena' bears double flowers. **Zones 3 to 8.**

TREE PEONIES

Besides the clump-forming herbaceous perennials that make up most of this genus, *Paeonia* also includes several species (the number is under debate) of deciduous shrubs or subshrubs that have been interbred for many centuries. Highly prized for their spring blossoms that range from immense doubles to more delicate singles and deeply incised leaves that provide fall color, the woody forms are almost always sold as cultivars or hybrids, rather than as species.

HOW TO GROW

Give tree peonies a bed of neutral to slightly acid soil, well amended both wide and deep with organic matter. High dappled shade is best, particularly during midday, as blooms will "melt out" quickly in full sun. Some growers strongly recommend fall planting, about six weeks before the first expected frost date. The bud union should be about ³/4 inch underground. Mulch well, especially in fall if you live where hardiness may be borderline. After the first year or so, the deep root system makes these plants drought tolerant. Use them as specimens or in a herbaceous or shrub border. In spring, prune back to remove dead wood above swelling buds. Propagate by layering or by dividing mature plants.

CULTIVARS AND HYBRIDS

Tree peony species are used primarily for breeding, rather than as

Paeonia 'Joseph Rock'

ornamental garden plants, since they tend not to be cold hardy and have small flowers that are hidden in the foliage. *P. suffruticosa* has been the source of most large-flowered selections. *P. rockii*, which has maroon flares at the base of its white petals, is sometimes considered a separate species, sometimes a botanical variety of *P. suffruticosa*, and is often sold as 'Joseph Rock' or in double forms called "double rocks." Nurseries may specialize in either Chinese or Japanese hybrids (called moutan or sometimes mudan) and will argue strongly for their superiority over the other type. A good tree peony has strong stems that hold the flowers well above the foliage. These hybrids come in white, pink, red, and purple, and shapes can range from single through "thousand petal."

In recent years, European and American breeders have used *P. lutea* to add yellow to the color palette. Many of these cultivars have a lemon fragrance. 'Age of Gold', 'Golden Era', 'Golden Isles', and 'High Noon' are among the most popular. 'Gauguin' is sunset colored, its orange petals streaked with gold. **Zones 4 to 8.**

Pancratium

pan-KRAY-tee-um. Amaryllis family, Amaryllidaceae.

Commonly called sea lilies, *Pancratium* species are tender bulbs grown for their fragrant flowers, which resemble daffodils as well as their close relatives in the genus *Hymenocallis*. About 16 species belong here, all of which grow from tunicate bulbs and are native from the Mediterranean region to tropical Asia and western Africa. They bear basal leaves that

are linear to strap shaped. The flowers have six narrow, spreading petal-like tepals that are joined at the base. The tepals surround a cup that resembles the cup of a daffodil but is properly called a staminal cup because it is formed by six stamens that are fused at the base. (A close look at the flowers reveals the stamens protruding from the cup.) One difference between *Hymenocallis* species and *Pancratium* species is the fact that the latter produce numerous unwinged seeds in each ovary compartment, while the former produce two or sometimes up to eight seeds per compartment.

HOW TO GROW

Select a site in full sun or partial shade with rich, evenly moist, well-drained soil. Where they are hardy, plant the bulbs outdoors in late summer or early fall. In the North, plant the bulbs outdoors in late spring or early summer after the soil has warmed up. Either way, set the tips of the bulbs 6 to 8 inches below the soil surface — slightly deeper if you are trying to grow them outdoors year-round at

Pancratium maritimum

Panicum virgatum

the northern limit of their hardiness. In containers, plant bulbs with the necks just above the soil surface. Keep the soil evenly moist while the plants are growing actively, and feed container-grown specimens every other week with a dilute, balanced fertilizer. To overwinter the plants where they are not hardy, dig the bulbs after a light fall frost or when the foliage turns completely yellow. Try to avoid damaging the roots when digging. Set the bulbs upside down to dry them off (this ensures that moisture from the foliage will drip away from the bulbs). Store the bulbs in nearly dry peat moss or vermiculite in a cool (55° to 60°F), dry spot. Propagate by separating the offsets in spring or fall when the plants are dormant or by seeds.

P. maritimum

p. mah-RIT-ih-mum. S ea L ily. A 12-inch-tall species from the Mediterranean region that bears umbels of fragrant white 4-inch-wide flowers in late summer. **Zones 8 to 11**.

Panicum

PAN-ih-kum. Grass family, Poaceae.

The genus *Panicum* contains some 470 species of annual and perennial grasses with narrowly lance-shaped or linear-ovate leaves and airy, branched panicles of flowers in late summer and fall.

HOW TO GROW

Select a site with full sun and rich, evenly moist, well-drained soil. *P. virgatum,* the species most often grown as an ornamental grass, tolerates dry, sandy conditions as

well as boggy soil and also grows in light shade. Propagate by dividing the clumps in late spring or early summer or by sowing seeds.

P. virgatum

p. ver-GAH-tum. S witch G rass. A 3-foot-tall warm-season native North American prairie grass forming 2¹/₂- to 3-foot-wide clumps of fine-textured leaves topped by silvery or pinkish 4- to 8-foot-tall flowers. In fall, flowers turn whitish or buff-brown and foliage turns yellow, then brown. 'Haense Herms' turns orange-red in fall. 'Heavy Metal' has metallic blue-green leaves and good yellow fall color. **Zones 5 to 9**.

Papaver

pah-PAH-ver. Poppy family, Papaveraceae.

Although many plants are commonly called poppies, *Papaver* is the genus of the true poppies, which are grown for their showy, bowl- or cup-shaped flowers with silky, crepe paper–textured petals. Some 70 species of annuals, biennials, and perennials belong here. They bear simple to deeply cut, fernlike leaves, and their stems exude a milky latex when cut. Blooms come in hot colors — oranges, orange-reds, scarlet, hot pink, and yellow — as well as soft pink, pale yellow, and white. The flowers are followed by distinctive, rounded seed capsules.

HOW TO GROW

Give poppies full sun and average to rich, evenly moist, well-drained soil. Alpine poppy (*P. alpinum*) requires excellent drainage and is a good choice for rock gardens or

Papaver croceum

Papaver orientale cultivar

along the tops of low walls where it will get very good soil drainage. For all poppies, a site protected from wind is best, and in areas with hot summers, a spot with morning sun and afternoon shade provides beneficial heat protection. Both *P. alpinum* and *P. croceum* grow best in areas with cool nights and warm days and die out in midsummer in regions with hot, humid summers. Oriental poppy (*P. orientale*) goes dormant in midsummer after it flowers, so combine it with plants that cover the space it leaves. Clumps of *P. orientale* have deep roots and are happiest if left undisturbed, but they usually spread enough to need dividing every 5 years or so. Divide them in late summer to early fall, just as the new leaves are beginning to emerge from summer dormancy. Poppies self-sow, and self-sown seedlings are a good option for propagating short-lived perennials — *P. alpinum* and *P. croceum* — so let some seedpods ripen.

Poppies make fine cut flowers, but the stems need to be seared to prolong vase life: Cut them when the buds begin to open. Recut the stems once they are in the house, and immediately dip the tips into an inch or two of boiling water for a few seconds. Or sear the ends with a match. Stand the flowers in cold water for several hours before arranging. Sear the ends of the stems again if you cut them while arranging.

P. alpinum

p. al-PIE-num. A lpine P oppy. Short-lived 6- to 10-inch-tall perennial with a 4- to 6-inch-wide tuft of fernlike leaves. Bears cup-shaped 1¹/₂-inch-wide flowers in early to midsummer in white, yellow, orange, or red. **Zones 4 to 7**.

P. commutatum

p. kom-mew-TAH-tum. A 1¹/₂-foot-tall annual bearing 3-inch-wide, brilliant red flowers with black spots at the base of each petal in summer. Cool-weather annual.

P. croceum

p. KRO-see-um. I celand P oppy, A rctic P oppy. Formerly *P. nudicaule*. A 1- to 2-foot short-lived perennial, hardy in **Zones 2 to 8**, usually grown as a biennial or annual. Bears showy, 3- to 5-inch-wide flowers in spring and early summer in the full range of poppy colors. Hardy perennial, biennial, or cool-weather annual.

P. orientale

p. or-ee-en-TAL-ee. O riental P oppy. Clump-forming perennial producing 1-foot-tall mounds of deeply divided, coarse-looking foliage and spreading by rhizomes to form 2- to 3-foot-wide drifts. Bears brilliant red-orange flowers with purple-black centers on 2- to 4-foot-tall stems for a few weeks in early summer. Blooms usually are 4 to 6 inches wide, but improved cultivars bear flowers that can reach 8 inches or more across and come in a range of colors, including red, pale salmon, pink, white, and scarlet-orange. Cultivars include 'Glowing Rose' (deep pink), 'Helen Elizabeth' (salmon pink), 'Snow Queen' (white), and 'Turkenlouis' (ruffled, orange-red). **Zones 3 to 7**.

P. rhoeas

p. ROE-ee-as. F landers P oppy, C orn P oppy, F ield P oppy. A 2- to 3-foot annual with 3-inch-wide, bowl-shaped, single or double flowers. The species bears brilliant red blooms, but cultivars in pastel shades also are available. The popular Shirley Se-

P

Papaver rhoeas Shirley Series

ries poppies bear single, semi-double, or double blooms in the full range of poppy colors, with petals that lack black spots at the base. Cool-weather annual.

P. somniferum

p. som-NIF-er-um. OPIUM POPPY, BREAD POPPY. A 3- to 4-foot annual with blue-green leaves and bowl-shaped, 3- to 4-inch-wide flowers in shades of pink, mauve, white, or red. Double-flowered forms are available. The seeds of this species are the source of poppy seeds, which are used in breads and other confections. Cool-weather annual.

Parrotia

pah-ROE-tee-uh. Witch-hazel family, Hamamelidaceae.

This genus has only one species, a deciduous tree that hails from an area of the Caucasus Mountains near the Caspian Sea, where it sometimes forms dense forests with *Carpinus betulus* (European hornbeam).

HOW TO GROW
Plant in full sun to light shade and well-drained, humus-rich, slightly acid to alkaline soil. Tolerates drought and urban conditions once established. Does not tolerate wet sites. Most attractive if the lower branches are not pruned off. Protect the trunk from mechanical injury. Japanese beetles may be a problem. Performs well in the South.

P. persica

p. PER-sih-kuh. PERSIAN PARROTIA, PERSIAN IRONWOOD. An attractive specimen throughout the year, Persian parrotia is a single- or multi-stemmed, rounded or spreading, low-branched tree that matures to 30 to 40 feet tall and wide. The flowers of this unusual tree have no petals but consist of tiny, mopheadlike clusters of dark red stamens. They cover the bare branches in late winter, well before the leaves emerge, and are splendid when viewed up close, although they may go unnoticed from a distance. The leaves are reddish purple when young, maturing to glossy, dark green, 2- to 5-inch-long wedges. Fall color is spectacular, a mixture of gold, orange, and scarlet late in the season. The dark reddish brown bark on the trunk and main branches flakes off to reveal a mottled pattern of green, silver gray, and cream, which is especially striking in winter. Use as a specimen in a border or garden where it can be seen in winter. Mulch the ground or plant a ground cover under its low branches, which will shade out grass. 'Biltmore' exhibits excellent fall color. 'Pendula' forms a weeping mound. 'Vanessa' is columnar. From Iran. **Zones 5 to 9**.

Parthenocissus

par-then-oh-SIS-us. Grape family, Vitaceae.

"Boston ivy," "Virginia creeper," and "woodbine" are the most common names for this genus's two ornamental deciduous vines that are adept at ascending trees, walls, and cliffs. Plants climb both by weaving young stems among supporting objects such as fences and by affixing tendrils to branches or walls. Once they are climbing, they also may root from the stems and nodes and require no further means of support. *Parthenocissus* leaves are lobed (as in Boston ivy, *P. tricuspidata*) or compound, with five to seven

Parthenocissus quinquefolia

leaflets per leaf (as in Virginia creeper, *P. quinquefolia*). Both species are noted for exceptionally fine autumn colors.

HOW TO GROW
These plants are not particular as to soil, but it should be of at least average fertility and not subjected to periodic flooding. Climbing vines will have the best color if they are grown where they get at least a half day of sun.

P. quinquefolia

p. kwink-eh-FOE-lee-uh. VIRGINIA CREEPER. This eastern North American species grows to 50 feet and produces adhesive disks at the ends of the tendrils that can cling to any surface (including trees, fences, and walls). The leaves turn flaming red in early autumn, before most trees start to change color. **Zones 4 to 9**.

P. tricuspidata

p. try-kus-pih-DAH-tuh. BOSTON IVY. This Asian species is the

Parrotia persica

Parthenocissus tricuspidata

Parthenocissus quinquefolia

Passiflora caerulea

"ivy" of the Ivy League colleges, where it traditionally covers numerous campus buildings. The leaves, which grow to 10 inches long, overlap like shingles. **Zones 4 to 9.**

Passiflora

pass-ih-FLOR-ah.
Passionflower family,
Passifloraceae.

The genus *Passiflora* contains about 400 species, most tender evergreen vines that climb by tendrils. The plants are grown for their exotic-looking flowers that are made up of colorful tepals (petals and petallike sepals) surrounding a ring of showy filaments. At the center of each flower is a stalk containing a prominent ovary and stamens. Flowers are usually borne singly and are followed by egg-shaped, edible fruits. While most passionflowers are tropicals that only can be grown in greenhouses, a few species are hardy.
HOW TO GROW
Select a site in full sun or partial shade with average to rich, moist soil that is well-drained. Where marginally hardy, select a protected site. Passionflowers require a trellis or other support upon which to climb. In warm climates, they are large enough to grow on arbors or up trees. Prune plants as necessary in spring to direct their growth and keep them in bounds. Propagate by layering stems in spring or fall or by cuttings taken in summer.

P. caerulea
p. see-RUE-lee-uh. BLUE
PASSIONFLOWER. A vigorous

climber that attaches to supports by tendrils and can reach 30 feet in height. Native to Central and South America. Bears deeply lobed leaves and 3- to 4-inch wide blue-and-white flowers that are bowl-shaped from summer to fall. Flowers are followed by edible, but not particularly tasty, orange-yellow fruit that is 2^1/$_2$ inches long. 'Grandiflora' bears 6-inch-wide flowers. 'Constance Elliott' bears fragrant white blooms. **Zones 6 to 9.**

P. incarnata
p. in-kar-NAH-tuh. MAYPOPS. A vigorous climber native to the Southeastern United States that attaches to supports by tendrils and can reach 6 feet in height. Bears deeply lobed leaves and 3-inch-wide, lightly scented flowers that

Patrinia scabiosaefolia

are pale purple to white. Flowers are followed by egg-shaped, 2^1/$_2$-inch-long fruit. **Zones 6 to 8.**

Patrinia

pah-TRIN-ee-uh. Valerian
family, Valerianaceae.

Some 15 species belong to the genus *Patrinia*, all clump-forming perennials native to Siberia and Japan. They produce low mounds of

Paulownia tomentosa

rounded leaves that usually are deeply cut in a pinnate or palmate fashion. The mounds of foliage are topped in late summer by branched panicles of small cup-shaped yellow or white flowers that have five petal lobes.
HOW TO GROW
Select a site in full sun or partial shade with average to rich, moist but well-drained soil. Plants tolerate heat and humidity. They need staking to remain erect, or they can be allowed to sprawl. Clumps can grow for years without needing division but can be dug and divided in either spring or fall for purposes of propagation. They also self-sow: cut off faded blooms to reduce the number of self-sown seedlings.

P. scabiosaefolia
p. scah-bee-oh-see-FOE-lee-uh.
Clump-forming 1- to 2-foot-tall species forming 2-foot-wide mounds of leaves and branched 3- to 7-foot-tall clusters of yellow flowers in late summer and fall. **Zones 4 to 8.**

Paulownia

paw-LOW-nee-uh. Figwort
family, Scrophulariaceae.

This genus contains six species of trees from eastern Asia. All are tall specimens with showy flowers and foliage. In China and Japan, the

P

lightweight, beautifully grained wood of *P. tomentosa* is sacred and highly prized for making furniture and jewelry boxes.

HOW TO GROW

Plant in full sun to partial shade. Tolerates most soils, from acid to slightly alkaline, although it does best in rich, moist soil. Tolerates both dry and wet conditions, as well as road salt. Train when young to a single leader. Usually pest-free.

P. tomentosa

p. toe-men-TOE-suh. EMPRESS TREE, PRINCESS TREE. Naturalized in many places in eastern North America, this Asian tree grows rapidly into an irregular pyramidal or rounded shape, reaching 35 to 50 feet tall and wide. Leaves are 5 to 10 inches long, somewhat downy, and deep green. Varying from heart shaped to three or five lobed, they create a bold tropical texture. They drop over several weeks in fall with little change in color. Dramatic 12-inch spires of fragrant lavender or purple, yellow-striped, foxglovelike flowers bloom at all the branch tips in midspring, before the leaves emerge, creating an unforgettable sight. Trunk bark is smooth and gray. Clusters of pale green, egg-shaped, 1- to 2-inch capsules ripen to brown in fall and last into winter as pretty ornaments. They release numerous seeds, which readily germinate in undisturbed or barren sites, sometimes causing a weed-seedling problem. Use this fast-growing tree in a difficult site (it might grow 20 feet tall in 2 years), with the intention of re-

placing it with a longer-lived specimen. Or use it as a dense shade tree in an open area where its litter will not be problematic. Also valuable for reforestation and land-reclamation projects.

In Zones 5 and 6, empress tree dies to the ground in winter but regrows from the roots in spring, sending up 10- to 14-foot-tall stems with 30-inch-wide leaves. In warmer zones, many landscape designers deliberately create this effect by "stooling" the tree. From China and Korea. Flower buds and branch tips may winterkill in Zones 6 and 7. Cold hardy in Zones 6 to 9.

CULTIVARS

'Lilacina' has paler flowers without spots.

Paxistima

pax-ISS-tih-muh. Bittersweet family, Celastraceae.

These two species of low-growing evergreen shrubs, native to North America and related to *Euonymus,* make a useful woody ground cover for shady gardens, where their glossy, leathery leaves can bring some much-needed sparkle.

HOW TO GROW

Growing naturally on limy, stony ground, these ground covers tolerate low fertility and high pH but need organic amendments to ensure that the soil is moisture retentive and well aerated. They thrive in partial shade, although growth may be denser in full sun. Site at the edge of a woodland, use as a ground cover in dappled shade, or include in a rock garden. Easily

Paxistima canbyi

Pelargonium peltatum

propagated by division or by semiripe cuttings collected in summer.

P. canbyi

p. KAN-bee-eye. CLIFF GREEN. Native to mountains of Virginia and West Virginia, this species, also called rat stripper and mountain lover, rarely reaches a foot tall. A single plant may spread up to 5 feet, as the stems root where they touch the ground. The narrow, serrated, evergreen leaves range from 1/4 to 1 inch long on erect stems and may turn bronze in winter. Clusters of 1/4-inch greenish white flowers bloom in summer. Zones 3 to 7.

P. myrtifolia

p. mer-tih-FOE-lee-uh. OREGON BOXWOOD. Formerly *P. myrsinites*. This western U.S. native is more upright and usually taller than *P. canbyi*, up to 3 feet, with finely serrated 1-inch leaves. It bears 1/4-inch greenish white flowers in spring and summer. Zones 5 to 8.

Pelargonium

pel-are-GO-nee-um. Geranium family, Geraniaceae.

Pelargonium contains about 230 species of tender perennials, subshrubs, shrubs, and succulents, including the popular garden plants widely known as geraniums. Most species are native to South Africa, but gardeners mostly grow cultivated varieties that belong to one of several horticultural groups, including zonal geraniums, ivy-leaved geraniums, regal or Martha Washington geraniums,

and scented-leaved geraniums. In general, *Pelargonium* species bear rounded to deeply cut or fernlike leaves that often are hairy and/or aromatic. The five-petaled, star- or saucer-shaped flowers are carried in rounded clusters that resemble umbels. Most geraniums bloom from spring to frost; in frost-free regions, many bloom year-round.

HOW TO GROW

Give most geraniums full sun to light shade and rich, well-drained soil. A neutral to slightly alkaline pH is best. In areas with very hot summers, give them partial shade during the hottest part of the day. Regal geraniums grow best in areas with cool summers and prefer partial shade. Where hardy, grow geraniums outdoors as perennials. Most are hardy only from Zone 10 south, but some species survive winters in colder climates, especially in a protected site with dry winter mulch. In the North, grow geraniums as bedding plants replaced annually or as tender perennials, wintered over indoors. Sow seeds indoors about 14 to 16 weeks before the last spring frost date at 70° to 75°F. Germination takes 1 to 3 weeks. Or propagate by 4-inch cuttings taken in late summer for overwintering or from overwintered plants in winter or early spring to grow plants for the garden. Pinch plants to encourage branching. Water container-grown plants regularly, and feed at least monthly. Deadhead plants regularly.

To overwinter, bring container-grown plants indoors in fall, and keep them nearly dry in a bright, cool (40°F), frost-free place. Or keep them slightly warmer (50° to 55°F), and keep the soil barely

Pelargonium × hortorum

Pelargonium × hortorum 'Pink Parfait'

moist. To root cuttings, remove all but three leaves, and let the cuttings dry for about 6 hours to seal the stem ends. Then dust the ends with rooting powder and stick them in pots filled with sterilized sharp sand. Water thoroughly, then keep the cuttings on the dry side, but do not allow them to wilt. Pot in individual 3-inch pots once they have rooted, and treat them as you would overwintered plants. Repot and cut back overwintered plants in late winter, then feed twice a month beginning in early spring once plants are growing actively. Scented types are appropriate additions to herb gardens. Hummingbirds will visit geranium flowers.

IVY GERANIUMS

Cultivars of *P. peltatum* with fleshy, lobed, ivylike leaves and trailing stems that can reach 3 to 4 feet. They bear 1¹/₂- to 2-inch-wide clusters of single or double flowers in shades of pink, mauve, lilac, and white and are ideal for hanging baskets. Summer Showers Series plants can be grown from seeds and come in a range of colors. Tender perennials. **Zones 10 and 11**.

REGAL GERANIUMS

A group of cultivars commonly listed as *P. × domesticum* and also called Martha Washington geraniums. They bear rounded, sometimes lobed or toothed, leaves on 1- to 4-foot plants. Single or sometimes double flowers are carried in 2- to 4-inch-wide clusters and come in solid colors or combina-

tions of red, purple, pink, white, maroon, and orange. Angel geraniums, the result of a cross between regal geraniums and *P. crispum*, bear showy, regal-like flowers and sometimes scented leaves. Tender perennials. **Zones 10 and 11**.

SCENTED GERANIUMS

A mix of species and cultivars fall into the scented group, most of which bear small clusters of single, 1-inch-wide flowers. 'Mabel Grey' produces lemon-scented, deeply cut leaves and 2-inch-wide clusters of pale purple flowers. Nutmeg geranium, sold as *P. × fragrans* and *P.* 'Fragrans', bears gray-green, nutmeg-scented leaves and 1- to 1¹/₄-inch-wide clusters of white flowers. Coconut-scented geranium *(P. grossularioides)* has lobed, coconut-scented leaves; red stems; and small, star-shaped, magenta-pink flowers. Other scented geraniums featuring the fragrances that their names imply include apple geranium *(P. odoratissimum)*, peppermint geranium *(P. tomentosum)*, rose geranium *(P. graveolens* or *P.* 'Graveolens'), 'Lemon Rose', 'Lime', 'Peppermint Lace', and 'Prince of Orange'. Tender perennials. **Zones 10 and 11**.

ZONAL GERANIUMS

Commonly listed as *P. × hortorum*, these are better known as bedding or common geraniums. They are succulent-stemmed tender perennials with rounded leaves that may or may not exhibit the dark maroon band, or "zone," that gave these plants their name. Showy, 3- to 5-inch-wide clusters of 1-inch-wide flowers appear from early summer to frost. Single-flowered types bear five petals per flower and are the most common. They include such seed-grown cultivars as 'Big Red', 'Freckles' (pink dotted with white), and 'Neon Rose'. "Rosebud" geraniums bear double flowers with centers that do not open, like rosebuds. "Stellar" geraniums have

single, star-shaped flowers; 'Bird Dancer' bears dark-zoned, maplelike leaves and star-shaped pink flowers in 3-inch-wide clusters. Fancy-leaved geraniums fall here, too, and are grown primarily for their showy leaves. 'Mr. Henry Cox' has leaves marked with cream, yellow, green, purple-maroon, and red. 'Vancouver Centennial' has lobed gold leaves with maroon-brown center splotches and red-orange, star-shaped flowers. Tender perennials. **Zones 10 and 11**.

Pennisetum

pen-ih-SEE-tum. Grass family, Poaceae.

Pennisetums, also called fountain grasses, are grown for their feathery, bottlebrush or bushy, foxtail-like seed heads, which are produced over clumps of arching, linear leaves. The botanical name refers to the feathery flowers: it is from the Greek *penna*, meaning "feather," and *seta*, "bristle." The genus contains about 120 species of annuals and hardy and tender perennials.

HOW TO GROW

Give pennisetums full sun and average to rich, well-drained soil. *P. alopecuroides* tolerates light shade. Cut back the foliage in late winter before growth resumes. Propagate by division in spring or early summer or by seeds. Species self-sow prolifically and can easily become invasive. Cut off the seed heads of perennials before they begin to

Pennisetum setaceum

shatter in late fall and/or pull up seedlings regularly.

p. alopecuroides

p. al-oh-peh-kure-OY-deez. FOUNTAIN GRASS. Clump-forming, warm-season perennial grass with rounded mounds, 2 to 3 feet tall and wide, of narrow ¹/₂-inch-wide leaves. Bears bottlebrush-like pinkish to white flowers in midsummer, and clumps are 3 to 4 feet tall in bloom. Compact cultivars include 2- to 3-foot-tall 'Hameln', 8- to 10-inch-tall 'Little Bunny', and 1¹/₂-foot-tall 'Little Honey', which has silver-variegated leaves. 'Moudry' bears black-purple flowers and reseeds especially prolifically. **Zones 6 to 9; to Zone 5 with winter protection**.

P. setaceum

p. seh-TAY-see-um. FOUNTAIN GRASS. A tender, 3-foot-tall perennial, hardy from **Zone 9 south**, with plumelike, 1-foot-long, pinkish or purplish flower heads in late summer and fall. 'Burgundy Giant' reaches 5 feet and has purple-maroon leaves. 'Purpureum', also listed as 'Atropurpureum', bears purple leaves and red-pink flowers. Tender perennial, or grow as a warm-weather annual.

P. villosum

p. vil-LOW-sum. FEATHERTOP. A tender, 2-foot-tall perennial, hardy from **Zone 9 south**, with plumy, cylindrical, 4- to 5-inch-long, green or white flowers that mature to purplish seed heads. Tender perennial, or grow as a warm-weather annual.

Penstemon

PEN-steh-mun. Figwort family, Scrophulariaceae.

Primarily native to North and Central America, *Penstemon* species are perennials and subshrubs with linear to lance-shaped leaves and panicles of tubular or bell-shaped, two-lipped flowers in shades of lavender, purple, purple-blue, lilac-blue, pink, red, yellow,

Penstemon barbatus

Penstemon digitalis

and white. The 250 species in the genus are found in a wide range of habitats — cool, moist, western mountains; dry plains and deserts; and both dry and moist woodlands and prairies in the eastern half of the country.

HOW TO GROW

Give the penstemons listed here full sun to partial shade and rich, very well drained, evenly moist soil. They grow best in areas with cool summers; in areas with hot summers, select a site with shade in the afternoon. *P. digitalis* tolerates heat and humidity well. Many penstemons are short-lived or will not grow well outside their native range, so for best results with these plants, match the requirements of the species to the existing site and soil conditions in your garden. Water during dry weather. Where plants are marginally hardy, in late fall cover them with a dry winter mulch such as evergreen boughs or weed-free straw. Divide plants every 5 to 6 years to keep them

Penstemon smallii

vigorous. Propagate by dividing plants in spring, taking cuttings in spring or summer, or by seeds. The flowers attract hummingbirds.

P. barbatus

p. bar-BAY-tuss. Common Beardtongue, Beardlip Penstemon. A 1¹/2- to 4-foot-tall species native to the western United States and Mexico. Produces low 2-foot-wide mounds of semievergreen leaves topped by panicles of pendent, tubular, 1¹/2-inch-long flowers from early summer to fall. Blooms are red with tinges of pink. 'Albus', from 1¹/2 to 4 feet in height, bears white flowers. 'Coccineus' produces red flowers on 1¹/2-foot-tall plants. 'Elfin Pink' bears pink flowers on 1-foot-tall plants. **Zones 4 to 9.**

P. campanulatus

p. kam-pan-yew-LAY-tus. A tender, 1- to 2-foot perennial that bears loose racemes of bell-shaped, violet or rose-purple, 1¹/2-inch-long flowers in early summer. Tender perennial. **Zones 7 to 10.**

P. digitalis

p. dih-jih-TAL-iss. A 2- to 4-foot species native to the eastern and southeastern United States. Bears 1¹/2-foot-wide rosettes of shiny, semievergreen leaves topped by panicles of tubular to bell-shaped,

1-inch-long white flowers from early to late summer. 'Husker Red' has leaves that are maroon-red when young and white flowers tinged with pink. **Zones 2 to 8.**

P. hirsutus

p. her-SUE-tus. A 1¹/2- to 2¹/2-foot-tall subshrub native to the Northeast that produces low 1- to 2-foot-wide mounds of evergreen leaves. In summer, bears loose racemes of tubular- to funnel-shaped, 1- to 2-inch-long flowers with white throats that are tinged with lavender or pale purple on the outside. Dwarf *P. h.* var. *pygmaeus* reaches 4 inches in height, spreads from 4 to 6 inches, and bears maroon-purple–tinged leaves. **Zones 3 to 9.**

P. hybrids

A wide variety of hybrids with variable hardiness and adaptability are available. Most cultivars offered are hardy from **Zone 7 south** and best in gardens on the West Coast because of their preference for cool summers. Treat them as biennials or short-lived perennials in the East. Hybrids bear tubular, bell-shaped flowers in summer that are 1 to 2 inches long. Plants range from 1¹/2 to 2 feet tall and spread about 1 to 1¹/2 feet. 'Prairie Dusk' has purple blooms. 'Prairie Fire' bears bell-shaped crimson flowers. 'Rose Elf' has rose-pink flowers. All three cultivars are

hardy in **Zones 3 to 8.** 'Sour Grapes', hardy in **Zones 6 to 8**, bears purple-pink flowers with white throats.

P. pinifolius

p. pin-ih-FOE-lee-us. An evergreen subshrub with needlelike leaves that reaches 1¹/2 feet tall and spreads about as far. Bears loose racemes of scarlet tubular flowers in summer. **Zones 4 to 10.**

P. smallii

p. SMALL-ee-eye. Small's Penstemon. Shrubby 1¹/2- to 2-foot-tall perennial native to the eastern United States that spreads to about 2 feet. In late spring, produces spikes of tubular, 1¹/2-inch-long rose- to lilac-pink flowers that have white-striped throats. **Zones 5 to 9.**

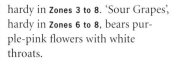

Pentas

PEN-tas. Madder family, Rubiaceae.

Of the 40 or so species of perennials, biennials, subshrubs, and shrubs that belong to this genus, one is a tender perennial grown for its showy flowers in shades of pale pink, mauve, magenta, purple-red, lilac, or white. Commonly called star clusters, *Pentas* species bear hairy, ovate or lanceolate leaves and rounded or

Penstemon 'Garnet'

Pentas lanceolata

flat clusters of tubular to bell-shaped flowers, each with five lobes, or "petals." They are native to tropical Africa, the Arabian Peninsula, and Madagascar.

HOW TO GROW

Star clusters thrive in full sun and rich, well-drained soil. They are hardy in **Zones 10 and 11**, where they can be grown outdoors year-round. In the North, grow them as bedding plants replaced annually or as tender perennials over-wintered indoors. Sow seeds in-doors 8 to 10 weeks before the last spring frost date at 60° to 65°F. *Pentas* species also are easy to grow from cuttings taken any time of year. Water during dry weather, and feed pot-grown plants monthly in summer. To over-winter, either take cuttings or keep plants in containers. Gradually withhold water in fall; set them in a bright, cool (55° to 60°F) spot; and keep plants on the dry side over winter. Prune to shape plants in late winter or early spring: cut them back hard, if necessary. Or use overwintered plants as stock plants and take cuttings. Star clus-ters make showy additions to beds and borders and fine container plants. Their flowers attract hum-mingbirds.

P. lanceolata

p. lan-see-oh-LAH-tuh. STAR CLUSTER, STAR FLOWER, EGYPTIAN STAR CLUSTER. A woody-based perennial or sub-shrub that can reach 6 feet in frost-free climates but generally is from 1 to 2 feet tall in northern gardens. Bears rounded, 3- to 4-inch-wide clusters of ½-inch-wide flowers. Tender perennial. **Zones 10 and 11**.

Perilla

peh-RIL-lah. Mint family, Lamiaceae.

Six species of annuals native from India to Japan belong to the genus *Perilla*. Closely related to coleus *(Solenostemon scutellarioides)*, these plants also are grown for their showy, often richly colored foliage. Like coleus, they bear erect spikes of insignificant, two-lipped flowers. One species is a vigorous annual grown as a foliage plant for the lush, tropical air it adds to gar-dens.

HOW TO GROW

Give perillas full sun to partial shade and very rich, moist, well-drained soil. Sow seeds indoors in individual pots 10 to 12 weeks be-fore the last spring frost date at 65° to 70°F. Or sow outdoors after the last frost date. When sowing, just press the seeds onto the soil sur-face, as light is required for germi-nation. Perillas also can be propa-gated by cuttings, which can be used to overwinter the plants in-doors. Or cut back plants, and pot them up for overwintering. Plants self-sow with abandon and can be-come invasive.

P. frutescens

p. fru-TESS-enz. BEEFSTEAK PLANT, CHINESE BASIL, FALSE COLEUS. A 1- to 3-foot annual with broadly ovate, deeply toothed leaves and 6-inch-tall spikes of tiny white flowers. The species has green leaves, but 'Atropurpurea' bears deep red-purple leaves and *P. f.* var. *crispa* (also listed as *P. nankinensis*) bears purple to bronze leaves with frilled, deeply toothed margins. Warm-weather annual.

Perovskia

per-OFF-skee-uh. Mint family, Lamiaceae.

Seven species of subshrubs, all na-tive to central Asia, belong to the genus *Perovskia*, one of which is a popular plant for perennial gar-dens. Commonly called Russian sage or simply perovskia, it pro-duces airy spikes of tiny lavender-blue flowers that create a cloudlike haze of color above silver- to gray-green, deeply cut leaves and silvery stems.

HOW TO GROW

Select a site in full sun with very well drained, poor to average, sandy or loamy soil. Plants grow well in dry soil and in alkaline soil and are good choices for seaside gardens. Well-drained soil is espe-cially important in winter. Newly planted specimens take a year or two to become established. After the first hard frost of fall, cut plants to within 1 foot of the ground. From the colder portions of Zone 5 north, plants are killed to the ground over winter but resprout in spring. In northern zones, cover them with evergreen boughs or straw over winter. For best results, do not divide Russian sage, because the woody crowns are hard to separate successfully. Propagate by taking cuttings from shoots that emerge from the base of the plants in spring or early summer. Or pot up small offsets that appear on the outside of es-tablished clumps.

P. atriplicifolia

p. ah-trih-plih-sih-FOE-lee-uh. RUS-SIAN SAGE. A 3- to 5-foot-tall subshrub, spreading from 3 to 4 feet, with silvery, deeply cut, gray-green, aromatic leaves. Bears showy panicles of small tubular vi-olet-blue flowers from late sum-mer to fall. 'Blue Spire' is a heavy-flowering selection with violet-blue flowers on 3-foot plants. 'Filagran' has very finely cut leaves. **Zones 5 to 9; to Zone 4 with winter pro-tection.**

Persicaria

per-sih-KARE-ee-uh. Buckwheat family, Polygonaceae.

Commonly known as knotweeds or smartweeds, *Persicaria* species

Perilla frutescens 'Atropurpurea'

Perovskia atriplicifolia

P

Phalaris arundinacea var. *picta*

are native to North America, Europe, Asia, and North Africa, but only one, *P. arundinacea*, is commonly used in gardens as a ground cover. Ribbon grass forms a thick mass of stems and leaves that can grow up to several feet tall. Several variegated forms have been selected over the centuries, and these are the ones most commonly seen in gardens. Plants are strongly stoloniferous and spread vigorously. In some parts of the country, ribbon grass is an invasive pest.

HOW TO GROW

Ribbon grass grows well in a number of difficult sites. It is excellent for erosion control in moist to nearly dry soils and thrives if periodically flooded. It will grow in full sun provided there is adequate moisture and will tolerate partial shade. Try planting it near the entrance to a driveway, especially if this is a moist or poorly drained area. The light green and white foliage of the variegated forms will catch car headlights at night, and the area can be mowed in midseason to encourage a flush of new growth. This is also an excellent choice for an area that needs to be seasonally cleared, perhaps for snow removal.

P. arundinacea

p. ah-run-din-AY-see-uh. RIBBON GRASS. This species spreads by underground runners. It will move quickly through rich, well-drained soils but will slow down in heavy wet soils. Plant it with care; once established, it is difficult to eradicate. At all times, ribbon grass

roots should be controlled, either by a physical barrier (such as a path, roadway, or watercourse) or by buried obstacles. *P. a.* var. *picta* has green-and-white foliage. 'Feesey' ('Feesey's Variety') is a notoriously vigorous spreading selection with narrow foliage that is pinkish as the new leaves emerge. **Zones 3 to 9.**

Phaseolus

phah-zee-OH-lus. Pea family, Fabaceae.

The best-known plants in this genus of 20 species of annuals and perennials are commonly grown in vegetable gardens — green beans and lima beans. *Phaseolus* species are primarily climbing plants with twining stems, three-part leaves, and clusters of pea-shaped flowers. One species is grown both as an ornamental for its showy flowers and as a food plant for its edible pods and seeds.

HOW TO GROW

Give scarlet runner bean (*P. coccineus*) full sun and average to rich, moist but well-drained soil. Plants require a trellis or strings to climb or can be trained over shrubs. They thrive in heat and humidity but stop setting seeds when temperatures are over 90°F. Sow seeds indoors in individual pots 4 to 6 weeks before the last spring frost date at 60° to 70°F. Germination takes 1 to 2 weeks. Or sow outdoors 2 weeks after the last frost date. Water plants regularly in dry weather. Keep beans picked to encourage new flowers to form.

They are most tender when harvested at 4 inches or less. Plants produce tuberous roots, and in areas where the ground doesn't freeze, they can be killed back by frost but will resprout from the roots. In addition to being handsome climbers, scarlet runner beans attract hummingbirds, butterflies, and bees to the garden.

P. coccineus

p. kok-SIN-ee-us. SCARLET RUNNER BEAN. A twining climber that can reach 8 to 12 feet in a single season. Loose racemes of 1¼-inch-wide scarlet flowers appear from early summer to frost. 'Albus' bears white flowers. 'Hammond's Dwarf' is a 1½-foot-tall, non-climbing cultivar suitable for pots. Warm-weather annual or tender perennial.

Phellodendron

fell-oh-DEN-dron. Rue family, Rutaceae.

About 3 to 10 very similar species of deciduous trees belong to this genus, which resemble *Ailanthus* (tree of heaven). The compound leaves are opposite each other and are aromatic when crushed or broken.

Phaseolus coccineus

HOW TO GROW

Plant in full sun and moist, well-drained, acid to alkaline soil. Tolerates some drought. Performs well in urban conditions only if space is plentiful. Prune during dormancy when young to develop a single trunk with well-spaced, high branches. Fruits of female trees can cause a weed-seedling

Phellodendron amurense

Philadelphus coronarius

problem; plant a fruitless form. Usually pest-free, but leaf scorch may develop in hot, dry situations.

P. amurense

p. ah-murr-EN-see. AMUR CORK TREE. This tough tree gets more picturesque as it matures into a wide-spreading or rounded, open-branched specimen, 30 to 45 feet tall and wide. It has a stout central trunk with deeply furrowed, gray-brown, corky bark, from which radiate a few sturdy horizontal branches studded with orange-yellow twigs. The boldly attractive compound leaves are 10 inches long and consist of 9 to 13 smooth-edged, oval, 2- to 4-inch-long leaflets. They are glossy dark green with lighter undersides and turn bright yellow in fall. The greenish white spring flowers are inconspicuous. The 1/2-inch, round, black fruits drop in large quantities, making a mess on walkways and roads. Seedless forms are preferred as street trees or in groomed lawns and parks. From western Europe and eastern Asia. **Zones 4 to 7.**

CULTIVARS AND SIMILAR SPECIES

'Macho' is upright and vase shaped, growing 25 to 30 feet tall; fruitless. 'Shademaster' is a fruitless form that grows 30 to 35 feet tall. *P. a.* var. *sachalinense* has less corky bark and is hardy in **Zones 3**

to 7. 'His Majesty' is seedless and has an open-branched vase shape.

Philadelphus

fill-uh-DEL-fuss. Saxifrage family, Saxifragaceae.

The heady orange-blossom scent of these old garden favorites is second only to that of lilacs in evoking nostalgia. This genus comprises 60 species of shrubs, commonly known as mock oranges, native to North America and from eastern Europe to East Asia. The origins of many hybrids and cultivars are somewhat unclear, but all offer gardeners an array of single and double white flowers, blooming in early summer with slightly varying scents.

HOW TO GROW

Mock orange blooms best in full sun but will grow in partial shade. Although quite adaptable to varied pH and drought, like most shrubs it does best in organically enriched soil that both retains moisture and drains well. Because it can become ragged looking, it benefits from regular judicious pruning to shape and remove unproductive branches. Propagate from seeds or softwood cuttings, treated with hormones, in early to midsummer.

P. 'Buckley's Quill'

A compact selection to 6 feet tall and 4 feet wide. The unusual flowers have about 30 quill-like petals. **Zones 4 to 7.**

P. coronarius

p. kor-oh-NAIR-ee-us. SWEET MOCK ORANGE. From southeastern Europe and Asia Minor, this species grows stiffly upright to 10 to 12 feet high and wide and slightly rounded. The fragrant

Philadelphus coronarius

Phlomis tuberosa (see page 300)

late-spring flowers have four petals and four sepals and bloom in racemes. For summer interest, look for yellow-foliaged 'Aureus' or 'Variegatus', which has leaves edged with white. **Zones 4 to 8.**

P. 'Galahad'

This relatively new selection is about 5 feet tall with a rounded habit. The fragrant single flowers have prominent yellow centers. **Zones 5 to 8.**

P. × lemoinei

p. × lem-WON-ee-eye. These hybrids grow 4 to 5 feet tall and wide with arching branches. The 2-inch leaves are tapered and sparsely toothed. Single cup-shaped, 1-inch flowers bloom in groups of three to five in midsummer. Popular selections include 'Belle Etoile' (wide-spreading habit and single flowers more than 2 inches across with pale purple markings in the center), 'Innocence' (upright to 10 feet, leaves mottled yellow), and 'Silver Showers' (rounded form, profuse strawberry-scented flowers). **Zones 5 to 8.**

P. microphyllus

p. my-kro-FILL-us. LITTLELEAF MOCK ORANGE. Native to the southwest United States, this species is 4 feet tall and bears 1/2-inch-long leaves and 1-inch, sweetly scented flowers. Needs full sun. **Zones 6 to 9.**

P. 'Natchez'

A cultivar with especially profuse flowering. **Zones 5 to 8.**

P. 'Snowgoose'

A cold-hardy selection with profuse, fragrant flowers on arching branches. **Zones 4 to 7.**

P. × virginalis

p. × ver-jin-AL-iss. An old-fashioned favorite growing 10 feet high and wide with fragrant double flowers. Most of the named selections are smaller. They include 'Bouquet Blanc' (6 feet tall, with a name that reflects its mix of garden scents), 'Minnesota Snowflake' (double flowers in racemes of up to seven, hardy to **Zone 4**), and 'Virginal' (to 10 feet tall and 8 feet wide with double, very fragrant flowers). **Zones 5 to 8.**

P

Phlomis

FLOW-mis. Mint family,
Lamiaceae.

Four-sided stems and dense
whorls, or tiers, of tubular, two-
lipped flowers characterize
Phlomis species. Sometimes referred to as Jerusalem sages, these
are somewhat sagelike perennials,
shrubs, and subshrubs native from
Europe and northern Africa to
Asia. Leaves are lance shaped to
ovate, gray-green in color, and often covered with hairs. About 100
species belong to the genus.

HOW TO GROW

Select a site in full sun with average to rich, well-drained soil. *P.
russeliana* will grow in light shade,
and in the South, shade during the
hottest part of the day is best for
all species. Plants are fairly
drought tolerant and also good
choices for seaside gardens, as they
tolerate salt. In zones where plants
are not killed to the ground over
winter, prune to shape immediately after flowering. Propagate by
dividing the clumps in spring or
fall, by cuttings of shoots taken in
summer, or by seeds.

P. fruticosa

p. fru-tih-KOH-suh. JERUSALEM
SAGE. A mounding 3- to 4-foot-
tall shrub that spreads from 4 to 5
feet. Bears gray-green leaves that
are woolly underneath. Erect
stems have dense whorls of golden
yellow 1¼-inch-long flowers that
appear from early to midsummer.
Plants are killed to the ground
north of Zone 7 and behave like
perennials. **Zones 4 to 8.**

P. lanata

p. lan-AY-tuh. This dense shrub
from Greece forms a mound
about 20 inches tall and 30 inches
wide and is a good choice for a
rock garden. The 1-inch leaves
have deep veins and a pebbly texture. Half-inch golden summer
flowers are covered with brown
hairs. **Zones 8 to 10.**

P. russeliana

p. rus-el-ee-AH-nuh. JERUSALEM
SAGE. A 3-foot-tall perennial
with 3-foot-wide clumps of hairy,
ovate leaves. Bears erect stems
with dense whorls of butter yellow, hooded, 1- to 1½-inch-long
flowers from late spring to early
fall. 'Edward Bowles', a hybrid between this species and *P. fruticosa*,
bears large gray-green leaves and
whorls of sulphur yellow 1¼-inch-

Phlox divaricata

long flowers in early to midsummer. **Zones 4 to 9.**

P. tuberosa

p. too-ber-OH-suh. A 4- to 5-foot-tall
perennial that produces small tubers on its roots and spreads to
form 3- to 4-foot-wide clumps.
Bears whorls of purplish pink ¾-
to 1-inch-long flowers in summer.
Zones 5 to 8.

Phlox

FLOX. Phlox family,
Polemoniaceae.

This well-known genus contains
70 species, including a variety of
handsome hardy perennials, popular annuals, and a few shrubs.
Nearly all are native North American wildflowers — one species is
from Siberia. They bear showy,
rounded clusters of flowers. The
individual blooms have a slender
tube at the base, an abruptly flared
and flattened face, and five lobes,
or "petals." Leaves are simple and
linear to ovate. The name *Phlox* is
from the Greek word for flame, a
reference to the fact that many
species bear hot-colored flowers.
Blooms come in crimson-red, ma-

Phlox divaricata

genta-pink, white, pale pink, lavender, lavender-blue, and purple.

HOW TO GROW

There are phlox suitable for sun
and shade and a wide range of soil
conditions. The most commonly
grown perennial species can be divided into three groups based on
both culture and bloom time.

SPRING/SUN

Give spring-blooming *P. bifida*, *P.
douglasii*, and *P. subulata* full sun
and average to rich, well-drained
soil. *P. bifida* will grow in poor,
very well drained soil. In areas
with hot, dry summers, dappled
afternoon shade is best. All three
species thrive for years without
needing to be divided unless they
outgrow their space, die out in the
centers of the clumps, or appear to
be less vigorous. Propagate by di-

viding plants in spring or by taking cuttings in early to midsummer of new shoots that arise near
the base of the plant.

SPRING/SHADE

P. divaricata and *P. stolonifera* both
thrive in light to full shade in a site
with rich, evenly moist, well-
drained soil. Both spread into
broad clumps via creeping stems
that root where they touch the
soil; *P. stolonifera* spreads more
quickly and widely than *P.
divaricata*. *P. divaricata* may be
disfigured by powdery mildew;
keep the soil evenly moist and thin
out the stems to help prevent this
disease. These species need dividing only if they outgrow their
space. Propagate by dividing
plants in spring after the flowers
fade, by digging up rooted

Phlox paniculata

plantlets that appear, or by taking cuttings in spring or early summer from shoots that arise near the base of the plant. Both self-sow.

SUMMER

Summer-blooming *P. carolina*, *P. maculata*, and *P. paniculata* all thrive in full sun or partial shade and rich, deeply prepared, evenly moist soil. All are best in areas with relatively cool summers. None tolerate drought. In southern zones, a site with light shade during the hottest part of the day is best. Feed plants in spring with a topdressing of compost or well-rotted manure. Deadhead spent flowers to prolong bloom and prevent self-sowing. (Named cultivars do not come true from seed, and seedlings, which generally have unattractive magenta-pink flowers, will overwhelm improved cultivars. Rogue out seedlings that do appear.) Tall phlox, especially *P. paniculata*, usually require staking. Dig and divide all of these species every 2 to 3 years in fall or spring to keep them vigorous. Propagate by division or by taking cuttings in spring or early summer from shoots that arise near the base of the plant.

Powdery mildew is a problem on *P. paniculata*, causing large white blotches on the leaves, which eventually drop off. To prevent this, select a site with good air circulation, plant resistant species and cultivars (both *P. carolina* and *P. maculata* resist this disease), thin stems in spring so air can circulate through the clumps, and keep plants well watered during dry spells. Clean up and destroy all mildew-infected plant debris in late summer. To prevent the disease, spray wettable sulfur on the foliage weekly once the first patch of white appears on the leaves.

P. bifida
p. BIFF-ih-duh. CLEFT PHLOX, SAND PHLOX. Mounding 6- to 8-inch-tall perennial that spreads as far. Bears needlelike, evergreen leaves and fragrant, star-shaped, $^3/_4$-inch-wide, lavender to white flowers with deeply cleft petal ends in spring. **Zones 4 to 8.**

P. carolina
p. kare-oh-LIE-nuh. CAROLINA PHLOX, THICK-LEAVED PHLOX. A 3- to 4-foot-tall perennial that spreads from 1$^1/_2$ to 2 feet. Features glossy oval leaves and clusters of purple to pink $^3/_4$-inch-

wide flowers in summer. **Zones 4 to 9.**

P. divaricata
p. dih-vair-ih-KAH-tuh. WILD BLUE PHLOX, WOODLAND PHLOX. A 10- to 14-inch-tall woodland native that spreads to 2 feet or more and has semievergreen leaves. Bears clusters of fragrant lavender, pale violet, or white flowers in spring. 'Clouds of Perfume' has especially fragrant pale lavender-blue flowers. 'Fuller's White' has white flowers. 'Louisiana Purple' bears purple flowers with magenta eyes. **Zones 3 to 9.**

P. douglasii
p. doug-LASS-ee-eye. DOUGLAS'S PHLOX. Mounding 3- to 8-inch-tall evergreen perennial that spreads to 1 foot. Bears white, lavender, or pink $^1/_2$-inch-wide flowers singly or in very small clusters from late spring to early summer. 'Crackerjack' produces magenta-red blooms on 5-inch plants. **Zones 4 to 8.**

P. drummondii
p. drum-MON-dee-eye. ANNUAL PHLOX, DRUMMOND PHLOX. A much-hybridized, 4- to 18-inch-tall annual with clusters of purple, lavender, salmon, pink, or red, single or double blooms that are 1 inch wide. Thrives in cool weather and dies out in heat and humidity. Dwarf Beauty Series plants are 8 inches tall; 'Dolly Mix', 4 inches tall. For cut flowers, look for taller cultivars, such as 1$^1/_2$- to 2-foot-tall 'Tapestry'. Cool-weather annual.

P. maculata
p. mak-yew-LAH-tuh. WILD SWEET WILLIAM, MEADOW PHLOX. An erect 2- to 3-foot-tall perennial that forms 1$^1/_2$-foot-wide clumps. Bears glossy leaves and elongated clusters of fragrant, $^3/_4$- to 1-inch-wide mauve-pink flowers in early to midsummer. 'Miss Lingard' (sometimes listed under *P. carolina*) has white flowers. 'Omega' is white with a lilac eye, and 'Rosalinde' is rose-pink. **Zones 4 to 8.**

P. paniculata
p. pan-ick-yew-LAH-tuh. GARDEN PHLOX. A popular, heavily hybridized 3- to 4-foot-tall perennial that forms 2- to 3-foot-wide clumps. Bears rounded clusters of fragrant $^1/_2$- to 1-inch flowers in summer to early fall. Many cultivars are available with pale to rose-pink, orange-red, crimson,

Phormium tenax

purple, lilac, or white flowers. Bicolor blooms are also available. Several cultivars that resist powdery mildew have been developed, including 'David' (white), 'Katherine' (lavender), 'Pax' (white), and 'Sandra' (scarlet). 'Bright Eyes' is a popular compact selection from 2 to 2$^1/_2$ feet tall with pink flowers. 'Nora Leigh' has white-edged leaves and pale lilac flowers. **Zones 3 to 8.**

P. stolonifera
p. stow-lahn-IF-er-uh. CREEPING PHLOX. A 4- to 6-inch-tall perennial spreading by stolons to form 1- to 2-foot-wide drifts. Bears loose clusters of pink, lilac-blue, or white flowers in spring. Cultivars include 'Blue Ridge' (lilac-blue), 'Bruce's White' (white), and 'Pink Ridge' (mauve-pink). **Zones 3 to 8.**

P. subulata
p. sub-yew-LAH-tuh. MOSS PHLOX, CREEPING PHLOX, MOSS PINK. Ground-hugging 2- to 6-inch-tall perennial that forms 1$^1/_2$- to 2-foot-wide mats. Has evergreen, needlelike leaves

and bears masses of $^1/_2$- to 1-inch flowers directly atop the leaves in mid- to late spring in shades of lavender, purple, pink, or white. Many cultivars with solid and bicolor blooms are available. 'Apple Blossom' has pale lilac-pink blooms with darker eyes. 'Blue Hills' has dark purple-blue flowers with notched petals. 'Fort Hill' bears dark pink blooms. 'Snowflake' features white blooms. **Zones 2 to 9.**

Phormium
FOR-mee-um. Agave family, Agavaceae.

This genus of tender perennials contains two species, both native to New Zealand, grown for their dramatic grassy or irislike clumps of sword-shaped leaves, each folded lengthwise in a V. They bear erect panicles of small flowers in summer. The Maori traditionally used fiber from the leaves in basket making, and the botanical name is from the Greek *phormos*, meaning "basket." The common

P

name New Zealand flax also refers to this use.

HOW TO GROW

Give these plants full sun and rich, moist, well-drained soil. Where hardy, generally from **Zone 9 south**, grow them outdoors as perennials. In areas where they are marginally hardy, select a sheltered, south-facing site and protect plants with a thick layer of dry mulch such as salt hay or weed-free straw over winter. Or grow plants in tubs or large containers and overwinter them indoors in a bright, cool (45° to 50°F) spot. Most garden-ers start plants from divisions, which is the only way to acquire the choice cultivars. Use phormiums as specimen plants and for vertical accents in contain-ers. Set pot-grown plants on ter-races, or sink them to the rim in garden soil.

P. tenax

p. TEN-ax. NEW ZEALAND FLAX. A tender, clump-forming perennial with leaves that range from 3 to 9 feet long and clusters of dark red, 2-inch-long flowers in summer. The species bears green leaves with red or orange edges. 'Bronze Baby' is a 2- to 3-foot plant with arching bronze leaves. 'Dazzler' reaches 3 feet and bears arching, bronze-maroon leaves with red and pink stripes. 'Sun-downer' reaches 6 feet and has leaves striped in bronze, green, and rose-pink. Tender perennial. **Zones 9 and 10.**

Photinia

foe-TIN-ee-uh. Rose family, Rosaceae.

A genus of about 40 species of de-ciduous and evergreen shrubs and trees native to East Asia, grown widely throughout the South for their colorful new foliage and ber-ries. They are closely related to hawthorn (*Crataegus*) and fire-thorn (*Pyracantha*) and have similar white midspring flower clusters. Some gardeners find the scent of the blossoms unpleasant and prune them off to stimulate new colorful leaves.

HOW TO GROW

Give photinia fertile, well-drained soil in full sun or partial shade. *P. villosa* prefers acid soil. Photinia is often defoliated by leaf spot in hu-mid climates but is otherwise a tough plant, most commonly used as a hedge or screen. Prune off ex-uberant new growth that spoils its shape. Propagate with cold-stratified seeds or root semiripe cuttings in summer.

P. × fraseri

p. × FRAY-zer-eye. An evergreen hy-brid growing 15 feet tall and wide. New coppery growth lasts up to a month, followed by midspring clusters of white flowers to 6 inches across. Berries are rare. 'Birmingham' has especially red new growth; 'Indian Princess' grows more slowly and has smaller leaves. Once on the verge of over-

Photinia × fraseri

Phygelius aequalis

use in the South, this species has declined in popularity because leaf spot is almost inevitable. **Zones 7 to 10.**

P. glabra

p. GLAY-bruh. JAPANESE PHO-TINIA. Smallest of the ever-greens, usually less than 12 feet tall, with smaller leaves that emerge red. The early-summer flower panicles, 4 inches across, are fol-lowed by red berries that turn black. Cultivars include 'Rosea Marginata' (leaves marbled with gray, white, and pink), 'Rubens' (especially red new leaves), and 'Variegata' (new leaves emerge pink, then turn green with white margins). **Zones 8 and 9.**

P. serrulata

p. seh-rue-LAY-tuh. CHINESE PHOTINIA. Formerly *P. serrati-folia*. Easily 25 feet tall and 16 feet

wide and often larger, this species is too big for most home land-scapes. The evergreen leaves, 4 to 8 inches long, remain bronzy purple as the flowers unfold in mid-spring, then turn shiny dark green. They are highly resistant to leaf spot. Bright red round fruits, 1/4 inch across, can remain from late summer through spring. **Zones 6 to 9.**

P. villosa

p. vil-OH-suh. ORIENTAL PHO-TINIA. A multistemmed decidu-ous shrub, to 15 feet tall and about 10 feet wide, that can be trimmed as a tree. Finely toothed leaves 1 1/2 to 3 inches long emerge bronzy red, turn dark green, then color yellow to orange-red or scarlet in fall. The round red fall fruits are popular with birds. Prone to fire blight. **Zones 4 to 7.**

Phygelius

fy-GEE-lee-us. Figwort family, Scrophulariaceae.

Commonly called Cape fuchsias, *Phygelius* species are tender shrubs or subshrubs native to South Af-rica that spread by suckers. They bear bluntly toothed, ovate-lan-ceolate leaves and racemes of

Photinia × fraseri

showy flowers, which appear from summer to fall. The flowers are tubular and have five lobes, or "petals," that curve backward. Two species belong to the genus. They are not closely related to fuchsias (*Fuchsia*), although the flowers bear a superficial resemblance. Botanically, they are more similar to other figwort-family members such as penstemons (*Penstemon*).

HOW TO GROW

Cape fuchsias thrive in full sun and rich, moist, well-drained soil. They tolerate hot, dry conditions, too. In very hot climates, a site with shade during the hottest part of the day is best. Where hardy, grow them outdoors as shrubs; in areas where they are marginally hardy, try growing them as perennials, since they can be killed to the ground and will resprout from the roots. For extra winter protection, try a site against a south-facing wall and cover them with a dry mulch such as salt hay or weed-free straw. In the North, grow them in containers and overwinter them indoors in a bright, cool (40° to 45°F) spot. Sow seeds indoors 6 to 8 weeks before the last spring frost date at 70° to 75°F. Germination takes about 2 weeks. Plants also can be propagated in spring either by cuttings or by digging up suckers that appear around the plants. Use Cape fuchsias in containers, shrub borders, and mixed plantings. Their flowers attract hummingbirds.

P. aequalis

p. ee-QUAL-iss. A tender, 3-foot-tall-shrub with 10- to 12-inch-long panicles of 2¹/₂-inch-long trumpets, which are pink with red petals and yellow throats. 'Yellow Trumpet' bears creamy yellow flowers. **Zones 7 to 10.**

P. × rectus

p. × REK-tus. A 3- to 5-foot tender shrub with 6- to 12-inch-long panicles of 2¹/₂-inch-long red flowers. Cultivars include 'African Queen', salmon-orange; 'Moonraker', with greenish yellow flowers; and 'Winchester Fanfare', shell pink. **Zones 8 to 10.**

Physalis

fy-SAL-iss. Nightshade family, Solanaceae.

Physalis species are commonly known as ground cherries because their tiny bell-shaped flowers are followed by berries encased in an

Physalis alkekengi

inflated calyx that resembles a papery, lanternlike husk. About 80 species of annuals and perennials belong to the genus. One hardy perennial species is grown for its showy, bright orange "lanterns," which are used in dried arrangements and other crafts.

HOW TO GROW

Select a site in full sun or partial shade with average, well-drained, evenly moist soil. Plants spread quickly by rhizomes and can become invasive, so select the site with care. Water during dry weather, especially as the "lanterns" are developing. Divide plants as needed to keep them in check or for propagation. Or sow seeds.

P. alkekengi

p. al-keh-KEN-jee. CHINESE LANTERN. Rhizomatous 2- to 3-foot-tall perennial that spreads to 3 feet or more. Bears rounded, arrow-head-shaped leaves and ³/₄-inch-long creamy white flowers in mid-summer followed by berries surrounded by red-orange 2-inch-wide "lanterns." 'Gigantea' ('Monstrosa') bears exceptionally large fruit. **Zones 5 to 8.**

Physocarpus

fy-so-KAR-pus. Rose family, Rosaceae.

A genus of 10 species of deciduous shrubs from North America and East Asia, grown for its ease of culture in difficult situations as well as seed capsules and bark that provide winter interest. The leaves look like a currant's, while the flowers resemble the related spirea, or perhaps a scaled-down snowball viburnum.

HOW TO GROW

Physocarpus adapts to acid or alkaline soils, drought, and pollu-tion, in full sun or partial shade. Because these plants have a somewhat coarse habit, their best uses are for naturalizing and in informal hedges. Prune them to the ground in late winter or early spring. Propagate from seeds or untreated semiripe cuttings taken in summer.

P. capitatus

p. kap-ih-TAY-tus. Native to the mountainous northwest United States, this species grows to 8 feet tall and bears three-lobed leaves similar to a currant's and 2-inch rounded clusters of white flowers. Prefers moisture-retentive soil. **Zones 5 to 7.**

P. monogynus

p. mon-oh-JY-nus. MOUNTAIN NINEBARK. This relatively diminutive species native from Texas to South Dakota averages 3 feet tall and wide and has toothed, lobed leaves to 1¹/₂ inches long. The late-spring flower clusters, which have fewer blooms than other species, are followed by reddish seed capsules that are touched with green. **Zones 5 to 7.**

P. opulifolius

p. op-yew-lih-FOE-lee-us. NINEBARK. Native to roughly the northeastern quadrant of the country and north into Quebec, ninebark grows 6 to 10 feet tall and wide. The leaves, which usually have three to five lobes, turn yellow or bronze in fall. Balls of small white flowers, with pink-tinged petals and stamens tipped with purple, bloom in late spring, followed in fall by reddish seed capsules (follicles). Its exfoliating bark is interesting in winter al-

P

Physocarpus opulifolius

Physostegia virginiana

though often hidden. 'Dart's Gold' grows to about 5 feet tall and has yellow foliage, 'Diablo' has reddish purple foliage, and 'Luteus' bears yellow-green leaves and grows to 8 feet or more. **Zones 2 to 7.**

Physostegia

fy-so-STEE-jee-uh. Mint family, Lamiaceae.

Physostegia species are native North American perennials that spread by rhizomes and bear showy racemes of tubular, two-lipped flowers. There are about 12 species in the genus — all perennials with square stems and lanceolate to somewhat oblong leaves. The species commonly grown in gardens, *P. virginiana*, is sometimes called false dragonhead, a reference to the shape of the flowers. "Obedient plant" is another common name that also refers to the flowers, which have uniquely jointed bases that allow them to be adjusted in position on the main stalk. Once moved, they obediently remain pointed in the direction selected.

HOW TO GROW

Select a site in full sun to partial shade with average, evenly moist soil. Plants tolerate wet conditions but will flop in very fertile soil. Compact cultivars, which range from 2 to 3 feet tall, usually stand without staking. Obedient plants spread quickly by rhizomes: divide the clumps every 2 to 3 years to keep them in bounds and for propagation. Or propagate by stem cuttings taken in early summer.

P. virginiana

p. ver-jin-ee-AH-nuh. OBEDIENT PLANT, FALSE DRAGON-HEAD. Rhizomatous 3- to 4-foot-tall perennial that easily spreads to 2 or 3 feet. Bears dense, erect spikes of two-lipped, 1-inch-long, lilac to rose-pink flowers from midsummer to early fall. 'Alba' and 'Summer Snow' have white flowers. 'Pink Bouquet' bears bright pink flowers. 'Variegata' has white-edged leaves and magenta flowers. 'Vivid' bears bright purplish pink flowers on 2- to 3-foot plants. **Zones 3 to 9.**

Picea

pye-SEE-ah. Pine family, Pinaceae.

The 40 species of evergreen, coniferous trees in this genus, the spruces, hail from North America, Europe, and Asia, mostly from cool, moist regions. They look very similar to the firs *(Abies)*, featuring a pyramidal to conical shape with whorled branches and maintaining the same symmetrical shape even with great age. Needles are usually four angled and spirally arranged on the branchlets. Cones are oval or elongated and typically hang down, remaining on the tree without shattering. (Spruce needles feel sharp; firs are softer. Spruce cones hang down; fir cones stand up.) Several species of these very formal looking conifers are popular in gardens and large-scale landscapes, where they are most attractive if the lower branches are left to sweep to the ground.

HOW TO GROW

Give spruces moisture-retentive, fairly neutral soil that drains well and full sun. Because of their shallow root system, you should amend a planting area that is wide but not especially deep. Mulch to improve moisture retention. They will tolerate clay soil but not heat, drought, or pollution. When young, most can benefit from wind protection.

P. abies

p. AY-beez. NORWAY SPRUCE. This pyramidal tree reaches 90 feet tall and 35 feet wide and is quite stiff looking when young, although it becomes more open and graceful as it matures. The wide-spreading side branches are almost horizontal but turn downward and then upward at their tips. They are decorated with weeping twigs and branchlets that are densely cloaked with needles. The $^{1}/_{2}$- to 1-inch-long needles are stiff and dark green and have a blunt point. Young cones are reddish purple in spring and ripen into 6-inch-long, light brown, cigar-shaped cylinders that hang from the upper branches all winter. Norway spruce has rough, reddish brown bark and is fast growing and very long-lived; it resists cold and wind. It grows to a large size that can dwarf many home landscapes, so plant it where it has plenty of room to expand, and take into account its dark, somber appearance. Useful as a specimen, screen, or windbreak. Large trees transplant well. From Europe. **Zones 3 to 7.**

CULTIVARS

Treelike forms include the following: 'Acrocona' has showy, raspberry pink cones in spring and forms a 12-foot-tall, 4-foot-wide pyramid. 'Cranstonii' is a sparsely branched, gaunt, full-size pyramid with long, weeping, snakelike branchlets. 'Cupressina' is a dense, broad column with tightly weeping branches and small needles and cones; reaches 50 feet tall.

Picea abies 'Asselyu'

Picea abies 'Pendula'

'Frohburg' is a vigorous, upright tree with strongly weeping branches and a tidy appearance. 'Inversa' has a straight main trunk with weeping branches and twigs on a small frame. 'Reflexa' spreads on the ground, with upward-reaching branch tips. 'Pendula' is a variable weeping form that may resemble 'Inversa' or 'Reflexa'.

Many dwarf, shrublike forms are available. These include 'Little Gem', a diminutive cushion-shaped cultivar to 2 feet high and 3½ feet wide with a depression in the middle. 'Nidiformis' (bird's-nest spruce) is a spreading plant slowly reaching 3 to 6 feet tall to twice as wide with a characteristic dip in the center. 'Repens' has the opposite characteristic, with a mounding in the middle.

P. glauca

p. GLAW-kuh. White Spruce. When young, white spruce forms a broad, dense pyramid with horizontal branches. It matures into a spirelike, pyramidal or columnar tree with ascending branches and ultimately grows to 50 feet tall and 20 feet wide. The ³/4-inch-long, pale blue-green needles are rigid with a barely sharp point. They have white bands on both sides, creating a less somber appearance than that of *P. abies*. The 2-inch-long cones are green in spring, ripen to pale brown in fall, and remain on the tree through the winter. Bark is rough and gray-brown. White spruce ultimately reaches a large size with branches all the way to the ground. Use it as a specimen or screen where it has plenty of room to grow. This is the most heat-tolerant spruce. It adapts to coastal conditions. From northern North America. **Zones 2 to 8.**

CULTIVARS

'Coerulea' has beautiful blue-green needles. 'Pendula' has light gray-green needles and forms a narrow, weeping pyramid; grows to 30 feet tall. *P. g.* var. *albertiana* 'Conica' (dwarf Alberta spruce) is a very popular dwarf form with tiny, feathery, light green needles; forms a slow-growing, dense cone that can reach 20 feet tall after many years; very susceptible to spider mites in hot locations. *P. g.* var. *densata* (Black Hills spruce) is a slow- to moderate-growing form that matures as a 30-foot-tall, broad pyramid with very dense, dark green or blue-gray needles; an exceptional ornamental in the North.

P. omorika

p. oh-MOR-ee-kuh. Serbian Spruce. Though not well known, this slow-growing spruce, with its narrow pyramidal shape and weeping branches, is perhaps the most elegant of the genus and one of the toughest, too. It reaches 60 feet tall and 20 feet wide, has short side branches that curve gracefully upward at their tips, and has somewhat pendulous branchlets, creating a distinctive silhouette. The dense, sharp-pointed, 1- to 1½-inch-long needles are dark blue-green on top and gray-white on their undersides, which lends a two-tone effect. The 2-inch-long, cylindrical cones are dark blue-purple when young and turn cinnamon brown when mature. Use this narrow tree as a strong vertical accent in a mixed border. Unlike most spruces, it tolerates heat, humidity, and dry air. From western Europe. **Zones 4 to 8.**

CULTIVARS

'Gnom' is conical to 5 feet tall. 'Nana' is more rounded, to 8 feet tall.

P. orientalis

p. or-ee-en-TAL-is. Oriental Spruce. Less commonly grown than *P. abies* or *P. glauca* and much more beautiful, Oriental spruce forms a slow-growing, broad cone that reaches 60 feet tall and 20 to 30 feet wide. It has horizontal or slightly pendulous branches and short, stiff branchlets that are less pendulous than those of other spruces. The blunt-tipped, four-sided needles are noted for their fine texture and glossy, dark black-green color. They are only ¼ inch long and are pressed tightly against the stems, creating very densely needled twigs. Cones are reddish purple in spring and mature to 3½-inch-long, dangling, brown cones in fall. This very formal-looking spruce is best used as a specimen in a lawn or border. The golden-needled forms look best against dark green evergreens. This is one of the best spruces where summers are hot and humid. From eastern Europe and Asia Minor. **Zones 4 to 8.**

CULTIVARS

'Atrovirens' has glossy, very dark green needles. 'Aurea' bears creamy yellow needles at the branch tips all year. 'Aurea Compacta' forms a very slow growing, dense, 30-foot-tall cone and has golden new growth. 'Aureo-spicata' has ivory-yellow new growth that turns green in summer. 'Skylands' features brilliant creamy yellow new growth that darkens to rich gold; forms a very slender, slow-growing pyramid.

P. pungens

p. PUN-jenz f. Colorado Blue Spruce. This extremely dense, blue-needled tree forms a very symmetrical, 60-foot-tall, 25-foot-wide pyramid made up of tiers of stiff, horizontal branches and short, nonweeping branchlets. The

Picea orientalis 'Aurea'

Picea pungens

sharp-pointed needles are about 1 inch long and encircle the stems. They range in color from blue-gray to steel blue to powder blue; the species itself has gray-green to dark green needles. Cones are green when young and mature to shiny, light brown, 4-inch-long cylinders. This popular tree has a very formal shape that does not lend itself to all landscapes. Plant in a lawn as a specimen, in groups as a windbreak, or as a screen where there's plenty of growing room. The best blue color develops in full sun. Looks best against dark green (not golden) evergreens. From western North America. **Zones 3 to 7.**

CULTIVARS

'Bakeri' has deep blue needles and forms a 30-foot-tall pyramid. 'Bizon Blue' is a dense pyramid with brilliant blue needles. 'Fat Albert' has pale silvery blue needles and forms a dense, 15-foot-tall pyramid. 'Hoopsii' is fast growing and has beautiful silver-blue, almost white needles. 'Iseli Fastigate' forms a 15-foot-tall, 2-foot-wide column with steel blue needles.

'Iseli Foxtail' grows into a narrow, 15- to 20-foot-tall pyramid with twisted blue needles that form tufted branch tips; an oddity to use as a specimen. 'Koster' has silver-blue or powder blue needles and a variable form. 'Moerheimii' is compact and narrow, with silver-blue needles.

Pieris

pee-AIR-iss. Heath family, Ericaceae.

These evergreen shrubs, five species native to North America and East Asia, provide year-round interest in gardens with colorful new foliage, urn-shaped flowers, and drooping tassels of beadlike buds that last from midsummer to the next spring's flowering. The fissured bark is attractive when exposed on older specimens.

HOW TO GROW

As with other members of the heath family, give pieris acid soil amended with peat moss or other organic matter for moisture retention and excellent drainage. It

grows in full sun but benefits from partial shade in the South. Protect from strong winds. Use in masses, interplanted with rhododendrons and azaleas, or, if compact, against a wall. Lace bugs can be a problem, especially on *P. japonica.* Pieris doesn't require pruning but can be trimmed lightly after flowering to remove seedpods. Older specimens are sometimes limbed up slightly to expose attractive bark. Seeds need light and mist to germinate; cuttings root readily.

P. 'Brouwer's Beauty'

A hybrid of *P. japonica* and *P. floribunda,* growing 6 feet tall and wide, with yellow-green new foliage and mahogany flower buds. **Zones 5 to 8.**

P. floribunda

p. flor-ih-BUN-duh. M O U N T A I N
P I E R I S. Native to the southeastern United States and sometimes called mountain fetterbush or mountain andromeda, this relatively compact species grows 2 to 6 feet tall and wide, bearing fragrant upright panicles of flowers in midspring. It resists the lace bug that often plagues Asian forms but doesn't like heat and humidity and will develop problems where drainage is poor. **Zones 4 to 6.**

P. 'Forest Flame'

A compact hybrid to 4 feet tall with especially bright red new shoots and heavy flower clusters. Does best in a mild climate. **Zones 7 and 8.**

P. japonica

p. juh-PON-ih-kuh. J A P A N E S E
P I E R I S. The species grows 9 to 12 feet tall, spreading 6 to 8 feet wide, and produces glossy oblong or lance-shaped leaves that emerge bronze to reddish. The white urn-shaped flowers are fragrant and borne in drooping panicles to 6 inches long in early to midspring. Cultivars allow gardeners to choose more spectacular new foliage, pink flowers, or more compact size. For pink flowers look for 'Christmas Cheer', 'Daisen', 'Dorothy Wycoff', 'Flamingo', or 'Valley Valentine'. Growing only 3 feet tall, 'Pygmaea' has tiny feathery leaves. The foliage of 'Bert Chandler' includes chartreuse, salmon, cream, and dark green. 'Mountain Fire' has bright red new growth unfolding earlier than others, so it is sometimes damaged by late frosts. **Zones 4 to 7.**

Pinus

PYE-nuss. Pine family, Pinaceae.

The roughly 90 species of evergreen, coniferous trees in this genus are distributed throughout the Northern Hemisphere. Pine needles are very distinctive: they are linear, sprout from papery brown sheaths, and are grouped along the stems in bundles of two, three, or five (sometimes four). Pines with bundles of five needles are called white pines or soft pines; those with two or three needles per bundle are called black pines or hard

Pieris floribunda

Pinus densiflora

pines. Spring growth consists of elongating stems, called candles, that reach their full length before their new needles mature. Pines can be pruned by cutting off half the length of the candles before the needles elongate. Limbs should be pruned back only to a fork in the branch because they will not resprout from leafless wood. Pines are popular landscape trees and offer gardeners a soft, informal texture as screens or specimens.

HOW TO GROW
In general, pines are tough, drought-resistant trees, with different species thriving in different regions. See the individual entries for specific needs.

P. aristata
p. air-is-TAH-tah. BRISTLECONE PINE. This very slow growing, open-branched pine is an irregular, spreading or flat-topped tree, 15 to 20 feet tall and wide, that stays in scale with a small garden for many years. It has one or more trunks and rough bark. Needles are 1 to 2 inches long and dark green, marked with dots of white resin. They are arranged in bushy bundles of five on sparsely branched stems. Individual needles live for 10 or more years before dropping, so the branches have a dense bottlebrush appearance that distinguishes them from those of other pines. The brown cones are 3 inches long and have sharp, spiny bristles at the tip of each scale. Wild bristlecone pines are the longest-lived trees known; some gnarled, weather-beaten specimens are at least 4,000 years old.

Plant this picturesque tree in full sun. It thrives in poor-soil areas and tolerates drought. From the high mountains of southwestern North America. **Zones 3 to 7 in the East; to Zone 9 on the West Coast.**

CULTIVARS
'Sherwood Compacta' has a compact, conical shape resembling that of Alberta spruce (*Picea glauca* var. *albertiana*).

P. bungeana
p. bun-jee-AH-nuh. LACEBARK PINE. This rare pine is admired for its open, flat-topped shape and for the showy bark that cloaks its multiple trunks. Lacebark pine grows very slowly but ultimately reaches 30 to 50 feet tall and wide. Bark is a patchwork of green, pink, and cream that is most colorful when the sun strikes the trunks, but it does not develop its distinctive colors until the tree is at least 10 years old. The glossy, dark green, 3-inch-long needles are sharp pointed and in bundles of three. Cones are 3-inch-long, light brown ovals with triangular spines. This pine is grown in temple gardens in China and makes a wonderful specimen in a border where it has plenty of space to grow and the bark can be admired up close.

Plant in full sun and acid or alkaline, well-drained soil. From China. **Zones 5 to 9.**

CULTIVARS
'Rowe Arboretum' forms a tight pyramid with glossy green needles.

P. densiflora
p. den-sih-FLOR-uh. JAPANESE RED PINE, TANYOSHO PINE. This sculptural, slow-growing pine features multiple trunks and layers of upturned, horizontal branches that form an irregular or flat-topped shape. It can reach 60 or more feet tall and wide, but its most popular form is half that size, and it has several dwarf forms that make handsome shrubs. Along with its striking silhouette comes a showy cloak of reddish orange bark that brightens a garden throughout the year. The 3- to 5-inch-long needles are bright light green, slightly twisted, and arranged in bundles of two in dense, upright tufts along the branches. Numerous clustered, yellowish, 2-inch-long cones adorn the branches all winter. Use the species or a smaller cultivar where it has plenty of room to grow, as a lawn specimen, in a border, or silhouetted in a distant view.

Pinus strobus

Like spruces and other conifers, many of the large pine species have handsome dwarf varieties that are easy to use as shrubs, in rock gardens, and in a variety of other garden settings. Among them are the following:

Pinus aristata 'Sherwood Compacta'
P. densiflora 'Aurea', 'Oculus Draconis', 'Soft Green'
P. koraiensis 'Pygmaea'
P. mugo 'Gnom', 'Mops'
P. parviflora 'Venus'
P. pumila
P. sylvestris 'Watereri'
P. taeda 'Nana'

Plant in full sun and any well-drained, slightly acid soil, from sandy to slightly heavy, with moderate moisture. Tolerates salt spray and seashore conditions. From China, Japan, and Korea. **Zones 5 to 7.**

CULTIVARS
'Aurea' is a bushy, 8-foot-tall dwarf; new needles are golden in spring, mature to lime-yellow in summer, and turn more golden in fall. 'Umbraculifera' (Tanyosho pine) is a popular slow-growing cultivar that reaches 15 to 30 feet tall and wide; has vase-shaped trunks and a mushroom-shaped, flattened top. 'Heavy Bud' resembles 'Umbraculifera' but has large red buds. 'Soft Green' is similar to, but more dwarf than, 'Umbraculifera'. 'Morris Arboretum' is beautifully irregular, with a pronounced flat top. 'Oculus Draconis' (dragon's-eye pine) has green needles with bright yellow bands; produces a creamy effect when seen from a distance. 'Pendula' ('Prostrata') weeps if staked and grafted to a tall, straight trunk.

P. flexilis
p. FLECK-sill-iss. LIMBER PINE. This stunning pine forms a loose pyramid when young and matures into a broad, flat-topped specimen that reaches 45 feet tall and 30 feet wide. Limber pine is not widely

Pinus strobus

Pinus sylvestris 'Rezek'

planted but ought to be used more in gardens, because it is quite beautiful and widely adapted. The slender, blue-green, 3-inch-long needles appear in bundles of five and are slightly twisted, giving the tree a dense, fluffy texture. Mature cones are 6 inches long, light brown, and pendulous. This pine may form single or multiple trunks that are covered with deeply fissured, dark gray bark. The young branches are so flexible that they can be bent in half without breaking. Use as a tall, soft-textured screen or specimen.

Plant in full sun to partial shade and moist, well-drained soil. Tolerates rocky soil and some drought or salt. Do not remove lower limbs. Performs best in the West and Midwest. From the Rocky Mountains. **Zones 3 to 7.**

CULTIVARS

'Extra Blue' forms a strong pyramid with very blue needles. 'Glauca' has bluish needles. 'Glauca Thume' features very blue needles on a compact, upright plant; good for a screen. 'Millcreek' has very blue needles and a full pyramidal shape. 'Temple' is upright and open branched; grows to 30 feet tall; has short, silvery blue-green needles. 'Vandewolf's Pyramid' is a fast-growing, narrow, pyramidal tree that reaches 25 feet tall and has long, silvery blue-green needles.

P. koraiensis

p. kor-ay-eye-EN-sis. KOREAN PINE. Loosely pyramidal, growing to 40 feet tall and 15 to 20 feet wide, this little-known pine is a beautiful, lush tree with long, densely needled, horizontal or upright branches. Korean pine resembles the much more common eastern white pine *(P. strobus)*, but it has longer needles and a more layered shape when young. The thick, stiff needles are arranged in bundles of five. They are 3½ to 4½ inches long and glossy dark green with white stripes, giving the tree an overall blue-green or gray-green hue. Blue-needled forms are the most striking. Dense, reddish brown hairs cloak the twigs between the bundles of needles, an identifying feature. Trunk bark is smooth and gray-brown. Cones are yellow-brown, upright, and about 5 inches long. They fall unopened to the ground, where birds and animals eat them and release the seeds. Use this somewhat formal tree in groves, as a windbreak, or as a specimen.

Plant in full sun to partial shade and almost any garden soil. From China, Japan, and Korea. **Zones 4 to 7; to Zone 8 in the West.**

CULTIVARS AND SIMILAR SPECIES

'Glauca' has blue-green needles and grows to 25 feet tall. 'Morris Blue' has excellent silver-blue needles and reaches 25 feet tall. 'Silveray' is identical to 'Morris Blue'. *P. cembra* (Swiss stone pine) looks similar but has shorter green needles and a dense cone shape when young, eventually becoming flat topped and spreading; grows to 35 feet tall; twigs have dense reddish hairs; cones are greenish violet, eventually turning purple-brown, and do not open; **Zones 3 to 7.** 'Pygmaea' forms a dense pyramid.

P. mugo

p. MEW-go. SWISS MOUNTAIN PINE. This variable shrublike species, which has blunt needles, is valued primarily for its dwarf cultivars. 'Gnom' forms a mound 15 inches tall and about twice as wide; 'Mops' is also a mound, about 3 feet tall and wide.

Plant in full sun and well-drained soil. Tolerates salt spray. **Zones 3 to 7.**

P. parviflora

p. par-vih-FLOR-uh. JAPANESE WHITE PINE. This elegant, slow-growing pine creates a fine-textured, silvery blue effect. Dense and conical when young, it becomes more open and wide spreading as it matures, with a flat top and tiers of horizontal branches. It eventually reaches 35 to 50 feet tall and 20 to 35 feet wide. The slightly twisted, blue-green needles are stiff and short — only 2 to 2½ inches long — and very narrow, with white bands. They are in groups of five, forming clustered tufts at the tips of branches. Reddish brown, 2- to 4-inch-long, oval cones form even on young trees and decorate the branches for several years. Bark on older trunks is scaly and dark gray. This pine makes an excellent specimen in a border, small-scale garden, or seaside site.

Plant in full sun and almost any well-drained, acid soil with moderate moisture. Tolerates salt and seashore conditions. From Japan and Korea. **Zones 5 to 9.**

'Glauca' has silvery blue-green, more twisted needles and numerous cones; grows slowly to 30 feet tall; more commonly grown than the species. 'Glauca Brevifolia' has shorter, more tufted, blue-green needles. 'Glauca Nana' has blue-green needles and forms a narrower, shorter tree. 'Templehof' grows faster and is bluer than 'Glauca'. 'Venus' has shorter, bluer needles and a compact shape. *P. pumila* (Japanese stone pine) is similar but more shrublike and low spreading; grows only 10 to 15 feet tall.

P. resinosa

p. rez-eh-NO-suh. RED PINE, NORWAY PINE. This very cold hardy, durable pine has a pyramidal or oval shape with heavy branches and grows to 50 or more feet tall and 25 feet wide. Though handsome, red pine is best used in cold, demanding sites where more beautiful pines perform poorly. The yellow-green needles are 6 inches long and arranged in pairs that form dense tufts along the branches. Needles are so brittle that they snap when bent, an identifying feature. Cones are light brown and 2 inches long. Older trunks have reddish brown bark that is broken into diamond-shaped plates, an attractive attribute that is revealed when lower limbs die naturally. Plant in groves or rows to use as a windbreak or screen in areas with demanding growing conditions. Makes a picturesque specimen to silhouette against the sky.

Plant in full sun and any well-drained, acid soil. Performs well in sandy or gravelly soil; sensitive to air pollution. Best in cold climates. From north-central and northeastern North America. **Zones 2 to 6.**

SIMILAR SPECIES

P. ponderosa (ponderosa pine, western yellow pine) grows into a narrow or irregular, 60- to 100-foot-tall, 25- to 60-foot wide pyramid; deeply fissured, reddish

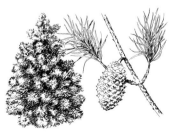

Pinus virginiana

brown bark; 5- to 10-inch-long needles in bundles of three; from western North America; tolerates drought and alkaline soil; **Zones 3 to 8.**

P. strobus

p. STROH-bus. EASTERN WHITE PINE. Probably the most beautiful and widely grown pine, eastern white pine features graceful, horizontally spreading branches and a pyramidal shape, growing 50 to 80 feet tall and 20 to 40 feet wide. The long, narrow, light green or blue-green needles are 2 to 5 inches long and arranged in bundles of five, giving the tree a lovely texture. Older trunks feature deeply furrowed, gray-brown bark. The 6- to 8-inch-long, brown cones are pendulous. Use this fast-growing pine as a fine-textured windbreak or specimen, or plant it in groves for a naturalistic effect. Can be pruned to develop a dense hedge.

Plant in full sun or partial shade. Does not tolerate heavy or poorly drained soil, road salt, air pollution, or seaside conditions. From eastern North America. **Zones 3 to 9.**

CULTIVARS

P. s. var. *glauca* has blue needles. 'Alba' has creamy white new growth that matures to blue-green. 'Contorta' is slow growing, with very twisted needles and contorted, ascending branches. 'Fastigiata' is columnar when young and broadens with age, reaching 60 feet tall and 8 feet wide; excellent for screening. 'Hillside Winter Gold' has green needles that turn a beautiful light yellow in winter. 'Pendula' forms a weeping specimen if staked and supported to the desired height. 'Torulosa' has twisted needles and a typical growth habit. 'White Mountain' is a vigorous grower with beautiful powder blue needles.

P. sylvestris

p. sil-VES-tris. SCOTCH PINE, SCOTS PINE. This widely grown pine has an open structure with wide-spreading branches and an irregular, flat top; it becomes attractively craggy with age. Scotch pine grows quickly to 30 to 60 feet tall and 30 to 40 feet wide. The pairs of 2- to 3-inch-long needles are stiff, twisted, and tinted blue-green to gray-green, often turning yellowish green in winter. The flaky bark is an eye-catching orange-brown on the limbs and up-

Pinus thunbergii

per trunks and gray or reddish brown and fissured on older trunks. Cones are gray-brown and 3 inches long. Scotch pine works well as a specimen in a small garden or can be grouped for a naturalistic effect in a large landscape.

Plant in full sun and any well-drained, acid to slightly alkaline soil. Tolerates infertile, dry sites and some road salt. Often attacked by pine wilt and tip blight in the East and Midwest. From northern and central Europe. **Zones 3 to 8.**

CULTIVARS

'Arctic' is very cold hardy (**Zone 2**); has blue-green summer needles and bright yellow winter needles. 'Aurea' has bright yellow new growth that turns light green in summer and bright yellow in winter; very slow growing; useful as a shrub for many years. 'Auvergne' has the best green winter color. 'East Anglia' has a straight trunk and deep green needles even in winter. 'Fastigiata' has blue-green needles and forms a slow-growing, narrow column; grows to 25 feet tall and 5 feet wide. 'French Blue' has brighter blue needles and a compact shape. 'Spaan's Fastigiate'

is a compact, vertical tree with blue-green needles; resists ice and snow damage. 'Waterii' is a favorite compact, rounded tree; grows 20 to 30 feet tall; blue-green needles and very orange bark.

P. taeda

p. TEE-duh. LOBLOLLY PINE. An important timber tree in the South, this native pine is pyramidal when young and becomes branched and rounded with age, maturing at 45 to 60 or more feet tall and half as wide. The dark yellow-green needles are 6 to 10 inches long and arranged in bundles of three. The narrow cones are 6 inches long and have sharp spines. Bark is gray and deeply furrowed and ridged. Though not as beautiful as many pines, this fast-growing, straight-trunked species adapts to adverse conditions and provides an effective screen in sites where other evergreens won't grow. Established native stands of loblolly pine should not be cleared, because they provide shade and protection.

Plant in full sun to partial shade and moist, acid clay. Tolerates

poor drainage and drought. From southeastern North America. **Zones 7 to 9.**

CULTIVARS AND SIMILAR SPECIES

'Nana' is a dwarf that grows slowly into a dense, rounded shape 15 feet tall. *P. elliotti* (slash pine), a southern native, reaches 80 feet tall; features pairs of 8- to 10-inch-long, yellow-green needles; tolerates poorly drained soil; **Zones 8 and 9.** *P. palustris* (longleaf pine) is another southern native that reaches 80 feet tall; slender, 8- to 18-inch-long, bright green needles are in bundles of three and form fluffy tufts on short branches; grows in sandy soil.

P. thunbergii

p. thun-BER-jee-eye. JAPANESE BLACK PINE. Formerly *P. thunbergiana*. Open branched, with an irregular curving main trunk, this attractive small pine grows 35 to 60 feet tall and is a perfect choice for a seaside or high-desert garden, because it thrives in sandy soil and salt spray. Unfortunately, insect and disease problems may preclude planting the tree in some areas. The shiny, dark green needles are 2½ to 4½ inches long and arranged in bundles of two. The very prominent, silvery buds are an identifying feature. Trunk bark is dark gray to black and broken up into large plates. The 3-inch-long cones are shiny light brown. Use Japanese black pine as a specimen or windbreak or to stabilize dunes in areas where pests are not a problem. Pinewood nematodes (carried by long-horned beetles) and blue-stain fungus (carried by black turpentine beetles) attack and kill trees that are 20 or more years old in some regions, especially the

P

Pinus wallichiana

Pistacia chinensis

East; check with local experts to see if pest problems preclude planting the tree in your area. From Japan and Korea. **Zones 6 to 9.**

CULTIVARS AND SIMILAR SPECIES
'Majestic Beauty' tolerates smog. 'Thunderhead' features extra-large silver buds and is fast growing, with an upright shape. *P. leucodermis* (*P. heldreichii* var. *leucodermis;* Bosnian pine) makes a good substitute for *P. thunbergii*; pairs of dark green, 3¹/2-inch-long needles; smooth, gray-green bark and white-barked twigs; grows slowly into a 45-foot-tall, upright tree; tolerates dry or alkaline soil; resists *Diplodia* tip blight; **Zones 5 to 8.** *P. nigra* (Austrian pine) grows 60 to 100 feet tall; very dark green, long, sharp, stiff needles; furrowed, mottled bark; tolerates salt spray, sandy or clayey soil, and alkaline soil; in some areas, *Diplodia* tip blight devastates 15- to 20-year-old trees; resists oak root rot fungus; **Zones 4 to 8.** 'Arnold Sentinel' is columnar to 25 feet tall.

P. virginiana
p. ver-jin-ee-AH-nuh. V IRGINIA P INE , S CRUB P INE , J ERSEY P INE . Pyramidal or flat topped and irregularly branching, Virginia pine grows 15 to 40 feet tall and 10 to 30 feet wide and is a durable pine where growing conditions challenge more attractive species. The stout green needles are somewhat twisted, 2 to 3 inches long, and arranged in pairs. In winter they may turn an unattractive yellowish green. The spiny cones are reddish brown, 2 inches long, and pendulous, with sharp spines. Bark is a colorful orange-brown. Use Virginia pine and similar species for a screen or specimen in a Xeriscape garden or in areas with infertile, dry soil. Virginia pine is also useful on reclamation sites.

Plant in full sun. Best in clayey, acid to slightly alkaline loam, but performs well in poor, clayey or sandy soil. Tolerates drought and seashore conditions. From eastern and central North America. **Zones 5 to 9.**

CULTIVARS AND SIMILAR SPECIES
'Watt's Gold' is slow growing; light green needles in summer, turning bright gold in winter. *P. banksiana* (jack pine) is a fast-growing, cold-hardy, northern native with a pyramidal or shrubby, rugged shape that can grow to 50 feet tall; the paired, 1- to 2-inch-long needles are olive green and slightly twisted; makes a good coastal or poor-soil plant; **Zones 2 to 6.** *P. edulis* (*P. cembroides* var. *edulis*) (pinyon pine) is a southwestern native that is bushy and stiff, growing 15 to 20 feet tall; 1- to 2-inch-long, dark green, paired needles; tolerates dry sites in the Midwest and West (in a Xeriscape or high-desert garden) but may be susceptible to insects in landscape situations; **Zones 5 to 7; to Zone 8 in the West.** *P. rigida* (pitch pine) is native to east-central North America; good for very poor, sandy sites; needles in bundles of three; susceptible to tip blight, tip moths, and pine needle scale; **Zones 4 to 7.**

P. wallichiana
p. wah-lik-ee-AY-nuh. H IMALAYAN P INE , B HUTAN P INE . Formerly *P. griffithii.* Perhaps the most beautiful of all the pines, Himalayan pine is a soft-textured, broadly pyramidal tree that reaches 30 to 50 or more feet tall and wide, with branches all the way to the ground. The sharp-pointed needles are 6 to 8 inches long and arranged in soft, cascad-

ing groups of five. They are gray-green with white stripes, giving the tree a silvery sheen from a distance and creating an outstanding landscape effect. Light brown, pendulous cones are 6 to 10 inches long and 2 inches wide. Use this elegant tree as a specimen in a border or lawn. It's particularly beautiful with a dark background such as dark green or steel blue evergreens.

Plant in full sun and moist, well-drained, fertile, acid, sandy loam. Does not tolerate drought. Shelter from wind. From northern India and Pakistan. **Zones 5 to 8.**

CULTIVARS
'Glauca' has very blue needles. 'Frosty' bears very silvery needles. 'Morton' is cold hardy to **Zone 4.** 'Zebrina' has unusual green needles with creamy yellow bands.

Pistacia
piss-TAY-she-uh. Cashew family, Anacardiaceae.

This genus of 10 species of trees and shrubs with compound leaves includes the commercial pistachio tree, valued for its nuts, as well as several ornamentals.

HOW TO GROW
Plant in full sun and moist, well-drained, acid to alkaline soil. Tolerates heat, drought, and urban conditions. Prune when young to develop a strong central leader. Usually pest-free. Performs well in the South and Southwest.

P. chinensis
p. chih-NEN-sis. C HINESE P ISTACHE , C HINESE P ISTA - CHIO . Prized for its dependable fall color in the South, where few trees put on outstanding displays, Chinese pistachio grows into a rounded, open-branched specimen, 25 to 35 feet tall and wide, with a lacy character. The 8-inch-long, compound leaves are deep green, with 10 to 12 lance-shaped, aromatic leaflets that turn flaming red and orange in late autumn. Greenish flowers bloom before the leaves open in spring but are not remarkable. Clusters of showy red fruits, which ripen to a bright metallic blue in autumn, develop on female trees. These are not messy because they are usually eaten by birds. The attractive, flaking, mottled trunk bark is gray and salmon-orange. Although this tree may look a bit awkward when young, it grows more attractive with age and is a good choice for casting light shade on a lawn, street, or patio. 'Keith Davey' has outstanding scarlet fall color. From China. **Zones 6 to 9.**

Pittosporum
pit-oh-SPOR-um. Pittosporum family, Pittosporaceae.

There are some 200 species in this genus from Australasia, South and East Asia, and Africa. They are mostly evergreen trees and shrubs grown primarily for their glossy, leathery leaves and secondarily for fragrant flowers or showy fruit.

HOW TO GROW
The species listed here adapt to a range of soils and tend to make good seaside plantings, withstanding salt, drought, and wind, in full sun or partial shade. Use as windscreens, as hedges, or in contain-

Pittosporum tobira

ers. Some species take to shearing. Head back *P. tobira* if you want to control its size or shape. Propagate from cuttings.

P. tenuifolium

p. ten-yew-ih-FOE-lee-um. Finely textured with dark green leaves and fragrant dark maroon spring flowers, this species can become a good-sized tree. Look for some of the many smaller cultivars, such as 'Irene Paterson', which grows slowly to about 8 feet tall and 4 feet wide. **Zones 9 to 10.**

P. tobira

p. toe-BY-ruh. JAPANESE MOCK ORANGE. A dense shrub or small tree, usually 6 to 15 feet tall, with shiny, dark green, leathery leaves. In early spring, creamy terminal flowers bloom in clusters and smell like orange blossoms. The round fruits turn brown and pop open to expose orange seeds. 'Variegatum', with gray-green white-edged leaves, usually remains under 5 feet, and 'Wheeler's Dwarf' stops growing at 2 feet. **Zones 9 and 10.**

Platanus

PLAT-ah-nus. Sycamore family, Platanaceae.

This genus contains nine species of large deciduous trees that have maplelike leaves and mottled bark. They are popular urban street trees.

HOW TO GROW

Plant in full sun to partial shade and deep, fertile, moist, acid soil. Tolerates drought, wetness, infertile or alkaline soil, heat, and air pollution. Messy fruits need to be raked up in spring. Remove lower branches to show off trunk bark. This tree is less susceptible to anthracnose than other sycamores, but it may be disfigured during wet seasons. Mildew, borers, and lace bugs are other pests.

P. × acerifolia

p. × aye-sir-ih-FOE-lee-uh. LONDON PLANE TREE. This well-known hybrid of *P. occidentalis* and *P. orientalis* is superior to both of them, combining each one's best characteristics into a tall, attractive, disease-resistant shade tree. Pyramidal when young, the tree grows into a rounded specimen reaching 50 to 60 feet tall and 30 to 40 feet wide. Its massive trunk and sturdy, wide-spreading scaffold branches create a rugged sil-

Platanus × acerifolia

houette. Leaves are 6 to 10 inches long, dark green, and lobed like those of a maple *(Acer)*. They turn yellowish brown in fall before dropping. Bark is striking, peeling to a patchwork of creamy white and gray. Curious 1- to 2-inch-wide, tan seed balls made up of tightly packed, prickly seeds develop in fall and hang on into winter before dropping. Kids call them "itchy balls" and like to torment each other with them. London plane tree is a durable urban dweller but also looks wonderful in an open, naturalistic setting, where its ghostly bark and craggy shape can be appreciated fully. **Zones 5 to 9.**

CULTIVARS AND SIMILAR SPECIES

Choose named cultivars to ensure disease resistance. 'Bloodgood' is the oldest and most common cultivar; highly resistant to anthracnose, but suffers from mildew. 'Columbia' is a pyramidal form with deeply lobed leaves from the National Arboretum; resists anthracnose (on the East, but not the West, Coast) and mildew. 'Liberty' is similar to 'Columbia', but the leaves are not as deeply lobed. 'Metroshade' is very tall and fast growing, with bronze new growth; anthracnose and mildew resistant. 'Yarwood' has large, light green leaves that resist powdery mildew and anthracnose on the West Coast. *P. occidentalis* (sycamore, American plane tree, buttonwood) is a fast-growing native that can reach 100 to 150 feet tall; bark is ghostly white and tan, and leaves are shallowly lobed; suffers from anthracnose and mildew; grows and looks best in a natural landscape with moist to wet soil; **Zones 5 to 9.** *P. orientalis* (Oriental plane tree) has deeply lobed leaves, is wide spreading, and grows to 25 feet tall; a useful, small street tree; resists scale. **Zones 7 to 9.**

Platycodon

plat-ee-KOE-don. Bellflower family, Campanulaceae.

A single species commonly known as balloon flower belongs to the genus *Platycodon*. It is a dependable, clump-forming perennial with inflated flower buds that split open into broad, shallow, bell-shaped flowers. The common name refers to the balloonlike buds, while the botanical name refers to the 3-inch-wide flowers themselves: *Platycodon* is from the Greek *platys*, meaning "broad," and *kodon*, "bell."

HOW TO GROW

Plant balloon flowers in full sun or light shade and average to rich, well-drained soil. In the South, a spot that receives afternoon shade is best. Plants in rich soil and partial shade are more likely to need staking. Deadheading spent blooms keeps plants blooming all summer long. Mark the location of clumps, as they are late to emerge in spring and thus easy to dig into by mistake. Established clumps seldom need dividing, and they resent disturbance, but they can be dug in spring or early fall for propagation or transplanting. Rooted shoots that sometimes ap-

Platycodon grandiflorus

Platycodon grandiflorus 'Sentimental Blue'

Plectranthus forsteri

pear at the base of the clumps offer another propagation option. Most cultivars also come true from seed, and plants self-sow.

P. grandiflorus

p. gran-dih-FLOR-us. BALLOON FLOWER. Long-lived 2-foot-tall species forming 1-foot-wide clumps. Bears attractive blue-green, oval- to lance-shaped leaves and 2-inch-wide purple, blue-violet, lilac-blue, pink, or white flowers from early to midsummer. *P. g.* ssp. *mariesii* (also sold as 'Mariesii') bears purple-blue flowers on 1- to 1¹/₂-foot plants. 'Sentimental Blue' has lilac-blue flowers on 10- to 14-inch plants. 'Shell Pink' bears pale pink flowers on 2-foot plants. Fuji Series plants are seed grown and have white, pink, or purple-blue flowers. 'Double Blue' bears double lilac-blue flowers on 1¹/₂- to 2-foot plants. **Zones 3 to 8**.

Platystemon

plat-ee-STEM-on. Poppy family, Papaveraceae.

Platystemon contains one species native to grasslands, deserts, and chaparral in the western United States. Commonly called cream-cups, it is an erect or sprawling annual with hairy, gray-green, linear to narrow, lance-shaped leaves and an abundance of small poppylike flowers.

HOW TO GROW

Plant creamcups in full sun and average, loose, well-drained soil. They tolerate dry soil, but extremely hot, humid weather may cause plants to die back (or die off); fortunately, they generally recover once cooler conditions return. Sow seeds outdoors in fall or several weeks before the last spring

frost date, when the soil is still cool. Barely cover the seeds with soil. Or sow indoors in individual pots 6 to 8 weeks before the last spring frost date and transplant with care. Outdoor sowing is generally best. Water during dry weather. Use creamcups as edgings, at the front of shrub borders, in rock gardens, and in mixed plantings. Plants self-sow.

P. californicus

p. kal-ih-FOR-nih-kus. CREAM-CUPS. A well-branched, 4- to 12-inch-tall annual that can spread to

Platystemon californicus

9 to 10 inches. Bears 1-inch-wide, six-petaled, creamy yellow flowers. Cool-weather annual.

Plectranthus

plek-TRAN-thus. Mint family, Lamiaceae.

Some 350 species of annuals, perennials, and shrubs belong to this genus from tropical Africa, Asia, Australia, and the Pacific islands. They have square, sometimes succulent stems that can be erect or trailing. Gardeners most

often value them for their showy leaves, which can be heart shaped to rounded with scalloped, toothed, or wavy margins. The foliage is often aromatic and somewhat hairy. The plants produce erect clusters of small, tubular, two-lipped flowers in shades of pale pink, mauve, white, or lilac in summer.

HOW TO GROW

Give these plants a site in dappled shade and average to rich, well-drained soil. Grow them as bedding plants replaced annually or as tender perennials overwintered in a bright, cool to warm (60° to 70°F) spot. (They also make fine houseplants.) Sow seeds indoors 8 to 10 weeks before the last spring frost date at 65° to 75°F. Transplant after the last frost date once temperatures remain above 45°F. They root easily from cuttings taken at any time of year, and cuttings (or simply digging up rooted stems) are the best way to propagate variegated forms. Use these plants to add foliage interest to mixed plantings and containers. Trailing types are effective cascading out of hanging baskets and large tubs.

P. amboinicus

p. am-BOY-nih-kus. MEXICAN MINT, CUBAN OREGANO, INDIAN BORAGE, SPANISH THYME. A 1-foot-tall tender perennial, spreading to 3 feet or more, with hairy, fleshy, rounded, 1³/₄-inch-long, aromatic leaves used in cooking for their spicy flavor, which has been likened to a mix of savory, thyme, and oregano. Bears 12- to 16-inch-long spikes of ¹/₂-inch-long lilac flowers. A form with white-edged leaves is available as 'Variegatus' or 'Marginatus'. Tender perennial or warm-weather annual.

P. argentatus

p. are-jen-TAY-tus. An erect, tender shrub, to 2 to 3 feet tall and wide, with ribbed, scallop-edged, gray-green, 2- to 4¹/₂-inch-long leaves. Produces 1-foot-long spikes of bluish white, ¹/₂-inch-long flowers. Tender perennial or warm-weather annual.

P. forsteri

p. FOR-ster-eye. Also listed as *P. coleoides*. A 10-inch-tall tender perennial that can spread to 3 feet or more. Bears hairy, rounded, scalloped-edged, 2¹/₂- to 4-inch-long leaves and 6- to 8-inch-long racemes of tiny, pale pink or white flowers. 'Marginatus' ('Iboza') has white-edged leaves. Tender perennial or warm-weather annual.

P. madagascariensis

p. mad-ah-gas-kar-ee-EN-sis. MINT-LEAF. A tender, 1-foot-tall perennial with brown stems that can spread 3 feet or more. The fleshy, rounded, scallop-edged, 1¹/₂-inch-long leaves smell of mint when crushed. Bears 4- to 6-inch-long flower spikes of pale lavender or white blooms. 'Variegated Mintleaf' has white-edged leaves. Tender perennial or warm-weather annual.

Pleione

plee-OH-nee. Orchid family, Orchidaceae.

Pleione species are small orchids native from western India to China and Japan that are sometimes grown for their showy flowers. Plants grow from bulblike organs called pseudobulbs and may be terrestrial (growing in soil) or epiphytic (growing on another plant, but not taking water or nutrients from that plant). Plants bear one or two deciduous leaves per pseudobulb; these are lance shaped to rounded and folded lengthwise like a fan. Flowers, which appear before the leaves, are solitary or borne in pairs, usually in shades of pink. They have a prominent, fringed, tubular lip marked with brown, maroon-red, or yellow on the inside, and five spreading petals. One terrestrial species, *P. formosana*, is sometimes offered in bulb catalogs.

HOW TO GROW

Give *P. formosana* a spot in partial to full shade with very well drained soil rich in organic matter. It is native to mountainous areas and prefers cool summer temperatures, so be sure to select a spot shaded from hot sun — a location on the north side of a house or wall with deep, organic soil is suitable. It also requires dry soil in winter, so be sure the soil is very well drained: in areas with rainy winters (as well as in the North), it is best overwintered indoors or grown in containers year-round. Plant the pseudobulbs in spring at a depth of 2 inches after the soil has warmed up. Where hardy, they can be left in the ground and protected over winter with a thick, coarse mulch such as evergreen boughs, salt hay, or pine needles. To grow them in containers, plant the pseudobulbs in spring in a light, fast-draining soilless mix, and set them with the top two-thirds above the soil surface.

In the ground or in containers, water sparingly at first, then keep the soil evenly moist once the plants are growing actively. In late summer or early fall, gradually withhold water. To overwinter the pseudobulbs indoors, dig them in fall just as the foliage disappears, and store them in dry peat moss or vermiculite in a cool (35° to 40°F), dry place; keep container-grown plants at that same temperature over winter. Repot container-grown plants in spring, discarding the old pseudobulbs. Individual pseudobulbs are short-lived, usually lasting one or at most two years: propagate these plants in spring by separating the small pseudobulbs that arise around the parent one.

P. formosana

p. for-moe-SAH-nuh. A 3- to 6-inch-tall terrestrial species bearing nearly round pseudobulbs, each of which produces a single pleated 5- to 6-inch-long leaf. Bears solitary 3-inch-wide flowers in spring that have rose-pink petals and a white lip mottled with pale red-brown to purplish pink on the inside. **Zones 8 to 10.**

Pleione formosana

Plumbago auriculata

Plumbago

plum-BAY-go. Sea-lavender family, Plumbaginaceae.

Plumbago includes 12 species of perennials, shrubs, and shrubby vines native to several warm regions around the world. They are commonly known as leadworts. Like the related sea lavenders (*Limonium*) and thrifts (*Armeria*), leadworts are native to and tolerant of salty, calcareous, rocky, and otherwise difficult, dry sites. They have simple, alternate leaves that are usually elliptic in outline, although they may be lobed at the base. Leaves are deciduous or semievergreen. Flowers are generally showy and clustered into headlike arrangements reminiscent of garden phlox. They range in color from white through a spectrum of blues. Flower color of a particular plant is fixed for life, but plants do vary in hue, so if precise color matching is critical, it is important to select individual plants when in bloom. In most parts of North America, when gardeners refer to "plumbago," they mean *Ceratostigma plumbaginoides*.

HOW TO GROW

P. auriculata requires perfect drainage and, once established, is quite drought tolerant. It is not particular as to soil provided it is in full to only partial sun.

P. auriculata

p. aw-rik-yew-LAH-tuh. CAPE PLUMBAGO. This South African native is adapted to mild, moist winters and hot, dry summers. It is a vigorous semievergreen shrub or vine that reaches 6 to 8 feet tall and spreads 10 to 12 feet. Occasional supplemental watering will keep the plants full. Flowers are blue and may be bleached out in hot desert areas. *P. a.* var. *alba* has white flowers. **Zones 9 and 10.**

Podocarpus

poe-doe-KARP-us. Podocarp family, Podocarpaceae.

This genus of about 100 species of evergreen, coniferous trees and shrubs hails from forested areas of the warm temperate and tropical zones of the Southern Hemisphere. The needlelike leaves are arranged spirally around the stems, and male and female catkins are borne on separate plants. Female plants develop showy, red or blue, berrylike, one-seeded cones. The several popular garden species are useful as specimens, screens, and hedges, because they take well to shearing.

HOW TO GROW
Plant in full sun to light shade. Best in moist, well-drained, fertile soil but tolerates well-drained sandy loam or clay. Tolerates heat and salt spray but not wet or alkaline soil. Stem tips may winterkill in sunny, windy sites in Zone 8. Shear in spring and midsummer for a hedge. Usually pest-free.

P. macrophyllus
p. mak-roe-FILL-us. YEW PINE, YEW PODOCARPUS. With a dense, upright or oval shape, yew pine matures at 20 to 30 feet tall and 10 to 15 feet wide and has many uses in the landscape, espe-

Podocarpus macrophyllus 'Maki'

cially in the South, where it is quite common. The lance-shaped, leathery needles, which are arranged spirally around the stems, are waxy dark green with two white bands on their undersides and measure 3 to 8 inches long and ¹/₂ inch wide. They densely cloak the twiggy branches, giving the tree an intriguing, feathery texture. Trunk bark is reddish brown. The berrylike, pea-sized fruits ripen in fall to bright blue on thick red stalks. Use this dark green evergreen as a specimen in a border or foundation planting or as a privacy screen, or shear it for a formal hedge. Useful in seaside gardens. 'Maki' is a 10-foot-tall dwarf form with 1¹/₂- to 2¹/₂-inch-long needles. From China and Japan. **Zones 8 and 9.**

Polemonium

poe-lih-MOAN-ee-um. Phlox family, Polemoniaceae.

Commonly called Jacob's ladders, *Polemonium* species are annuals or perennials bearing tubular or bell-, saucer-, or funnel-shaped flowers in spring or summer. Blooms are borne either in branched clusters or singly and usually come in shades of lavender-blue or white, but also purple, pink, or yellow. The plants produce clumps of leaves divided in a pinnate fashion. Some 25 species belong to the genus.

HOW TO GROW
For the species listed here, select a site in full sun or partial shade with rich, well-drained, evenly moist soil. *P. reptans* is best in par-

tial shade. Neither of the species described here tolerates heat and humidity, and in areas with warm summers both require a site with shade during the hottest part of the day. Plants seldom need division, but they can be divided in spring for propagation. They also self-sow and can be grown from seeds.

P. caeruleum
p. see-RUE-lee-um. JACOB'S LADDER, GREEK VALERIAN. Clump-forming 1- to 3-foot-tall perennial native to western North America as well as Europe and northern Asia. Forms handsome 1-foot-wide mounds of leaves topped by clusters of bell-shaped lilac-blue flowers in early summer. 'Brise d'Anjou' bears leaves variegated with creamy to pale yellow. *P. c.* var. *lacteum,* also listed as var. *album,* bears white flowers. **Zones 4 to 7.**

P. reptans
p. REP-tanz. CREEPING JACOB'S LADDER. Mounding species native to the eastern United States that reaches about 1 foot in height and spreads to 1¹/₂ feet. Bears clusters of bell-shaped, sky blue, ¹/₂-inch-wide flowers in late spring and early summer. 'Alba' has white flowers. 'Lambrook Mauve', also sold as 'Lambrook Manor', bears ¹/₂- to ³/₄-inch-wide lilac-blue flowers. **Zones 2 to 8.**

Polianthes

pah-lee-AN-theez. Agave family, Agavaceae.

All of the 13 species that belong to the genus *Polianthes* are tender perennials native to Texas and Mexico. They have tuberous, bulblike bases and thick roots, both of which grow from short rhizomes. Plants bear succulent, lance-shaped or linear leaves and erect spikelike racemes of flowers. Individual flowers are tubular to narrowly funnel shaped and have six lobes. Blooms come in orange-red or white. Surprisingly, as members of the agave family, they are closely related to century plants *(Agave)* as well as yuccas *(Yucca).* One species of *Polianthes* is treasured for its incredibly fragrant white flowers — common tuberose, *P. tuberosa.*

HOW TO GROW
Select a site in full sun with light, evenly moist soil rich in organic matter. Plant the tubers outdoors

Polemonium reptans

Polianthes tuberosa

in spring with the tops about 2 to 3 inches below the soil surface. Where hardy, they can be grown outdoors year-round, and in areas with fairly long growing seasons (roughly Zones 6 and 7), plants will have plenty of time to bloom when planted directly outdoors. Work a balanced fertilizer into the soil at planting time. In areas with shorter growing seasons, start them indoors in containers 5 to 6 weeks before the last spring frost date; setting containers on a heat mat speeds them along. Set plants outside — or sink containers to the rim in the garden — once the soil has warmed up and nighttime temperatures remain above about 60°F. Once leaves appear, water regularly. Feed container-grown plants every 2 weeks until flowers fade.

Tubers may survive Zone 7 winters with an extra-heavy layer of coarse mulch such as evergreen boughs, salt hay, or pine needles. To overwinter the tubers indoors, gradually withhold water as the leaves begin to turn yellow. Dig them after the first light fall frost; allow them to dry out in a warm, shaded place; then cut off the foliage. Store the tubers in dry peat moss or vermiculite in a cool (65°F), dry place over winter. Propagate by separating the offsets in spring.

P. tuberosa

p. too-ber-OH-suh. TUBEROSE. A 2- to 4-foot-tall species with rosettes of basal leaves. From summer to fall, bears erect spikes of 20 or more waxy white 1¼- to 2½-inch-wide flowers that are intensely fragrant. 'The Pearl' produces fragrant, semidouble or double creamy white flowers. **Zones 8 to 10; to Zone 7 with winter protection.**

Polygala

pah-LEE-gah-luh. Milkwort family, Polygonaceae.

This genus comprises more than 500 widely distributed species of annual and perennial herbs and shrubs. Just a handful of species have been cultivated for gardens,

Polygala × dalmaisiana

Polygonatum odoratum 'Variegatum'

and they are valued for their racemes of colorful, intricate pea-like flowers with winged sepals and petals that form fringed "keels."

HOW TO GROW

Give polygala moisture-retentive but well-aerated acidic soil. It prefers full sun but will grow in light shade. Species vary in size and habit and thus in landscape use and pruning needs. Propagate from green or semiripe cuttings.

P. chamaebuxus

p. kam-ay-BUX-iss. A mat-forming evergreen shrub, to 6 inches tall and 12 inches wide, often used in rock gardens. Its small leathery leaves resemble those of boxwood (*Buxus*). The ½-inch white-and-yellow flowers, sometimes with a keel that turns purple-red, bloom in late spring. Those of *P. c.* var. *grandiflora* have magenta wings and yellow lips. **Zones 6 to 9.**

P. × dalmaisiana

p. × dal-mays-ee-AH-nuh. An erect evergreen shrub averaging 5 feet tall, round in youth and then spreading, with sparse foliage at the base. Racemes of 1-inch magenta flowers with pale pink keels bloom midsummer to autumn. Best positioned at the back of a border to hide the bare lower branches. **Zones 9 to 11.**

Polygonatum

pah-lig-oh-NAY-tum. Lily family, Liliaceae.

Grown primarily for their handsome foliage, *Polygonatum* species are rhizomatous perennials with unbranched, erect or arching stems that bear linear to ovate leaves. The foliage of most commonly cultivated kinds is feather- or plumelike in effect. Plants bear small, pendent, bell-shaped or tubular flowers beneath the leaves either singly or in small clusters. The flowers, which usually are creamy colored or white with green markings, are followed by round, usually black berries. The plants grow from many-jointed rhizomes: the botanical name, from the Greek *polys*, meaning "much," and *gony*, "knee," refers to this fact. The common name "Solomon's seal" refers to the joints as well, which resemble the wax seals sometimes applied to official documents.

HOW TO GROW

Plant Solomon's seals in partial to full shade and rich, moist, well-drained soil. They tolerate full sun in northern zones but require shade during the hottest part of the day in the South. Most species tolerate dry soil. They spread steadily, but not invasively, to form handsome drifts. Divide plants in spring or fall to propagate or to keep them from outgrowing their space.

P. biflorum

p. bi-FLOR-um. SOLOMON'S SEAL. A 1½- to 7-foot-tall species forming 2- to 3-foot-wide clumps. Bears pendent, ½- to 1-inch-long, greenish white flowers either singly or in clusters of two or four from late spring to early summer.

Polygonatum biflorum

Polystichum munitum

The enormous 4- to 7-foot-tall plants commonly listed as *P. commutatum,* and sometimes called great Solomon's seal, are currently classified as forms of *P. biflorum.* **Zones 3 to 9.**

P. humile

p. hue-MILL-ee. Dwarf Solomon's Seal. Dwarf 8-inch-tall species forming loose 2-foot-wide clumps. Bears solitary or paired, pendent, ³/4-inch-wide white flowers in spring. **Zones 5 to 8.**

P. odoratum

p. oh-door-AH-tum. Fragrant Solomon's Seal. A 2¹/2- to 3-foot-tall species with pendent 1¹/4-inch-long white flowers borne singly or in pairs. Blooms late spring to early summer. 'Variegatum', which has leaves striped at the edges with white, is most often grown. **Zones 4 to 8.**

Polystichum

pol-ISS-tih-kum. Woodfern family, Dryopteridaceae.

Commonly called shield or sword ferns, *Polystichum* species bear leathery, often evergreen fronds that are once-, twice-, or thrice-cut. Most are 1 to 4 feet or more in height. The plants usually form graceful, vase-shaped clumps.

HOW TO GROW
Select a site in partial shade with evenly moist soil rich in organic matter. Christmas fern (*P. acrostichoides*) also grows in dry soil, on slopes, or among rocks, making it an excellent ground cover for shade. The fronds of evergreen species usually become prostrate by early winter. Either leave them in place from year to year or remove them in late winter before the new fronds unfurl. *Polystichum* species grow from erect, branched rhizomes that form crowns. Propagate them by digging the plants in spring and carefully separating the rhizomes.

P. acrostichoides

p. ack-roe-stick-OY-deez. Christmas Fern. A 1¹/2-foot-tall fern native to the northeastern United States that forms 3-foot-wide clumps with time. Bears once-cut, evergreen fronds that have stocking-shaped leaflets. **Zones 3 to 9.** Gardeners in the Northwest should grow western sword fern (*P. munitum*) instead of Christmas fern. Also evergreen, it ranges from 1¹/2 to 5 feet tall. Although hardy in **Zones 6 to 9**, it does not do well in the East.

P. setiferum

p. seh-TIFF-er-um. Soft Shield Fern, Hedge Fern. A 4-foot-tall evergreen species native to Europe. It forms 3-foot-wide clumps of shiny, twice-cut fronds. Many cultivars with crested or heavily divided fronds are available. **Zones 5 to 8.**

Poncirus

pon-SEAR-us. Rue family, Rutaceae.

This genus contains only one species, a small ornamental tree with vicious spines.

HOW TO GROW
Plant in full sun to partial shade and moist, well-drained, acid soil. Tolerates heat and drought. Locate where the thorns won't pose a hazard to gardeners and passersby. May be pruned into a dense screen or hedge; prune immediately after blooming. Usually problem-free, but develops chlorosis if the soil pH is above 7.5.

P. trifoliata

p. try-foe-lee-AH-tuh. Trifoliate Orange, Hardy Orange. This small thorny tree, a cold-hardy relative of the orange tree, has an oval shape and grows 10 to 20 feet tall. Bark on trunk and branches is an attractive green. Star-shaped, 2-inch-wide, white flowers decorate the branches in spring and have a sweet perfume. The 3-inch-long leaves are divided into three leaflets on winged stalks. They are bright yellow-green when young, mature to glossy mid-green, and turn glowing yellow in fall. Leaves drop in autumn to reveal bright golden orange, 2-inch, citruslike fruits. These sour-tasting fruits adorn the branches through the winter, standing out beautifully against the green branches. This tree's main attraction or detraction, depending on your point of view, is its 2-inch-long, extremely sharp, stout, green thorns, which make it very useful as a security barrier when planted on boundaries or under windows. When using the tree as an ornamental, be sure to locate it where it is visible in winter. 'Monstrosa' is a dwarf with twisted branches that is useful as an ornamental shrub. From China and Korea. **Zones 6 to 9.**

Populus

POP-yew-lus. Willow family, Salicaceae.

About 35 species of poplar and aspen trees belong to this genus, which is native throughout the northern temperate zones. These are the fastest-growing trees in temperate climates and often have ornamental white or gray bark, male and female catkins on sepa-

Poncirus trifoliata

Populus tremuloides

rate trees, and leaves that flutter gracefully on long, flattened stems.

HOW TO GROW

Plant in full sun and moist but well-drained soil. Poplars have invasive root systems and should be planted at least 30 feet from foundations, water pipes, sewer pipes, or septic systems. Their great thirst for water makes them invaluable in cleaning up sites damaged by polluted groundwater. Most poplars are weak wooded and susceptible to storm damage. Some are also susceptible to canker, so they are often short-lived. In some regions, they are grown and harvested for firewood.

P. alba

p. AL-buh. WHITE POPLAR. Often grown as a graceful, multi-trunked clump, white poplar is a round-topped, spreading tree that grows quickly to 40 to 70 feet tall and wide. Leaves are 3 to 5 inches across and three lobed, rather like a maple's *(Acer)*. They are shiny dark green on top, with a felt of white hairs on the undersides. The slightest breeze sets the leaves in motion, flashing a silvery light. Fall color is yellow. Trunk bark is a showy, grayish white and attracts attention all year. As trunks mature, they become marked with black. Though attractive, this tree is soft wooded, short-lived, and a bit messy, continually dropping leaves during summer and fall. It is best used to create quick shade in the Midwest and West, where few shade trees thrive. From Central Europe and Asia. **Zones 4 to 9.**

CULTIVARS AND SIMILAR SPECIES

'Nivea' is the most common form sold (although it may not be labeled with its cultivar name); three- to five-lobed leaves with very silvery undersides. 'Pyramidalis' ('Boleana') is very narrow and does not sucker, but its leaves are less silvery; an excellent substitute for Lombardy poplar (*P. nigra* 'Italica') for screens and windbreaks. 'Raket' is similar to 'Pyramidalis' but has more silvery fo-

Populus nigra 'Italica'

liage. *P. angustifolia* (willowleaf poplar) is an upright native with willowlike leaves and excellent gold fall color; grow in moist soil at high elevations to 10,000 feet. *P. × canescens* 'Tower', a hybrid with *P. tremula,* grows to 45 feet tall and 10 feet wide; excellent disease resistance; makes a good substitute for Lombardy poplar. *P. tremuloides* (quaking aspen) is native to the Rockies and has bright white to gray-green bark and small, wedge-shaped leaves with silver undersides that turn a beautiful yellow in fall; performs well only in the Mountain States above 7,000 feet; otherwise it is short-lived and disease prone; **Zones 2 to 6.** 'Pike's Bay' has lighter bark and is canker resistant.

P. deltoides

p. del-TOY-deez. COTTONWOOD. Pyramidal when young and becoming irregularly open and vase shaped with age, this tree has a low-branching trunk and grows 75 to 100 feet tall and 50 to 75 feet wide along watercourses in the West and Midwest. It has a rugged character and a massive silhouette, with its tall, stout trunk and big branches covered with deeply furrowed, brown bark. Leaves are tri-

angular, 3 to 5 inches across, bright green on top, and blue-green on the undersides. They turn yellow, gold, or brown before dropping in autumn. Male trees produce a lot of pollen, which can irritate al-

lergy sufferers. Female trees produce enormous amounts of cottony white seeds that float great distances and create quite a mess. Numerous seedlings can invade open areas and grow in seemingly hostile sites. Despite its drawbacks, cottonwood is one of the hardiest shade and shelterbelt trees for the cold climates of the North, Plains, and Mountain States, where most trees have a difficult time growing. In the home landscape, a male, cottonless form is best, used only in large-scale situations and away from drainpipes. From central and western North America. **Zones 3 to 9.**

CULTIVARS AND SIMILAR SPECIES

'Robusta' is cottonless and has coppery new leaves; broadly oval, growing to 60 feet tall. 'Siouxland' is pyramidal, cottonless, and rust and storm resistant; grows to 75 feet tall. *P. × acuminata* (lanceleaf poplar) is a common natural hybrid with very narrow leaves, excellent fall color, and a rounded form. *P. × canadensis* (*P. × euroamerica*) and its cultivars are superior cottonless hybrids with *P. nigra;* they have smooth bark and triangular leaves. 'Imperial' is disease resistant and narrowly pyramidal, growing to 60 feet tall. 'Prairie Sky' is very narrow, growing to 40 feet tall and 8 feet wide, with smooth gray bark and very good resistance to canker and storm damage. 'Robusta' has cop-

Populus tremuloides

Primula vulgaris

stems and come in red, white, and shades of pink. Plants require partial to full shade (but good light) and constantly moist to wet soil but will not grow in stagnant conditions: plant them where there is at least gentle water movement. Set the crowns slightly above the water line. Plants self-sow. 'Miller's Crimson' bears bright red blooms; 'Potsford White', white blooms; and 'Rosea', pink blooms. **Zones 5 to 8.**

P. juliae
p. JUL-ee-eye. A diminutive species with 2- to 3-inch-tall rosettes of leaves that spreads slowly to form 10- to 12-inch-wide clumps. Bears solitary magenta-pink 1-inch-wide flowers in early spring. 'Wanda' is a robust selection with red-purple flowers. **Zones 3 to 8.**

P. malacoides
p. mal-ah-KOY-deez. FAIRY PRIMROSE. A 6- to 8-inch-tall tender perennial, hardy only from **Zone 8 south**, with tiers of whorled, ¹/₂-inch-wide, single or double flowers in shades of lavender-pur-

Primula vulgaris

ple, reddish pink, or white. Tender perennial, or grow as a cool-weather annual.

P. obconica
p. ob-KON-ih-kuh. FAIRY PRIMROSE, GERMAN PRIMROSE. A 9- to 16-inch-tall tender perennial, hardy only in **Zones 10 and 11**, with tiers of whorled, 1- to 2-inch-wide flowers that sometimes have frilled petal edges. Flowers come in shades of pink, red, lilac-blue, and white. Touching the foliage can cause a skin rash. Tender perennial, or grow as a cool-weather annual.

P. Polyanthus Group
These hybrids are also listed as *P. × polyanthus* and are crosses between various hardy primroses. Plants form low 8- to 12-inch-wide rosettes of evergreen to semievergreen, rough-textured leaves and, in midspring, clusters of showy 1- to 2-inch-wide flowers on 6-inch-tall stems in a wide range of colors, including pale to deep yellow, red, orange, violet-blue, white, and pink. They often have yellow eyes. Depending on the cultivar, they can be hardy to Zone 3, but florist's types are usually less hardy — to Zone 6. **Zones 3 or 6 to 8.**

P. sieboldii
p. see-BOLD-ee-eye. SIEBOLD PRIMROSE. Produces 8- to 12-inch-wide rosettes of leaves topped in early spring by 1-foot-

tall clusters of delicate, lacy-looking, 1-inch-wide flowers. Flowers come in pale pink, rose, white, pale purple, and purple-red. **Zones 3 to 8.**

P. veris
p. VAIR-iss. COWSLIP PRIMROSE. Produces low 5- to 6-inch-wide rosettes of evergreen or semievergreen leaves and 1-inch-tall clusters of fragrant, nodding, 1-inch-wide yellow flowers in early to midspring. **Zones 4 to 8.**

P. vulgaris
p. vul-GAIR-iss. ENGLISH PRIMROSE, COMMON PRIMROSE. Formerly *P. acaulis*. Produces 6- to 8-inch-wide rosettes of evergreen to semievergreen 9- to 10-inch-long leaves and clusters of pale yellow 1- to 1¹/₂-inch-wide flowers in early spring. Many cultivars are available, with either single or double flowers, in white, orange, magenta, purple-pink, and yellow. **Zones 4 to 8.**

Proboscidea
pro-bos-SIH-dee-uh. Pedalium family, Pedaliaceae.

Both the botanical and common names for *Proboscidea* species are based on their woody seed capsules, which have hornlike beaks or protrusions at one end. The botanical name is from the Greek *proboskis*, meaning "snout" or "nose," and common names include unicorn plant, devil's claw, ram's horn, elephant's tusk, and proboscis flower. The genus contains nine species of annuals and

perennials native to the Americas. They are grown for their tropical foliage; racemes of five-lobed, funnel- to bell-shaped flowers; and interesting seedpods.

HOW TO GROW
Select a site in full sun to very light shade with rich, well-drained soil. Established plants tolerate dry soil but do better with regular watering during dry spells. Sow seeds indoors 6 to 8 weeks before the last spring frost date at 70° to 75°F. In areas with long growing seasons, roughly Zone 8 south, sow outdoors a week or two after the last frost date. Use these annuals to add a lush, tropical effect to mixed plantings. The seedpods are attractive in dried arrangements.

P. louisianica
p. loo-ee-see-AN-ih-kuh. UNICORN PLANT, DEVIL'S CLAW. Sometimes listed as *P. jussieui*, *P. proboscidea*, and *Martynia fragrans*. An erect to spreading annual that can reach 1¹/₂ feet tall and spread to 3 feet. Bears softly hairy, 2¹/₂- to 8-inch-long leaves and funnel-shaped, 1¹/₂- to 2-inch-long, creamy white to purplish flowers with yellow throats and spotted with red-purple. The flowers are followed by curved, 4- to 8-inch-long seedpods. Warm-weather annual.

Prunella
proo-NELL-uh. Mint family, Lamiaceae.

Seven species of semievergreen perennials belong to this genus of mint-family plants. All bear dense

Proboscidea louisianica

spikes of two-lipped tubular flowers in shades of violet, pink, or white. Leaves range from linear to lance shaped or ovate and may be entire or lobed. Plants spread to form thick mats of foliage.

HOW TO GROW

Select a site in full sun or partial shade with average soil that remains evenly moist. These plants do not tolerate dry soil. Since they root easily at the leaf nodes and also self-sow, they can be quite invasive: *P. vulgaris* is a common weed of lawns and waste places. Especially in areas with cool summers, select a site with care to keep them in bounds, and watch for and dig up plants that spread too far. Shear the plants to remove flowers as they fade to curtail self-sowing. Divide in spring or fall as needed for propagation.

P. grandiflora

p. gran-dih-FLOR-uh. LARGE SELF-HEAL. Vigorous 6-inch-tall perennial that spreads to form 3-foot-wide mats. Bears rounded, slightly toothed leaves and upright spikes of $1^1/4$-inch-long purple flowers in summer. 'Loveliness' has pale lavender-purple blooms; 'Pink Loveliness', pink flowers; 'White Loveliness', white ones. **Zones 5 to 8.**

Prunus

PROO-nuss. Rose family, Rosaceae.

This large genus contains about 400 species of deciduous and evergreen trees and shrubs, many of them ornamental cherries. *Prunus* members have five-petaled (or

Prunus × subhirtella 'Eureka Weeping'

double) pink or white flowers, often borne in large rounded or elongated clusters; single-seeded fruits; and alternate, pointed, oval leaves.

HOW TO GROW

The genus as a whole is adaptable to most soils as long as they are well drained, although organic amendments will ensure health and hasten growth. Evergreen species need full sun or partial shade; deciduous species require full sun. In general, the tree forms are short-lived, about 20 years, because they are prone to numerous diseases and insect pests, including borers, scale, aphids, tent caterpillars, canker, and leaf spot. However, these trees' exceptional beauty and utility far surpass any concern over their longevity.

TREES

P. cerasifera 'Atropurpurea'

p. sair-ah-SIFF-er-uh. PURPLE-LEAVED PLUM, CHERRY PLUM. This deciduous small tree is one of the most cold-hardy purple-leaved plants available and grows into a rounded or vase-shaped form, 15 to 30 feet tall and wide, with gently arching branches. In early spring, fragrant, pale to dark pink, $1/2$-inch flowers cover the limbs, blooming just as the richly colored new leaves begin to unfold. The leaves are vivid ruby red in spring and mature to greenish bronze-purple by midsummer, although some other cultivars remain more vibrantly purple through the summer. Fall color is reddish purple. Small, purple, plumlike fruits ripen in midsummer, attract birds, and can be messy if they drop to the ground. This pretty little tree makes an eye-catching focal point in a border or foundation planting. Somewhat drought tolerant. Pests are less of a problem on this species than on others. From Eurasia. **Zones 4 to 9.**

CULTIVARS AND SIMILAR SPECIES

'Thundercloud' has very deep purple foliage all summer and purple fruits; the most widely grown cultivar. 'Krater's Vesuvius' is very similar to 'Thundercloud' but has deeper red new growth, is a bit purpler in summer, and has almost no fruits; excellent in the Southwest. 'Mt. St. Helens' is rounded, has light pink flowers, and has rich purple leaves all summer and fall. 'Newport' has light pink flowers, few fruits, and dark purple foliage all summer, with reddish fall color. *P. × blireana* (blireana plum) is widely vase shaped and twiggy, growing 15 to 20 feet tall and wide; very early, bright pink, double, 1-inch flowers; **Zones 6 to 9.**

P. maackii

p. MAK-ee-eye. AMUR CHERRY, GOLDBARK CHERRY. Grown for its gorgeous bark, Amur cherry is pyramidal when young and grows into a rounded, single- or multitrunked, 30-foot-tall tree. Bark is smooth or exfoliating and is a glistening, metallic honey gold with lighter horizontal bands. It attracts attention all year but is especially beautiful when the tree is leafless. Dangling, 3-inch clusters of tiny white flowers bloom in mid- to late spring but are partly obscured by the leaves. The medium green leaves, which measure 2 to 4 inches long and have tiny teeth on the margins, turn yellowish and drop in early autumn. Small black fruits ripen in summer but are eaten by birds, so they are not usually messy. Use this medium-size tree to shade a patio, in a winter border, or as a street tree where it can be seen up close. It is an especially good ornamental

Prunella grandiflora

Prunus serrulata

choice for cold climates, where it is relatively pest-free. From Manchuria and Korea. **Zones 3 to 7.**

SIMILAR SPECIES

P. serotina (black cherry, wild black cherry) has rough, peeling, black bark on the trunk and main branches but shiny bark on young branches; 5-inch-long, drooping clusters of creamy flowers; leathery leaves turn orange in fall; ¹/₂-inch fruits ripen from green to red to black in summer and provide food for birds but stain concrete if they drop to the ground; the tallest cherry, growing 80 to 100 feet tall; **Zones 3 to 9.** *P. serrula* (paperbark cherry, birchbark cherry) is a pyramidal or rounded, 20- to 30-foot-tall tree; gleaming, dark red-brown bark with horizontal brown bands; narrow, willowlike leaves; white flowers in late spring; **Zones 5 to 8.**

P. 'Okame'

p. oh-CALM-ee. OKAME CHERRY. This award-winning deciduous cultivar is a hybrid between *P. incisa* and *P. campanulata* and is the earliest- and longest-blooming of all the cherries. It grows into a gracefully spreading, 20- to 30-foot-tall vase shape. Opening from dark pink buds set into red calyxes, the profuse, clear pink flowers have jagged petals and bloom before the leaves unfold; they remain showy for about 3 weeks until the leaves mature. Blooming is early, often starting in late winter when the magnolias are still in bloom. Leaves are 1 to 2¹/₂ inches long, dark green, fine textured, and sharp toothed. They turn bright yellow and orange in fall. Use as a small specimen in a garden or plant in groups. **Zones 6 to 9.**

SIMILAR CULTIVARS AND SPECIES

'Hally Jolivette' is a shrubby hybrid that grows 15 to 20 feet tall; profuse, semidouble, 1¹/₄-inch, white flowers with pink centers open over 3 weeks in early spring on slender branches; **Zones 5 to 8.** *P. mume* (Japanese flowering apricot) has very early, single, pink

Prunus besseyi

flowers; double forms with dark pink, red, or white flowers also are available; **Zones 7 to 9.**

P. sargentii

p. sar-JEN-tee-eye. SARGENT CHERRY. Perhaps the loveliest of all the cherries, Sargent cherry grows into a rounded or vase-shaped specimen, 30 to 50 feet tall and wide, that is a mist of pink when in bloom. Flowers are single and delicate rose-pink, or sometimes white, 1 to 1¹/₂ inches across, and borne in groups of two or three. They bloom before the leaves open, enhancing their appeal. The toothed leaves are about 6 inches long and 3 inches wide, wider than most cherry leaves. They are a shiny reddish green when they open, mature to dark green, and finally turn orange-red and yellow in fall. This is one of the best cherries for reliable fall color. The black fruits are small and not messy. Bark is a very attractive polished, chestnut brown with prominent horizontal bands. Sargent cherry makes a beautiful flowering shade tree for year-round interest. Use in a lawn or garden or as a street tree where there is plenty of soil. This is the most cold hardy of the flowering cherries. Japanese beetles are a serious problem, but other pests are not and the tree is longer-lived than most. From Japan and Korea. **Zones 4 to 9.**

CULTIVARS

'Columnaris' ('Rancho') is narrowly upright, growing to 30 feet.

P. serrulata Sato-zakura Group

p. sair-yew-LAH-tah. ORIENTAL CHERRY, JAPANESE FLOWERING CHERRY. These double- or single-flowered deciduous hybrids have few equals, as they provide dramatic spring beauty coupled with great foliage and bark. Oriental cherries are usually flat topped and wide spreading, growing 50 to 75 feet tall and wide. In midspring, large clusters of 2-inch-wide flowers with 10 to 30 petals hang down from the limbs beneath the unfolding leaves, blooming in white or shades of pink. The single-flowered types are more delicate, while the double-flowered ones are more sensational. The oval or lance-shaped, 3- to 5-inch-long, glossy leaves usually emerge with a soft bronze tinge, mature to dark green, and then turn rich orange, red, or scarlet in fall. The reddish brown bark on the stout trunk and branches is shiny and marked with light horizontal bands. Susceptible to many insects and diseases, including viruses, so may be short-lived. From Korea and Japan. **Zones 6 to 8.**

CULTIVARS

'Amanogawa' has light pink, semidouble flowers with 5 to 15

petals and yellow-bronze new growth; columnar, reaching 20 feet tall and 5 feet wide. 'Kwanzan' has amazingly large clusters of shocking pink, double flowers with 20 to 30 petals in late spring (some gardeners find it too aggressive a color); one of the cherries planted in the Washington, D.C., tidal basin; **Zones 5 or 6 to 8.** 'Royal Burgundy' is like 'Kwanzan' but has shiny red-purple leaves. 'Shirofugen' is perhaps the best cultivar; the large clusters of 30-petaled, blush pink blossoms fade to pure white, then become deep pink again before dropping after a 3-week bloom; new growth is bronze; flat topped and wide spreading to 25 to 30 feet tall. 'Shirotae' ('Mt. Fuji') has large clusters of pure white, fragrant flowers with 12 petals; new growth is green; grows 15 to 20 feet tall. 'Shogetsu' has 30-petaled, white flowers and green new growth; reaches 15 feet tall with a flat top. 'Tai Haku' has white, 2¹/₂-inch, five-petaled flowers opening from pale pink buds; coppery bronze new growth; a broad vase shape, growing to 35 feet tall.

P. × subhirtella var. pendula

p. × sub-her-TELL-ah var. PEN-due-luh. HIGAN CHERRY, WEEPING CHERRY. Formerly *P. pendula.* This graceful weeping tree grows rapidly to 20 to 40 feet tall and 15 to 30 feet wide and is most dramatic in early spring, when its leafless branches become a waterfall of single or double, pink or white, 1¹/₂-inch blossoms. The glossy, dark green leaves measure 3 inches long, are deeply toothed, and usually remain green well into fall before dropping without changing color. In some cases, however, they may change briefly to yellow. The tree's silhouette is wonderful in winter, especially when outlined against the sky or dusted with snow or ice. Locate it where it can be reflected in a pool of water, or plant it at the top of a slope to emphasize its cascading branches. More pest tolerant than Oriental cherries if the

Prunus laurocerasus

Prunus glandulosa

soil is kept moist. From Japan. **Zones 5 to 8.**

CULTIVARS AND SIMILAR SPECIES

'White Fountain' ('Snow Fountains', 'Wayside White Weeper') is a naturally weeping (not grafted) hybrid that grows 12 to 15 feet tall and has large white flowers, shiny bark, and gold fall color. 'Yae-shirdare-higan' ('Plena Rosea') bears long-lasting, double, dark pink, 1-inch flowers. *P. × s.* 'Autumnalis' has semidouble pink flowers that bloom in early spring and again lightly in autumn; more rounded and less weeping.

P. × yedoensis

p. × yeh-doe-EN-sis. Y O S H I N O C H E R R Y, P O T O M A C C H E R R Y. One of the cherries that made Washington, D.C., famous for its cherry blossoms, Yoshino cherry is a graceful, medium-size, broadly rounded deciduous tree that grows 40 to 50 feet tall. It's extremely showy when in bloom, as the fragrant, single, 1¼-inch-wide blossoms are so profuse before the leaves emerge that they turn the tree into a translucent cloud. Flowers open pale pink and then turn snowy white. They are borne in clusters of three to six. The dark green leaves are 2 to 4 inches long and turn yellowish before dropping. Tiny black fruits ripen in early summer. Use this dramatic tree where its spring bloom can be appreciated — in a border, garden, or lawn, or even as a street tree where there is plenty of room for root growth. From Japan. **Zones 6 to 8.**

CULTIVARS

'Afterglow' has rich pink flowers that do not fade to white. 'Akebono' has soft pink flowers and a rounded shape; very vigorous. 'Shidare-yoshino' is a dwarf weeping form with small white flowers.

S H R U B S

P. americana

p. ah-mair-ih-KAH-nuh. W I L D P L U M. Native from New England to the southwestern United States, this deciduous shrub or small tree averages 15 to 20 feet tall, suckering to form colonies. Umbels of 1-inch sweet-scented white flowers bloom before the leaves emerge in early spring. Round red or yellow fruits with a tart flavor ripen in midsummer and can be used to make jams and jellies. **Zones 3 to 8.**

P. angustifolia

p. an-gus-tih-FOE-lee-uh. C H I C K A - S A W P L U M. An evergreen, suckering shrub with thorny side branches, it is often the first woody plant to flower in its native range, from the Mid-Atlantic to Florida and west to Kansas and Texas. White ½-inch flowers appear before leaves in late winter to early spring, followed by small dark berries used for jelly. **Zones 5 to 9.**

P. besseyi

p. BESS-ee-eye. W E S T E R N S A N D C H E R R Y. Native to the central United States, this deciduous shrub suckers and spreads to about 5 feet tall and wide and has gray-green leaves. Midspring white flowers are followed in midsummer by sweet, blue-black ¾-inch berries used in jellies and desserts. **Zones 3 to 6.**

P. caroliniana

p. kar-oh-lin-ee-AH-nuh. C A R O L I N A C H E R R Y. A southeastern native evergreen tree or shrub to 30 feet tall, about half as wide. Intensely fragrant flowers bloom in early spring, followed by shiny black berries that may last through winter if not eaten by birds. Stems are fragrant when crushed or pruned. Compact cultivars are available. **Zones 7 to 10.**

P. × cistena

p. × sis-TEEN-uh. P U R P L E L E A F S A N D C H E R R Y. A deciduous hybrid to 10 feet tall and narrower with reddish purple foliage and fragrant pink flowers that appear with the leaves in midspring, followed by purple-black fruits. 'Minnesota Red' has a deeper color. **Zones 4 to 7.**

P. glandulosa

p. glan-due-LOH-suh. D W A R F F L O W E R I N G A L M O N D. A commonly available deciduous shrub from Asia, growing to 5 feet tall and wide, with light green 4-inch leaves and white or pink flowers in midspring, rarely fruiting. 'Alba Plena' and 'Rosea Plena' ('Sinensis') have double white and pink flowers, respectively. **Zones 4 to 8.**

Prunus maritima

P. laurocerasus 'Otto Luyken'

p. lahr-oh-SER-uh-sus. O T T O L U Y K E N C H E R R Y L A U R E L. This cultivar of an evergreen species from southeast Europe and Asia Minor grows to about 4 feet tall and twice as wide and has 4-inch dark green leaves held at an acute angle to the stem. The white midspring flowers, borne in racemes, have numerous stamens and a strong fragrance. It tolerates heavy shade but must have good drainage. It may develop insect problems as a result of overhead watering or summer rain. **Zones 6 to 8.** Considered hardy to **Zone 5** is 'Schipkaensis', which differs primarily in holding its leaves perpendicular to the stem.

P. lusitanica

p. loo-sih-TAN-ih-kuh. P O R T U - G U E S E C H E R R Y L A U R E L. A large evergreen shrub that may eventually reach 20 feet tall, it has slightly toothed, glossy leaves to 5 inches long. The fragrant white flowers are borne in racemes 6 to 10 inches long in mid- to late spring, from both terminals and axils. The dark purple fruits are cone shaped. **Zones 7 to 9.**

P. maritima

p. mah-RIT-ih-muh. B E A C H P L U M. A dense suckering shrub to 6 feet tall with white flowers in midspring, followed in late summer by dull purple fruits that are used in jams and jellies. Native along the coast from Canada to Virginia, it flourishes in salt and sand. **Zones 3 to 7.**

P. tenella

p. teh-NEL-uh. D W A R F R U S S I A N A L M O N D. A deciduous shrub with upright, suckering shoots 2 to 5 feet tall. Glossy leaves and deep pink flowers open together in midspring. 'Fire Hill' has bright red flowers on a plant that remains 2 feet tall. **Zones 2 to 6.**

Pseudolarix

sue-doe-LAR-ix. Pine family, Pinaceae.

Only one species belongs to this genus, an uncommon deciduous conifer that makes an unusual landscape specimen featuring beautiful, delicate foliage.

HOW TO GROW

Plant in full sun to partial shade and moist, well-drained, acid to neutral, sandy loam. Intolerant of

P

Pseudolarix amabilis

alkaline conditions. Shelter from wind. Allow branches to remain to the ground. Usually pest-free. Performs well in the South.

P. amabilis

p. ah-MAB-ih-liss. GOLDEN LARCH. Formerly *P. kaempferi.* Although it's a member of the pine family, this conifer drops its needles and stands leafless in winter. It grows slowly but after many years forms a 50-foot-tall, 40-foot-wide, open-branched pyramid with a straight central trunk and horizontally spreading branches. The very narrow, flattened needles are 1 to 2½ inches long. They are light green in spring, mature to soft green in summer, and finally turn a stunning yellow or russet-gold before dropping in autumn. They are arranged spirally around the young stems and in rosettes on the short spurs of older wood. The 3-inch-long, yellow-green cones ripen to reddish brown in autumn and are showy but soon shatter and drop off. Use golden larch as a specimen where it has plenty of room to grow. From China.
Zones 6 to 8.

Pseudotsuga

sue-doe-SUE-guh. Pine family, Pinaceae.

This genus of six to eight evergreen, firlike trees from North America and Asia is identified by its pendulous cones, which have conspicuous protruding bracts, and its pointed, many-scaled buds. These very important timber trees can grow to gigantic heights but are smaller in home landscapes. One species is a graceful landscape tree.

HOW TO GROW

Plant in full sun and moist, well-drained, deep, acid to neutral soil. Blue types tolerate slightly alkaline soil. Sensitive to road salt. Protect from strong wind. Allow branches to remain to the ground. Branches may break if laden with snow or ice. Shear new growth annually for a hedge. May be troubled by canker, bark beetles, twig blight, budworms, gypsy moths, scale, tussock moths, and root weevils. Do not plant within 200 feet of Colorado spruce (*Picea pungens*), as they are alternate hosts for Cooley spruce gall aphids.

P. menziesii

p. men-ZEE-see-eye. DOUGLAS FIR. In the wild, this is one of the tallest trees in North America, reaching 200 feet in height. In home landscapes, it usually grows into a spirelike, 50- to 80-foot-tall, 15- to 25-foot-wide pyramid. The branches are mostly horizontal — downswept at the bottom and upturned near the top of the single main trunk. The fine-textured, 1- to 1½-inch-long needles are arranged spirally in two ranks around the twigs. They are dark green in *P. m.* ssp. *menziesii*, which is from coastal areas, and blue-green or blue-gray in *P. m.* ssp. *glauca* which is from the Rocky Mountains. The mountain trees are more cold hardy than the coastal trees and are more commonly used in gardens. Douglas fir's young cones are a pretty rose-red and ripen to cinnamon brown, with forked bracts protruding from between the scales. Trunk bark is reddish and deeply fissured, becoming dark brown and corky on older trees. Use this attractive, fast-growing tree as a soft-textured specimen or screen, or plant in groups for a naturalistic effect. From western North America. Rocky Mountain forms grow in **Zones 3 to 6** and cool areas of **Zones 7 and 8**; coastal forms grow in **Zones 6 to 8**.

CULTIVARS

'Blue' has bright blue needles, like those of Colorado blue spruce (*Picea pungens* f. *glauca*). 'Fastigiata' is a narrow, columnar, green-needled form. 'Glauca' is a slow-growing, narrower form with blue-green needles. 'Glauca Pendula' has soft blue-green needles and a tall, narrow, weeping shape. 'Pendula' has weeping branches, a twisted leader, and green needles; wide spreading.

Psylliostachys

sil-ee-oh-STACK-eez. Plumbago family, Plumbaginaceae.

Psylliostachys contains from six to eight species of annuals that once belonged to *Limonium,* better known to gardeners as statice. They bear deeply lobed to rounded or lance-shaped leaves that generally are clustered in a rosette at the base of the plant. From summer to fall, they produce branched or unbranched panicles of tiny, pink or white, tubular flowers.

HOW TO GROW

Grow statice in full sun and average, well-drained soil. Plants grow well in sandy soil and are good choices for seaside gardens. Sow seeds indoors 6 to 8 weeks before the last spring frost date at 65° to

Pseudotsuga menziesii

Psylliostachys suworowii

75°F. Germination takes 2 to 3 weeks. Or sow outdoors after the last frost date. Add statice to mixed plantings. They are ideal candidates for cutting gardens and are top-notch dried flowers. Harvest when most of the flowers in the spray have opened fully, and hang in small bunches in a warm, dark place to dry.

P. suworowii

p. suh-vo-ROW-vee-eye. RATTAIL STATICE, RUSSIAN STATICE. Formerly *Limonium suworowii*, *Statice suworowii*. A 1- to 1¹/₂-foot-tall annual producing narrow, 8-inch-long, branched, cylindrical spikes of rose-pink flowers from summer to early fall. 'Pink Poker', sometimes used as a cultivar name, actually is another common name for the species. Warm-weather annual.

Pulmonaria

pull-moe-NAIR-ee-uh. Borage family, Boraginaceae.

Commonly called lungworts, Bethlehem sages, or simply pulmonarias, *Pulmonaria* species are underappreciated perennials that add season-long interest to the garden. Among the earliest perennials to bloom, they produce small clusters of dainty, bell-shaped flowers from late winter to late spring before or just as the leaves begin to emerge. Blooms come in shades of lavender- and violet-blue as well as white, pink, and red. Most cultivated pulmonarias produce mounds of broadly oval green leaves splashed with white or silver. The largest leaves are produced in a low rosette at the base of the plant, and smaller leaves are borne on the flower stems as well. The foliage remains attractive until early winter, and in mild-climate areas, some lungworts are evergreen. About 14 species belong to the genus.

HOW TO GROW

Grow lungworts in partial to full shade in a site with rich, evenly moist soil. A site with morning sun and afternoon shade also is suitable. Plants self-sow, and seedlings may be very attractive, although pulmonarias hybridize freely, so they will not be identical to the parents. They make lovely manageable ground covers. Established plants tolerate drought, but watering during dry weather keeps the foliage looking its best. Plants thrive for years without needing to be divided, but for propagation the clumps can be dug in spring, after they flower, or in early fall.

Pulmonaria saccharata 'Mrs. Moon'

P. angustifolia

p. an-gus-tih-FOE-lee-uh. BLUE LUNGWORT, BLUE COWSLIP. A 10- to 12-inch-tall species that spreads by rhizomes to form 1¹/₂-foot-wide clumps. Bears unspotted dark green leaves and funnel-shaped ³/₈-inch-wide blue flowers in early spring. *P. a.* ssp. *azurea* has rich blue flowers with red-tinted buds. **Zones 4 to 8.**

P. hybrids

Many hybrid lungworts with outstanding foliage or spring-borne flowers are available. They are 9 to 14 inches tall and spread to 18 inches. 'Janet Fisk', with white-marbled leaves, has pink flowers that age to blue and is hardy in **Zones 3 to 8.** 'Roy Davidson', hardy in **Zones 5 to 8,** bears mid-green leaves evenly blotched with silver and sky blue flowers. 'Sissinghurst White', **Zones 4 or 5 to 8,** is grown for its white flowers. 'Spilled Milk', **Zones 5 to 8,** has leaves that are mostly silver-white and pink flowers that age to blue.

P. longifolia

p. lon-jih-FOE-lee-uh. LONGLEAF LUNGWORT. Forms 9- to 12-inch-tall mounds of lance-shaped, 18-inch-long leaves with silver spots and spreads by rhizomes to form 2¹/₂-foot-wide clumps. It bears showy clusters of purple-blue flowers in early spring. **Zones 4 to 8.**

P. rubra

p. RUE-bruh. RED LUNGWORT. A 1- to 1¹/₂-foot-tall species forming mounds of solid green leaves that reach 2 feet in length. Spreads by rhizomes to form 3-foot-wide clumps. Bears reddish pink flowers in early spring. **Zones 5 to 8.**

P. saccharata

p. sak-ah-RAH-tuh. BETHLEHEM SAGE. Produces 8- to 12-inch-tall mounds of silver-spotted leaves and spreads by rhizomes to form 2-foot-wide clumps. In early spring, bears pink flower buds that open to purple-blue or red-violet flowers. Evergreen in areas with mild winters. 'Mrs. Moon', with pink buds and bluish lilac flowers, is the most commonly available cultivar. 'Pierre's Pure Pink' has shell pink flowers. **Zones 3 to 8.**

Pulsatilla

pul-sah-TILL-uh. Buttercup family, Ranunculaceae.

Commonly called pasqueflowers, *Pulsatilla* species are clump-forming perennials with very finely cut leaves that have a fernlike texture and cup- or bell-shaped flowers, which are borne in spring and early summer. The flowers are followed by silvery-hairy pomponlike seed heads that also are ornamental. About 30 species belong to the genus.

HOW TO GROW

Plant pasqueflowers in full sun and rich, very well drained soil. The plants go dormant in early summer, so mark their locations to avoid digging into the clumps by mistake. In general, they are slow to establish and resent transplanting, so select a permanent location. (Small plants often are easier to establish than large ones.) Avoid digging or dividing plants unless absolutely necessary, because the roots are easily damaged. Plants self-sow, and seedlings, which are easy to move when small, are a good propagation option. Or, take root cuttings in winter.

P. vulgaris

p. vul-GAIR-iss. PASQUEFLOWER. Formerly *Anemone vulgaris*. A 6- to 10-inch-tall species with feathery, silvery-hairy leaves that emerge after the plants have nearly finished blooming. Bears 1¹/₂- to 3¹/₂-inch-wide flowers in shades of

Pulmonaria saccharata

P

rosy purple, blue-violet, or white in very early spring. **Zones 5 to 8.**

Punica

POO-nih-kuh. Pomegranate family, Punicaceae.

This genus includes only two species of deciduous shrubs or trees. The most commonly grown species is native to Southwest Asia, southeast Europe, and the Himalayas and is cultivated for its colorful funnel-shaped flowers and edible fruits.

HOW TO GROW

Pomegranate will do best in fertile, moisture-retentive soil but adapts to both sandy and clay soils in a wide pH range as long as it has good drainage. It tolerates some shade but will flower and fruit best in full sun. Use in a shrub border, in a mass, or in a container. Where hardiness is borderline, grow it against a warm wall. Prune in spring to shape and to encourage summer flowers on new growth. Propagate from seeds or softwood cuttings.

P. granatum

p. gran-AY-tum. POMEGRANATE. Upright, slightly rounded in habit, with most popular varieties about 10 feet tall and wide or slightly narrower. The glossy oblong leaves may be bronzed when new, chartreuse in autumn. The species has orange-red funnel-shaped flowers with five crinkled lobes, first appearing in mid- to late summer and continuing into fall. That's when the round, edible, yellow-brown fruits (sometimes shades of red) begin developing, up to 5 inches in diameter. *P. g.* var. *nana*

Punica granatum

Pulsatilla vulgaris

gets only 3 feet tall; 'Wonderful' has a fountainlike habit with red fruit. **Zones 8 to 10.**

Puschkinia

push-KIN-ee-uh. Lily family, Liliaceae.

Puschkinia contains a single species of spring-blooming bulb — *P. scilloides*, commonly known as striped squill. Closely related to both *Chionodoxa* and *Scilla*, it hails from the Middle East and grows from a small tunicate bulb. Plants bear basal, linear to strap-shaped leaves and dense racemes of small flowers, which appear in spring. The flowers are borne on leafless stalks and consist of six petal-like tepals.

HOW TO GROW

Select a site with average, well-drained soil that is in full sun or in partial to full shade under deciduous trees so plants receive full sun in spring when they are actively growing. A site that dries out in summer when plants are dormant is beneficial but not required. Plant the bulbs in fall with the bases at a depth of about 3 inches. For best effect, arrange them in drifts — a plant or two here and there will be lost in the spring garden. Propagate by digging and dividing the clumps and/or separating the offsets and seedlings in early summer just as the foliage dies back.

P. scilloides

p. sil-OY-deez. STRIPED SQUILL. A 6- to 8-inch-tall species bearing erect racemes of 4 to 10 densely packed flowers in spring. Individual blooms are bell shaped, $1/2$ inch wide, and very pale bluish white in color with a darker stripe on each tepal. *P. s.* var. *libanotica* (formerly *P. libanotica*) bears

racemes of small $1/4$- to $3/8$-inch-wide white flowers that usually lack darker stripes and have pointed tepals. **Zones 3 to 9.**

Pyracantha

pye-ruh-KAN-thuh. Rose family, Rosaceae.

A genus of seven spiny evergreens, mostly shrubs, native to East Asia and southeast Europe. From late spring to early summer they bear clusters of small white flowers, but the main attraction is the colorful persistent berries that follow.

HOW TO GROW

A good plant for hot, dry climates, pyracantha prefers neutral to somewhat acid, well-drained soil. It needs full sun for best fruiting and doesn't transplant well once established. Grow as a specimen or in a shrub border. It's too thorny for an entire hedge, except as a security barrier. It is often espaliered since it tolerates hard pruning at any time and needs regular hard pruning to maintain an attractive shape. Propagate from cold-stratified seeds or semiripe cuttings.

P. coccinea

p. kok-SIN-ee-uh. SCARLET FIRETHORN. An evergreen 6 to 18 feet tall and wide with stiff, sparse branches, long thorns, and glossy 2-inch dark green leaves. Clusters of $1/3$-inch white flowers bloom along the previous season's stems in mid- to late spring. The orange-red pea-sized berries ripen in early fall and may last through winter. Lace bug can be a pest, but the biggest problems are scab and fire blight. Some resistant cultivars are 'Apache' (to 4 feet, with red persistent fruits), 'Fiery Cascade' (upright, with orange berries turning red, cold tolerant), 'Goldrush' (densely branched, with yellow-orange fruits), 'Mohave' (upright with heavy flowering and fruiting), 'Navaho' (6 feet, dense branching), 'Pueblo' (wide spreading, with profuse persistent fruits), 'Rutgers' (4 feet tall, wide spreading, cold tolerant), and 'Teton' (upright, yellow-orange fruits). 'Lalandei' is hardy to **Zone 5** but susceptible to scab. **Zones 6 to 9.**

P. koidzumii

p. koyd-ZOOM-ee-eye. FORMOSA FIRETHORN. Semievergreen to evergreen shrub with upright branching 8 to 12 feet high and wide. Racemes of $1/4$-inch white flowers bloom in midspring, followed by persistent red berries beginning in early fall. Disease-resistant cultivars include 'Santa Cruz' (horizontal form to 3 feet tall and 6 feet wide) and 'Victory' (upright and arching, with dark red fruits). **Zones 8 to 10.**

P. × watereri

p. × WAH-ter-er-eye This hybrid grows 8 feet tall and wide and has fewer thorns and profuse, long-lasting dark red berries. **Zones 7 to 10.**

Puschkinia scilloides

P

Pyrus

PYE-russ. Rose family,
Rosaceae.

This genus contains about 30 species of Old World trees that produce small clusters of white flowers in spring and usually small, seedy, inconspicuous fruits, although several are orchard trees that produce edible pears. The leaves are glossy ovals with toothed or scalloped edges; branches are sometimes thorny. Several species are popular for their ornamental flowers and handsome leaves. One, *P. calleryana* 'Bradford' (Bradford pear), has been overplanted as a street tree, and its susceptibility to storm damage has become an expensive problem for many municipalities.

HOW TO GROW

Plant in full sun to partial shade and almost any well-drained soil. Best with even moisture, but tolerates drought and intermittently wet soil. Performs well in urban settings; tolerates air pollution. Large limbs of cultivars with tight branch angles may be susceptible to storm damage. Choose improved cultivars or prune when young to develop strong crotch angles. Susceptible to several insects and diseases; the worst problem is fire blight in the South.

P. calleryana

p. kal-ler-ee-AH-nuh. CALLERY PEAR, FLOWERING PEAR. Cold hardy and beautiful in bloom and in leaf, Callery pear and its many cultivars have become popular as garden and street trees because they grow into manageable oval or rounded shapes 30 to 50

Pyracantha coccinea 'Mohave'

feet tall and 20 to 35 feet wide. In early spring, fluffy clusters of white, five-petaled, 1-inch flowers with dark-tipped anthers transform the tree into a snowy mass. Most cultivars have an offensive odor up close that can permeate a yard, especially when several trees are grown together. The dark green, oval leaves have a high polish and lovely scalloped edges. They open when the flowers begin to fade and are 4 to 5 inches long. Color is spectacular in late fall and often lasts for several weeks. A single tree may include red, purple, orange, and scarlet foliage. The green or russet, $^1/_4$- to $^1/_2$-inch fruits ripen in summer and are attractive to birds; although the fruits themselves are not messy, the resulting bird droppings may be. Most cultivars tend to have a stiff oval shape, which makes them good street trees, because the limbs do not interfere with traffic. But the shape is often too formal for their use as shade trees in home landscapes. An excellent performer in the Midwest and North. From Asia. **Zones 5 to 9**, but may vary, depending on the cultivar.

CULTIVARS AND SIMILAR SPECIES

'Aristocrat' is fast growing and pyramidal when young, and rounded with strong, more horizontal branches as it ages; leaves are narrow, turning red and yellow in fall; does not flower well when young. 'Autumn Blaze' has strong, wide crotch angles and the widest, most informal crown of any cultivar; grows to 35 feet tall and 20 feet wide; excellent, long-lasting, cardinal red early-fall color and bad-smelling flowers; susceptible to fire blight. 'Bradford' has a uniform oval shape, growing to 45 feet tall; prone to storm damage because of its crowded, narrow crotch angles; widely planted but now out of favor. 'Burgundy Snow' bears profuse white flowers with burgundy centers; pyramidal, growing to 40 feet tall; **Zones 4 to 9**. 'Capital' is columnar, has a strong central leader, and grows to 40 feet tall and 12 feet wide; purple and bright red early-fall color. 'Chanticleer' ('Cleveland Select') is a 35-foot-tall, formal pyramid or oval with strong branches and a central leader if properly pruned; abundant, bad-smelling flowers; gold, red, and purple early-fall color; fire blight resistant; **Zones 4 to 9**. 'Frontier' is narrow and upright, growing to 35 feet tall and 20 feet

Pyrus calleryana 'Chanticleer'

wide, and is the most cold-hardy selection, to **Zone 3**. 'Metropolitan' has a wide-spreading shape, growing to 45 feet tall, with strong branch angles. 'Redspire' is a dense, narrow pyramid, growing to 35 feet tall and 15 feet wide; strong branches, large flowers, and yellow, red, and maroon early-fall color; somewhat susceptible to fire blight. 'Valiant' is short and compact, reaching 30 feet tall and 20 feet wide; crimson early-fall color; **Zones 4 to 9**. 'Whitehouse' is a narrow, pyramidal oval reaching 40 feet tall and 18 feet wide; reddish purple early-fall color.

P. ussuriensis (Ussuri pear) is a very cold hardy, fire blight–resistant Asian species; rounded and growing 40 to 50 feet tall; prolific white flowers, leathery leaves, and reddish purple fall color; **Zones 3 to 6**. 'Mountain Frost' is vigorous and upright, reaching 30 feet tall. 'Prairie Gem' is smaller and more rounded, reaching 18 to 25 feet tall.

P. salicifolia 'Pendula'

p. sal-ih-sih-FOE-lee-uh. WEEPING WILLOW-LEAVED PEAR. This graceful weeping tree grows to 25 feet tall and makes a spectacular light-reflecting focal point against a dark background. Its main attraction is its narrow silvery leaves, which are $3^1/_2$ inches long and covered with white fuzz. Combined with the cascading branches, these leaves create the same effect as a weeping Russian olive (*Elaeagnus angustifolia*). The spring-blooming flowers are white and showy, but they are obscured by the leaves. The green, pear-shaped, $1^1/_2$-inch fruits are sparse and also go unnoticed. Plant this specimen as a focal point at the axis of a path or near a patio where its silvery glow can stand out against a background of evergreens or a dark wall. It is subject to fire blight. From southwestern Asia. **Zones 5 to 8**.

CULTIVARS AND SIMILAR SPECIES

'Silver Frost' is the same as 'Pendula'. *P. betulaefolia* (birch-leaf pear) has an oval shape with strong, slightly pendulous branches; grows to 35 feet tall; coarse-toothed leaves are green on top and silvery on their undersides; white spring flowers are partly hidden by the leaves; resists fire blight. 'Dancer' has silvery leaves that flutter like an aspen's (*Populus*) in the slightest breeze. 'Edgedell' is a hybrid with purple-tinged new leaves that mature to silver.

Q

Quercus

KWER-kus. Beech family, Fagaceae.

This large genus of 450 species contains both evergreen and deciduous trees and shrubs that hail mostly from the Northern Hemisphere and are particularly abundant in Mexico, which claims more than 100 native species. Most North American species are large, long-lived trees that make an impressive statement in the landscape. Flowers are usually inconspicuous male and female catkins. Fruits are highly recognizable acorns — the seeds rest in a rough, caplike cup. Leaves are alternate and usually lobed, with blunt or pointed tips, but some species have unlobed leaves. Deciduous oaks are divided into two groups: black (red) oaks, with bristle-tipped pointed lobes and acorns that take 2 years to mature, and white oaks, with rounded lobes and acorns that take 1 year to mature. (Evergreen oaks are listed separately after the deciduous species.) Many of these forest dwellers are important for lumber and wildlife, but they also are popular and useful shade trees for home

and public landscapes. Until recently, most species were not widely propagated by nurseries because cuttings were difficult to root and many species have taproots. Modern growing techniques are overcoming these problems, and oaks are now more widely available.

Many diseases and insects attack oak trees, although most are not life threatening. Gypsy moths defoliate oaks during epidemic years. Red oaks are highly susceptible to oak wilt; they should not be pruned during the growing season, because beetles carrying this deadly fungus can easily enter the wounds; infected trees should be destroyed. White oaks are susceptible to mildew during wet years. See individual descriptions for specific requirements.

BLACK (RED) OAKS

Q. coccinea

q. kok-SIN-ee-uh. SCARLET OAK. This pyramidal or rounded tree is beloved for its scarlet fall color and grows to 75 feet tall and 40 feet wide. More reliable and more colorful than most oaks in autumn, scarlet oak turns maroon to brilliant scarlet in midfall, in a

good year rivaling the best of the maples (*Acer*). Leaves are deeply cut into seven to nine C-shaped lobes with bristly points. They measure 3 to 6 inches long and $2^{1}/_2$ to $4^{1}/_2$ inches wide, emerging bright red and maturing to a glossy dark green on top with waxy, dull green undersides. The reddish brown acorns are $^{1}/_2$ to 2 inches long and are mostly covered by a bowl-like cup. Like many native oaks, this one was difficult to find in nurseries until recently. It should be saved during development and makes an excellent lawn or street tree.

Grow it in full sun. It does best in moist, acid, sandy soil but tolerates slightly alkaline, clayey, or dry soil. From eastern and central North America. **Zones 5 to 9.**

Q. palustris

q. pal-US-tris. PIN OAK. This strongly pyramidal tree grows 60 to 70 or more feet tall and 25 to 40 feet wide. It has a distinctive straight trunk and a strong horizontal branching pattern, with the lowest branches sweeping downward and creating a skirt near the base of the tree. The yellow-green catkins bloom along with the emerging foliage. The 3- to 6-inch-

long, deep green leaves are deeply cut into five to seven U-shaped lobes with sharp points. In fall the leaves change to yellow or coppery red, then become paper-bag brown and may remain on the tree through the winter. Pin oak produces numerous crops of round, $^{1}/_2$-inch, light brown acorns with thin, shallow cups. This is probably the oak that is most widely planted as a lawn and street tree. However, it needs plenty of room for its low, ascending branches and therefore actually makes a poor street tree.

Pin oaks like full sun and moist, well-drained, rich, acid soil. They tolerate wet sites, air pollution, and drought, but the acorns may be a litter problem. The tree is easy to transplant because of its shallow, fibrous root system. Chlorosis is serious in neutral to alkaline soil, so the tree performs poorly in the Plains and Midwest. From eastern North America.
Zones 5 to 8.

CULTIVARS AND SIMILAR SPECIES

'Crownright' has strongly horizontal branches that do not droop, but it is subject to breakage and so is no longer recommended. *Q. ellipsoidalis* (northern pin oak) is

Quercus coccinea

Quercus palustris

Quercus falcata

very similar to pin oak but is native to a more northerly area; **Zones 3 to 6**. *Q. nuttallii (Q. texana)* (Nuttall's oak) resembles pin oak but hails from the South; a very fast grower with a pyramidal shape and red fall color, it withstands the wet soil and urban conditions of the South and Midwest; **Zones 5 to 9**.

Q. rubra
q. RUE-bruh. NORTHERN RED OAK. Formerly *Q. borealis*. Upright with horizontal branching, northern red oak grows to 70 feet tall and wide and can rival *Q. coccinea* for fall color. The 4- to 8-inch-long leaves are deeply cut into 7 to 11 shallow lobes with sharp points. They unfold pinkish red in spring and mature to dark green with gray-green undersides. In autumn they turn russet-red to bright red. The 1-inch acorns are dark brown with smooth ridges and gray stripes. Bark on mature trees is deeply furrowed and quite ornamental. Use this fast-growing, long-lived oak as a shade tree for a lawn or park. Makes a good street tree except under power lines.

Grow it in full sun to partial shade and well-drained, light, acid to neutral soil. It tolerates drought and urban conditions. Acorns may be a litter problem. Train to develop a strong central leader with evenly spaced branches. Chlorosis can develop in alkaline soil. From eastern and midwestern North America. **Zones 3 to 9**.

SIMILAR SPECIES
Q. falcata (southern red oak, Spanish oak) has red-orange to russet-orange fall color and can grow in very poor soil; **Zones 6 to 9**. *Q. shumardii* (shumard oak) is very similar to *Q. rubra* in its red

fall foliage, but it is native to southeastern and south-central North America; fast growing, it performs well in its native regions in wet or dry soil; **Zones 5 to 9**. *Q. velutina* (black oak) is native to eastern and midwestern North America; not widely available commercially, but should be saved during development; the seven- to nine-lobed, stiff, shiny green leaves turn russet in autumn; $1/2$-inch, light brown acorns; grows in sandy to heavy soil but performs best in a rich, moist site; **Zones 4 to 8**.

WHITE OAKS

Q. acutissima
q. ah-kew-TISS-ih-muh. SAWTOOTH OAK. Pyramidal when young, sawtooth oak becomes rounded with age, growing 35 to 45 feet tall and wide, with large, low branches. The leaves of this beautiful, fine-textured shade tree resemble chestnut leaves: unlobed and oblong (7 inches long and $2^{1}/4$ inches wide), with softly bristled edges. They open light golden green in spring and mature to shiny dark green. Fall color is bright yellow to gold and develops late; dry leaves often persist through the winter. Attractive, golden, 4-inch-long catkins decorate the tree in spring when the leaves open. One-inch-long, round, rich brown acorns with shaggy caps are borne profusely, providing excellent food for wildlife but posing a cleanup problem if not eaten. Bark is deeply ridged and furrowed, becoming corky with age. This heat-tolerant tree makes an exceptional shade tree in the South.

Grow it in full sun and rich, moist, well-drained, acid to neutral soil. It tolerates intermittent

poor drainage, drought, and salt spray. Train it to a single leader with evenly spaced main branches. May be defoliated by oakworms and become chlorotic in an alkaline site. From Asia. **Zones 5 to 9**.

CULTIVARS AND SIMILAR SPECIES
'Gobbler' has an especially reliable, heavy crop of acorns and is very cold hardy. The following North American trees are valuable natives with similar leaves. Though not widely sold, they should be preserved during site development. *Q. muehlenbergii* (yellow chestnut oak) is native to east-central and southwestern North America and is often found on limestone outcroppings; its yellow-green leaves are unlobed with round-toothed edges and have felty white undersides; the tree's shape is narrow and vaselike; grows to 50 or more feet tall; a good choice for neutral to alkaline soil; **Zones 5 to 8**. *Q. prinus* (chestnut oak) is native to eastern North America; it forms a dense, rounded tree that reaches 60 feet tall; its leaves measure up to 7 inches long, open pale green, mature to dark green, and turn red-orange and golden brown in autumn; acorns are large and can pose a cleanup problem; excels in dry, rocky, acid soil; **Zones 5 to 9**. *Q. michauxii* (swamp chestnut oak) is very similar to *Q. prinus* but is native to wet sites in southern and central North America; **Zones 6 to 9**.

Q. bicolor
q. BI-kul-or. SWAMP WHITE OAK. The winter silhouette of this mighty oak is rugged and coarse, with a round, low, open canopy that grows 50 to 60 feet tall and spreads even wider. Leaves are 3 to 7 inches long, blunt lobed or

Quercus alba

wavy edged, and shiny dark green on top with velvety gray-green undersides. They form a dense foliage that turns yellow-brown to red in autumn. The bark on the branches peels like that of a birch (*Betula*), and the trunk bark is roughly furrowed and marked with white. Light brown acorns ripen in early fall and are about 1 inch long. Native to swampy sites, this massive oak also tolerates drought and is one of the easiest white oaks to transplant. It makes an excellent choice for parks, wetlands, and open spaces.

Grow in full sun to partial shade. Best in moist, acid to neutral soil but also grows well in wet sites and tolerates drought. Suffers from chlorosis in highly alkaline soil. Trees saved during development are very sensitive to soil compaction or disturbance during construction and should be mulched heavily rather than having grass planted beneath them. Usually not bothered by pests, except for gypsy moths. Performs well in the Midwest and Mountain States. From eastern North America. **Zones 4 to 8**.

CULTIVARS AND SIMILAR SPECIES
Q. alba (white oak) is a massive, spreading, slow-growing native oak that has only recently been offered by nurseries; it has upright to horizontal branches and a picturesque, rugged, 80- to 100-foot-tall silhouette; trunk and limbs are covered with light brown or gray shaggy bark; leaves are 4 to 8 inches long with rounded lobes; they emerge pinkish, mature to a deep matte blue-green, and usually turn purplish or crimson before dropping in fall; one of the finest fall displays of any oak; leaves are mildew resistant; tolerates alkaline and occasionally wet soil; **Zones 4 to 9**. *Q. macrocarpa* (bur oak, mossycup oak) is slow growing to 60 to 80 feet tall; it has a straight trunk and low branches; leaves are blunt lobed; twigs are corky; acorns are 2 inches around and provide food for wildlife; tolerates drought and wet soil; an excellent shade tree or windbreak in acid or alkaline soil in its native midwestern Plains and Rocky Mountains; **Zones 3 to 9**. 'Boomer' is more upright, with spreading branches and vigorous growth.

Q. nigra
q. NYE-gruh. WATER OAK, POSSUM OAK. This upright or rounded tree is a fast-growing,

rough-barked native that reaches 50 to 80 feet tall and half as wide. It is a popular street and shade tree in the South because of its shape and slender branches. Its fine-textured, dull blue-green leaves measure 2 to 4 inches long and half as wide and vary from unlobed to slightly lobed to paddle shaped. They stay green until they drop in early winter and may be semievergreen in the Deep South. Acorns are $1/2$ inch long, are striped brown and black, have shallow caps, and require little cleanup, although they can stain concrete when they drop. Use this tall tree where there is plenty of room for it to grow.

It needs full sun; is best in moist, well-drained soil but tolerates wet sites and heavy, compacted soil. Mistletoe, aphids, scale, and borers can be problems. From southeastern North America. **Zones 6 to 10.**

Q. phellos

q. FILL-loos. WILLOW OAK. This fine-textured oak is pyramidal with weeping lower branches when young and becomes rounded with age, growing 50 to 90 feet tall and 40 feet wide. The leaves are unusual for an oak — long, slender, and unlobed, measuring about 4 inches long and 1 inch wide. These shiny, dark green leaves create a much more refined texture than that of most oaks. In the coldest zones of its range, the leaves often turn red or yellow in fall, but in the warmest zones, they remain green into winter. The tree produces copious $1/2$-inch acorns, which are excellent food for wildlife and, because of their small size, do not pose a cleanup problem in groomed landscapes. Use this graceful tree to shade a lawn or street. It is easily transplanted and readily available.

Grow in full sun and moist, well-drained, acid soil. Tolerates intermittent poor drainage. The small leaves are easy to rake. Chlorosis develops in alkaline soil; otherwise it is problem-free. From southeastern North America. **Zones 6 to 9.**

Q. robur

q. ROE-bur. ENGLISH OAK. This distinguished European oak is broad and rounded, with a short massive trunk and huge low branches, making an impressive specimen 50 to 100 feet tall and wide. The dark, matte green leaves are 2 to 5 inches long, with three

Quercus virginiana

to seven rounded lobes. They drop in early winter without changing color. The 1-inch-long, shiny, dark brown acorns have a distinctive narrow shape and grow on long stalks. Trunk bark is rugged, deeply furrowed, and gray-black. The species grows quite large and is best used in parks. Smaller and narrower cultivars perform well as screens, windbreaks, and garden shade trees.

Grow in full sun and well-drained soil. Tolerates clayey or slightly alkaline soil, urban conditions, and drought. It is excellent in the Midwest and Mountain States. From Europe and western Asia. **Zones 5 to 9.**

CULTIVARS AND SIMILAR SPECIES

'Crimson Spire' is a tight, columnar hybrid with *Q. alba,* growing to 45 feet tall and 15 feet wide; mildew-resistant leaves and rusty red fall color. 'Rosehill' is a narrow oval that reaches 40 feet tall and 20 feet wide; glossy, mildew-resistant leaves. 'Skymaster' has very dark green leaves and is narrowly pyramidal, with a strong central leader; grows to 50 feet tall and 15 feet wide. 'Skyrocket' ('Fastigiata') grows to 50 feet tall and 15 feet wide. 'Westminster Globe' is rounded and symmetrical, with a strong branch structure; grows to 45 feet tall and wide. *Q.* × *warei* 'Regal Prince' is an upright, oval hybrid with *Q. bicolor* that grows to 50 feet; dark green leaves with

silvery undersides; tolerates wet or dry sites.

EVERGREEN OAKS

Q. chrysolepis

q. kry-so-LEP-iss. CANYON OAK. This round-headed or spreading evergreen grows 20 to 60 feet tall and 20 feet wide. The shiny, dark green leaves are 4 inches long and $2^{1}/2$ inches wide and unlobed, with or without spines along the margins. Their undersides are coated with a dense gold or gray felt. Trunk bark is smooth and whitish gray when young, becoming darker and scaly with age. The oblong or oval, 1- to 2-inch-long acorns have gold-felted caps. Use as a shade tree in a naturalistic or informal site. This native tree should be saved during site development, but do not irrigate it, as it is adapted to little water.

Grow in full sun and well-drained soil. Tolerates drought. Prune deadwood only if dangerous, because pruning cuts allow fungal diseases to enter the tree. From western North America. **Zones 7 to 9.**

Q. virginiana

q. ver-jin-ee-AH-nuh. LIVE OAK. One of the white oaks, this fast-growing, long-lived tree grows slowly into an irregularly shaped specimen with a stout trunk and massive outstretched branches that sometimes sweep sinuously

Quercus virginiana

downward to rest on the ground. Trees grow to at least 80 feet tall and 120 feet wide. The 3-inch-long, 1-inch-wide, oval leaves are leathery and have smooth, unlobed edges. Leaves are bright olive green in spring and mature to dark green with gray-green, felt-covered undersides. Older leaves drop in spring when the new leaves emerge, making the tree essentially evergreen. Long, yellowish brown catkins bloom in spring. Clusters of 1-inch-long, black acorns ripen in late summer and provide food for wildlife. Trunk bark is dark brown to black and fissured into large blocks. Use as a lawn specimen, for shade, or to line a long driveway or a street where there is plenty of room for the tree to grow.

Grow in full sun to partial shade and well-drained, acid to alkaline soil. Tolerates sandy soil and drought once established and withstands seashore conditions. Remove deadwood as the tree ages. Spanish moss hanging from the branches does no harm, but do not allow ivy to grow too high into the tree, as its weight may contribute to storm damage. Grows best in warm, humid coastal areas; performs poorly inland. From southeastern coastal North America. **Zones 7 to 9.**

CULTIVARS AND SIMILAR SPECIES

'Heritage' is fast growing and performs well in low desert areas. 'Highrise' has an upright, rather than a spreading, shape, making it a better street tree. 'Southern Shade' has excellent foliage and is fast growing, with the typical spreading shape. *Q. agrifolia* (coast live oak) is native to the coastal ranges of western North America; it grows to 70 feet tall and at least as wide and has dense, hollylike leaves. *Q. engelmanii* (mesa oak) is another evergreen, wide-spreading oak that is native to southern California. *Q. fusiformis* (upland live oak) is very similar to live oak and is native to central Texas; resists oak wilt but is susceptible to root rot.

Q

Ranunculus

rah-NUN-kew-liss. Buttercup family, Ranunculaceae.

Best known as buttercups, *Ranunculus* species are primarily perennials, although there are some annuals and biennials among the 400 species in the genus. Most bear cup-, bowl-, or saucer-shaped flowers with five petals around a cluster of showy stamens. There also are garden-grown forms with double flowers, as well as species that lack petals altogether. Blooms are solitary or carried in clusters. Yellow is by far the most common flower color, although a few species feature white, pink, orange, or red blooms. Buttercups produce a rosette of leaves that vary greatly in shape: they range from deeply cut or lobed in a pinnate fashion to simple with entire or toothed leaf margins. There are buttercups suitable for a wide range of conditions, including boggy spots, rock gardens, shady moist woodlands, and sites with rich soil in full sun or partial shade. Depending on the species, plants have fibrous or tuberous roots, and there are species that spread by rhizomes, runners, or stolons. Some can be aggressive spreaders.

HOW TO GROW
Cultivation requirements of the bulbs listed here vary. *R. aconitifolius* is best in partial to full shade with constantly moist soil. Give *R. asiaticus* full sun and light, rich, well-drained soil that is evenly moist when the plants are actively growing and dry during the summer, when they are dormant. In areas with mild climates that offer these conditions, including southern California, *R. asiaticus* can be grown outdoors year-round. Elsewhere, grow this species in containers. It is often treated as an annual. Water sparingly at planting time and until foliage appears. Once buds appear, feed each time you water with a dilute liquid fertilizer and keep the soil evenly moist.

R. bulbosus thrives in a site with full sun or partial shade and rich, moist, well-drained soil. *R. ficaria* requires partial to full shade and rich, moist soil. Plant these two species outdoors in fall, where they're hardy, or plant in spring at a depth of 2 inches. For all three species, where they're marginally hardy, cover the beds with mulch over winter, but remove it in late winter. Propagate tuberous species by dividing plants in spring or fall. *R. bulbosus* and *R. ficaria* self-sow.

R. aconitifolius
r. ack-oh-nye-tih-FOE-lee-us. ACO-NITE BUTTERCUP, BACHE-LOR'S BUTTONS. A 2-foot-tall clump-forming perennial that spreads to about 1^1/$_2$ feet. Bears white ^{1}/$_2$- to ^{3}/$_4$-inch-wide flowers in late spring and early summer. 'Flore Pleno', with double flowers, is more often grown than the species. **Zones 5 to 9.**

R. acris
r. AY-kris. TALL BUTTERCUP, MEADOW BUTTERCUP. A 1- to 3-foot-tall perennial native to Europe that has naturalized in North America. Plants spread to 1 to 1^1/$_2$ feet and bear 1-inch-wide golden yellow flowers from early to midsummer. 'Flore Pleno', also sold as 'Plena' and 'Multiplex', bears double flowers and is more often grown than the species, which is fairly weedy. **Zones 3 or 4 to 8.**

R. asiaticus
r. ay-see-AT-ih-kus. PERSIAN BUT-TERCUP. An 8- to 18-inch-tall tuberous-rooted species with rounded, three-lobed, 5^1/$_2$-inch-long leaves. Bears branched stems of one to four cup-shaped 1^1/$_4$- to 2-inch-wide flowers in late spring and early summer. Blooms come in yellow, red, pink, and white and have purple-black centers. Teco-lote Mixed cultivars bear double or single 4-inch-wide flowers in shades of yellow, orange, pink, and white. Turban Group cultivars also bear double flowers in a range of colors. **Zones 7 to 11.**

R. bulbosus
r. bul-BO-sus. BULBOUS BUT-TERCUP. A 6- to 16-inch-tall species native to Europe and North Africa that has naturalized in North America. Grows from a swollen base that resembles a corm. Bears three-lobed 5-inch-long leaves that are further toothed and divided. In late spring and early summer, plants produce clusters of golden yellow ^{3}/$_4$- to 1^1/$_4$-inch-wide flowers. 'F. M. Burton', sometimes sold as *R. b.* var. *farreri*, bears glossy, creamy yellow flowers. **Zones 7 to 9.**

R. ficaria
r. fih-KAH-ree-uh. LESSER CELAN-DINE. A 2- to 6-inch-tall tuberous species native from Europe and North Africa to southwestern Asia that has naturalized in parts of North America. Bears handsome heart-shaped leaves with toothed or scalloped margins and often marked with silver, bronze, or black-purple. In early spring, solitary, cup-shaped golden yellow flowers with shiny petals appear. Blooms are ^{3}/$_4$ to 1^1/$_4$ inches wide. Leaves die down in early summer after the plants flower. Produces offsets and self-sown seedlings with abandon, and may become invasive. Double-flowered forms produce fewer seeds. Many cultivars are available, including 'Brazen Hussy', with black-purple leaves and golden flowers; 'Collarette', with silver-marbled leaves and yellow flowers with a ruff of petaloid stamens in the center; 'Double Bronze', bearing double golden yellow blooms and

Ranunculus asiaticus

Ratibida pinnata

leaves marbled in purple and silver; 'Flore Pleno', with double yellow flowers; 'Randall's White', with creamy white flowers and marbled leaves; and 'Salmon's White', with white flowers and leaves veined in dark purple. **Zones 4 to 8.**

R. montanus
r. mon-TAN-us. A low-growing 3- to 6-inch-tall perennial that spreads by rhizomes to form 1-foot-wide mats. Bears ³/₄- to 1-inch-wide yellow flowers in early summer. Spreads, but is not as invasive as *R. repens*. 'Molten Gold' has 1- to 1¹/₄-inch-wide golden yellow flowers. **Zones 4 to 8.**

R. repens
r. REP-enz. CREEPING BUTTERCUP. Fast-spreading 1- to 2-foot-tall perennial that spreads by stolons to form drifts 6 feet or more across. Bears clusters of ¹/₂- to ³/₄-inch-wide yellow flowers from late spring to midsummer. Dig up clumps if they outgrow their places. Double-flowered 'Pleniflorus', sometimes sold as 'Flore Pleno', is somewhat less invasive and more commonly grown than the species. **Zones 3 to 8.**

Ratibida
rah-tih-BID-uh. Aster family, Asteraceae.

Native to North America and Mexico, *Ratibida* species are woody-based biennials and perennials grown for their daisylike blooms. Commonly called Mexican hat or prairie coneflowers, they bear flower heads with long drooping ray florets, or "petals," surrounding prominent, conelike centers of disk florets. Ray florets are yellow, orange, or purple-brown; conelike centers are generally brown. The leaves are deeply cut in a pinnate fashion. There are about five or six species of *Ratibida*, which are closely related to orange coneflowers *(Rudbeckia)* and were once included in that genus.

HOW TO GROW
Select a site in full sun with average, well-drained soil. Plants tolerate dry soil as well as heat and humidity. Neutral to alkaline pH is best. Propagate by dividing plants in spring, but divide only young plants, as the roots and crowns become woody with age. Or start from seeds. Both species listed here are sometimes grown as annuals or biennials.

R. columnifera
r. kol-um-NIFF-er-uh. PRAIRIE CONEFLOWER. Formerly *Lepachys columnifera, Rudbeckia columnifera*. A 3-foot-tall native North American wildflower that spreads to about 1 foot. From early summer to fall, bears yellow daisy-like 3-inch-wide flower heads with conelike 2-inch-tall centers that turn from green to brown. *R. c. f. pulcherrima* produces flower heads with purple- or red-brown ray florets. **Zones 3 to 10.**

R. pinnata
r. pin-NAH-tuh. DROOPING CONEFLOWER, GRAY-HEAD CONEFLOWER. Formerly *Lepachys pinnata, Rudbeckia pinnata*. A 3- to 4-foot-tall species native to North America that forms 1¹/₂-foot-wide clumps. Has blue-green leaves and, from summer to fall, bears 5-inch-wide daisylike flower heads with yellow ray florets surrounding red-brown cones. **Zones 3 to 10.**

Rehmannia
reh-MAH-nee-uh. Figwort family, Scrophulariaceae.

Native to China, the 10 species of *Rehmannia* are tender perennials that gardeners grow for their showy racemes of foxglove-like, two-lipped flowers. They bear a rosette of large leaves that are rounded or oblong, toothed or lobed.

HOW TO GROW
Select a site in full sun to dappled shade with average to rich, evenly moist, well-drained soil. Plant in a sheltered site. *Rehmannia* species require cool conditions: Grow them as perennials in areas with cool summers and mild winters (Zone 9 south) — the Pacific Northwest and California. Elsewhere, grow them as biennials or tender perennials. Sow seeds indoors 6 to 8 weeks before the last spring frost date at 60° to 65°F. Or propagate by root cuttings in fall or cuttings taken from shoots at the base of the plant. Take cuttings either before flowering in spring or from new shoots that arise when the plants are cut down after flowering. To overwinter, pot up or propagate plants and keep them in a bright, cold (40° to 45°F) spot. Use *Rehmannia* species in mixed plantings and in containers.

R. elata
r. eh-LAH-tuh. CHINESE FOXGLOVE. Also listed as *R. angulata*. A tender, 3- to 5-foot perennial with racemes of tubular rosy purple flowers with red-spotted

Rehmannia elata

throats. Biennial or tender perennial. **Zones 9 and 10.**

Reseda
reh-SEE-duh. Mignonette family, Resedaceae.

One of the 55 to 60 species of annuals and perennials in this genus is an old-fashioned annual beloved for its intensely fragrant flowers. Native from the Mediterranean region to North Africa and central Asia, plants in this genus bear clusters of star-shaped greenish, yellow, or white flowers from spring to fall.

HOW TO GROW
Resedas prefer cool conditions and will stop blooming when hot weather arrives. They will grow in full sun in areas with cool summers, but elsewhere a site that receives dappled shade during the hottest part of the day is best. Grow them in average, well-drained soil; plants prefer, but do not require, an alkaline pH. Sow seeds outdoors several weeks before the last spring frost date, when the soil is still cool. Sow new crops every 3 weeks until early summer for a long season of bloom. From Zone 9 south, sow seeds outdoors in late summer or fall for bloom the following spring. When sowing, just press the seeds into the soil surface, as light is required for germination. Pinch seedlings to encourage branching and bushy growth. Use mignonettes in mixed plantings and to provide cut flowers for fresh and dried bouquets. The

Reseda odorata

Rhaphiolepis 'Ballerina'

flowers, which are attractive to bees and butterflies, hold their fragrance even when dried. For drying, harvest when most of the flowers have opened but before those at the bottom of the stalk have started to fade.

R. odorata

r. oh-door-AH-tuh. C O M M O N M I-
G N O N E T T E. An erect to spreading, 1- to 2-foot-tall annual with rounded spikes of ¼-inch-wide flowers in yellowish green, white, or reddish green. Newer cultivars with brighter-colored flowers usually are less fragrant than the species. Cool-weather annual.

Rhaphiolepis

raf-ee-oh-LEE-pis. Rose family, Rosaceae.

Rhaphiolepis comprises up to 15 species of evergreen shrubs and small trees native to subtropical areas of East Asia. They are popular in mild-climate areas for their glossy, leathery leaves and their midwinter to spring flowers that come in colors ranging from white through all shades of pink.

HOW TO GROW

These shrubs do best in neutral to slightly acid soils that are well drained yet moisture retentive; they will tolerate some drought and salt. Full sun will increase flowering and keep the habit com-

pact. Good for a low hedge or walkway edging, they also adapt well to containers. Pinch or prune lightly after flowering to encourage compact growth, or thin interior branches for a more open shape. Propagate from seeds cleaned of pulp.

R. cultivars

The many cultivars include 'Ballerina', less than 2 feet tall with deep rose-colored flowers; 'Enchantress', 3 feet tall and 5 feet wide with rosy pink flowers in late winter through early summer; 'Indian Princess', 3 feet tall with pale pink flowers; 'Majestic Beauty', an especially vigorous form that grows from 8 to 15 feet tall, is often trained as a standard, and bears 4-inch leaves and fragrant, pale pink flowers in clusters up to 10 inches across; 'Snow White', dwarf with pure white flowers from early spring to early summer; and 'Springtime', 4 to 6 feet tall with pink flowers in late winter to early spring. **Zones 8 to 10.**

R. indica

r. IN-dih-kuh. I N D I A N H A W-
T H O R N. The species, to 5 feet tall with pink-tinged white flowers, is less well known than its hybrids or cultivars. The cultivars are listed separately above because of confusion about origins, many possibly stemming from a hybrid, R. × *delacourii*. **Zones 8 to 10.**

R. umbellata

r. um-bel-LAH-tuh. Y E D D O H A W-
T H O R N. The most common forms are dense mounds to 6 feet tall and wide, with leaves at the ends of branches. The leaves are broad ovals, gray-green when new and then turning dark blue-green, sometimes bronzy purple in winter. The five-petaled white flowers are slightly fragrant and borne in upright panicles to 3 inches across in midspring. **Zones 8 to 10.**

Rheum

REE-um. Buckwheat family, Polygonaceae.

Of the 50 species that belong to this genus, common rhubarb (R. × *hybridum*, formerly R. *rhabarbarum*) is undoubtedly the best known, but there also are rhubarbs grown for their ornamental value. All rhubarbs are rhizomatous perennials native from Europe to Asia and China. They bear clumps of large, often coarsely toothed leaves that are either rounded or lobed in a palmate fashion. While the individual flowers are tiny and petalless, they are borne in enormous, showy panicles that resemble huge astilbe (*Astilbe*) blossoms.

HOW TO GROW

Select a spot in full sun or partial shade with deeply prepared, rich soil that remains evenly moist. Top-dress plants annually with compost, composted manure, or other organic matter to keep the soil rich. Plants do not tolerate drought or heat. Water deeply during dry weather. In the South, constant moisture and shade during the hottest part of the day are essential. Cut the bloom stalks to

the ground after the flowers fade. Propagate by dividing the clumps in spring or severing small offsets that appear around the outside of the clumps.

R. palmatum

r. pal-MAY-tum. C H I N E S E R H U-
B A R B. Enormous, bold, clump-forming plant producing 3- to 4-foot-tall mounds of 3-foot-long leaves that easily reach 6 feet in width. Bears 4- to 6-foot-tall panicles of tiny flowers in early summer that range from creamy green to red, and in bloom plants are 7 to 8 feet tall. 'Atrosanguineum' has leaves that are red-purple when young and reddish pink blooms. 'Bowles' Crimson' bears red flowers and leaves that are red underneath. **Zones 5 to 9.**

Rhodanthe

roe-DAN-thee. Aster family, Asteraceae.

Commonly called strawflowers or everlastings, *Rhodanthe* species are annuals and perennials from Australia grown for their daisylike flower heads that are outstanding for dried bouquets. They bear linear to rounded leaves that often are gray-green in color. The flower heads consist of all disk florets — they lack the ray florets, or "petals," of many aster-family plants. The showy "petals" in this case are papery, petal-like bracts in yellow, pink, or white that surround yellow centers.

HOW TO GROW

A site with full sun and poor to average, well-drained soil is ideal for these drought-tolerant plants, which also grow well in sandy soil. Sow seeds indoors in individual

Rheum palmatum 'Atrosanguineum'

Rhodanthe chlorocephala ssp. *rosea*

pots 6 to 8 weeks before the last spring frost date at 60° to 70°F. Germination takes 2 to 3 weeks. In the South, strawflowers can be sown outdoors in spring. When sowing, just press the seeds into the soil surface, as they need light to germinate. Wait to transplant until after the last frost. Stake with twiggy brush. To dry the flower heads, pick them before they are fully open, then hang them in small bunches in a warm, dark, dry place. Or simply pull up the entire plant and hang to dry.

R. chlorocephala ssp. rosea

r. chlor-oh-SEFF-ah-luh ssp. ROSE-ee-uh. Formerly *Acroclinium roseum*, *Helipterum roseum*. A fast-growing, 1- to 2-foot-tall annual with 1- to 3-inch-wide, papery daisies that close in cloudy weather. Flower heads have white or pink bracts surrounding yellow centers in summer. Warm-weather annual.

R. manglesii

r. man-GLEH-see-eye. SWAN RIVER EVERLASTING. Formerly *Helipterum manglesii*. A bushy, 2-foot-tall annual producing clusters of 1¼-inch-wide flower heads with yellow centers and white, pink, or red bracts. Warm-weather annual.

Rhodochiton

roe-doe-KYE-ton. Figwort family, Scrophulariaceae.

Three species of climbing perennials, commonly called purple bell vines, belong to this genus

of unlikely looking snapdragon relatives. Both the common and botanical names — *Rhodochiton* is from the Greek *rhodon*, meaning "rose," and *chiton*, "cloak" — refer to the unusual pendent flowers. Each bloom has an inflated, cup- or bell-shaped calyx (sepals) from which a tubular corolla (petals) emerges. The "bell," or calyx, opens before the corolla, which forms the "clapper." The bell-like calyx also remains on the plant after the corolla drops. The leaves are heart shaped or roughly triangular, and the plants climb by both twining leafstalks and stems.

HOW TO GROW

These vines require full sun and rich, evenly moist, well-drained soil, as well as a trellis, strings, or

Rhodochiton atrosanguineus

other supports upon which to climb. They grow in light, sandy soil as well. Sow seeds indoors 6 to 8 weeks before the last spring frost date at 60° to 65°F. Seeds can be slow to germinate, taking from 12 to 40 days; fresh ones germinate fastest. From Zone 9 south, seeds can be sown outdoors after the last frost date. Seedlings will need thin stakes upon which to climb. While purple bell vines are most often grown as annuals, they can be treated as tender perennials. They are hardy from about Zone 10 south but may overwinter (but be killed to the ground) in warmer parts of Zone 9 if given a protected, south-facing site and covered with a dry mulch such as salt hay or weed-free straw over winter. In the North, pot-grown plants can be overwintered in a bright, cool (60° to 65°F) spot. Water regularly during the summer months, but keep them barely moist over winter. Cut plants back and repot in spring. Plants also can be propagated by cuttings taken in spring or summer, which can be used to overwinter the plants. Use these vines to cover trellises or other supports. They also are attractive in hanging baskets.

R. atrosanguineus

r. at-roe-san-GWIN-ee-us. PURPLE BELL VINE. Also listed as *R. volubile*. A tender vine that commonly reaches 10 feet in northern gardens, more in frost-free regions. Bears 1¾-inch-long, dark maroon-purple flowers with lighter, mauve-pink calyxes from summer to fall. Tender perennial, or grow as a warm-weather annual.

Rhododendron

roe-doe-DEN-dron. Heath family, Ericaceae.

With the exception of roses, these have to be gardeners' favorite shrubs, including not only those commonly called "rhodies" but also azaleas. In all, the genus contains more than 900 species of deciduous and evergreen shrubs and trees native to North America, Asia, Europe, and Australasia. They are grown primarily for their colorful flowers, often spotted inside, borne singly or in clusters called trusses. The list below, although a long one, barely skims the surface of available shrubs, as these plants have been widely hybridized by both bees and hu-

mans. Sizes range from tree-size ("rhododendron" is derived from Greek words meaning "red tree") to prostrate forms with pinhead leaves; colors include yellows and dark reds as well as the more familiar pinks, purples, and white; fragrances can rival a daphne's; and bloom can occur not only in spring but also in midsummer and even fall. It is well worth looking for specialty nurseries that offer a wide range of these shrubs.

(So what is the difference between rhododendrons and azaleas? Even the experts may hem and haw. Rhododendrons *tend* to be evergreen and have flowers shaped liked bells, and azaleas *tend* to be deciduous and have funnel-shaped flowers. But there are obviously exceptions. The best rule is to simply enjoy them.)

HOW TO GROW

All rhododendrons need excellent drainage and an acidic soil that is rich in organic matter. They will not tolerate hot, dry, or windy conditions, and a combination of these is lethal. High, dappled shade is best, but many will grow in full sun given moderate temperatures and adequate moisture. Make the planting hole shallow, as appropriate for their fine, surface-feeding roots, and mulch well with pine needles or leaf mold rather than cultivating near the base. Rhododendrons have endless uses in a semishady garden, from hedging and defining paths to brightening dark corners, as specimens, and mixed in borders with other acid-loving plants. Dwarf varieties are suitable for rock gardens. Pruning is rarely necessary except to renew neglected plants. Spent flowers should be pinched off to prevent seed formation. Propagate by planting the tiny seeds under plastic or misting daily, by layering, or by softwood or semi-hardwood cuttings treated with hormone powder.

R. alabamense

r. al-uh-bam-EN-see. ALABAMA AZALEA. A fairly compact deciduous native of the southeast United States, growing to 8 feet tall

Rhododendron catawbiense

Rhododendron maximum

and suckering to form colonies. The early to midspring flowers are usually white with a yellow blotch and prominent stamens and exude a lemony spice scent. **Zones 6 to 8.**

R. arborescens
r. are-bore-ESS-enz. SWEET AZA-LEA. This deciduous native of an area ranging from the Mid-Atlantic south to Georgia and Alabama grows anywhere from 10 to 20 feet tall, with foliage often turning red in fall. In midsummer, white flowers with pink stamens emit a heliotrope-like fragrance. **Zones 5 to 8.**

R. atlanticum
r. at-LAN-tih-kum. COAST AZA-LEA. This suckering deciduous Mid-Atlantic species is also called dwarf azalea because it usually stays under 3 feet tall. In early to midspring, white to pale pink, sweetly scented flowers with prominent stamens bloom as the leaves unfurl. **Zones 6 to 8.**

R. austrinum
r. aws-TRY-num. FLORIDA FLAME AZALEA. This deciduous species from the Deep South grows to about 10 feet tall with an open habit. The yellow-orange tubular blossoms that open from early to midspring have long sta-

Rhododendron austrinum

mens and a fruity sweet scent. **Zones 7 to 9.**

R. calendulaceum
r. kal-en-doo-LAY-see-um. FLAME AZALEA. Ranging anywhere from 6 to more than 12 feet tall and equally wide, this deciduous species is native to mountainous areas from Pennsylvania to Georgia. The foliage may color yellow in fall. The unscented late-spring flowers are generally yellow-orange but may include pink tones. **Zones 6 and 7.**

R. canescens
r. kan-ESS-enz. PIEDMONT AZA-LEA. This is the Southeast's most common native azalea, deciduous and growing to 12 feet or taller, with sweet-scented light pink flowers from early to midspring. It can sucker to form colonies and so needs a firm hand with the pruners. **Zones 6 to 8.**

R. catawbiense
r. kat-ah-bee-EN-see. CATAWBA RHODODENDRON. This evergreen species gets its name from a river in the Carolinas, not from the wine-making grape, although its purple-pink color is that of a watered-down rosé. Native to mountainous areas from Alabama to West Virginia, it grows to around 10 feet tall and often as wide with oblong evergreen leaves 3 to 6 inches long. The rosy to pinkish purple flowers are streaked brown inside, in spectacular trusses up to 6 inches across in mid- to late spring. There are many cultivars and hybrids with flowers of purple, red, pink, white, or yellow, with some variation in cold hardiness. **Zones 5 to 8.**

R. Exbury, Knap Hill Hybrids
These hybrids of native East and West Coast and Asian species are deciduous, upright plants, with often fragrant flowers in sunset tones as well as white, pastels, and bicolors. Of the many cultivars, only a few are heat resistant. This group is also more prone than most to powdery mildew and lace bug. **Zones 5 to 7.**

R. flammeum
r. FLAM-ee-um. OCONEE AZA-LEA. A deciduous southeastern U.S. native growing to about 8 feet tall with early to midspring tubular orange or red flowers in clusters of a dozen or more. **Zones 6 to 8.**

R. Kurume Group
Compact and dense, these shrubs bear small evergreen leaves and profuse small flowers, many with the double flower form called hose-in-hose. They vary in cold hardiness, most **Zones 7 to 9.**

R. maximum
r. MAX-ih-mum. ROSEBAY RHO-DODENDRON. This evergreen native from eastern North America earns its species name with elliptic leaves up to 8 inches long and its overall treelike proportions. It will grow up to 30 feet in the wild but usually half that in cultivation. It can make a dramatic hedge if you have space for it. In spring it produces 5-inch trusses of white flowers, sometimes blushing pink in the cooler parts of its range. **Zones 5 to 8.**

R. Northern Lights Group
Shrubs in this series, developed at the University of Minnesota, are exceedingly cold hardy. They grow about 10 feet tall and wide, and the fragrant flowers of white, pink, lavender, yellow, and orange bloom before the leaves emerge in late spring. Most of the cultivar names include the word "Lights." **Zones 4 to 7.**

R. North Tisbury Group
A group of low-growing evergreen hybrids, primarily from the Japanese *R. nakahari*, bred as ground covers and rock-garden plants. Most flowers are pink or brick red. **Zones 6 to 8.**

R. occidentale
r. ox-ih-den-TAL-ee. WESTERN AZALEA. Native to slopes in Oregon and California, this deciduous shrub grows to 10 feet tall and wide. It bears white to palest pink flowers, blotched with yellow inside, in trusses of 6 to 12. **Zones 7 to 9.**

R. periclymenoides
r. pair-ih-kly-men-OY-deez. PINX-TERBLOOM AZALEA. Native to hills and piedmont from Maine to Georgia, this deciduous species was formerly called *R. nudiflorum* because its pink or white tubular flowers bloom on bare branches. (The shape of the flowers inspired another common name, wild honeysuckle.) **Zones 4 to 8.**

R. PJM Group
A cold-hardy group developed from crossing the native evergreen

Rhododendron prunifolium

R

R. carolinianum with an Asian deciduous species. The resulting plants are evergreens with a rounded habit to 6 feet tall and wide. Leaves may bronze in the fall. Bright lavender-pink flowers appear reliably in midspring. Some selections offer flowers of white, darker pink, or magenta, as well as fragrance. **Zones 4 to 8.**

R. prinophyllum (syn. R. roseum)

r. prin-oh-FILL-um. ROSESHELL AZALEA. Native to the Mid-Atlantic and the northeastern United States, this deciduous species grows to 6 feet tall and wide and bears pure pink tubular flowers that have a distinctive clove scent. **Zones 4 to 7.**

R. prunifolium

r. proo-nih-FOE-lee-um. PLUMLEAF AZALEA. A southeastern U.S. native evergreen growing to about 10 feet tall. It blooms in mid- to late summer with brick red flowers that attract hummingbirds. **Zones 6 to 8.**

R. schlippenbachii

r. schlip-en-BOK-ee-eye. ROYAL AZALEA. A deciduous native of Korea and Manchuria growing 6 to 8 feet tall. The leaves are red, orange, and yellow in autumn. Fragrant, delicate pale pink flowers expand in midspring with the leaves. **Zones 4 to 6.**

R. vaseyi

r. VAY-zee-eye. PINKSHELL AZALEA. This deciduous native of North Carolina's Blue Ridge Mountains usually grows to about 6 feet tall, although it can reach more than twice that height. It tolerates moderately dry soil and is unusual in offering burgundy fall foliage. Rich pink flowers (occasionally white or paler pink) bloom in clusters of half a dozen before the leaves emerge in early to late spring. **Zones 5 to 7.**

R. viscosum

r. viss-KOH-sum. SWAMP AZALEA. A deciduous species native to wetlands from Maine into Georgia and Alabama, averaging about 5 feet tall with an open habit and shiny leaves. White spicy-scented flowers bloom in late spring. **Zones 5 to 8.**

R. yakushimanum

r. yak-oo-shee-MAH-num. A Japanese evergreen species growing to 3 feet tall and wide with rosy pink buds opening to white flowers. Its many cultivars include 'Mist Maiden', with trusses of up to 17 flowers, and 'Yaku Princess', with flowers spotted pink and green. **Zones 5 to 8.**

Rhodophiala

roe-doe-fee-AL-uh. Amaryllis family, Amaryllidaceae.

Closely related to amaryllis (*Hippeastrum*), *Rhodophiala* species are tender bulbs native to South America that produce trumpet- or funnel-shaped flowers. About 35 species belong here, all of which grow from small tunicate bulbs that have a neck. They bear basal, linear leaves and umbels of lilylike flowers atop leafless stems. The flowers have six petal-like tepals.

Rhodophiala bifida

HOW TO GROW

Where they are hardy, give these plants a site in full sun to partial shade with deeply prepared, rich, well-drained soil. Plant the bulbs in spring or fall at a depth of 6 to 8 inches. At the northern limit of hardiness, mulch heavily with evergreen boughs, pine needles, or salt hay over winter. In most of the country, they are best grown in containers: plant them in winter or early spring as you would *Hippeastrum*. Set the bulbs so the top two-thirds are above the soil surface. Keep the soil barely moist and set the pots in a cool (55° to 60°F) room until the bulbs begin growing actively. Once they flower, remove the flower stalks and feed the plants with a dilute, balanced fertilizer every 2 weeks until mid- to late summer. Then begin to withhold water gradually to encourage the leaves to go dormant. Once the leaves die back, store the bulbs (still in their pots) dry at about 55°F. Let them rest for at least 8 weeks. Top-dress the bulbs in midwinter and begin watering again — very sparingly until plants are growing actively.

Like *Hippeastrum* species, these plants have permanent, perennial roots and resent root disturbance. To minimize root disturbance, repot bulbs only as necessary — every 3 to 4 years — and when top-dressing, disturb the roots as little as possible. When growing these plants in the ground, dig them only if absolutely necessary. Propagate by removing offsets in fall.

R. advena

r. ad-VEE-nuh. Formerly *Hippeastrum advenum*. A 1- to 2-foot-tall species bearing umbels of two to six funnel-shaped 2-inch-long flowers in late summer or early fall. The flowers come in red, pink, or yellow and appear just before the linear leaves appear. **Zones 9 to 10.**

R. bifida

r. BIFF-ih-duh. Formerly *Hippeastrum bifidum*. A 12-inch-tall species bearing showy umbels of two to six narrowly funnel-shaped, 2-inch-long deep red flowers in summer that appear either just as, or just before, the leaves linear emerge. **Zones 9 and 10.**

Rhodotypos

roe-doe-TY-pohs. Rose family, Rosaceae.

There is only one species in this genus, a deciduous shrub native to woods and scrublands in Japan and China. It rewards gardeners not only with its four-petaled white flowers and the persistent shiny black fruits from which it

Rhododendron yakushimanum

Rhodotypos scandens

Rhus copallina

gets its common name, jetbead, but also an ability to shrug off the less than ideal circumstances of urban life.

HOW TO GROW

Jetbead is easy to grow in a wide range of soil types, in sun or shade, and tolerates pollution and other stressful situations. Useful in borders or massed in shade. Doesn't require much pruning, but one-third of old growth can be removed in early spring to promote new shoots. Propagate by softwood cuttings after the plant has leafed out.

R. scandens

r. SCAN-denz. JETBEAD. Sometimes called white kerria, this shrub grows rounded and slightly arching from 3 to 6 feet tall and up to 8 feet wide. Leaves up to 4 inches long are toothed and prominently veined and may be touched with yellow in autumn. The white flowers are 1^{1}/$_{2}$ inches across, borne in late spring at the ends of branches, and rebloom sporadically. The ^{1}/$_{2}$-inch fruits are hard and beadlike, unusual although not particularly showy. **Zones 5 to 8.**

Rhus

RUS. Sumac family, Anacardiaceae.

It's often said that European gardeners appreciate America's native plants far more than we do, and our sumacs are a case in point. Despite their dramatic fall color and berries, they have often been tarred with the unpleasant brush of their close relatives poison ivy, poison oak, and poison sumac — all of which belong to the genus *Toxicodendron. Rhus* includes a total of 200 deciduous or evergreen shrubs, trees, and vines from throughout much of North America as well as East Asia, South Africa, and parts of Australia. Gardeners in the know appreciate the species listed here for their graceful dissected foliage that sets au-

Rhus glabra

tumn ablaze and their often interesting, persistent fruits.

HOW TO GROW

Most sumacs are tough, adaptable shrubs, needing only excellent drainage and a neutral to acid pH. They tolerate low fertility and pollution and will grow in shade but usually color best in full sun. Depending on size they can be massed or used for naturalizing, as ground covers, or in a shrub border. They can be pruned hard: *R. glabra, R. × pulvinata,* and *R. typhina* are often cut to the ground in spring to stimulate new growth.

R. aromatica

r. air-oh-MAT-ih-kuh. FRAGRANT SUMAC. Native to eastern North America from Ontario to Florida and Louisiana and west to Minnesota, this variable deciduous species can grow 2 to 6 feet tall and spread to 8 feet. The three-part oval leaves are toothed and turn orange-red or reddish purple in fall. The flower is a catkin, on male plants appearing from late summer through winter. Females produce a hairy red fruit. Fall foliage is orange-red and purple. 'Grolow' is a spreading cultivar to 2 feet tall, useful as a ground cover. **Zones 3 to 9.**

R. chinensis

r. chih-NEN-sis. CHINESE SUMAC. At 20 feet or taller and suckering aggressively, this deciduous shrub may be too large for most gardens. Valuable in open natural sites for its late-summer cream-colored flower panicles, which average 8 inches long and wide, often much larger, especially in the cultivar 'September Beauty'. These are followed by orange-red

fruits and golden orange foliage. **Zones 5 to 7.**

R. copallina

r. koh-pawl-EEN-uh. FLAMELEAF SUMAC. Another deciduous species from eastern North America, sometimes called shining sumac, this one can grow 25 feet tall and wide but is useful for dry, rocky sites. It also tolerates salt and wind and so is excellent in a coastal garden. It has picturesque branching and shiny, pinnate leaves that turn bright red and burgundy in fall. **Zones 4 to 9.**

R. glabra

r. GLAY-bruh. SMOOTH SUMAC. Found throughout the lower 48 states, this deciduous species grows 10 to 15 feet tall, suckering and forming colonies. The compound leaves turn yellow to reddish purple in autumn, and the female bears a conical cluster of

Rhus typhina 'Laciniata'

persistent, hairy, bright red fruits. **Zones 3 to 9.**

R. integrifolia

r. in-teh-grih-FOE-lee-uh. LEMONADE BERRY. An evergreen species native to southern California, generally under 10 feet tall and wide. The leathery leaves are almost round. Clusters of pink or white flowers bloom in late winter, followed by soft red fruits used to give drinks a tart taste. Best in coastal conditions. **Zones 9 and 10.**

R. ovata

r. oh-VAH-tuh. SUGARBUSH. Another evergreen native to southern California, as well as Arizona, that grows up to 10 feet tall, often spreading, with pointed glossy leaves. White or pink flower clusters bloom for a long period in spring, followed by hairy, reddish fruits. Tolerates drought but not salt or wind. **Zones 9 and 10.**

R. × pulvinata 'Red Autumn Lace'

r. × pul-vin-AH-tuh. A female selection of a cross between *R. glabra* and *R. typhina,* it bears deeply cut, lobed leaves that give it a ferny appearance. The fall color is orange and reddish purple, and the hairy fruits are bright red. **Zones 3 to 8.**

R. trilobata

r. try-loh-BAH-tuh. SKUNKBUSH SUMAC. Native to the western half of the United States, this species grows 3 to 6 feet tall and suckers to form a dense hedge. Good for alkaline soils. The common name comes from the leaves, which smell somewhat unpleasant when bruised. 'Autumn Amber' remains about 18 inches tall and has yellow and red fall color but no fruit. **Zones 4 to 6.**

R. typhina

r. ty-FEEN-uh. STAGHORN SUMAC. A deciduous shrub or small tree growing to 20 feet tall or more and suckering for an equal spread. It gets its common name from the reddish brown fuzz that covers its

Rhus trilobata

Ribes sanguineum

Ribes sanguineum

shoots, like the velvet on a deer's horns. The compound leaves have 13 to 27 leaflets up to 5 inches long and turn red, orange, and yellow in fall. Large panicles of yellow-green flowers are followed by a cone of red fruits that turn brown over winter. 'Dissecta' and 'Laciniata' have deeply divided leaves. **Zones 4 to 8**.

Ribes

RYE-beez. Saxifrage family, Saxifragaceae.

A genus of about 150 usually deciduous shrubs, sometimes spiny, found primarily in temperate areas. Several are cultivated for their edible berries, while others are grown for their colorful flowers. The leaves are usually lobed and toothed.

HOW TO GROW

Most currants and gooseberries are easy to grow in ordinary soil, preferably in full sun but also in partial shade. *R. speciosum* is often grown against a wall and does best with some shade where the climate is dry. Good for massing in difficult sites. Many members of the genus are prone to rust and other problems and do best where air circulation is good and humidity low. To rejuvenate mature plants, cut back a portion of producing shoots after flowering or fruiting. *R. alpinum* can be sheared as a formal hedge.

R. alpinum

r. al-PIE-num. ALPINE CURRANT. A dense deciduous European species with upright branching, growing to about 5 feet tall

and wide, popular as a hedge in cold climates. Inconspicuous yellow-green catkins bloom in early spring, followed by bright red berries that are quickly stripped by birds. 'Green Mound' remains under 3 feet tall. **Zones 2 to 7**.

R. aureum

r. AW-ree-um. GOLDEN CURRANT. A native of the Plains and Rocky Mountains, this deciduous species is upright, ranging from 3 to 9 feet tall. The clove-scented spring flowers are yellow tubes with a touch of red. The summer berries can be black, red, or yellow. **Zones 2 to 7**.

R. odoratum

r. oh-dor-AH-tum. CLOVE CURRANT. Native to the central United States, this species has arching upright shoots about 7 feet tall, usually suckering. The blue-green leaves can turn a rich burgundy in fall. From early to midspring, yellow flowers smelling of cloves bloom in racemes. The edible ¹/₃-inch berries are black. 'Crandall' has yellow fruit. **Zones 4 to 6**.

R. sanguineum

r. san-GWIH-nee-um. WINTER CURRANT. Native to western North America, this deciduous shrub grows 4 to 12 feet tall with foliage that resembles small maple leaves. Dark pink to red flowers droop in racemes from early to late spring, followed by ¹/₃-inch berries. **Zones 5 to 7**.

R. speciosum

r. spee-see-OH-sum. FUCHSIA-FLOWERED GOOSEBERRY. A

California native with semievergreen foliage and spiny stems, growing 3 to 6 feet tall. Scentless, bright red fuchsia-like flowers with protruding stamens are borne over a long period, from winter to spring. Cultivars offer pink and white flowers. 'Brocklebankii' has yellow foliage. **Zones 8 to 10**.

Ricinus

rye-SINE-us. Euphorbia family, Euphorbiaceae.

Castor bean, the only species in this genus, is a tender shrub of considerable commercial importance as well as a dramatic addition to ornamental gardens. In gardens, it is valued primarily for its large, glossy, palmately lobed leaves. The small, cup-shaped, greenish yellow flowers are borne in spikes but are fairly insignificant, although the spiny, round, red-brown seed capsules are interesting and attractive. All parts of the plant, especially the seeds, are quite poisonous if ingested.

HOW TO GROW

A site with full sun and rich, well-drained soil is ideal, although plants also tolerate partial shade. Castor beans grow in a range of soils, but poor, infertile soil yields plants that bear small, less attractive foliage. A protected site is best; otherwise stake plants to help them withstand wind. Sow seeds indoors in individual pots 6 to 8 weeks before the last spring frost date at 70°F. Germination takes 2 to 3 weeks. From Zone 8 south, sow outdoors after the last frost

date. Before sowing, soak seeds in warm water for 24 hours to speed germination. Transplant seedlings a few weeks after the last frost date once the weather has settled and temperatures remain above 50°F. Castor beans are shrub-size annuals that add a lush, tropical look to mixed plantings. They also can be grown in containers.

R. communis

r. kuh-MEW-nis. CASTOR BEAN. A tender shrub, hardy from **Zone 9 south**, that can reach 6 to 10 feet in a single season. The leaves have 5 to 12 lobes, range from ¹/₂ to 1¹/₂ feet long, and come in green, red-purple, or bronze-red. 'Carmencita' has bronze-red leaves. 'Zanzibarensis' bears green leaves that can reach 3 feet across. Tender perennial or warm-weather annual.

Ricinus communis 'Zanzibarensis'

Robinia

roe-BIN-ee-uh. Pea family, Fabaceae.

The four species of deciduous trees and shrubs in this North American genus have alternate, pinnately compound leaves and clusters of fragrant flowers. They can fix their own nitrogen from the soil, so they adapt well to poor, infertile sites.

HOW TO GROW

Plant in full sun. Best in fertile, moist soil but adapts to poor, infertile soil. Tolerates drought and urban conditions. Fast-growing suckers can sprout at great distances from the trunk, especially in poor-soil sites, and should be cut out promptly. The tree described here has shallow roots and can topple during high winds if the ground is soggy. Prune in fall or winter to develop a single leader; multiple trunks are weak.

R. pseudoacacia

r. sue-doe-ah-KASE-ee-ah. BLACK LOCUST. Varying within its native range from a very narrow tree with an arrow-straight, 75-foot-tall trunk to an irregularly branched, spreading, 45-foot tall tree, black locust casts dappled shade that's perfect for many garden situations. The fine-textured leaves appear in late spring and are divided into 15 rounded, 1- to 2-inch-long, blue-green leaflets, which fold up at night. Some trees have yellow fall color; others lose leaves without changing color. In late spring and early summer, 8-inch-long clusters of very fragrant, creamy white flowers hang beneath the foliage. They can ripen into flat, 6-inch-long, brown seedpods. The branches have a zigzag pattern and are slightly thorny. Trunk bark is deeply furrowed and light brown, with a lot of winter character. Although the branches are brittle, the trunk wood is very durable, and tall trunks are used for ships' masts and fence posts. Use this fast-growing tree in difficult, poor-soil sites and to create light shade in a lawn. From eastern and central North America and naturalized throughout most of the continent. Zones 4 to 9.

CULTIVARS AND SIMILAR SPECIES

'Appalachia' has a straight trunk and resists borers. 'Bessoniana' is thornless, compact, and oval; grows to 30 feet tall. 'Frisia' has lovely chartreuse leaves all season

Robinia pseudoacacia 'Frisia'

and makes an outstanding focal point against a dark background; grows 30 to 50 feet tall; provides afternoon shade in hot climates. 'Inermis' is thornless, dense, and rounded; grows to 20 feet tall and wide. 'Purple Robe' is a dense hybrid with bronze-red new growth, bronze-green mature leaves, and beautiful rose-pink spring flowers; grows 30 to 50 feet tall, with variable thorniness. 'Pyramidalis' is thornless and columnar; grows to 40 feet tall and 15 feet wide. 'Umbraculifera' is a dense, rounded, thornless, shrublike form; grows to 15 feet tall with few flowers. *R.* × *ambigua* 'Idahoensis' is a hybrid with purple-pink flowers and an upright, oval shape; grows to 35 feet tall; good in places with hot, dry summers and cold winters.

Rodgersia

roe-JER-zee-uh. Saxifrage family, Saxifragaceae.

Rodgersia species, perennials that are closely related to astilbes *(Astilbe),* are grown for their handsome, bold foliage as well as their fluffy, branched panicles of tiny flowers. The individual flowers are petalless, star shaped, and quite small — about $1/4$ inch wide — but are borne in large branched panicles above the foliage. The leaves are compound, with leaflets arranged in a palmate or pinnate fashion, and often distinctively textured. Some species feature foliage with a bronze or

Robinia pseudoacacia (flowers)

purple tint, and several exhibit excellent fall color. The genus contains six species native to China, Japan, and other parts of Asia. All are vigorous, rhizomatous perennials native to areas with moist soils.

HOW TO GROW

Select a site in light to full shade with rich, evenly moist — even constantly wet — soil. Plants tolerate drier conditions provided they are planted in shade, and full sun provided they receive ample moisture and are growing in an area where summers do not get too hot. They are best planted along a pond or stream, or in a bog garden, to ensure they receive ample moisture. To propagate, divide plants in early spring or fall or sow seeds.

R. aesculifolia

r. ess-kew-lih-FOE-lee-uh. FINGERLEAF RODGERSIA. Clumping species forming 3-foot-

Rodgersia pinnata 'Superba'

tall mounds of foliage that spread to 3 feet or more. The leaves, which are palmate and resemble those of horse chestnut (*Aesculus*), have a corrugated or crinkled texture and can be 2 feet across. Plants bear 2-foot-long panicles of white flowers in mid- to late summer and reach 6 feet tall in bloom. **Zones 5 to 8**.

R. pinnata

r. pin-NAH-tuh. FINGERLEAF RODGERSIA. A species producing 2- to 3-foot-tall mounds of heavily veined, rough-textured leaves that spread to 3 to 4 feet. The 3-foot-long leaves are pinnate but sometimes look palmate. Plants bear 1- to 2-foot-long panicles of yellowish white, pink, or red flowers in mid- to late summer and reach 3 to 4 feet tall in bloom. 'Superba' produces leaves that are bronze-purple when young and rose-pink flowers. **Zones 5 to 8**.

R. podophylla

r. poe-doe-FILL-uh. BRONZE-LEAVED RODGERSIA. Formerly *R. japonica*. A bold-leaved species forming 4-foot-tall mounds of leaves that spread to 6 feet. Leaves are 1 to 1¹/2 feet long and turn bronze-red in fall. Plants bear 1-foot-long panicles of creamy flowers in mid- to late summer and reach 5 feet tall in bloom. **Zones 5 to 8**.

R. sambucifolia

r. sam-buke-ih-FOE-lee-uh. ELDER-BERRY RODGERSIA. A species with pinnate 2¹/2-foot-long leaves forming 2-foot-tall clumps of leaves that spread to 3 feet. Plants reach 3 feet tall in bloom and bear 1¹/2-foot-tall panicles of white or pink flowers from early to mid-summer. **Zones 5 to 8**.

Rosa

ROE-suh. Rose family, Rosaceae.

Few plants offer the romance and allure of roses, so it's little wonder they have such an appeal for gardeners. At the same time, there are few plant groups with such an aura of mystery and a reputation for being difficult to grow. Although some are indeed difficult to bring to show-quality perfection, there are thousands of roses that the average gardener can grow and enjoy. It helps to understand the different kinds of roses that

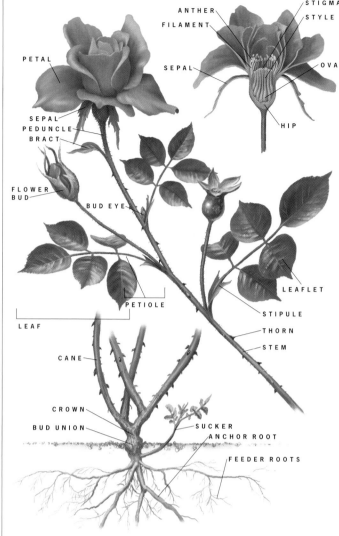

you might want to include in your garden.

ROSES BY CLASS

One convenient way to group them is to divide them by their date of introduction.
Species roses: These roses have been growing in the wild for hundreds or thousands of years.
Old garden roses: These roses were introduced before 1867, the year when the hybrid tea rose 'La France' was introduced.
Modern roses: These roses were introduced in 1867 or afterward.

Within these three divisions, roses are subdivided by their physical characteristics, such as their growth habits, foliage traits, and flower forms.

OLD GARDEN ROSES

The main subdivisions of old garden roses include the following.
ALBA: Their flowers are generally white or pale pink against gray-green leaves; once-flowering.
BOURBON: The first repeat-flowering roses, they originated on the Indian Ocean island called the

Isle of Bourbon, now known as Reunion Island. They are very fragrant.
CENTIFOLIA: Also referred to as "cabbage roses," these full flowers often have more than 100 petals; once-blooming.
DAMASK: Intensely fragrant flowers that are usually white, pink, or red; some bloom once, while others repeat.
HYBRID CHINA: These open plants are rather tender, needing winter protection north of Zone 7. They are usually repeat-flowering.
HYBRID GALLICA: These flowers are usually pink, red, or purple and have intense fragrance. The plants generally have few thorns and are once-flowering.
HYBRID PERPETUAL: These repeat-flowering roses have fragrant flowers that are usually pink or red (sometimes white).
MOSS: Centifolia roses that produce a slightly sticky green or brown mosslike growth on their flower stems and buds; fragrant and mostly once-blooming.
NOISETTE: Large, rather sprawling plants with clustered, fragrant flowers; somewhat cold-tender.

PORTLAND: Very fragrant, usually pink blooms; sometimes called damask perpetuals; repeat-flowering.
TEA: The flowers are in the light yellow, pink, or white range and are borne on canes that have few thorns; are best in Zone 7 and south; repeat-flowering.

MODERN ROSES

The class known as modern roses is also divided into a number of subdivisions. Here are some of the main ones (most of which are repeat-flowering).
CLIMBERS: This is a mixed group of roses with long, arching canes that need some kind of support. This group includes the climbing hybrid tea, climbing floribunda, climbing grandiflora, hybrid wichurana, large-flowered climber, and climbing miniature classes.
FLORIBUNDA: High-centered flowers are produced in clusters, usually with nearly continuous bloom. These plants tend to be hardier than hybrid teas.
GRANDIFLORA: These plants have high-centered flowers held singly or in clusters on rather tall plants; otherwise they are very similar to hybrid teas.
HYBRID TEA: High-centered, long-stemmed flowers, generally one per stem, bloom on rather upright, narrow plants, usually in flushes every 6 weeks or so. This is the classic rose used for cut flowers.
MINIATURE AND MINI-FLORA: Scaled-down versions of larger modern roses, these plants can range in size from 6 inches to 6 feet tall, though they normally are in the 1- to 2-foot range. Their leaves and flowers are proportionately diminutive. Mini-floras have flowers and leaves that are in between those of miniatures and floribundas in size.
POLYANTHA: Small blooms appear in large clusters on relatively compact, free-flowering plants.
SHRUB: This large group actually contains several classes, including the hybrid kordesii, hybrid moyesii, hybrid musk, hybrid rugosa, and shrub classes. These plants vary widely in height and habit. This also includes the popular group known as English or Austin roses, which were hybridized in England by the rose breeder David Austin.
HOW TO GROW
Roses need full sun and an open site. Soil should be moderately

Rosa 'Alba Meidiland'

Rosa 'Betty Prior'

rich, well drained, and generously amended with organic matter. The species and cultivars listed here are generally resistant to black spot and other fungal diseases to which some roses are prone. Good air circulation, full sun, and attentive garden hygiene will go a long way toward preventing problems. Companion planting with alliums (these include onions and garlics, but also many purely ornamental species) will also help deter some rose pests. Avoid giving roses too much nitrogen, which can make their growth succulent and delicious to pests.

Everblooming roses should be pruned in spring, removing one-third to half the length of flowered canes on mature plants. Prune once-blooming roses lightly after flowering, removing old unproductive stems on mature plants. Deadhead spent flowers except on roses grown for their hips.

R. 'Alba Meidiland'

SHRUB. MEILLAND, 1987.
If you are looking for a low-growing, low-maintenance shrub rose, 'Alba Meidiland' might be just the right one for you. The pure white, double, cupped flowers are on the small side (about 2 inches across), but they bloom in large clusters. The first flush of bloom in early to midsummer is profuse; flowers continue to appear into fall. The glossy, dark green leaves make a handsome backdrop for the white flowers. **Zones 4 to 9.**
HOW TO USE
'Alba Meidiland' produces a vigorous low-spreading bush reaching 2 to 3 feet tall and 4 to 6 feet wide. It is an excellent choice for use as a mounding ground cover. Hardy and disease resistant, it also makes a good space filler in a border, and

it grows well in containers, too. Its lack of scent is a small drawback, but it makes up for that with its generous display of blooms, which drop off cleanly when they are finished, essentially eliminating the need for deadheading to keep the bush looking good all season.

R. 'Bantry Bay'

LARGE-FLOWERED CLIMBER.
MCGREDY, 1967.
'Bantry Bay' is a handsome climber with a long bloom season. It offers clusters of loosely double, slightly fragrant blooms up to 4 inches across. The cupped flowers open to a flattened form, revealing a cluster of golden stamens surrounded by rich rosy pink petals. Flowering usually starts in early summer and repeats through summer into fall. Held on vigorous, branching stems, the shiny, dark green leaves make a lovely background for the beautiful blooms. **Zones 5 to 9.**
HOW TO USE
'Bantry Bay' is a moderately vigorous climber, usually reaching 10

feet but sometimes stretching to 15 feet in height. Train it up an arbor or try it on a pergola post for a long season of bloom. It also looks handsome trained against a fence or wrapped around a pillar. Offers good disease resistance.

R. 'Betty Prior'

FLORIBUNDA. PRIOR, 1935.
'Betty Prior' is a rose for people who think they can't grow roses. With a minimum of basic good care, this tough, trouble-free floribunda blooms freely for months and is rarely bothered by diseases — a big plus. Reddish, rounded buds open to single, cupped to saucer-shaped blooms about 3½ inches across. The petals are bright reddish pink, fading to nearly white at the base, where they are accented with a cluster of golden stamens. 'Betty Prior' has little or no scent, but it makes up for that by producing dazzling clusters of flowers from late spring or early summer well into fall. The vigorous, upright, moderately thorny canes

carry medium green, semiglossy foliage. **Zones 5 to 9.**
HOW TO USE
'Betty Prior' forms a bushy shrub, usually reaching 3 to 4 feet tall and about as wide. Its compact size and long flowering season make it a good partner for perennials, annuals, and shrubs in a mixed border or foundation planting. Plant a single bush by itself as an accent, or enjoy the display of multiple plants in a mass or hedge. Usually has excellent disease resistance.

R. 'Bonica'

SHRUB. MEILLAND, 1985.
"Sturdy but stunning" sums up the strong points of this justly popular shrub rose. 'Bonica' produces generous clusters of oval buds that

Rosa 'Bonica'

Rosa 'Bantry Bay'

Rosa 'Champneys' Pink Cluster'

Rosa 'Earth Song'

open to double, 1- to 2-inch, cupped blooms. The petals are a rich, warm rosy pink when just opened, gradually aging to a soft pink. Plants begin flowering in early summer, with moderate summer rebloom and another flush of flowers in fall. There is no scent, but on the plus side, there is a crop of small orange hips scattered over the bush in fall. Arching canes bear a dense covering of glossy, dark green leaves.
Zones 5 to 9.

HOW TO USE
'Bonica' produces a bushy, spreading shrub that is 3 to 5 feet tall and about 4 feet wide. Try it alone or in groups as a landscape accent, or in a row for a flowering hedge. Tuck it into a foundation planting, or pair it with perennials, annuals, and other shrubs in a mixed border. Generally touted as being disease-free but can develop black spot in humid conditions if you don't use preventive measures.

'Royal Bonica' is a more recent introduction, with fuller flowers in a deeper shade of pink.
All-America Rose Selection 1987

R. 'Champneys' Pink Cluster'

NOISETTE. CHAMPNEYS, 1811.
The development of this lovely rose by John Champneys in South Carolina ushered in the group of roses later known as noisettes, named for the French nurserymen who used its offspring to breed other vigorous, fragrant, free-flowering roses. 'Champneys' Pink Cluster' produces large clusters of dark pink buds that open to small, double, cupped flowers up to 2 inches across. The clustered

blooms are pale pink and have a pleasing scent. Flowering begins with a generous show in spring, with moderate rebloom in summer and another flush in fall. The almost thornless canes carry glossy, light green leaves.
Zones 7 to 10.

HOW TO USE
This rose generally grows as an upright shrub reaching 6 to 8 feet tall and about as wide. It makes a good hedge but also works well in shrub borders or mixed borders. If your space is limited, try training the flexible stems to grow on a fence or up a post or pillar; it can reach 10 to 12 feet this way. Usually quite disease resistant but may develop mildew or black spot by the end of the growing season in some areas.

R. 'Double Delight'

HYBRID TEA. SWIM & ELLIS, 1977.
'Double Delight' produces long, tapered buds that unfurl into large, high-centered, double blooms about 5 inches in diameter.

As they open, the creamy white petals gradually develop a distinct, cherry red edge, creating a dramatic contrast. The amount of color that develops depends on the amount of sunlight and the age of the bloom, so each flower is slightly different. Usually held singly on long stems, the blooms are also graced with a moderate to strong scent that some describe as spicy and others refer to as fruity. Flowers first appear in late spring to early summer, typically with good repeat through the rest of the season. The moderately thorny canes bear semiglossy, deep green leaves. **Zones 6 to 10.**

HOW TO USE
'Double Delight' forms a somewhat spreading bush that generally reaches 3 to 5 feet in height and 2 to 4 feet in width. Its bold color combination makes it an eye-catching addition to any garden. Also a good cut flower; just be aware that the blooms need some sunlight to develop their showy red edging. Susceptible to powdery mildew, particularly in cooler cli-

mates; be prepared to apply preventive sprays if this problem is common in your garden.

'Climbing Double Delight' is a once-blooming climber that makes quite a show against a wall or fence. It shares its parent's showy blooms but also its disease susceptibility.
All-America Rose Selection 1977; World Rose Hall of Fame 1985; James Alexander Gamble Fragrance Medal 1986

R. 'Earth Song'

GRANDIFLORA. BUCK, 1975.
Considered by many to be one of Dr. Griffith Buck's best roses, 'Earth Song' is a favorite with many gardeners in both warm and cool climates. This grandiflora produces elegant, tapered, reddish buds that open to high-centered, double flowers up to 4½ inches across, held singly or in small clusters. As the blooms age, their deep rosy pink petals age to a lighter pink, and they develop a cupped form that is accented with a cluster of yellow stamens. The flowers have a light to moderate, sweet scent. Bloom starts in late spring or early summer and continues freely until heavy frost. The thorny stems carry glossy, dark green leaves that have a leathery texture.
Zones 4 to 9.

HOW TO USE
'Earth Song' forms an upright, bushy shrub reaching 3 to 5 feet tall and about as wide. Plant it by itself as a landscape accent or in groupings as a mass planting or hedge. This rose makes a valuable addition to a mixed border, adding months of color to complement perennials, grasses, and other plants. Its rich rose-pink flowers

Rosa 'Double Delight'

R

Rosa 'Félicité Parmentier'

Rosa 'Gourmet Popcorn'

look especially good with purple and blue blooms, such as those of sages *(Salvia)* and bellflowers *(Campanula)*. Shares the excellent disease resistance that Buck roses are known for.

R. 'Félicité Parmentier'

ALBA. PARMENTIER, 1834. 'Félicité Parmentier' offers the delicate colors and scent of alba roses on a compact shrub. Plump, creamy white buds tinged with yellow or light green open into rather flattened to nearly rounded, very double, 2-inch flowers packed with many folded petals. Clear, light pink when newly opened, the flowers fade to blush white around the edges; in hot weather, the entire bloom may quickly bleach to almost white. The flowers appear in one main flush, normally starting in late spring or early summer and lasting 4 to 6 weeks. The sturdy, thorny canes carry an abundant covering of handsome, dark green leaves that have a bluish tint. Among the best of the old garden roses for scent. **Zones 4 to 8.**

HOW TO USE

'Félicité Parmentier' is a vigorous but relatively compact rose, usually reaching just 4 to 5 feet in height and 3 to 4 feet in spread. Its more restrained size and upright habit make it an excellent alba for a smaller garden. Grow it as a low hedge, or add it to mixed borders or cottage gardens. It looks good combined with early-summer perennials, such as foxgloves *(Digitalis)* and catmints *(Nepeta)*. It even grows well in a large container. 'Félicité Parmentier' appreciates a bit of afternoon shade in warm climates. Like other albas, this one can tolerate some shade in other areas as well, but it's more prone to mildew there than its relatives. May also develop rust in ar-

eas where this fungal disease is common.

R. gallica var. officinalis

r. GAL-ick-uh var. oh-fih-shih-NAL-iss. SYNS. 'OFFICINALIS'; R. × *centifolia provincialis, R. gallica maxima, R. gallica plena, R. officinalis, R. provincialis;* APOTHECARY'S ROSE, DOUBLE FRENCH ROSE, RED ROSE OF LANCASTER, ROSE OF PROVINS SPECIES. CULTIVATED BEFORE 1600. This classic rose has been cultivated for centuries for use in medicines and perfume. But this species isn't just practical: it's very pretty, too, offering several seasons of interest on a relatively compact bush. The show starts in late spring to early summer, with three to four weeks of bloom. The semidouble flowers are a rich, deep reddish pink; they start out cupped and open almost flat, up to 4 inches across. The fresh blooms are moderately fragrant; the dried petals are heavily scented. In fall, this rose offers another showy display, this time of abundant, rounded to oval, or-

ange-red hips. Throughout the growing season, rough, dark green leaves with a grayish cast are carried on upright stems. The canes have bristles but few true thorns. **Zones 3 to 10.**

HOW TO USE

R. gallica var. *officinalis* forms a rounded bush that's usually 3 to 4 feet tall and wide. When grown on its own roots (not grafted), it can spread by suckers. The compact plants are excellent for small properties, in beds and borders, herb gardens, and cottage-garden plantings. This versatile rose also makes a great low, dense hedge. Resistant to black spot but may get some mildew, particularly in fall.

R. g. versicolor (also known as *R. g. var. rosa mundi, R. g. var. variegata, R. mundi,* and 'Rosa Mundi') has irregular white striping on the reddish pink petals; otherwise, it is similar to *R. g. officinalis.*

R. 'Gourmet Popcorn'

MINIATURE. DESAMERO, 1986. This miniature displays hundreds of tiny, rounded, ivory buds that

open to small, semidouble, 1-inch rosettes. The flowers are bright white accented with a cluster of golden yellow stamens, and they're held in large, puffy clusters that look rather like masses of popped popcorn. Reports on the fragrance vary. Bloom season lasts from late spring or early summer well into fall. Glossy, dark green leaves are held on somewhat slender stems that arch under the weight of the flower clusters. **Zones 4 to 9.**

HOW TO USE

'Gourmet Popcorn' has a compact, bushy, mounded habit, generally reaching 18 to 30 inches in height and 15 to 24 inches in spread. It produces a show of white blooms all season long. Let it cascade out of a container planting or over a low wall, tuck it into beds and borders, or plant it in a drift of three or more for a low landscape accent. An easy-care rose that seldom has any disease problems.

R. 'Königin von Dänemark'

SYN. 'BELLE COURTISANE' ALBA. BOOTH, 1826. This lovely old alba is prized for its

R

Rosa gallica var. *officinalis*

Rosa 'Königin von Dänemark'

beautiful blooms and exquisite fragrance. It produces red-tinged, light pink buds that open into fully double, 2¹/2- to 3¹/2-inch flowers filled with folded, clear pink petals that age to pale pink or nearly white. Fully opened flowers have a rather flattened form, with outer petals that fold back and center petals that curl in tightly to form a "button" eye. The sweetly scented blooms appear in one glorious show in late spring or early summer, followed by large red hips in late summer to fall. The blue-green leaves are carried on thorny, arching stems. **Zones 4 to 8.**

HOW TO USE

'Königin von Dänemark' has an upright, slender habit that can become somewhat open when the heavy blooms weigh down the stems. It generally grows 4 to 6 feet tall and 4 to 5 feet wide. Use alone as a landscape accent, or group in multiples for a mass planting or hedge. Excellent disease resistance.

R. 'Magic Carrousel'

MINIATURE. MOORE, 1972.
It's been around for decades, but 'Magic Carrousel' retains the charm that has made it one of the most popular miniature roses produced to date. Small, pointed, creamy yellow buds tipped with red unfurl into semidouble to double, cupped rosettes that open to flat, 2- to 2¹/2-inch flowers with golden stamens in the center. The creamy white or pale yellow petals are distinctly marked with a red or dark pink edge. The color contrast tends to be most intense in cool weather. The clustered flowers have little or no scent, but they're produced generously in late spring or early summer, with good repeat

Rosa 'Magic Carrousel'

through the rest of the growing season. Branching, thorny canes carry glossy, medium to dark green leaves. **Zones 5 to 10.**

HOW TO USE

'Magic Carrousel' has an upright, bushy habit. Left alone, it can grow 24 to 30 inches tall and 18 to 24 inches wide; with regular pinching, it will stay much more compact (12 to 18 inches tall and about 9 to 12 inches wide). This distinctive miniature makes an eye-catching addition to many parts of the garden: in beds and borders, as a low hedge, around a deck or patio, or in a planter. Moderate disease resistance; black spot may be a problem if you don't take preventive measures. *ARS Award of Excellence for Miniature Roses 1975; Miniature Rose Hall of Fame 1999*

R. 'Mister Lincoln'

HYBRID TEA. SWIM & WEEKS, 1964.
Introduced well over 30 years ago, 'Mister Lincoln' is still beloved by

gardeners for its color and fragrance. Elegant, maroon buds unfurl to reveal double, velvety maroon-red to cherry red flowers that are 4 to 6 inches across. Held singly on long stems, the powerfully perfumed blooms start out with high centers, opening to a cupped form accented with yellow stamens. Flowering starts in late spring or early summer, with good repeat through summer and into fall. Tall, thorny stems bear matte, dark green foliage. **Zones 5 to 9.**

HOW TO USE

'Mister Lincoln' produces gorgeous flowers, but the bush itself isn't particularly pretty. It has a fairly stiff, upright habit, generally growing 4 to 6 feet tall and 2 to 3 feet wide. In the garden, it looks best planted in groups of three or more to create a bushier effect at the back of a border. Disease resistance is usually just moderate — consider taking preventive measures against powdery mildew, black spot, and rust. *All-America Rose Selection 1965*

R. 'Mme. Hardy'

DAMASK. HARDY, 1832.
'Mme. Hardy' is officially classified as a damask rose, although some experts detect traits of other roses in its form and habits. Whatever its classification, it's a splendid old

rose. Pink-tinted, cream or yellow buds enclosed in ferny, leaflike sepals open to display fully double flowers that are 2¹/2 to 3¹/2 inches across. Cupped when new, the pleasingly perfumed blooms become flattened as they age, showing a center with incurved petals surrounding a green eye. There's only one bloom season, starting in late spring or early summer and lasting anywhere from 3 to 6 weeks, but it's definitely worth waiting for. Moderately thorny, upright to arching stems carry light green to gray-green leaves. **Zones 5 to 8.**

HOW TO USE

'Mme. Hardy' has an upright-spreading to somewhat sprawling habit. As a shrub, it usually grows 4 to 6 feet tall and 3 to 5 feet wide. Try it in a mixed border or cottage garden, or as an accent plant or hedge. Planted alone, it looks best with some kind of support, such as a tripod of stakes; set at 3-foot spacings for a hedge, the bushes will hold each other up. This rose also works well as a 7- to 10-foot climber trained on a wall, fence, post, or pillar. Disease resistance is generally excellent; black spot may cause a bit of leaf discoloration but seldom seriously affects the rose's health.

R. 'New Dawn'

LARGE-FLOWERED CLIMBER. DREER, 1930.
One of the most popular roses of all time, 'New Dawn' has pointed, medium pink buds that open into loosely double, 3-inch blooms that are creamy pink with high centers. As they age, the color fades to pale pink or nearly white (especially in strong sun). Opinions vary on its fragrance, but most agree it has at least a moderate sweet or fruity scent. Held singly or in clusters, the flowers appear in glorious profusion in late spring or early summer, usually followed by fair summer rebloom and another good show in fall. Moderately thorny stems carry medium to deep green, glossy foliage. **Zones 5 to 10.**

HOW TO USE

'New Dawn' has a vigorous growth habit. Left unsupported, it forms a large, mounding shrub that can reach 8 to 10 feet tall and wide; regular pruning can keep it somewhat smaller. This rose really shines when used as a 10- to 20-foot climber adorning an arbor, arch, wall, trellis, pillar, or pergola post. It also looks lovely when allowed to scramble into a tree. Dis-

R

Rosa 'Mister Lincoln'

Rosa 'Mme. Hardy'

Rosa 'New Dawn'

ease resistance is usually excellent, although a bit of powdery mildew has been reported in some regions.

World Rose Hall of Fame 1997

R. 'Reine des Violettes'

HYBRID PERPETUAL. MILLET-MALET, 1860.
This hybrid perpetual is a classic, prized by generations of gardeners for its unique color and intense fragrance. Plump buds open to reveal fully double, 3- to 5-inch flowers that have a flattened rosette form with a cluster of short, tightly incurved petals in the center. The flower color varies somewhat but is usually violet-red to rosy purple at first, aging to a soft purple; cool weather tends to bring out the richest hues. Held

singly or in small clusters, the individual blooms aren't long lasting, but they are glorious when the bush is in full flower. The show is typically best in late spring to early summer, with good repeat through the rest of the season in some areas and only sparse rebloom in others. Matte, grayish green leaves are carried on nearly thornless stems. Zones 5 to 9.

HOW TO USE

'Reine des Violettes' has a somewhat bushy, upright habit. As a shrub, it can range from 5 to 8 feet tall and 3 to 6 feet wide, although hard pruning during the dormant season can encourage more compact growth. It also adapts to training as an 8- to 12-foot climber on a wall, trellis, or pillar. If you don't take preventive measures, black spot can be a problem in some areas, but the bush usually recovers, particularly when kept vigorous with good soil care and regular watering.

R. 'Sun Flare'

FLORIBUNDA. WARRINER, 1981.
A descendant of the equally excellent floribunda 'Sunsprite', 'Sun Flare' is a spectacular addition to any landscape. Clustered, pointed buds open into double, 4-inch blooms with clear, medium yellow petals surrounding a crown of orange-gold stamens. Newly opened flowers have a high center, but they develop a loosely ruffled to nearly flat form as they age. Opinions vary on the fragrance: some say it is slight at best, while others claim this cultivar has an exceptional, licorice-like scent; most say

Rosa 'Sun Flare'

the perfume is at least moderate. 'Sun Flare' produces a profuse flush of bloom in late spring to early summer, with generous repeat through the rest of the growing season. Thorny canes bear shiny, deep green foliage. Zones 5 to 10.

HOW TO USE

'Sun Flare' has a bushy, somewhat spreading habit. It generally grows 2 to 4 feet tall and about as wide, though long-established bushes can get larger. It's a winner in beds, borders, and foundation plantings, adding months of bright, easy-care color. May develop a touch of black spot if you don't take preventive measures, but otherwise it's normally quite disease resistant.

'Climbing Sun Flare' is usually offered under the name 'Yellow

Blaze'; it generally grows 10 to 14 feet in height.

All-America Rose Selection 1983

R. 'The Fairy'

POLYANTHA. BENTALL, 1932.
It's difficult to say enough good things about this charming little polyantha. It has just about everything you could want in a rose, with the exception of fragrance. 'The Fairy' produces rounded, dark pink buds that open to ruffled, cupped rosettes that are just 1 to 1¹/₂ inches in diameter, in a light rosy pink that ages to near white in strong sun. The individual blooms may be small, but they're held in large clusters that make quite a show. Flowering usually begins in early summer (a bit

Rosa 'Reine des Violettes'

Rosa 'The Fairy'

R

earlier in warm climates, a little later in cool areas) and continues freely through the rest of the summer into fall. Very thorny stems carry an abundant covering of small, shiny, bright green leaves. Excellent disease resistance. **Zones 4 to 9.**

HOW TO USE

'The Fairy' has a low, spreading habit, generally growing just 2 to 3 feet in height but stretching 3 to 6 feet in width. Its low growth and long flowering season make it a splendid choice for a mixed border; it also makes a pretty low hedge. Use it to edge a deck or patio or to add months of easy-care color to a foundation planting. Its arching stems also show off to advantage when planted atop a low wall, on a gentle slope, or in a container. Rarely has disease problems; can even tolerate a bit of shade.

Rosmarinus

rohs-MAIR-in-us. Mint family, Lamiaceae.

The ancient Greeks thought rosemary improved the memory, and modern science says that consuming rosemary leaves may actually ward off senility. The genus contains just two species of evergreen shrubs from the Mediterranean region (the botanical name means "dew of the sea"), one of which is popular in warm-climate gardens for the fragrant foliage we use as a seasoning, as well as for its tiny, usually bright lavender-blue flowers.

HOW TO GROW

Rosemary must have full sun, excellent drainage, and only moderately fertile soil. It is an excellent container plant and works well in a perennial border or herb garden, or as a low hedge. More prostrate varieties can be used on banks to control erosion or as ground covers. Pinch tips or prune lightly to keep shrubs compact. Root from semiripe cuttings or by layering.

R. officinalis

r. oh-fih-shih-NAL-iss. ROSEMARY. The species grows 2 to 6 feet tall and bears leathery, needlelike leaves that are white underneath and smell of pine. The tubular, two-lipped blue flowers bloom in the leaf axils in late spring or early summer, often reblooming when weather cools in fall. Popular cultivars include 'Arp' (white flowers, hardy to at least **Zone 7**), 'Benenden Blue' (bright blue flowers), 'Golden Rain' (new leaves edged in gold), 'Majorca Pink' (pink flowers), 'Lockwood de Forest' (1 foot tall, 3 feet wide), and 'Tuscan Blue' (upright to 6 feet tall, deep blue flowers). There is also a weeping form, 'Prostratus'. **Zones 8 to 10.**

Rubus

ROO-bus. Rose family, Rosaceae.

A genus of some 250 species of bristly or prickly deciduous or evergreen shrubs and climbers (and a few herbaceous perennials) native to a wide range of habitats throughout the world. Known primarily for bearing edible fruits, this group also includes plants grown for flowers or eye-catching shoots in winter.

HOW TO GROW

Plant in ordinary, well-drained soil in full sun. Grow those with winter interest against a background of dark conifers or where they will

Rubus odoratus

catch early-morning or late-afternoon light. Prune in early spring. Propagate from suckers.

R. 'Benenden'

A deciduous, sterile hybrid shrub with thornless arching branches to 8 feet tall and peeling bark that provides winter interest. The dark green leaves are shallowly lobed, while the solitary, five-petaled flowers — which look like single white roses with yellow centers — are 3 inches across and bloom in late spring and early summer. **Zones 5 to 8.**

R. cockburnianus

r. kok-burn-ee-AY-nus. GHOST BRAMBLE. This deciduous shrub forms thickets of prickly arching canes to 8 feet tall. The leaves are pinnately compound, green above and fuzzy white underneath. Terminal racemes of $1/2$-inch purple flowers in summer are followed by $1/2$-inch inedible black fruits. The chief attraction is its silvery white shoots, which glow like "ghosts" in winter. **Zones 5 to 8.**

R. odoratus

r. oh-dor-AH-tus. FLOWERING RASPBERRY. Also called thimbleberry, this deciduous shrub is native to eastern North America as far west as Michigan and south to Georgia. It grows to 6 feet high with erect, suckering, thornless branches. The lobed, maple-shaped leaves are velvety, turning red in autumn in the northern part of its range. Fragrant mauve, five-petaled flowers bloom in 2-inch clusters in mid- to late summer. **Zones 5 to 8.**

R. spectabilis

r. spek-TAB-ih-liss. SALMONBERRY. A deciduous, thicketforming shrub of prickly shoots to about 6 feet tall. It has 6-inch

Rosmarinus officinalis var. *angustissimus*

Rudbeckia hirta var. *pulcherrima*

R

Rudbeckia fulgida 'Goldsturm'

palmate leaves with three glossy leaflets and fragrant purple-pink midspring flowers. Those of 'Olympic Double' are frilly and 2 inches across. **Zones 5 to 8.**

R. thibetanus

r. tih-bet-AY-nus. The erect prickly shoots of this deciduous shrub form a thicket to 8 feet tall. The pinnately divided leaves have 7 to 13 gray fuzzy leaflets; 1/2-inch reddish purple summer flowers are followed by 1/2-inch black berries, lightly "frosted." The shoots are silver in winter. **Zones 6 to 9.**

R. tricolor

r. TRY-kuh-lor. A prostrate bramble with arching shoots to 2 feet tall, spreading to 10 feet and covered with red bristles. The 4-inch leaves have three to five lobes; 1-inch white flowers borne in summer are followed by edible red berries. **Zones 6 to 9.**

Rudbeckia

rude-BEK-ee-uh. Aster family, Asteraceae.

Commonly known as black-eyed Susans, orange coneflowers, or simply rudbeckias, these aster-family plants are native North American wildflowers grown for their showy, summer-borne, daisylike flower heads. Some 20 species of annuals, biennials, and perennials belong to the genus, all of which bear flower heads consisting of ray florets, or "petals," surrounding spiny black, brown, or green centers of disk florets, which produce the seeds. Most have ray florets in shades of yellow to yellow-orange, but one popular species comes in a wider range of colors, including yellows as well as red-brown and rusty orange. Leaves may be lance shaped and simple or toothed, deeply lobed or cut in a pinnate fashion.

HOW TO GROW

Give coneflowers full sun to light shade and average to rich soil. While evenly moist soil is ideal, plants are drought tolerant once established. Most stand without staking, although *R. laciniata* may need some support. Coneflowers also don't need dividing regularly. Dig them in spring or fall if they outgrow their space, die out in the centers of the clumps, or for propagation. Or propagate by seeds. Plants self-sow.

R. fulgida

r. FUL-jih-duh. ORANGE CONE-FLOWER. A 1 1/2- to 3-foot-tall perennial that spreads to 1 1/2 feet. Bears 2- to 2 1/2-inch-wide daisies with orange-yellow ray florets and chocolate brown centers from midsummer to early fall. 'Goldsturm' (*R. f.* var. *sullivantii* 'Goldsturm') produces 3- to 4-inch flowers on 2-foot plants. **Zones 3 to 9.**

R. hirta

r. HUR-tuh. BLACK-EYED SU-SAN. An erect, well-branched biennial or short-lived perennial ranging from 1 to 3 feet in height and spreading from 1 to 1 1/2 feet. Bears 3- to 6-inch-wide single or semidouble flowers from summer to early fall. Many cultivars are available (and gloriosa daisies belong here). They bear 3- to 6-inch-wide flowers in shades of red-brown, yellow, gold, bronze, or rusty orange; many flowers have

Rudbeckia fulgida 'Goldsturm'

bicolor "petals." 'Becky Mixed' is a dwarf mix, to 1 foot tall, that comes in similar colors. 'Indian Summer' has golden yellow 6- to 9-inch-wide blooms. 'Toto' bears golden flowers on 10-inch plants. **Zones 3 to 9.**

R. laciniata

r. lah-sin-ee-AH-tuh. RAGGED CONEFLOWER, GREEN-HEADED CONEFLOWER, CUT-LEAVED CONEFLOWER. Robust 3- to 6-foot-tall perennial that spreads by rhizomes to form 3- to 4-foot-wide clumps. Bears 3- to 6-inch-wide flower heads with yellow ray florets and green centers from midsummer to fall. 'Golden Glow' produces double flowers on 5- to 6-foot plants. 'Goldquelle', also double, stays between 3 and 4 feet. **Zones 3 to 9.**

R. maxima

r. MAX-ih-muh. GIANT CONE-FLOWER. A 5- to 9-foot-tall perennial that makes 2- to 3-foot-wide clumps of handsome gray-green, 1-foot-long leaves. Bears 3- to 5-inch-wide flower heads in late summer with orange-yellow ray florets and cone-shaped 1 1/2-inch-tall brown centers. **Zones 3 to 9.**

R. nitida

r. NIT-ih-duh. Clump-forming 5- to 6-foot-tall perennial that forms 3-foot-wide clumps. Bears 4-inch-wide flower heads in late summer and early fall with yellow ray florets surrounding green centers. 'Autumn Glory' produces gold flowers on 5-foot plants. 'Herbstsonne', a 6-foot hybrid between this species and *R. laciniata*, bears yellow 4- to 5-inch-wide flower heads from midsummer to fall with green to yellow-brown centers. **Zones 3 to 9.**

Ruta

ROO-tuh. Rue family, Rutaceae.

This genus embraces eight species of perennials and shrubs from the Mediterranean region. The single species listed here, once thought to repel witches and safeguard eyesight, came to symbolize repentance. Known as the "herb of grace," it was used in the Roman Catholic Church to sprinkle holy water and, because of this history of symbolism, is often found in herb gardens today. It has a place in the ornamental garden because of its feathery, bluish foliage and airy cymes of summer flowers.

HOW TO GROW

Give rue average, well-drained, neutral to slightly alkaline soil in full sun. Handle the plants with caution, as they can cause an allergic reaction in some people. In spring, prune back flowered shoots just above last year's growth. Plant in herb or perennial beds for contrast in foliage color and texture, or use as low hedging. The seedpods are used in arrangements. Propagate from seeds, cuttings, or division.

R. graveolens

r. grav-ee-OH-lenz. RUE. This subshrub grows 2 to 3 feet tall and bears pungent, blue-green leaves coated with white, which are much divided and ferny. The tiny greenish yellow leaves bloom in flat clusters for a long period beginning in midsummer. 'Jackman's Blue' is compact and has bluer foliage. **Zones 4 to 9.**

Ruta graveolens

Salix

SAY-liks. Willow family, Salicaceae.

In landscapes, the most familiar willows are the huge weeping forms that so often hang over ponds and streams. Herbalists know that the white willow (*S. alba*) and several other species contain the active ingredient in aspirin (salicin). The little pussy willow is regarded as a harbinger of spring, but it is probably seen in arrangements more often than in gardens. Although 100 or so willow species are native to North America, the popular landscape trees are from Europe. These garden specimens are weak wooded and messy, so site them with care. The shrub species are showy for their graceful habit and foliage, furry spring catkins, and colorful winter shoots.

HOW TO GROW

Most willows tolerate damp conditions. Give them full sun in moderately fertile soil. Use them for hedges, screens, specimens, or shrub borders, and for cutting for arrangements. They are handsome in pondside plantings, but their aggressive roots can tear rubber liners. Keep them away from water mains and septic systems. They are also prone to developing cankers and fungal diseases. Species grown for their colorful winter shoots need old branches removed regularly. Willows propagate easily from cuttings.

S. alba 'Tristis'

s. AL-buh. NIOBE WILLOW, GOLDEN WEEPING WILLOW. Also listed as *S. × sepulcralis* 'Chrysocoma'. This popular tree forms a large, rounded canopy of long, gracefully weeping branches and grows 50 to 70 feet tall and wide. The trunk and main branches are massive and cloaked in rough brown bark. The slender weeping branches and twigs feature bright gold bark that is especially pretty in winter. Leaves are narrow and lance shaped, measure 4 inches long and $1/2$ inch wide, and have whitish undersides. They are bright yellow-green very early in spring, mature to dark green with silver undersides in summer, and change to golden yellow in late fall. Plant Niobe willow beside a pond or stream, where its form will be reflected in the water, or use it in any informal site with moist to wet soil. Avoid groomed areas, as it is messy, and keep away from water mains. Attacked by many insects and diseases, including twig blight, gall, canker, aphids, borers, and sawflies. From Europe, northern Africa, and western and central Asia. **Zones 3 to 9.**

CULTIVARS AND SIMILAR SPECIES

'Niobe' is another name for 'Tristis'. 'Prairie Cascade' is a 45-foot-tall hybrid with glossy, leathery, green leaves and gold weeping branches; **Zones 3 to 7.** *S. alba* (white willow) is an upright tree with greenish twigs. *S. a.* var. *vitellina* (golden willow) is round headed and nonweeping, with gold to bright yellow twigs and very narrow leaves. *S. babylonica* (weeping willow) is very similar to Niobe willow but is even more pendulous, with green twigs; **Zones 7 to 9.**

S. caprea

s. KAP-ree-uh. FRENCH PUSSY WILLOW. The Latin-derived species name refers to goats, since this plant was once used for fodder, and another common name is goat willow. It is upright and often treelike at 25 feet tall and 15 feet wide and bears pink-gray woolly catkins in early spring. 'Pendula' (Kilmarnock willow) and 'Weeping Sally' are weeping forms that require staking when young. **Zones 4 to 8.**

S. chaenomyloides

s. ky-noh-my-LOY-deez. JAPANESE PUSSY WILLOW. This species grows quickly into a large shrub 12 to 15 feet tall with stunning catkins more than 2 inches long. Emerging from red buds, they are tinged with deep pink and are set off by yellow-orange anthers. **Zones 6 to 8.**

S. exigua

s. eks-IG-ew-uh. COYOTE WILLOW. A western U.S. native shrub growing 10 to 12 feet tall, suckering and spreading to 15 feet. The narrow silvery leaves are 4 inches long and hairy when new. Spring catkins about 2 inches long appear with the leaves. It does well in sandy soil. **Zones 4 to 6.**

S. fargesii

s. far-GEE-see-eye. A Chinese shrub species to 8 feet tall with shiny reddish brown shoots and bright red buds. The 6-inch leaves are

Salix chaenomyloides

Salix alba 'Tristis'

Salpiglossis sinuata

glossy with prominent veins. Green spring catkins averaging 6 inches long appear with the leaves. **Zones 6 to 8.**

S. gracilistyla

s. gras-il-IS-til-uh. ROSE-GOLD PUSSY WILLOW. Upright shrub to 6 to 10 feet tall with gray-green leaves. The common name comes from the gold and rose stamens on the gray 1¹/2-inch early-spring catkins. S. 'Melanostachys' (black pussy willow), sometimes listed as a botanical variety or a separate species, has purple-black stems and black catkins with red anthers that turn yellow. **Zones 5 to 7.**

S. hastata 'Wehrhahnii'

s. has-TAH-tuh. An upright shrub to 4 feet tall and wide with dark purple-brown shoots, bright green oval leaves, and silvery catkins in spring before the leaves. **Zones 5 to 8.**

S. lanata

s. lan-AH-tuh. WOOLLY WILLOW. A low-growing native of Europe and Asia to 4 feet tall and a bit wider, with silvery, hairy, oval leaves 1 to 2 inches long. The 2- to 4-inch-long catkins are yellow with some gray and bloom with the leaves in spring. **Zones 2 to 4.**

S. matsudana

s. mat-sue-DAY-nuh. HANKOW WILLOW, PEKING WILLOW. Also listed as S. babylonica var. pekinensis. This large willow is a nonweeping tree with a rounded or oval shape, bright green twigs, and fine-textured branches. It matures to 40 to 50 feet tall and wide and looks very similar to S. babylonica, except that it does not

weep. Forms with twisted branches are the most common landscape types, and they make unique accent plants that stand out in the winter garden. From northern China. **Zones 5 to 9.**

CULTIVARS

'Golden Curls' is a hybrid with slightly twisted, gold stems and somewhat curled leaves; rather shrubby, growing to 30 feet tall and half as wide. 'Scarlet Curls' has semipendulous, slightly twisted branches, red twigs, and curly leaves; grows to 30 feet tall and 15 to 20 feet wide. 'Torulosa' (corkscrew willow) has ornamental, very twisted branches and twigs and curled leaves; train to a single trunk; grows 20 to 30 feet tall.

S. sachalinensis 'Sekka'

s. sak-uh-lih-NEN-sis. JAPANESE FANTAIL WILLOW. A male cultivar with contorted branches, sometimes curled and flattened. It forms a broad and graceful shrub that grows 10 to 15 feet tall and wide, with 4-inch leaves that are dark green and shiny on top, silver beneath. Gray ¹/2-inch catkins appear in March. **Zones 4 to 7.**

Salpiglossis

sal-pih-GLOSS-iss. Nightshade family, Solanaceae.

Two species belong to the genus *Salpiglossis*, both annuals or short-lived perennials native to the southern Andes in Chile. They have oval to lance-shaped leaves covered with sticky hairs, and funnel-shaped, velvety-textured flowers in a rich array of colors, including yellow, red, purple-pink,

and orange, from summer to fall. In many cases, the blooms are striped or veined with contrasting colors. One species, commonly known as painted tongue, is a popular bedding plant.

HOW TO GROW

Select a site with full sun and average to rich, well-drained soil that is evenly moist. Plants grow best in areas where summers are not excessively hot. In areas with hot summers, start plants early so they have time to bloom before warm weather arrives; also give them a spot with light shade during the afternoon to help them cope with heat. Sow seeds indoors in individual pots 8 to 10 weeks before the last spring frost date at 70° to 75°F. Germination takes 1 to 4 weeks. Hardened-off seedlings can be moved to the garden 2 weeks before the last frost date, but transplant with care, as they resent being moved. Or sow outdoors on or just before the last frost date. When sowing, just press the tiny seeds into the soil surface, but since they need darkness to germinate, cover them with black plastic or an overturned seed flat until seedlings appear. Mulch plants when they are several inches tall to help keep the soil cool. Let the soil dry out slightly between waterings. Stake plants with twiggy brush. Deadhead regularly. Use painted tongues in mixed plantings and containers. They are excellent cut flowers.

S. sinuata

s. sin-yew-AH-tuh. PAINTED TONGUE. An erect, somewhat weak-stemmed annual bearing five-lobed, 2-inch-wide flowers from summer to fall. 'Casino Mix'

plants are densely branched and 1¹/2 to 2 feet tall, with flowers in a full range of rich colors. Cool-weather annual.

Salvia

SAL-vee-uh. Mint family, Lamiaceae.

The large salvia clan comprises some 900 species of widely distributed annuals, biennials, perennials, and shrubs. Commonly called sages as well as salvias — the popular culinary herb common sage (*S. officinalis*) belongs here — they bear erect spikes of tubular two-lipped flowers in shades of violet, purple, lilac, mauve-purple, scarlet, pink, white, and rich true blue. Each flower has a tubular, bell-, or funnel-shaped calyx at the base, which in some species is quite showy in its own right. Like other mint-family plants, most species feature square stems. Leaves are usually simple, ranging from linear and lance shaped to heart shaped and ovate. They are generally toothed or scalloped and are often aromatic and hairy. The flowers attract hummingbirds and butterflies.

HOW TO GROW

Grow salvias in full sun to light shade and average to rich, well-drained soil that is evenly moist. In areas with hot summers, a site with dappled afternoon shade is best. Most species are very drought tolerant once established. Good soil drainage is especially important in winter. *S. officinalis* needs very well drained soil and is best in full sun. In areas where salvias are marginally hardy, grow them against a south-facing wall for extra winter protection or take

Salvia argentea

Salvia farinacea

cuttings in late summer and overwinter them indoors. Hardy perennial salvias seldom need dividing, but they can be dug in spring or early fall if they outgrow their space or for propagation. Propagate by division, cuttings taken from spring through early fall, or seeds. To grow annual or biennial salvias, sow seeds indoors 6 to 8 weeks before the last spring frost date.

S. argentea
s. are-JEN-tee-uh. SILVER SAGE, SILVER SALVIA. A biennial or short-lived perennial grown for its rosette of large, rounded, 8-inch-long, gray-green leaves covered with silvery hairs. Bears white to pinkish flowers on 2- to 3-foot-tall spikes in summer. Plants do not tolerate wet soil in winter. **Zones 5 to 8.**

S. azurea
s. ah-ZURE-ee-uh. BLUE SAGE, AZURE SAGE. Shrubby 3- to 4-foot-tall perennial that spreads from 2 to 3 feet. Bears dense racemes of $3/4$-inch-long blue or white flowers from late summer to fall. **Zones 5 to 9.**

S. buchananii
s. bue-kah-NAN-ee-eye. A tender, 2-foot-tall perennial with a somewhat sprawling habit. Bears loose racemes of 2-inch-long, magenta-red flowers from summer to fall. Tender perennial or warm-weather annual. **Zones 9 and 10.**

S. coccinea
s. kok-SIN-ee-uh. A bushy, $1^1/2$- to 3-foot-tall annual with spikes of $3/4$-inch-long flowers that have flaring lower lips. Flowers are borne from summer to fall and come in pink, red, or white. 'Coral Nymph', also sold as 'Cherry Blossom', bears flowers with a white upper lip and a salmon-pink lower one. 'Lady in Red' has scarlet flowers. Both are compact, $1^1/2$-foot-tall selections. Warm-weather annual.

S. elegans
s. EL-eh-ganz. PINEAPPLE SAGE. A shrubby tender peren-

Salvia farinacea

nial ranging from 3 to 6 feet or more in height. Bears softly hairy, pineapple-scented leaves and loose panicles of 1-inch-long scarlet flowers in late summer and fall. 'Scarlet Pineapple' has more strongly scented leaves than the species and larger, $1^1/2$-inch-long flowers. Tender perennial or warm-weather annual. **Zones 8 to 10.**

S. farinacea
s. fair-ih-NAY-see-ah. MEALYCUP SAGE. A bushy, 2-foot-tall tender perennial. Bears dense spikes of $3/4$-inch-long flowers on purple stems from summer to fall. Flowers come in violet, violet-blue, or white. S. 'Indigo Spires', a hybrid of this species and *S. longispicata*, bears spikes of purple, $1/2$-inch-long flowers with blue bracts. The spikes can reach as much as 3 feet in length. Tender perennial or warm-weather annual. **Zones 8 to 10.**

S. greggii
s. GREG-ee-eye. GREGG SAGE, AUTUMN SAGE. A 1- to 2-foot shrub or perennial with $3/4$-inch-long flowers in shades of red, purple, violet, pink, or yellow from late summer to frost. **Zones 7 to 10.**

S. guaranitica
s. gwar-ah-NIH-tih-kuh. A shrubby, 5-foot-tall tender perennial. Bears deep blue, 2-inch-long flowers with purple-blue calyxes from late summer to fall. Tender perennial

or warm-weather annual. **Zones 8 to 10.**

S. leucantha
s. lew-KAN-thuh. MEXICAN BUSH SAGE. A 2- to $3^1/2$-foot-tall subshrub with gray-green leaves. Bears dense spikes of white or purple, $1/2$- to $3/4$-inch-long flowers with showy purple calyxes in fall. Tender perennial or warm-weather annual. **Zone 10.**

S. officinalis
s. oh-fih-shih-NAL-iss. COMMON SAGE, GARDEN SAGE. Shrubby 2- to $2^1/2$-foot-tall perennial that spreads to about 3 feet. Bears evergreen, aromatic leaves used in cooking that are woolly and gray-green. Produces branched racemes of $1/2$-inch-long lavender-blue flowers in midsummer. Compact 1-foot-tall 'Aurea' has yellow leaves. 'Icterina' has leaves splashed with yellow and green. 'Purpurascens' bears leaves that are reddish purple when young. 'Tricolor' has variegated leaves marked with green, purple, pink, and cream. **Zones 5 to 9; to Zone 4 with winter protection;** cultivars may be less hardy than the species.

S. patens
s. PAY-tens. BLUE SAGE, GENTIAN SAGE. A tender, $1^1/2$- to 2-foot perennial. Bears loose racemes of 2-inch-long deep blue flowers from midsummer to fall. Tender perennial or warm-weather annual. **Zones 8 to 10.**

S. pratensis
s. pray-TEN-sis. MEADOW SAGE, MEADOW CLARY. Shrubby 1- to 3-foot-tall perennial that spreads as far. Bears oval, wrinkle-textured leaves and branched clusters of 1-inch-long violet flowers from early to midsummer. 'Haematodes' has blue-violet flowers. 'Rosea' has rose-pink blooms. **Zones 3 to 9.**

S. splendens
s. SPLEN-denz. SCARLET SAGE. A tender, 1- to 2-foot perennial popular as an annual bedding plant. Bears dense spikes of $1/2$- to 2-inch-long flowers with showy bracts from summer to fall in scarlet, mauve-purple, creamy white, or pink. Sizzler Series plants reach 16 inches and come in a wide range of colors, including red, salmon, burgundy, pink, lavender, and purple. 'Red Hot Sally' bears scarlet flowers on 10-inch plants. 'Van Houttei' produces rose-red flowers with burgundy calyxes on 4-foot plants. Red-flowered forms are best in full sun, while pastels benefit from partial shade. Tender perennial or warm-weather annual. **Zone 10.**

S. × sylvestris
s. × sil-VES-tris. HYBRID SAGE. A 2- to 3-foot-tall hybrid perennial (*S. nemorosa* × *S. pratensis*) forming 1-foot-wide clumps. Bears dense racemes of $1/2$-inch-long pinkish purple flowers from early to midsummer. 'Blue Queen', also sold as 'Blaukönigin', produces blue-violet flowers on 2-foot plants. 'East Friesland', also sold as

Salvia greggii

S

'Ostfriesland' and sometimes listed as a cultivar of *S. nemorosa*, bears violet-blue flowers on 1¹/₂-foot plants. 'May Night', also sold as 'Mainacht', has ³/₄-inch-long indigo flowers on 2-foot plants. 'Rose Queen' bears pink flowers and grayish green leaves on 2¹/₂-foot plants. **Zones 4 to 9.**

S. uliginosa

s. yew-lih-gih-NO-suh. Bog Sage. A tender, shrubby perennial from 4 to 6 feet tall and spreading to 3 feet. Bears spikes of ³/₄-inch-long, sky blue flowers from late summer to fall. Plants thrive in moist, well-drained soil but also do well in wet conditions. Tender perennial or warm-weather annual. **Zones 8 to 10.**

S. viridis

s. VEER-ih-dis. Annual Clary Sage. Formerly *S. horminum*. A bushy, 1¹/₂- to 2-foot-tall annual with spikes of insignificant, pink to purplish flowers and showy, 1¹/₂-inch-long bracts. The bracts are mauve-pink, purple, or white and have darker veins. Warm-weather annual.

Sambucus

sam-BUE-kus. Honeysuckle family, Caprifoliaceae.

Elders may be better known for their folk uses — elderberry wine, pancakes, and an herbal pain reliever — than they are in the ornamental landscape. They represent a genus of about 25 herbaceous perennials and deciduous shrubs and trees widely distributed throughout temperate and subtropical areas. Some are a bit shaggy for a formal garden, but they work well for naturalizing and attracting birds. Some cultivars have striking divided foliage.

HOW TO GROW

Elders do best in moisture-retentive, well-drained soil but adapt to some drought and a wide range of pH. The yellow-foliaged types need dappled shade to prevent fading. European species are not heat tolerant. Use species for naturalizing or for windbreaks; cultivars, in a shrub border. They tolerate hard pruning and require it to keep from becoming unkempt. Propagate from seeds or cuttings, or by dividing suckers.

S. canadensis

s. kan-uh-DEN-sis. American Elder. A variable shrub from 5 to 12 feet high and wide with pinnately compound leaves and, in midsummer, profuse flat-topped clusters of white flowers with prominent yellow stamens. The late-summer berries are purple-black, eaten by birds but also used for jelly, pies, and juice. 'Aurea' has yellow foliage and red fruit. **Zones 3 to 9.**

S. mexicana

s. mex-ih-KAN-uh. Blue Elderberry. Also listed as *S. caerulea*. Native from British Columbia into southern California and east to the Rockies, this species ranges from a large shrub to a tree 30 feet or taller. Five to nine leaflets form leaves up to 8 inches long. The flat-topped clusters of creamy

Sambucus nigra

white flowers bloom late spring to midsummer, followed by blue-black ¹/₄-inch berries. **Zones 5 to 7.**

S. nigra

s. NYE-gruh. European Elder. The species grows 10 to 20 feet tall and bears early-summer clusters of white flowers, smaller than those of *S. canadensis*. There are almost 30 cultivars offering foliage that is golden ('Aurea'), variegated ('Marginata'), finely cut ('Laciniata'), or even purple ('Guincho Purple'). **Zones 5 to 7.**

S. racemosa 'Plumosa Aurea'

s. rass-eh-MOE-suh. European Red Elder cultivar. A multistemmed shrub 8 to 12 feet tall and wide with finely cut, compound, toothed leaflets of bright yellow or chartreuse. Tiny yellow flowers bloom in round-topped clusters in midspring, followed by bright red, ¹/₄-inch berries. **Zones 5 to 7.**

Sandersonia

san-der-SO-nee-uh. Lily family, Liliaceae.

Sandersonia contains a single species native to South Africa grown for its charming, lanternlike flowers. A climber that grows from tuberous roots, *S. aurantiaca* bears lance-shaped leaves often tipped with tendrils. The nodding, nearly round flowers are bell to urn shaped and borne on slender, fairly long stalks in the leaf axils.

HOW TO GROW

Select a site in full sun with rich, well-drained soil. In areas with hot summers, shade during the hottest part of the day is best. Plants need a trellis or other support to climb.

Sandersonia aurantiaca

Where they are hardy, grow plants outdoors year-round; in areas where they are marginally hardy, look for a protected, south-facing site and mulch heavily over winter with evergreen boughs, pine needles, or salt hay. Mulch in summer to keep the root run fairly cool, and water regularly when plants are growing actively. In the North, grow plants in containers or plant the tubers outdoors in spring on or slightly after the last frost date. Indoors or out, handle the brittle tubers very carefully. Plant them with the tips 5 to 6 inches beneath the soil surface. Although the tubers can be dug in fall after the first light frost and stored indoors over winter in dry peat moss or sand, plants are happiest when left undisturbed for several years, and digging the brittle tubers can damage them. For this reason, in the North keeping them in containers year-round is easiest. Overwinter container-grown plants by gradually allowing the soil to dry out at the end of the season and storing plants — pot and all — in a cool (50° to 55°F), dry place. Repot or top-dress container-grown plants in spring.

S. aurantiaca

s. aw-ran-tee-AH-kuh. A 2- to 3-foot-tall climber with lance-shaped leaves. Bears pendent 1-inch-long orange flowers that are nearly round or bell or urn shaped in summer. **Zones 7 to 10.**

Sanguinaria

san-gwih-NAIR-ee-uh. Poppy family, Papaveraceae.

A single species of woodland wildflower native to eastern North America belongs to this genus. Commonly called bloodroot, it

S

Sanguinaria canadensis

grows from a fleshy rhizome that exudes red bloodlike sap when cut. The dainty white flowers, which resemble daisies more than the poppies to which this plant is related, emerge in spring shortly before the leaves.

HOW TO GROW
Select a site in partial to full shade with rich, evenly moist, well-drained soil. Plants go dormant and disappear by midsummer, so mark the locations of the clumps to avoid digging into them by mistake. Propagate by seeds or by dividing the clumps immediately after they flower. Double-flowered forms must be propagated by division.

S. canadensis
s. kan-uh-DEN-sis. BLOODROOT, RED PUCCOON. A slowly spreading, rhizomatous species that reaches 4 to 6 inches in height and spreads to 1 foot. Bears cup-shaped 2¹/2- to 3-inch-wide white flowers in spring that open before the scalloped, kidney-shaped leaves unfurl. 'Flore Pleno' ('Multiplex') bears long-lasting double white flowers. **Zones 3 to 9.**

Sanguisorba
san-gwih-SOR-buh. Rose family, Rosaceae.

Commonly called burnets, these unlikely-looking rose-family plants bear handsome pinnate leaves and bottlebrush-like spikes of tiny flowers on wiry, erect stems. Blooms come in white, pink, or red and lack petals but have prominent stamens. About 18 species belong to the genus, all of which are rhizomatous perennials.

HOW TO GROW
Plant burnets in full sun or partial shade and well-drained soil that is fairly rich in organic matter and remains evenly moist. In the South, a spot with shade during the hottest part of the day is best. *S. canadensis* is a vigorous spreader and can become invasive in wet-soil sites. Tall species require staking. Propagate by division in spring or fall or by seeds.

S. canadensis
s. kan-uh-DEN-sis. CANADIAN BURNET. A 6-foot-tall species native to North America that easily spreads by rhizomes to 3 to 4 feet. Bears fluffy 6- to 8-inch-long spikes of white flowers from midsummer to fall. **Zones 3 to 8.**

S. obtusa
s. ob-TOO-suh. JAPANESE BURNET. A 2-foot-tall species that forms 2- to 3-foot-wide clumps. Bears handsome 1¹/2-foot-long gray-green leaves and 3-inch-long

Sanguisorba canadensis

Sanguinaria canadensis

spikes of fluffy deep pink flowers from midsummer to fall. **Zones 4 to 8.**

S. officinalis
s. oh-fih-shih-NAL-iss. GREAT BURNET. A 4-foot-tall species that spreads to 2 to 3 feet. Bears nearly 2-foot-long leaves and maroon to purple-brown flowers that are carried in short, rounded 1-inch-long spikes from early summer to fall. **Zones 4 to 8.**

Santolina
san-toe-LEE-nuh. Aster family, Asteraceae.

Santolina species are actually shrubs and subshrubs rather than herbaceous perennials, but most gardeners use them as perennials in sunny beds and borders as well as herb gardens. About 18 species belong to the genus, all evergreens native to the Mediterranean region. They bear aromatic leaves usually finely cut in a pinnate fashion and petalless, rounded, buttonlike flower heads consisting of all disk florets.

HOW TO GROW
Select a site in full sun with poor to average, very well drained soil. Sandy soil is ideal. Plants tolerate

heat but because of fungal diseases do not fare well in areas with wet, humid summers. Some gardeners shear off the flowers to highlight the foliage. Prune plants hard in spring to keep them compact, and/or cut them back hard immediately after flowering. Propagate by cuttings in late summer.

S. chamaecyparissus
s. kam-ee-sip-ah-RISS-uss. LAVENDER COTTON. A 1- to 2-foot-tall shrub that forms 2- to 3-foot-wide mounds of finely cut, woolly gray-white leaves. Bears ¹/2- to ³/4-inch-wide yellow flowers from mid- to late summer. 'Lambrook Silver' has silvery gray foliage. 'Lemon Queen' is compact, to 2 feet tall and wide, with lemon yellow flower heads. 'Weston' is a dwarf form that reaches about 6 inches tall and spreads to 8 inches. **Zones 6 to 9.**

S. rosmarinifolia
s. rose-mah-rin-ih-FOE-lee-uh. GREEN LAVENDER COTTON. Formerly *S. viridis*. Mounding shrub reaching 2 feet in height and spreading to 3 feet. Bears bright green leaves and yellow ³/4-inch-wide flower heads in midsummer. 'Primrose Gem' has pale yellow flower heads. **Zones 6 to 9.**

Sanvitalia
san-vih-TAL-ee-uh. Aster family, Asteraceae.

Sanvitalia contains seven species of creeping annuals and perennials with oval leaves and small daisylike flowers, all native to the southwestern United States and

Santolina chamaecyparissus

S

Sanvitalia procumbens

Sarcococca humilis

Mexico. One species is an easy-to-grow annual with tiny zinnia- or sunflower-like blooms.

HOW TO GROW

Give creeping zinnia (*S. procumbens*) a site with full sun and average to rich, well-drained soil. Plants tolerate dry and sandy soil. Sow seeds outdoors several weeks before the last spring frost date. From Zone 9 south, sow outdoors in fall for bloom the following spring. Or sow indoors in individual pots 6 to 8 weeks before the last frost date at 70°F. Germination takes 2 to 3 weeks. Transplant with care. Outdoor sowing is generally best, since plants resent being disturbed. When sowing, just press the seeds into the soil surface, as light aids germination. Use creeping zinnias as edgings, in rock gardens, as ground covers, and in mixed plantings. They are attractive container plants and will trail over the edges of a hanging basket.

S. procumbens

s. pro-KUM-benz. CREEPING ZINNIA. A mat-forming annual that reaches 6 to 8 inches in height and can spread 2¹/₂ feet. Bears ³/₄-inch-wide daisylike flowers with black centers and golden ray florets, or "petals," from early summer to fall. Warm-weather annual.

Saponaria

sap-oh-NAIR-ee-uh. Pink family, Caryophyllaceae.

Soapworts, as *Saponaria* species are commonly called, bear clusters of five-petaled flowers usually in shades of pink. Leaves are simple and usually lance shaped. Some 20

species — both annuals and perennials — belong to the genus. They are native from Europe to southwestern Asia and closely related to *Lychnis* and *Silene*, both commonly referred to as catchflies. The botanical name is from the Latin *sapo*, meaning "soap," and refers to the fact that the leaves of some species produce a lather when rubbed in water.

HOW TO GROW

Plant soapworts in full sun in average, well-drained soil, preferably with a neutral to alkaline pH. Plants do not do well in areas with very hot, humid summers. Sandy soil is fine, and too-rich soil causes plants to flop over. *S. officinalis* tolerates partial shade but is more likely to flop there. Cut soapworts, especially *S. ocymoides*, back hard

after flowering to keep the plants compact. The perennials spread readily to form broad clumps because they grow from fleshy white roots that creep, and stems sometimes root where they fall over and touch the soil. Except for double-flowered forms, plants also self-sow. Dig clumps in spring or fall to keep them in bounds or for propagation. Or propagate by rooting cuttings in summer. Plants can be grown from seeds, but double-flowered forms do not come true and must be propagated vegetatively.

S. × lempergii

s. × lem-PER-jee-eye. SOAPWORT. Sprawling hybrid perennial that forms ¹/₂- to 1-foot-tall clumps that spread to 1¹/₂ feet. Bears clus-

ters of hot pink 1-inch-wide flowers from midsummer to fall. 'Max Frei' has paler pink flowers than the species. **Zones 5 to 8.**

S. ocymoides

s. oh-sih-MOY-deez. ROCK SOAPWORT. Low-growing 3- to 6-inch-tall perennial that spreads to 1¹/₂ feet. Bears loose clusters of ¹/₂-inch-wide pink flowers in summer. 'Alba' has white flowers. 'Rubra Compacta' bears red flowers on low, dense plants. **Zones 4 to 8.**

S. officinalis

s. oh-fih-shih-NAL-iss. BOUNCING BET, SOAPWORT. Fast-spreading 1- to 2¹/₂-foot-tall perennial that spreads by rhizomes to form 2-foot-wide clumps. Bears clusters of ³/₄-inch-wide white, pink, or red flowers from summer to fall. 'Alba Plena' has double white flowers. 'Rosea Plena' bears fragrant double pink flowers. 'Rubra Plena' has double red flowers that fade to pink. **Zones 3 to 9.**

Sarcococca

sar-koh-KOKE-uh. Boxwood family, Buxaceae.

This is a genus of 14 evergreen Asian shrubs, surprisingly underused in gardens given the plants' many attributes: fragrant, petalless winter flowers; glossy lance-shaped or elliptical leaves; tolerance of shade and shearing; and generally trouble-free nature.

HOW TO GROW

Give sarcococca soil that is organically amended, slightly acid, and moisture retentive but well aerated. It will not tolerate both full

Saponaria × lempergii

sun and dry soil. Grow as a low hedge, tall ground cover, edging for a path, in a foundation, or to face down shrubs of contrasting texture in a shrub border.

S. confusa

s. kon-FEW-suh. A dense, rounded shrub to 6 feet tall and 3 feet wide with elliptical, glossy leaves and clusters of fragrant white spring flowers borne in the leaf axils. The 1/4-inch fruits are round and glossy black. **Zones 6 to 10.**

S. humilis

s. hew-MIL-us. SWEETBOX. Formerly *S. hookeriana* var. *humilis.* This is the most commonly available variety. Averaging 18 inches tall, it suckers to form a non-aggressive, mounded colony. The 3-inch dark green leaves usually hide the 1/2-inch flowers, white and sweetly aromatic, that bloom late winter to early spring. The fruits are glossy and blue-black. **Zones 5 to 10.**

S. ruscifolia

s. rus-kih-FOE-lee-uh. FRAGRANT SARCOCOCCA. This species grows slowly to form a mound about 5 feet high, varying in width from 3 to 7 feet. Arching shoots bear lance-shaped, pointed, glossy leaves. The fragrant white early-spring flowers are followed by 1/4-inch dark red fruits. **Zones 7 to 10.**

Satureja

sah-tur-EE-juh. Mint family, Lamiaceae.

Commonly known as savories, *Satureja* species are aromatic-leaved annuals, perennials, and subshrubs with spikes of tiny two-lipped tubular flowers. The pungent leaves are linear, lance shaped, or rounded. About 30 species belong to the genus, one of which is a popular perennial herb.

HOW TO GROW

Grow satureja in full sun and loose, average to rich, well-drained soil. Neutral to slightly alkaline pH is best. Cut plants back in early spring. Plants become woody and need to be renewed every 2 to 3 years: propagate them by starting from cuttings taken in summer, by dividing in early spring, or by seeds.

S. montana

s. mon-TAHN-uh. SUMMER SAVORY. Shrubby 16-inch-tall perennial with lance-shaped leaves

Satureja montana

that spreads from about 8 inches to 1 foot. Bears upright spikes with whorls of tiny lavender-pink flowers in summer. **Zones 5 to 8.**

Saxifraga

saks-ih-FRAY-juh. Saxifrage family, Saxifragaceae.

Saxifraga is a large, very diverse genus containing about 440 species and hundreds of cultivars. Leaves vary greatly in shape, but most plants produce only basal leaves. The individual flowers, which usually have five petals, are small, but most species bear them in abundance in racemes or panicles. Plants are semievergreen or evergreen and usually perennial, although the genus contains a few

Saxifraga umbrosa var. *primuloides*

biennials and annuals. Most are mat- or cushion-forming plants — some are almost mosslike — native to mountainous regions in the Northern Hemisphere and are most often grown in rock gardens. The botanical name is from the Latin *saxum,* meaning "rock," and *frango,* "break," and alludes to the fact that many saxifrages grow naturally in rock crevices.

HOW TO GROW

The cultural requirements of saxifrages vary widely: most species need rock-garden conditions and grow well only in the Pacific Northwest, New England, and adjacent parts of Canada, because they do not tolerate summer heat and humidity. The species listed here are exceptions to that rule and grow well in partial to full shade and well-drained, moist soil that is rich in organic matter. Well-drained soil is essential to success. Propagate by dividing plants in spring, separating individual rosettes of foliage and rooting them, or by seeds.

S. stolonifera

s. stow-lon-IF-er-uh. STRAWBERRY GERANIUM, MOTHER OF THOUSANDS. Formerly *S. sarmentosa.* Stoloniferous species that produces low 2- to 4-inch-tall mounds of hairy, kidney-shaped, 1 1/2- to 3 1/2-inch-long leaves. Plant spreads to 1 foot or more. Bears loose panicles of small 1-inch-wide white flowers in summer. 'Tricolor' has leaves variegated with pink, white, and green. **Zones 6 to 9.**

S. umbrosa var. primuloides

s. um-BRO-suh var. prim-yew-LOY-deez. DWARF LONDON PRIDE. Formerly *S. primuloides.* An 8-inch-tall evergreen with rosettes of leathery, ovate to spoon-shaped leaves with scalloped edges. Bears loose panicles of starry, pale pink 1/4- to 3/8-inch flowers in spring. **Zones 4 to 7.**

S. × urbium

s. × UR-bee-um. LONDON PRIDE. Vigorous 12-inch-tall species that spreads to 2 feet. Bears rosettes of evergreen, spoon-shaped, leathery leaves and loose panicles of starry 3/8-inch-wide white flowers flushed with pink in summer. **Zones 5 to 7.**

Scabiosa

scah-bee-OH-suh. Teasel family, Dipsacaceae.

Commonly known as pincushion flowers or scabious, *Scabiosa* species are annuals, biennials, or perennials. As their common name suggests, they bear rounded flower heads that somewhat resemble pincushions. The blooms, which can be single or double, also look somewhat like daisies or asters and actually are constructed in a similar fashion. They have small central florets that form the "pincushion" surrounded by larger petal-like florets. The leaves are either entire, lobed, or deeply cut in a featherlike fashion. About 80 species belong to the genus.

HOW TO GROW

Pincushion flowers thrive in full sun and average, well-drained soil.

S

Scabiosa stellata

A neutral to slightly alkaline pH is best. Plants do not tolerate soil that is too moist, especially in winter. In the South, select a site that receives afternoon shade. Deadhead regularly to prolong bloom. Divide clumps in spring if they outgrow their space or become too crowded, or for propagation.

Sow the annuals listed here indoors 4 to 5 weeks before the last spring frost date at 70° to 75°F. Germination takes about 2 weeks. Or sow outdoors after the last frost date. From Zone 8 south, sow outdoors in fall. Stake plants with twiggy brush. Deadhead regularly to encourage new flowers to form. Use pincushion flowers in mixed plantings, cottage gardens, and containers. Both hummingbirds and butterflies visit the blooms. The seed heads of *S. stellata* are attractive in dried arrangements.

S. atropurpurea

s. ah-tro-pur-PUR-ee-uh. SWEET SCABIOUS, PINCUSHION FLOWER. A 2- to 3-foot annual with feathery leaves and fragrant, 2-inch-wide flower heads in shades of purple, lavender, white, pink, or purple-blue. 'Dwarf Double' is a 1¹/₂-foot-tall, double-flowered plant. Warm-weather annual.

S. caucasica

s. kaw-KASS-ih-kuh. PINCUSHION FLOWER, SCABIOUS. Clump-forming perennial that reaches 2 feet when in bloom and spreads as far. Bears featherlike leaves and rounded 3-inch-wide flower clusters in lavender, white, yellow, or rose-purple from summer to early fall. 'Alba' and 'Miss Willmott' both bear white flowers. **Zones 4 to 9.**

S. columbaria

s. kol-um-BAR-ee-uh. Clump-forming perennial reaching 2 feet in bloom and spreading to 3 feet. Bears featherlike leaves and lilac-blue 1¹/₂-inch-wide flower heads from summer to fall. 'Butterfly Blue' and 'Pink Mist', also sold as 'Butterfly Pink', are outstanding, long-blooming cultivars sometimes listed under *S. caucasica*. **Zones 3 to 8.**

S. stellata

s. steh-LAH-tah. STAR FLOWER. A 1¹/₂-foot-tall annual with wiry stems and rounded, 1¹/₄-inch-wide, pale bluish white or pink flowers. The flowers are followed by round, 3-inch-wide seed heads consisting of cup-shaped, creamy tan to brown bracts. Warm-weather annual.

Scadoxus

ska-DOX-us. Amaryllis family, Amaryllidaceae.

Grown for their showy, rounded brushlike flower heads, *Scadoxus* species share the common name "blood lily" with their close relatives in the genus *Haemanthus*. Nine species of perennials, all native to tropical regions of Africa, belong here. They grow from either tunicate bulbs or rhizomes and bear umbels of 10 to as many as 200 tiny, tightly packed, tubular flowers. The individual flowers have six petal-like tepals as well as six showy, protruding stamens that add to the brushlike appearance. The leaves are arranged in a spiral (those of *Haemanthus* species are borne in two rows), and flowers appear either before or as the leaves emerge. Flowers are followed by showy round berries.

HOW TO GROW

Select a spot in full sun or partial shade with rich, well-drained soil. Neutral to alkaline soil pH is best. These plants require evenly moist soil when they are growing actively and dry conditions when dormant. Where they are marginally hardy, look for a protected, south-facing site and mulch the plants heavily in late fall. Elsewhere, plant them in containers or outdoors in spring after the last frost date once the soil has warmed up and nighttime temperatures stay above 60°F. In the ground or in containers, set the bulbs with the necks just above the soil surface. Water regularly when the plants are growing actively.

To overwinter the bulbs indoors, gradually withhold water toward the end of the season and either bring containers indoors or dig the bulbs before the first light frost of fall. Keep the soil of container-grown plants dry, or pack bulbs in dry peat moss and store them in a cool, dry spot where temperatures do not drop below 50°F. Plants are happiest when their roots and bulbs are left undisturbed, so keeping them in containers year-round usually is a better option than digging them annually in fall. Where they're hardy, they thrive for years without needing to be divided. Container-grown blood lilies bloom best when they are pot-bound, so repot only if necessary just when new growth resumes in spring. Propagate by separating offsets in early spring or by seeds.

S. multiflorus

s. mul-tih-FLOR-us. BLOOD LILY. Formerly *Haemanthus multiflorus*. A 1¹/₂- to 2-foot-tall species from tropical and South Africa with broad, basal, lance-shaped leaves. In summer, bears round 4- to 6-inch-wide red flower heads followed by orange berries. *S. m.* ssp. *katherinae* (formerly *Haemanthus katherinae*) has wavy-edged leaves. **Zones 9 to 11; to Zone 8 with winter protection.**

S. puniceus

s. pew-NIH-see-us. ROYAL PAINT BRUSH, GIANT STOVE BRUSH. Formerly *Haemanthus puniceus*. A 20-inch-tall species from eastern and southern Africa with rounded, basal, wavy-edged leaves. From spring to early summer, bears 4-inch-wide cone-shaped flower heads that are pink or red and surrounded by conspicuous red bracts (actually spathe valves). Yellow berries follow the flowers. **Zones 9 to 11.**

Scaevola

skuh-VOL-ah. Goodenia family, Goodeniaceae.

Some 96 species of tender perennials, climbers, shrubs, and small trees belong to this genus of plants that are found from Australia to Polynesia in a wide range of

Scadoxus multiflorus

Scaevola aemula 'Blue Wonder'

habitats, including coastal dunes and beaches and damp, subalpine mountains in the tropics. They bear unusual fan-shaped flowers with five fingerlike lobes, or "petals"; the botanical name is from the Latin *scaeva,* meaning "left-handed," and is a reference to their one-sided, handlike shape. Flowers are carried either singly or in small clusters.

HOW TO GROW
Give fan flower (*S. aemula*) full sun or dappled shade and average, evenly moist soil that is well drained. In Zones 10 and 11, it can be grown outdoors as a perennial; in the North, grow it as a bedding plant replaced annually or as a tender perennial. They are easy to grow from cuttings taken in summer, which can be used to overwinter the plants. Sow seeds indoors 6 to 8 weeks before the last spring frost date. To overwinter, take cuttings or pot up plants; keep them barely moist over winter. Use fan flower in mixed plantings and in containers.

S. aemula
s. eye-MULE-ah. FAN FLOWER, AUSTRALIAN BLUE FAN FLOWER, FAIRY FAN FLOWER. A sprawling, ^{1}/2- to 2-foot-tall perennial that can spread from 4 to 5 feet. Bears spoon-shaped leaves on succulent stems and racemes of 1-inch-wide, purple-blue flowers in summer. 'Blue Wonder' produces an abundance of ^{1}/2-inch-wide, lilac-blue flowers. Tender perennial or warm-weather annual. **Zones 10 and 11**.

Schizanthus

skih-ZAN-thus. Nightshade family, Solanaceae.

Schizanthus species are annuals and biennials with deeply cut, fernlike leaves and clusters of tubular, two-lipped flowers. From 12 to 15 species belong here, all of which are native to Chile. Their showy flowers have been compared to various butterflies and orchids — thus the common names "butterfly flower" and "poor-man's orchid" — despite the fact that they are more closely re-

lated to petunias (*Petunia*) and flowering tobaccos (*Nicotiana*).

HOW TO GROW
Select a site in full sun with rich, evenly moist, well-drained soil. Butterfly flowers grow well only in areas with cool summers, where night temperatures consistently drop below 65°F. Sow seeds indoors 8 to 10 weeks before the last spring frost date at 60° to 65°F. Germination takes from 1 to 3 weeks. From Zone 9 south, sow seeds outdoors in spring, several weeks before the last frost date. When sowing, barely cover the seeds with soil, as darkness is required for germination. Pinch seedlings to encourage branching and bushy growth. Stake with twiggy brush. Water regularly. Use butterfly flowers in mixed plantings as well as containers.

S. pinnatus
s. pin-AY-tus. BUTTERFLY FLOWER, POOR-MAN'S ORCHID. A ^{1}/2- to 1^1/2-foot-tall annual with fernlike leaves and clusters of tubular, 3- to 4-inch-wide flowers with flaring lips in shades of pink, purple, red, yellow, or white. The blooms often have throats marked in contrasting colors. Cool-weather annual.

Schizostylis

skih-zoh-STY-liss. Iris family, Iridaceae.

A single species commonly called crimson flag or kaffir lily belongs to the genus *Schizostylis*. Native to South Africa, it grows from a rhi-

Schizostylis coccinea

zome — unlike many of its close relatives from that country, including *Gladiolus* and *Ixia* species, both of which grow from corms. Plants bear dense, unbranched spikes of cup-shaped flowers that resemble gladiolus from late summer to fall and into winter in mild climates. Individual blooms have six petal-like tepals. The sword-shaped leaves are produced in fans and are evergreen.

HOW TO GROW
Give these plants a site in full sun or partial shade with average to rich, moist, well-drained soil. In the wild, they are found along streams and rivers, making them good choices for bog gardens or other spots where the soil remains constantly moist but is not completely waterlogged. Where they are hardy, grow them outdoors year-round. Toward the northern limits of their hardiness, look for a sheltered, south-facing site and

S

Schizanthus pinnatus

protect them in fall with an insulating mulch of evergreen boughs, coarse leaves, pine needles, or salt hay. Elsewhere, grow them in containers year-round and move them outdoors in spring after the last frost date. To overwinter them, bring the containers indoors before the first fall frost and keep them in a cool (45° to 50°F) spot over winter. Plants bloom best when they are left undisturbed. Divide or repot in spring when the roots become overcrowded. Propagate by division.

S. coccinea

s. kok-SIN-ee-uh. CRIMSON FLAG. A rhizomatous 1¹/₂- to 2-foot-tall species that spreads to about 1 foot. Bears showy spikes of 1 to as many as 14 cup-shaped ³/₄-inch-wide red flowers in late summer or fall. 'Major' ('Grandiflora') has 2- to 2¹/₂-inch-wide red flowers. 'Sunrise' bears 2- to 2¹/₂-inch-wide pink flowers. 'Viscountess Byns' features pale pink 1¹/₄-inch-wide flowers. *S. c.* var. *alba* has white flowers. **Zones 7 to 9; to Zone 5 or 6 with winter protection.**

Sciadopitys

sy-uh-DOP-it-iss. Bald-cypress family, Taxodiaceae.

The only species in this genus is a rare and unusual conifer that draws attention wherever it grows.

HOW TO GROW

Plant in full sun to partial shade; afternoon shade in the North and light shade in the South prevents desiccation. Best in fertile, moist, well-drained, acid soil. Protect from drying wind and full winter sun. Train to a single trunk if necessary. Allow low branches to remain to the ground. Usually pest-free and deer-proof.

S. verticillata

s. ver-tih-sil-LAH-tuh. JAPANESE UMBRELLA PINE. Highly variable, depending on the seed source, this evergreen can grow into a narrow cone or a broad pyramid at least 25 to 30 feet tall and 15 to 20 feet wide, with symmetrical branches all the way to the ground. The flattened, thick needles are glossy dark green, 4 to 5

Sciadopitys verticillata

Scilla siberica

inches long, and ¹/₈ inch wide. They form dense whorls that spiral out from the branch tips, creating a billowy effect. Needles on some plants may turn bronze-green in winter. The 4-inch-long, egg-shaped, green cones ripen to dark reddish brown. The trunk is covered with shredding, reddish brown bark, which is not very noticeable because of the dense branches. Umbrella pine grows very slowly and is thus rare and costly. Use it as a focal point in a border or foundation planting, but allow room for it to mature into a noble specimen. From Japan. **Zones 6 to 8.**

CULTIVARS

'Aurea' has golden needles. 'Wintergreen' retains an excellent dark blue-green color throughout the year.

Scilla

SIL-uh. Lily family, Liliaceae.

Spring-blooming *Scilla* species, commonly called squills, are treasured for the erect clusters of rich blue flowers they bring to the garden. The flowers appear in spring, late summer, or fall, depending on the species (spring-blooming species are the best known). They are bell shaped or starry and carried in few- to many-flowered clusters. The individual flowers consist of six petal-like tepals. The tepals are split all the way to the base of the flower; in *Chionodoxa*, with which *Scilla* species are often confused, the tepals are united at the base to form a tube. *Scilla* flowers also have wide-spreading stamens. While blue is the most common color, selections with purple,

white, or pink flowers also are available. Plants grow from small, usually tunicate bulbs and produce a few to several grassy, basal, linear to somewhat rounded leaves. About 90 species belong to the genus, native to Europe, Africa, and Asia.

HOW TO GROW

Select a site with average, well-drained soil that is in full sun or in partial to full shade under deciduous trees so plants receive full sun in spring when they are actively growing. Plant the bulbs in fall with the bases at a depth of 3 to 4 inches. For best effect, arrange them in drifts — a plant or two here and there will be lost in the spring garden, while drifts of 20 to 50 or more bulbs are stunning. Plants produce offsets freely and also self-sow: they are ideal for naturalizing and when left undisturbed form large showy colonies. Propagate by digging and dividing the clumps and/or separating the offsets and seedlings in early summer as the foliage dies back.

S. bifolia

s. bi-FOE-lee-uh. TWIN-LEAF SQUILL. A 3- to 6-inch-tall species bearing two linear leaves and starry-shaped purple-blue flowers in early spring. The 1- to 1¹/₂-inch-wide flowers are carried in loose, one-sided racemes of up to 10 blooms. **Zones 4 to 8.**

S. litardierei

s. lih-tar-DEE-er-ee-eye. Formerly *S. amethystina*, *S. pratensis*. A 4- to 8-inch-tall species with up to six basal leaves that appear in late spring or early summer with pale bluish violet ¹/₄-inch-wide flowers. The starry flowers are carried

Scilla peruviana

in racemes of 15 to 30 or more. **Zones 4 to 9.**

S. mischtschenkoana

s. mis-shenk-oh-AH-nuh. S Q U I L L. Formerly *S. tubergeniana*. A 4- to 6-inch-tall species with up to five leaves that appear in late winter or early spring with racemes of starry 3/4-inch-wide flowers. Blooms are borne in two- to six-flowered racemes and are silvery blue with darker stripes. **Zones 4 to 8.**

S. peruviana

s. per-oo-vee-AH-nuh. C U B A N L I L Y, P E R U V I A N J A C I N T H. A tender, nearly evergreen 6- to 18-inch-tall species from the Mediterranean region and southern Africa with up to 15 basal leaves; new leaves develop in fall. Bears rounded racemes of 50 to 100 star-shaped 1/2-inch-wide flowers in early summer. Blooms come in white and purplish blue. **Zones 8 and 9.**

S. scilloides

s. sil-OY-deez. C H I N E S E S C I L L A. Formerly *S. chinensis, S. japonica*. A 6- to 8-inch-tall species with up to seven leaves that appear in late summer or early fall with starry 1/8-inch-wide mauve-pink flowers. Blooms are borne in racemes of 40 to as many as 80 flowers. **Zones 4 to 8.**

S. siberica

s. sye-BEER-ih-kuh. S I B E R I A N S Q U I L L, S P R I N G S Q U I L L. A 4- to 8-inch-tall species with two to four leaves that appear in spring with deep blue nodding, bell- to bowl-shaped flowers. Blooms are borne in loose clusters of four or five. 'Alba' has white flowers.

'Spring Beauty' is a vigorous cultivar with dark blue blooms on 8-inch-tall plants. **Zones 4 to 8.**

Sedum

SEE-dum. Stonecrop family, Crassulaceae.

Tough, drought-tolerant sedums are annuals, biennials, perennials, subshrubs, and shrubs with fleshy leaves that are either oval and somewhat flattened or rounded. Also called stonecrops, they produce tiny, star-shaped, five-petaled flowers carried in dense, showy clusters ranging from 1/2 inch to 8 inches or more across. Perennial species range from mat-forming 1-inch-tall ground covers to 2-foot-tall mounding specimens for beds and borders. Some species are evergreen, others deciduous. Many feature ornamental foliage. About 400 species belong to this genus.

HOW TO GROW

Plant sedums in full sun in well-drained, average to rich soil. They also grow in poor, dry soil. Wet soil leads to root or crown rot and death. Some low-growing sedums can become quite invasive and are best used alone as ground covers where they can spread as they will. Dig or cut back spreading types as needed to keep them in bounds. In late winter or early spring, cut clump-forming sedums such as 'Autumn Joy' to the ground. Dig the clumps if they outgrow their space or begin to look over-crowded, but otherwise the plants don't need regular division. Propagate by dividing the clumps in spring or fall or by taking cuttings anytime the plants are not in flower. Some species self-sow.

S. acre

s. AY-ker. G O L D M O S S S E D U M. Fast-spreading 2-inch-tall perennial that easily spreads to several feet. Bears evergreen leaves and small 1/2-inch-wide clusters of starry yellow-green flowers in summer. 'Aureum', with yellow leaves, is a more modest spreader. **Zones 4 to 9.**

S. aizoon

s. eye-ZOON. A I Z O O N S T O N E-C R O P. Rhizomatous 1 1/2-foot-tall perennial that spreads as far. Bears flat 3- to 4-inch-wide clusters of 1/2-inch-wide yellow flowers in early summer. **Zones 4 to 9.**

S. album

s. AL-bum. W H I T E S T O N E-C R O P. Spreading 4- to 6-inch-tall perennial that forms 1 1/2-foot-wide mats. Bears evergreen leaves and 1- to 2-inch-wide clusters of small white flowers in summer. 'Coral Carpet' has pink leaves on 4-inch plants; 'Murale' has bronze-green leaves. **Zones 3 to 9.**

S. hybrids

By far the best-known hybrid sedum is 'Autumn Joy', also sold as 'Herbstfreude'. It produces 2-foot-tall, 2-foot-wide clumps with 8-inch-wide heads of densely packed flowers. The flowers start out as pale green buds in midsummer, open to dark pink and gradually age to red-brown from late summer through fall, and stand though winter; **Zones 3 to 9.** 'Ruby Glow', another excellent hybrid, is

Sedum 'Autumn Joy'

a 10-inch-tall plant with purplish green leaves and 2 1/2-inch-wide clusters of pinkish red flowers from midsummer to early fall; **Zones 5 to 9.** 'Vera Jameson', also 10 inches tall, bears 2 1/2-inch-wide clusters of rose-pink flowers in late summer and fall and has purplish to burgundy leaves; **Zones 4 to 9.**

S. kamtschaticum

s. kamt-SHAH-tih-kum. A 4-inch-tall perennial that spreads modestly by rhizomes to form 1-foot-wide clumps. Bears 1- to 2-inch-wide clusters of golden yellow flowers in late summer. 'Variegatum' has white-edged leaves. **Zones 4 to 9.**

S. sieboldii

s. see-BOLD-ee-ee. O C T O B E R D A P H N E. A 6- to 9-inch-tall perennial with arching stems of fleshy blue-green leaves edged in pink. Bears 2 1/2-inch clusters of pink flowers in fall. **Zones 3 to 8.**

S. spathulifolium

s. spath-yew-lih-FOE-lee-um. A 4-inch-tall perennial that tolerates light shade and spreads modestly to form mats about 2 feet wide. Bears tiny, fleshy, evergreen leaves and 1/2- to 1-inch-wide clusters of starry yellow flowers just above the foliage in summer. 'Cape Blanco' has silver-blue leaves; 'Purpureum' has red-purple and silver ones. **Zones 5 to 9.**

S. spectabile

s. spek-TAB-uh-lee. S H O W Y S T O N E C R O P. Clump-forming 1 1/2-foot-tall perennial that spreads as far. Bears rounded 1 1/2-inch-wide clusters of pink flowers in late summer. Hot pink–flowered 'Brilliant' is its best-known cultivar. 'Carmine' bears dark pink flowers. 'Variegata' has pale pink flowers and leaves with creamy yellow centers. **Zones 3 to 9.**

S. spurium

s. SPUR-ee-um. T W O - R O W S E D U M. Fast-spreading 4-inch-tall perennial that rapidly forms mats 2 to 3 feet or more in width. Bears fleshy, evergreen leaves and

Sedum 'Autumn Joy'

Sedum spurium 'Schorbuser Blut'

loose 1¹/₂-inch-wide clusters of pinkish purple or white star-shaped flowers in late summer. 'Dragon's Blood' ('Schorbuser Blut') has purple-tinted leaves and dark pink flowers. 'Elizabeth' has bronze and maroon leaves; 'Tricolor' produces pink-, white-, and green-striped ones. **Zones 4 to 9.**

S. telephium

s. tel-EH-fee-um. Clump-forming 2-foot-tall perennial that spreads to about 1 foot. Bears gray-green 3-inch-long leaves and loose 3- to 5-inch-wide clusters of small starry purple-pink flowers in late summer and early fall. *S. t.* ssp. *maximum* 'Atropurpureum' has dark purple stems and leaves and pink flowers; it reaches 1¹/₂ to 2 feet in height. **Zones 4 to 9.**

Sempervivum

sem-per-VYE-vum. Stonecrop family, Crassulaceae.

Commonly known as hens-and-chicks or houseleeks, *Sempervivum* species are rosette-forming perennials with succulent, evergreen leaves. The plants spread slowly but steadily to form low, dense mats by producing new off-sets at the ends of runners. In summer, full-grown rosettes produce a loose panicle of small pink, purplish, or white flowers that are star shaped or almost resemble small daisies. The rosettes, commonly referred to as the "hens," or mother plants, die after they flower, but new rosettes, or "chicks," quickly fill in the space they leave.

HOW TO GROW
Select a site in full sun or light shade with poor to average, well-drained soil. Plants are quite drought tolerant and will happily thrive with their roots in a crevice between rocks, in spots with only 2 to 3 inches of soil (provided the soil doesn't remain wet), in raised beds, and in containers. Extremely dry conditions cause plants to shrivel and become dwarfed. Pull up the mother plants after they bloom to make room for surrounding plantlets. To propagate, divide the clumps or pick off individual "chicks" and plant them anytime during the growing season.

S. arachnoideum

s. ah-rak-NOY-dee-um. COBWEB HOUSELEEK. Mat-forming species forming 2- to 3-inch-tall, ¹/₂- to 1-inch-wide rosettes of leaves that are covered with spider-weblike hairs. Spreads to form 1-foot-wide mounds. Bears 1-inch-wide clusters of reddish pink flowers on 1-foot-tall stems in summer. **Zones 4 to 8.**

Sempervivum arachnoideum

S. tectorum

s. tek-TOR-um. HENS-AND-CHICKS, ROOF HOUSELEEK. Forms 2- to 4-inch-tall rosettes of succulent leaves that are green to blue-green and sometimes flushed with purple or maroon in summer. Rosettes are 2 to 4 inches across and plants spread to form 2-foot-wide mounds. Bears 12- to 15-inch-tall stems topped by 2- to 4-inch-wide clusters of small red-purple flowers in summer. Many cultivars are available, with vari-ous-sized rosettes and leaves ranging from green with dark tips to maroon or red. **Zones 4 to 8.**

Senecio

seh-NEE-see-oh. Aster family, Asteraceae.

Senecio is a large, diverse genus of over 1,000 species of annuals, bi-ennials, perennials, climbers, shrubs, and small trees found all around the world. The genus contains species grown as bedding plants, tender perennials, and houseplants, as well as weeds, all of which bear daisylike flowers. The flowers are usually carried in clusters, but sometimes are borne singly, and consist of densely packed centers, or eyes, of disk florets that produce seeds. In most, but not all, species, the eyes are surrounded by ray florets, or "petals." Foliage is especially diverse, and leaf shapes include rounded, triangular, and deeply cut or fernlike. Foliage also can be fleshy or succulent, and several species bear hairy to woolly white leaves.

HOW TO GROW
The *Senecio* species listed here grow in full sun to very light shade and average to rich, well-drained

Senecio cineraria 'Silver Queen'

soil. Sow seeds indoors 6 to 8 weeks before the last spring frost date at 65° to 70°F. Damping off is a common problem, so sow in a sterile seed-starting mix and water from below, keeping the medium barely moist, never dry or wet. Or sow outdoors several weeks before the last frost date. From Zone 9 south, sow seeds outdoors in fall. When sowing, just press the seeds into the soil surface, as light is required for germination. To overwinter perennial species, consider taking cuttings in mid- to late summer. Keep them on the dry side over winter, and grow them in a bright, cool (minimum 45° to 50°F) spot. Use these plants in mixed plantings or in containers. Dusty miller (*S. cineraria*) is a good edging plant and also adds texture to other plant combinations. Give vining types a trellis to climb, or let them cascade out of a hanging basket.

S. cineraria

s. sin-er-AIR-ee-uh. DUSTY MILLER. Formerly *S. maritimus*. A tender, 1- to 2-foot-tall shrub grown for its deeply cut, woolly white leaves. Plants bear clusters of 1-inch-wide, mustard yellow flower heads, which many garden-ers remove. 'Silver Dust' is a 12-inch-tall cultivar with very lacy white leaves; 'Silver Queen' bears similar foliage on 8-inch-plants. Cool-weather annual or tender perennial. **Zones 8 to 10.**

S. confusus

s. kon-FEW-sus. ORANGE GLOW VINE. Formerly *Pseudogynoxys chenopodioides*. This tender climber can reach 20 feet in frost-free climates. It bears thick, toothed, lance-shaped leaves and in summer produces clusters of fragrant, 2-inch-wide, orange flower heads that fade to red. Tender perennial. **Zone 10.**

S. elegans

s. EL-eh-ganz. PURPLE SENECIO, PURPLE RAGWORT. A 2-foot-tall annual with lobed or toothed leaves and 1-inch-wide flower heads with yellow eyes and petals that are purple, red-purple, or sometimes white. Cool-weather annual.

Setaria

seh-TAIR-ee-uh. Grass family, Poaceae.

About 100 species of annual and perennial grasses belong to the genus *Setaria*. They bear leaves that range from linear or narrow and lance shaped to ovate. Narrow, arching flower heads with prominent bristles are carried above the foliage in summer. The botanical name is derived from the Latin *seta*, meaning "bristle."

HOW TO GROW
Give these grasses full sun to partial shade and average to rich, well-drained soil. Sow seeds outdoors after the last spring frost date. When sowing, just press the seeds into the soil surface, as light

is required for germination. Use foxtail millet (*S. italica*) in informal plantings or meadow gardens. The seed heads are attractive to birds and can be added to dried arrangements.

S. italica

s. ih-TAL-ih-kuh. FOXTAIL MILLET. A 3- to 5-foot annual with linear leaves and brownish to purplish, cylindrical flower heads that reach 1 foot or more in length. Warm-weather annual.

Shepherdia

shep-HER-dee-uh. Oleaster family, Elaeagnaceae.

This genus comprises three species of evergreen or deciduous shrubs and trees native to North America, grown for silvery foliage and tolerance of difficult conditions. Gardeners who are discovering their regional natives appreciate these rugged species, which have adapted to the rigors of the Plains.

HOW TO GROW
Shepherdia thrives in full sun and dry, alkaline soils and tolerates the cold wind and salt of coastal situations. You need to have both male and female plants to produce berries. Use for naturalizing, for attracting birds, or as a hedge in a harsh climate. Does not need pruning. Propagate from cold-stratified seeds or root cuttings.

S. argentea

s. ar-JEN-tee-uh. SILVER BUFFALOBERRY. Native from Can-

Sidalcea malviflora

ada south to Kansas and west to Nevada, this deciduous shrub has thorny, erect branches and usually grows 6 to 10 feet tall and spreads by suckering. The 1-inch leaves are silvery and scaly. Inconspicuous yellow springtime flowers are followed on female plants by tart red oval berries appreciated by birds and used for jellies. **Zones 3 to 6.**

S. canadensis

s. kan-uh-DEN-sis. RUSSET BUFFALOBERRY. Native to the contiguous northern states and Alaska, this deciduous shrub is usually 8 feet tall or less and has more gray-green foliage and yellower fruits than *S. argentea*. **Zones 2 to 6.**

Sidalcea

sid-AL-see-uh. Mallow family, Malvaceae.

Sidalcea species are native North American wildflowers closely related to hollyhocks (*Alcea*) as well as a less well known genus, *Sida*. This relationship is commemorated by the botanical name, which combines the two names — *Sida* and *Alcea*. The genus contains between 20 and 25 species of annuals and perennials, all bearing

erect racemes of five-petaled, hollyhock-like flowers. Blooms come in shades of pink, purple-pink, and white. The leaves are rounded and usually lobed or divided in a palmate fashion.

HOW TO GROW
Select a site in full sun or light shade with average to somewhat rich, moist but well-drained soil. A spot with shade during the hottest part of the day is best in the South, as plants do not tolerate heat and humidity well. Plants thrive in a wide range of soils — from sandy to loamy — provided the soil is well drained. Cut the flowering stems back hard after the flowers fade to encourage compact growth and a second flush of blooms, as well as to curtail self-seeding. Dig and divide the clumps in spring or fall if they die out in the center or outgrow their space, or for propagation. Or propagate from seeds.

S. malviflora

s. mal-vih-FLOR-uh. CHECKERBLOOM. A 2- to 4-foot-tall, 1 1/2-foot-wide perennial with erect racemes of 2-inch-wide pink or lavender-pink flowers from early to midsummer. Most available cultivars are hybrids between this species and *S. candida*. 'Brilliant'

Setaria italica

Shepherdia canadensis

S

Silene virginica

bears carmine red flowers. 'Elsie Heugh' has purple-pink flowers. 'Party Girl' produces gray-green leaves and pink flowers on a 2- to 3-foot plant. **Zones 5 to 8.**

Silene

sy-LEE-nee. Pink family, Caryophyllaceae.

Commonly known as campions or catchflies, *Silene* species are annuals, biennials, or perennials found mostly in the Northern Hemisphere, especially in the Mediterranean region. About 500 species belong to the genus, all with flowers that have five notched or cleft petals in shades of pink, white, and red. The flowers are carried singly or in clusters and in many species have an inflated calyx at the base of the corolla (petals). Leaves are opposite and linear to rounded. *Silene* species are quite similar to *Lychnis* species, which are also commonly called campions and catchflies.

HOW TO GROW

Select a site in full sun or partial shade with average, well-drained soil. Neutral to slightly alkaline pH is best. Good drainage is essential. Plants tolerate dry soil and sandy or even rocky conditions. Perennials commonly are short-lived, especially in areas with hot, humid summers, but they do self-sow. Propagate by division in spring, by taking cuttings from shoots that arise from the base of the plants in spring, or by seeds. Sow seeds of annual species outdoors several weeks before the last spring frost

date or in fall. Or sow them indoors 8 to 10 weeks before that date. The flowers attract hummingbirds.

S. acaulis

s. aw-KAUL-iss. MOSS CAMPION. Mosslike 2-inch-tall perennial, native to the Arctic in North America, Europe, and Asia, that spreads to about 8 inches. Bears evergreen leaves and solitary ¹/₂-inch-wide pink flowers from late spring to summer. **Zones 3 to 6.**

S. armeria

s. are-MEER-ree-uh. SWEET WILLIAM CATCHFLY. This gray-green–leaved annual is 1 foot tall

Silene coeli-rosa

and bears showy, rounded clusters of deep magenta-pink, ¹/₂-inch-wide flowers in late summer. Cool-weather annual.

S. caroliniana

s. kare-oh-lin-ee-AH-nuh. CAROLINA CAMPION. An 8-inch-tall evergreen perennial native to North America. Forms 6-inch-wide clumps and bears clusters of 1-inch-wide pink flowers in early summer. **Zones 5 to 8.**

S. coeli-rosa

s. KOE-lee-ROE-suh. ROSE OF HEAVEN. Formerly *Agrostemma coeli-rosa*, *Lychnis coeli-rosa*. A 10- to 20-inch-tall annual with gray-green leaves and loose clusters of 1-inch-wide, rose-pink flowers with white centers and deeply notched petals. Cool-weather annual.

S. regia

s. REE-jee-uh. ROYAL CATCHFLY. A 2- to 5-foot-tall North American native wildflower that spreads to 1 foot and bears ¹/₂- to 1-foot-wide clusters of brilliant red 1-inch-wide flowers in spring and early summer. **Zones 5 to 8.**

S. schafta

s. SHAFF-tuh. SCHAFTA CAMPION, SHAFTA PINK. A 3- to 6-inch-tall perennial that spreads to 1 foot and bears clusters of ³/₄-inch-wide magenta-pink flowers from late summer to fall. **Zones 5 to 7.**

S. virginica

s. ver-JIN-ih-kuh. FIRE PINK. Short-lived 2- to 3-foot-tall perennial native to North America that forms 1-foot-wide clumps. Bears clusters of brilliant red ³/₄-inch-wide flowers in spring and early summer. **Zones 4 to 7.**

Silphium

SIL-fee-um. Aster family, Asteraceae.

Silphium species are robust native North American wildflowers that bear branched clusters of flower heads that resemble sunflowers or yellow daisies. The common name "rosinweed" comes from the fact that when cut, the stems exude a rosinlike sap that smells like turpentine. Unlike those of most aster-family plants, *Silphium* flower heads have sterile disk florets (the "eyes"): the seeds are produced by fertile ray florets, or "petals."

HOW TO GROW

Select a site in full sun or light shade with average, deeply prepared, evenly moist soil. Soil that

Silphium perfoliatum

Silybum marianum

is too rich encourages rank growth and plants that are likely to flop. These are tall, bold perennials, best for wild gardens or the backs of borders; site them with care, as they can take up considerable space and will thrive for years without needing to be divided. Propagate by dividing the clumps in spring or early fall or by sowing seeds. Plants self-sow.

S. laciniatum
s. lah-sin-ee-AH-tum. Compass Plant. A 5- to 10-foot-tall perennial forming 2- to 3-foot-wide clumps. The common name refers to the fact that the 1¹/₂-foot-long pinnately lobed leaves orient themselves north and south on the stems (flat sides facing east and west). From midsummer into fall, plants bear clusters of 5-inch-wide flower heads with yellow ray florets and darker yellow centers. Zones 5 to 9.

S. perfoliatum
s. per-foe-lee-AH-tum. Cup Plant. Bold 5- to 8-foot-tall perennial forming 3-foot-wide clumps. The common name refers to the fact that older leaves are connate-perfoliate, meaning their bases join across the stems and form a "cup" that holds water. Bears branched clusters of 3-inch-wide yellow flowers with darker yellow centers. Blooms from midsummer to fall. Zones 5 to 9.

Silybum
sih-LIH-bum. Aster family, Asteraceae.

Spiny leaves and thistlelike flower heads characterize the two species that belong to this genus. *Silybum* species are annuals or biennials with a rosette of glossy, prickly leaves topped by rounded, spiny, purple-pink flower heads. One species is grown in gardens for its ornamental leaves.

HOW TO GROW
Give *Silybum* full sun and poor to average, well-drained soil. Neutral to slightly alkaline pH is best, and plants prefer cool weather. Sow seeds indoors 6 to 8 weeks before the last spring frost date at 55° to 60°F. Germination takes 2 to 3 weeks. Plants started early bloom the first year. Or sow outdoors in spring after the last frost date or in early summer. If you want plants to overwinter, be sure drainage is perfect, as they resent wet soil in winter. Some gardeners remove flowers as they appear to show off the foliage to best effect. Plants self-sow and can become weedy; deadheading helps control them. Use these plants to add interesting foliage texture and color to mixed plantings.

S. marianum
s. mair-ee-AY-num. Mary's Thistle, Our Lady's Thistle, Holy Thistle, Milk Thistle. A biennial with a low rosette of spiny, dark green leaves attractively veined and mottled with white. In sum-

Skimmia japonica

mer, it bears 2-inch-wide, purple-pink flower heads on stems that can range from 2 to 5 feet tall. Zones 6 to 9.

Sisyrinchium
sis-eh-RINK-ee-um. Iris family, Iridaceae.

Commonly known as blue-eyed or golden-eyed grasses, *Sisyrinchium* species are clump-forming or rhizomatous plants native to North and South America. About 90 species of annuals and semievergreen perennials belong to the genus, all producing grassy clumps of linear to lance-shaped leaves that often are arranged in fans. They bear small star- or cup-shaped flowers in spring and summer. Blooms are carried singly or in clusters above

the foliage and come in shades of purple-blue, yellow, mauve, and white.

HOW TO GROW
Select a site in full sun with poor to average soil that is well drained. Neutral to slightly alkaline pH is best. The plants will grow in evenly moist soil but require good drainage, especially in winter. Propagate by dividing the clumps in spring or fall or by seeds. Plants self-sow.

S. graminoides
s. gram-in-OY-deez. Blue-eyed Grass. Formerly *S. angustifolium;* plants grown as *S. bermudiana* and *S. birameum* also belong here. A ¹/₂- to 1¹/₂-foot-tall perennial forming grassy ¹/₂- to 1-foot-wide clumps of linear leaves. Bears starry purple-blue ³/₄-inch-wide flowers with yellow throats over a long period in summer. Zones 3 to 9.

Skimmia
SKIM-ee-uh. Citrus family, Rutaceae.

A genus of four evergreen shrubs and trees from Asia, grown for their aromatic foliage, often fragrant flower clusters, and, on some

Sisyrinchium graminoides

Sisyrinchium graminoides

Smilacina racemosa

species, ornamental fruits. A good choice for small shady gardens.

HOW TO GROW

Give skimmia organically rich, acidic soil that retains moisture and drains well, in either partial or full shade. It will discolor in full sun and does not tolerate heat well. Use in woodland gardens, along foundations, or in borders with other shade-loving evergreen shrubs. Does not need pruning. Propagate from cleaned seeds or cuttings taken in fall.

S. japonica

s. juh-PON-ih-kuh. JAPANESE SKIMMIA. A dense, rounded shrub, to about 4 feet tall, with glossy elliptic leaves that are slightly fragrant when bruised and held in whorls near the ends of the branches. Males are somewhat smaller and denser than females and have smaller leaves. Red buds open to small white fragrant flowers in 3-inch upright panicles in early to midspring. If both male and female plants are present, females produce 1/3-inch bright red berries held at the ends of branches from midautumn to spring; flowers and fruits are sometimes present at the same time. **Zones 7 and 8**.

S. reevesiana

s. reev-see-AY-nuh. REEVES SKIMMIA. A compact shrub, to about 2 feet tall, with both male and female flowers on a single plant. **Zones 6 and 7**.

Smilacina

smile-ah-SEEN-uh. Lily family, Liliaceae.

Commonly called Solomon's plume or false Solomon's seal, *Smilacina* species are rhizomatous perennials producing erect or arching, unbranched stems. Plants bear ovate to lance-shaped leaves and large fluffy clusters of flowers at the tips of the branches. The individual flowers, which are star shaped and creamy white in color, are followed by clusters of round green berries that ripen to red.

HOW TO GROW

Select a site in partial to full shade with rich, moist, well-drained soil. Plants require shade during the hottest part of the day in the South and regular watering in dry weather to look their best. Plants spread steadily, but not invasively, to form handsome drifts. Propagate by dividing clumps in spring or fall. Plants also self-sow, and seedlings are easy to move at any time during the growing season.

S. racemosa

s. rass-eh-MOE-suh. SOLOMON'S PLUME, FALSE SOLOMON'S SEAL. A 1 1/2- to 3-foot-tall native North American wildflower with arching stems that end in a 6-inch-long plume of tiny, 1/4-inch-wide, creamy white flowers in spring. Red berries follow the flowers in late summer or fall. **Zones 4 to 9**.

Solanum

so-LAH-num. Nightshade family, Solanaceae.

Both vegetable and ornamental gardeners have reason to grow members of this genus, which comprises some 1,400 species of annuals, biennials, perennials, shrubs, trees, and climbers. Along with a number of species grown as ornamentals, *Solanum* contains two well-known vegetable crops — eggplant and potato. Plants in the genus bear entire, lobed, or pinnate leaves and clusters of small, five-lobed flowers that can be bell-, trumpet-, or star-shaped and come in shades of lavender-blue, purple, lilac, or white. The flowers are followed by fruits (berries) that are sometimes ornamental. Keep in mind that all parts of these nightshade-family plants can be poisonous if ingested; the vegetable members of the genus are happy exceptions.

HOW TO GROW

Select a site in full sun with average to rich, well-drained soil that remains evenly moist. Neutral to slightly alkaline pH is ideal. Climbers require a trellis or can be trained over shrubs. Sow seeds indoors 6 to 10 weeks before the last spring frost date at 65° to 70°F. Germination takes 1 to 2 weeks. Transplant once the soil has warmed to 60°F and the weather has settled. Stake plants, and tie climbers to supports as they grow. Water regularly and feed monthly during the growing season. To overwinter perennial species, consider taking cuttings in mid- to late summer. Keep them on the dry side over winter, and grow them in a bright, cool (50°F) spot.

S. aviculare

s. ah-vih-kew-LAH-ree. KANGAROO APPLE. A tender shrub that can reach 6 to 11 feet in frost-free areas. Bears small clusters of 1 1/2-inch-wide, bluish purple or white flowers in spring and summer. Flowers are followed by 1/2-inch-long, oval fruits that turn from green to yellow. Tender perennial or warm-weather annual. **Zone 10**.

S. jasminoides

s. jazz-mih-NOY-deez. POTATO VINE. A scrambling climber that can reach 20 feet in warm cli-

Solanum jasminoides

Solenopsis axillaris

S

mates. Bears small clusters of fragrant, 1-inch-wide, bluish white flowers from summer to fall, followed by small black berries. 'Album' has white flowers. 'Aurea' bears leaves variegated with green and yellow. Tender perennial or warm-weather annual. **Zones 8 to 10.**

Solenopsis

so-leh-NOP-sis. Bellflower family, Campanulaceae.

Solenopsis contains some 25 species of annuals and perennials native to Central and South America as well as Australia. They bear lobed to deeply cut, fernlike leaves and salverform flowers, which have a slender tube with a flattened "face" consisting of five narrow lobes, or "petals," arranged in a star-shaped pattern.

HOW TO GROW

Select a site in full sun with average, well-drained soil. Grow *Solenopsis* species as bedding plants replaced annually or as tender perennials overwintered indoors. In frost-free areas, they can be grown outdoors year-round. Sow seeds indoors 8 to 10 weeks before the last spring frost date at 65° to 75°F. Transplant once the weather has settled and temperatures remain above 40°F. Perennials also can be propagated from cuttings taken in summer, which can be used to overwinter the plants. Or keep them in containers year-round. To overwinter, set plants in a bright, cool (50°F) spot, and keep them on the dry side while they are dormant.

S. axillaris

s. ax-il-LAIR-iss. Formerly *Isotoma axillaris, Laurentia axillaris.* A 1-foot-tall tender perennial with lacy, fernlike leaves. Bears an abundance of starry, 1½-inch-wide flowers in pale to deep lavender-blue from early summer to fall. Tender perennial or warm-weather annual. **Zone 10.**

Solenostemon

so-leh-NAH-stem-on. Mint family, Lamiaceae.

The plants in this genus of 60 species of tender, subshrubby perennials are far better known by their former botanical name, *Coleus,* which no doubt will continue to serve as the common name for both gardeners and nongardeners

Solenostemon scutellarioides 'Solar Summer'

alike. Native to tropical Africa and Asia, they bear opposite, rounded, generally toothed leaves on square stems. Spikes of tiny, two-lipped, tubular flowers appear in summer. The cultivars of one species are grown for their wonderfully varied, colorful leaves.

HOW TO GROW

Give coleus a site in partial shade to full sun with rich, well-drained soil that is evenly moist. A site protected from wind is best, and in areas with hot summers the plants benefit from shade during the hottest part of the day. Coleus can be grown as perennials only in Zones 10 and 11. In the North, grow them as bedding plants replaced annually or as tender perennials. Sow seeds indoors 10 to 12 weeks before the last spring frost date at 65° to 70°F. Germination takes about 2 to 3 weeks. In areas with very long summers — Zone 9 south — seeds can be sown outdoors after the last frost date. When sowing, just press the seeds into the soil surface, as light is required for germination.

Coleus are extremely easy to propagate from cuttings, which will root in water or any conventional medium for cuttings, such as a 50-50 mix of peat moss and perlite. Since young plants are the most vigorous — the older ones become woody — consider growing new ones from cuttings taken annually or every other year. Also, many of the best cultivars can be grown only from cuttings. Take cuttings in late summer for overwintering, or from overwintered plants in winter or early

spring, to grow plants for the garden. Wait to transplant plants until temperatures remain above 50°F. Pinch plants to encourage branching. Water container-grown plants regularly, and feed at least monthly. Remove flowers when they appear.

S. scutellarioides

s. skew-tel-air-ee-OY-deez. COLEUS, FLAME NETTLE, PAINTED NETTLE. Formerly *Coleus blumeii* var. *verschaffeltii.* A bushy, 1- to 3-foot-tall tender perennial with leaves that are usually toothed and sometimes heart shaped at the base. Cultivars come with leaves in a mix of colors and patterns, usually with two or more colors as edgings, irregular splotches, or veining. Colors include green, cream, chartreuse, maroon, purple-black, red, orange, and pink. Bears 6-inch-tall spikes of ½-inch-long, pale purple-blue or white flowers, which are usually removed. Many cultivars are available. 'Wizard Mix' is a dwarf (to 10 inches), seed-grown strain that comes in a full range of colors. 'Rainbow Blend', also in a range of colors, reaches 1½ feet. The selection of cultivars that are cutting-propagated — some named, others unnamed — is seemingly endless. 'India Frills' bears small, deeply lobed leaves marked with rose-purple, green, and yellow on compact, 8- to 10-inch plants. 'The Line' has chartreuse leaves with a maroon stripe down the center. Tender perennial or warm-weather annual. **Zones 10 and 11.**

Solidago

sol-ih-DAY-go. Aster family, Asteraceae.

Classic harbingers of fall, *Solidago* species — better known as goldenrods — are well-known wildflowers that all too often are overlooked by gardeners. There are about 100 species in the genus, all woody-based perennials. Most are native to North America, but a few species are from South America and one is native to Europe. They bear undivided or toothed, lance-shaped leaves on stiff stems. Like other aster-family plants, goldenrods bear flower heads consisting of tiny ray and disk florets.

Solidago sempervirens

S

In this case, the individual flower heads usually are yellow and quite small. They consist of a cluster of disk florets that are bisexual, surrounded by a row of small ray florets that are all female, so all can produce seeds. (In many aster relatives, the ray florets, or "petals," are sterile.) Flower heads are carried in showy, plumelike panicles; racemes; or spikes from midsummer to fall. The flowers *do not* cause hay fever. Goldenrods bloom at the same time as ragweeds (the primary hay fever culprit), but their pollen is too heavy to be dispersed in the air.

HOW TO GROW

Plant goldenrods in full sun and poor to average soil that is moist but well drained. Most tolerate dry soil, except *S. virgaurea*. Too-rich soil causes rank growth and plants that tend to flop, as well as rampant spreading. *S. caesia* grows in full sun or partial shade; *S. odora*, *S. sempervirens*, and *S. sphacelata* grow in poor, even sandy soil and also tolerate salt, making them good choices for seaside gardens. Select goldenrods with care, as many species spread quite quickly by rhizomes and become very invasive. The species listed here are well-behaved garden residents. Like asters, goldenrods are best divided every 2 to 3 years. Cut the seed heads off after the flowers fade if self-sowing becomes a problem. Propagate by dividing the clumps in spring or fall or taking cuttings in early summer.

S. caesia

s. SEE-see-uh. WREATH GOLDENROD. Native 1- to 3-foot-tall species that spreads by short, thick rhizomes to 2 to 3 feet. Bears blue-green leaves on wandlike, bluish purple stems. Yellow flower heads are borne in small tufts or clusters in the leaf axils all along the stems from late summer to fall. **Zones 4 to 8.**

S. odora

s. oh-DOR-uh. SWEET GOLDENROD. Native 1½- to 3-foot-tall species that forms 3-foot-wide clumps. Bears lance-shaped leaves that are anise scented when crushed. Yellow flower heads are carried in late summer in a series of one-sided panicles that form a plumelike cluster. **Zones 3 to 9.**

S. rugosa

s. rue-GO-suh. ROUGH-LEAVED GOLDENROD, ROUGH-STEMMED GOLDENROD. Na-

× *Solidaster luteus*

tive 4- to 5-foot-tall species that spreads steadily, but not invasively, to form 2- to 3-foot-wide clumps. Bears wrinkled, hairy, toothed leaves and large plumelike panicles of golden yellow flowers in fall. 'Fireworks' has panicles with lacy, arching branches and is more compact than the species, to 3 to 4 feet. **Zones 4 to 9.**

S. sempervirens

s. sem-per-VIE-renz. SEASIDE GOLDENROD. Native 4- to 6-foot-tall species forming 2- to 3-foot-wide clumps. Bears lance-shaped leaves and showy panicles of ¼-inch-wide flower heads from late summer to fall. **Zones 4 to 9.**

S. sphacelata

s. sphay-sel-LAH-tuh. DWARF GOLDENROD. Native 2-foot-tall species that spreads 1 to 2 feet. Bears rounded leaves and arching, branched panicles of flowers in fall. 'Golden Fleece', a heavy-blooming, dwarf 1½-foot-tall cultivar, is more commonly grown than the species. **Zones 4 to 9.**

S. virgaurea

s. ver-GAR-ee-uh. EUROPEAN GOLDENROD. A 2- to 3-foot-tall species that spreads to about 1½ feet. Bears lance-shaped, toothed leaves and dense spikelike racemes of golden flowers from late summer to fall. 'Cloth of Gold' is a vigorous 1½- to 2-foot-tall cultivar with golden yellow flowers. 'Crown of Rays' produces

2- to 3-foot stems and does not require staking. 'Goldenmosa' is a compact 2½-foot-tall selection. **Zones 3 to 9.**

× *Solidaster*

× sol-ih-DAS-ter. Aster family, Asteraceae.

This is a hybrid genus consisting of a single species, the result of a natural cross between upland white aster (*Aster ptarmicoides*) and a species of goldenrod — Canada goldenrod (*Solidago canadensis*) or perhaps Missouri goldenrod (*S. missouriensis*). Although both parents are native North American wildflowers, oddly enough the cross occurred in a nursery in France. Plants bear large clusters of small yellow daisylike flower heads from midsummer to fall. Leaves are lanceolate to linear-elliptic.

HOW TO GROW

Select a site in full sun with average to somewhat rich, well-drained soil. Propagate by dividing the clumps in spring or fall or by taking cuttings from shoots at the base of the plant in spring.

× S. luteus

× s. LOO-tee-us. Also listed as *S. × hybridus*. A 2- to 3-foot-tall perennial that forms 1-foot-wide clumps. Bears branched clusters of daisylike ½-inch-wide flower heads with pale yellow ray florets surrounding darker yellow centers. **Zones 5 to 8.**

Sophora

so-FOR-ah. Pea family, Fabaceae.

This varied genus includes 50 to 80 species of trees, shrubs, and herbs. The leaves are pinnately compound, and the seedpods are rounded or winged and tightened between the seeds. One species is an increasingly popular landscape tree.

HOW TO GROW

Plant in full sun and fertile, moist, acid to alkaline soil. Tolerates drought, heat, air pollution, and urban conditions but not poorly drained soil. Fall cleanup is minimal due to the small leaflets. Flowers fall in late summer; pods fall in winter and may be slippery. Train when young to develop a single tall trunk with well-spaced branches. Cable large scaffold branches of mature trees to prevent storm damage, or prune back side branches in late summer to reduce weight. Usually pest-free, but leafhoppers, mildew, and twig blight are sometimes troublesome.

S. japonica

s. juh-PON-ih-kuh. JAPANESE PAGODA TREE, CHINESE SCHOLAR TREE. Fifty to 75 feet tall and wide, with a rounded spreading crown, this graceful, fine-textured summer bloomer has become a recent favorite as an urban street tree. Leaves can reach 9 inches in length and are shiny, bright green, and divided into 7 to

Sophora japonica

17 pointed, 1-inch-long leaflets, which drop in late fall with no color change. In mid- to late summer, large, airy, pyramidal clusters of small creamy flowers adorn the tree for 2 to 3 weeks, creating a lovely lacy look, but flowering may not commence until the tree is 10 years old. As with all trees in the pea family, the 4- to 8-inch-long seedpods are a showy yellow in fall, ripen to dark brown, and remain on bare branches during the winter, dropping intermittently. Trunk bark is dark gray and corrugated on mature trees. Use this tree to cast light shade on a house, patio, or lawn or to line a street away from power lines. From China and Korea. **Zones 5 to 8.**

CULTIVARS

Seed-grown trees are variable in form and often slow growing; choose a named cultivar. 'Princeton Upright' is upright and compact, growing 40 to 50 feet tall; a good street tree. 'Regent' has an oval crown, reaches 40 to 50 feet tall, is disease resistant, and blooms well when young.

Sorbus

SOR-bus. Rose family, Rosaceae.

This large genus contains 120 species of deciduous trees and shrubs from North America and Europe. The flowers are usually creamy white; are borne in flattened, elderlike heads; and ripen into clusters of small, showy, red apples. The leaves are variable, from compound to simple. Species with compound leaves are called mountain ashes; those with simple leaves are called whitebeams. Most hail from cool, moist, northern climates and do not fare well when grown in hot sites or in poor, dry soil, hence their reputation for being disease ridden. When planted in a favorable climate, however, they are very showy and desirable garden trees that offer year-round beauty.

HOW TO GROW

Full sun is best for fall color, but sorbus tolerates light shade. Likes moist, well-drained, acid to alkaline soil. Mulch to keep the roots cool and moist. Grow as a single- or multitrunked tree. Resists borers, but may suffer from scab and fire blight in hot, humid areas. Highly disease resistant in cool, dry climates.

S. alnifolia

S. al-nih-FOE-lee-uh. KOREAN MOUNTAIN ASH. This pest-resistant tree has an upright or pyramidal shape when young and becomes rounded with age. It grows 40 to 50 feet tall and 20 to 30 feet wide and draws attention throughout the year. In late spring, 3-inch, lacy clusters of white flowers bloom above the foliage, creating a show for a week or so. The leaves are 4-inch-long, pointed ovals with slightly toothed edges. They turn glorious colors in autumn — first yellow-green, then yellow, and finally deep coral red. When the leaves drop, the ripened clusters of pendulous, shiny, rose-red or scarlet berries are displayed to full advantage. The berries remain on the tree well into winter and provide food for birds. The silver gray trunk and limbs are very attractive in winter. Grow as a low-branched border tree so that you can appreciate the flowers and fruits at eye level. This species may bloom and fruit well only every other year. 'Redbird' forms a narrow column, growing to 25 feet

Sorbus alnifolia

Sorbus aucuparia

tall; it has numerous red berries and golden yellow fall color. From Asia. **Zones 3 to 7.**

S. aucuparia

S. aw-kew-PAR-ee-uh. EUROPEAN MOUNTAIN ASH. Growing 35 feet tall and 20 feet wide, this species makes a fine, medium-size shade tree for a lawn or border, but only in cool climates, where it is most pest-free. The leaves are 9 inches long, dark green, and divided into 11 to 17 fernlike, rounded leaflets with toothed edges. Flattened, 5-inch-wide clusters of white flowers bloom in late spring and ripen by fall into orange berries that turn dark red. The berries are quite showy against the green leaves in late summer, but they blend into the fiery shades of the leaves as they change to orange and red in midfall. Berries do not usually remain on the tree into winter because they are eaten by birds, but the shiny bark adds winter interest. Grow in northern or high-elevation regions to avoid fire blight and other problems. From Europe and Asia. **Zones 2 to 6.**

CULTIVARS AND SIMILAR SPECIES

'Black Hawk' is somewhat columnar, growing to 30 feet tall and 20 feet wide and featuring large orange fruits and green fall color. 'Brilliant Yellow' bears large clusters of yellow berries. 'Cardinal Royal' is vigorous and tightly upright, with very dark green leaves, bright white flowers, and outstanding red fruits. 'Rossica' is a uniform oval, growing to 30 feet tall and offering bright red fruits and rusty fall color. *S. americana* (American mountain ash) is very similar to European mountain ash but is bushier and more disease resistant; not widely grown by nurseries. 'Belmonte' is tightly upright. *S. decora* (showy mountain ash) is native to Canada and grows 20 to 30 feet tall; free of fire blight; has an oval shape, showy flowers, red fruits, and red fall foliage; **Zones 2 to 6**. *S. rufoferrugenia* 'Longwood Sunset' resembles European mountain ash but is highly disease resistant and tolerates heat and drought; it features large clusters of orange berries and stunning burgundy fall color on a rounded, 30-foot-tall tree; **Zones 4**

S

Sparaxis tricolor

to 7. *S.* × *thuringiaca* 'Fastigiata' (oakleaf mountain ash) is disease resistant; it has 5-inch white flower clusters, bright red berries, and 6-inch-long, divided, leathery, green leaves; it forms a broad, 30-foot tall dome and is often mislabeled *S.* × *hybrida;* **Zones 5 to 8.**

S. reducta

s. reh-DUK-tuh. D WARF M OUN-TAIN A SH. This diminutive Chinese native forms a thicket of upright shoots about 3 feet tall. The dark green leaves are composed of 9 to 15 leaflets that in fall turn bronze, orange-red, and purple-red. The late-spring flowers, held in terminal clusters, are white, and the 1/4-inch berries are pink. **Zones 5 to 8.**

Sparaxis

spah-RAX-iss. Iris family, Iridaceae.

Commonly known as wandflowers or harlequin flowers, *Sparaxis* species are grown for their showy, brightly colored, funnel-shaped flowers that are carried in loose spikes in spring or summer. The individual blooms, which are often marked with contrasting colors, have six petal-like tepals that are joined at the base to form a short tube. Each corm bears two or more stems with anywhere from 2 to about 10 flowers. Plants grow from small rounded corms and produce lance- or sickle-shaped leaves, usually arranged in fans.

About six species belong here, all perennials and native to South Africa.

HOW TO GROW

Plant wandflowers in a site with full sun and average to rich, well-drained soil. Where they are hardy, grow them outdoors year-round and plant the corms in fall at a depth of 3 to 4 inches. Like many South African species, they prefer warm days, cool nights, and dry soil conditions when they are dormant. In areas with wet winters, select a site with very well drained soil, such as a raised bed. Toward the northern limits of their hardiness, look for a protected spot, such as at the base of a south-facing wall, and mulch heavily in fall with a coarse mulch.

Where wandflowers are not hardy, grow them in containers or treat them like gladiolus. Pot the corms in late summer, setting them at a depth of about 1 to 2 inches, and keep the containers in a cool (45° to 50°F), well-ventilated place, such as a cold frame, over winter. Or plant the corms outdoors in late spring. Either way, move them to the garden only after the last frost date. Replace the corms annually (they are inexpensive) or, to hold them for another year's bloom, continue watering and feeding after the plants flower. When the leaves begin to turn yellow and die back, allow the soil to gradually dry out and store the corms — still in their containers — in a fairly warm (60° to 75°F), dry, airy spot. Corms also can be dug and stored dry, like gladiolus.

S. elegans

s. EL-eh-ganz. W ANDFLOWER, H ARLEQUIN F LOWER. Formerly *Streptanthera cuprea, Streptanthera elegans.* A 4- to 12-inch-tall species bearing up to five flower spikes per corm and up to five flowers per stem in spring to summer. Individual blooms are funnel shaped, 1½ inches wide, and come in shades of red, orange, or sometimes white marked with yellow or violet. **Zones 9 to 11; to Zone 7 or 8 with winter protection.**

S. tricolor

s. TRY-kuh-lor. W ANDFLOWER, H ARLEQUIN F LOWER. A 4- to 16-inch-tall species that bears from one to five flowering stems per corm in late spring to early summer. Individual blooms are funnel shaped, 2 to 3 inches wide, and come in shades of red, orange, or purple with dark red or black central blotches. **Zones 9 to 11; to Zone 7 or 8 with winter protection.**

Spartium

SPAR-tee-um. Pea family, Fabaceae.

This genus consists of a single species of deciduous shrub native to the Mediterranean region and related to *Cytisus* species, which are also commonly called brooms. It is grown primarily for its fragrant, pealike flowers that bloom for several months.

HOW TO GROW

Spanish broom needs full sun and tolerates poor, dry, rocky or sandy soil. Because it spreads by under-ground stems, it can be used to stabilize banks, but it also can become invasive. It is crowding out native species in the foothills of the California chapparal and has also escaped into the wild in Oregon. Gardeners in those states should avoid it. Elsewhere, remove shoots to keep it under control in the garden, and prune hard to keep it from becoming leggy.

S. junceum

s. YUN-kee-um. S PANISH B ROOM. An almost leafless shrub of erect green stems 6 to 10 feet tall. The bright yellow 1-inch flowers, borne at the end of branches from early summer to early autumn, have a citrusy scent that adds to their charm as cut flowers. They are followed by hairy brown seedpods up to 3 inches long. **Zones 8 to 10.**

Spigelia

spy-JEE-lee-uh. Logania family, Loganiaceae.

About 50 species of annuals and perennials native to North and South America belong to the genus *Spigelia*. They bear ovate, entire leaves and clusters of tubular to funnel-shaped flowers in shades of red, yellow, and purple. One species is sometimes grown in gardens.

HOW TO GROW

Select a site in partial shade with rich, moist, well-drained soil. A spot in full sun also is suitable provided the soil remains moist. Propagate by dividing the clumps

Spartium junceum

Spigelia marilandica

in spring or from seeds. *S. marilandica* is native to the southeastern United States: when buying plants, be sure they are seed grown and not wild collected.

S. marilandica

s. mair-ih-LAN-dih-kuh. INDIAN PINK, MARYLAND PINK-ROOT. A 2-foot-tall clump-forming perennial that spreads to 1 1/2 feet. Bears clusters of erect 2-inch-long red flowers from spring to summer. **Zones 6 to 9.**

Spiraea

spy-REE-uh. Rose family, Rosaceae.

This genus comprises about 80 generally deciduous shrubs found in a diversity of habitats throughout North America, Asia, and Eu-

rope. Some cultivars are old garden favorites for their profuse clusters of small spring or summer flowers or, in a few cases, colorful foliage, and breeders continue to develop new variations on these themes. Two of the species, *S. japonica* and *S. prunifolia,* are invading natural habitats.

HOW TO GROW

Given full sun, spireas are easy to grow in any soil as long as it isn't waterlogged. They can be used as hedges or in a mixed shrub border. Some gardeners use the smallest cultivars in rock gardens or massed as a tall ground cover. Prune back summer-flowering varieties *(S. × bumalda* and *S. japonica)* in early spring; selectively remove shoots of spring-flowering spireas when their bloom is finished. They propagate easily by softwood cuttings in summer.

S. × arguta 'Compacta'

s. × ar-GEW-tuh. DWARF GARLAND SPIREA CULTIVAR. The species grows 6 to 8 feet tall, but this cultivar stops at about 3 feet. White flowers are clustered along the graceful arching shoots in midspring. The bright green leaves are serrated. **Zones 5 to 8.**

S. × bumalda

s. × bew-MAWL-duh. BUMALD SPIREA. A flat-topped twiggy shrub, slightly mounded, growing 3 to 4 feet tall and 5 to 6 feet wide. 'Anthony Waterer' has reddish new foliage that turns blue-green, then reddish purple in fall. Some of its leaves have yellow or white markings. The flat-topped rosy pink flowers bloom for several weeks in summer. 'Froebelii' is slightly taller, more upright, and cold tolerant. Popular 'Goldflame' has bronze new growth that turns yellow, then green (more so in hot climates), and reddish again in autumn. 'Limemound' stays about a foot smaller, with chartreuse leaves. **Zones 4 to 8.**

S. cinerea 'Grefsheim'

s. sin-eh-REE-uh. GREFSHEIM SPIREA. A 5-foot shrub with arching shoots, narrow soft green leaves that turn yellow in fall, and spikes of fragrant white flowers that smother the branches before the leaves unfurl in midspring. **Zones 4 to 8.**

S. japonica

s. juh-PON-ih-kuh. JAPANESE SPIREA. Some consider this the same as *S. × bumalda,* while others de-

Spiraea japonica

scribe it as more upright (to 4 to 5 feet) with leaves that are more serrated. The flat-topped summer flowers are usually pink. 'Gold Mound' averages 3 feet tall and bears golden yellow leaves. 'Shirobana' ('Shiburi') has blooms of pink and white, sometimes on the same flower cluster, and reblooms. Dwarf cultivars are 'Alpina' (sometimes called daphne spirea, 1 to 2 feet) and 'Little Princess' (to about 2 1/2 feet). **Zones 3 to 8.**

S. nipponica 'Snowmound'

s. nip-PON-ih-kuh. NIPPON SPIREA CULTIVAR. Dense with a rounded mature habit, to 3 to 5 feet tall and wide, this has blue-green leaves and is heavily clothed in white flowers in late spring. **Zones 4 to 8.**

S. prunifolia

s. proo-nih-FOE-lee-uh. BRIDAL-WREATH SPIREA. This old favorite has an open habit from 6 to 9 feet tall. The dark green leaves are toothed and somewhat shiny and turn bronzy yellow or red in fall. Double white 1/3-inch

Spiraea × bumalda 'Anthony Waterer'

Spiraea thunbergii

Stachys byzantina

flowers bloom on old wood in midspring before the plant leafs out. **Zones 4 to 8.**

S. thunbergii

s. thun-BER-jee-eye. T H U N B E R G S P I R E A. This is a dense shrub, to 5 feet tall and 6 feet wide, given a delicate appearance by arching branches and willowlike, light green leaves. They turn bronzy orange in fall. Round 2-inch clusters of white flowers march down the branches in early to midspring. **Zones 4 to 8.**

S. tomentosa

s. toe-men-TOE-suh. H A R D H A C K. This species, native from Nova Scotia to the mountains of Georgia, is similar to *S. japonica*, except that the rosy purple or deep pink summer flowers appear in a more rounded plume. Growing 3 to 4 feet tall, it looks best in a sunny wildflower border. It tolerates considerable moisture but not drought or shade. **Zones 4 to 8.**

S. × vanhouttei

s. × van-HOO-tee-eye. V A N - H O U T T E S P I R E A. A ubiquitous shrub, fountainlike to 6 to 8 feet tall and 10 to 12 feet wide, with blue-green three-lobed leaves. After the leaves emerge, clusters of cup-shaped white flowers bloom on old wood in midspring to early summer. **Zones 4 to 8.**

S Stachys

STAY-kuss. Mint family, Lamiaceae.

Stachys contains about 300 species of annuals, perennials, and shrubs that have square stems and hairy, often aromatic, lance-shaped to ovate leaves. The leaves have entire, toothed, or scalloped margins and prominent veins. Plants bear small tubular, two-lipped flowers either in spikes or racemes, or in whorls in the leaf axils.

HOW TO GROW

Select a site in full sun or partial shade with very well drained, average soil. Lamb's ears (*S. byzantina*)

Stachys byzantina 'Countess Helene von Stein'

grows well in sandy soil. A site with shade during the hottest part of the day is best in the South. In areas with hot, humid, rainy summers, plants are frequently subject to crown rot. Cut plants back in midsummer if the foliage looks diseased or the stems appear to be rotting. They will recover in fall when cooler weather arrives. Some gardeners consider the flowers unattractive and remove them as they appear. Cut plants to the

ground in fall or early spring: fall is best in areas with wet winters, because it prevents the leaves from smothering the crowns. Divide plants in spring if they outgrow their space, become overcrowded and die out in the middle, or for propagation.

S. byzantina

s. bih-zan-TEE-nuh. L A M B ' S E A R S, W O O L L Y B E T O N Y. Formerly *S. lanata*, *S. olympica*. Mound-forming perennial primarily grown for its ¹/₂- to 1-foot-tall rosettes of white-woolly leaves that form clumps spreading to 2 feet or more. Bears woolly, erect 1¹/₂-foot-tall spikes of ¹/₂-inch-long purple-pink flowers from early summer to fall. 'Countess Helene von Stein' ('Big Ears') has large 10-inch-long greenish white leaves with a felt-like texture. 'Primrose Heron' has yellow-gray leaves. 'Silver Carpet' has gray-white leaves and does not flower. **Zones 4 to 8.**

S. macrantha

s. mah-KRAN-thuh. B E T O N Y. Formerly *S. grandiflora*. A 1- to 2-foot-tall perennial that forms 1-foot-wide clumps of hairy green leaves with scalloped margins. Bears showy, dense spikes of pinkish purple 1¹/₄-inch-long flowers from early summer to fall. **Zones 3 to 8.**

S. officinalis

s. oh-fih-shih-NAL-iss. W O O D B E T - O N Y, B I S H O P ' S W O R T. A 2-foot-tall perennial that spreads to 1 foot. Bears nearly hairless, scallop-edged leaves and showy spikes of ¹/₂-inch-long flowers from early summer to fall in shades of purple, pink, or white. **Zones 5 to 8.**

Stachyurus

stah-kee-YEW-rus. Stachyurus family, Stachyuraceae.

This Asian genus boasts half a dozen species of deciduous or semievergreen shrubs or small trees. The one described here is a winter garden conversation piece grown for its unusual beadlike clusters of flowers.

HOW TO GROW

This shrub needs acid soil that is high in organic matter and that holds moisture and drains well. Situate it in partial or high shade, sheltered from heavy frost. Use in an informal, shady shrub border, or as a specimen against a dark background. Does not require pruning, but a proportion of flowered branches can be pruned to the ground for rejuvenation. Propagate by sowing fresh seeds or by layering.

S. praecox

s. PREE-koks. E A R L Y S P I K E - T A I L. An upright deciduous shrub growing 6 to 10 feet tall. The bright green, toothed leaves grow 3 to 7 inches long with a sharp tip

Stachyurus praecox

Staphylea colchica

and turn yellow or pinkish red in autumn. In late winter to early spring, 3- to 4-inch racemes of buds hang from the branches, opening to bell-shaped, pale yellow-green flowers. Berrylike fruits follow in late summer. **Zones 6 to 8.**

Staphylea

staf-ih-LEE-uh. Bladdernut family, Staphyleaceae.

This genus consists of 11 species of deciduous shrubs and small trees found in the woods of northern temperate climates. Cultivated varieties are grown for both their bell-shaped flowers and their unusual bladderlike fruit capsules.

HOW TO GROW

Bladdernuts need moisture-retentive but well-drained soil in either full sun or partial shade. Use them for naturalizing, in the shrub border, or at the edge of a woodland. They need minimal pruning, but shoots can be selectively trimmed back to promote new growth and suckers removed to restrict size. Seeds have double dormancy; propagation is easier from cuttings.

S. colchica

s. KAHL-keh-kuh. COLCHIS BLADDERNUT. A species from the Caucasus growing to 10 feet tall, suckering and spreading wider. The compound leaves have three or five leaflets. In mid- to late spring, bears fragrant white

bell-shaped flowers in upright panicles up to 5 inches long, followed by light green 4-inch fruit capsules. **Zones 6 and 7.**

S. trifolia

s. try-FOE-lee-uh. AMERICAN BLADDERNUT. Native from Ontario to Georgia, west to Minnesota and Missouri, this upright, brushy, suckering shrub grows 10 to 15 feet tall and usually about half as wide. The bark is smooth with white stripes. The pinnate leaves, with three sharply pointed leaflets, are dark green, then dull yellow in autumn. Bell-shaped greenish white flowers are produced in abundant 2-inch panicles in midspring. Pale green fruit cap-

Stenanthium gramineum

sules, to 1 1/2 inches long and often used in dried arrangements, form in early fall. **Zones 3 to 8.**

Stenanthium

steh-NAN-THEE-um. Lily family, Liliaceae.

Five species belong to this genus of lily-family relatives, all perennials native to North America as well as Russia's Sakhalin Island. Plants grow from tunicate bulbs and bear arching, grasslike, primarily basal leaves. They produce racemes or panicles of bell- or star-shaped flowers in summer that are white, greenish white, or purple. Individual blooms have six

petal-like tepals. The botanical name refers to the fact that the tepals are narrow: it is from the Greek *stenos*, meaning "narrow," and *anthos*, "flower."

HOW TO GROW

Select a site in partial shade with deeply prepared, moist, well-drained soil that is rich in organic matter. A sheltered spot protected from wind is best. Plants do not do well in hot, dry sites, and shade during the hottest part of the day is important. Neutral to slightly acid pH is best for *S. gramineum;* species native to western North America prefer neutral to slightly alkaline soil. Plant bulbs in fall at a depth of 4 inches. Mulch with compost or chopped leaves to keep the soil moist and cool. Plants are best left undisturbed unless the clumps become overcrowded. Propagate by seeds sown as soon as they are ripe.

S. gramineum

s. grah-MIN-ee-um. FEATHER-FLEECE. A 3- to 6-foot-tall species native to the eastern United States from Pennsylvania to Illinois. Bears arching 2-foot-long panicles of fragrant, densely packed flowers in summer. Individual flowers are star shaped, 1/2 to 3/4 inch wide, and white, greenish white, or purple in color. **Zones 7 to 9.**

Stephanandra

stef-uh-NAN-druh. Rose family, Rosaceae.

This genus comprises four species of deciduous shrubs from eastern Asia, closely related to *Spiraea.* The cultivar described here is

Stephanandra incisa

Sternbergia candida

probably the most widely available representative of the group, admired for its graceful habit, finely textured leaves, and fall color.

HOW TO GROW

Give stephanandra acidic soil, well amended with organic matter to retain moisture and improve drainage, in full sun or partial shade. It makes a good low hedge, or it can be massed for a tall, low-maintenance ground cover, or for erosion control. Pruning stimulates new growth and is sometimes required when tips are winter-burned in exposed areas. Propagate from suckers or cuttings.

S. incisa

s. in-SY-zuh. This dense shrub grows from 4 to 7 feet tall and has arching shoots that root along their length. The bright green, triangular leaves are deeply cut and serrated, touched with bronzy red when new and turning reddish orange in fall. Small greenish white flowers appear in 3-inch panicles in late spring. 'Crispa' grows to only 1¹/₂ to 3 feet tall. **Zones 5 to 8.**

Sternbergia

stern-BER-jee-uh. Amaryllis family, Amaryllidaceae.

Although *Sternbergia* species are commonly known as autumn daffodils, at first glance their flowers look more like crocuses. In addition, not all species bloom in fall. The flowers usually are funnel to goblet shaped, although some species bear more star-shaped blooms. The flowers consist of six petal-like tepals. Unlike crocuses, which belong in the iris family and have three stamens, the flowers of *Sternbergia* species have six stamens. And while crocuses grow from corms, *Sternbergia* species grow from tunicate bulbs. The basal leaves are linear to strap shaped and appear with or just after the flowers. About eight species belong to the genus, and they are native from southern Europe and Turkey to Central Asia.

HOW TO GROW

Select a site in full sun to partial shade with very well drained, average to rich soil. Well-drained soil is especially important in winter; a spot in a raised bed or rock garden provides the conditions these plants prefer. Plant the bulbs in late summer — for best results as early as you can obtain them — setting them at a depth of 6 inches. Plant *S. candida* 8 inches

Stewartia pseudocamellia var. *koreana*

deep. Be sure to loosen the soil several inches below this depth to encourage the roots to spread out. Once planted, sternbergias are best left undisturbed. They will form large clumps with time, and plants also self-sow. Propagate by seeds or by separating the offsets just as the leaves die down.

S. candida

s. kan-DEE-duh. A late-winter– to spring-blooming species that is 4 to 8 inches tall. Bears fragrant, funnel- to goblet-shaped, 2-inch-wide white flowers that appear shortly after the leaves. **Zones 8 to 10.**

S. lutea

s. LOO-tee-uh. AUTUMN DAFFODIL, WINTER DAFFODIL. A fall-blooming 6-inch-tall species bearing golden yellow, goblet-shaped, 1¹/₂-inch-wide flowers in fall. The narrowly lance-shaped leaves appear with the flowers and last through the winter. **Zones 6 to 9.**

S. sicula

s. SIK-yew-luh. A fall-blooming 3-inch-tall species. Bears ¹/₂- to 1¹/₂-inch-wide flowers that are star shaped and dark yellow in color. **Zones 6 to 9.**

Stewartia

stew-ARE-tee-uh. Tea family, Theaceae.

Related to *Camellia* and *Franklinia*, the 15 members of this genus, which are deciduous or evergreen trees or shrubs, bloom in summer and have lovely, camellia-like flowers. Several species are valued in temperate gardens for their ornamental bark, fine foliage, and unusual summer blossoms.

HOW TO GROW

Give stewartia light afternoon shade and humus-rich, moist, acid soil. Easy to grow and pest-free as long as soil and light requirements are met. Train to a single trunk or several trunks and remove lower branches to expose the attractive trunk bark. Faded flowers drop and require daily cleanup.

S. pseudocamellia

s. sue-doe-kah-MEEL-ee-uh. JAPANESE STEWARTIA, KOREAN STEWARTIA. Open branched and oval or vase shaped, this pretty garden tree grows slowly to 30 feet tall and 20 feet wide. The oval, pointed leaves are 2 to 4 inches long and dark green. Bloom commences in early to midsummer. The 2- to 3-inch-wide, cup-shaped, yellow-centered white blossoms open from prominent round buds and have slightly crinkled petals. Each lasts only 1 day, but many flowers bloom each day for 2 to 3 weeks. Fall foliage is luscious, turning many shades of orange, gold, and red, depending on sun exposure. After the dense leaves drop, the flaky bark on the

Stewartia pseudocamellia var. *koreana*

Stokesia laevis

trunk and branches is displayed to perfection as an orange, tan, and apricot patchwork. From Japan and Korea. **Zones 5 to 8**.

CULTIVARS AND SIMILAR SPECIES

'Ballet' has 3¹/₂-inch flowers and graceful downturned branches. 'Korean Splendor' (*S. p.* var. *koreana, S. koreana;* Korean stewartia) is very similar to the species, but flowers are 3 inches across and open more widely. *S. monodelpha* (tall stewartia) has metallic orange bark and is blanketed with 1¹/₂-inch, violet-centered white flowers through the summer; grows 40 to 50 feet tall.

Strobilanthes dyerianus

S. ovata (mountain stewartia) is a southeastern native that forms a bushy, 20-foot-tall tree; the 6-inch-long leaves have downy undersides; 4-inch, cup-shaped white flowers bloom in mid- to late summer.

Stokesia

STOKE-see-uh. Aster family, Asteraceae.

Stokesia contains a single species of perennial native to the southeastern United States. Commonly called Stokes' aster, it bears rosettes of rounded, lance-shaped, evergreen leaves and cornflower- or asterlike flowers from midsummer to early fall.

HOW TO GROW

Plant in full sun or light shade in rich, evenly moist, well-drained soil. Poorly drained soil leads to crown rot and death. Plants generally require staking. Deadheading encourages plants to rebloom. Propagate by dividing the clumps in spring or fall, by root cuttings taken in late winter or early spring, or by sowing seeds.

S. laevis

s. LEE-vis. S T O K E S' A S T E R. A 1- to 2-foot-tall species that forms 1¹/₂-foot-wide clumps. Bears 2- to 3-inch-wide flower heads with two rows of fringed ray florets, or "petals," around fuzzy centers of disk florets. Flowers come in shades of violet-blue, pink, and white. 'Alba' has white flowers. 'Blue Danube' bears showy 4-inch-wide lavender-blue flowers. **Zones 5 to 9**.

Strobilanthes

stro-bih-LAN-theez. Acanthus family, Acanthaceae.

Strobilanthes contains some 250 species of tender perennials and shrubs from Madagascar and Asia, most of which grow naturally on woodland edges. They bear clusters of tubular to funnel-shaped, two-lipped flowers and lance-shaped to rounded leaves. While some are grown for their flowers, the most popular species is primarily valued for its silver-and-purple-patterned foliage.

HOW TO GROW

Give Persian shield (*S. dyerianus*) a site in partial shade to full sun with rich, well-drained soil that remains evenly moist. Rich soil and even moisture yield lush growth and thus the best foliage display. This species thrives in heat and humidity but benefits from a spot with some shade during the hottest part of the day, especially in areas with hot summers. North of Zone 10, grow Persian shield as a bedding plant replaced annually or as a tender perennial. Plants usually are grown from cuttings. Since young plants have the best foliage — the older ones become woody stemmed — consider growing new ones from cuttings taken annually or every other year in spring or early summer. Pinch to encourage branching. Water container-grown specimens regularly and feed at least monthly. To overwinter, bring plants indoors in fall and keep them in a bright, warm (minimum 60° to 65°F) place. Prune overwintered plants in early spring as necessary to shape them.

S. dyerianus

s. dy-er-ee-AY-nus. P E R S I A N S H I E L D. A tender shrub that can reach 4 feet in frost-free climates but is usually smaller when grown in the North. Bears toothed, 6-inch-long, dark green leaves marked with purple and overlaid with a silvery sheen. Small spikes of 1¹/₄-inch-long, pale lilac-blue flowers bloom in fall. Tender perennial. **Zone 10**.

Stylophorum

sty-LOFF-or-um. Poppy family, Papaveraceae.

Three species belong to this genus in the poppy family. All are perennials with pinnately lobed leaves. They produce clusters of saucer-shaped, four-petaled, poppylike flowers in shades of yellow or orange.

HOW TO GROW

Select a spot in partial to full shade with average to rich, moist soil. Plants survive in full sun but generally have unattractive, scorched foliage there. Propagate by dividing the plants very carefully in spring or, better yet, start from seeds. Where happy, the plants self-sow with enthusiasm.

S. diphyllum

s. die-FILL-um. C E L A N D I N E P O P P Y. A 1- to 1¹/₂-foot-tall species native to the eastern United States that forms 1-foot-wide mounds. Bears deeply lobed 8- to 12-inch-long leaves with scalloped margins and clusters of golden yellow 1- to 2-inch-wide flowers from spring to summer. **Zones 4 to 8**.

Stylophorum diphyllum

S

Styrax

STY-rax. Styrax family, Styraceae.

This genus, a relative of *Italesia*, contains about 100 species of trees and treelike shrubs native to warm areas of the Northern Hemisphere. A few are grown in North American gardens, prized for their bell-like white flowers that waft a welcome light fragrance in spring.

HOW TO GROW
Styrax blooms best in full sun, but light afternoon shade is preferable in hot climates. Except for *S. americanus*, which can stand in water, the Asian species listed here need good drainage. Amend the soil heavily with peat moss to ensure acidity and moisture retention, and mulch well to keep the roots cool.

S. americanus

s. ah-mair-ih-KAH-nus. AMERICAN SNOWBELL. Native from Virginia to Florida and west to Missouri, this deciduous shrub is rounded to about 10 feet with slender stems and elliptic bright green leaves 3 inches long. The white bell flowers, which have petals that curve sharply backward and a sweet fragrance, are borne in the leaf axils in late spring. Gray oval fruits appear in early fall. Found naturally along streambanks, the native snowbell is one of the few shrubs that will tolerate water around their roots. **Zones 6 to 8.**

S. japonicus

s. juh-PON-ih-kus. JAPANESE SNOWBELL. Rounded to spreading, with distinctive horizontal branches, this small, multitrunked deciduous tree reaches 20 to 30

Styrax japonicus 'Issai'

feet tall and wide and puts on a pretty show of white flowers in late spring or early summer, when most other trees are done blooming. The leaves are 3 inches long and glossy dark green, turning yellowish to rusty red in fall. The flowers are $3/4$-inch-long, fragrant white bells that dangle in clusters from the outstretched branches. If possible, plant this tree on a slope or where it can be seen from below, or use it in a border or to shade a patio. Do not plant it near a walkway, because the fallen pods are messy in late winter. 'Carillon' is a smaller, 10-foot-tall tree with pendulous branches. 'Pink Chimes' has charming pale pink flowers. 'Sohuksan' has larger flowers and leaves. From Asia. **Zones 6 to 8.**

S. obassia

s. oh-BASS-ee-uh. FRAGRANT SNOWBELL. With the largest flower clusters of any *Styrax*, this deciduous tree grows to 30 or more feet tall and wide and has spreading branches that form an upright or rounded crown. One-inch, bell-shaped, fragrant white flowers bloom in 6- to 8-inch-long clusters in early summer. They hang beneath the foliage and are partially obscured, so they are best viewed from underneath. The rounded, 8-inch-long, dull green, fuzzy leaves have silvery green undersides and are quite striking because of their bold texture and color. Unfortunately, they have only a slight yellow color in fall. Use this tree in a border or lawn. From China, Japan, and Korea. **Zones 6 to 8.**

Symphoricarpos

sim-for-ih-KAR-pos. Honeysuckle family, Caprifoliaceae.

This genus comprises 17 species of deciduous shrubs native to North America, Mexico, and China. Although they have been in and out of style over the years, their showy fruits consistently make them desirable to collectors.

HOW TO GROW
These shrubs are tolerant of almost any soil, in full sun as well as relatively heavy shade. They are

Symphoricarpos albus

most useful for erosion control or naturalizing difficult areas. They don't need pruning except for shaping, and they propagate easily from cuttings.

S. albus

s. AL-bus. COMMON SNOWBERRY. Native to most of Canada south to Minnesota and Virginia, this bushy, rounded 3- to 6-foot shrub has numerous upright arching shoots and 2-inch dark green leaves, occasionally lobed. Relatively inconspicuous spikes of small pink flowers bloom in late spring, followed by $1/2$-inch white berries that can last until late fall. *S. a.* var. *laevigatus* is more vigorous and has larger leaves. **Zones 3 to 7.**

S. × chenaultii 'Hancock'

s. × shen-OH-ee-eye. CHENAULT CORALBERRY CULTIVAR. A low- and wide-growing selection, to 2 feet tall and 12 feet wide, with small blue-green leaves. Gardeners grow it for its graceful arching habit rather than the dark pink flowers or small greenish white fruits. **Zones 4 to 7.**

S. × doorenbosii

s. × dor-en-BOH-see-eye. This hybrid blooms in early summer with greenish white flowers sometimes tinged with pink, but it is primarily grown for the dense fruit clusters, which range from rosy lilac to off-white blushed with pink. **Zones 4 to 7.**

S. orbiculatus

s. or-bih-kew-LAY-tus. INDIAN CURRANT CORALBERRY. Native from the central United States to New Jersey and Georgia, this shrub has arching branches and grows 2 to 6 feet tall. The early- to midsummer flowers are off-white touched with rose, borne in axils and at the ends of branches. Persistent reddish purple fruits develop in midautumn. **Zones 2 to 7.**

Symphytum

sim-FYE-tum. Borage family, Boraginaceae.

Commonly known as comfrey, *Symphytum* species bear clusters of nodding, tubular flowers that resemble bluebells *(Mertensia)*. Blooms have five lobes, or petals, and come in shades of blue, purple, pink, and white. The plants produce mounds of hairy, oblong to lance-shaped leaves with promi-

Symphoricarpos albus

Symphytum × uplandicum 'Variegatum'

nent veins and a wrinkled texture. Comfreys are rhizomatous perennials with fleshy roots and can become invasive. Between 25 and 35 species belong to the genus. Common comfrey (*S. officinale*) has traditionally been used in a variety of herbal preparations, but its leaves and roots cause severe indigestion if ingested, and contact with the foliage can cause skin irritation. Both the botanical and the common names refer to the traditional herbal use for this plant, which was once used to heal broken bones: the botanical name is from the Greek *symphio,* meaning "to grow together," while "comfrey" is from the Latin word *conferva,* "join together."

HOW TO GROW

Select a site in full sun or partial shade with average to rich, moist soil. Even moisture is essential if the plants are to look their best in sun. Comfreys are very vigorous spreaders, so select a site with care. They make excellent ground covers in shade but quickly overtake less robust companions, and even small sections of root left in the soil will give rise to new plants. Variegated forms tend to be less vigorous than green-leaved ones. Some gardeners remove the flowers of variegated forms to enhance the foliage. Taller species require staking. Propagate by dividing the clumps in spring, by taking root cuttings in late fall, or by seeds.

S. caucasicum

s. kaw-KASS-ih-kum. CAUCASIAN COMFREY. A 1½- to 2-foot-tall species that spreads to 2 feet. Bears clusters of bright blue ½-inch-long flowers from early to late summer. Zones 3 to 9.

S. hybrids

A variety of hybrids of uncertain parentage are available. 'Goldsmith' bears leaves patterned with gold and creamy white and pale blue, pink, or cream flowers in spring on 1-foot plants. 'Hidcote Blue', 1½ feet tall, has red buds that open into ½-inch-long pale blue flowers, also in spring. 'Hidcote Pink' bears clusters of pale pink and white ½-inch-long flowers in spring on 1½-foot plants. Zones 5 to 9.

S. officinale

s. oh-fih-shih-NAL-ee. COMMON COMFREY. Vigorous 3- to 4-foot-tall species that spreads to form 5- to 6-foot-wide mounds.

Bears branched clusters of ¾-inch-long flowers from late spring to summer in shades of violet purple, pink, or creamy yellow. 'Variegatum' has white-edged leaves. Zones 3 to 9.

S. × uplandicum

s. × up-LAN-dih-kum. RUSSIAN COMFREY. A 4- to 6-foot-tall species that spreads to 4 feet. Bears clusters of pinkish blue buds that open into ¾-inch-long purple-blue flowers from late spring to late summer. 'Variegatum' has gray-green leaves with white margins on 3-foot-tall plants that spread to 2 feet. Zones 3 to 9.

Symplocos

sim-PLOH-kos. Sweetleaf family, Symplocaceae.

This is a genus of some 250 species of widely distributed evergreen and deciduous trees and shrubs. Only one species, known for its showy berries and easy care, is commonly grown in gardens.

HOW TO GROW

Give sapphireberry soil that is fertile, moist but well aerated, and acid to neutral, in full sun or light shade. It can be grown as a specimen, but more than one plant will ensure better fruiting. Try it as an informal hedge or screen. It should not require pruning. Propagate from softwood cuttings.

S. paniculata

s. pan-ick-yew-LAH-tuh. SAPPHIRE-BERRY. From China, Japan, and the Himalayas, this deciduous

Symplocos paniculata

species forms a large spreading shrub or small tree at 10 to 20 feet. The upright branches are covered with gray furrowed bark and finely toothed, somewhat hairy 3-inch leaves. Fragrant white star-shaped flowers, each with 30 prominent yellow stamens, are borne profusely in late spring to early summer. The bright turquoise berries ripen in early fall and last several weeks before being stripped by birds. Zones 4 to 8.

Syringa

sih-RING-guh. Olive family, Oleaceae.

Approximately 20 species of deciduous shrubs native to Europe and Asia have been hybridized and selected to produce an estimated 1,600 named varieties of lilacs, grown for their strongly fragrant, tubular spring flowers, borne in cone- or pyramid-shaped clusters.

HOW TO GROW

Lilacs do best in neutral to alkaline soil that is moist but well drained, in open areas where they will have full sun and good air circulation. In cool, dry climates where mildew doesn't mar the foliage in summer, all lilacs make good specimen shrubs. They are also often used in masses, against buildings, or in shrub borders.

In humid regions, all lilacs (although some more than others) are prone to develop powdery mildew, which coats the leaves with an unsightly white powder but won't kill the plant. More serious are blights, which first appear as brown blotches on the foliage. They can be prevented by pruning to provide good air circulation and keeping tools sterile, and they can be treated with a spray of Bordeaux mix. Scale and lilac borers, which look like wasps, are the most common insect pests.

Lilac stems should be pruned out in winter so they don't rub each other. Remove spent blooms to prevent seed formation. Propagate from stratified seeds, cuttings treated with hormone powder, or suckers.

S. × chinensis

s. × chih-NEN-sis. CHINESE LILAC. An old hybrid 8 to 15 feet tall and wide with arching branches and fragrant lilac-colored flowers. More delicate looking and less mildew-prone than common lilac (*S. vulgaris*). 'Lilac Sunday', from the Arnold Arboretum, forms a

S

Syringa × hyacinthiflora

fountain of pale purple panicles both at the branch tips and along the willowy stems. **Zones 3 to 7.**

S. × hyacinthiflora
s. × hy-uh-sin-thih-FLOR-uh. Hybrid of Chinese *S. oblata* and *S. vulgaris* growing to 10 or even 12 feet tall and wide with bronze new growth and purple foliage in fall. Blooms 1 to 2 weeks sooner than *S. vulgaris* with slightly more open panicles. There are many cultivars, offering single or double flowers in white, lavender, pink, or magenta. 'Blanche Sweet' has blue buds opening to palest lavender-pink flowers with an almost sugary scent. **Zones 3 to 7.**

S. × josiflexa
s. × joe-sih-FLEX-uh. Vigorous, upright shrub to 20 feet but usually maintained at about half that. Blooms somewhat later than other lilacs. 'Bellicent' is pink, while 'Royalty' is a popular lavender selection. **Zones 4 to 7.**

S. × laciniata
s. × lah-sin-ee-AH-tuh. CUTLEAF LILAC. Growing 6 to 8 feet tall and up to 10 feet wide with slender arching stems and leaves with up to nine lobes. Resistant to mildew. The pale lilac flowers bloom in mid- to late spring. **Zones 4 to 8.**

S. meyeri
s. MY-er-eye. MEYER LILAC. Uniform, dense, rounded shrub 4 to 8 feet tall and spreading wider with small rounded leaves. It flowers when quite young, covering the plant with violet panicles up to 4 inches long in midspring. 'Palibin' is especially compact and has reddish purple buds opening

Syringa vulgaris

to pink flowers tinged with white or lavender-pink. **Zones 4 to 7.**

S. microphylla
s. my-kro-FILL-uh. LITTLELEAF LILAC. Also listed as *S. pubescens* ssp. *microphylla*. A dense shrub growing to 6 feet or taller and twice as wide. The lilac-pink flowers open in mid- to late spring, with some rebloom in early fall. 'Superba' has lighter pink flowers and a longer bloom period. **Zones 4 to 7.**

S. patula 'Miss Kim'
s. PAT-yew-luh. MANCHURIAN LILAC CULTIVAR. Upright and vigorous to about 8 feet and not as wide with leaves up to 5 inches long. Pale lilac-blue flowers are borne in upright panicles in mid- to late spring. **Zones 4 to 7.**

S. × pekinensis
s. × pee-kin-EN-sis. PEKIN LILAC. Upright to 15 or 20 feet with many slender stems. Blooms in

Syringa reticulata

late spring with cream-colored 3- to 6-inch panicles. The reddish brown bark can be cherrylike with horizontal lines, or exfoliating. **Zones 4 to 7.**

S. × persica
s. × PER-sih-kuh. PERSIAN LILAC. Relatively small shrub at 4 to 8 feet tall and slightly wider. The fragrant pale lilac flowers appear in midspring. **Zones 3 to 7.**

S. reticulata
s. reh-tik-yew-LAY-tuh. JAPANESE TREE LILAC. A huge shrub or broad tree up to 30 feet tall and 25 feet wide with cherrylike bark. Creamy white flowers bloom in fragrant panicles up to 12 inches long and 10 inches wide in late spring to early summer. Good disease and pest resistance. **Zones 4 to 7.**

S. vulgaris
s. vul-GAIR-iss. COMMON LILAC. An upright, suckering shrub, native to southeastern Europe, with an irregular habit. It loses its lower branches with maturity, exposing often picturesque rough bark. May be defoliated by mildew in hot, humid climates. There are virtually hundreds of cultivars, all with intensely fragrant midspring flowers of lavender, purple, pink, white, or bicolors. **Zones 3 to 7.**

Syringa patula 'Miss Kim'

Tagetes

TAH-jeh-teez. Aster family, Asteraceae.

Tagetes species, better known as marigolds, are a familiar sight in summer gardens everywhere. Approximately 50 species of annuals and perennials belong to this genus, most with aromatic foliage deeply cut in a featherlike fashion. With the exception of one species, which is native to Africa, all are native from New Mexico through Central and South America. Like other aster-family plants, marigolds bear flower heads with disk florets and larger, petal-like ray florets. Flowers can be single, semidouble, or double and are borne either singly or in clusters. Colors include yellow, orange, mahogany, rust, maroon, and creamy yellowish white.

HOW TO GROW

Give easy-to-grow marigolds a spot in full sun with average, well-drained soil. In areas with hot summers, a site with afternoon shade is best. Plants tolerate drought but bloom best with regular watering. Too-rich soil yields plants with plenty of foliage but few flowers; it also makes the plants more prone to disease. Too much water causes similar problems. Sow seeds indoors 6 to 8 weeks before the last spring frost date at 70° to 75°F. Germination takes 1 to 2 weeks. Or sow seeds outdoors around the last spring frost date. Plants grown from indoor sowings bloom earlier in the season, and indoor sowing is best with African-type marigolds, which are slow to bloom from seeds.

Pinch plants to promote branching and bushy growth. Deadhead regularly to encourage new buds to form. Some marigolds, especially French types, stop blooming during very hot weather; keep them watered, and they will resume blooming when cooler fall weather arrives. African marigolds may rot in wet, humid weather. Both butterflies and hummingbirds will visit marigold flowers.

T. erecta

t. ee-RECK-tuh. AFRICAN MARIGOLD, AMERICAN MARIGOLD. A Central American, not African, species with pinnate leaves on 1½- to 3-foot-tall plants. Bears showy, carnation-like, double flowers that are 4 to 5 inches across, in shades of yellow, gold, and orange. Compact cultivars stay under 1½ feet tall and include Gold Coin Series, Inca Series, and Lady Series. Warm-weather annual.

T. patula

t. PAH-tyew-luh. FRENCH MARIGOLD. A compact, 6- to 12-inch-tall, well-branched species with pinnate leaves and usually double flowers, although cultivars with single, semidouble, and crested flowers are available. French types include Hero Series, Bonanza Series, and Janie Series. Warm-weather annual.

Triploid Marigolds

These are vigorous hybrid plants developed by crossing African and French marigolds. They have more dwarf, French-type habits (to about 1 foot in height) and single or double flowers that range from 2 to 3 inches across. They don't set seeds and thus continue blooming even in hot weather or under other stressful conditions. Zenith Series and Nugget Series are triploid selections. Warm-weather annual.

T. tenuifolia

t. ten-yew-ih-FOH-lee-uh. SIGNET MARIGOLD. Bushy, mound-forming, 9- to 12-inch plants with lacy, finely divided leaves. Bears an abundance of dainty, single, ¾-inch-wide flowers. Gem Series cultivars, in gold, lemon yellow, or orange, are most common. Warm-weather annual.

Tamarix

TAM-ar-iks. Tamarix family, Tamaricaceae.

A genus of about 50 species of deciduous shrubs and trees from Europe, Asia, and North Africa. A half dozen or so are cultivated for delicate foliage and flowers and resistance to difficult situations, including drought, salt, and wind. Aggressive roots can overcome other species. The species below has outspread its welcome and wiped out native wetland species in the American West; its cultivation is discouraged in areas where it can become a problem. There are some reports of invasiveness in the East as well.

HOW TO GROW

Give tamarix full sun in almost any type of soil. Prune after flowering, since the blooms appear on the previous season's growth. May need heavy pruning to prevent its becoming top-heavy. Tamarix is sometimes pruned to

Tagetes patula 'Tiger Eyes'

Tamarix ramosissima

Tanacetum parthenium

the ground for increased foliage effect in mixed borders and masses or as specimens. Propagate from seeds or cuttings.

T. ramosissima

t. ram-oh-SISS-ih-muh. SALT CEDAR. A native of Europe and Asia, usually growing to about 15 feet tall and wide with a loose, open habit and long, slender, reddish brown shoots clothed with ⅛-inch leaves and, in midspring or early summer, in airy racemes of rose-pink flowers. **Zones 3 to 8.**

Tanacetum

tan-ah-SEE-tum. Aster family, Asteraceae.

Tanacetum contains some 70 species of annuals, perennials, and subshrubs with leaves that are entire, toothed, lobed, or deeply cut in a feathery fashion. The foliage often is aromatic. The flowers are daisy- or buttonlike and carried singly or in clusters. The centers, or "eyes," which may or may not be surrounded by petal-like ray florets, consist of a dense cluster of yellow disk florets that produce the seeds. Over the years members of this genus have been classified in various genera, including *Chrysanthemum*, *Pyrethrum*, and *Matricaria*.

HOW TO GROW

Select a site in full sun with average, well-drained soil. Sandy soil is ideal, although plants will thrive in any soil provided it is well drained. Deadhead plants regularly to keep them neat and prevent an abundance of self-sown seedlings. (*T. parthenium* is especially prolific.) Cut back *T. coccineum* hard after flowering to encourage plants to produce a second flush of bloom. Divide plants in spring or fall if they outgrow their space or die out in the middle of the clumps. In addition to division, plants can be propagated by rooting cuttings of shoots that appear at the base of the plants in spring, taking cuttings in early summer, or sowing seeds.

T. coccineum

t. kock-SIN-ee-um. PAINTED DAISY, PYRETHRUM. Formerly *C. coccineum*, *P. coccineum*, *P. roseum*. Bushy 1½- to 2½-foot-tall perennial spreading to 1½ feet. Bears deeply cut leaves and 3-inch-wide, daisylike flowers in early summer with ray florets in shades of pink, red, yellow, and white. 'Eileen May Robinson' bears single pink blooms. 'James Kelway' produces single red flowers. **Zones 3 to 7.**

T. parthenium

t. par-THEN-ee-um. FEVERFEW. Formerly *C. parthenium*, *M. parthenium*, and *P. parthenium*. Bushy 1½- to 2-foot-tall species that spreads to 1 foot. Bears aromatic, feathery leaves and small 1-inch-wide, daisylike flowers in summer with yellow centers and white ray florets. 'Aureum' bears golden foliage and comes true from seeds. 'Flore Pleno', 'Snowball', and 'Tetra White' all bear double white flowers. **Zones 4 to 9.**

T. vulgare

t. vul-GAH-ree. COMMON TANSY. Vigorous 2- to 3-foot-tall perennial spreading to 1½ feet. Bears mounds of pinnately lobed (featherlike) or toothed leaves topped by clusters of bright yellow, ½-inch-wide, buttonlike flower heads in summer. **Zones 3 to 8.**

Taxodium

taks-OH-dee-um. Bald cypress family, Taxodiaceae.

This genus of deciduous and semievergreen conifers contains two species from the swampy areas of southern North America. Although they grow naturally in wet areas, these trees adapt readily to normal garden conditions and grow to stately size even in climates colder than those in their natural range.

HOW TO GROW

Taxodium thrive in full to partial sun and deep, moist, acid, sandy loam or wet, swampy conditions. They adapt readily to average moisture, and even to harsh midwestern sites, but will drop needles during a drought. Need no pruning other than to remove any competing leaders. Although usually problem-free, these trees may suffer from twig blight, wood rot, or spider mites. They become chlorotic in alkaline soil.

T. distichum

t. DIS-tih-kum. BALD CYPRESS, SWAMP CYPRESS. A deciduous conifer that grows to about 60 feet tall and 25 feet wide, bald cypress has a beautiful, symmetrical shape and delicate foliage that make it an eye-catching choice for a home landscape.

The ½-inch-long, narrow, pointed needles are flattened and

Taxodium distichum

arranged in two-ranked sprays on delicate green twiglets that drop to the ground in autumn. Needles emerge bright green in spring, mature to gray-green, and turn golden rust-brown in autumn before dropping. (Bald cypress can be distinguished from dawn redwood by the needle arrangement: bald cypress needles are arranged alternately, while dawn redwood's needles are opposite.) The trunk is very straight, buttressed at the base, and cloaked in pale brown, shredding bark. Found growing naturally along streams or in other wet sites, bald cypress sends up odd, knobby growths called knees from its wide-spreading roots where soil is wet, but not in aver-

Taxodium distichum

age or dry soil. Cones are round, dark brown and about 1 inch in diameter. Use this fast-growing tree as a specimen in a lawn or near water, or plant it in a grove in a wet or swampy site on a large property. From southern North America. **Zones 4 to 9.**

CULTIVARS

'Shawnee Brave' has a tight pyramidal form with short branches and bronze-orange fall color. 'Monarch of Illinois' is much more wide-spreading than the species. *T. distichum* var. *imbricarium* (*T. ascendens*) (pond cypress) is very similar, with light brown bark and small, scalelike leaves that are held close to the upright twigs, creating a threadlike effect; **Zones 6 to 9.** 'Nutans' has weeping branchlets. 'Prairie Sentinel' has a threadlike leaf arrangement and very short, regularly spaced, horizontal branches that form a narrow column.

Taxus

TAKS-uss. Yew family, Taxaceae.

This is a genus of 5 to 10 evergreen conifers found from northern temperate zones south to Central America and grown for its handsome, problem-free foliage and, on some types, attractive red fruits.

HOW TO GROW

Yews can handle any kind of soil as long as the drainage is excellent. They grow in full sun to dense shade and tolerate pollution and drought, although most need some protection from harsh winds and extreme heat. Yews can take heavy pruning, but the cultivars listed here should not need it ex-

Taxus cuspidata 'Capitata'

cept to remove browned or broken stems. Propagate by cuttings collected in winter. Although all parts of the yew are toxic except the seed covering, deer find them irresistible.

T. baccata

t. buh-KAH-tuh. ENGLISH YEW. The species, native to Europe, Africa, and Asia, can grow 60 feet tall and 25 feet wide with dark, spirally arranged needles. Low-growing cultivars include 'Fowle' (sometimes called 'Adpressa Fowle'), the midget boxleaf English yew, compact and dense, that grows slowly to 7 feet tall and 16 feet wide; and 'Repandens', a low-growing female 2 to 4 feet tall and spreading 12 to 15 feet wide with sickle-shaped leaves and drooping branch tips. **Zones 5 to 7.**

T. cuspidata

t. kus-peh-DAH-tay. JAPANESE YEW. Because it is so cold hardy, Japanese yew is the most common yew grown in North American landscapes. It can form a multitrunked, 25- to 40-foot-tall tree with upright or spreading branches, but dwarf types are grown more often than the species. Needles are 1 inch long and pointed. They emerge bright green in spring, creating an eye-catching contrast against the very dark green older needles, which have yellowish green undersides. Needles are arranged in two irregular ranks on all the shoots, which have brown bark. This yew makes an excellent hedge or screen. It can also be used as a specimen in a mixed border or shady garden. From Japan and Korea. **Zones 4 to 7.**

T. × media

t. × MEE-dee-uh. These hybrids of *T. cuspidata* and *T. baccata* have produced numerous shrub-sized cultivars that are useful for smaller gardens and low to medium hedges. They include 'Brownii', with a rounded form 9 to 12 feet tall; 'Densiformis', a 4-foot ball; 'Green Wave', low and mounding to 4 feet tall and 8 feet wide with graceful arching branches; and 'Hatfieldii', forming a column or pyramid about 10 feet tall and wide. 'Tauntonii' is a 3-foot-high spreader that tolerates both cold and heat. **Zones 4 to 7.**

Tecophilaea

tek-oh-FILL-ee-ee. Lily family, Liliaceae.

Two species, sometimes called Chilean crocuses, belong to this genus in the lily family. In spring they bear small, crocuslike flowers in rich, true blue or violet. Flowers have six petal-like tepals. They grow from corms and have basal, grassy, narrowly lance-shaped leaves. Both of the species in this genus are native to high altitudes in South America.

HOW TO GROW

Select a site in full sun with sandy, well-drained soil rich in organic matter. Perfect drainage is essential: these are plants best suited to rock gardens and require warm, dry conditions when they are dormant in summer. They also do best in areas with cool summers and mild winters, conditions that duplicate their native Andes.

Plant the corms in fall at a depth of 2 inches. In areas where they are not hardy or where winters are excessively rainy, keep them in containers set in a cold frame. Chilean crocuses tend to emerge very early in spring and often are cut down by late frosts,

Taxus × media

Taxus baccata 'Repandens'

Tecophilaea cyanocrocus

Tetrapanax papyrifer

so even in areas where they are hardy, connoisseurs often grow them in containers kept in a cold frame and move them out after the weather has settled in spring. Mulch with pea gravel or granite chips to retain soil moisture and ensure perfect drainage. Keep the soil evenly moist while plants are actively growing, then gradually dry them off in summer as the leaves die back. Propagate by seeds or offsets.

T. cyanocrocus

t. sy-an-oh-KRO-kus. CHILEAN BLUE CROCUS. A 3- to 4-inch-tall species bearing 1¹/₂- to 2-inch-long funnel-shaped flowers in spring that are rich gentian blue with white striping at the throat. **Zones 7 to 9.**

Tellima

tel-LY-muh. Saxifrage family, Saxifragaceae.

The one species of *Tellima*, commonly called fringecups, is a wildflower native from California to Alaska that is useful in woodland and naturalistic gardens throughout the Northern Hemisphere. Its cultural conditions are similar to those of its close relatives *Heuchera* and *Tiarella*. The leaves of fringecups are deciduous, up to several inches long, and shallowly lobed or toothed. They are produced on short, rhizomatous rootstocks, resulting in a low, leafy crown and, where conditions are right, a vigorously spreading mat. Flowers are small, greenish white, and not very showy, but they are fragrant.

HOW TO GROW

Fringecups thrive in moist, organic, acid, woodland soil and partial shade. Plants should not be allowed to dry out, or the leaves will burn and the plants will go dormant prematurely.

T. grandiflora

t. gran-deh-FLOR-uh. FRINGE-CUPS. This Pacific Northwest native grows in partial shade to shade and in cool, moist, woodland soil. It quickly forms clumps that reach 12 inches tall and spread much farther. Although similar to its eastern cousin *Tiarella* the flowers of *T. grandiflora* are less showy. 'Forest Frost' is a charming copper-leaved selection growing to 2 feet tall. Flowers are greenish white in spring and then fade to pink. **Zones 4 to 7**; farther south in maritime climates.

Ternstroemia

tern-STROH-mee-uh. Tea family, Theaceae.

A genus of about 85 evergreen shrubs and trees, most of them tropical. This hardy species is grown primarily for its handsome foliage, summer and fall.

HOW TO GROW

Site this camellia relative in partial shade and give it acidic soil that has been generously amended with organic matter to retain moisture and enhance drainage. It can be grown as both a specimen and a hedge or screen. Trim lightly after flowering. Propagate from fresh seeds planted in fall or from cuttings collected in late summer or early autumn.

T. gymnanthera

t. jim-NAN-ther-uh. Often incorrectly sold as *Cleyera japonica*, this densely branched shrub has an oval habit and grows slowly to 8 feet, though more often about half that. The evergreen leaves are lustrous and leathery to 4 inches long, bronzy when new and turning reddish purple in fall. Cream-colored ¹/₂-inch flowers, borne in late spring to early summer, are fragrant but not showy. There are variegated and gold-leaved cultivars. **Zones 7 to 10.**

Tetrapanax

tet-ruh-PAN-aks. Aralia family, Araliaceae.

This is one of those plants that landscape designers call "architectural." An evergreen native to China and Taiwan and the only species in its genus, rice-paper plant is bold in both habit and leaf and produces unusual flowers as well.

HOW TO GROW

This shrub grows in any average soil with good drainage, in full sun. Its best use is in a shrub border. It may die to the ground in the north of its range and can be pruned to the ground to stimulate larger new foliage. Propagate from suckers.

T. papyrifer

t. pah-pih-RIH-fer. RICE-PAPER PLANT. The thick, nearly unbranched shoots sucker and form thickets to 15 feet tall and wide. The leaves, which have 5 to 11

Tellima grandiflora

Ternstroemia gymnanthera 'Burnished Gold'

T

Teucrium chamaedrys

lobes, can be almost 2 feet across, scaly on top and white and felted underneath, held at the ends of the shoots. Small, creamy white flowers in panicles up to 20 inches long bloom in fall, followed by ¹/₈-inch yellow or red-orange berries that split to reveal glossy black seeds. Fuzz on new stems and leaves can irritate skin. **Zones 7 to 10.**

Teucrium

TOO-cree-um. Mint family, Lamiaceae.

Commonly called germanders, *Teucrium* species are perennials, subshrubs, or shrubs with handsome, aromatic, simple or lobed leaves that can be evergreen or deciduous. They bear whorled clusters or racemes of small bell-shaped to tubular flowers that are sometimes, but not always, two lipped. About 100 species belong to the genus, most native to the Mediterranean. Germanders have a long history of medicinal use — the botanical name honors Teucer, the first king of Troy, who is believed to have been the first to use the plants medicinally.

Thalictrum rochebruneanum

HOW TO GROW
Select a site in full sun with poor to average, well-drained soil. Neutral to slightly alkaline pH is best. *T. chamaedrys* can be used as a low hedge, which can be kept compact by pruning or shearing the plants in spring to within about 2 inches of the ground. Propagate by taking cuttings in early or midsummer or start from seeds.

T. chamaedrys
t. kam-EE-drus. WALL GERMANDER. This subshrub was once so popular as a low hedge in knot gardens that it was called "poor man's box," since it could substitute for more expensive boxwood. As an herb in its own right, it was recommended for curing gout. Germander grows about 18 inches tall with glossy, aromatic, dark green leaves that are evergreen to about Zone 7. From midsummer to fall it bears racemes of rose-pink or magenta flowers. **Zones 5 to 10.**

T. fruticans
t. FROO-tih-kanz. SHRUBBY GERMANDER. A bushy evergreen that grows to 3 feet tall and 1 foot wide with fuzzy white shoots. The aromatic, gray-green oval to lance-shaped leaves are shiny on top, white and felted underneath. Terminal whorls of pale blue flowers bloom for several weeks in summer. **Zones 8 to 10.**

Thalictrum

thah-LICK-trum. Buttercup family, Ranunculaceae.

Although their relationship is not immediately apparent to the nonbotanist, *Thalictrum* species are closely related to buttercups (*Ranunculus* spp.), clematis (*Clematis* spp.), and columbines (*Aquilegia* spp.). Commonly called meadow rues, *Thalictrum* species produce mounds of handsome, lacy-textured, blue-green leaves that usually are divided several times in a pinnate (featherlike) fashion and have lobed or toothed leaflets. The flowers are petalless, but they create a showy, delicate

Thalictrum aquilegifolium

effect because they are borne in large branched clusters above the foliage and usually have prominent clusters of stamens. About 130 species belong to the genus, all of which are perennials.

HOW TO GROW
Plant meadow rues in partial shade with rich, moist soil. They tolerate full sun provided the soil remains constantly moist, but a site with some shade is best. In areas with warm summers, site them where they receive shade during the hottest part of the day. Plants tend to be late to emerge in spring, so mark the clumps to avoid digging into the crowns by accident early in the season. Water during dry weather. Taller species generally need staking. Plants thrive for years without needing to be divided but can be dug and divided if necessary in early spring or fall for propagation. Meadow rue can also be propagated by seeds.

T. aquilegifolium
t. ack-wih-lee-jih-FOH-lee-um. COLUMBINE MEADOW RUE. Rhizomatous, 2- to 3-foot-tall species forming 1¹/₂- to 2-foot-wide mounds of columbine-like leaves with rounded leaflets. In early summer it bears 6- to 8-inch-wide clusters of fluffy ¹/₂-inch-long flowers with showy purple or white stamens. **Zones 4 to 8.**

T. delavayi
t. deh-LAH-vay-eye. YUNAN MEADOW RUE. A 2- to 4-foot-tall species that forms 2-foot-wide clumps. From summer to fall, it bears branched panicles of fluffy flowers with purple sepals and creamy yellow stamens. 'Hewitt's Double' has rounded, mauve-purple flowers consisting of many petal-like sepals. **Zones 4 to 9.**

T. dioicum
t. die-OH-ih-kum. EARLY MEADOW RUE. A 1- to 3-foot-tall species native to North America that spreads to 2 feet. Bears panicles of yellow to yellowish green flowers. Male and female flowers are borne on separate plants, and male plants have the showiest blooms. **Zones 4 to 9.**

T. flavum
t. FLAY-vum. YELLOW MEADOW RUE. Vigorous 1- to 3-foot-tall species that spreads by rhizomes to form mounds 2 to 4 feet wide. Bears panicles of lightly fragrant ¹/₄-inch-long yellow flowers in summer. *T. flavum* ssp. *glaucum*,

Thermopsis villosa

which has blue-green leaves and stems, bears large clusters of pale sulphur yellow flowers. **Zones 5 to 9.**

T. rochebruneanum

t. roh-cheh-broo-nee-AH-num. Lavender Mist. A 3- to 5-foot-tall species forming 2- to 3-foot-wide mounds of foliage topped in summer by loose panicles of $^{1}/_{2}$-inch-long lilac-pink or white flowers. **Zones 4 to 7.**

Thermopsis

ther-MOP-siss. Pea family, Fabaceae.

Commonly called false lupines, *Thermopsis* species are rhizomatous perennials bearing erect racemes of flowers that resemble lupines (*Lupinus* spp.) or baptisias (*Baptisia* spp.). Most species bear yellow flowers, but some have purple ones. Leaves are palmate (handlike) and have three leaflets. Flat seedpods follow the petal-like flowers, and this is the main characteristic that distinguishes these plants from baptisias, which bear rounded, inflated pods. Some 20 species belong to the genus, all perennials native from North America, Russia, eastern Asia, and India. The botanical name is from the Greek *thermos,* lupine, and *opsis,* appearance.

HOW TO GROW

Select a site in full sun or very light shade with average, well-drained soil that remains evenly moist. In areas with hot summers, a site with shade during the hottest part of the day is best. Stake in early spring to keep them erect. These drought-tolerant plants

have deep taproots and thrive for years without needing to be divided. Since they resent being disturbed and are slow to recover (digging breaks the deep roots), dig them only if necessary in early spring. Propagate by division (or by severing and potting up or replanting portions of the clumps that spread too far), taking cuttings in early summer, or starting from seeds.

T. villosa

t. vil-LOH-suh. Carolina Lupine. Formerly *T. caroliniana.* Native North American wildflower, found from the Carolinas to Georgia, that ranges from 3 to 5 feet in height and with time spreads as far. Bears dense 8- to 12-inch-long racemes of $^{3}/_{4}$-inch-long

Thuja occidentalis 'Hetz Midgit'

yellow flowers in late spring and early summer. **Zones 3 to 9.**

Thuja

THEW-yuh. Cypress family, Cupressaceae.

These evergreen trees and shrubs from North America and eastern Asia have small, rounded, brown cones and scalelike or needlelike leaves that are aromatic and borne on frondlike branches. Many cultivars are very popular landscape plants in cooler regions. They are ideal for screens and look better than most conifers when mass planted because they have a softer, more informal outline.

HOW TO GROW

Site in full sun to light shade. (Gold-leaved forms need sun.) Arborvitae does best in fertile, moist, acid to alkaline, mulched soil but tolerates wet soil and clay; it tolerates dry soil that is cool and mulched. These trees adapt best to humid areas. Avoid storm damage by pruning young trees to a single leader or by tying multitrunked trees with an encircling support of twine for the winter. Trees are shallow rooted in wet soil and thus more likely to blow over in a storm.

T. occidentalis

t. oks-seh-den-TAY-liss. Arborvitae, Eastern White Cedar, White Cedar. A columnar, 30- to 40-foot-tall, 15-foot-wide native evergreen, arborvitae is a common and very adapt-

Thuja occidentalis 'Smaragd'

able landscape plant with sprays of soft, aromatic foliage. Leaves are shiny, $^{1}/_{2}$-inch-long scales that are tightly pressed to the twigs, which form flat, horizontal fans. The glossy green foliage cloaks the tree all the way to the ground. Foliage may remain green all winter or turn bronze, especially if exposed to full sun. In nature the tree usually forms a single trunk; because nursery-grown specimens are often multitrunked, they are more likely to split under ice or snow. Trunk bark is dark grayish brown and shredding. Cones are $^{1}/_{2}$ inch long and ripen from yellow-green to light brownish yellow, with 8 to 10 woody scales. Use arborvitae as a screen or a vertical accent in a border. Many dwarf, shrublike forms are available. From northeastern and north-central North America. **Zones 3 to 10.**

T. plicata

t. ply-KAY-tuh. Western Red Cedar, Giant Arborvitae. In cultivation, this beautiful, fast-growing, native evergreen forms a narrow, 50- to 60-foottall, 15- to 20-foot-wide pyramid with a dominant single trunk and horizontal branches all the way to the ground. In the wild, it can reach 120 feet tall.

Western red cedar has an attractive, buttressed trunk with shredding, reddish brown bark. The horizontal, fanlike sprays of aromatic foliage consist of glossy, green, scalelike leaves with white

T

Thunbergia alata

markings on their undersides. Foliage is coarser and darker and grows in narrower sprays than that of arborvitae and may turn bronze in winter. Cones are ¹/₂ inch long, have 10 to 12 woody scales, and ripen from green to brown.

This tree's tall, narrow shape makes it suitable as a screen or as a vertical accent in a border or near a building. Many cultivars, including shrubs, are available. From the Pacific Northwest. **Zones 4 to 8.**

Thunbergia

thun-BER-gee-uh. Acanthus family, Acanthaceae.

Many of the 100 species of annuals and perennials that belong to *Thunbergia* are twining climbers, although a few shrubs are classified here as well. Native to tropical and southern Africa as well as Madagascar, they bear ovate to nearly round leaves and tubular flowers that are trumpet-shaped or salverform, meaning they have a tubular base with a flattened "face" consisting of five spreading lobes, or "petals."

HOW TO GROW

Select a site in full sun with rich, evenly moist, well-drained soil. In hot climates, a spot that receives partial shade in the afternoon is best. Sow seeds indoors 6 to 8 weeks before the last spring frost date at 60° to 70°F. Germination takes 2 to 3 weeks. Water regularly throughout the growing season; container-grown plants may need daily watering in hot weather.

Commonly grown *Thunbergia* species are perennials and can be propagated by taking cuttings from spring to midsummer, as well as by layering. Use cuttings or layers to propagate plants for the garden or for overwintering. Although black-eyed Susan vine *(T. alata),* the most popular species, is usually treated as an annual, it can be overwintered, and second-year plants are more vigorous than first-year ones. Overwinter in a sunny, warm (60° to 70°F) spot. Prune as necessary in early spring before new growth begins. Use these vines to cover trellises or other supports. Black-eyed Susan vine is especially effective trailing over the sides of a hanging basket or other container.

T. alata

t. ah-LAH-tuh. Black-eyed Susan Vine. A tender perennial, hardy only in frost-free climates, where it can reach 8 feet. Bears arrowhead-shaped to triangular leaves and solitary, salverform,

Thymus pseudolanuginosus

1¹/₄- to 1¹/₂-inch-wide flowers from summer to fall. Flowers are orange, orange-yellow, yellow, or creamy white with dark black to brownish black centers. Tender perennial or warm-weather annual.

Thymophylla

ty-moh-FILL-uh. Aster family, Asteraceae.

Daisylike flowers and strongly aromatic foliage characterize the 10 to 12 species of annuals, biennials, perennials, and subshrubs that belong to this genus. Native from prairies and dry slopes in the United States through Central America, they have very finely cut, feathery leaves and produce an abundance of small, yellow to yellow-orange flower heads from spring to summer.

HOW TO GROW

Select a site in full sun with average, well-drained soil that is not too rich. *Thymophylla* species thrive in heat and tolerate dry soil. Sow seeds outdoors a few weeks before the last spring frost date. For earlier flowers, sow indoors 6 to 8 weeks before the last frost date at 50° to 55°F. Use them as edgings, in mixed plantings, in rock gardens, and in containers. Plants self-sow.

T. tenuiloba

t. ten-yew-ih-LOH-buh. Dahlberg Daisy, Golden Fleece. Formerly *Dyssodia tenuiloba.* A well-branched, mounding, ¹/₂- to 1-foot-tall annual or short-lived perennial with fragrant leaves cut into threadlike segments. Bears starry, ¹/₂-inch-wide, yellow, daisylike flowers from spring to summer. Cool-weather annual.

Thymus

TY-muss. Mint family, Lamiaceae.

Handsome, useful thymes are valued as cooking herbs, ground covers, and ornamentals. About 350 species belong to this genus, including woody-based perennials, subshrubs, and shrubs. Rounded,

Thymophylla tenuiloba

lacy-looking clusters of pink, rose-purple, or white flowers cover the plants in late spring or early summer. The tiny individual flowers are two lipped and range from about $^1/_8$ to $^3/_8$ inch in length. Plants bear very aromatic, evergreen, oval to linear leaves that are also small, about $^1/_2$ inch or less.

HOW TO GROW
Select a site in full sun or very light shade with well-drained soil. Plants prefer warm, dry, poor, sandy or gravelly soil but also grow in rich soil or even in heavy clay, provided drainage is excellent. Moist soil or poorly drained conditions lead to fungal diseases and rot, while too-rich soil causes rampant growth and foliage that has less fragrance and flavor. A spot with good air circulation is best, especially for *T. pseudolanuginosus*.

Mulch with gravel to control weeds but maintain soil drainage. Toward the northern part of their range, protect shrubby thymes in winter with evergreen branches placed over the plants after the ground freezes in late fall. Trim shrubby species in mid- to late summer after they flower to keep them looking neat. On variegated or golden-leaved forms, prune or dig out any growth that reverts to all-green. Divide (or propagate and replace) shrubby thymes every 3 or 4 years, since they tend to become woody and less vigorous. Divide mat-forming thymes only if they die out in the centers of the clumps or for propagation. With either type, divide plants in spring or early fall or propagate by cut-tings taken in spring or summer or by mound layering in spring. Seed-grown thymes seldom resemble their parents.

T. × citriodorus
t. × sih-tree-oh-DOR-uss. LEMON THYME. Shrubby, rounded 10- to 12-inch-tall plant that spreads to about 2 feet. Mounds of lemon-scented leaves are topped by clusters of pale lilac flowers in summer. 'Aureus' bears yellow leaves, while 'Argenteus' has silver-edged leaves. **Zones 5 to 9.**

T. pseudolanuginosus
t. SUE-doe-lah-nyew-jih-NOH-suss. WOOLLY THYME. Mat-forming 1- to 3-inch-tall species that spreads from 1 to 3 feet. Bears silvery-hairy leaves and sparse pale pink flowers in summer. Tolerates a certain amount of foot traffic. Requires perfect drainage. **Zones 5 or 6 to 8.**

T. pulegioides
t. pull-ed-jee-OY-deez. MOTHER OF THYME. A 3-inch-tall subshrub that spreads to 1 foot or more and bears mauve-pink flowers in late spring and early summer and lemon-scented leaves. **Zones 4 to 9.**

T. serpyllum
t. ser-PILL-um. WILD THYME, CREEPING THYME. Ground-hugging subshrub ranging from 1 to 10 inches in height and spreading to about $1^1/_2$ feet. Bears aromatic leaves and purple flowers in summer. Dwarf cultivars, such as 1-inch-tall 'Pink Chintz', are especially handsome as ground covers. *T. serpyllum* var. *coccineus* (formerly *T. praecox* 'Coccineus') is a 3-inch-tall creeper with purple-red flowers. **Zones 4 to 9.**

T. vulgaris
t. vul-GAIR-iss. COMMON THYME, GARDEN THYME. A 6- to 12-inch-tall subshrub forming a spreading, $1^1/_2$-foot-wide mound of twiggy branches covered with gray-green aromatic leaves. White or rose-purple flowers appear from late spring to early summer. **Zones 4 to 8.**

Tiarella
tee-uh-RELL-uh. Saxifrage family, Saxifragaceae.

Tiarella species, commonly known as foamflowers, are shade-loving perennials native to North America as well as eastern Asia. About seven species belong to the genus, all of which produce mounds of toothed, primarily basal leaves that are either simple in outline or, more often, lobed in a palmate (handlike) fashion. The leaves have prominent veins and are covered with bristly hairs. Plants bear airy panicles or racemes of tiny $^1/_4$- to $^1/_2$-inch-wide white or pinkish white flowers from spring to summer.

HOW TO GROW
Plant foamflowers in partial to full shade with rich, evenly moist, well-drained soil. A slightly acid pH is best. Plants grow naturally in damp woodlands and along streambanks, but constantly wet soil usually is fatal, especially in winter. Propagate by digging and dividing the clumps in spring or fall, by digging up individual plantlets that emerge at the end of runners, or by sowing seeds.

T. cordifolia
t. kore-dih-FOH-lee-uh. ALLEGHENY FOAMFLOWER. A 6- to 10-inch-tall native North American wildflower that spreads vigorously by runners and rhizomes to form 1- to 2-foot-wide clumps. Bears fluffy, spikelike racemes of white flowers in spring above attractive maplelike leaves. 'Brandywine' bears leaves with showy red veins. 'Tiger Stripe' also has red-veined leaves with a prominent central stripe. 'Slickrock' bears very deeply cut, dark green leaves. 'Eco Red Heart', sometimes listed as a cultivar of *T. wherryi*, has leaves with a reddish central blotch. **Zones 3 to 8.**

T. wherryi
t. WHERE-ee-eye. WHERRY'S FOAMFLOWER. Compact perennial, similar to *T. cordifolia*, that reaches 6 to 10 inches in height but spreads much more slowly, eventually forming 6- to 10-inch-wide clumps. Bears fluffy, spikelike racemes of white or pink-tinged flowers in spring above attractive maplelike leaves. 'Oakleaf' bears oakleaf-shaped foliage and pink flowers. 'Dunvegan' forms clumps of deeply lobed leaves topped by pink flowers. **Zones 3 to 8.**

Tibouchina
tih-boo-CHEE-nuh. Melastoma family, Melastomataceae.

Tibouchina contains about 350 species of perennials, subshrubs, shrubs, and climbers native to the rain forests of South and Central America. They are commonly called glory bushes, and the botanical name is based on a native South American name for these tropical plants. Although many are quite showy, few are cultivated.

Tiarella wherryi

Tiarella cordifolia

Tibouchina urvilleana

They bear ovate to lance-shaped leaves and five-petaled, cup- to saucer-shaped flowers from summer to fall.

HOW TO GROW

Select a site in full sun or dappled shade with rich, evenly moist soil. Plants usually are propagated by cuttings taken in spring or summer but also can be grown from seeds sown about 8 to 10 weeks before the last spring frost date at 65° to 70°F. From Zone 10 south, grow *Tibouchina* outdoors as shrubs; where marginally hardy, try them in a protected, south-facing site and mulch over winter. In the North, grow them in containers either set on terraces or sunk to the rim in the soil over the summer. They also can be treated as bedding plants replaced annually, but plants treated as tender perennials will be showier and make outstanding specimens. They also can be trained as standards.

Water regularly during the summer months, and feed pot-grown plants monthly. Overwinter them indoors in a bright, somewhat cool (50° to 60°F) spot, and keep them on the dry side over winter. Prune to shape plants in late winter or early spring.

T. urvilleana

t. ur-vill-ee-AH-nuh. Glory Bush, Brazilian Spider Flower. Sometimes listed as *Pleroma macrantha* or *T. semidecandra*. A tender shrub that can range from 10 to 20 feet in frost-free regions. Bears dark green, 2- to 3-inch-long leaves covered with velvety hairs and satiny-textured, 2-inch-wide, violet-purple flowers. Tender perennial or warm-weather annual.

Tigridia

tih-GRIH-dee-uh. Iris family, Iridaceae.

Easy-to-grow, summer-blooming tigridias have a number of colorful common names, including tiger flower, peacock flower, and Mexican shell flower. The showy flowers have six petal-like tepals. The three outer tepals are large and showy: they flare out at the top, giving the blooms a somewhat triangular outline, and come together at the base to form a deep cup or shallow saucer. The three inner tepals are much smaller and point up or out. The botanical name, from the Latin *tigris* (tiger), refers to the fact that the centers of the blooms are prominently spotted. In this case, however, "tiger" refers to the Central American tiger, better known as the jaguar, since tigridias are native to Mexico and Guatemala. Individual flowers last only a day but are borne in succession for several weeks in summer. Plants grow from tunicate bulbs and bear fans of lance- to sword-shaped leaves.

HOW TO GROW

Select a site in full sun with light, evenly moist soil rich in organic matter. Tigridias are grown much like gladiolus: plant bulbs in spring after the soil has warmed up and nighttime temperatures remain above 55°F. Set bulbs 4 to 5 inches deep; in heavy or clayey soil, plant them at a depth of about 3 inches. Plant small bulbs shallowly — from $^1/_2$ to 1 inch deep — until they reach full size. For best results, dig the soil deeply and work organic matter and a balanced organic fertilizer into the soil at planting time. Then set the bulbs in a shallow trench and fill it gradually with soil as the plants grow. Deep planting helps eliminate the need to stake plants. Plant new bulbs every two weeks to extend the bloom season.

In areas where the plants are not hardy, let the foliage ripen for 6 weeks after flowering. Then dig the bulbs after the leaves turn yellow, cut off the foliage, and set them in a warm, dry place for a few hours. Store the bulbs in a cool (40° to 50°F), dry place over winter. Tigridias are quite inexpensive and often are grown as annuals. They also are effective in containers. Propagate by separating the offsets or by sowing seeds.

T. pavonia

t. pah-VOH-nee-uh. Peacock Flower, Tiger Flower. A $1^1/_2$- to 2-foot-tall species bearing somewhat irislike 4- to 6-inch-wide flowers in summer. Blooms come in a range of showy colors, including red, pink, orange, yellow, and white with contrasting, spotted centers. Many cultivars are available, including 'Alba Grandiflora', white with red-spotted centers; 'Aurea', yellow with red-spotted centers; and 'Canariensis', yellow with red centers. Mixtures of many colors are often available. **Zones 8 to 10.**

Tilia

TILL-ee-uh. Linden family, Tiliaceae.

Members of this genus usually have bold, toothed, alternate leaves that are heart-shaped or rounded; clusters of small, creamy, fragrant flowers attached to winglike, spoon-shaped, green bracts; and clusters of green, pea-shaped fruits. The flowers attract bees, which make a flavorful honey from the nectar. Several species are important landscape subjects, despite a host of disease and insect problems, including leaf blight,

T

Tigridia pavonia 'Aurea'

Tilia cordata 'Greenspire'

mildew, verticillium wilt, anthracnose, rust, borers, gypsy moth caterpillars, aphids, and Japanese beetles. Most of these problems are usually not life threatening. Aphids are the most annoying problem, because they secrete a sticky honeydew that collects on pavement, cars, or lawn furniture beneath infested trees.

HOW TO GROW

Plant in full sun to light shade and in deep, rich, moist, alkaline or acid soil. Tolerates some drought when established. Train when young to develop a strong branch structure. Remove competing leaders and suckers.

T. americana

t. ah-mare-eh-KAH-nuh. BASS-WOOD, AMERICAN LINDEN. This native grows 50 to 80 feet tall and has a decidedly oval shape created by a strong, straight trunk and a skirt of low, down-swept branches. The coarse-textured, toothed, heart-shaped leaves are 4 to 8 inches long and dark green, turning yellowish before dropping in autumn. In early summer, 2- to 3-inch-wide clusters of pale greenish yellow flowers hang among the leaves, giving off a pleasant spicy-sweet scent. Give this large tree plenty of growing space in a park or lawn where it will cast dense shade. It's ideal in a naturalistic setting. Aphids, with subsequent sooty mold, are the worst pests. Leaf scorch occurs in dry years,

rust in wet ones. From eastern North America. **Zones 3 to 8.**

CULTIVARS

'Boulevard' is narrower than the species, growing to 60 feet tall and 30 feet wide, with a strong central leader. 'Frontyard' forms a very symmetrical, uniform pyramid with a strong central leader. 'Legend' is broad and has glossy, rust-resistant leaves. 'Redmond' is a fast-growing hybrid with large glossy leaves, bright yellow fall color, and a compact, tight, 70-foot-tall, pyramidal form. 'Lincoln' forms a compact pyramid, growing to 35 feet tall and 25 feet wide.

T. cordata

t. kore-DAH-tuh. LITTLELEAF LINDEN. A favorite street tree because of its dense, symmetrical shape, littleleaf linden is pyramidal when young but matures into a rounded, 60- to 70-foot-tall, 40-foot-wide tree. Most cultivars are uniform and formal looking. Leaves are tidy, bright green, 2- to 4-inch-long hearts with lighter undersides and unremarkable yellowish fall color. Three-inch clusters of creamy yellow flowers bloom in midsummer, dangling beneath the dense leaves in such profusion that from a distance the tree has a two-tone effect. Trunk bark is gray-brown, ridged, and roughly furrowed. Tolerates air pollution, and urban conditions. Usually trouble-free, although aphids and Japanese beetles are common. Use as a street, lawn, or park tree. From Europe. Tolerates air pollution, and urban conditions. Train when young to develop a single leader and a strong branch structure. Thin branches, pruning when dormant, to reduce overcrowding in the dense canopy.

Tilia cordata

Usually trouble-free, although aphids and Japanese beetles are common. **Zones 3 to 8.**

CULTIVARS AND SIMILAR SPECIES

'Chancellor' forms a 50-by-20-foot, narrow pyramid with golden yellow fall color. 'Corinthian' forms a 45-by-15-foot pyramid with small, very shiny leaves. 'Fairhaven' has a straight trunk, uniform branches, and slightly larger leaves. 'Glenleven' is a fast-growing hybrid that forms an open pyramid, growing to 50 feet tall with a strong central leader; with golden fall color, it thrives in the Mountain States. 'Greenspire' is the best-known cultivar; it has a straight trunk and well-spaced branches, forming a symmetrical, 50-foot-tall pyramid. 'Olympic' grows 40 feet tall and 30 feet wide; with a looser shape than most cultivars, it looks better in informal settings. 'Rancho' has small leaves and a beautiful, narrow form. 'Shamrock' is similar to 'Greenspire' but grows faster and is a bit more open. *T. × euchlora* (Crimean linden) has beautiful, fine-textured, glossy foliage that turns bright yellow in fall; it grows to 40 feet tall and 35 feet wide, forming a broad pyramid; **Zones 5 to 8.**

T. tomentosa

t. toh-men-TOH-suh. SILVER LINDEN. Pyramidal or rounded and growing to 70 feet tall, silver linden has a formal shape that's suitable for manicured gardens. Its 5-inch-long leaves are outstanding — glossy dark green on top with silver gray, woolly undersides. They shimmer and flash in the sun and turn an attractive golden yellow in fall. Fragrant flowers bloom in early summer but are obscured by the dense leaves. Branches and young trunks are covered with smooth, silver gray bark. Older trunks become gray-brown and are ridged and furrowed. Use as a street or lawn tree. Bothered much less than other lindens by diseases and pests, especially Japanese beetles and gypsy moths. From Europe. **Zones 5 to 8.**

CULTIVARS

'Green Mountain' grows rapidly to 45 feet tall and 35 feet wide and has thick leaves that tolerate heat and drought. 'Sterling Silver' grows to 45 feet tall and 35 feet wide, forming a neat, symmetrical oval, and has silvery new growth. 'Satin Shadow' forms a 50-by-40-foot uniform oval and has silvery leaves.

T

Tithonia

tih-THOH-nee-uh. Aster family, Asteraceae.

Commonly called Mexican sunflowers, *Tithonia* species are native from Mexico through Central America. About 10 species belong to this genus, most of which are annuals, although some are perennials or shrubs. One is a popular annual. Mexican sunflowers, or tithonias, as they also are called, bear entire or lobed leaves and daisylike flower heads in shades of yellow, orange, or red from late summer to fall.

HOW TO GROW

Give Mexican sunflower *(T. rotundifolia)* full sun and poor to average, well-drained soil. Plants thrive in heat. Too-rich soil yields abundant foliage but few flowers. Sow seeds indoors 6 to 8 weeks before the last spring frost date at 60° to 70°F. Germination takes 1 to 2 weeks. Or sow seeds outdoors after the last frost date.

Stake plants to keep them erect during windy weather. Deadhead regularly to encourage new flowers to form. Water during dry weather. Use these plants at the back of perennial borders or mixed plantings. Butterflies and hummingbirds are attracted to tithonia, which also make excellent, long-lasting cut flowers.

T. rotundifolia

t. roh-tun-dih-FOH-lee-uh. MEXICAN SUNFLOWER. A vigorous, somewhat coarse, 3- to 6-foot-tall annual bearing 3-inch-wide daisies in shades of orange or orange-red from late summer to frost. 'Torch' bears 4-inch-wide orange-red

Tithonia rotundifolia

Torenia fournieri 'Summer Wave'

flowers. 'Goldfinger' bears burnt orange flowers on compact, 30-inch-tall plants. Warm-weather annual.

Torenia

tor-REE-nee-uh. Figwort family, Scrophulariaceae.

Of the 40 to 50 species that belong to the genus *Torenia*, two are commonly grown in gardens. All *Torenia* species bear clusters of tubular flowers that somewhat resemble monkey flowers *(Mimulus* spp.). They have two flaring, lobed lips and are marked with combinations of violet, purple, pink, white, and yellow. Leaves are ovate to lance shaped.

HOW TO GROW

Select a site with partial shade and rich, well-drained, evenly moist soil. Plants that receive shade in

the afternoon tend to have brighter flowers. Sow seeds indoors 6 to 8 weeks before the last spring frost date and germinate at 65° to 70°F. Germination takes 1 to 4 weeks. Grow seedlings at about 55°F to keep them compact. Or sow outdoors a week before the last frost date. When sowing, just press the seeds into the soil surface, as light aids germination. Transplant seedlings about 2 weeks after the frost date, once the weather is settled. Pinch plants when they are 2 to 3 inches tall to encourage branching and bushy growth. Use *Torenia* species in shady gardens as well as containers. Hummingbirds will visit the flowers.

T. fournieri

t. FOR-nee-AIR-ee. WISHBONE FLOWER. An erect, 1-foot-tall annual with 1½-inch-long purple

flowers with deep violet lobes and a yellow blotch on the throat. 'Clown Mix' bears lavender and white, violet and purple, and pink and white flowers, all with yellow throats, on 8-inch-tall plants. Warm-weather annual.

T. flava

t. FLAY-vuh. YELLOW WISHBONE FLOWER. Also listed as *T. baillonii*. An 8- to 12-inch-tall annual with ³/4- to 1-inch-long, golden yellow flowers that have dark purple-red throats. 'Suzie Wong' bears 1-inch-long flowers on 8-inch plants. Warm-weather annual.

Trachelium

tray-KEL-lee-um. Bellflower family, Campanulaceae.

Trachelium contains seven species, all tender perennials, that are native to the Mediterranean. They bear tubular flowers with five spreading "petals," more properly called lobes, and leaves that range from lance shaped to nearly round. They are commonly called throatworts, and the botanical name is from the Greek *trachelos* ("neck"). Both names are references to the plants' supposed virtues in treating diseases of the trachea.

HOW TO GROW

Give blue throatwort *(T. caeruleum)* full sun to partial shade and average, very well drained soil that remains evenly moist. A spot that receives shade during the hottest part of the day is best. This species can be grown as an annual or a biennial. To grow it as an annual, sow seeds indoors 8 to 10 weeks before the last spring frost date at 55° to 60°F. Germination takes 2 to 3 weeks. To grow it as a biennial, sow seeds in midsummer into pots, then overwinter the plants in a bright, cool (45°F) spot. Transplant to the garden after the last frost the following spring. Water regularly in dry weather. These plants also can be propagated by cuttings taken in early summer. Use throatworts in mixed plantings. They also make attractive cut flowers.

T. caeruleum

t. see-RUE-lee-um. BLUE THROATWORT. An erect, 3- to 4-foot tender perennial, hardy from **Zone 9 south.** Bears dense, flattened clusters of starry, ¹/4-inch-wide, violet-blue, white, or

Trachelium caeruleum

lavender-mauve flowers that have a slight fragrance. Warm-weather annual or biennial.

Trachelospermum

trah-kee-loh-SPER-mum. Dogbane family, Apocynaceae.

The 30 species of Confederate jasmine include fragrant-flowered vines native from India to Japan as well as in the southern United States. The genus is useful both as a ground cover and a vine that climbs by twining stems. The dark green leaves are evergreen, opposite, and rather tough without being coarse. The fragrant flowers are five lobed, with the narrow lobes joined atop a long tube. In the wild, these flowers are undoubtedly pollinated by moths that use the fragrance and pale color to locate them in twilight hours.

HOW TO GROW
Trachelospermums thrive in partial shade and fertile soil that is never fully dry. Given these conditions, they will form extensive, weed-choking carpets of dark green or variegated foliage. For best flowering, stems need to climb, such as over a trellis or trained on a wall.

T. asiaticum (T. majus)
t. ay-see-AH-tih-kum. STAR JASMINE. This species is ubiquitous in southern landscapes. When the temperature falls to freezing, it dies back, but then returns from the roots. Flowers are yellow. In light frosts, the foliage turns dark red. It is hardy and reliably attrac-tive in moist, well-drained soils that never fully dry out. Zones 8 to 10.

T. jasminoides
t. jaz-mih-NOY-deez. CONFEDERATE JASMINE. This well-known vine spreads 10 to 15 feet as a ground cover and is not always a strong climber. The fragrant white flowers are produced in spring, mostly on branches that climb or are draped over walls and structures. Plants do best in moist, rich, loamy soils. 'Variegatum' has leaves mottled with white. Zones 9 and 10.

Trachymene

tray-KEH-men-ee. Carrot family, Apiaceae.

Native to Australia and the islands of the western Pacific, *Trachymene* species are annuals, biennials, and perennials with three-part leaves that usually have narrow leaflets and dainty umbels of tiny, star-shaped flowers. Of the approximately 12 species that belong to the genus, one is grown for its lacy flowers.

HOW TO GROW
Give blue lace flower (*T. coerulea*) full sun and average, well-drained soil. The plants tolerate dry soil but grow best in evenly moist, not wet, conditions. A site sheltered from wind is best. Sow seeds indoors in individual pots 8 to 10 weeks before the last frost date at 60° to 70°F. Germination takes 2 to 4 weeks. Transplant with care. Or sow outdoors after the last frost date. When sowing, barely cover the seeds with soil, as darkness is required for germination. Pinch seedlings when they are several inches tall to encourage branching. Stake with twiggy brush. Blue lace flower can be used in beds and borders and makes an excellent cut flower.

T. coerulea
t. see-RUE-lee-uh. BLUE LACE FLOWER. Formerly *Didiscus coeruleus*. A 2-foot-tall annual or biennial with lacy, 2-inch-wide umbels of lightly fragrant, lavender-blue flowers in summer. Warm-weather annual.

Trachymene coerulea

Tradescantia

trad-ess-CAN-tee-uh. Spiderwort family, Commelinaceae.

Commonly known as spiderworts, *Tradescantia* species are hardy and tender perennials bearing clusters of saucer-shaped flowers that have three petals and three sepals. While the individual flowers last only half a day, they are produced in clusters, each with a pair of boat-shaped bracts at the base, and appear over a long season. Leaves are usually strap to lance shaped but also can be linear or ovate. They are attached to the stems by a sheath that clasps the stem. About 65 species of spiderwort native to North, South, and Central America belong to this genus. The hardy perennials commonly grown in gardens usually are hybrids.

HOW TO GROW
Select a site in light to full shade with rich, moist, well-drained soil. Cut plants to the ground after the main flush of flowers to discourage reseeding, encourage rebloom, and keep plants looking neat. In areas with cool summers, they regrow fairly quickly; in areas with warm summers, they reemerge in fall. Plants spread vigorously to form dense clumps. For propagation and to keep plants in bounds, dig and divide them every 3 to 4 years in spring or fall. Spiderworts self-sow with enthusiasm, but hybrids do not come true from seeds.

Tradescantia virginiana

Trachelospermum jasminoides

T. Andersoniana Group

Clump-forming hybrid spiderworts that produce 1¹/₂- to 2-foottall mounds of lance-shaped leaves and spread from 2 to 3 feet. Bears clusters of saucer-shaped, 1-inchwide, three-petaled flowers from early to midsummer. Blooms come in violet, lavender-blue, pink, rose-red, and white. 'Iris Prichard' bears white flowers with pale lavender-blue shading. 'Red Cloud' has bright rose-red flowers. 'Purple Dome' bears violet-purple blooms. 'Snowcap' has large white blooms. 'Purple Profusion' bears violet-blue leaves on 1- to 1¹/₂-foot-tall plants. 'Concord Grape,' also 1 to 1¹/₂ feet tall, bears rosy purple blooms. **Zones 4 to 9, to Zone 3 with winter protection.**

T. virginiana

t. vir-jin-ee-AH-nuh. VIRGINIA SPIDERWORT. Native North American wildflower forming 1- to 2-foot-tall mounds of strapshaped leaves that spread from 2 to 3 feet. Bears clusters of 1-inchwide, purple-blue flowers. **Zones 4 to 9.**

Tricyrtis

try-SIR-tiss. Lily family, Liliaceae.

Tricyrtis species, or toad lilies as they are also called, are perennials

Tricyrtis hirta

Trillium grandiflorum

native from the Himalayas to Japan and the Philippines. They form clumps of erect or arching stems clothed in ovate to somewhat oblong leaves. The leaves clasp the stems at the base. Toad lilies have unusual, waxy-textured flowers that are borne either singly or in clusters in the leaf axils or, less often, at the stem tips. Blooms have six tepals and may be star, funnel, or bell shaped. About 16 species belong to the genus.

HOW TO GROW

Select a site in light to full shade with rich, moist, well-drained soil. Plants thrive for years without needing to be divided. Propagate by dividing plants in spring. Toad lilies self-sow in areas with summers that are long enough for the seeds to ripen.

T. formosana

t. for-moh-SAH-nuh. FORMOSA TOAD LILY. Also listed as *T. stolonifera*. Rhizomatous 1- to 2-foot-tall species also spreading by stolons to form 2-foot-wide clumps with time. Bears glossy dark green leaves with purplegreen spots on somewhat zigzagged stems. From late summer into fall, plants produce clusters of upward-facing, starry, 1-inch-wide flowers in white, pinkish white, or pinkish purple with red-purple spots. **Zones 4 to 9.**

T. hirta

t. HUR-tuh. Toad Lily. Also listed as *T. japonica*. A 2- to 3-foot-tall spe-

cies that spreads by rhizomes to form 2-foot-wide clumps. Bears clusters of white, purple-spotted flowers in late summer and fall in the leaf axils along the stems. 'Variegata' bears leaves with yellow margins. 'Miyazaki' bears white flowers with lilac-purple spots on 3-foot plants. **Zones 4 to 9.**

Trillium

TRIL-ee-um. Lily family, Liliaceae.

Trilliums are spring-flowering perennials native to woodlands in North America as well as eastern Asia. They grow from tuberlike rhizomes and form clumps of erect stems, each topped by a single set of rounded to ovate or diamond-shaped leaves. The flowers are solitary and borne above the whorl of leaves. The botanical name *Trillium* is from the Latin *tres*, a reference to the normal number of leaves borne on each stem as well as the number of sepals and petals on each flower.

HOW TO GROW

Select a site in partial to full shade with moist, well-drained soil rich in organic matter. Soil with an acid to neutral pH is best for most species. Mulch plants annually with chopped leaves to keep the soil moist and replenish organic matter. Trilliums are spring ephemerals, meaning they die back after flowering, generally by early summer, so mark the loca-

tions of plants to avoid digging into them accidentally. *Do not collect trilliums from the wild or purchase plants that have been wild collected.* Propagate by dividing the rhizomes in spring after the plants flower. The divisions may be slow to reestablish. Trilliums also selfsow where happy, although plants take several years to bloom from seeds.

T. erectum

t. ee-RECK-tum. STINKING BENJAMIN. A 1- to 1¹/₂-foot-tall native North American wildflower that spreads to about 1 foot. Bears 2- to 3¹/₂-inch-wide flowers with foul-smelling maroon to maroonbrown petals in spring. Blooms are on long stalks and point up or out. **Zones 4 to 9.**

T. grandiflorum

t. gran-dih-FLOR-um. GREAT WHITE TRILLIUM, WOOD LILY, WAKE-ROBIN. A 1- to 1¹/₂-foot-tall native North American wildflower that eventually forms 2-foot-wide clumps. In spring, bears showy, short-stalked, 3-inch-wide white flowers that change to pink. **Zones 4 to 8.**

Triteleia

trih-TEL-ay-uh. Lily family, Liliaceae.

Triteleia contains about 15 species of perennials native to the western United States. Like their close relatives in the genus *Brodiaea*, they are grown for their showy umbels of funnel-shaped flowers borne atop thin, leafless stalks. The flowers in the umbel are borne on individual stalks and have six petal-like tepals. The tepals are joined at the base to form a short tube. The long leaves are basal and grassy or linear and generally die back as the flowers appear. Like crocuses and gladiolus, triteleias grow from corms, which last only

Triteleia ixioides

Tritonia crocata

one year but are replaced annually as new ones develop during the growing season.

HOW TO GROW

Select a site in full sun or partial shade that has rich, well-drained soil. Light, sandy loam is ideal. Plant corms in early fall, setting them 3 to 5 inches deep, depending on the size. Triteleias are most effective planted in drifts or clumps with fairly close spacing — 2 to 3 inches apart. Work sand or grit into the soil to improve drainage. Plants require even moisture when they are actively growing, but once the plants go dormant in summer, they require warm, dry conditions.

In the West, where triteleias grow naturally in dry grasslands and woodlands, these plants are ideal for naturalizing. In areas where they are marginally hardy, look for a protected, south-facing site and cover the plants over winter with a loose mulch of evergreen branches, pine needles, or salt hay. In the North and in areas with rainy summers, grow them in containers or try them in rock gardens, raised beds, or other sites that offer the excellent drainage and dry summer conditions they require. Container-grown plants are easy to move to a warm, dry site protected from rain to ensure a dry dormancy. Overwinter container-grown plants indoors in a cool (40° to 45°F), dry spot, then repeat the cycle in spring.

Since the foliage often is dying back when the plants are flowering, underplant with shallow-rooted annuals to fill in around them. Propagate by separating offsets just as the plants go dormant or by sowing seeds.

T. hyacinthina

t. hy-ah-sin-THY-nuh. W ILD H YA - CINTH . Formerly *Brodiaea hyacinthina, B. lactea.* A 2-foot-tall species bearing 4-inch-wide umbels of 20 or more ^{1}/$_2$-inch-long flowers in late spring or early summer. Flowers are either white or pale lilac-blue. **Zones 7 to 10.**

T. ixioides

t. iks-ee-OH-deez. P RETTY F ACE , G OLDEN S TAR . Formerly *Brodiaea ixioides, B. lutea.* A 2-foot-tall species bearing 5-inch-wide umbels of 20 to 25 ^{1}/$_2$- to 1-inch-wide flowers in early summer. Flowers are yellow with a purple stripe down the center of each tepal. **Zones 7 to 10.**

T. laxa

t. LAKS-uh. G RASS N UT , T RIP - LET L ILY , I THURIEL'S S PEAR . Formerly *Brodiaea laxa.* A 2-foot-tall species bearing loose, 6-inch-wide umbels of 20 to 25 flowers in early summer. Individual blooms are ^{3}/$_4$ to 2 inches wide and pale lavender to dark purple-blue in color. 'Queen Fabiola' (also listed as 'Koningin Fabiola') bears 2-inch-long purple-blue flowers. **Zones 6 to 10; to Zone 5 with winter protection.**

Tritonia

trih-TOH-nee-uh. Iris family, Iridaceae.

These South African natives are grown for their showy clusters of flowers that come in a range of bright colors and are carried from spring to summer on thin, wiry stems. Individual blooms are funnel to cup shaped with tubular bases that split into 6 lobes, or petal-like tepals. The plants, which grow from corms, produce fans of linear to lance-shaped, mostly basal leaves. About 28 species belong to this genus.

HOW TO GROW

Select a site with full sun and rich, well-drained soil. Where hardy, they can be grown outdoors year-round. Like many South African species, they need dry soil conditions when dormant. Especially in areas with wet winters, a site with very well drained soil (such as a raised bed) is essential. When growing these corms outdoors, plant them in fall at a depth of 2 to 4 inches. Where they are marginally hardy, look for a protected spot, such as at the base of a south-facing wall, and mulch

heavily in fall with a coarse mulch such as evergreen boughs, salt hay, or pine needles.

In the North, treat the corms like those of gladiolus: plant them outdoors in spring after all danger of frost has passed, dig them in summer after the leaves have died back, and store them dry in net or paper bags in a warm (60° to 75°F), dry, well-ventilated spot. Or grow them in containers by potting the corms in spring at a depth of about 1 to 2 inches. Water carefully until plants begin to flower: the soil should stay barely moist but never become wet or completely dry. Replace the corms annually or, to hold them for another year's bloom, continue watering after plants flower and feed every other week with a dilute, balanced fertilizer. When the leaves begin to turn yellow and die back, gradually dry off the plants and store the containers in a cool (50° to 60°F), dry, well-ventilated spot. Or clean the soil off the corms and store them in paper bags. Propagate by seeds or by separating offsets in late summer just as the leaves die down.

T. crocata

t. kroh-KAH-tuh. Formerly *T. fenestrata, T. hyalina.* An 8- to 12-inch-tall species bearing arching spikes of about 10 flowers in spring. Individual blooms are cup shaped, ^{1}/$_2$ inch long, and orange to pinkish red in color. **Zones 8 to 10; to Zone 7 with winter protection.**

T. disticha

t. DIS-tih-kuh. Formerly *Crocosmia rosea.* A 2- to 3-foot-tall species

bearing arching spikes of many ^{3}/$_4$-inch-long flowers in mid- to late summer. Individual flowers are funnel shaped and come in shades of orange-red, red, and pink. *T. disticha* ssp. *rubrolucens* (formerly *T. rosea, T. rubrolucens*) bears funnel-shaped, 1- to 1^1/$_2$-inch-long pink flowers. **Zones 9 to 10; to Zone 8 with winter protection.**

Trollius

TROLL-ee-uss. Buttercup family, Ranunculaceae.

Trollius species, commonly called globeflowers, are perennials native to areas with damp to wet soils in Europe, Asia, and North America. The plants bear buttercup-like flowers that may be cup shaped, bowl shaped, or rounded and come in shades of yellow, orange, white, and pink. The flowers consist of showy, petal-like sepals: the petals resemble the stamens and form a small cluster in the centers of the flowers. The plants produce low mounds of mostly basal leaves that are palmately lobed (divided in a handlike fashion) and usually toothed.

HOW TO GROW

Select a site in full sun or partial shade with very rich soil that is constantly moist or wet. A site in a bog garden or along a pond or stream is ideal; globeflowers prefer heavy, clayey soil rather than sandy conditions. Globeflowers are best in areas with cool summers. In Zones 6 and 7, give them a site with shade during the hottest part of the day. Water regularly in dry weather. Cut the plants back after

Trollius × cultorum 'Golden Queen'

Tropaeolum majus 'Empress of India'

the first flush of flowers and feed them to encourage a second flush of flowers. To propagate, divide clumps in spring or fall or start from seeds.

T. × cultorum

t. × kul-TOR-um. HYBRID GLOBEFLOWER. A group of hybrid cultivars ranging from 2 to 3 feet in height and forming 2-foot-wide clumps. They bear 1- to 3-inch-wide flowers from spring to midsummer. 'Alabaster' bears creamy yellow flowers in spring. 'Earliest of All' has orange-yellow blooms in spring. 'Goldquelle', also sold as 'Gold Fountain', bears 3-inch-wide yellow blooms. 'Orange Princess' has 2¹/₂- to 3-inch orange blooms. 'Golden Queen' bears 2-inch-wide orange flowers on 2-foot-tall plants. 'Pritchard's Giant' has yellow blooms on 3-foot plants. **Zones 3 to 6.**

T. europaeus

t. yew-roh-PAY-uss. COMMON GLOBEFLOWER. A 2-foot-tall species that forms 2-foot-wide clumps and bears rounded, 2-inch-wide yellow flowers from early to midsummer. 'Superbus' bears an abundance of 4-inch-wide sulphur yellow blooms. **Zones 4 to 7.**

Tropaeolum

troh-pee-OH-lum. Nasturtium family, Tropaeolaceae.

The genus *Tropaeolum* contains from 80 to 90 species of annuals and perennials native from Mexico to Chile. The plants can be bushy, trailing, or climbing, and many have tuberous roots, which can be lifted for overwintering. Commonly called nasturtiums, they are grown for their showy, spurred, five-petaled flowers, usually in shades of red, scarlet, orange, yellow, or cream. The leaves are rounded or lobed and peltate, meaning the stem is attached near the center of the leaf, rather than on the edge.

In a confusing twist of nomenclature, nasturtium is the botanical name for watercress, *Nasturtium officinale*. Like watercress, *Tropaeolum* species bear edible leaves that have a peppery taste. The flowers are edible and also attract hummingbirds.

HOW TO GROW

While all *Tropaeolum* species grow in full sun, soil preferences vary. Plant common nasturtiums (*T. majus*) in poor, well-drained soil; rich soil yields foliage but few flowers. Give flame nasturtium (*T. speciosum*) well-drained, evenly moist soil that is rich in organic matter; it also will grow in partial shade. Plant the other species in well-drained, evenly moist soil of average fertility.

Tropaeolum species are best in areas with relatively cool summers and do not grow well in the hot, humid Southeast. Where hardy, grow the perennials outdoors. In the North, treat these plants as annuals or tender perennials. Sow seeds outdoors 1 week after the last spring frost date. Or sow indoors in individual pots 4 to 5 weeks before the last frost date at 55° to 65°F. Transplant with care.

Seeds of perennial species often germinate erratically. Plants also can be propagated by cuttings taken in spring or early summer to propagate plants for the garden, or in late summer to overwinter the plants. Double-flowered forms must be propagated by cuttings. Or propagate tuberous-rooted species by dividing the tubers in fall. Overwinter perennials by bringing pot-grown plants indoors and growing them in a sunny, cool (50° to 60°F) spot. Or dig the tubers in fall and store them in a frost-free spot, as you would dahlias. Train climbing types onto strings, trellises, shrubs, or other supports.

T. azureum

t. ah-ZUR-ee-um. A tender perennial climber, hardy from **Zone 9 south,** with palmate or palmately lobed leaves. Plants climb to 7 feet and bear short-spurred, pale blue, ¹/₂- to ³/₄-inch flowers in late spring. Warm-weather annual or tender perennial.

T. majus

t. MAY-juss. COMMON NASTURTIUM, INDIAN CRESS. A climbing annual with nearly round, wavy-margined leaves. Bears 2- to 2¹/₂-inch-wide, long-spurred flowers from summer to fall in shades of red, orange, or yellow. Both bushy and climbing cultivars are available; many are hybrids with other species and sometimes are listed as *T. nanum*. Whirlybird Series plants are bushy rather than climbing and grow 10 inches tall, bearing spurless flowers well above the foliage. Alaska Series plants reach 1 foot tall and bear leaves variegated with cream. Gleam Series plants are about 1¹/₂ feet tall and trail to 2 feet wide. 'Jewel of Africa' climbs to 8 feet and has leaves variegated with creamy white. 'Tip Top Mahogany' bears chartreuse leaves with mahogany flowers on 1-foot-tall plants. 'Empress of India' bears semidouble scarlet blooms on 1-foot-tall plants. Warm-weather annual.

T. peregrinum

t. peh-reh-GRY-num. CANARY VINE, CANARY CREEPER. A vigorous annual or tender perennial, hardy from **Zone 9 south,** that climbs to 12 feet in a single season. Leaves are lobed and grayish green. Bears yellow, 1-inch-wide flowers with fringed petals from summer to fall. Tender perennial or warm-weather annual.

T. polyphyllum

t. pah-lee-FILL-um. A trailing annual or tender perennial, hardy from **Zone 8 south,** with a fleshy, rhizomelike tuber and deeply lobed, blue-green leaves. Plants are 2 to 3 feet tall and spread to 3 feet. Bears spurred, 1¹/₂-inch-wide, deep yellow flowers over a long season in summer. Warm-weather annual or tender perennial.

T. speciosum

t. spee-see-OH-sum. FLAME FLOWER, FLAME NASTURTIUM. A tender climbing perennial, hardy from **Zone 8 south,** that climbs to 10 feet and has a fleshy rhizome. Bears palmate, dark green leaves and brilliant scarlet flowers from summer to fall. Warm-weather annual or tender perennial.

Tsuga

TSUE-gah. Pine family, Pinaceae.

This genus contains 14 species of trees from North America and Asia and has the smallest needles

Tropaeolum speciosum

Tsuga canadensis

and cones of any member of the pine family. Needles are short, flat, and fine-textured. They have two white bands on their undersides and are arranged on slender, flexible twigs. Cones ripen in autumn and resemble miniature pine cones. All species do best in a cool, moist climate and look less formal than many other evergreens in a garden or home landscape. Unfortunately, a pest introduced from Asia in 1924 has been slowly migrating through the Mid-Atlantic States and New England, devastating cultivated and native Canada hemlocks. All American species are susceptible to this pest, called the woolly adelgid, but the Japanese species are probably immune. A parasitic mite that preys on this pest may offer biological control. Otherwise, a properly timed horticultural oil spray can be used to control and prevent the adelgid. It must be applied so as to drench the tree and coat the undersides of the needles in late winter and again in early summer, to coincide with the pest's life cycle. A professional arborist may be needed to treat large trees.

HOW TO GROW
Plant in full to partial shade; these trees tolerate sun in a protected location where soil does not dry out. They need moist, well-drained, acid, humus-rich soil and are sensitive to drought, heat, air pollution, and drying wind. Mulch to keep soil cool and moist. Protect from wind. Remove multiple leaders on new plants that are grown as trees. Allow limbs to remain to the ground. May be thinned or sheared as a hedge. Highly susceptible to woolly adelgids.

T. canadensis
t. kan-uh-DEN-siss. CANADA HEMLOCK, EASTERN HEMLOCK. This elegant evergreen has wide-spreading, slightly pendu-

Tsuga canadensis

lous, horizontal branches that cloak the central trunk from the top of its nodding leader all the way to the ground, creating a soft-textured, refined pyramid that can grow to 75 feet tall and 30 feet wide in a garden setting. The blunt-tipped needles are $2/3$ inch long and shiny dark green or dark gray-green. They have two white stripes on their undersides and are arranged in two opposite rows along hairy, yellowish brown branchlets. Mature trees feature deeply furrowed, brown bark. The pretty cones are about $3/4$ inch around and resemble miniature pine cones, ripening to brown in autumn.

A beloved forest and landscape tree, Canada hemlock is perhaps the most fine-textured evergreen commonly planted in gardens and also one of the few conifers that thrive in shade. Use it in a cool, lightly shaded location for a screen or hedge or in a naturalistic site or border. It does not work well in a lawn unless it is planted in a mulched bed. From northeastern North America. **Zones 3 to 8.**

CULTIVARS AND SIMILAR SPECIES
Shrublike forms: Among more than 50 cultivars are 'Jeddeloh', hemispherical with a central depression, about 4 feet tall and 6 feet wide; 'Jervis', twiggy, dense, and irregular to about 2 feet; and 'Pendula' (Sargent's weeping hemlock), broadly spreading and about 12 feet tall. **Zones 3 to 7.**

Tsuga canadensis 'Jeddeloh'

'Albospica' grows into a small, compact tree with bright white new growth; it needs some afternoon shade. More attractive than 'Albospica' is 'Summer Snow,' which has dark green needles that contrast beautifully with its bright white new growth. 'Emerald Fountain' forms a narrow, rich green column with weeping branches. 'Emerald King' has rich green foliage all year. 'Golden Splendor' is a fast-growing form with golden needles. 'Pendula', which can be variable, is an upright tree with weeping branches. 'Westonigra' is a fast-growing, compact tree with exceptionally dark green foliage. *T. caroliniana* (Carolina hemlock), native to southeastern North America, has a more open-branched, compact shape than Canada hemlock; it grows to 50 feet tall, has $3/4$-inch-long needles arranged radially around reddish brown, hairy branchlets, and tolerates more heat and is less susceptible (but not immune) to woolly adelgids; **Zones 5 to 7.** *T. heterophylla* (western hemlock) is native to the Pacific Northwest and grows best in sites with moist, cool summers; **Zones 6 to 8.**

T. sieboldii
t. see-BOLE-dee-eye. SOUTHERN JAPANESE HEMLOCK. This broadly conical tree has a graceful, open shape and often multiple trunks. It grows to 50 feet tall and 25 feet wide. The shiny, dark green needles are about $3/4$ to 1 inch long and are broader than those of most other hemlocks. They have rounded, notched tips and are borne on waxy, yellowish brown branchlets. The attractive cones are about $1^1/4$ inches long. This tree is not widely grown in North America, but it is being used more often as a replacement for Canada hemlock because of its resistance to pests and greater tolerance of adverse growing conditions. From Japan. **Zones 5 to 8.**

Tulbaghia
tul-BAHG-ee-uh. Lily family, Liliaceae.

About 24 species, all native to tropical and southern Africa, belong to the genus *Tulbaghia*. They produce grassy to strap-shaped leaves that have a garlic- or onionlike odor, along with dainty umbels of starry, tubular flowers in lilac-purple or white.

T

Tulbaghia violacea

HOW TO GROW

Select a site in full sun and average to rich, well-drained soil. Where hardy, grow *Tulbaghia* species outdoors; in areas where they are marginally hardy, try a site against a south-facing wall for extra winter protection. In the North, grow them in containers either set on terraces or sunk to the rim in the soil. Water regularly in summer and feed pot-grown plants monthly. Gradually withhold water in fall, and keep them nearly dry over winter. Overwinter them in a bright, cool (40° to 50°F) spot, and water sparingly until active growth resumes in spring. Propagate by dividing the clumps or sowing seeds (germinate at 55° to 60°F). Repot or divide in late winter or early spring as necessary.

T. violacea

t. vee-oh-LAY-see-uh. SOCIETY GARLIC, PINK AGAPANTHUS. A clump-forming, 1¹/₂- to 2-foot-tall, tender perennial with linear, gray-green leaves. Bears small umbels of fragrant, ³/₄-inch-long, lilac flowers from midsummer to fall. 'Variegata,' or 'Silver Lace,' bears leaves striped in gray-green and cream. **Zones 7 to 10**; or grow as an annual.

Tulipa

TOO-lip-uh. Lily family, Liliaceae.

These classic spring-blooming bulbs are treasured for their showy flowers, which come in a wide range of colors, from bold deep reds, violet-purple, golden yellow, and orange to pastel mauve, pink, lavender, and white — everything except true blue. Many tulips feature bicolor blooms — red-and-white- or red-and-yellow-striped, for example — or flowers may have a contrasting eye, or center. The most familiar tulips have cup-shaped blooms, but bowl-shaped and double-flowered cultivars are also available, as well as selections with goblet- or star-shaped blooms. There also are tulips with fringed petal edges, ones with ruffled petals, and ones that bear several blooms per stem.

Like other plants in the lily family, the individual flowers consist of six petal-like tepals. Tulips grow from somewhat teardrop-shaped, tunicate bulbs and have basal leaves that usually are broadly oval and bluish or gray-green, although some species have strap-shaped or long, very narrow leaves.

There are about 100 species of tulips and hundreds of named cultivars, all of which have been organized into 15 divisions based on flower shape and origin. Catalogs and well-labeled nursery displays use these divisions to organize their offerings, and planting tulips from several divisions helps ensure you will have a variety of shapes and sizes of flowers to enjoy. In addition, bloom times vary from division to division — although not all cultivars in a division bloom at the same time and there is plenty of overlap. Still, with careful selection, it's possible to have tulips in bloom for 8 weeks or more in spring.

HOW TO GROW

Plant tulips where they will receive at least 5 hours of full sun daily and light shade for the rest of the day. Morning sun and afternoon shade is beneficial in the South, because it protects the flowers from heat. Rich, well-drained soil is best, although plants will bloom satisfactorily for a year or two in a wide range of well-drained soils.

For best growth, tulips require a cool, moist winter and a warm, dry summer. Most can be grown in Zones 3 to 8 but actually perform best in Zones 4 to 6. In the Southeast, summer heat and rain tend to diminish their performance. (Some cultivars are better performers in the South than others; a reputable garden center will stock good selections for your area.) In Zones 8 or 9 to 10, where the bulbs don't receive cold

Gardeners are often disappointed with tulips that bloom wonderfully well the first year, then gradually decline in size and numbers in succeeding years. In Zones 3 to 7, you can perennialize tulips by choosing the right bulbs and planting them properly.

Species tulips are known for behaving like perennials, but some hybrids can also give you good repeat performances. Look for cultivars in the following groups and experiment to see which work best for you:

Darwin Hybrid Tulips
Triumph Tulips
Kaufmanniana Tulips
Fosteriana Tulips
Greigii Tulips

The following species are good perennials:

Tulipa batalini
T. humilis
T. saxatilis
T. tarda

Plant the bulbs 8 to 10 inches deep, let the foliage ripen, and feed the bulbs annually. Choosing a site that is dry in summer after the flowers bloom will help your tulips live a long, healthy life.

enough temperatures in winter to bloom, buy precooled bulbs and treat them as annuals. *T. clusiana, T. saxatilis, T. sylvestris,* and *T. tarda* are species tulips that can be grown in southern zones and do not require a cold treatment to flower.

When buying tulips, look for fat, fleshy bulbs with no signs of mold or black, rotted blotches. The brown tunic should be on the bulb and intact. Avoid buying cheap bulbs, which may not have been stored or handled properly. This is especially important because the bulbs resent being exposed to temperatures above 70°F, both in the ground and any time they are stored. Storage at high temperatures reduces or destroys the quality of the bulbs and the flowers they produce.

Plant tulips in fall as soon as they are available — early fall in northern zones, toward early winter in the South. Dig the soil deeply at planting time, and work in plenty of organic matter such as compost or leaf mold. Also incorporate a balanced organic fertilizer into the soil. Deep soil preparation is important because the soil several inches below the bulbs needs to be improved and well drained. (Improving the soil around the bulbs doesn't benefit the roots, which emerge from the base of the bulbs.)

Set the bulbs with their bases at least 8 inches below the soil surface — 10 inches is better. This keeps them cool in summertime and discourages them from breaking up into lots of smaller nonflowering bulbs after the first year. If you are growing the bulbs as annuals, a depth of 5 or 6 inches is fine. Deep planting also makes it easy to fill in on top of the bulbs with annuals or shallow-rooted perennials.

For a planting that blooms uniformly at one time and at one height, excavate the entire bed and plant all the bulbs at the same

Tulipa 'Abba'

T

Tulipa 'Heart's Delight'

mainly from that species. The species bears creamy white flowers with a yellow base and tepals often streaked with rose-pink. Both species and cultivars bear single, cup- or bowl-shaped blooms that have a starry or waterlily-like appearance when fully open. The individual blooms range from 2 to 5 inches across, often feature a multicolored base, and are borne singly or in small clusters of two to five blooms. Kaufmanniana tulips are dependable perennials that bloom from very early to midspring and often feature handsome, mottled leaves. Plants usually range from 6 to 12 inches tall.

Cultivars include 'Ancilla', rose-red and soft pink on the outside and white with a yellow eye circled in red on the inside; 'Heart's Delight', red, rose-pink, and yellow blooms coupled with handsomely mottled leaves; 'Shakespeare', red with salmon tepal edges on the outside and salmon flushed with red on the inside with a yellow central blotch; 'Showwinner', bright red with a yellow base; and 'Stresa', red edged with yellow on the outside and yellow marked with red at the base on the inside. **Zones 3 to 8.**

Fosteriana Tulips (Division 13)

This division includes *T. fosteriana* and cultivars derived from that species. The species bears solitary, red, bowl-shaped flowers with a purple-black central blotch edged in yellow. Cultivars that fall in this division bear single, 5-inch-wide blooms in white, yellow, or red that have contrasting blotches or bases. Plants bloom in midspring and carry flowers on 8- to 26-inch-tall stems. Fosteriana tulips are reliable perennials in the garden. Included in this division are the classic, well-known Emperor cultivars, among them, 'Golden Emperor', yellow; 'Red Emperor', red with a black heart; 'Orange Emperor', orange with a yellow base; and 'White Emperor' and 'Purissima', both white with a creamy yellow base and heart. Other cultivars include 'Juan', orange flowers with a yellow base and attractively purple-mottled leaves; 'Solva', pinkish red flushed with pink; and 'Sweetheart',

creamy yellow brushed with creamy white along the edges of the tepals. **Zones 3 to 8.**

Greigii Tulips (Division 14)

This division includes *T. greigii* and cultivars derived from that species. While the species usually bears red flowers with a black blotch, the cultivars come in a range of shades from yellow to red, usually with a blotch or base and often with tepal edges marked with a contrasting color. Greigii tulips bear single, 4-inch-wide, bowl-shaped flowers in early to midspring on compact 6- to 12-inch-tall plants. They also feature leaves handsomely mottled or striped with purple and are reliable perennials.

Cultivars include 'Czar Peter', pinkish red tepals edged in white with burgundy-striped leaves; 'Cape Cod', yellow to apricot tepals flamed with red and purple-mottled leaves; 'Oratorio', watermelon to coral-pink flowers and purple-mottled leaves; 'Pinocchio', creamy white blooms marked with red flames and a bronzy heart atop heavily mottled leaves; 'Red Riding Hood', red blooms with a small black heart and leaves heavily mottled with purple; 'Sweet Lady', pink blooms blushed with apricot-pink and yellow-tinged bronze bases atop leaves striped with dark maroon; and 'Turkish Delight', red blooms that are creamy white inside with a central black blotch marked with red and yellow. **Zones 3 to 8.**

Miscellaneous Tulips (Division 15)

As the name of this division suggests, it contains a wide range of plants: all species tulips fall here,

as do hybrids that are not included in other divisions. Following is information on species tulips and their cultivars.

Tulip Species

T. acuminata

t. ah-kew-mih-NAH-tuh. A 16- to 18-inch-tall species with linear- to lance-shaped gray-green leaves. Bears solitary 4-inch-long flowers in midspring. Blooms are red or yellow streaked with red and have very narrow tepals with long pointed tips. **Zones 3 to 8.**

T. albertii

t. al-BER-tee-eye. A 6- to 8-inch-tall species that produces glaucous blue leaves and orange-red blooms in early spring with tepals that have a yellow-edged, black to purple blotch at the base. **Zones 6 to 8.**

T. altaica

t. al-TAY-ih-kuh. A 10- to 12-inch-tall species that blooms in midspring and bears cup-shaped, rich yellow flowers with pointed tepals that are tinged with red on the outside. **Zones 3 to 8.**

T. aucheriana

t. aw-sher-ee-AH-nuh. A 6- to 8-inch-tall species blooming in midspring. Bears starry, 3-inch-wide pink flowers that open flat and have a yellow to yellow-brown central blotch. Blooms are usually solitary but are sometimes borne in clusters of two or three. **Zones 4 to 8.**

T. bakeri

t. BAY-ker-eye. An 8- to 10-inch-tall species that spreads by runners and is very similar to *T. saxatilis*. Plants bear fragrant, star-shaped flowers in mid- to late spring that

Tulipa acuminata

Tulipa clusiana

are 2¹/₂ to 3 inches across and come in dark pink to purple-pink. Plants sold under this name are currently thought to be *T. saxatilis*. *See T. saxatilis.* **Zones 5 to 9.**

T. batalinii
t. bah-tah-LIN-ee-eye. A 4- to 8-inch-tall species with sickle-shaped gray-green leaves. Blooms in mid- to late spring and produces bowl-shaped, 3-inch-wide, pale yellow flowers marked with bronze or dark yellow inside. Cultivars include 'Apricot Jewel', apricot-orange blooms that are yellow on the inside; 'Bright Gem', with sulphur yellow blooms flushed with orange; 'Bronze Charm', yellow blooms flushed with bronze; and 'Red Gem', red blooms blushed with apricot pink. **Zones 3 to 8.**

T. biflora
t. by-FLOR-uh. Formerly *T. polychroma*. Diminutive 3- to 5-inch-tall species bearing gray-green leaves and starry, fragrant, 1¹/₂-inch-wide white flowers that are yellow at the base. Blooms are solitary or borne in clusters of two or three in early spring. **Zones 5 to 9.**

T. clusiana
t. kloo-see-AN-uh. LADY TULIP. Formerly *T. aitchisonii*. A 10- to 12-inch-tall species that has gray-green leaves and blooms in early to midspring. Bowl-shaped, 4-inch-wide flowers, borne singly or two to a stem, are starry shaped

once they are fully open. Blooms are white with a dark pink stripe on the outer tepals and marked with red at the base on the inside. *T. clusiana* var. *chrysantha* bears clusters of up to three yellow flowers with outer tepals tinged red or brown-purple on the outside. *T. clusiana* var. *chrysantha* 'Tubergen's Gem' bears yellow flowers with red outer tepals. **Zones 3 to 8.**

T. greigii
t. GREG-ee-eye. *See* Greigii Tulips.

T. hageri
t. HAH-ger-eye. An 8- to 10-inch tall species that blooms in early to midspring. Bears lance-shaped leaves and star-shaped 2¹/₂- to 3¹/₂-inch-wide blooms that are dull red with green flames and tepal tips and blue-black centers. Blooms are solitary or produced in clusters of up to four. 'Splendens' bears clusters of three to five flowers that are red flecked with green outside and copper- to bronze-red inside. **Zones 3 to 8.**

T. humilis
t. HEW-mill-iss. A 4- to 6-inch-tall species bearing gray-green linear leaves and starry, 3-inch-wide, crocuslike flowers in early spring. Blooms are rose-pink with a yellow base. Cultivars include 'Lilliput', with scarlet flowers that have violet bases; 'Persian Pearl', with magenta blooms that are yellow at the base and purple-pink inside; and 'Violacea', purple-red with a green-black base. **Zones 4 to 8.**

T. kaufmanniana
t. kawf-man-ee-AH-nuh. WATER-LILY TULIP. *See* Kaufmanniana Tulips.

T. kolpakowskiana
t. kole-pack-ow-skee-AH-nuh. A 6- to 8-inch-tall species bearing gray-green leaves and bowl-shaped, 1¹/₂- to 3-inch-wide flowers in early to midspring. Blooms are yellow with a red stripe on the outside and solid yellow inside. **Zones 3 to 8.**

T. linifolia
t. lih-nih-FOH-lee-uh. A 3- to 6-inch-tall species with linear, sickle-shaped leaves and red, 3-inch-wide, bowl-shaped blooms that have a black blotch at the base. Flowers open nearly flat on sunny days. Leaves are edged in red. **Zones 4 to 8.**

T. maximowiczii
t. maks-ih-moh-WICK-zee-eye. A 3- to 6-inch-tall species with linear, sickle-shaped leaves and red flowers that have a dark blue blotch at the center. Flowers open nearly flat on sunny days. **Zones 4 to 8.**

T. neustruevae
t. new-STROO-vee. A 3- to 4-inch-tall species that bears yellow crocuslike flowers in early spring that have outer tepals marked with greenish brown. **Zones 3 to 8.**

T. orphanidea
t. ore-fah-NID-ee-uh. An 8- to 10-inch-tall species that bears lance-shaped leaves, sometimes edged in maroon, and solitary or clusters of up to four red flowers in early to midspring that are marked with buff blushed with green or purple on the outside of the outer tepals. 'Flava' bears brilliant yellow flowers that shade to red at the tops of the tepals. The insides of the flowers are lemon yellow shading to garnet red. **Zones 5 to 8.**

T. polychroma
t. pah-lee-KRO-muh. An early spring–blooming 3- to 4-inch-tall tulip listed and sold as a separate species by some sources but currently thought to belong in *T. biflora*. The starry blooms, borne singly or in clusters of up to three, are white with a yellow center and have violet-purple at the tips of the tepals. *See T. biflora.* **Zones 5 to 9.**

T. praestans
t. PRAY-stanz. An 8- to 12-inch-tall species bearing bowl-shaped red-orange blooms in early spring. The 4- to 5-inch-wide flowers are

Tulipa humilis

T

Tulipa saxatilis 'Lilac Wonder'

Tweedia caerulea

borne singly or in clusters of up to five. A good perennializer where happy. 'Fusilier' bears brilliant red flowers. 'Unicum' bears red flowers and leaves edged in creamy white. **Zones 4 to 8.**

T. pulchella

t. pull-KEL-luh. A 10- to 12-inch-tall species bearing starry, 3-inch-wide flowers in early to midspring. Blooms are red to purple with blue-black central blotches and are solitary or sometimes carried in clusters of up to three. **Zones 4 to 8.**

T. saxatilis

t. saks-AH-tih-liss. An 8- to 10-inch-tall species that spreads by runners. Produces fragrant, star-shaped flowers in mid- to late spring that are 2¹/2 to 3 inches across. The pink to purplish pink blooms are carried singly or in

clusters of up to four. Plants sold as *T. bakeri* have darker pink to purple-pink blooms. 'Lilac Wonder' has lilac-pink to rose-purple flowers with yellow centers. Plants need poor soil, mild winters, and hot summers. Requires no cold period to bloom. **Zones 5 to 9 or 10.**

T. sprengeri

t. SPRING-er-eye. A 12- to 14-inch-tall species bearing linear leaves and solitary, goblet-shaped, 2- to 2¹/2-inch-long flowers in late spring. Blooms are red or orange-red and yellow at the base. **Zones 4 to 8.**

T. sylvestris

t. sil-VES-triss. Formerly *T. australis*. A 14- to 16-inch-tall stoloniferous species bearing linear leaves and starry, fragrant flowers in mid-spring that are yellow and 2¹/2 to 3 inches across. Blooms are solitary or borne in pairs. Plants do not require a cold period to bloom. **Zones 4 to 10.**

T. tarda

t. TAR-duh. Formerly *T. dasystemon*. A 4- to 6-inch-tall species with lance-shaped leaves and clusters of star-shaped, 2¹/2-inch-wide blooms borne in midspring. Blooms, carried in clusters of four to six, are golden yellow with white tips. **Zones 3 to 8.**

T. turkestanica

t. ter-kess-TAN-ih-kuh. A 6- to 10-inch-tall species bearing linear gray-green leaves and clusters of up to 12 starry, 1- to 2-inch-wide flowers in early to midspring. Blooms are white with yellow or orange at the center, have an un-

pleasant odor, and close at night and on cloudy days. **Zones 4 to 8.**

T. uruminensis

t. yew-room-ih-NEN-siss. A 4- to 6-inch-tall species with linear leaves and starry, yellow, 2- to 3-inch-wide flowers borne singly or in pairs. Blooms are flushed with cream, lilac, or red-brown on the outside and are borne in early spring. **Zones 4 to 8.**

T. vvedenskyi

t. veh-DEN-skee-eye. A 10- to 12-inch-tall species with lance-shaped gray-green leaves. Bears red blooms in early to midspring that have black or red blotches at the base. **Zones 5 to 8.**

T. whittallii

t. whih-TAHL-lee-eye. An 8- to 10-inch-tall species with lance-shaped leaves sometimes edged in red-purple. Bears star-shaped, 1¹/4- to 2¹/2-inch-wide, bronzy orange flowers in early to midspring. Blooms are carried singly or in clusters of up to four and have central black basal blotches sometimes edged in yellow. **Zones 5 to 8.**

T. wilsoniana

t. will-sun-ee-AH-nuh. A 4- to 6-inch-tall species with wavy-edged gray-green leaves blushed with red. Bears dark blood red flowers that have pointed outer tepals and a central black blotch. **Zones 5 to 8.**

Tweedia

TWEE-dee-uh. Milkweed family, Asclepiadaceae.

A single species belongs to this genus: *Tweedia caerulea*, which is na-

tive to Brazil and Uruguay. The plants are shrubby at the base but bear twining stems higher up on the plant and are grown for their clusters of sky blue flowers.

HOW TO GROW

Select a site in full sun with average to rich, evenly moist, well-drained soil. Plants tolerate poor, dry soil. Sow seeds 6 to 8 weeks before the last spring frost date at 60° to 70°F. Germination takes 2 to 3 weeks. Pinch seedlings once or twice to encourage branching and bushy growth. Move them to the garden a few weeks after the last frost date, once the weather has settled and temperatures remain above 40°F. Twining stems require a trellis or other support. Water regularly and feed monthly, especially container-grown specimens.

Grow *Tweedia* as an annual or a tender perennial overwintered indoors. Take cuttings in spring to propagate plants for the garden or in summer to bring them in for overwintering. To bring container-grown specimens indoors, dry them off gradually in fall and keep them on the dry side over winter. In winter, give plants a bright, cool (55° to 65°F) spot. Prune plants as necessary in early spring.

T. caerulea

t. see-RUE-lee-uh. Formerly *Oxypetalum caeruleum* and *Amblyopetalum caeruleum*. A 2- to 3¹/2-foot tender subshrub, hardy in **Zones 10 and 11**, with oblong to lance-shaped leaves that have heart-shaped bases. Bears three- to four-flowered clusters of five-petaled, ³/4- to 1-inch-wide flowers that are pinkish in bud and open to sky blue. Warm-weather annual or tender perennial.

Tulipa tarda

Ulmus

ULL-muss. Elm family, Ulmaceae.

This large genus includes trees from Europe, Asia, and North America. Leaves are oval or oblong and pointed, with double-toothed margins and many prominent veins. Fruits are winged nutlets that ripen soon after the inconspicuous flowers bloom. One species in particular, *U. americana* (America elm), was a beloved street tree that lined boulevards across America at the beginning of the twentieth century. In the 1930s, Dutch elm disease (DED), a fungus so named because Dutch researchers identified it, was accidentally introduced into New York on a shipment of logs from France. The fungus was spread to native trees by elm bark beetles (both an American and an introduced European species), and within 30 years most of the elms in the Northeast and Midwest were wiped out. To make matters worse, a new, more virulent strain of DED has recently appeared, killing the remaining trees at an even faster clip.

All American species of elms are highly susceptible to DED. European species are highly resistant, and Asian ones are usually immune. Plant geneticists at the National Arboretum and the Morton Arboretum have been selecting and hybridizing among these species with the goal of developing a tree that looks like our cherished elm while warding off DED and other serious pests. Several hybrids with great potential are now available, and more are on the way.

Meanwhile, existing American elms and other susceptible elms can be protected from DED with good sanitation. Pruning out infected limbs can sometimes stop the disease. Dead or dying trees should be removed immediately. The beetles that spread the fungus burrow between bark and wood, so logs from infected elm trees should be either stripped of their bark or burned, chipped, or buried to prevent further transmission. Never stack this wood in piles with the bark intact. Elms should be separated by at least 500 feet to stop beetles from moving from tree to tree, and a pesticide program to control beetles should be considered. The fungus also is spread by root contact, so wide spacing can prevent transmission via this method. Infected trees may be saved with a fungicide or biological serum injections.

HOW TO GROW

Select a site in full sun, with humus-rich, moist soil. Elms are quite drought tolerant, however, once established. They also tolerate acid or alkaline soil and urban conditions.

U. americana

u. ah-mare-eh-KAH-nuh. AMERICAN ELM, WHITE ELM. This elegant, vase-shaped, 80-foot-tall, 60-foot-wide native has a distinctive, picturesque shape. The tall, stout trunk splits into several leaders that grow upward, eventually arching out to create the tree's unmistakable fountainlike silhouette. The leaves emerge reddish in very early spring, mature to glossy dark green, and change to bright yellow in fall. They measure 3 to 6 inches long and have toothed edges and asymmetrical bases. Flowers are small and reddish, blooming very early, well before the leaves. Winged seeds are insignificant but can cause a litter problem on sidewalks and a weed seedling problem in beds. This tree's high, spreading canopy makes it ideal for shading streets because traffic can flow easily beneath its branches. It also makes an excellent lawn tree, but it has become a rarity in many parts of the country, especially the Northeast and Midwest, due to severe infestations of DED, elm yellows, and elm leaf beetles. Plant only disease-resistant cultivars or hybrids. From eastern and midwestern North America. Zones 2 to 9.

CULTIVARS AND SIMILAR SPECIES

Though not totally immune, the following cultivars and hybrids are highly resistant to DED. 'American Liberty' has an excellent vase shape but is susceptible to elm yellows. 'Delaware' is vigorous and wide spreading, growing 70 to 80 feet tall. 'New Harmony' was developed by the National Arboretum and is vase shaped and resistant to elm yellows and leaf beetles; Zones 5 to 9. 'Princeton' grows quickly to 60 to 70 feet tall, has a uniform vase shape, and resists elm leaf beetles. 'Urban' is vase shaped and tolerates compacted soil, restricted root space, and drought. 'Valley Forge' was developed by the National Arboretum, is vase shaped, and resists elm leaf beetles and elm yellows; Zones 5 to 9. *U. davidiana* is an Asian look-alike of American elm. *U. davidiana* var. *japonica* 'Discovery' has a strong, upright vase shape, grows to 40 feet tall and 35 feet wide, is very cold hardy, and resists elm leaf beetles; Zones 3 to 6. *U. wilsoniana* 'Prospector', a tough

Ulmus americana

Ulmus parvifolia

Ulmus glabra 'Camperdownii'

cultivar from the National Arboretum with the same vase shape as American elm, grows to 40 feet tall and resists DED, elm yellows, and elm leaf beetles; **Zones 4 to 9**. *U. × wilsoniana* 'Accolade', a hybrid from the Morton Arboretum with a good vase shape, grows to 70 feet tall and 40 to 50 feet wide; **Zones 4 to 7**. 'Danada' is similar, with red-tinted new growth and a graceful shape.

U. carpinifolia (U. minor)
u. kar-pin-eh-FOH-lee-uh. SMOOTH-LEAF ELM. This cold-hardy elm features a tall, straight main trunk and graceful, ascending, narrow branches that create a 70- to 90-foot-tall, 30-foot-wide pyramid. Leaves are more rounded than those on most elms. Up to 4 inches long, they are shiny dark green and have fine-toothed edges and unequal bases, giving the tree a fine-textured cloak. This is Europe's most common elm and makes a useful street or lawn tree. The species is somewhat susceptible to DED; the hybrids are more valuable in North America because they are highly disease resistant. From Europe, northern Africa, and western Europe.
Zones 5 to 9.
CULTIVARS
All of these hybrids resist DED and elm yellows. 'Frontier' is a 45-foot-tall hybrid with *U. parvifolia;* it has a narrow oval shape and long-

lasting, burgundy fall color; resistant to elm leaf beetles. 'Homestead' is a complex hybrid from the USDA that forms an arching, narrow oval growing to 55 feet tall. 'Pioneer' is a vigorous grower with a rounded canopy; grows to 50 feet tall; a hybrid with *U. glabra* from the USDA.

U. glabra 'Camperdownii'
u. GLAY-bruh. CAMPERDOWN ELM. This unusual specimen tree forms an umbrella-like canopy of slender, weeping branches that can reach to the ground. It matures at 20 to 25 feet tall and 18 to 20 feet wide. Leaves are large for an elm (6 to 8 inches long), lobed at the tips, and dark green. As the new leaves mature, they are joined by winged, pale yellow-green fruits that give the tree an enchanting two-tone appearance. Use this tree as a specimen to create a focal point in the garden. The silhouette is most striking when leafless in winter, so locate it where it can be seen from indoors. These trees are usually grafted, so remove any suckers that might arise from the rootstock. The trees are resistant to DED but susceptible to elm leaf beetles, which disfigure the leaves but don't destroy the tree. From eastern Europe, western Asia, and northern Africa. **Zones 4 to 7.**
SIMILAR SPECIES
U. alata 'Lace Parasol' ('Pendula') is a weeping tree with corky,

winged branches and an irregular, twisted branching pattern reminiscent of cut-leaved maple. It grows to 10 feet tall and 12 feet wide, is fairly resistant to DED and elm leaf beetles, and adapts to sandy or clayey soil. **Zones 6 to 9.**

U. parvifolia
u. par-veh-FOH-lee-uh. LACEBARK ELM, CHINESE ELM. Rounded or slightly vase shaped and growing to 50 feet tall and wide, this pest-resistant Asian tree is beautiful but not commonly grown. Some cultivars and hybrids closely resemble American elm in shape and are being promoted as substitutes for the native tree. Leaves are glossy dark green, measure 3 inches long, have finely toothed edges with equal bases, and are borne in dense clusters. They turn yellowish to reddish purple in late autumn in northern areas and are almost evergreen in the South. Colorful orange, tan, and gray bark cloaks the trunk and branches with a fine-textured patchwork that is especially attractive in winter. Use this large tree to cast shade in tough sites. It tolerates urban conditions, alkaline soil, and drought. Highly resistant to DED, elm leaf beetles, and Japanese beetles. **Zones 5 to 9.**
CULTIVARS
'Allee' has a tall vase shape, growing to 50 feet tall. 'Athena' is a highly recommended, drought-

tolerant, dense, rounded tree that reaches 50 feet tall; shiny, dark green leaves and unusual burgundy fall color; very colorful flaking bark; **Zones 4 to 9**. 'Drake' has almost evergreen leaves and grows to 35 feet tall. 'Dynasty' is a hybrid with a strong vase shape and red fall color. 'Elsmo' is fast growing, with a rounded vase shape, and resists elm yellows. 'Emerald Vase' grows to 70 feet tall and closely resembles American elm. 'King's Choice' is similar to American elm, with furrowed bark. 'Milleken' is rounded and spreading, reaching 50 feet tall and wide, with colorful bark. 'Pathfinder' grows broadly upright to 50 feet tall and has glossy yellow-green leaves, reddish fall color, and especially colorful bark.

U. pumila
u. poo-MILL-uh. SIBERIAN ELM, CHINESE ELM. This tough, drought-resistant, cold-hardy, fast-growing, disease-resistant tree has an upright oval or vase shape and matures to 50 to 70 feet tall and 35 to 50 feet wide. The 3-inch-long leaves are oval or lance shaped, with toothed margins and equal bases. It makes a useful tree in shelterbelts and reclamation projects in the cold, dry regions of the Plains and Mountain States. It tolerates cold, heat, drought, and urban conditions but is susceptible to elm leaf beetles. Despite its many assets, it is weak wooded and drops a lot of litter. From Korea, China, and Siberia.
Zones 2 to 9.
CULTIVARS
'Cathedral' is an attractive, disease-resistant hybrid with *U. japonica* that resembles American elm. **Zones 4 to 7.**

Ursinia
ur-SIH-nee-uh. Aster family, Asteraceae.

Commonly called African daisies, *Ursinia* species are annuals, perennials, or subshrubs grown for their showy, daisylike flowers.

u

The 40 species in the genus are found growing in dry grasslands, mostly in South Africa, but also in Namibia, Botswana, and Ethiopia. The leaves are usually cut or divided in a fernlike fashion and often are aromatic. The flower heads are borne on tall stems above the foliage, usually singly but sometimes in small clusters. They come in shades of yellow, red, or orange. The flowers close at night and also tend to close during overcast weather.

HOW TO GROW

Select a site in full sun with poor to average, light, very well drained soil. Plants are drought-tolerant. They do not grow well in heat and humidity, so in areas with hot summers, start them early enough to bloom before hot weather arrives, then pull them up and replace them when they begin to die out. Sow seeds indoors 6 to 8 weeks before the last spring frost date at 55° to 60°F. Germination takes 2 to 4 weeks. Or sow outdoors after the last frost. Deadhead to prolong the bloom season. Plants need staking, especially in rich soil. The species listed here is an annual, but perennial species are hardy in **Zones 10 and 11**. Use *Ursinia* species in beds and borders as well as in containers.

U. anthemoides

u. an-them-OY-deez. A 1- to 1¹/₂-foot-tall annual with aromatic, deeply cut leaves and 2¹/₂-inch-wide daisies in summer. Flowers are yellow-orange with purple centers. Warm-weather annual.

Uvularia

yew-view-LAIR-ee-uh. Lily family, Liliaceae.

Commonly known as merry bells or bellworts, *Uvularia* species are spring-blooming wildflowers native to eastern North America. Five species belong to the genus, all rhizomatous perennials with pendent, bell-shaped flowers consisting of six tepals. The blooms are carried on erect branched or unbranched stems clothed with lance-shaped leaves. Both species listed here bear perfoliate leaves.

HOW TO GROW

Select a site in partial to full shade with rich, moist, well-drained soil. Mulch with compost or chopped leaves in spring. Water during dry weather. Plants spread by rhizomes to form handsome clumps with time, and they can grow for

Ursinia anthemoides

years without needing division. Propagate by dividing the clumps in spring or fall or by sowing seeds.

U. grandiflora

u. gran-dih-FLOR-uh. LARGE MERRYBELLS, GREAT MERRYBELLS. A clumping 1- to 1¹/₂-foot-tall perennial that spreads to about 1 foot. Bears yellow to orange-yellow 2-inch-long flowers, either singly or in pairs, in mid- to late spring. The flowers of this species have few, if any, granules inside (see *U. perfoliata*), stamens that are longer than styles, and leaves with downy undersides. **Zones 3 to 9.**

U. perfoliata

u. per-foh-lee-AH-tuh. PERFOLIATE BELLFLOWER, STRAWBELL. A 1- to 2-foot-tall species with 1- to 1¹/₂-inch-long pale yellow flowers in spring. The flowers of this species have orange granules inside, stamens shorter than styles, and leaves that are smooth underneath. **Zones 4 to 8.**

Uvularia grandiflora

U

V

Vaccinium

vaks-SIN-ee-um. Heath family, Ericaceae.

A genus of 450 deciduous and evergreen shrubs and trees primarily from the Northern Hemisphere, usually cultivated for their edible fruits. Breeders are just beginning to develop plants with greater ornamental potential, stressing their usually white, urn-shaped flowers and colorful fall foliage.

HOW TO GROW
These shrubs must have acid soil (pH 4.5 to 5.5) that retains moisture but drains well; a peat-sand mix is excellent. Growing in sun or partial shade, they make a handsome hedge and mix well in a border with other acid-lovers. Plant more than one cultivar for best pollination. Prune lightly after fruiting. Propagate from cuttings.

V. ashei

v. ASH-ee-eye. RABBITEYE BLUEBERRY. A deciduous southeastern U.S. native growing upright 8 to 10 feet tall, similar to the better-known highbush blueberry but better suited to southern gardens. **Zones 8 to 9.**

V. corymbosum

v. kor-im-BOH-sum. HIGHBUSH BLUEBERRY. Upright and many branched, 6 to 12 feet high and as wide, with lustrous often blue-green leaves turning bronze, orange, reddish, and purple in fall. Racemes of pink-tinged white flowers that are urn shaped and bloom in midspring, followed by the blue-black edible fruits. **Zones 3 to 7.**

Vaccinium corymbosum

Vancouveria

van-coh-VAIR-ee-uh. Barberry family, Berberidaceae.

Close relatives of epimediums, *Vancouveria* species are perennial wildflowers native to western North America. Three species belong to the genus, all rhizomatous, spring-blooming perennials that form handsome mounds of delicate-looking, fernlike foliage. The leaves are twice or thrice divided into rounded, shallowly lobed leaflets. Blooms have 6 to 9 sepals that drop quickly once the flowers open, plus 6 reflexed petals and 12 petal-like sepals that are reflexed like the true petals.

HOW TO GROW
Select a site in partial shade with rich, evenly moist, well-drained soil. Water during dry weather. Mulch annually with chopped leaves or compost to replenish soil and retain moisture. Propagate by dividing the clumps in spring or fall.

V. hexandra

v. hecks-AN-druh. VANCOUVERIA, AMERICAN BARRENWORT. Formerly known as *Epimedium hexandra*. A 10- to 14-inch-tall woodland wildflower native to the Pacific Northwest that forms 1-foot-wide clumps of fine-textured leaves. Bears white flowers in spring. A slow-spreading ground cover for shade. **Zones 5 to 7.**

Vaccinium corymbosum

Veltheimia

vel-THY-mee-uh. Lily family, Liliaceae.

Veltheimia species are tender, bulbous perennials that, unlike many bulbs, are grown for their handsome leaves as well as their flowers. Two species belong here, both native to South Africa. They produce rosettes of thick, strap-shaped leaves with wavy margins. Dense, rounded clusters of flowers — somewhat resembling those of red-hot pokers (*Kniphofia* spp.) — are carried on erect stalks above the leaves. Individual flowers are pendent and tubular with six small lobes at the top.

HOW TO GROW
Select a spot in full sun with average, well-drained soil. A spot with shade during the hottest part of the day helps protect the flowers. They can be grown outdoors year-round only in mild climates (Zones 10 and 11, or to Zone 9 with winter protection) that offer dry conditions when the plants are dormant in summer. To grow them outdoors, plant the bulbs in fall with the neck above the soil surface. Where they are marginally hardy, look for a protected, south-facing site and mulch the plants heavily in fall with evergreen boughs, salt hay, coarse leaves, or pine needles.

Elsewhere, grow them in containers — they make outstanding container plants, growing indoors from fall to spring, when they bloom reliably. Pot the bulbs in fall, setting them with the tops about halfway out of the soil in pots that allow at least 1 inch on all sides. These are not tropical plants, and they are best kept over winter in a spot where nighttime temperatures range between 50° and 55°F. Water very carefully until leaves appear, then keep the soil evenly moist but never wet. Feed container-grown plants every few

Vancouveria hexandra

Veltheimia bracteata

weeks with a balanced fertilizer. Once leaves begin to turn yellow — generally by midsummer — gradually withhold water until the leaves die back completely. Rest plants for at least two months by keeping the soil completely dry. Resume watering in fall.

Plants are happiest when their roots and bulbs are left undisturbed, and plants growing in the ground thrive for years without needing to be divided. Repot container-grown plants in late summer or fall only if they become overcrowded. Propagate by separating offsets in late summer or early fall or by seeds. *Veltheimia* species also can be propagated by leaf cuttings: pull off entire mature leaves and root them in sand or vermiculite.

V. bracteata

v. brack-tee-AH-tuh. Formerly *V. viridifolia.* A vigorous 1¹/₂-foot-tall species with rosettes of glossy, strap-shaped 12- to 14-inch-long leaves with wavy margins. Bears dense rounded racemes of tubular, 1¹/₂-inch-long, pinkish purple flowers in spring. **Zones 10 and 11; to Zone 9 with winter protection.**

Veratrum

ver-AH-trum. Lily family, Liliaceae.

Commonly called false hellebores, *Veratrum* species are vigorous perennials that produce handsome clumps of bold, pleated, broadly ovate to nearly round leaves with prominent veins. They produce erect panicles of small, densely packed, starry to bell-shaped flowers in summer. Blooms may be greenish, white, reddish, brown, or nearly black. About 45 species belong to the genus, all of which are perennials that grow from stout, poisonous black rhizomes. The leaves and seeds are poisonous as well.

HOW TO GROW

Select a site in partial shade with deep, very rich, moist but well-drained soil. Plants tolerate full sun in constantly moist soil, but in areas with warm summers, select a site with shade during the hottest part of the day. Water as necessary during dry weather; if the soil dries out, the edges of the leaves become scorched and crisp. Propagate by dividing plants in early spring or fall.

V. viride

v. VEER-ih-day. INDIAN POKE. A 2- to 6-foot-tall perennial native to North America that spreads to about 2 feet. Bears 2-foot-tall panicles of starry green to greenish

Veratrum viride

yellow flowers from early to midsummer. **Zones 3 to 8.**

Verbascum

ver-BAHS-kum. Figwort family, Scrophulariaceae.

Commonly known as mulleins, *Verbascum* species produce erect, spirelike bloom stalks covered with small flowers that have a short, tubular base and five spreading lobes or petals. About 360 species belong to this genus, and most are biennials, although the genus also contains some annuals, perennials, and subshrubs. Most species have hairy to woolly leaves borne in a large rosette at the base of the plant. Mulleins are native from Europe to northern Africa and Asia and are also widely naturalized in North America.

HOW TO GROW

Select a site in full sun with poor to average, well-drained soil. Neutral to slightly alkaline pH is ideal. Established plants tolerate dry soil. The species listed here are grown as biennials or perennials. Plants have deep taproots and are happiest if left undisturbed once planted. Propagate by division in spring, by taking root cuttings in late fall or winter, or by sowing seeds. Plants self-sow.

V. chaixii

v. SHAKE-see-eye. NETTLE-LEAVED MULLEIN. A 3-foot-tall perennial forming a low, 1¹/₂-foot-wide rosette of 2- to 10-inch-long gray-green leaves. Bears narrow, branched panicles of densely packed, 1-inch-wide yellow flowers from mid- to late summer.

V. chaixii f. *album* bears white flowers with mauve-purple eyes. **Zones 4 to 8.**

V. olympicum

v. oh-LIMP-ih-kum. OLYMPIC MULLEIN. A 6-foot-tall perennial with a 2-foot-wide rosette of silvery white woolly leaves and stems. Bears branched, candelabra-like bloom stalks that reach 3 feet in length with 1¹/₄-inch-wide golden yellow blooms from early to late summer. Plants often die after flowering. **Zones 6 to 8.**

Verbena

ver-BEE-nuh. Vervian family, Verbenaceae.

Some 250 species of annuals, perennials, and subshrubs, both hardy and tender, belong to the genus *Verbena.* Most are native to the Americas, although a few species are found in southern Europe. They have square stems and usually opposite leaves that range from toothed to deeply lobed. Their small flowers have a slender tube at the base and an abruptly flared and flattened face that has five lobes, or "petals." Blooms are carried in showy spikes or clusters over a long season and come in shades of purple, violet, pink, cream, scarlet, and magenta.

HOW TO GROW

Select a site in full sun to light shade with poor to average, well-drained sandy or loamy soil. Shade during the hottest part of the day is best in the South. Plants tolerate both heat and drought. *V. hastata* will grow in evenly moist, well-drained soil. Trim back creeping

Verbascum chaixii f. *album*

Verbena canadensis

species to control their spread and keep them bushy. Deadhead or shear the plants after the main flush of flowers to encourage rebloom. Dig and divide the plants in spring if they outgrow their space or die out in the centers of the clumps, or for propagation. Or propagate by taking cuttings in late summer or by sowing seeds. Flowers will attract hummingbirds and butterflies.

V. bonariensis

v. bah-nair-ee-EN-siss. Formerly *V. patagonica*. A tender, shrubby perennial that reaches 6 feet in southern areas but is about 3 feet tall in the North. The lance-shaped leaves are borne at the base of the plant and topped by erect, branching stems with 2-inch-wide clusters of $^1/_4$-inch-wide purple flowers from midsummer to fall. **Zones 7 to 11**, or grow as a warm-weather annual.

V. canadensis

v. kan-uh-DEN-siss. Rose Verbena, Rose Vervian. A $^1/_2$- to 1$^1/_2$-foot-tall perennial native to North America that spreads to 3 feet by stems that root where they

Verbena bonariensis

touch the soil. Bears dense, rounded, 2$^1/_2$-inch-wide clusters of rose-pink flowers in early summer and then blooms sporadically until fall if spent flowers are removed. 'Homestead Purple' is a mildew-resistant, purple-flowered cultivar. **Zones 6 to 10**.

V. hastata

v. hahs-TAH-tuh. Blue Vervain. A 3- to 5-foot-tall perennial with stiff, branched, 2- to 4-inch-wide clusters of flowers from early sum-

mer to early fall in shades of violet, purple, and sometimes white. **Zones 3 to 7**.

V. × hybrida

v. × HY-brih-duh. Common Garden Verbena. Also listed as *V. × hortensis*. A tender 1$^1/_2$-foot-tall perennial, hardy from Zone 9 south, that can be erect and bushy or mat-forming, depending on the cultivar. Leaves are oblong and toothed. Flowers are borne in rounded, 3-inch-wide clusters

from summer to fall. Individual flowers are $^1/_2$ to 1 inch wide and come in violet, purple-blue, scarlet, rose, wine red, and white, most with a white eye. Some cultivars are fragrant. 'Peaches and Cream' bears pastel apricot and salmon flowers on 9-inch-tall plants. Romance Series and Novalis Series bear flowers in a range of colors on 10-inch-tall plants. **Zones 9 and 10**, or grow as a warm-weather annual.

V. rigida

v. RIH-jih-duh. Vervain. Also listed as *V. venosa*. A 1$^1/_2$- to 2-foot-tall tender perennial, with oblong, toothed leaves and loose, 2-inch-wide clusters of fragrant, purple or magenta, $^1/_4$-inch-wide flowers. **Zones 8 to 10**, or grow as a warm-weather annual.

V. tenuisecta

v. ten-yew-ih-SECK-tuh. Moss Verbena, Cut-leaf Verbena. A 1$^1/_2$-foot-tall annual or tender perennial, with aromatic, three-lobed leaves and 3-inch-wide clusters of flowers in lavender, mauve, purple, lilac-blue, and white from summer to fall. 'Alba' bears white flowers on 6-inch plants. **Zones 8 to 10**, or grow as a warm-weather annual.

Vernonia

ver-NOH-nee-uh. Aster family, Asteraceae.

Vernonia is a vast genus containing about 1,000 species of annuals, perennials, vines, subshrubs, shrubs, and trees. Many of the species that belong here are tropical or subtropical, but about 19 species of fall-blooming herbaceous perennials are hardy and native to North America. The perennial species have erect stems clothed in simple leaves that are either toothed or toothless. They bear large, branched, somewhat rounded flower clusters that are made up of buttonlike flower heads in shades of purple, violet, reddish pink, and sometimes white. The individual flower heads consist of small tubular disk florets; they lack ray florets, or "petals."

HOW TO GROW

Select a site in full sun with average, evenly moist, well-drained soil. Plants tolerate drought. *V. noveboracensis* also grows naturally in damp to wet soil. Cutting the stems back hard once or twice

Verbena × hybrida

Vernonia noveboracensis

Veronicastrum virginicum

early in the season encourages branching and keeps plants shorter and more compact. Clumps benefit from being divided every 3 or 4 years. Propagate by division in spring or fall or by seeds.

V. noveboracensis

v. noh-vay-bore-ah-SEN-siss. IRON-WEED. An East Coast native wildflower ranging from 3 to 7 feet in height and forming 2- to 3-foot-wide clumps. From late summer to fall, bears 6- to 8-inch-wide flower clusters consisting of many reddish purple, ^{1}/$_2$-inch-wide flower heads. **Zones 5 to 9.**

Veronica

ver-AH-nih-kuh. Figwort family, Scrophulariaceae.

Best known as speedwells, *Veronica* species are vigorous, easy-to-grow plants that offer flowers in a rich palette of colors, including true blue, violet-blue, pink, and white. The genus contains about 250 species of annuals, perennials, and a few subshrubs native primarily to Europe. All bear linear to lance-shaped or rounded leaves and showy bottlebrush-like spikes of flowers. The individual blooms are tiny — from ^{1}/$_4$ to ^{1}/$_2$ inch wide. While the most popular speedwells are upright plants, some low-growing, mat-forming species are useful as ground covers or rock garden plants. Most speedwells are quite vigorous, though still well behaved enough for the garden, but creeping speedwell (*Veronica filiformis*), a mat-forming, 2-inch-tall species with pale blue flowers, becomes a serious weed in gardens and lawns.

HOW TO GROW

Plant speedwells in full sun or partial shade and average to rich soil that is moist but well drained. Plants will not tolerate constantly moist conditions, especially in winter, but since they are fairly shallow rooted they also are not particularly drought tolerant. Water during dry weather. Taller-growing speedwells may need staking — very rich soil increases the likelihood they will flop. Cut plants back after they flower, as some species may rebloom. Most benefit from being divided regularly — about every 3 or 4 years. Propagate by dividing the clumps in spring or fall, by taking cuttings in late spring or early summer, or by sowing seeds.

V. austriaca ssp. teucrium

v. aw-stree-ACK-uh ssp. TOO-cree-um. HUNGARIAN SPEEDWELL.

Veronica longifolia

Formerly *V. teucrium* and *V. latifolia*. A ^{1}/$_2$- to 2-foot-tall species that spreads to 2 feet. Bears rich, deep blue flowers in 4- to 6-inch-long spikes from late spring to early summer. 'Crater Lake Blue', from 1 to 1^1/$_2$ feet tall, bears intensely blue flowers in early summer. **Zones 3 to 8.**

V. gentianoides

v. jen-shan-OY-deez. GENTIAN SPEEDWELL. A ^{1}/$_2$- to nearly 2-foot-tall species that forms dense mats of foliage about 1^1/$_2$ feet wide. Bears loose 10-inch-long spikes of pale blue to white flowers in late spring to early summer. **Zones 4 to 8.**

V. longifolia

v. lahn-jih-FOH-lee-uh. LONG-LEAVED SPEEDWELL. A 2- to 4-foot-tall species that spreads to 2 feet. Bears dense 10- to 12-inch-

long clusters of small lilac-blue flowers in late summer and early fall. 'Icicle' bears white flowers, and 'Rosea' has pink blooms. 'Blauriesen', sometimes sold as 'Foerster's Blue', bears deep blue flowers. **Zones 3 to 8.**

V. prostrata

v. prahs-TRAH-tuh. HAREBELL SPEEDWELL. Low-growing 3- to 6-inch-tall species that spreads to 1^1/$_2$ feet. Produces short spikes of starry blue flowers in late spring or early summer. 'Heavenly Blue' bears intensely blue flowers on 3-inch plants. **Zones 5 to 8.**

V. spicata

v. spy-KAH-tuh. SPIKE SPEEDWELL. A 1- to 3-foot-tall species that spreads as far. Bears dense, foot-long spikes of flowers from early to late summer in shades of purple, blue, pink, and white. 'Blue Charm' bears pale lavender-blue flowers on 3-foot plants. 'Red Fox', also sold as 'Rotfuchs', has deep pink flowers and reaches 1 foot. 'Icicle' bears white flowers on 2-foot plants. 'Goodness Grows' bears dark violet-blue flowers on 1- to 1^1/$_2$-foot plants. Woolly speedwell (*V. spicata* ssp. *incana*, formerly *V. incana*) features spike-like flowers borne over densely hairy gray-green leaves. Woolly speedwell does not do well in areas with hot, wet summers; give it especially well drained conditions and avoid getting the leaves wet when watering. **Zones 3 to 8.**

V. 'Sunny Border Blue'

A 1^1/$_2$- to 2-foot-tall hybrid that spreads to 1 foot or more and bears showy, violet-blue, 7-inch-long spikes of flowers from early summer to late fall. **Zones 4 to 8.**

Veronicastrum

ver-ah-nih-KAHS-trum. Figwort family, Scrophulariaceae.

Two species belong to this genus in the figwort family, one native to Siberia and the other to North America. Both are perennials with whorls of simple, toothed leaves and spikes of small flowers that resemble those of speedwells (*Veronica* species). The individual blooms have a long slender tube at the base that opens into flared lobes, or "petals." (*Veronica* species have short-tubed flowers with petal lobes that are longer than the tube, while *Veronicastrum* flowers have a tube longer than the petal lobes.) The botanical name marks this resemblance: it is derived from the name *Veronica* and the suffix -*astrum*, which indicates an incomplete resemblance.

HOW TO GROW
Select a site in full sun to partial shade with average to rich, moist soil. Plants usually have a laxer habit in shade and need staking. Water in dry weather, and feed annually. Divide clumps every 4 years or so to keep them from becoming overcrowded. Propagate by division in spring or fall, by cuttings taken from nonflowering stem tips in early summer or by sowing seeds.

V. virginicum

v. vir-JIH-nih-kum. CULVER'S ROOT, CULVER'S PHYSIC. Formerly *Veronica virginica*. Robust 4- to 6-foot-tall perennial native to North America that forms 2- to 4-foot-wide clumps. From midsummer to early fall, bears fluffy, bottlebrush-like racemes of densely packed, 1/4-inch-long flowers that can be white or pinkish or pale bluish purple. Zones 3 to 8.

Viburnum

vy-BURN-um. Honeysuckle family, Caprifoliaceae.

A genus of 150 species of deciduous to evergreen shrubs and trees from northern temperate zones, with a few from Southeast Asia and South America. Many are garden worthy for their fragrant flower clusters, ornamental fruits, colorful fall foliage, or, often, a combination of these qualities. The species listed here are deciduous unless otherwise noted.

HOW TO GROW
Most viburnums are easy to grow given slightly acid, moisture-retentive, but well-drained soil in sun to partial shade. They are generally not wind tolerant. Depending on size and habit, they are excellent for naturalizing, hedges, massing, shrub borders, or as specimens. Prune only to restrict size or remove suckers. Propagate from semiripe cuttings in summer.

V. acerifolium

v. ay-ser-ih-FOH-lee-um. MAPLE-LEAF VIBURNUM. An eastern U.S. native growing to 6 feet tall and 4 feet wide. Suckering to form thickets, it gets its common name from its three-lobed, 4-inch leaves that turn reddish purple in autumn. Creamy flowers bloom in flat-topped terminal clusters in late spring, followed by black elliptical, persistent fruits. Tolerates shade and drought. Zones 4 to 8.

V. × burkwoodii 'Mohawk'

v. × burk-WOOD-ee-eye. BURK-WOOD VIBURNUM CULTIVAR. An upright compact shrub that grows to 7 feet high and wide with rough leaves that turn orange-red to reddish purple in autumn. In early to midspring, dark pink flower buds open to domed clusters of tubular white, intensely clove-scented flowers. Semievergreen in the South. A recipient of the Pennsylvania Horticultural Society Gold Medal. Zones 5 to 8.

V. carlesii

v. kar-LEE-see-eye. KOREAN SPICE VIBURNUM. A compact shrub that grows slowly to about 6 feet tall and wide with leaves that may turn red in fall. In midspring, pink buds open to 1/2-inch, white, intensely fragrant flowers in domed clusters, followed by red fruits that turn black. Zones 5 to 8.

V. 'Cayuga'

A deciduous shrub that grows to 5 feet or taller, with pink buds that open midspring to waxy white, beginning from one side of a rounded cluster. Slightly fragrant. Zones 5 to 8.

V. 'Conoy'

An evergreen growing 4 to 5 feet tall and 7 feet wide, with small, shiny, leathery leaves that sometimes bronze. Red buds open to white clusters of up to 70 flowers in midspring, followed in late summer by red fruits that turn black and remain for many weeks.

Gardeners who want to grow native plants will find a number of attractive species among the viburnums, including the following:

> *Viburnum acerifolium,* mapleleaf viburnum, native to the eastern U.S.
> *V. dentatum,* arrowwood viburnum, eastern U.S.
> *V. lantanoides,* hobblebush, Maine to Georgia
> *V. lentago,* nannyberry, northeastern states south to Georgia and Mississippi
> *V. nudum* var. *cassinoides,* witherod viburnum, Canada to Minnesota, south to Florida
> *V. opulus* var. *americanum,* American cranberrybush, Canada and northern states
> *V. prunifolium,* blackhaw viburnum, eastern U.S.

A 1997 winner of the Pennsylvania Horticultural Society Gold Medal. Zones 7 to 8; will survive as a deciduous shrub in Zone 6.

V. dentatum

v. den-TAY-tum. ARROWWOOD VIBURNUM. A suckering, spreading shrub native to much of the eastern United States, with toothed dark green leaves that turn yellow, red, or purple-red in autumn. The late-spring flowers are white with prominent yellow stamens in flat-topped clusters, followed by blue-black fruits that attract birds. The species can grow more than 10 feet wide and tall, but compact selections are being introduced. Zones 3 to 8.

V. dilatatum

v. dil-ih-TAY-tum. LINDEN VIBURNUM. East Asian species growing to about 9 feet tall and 6 feet wide, with toothed leaves that turn dark red or bronze in fall. Cream-colored flowers bloom profusely in 4-inch flat clusters in mid- to late spring. Bright red fruits last from early to late fall. Cultivars include 'Erie', a Pennsylvania Horticultural Society award winner, with yellow, orange, and red fall foliage and red berries persisting as coral; and 'Iroquois', with thick leaves, heavy flowering, and large fruits. Zones 5 to 7.

V. 'Eskimo'

Dense, semievergreen that grows to 5 feet tall and wide with shiny dark green leaves. White "snowballs" of more than 100 cream-colored florets tinged with pink open in midspring, followed in late summer by elliptical dark red fruits that turn black. Another Pennsylvania Horticultural Society award winner. Zones 6 to 8.

V. × juddii

v. × JUD-ee-eye. SPICE VIBURNUM. This hybrid grows 6 to 8 feet tall. In midspring, white snowball flowers tinged with pink invite gardeners out to sample

Viburnum × *burkwoodii* 'Mohawk'

Viburnum opulus 'Roseum'

Viburnum dilatatum 'Erie'

their fragrance or snip some samples to bring indoors. **Zones 5 to 8**.

V. lantana 'Mohican'

v. lan-TAN-uh. WAYFARING TREE CULTIVAR. Deciduous shrub that grows to 7 feet tall and 9 feet wide with thick, oval 4-inch leaves. Cream-colored flowers bloom in flat-topped clusters as leaves emerge in midspring, followed in late summer by yellow berries that turn red then black, with all colors in a single cluster. Tolerates some drought and alkalinity. **Zones 4 to 7**.

V. lantanoides

v. lan-tan-OY-deez. HOBBLEBUSH. Native from Maine down through the mountains of Georgia, this species grows to 6 (rarely 12) feet tall, with drooping outer branches that may take root. Toothed leaves to 8 inches long turn wine red in fall. Lacy white flower clusters in

mid- to late spring are followed by red berries that turn purple-black. **Zones 4 to 7**.

V. lentago

v. len-TAH-goh. NANNYBERRY. Native from the Northeast into Georgia and Mississippi, nannyberry is a large shrub or small tree that opens and arches to 15 feet or taller and about 10 feet wide, with finely toothed glossy green leaves, sometimes coloring red in fall. Creamy white flowers in flat clusters bloom midspring, followed by $1/2$-inch fruits that are deep pink or somewhat yellow before turning blue-black. Good for attracting birds. **Zones 3 to 7**.

V. macroencephalum

v. mack-roh-en-SEF-ah-lum. CHINESE SNOWBALL VIBURNUM. A rounded shrub ranging from deciduous to evergreen and

from 8 feet to more than 15 feet tall. In mid- to late spring it bears white flowers in balls up to 8 inches across. **Zones 6 to 10**.

V. nudum var. cassinoides

v. NOO-dum var. kass-in-OY-deez. WITHEROD VIBURNUM. Native to moist habitats from Canada to Minnesota and south into Florida, this dense rounded shrub can exceed 10 feet but usually grows about 6 feet tall and wide. New leaves emerge bronze and in fall may be dark red, orange-red, or purple. Midsummer flowers are white in flat clusters to 5 inches across, followed by fruits that turn green, then pink, red, blue, and black, often with several colors in the same cluster. **Zones 3 to 8**.

V. nudum 'Winterthur'

v. NOO-dum. SMOOTH WITHEROD CULTIVAR. Compact to about 10 feet with shiny leaves that turn red to purple in autumn. Off-white flowers bloom in flat clusters in midsummer, followed by pink berries that turn blue. Tolerates wind better than most viburnums. Another Pennsylvania Horticultural Society award winner. **Zones 5 to 9**.

V. opulus

v. op-YEW-luss. CRANBERRYBUSH VIBURNUM. This native of Europe, northern Asia, and Africa grows 8 to 12 feet high and

wide. The coarse, somewhat shiny, rounded 3-inch leaves have three lobes and may color red in fall. Flowers bloom in lacecap clusters, followed by $1/4$-inch fruit that turns from yellow to red. It tolerates wet soil but is prone to aphids. *V. opulus* 'Roseum' is a sterile form with large balls of white flowers, also known as snowball bush. **Zones 3 to 8**.

V. opulus var. americanum

v. op-YEW-lus var. uh-mair-ih-KAY-nuh. AMERICAN CRANBERRYBUSH VIBURNUM. Native to Canada and the northern United States, this deciduous species grows 8 to 12 feet tall and wide with broad, three-lobed leaves that turn yellow to reddish purple in fall. The white midspring lacecap flowers are followed by $1/3$-inch bright red fruits that last from early fall into late winter. **Zones 2 to 7**.

V. plicatum var. tomentosum

v. plih-KAH-tum var. toh-men-TOH-sum. DOUBLEFILE VIBURNUM. Strong horizontal branching to 6 feet tall and twice as wide. Leaves are toothed and prominently veined, turning reddish purple in fall. In midspring, double rows of white 4- to 6-inch flower clusters resembling those of lacecap hydrangea march down the branches. Oval fruits are bright red turning black. 'Shasta' won a Pennsylvania Horticultural Society award in 1991. 'Shoshoni' is somewhat smaller in all respects. **Zones 5 to 8**.

V. × pragense

v. × prah-GEN-see. PRAGUE VIBURNUM. A hardy, fast-growing evergreen hybrid with shiny ellip-

Viburnum plicatum var. tomentosum

Viburnum plicatum

Vinca minor

Vinca minor f. *alba*

tic leaves to 4 inches long and lightly fragrant, flat-topped clusters of white flowers that open from pink buds in midspring. **Zones 5 to 8.**

V. prunifolium

v. proo-nih-FOH-lee-um. BLACK-HAW VIBURNUM. Native throughout the eastern United States, this shrub grows to more than 12 feet tall and almost as wide with leaves that turn purple-red in fall. Cream-colored flowers are borne in flat-topped clusters in midspring, followed by edible fruits that turn from dark pink to blue-black. Don't plant near ponds or similar sites, since the fallen leaves can develop an unpleasant aroma when wet. **Zones 3 to 9.**

V. × rhytidophylloides 'Alleghany'

v. × ry-tih-doh-fy-LOY-deez. Upright, coarse shrub with leathery leaves that are gray and fuzzy underneath. White or off-white flowers bloom in flat-topped clusters in midspring, followed by red fruits that turn black. **Zones 5 to 8.**

V. rhytidophyllum

v. ry-tih-doh-FY-lum. LEATHER-LEAF VIBURNUM. A vigorous evergreen that grows up to 15 feet tall and about 12 feet wide with narrow, wrinkled leaves up to 7 inches long. A prominent knot of rusty flower buds is borne through winter. In late spring they open as domed umbels of small creamy flowers with prominent stamens. Oval red fruits ripen to black. This

shrub loses its leaves and may even be killed to the roots in Zone 5. **Zones 5 to 9.**

V. sargentii 'Onondaga'

v. sar-GEN-tee-eye. SARGENT VIBURNUM CULTIVAR. Compact selection growing about half the size of the 12-foot Asian species. Three-lobed, maplelike leaves retain a maroon tinge and may turn red in fall. Red buds open to white flowers in lacecap clusters, followed by $^1/_2$-inch red fruits. **Zones 4 to 7.**

Vinca

VINK-uh. Dogbane family, Apocynaceae.

The seven species that belong to the genus *Vinca* are hardy or tender subshrubs native from Europe and northern Africa to central Asia. Commonly called periwinkles or vinca, they bear opposite, ovate to lance-shaped leaves and flowers that have a slender tube at the base and an abruptly flared and flattened face. The flowers have five lobes, or "petals."

HOW TO GROW

Select a site in full sun or partial shade with average to rich, well-

Viola canadensis

drained soil. *V. minor*, a popular evergreen ground cover, grows best in partial shade. The plants have slender stems that spread widely and root at the nodes wherever they touch the ground. Cut back plants hard in spring to shape them and control their spread. Propagate by taking cuttings in summer or dividing the clumps in spring or fall. Another option is to separate and dig up small plants that arise where stems have touched the soil and rooted.

V. major

v. MAY-jer. GREATER PERIWINKLE. A tender, $1^1/_2$-foot-tall perennial, hardy to **Zone 7**, that can spread indefinitely in frost-free areas. Bears purple-blue, 2-inch-wide flowers from spring to fall but is primarily grown as a foliage plant in variegated forms. 'Variegata' bears leaves with creamy white margins and blotches. 'Maculata' bears leaves with yellow-green centers. Tender perennial or warm-weather annual.

V. minor

v. MY-ner. COMMON MYRTLE, LESSER PERIWINKLE, COMMON PERIWINKLE. Spreading 4- to 6-inch-tall subshrub that forms mats of foliage several feet

wide. Bears oval leaves and lavender-blue $^3/_4$- to 1-inch-wide flowers in spring and sporadically later in the season. *V. minor* f. *alba* bears white blooms. 'Bowles' Variety' has $1^1/_4$-inch-wide lavender flowers. 'Alba Variegata' has leaves with creamy white edges. 'Atropurpurea', also sold as 'Purpurea' and 'Rubra', bears red-purple flowers. **Zones 4 to 9.**

Viola

vy-OH-luh. Violet family, Violaceae.

Viola is a large genus of beloved garden plants commonly known as violets, violas, and pansies. The genus contains some 500 species of annuals, biennials, and perennials (both hardy and tender), along with a few subshrubs. They bear flowers with five petals: a spurred lower petal that is the lower "lip," two petals that point up, and two more that point sideways. Leaves range from rounded and toothed or lobed to heart-shaped but also can be cut in a pinnate (featherlike) fashion.

HOW TO GROW

Select a planting site in partial to full shade with rich, moist, well-drained soil. Violets tolerate full sun with consistent soil moisture but generally are happier with some shade. *V. pedata* is an exception: it requires very well drained, sandy soil that is high in organic matter and has an acid pH. All violets grow best during seasons when temperatures are cool, from late winter to early summer and again in fall. Plants spread by creeping rhizomes and also self-

Viola tricolor

V

Viola pedata

Viola pedata

sow: they can become quite weedy and invasive but make a dense, weed-smothering ground cover in the right site. Pull up unwanted seedlings wherever they appear. Propagate by division in spring or fall or by seeds. The species hybridize readily, so self-sown seedlings may not resemble their parents.

V. canadensis
v. kan-uh-DEN-siss. CANADA VIOLET. Native 6- to 12-inch-tall wildflower that forms 1-foot-wide mounds of heart-shaped leaves. Bears white $^1/_2$- to $^3/_4$-inch-wide flowers with yellow eyes in spring. The backs of the petals are blushed with purple. **Zones 3 to 8.**

V. cornuta
v. kore-NEW-tuh. HORNED VIOLET. A 4- to 12-inch-tall species that spreads by rhizomes to form 12- to 14-inch-wide mounds of evergreen, oval, toothed leaves. From spring to summer, plants bear 1- to 1$^1/_2$-inch-wide lilac-blue flowers that look like small pansies. 'Chantreyland' bears apricot flowers; 'Jersey Gem', purple-blue blooms; 'Alba' and 'White Perfection', white flowers; and 'Blue Perfection', sky blue blooms. **Zones 6 to 9.**

V. labradorica
v. lab-rih-DOR-ih-kuh. LABRADOR VIOLET. Native 1- to 4-inch-tall species that spreads via prostrate stems to form mounds 1 foot or more wide. Bears kidney- to heart-shaped leaves and pale purple, $^1/_2$-inch-wide flowers in spring and summer. One of the best species to use as a ground cover. **Zones 2 to 8.**

V. odorata
v. oh-dor-AH-tuh. SWEET VIOLET, ENGLISH VIOLET, GARDEN VIOLET. Rhizomatous 2- to 8-inch-tall species that spreads to 1$^1/_2$ feet. Bears rounded to heart-shaped leaves and $^3/_4$-inch-wide lavender-blue or white flowers in spring. Cultivars include 'Czar', which bears dark violet flowers, and 'White Czar', which bears white blooms. **Zones 6 to 8.**

V. pedata
v. peh-DAH-tuh. BIRD'S-FOOT VIOLET, CROW-FOOT VIOLET. Native 2- to 6-inch-tall wildflower that spreads by rhizomes to form 1-foot-wide mounds of deeply cut leaves with very narrow lobes. Bears 1$^1/_4$-inch-wide pale lavender blooms in late spring and early summer. **Zones 4 to 8.**

V. sororia
v. sor-OR-ee-uh. WOOLLY BLUE VIOLET. Native 3- to 6-inch-tall species that spreads by rhizomes and forms 8-inch-wide mounds of rounded, scalloped, densely hairy leaves. In spring and summer, bears $^3/_4$-inch-wide white flowers speckled and streaked with purple. Some forms have violet-blue flowers. **Zones 4 to 8.**

V. tricolor
v. TRY-cuh-ler. JOHNNY-JUMP-UP, HEARTS-EASE. A 3- to 5-inch-tall annual, biennial, or short-lived perennial with 1-inch-wide flowers from early spring to fall, marked with deep violet, purple, white, or yellow in a facelike pattern. Cool-weather annual, biennial, or short-lived perennial.

V. × wittrockiana
v. × wit-rock-ee-AH-nuh. PANSY. A 6- to 9-inch-tall perennial with showy, 2$^1/_2$- to 4-inch-wide flowers in a wide variety of patterns and colors, including violet, maroon, bronze, yellow, orange, lavender, wine purple, lilac-blue, and white. Traditional types, such as Swiss Giant Series plants, have a dark, velvety, facelike blotch at the center, but solid colors also are available. 'Padparadja' bears orange flowers. Clear Crystal Series and Crystal Bowl Series plants come in a range of solid colors without faces. Cool-weather annual or biennial.

Vitex

VY-tecks. Verbena family, Verbenaceae.

This is a genus of 250 primarily tropical evergreen and deciduous trees and shrubs. The two deciduous species listed here are cultivated in gardens for their mid- to late-summer purple flower spikes and aromatic silvery foliage. There are some white-flowering cultivars. The shrubs get their common name of chasteberry or chaste tree from the days when monks would season their food with the peppery seeds in the belief that they inhibited carnal desire. Modern herbalists use them to treat problems related to menstruation.

HOW TO GROW
Chaste trees need full sun in any well-drained soil. They can be pruned hard, to within a few inches of the ground, to reshape or rejuvenate, or trained to a single trunk. Grow as a specimen, in a shrub border, or as a flowering hedge. Propagate from seeds or from softwood cuttings. May self-sow.

V. agnus-castus
v. AG-nuss-KAS-tuss. CHASTE TREE. A native of western Asia and southern Europe, this open species will form a shrub about 10 feet tall and wide but can be pruned as a tree up to 20 feet tall. The compound palmate leaves are gray-green, silvery underneath, and aromatic. Lavender flowers are borne in spiky panicles from mid- to late summer. **Zones 7 to 10.**

V. negundo
v. neh-GUN-doh. CHASTE TREE. Native from East Asia to southeast Africa, this shrub is openly branched and grows 10 to 15 feet tall and wide. The grayish green compound palmate leaves have three to seven leaflets, often serrated. The blue to lavender flowers bloom in spikes from mid- to late summer. **Zones 6 to 10.**

Vitex agnus-castus

W

Waldsteinia

wald-STINE-ee-uh. Rose family, Rosaceae.

This small genus in the rose family contains about six species that bear three-parted leaves and yellow saucer-shaped, five-petaled blooms that reveal a close relationship to potentillas or cinquefoils (*Potentilla* spp.). The common name barren strawberry refers to the fact that the flowers, which are borne singly or in small clusters, are followed by small dry, inedible fruits. While *Waldsteinia* species are vigorous, they are not to be confused with *Duchesnea indica,* a closely related, similar species commonly called mock strawberry. It is a very invasive weed that spreads quickly by runners.

HOW TO GROW

Select a site in partial to full shade with average to rich soil. Even soil moisture is best, although plants tolerate drought and are useful ground covers for dry shade. They also will grow in full sun, provided the soil remains moist. Propagate by dividing the clumps in spring or fall.

W. fragarioides

w. fray-gair-ee-OY-eye-deez. BARREN STRAWBERRY. Rhizomatous 4- to 10-inch-tall native wildflower that spreads to form 2-foot-wide mats. Bears clusters of saucer-shaped ³/4-inch-wide golden yellow flowers in spring and summer. **Zones 3 to 8.**

W. ternata

w. ter-NAY-tuh. BARREN STRAWBERRY. Rhizomatous, semievergreen species native to Siberia, China, and Japan that reaches 4 inches and spreads to 2 feet. Bears bright yellow ¹/2-inch-wide flowers in late spring and early summer. **Zones 3 to 8.**

Watsonia

wat-SO-nee-uh. Iris family, Iridaceae.

Watsonias are grown for their showy spikes of flowers that usually resemble those of *Gladiolus.* About 60 species native to South Africa as well as Madagascar belong to the genus, all of which grow from corms and produce basal, sword-shaped leaves. The individual flowers are tubular and curved at the base with six spreading lobes, or petal-like tepals. *Watsonia* flowers, unlike those of *Gladiolus,* are nearly symmetrical: the tube at the base is slender and has enlarged lobes, or tepals, at the top, while *Gladiolus* flowers are more evenly funnel shaped.

HOW TO GROW

Select a site in full sun with light, evenly moist soil rich in organic matter. Grow these plants as you would glads: plant corms in spring, setting small corms 3 inches deep and large corms 6 to 8 inches deep. Where hardy, they can be planted in fall. For best results, dig a shallow trench and fill it with soil as the plants grow. Deep planting helps minimize the need to stake plants, but stake them if necessary. In areas where the plants are not hardy, let the foliage ripen for at least 6 weeks after flowering. Then dig the corms after the leaves turn yellow, cut off the foliage, and set them in a

Waldsteinia fragarioides

Watsonia borbonica

Weigela florida

warm, dry place for a few hours to dry. Separate the new corms and small cormels from the old withered one, which will not bloom again. Dust the corms with sulfur or another fungicide and store them in a cool (40° to 50°F), dry place over winter.

W. borbonica

w. bor-BON-ih-kuh. Formerly *W. pyramidata*. A 3- to 5-foot-tall species bearing branched spikes of up to 20 pink 1¼-inch-long flowers that have spreading lobes. **Zones 9 and 10.**

Weigela

wy-GEE-luh. Honeysuckle family, Caprifoliaceae.

From a genus of a dozen deciduous Asian shrubs, one species has been plumbed exhaustively by breeders to develop variations on the funnel-shaped, late-spring to summer flowers.

HOW TO GROW
As long as it has full sun and good drainage, weigela is happy in any soil and tolerates pollution well. Mix with other shrubs in the border, since it is not particularly interesting when out of bloom. Prune after flowering to reshape young branches, removing a portion of old growth to the ground. Propagate from seeds or softwood cuttings.

W. florida

w. FLOR-ih-duh. A spreading shrub 6 to 9 feet tall and about 10 feet wide with coarse branches that arch to the ground. In late spring to early summer it is smothered in the funnel-shaped flowers, lavender pink in the species while usually various shades of pink or red in the cultivars. It reblooms lightly through fall. Cultivars include 'Canary' (yellow flowers, sometimes mixed with pink), 'Eva Rathke' (red flowers, good reblooming), 'Evita' (3 feet tall with red flowers), and 'Variegata' (light pink flowers, leaves with cream edge). Rated hardy to Zone 4 are 'Red Prince' (rich red flowers, upright, long blooming) and 'Alexandra' (trademarked as Wine and Roses, with disease-resistant dark burgundy-purple leaves). The latter is a Pennsylvania Horticultural Society award winner. **Zones 4 to 8.**

Wisteria

Wis-TEER-ee-uh. Pea family, Fabaceae.

There are 10 species of these deciduous plants, which grow naturally as woody vines, to 30 feet or higher, but are often trained to a shrubby form. The large leaves are pinnately compound. Racemes of purple, sweetpea flowers bloom in spring, followed by long pods. Asian forms, particularly *W. floribunda*, have become highly invasive, and their weight and shade is able to topple trees. Don't plant them near parks or wild lands, and prune them heavily to prevent seed formation or rooting from shoots. There are two native species that are less problematic.

HOW TO GROW
Give wisteria full sun. It grows in a wide range of soils, as long as they

Wisteria sinensis

are of moderate fertility (as a legume, wisteria makes its own nitrogen) and pH isn't extreme. Oriental wisterias are more invasive in areas with abundant rainfall and trees that they can climb. Use one as a specimen shrub or grow against a wall. Native wisterias are best viewed from the side or above. Because they leaf out later in the year than Asian species they are less prone to frost damage. They also differ in developing terminal flowers on new growth. To develop shrublike forms, prune off vigorous upward-growing shoots to promote a strong woody framework at the desired height. They may root where branches touch the ground or spread by root sprouts or seeds. To prevent escape, remove spent racemes and any seedpods. Prune the most vigorous new shoots back to two or three leaves in spring, and in late summer, prune off new shoot growth not conforming to the shape of your shrub. Mow or clip any root sprouts.

W. floribunda

w. flor-ih-BUN-duh. JAPANESE WISTERIA. Blooms in midspring on old wood, after leaves appear, but can be damaged by late frosts. Twines clockwise. The species has violet, slightly fragrant flowers in racemes 8 to 20 inches long. There are many cultivars selected for pink or white flowers, longer racemes, or stronger fragrance. **Zones 5 to 9.**

W. frutescens

w. froo-TESS-ens. AMERICAN WISTERIA. This eastern U.S. native bears blue-violet flowers in abundant racemes of 30 to 65 in late spring. 'Amethyst Falls' begins blooming when young and may rebloom later in the season. There is also a white-flowered form. **Zones 5 to 9.**

W. macrostachys

w. mak-roh-STAK-eez. KENTUCKY WISTERIA. In late spring or early summer this native produces lightly scented soft violet flowers in racemes of 70 to 80. It is more cold hardy and tolerant of wet soil than *W. frutescens*. Cultivars include white-flowered, heavy-blooming 'Clara Mack', cold-hardy and vigorous 'Aunt Dee', and cold-hardy, reblooming 'Blue Moon'. **Zones 4 to 8.**

W. sinensis

w. sin-EN-siss. CHINESE WISTERIA. Similar to the Japanese species, but blooming a couple of weeks later with blue-violet flowers. Racemes are shorter with less fragrance, and it twines counterclockwise. Cultivars offer deeper purple, dark pink, double, or bicolored flowers. **Zones 5 to 8.**

Wisteria sinensis

X, Y, Z

Xeranthemum

zer-AN-thuh-mum. Aster family, Asteraceae.

Xeranthemum contains six species of annuals grown for their papery, daisylike flowers, which are used in dried bouquets. The botanical name — from the Greek *xeros*, "dry," and *anthos*, "flower" — refers to the texture of the flower heads, which consist of a cluster of small florets surrounded by showy, stiff, petal-like bracts in pink, mauve, lilac, white, and red. Leaves are entire and linear to linear-elliptic, and both leaves and stems are woolly white.

HOW TO GROW

Select a site in full sun with poor to average, well-drained soil. Plants tolerate dry soil, and too-rich soil yields lots of foliage but few flowers. Sow seeds indoors in individual pots 6 to 8 weeks before the last spring frost date at 60° to 70°F. Germination takes 2 to 3 weeks. Or sow outdoors after the last frost date; plants take about 10 weeks to bloom from seeds, so in areas with short growing seasons, it's best to give them a head start indoors. Stake plants with twiggy brush. They are attractive addi-tions to mixed plantings and are also good for fresh or dried ar-rangements. Harvest the flowers just before they open fully, and use fresh or hang in bunches in a cool, dry, dark place.

X. annuum

x. AN-yew-um. IMMORTELLE. A 1- to 3-foot-tall annual with silvery leaves and 2-inch-wide, single or double flower heads in shades of bright pink, purple, or white from summer to fall. *X. cylindraceum* is a 1¹⁄₂- to 2-foot annual with pink flowers. Warm-weather annual.

Yucca

YUCK-uh. Agave family, Agavaceae.

Rugged, adaptable yuccas are perennials, shrubs, and trees na-tive to North and Central Amer-ica. Some 40 species belong to the genus, and the perennials grown in gardens are tough, woody-based plants that produce large dense clumps of bold, linear to lance-shaped evergreen leaves. The clumps are topped in summer by showy, erect spikes of creamy white flowers that are waxy tex-tured, nodding, and bell shaped. Bloom spikes rise to a height of 5 to 10 feet or more, well above the 2- to 2¹⁄₂-foot-tall mounds of sword-shaped leaves.

HOW TO GROW

Plant yuccas in full sun or very light shade. They grow in a wide range of soils, including average to rich well-drained soil and dry, sandy soil. Plants do not tolerate wet conditions but will grow in clay soil provided it is well drained. Cut off the flower stalks at the base after the blooms fade. The individual crowns die after they flower, so cut them out of the clumps when the leaves begin to fade. Clumps, which can be left for years without needing division, form broad mounds with time. They are quite deep rooted and difficult to dig, so give them plenty of space at planting time. Divide plants in spring or fall if they out-grow their space or for propaga-tion.

Y. aloifolia

y. al-loh-ih-FOH-lee-uh. DAGGER PLANT. This southeastern U.S. native, sometimes misleadingly called Spanish bayonet, is capable of growing to more than 20 feet but in cultivation usually remains at about half that height, with ei-ther one or multiple trunks. The dense leaves are 2 feet long and 2 inches wide with a sharp point. White 4-inch flowers bloom in 18-inch panicles in summer. **Zones 7 to 10.**

Y. filamentosa

y. fill-uh-men-TOH-suh. ADAM'S NEEDLE. North American native species with stiff, blue-green, 2¹⁄₂-foot-long evergreen leaves. Forms 2¹⁄₂-foot-tall clumps of foliage that spread to 4 or 5 feet wide. Bears 5- to 6-foot-tall panicles of 2-inch-wide green or cream flowers in summer. Variegated cultivars, which add year-round color to the garden, include 'Bright Edge' and 'Color Guard', which have leaves with yellow margins, and 'Golden Sword' and 'Garland Gold', which have yellow-centered leaves. *Y. flaccida* resembles *Y. filamentosa* but has leaves that are less rigid and tend to droop at the tips. Both species are hardy in **Zones 4 to 10.**

Y. flaccida

y. FLASS-ih-duh. WEAKLEAF YUCCA. This Southeast native is similar to *Y. filamentosa*, but the leaves are shorter, narrower, and bent near the middle, and the marginal threads are straight. **Zones 4 to 9.**

Y. gloriosa

y. glor-ee-OH-suh. SPANISH BAY-ONET. A Southeast native devel-oping multiple branches to 10 feet tall, with 2-foot, soft-pointed leaves in whorls at the branch ends. Panicles of white flowers to 8 feet long bloom in late summer. Leaves of 'Variegata' have white edges. **Zones 7 to 9.**

Xeranthemum annuum

Yucca aloifolia

Yucca filamentosa

X
Y
Z

Y. recurvifolia

y. ree-ker-vih-FOH-lee-uh. A native of the south-central United States that tends to be single-trunked and grows 6 to 10 feet tall. Pliable blue-green leaves up to 3 feet long curve downward. The white 3-inch flowers bloom in upright panicles from mid- to late summer. **Zones 7 to 9.**

Zantedeschia

zan-teh-DESS-kee-uh. Arum family, Araceae.

Zantedeschia species are commonly called calla lilies, although they are not related to true lilies (*Lilium* spp.), which belong to the lily family. Instead, the six species of tender perennials in *Zantedeschia*, sometimes also called arum lilies, are more closely related to Jack-in-the-pulpits (*Arisaema* spp.) and caladiums (*Caladium* spp.). The plants bear fleshy, lance- to arrowhead-shaped leaves and grow from fleshy, tuberous rhizomes. Plants are evergreen or deciduous. Like other arum-family plants, calla lilies bear flowers that are actually an inflorescence consisting of many tiny flowers clustered on a central stalk, called a spadix. The spadix is surrounded by a showy modified leaf, called a spathe. *Zantedeschia* species are native to southern and eastern Africa.

HOW TO GROW

Select a site in full sun or partial shade with rich, moist soil. A spot protected from sun during the hottest part of the day is best. *Z. aethiopica* will grow in boggy soil and in standing water up to a depth of 12 inches; it is commonly used as a marginal plant along the edges of water gardens. Where hardy, calla lilies can be grown outdoors year-round; elsewhere, plan on overwintering them indoors by keeping them in containers or digging them annually in fall. Where they are marginally hardy, look for a protected site and mulch heavily in fall with a dry, coarse mulch such as evergreen boughs, salt hay, or pine needles.

Plant the fleshy rhizomes in spring: set them just under the soil surface — on their sides if you cannot tell top from bottom. Water carefully until the plants are growing actively, then keep the soil evenly moist. Feed container-grown plants every 2 weeks with a balanced fertilizer. In the North, start plants indoors in late winter

Zantedeschia 'Carmine Red'

or early spring and move them to the garden after all danger of frost has passed. To overwinter the rhizomes indoors, dig them in early fall, dry them off, and store them in dry peat or vermiculite in a cool (50° to 55°F), dry, airy place. Or keep plants in containers year-round and gradually reduce watering in late summer until the leaves die back, then store the plants in a cool, dry spot — still in their pots — over winter. Propagate by removing offsets or dividing the rhizomes in spring.

Z. aethiopica

z. ee-thee-OH-pih-kuh. CALLA LILY. A 2- to 3-foot-tall species that bears glossy, 16-inch-long, arrowhead-shaped leaves that are evergreen in mild climates. From late spring to midsummer, plants produce showy flowers with white 4- to 10-inch-long spathes surrounding a yellow spadix. 'Crowborough' has 4- to 6-inch-long spathes and is supposedly hardier than the species. 'Green Goddess' bears white 6- to 8-inch-long spathes marked with green. 'Pink Mist' bears white spathes blushed with pink. **Zones 8 to 11; to Zone 7 or even 6 with winter protection.**

Z. albomaculata

z. AL-boh-mack-yew-LAH-tuh. SPOTTED CALLA. A 12- to 16-inch-tall species bearing dark green, arrow-shaped, 12- to 18-inch-long leaves spotted with white. Handsome flowers with 5-inch-long white spathes surrounding a yellow spadix appear in sum-

Zantedeschia rehmannii

mer. **Zones 8 to 11; to Zone 7 with winter protection.**

Z. elliottiana

z. el-lee-ah-tee-AH-nuh. GOLDEN CALLA, YELLOW CALLA. A 2- to 3-foot-tall species bearing dark green, heart-shaped, 12- to 18-inch-long leaves spotted with white. In summer, bears blooms with 6-inch-long yellow spathes surrounding a yellow spadix. **Zones 9 to 11.**

Z. hybrids

Several hybrids are available, many with *Z. elliottiana* as an important parent. 'Black-eyed Beauty' bears heavily spotted leaves and creamy white spathes that have a black eye. 'Cameo' and 'Pacific Pink' bear pink blooms. 'Golden Affair' bears solid green leaves and bright

yellow spathes. 'Mango' bears red-orange spathes. **Zones 9 and 10; to Zone 8 with winter protection.**

Z. pentlandii

z. pent-LAN-dee-eye. Formerly *Z. angustiloba*. A 2- to 3-foot-tall species with rounded, lance-shaped, 12-inch-long leaves that are only rarely spotted. Bears flowers with bright gold to lemon yellow 5-inch-long spathes in summer that are marked with purple inside at the base and surround a yellow spadix. **Zones 8 to 11.**

Z. rehmannii

z. reh-MAH-nee-eye. PINK CALLA. A 12- to 16-inch-tall species with lance-shaped, 12-inch-long, dark green leaves. Bears flowers in summer that have pink, white, or purple 5-inch-long spathes surrounding a yellow spadix. **Zones 9 to 11.**

Zauschneria

zawsh-NER-ee-uh. Evening primrose family, Onagraceae.

California fuchsia is the common name for the few species in this gloriously showy genus. All are native to the western United States and Mexico, primarily California and Baja California. *Zauschneria* is related to *Fuchsia* (true fuchsias) and *Oenothera* (evening primroses). Leaves are very narrow, usually 1/2 to just over 1 inch long. They are green to silvery gray and deciduous or semievergreen, depending on the species and where the plants are grown. The riotously bright red flowers are tubular, up to 2 inches long, and held prominently in front of the lax branches. They are absolute magnets for hummingbirds.

Zauschneria californica

X Y Z

Zelkova serrata

HOW TO GROW

Zauschnerias require full sun and warm, well-drained soil. Plants will rot if moisture is allowed to stand in the soil at any time of the year. Where plants are marginally hardy they may benefit from a light cover of branches in winter, provided this does not trap water and moisture.

Z. californica

z. kal-ih-FOR-nih-cuh. CALIFORNIA FUCHSIA. This species, 16 inches tall, spreads by rhizomes that send up wiry stems topped by tubular, scarlet flowers; it makes a handsome ground cover. Foliage is green, gray-green, or even very felted white, depending on the degree of hairiness. A number of named selections are available. 'Catalina' is unusually tall and broad, with nearly white leaves and brilliant flowers. 'Cloverdale' is a prostrate form with bright gray leaves and typical flowers. 'Dublin' (also known as 'Glasnevin', for the famous National Botanic Garden in Ireland) grows to 8 inches tall. It has scarlet flowers held above small, bright green leaves. 'Etteri' makes low mats of silvery leaves and scarlet flowers. 'Mattole Select' makes low mounds of silvery foliage and scarlet flowers, but it does not spread readily. Zones 8 to 10.

Zelkova

zell-KOH-vuh. Elm family, Ulmaceae.

Zelkovia is a genus of six deciduous trees grown for their handsome shape and colorful fall color. The species are related to the elms, and sometimes confused with them. They can be used as a replacement for the American elm.

HOW TO GROW

Select a site in full sun. These trees do best in humus-rich, moist, well-drained soil but adapt to poor or alkaline soil. They tolerate drought, air pollution, and urban conditions. Train when young to develop a strong central leader and

Zelkova serrata

evenly spaced branches. Resistant to Dutch elm disease and elm leaf beetles; susceptible to Japanese beetles. Protect the trunk from injury, as wounds can invite canker.

Z. serrata

z. sir-AY-tuh. JAPANESE ZELKOVA. The species is rounded or broadly spreading and matures to 50 to 80 feet tall and wide. Some cultivars are tall and vase shaped with ascending branches, making them good replacements for American elm. The 2-inch-long, narrow, pointed leaves resemble elm leaves and are oval or oblong, with toothed margins and equal bases. They open pale green in spring, mature to dark green, and turn russet-orange or purplish red in midfall. The bark exfoliates into a mottled orange-and-gray patchwork. Use as a street tree or to shade a lawn, garden, or patio. From Japan and Korea. Zones 6 to 9.

CULTIVARS

'Green Vase' is very fast growing to 60 to 70 feet tall, with a graceful vase shape; orange-brown to rust-red fall color. 'Green Veil' is a narrow tree with weeping branch tips. 'Halka' is very fast growing to 50 feet tall and 30 feet wide, with a strong central leader; yellow fall color; most resembles American elm. 'Village Green' has an upright, rounded vase shape; grows 50 to 60 feet tall and wide; rust-red fall color; cold hardy to Zone 5.

Zenobia

zen-OH-bee-uh. Heath family, Ericaceae.

This genus is a lone deciduous or semievergreen shrub species native to streambanks and other damp environs from North Carolina to Florida. These shrubs are grown by gardeners for their fragrant bell-shaped white flowers and, on cultivars, blue-green foliage.

HOW TO GROW

Give zenobia acidic, moist soil in sun or partial shade. Excellent for natural pondsides or low-lying moist areas. Prune in early spring

Zenobia pulverulenta

to control height and stimulate new growth. Propagate from seeds collected while light brown and dried in a paper bag, then sown on top of peat. Semihard cuttings collected in midsummer will root in a well-drained medium.

Z. pulverulenta

z. pull-ver-YEW-len-tuh. DUSTY ZENOBIA. Irregular, with stems upright then arching, from 2 to 6 feet tall and 6 feet wide. Gray-green or blue-green leaves are covered with a waxy bloom (hence the common name) and in fall turn yellow-orange or burgundy. May lose its leaves north of Zone 8. The white $1/2$-inch flowers dangle from the shoot tips in long racemes in midsummer. 'Woodlander's Blue' is a blue-foliaged form growing to 4 feet. Zones 6 to 9.

Zephyranthes

zeh-fer-RAN-theez. Amaryllis family, Amaryllidaceae.

The charming plants in this genus have a variety of common names, including rain lilies, rain flowers, zephyr lilies, and fairy lilies. About 70 species belong here, all perennials native from North to South America that grow from tunicate bulbs and produce grassy leaves that are either deciduous or evergreen. The tubular flowers, which point upward, are either funnel shaped and resemble small lilies or more rounded, in which case they look more like crocuses. Flowers appear from spring to fall and, as the name "rain lily" suggests, often appear after a period of rainy weather. They come in shades of pink, red, yellow, and white.

HOW TO GROW

Select a site in full sun with rich, moist soil that is very well drained. Where hardy, these bulbs can be grown outdoors year-round. Where they are marginally hardy, look for a warm, sheltered spot such as at the base of a south-facing wall. They require fairly dry soil in winter when they are dormant, so plant them in raised beds or rock gardens and amend the soil with grit when planting to improve drainage. In the North, grow them in containers, which will make it easy to move plants outdoors for summer and indoors in fall. Or dig them annually in fall and overwinter them indoors. Where hardy, plant the bulbs in

X
Y
Z

Zephyranthes rosea

fall; elsewhere, plant in spring, setting them at a depth of about 2 inches.

Keep the soil evenly moist once plants are growing actively. Gradually withhold water as the leaves begin to die back. To overwinter bulbs indoors, bring the containers indoors after the foliage has died back and keep them in a cool (50° to 55°F), dry place. Dig the bulbs, dry them off, and store them in barely moist peat moss or vermiculite. Container-grown plants need repotting only every four years or so — they bloom best when slightly potbound. Propagate by offsets in spring or by seeds.

Z. atamasco

z. ah-tah-MASS-koh. ATAMASCO LILY. Wildflower native to the southeastern United States that ranges from 8 to 12 inches tall. Bears white, 3-inch-long, funnel-shaped flowers in spring or summer. **Zones 10 and 11.**

Z. candida

z. kan-DEE-duh. Heavy-blooming 4- to 8-inch-tall South American species bearing creamy white, crocus-like, 1¹/4-inch-long flowers from summer to early fall. **Zones 8 to 10; to Zone 7 with winter protection.**

Z. citrina

z. sih-TRY-nuh. A 4- to 6-inch-tall South American species with bright yellow, 2-inch-long, crocuslike flowers from late summer to fall. **Zones 9 to 11.**

Z. grandiflora

z. gran-dih-FLOR-uh. RAIN LILY, RAIN FLOWER, ZEPHYR LILY, FAIRY LILY. Formerly *Z.*

carinata. An 8- to 10-inch-tall species from Mexico bearing pink, funnel-shaped, 3-inch-long flowers from late summer to fall. **Zones 9 to 11.**

Z. rosea

z. ROH-see-uh. RAIN LILY, RAIN FLOWER, ZEPHYR LILY, FAIRY LILY. A 6- to 8-inch-tall species from Central America as well as the West Indies and Cuba. Bears pink, funnel-shaped, 1¹/4-inch-long flowers with white throats in fall. **Zones 10 and 11.**

Zinnia

ZIN-nee-uh. Aster family, Asteraceae.

Few flowers are as familiar or as easy to grow as zinnias. The genus contains about 20 species of annuals, perennials, and subshrubs that are primarily native to Mexico but also southwestern North America, as well as farther south in Central and South America. They bear leaves that range from linear to ovate or rounded and showy, daisylike flowers that can be single or double. Hot colors predominate in the zinnias: they come in shades of orange, red, bronze, hot pink, orange-red, and yellow-orange, as well as cooler colors such as white, pale pink, cream, and green.

HOW TO GROW

Select a site in full sun with average to rich, well-drained soil. A site with good air circulation is best; otherwise, powdery mildew can be a problem. Gardeners in areas with hot, humid summers should consider some of the newer disease-resistant selections. Sow seeds outdoors after the last frost date. Or sow indoors 6 to 8 weeks before the last frost at 60° to 65°F. Transplant with care. For season-long bloom, sow new crops of seeds every 3 to 4 weeks until midsummer. Pinch plants to encourage branching, unless you are growing exclusively for cut flowers and want long stems. Tall plants may need staking. Use zinnias in mixed plantings or in cottage gardens. Dwarf types make great edging plants and can be used in containers. The flowers attract both hummingbirds and butterflies and also make excellent cut flowers.

Z. elegans

z. EL-eh-ganz. COMMON ZINNIA. A bushy, ¹/2- to 4-foot-tall annual with lance-shaped leaves. Many cultivars are available, with single or double flowers ranging from 1¹/2 to 5 inches wide. Cactus-flowered cultivars, including Zenith Series, bear double and semidouble, 4-inch-wide flowers with narrow, curved petals, generally on 2¹/2- to 3-foot plants. Dahlia-flowered cultivars have semidouble to double, 3- to 5-inch-wide blooms in both full-size

Zinnia elegans 'Peppermint Stick'

Zinnia peruviana

and dwarf plants. 'Blue Point Mix' bears 5- to 6-inch, dahlia-like blooms on 4-foot plants. Dasher Series and Dreamland Series bear 3¹/2- to 4-inch-wide, double blooms on compact, 10- to 12-inch-tall plants. Oklahoma Series plants bear double, 2¹/2-inch-wide flowers and were developed for their "cut and come again" performance as cut flowers. Pulchino Series plants are 1 to 1¹/2 feet tall with 2- to 3-inch-wide flowers; they are more disease-resistant than most cultivars. Warm-weather annual.

Z. haageana

z. hah-gee-AH-nuh. NARROW-LEAVED ZINNIA, MEXICAN ZINNIA. Also listed as *Z. angustifolia* and *Z. linearis.* A bushy, 1- to 2-foot-tall annual with outstanding resistance to diseases as well as heat and drought tolerance. Bears linear to lance-shaped leaves covered in bristly hairs and daisylike, 1¹/2-inch-wide flower heads in summer. Star Series plants bear 2-inch-wide flowers in gold, orange, and white. Profusion Series produces 2- to 2¹/2-inch-wide flowers in cherry pink and orange. Warm-weather annual.

Z. peruviana

z. peh-roo-vee-AH-nuh. Formerly *Z. pauciflora.* A 2- to 3-foot-tall annual with linear to lance-shaped leaves that resist mildew. Bears 1- to 1¹/2-inch-wide, daisylike flowers with dark centers and red or yellow petals. 'Bonita Red' has brick to soft orange-red blooms, while 'Bonita Yellow' bears yellow to gold blooms. Warm-weather annual.

Propagating Plants

Glossary

Common Name Index

Photo Credits

Hardiness Zone Map

Propagating Plants

Many of the plants in this encyclopedia can be propagated by home gardeners. Where appropriate, the proper techniques are given in the "How to Grow" section of the plant descriptions. The drawings here will help gardeners who are unfamiliar with these techniques. For a fuller explanation, see *Taylor's Weekend Guide to Easy Plant Propagation*.

Growing from Seed

SOWING SEEDS IN CONTAINERS

Certain seeds benefit from being grown indoors in containers, such as those that need extra warmth to sprout or grow well, annuals that need a long growing season to bloom well, perennials that may bloom the first summer if given a head start, and summer sowings of perennial seeds.

Fill a pot to within ¼ to ½ inch of the rim with moist seed-starting medium.

Firm the surface with the back of your fingers, then scatter seeds evenly over the medium.

Sprinkle a little additional medium over seeds and add a label with the plant name and date.

Cover the finished pots with plastic and set them in a warm, bright place or under lights.

CONTAINER SOWING OUTDOORS

Outdoor sowing in containers is a good option for perennials, shrubs, and other plants that require a period of cold temperatures in order to germinate.

Scatter the seeds evenly over the medium and cover with ⅛ inch of medium followed by a ¼-inch layer of fine washed gravel.

Set labeled pots in a cold frame or sink them to their rims in a nursery bed.

TRANSPLANTING SEEDLINGS

Seedlings are ready to be moved to a larger pot when the first pair of true leaves has developed.

Tip out the potful of seedlings and soil and tease out the seedlings with a pencil.

Holding each seedling by a leaf (not the stem), plant it in an individual pot.

THINNING SEEDLINGS IN A BED

Use a blunt knife to lift out clumps of small seedlings, then transplant them to bare spots.

Thin larger seedlings by snipping off the stems at ground level.

PROTECTING SEEDLINGS FROM PESTS

A circle of diatomaceous earth can protect seedlings from slugs.

To guard seedlings against animal pests, set a low chicken-wire cage over the area or insert brushy prunings around the seedlings.

Multiplying by Dividing

ENCOURAGING RUNNERS TO ROOT

To speed the natural tendency of runners to root, pin them to the ground with a U-shaped piece of wire. Keep the soil moist to encourage rooting.

PROPAGATING FROM SUCKERS

Nothing could be easier. Dig up the rooted plantlets and move them to a nursery bed or another part of the garden.

DIVIDING IRIS RHIZOMES

Lift the rhizomes from the soil with a spading fork and cut or break young branching rhizomes from the parent plant. Inspect for borers or soft rot.

Select the youngest healthy sections for replanting at their previous depth. Discard older portions of the clump.

DIVIDING BULBS

Dig bulbs after the foliage has turned yellow and pull them apart. Replant them twice as deep as their height.

PROPAGATING LILIES FROM BULBLETS AND BULBILS

Dig lilies in the fall after the stem has yellowed and pick off the small bulblets that have formed along the stem below the soil's surface. Plant them in pots or a nursery bed.

Bulbils, found along the stem, may also be picked off and potted.

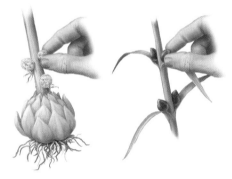

DIVIDING GLADIOLUS CORMS

Dig the corms after the foliage has turned yellow. Discard the withered old corm and pick off the small cormels. Store them in a cool, dark place until spring, then plant outdoors.

DIVIDING DAHLIAS

Cut the clump into sections so that each has at least one root. Dust the cuts with sulfur to prevent fungal diseases, then plant the divisions in pots or, after the last frost, in the garden.

Taking Cuttings

TAKING CUTTINGS OF ANNUALS AND PERENNIALS

Snip off healthy shoots 3 to 4 inches long. Remove the leaves from the bottom half of the cutting.

Insert the cutting about halfway into a pot of moist growing medium, using a pencil to make the hole. Firm the medium around the cutting and water well.

TAKING HARDWOOD CUTTINGS

Trim an inch off the top and cut the rest into 4- to 6-inch lengths.

Make a straight cut above a bud at the top of each piece and an angled cut at the bottom.

Cut pencil-thick shoots to about 10 inches long.

In warm zones, plant immediately. In northern zones, store the bundles in boxes of moist vermiculite in an un-heated room or bury them outdoors.

In early spring, plant the cuttings in moist soil deep enough to cover all but the top one or two buds.

TAKING CUTTINGS OF BROAD-LEAVED EVERGREENS

After the plant's new growth has finished and the stems are starting to harden, collect 4- to 6-inch pieces of tip growth.

Remove leaves from the bottom half of the stems and insert them in moist growing medium.

Glossary

Acid soil (or sour soil) Soil with a pH below 7.0. Soils that are slightly acid, with a pH between 6.5 and 7.0, are ideal for growing a wide range of plants. At pH levels below 6.0, minerals such as calcium, magnesium, and potassium are less available to plants, while iron, manganese, and aluminum may be too available. Soil organisms are not as active in acid soils. To raise pH, apply very finely ground limestone (calcium carbonate) or dolomitic limestone. Have the soil tested first and follow the application recommendations from the test. To raise soil pH more than one point (from 5.0 to 6.0, say), apply lime over two or three years instead of making the change in one year. Lime can be applied at any season, but fall is the best time. Wood ashes also raise pH. Another way to deal with acid soil is to grow acid-loving plants such as azaleas, rhododendrons, and blueberries (*Vaccinium* spp.), which tolerate soil pH as low as 4.5.

Air layering A propagation technique that causes roots to form on aboveground stems or branches still attached to the parent plant. Houseplants such as dumb cane (*Dieffenbachia* spp.) and figs (*Ficus* spp.) are commonly propagated by air layering, as are hardy shrubs. To air layer, remove the leaves on a section of stem or branch and make a shallow, thin, flap- or tongue-like cut partway through the stem with a sharp knife. Wrap moist sphagnum moss around the stem, sticking a piece or two under the flap to keep it open. Wrap the stem in plastic and fasten it at top and bottom with waterproof tape or twist ties. Remoisten the moss as necessary. When roots are visible through the plastic, cut the stem below the area where the roots have formed and pot up the new plant. Rooting takes from three months to a year, depending on the plant being propagated.

Alkaline soil (sweet or chalky soil) Soil with a pH above 7.0. To lower pH, apply elemental sulfur, also called flowers of sulfur. Have the soil tested and follow the application recommendations provided. To keep pH at the new level, reapply sulfur every 6 to 12 months. Even if garden soil is slightly acid or neutral, soil close to the foundation of a house may be alkaline because lime leached from the cement raises the pH.

Alternate Arranged on alternating sides, as leaves or buds along a stem. Alternate leaves have one leaf per leaf node.

Anchor root A main root with the primary function of holding the plant in place in the soil. Feeder roots branch off from the anchor root.

Annual Technically, a plant that germinates from seed, grows, flowers, sets seed, and dies all in one season. Gardeners also use the term to describe any plant that grows and flowers in a single season, a definition that includes tender perennials killed by frost at the end of the season. In this sense, a plant that is an annual in northern zones may be a perennial in frost-free regions.

Anther The pollen-bearing portion of a stamen, which is the male reproductive organ of a flower. Each anther is usually attached to the flower by a filament.

Anthracnose Also called bird's-eye spot, a fungal disease that causes dark, sunken lesions with pinkish centers on leaves. Leaf spots may have concentric rings of pink and brown.

Aphids Tiny pest insects that cluster on buds, shoots, and the undersides of leaves. They are soft and pear-shaped, may have wings or be wingless, and may be green, black, brown, or reddish. Aphids damage plants by sucking the juices, and their feeding causes stunted or deformed blooms and leaves. They also produce a sticky honeydew, which supports the growth of sooty mold fungus on leaves and stems. Control aphids by introducing lacewings or lady beetles or by spraying with insecticidal soap, pyrethrins, or a strong spray of water.

Asexual propagation *See* Vegetative propagation.

Axil The upper angle between a leaf stalk and the stem from which it arises. Flower stalks, shoots, and branches also form axils with stems or branches.

Balled-and-burlapped (B&B) Of a plant, dug from the ground with soil around the root ball and wrapped in burlap. To plant a B&B plant, set it in the hole and remove any staples or rope holding the burlap. Cut away as much of the burlap as possible without disturbing the root ball, then push the rest down to the bottom of the hole. If the burlap is made of synthetic fiber, carefully remove it completely before refilling the hole.

Bare-root Without soil around the roots. Roses, some shrubs, fruit trees, and many perennials are sold this way. Bare-root plants are dormant, or should be, and are normally planted in spring. Ideally, plant them as soon as possible after bringing them home. Soak the roots in water for several hours before planting, and if the plants have sprouted, cut back new top growth by about one-third. Water deeply when planting and weekly for the entire first season in the garden.

Basal leaf A leaf borne at the base of a plant near the soil line.

Bedding plant An annual, biennial, or tender perennial grown temporarily for its flowers or foliage. Bedding plants may be displayed in the garden for an entire season or for a few weeks. Plants are nearly flowering size at planting time and are normally arranged in blocks or patterns.

Beneficial insects Insects that help the garden by pollinating flowers or controlling pests. Beneficials include various wasps, flies, beetles, and other insects that parasitize and/or feed on pests such as aphids, caterpillars, mealybugs, mites, and tomato hornworms. Other beneficial insects are braconid and ichneumon wasps, lady beetles, tachinid flies, syrphid flies, dragonflies, minute pirate bugs, spined soldier bugs, soldier beetles, rove beetles, and various predatory mites.

Biennial A plant that takes two years to germinate, flower, set seed, and die. Most biennials produce a low rosette of leaves the first year and flowers the second year. Gardeners sometimes grow short-lived perennials as biennials, because these plants usually produce a large display of flowers the first year and fewer in the following years. True biennials include parsley (*Petroselinum crispum*) and Canterbury bells (*Campanula medium*). Common foxglove (*Digitalis purpurea*) and hollyhocks (*Alcea rosea*) are short-lived perennials often grown as biennials.

Bipinnate (twice-cut or twice-pinnate) Having paired leaflets arranged in a featherlike, or pinnate, fashion, with each individual leaflet further divided into pairs.

Black spot A fungal disease that attacks roses, causing black spots to appear on the leaves, which eventually turn yellow and drop. To control it, choose cultivars that are resistant to the disease, pick off infected leaves and throw them away, and prune away infected canes. At the first sign of the disease, spray infected plants weekly with fungicidal soap or sulfur.

Blood meal (or dried blood) An organic fertilizer that is an excellent source of nitrogen. Blood meal sprinkled on the ground helps repel rabbits and other animal pests.

Bone meal An organic fertilizer containing phosphate, calcium, and some nitrogen.

Borers Insect larvae that bore into the leaves, stalks, branches, or trunks of plants to feed. The wormlike larvae of moths or beetles often leave gummy, sawdust-like material around their entry holes. Borer-infested plants, stems, or plant parts tend to wilt even if the soil is moist. Borer holes on trunks are usually close to the soil line, and the infestation weakens or kills the plant.

Boss A showy, dense cluster of petal-like stamens or petaloids in the center of a flower.

Bract A modified leaf, usually small and scalelike, often borne at the base of a flower or flower cluster. Bracts may resemble petals, as in the case of dogwoods (*Cornus* spp.) and poinsettias *(Euphorbia pulcherrima)*. Sea hollies (*Eryngium* spp.) feature large, spiny, silver-gray bracts at the base of rounded flower clusters.

Branch collar The ridged, slightly bulging area at the base of a branch where it joins the trunk or main branch. When pruning, make cuts just *outside* the branch collar to promote healing.

Bud An immature or undeveloped organ enclosing an embryonic flower, leaf, shoot, or other plant part.

Bud eye A primary bud or a bud that has begun to swell.

Bud union On a grafted plant, the point on the stem where the scion, or upper portion of the plant, is joined to the rootstock.

Bulb A storage organ consisting of fleshy scales (actually modified leaves) attached to a basal plate. The bulb gives rise to the roots and contains a compressed stem with an embryonic shoot or flower. Onions (*Allium* spp.), daffodils (*Narcissus* spp.), and tulips (*Tulipa* spp.) all grow from true bulbs made up of tightly packed scales, called tunicate bulbs. The nontunicate bulbs of lilies (*Lillium* spp.) have loose scales; these dry out more quickly and are more easily damaged than tunicate bulbs. Gardeners often use the term "bulb" more generally to refer to various storage structures, including corms and tuberous roots.

Bulbil A small bulb that forms aboveground along the stem or in leaf axils. Bulbils can be picked off and planted, much like seeds, to propagate the parent plant.

Bulblet A small bulb that forms belowground along a stem or around or between the scales of the mother bulb. Bulblets can be picked off and planted, much like seeds, to propagate the parent plant.

Calyx (pl. **calyxes**) A collective term for all of a flower's sepals, which are located just outside the corolla (the ring of petals). A calyx may consist of individual sepals or of sepals fused together to form a tube.

Cane A main stem that grows from the base of a plant. Rose stems are usually called canes.

Carpet bedding A planting style in which masses of very low-growing bedding plants are arranged in colorful patterns of flowers or foliage.

Catkin A spike or spikelike flower cluster, usually cylindrical and pendulous, consisting of scalelike bracts and densely packed flowers, which usually lack petals.

Chlorosis An unhealthy condition caused by lack of chlorophyll, which occurs when certain nutrients used to make chlorophyll are unavailable. Chlorotic leaves are very pale green, yellow, or nearly white with green veins.

Cold frame An unheated box used to germinate seeds of hardy plants during the winter, grow seedlings, root cuttings, harden off plants before they are moved to the garden, or overwinter plants that are not quite hardy. A cold frame is usually made of wood with a sloping, hinged glass or Plexiglas roof. Traditionally it is constructed over a foundation dug a foot or more into the ground, but a cold frame can be built on the soil surface. Shallow, portable cold frames are available as well.

Cool-weather annual An annual that grows best in cool conditions. Sometimes called hardy or half-hardy, these plants generally die out in hot summer weather. In the deep South they are often grown for winter or very early spring bloom. Where summers are cool they usually will bloom for much or all of the season. Pansies and Johnny-jump-ups (*Viola* spp.), larkspur *(Consolida ajacis)*, and pot marigolds *(Calendula officinalis)* are cool-weather annuals.

Come true To produce seeds that grow into plants that are identical or very similar to the parent plant in such characteristics as flower color, foliage form, and habit.

Compost The decomposed remains of various organic materials, including garden trimmings, grass clippings, kitchen scraps, leaves, wood shavings, and manure. Compost is a valuable soil amendment as well as an excellent material for mulching. The organic materials are gathered in a pile or combined in a cage, bin, or other structure, then kept moist and turned once or twice a year to promote decomposition. Turning the pile every two to three weeks speeds the process even more. Avoid adding the following items to a compost pile: cat or dog droppings, diseased plant materials, weeds that have gone to seed, and meat, bones, or fat from the kitchen.

Compound Divided into two or more separate leaflets.

Conifer A tree or shrub that bears cones. Most conifers are evergreens, including such popular landscape plants as pines (*Pinus* spp.), spruces (*Picea* spp.), and junipers (*Juniperus* spp.). Larches (*Larix* spp.), bald cypress *(Taxodium distichum)*, and ginkgo *(Ginkgo biloba)* are deciduous conifers.

Cool-season grass Any variety of grass that grows best during spring and fall, when temperatures are between 60° and 75°F. Cool-season grasses are dormant or grow slowly during hot summer weather and usually remain green in winter.

Corm A structure resembling a true bulb (*see* Bulb) that is actually a solid, swollen underground stem. A corm is usually covered with a papery tunic. Most corms, including those of gladiolas (*Gladiolus* spp.) are annuals: after the plant blooms, the old corm dies and a new one grows on top of it. Tender corms must be dug in fall, allowed to dry, and overwintered indoors. Those that are hardy can be left in the garden over the winter.

Cormel A small corm that develops around the parent corm. Cormels can be planted in pots, much like seeds, and grown on to propagate the parent plant. A cormlet is a small, secondary cormel.

Corolla The collective term for all of a flower's petals. The corolla, located just inside the calyx, or sepals, may consist of separate petals or of the petals fused together to form a tube or trumpet.

Corona A usually petal-like flower part that is crown- or cup-shaped, such as the flower of a daffodil (*Narcissus* spp.).

Corymb A broad, shortened flower cluster that is either flat or slightly rounded on top. The individual flowers open first on the outside of the corymb, and the central stalk continues to elongate as new flowers open. The flower clusters of yarrows (*Achillea* spp.) and bigleaf or florist's hydrangeas *(Hydrangea macrophylla)* are corymbs.

Crown A term with several botanical meanings: 1) The base of a herbaceous perennial, shrub, or tree, where the stems and roots meet. The crown produces new stems and contains dormant buds. In herbaceous plants the crown can be divided to propagate the plant. 2) A piece of rhizome that has roots and one or more buds. 3) The corona, or cup, of a daffodil flower. 4) The branches and foliage of a tree or shrub.

Cultivar A cultivated variety of a plant species. The term refers to a unique form of a particular plant that originated under cultivation and is maintained by asexual propagation or by seed. (In books and catalogs, cultivar names are set in roman type and set off with single quotes.) The cultivar name may be used with either the common or the botanical name of the parent plant: thus, both *Geranium sanguineum* 'Shepherd's Warning' and bloody cranesbill 'Shepherd's Warning' are acceptable. Cultivars that are the result of complex or unknown crosses are called hybrids, and their names are listed without a specific epithet — *Paeonia* 'Bowl of Cream' and *Hosta* 'Francee', for example.

Cyathium (pl. **cyathia**) A usually showy flower cluster consisting of one female flower surrounded by several male flowers; together they resemble a single flower. The cyathium is characteristic of euphorbias (*Euphorbia* spp.).

Cyme A flat-topped or rounded inflorescence in which the flower at the tip of the central stem opens first, followed by the secondary flowers, which are borne on stems beneath the terminal flower. Once the first flower opens, the main stem stops growing, and the secondary flowers may be higher than the terminal. *Viburnum plicatum* bears cymes.

Damping-off A fungal disease that rots seedling stems at the soil line, causing them to fall over and die. It can also rot seeds before they sprout. To prevent damping-off, use a disease-free seed-starting medium, sow thinly to avoid overcrowding, provide good air circulation, and water pots from below to keep the soil surface relatively dry.

Deadheading Pinching or cutting off spent flowers to encourage the plants to form new buds, keep them looking neat, and prevent seed set and self-sowing. Plants with many very small flowers can be

deadheaded by shearing, cutting the entire plant back by one-third to one-half.

Deciduous Falling off at the end of a season or period of growth, as a tree or shrub that loses its leaves in fall.

Dioecious Bearing male and female flowers on separate plants. Hollies (*Ilex* spp.) are perhaps the best-known dioecious plants. Only the female holly produces berries, but the pollen of a male plant of the same species or a compatible cultivar is required to fertilize the female.

Disk florets (or disk flowers) Small, usually densely packed flowers in the center, or "eye," of a sunflower, daisy, or other member of the aster family, Asteraceae. When fertilized, they produce the seeds.

Division (or crown division) A technique of pulling or cutting plants apart to make new, smaller plants. A plant may be divided to propagate it, to keep it from spreading, or to rejuvenate a clump that has died out in the center. To divide a clump, dig around it and lift it, with its roots, out of the hole. Pull it apart with your fingers, if possible, or cut it into sections with a knife, or force it apart with two garden forks set back to back. Keep the roots moist, and replant or pot up the new plants as soon as possible. Discard old, woody portions of the clump in favor of younger, more vigorous growth.

Dormancy A period during which a plant or seed stops growing and/or metabolic processes slow down (become dormant). Deciduous plants drop their leaves during dormancy, and herbaceous plants are often killed to the ground, then spend their dormancy as crowns with resting buds that will grow again in spring. Seeds that do not germinate even when given optimal warmth and moisture are considered dormant. Several factors can cause seed dormancy, including hard seed coats and chemicals in the seed that must be washed away by a season or two of rain. Some dormant seeds require cycles of cool, moist storage and/or warm, moist storage before they will germinate.

Double flower One that has more than the usual number of petals and/or has petal-like stamens or other flower parts.

Dutch elm disease (DED) A fungal disease spread by bark beetles that has killed off American elms (*Ulmus americana*) across the country. The leaves of infected plants turn yellow and drop, and twigs and branches gradually die off. American elms are very susceptible to DED, but some other elm species have exhibited resistance to the disease, and hybridizers are trying to develop DED-resistant American elms. Keeping uninfected trees healthy and vigorous and combating the beetles that spread the disease are the best courses of action.

Dwarf A plant that has a naturally compact or small habit, usually because of a mutation.

Edging 1) Trimming grass along the edges of a lawn; or 2) cutting through grass roots with a spade or other tool to make a neat, clean edge between lawn and flower beds or walkways. Edging strips are metal or plastic barriers that keep grass from spreading into flower beds or keep vigorous ground covers from invading the lawn. The term "edging" is also used for a row of low hedge plants planted close together along the front of a bed or border.

Ephemeral A plant or flower that lasts only a short time — usually only a day. Daylily (*Hemerocallis* spp.) flowers are ephemeral. The term is also used to describe a plant's life cycle. A spring ephemeral is a plant that produces leaves and flowers in spring, then goes dormant, usually by early summer. Many spring bulbs and native wildflowers are ephemerals, including winter aconite (*Eranthis hyemalis*) and spring beauties (*Claytonia virginica*).

Epiphyte A plant that grows on another plant but takes no water or nutrients from it. Many orchids and bromeliads are epiphytes.

Espalier As a noun, a tree or shrub that has been trained to grow in a flat plane, with a central trunk and branches trained in various two-dimensional patterns. As a verb, the term means the process of training such a tree or shrub by tying, pinching, and pruning the branches to keep the pattern visible. Fruit trees are good candidates for espaliers.

Etiolate (or blanch) To cause a plant part to develop without chlorophyll, and thus without normal green coloring, by blocking sunlight.

Evergreen Remaining green year-round. Plants that retain their leaves or needles through the winter months, such as pines (*Pinus* spp.) and spruces (*Picea* spp.), are evergreen. Some herbaceous perennials, such as hellebores (*Helleborus* spp.) and Christmas ferns (*Polystichum acrostichoides*), also are evergreen, although their leaves may be fairly tattered by late winter.

Eye 1) A dormant bud on a tuber or tuberous root; 2) a bud on a perennial clump (peonies are priced and sold by the number of eyes on each piece); 3) a stem cutting that has only one bud; and 4) the central zone of a flower that has a different color from the rest of the petals.

Feeder roots Small roots whose primary function is gathering nutrients and taking up water.

Filament The threadlike stalk that supports the pollen-carrying anther. Together, anther and filament make up the stamen, the male organ of a flower.

Flower bud An immature organ that encloses an embryonic or undeveloped flower.

Forcing Causing bulbs, plants, or cut shoots to produce flowers by manipulating their environment. Hardy spring bulbs can be forced by planting them in pots that are placed outdoors and exposed to cold temperatures (35° to 40°F) for several months in winter. You can force branches of early-blooming shrubs such as forsythia and pussy willow in late winter by cutting them and placing the stems in water in a cool (60°F) spot until the flowers begin to open.

Frond The leaf of a fern; also a very large compound leaf, like that of a palm.

Frost date The beginning or end of a growing season. The last spring frost date, also called the last frost date or the spring frost date, is the *average* date when gardeners can expect the last freezing temperatures. The first fall frost, often called the first frost or the fall frost date, is the *average* date when freezing temperatures first damage or kill tender plants. To find spring and fall frost dates for your region, call the local Cooperative Extension Service office.

Frost heaving A process caused by alternating cycles of freezing and thawing, which can push a perennial or other plant out of the ground during winter. Newly planted perennials and shrubs are most susceptible to frost heaving.

Frost pocket An area where cold air collects and, as a result, has later spring frosts and earlier fall frosts than surrounding areas. A frost pocket may occur at the bottom of a slope or just uphill from a fence, building, or other obstruction.

Full shade A site that does not receive direct sun anytime during the day. To be suitable for gardening, a site in full shade should receive good indirect light all day long. Sites that do not, such as those under evergreens, will not support plants.

Full sun A site that receives 10 hours of direct, uninterrupted sunlight per day. Many plants that need full sun will grow well with 8 hours of direct sun.

Fungicide A liquid or powder used to control fungi. Baking soda spray — 1 teaspoon baking soda and a dash of dishwashing liquid per quart of water — makes an effective organic fungicide. Other organic fungicides include sulfur, Bordeaux mix (a wettable powder combining copper sulfate and hydrated lime), and copper.

Genus (pl. **genera**) A group of plant species having similar characteristics within a botanical family. A genus may include one or many individual species. *Rosa, Acer, Hosta,* and *Tulipa* are all genus names.

Germination The process that transforms the embryonic plant inside a seed into a seedling. When the seed absorbs water, the embryo can begin to grow, using the food stored in the seed. The root pushes down first, to anchor the seedling and take up water and nutrients, followed by the upward growth of the shoot.

Glaucous Of leaves, having a waxy or powdery, blue-gray, gray, or whitish covering that is easily rubbed off. Blue-leaved hostas such as *Hosta sieboldiana* 'Elegans' have glaucous leaves.

Granule A grain of dry fertilizer.

Ground cover A low-growing perennial, shrub, or other plant that is grown for the purpose of covering an area with a mass of foliage. Ground covers usually spread by rhizomes or other structures to form a covering dense enough to keep weeds in check, prevent soil erosion, and serve as a low-maintenance alternative to lawn grass.

Typically, the plants are less than 1 foot in height, but taller plants make fine ground covers as well.

Habit The size, shape, and general appearance of a plant.

Half-hardy annual An annual that can survive light frost but will be damaged or killed outright by longer periods of freezing weather. *See* Cool-weather annual.

Hardening off Gradually exposing seedlings, cuttings, or other young plants grown indoors to the harsher conditions they will encounter in the garden. Typically, the plants are set in a shady, protected spot for an hour on the first day of hardening off, then are gradually exposed to brighter sunshine and longer periods outdoors over the course of a week. After that they are ready to be planted in the garden.

Hardiness A plant's ability to survive cold winter weather. While survival at low temperatures is a primary factor, other conditions contribute to a plant's success in a particular site. Some species can survive extremely low temperatures if protected by a blanket of snow all winter. In warmer zones these same plants may become desiccated by winter winds or succumb to winter rain, cold wet soil, or alternate periods of freezing and thawing. Hot summer weather also can weaken a plant, causing it to die over the winter. Hardiness ratings based on the USDA Hardiness Zone Map (*see* pages 446–47) have been assigned to perennials, shrubs, and trees.

Hardiness is normally judged without protection such as mulch. To experiment with growing a plant that may not be hardy in your area, cover it after the ground freezes with a loose blanket of winter mulch, such as oak leaves or straw. Carefully remove the mulch in late winter or early spring.

Hardwood cutting A cutting taken from fully mature, hardened wood of a shrub, tree, or other plant. Hardwood cuttings can be taken from fall, after the plants have dropped their leaves, to midwinter. Vigorous, pencil-thick shoots from new wood (the current year's growth) will root best, but older wood can be rooted. Cut 4- to 8-inch-long shoots with at least two buds. Mark the bottom of the shoot with a slanted cut, the top with a straight cut; an upside-down cutting will not root. From Zone 6 south, dip the base of each cutting in rooting hormone and plant it immediately, either in a nursery bed or in a pot set outdoors in a protected spot. Mulch the cuttings to protect them from cycles of freezing and thawing. In the North, dip cuttings in rooting hormone, bundle them together, and bury them *upside down* outdoors in a spot with well-drained, sandy soil for the winter. Or you can pack them in boxes filled with moistened sand or sawdust and keep them in an unheated area or in the refrigerator. Unbury the stored cuttings in early spring and plant them.

Heading cut A pruning cut that removes the tip of a stem or branch or that cuts across the stem just above a bud anywhere along its length.

Heel cutting A cutting that includes at its base a small strip of bark and wood from the stem. That strip is the heel, which helps promote rooting. Heel cuttings are usually taken from semiripe or hardwood and are pulled or cut off the parent plant.

Herbaceous perennial A plant that lacks woody growth and persists for more than two years. Gardeners usually refer to herbaceous, or nonwoody, species as perennials. The terms "herbaceous perennial" and "perennial" are interchangeable.

Hip The rounded fruit of a rose (*Rosa* spp.), usually red or orange-red when ripe.

Hybrid The result of cross-pollination of two genetically different parent plants or lines. Hybrids can be produced naturally, by bees or wind, for example. They also are created by plant breeders deliberately transferring pollen from one plant to another. In a botanical name, a multiplication sign (×) between the genus and species names indicates a hybrid: *Geranium × magnificum* is a cross between *G. ibericum* and *G. platypetalum,* for example. The term "hybrid" also refers to cultivars that are the result of complex crosses.

Inflorescence A flower cluster; also the arrangement of flowers on a plant, such as a cyme, corymb, or raceme.

Internode The length of stem between two nodes.

Introduced Nonnative, brought from another area. This term is usually applied to garden escapees that are now found growing in the wild.

Invasive Vigorous, fast-spreading, with wide-ranging roots. Once established, invasive plants are difficult to keep under control or eradicate.

Involucre A series of bracts borne in a whorl or spiral beneath a flower cluster or other plant part. Plants in the aster family, Asteraceae, have involucres on the back of the flower heads.

Knees Woody root projections produced by some tree species, such as bald cypress (*Taxodium distichum),* especially in damp or wet soil. Knees project above the surface of the soil or water all around the tree.

Knot garden A garden that features a pattern of low, closely clipped hedges arranged in a knot- or mazelike pattern. Areas enclosed by the hedges are filled with annuals or herbs or are spread with gravel.

Layering A vegetative propagation technique that induces a shoot still attached to the parent plant to produce roots and grow a new plant. The shoot can be induced to form roots along its length, or the tip of the stem can be made to root, a process called tip layering. To tip layer a plant, in late winter or early spring, select a long, flexible stem that is close to the soil. Bend the shoot to the ground and loosen the soil where it touches. Remove the leaves along the stem but not at the tip, and make a shallow cut at a leaf node to form a thin flap. Put a toothpick under the flap to keep it open, then bury that portion of the stem, pinning it down with a U-shaped piece of wire. Stake the stem tip if necessary. Keep the area well watered all summer. In fall or spring, check for roots; if they have formed, sever and pot up the plant.

Leader The main, central shoot or trunk of a tree.

Leaf A plant part that carries out the process of photosynthesis. Leaves are usually green and flattened and are borne on a shoot or stem.

Leaf blight Any fungal or bacterial disease that causes leaf spots or blotches, which can eventually kill entire leaves.

Leaflet The individual "leaves" that make up a compound leaf.

Limbing up Pruning away a tree's lower branches to make it possible to walk beneath the tree.

Little bulbs (minor bulbs) Plants smaller than standard-size tulips and daffodils that grow from bulbs, corms, or other similar structures. Little bulbs include crocuses (*Crocus* spp.), autumn crocuses (*Colchichum* spp.), species daffodils (*Narcissus* spp.) and tulips (*Tulipa* spp.), glory-of-the-snow (*Chionodoxa* spp.), winter aconites (*Eranthis* spp.), snowflakes (*Leucojum* spp.), grape hyacinths (*Muscari* spp.), squills (*Puschkinia* spp.), and scillas (*Scilla* spp.).

Loam Soil consisting of nearly equal quantities of sand, silt, and clay particles. Loam is the ideal soil type for gardening.

Lobe A rounded edge of a leaf or other plant part. A lobed leaf is divided into rounded segments.

Mallet cutting A cutting that includes a short piece of the main stem still attached at the base. Usually collected from semiripe wood, mallet cuttings are often used to root plants that have pithy or hollow stems.

Microclimate A site with growing conditions that differ from those of the surrounding area, such as an unusually warm spot on the south side of a building or wall.

Mildew A group of fungal diseases characterized by powdery white or grayish patches on plant leaves, stems, flower buds, and flowers. Powdery mildew and downy mildew are the most common forms. To prevent mildew problems, choose resistant cultivars, keep leaves dry by avoiding overhead watering, and allow plants enough space. If signs of mildew appear, pick off infected leaves and spray plants with a fungicide weekly.

Minor bulbs *See* Little bulbs.

Monocarp A plant that dies after blooming once and setting seed. Monocarpic species often produce foliage for several years before blooming. Giant lilies (*Cardiocrinum* spp.) are monocarpic.

Monoecious A plant that produces separate male and female flowers on the same plant. Wax begonias and tuberous begonias (*Begonia* spp.) are monoecious.

Mulch A layer of organic or inorganic material added to the soil surface to control weeds, prevent erosion, and hold in moisture. Organic mulches include compost, ground bark, wood chips, chopped leaves, pine needles, and grass clippings. Inorganic mulches include black plastic, crushed stone, and landscape fabric.

Native Growing naturally in, or indigenous to, a particular area.

Naturalize To plant perennials, bulbs, wildflowers, or other plants in such a way that they appear to be growing naturally. An alien or nonnative plant that has been introduced to an area or has escaped from gardens and is now growing wild is said to have naturalized.

New wood Shoots or other growth produced during the current growing season. Shrubs that flower on new wood usually produce buds in late spring and bloom in mid- to late summer or fall. In general, prune these plants in late winter or early spring, while they are dormant.

Nursery bed A garden bed in which new plants are given extra care until they are large and vigorous enough to be moved out to the garden. Keeping seedlings, rooted cuttings, divisions, and other small plants all together in a nursery bed makes it easy to keep them watered and give them other needed attention.

Nursery-grown Of wildflowers, grown for a season or two in a nursery, though possibly collected in the wild.

Nursery-propagated Of wildflowers, not collected from the wild but grown from seeds or propagated in a nursery.

Nutrients Elements necessary for plant growth. Plants need relatively large amounts of the macronutrients — calcium, carbon, hydrogen, magnesium, nitrogen, oxygen, phosphorus, potassium, and sulfur — but only very small amounts of the micronutrients — boron, chlorine, copper, iron, manganese, molybdenum, and zinc. Plants take up most nutrients from the soil, but acquire carbon, hydrogen, and oxygen from the air.

Obovate Of a leaf, egg-shaped with a wide, rounded tip and a narrower base.

Offset (or offshoot) A small shoot, bulb, or plant produced from the main crown or stem of a parent plant, to which it is identical. Offsets can be severed from the parent, potted up, and grown on as new plants.

Old wood Shoots or other growth produced during a previous growing season. Shrubs that flower on old wood usually bloom in spring or early summer, then form flower buds for the following year. In general, prune these shrubs immediately *after* flowering; late-winter pruning will remove the flower buds for the coming season.

Opposite Arranged in pairs on opposite sides along a stem. The term describes the placement of leaves, buds, or other plant parts.

Organic matter An essential ingredient in any good garden soil. Organic matter improves soil structure, helps soil retain water, and helps neutralize pH. Adding organic matter to build good garden soil is an ongoing activity. Sources include compost, chopped leaves, well-rotted manure, and grass clippings, all of which can be dug or tilled into the soil or spread on top as mulch.

Ovary The portion of a flower where seeds form. It is part of the pistil, the flower's female reproductive organ.

Ovate Rounded, egg-shaped. An ovate leaf has a wide rounded base and a narrower rounded tip.

Overwintering Holding plants that are not hardy in a frost-free area over winter. Plants can be overwintered in several ways. Whole plants can be brought indoors, either in pots or simply with a root ball, and stored in a cool, frost-free spot. Or cuttings can be taken and rooted in late summer or fall.

Palmate Of leaflets, leaf lobes, or leaf veins, radiating out from a single point in a palmlike or handlike arrangement.

Panicle A flower cluster with a main stem and branched side stems. (In contrast, a raceme has unbranched side stems.) The flowers open from the bottom of the panicle to the top, and the main stem continues to grow longer as new flowers open. Lilacs (*Syringa* spp.) and astilbes (*Astilbe* spp.) bear panicles.

Partial shade A site that is in shade for part of the day and full sun for the remaining daylight hours. The amount of light received by a partially shaded site varies greatly. A high canopy of trees casts bright, dappled shade, while a building may create deep shade. Although there is no standard definition, in general a site in partial shade receives more shade than sun.

Partial sun A site that is in sun for part of the day and shade for the remaining daylight hours. In general, a site in partial sun receives more sun than shade.

Pea stakes (pea brush, brushy twigs, twiggy brush) Twiggy branches, cut from woody shrubs, used to stake weak-stemmed plants such as peas. The branches are pushed into the ground around small, lightweight plants, which grow up and through the twigs.

Peat moss The partially decomposed remains of sphagnum moss and/or other plants found in bogs or marshes. Peat moss can hold up to 10 times its dry weight in water and has an acid pH — from 3.8 to 4.5. It is commonly used in seed-starting and potting mixes. Do not use it as mulch, since it can form a crust that prevents water from percolating into the soil. Peat can be used as a soil amendment to lower pH, but because it is a mined product that cannot readily be renewed, many gardeners avoid using it.

Pedicel The stalk of an individual flower in an inflorescence.

Peduncle The stalk of a single flower or of an inflorescence.

Peltate Having a stem attached near the center, rather than at an outer edge, of a round or rounded leaf or bract. Nasturtiums (*Tropaeolum majus*) have peltate leaves.

Pendent Drooping or hanging down.

Perennial A plant that lives for more than two years. While this definition encompasses trees, shrubs, and woody vines, gardeners typically use the term to refer to nonwoody plants, that is, herbaceous perennials. A short-lived perennial lives for two or three years.

Perfoliate Of a leaf or bract, having lobes at the base that encircle the stem so that the stem seems to be inserted through the leaf. Bellworts or merrybells (*Uvularia* spp.) bear perfoliate leaves.

Petal A single segment of the corolla of a flower. Petals are usually brightly colored or white. They may be entirely separate or fused together into a tube form.

pH The measure of a soil's acidity or alkalinity, as indicated on a scale of 0 to 14. The pH determines which nutrients are dissolved in the soil and are thus available to plants. Soil with a pH of 7 is neutral. A pH above 7 indicates alkaline soil, while pH values below 7 are acid. Each whole number on the scale differs from the next by a factor of 10, meaning that pH 4 is ten times more acid than pH 5. To determine soil pH, collect a soil sample and have it tested by a private soil-testing lab, the Cooperative Extension Service, or a home soil test.

Pinching Pruning by snapping off stem tips with the thumb and forefinger. Stem tips that are too thick or woody to be pinched can be removed with pruning shears or a sharp knife. Pinching encourages plants to branch, thus developing denser, more compact growth.

Pinnate Of a leaf, compound, with pairs of leaflets arranged along a main stem in featherlike fashion. Many ferns have pinnate leaves.

Pistil The female portion of a flower, which produces seed and is made up of the stigma, style, and ovary.

Propagation The process of creating new plants from existing ones. Vegetative, or asexual, propagation techniques include layering, taking and rooting cuttings, and dividing. Sowing seeds is a sexual propagation technique.

Prune To remove growth from a tree, shrub, or other plant for a particular purpose. Plants are pruned to direct their size and shape, remove diseased or damaged wood, maintain health and vigor, and control flowering and/or fruiting.

Raceme A single-stemmed inflorescence with flowers on individual stalks all along the stem. The flowers at the bottom open first, and the main stalk continues to elongate as the flowers open. Snapdragons (*Antirrhinum majus*) bear racemes.

Ray floret A small flower that is one of the "petals" surrounding the center florets of a daisy or aster. The single, strap-shaped corolla of a ray floret looks like a petal.

Remontant Blooming repeatedly through the season or producing two or more flushes of bloom in a single growing season.

Rhizome A specialized horizontal stem that runs either underground or along the soil surface. Like any stem, a rhizome has nodes, which can produce roots. Rhizomatous plants can be propagated by cutting the rhizome into sections with at least one node apiece.

Root cuttings Pieces of roots that are induced to form new shoots and grow into individual plants. Root cuttings can be taken from late winter to early spring. Like all cuttings, they exhibit polarity and must be planted right side up in order to grow. When gathering roots, be sure to mark the top — the end that was closest to the crown of the plant. Keep the cuttings moist and plant them in pots filled with moistened seed-starting mix. Thin roots should be placed on the surface, then covered with $^1/_2$ inch of mix. Put pencil-size roots into the mix vertically, with the tops even with or just below the surface. Set the pots in a cold frame or a cool, bright room and keep the mix evenly moist. Root cuttings are well established when roots protrude from the holes in the bottom of the pot.

Rootstock In general, the thick, fleshy roots of a plant. On a grafted or budded plant, the rootstock is the plant that provides the root system.

Rosette A low-growing cluster of leaves radiating out from the crown of a plant.

Runner A long, slender stem that runs along the ground horizontally and produces roots and small plants at the tip and/or at leaf nodes along its length. A stolon, in contrast, forms plantlets only at the tip; however, many gardeners use the terms "runner" and "stolon" interchangeably. The plantlets can be severed and used to propagate the parent plant.

Rust A common fungal disease that produces rusty, powdery, yellow to orange spots on the underside of leaves of susceptible species. Whitish or yellowish spots appear on the upper side directly above the rusty patches. Infected leaves eventually turn completely yellow and dry up. The best way to prevent this disease is to plant resistant cultivars. If you see signs of rust, pick off and throw away infected leaves and keep foliage as dry as possible by watering with soaker hoses. Apply sulfur dust every 1 to 2 weeks.

Salverform Of a flower, slender-tubed with an abruptly flattened and flared end, as in a trumpet. Phlox (*Phlox* spp.) flowers are salverform.

Scale insects Pests that infest stems, stem tips, and leaves, sucking plant juices and causing stunted, yellowed, or off-color growth. The sticky honeydew they exude causes the growth of sooty mold on leaves below where they are feeding. The female insects are small, with soft or hard bodies that look like nothing more than bumps on the infested plant parts. They may be red, white, brown, black, or gray. Controls include cutting off infested growth and spraying with horticultural oil diluted for growing-season use.

Scape A leafless flower stalk, sometimes having leafy bracts, that rises directly from the ground. Daffodils (*Narcissus* spp.) and daylilies (*Hemerocallis* spp.) bear flowers on scapes.

Scarifying Nicking, sanding, or otherwise wearing down a hard seed coat to hasten the uptake of water and speed germination.

Self-sow, self-seed To grow from naturally distributed seed. Plants such as larkspur (*Consolida ajacis*) and love-in-a-mist (*Nigella damascena*) are self-sowing annuals, meaning they appear in the garden year after year without being planted anew.

Semievergreen Retaining some green leaves through the winter. A single species or cultivar may be semievergreen, evergreen, or deciduous in different climate zones. Sweet bay magnolia (*Magnolia virginiana*) is evergreen in warm climates, deciduous in northern zones, and semievergreen in between.

Semiripe cutting A stem cutting taken from fairly new, partially matured growth on a woody plant. The base of the cutting is woody, while the growth at the tip is still soft and flexible. Deciduous woody plants are usually easiest to root from softwood cuttings, but semiripe cuttings are an especially effective way to propagate needled evergreens like conifers and broad-leaved evergreens such as rhododendrons and azaleas (*Rhododendron* spp.) and hollies (*Ilex* spp.). For instructions on collecting and rooting semiripe cuttings, *see* Softwood cuttings.

Sepal A single segment of a flower's calyx, located just outside the petals and usually green and leaflike.

Shelterbelt A planting of trees and shrubs, usually arranged in ranks by height, along one or more edges of a property to provide protection from wind. A shelterbelt may contain both deciduous and evergreen plants.

Shoot A new stem that arises from the ground or a new branch or twig that appears on an existing plant.

Simple Not compound or divided into separate leaflets. A simple leaf may be deeply lobed, however.

Slip A cutting or shoot that has already grown some roots.

Softwood cutting A cutting taken from the flexible new growth at a stem tip. Take softwood cuttings from actively growing shoots in summer. They wilt quickly, so put them in a jar of water as you collect them or wrap them in moist paper towels in a plastic bag. The best cuttings come from turgid shoots that snap off cleanly. Stems that bend, crush, or shatter when they break will not root well. Cuttings should be 4 to 6 inches long and have at least two leaf nodes. Make the cut just *below* a leaf node. Remove any flower buds and all the leaves at the bottom of the stem, leaving two to four leaves at the tip. For fastest rooting, dip the stem end in rooting hormone. Poke your finger into the planting medium to make a hole, then stick the cutting in and firm the medium around it. Root cuttings in an old aquarium or on a tray tented with a large, clear plastic bag to maintain high humidity. Set the cuttings in a warm (65° to 75°F), bright spot out of direct sun and keep the medium moist. When the cuttings begin to grow, check for roots by gently tugging on the stem.

Spadix A flower spike with a thickened stem covered with tiny, densely packed flowers. The "jack" of a jack-in-the-pulpit (*Arisaema triphyllum*) is a spadix.

Spathe The large bract that wraps around a spadix. It may be green and leaflike, mottled in color, or showy and petal-like, as in calla lilies (*Zantedeschia* spp.). The "pulpit" of a jack-in-the-pulpit (*Arisaema triphyllum*) is a spathe.

Species A group of closely related plants having similar characteristics within a genus. A plant's botanical name consists of the genus name coupled with a specific epithet, or species name. In the name *Hosta sieboldiana*, *Hosta* is the genus, and *sieboldiana* is the species.

Spike A single stem with flowers attached directly to it. The flowers on a spike open from bottom to top, and the stem continues to lengthen as the flowers open. Gladiolus (*Gladiolus* spp.) produce spikes.

Stamen The male, pollen-producing portion of a flower, consisting of an anther and a filament.

Staminode A sterile stamen or similar structure that in some flowers is modified to look like a petal. Many peony cultivars feature clusters of showy, curled staminodes at the center of the bloom.

Stem A shoot that supports plant parts such as leaves, flowers, and/or fruit.

Stem cutting Any cutting taken from a stem, including semiripe, softwood, and hardwood cuttings.

Sterile Not fertile, such as a flower that does not bear seeds or a shoot that has only vegetative growth.

Stigma The top of the pistil, on which pollen lands to fertilize the flower.

Stipule A small appendage resembling a leaf or bract borne at the base of a leaf stalk. The stipule falls off after the leaf opens.

Stolon A long, slender stem that runs horizontally, usually aboveground, and forms roots and a small plant at the tip. The plantlet can be severed and used for propagation. Many gardeners use the terms "stolon" and "runner" interchangeably, even though a runner can form roots at nodes along its length as well as at the tip.

Stooling (or mound layering) A propagation technique, commonly used on shrubby herbs, in which loose soil is mounded over a plant to encourage the formation of many new plants. Cover the plant with a 3- to 5-inch mound of loose, sandy soil or a mixture of mulch, loose soil, and compost. Leave the top 3 to 4 inches of each shoot tip exposed. Keep the mound evenly moist and add more soil as needed through the summer. In late summer or early fall, gently brush away the soil to check for roots. If roots have formed at the stem bases, sever and pot up the individual plants. If not, rebury the plant and check again in spring.

Stratification A technique for overcoming seed dormancy and aiding germination by storing seeds in cool-moist and/or warm-moist conditions. Seeds requiring cool-moist stratification usually need 1 to 3 months at 32° to 45°F. The easiest way to do this is to sow the seeds in pots and keep them in the refrigerator. Seeds that require warm-moist stratification need a period at 68° to 86°F, usually followed by a cool-moist period.

Style The stalk that links the stigma and ovary of a pistil, the female reproductive organ of a flower.

Subshrub A low-growing woody-stemmed plant or a plant with a woody base and soft, herbaceous stems.

Succulent A plant that has firm, juicy, fleshy leaves or stems, such as many sedums (*Sedum* spp.).

Sucker A shoot that grows from the roots, crown, or underground stem of a plant; also, any upright, fast-growing shoot. Suckers can be severed from the parent plant for propagation. Those that arise from the rootstock of a grafted plant, such as a rose, should be removed.

Taproot A root system that has a single main root with smaller roots branching off it. Plants with taproots, such as baptisias (*Baptisia* spp.), are drought tolerant but are difficult to transplant.

Tender perennial Any plant — herbaceous perennial, vine, tree, or shrub — that is killed by cold temperatures at the end of the growing season. In areas where they are not hardy, tender perennials are either grown as annuals or overwintered indoors.

Tetraploid Having four sets of chromosomes. Most plants and other organisms are diploid; that is, they have two sets of chromosomes, but hybridizers have developed cultivars with extra chromosomes. Tetraploid cultivars of daylilies (*Hemerocallis* spp.), for example, feature larger flowers with heavier substance than normal diploid ones.

Thinning cut A pruning cut that removes an entire branch or shoot at its base, where it arises from a larger branch or the tree trunk. Thinning cuts should be made just outside the branch collar.

Thorn A stiff, sharp-pointed outgrowth of a branch or stem.

Tip cutting A cutting taken from the tip of a shoot or stem.

Toothed Of a leaf, sharply indented or cut.

Top-dress To spread soil amendments, fertilizers, or other materials evenly over the soil surface. Top-dressing can be applied by hand or with a spreader.

Topdressing Any material, such as compost or dry fertilizer, that is spread over the soil surface to improve the soil or feed plants.

Tuber A fleshy, swollen underground stem that develops to store food and/or reproduce the parent plant. Like a typical stem, a tuber has leaf nodes and buds, or "eyes." Potatoes (*Solanum tuberosum*) and Jerusalem artichokes (*Helianthus tuberosus*) are edible tubers.

Tuberous root The swollen, fleshy section of a root that stores food and allows a plant to survive the dormant season. Dahlias (*Dahlia* spp.) have tuberous roots.

Tunicate Enclosed in a loose, usually papery membrane. Onions (*Allium* spp.) and daffodils (*Narcissus* spp.) bear tunicate bulbs, as do most corms.

Umbel A flat or rounded flower cluster in which the individual flowers are carried on stalks that arise from a single point. Queen Anne's lace *(Daucus carota)*, dill *(Anethum graveolens)*, and onions (*Allium* spp.) bear umbels.

Variegated Of a leaf, marked with stripes, edges, bands, spots, or blotches of cream, white, or another color.

Vegetative propagation (or asexual propagation) Any method of increasing plants that does not involve seeds. Vegetative propagation techniques include taking cuttings, layering, division, and tissue culture, all of which yield plants that are identical to the parent plant.

Verticillium wilt A fungal plant disease that causes leaves to turn yellow and drop and causes plant stems to wilt.

Warm-season grass A grass that grows best at temperatures between 80° and 95°F. Warm-season grasses turn brown in fall and are dormant in winter.

Warm-weather annual An annual that thrives in heat and is typically planted in the garden in late spring or early summer, after all danger of frost has passed.

Whorl A group of three or more leaves, flowers, petals, or other plant parts arranged in a circle around a stem and attached at a single point.

Wildflower A flowering plant that grows in an uncultivated area. Native, or indigenous, wildflowers are those that grow naturally in a given area, while nonnative, introduced, alien, or naturalized plants are those brought from somewhere else. The term usually refers to annuals, perennials, biennials, and bulbs, although flowering shrubs and vines are also sometimes called wildflowers.

Golden weeping willow, *Salix alba*, 351

Goldflame honeysuckle, *Lonicera × heckrottii*, 245

Gold moss sedum, *Sedum acre*, 361

Good luck plant, *Ostrya tetraphylla*, 285

Gooseberry, *Ribes*, 340

Gooseneck loosestrife, *Lysimachia clethroides*, 250

Gopher spurge, *Euphorbia lathyris*, 155

Goutweed, *Aegopodium*, 14

Graceful wattle, *Acacia decora*, 3

Grancy graybeard, *Chionanthus virginicus*, 92

Grand crinum, *Crinum asiaticum*, 117

Grape hyacinth, *Muscari*, 267

Grape-leaf anemone, *Anemone tomentosa*, 29

Grass nut, *Triteleia laxa*, 392

Grass pink, *Dianthus plumarius*, 134

Grassy bells, *Dierama pendulum*, 137

Grassy-leaved sweet flag, *Acorus gramineus*, 12

Gray dogwood, *Cornus racemosa*, 110

Gray-head coneflower, *Ratibida pinnata*, 334

Grayleaf cranesbill, *Geranium cinereum*, 173

Gray's lily, *Lilium grayi*, 239

Great bellflower, *Campanula latifolia*, 71

Great blue lobelia, *Lobelia siphilitica*, 244

Great burnet, *Sanguisorba officinalis*, 355

Greater celandine, *Chelidonium majus*, 91

Greater periwinkle, *Vinca major*, 411

Greater wood rush, *Luzula sylvatica*, 248

Great leopard's bane, *Doronicum pardalianches*, 140

Great merrybells, *Uvularia grandiflora*, 403

Great white trillium, *Trillium grandiflorum*, 391

Grecian windflower, *Anemone blanda*, 28

Greek valerian, *Polemonium caeruleum*, 314

Green-and-gold, *Chrysogonum virginianum*, 95

Green ash, *Fraxinus pennsylvanica*, 163

Green-banded mariposa, *Calochortus macrocarpus*, 68

Green dragon, *Arisaema dracontium*, 36

Green-flowered corn lily, *Ixia viridiflora*, 213

Green hawthorn, *Crataegus viridis*, 116

Green-headed coneflower, *Rudbeckia laciniata*, 349

Green lavender cotton, *Santolina rosmarinifolia*, 355

Green-stem forsythia, *Forsythia viridissima*, 161

Grefsheim spirea, *Spiraea cinerea* 'Grefsheim', 371

Gregg sage, *Salvia greggii*, 353

Griffith's spurge, *Euphorbia griffithii*, 155

Ground cherry, *Physalis*, 303

Ground clematis, *Clematis recta*, 99

Groundsel bush, *Baccharis halimifolia*, 47

Guernsey lily, *Nerine sarniensis*, 275

Guinea-hen flower, *Fritillaria meleagris*, 165

Gum tree, *Liquidambar styraciflua*, 242

Hackberry, *Celtis*, 82

Hankow willow, *Salix matsudana*, 352

Hardhack, *Spiraea tomentosa*, 372

Hair grass, *Deschampsia*, 132

Hakone grass, *Hakonechloa macra*, 184

Handkerchief tree, *Davidia involucrata*, 130

Hard maple, *Acer saccharum*, 9

Hardy ageratum, *Eupatorium coelestinum*, 154

Hardy amaryllis, *Lycoris squamigera*, 250

Hardy begonia, *Begonia grandis* ssp. *evansiana*, 49

Hardy cactus, *Opuntia compressa*, 281

Hardy cyclamen, *Cyclamen coum*, 123

Cyclamen hederifolium, 123

Cyclamen repandum, 124

Hardy fall mum, *Chrysanthemum × morifolium*, 95

Hardy fuchsia, *Fuchsia magellanica*, 166

Hardy geranium, *Geranium*, 172

Hardy gladiolus, *Gladiolus communis* ssp. *byzantinus*, 177

Hardy gloxinia, *Incarvillea*, 207

Hardy kiwi, *Actinidia arguta*, 13

Hardy orange, *Poncirus trifoliata*, 316

Harebell, *Campanula rotundifolia*, 71

Hyacinthoides non-scripta, 200

Harebell speedwell, *Veronica prostrata*, 408

Hare's tail grass, *Lagurus ovatus*, 225

Harlequin glory bower, *Clerodendrum trichotomum*, 100

Harlequin flower, *Sparaxis*, 369

Harry Lauder's walking stick, *Corylus avellana*, 111

Hawaiian heather, *Cuphea hyssopifola*, 121

Hawk's beard, *Crepis rubra*, 116

Hawkweed, *Crepis rubra*, 116

Hawthorn, *Crataegus*, 115

Hay-scented fern, *Dennstaedtia punctilobula*, 132

Heart-leaved aster, *Aster cordifolius*, 42

Heart-leaved bergenia, *Bergenia cordifolia*, 52

Heart's-ease, *Viola tricolor*, 412

Heart seed, *Cardiospermum*, 74

Heath, *Erica*, 148

Heath aster, *Aster ericoides*, 43

Heather, *Calluna*, 66

Heath spotted orchid, *Dactylorhiza maculata*, 127

Heavenly bamboo, *Nandina domestica*, 269

Hedge cotoneaster, *Cotoneaster lucidus*, 114

Hedge fern, *Polystichum setiferum*, 316

Hedge maple, *Acer campestre*, 6

Heliotrope, *Heliotropium arborescens*, 190

Hemlock, *Tsuga*, 393

Henry anise tree, *Illicium henryi*, 206

Henry lily, *Lilium henryi*, 239

Hens-and-chicks, *Sempervivum*, 362

Herbaceous clematis, *Clematis integrifolia*, 99

Hickory, *Carya*, 76

Higan cherry, *Prunus × subhirtella* var. *pendula*, 322

Highbush blueberry, *Vaccinium corymbosum*, 405

Himalayan cinquefoil, *Potentilla atrosanguinea*, 318

Himalayan foxtail lily, *Eremurus himalaicus*, 148

Himalayan honeysuckle, *Leycesteria formosa*, 234

Himalayan jewelweed, *Impatiens glandulifera*, 206

Himalayan knotweed, *Persicaria affinis*, 296

Himalayan pine, *Pinus wallichiana*, 310

Hinoki false cypress, *Chamaecyparis obtusa*, 89

Hobble bush, *Viburnum lantanoides*, 410

Hollow Joe-Pye weed, *Eupatorium fistulosum*, 154

Holly, *Ilex*, 203

Holly fern, *Cyrtomium falcatum*, 126

Hollyhock, *Alcea*, 18

Hollyhock mallow, *Malva alcea*, 258

Holly olive, *Osmanthus heterophyllus*, 283

Holly osmanthus, *Osmanthus heterophyllus*, 283

Holy thistle, *Silybum marianum*, 365

Honesty, *Lunaria annua*, 247

Honey bush, *Melianthus major*, 260

Honey garlic, *Nectaroscordum siculum*, 273

Honey locust, *Gleditsia*, 178

Honeysuckle, *Lonicera*, 245

Hoop petticoat daffodil, *Narcissus bulbocodium*, 272

Hop hornbeam, *Ostrya virginiana*, 284

Hops, *Humulus*, 199

Horned poppy, *Glaucium*, 177

Horned violet, *Viola cornuta*, 412

Horse chestnut, *Aesculus*, 14

Houseleek, *Sempervivum*, 362

Hummingbird mint, *Agastache cana*, 16

Hungarian speedwell, *Veronica austriaca* ssp. *teucrium*, 408

Hyacinth, *Hyacinthus orientalis*, 200

Hyacinth bean, *Lablab purpureus*, 223

Hyacinth bletilla, *Bletilla striata*, 55

Iceland poppy, *Papaver croceum*, 289

Ice plant, *Delosperma nubigerum*, 130

Immortelle, *Xeranthemum annuum*, 415

Incense cedar, *Calocedrus decurrens*, 66

Indian bean, *Lablab*, 223

Indian blanket, *Gaillardia pulchella*, 167

Indian borage, *Plectranthus amboinicus*, 312

Indian chocolate, *Geum rivale*, 175

Indian cress, *Tropaeolum majus*, 393

Indian currant coralberry, *Symphoricarpos orbiculatus*, 376

Indian hawthorn, *Rhaphiolepis indica*, 335

Indian physic, *Gillenia stipulata*, 175

Gillenia trifoliata, 175

Indian pink, *Spigelia marilandica*, 371

Indian plum, *Oemleria cerasiformis*, 279

Indian poke, *Veratrum viride*, 406

India rubber tree, *Ficus elastica*, 159

Inkberry, *Ilex glabra*, 204

Inland ceanothus, *Ceanothus ovatus*, 80

Intermediate shield fern, *Dryopteris intermedia*, 141

Interrupted fern, *Osmunda claytoniana*, 283

Irish heath, *Daboecia cantabrica*, 127

Ironweed, *Vernonia noveboracensis*, 408

Ironwood, *Ostrya virginiana*, 284

Italian alkanet, *Anchusa azurea*, 27

Italian arum, *Arum italicum*, 39

Italian aster, *Aster amellus*, 42

Italian bellflower, *Campanula isophylla*, 71

Italian bugloss, *Anchusa azurea*, 27

Italian clematis, *Clematis viticella*, 100

Italian crocus, *Crocus imperati*, 119

Italian squill, *Hyacinthoides italica*, 199

Italian yellow jasmine, *Jasminum humile*, 215

Ithuriel's spear, *Triteleia laxa*, 392

Ivy, *Hedera*, 186

Ivy-leaved geranium, *Pelargonium peltatum*, 293

Jack-in-the-pulpit, *Arisaema*, 36

Jack pine, *Pinus banksiana*, 310

Jacob's ladder, *Polemonium caeruleum*, 314

Jacob's rod, *Asphodeline*, 41

Jamaica crinum, *Crinum bulbispermum*, 117

Japanese anemone, *Anemone × hybrida*, 29

Japanese angelica tree, *Aralia elata*, 33

Japanese aucuba, *Aucuba japonica*, 45

Japanese beautyberry, *Callicarpa japonica*, 65

Japanese black pine, *Pinus thunbergii*, 309

Japanese burnet, *Sanguisorba obtusa*, 355
Japanese camellia, *Camellia japonica*, 70
Japanese cedar, *Cryptomeria japonica*, 120
Japanese clethra, *Clethra barbinervis*, 101
Japanese dogwood, *Cornus kousa*, 109
Japanese fantail willow, *Salix sachalinensis* 'Sekka', 352
Japanese flowering cherry, *Prunus serrulata*, 322
Japanese flowering crab apple, *Malus floribunda*, 256
Japanese flowering quince, *Chaenomeles japonica*, 87
Japanese garden juniper, *Juniperus procumbens*, 217
Japanese holly, *Ilex crenata*, 204
Japanese honeysuckle, *Lonicera japonica*, 246
Japanese hops, *Humulus japonicus*, 199
Japanese iris, *Iris ensata*, 212
Japanese kerria, *Kerria japonica*, 220
Japanese larch, *Larix kaempferi*, 227
Japanese laurel, *Aucuba*, 45
Japanese lily, *Lilium speciosum*, 239
Japanese mahonia, *Mahonia japonica*, 254
Japanese maple, *Acer palmatum*, 10
Japanese meadowsweet, *Filipendula purpurea*, 160
Japanese mock orange, *Pittosporum tobira*, 311
Japanese pagoda tree, *Sophora japonica*, 368
Japanese painted fern, *Athyrium niponicum*, 44
Japanese photinia, *Photinia glabra*, 302
Japanese pieris, *Pieris japonica*, 306
Japanese plum yew, *Cephalotaxus harringtoniana*, 84
Japanese primrose, *Primula japonica*, 319
Japanese privet, *Ligustrum japonicum*, 235
Japanese pussy willow, *Salix chaenomyloides*, 351
Japanese red pine, *Pinus densiflora*, 307
Japanese silver grass, *Miscanthus sinensis*, 263
Japanese skimmia, *Skimmia japonica*, 366
Japanese snowbell, *Styrax japonicus*, 376
Japanese spicebush, *Lindera obtusiloba*, 241
Japanese spindle tree, *Euonymus japonicus*, 154
Japanese spirea, *Spiraea japonica*, 371
Japanese stewartia, *Stewartia pseudocamellia*, 374
Japanese tree lilac, *Syringa reticulata*, 378
Japanese umbrella pine, *Sciadopitys verticillata*, 360
Japanese white pine, *Pinus parviflora*, 308
Japanese winterberry, *Ilex serrata*, 205
Japanese wisteria, *Wisteria floribunda*, 414
Japanese yew, *Taxus cuspidata*, 381
Japanese zelkova, *Zelkova serrata*, 417
Jasmine, *Trachelospermum*, 390
Jersey pine, *Pinus virginiana*, 310
Jerusalem artichoke, *Helianthus tuberosus*, 189
Jerusalem cross, *Lychnis chalcedonica*, 249
Jerusalem sage, *Phlomis*, 300
Jetbead, *Rhodotypos*, 339
Jewel of Burma, *Curcuma roscoeana*, 123
Jewelweed, *Impatiens capensis*, 206
Job's tears, *Coix lacryma-jobi*, 102
Joe-Pye weed, *Eupatorium purpureum*, 154
Johnny-jump-up, *Viola tricolor*, 412
Jonquil, *Narcissus*, 269
Joseph's coat, *Acalypha wilkesiana*, 4
  Amaranthus tricolor, 23
Juniper, *Juniperus*, 216
Jupiter's beard, *Centranthus ruber*, 84

Kaffir lily, *Schizostylis*, 359
Kahili ginger, *Hedychium gardnerianum*, 187
Kalm's St. Johnswort, *Hypericum kalmianum*, 202
Kamchatka bugbane, *Cimicifuga simplex*, 95
Kangaroo apple, *Solanum aviculare*, 366
Kansas gayfeather, *Liatris pycnostachya*, 235
Katsura tree, *Cercidiphyllum japonicum*, 86
Keeled garlic, *Allium carinatum*, 20
Keisk's leucothoe, *Leucothoe keiskei*, 233
Kentucky coffee tree, *Gymnocladus dioica*, 180
Kentucky wisteria, *Wisteria macrostachys*, 414
Kingfisher daisy, *Felicia bergeriana*, 159
King's spear, *Asphodeline lutea*, 41
Kinnikinick, *Arctostaphylos uva-ursi*, 34
Kiss-me-over-the-garden-gate, *Persicaria orientale*, 296
Kiwi, *Actinidia*, 13
Knapweed, *Centaurea*, 83
Knife acacia, *Acacia cultriformis*, 3
Knotweed, *Persicaria*, 295
Korean barberry, *Berberis koreana*, 41
Korean dogwood, *Cornus kousa*, 109
Korean fir, *Abies koreana*, 2
Korean mountain ash, *Sorbus alnifolia*, 369
Korean pine, *Pinus koraiensis*, 308
Korean spice viburnum, *Viburnum carlesii*, 409
Korean stewartia, *Stewartia pseudocamellia*, 374
Kousa dogwood, *Cornus kousa*, 109

Lablab, *Lablab purpureus*, 223
Labrador tea, *Ledum groenlandicum*, 230
Labrador violet, *Viola labradorica*, 412
Lacebark elm, *Ulmus parvifolia*, 402
Lacebark pine, *Pinus bungeana*, 307
Lace flower, *Ammi majus*, 25
Ladies' bedstraw, *Galium odoratum*, 168
Lad's love, *Artemisia abrotanum*, 38
Ladybells, *Adenophora*, 13
Lady fern, *Athyrium filix-femina*, 44
Lady's mantle, *Alchemilla*, 19
Lady's smock, *Cardamine pratensis*, 73
Lady tulip, *Tulipa clusiana*, 399
Lamb's ears, *Stachys byzantina*, 372
Lanceleaf poplar, *Populus acuminata*, 317
Lance-leaved coreopsis, *Coreopsis lanceolata*, 107
Lantana, *Lantana camara*, 227
Larch, *Larix*, 227
Large-flowered calamint, *Calamintha grandiflora*, 64
Large fothergilla, *Fothergilla major*, 161
Large-leaved aster, *Aster macrophyllus*, 43
Large merrybells, *Uvularia grandiflora*, 403
Large selfheal, *Prunella grandiflora*, 321
Larkspur, *Consolida ajacis*, 105
Laudanum, *Cistus × ladanifer*, 96
Lavender, *Lavandula*, 228
Lavender cotton, *Santolina chamaecyparissus*, 355
Lavender globe lily, *Allium tanguticum*, 21
Lavender mist, *Thalictrum rochebruneanum*, 384
Lavender starflower, *Grewia occidentalis*, 180
Lawson false cypress, *Chamaecyparis lawsoniana*, 88
Leadwort, *Ceratostigma plumbaginoides*, 85
  Plumbago, 313

Leatherleaf mahonia, *Mahonia bealei*, 254
Leatherleaf viburnum, *Viburnum rhytidophyllum*, 411
Leatherwood, *Cyrilla racemiflora*, 125
Leichtlin quamash, *Camassia leichtlinii*, 69
Lemoine deutzia, *Deutzia × lemoinei*, 132
Lemonade berry, *Rhus integrifolia*, 339
Lemon lily, *Hemerocallis lilioasphodelus*, 192
Lemon thyme, *Thymus × citriodorus*, 386
Lenten rose, *Helleborus × hybridus*, 191
Leopard flower, *Belamcanda chinensis*, 50
Leopard lily, *Lilium pardalinum*, 239
Leopard's bane, *Doronicum*, 140
Lesser calamint, *Calamintha nepeta*, 64
Lesser celandine, *Ranunculus ficaria*, 333
Lesser periwinkle, *Vinca minor*, 411
Leyland cypress, × *Cupressocyparis leylandii*, 121
Licorice plant, *Helichrysum petiolare*, 189
Lilac, *Syringa*, 377
Lilac daphne, *Daphne genkwa*, 129
Lilac geranium, *Geranium himalayense*, 173
Lilies-of-the-Nile, *Agapanthus*, 15
Lily, *Lilium*, 136
Lily-flowered magnolia, *Magnolia liliiflora*, 252
Lily leek, *Allium moly*, 29
Lily-of-the-Amazon, *Eucharis × grandiflora*, 152
Lily-of-the-Incas, *Alstroemeria aurea*, 23
  Alstroemeria ligtu, 23
Lily-of-the-valley, *Convallaria majalis*, 106
Lilyturf, *Liriope*, 243
  Ophiopogon, 281
Limber pine, *Pinus flexilis*, 307
Linden, *Tilia*, 387
Linden viburnum, *Viburnum dilatatum*, 409
Lion's ear, *Leonotis*, 231
Littleleaf box, *Buxus microphylla*, 62
Littleleaf lilac, *Syringa microphylla*, 378
Littleleaf linden, *Tilia cordata*, 388
Littleleaf mock orange, *Philadelphus microphyllus*, 299
Little quaking grass, *Briza minor*, 58
Live oak, *Quercus virginiana*, 331
Livingstone daisy, *Dorotheanthus bellidiformis*, 140
Loblolly pine, *Pinus taeda*, 309
Locust, *Gleditsia*, 178
  Robinia, 341
Loebner magnolia, *Magnolia × loebneri*, 252
Lombardy poplar, *Populus nigra*, 317
London plane tree, *Platanus acerifolia*, 311
London pride, *Saxifraga × urbium*, 357
Longleaf lungwort, *Pulmonaria longifolia*, 325
Long-leaved speedwell, *Veronica longifolia*, 408
Long-spurred columbine, *Aquilegia longissima*, 33
Long-spurred epimedium, *Epimedium grandiflorum*, 147
Longstalk holly, *Ilex pedunculosa*, 205
Loosestrife, *Lysimachia*, 250
Lords and ladies, *Arum maculatum*, 39
Lotus vine, *Lotus berthelotii*, 247
Louisiana irises, *Iris* Louisiana hybrids, 212
Love-in-a-mist, *Nigella damascena*, 277
Love-in-a-puff, *Cardiospermum halicacabum*, 74
Love-lies-bleeding, *Amaranthus caudatus*, 23
Lungwort, *Pulmonaria*, 325
Lupine, *Lupinus*, 247

Shumard oak, *Quercus shumardii*, 330
Siam tulip, *Curcuma alismatifolia*, 123
Siberian bugloss, *Brunnera macrophylla*, 60
Siberian carpet juniper, *Microbiota decussata*, 262
Siberian catnip, *Nepeta sibirica*, 274
Siberian crab apple, *Malus baccata*, 256
Siberian cypress, *Microbiota*, 262
Siberian elm, *Ulmus pumila*, 402
Siberian iris, *Iris sibirica*, 212
Siberian meadowsweet, *Filipendula palmata*, 160
Siberian squill, *Scilla siberica*, 361
Siebold primrose, *Primula sieboldii*, 320
Signet marigold, *Tagetes tenuifolia*, 379
Silk-tassel tree, *Garrya elliptica*, 170
Silk tree, *Albizia julibrissin*, 18
Silky dogwood, *Cornus amomum*, 108
Silverberry, *Elaeagnus commutata*, 145
Silver buffaloberry, *Shepherdia argentea*, 363
Silverbush, *Convolvulus cneorum*, 106
Silver dollar, *Lunaria*, 247
Silver fleece vine, *Fallopia aubertii*, 157
Silver lace vine, *Fallopia aubertii*, 157
Silver-leaved sunflower, *Helianthus argophyllus*, 188
Silver linden, *Tilia tomentosa*, 388
Silver maple, *Acer saccharinum*, 9
Silvermound artemisia, *Artemisia schmidtiana*, 38
Silver sage, *Salvia argentea*, 353
Silver salvia, *Salvia argentea*, 353
Siskiyou lily, *Fritillaria glauca*, 165
Skunkbush, *Rhus trilobata*, 339
Sky lupine, *Lupinus nanus*, 248
Skyrocket, *Ipomopsis aggregata*, 210
Small anise, *Illicium parviflorum*, 206
Small globe thistle, *Echinops ritro*, 144
Small's penstemon, *Penstemon smallii*, 294
Smartweed, *Persicaria*, 295
Smoke bush, *Cotinus coggygria*, 113
  Cotinus obovatus, 113
Smoke tree, *Cotinus coggygria*, 113
Smooth hydrangea, *Hydrangea arborescens*, 200
Smoothleaf elm, *Ulmus carpinifolia*, 402
Smooth sumac, *Rhus glabra*, 339
Smooth witherod, *Viburnum nudum*, 410
Snakeberry, *Actaea rubra*, 13
Snake palm, *Amorphophallus konjac*, 26
Snakeroot, *Cimicifuga*, 95
Snake's-head fritillary, *Fritillaria meleagris*, 165
Snakeshead turtlehead, *Chelone glabra*, 92
Snakeweed, *Persicaria bistorta*, 296
Snapdragon, *Antirrhinum*, 31
Sneezeweed, *Helenium*, 187
Sneezewort, *Achillea ptarmica*, 11
Snowberry, *Symphoricarpos albus*, 376
Snow crocus, *Crocus chrysanthus*, 118
Snowdrop anemone, *Anemone sylvestris*, 29
Snowdrops, *Galanthus*, 167
Snowflake, *Leucojum*, 232
Snow-in-summer, *Cerastium tomentosum*, 85
Snow-on-the-mountain, *Euphorbia marginata*, 155
Snowy wood rush, *Luzula nivea*, 248
Soapwort, *Saponaria*, 356
Society garlic, *Tulbaghia violacea*, 395
Soft shield fern, *Polystichum setiferum*, 316
Solomon's plume, *Smilacina*, 366
Solomon's seal, *Polygonatum biflorum*, 315

Sonoma manzanita, *Arctostaphylos densiflora*, 34
Sorrel tree, *Oxydendrum arboreum*, 285
Sour gum, *Nyssa sylvatica*, 278
Sourwood, *Oxydendrum arboreum*, 285
Southern blue flag, *Iris virginica*, 213
Southern bush honeysuckle, *Diervilla sessilifolia*, 137
Southern Japanese hemlock, *Tsuga sieboldii*, 394
Southern magnolia, *Magnolia grandiflora*, 253
Southern red oak, *Quercus falcata*, 330
Southern swamp lily, *Crinum americanum*, 117
Southern wax myrtle, *Myrica cerifera*, 268
Southernwood, *Artemisia abrotanum*, 38
Spanish bayonet, *Yucca aloifolia*, 415
  Yucca gloriosa, 415
Spanish bluebell, *Hyacinthoides hispanica*, 199
Spanish broom, *Spartium junceum*, 370
Spanish flag, *Ipomoea lobata*, 209
Spanish iris, *Iris xiphium*, 213
Spanish oak, *Quercus falcata*, 330
Spanish thyme, *Plectranthus amboinicus*, 312
Speedwell, *Veronica*, 408
Spicebush, *Lindera benzoin*, 241
Spice viburnum, *Viburnum × juddii*, 409
Spider flower, *Cleome hassleriana*, 100
Spider lily, *Crinum*, 116
  Hymenocallis caribaea, 201
  Hymenocallis harrisiana, 201
Spiderwort, *Tradescantia*, 390
Spike gayfeather, *Liatris spicata*, 235
Spike speedwell, *Veronica spicata*, 408
Spiketail, *Stachyurus praecox*, 372
Spike winter hazel, *Corylopsis spicata*, 111
Spiral bellflower, *Campanula cochleariifolia*, 70
Spotted bee balm, *Monarda punctata*, 265
Spotted calla, *Zantedeschia albomaculata*, 416
Spotted dead nettle, *Lamium maculatum*, 226
Spotted geranium, *Geranium maculatum*, 174
Spotted horsemint, *Monarda punctata*, 265
Spotted Joe-Pye weed, *Eupatorium maculatum*, 154
Spotted laurel, *Aucuba*, 45
Spotted orchid, *Dactylorhiza*, 127
Spreading cotoneaster, *Cotoneaster divaricatus*, 113
Spring meadow saffron, *Bulbocodium vernum*, 62
Spring snowflake, *Leucojum vernum*, 232
Spring starflower, *Ipheion uniflorum*, 208
Spring squill, *Scilla siberica*, 361
Spring vetchling, *Lathyrus vernus*, 228
Spruce, *Picea*, 304
Spurge, *Euphorbia myrsinites*, 155
Spurred snapdragon, *Linaria*, 241
Squill, *Scilla*, 360
Squirrel-tail grass, *Hordeum jubatum*, 197
Staff vine, *Celastrus scandens*, 82
Staghorn sumac, *Rhus typhina*, 339
Standing cypress, *Ipomopsis rubra*, 210
Star anise, *Illicium anisatum*, 205
Star astilbe, *Astilbe simplicifolia*, 44
Star cluster, *Pentas lanceolata*, 295
Star flower, *Pentas lanceolata*, 295
  Scabiosa stellata, 358
Star glory, *Ipomoea quamoclit*, 209
Star jasmine, *Trachelospermum asiaticum*, 390
Star lily, *Lilium concolor*, 239
Star magnolia, *Magnolia stellata*, 253
Star morning glory, *Ipomoea coccinea*, 209

Star-of-Bethlehem, *Campanula isophylla*, 71
  Ornithogalum, 282
Star of Persia, *Allium cristophii*, 20
Star of the veldt, *Dimorphotheca sinuata*, 138
  Osteospermum, 283
Starved aster, *Aster lateriflorus*, 43
Statice, *Limonium sinuatum*, 240
  Psylliostachys, 324
Stellar dogwood, *Cornus × rutgersensis*, 110
Sticktight, *Bidens*, 54
Stinking Benjamin, *Trillium erectum*, 391
Stinking hellebore, *Helleborus foetidus*, 191
Stinking iris, *Iris foetidissima*, 212
St. Johnswort, *Hypericum*, 202
Stock, *Malcolmia*, 255
  Matthiola, 259
Stokes' aster, *Stokesia*, 375
Stonecrop, *Sedum*, 361
Strawbell, *Uvularia perfoliata*, 403
Strawberry, *Fragaria*, 161
Strawberry begonia, *Saxifraga stolonifera*, 357
Strawberry bush, *Euonymus americanus*, 153
Strawberry foxglove, *Digitalis × mertonensis*, 138
Strawberry geranium, *Saxifraga stolonifera*, 357
Strawberry shrub, *Calycanthus floridus*, 69
Strawberry tree, *Arbutus unedo*, 33
Strawflower, *Bracteantha bracteata*, 57
  Rhodanthe, 335
Striped maple, *Acer pensylvanicum*, 7
Striped squill, *Puschkinia*, 326
Sugarbush, *Rhus ovata*, 339
Sugar maple, *Acer saccharum*, 9
Sulfur cinquefoil, *Potentilla recta*, 319
Sumac, *Rhus*, 339
Summer cypress, *Bassia scoparia* f. *trichophylla*, 49
Summer forget-me-not, *Anchusa capensis*, 27
Summer hyacinth, *Galtonia candicans*, 169
Summer lilac, *Buddleia davidii*, 61
Summer savory, *Satureja montana*, 357
Summer snowflake, *Leucojum aestivum*, 232
Summersweet, *Clethra alnifolia*, 101
Sundrops, *Oenothera*, 279
Sunflower, *Helianthus*, 188
Sunflower heliopsis, *Heliopsis*, 189
Sun rose, *Helianthemum*, 187
Sunset hibiscus, *Abelmoschus manihot*, 1
Sutherland begonia, *Begonia sutherlandii*, 50
Swamp azalea, *Rhododendron viscosum*, 338
Swamp cedar, *Chamaecyparis thyoides*, 89
Swamp chestnut oak, *Quercus michauxii*, 330
Swamp cypress, *Taxodium distichum*, 380
Swamp lily, *Crinum*, 117
Swamp maple, *Acer rubrum*, 8
Swamp milkweed, *Asclepias incarnata*, 40
Swamp rose mallow, *Hibiscus coccineus*, 194
Swamp spurge, *Euphorbia palustris*, 155
Swamp sunflower, *Helianthus angustifolius*, 188
Swamp white oak, *Quercus bicolor*, 330
Swan river daisy, *Brachyscome iberidifolia*, 57
Swan river everlasting, *Rhodanthe manglesii*, 336
Sweet alyssum, *Lobularia maritima*, 244
Sweet Annie, *Artemisia annua*, 38
Sweet autumn clematis, *Clematis terniflora*, 100
Sweet azalea, *Rhododendron arborescens*, 337
Sweet bay, *Laurus nobilis*, 228
Sweet bay magnolia, *Magnolia virginiana*, 253
Sweetbells leucothoe, *Leucothoe racemosa*, 233
Sweet box, *Sarcococca humilis*, 357

Photo Credits

RICH BAER: 343 top L, 343 top R, 346 bottom R, 347 bottom R

BERRY BOTANIC GARDENS: 405 R

BLOOMS OF BRESSINGHAM: 194 top

BRENT AND BECKY'S BULBS: 20 top, 22 bottom L, 23 bottom R, 50 top R, 52 bottom, 55 top, 58 bottom L, 62 top L, 67 bottom R, 69 top, 72, 90 bottom R, 103 top, 104 R, 117, 119 top, 123, 126 top, 135 bottom, 178 top, 179 top, 195 top, 199 top, 201 bottom R, 202 top L, 213 bottom, 232 bottom, 236 bottom, 249, 270 top, 270 bottom, 271 top L, 272 bottom, 274 bottom, 282 top, 288 bottom, 313 bottom, 338 top, 374 top, 382 top L, 387 bottom, 392 top, 397 top, 399 top, 399 bottom, 400 top L, 416 top L, 416 top R

ALBERT BUSSEWITZ/MASSACHUSETTS AUDUBON SOCIETY: viii R, ix R, 41 top L, 75 bottom R, 78 bottom, 81 bottom, 162 bottom, 285 bottom, 330 top, 376 bottom

DAVID CAVAGNARO: 18 bottom R, 23 top, 29 bottom, 31 top, 48 top L, 51 bottom, 57 bottom, 83 top, 102 top, 106 bottom, 130 bottom L, 141 top, 156 top R, 159 top L, 198 top R, 202 top R, 206 bottom, 208 bottom R, 209 top, 209 bottom, 223 L, 255 bottom, 258 bottom L, 275 top, 276 bottom, 320 bottom, 363 bottom L, 367 top, 393 top, 418 top R, 418 bottom

WILLIAM CULLINA: iv–v, x–xi, 68 bottom, 92 top, 101 top, 167, 205 top, 227 top, 245 bottom R, 290 bottom R, 306 top, 324 bottom, 337 bottom, 394 top

R. TODD DAVIS: 43 top, 55 bottom R, 63 L, 71 bottom, 210 bottom, 211 top, 259 top, 280 bottom R, 287 R, 296 bottom, 365 bottom, 366 top, 398 top, 398 bottom

ALAN AND LINDA DETRICK: 285 top

MICHAEL DIRR: 85 top L, 251 far L, 251 center L, 310 top, 314 top

KEN DRUSE: 25 top L, 188 top L, 268 top, 410 bottom

BARBARA ELLIS: 250 top L, 355 top, 384 top L

THOMAS ELTZROTH: 15 bottom, 36 top, 54 bottom R, 58 bottom R, 59 top, 64 bottom R, 66 top, 67 bottom L, 76 bottom, 107 bottom, 114 top R, 120 top, 124 bottom, 134 top, 136 top L, 181 bottom, 245 bottom L, 260 top L, 260 bottom, 267 top, 280 top, 297 top, 312 bottom, 318 top, 347 top R, 347 bottom L, 358 top, 364 bottom L, 379 L, 385 bottom

DEREK FELL: i, 1 R, 2 bottom L, 3 bottom L, 6, 7, 10 top, 11 top, 15 top, 17 top, 17 bottom, 20 bottom, 22 top, 24 bottom, 27 top, 34 top R, 35 top L, 35 top R, 36 bottom R, 45 top R, 50 top L, 51 top L, 54 top, 59 bottom, 61 bottom R, 62 bottom, 66 bottom, 74 L, 75 top, 76 top, 77 top, 77 bottom R, 80 top R, 86 top, 93 bottom, 94 top, 96 bottom R, 97 top, 103 bottom L, 103 bottom R, 114 bottom, 115 top, 115 bottom, 116 top, 116 bottom, 121 top, 121 bottom, 122 top, 126 bottom R, 136 bottom, 137 top, 139 top L, 140 bottom L, 141 bottom L, 145 top, 145 bottom L, 146 bottom, 148 bottom, 153 top, 153 bottom R, 157, 158 top L, 160 bottom, 163 top, 163 bottom, 164 top, 165 top, 168 top, 172 top, 175 top, 176 top, 176 bottom, 177 top, 180 top, 183 L, 184 bottom, 186 top, 192 R, 195 bottom R, 199 bottom, 202 bottom, 204 bottom, 208 bottom L, 215 R, 216 bottom, 217 bottom, 235 top R, 237, 243 bottom L, 251 center R, 252 top, 253 top, 253 bottom R, 256 top, 259 bottom, 264 top R, 265, 266 bottom, 274 top, 277 bottom, 278 top, 278 bottom, 281 top, 282 bottom, 284 bottom, 291 top R, 292 bottom, 303 top, 307 bottom, 309 top, 311, 315 top, 317 top, 322, 323 top, 324 top, 327 bottom, 329 L, 329 R, 331, 334 bottom R, 336 top, 338 bottom R, 339 top, 340 bottom, 341 top R, 343 bottom L, 345 bottom R, 348 top, 351 R, 352 top, 354 top, 362 bottom, 363 top, 366 bottom L, 368 bottom, 374 bottom, 379 R, 386, 388 top, 389 bottom R, 390 top, 393 bottom, 396 top, 400 top R, 402 top, 403, 411 top, 412 bottom, 415 R, 417 top, 418 top L

CHARLES MARDEN FITCH: 12 L, 19 bottom, 25 top R, 26 bottom, 38 top R, 41 top R, 50 bottom, 57 top, 58 top, 62 top R, 91 bottom, 94 bottom, 101 bottom L, 102 bottom, 128 top L, 140 bottom R, 169 bottom, 191 bottom, 194 bottom L, 219 L, 277 top inset, 281 bottom R, 284 top, 297 bottom L, 325 top, 359 bottom, 360 top, 391 bottom R

MARGE GARFIELD: 13 top R, 14 bottom L, 61 bottom L, 131 top L, 289 top R, 326 top, 355 bottom L, 356 bottom, 392 bottom, 406 bottom R

P. A. HARING: 344 top L, 344 top R, 344 bottom, 345 top L, 345 top R, 345 bottom L, 346 top, 346 bottom L, 347 top L

JESSIE HARRIS: 37 bottom, 47 R, 75 bottom L, 87 bottom L, 262 top L, 377 bottom, 409, 410 top R

DENCY KANE: 3 top, 385 top L, 389 top

CHARLES MANN: 4 bottom, 10 bottom, 11 bottom, 23 bottom L, 28 bottom R, 32 top L, 32 top R, 32 bottom, 37 top, 38 top L, 39 R, 40 top, 45 bottom R, 48 bottom, 55 bottom L, 63 R, 70 top, 70 bottom, 71 top, 77 bottom L, 82 bottom, 83 bottom, 85 top R, 97 bottom, 105 top R, 106 top R, 110 bottom, 130 bottom R, 132 top, 133 top R, 136 top R, 137 bottom, 140 top, 144 top, 149 top, 150 top, 168 bottom, 170 bottom, 177 bottom, 184 top, 187 bottom, 188 bottom, 189 L, 189 R, 190 top R, 193 top, 211 bottom, 220 bottom R, 221 top L, 226 top L, 232 top, 235 top L, 235 bottom, 247 bottom, 248 top L, 248 top R, 250 bottom, 258 bottom R, 262 bottom, 273 top, 281 bottom L, 288 top L, 289 top L, 294 bottom, 295 bottom R, 317 bottom, 318 bottom, 349 top, 355 bottom R, 365 top L, 387 top, 407 top, 411 bottom, 416 bottom

DR. LARRY MELLICHAMP: 53

NEW ENGLAND WILD FLOWER SOCIETY/JEAN S. BAXTER: 367 bottom

NEWFS/FRANK BRAMLEY: 9, 28 bottom L, 364 top, 406 bottom L

NEWFS/ALBERT BUSSEWITZ: 91 top R, 95 bottom, 294 top, 314 bottom

NEWFS/WILLIAM CULLINA: 300 top

NEWFS/CAROL FYLER: 150 bottom

NEWFS/WILLIAM LARKIN: vi–vii, 412 top

NEWFS/DOROTHY S. LONG: 42 bottom, 48 top R, 230 top R, 244 top, 260 top R

NEWFS/JOHN A. LYNCH: viii L, ix L, 108 top, 129 top R, 143 R, 149 bottom, 160 top, 161 bottom, 190 top L, 242 bottom, 300 bottom, 304 top, 330 bottom, 334 top, 337 top, 348 bottom R, 364 bottom R, 405 L, 413 L

NEWFS/LAWRENCE NEWCOMB: 73 top, 373 bottom L

NEWFS/WALT AND LOUISEANN PIETROWITZ: 375 bottom R

NEWFS/ADELAIDE M. PRATT: 255 top L, 323 bottom

NEWFS/LUCIEN TAYLOR: 29 top R, 31 bottom

STEVEN NIKKILA C/O PERENNIAL FAVORITES: 44 top, 162 top, 198 bottom, 250 top R

NANCY J. ONDRA: 261 bottom

JERRY PAVIA: ii–iii, 1 L, 2 top, 2 bottom R, 3 bottom R, 4 top, 5, 8, 12 R, 13 top L, 13 bottom, 14 top, 14 bottom R, 16 top, 16 bottom L, 16 bottom R, 18 top, 18 bottom L, 19 top, 21 top, 21 bottom, 25 bottom, 26 top R, 27 bottom L, 27 bottom R, 29 top L, 30 top, 30 bottom L, 30 bottom R, 33 top, 33 bottom L, 34 top L, 39 L, 40 bottom, 41 bottom, 42 top, 43 bottom, 44 bottom, 45 bottom L, 47 L, 49 top, 49 bottom, 51 top R, 56 top, 56 bottom L, 56 bottom R, 60 top L, 60 top R, 60 bottom, 64 top, 64 bottom L, 67 top, 68 top, 74 R, 78 top, 79 top, 79 bottom, 80 top L, 80 bottom, 81 top, 82 top, 84 top, 84 bottom, 85 bottom, 86 bottom, 87 bottom R, 90 bottom L, 91 top L, 93 top, 95 top, 96 top, 96 bottom L, 98 top, 98 bottom, 99 top, 99 bottom, 100 top, 100 bottom, 101 bottom R inset, 104 L, 105 top L, 107 top, 108 bottom R, 111 top, 111 bottom, 112 top, 112 bottom, 113 top, 114 top L, 119 bottom, 120 bottom, 122 bottom, 124 top, 125 top, 125 bottom, 126 bottom L, 127 R, 128 bottom, 129 top L, 129 bottom, 130 top, 131 top R, 133 top L, 133 bottom, 135 top, 138 L, 138 R, 139 top R, 143 L, 144 bottom, 145 bottom R, 147 top, 148 top, 152 top, 152 bottom, 153 bottom L, 154 top, 154 bottom, 155 top, 155 bottom, 156 top L, 158 bottom R, 159 top R, 159 bottom, 161 top L, 161 top R, 165 bottom, 166 top, 166 bottom, 169 top R, 170 top L, 171 top, 172 bottom L, 173 top, 173 bottom, 174 top, 174 bottom, 175 top, 178 bottom, 179 bottom, 180 bottom, 181 top, 183 R, 185 top L, 185 top R, 186 bottom, 188 top R, 190 bottom, 191 top, 192 L, 194 bottom R, 196 top, 196 bottom, 197 top, 197 bottom, 200 L, 200 R, 201 top, 201 bottom L, 203 center, 203 R, 206 top, 207 top L, 207 bottom, 210 top, 212, 213 top, 216 top, 220 bottom L, 221 top R, 221 bottom, 223 R, 224 top, 224 bottom, 225, 226 top R, 226 bottom, 227 bottom, 228 top, 228 bottom, 229 top, 229 bottom, 230 top L, 230 bottom, 231 top, 234 top, 236 top, 240 top, 240 bottom L, 240 bottom R, 241 top, 242 top, 243 top, 243 bottom R, 244 bottom L, 244 bottom R, 245 top, 246 bottom, 247 top, 251 far R, 254 top, 255 top R, 256 bottom, 257, 258 top, 263 top R, 263 bottom, 264 top L, 264 bottom, 267 bottom, 268 bottom, 269 L, 271 top R, 271 bottom, 273 bottom L, 273 bottom R, 275 bottom, 276 top, 277 top, 279 R, 283 top, 287 L, 289 bottom, 290 top, 290 bottom L, 291 top L, 291 bottom, 292 top, 293 top, 293 bottom, 295 top, 295 bottom L, 296 top, 297 bottom R, 298 top R, 299 top, 299 bottom, 301, 302 top, 303 bottom, 304 bottom, 305 top, 305 bottom, 306 bottom, 307 top, 308, 309 bottom, 310 bottom, 312 top L, 312 top R, 315 bottom R, 316 top, 316 bottom, 319 top, 319 bottom, 320 top, 321 top, 326 bottom L, 326 bottom R, 327 top, 333, 334 bottom L, 335 top, 335 bottom, 336 bottom, 339 bottom, 340 top, 341 top L, 341 bottom, 348 bottom L, 349 bottom, 352 bottom, 353 top, 353 bottom, 354 bottom, 356 top L, 357 top, 357 bottom, 358 bottom, 360 bottom, 361 top, 361 bottom, 362 top R, 363 bottom R, 365 top R, 360 bottom R, 368 top, 369 top, 369 bottom, 370 top, 370 bottom, 371 top, 371 bottom L, 372 top, 375 top, 375 bottom L, 376 top, 377 top, 378 top L, 378 top R, 380 top, 380 bottom, 381 top, 381 bottom, 382 top R, 382 bottom R, 383 bottom, 384 top R, 384 bottom, 388 bottom, 389 bottom L, 390 bottom R, 391 bottom L, 394 bottom, 395 top, 395 bottom, 396 bottom, 402 bottom, 406 top, 407 bottom, 408 top L, 408 top R, 408 bottom, 413 R, 414 top, 414 bottom, 415 L, 419

SUSAN ROTH: 54 bottom L, 88 top, 261 top, 298 bottom

PAUL SOMERS: 90 top

STEVEN STILL: 35 bottom, 45 top L, 65 top, 109, 113 bottom, 127 L, 131 bottom, 141 bottom R, 171 bottom, 187 top, 193 bottom, 198 top L, 207 top R, 217 top, 248 bottom, 262 top R, 321 bottom, 325 bottom, 362 top L, 385 top R

MICHAEL S. THOMPSON: 22 bottom R, 24 top, 33 bottom R, 34 bottom, 36 bottom L, 38 bottom, 38 bottom inset, 52 top, 61 top, 65 bottom, 73 bottom, 87 top, 88 bottom, 89, 92 bottom, 101 bottom R, 105 bottom, 106 top L, 108 bottom L, 110 top, 118 top, 118 bottom, 128 top R, 132 bottom, 134 bottom, 139 bottom, 146 top, 147 bottom, 151 top, 151 bottom, 156 bottom, 158 top R, 158 bottom L, 164 bottom, 169 top L, 170 top R, 172 bottom R, 185 bottom, 195 bottom L, 203 L, 204 top, 205 bottom, 208 top, 215 L, 219 R, 220 top, 231 bottom, 233 top, 233 bottom, 234 bottom, 238, 239, 241 bottom, 246 top, 252 bottom, 254 bottom, 263 top L, 266 top, 269 R, 272 top, 279 L, 280 bottom L, 283 bottom, 288 top R, 290 bottom center, 298 top L, 302 bottom, 313 top, 315 bottom L, 338 bottom L, 343 bottom R, 351 L, 356 top R, 359 top L, 359 top R, 371 bottom R, 372 bottom, 373 top, 373 bottom R, 378 bottom, 382 bottom L, 383 top, 390 bottom L, 391 top, 397 bottom, 400 bottom, 401, 410 top L, 417 bottom

MARK TURNER: 1 center, 28 top, 69 bottom, 161 top R inset

JOANNE WALKOVIC: 26 top L

Hardiness Zone Map

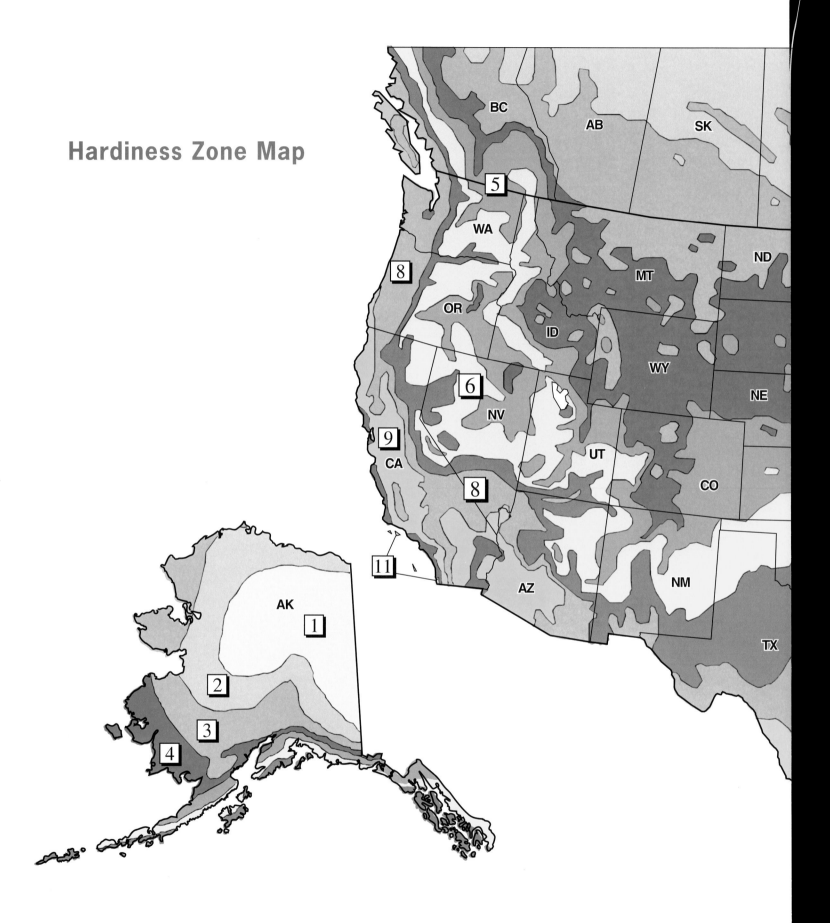

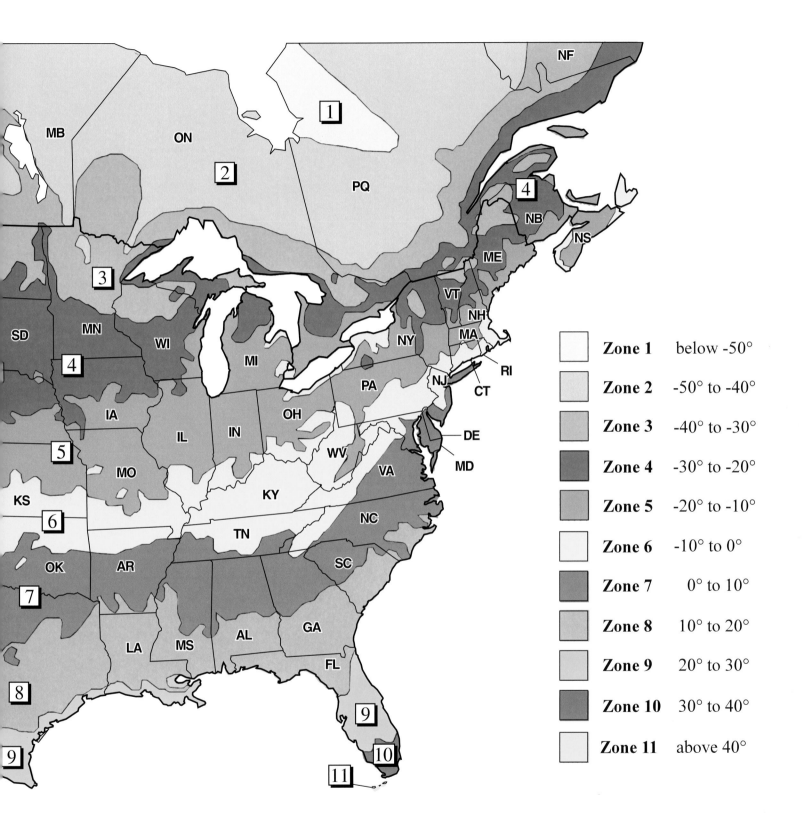

	Zone 1	below -50°
	Zone 2	-50° to -40°
	Zone 3	-40° to -30°
	Zone 4	-30° to -20°
	Zone 5	-20° to -10°
	Zone 6	-10° to 0°
	Zone 7	0° to 10°
	Zone 8	10° to 20°
	Zone 9	20° to 30°
	Zone 10	30° to 40°
	Zone 11	above 40°